SCRIBNER LIBRARY OF DAILY LIFE

ENCYCLOPEDIA OF FOOD AND CULTURE

EDITORIAL BOARD

France Detail of a painting by Charles Giraud called *La Salle à manger de la Princesse Mathilde* (1854), showing the interior of a grand salon fitted out with carpets, plants, and a sumptuous dinner service under silver covers. Courtesy of the Musée national du Château Compiègne, France. ©Réunion des Musées Nationaux/Art Resource, New York.

SCRIBNER LIBRARY OF DAILY LIFE

ENCYCLOPEDIA OF FOOD AND CULTURE

VOLUME 3:
Obesity to Zoroastrianism, Index

Solomon H. Katz, Editor in Chief

William Woys Weaver, Associate Editor

CHARLES SCRIBNER'S SONS®

THOMSON

GALE

12223

New York • Detroit • San Diego • San Francisco • Cleveland • New Haven, Conn. • Waterville, Maine • London • Munich

Encyclopedia of Food and Culture

Solomon H. Katz, Editor in Chief

William Woys Weaver, Associate Editor

LIBRARY OF CONGRESS CATALOGING-IN-PUBLICATION DATA

Encyclopedia of food and culture / Solomon H. Katz, editor in chief ;
William Woys Weaver, associate editor.
    p. cm.
Includes bibliographical references and index.
    ISBN 0-684-80568-5 (set : alk. paper) — ISBN 0-684-80565-0 (v. 1) —
ISBN 0-684-80566-9 (v. 2) — ISBN 0-684-80567-7 (v. 3)
    1. Food habits—Encyclopedias. 2. Food—Encyclopedias. I. Katz, Solomon H., 1939-
II. Weaver, William Woys, 1947-   III. Title.
GT2850 .E53 2003
394.1'2'097303—dc21   2002014607

Printed in the United States of America
10 9 8 7 6 5 4 3 2 1

SCRIBNER LIBRARY OF DAILY LIFE

ENCYCLOPEDIA OF
FOOD
AND CULTURE

O

OATS. *See* **Cereal Grains and Pseudo-Cereals.**

OBESITY. Obesity and overweight now affect more than 50 percent of adult Americans. Diabetes mellitus, hypertension, heart disease, gallbladder disease, and some forms of cancer result from obesity. Whether these diseases are yet present or not, the obese individual should be encouraged to lose weight by appropriate methods to reduce the future likelihood that they will develop. Methods of weight loss include diet, nutritional education, self-help groups, and behavioral change. Under some circumstances drugs or surgery may be considered.

Definition and Measurement of Obesity

Obesity and overweight are best defined using the body mass index (BMI). This index is determined by dividing body weight in kilograms by the square of the height in meters: $BMI = W/H^2$. The normal rate for BMI is 18.5 to 25. A BMI between 25 and 30 kg/m² is defined as overweight and a BMI above 30 kg/m² is defined as obesity (Table 1). Visceral fat can be used as an index of central adiposity. An increase in visceral fat reflects central obesity and increases health risks. The waist circumference is used to assess the amount of visceral obesity. A waist circumference in men of 40 inches (102 cm) or more, and in women, of 35 inches (88 cm) or more, is the threshold for defining central obesity (Table 1).

Prevalence of Overweight

More females than males are overweight at any age. The frequency of overweight increases with age to reach a peak at forty-five to fifty-four years in men and at age fifty-five to sixty-four in women. The National Health and Nutrition Examination Survey (NHANES) conducted by the U.S. government (published in 1993) found a BMI of 25 or more in 59.4 percent of men age twenty years or older and in 50.7 percent of women over the age of twenty years. The prevalence of obesity (BMI 30 or more) was 19.5 percent in men and 25.0 percent in women. The incidence of obesity continues to increase dramatically in the United States and elsewhere. A number of factors including age, sex, and physical inactivity influence the amount of body fat.

At birth, the human infant contains about 12 percent body fat. During the first years of life, body fat rises rapidly to reach a peak of about 25 percent by six months of age and then declines to 18 percent over the next ten years. At puberty, there is a significant increase in the percentage of body fat in females and a decrease in males. By age eighteen, males have approximately 15 to 18 percent body fat, and females have 25 to 28 percent. Be-

TABLE 1

Classification of overweight and obesity by BMI, waist circumference, and associated disease risk

	BMI kg/m²	Obesity class	Disease risk* relative to normal weight and waist circumference	
			Men = 102 cm (= 40 in) Women = 88 cm (= 35 in)	>102 cm (>40 in) >88 cm (>35 in)
Underweight	18.5		–	–
Normal +	18.5–24.9		–	–
Overweight	25.0–29.9		Increased	High
Obesity	30.0–34.9	I	High	Very High
	35.0–39.9	II	Very High	Very High
Extreme Obesity	= 40	III	Extremely High	Extremely High

*Disease risk for type 2 diabetes, hypertension, and CVD.
+Increased waist circumference can also be a marker for increased risk even in persons of normal weight.
*Clinical Guidelines on the Identification, Evaluation, and Treatment of Overweight and Obesity in Adults—The Evidence Report. National Institutes of Health.
Obes Res 1998;6 Suppl 2:51S–209S.*

Due to his enormous size, Frank Williams, age 16, weight 442 pounds, was placed on display at the St. Louis Exposition in 1893. Obese teenagers are now a much more common sight. Photo by McKnight, Paducah, Kentucky, circa 1893. ROUGH-WOOD COLLECTION.

tween ages twenty and fifty, the fat content of males approximately doubles and that of females increases by about 50 percent. Total body weight, however, rises by only 10 to 15 percent: fat now accounts for a larger part of the body weight and lean body mass decreases.

Risks Related to Obesity

As the BMI increases, there is a curvilinear rise in excess mortality. This excess mortality rises more rapidly when the BMI is above 30 kg/m². A BMI over 40 kg/m² is associated with a further increase in overall risk and for the risk of sudden death. The principal causes of the excess mortality associated with overweight include hypertension, stroke, and other cardiovascular diseases, diabetes mellitus, certain cancers, reproductive disorders, gall-bladder disease, and sudden death.

The insulin-resistant state or metabolic syndrome is strongly associated with visceral fat. It may include consequences such as glucose intolerance or type 2 diabetes mellitus, hypertension, polycystic ovarian syndrome, dyslipidemia (the state of abnormal—either higher or lower—values for blood fats), and other disorders. These are often responsive to weight loss, especially when this is achieved early and the loss is maintained.

Development of Obesity

Several mechanisms lead to obesity, including neuroendocrine imbalances, particular drugs, diet, reduced energy expenditure, and genetic factors that lead to certain syndromes and predisposition to obesity. Obesity can follow damage to the hypothalamus in the brain, but this is rare. Cushing's disease is somewhat more common and can result in obesity. Treatment should be directed at the cause of the increased formation of adrenal corticosteroids.

Treatment of diabetics with insulin, sulfonylureas, or thiazolidinediones (but not metformin) can increase hunger and food intake, resulting in weight gain. Treatment with some antidepressants, anti-epileptics, and neuroleptics can also increase body weight, as can cyproheptadine (a serotonin antagonist that produces weight gain), probably through effects on the monoamines (including norepinephrine, epinephrine, dopamine, histamine, and serotonin) in the central nervous system.

Eating a high-fat diet and excessive consumption of sugar-sweetened beverages and the prevalence of abundant varieties of food in cafeterias or supermarkets are dietary factors in the development of obesity. Reduced energy expenditure relative to energy intake is another major component. Energy expenditure can be divided into four parts.

An inactive individual at rest burns between 800 and 900 kilocalories during a twenty-four hour period. This rate is lower in females than in males, and declines with age, and could account for much of the increase in fat stores if food intake does not decline similarly. The effect of physical exercise on metabolism is variable but on average is responsible for about one-third of the daily energy expenditure. From a therapeutic point of view this component of energy expenditure is most easily manipulated. Dietary thermogenesis is the energy expenditure that follows the ingestion of a meal. Heat produced by eating may dissipate up to 10 percent of the ingested calories. These thermic effects of food are one type of metabolic "inefficiency" in the body, that is, where dietary calories are not available for "useful" work. In the obese, the thermic effects of food are reduced particularly in individuals with impaired glucose tolerance or diabetes. Acute over- or underfeeding will produce corresponding shifts in overall metabolism, which can be as large as 15 to 20 percent.

Genetic factors can produce some types of obesity that are easily recognized. Among these types of obesity are: (1) the Bardet-Biel syndrome, characterized by retinal degeneration, mental retardation, obesity, polydactyly, and hypogonadism; (2) the Alstrom syndrome, characterized by pigmentary retinopathy, nerve deafness, obesity, and diabetes mellitus; (3) Carpenter syndrome, characterized by acrocephaly (abnormalities in the facial and head bones), mental retardation, hypogonadism, obesity, and preaxial syndactyly (extra fingers or toes on one hand or foot); (4) the Cohen syndrome, characterized by mental retardation, obesity, hypotonia (reduced tone of the muscles, resulting in a "floppy" muscle mass), and characteristic facies (an appearance of the face that is typical of specific genetic diseases); (5) the Prader-Willi syndrome, characterized by hypotonia, mental retardation, hypogonadism, and obesity; and (6) the pro-opiomelanocortin (POMC) syndrome, characterized by defective production of POMC that is recognized as a red-headed fat child with a low plasma cortisol (a value that is below the normal range).

If both parents are obese, about 80 percent of their offspring will be obese. If only one parent is obese, the likelihood of obesity in the offspring falls to less than 10 percent. Studies with identical twins suggest that inheritance accounts for about 70 percent and environmental factors (diet, physical inactivity, or both) account for 30 percent of the variation in body weight. Deficiency of the gene leptin and deficiency of the leptin receptor are rare, but are associated with massive human obesity. Absence of convertase I has also been associated with obesity in one family. The most common defects associated with massive obesity are abnormalities in the melanocortin receptor system—up to 4 percent of massively obese people may have this type of defect.

Evaluation of the Obese Patient

A medical evaluation should include the expected medical history, family history, personal and social history, and review of the systems of the body with a particular focus on the medications that can cause weight gain. A physical examination should include an assessment of the patient's height, weight, waist circumference, blood pressure, and level of health risk due to obesity. Laboratory tests should include a lipid panel, glucose level, chemistry panel for hepatic (liver) function and uric acid, thyroid function testing, and, if indicated a cortisol level.

Evaluating Risk Using the Body Mass Index (BMI)

Individuals with a normal BMI (20–25 kg/m^2) have little or no risk from obesity. Any individual in this weight range who wishes to lose weight for cosmetic reasons should do so only with conservative methods. Individuals with a BMI of greater than 25 to 29.9 kg/m^2 are in the low-risk group for developing heart disease, hyper-

tension, gallbladder disease, and diabetes mellitus associated with obesity. They too should be encouraged to use low-risk treatments, such as caloric restriction and exercise. Individuals with a BMI of 27 to 30 kg/m^2 or more who have diseases related to obesity may use adjunctive pharmacotherapy for weight loss.

Individuals with a BMI of 30 to 40 kg/m^2, have moderate risk for developing diseases associated with obesity. Diet, drugs, and exercise would all appear to be appropriate forms of treatment. Individuals with significant degrees of excess weight often find exercise difficult. However, exercise is very important in helping to maintain weight loss. The use of weight loss medications, as an adjunct to treatment, may also be useful in this group. Individuals who have a BMI above 40 kg/m^2 have a high risk of developing diseases associated with their obesity. Moderate to severe restriction of calories is the first line of treatment, but for some of these patients surgery may be advisable.

Treatment of Obesity

Any diet must reduce an individual's caloric intake below daily caloric expenditure if it is to be successful. This requires an assessment of caloric requirements, by estimating caloric expenditure from desirable weight tables; for men, multiply desirable weight by 30 to 35 kilocalories/kilogram, (14–16 kilocalories/lb.); for women, multiply desirable weight by 25 to 30 kilocalories/kilogram (12–14 kilocalories/lb.). After assessing caloric requirements, a reasonable calorie deficit can be prescribed. A caloric deficit of 500 kilocalories/day (3,500 kilocalories/week) will produce the loss of approximately one lb. (0.45 kilograms) of fat tissue each week. Table 2 gives a list of diets divided into different levels of energy.

The very low calorie diet (below 800 kilocalories) was developed to facilitate the rate of weight loss since lower energy intake should lead to greater energy deficit. In free living people, however, diets with 400 kilocalories/day have not produced greater weight loss than those with 800 kilocalories/day, suggesting either that they are harder to adhere to or that there is an adaptation in energy expenditure. In either case, these diets should only be used under appropriate medical supervision.

TABLE 2

Characterization of diets by composition

Type of diet	Calories	Fat g (%)	Carbohydrate g (%)	Protein g (%)
Typical American	2,200	85 (35)	274 (50)	82 (15)
High-fat, low carbohydrate	1,400	94 (60)	35 (10)	105 (30)
Moderate-fat	1,450	40 (25)	218 (60)	54 (15)
Low & very low fat	1,450	16–24 (10–15)	235–271 (65–75)	54–72 (15–20)

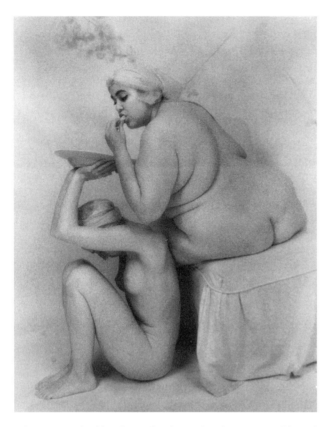

Obesity is a highly charged subject that has assumed broad sociological implications. In this 1998 photographic study called "Servitude I" by American artist Lynn Bianchi, several issues are exposed through novel inversions of female roles: body image, incessant snacking, and anorexia, to name three. Here it is the overly thin female who acts the role of caryatid-slave to an Earth Mother figure who never stops eating. PHOTO COURTESY OF THE ARTIST AND THE RALLS COLLECTION, INC., WASHINGTON, D.C.

Types of diets. There are several types of diets with more than 800 kilocalories/day that usually have more than 1,200 kilocalories/day. They can be divided into several categories. These categories are based on the relative proportion of macronutrients included in the diet and whether they use special foods. For all diets it must be true that they reduce the calorie intake to produce a negative energy balance. Low-carbohydrate diets are touted because they produce ketosis (a state of increased ketones associated with diabetes and fasting) and allow you to eat all of the protein and fat you want. This ends up reducing total calorie intake to about 1,500 kilocalories/day. Since these diets generally have carbohydrate levels below 50 g./day they are ketogenic and can be monitored clinically by the appearance of ketones in the urine. They vary in the level of fiber that is employed. The Atkins diet has low fiber levels, the Sugar Busters diet higher fiber levels.

Low-fat diets recommend fat intake in the range of 10 to 20 percent of calories. The higher carbohydrate in-

creases fiber intake. These diets were developed in a setting designed to reverse the atherosclerotic plaques associated with risks for heart disease, but because of the high fiber content they were often associated with weight loss. Moderate fat levels with higher carbohydrates are characteristic of many widely recommended "healthy diets." For weight loss, the New York Health Department recommends the Prudent Diet, which has stood the test of time.

The portion-controlled diet makes use of prepared foods that have a narrow range of calories. This includes liquid or powdered drinks as well as frozen or canned entrees that have about 300 kilocalories/meal. These can be combined conveniently and thus removes the problem of counting calories from the individual. A number of popular diets focus on a single food, and although nutritionally unbalanced, they are simple to follow and the monotony of single items tends to limit food intake.

Food Guide Pyramid. The Food Guide Pyramid provides an approach to evaluating the quality of your diet. At the bottom of the pyramid are the grains, beans, and starchy vegetables that provide vitamins, minerals, fiber, and energy; six or more servings are recommended. On the next level are the vegetables (3–5 servings) and the fruits (3–4 servings). On the third level are the meats, fish, poultry, and nuts (2–3 servings) along with the milk and yogurt (2–3 servings). At the top are the fats, sweets, and alcohol. Reducing the number of servings proportionally will provide you with a calorie-reduced diet. Most important for the dieter, however, is to sharply reduce the fats and sugar at the top of the pyramid and to reduce or eliminate alcoholic beverages. Not only do alcoholic beverages have calories, their consumption tends to reduce the individual's control in selecting the quality and quantity of foods to eat.

Changing behavioral patterns of eating. The basic principles of behavioral approaches for obesity can be summarized under the ABCs of eating.

- The A stands for antecedent. If one looks at eating as the response to events in the environment, then the antecedent events are those that trigger eating.

- The B stands for the behavior of eating. This includes among other things the place, the rate, and the frequency with which an individual eats. If the act of eating can be focused at one place with one plate and place setting it can help to provide control over eating.

- The C is the consequence of the eating. The feelings an individual has about eating can be altered, and rewards for changing eating patterns can be instituted.

Exercise and physical activity. The only part of energy expenditure that is amenable to significant manipulation is physical activity. During sleep, the lowest level of activity, approximately 0.8 kilocalories/minute is consumed. Thus, if an individual sleeps for an entire 24 hours, approximately 1,150 calories will be expended. Reclining increases this level to approximately 1.0-1.4 kilocalories/minute. Obese and diabetic patients should be encouraged to increase their physical activity for two reasons: First, it consumes calories, but second, and more important, exercise increases glucose utilization and may improve insulin sensitivity.

Drug treatment of obesity.   Only a few drugs have been approved by the Food and Drug Administration for treatment of obesity. Studies following individuals who have used these drugs for two years have been published for sibutramine (Meridia) and orlistat (Xenical). Weight-loss drugs should be reserved for patients with moderate- or high-risk obesity (BMI > 30 kg/m^2) or a BMI above 27 if they have other significant diseases related to obesity. They should be considered for the patient who has failed to lose weight with other methods. Herbal products containing ephedra and an herbal source of caffeine can also produce weight loss when used in accordance with the package instructions.

Surgery.   Gastric operations reduce the size of or bypass the stomach, but should be reserved for people with a BMI above 40 or when recommended by a physician.

The Obese Child

Estimates of the prevalence of obesity in children range from 3 to 15 percent. This figure has been rising more rapidly than in the rest of the population. The appearance of obesity in childhood and particularly adolescence is important because it most often persists into adult life. It may be a precursor to the appearance of type 2 diabetes in adolescents. The possibility of treatment should be considered for children who are above the seventy-fifth percentile of weight for height, and might be encouraged for those who are above the ninety-fifth percentile of weight for height. The treatment of prepubertal children should probably involve both parents and child since at this age the principal control of food availability is in the hands of the parents. For adolescents, however, it may be better to separate patient and parents, since the interaction between these groups may be part of the problem. Where growth has not reached its fullest extent, dietary restriction should attempt to reduce further weight gain. Severe caloric restriction and the use of appetite-suppressing drugs may slow height growth. For both children and adolescents, involvement in a regular exercise program is probably the first line of treatment.

See also **Anorexia, Bulimia; Body; Body Composition; Caloric Intake; Eating: Anatomy and Physiology of Eating; Fasting and Abstinence; Fats; Fiber, Dietary; Hunger, Physiology of.**

BIBLIOGRAPHY

Bessesen, D. H., and R. Kushner. *Evaluation and Management of Obesity.* Center for Obesity Research and Education. Philadelphia: Hanley and Belfus, 2002.

Bray, George A. *Contemporary Diagnosis and Management of Obesity.* Newtown, Pa.: Handbooks in Health Care, 1998.

National Heart, Lung, and Blood Institute (NHLBI). *Clinical Guidelines on the Identification, Evaluation, and Treatment of Overweight and Obesity in Adults.* Bethesda, Md., 1998.

Yanovski, J., and S. Z. Yanovski. "Obesity." *New England Journal of Medicine* 346, no. 8 (21 February 2002): 591–602.

George Bray

OCTOPUS. *See* **Mollusks.**

OIL.   Oil is liquid fat, usually plant-derived, used as a cooking medium, as a lubricant to keep food from sticking to pans, and as a source of flavor. Oil from animal sources, particularly fish oil, is also used as a nutritional supplement. Oil is also ubiquitous in processed foods.

The difference between oil and fat is that oil is liquid at room temperature while fat is solid. Chemically, both are composed of hydrocarbon chains and are potent sources of energy. The strong molecular bonds of fats and oils make them relatively resistant to heat and thus suitable for high-heat cooking methods such as deep-frying. Oil can be used in conjunction with other fats, such as butter, to raise the temperature of the other fat at which it would otherwise begin to break down and smoke.

History of Oil

Olive oil and sesame oils are among the most ancient oils in the Western world, dating back to 4,000 years or more. Olive trees are relatively simple to cultivate and, once the olives are prepared, the oil can be obtained by pressing. Both olive oil and sesame oil were used in southern Europe, while northern countries typically used animal fats such as lard or goose fat.

In the Orient, oil was pressed from soybeans, while sesame, mustard seed, and safflower oils were used in India and ancient Egypt. Peanuts, corn, and sunflower seeds were available in the New World, but oil was generally extracted only from squash seeds, especially squash belonging to the species *Cucurbita pepo*.

The nineteenth century saw the rise of international trade in tropical oils, particularly palm and coconut oil. The raw materials, which included hearts of palm and dried coconut meat (copra), were exported from Africa and the Pacific islands to industrial countries to be pressed for oil. The vast production of corn in the United States provided a source of oil to be used in cooking and in the manufacture of oleomargarine.

Olive oil is one of the major culinary oils employed in the Mediterranean region. This home-pressed oil is being bottled for private use at Dolcedo, Italy. © OWEN FRANKEN/CORBIS.

In nineteenth-century Africa, both the French and British introduced larger-scale peanut farming specifically for peanut oil, which was used as an adulterant in cheap grades of olive oil, and as a base ingredient in soap.

Composition of Oils

Oils, like other fats, consist mostly of triglycerides, which are three fatty acids attached to a molecule of glycerol (an alcohol built around three atoms of carbon). A fatty acid consists of a carboxyl group (carbon, oxygen, and hydrogen linked together), which in turn is linked to a hydrocarbon chain. The more the hydrocarbon chain is filled with hydrogen atoms, the more chemically stable it will be. A fatty acid fully loaded with hydrogen is said to be "saturated," while a less hydrogen-rich acid is "monounsaturated" or "polyunsaturated," depending on its structure. Oleic acid is a common monounsaturated fat, while linoleic acid is the most common polyunsaturated fatty acid.

The more saturated a fat is, the more likely it is to be solid at room temperature (such as lard or shortening). Oils are liquid because they are less saturated than fats. They are also less shelf-stable because their chemical structures are more likely to be affected by exposure to oxygen, causing them to become rancid or develop off-flavors. To make the product more stable, food processors pump hydrogen through the oil to fill in the gaps in its chemical structure, a process known as "hydrogenation." Highly hydrogenated oil is creamy or solid at room temperature, useful for making oleomargarine or other processed food products.

Oils generally have about the same caloric value of approximately 120 calories per tablespoon whether the fatty acids are saturated or not. More important to health-conscious consumers is the role of fatty acids in raising or lowering the presence in the bloodstream of the high-density lipoprotein (HDL) or low-density lipoprotein (LDL) associated with cholesterol. HDL (the "good cholesterol") is a beneficial substance that helps the body get rid of excess cholesterol, while LDL (the "bad cholesterol") builds up in the arteries and can increase the risk of heart disease. Eating foods high in monounsaturated fatty acids is believed to help lower LDL cholesterol levels and decrease the risk of heart disease, while the consumption of saturated fats may increase levels of LDL and total cholesterol. The consumption of polyunsaturated fats in place of saturated fats decreases LDL cholesterol levels. The American Heart Association recommends the consumption of oils that have no more than two grams of saturated fat per tablespoon.

Unsaturated fat content is a major selling point for household oils. One of the major oils on the market, canola oil, was developed specifically to appeal to consumers concerned about fat content. Canola—short for "Canadian oil"—is a variety of the rapeseed plant developed in Canada with less fatty acid than the traditional variety and thus a lower level of saturated fat than most other oils.

The chemical structure of oils makes them relatively stable at high temperatures, but at some point oil begins to break down and give off smoke; beyond this point there is danger of fire. The smoke point for most oils is around 410°F (210ºC), although some oils have even higher smoke points. The smoke point gets lower as oil is re-used due to degradation of chemical bonds and contamination of the oil with food particles. Commercial operations that re-use oil will pass it through a filter to take out the contaminants.

Sources of Oil

In addition to olives, oil is obtained from legumes such as peanuts and soybeans; from the seeds of many plants, including corn, rapeseed (canola), sesame, cottonseed, sunflower, palm, safflower, coconut, grapeseed, mustard, pumpkin, and avocado; and from tree nuts such as wal-

TABLE 1

Smoke Points of Common Oils

Oil	Smoke point (degrees F)
Sunflower	392
Olive	410
Corn	410
Peanut	410
Soybean	410
Cottonseed	435
Avocado	435
Canola	437
Grapeseed	446

SOURCE: *The Simon and Schuster Pocket Guide to Oils, Vinegars, and Seasonings*

TABLE 2

Fat Content of Major Household Oils

Oil	Calories per tablespoon	Saturated fatty acids (grams per tablespoon)	Polyunsaturated fatty acids (grams per tablespoon	Monounsaturated fatty acids (grams per tablespoon)
Olive	119.3	1.8	1.1	9.9
Corn	120.2	1.7	8.0	3.3
Canola	123.8	1.0	4.1	8.2
Peanut	119.3	2.3	4.3	6.2
Sesame	120.2	1.9	5.7	5.4
Soybean	120.2	2.0	8.0	3.2
Soybean, hydrogenated	120.2	2.0	5.1	5.8
Sunflower, 70% oleic and over	123.8	1.4	0.5	11.7
Sunflower, less than 60% linoleic	120.2	1.4	5.5	5.5
Sunflower, 60% linoleic and over	120.2	1.4	8.9	2.6
Sunflower, linoleic, hydrogenated	120.2	1.8	4.9	6.3
Grapeseed	120.2	1.3	9.5	2.2
Cottonseed	120.2	3.5	7.1	2.4
Safflower, over 70% linoleic	120.2	0.8	10.1	1.9
Almond	120.2	1.1	2.4	9.5
Rice bran	120.2	2.7	4.8	5.3
Avocado	123.8	1.6	1.9	9.9
Palm	120.2	6.7	1.3	5.0
Fish oil, menhaden, fully hydrogenated *	112.7	11.9	0.00	0.00

Unlike oils from plant sources, fish oil contains cholesterol. Fully hydrogenated menhaden oil contains 62.5 milligrams of cholesterol per tablespoon.

SOURCE: U.S. Department of Agriculture, Agricultural Research Service. 2001. USDA Nutrient Database for Standard Reference, Release 14. Nutrient Data Laboratory Home Page, http://www.nal.usda.gov/fnic/foodcomp.

nuts, almonds, hazelnuts, and pistachios. Tree nut oils are usually expensive and do not respond well to high heat, so they are used primarily to dress salads or to add flavor to baked goods.

The finest oils are simply extracted from the raw material (such as olives or nuts) by pressure. This is called "cold pressed" or "first pressed" oil. Oil that remains bound up in the raw material can be extracted by heat or chemical solvents.

Oils labeled by specific names, such as peanut oil, are obtained from those particular plants; a product labeled merely "vegetable oil" is a blend of various oils. In the production of vegetable oils, seeds are cracked, cooked, and run through a press to extract readily obtainable oil. The pulp is further processed to obtain the rest of the oil, which is neutral and tasteless; if flavor is desired, the oil can be mixed with the product of the first pressing to restore flavor and color.

Uses of Oil

Oil has a variety of uses in cooking, most of them based on its ability to transfer heat to the food while remaining stable itself. Asian food is often stir-fried in a little hot oil, just enough to keep the food from sticking to the pan. Chicken can be sautéed or fricasseed in a few tablespoons of oil, while pieces of breaded fish can be fried in shallow oil—perhaps a quarter of an inch deep.

Frying large pieces of food in deep oil requires a temperature of 350° to 375°F (177° to 191°C). At that temperature, the hot oil will sear the surface of the food being fried, trapping moisture within the food. The food thus cooks in its own moisture rather than in the oil, which is why properly fried food is not greasy. Greasiness results from frying at a temperature lower than optimal.

In Italy, olive oil is used as a dipping sauce for bread at the table. Olive oil is preferred as a salad dressing because it has its own flavor to contribute to the dish.

In food manufacturing, oils are used in a host of products, ranging from soups and gravies, salad dressings, bread and rolls, and fried foods to nondairy toppings and frozen desserts, coffee creamers and cocoa mixes, candy bars and cakes, and in most processed snack foods.

Fish Oil

Some species of fish such as Atlantic menhaden have high levels of certain essential fatty acids, called omega-3 fatty acids, which the human body is not able to synthesize by itself and must obtain from food. Oil made from these fish is sold as a nutritional supplement. Menhaden oil is used in the production of margarine and shortening in Europe and has been approved for use in the United States.

See also **Butter**; **Cooking**; **Fats**; **Fish**; **Frying**; **Snacks**.

BIBLIOGRAPHY

Lane, Mark, and Judy Ridgway. *The Simon and Schuster Pocket Guide to Oil, Vinegars, and Seasonings.* New York: Simon and Schuster, 1990.

McGee, Harold. *On Food and Cooking: The Science and Lore of the Kitchen.* New York: Fireside Books, 1984.

Pehaut, Yves. "The Invasion of Foreign Foods." In *Food: A Culinary History from Antiquity to Present*, edited by Jean-Loius Flandrin and Massimo Montanari, pp. 457–463. New York: Penguin Books, 1999.

Tannahill, Reay. *Food in History.* New York: Three Rivers Press, 1988.

Richard L. Lobb

ONIONS AND OTHER *ALLIUM* PLANTS. *Allium* crops have been cultivated for millennia by people worldwide for sustenance, flavor, and medicinal purposes. Each of these three properties is closely connected to a suite of unique organosulfur compounds present in *Allium* crops that make them distinct from other wild and cultivated food plants. These compounds impart the characteristic flavors and odors of edible alliums. A substantial body of scientific literature suggests that these organosulfur compounds likely arose through natural selection for pest resistance. In a fortuitous circumstance, humans find these odors and flavors appealing, thus what confers functional significance to the *Allium* crop for its survival also confers culinary significance to the *Allium* consumer for gastronomic pleasure.

Seven major allium crop complexes are recognized, five of which contain a single allium crop (Table 1). These five are bunching onion (*fistulosum*), chives (*schoenoprasum*), Chinese chives (*tuberosum*), garlic (*sativum*), and rakkyo (*chinense*). The remaining two complexes contain four separate crops (leek, kurrat, great-headed garlic, and pearl onion) in the case of *ampeloprasum* and two different crops (onion and shallot) in the case of *cepa*. Each of these crops represents a unique modification of the leaf. In the allium crops where bulbs are prominent, leaf bases are swollen due to the accumulation of carbohydrates from photosynthesis. In those crops where pseudostems are the edible portion, overlapping leaf bases form a hollow column that has the appearance of a stem, such as the base of the leek. For other allium crops the edible portion is the leaf blade, which also serves as the primary photosynthetic organ. These seven crop complexes are grown and consumed worldwide for a multiplicity of uses.

TABLE 1

The seven primary edible allium crop complexes

Species Complex	Crop	Variety	Storage Organs
cepa	bulb onion shallot	cepa ascolonicum	foliage leaf bases and bladeless leaf sheaths
fistulosum	bunching onion	NA	foliage leaf bases, bulbs absent
schoenoprasum	chives	NA	foliage leaf bases, bulbs absent
tuberosum	Chinese chives	NA	rhizomes, bulbs absent
ampeloprasum	leek kurrat great-headed garlic pearl onion	porrum kurrat holmense sectivum	bulbs generally absent, cloves like garlic in great-headed garlic and pearl onion; pseudostem in leek and kurrat
sativum	garlic	sativum	swollen, bladeless sheaths (cloves)
chinense	rakkyo	NA	swollen, foliage leaf bases, bulbs prominent

NA = not applicable

SOURCE: Brewster, 1994, as redrawn from Jones and Mann, 1963

Taxonomic History

The genus *Allium* contains more than five hundred species, including many ornamental and edible plants. The genus has been assigned to the family Alliaceae, although for many years it was classified with both the Amarylidaceae and the Liliaceae. Edible alliums are important staples in the diets of many of the world's cultures. Most of the edible alliums are native to the mountains of central Asia, and a number of alliums are still collected from the wild in this region. Distribution of *Allium* crops ranges widely throughout the Northern Hemisphere and in mountainous regions of the tropics. The area of greatest diversity is the mountains of central Asia, including Afghanistan, Tajikistan, Pakistan, and parts of Siberia and China.

Many edible alliums are classified into two subgenera, *Rhizirideum* and *Allium*. In subgenus *Rhizirideum* the sections Cepa, Schoenoprasum, and Rhizirideum are comprised of the species *cepa*, *fistulosum*, *schoenoprasum*, and *tuberosum*. In the subgenus *Allium* the section Allium is comprised of the species *ampeloprasum*, *sativum*, and *chinense* (Hanelt, 1990; Brewster, 1994). Together these seven species contain the primary edible alliums consumed throughout the world. G. R. Fenwick and A. B. Hanley (1985) also describe a number of other minor alliums consumed as vegetables or herbs, including the topset onion, the tree onion, the Wakegi onion, and others. These minor alliums are primarily from the *Allium cepa* group and are discussed in some detail in Henry A. Jones and Louis K. Mann's *Onions and Their Allies* (1963).

The topset onion, tree onion, and Egyptian topset onion (*A. cepa* subvarieties *viviparum*, *bulbiferum*, and *proliferum* respectively) form bulbils in their inflorescences. Bulbils are small, bulblike structures used as vegetative propagules for these alliums.

Crop Histories

Onion and shallot. The wild progenitor of onion is not known, although P. Hanelt (1990) and M. J. Havey (1995) have suggested it may be *Allium vavilovii*. Bulb onion was domesticated from a plant that likely had a long juvenile phase and grew as a perennial. Selection pressure during domestication was for larger bulbs that grew more rapidly, a biennial life cycle that concentrated vegetative growth into one season, and barriers to crossing with other wild species (Brewster, 1994). The cultivated *Allium cepa* has been placed into two horticultural groups by Hanelt (1990), the Common Onion group and the Aggregatum group. The Common Onion group includes the typical bulb onion, while the Aggregatum group consists of those subspecies or varieties of *A. cepa* whose lateral buds have been active, thereby forming clusters of smaller bulbs. These types of *A. cepa* have been further subdivided into multiplier or potato onions and shallots. Multiplier onions may possess as many as twenty small bulbs that are short and wide, whereas shallots form clusters of smaller, narrow separate bulbs (Jones and Mann, 1963). Most of the plants in the Aggregatum group are vegetatively propagated for horticultural use. Aggregatum group crops are found at extreme northern latitudes, such as Finland and Russia, and also in the tropics, but for different reasons. The short life cycle of Aggregatum group crops favors the short growing season in northern latitudes, whereas the intense pest pressure of tropical environments favors a short-season crop that can be grown from a vegetative propagule rather than from seed (Brewster, 1994).

Onion plants form bulbs in response to specific day lengths and temperatures. This photoperiodic response includes two primary categories, long day and short day. The long-day onion plant requires a day length of at least fourteen hours (actually a night length of less than ten hours) to initiate bulb formation, while short day onion plants require between twelve and fourteen hours of day length to form bulbs. Long-day onions are grown in the northern latitudes, often from seed or transplants sown in early spring. Bulb formation takes place during the summer months, and bulb harvest is during the later summer and the fall. The short-day onion is grown in warmer climates, where it may be sown in the fall and overwintered in the field. Bulb formation is in the spring, and harvest is in early summer.

Long-day onions were cultivated in Europe for many centuries and adapted to northern latitudes. Like many root vegetables developed for consumption during winter months in cold climates, these long-day onions were harvested in late summer and fall and stored at cold tem-

peratures. For this reason these cultivars or landraces became known as storage onions. Populations of storage onions developed in England and other parts of northern Europe and in the early seventeenth century were taken to the New World, where they were planted in the area around Salem, Massachusetts (Goldman et al., 2000). Selection for proper bulb formation and storability led to the development of popular cultivars, such as the Danvers Yellow Globe, which became a progenitor population for virtually all long-day storage onions in the United States during the nineteenth and twentieth centuries.

Short-day onions were cultivated in the Middle East and in many southern European countries for centuries, and immigrants from Italy and Spain brought these cultivars and landraces to the United States in the late nineteenth century (Goldman et al., 2000). The first southern European onions in the United States were likely the

Giant-sized onions became popular toward the end of the nineteenth century, due in part to the fame of the Giant Zittau onion of Germany. Burpee's Giant Gibraltar onion was an attempt to breed an American counterpart to that highly successful variety. Chromolithographic advertisement from a Burpee seed catalog. © CYNTHIA HART DESIGNER/CORBIS.

Topsetting onions are also called Egyptian onions, tree onions, and Catawissa onions. Contrary to popular belief, they are not from Egypt, and began to appear in English and American kitchen gardens only in the 1790s. They were highly valued for their early spring greens and for the bulbils shown here, which were used like pearl onions in pickles. Zammit-Havermann Garden, Toronto, Canada. PHOTO ROB CARDILLO.

Bermuda types, which originated in Italy and were first grown in the United States in southern Texas. The second type of onion introduced from southern Europe was the Babosa onion from Valencia, Spain, which was likely introduced early in the twentieth century. Fabian Garcia's early breeding work at the New Mexico Agricultural Experiment Station developed the Early Grano onion, an important progenitor of many of the sweet, mild onions grown in the southern United States (Brewster, 1994; Goldman et al., 2000). These onions were further selected into a number of important populations, including the Texas Early Grano and Granex series, which are important short-day onions in the U.S. market.

Garlic. Garlic almost certainly originated in the mountains of central Asia. Although its exact progenitor is unknown, it may be *A. longicuspis*. For thousands of years garlic has been propagated by asexual means because fer-

tile flowers were extremely rare. At the end of the twentieth century several reports of fertile garlic clones, both in the wild and in cultivation, initiated intense interest in seed propagation of garlic, which appears to be a realistic proposition (Pooler and Simon, 1994). Seed production is important for several reasons, including the possibility of reducing the spread of viral diseases by going through a reproductive phase and the potential for breeding garlic for improved characteristics. Despite the fact that little to no sexual reproduction of garlic has taken place under cultivation, much phenotypic variation exists among cultivars, likely due to the selection of interesting and favorable mutants.

Leek, kurrat, great-headed garlic, and pearl onion. The *ampeloprasum* group includes four primary crops, all of which can be freely crossed and interbred. Wild *A. ampeloprasum* is found in a broad geographic range that includes western Iran through the Mediterranean to Portugal (Brewster, 1994).

The leek group is characterized by the development of a pseudostem, which is actually the edible part of the leek plant. The pseudostem is so called because the concentric overlapping leaf bases fold over each other to create a hollow stemlike structure, although botanically the edible portion of the leek is not a stem. Leeks are well adapted to cool climates and are grown throughout northern Europe. Unlike bulb onions, leeks do not have specific photoperiodic requirements for pseudostem formation and can thus be grown in a wide range of latitudes.

The kurrat group includes those *A. ampeloprasum* selected for edible leaves and short pseudostems. The crop is popular in Egypt, where the leaves are repeatedly cut and harvested every three to four weeks over an eighteen-month period (Brewster, 1994).

The great-headed garlic group includes plants that form large cloves similar to garlic cloves, however the inflorescence is large and leeklike. Called elephant garlic by many commercial growers, it typically is much larger than a garlic plant and can produce up to six large cloves at the base of the flower stalk. When the plant does not flower, only a single large clove, known as a "round," is produced.

Pearl onion is a minor *Allium* crop grown in certain parts of Europe. The plant forms a cluster of small, spherical, white-skinned bulbs. In the United States, products marketed as pearl onion may in fact be small bulbs of *A. cepa* rather than the true pearl onion. Among U.S. horticulturists, the true pearl onion is often called Portuguese leek.

Bunching onion. The bunching onion has been the primary *Allium* crop in many parts of Asia for millennia and is still a major component in the diet in China and Japan. Bunching onions appear similar to bulb onions during early growth stages, but bunching onions do not form bulbs and instead are harvested for their green foliage.

Allium fistulosum may derive from the wild *Allium altaicum*, which grows in the mountains of southern Siberia and Mongolia and is interfertile with *A. fistulosum*.

In the U.S. market the consumer is usually presented with green onions or scallions that are likely the bulb onion *A. cepa* harvested for its green foliage. It is also possible that these green onions were produced from an interspecific hybrid between *A. cepa* and *A. fistulosum* known as "Beltsville Bunching" that has been a mainstay of bunching onion production in the United States for more than fifty years. Thus the green onions or bunching onions in the U.S. market may be of several different genetic backgrounds.

Bunching onion cultivars have been developed for a variety of market classes. These classes are primarily separated by the geographic areas in which the plants can be grown and by the quality of the foliage. Certain consumers prefer blanched pseudostems instead of green pseudostems. Cultivation of the former is accomplished by mounding soil on the developing plants, thereby reducing the amount of chlorophyll and producing a more tender, lighter-colored pseudostem.

Rakkyo. This allium crop is grown mainly in Japan and China, where it produces small bulbs that are mostly consumed pickled. The plants resemble chives but develop elongated bulbs in the summer.

Chives. Chives, which grows wild in Eurasia and in America, is the most widely distributed allium species. It is extremely cold hardy and is winter dormant, and it can grow in latitudes as high as 70° (Brewster, 1994). Chives form a cluster of low-growing, narrow, hollow leaves. After every two or three leaves have formed, axillary buds form side shoots that then allow for the development of a cluster of shoots (Brewster, 1994). The shoots are attached to each other on a rhizome.

Chinese chives. *Allium tuberosum* grows wild in East Asia and is cultivated for its garlic-flavored leaves and immature flowers. It forms rhizomes similar to those of chives, and the leaves arise as dense clumps from these rhizomes (Brewster, 1994). Unlike true chives, which has a hollow stem, the leaves of Chinese chives are flat.

Chemical Constituents and Culinary Significance

The word "allium" derived from the Greek phrase "to leap out," thereby suggesting a strong interaction between the crop and its consumer. Worldwide the edible alliums are prized for their unique flavors. These flavors are derived from a suite of unique organosulfur compounds that likely have their origin as a defense strategy, protecting allium plants from pests. Although they possess some toxicity for insect and microbial pests, their levels of toxicity for humans and larger animals is far less and in most cases nonexistent. Several exceptions exist, however, and these are discussed under the pharmacological properties of allium crops below.

Like all plants, alliums uptake the necessary element sulfur as sulfate from the soil. Sulfate is then used to form the amino acids cysteine and glutathione, which in turn form the gamma glutamyl peptides. These peptides serve as building blocks for the allium flavor precursors, known collectively as the alk(en)yl-L-cysteine sulfoxides or ACSOs. The ACSOs are present in the mesophyll storage cells, inside the cell's cytoplasm. Each allium crop is characterized by a different number and ratio of these ACSOs, which ultimately determine its flavor. For example, onion contains three ACSOs, while garlic contains four. The balance of these ACSOs in onion and garlic are different, resulting in flavor differences between the vegetables. Knowing the ACSO profile can help predict the flavor of an allium, because they are directly responsible for the flavor components as described below.

The ACSOs are considered flavor precursors because they do not impart flavors directly. Rather, it is only upon tissue disruption that allium crops yield their unique flavors and odors. This is accomplished through a chemical reaction that begins when the enzyme alliinase, stored in the bundle sheath cells and protected from the ACSOs by a membrane, comes into contact with the ACSOs after tissues are cut. Thus the scent of an unchopped onion bulb is completely different from the scent after tissues have been chopped, because the enzymatic lysis of the ACSOs initiates the development of the thiosulfinates, which are actually responsible for allium flavors.

As soon as allium tissues are disrupted, such as by a kitchen knife, the transient sulfenic acids are formed as well as the by-product pyruvic acid. Pyruvic acid has been used extensively as an indirect measure of onion pungency because the amount of enzymatically formed pyruvate is positively correlated significantly with a taste perception of pungency (Wall and Corgan, 1992). In all alliums except onions the sulfenic acids are rapidly converted into thiosulfinates, which are the compounds responsible for the flavors of allium vegetables. This conversion also takes place in onions, however, immediately prior to thiosulfinate formation, the compound propanethiol sulfoxide is formed. Propanethiol sulfoxide, also known as the lachrymatory factor, is responsible for the formation of tears in the eyes of those close enough to the chopped onion to intercept the airborne compound. Presumably the formation of tears is caused by the interaction of this sulfur compound with the eye's nerve cell membrane, causing the formation of sulfuric acid.

Thiosulfinate accumulation in crushed or cut allium tissues is perceived by the nose, the eyes, the tongue, and the skin. Because allium crops contain different ACSOs, they also contain different kinds and amounts of thiosulfinates, which in turn leads to different flavors. Thiosulfinate formation at room temperature is complete after thirty minutes (Thomas and Parkin, 1994). Chopped allium tissues therefore have differential thiosulfinate profiles depending upon the length of time they have been allowed to sit and the temperature at which they have been prepared.

Typically most consumers process cut alliums by boiling or by frying or sautéing in oil. These two processes yield different by-products. Boiling chopped garlic results in the formation of various sulfides, including diallyl disulfide and diallyl trisulfide. Sautéing in oil produces the vinyl dithiins and ajoene (Lawson, 1998). The transformation of sulfur compounds into thiosulfinates and downstream reactions that transform the thiosulfinates into sulfides and dithiins is an area of great interest and investigation in the allium research community.

Biology of Vegetable Alliums

Most of the edible alliums possess some variation of the leaf that creates their vegetable form. Those that form bulbs do so because the base of the leaf begins to swell with carbohydrates from photosynthesis. The concentric swollen leaf bases make up the structure of the onion bulb. Similarly the swollen leaf base and its protective leaf sheath make up the clove that is a part of the garlic bulb. Thus the bulb is nothing more than fleshy leaves or leaf bases on top of a short, flattened stem. Those alliums that form a pseudostem, such as leek, do so because the overlapping leaf bases form a hollow stemlike structure. These leaf bases do not swell but make up the edible portion of the crop just the same. And of course those vegetable alliums that are consumed for their leaf blades typically do not form swollen structures such as bulbs. In all cases a short, flattened stem is found under these leaf bases. It is likely that this stem has been shortened during the evolution of these allium crops, resulting in larger and more-prominent leaf bases and storage tissues.

These many variations on leaf morphology illustrate an important principle of crop domestication. Many of our most important crop plants occur in complexes where multiple morphological forms of a single species have been selected by humans to serve a variety of different needs. For example, the crop species in the *Brassica oleracea* complex, including cabbage, broccoli, cauliflower, kale, collards, and Brussels sprouts, all possess variations that partition their photosynthate into different storage organs. In the case of cabbage the photosynthate is stored in leaf tissue packed into a compact rosette. In the case of Brussels sprouts the axillary buds are activated, and smaller headlike structures become the item of commerce. In the case of broccoli photosynthates are partitioned into the thickened stem and immature inflorescence. Similar to allium crops, the variations in morphology serve the purpose of producing different crops for different uses. Among cultivated plants the alliums are unique in that their multiplicity of forms is based on how and where the photosynthate is partitioned in the leaf.

Another unique biological feature of the alliums is the presence of bulbils in the inflorescence. Bulbils are simply small bulblike structures that form in leaf axils, particularly in the inflorescence, of many allium crops. Bulbils are also comprised of leaf tissue but are not formed from swollen leaf bases as onion and garlic bulbs are. Rather, they represent a unique form of propagule from which alliums can be vegetatively propagated in a clonal fashion. The presence of bulbils in the inflorescence can also be a diagnostic character for differentiating alliums. They are common in garlic, are not present at all in Chinese chives and rakkyo, and occasionally are present in leek and kurrat.

Pharmacological Properties

> And if the boy have not a woman's gift to rain
> a shower of commanded tears,
> An onion will do for such a shift,
> which in a napkin being close conveyed,
> Shall in despite enforce a watery eye.

(William Shakespeare, *The Taming of the Shrew*, cited in Block, 1992)

Alliums may have been cultivated originally for their medicinal properties and only later developed into flavorants, although it is possible these two discoveries occurred simultaneously or in close proximity. Many of the most common vegetable crops, such as lettuce, tomato, and others, were originally used as medicinal plants prior to their widespread use as food (Rubatzky and Yamaguchi, 1997).

The Egyptians made extensive use of alliums to treat a variety of ailments, many of which are recorded in the Codex Ebers, a document at least 3,500 years old (Block, 1985). Documentation of their use in ayurvedic medicine in India, Western-style medicine in Greece, and Eastern-style medicine in China abounds (Lawson, 1998). Evidence also indicates that early Olympic athletes were fed alliums to promote blood circulation and to attain peak performance and that Europeans have used alliums to treat blood clots in horses and other domestic animals for many centuries (Block, 1985, 1992). Alliums were important in warding off plague and other microbial infections over the centuries (Lawson, 1998) and in treating dysentery, smallpox, and many other maladies during the twentieth century. Indeed edible alliums have been more widely used than many synthetic medicines for an incredibly diverse array of conditions.

The rising importance of synthetic, mono-molecular drugs during the twentieth century, particularly in the United States, resulted in a dearth of interest in naturally derived whole foods as medicines during that period. However, in the last decade of the century many people in the West became increasingly interested in the potential health functionality of food. In fact many consumers began to purchase food for these very properties (Sloan, 2000). The folkloric documentation of these crops as curatives is highly informative with respect to the potential health functionality of alliums in the diet. Many properties mentioned in this way have been partially confirmed by modern medical investigation.

Historically allium crops have been used to treat a wide range of ailments, but the most prominent has been cardiovascular disease. Within the rubric of this disease, allium intake has been associated with significant reductions in blood pressure, cholesterol, and platelet aggregation (Block, 1992). Reductions in each of these parameters have been measured in clinically relevant feeding trials (Lawson, 1998), suggesting the potential for dietary intervention with edible alliums for cardiovascular disease. The antiplatelet, or antiothrombotic, potential of onions appears to be quite potent in vivo following onion administration in canines (Briggs et al., 2000).

Significant applications also have been noted for the antimicrobial property of allium extracts, which extends to bacteria, fungi, and viruses; reductions in carcinogenesis; reductions in blood sugar and increases in insulin; and general antioxidant activity (Lawson, 1998). For many of these properties the thiosulfinates have been implicated as the suspected causal agents, although much work is required to determine the involvement of other compounds with significant potential for biological activity. One such example is the flavonoids, which are present in high concentrations in colored onion tissues and have significant potential as antioxidants, show reductions in tumorigenesis, and remain at relatively high levels following thermal processing. Among the most prominent flavonoid in onions is the flavonol known as quercetin, which has shown great promise as an in vivo antioxidant and platelet inhibitor but less promising results when studied in vivo (Janssen et al., 1998).

It is important that the conversion of the ACSOs into thiosulfinates is enzymatically controlled. Therefore this reaction may be significantly hindered by cooking. Furthermore the thiosulfinates are volatile compounds that are likely altered and possibly reduced in concentration with thermal processing. For these reasons evaluation of the above-mentioned medicinal properties in feeding studies with cooked alliums are important in determining the extent of the health implications of dietary alliums.

Nutritional Components and Utilization

The dry matter content of many allium vegetables is in the range of 7 to 15 percent, with the exception of the 35 to 50 percent dry matter found in garlic (Brewster, 1994). Approximately 1 to 2 percent is protein, 0.2 percent is fat, and 5 to 12 percent is carbohydrates. Garlic bulbs may contain up to 6 percent protein. The caloric value is approximately 35 calories per 100 grams but is much higher for garlic. Onion contains a variety of secondary compounds, such as flavonols, anthocyanin pigments, sterols, and saponins (Brewster, 1994).

Just as in ancient times, onion growing is still a specialized branch of farming. This onion farmer in Costa Rica is grading the onions in her barn. © CARL & ANN PURCELL/CORBIS.

A large number of processed products are made from vegetable alliums, and these find their way into a wide array of processed foods. Concentrated oils are produced from steam distillation of fresh onion and garlic, and these are used to deliver onion or garlic flavor to processed foods. Dehydrated products make up a sizable portion of the onion and garlic processing industry. Dehydration requires fairly low temperatures due to the potential for carmelization under high heat. The fresh product is ultimately dried to 4 percent moisture. The resultant dried flakes can be further ground into powder and mixed with salt and calcium stearate to produce onion or garlic salt. In a number of countries, particularly in Asia, pickled allium bulbs are consumed. These are produced in a fermentation process and then bottled in vinegar and salt to make a sour pickle or vinegar and sugar to make a sweet pickle.

During the late twentieth century the popularity of mild, sweet onion bulbs rose dramatically in many markets around the world, indicating a desire for a less-pungent onion. Reduced pungency can be obtained through a combination of genetic backgrounds and favorable environments, in particular those soils where sulfur supply is low or is deliberately reduced. As discussed above, since the flavor pathway in alliums begins with the uptake of sulfate, high levels of soil sulfur can result in the production of more pungent onion bulbs (Randle et al., 1995). Only certain short-day onion cultivars grown in the southern United States have made significant inroads into the consumer market as a sweet or mild product, and these are not available year round in many markets. Since the accumulation and partitioning of sulfur and organosulfur compounds in alliums is not fully understood, it is difficult to predict the potential for mild onion cultivars in other market classes.

See also **Vegetables**.

BIBLIOGRAPHY

Block, E. "The Chemistry of Garlic and Onions." *Scientific American* 252 (1985): 114–119.

Block, E. "The Organosulfur Chemistry of the Genus *Allium*: Implications for Organic Sulfur Chemistry." *Angewande Chemie*, International Edition, English. 31 (1992): 1135–1178.

Brewster, J. L. *Onions and Other Vegetable Alliums*. Wallingford, U.K.: CAB International, 1994.

Briggs, W. H., J. D. Folts, H. E. Osman, and Irwin L. Goldman. "Administration of raw onion inhibits platelet-mediated thrombosis in dogs." *Journal of Nutrition* 131 (2001): 2619–2622.

Fenwick, G. R., and A. B. Hanley. "The Genus *Allium*." *Critical Reviews of Food Science and Nutrition* 22 (1985): 1199–1271.

Goldman, Irwin L., G. Schroeck, and M. J. Havey. "History of Public Onion Breeding Programs in the United States." *Plant Breeding Reviews* 20 (2000): 67–103.

Hanelt, P. "Taxonomy, Evolution, and History." In *Onions and Allied Crops*, edited by Haim D. Rabinowitch and James L. Brewster, 1–26. Boca Raton, Fla.: CRC Press, 1990.

Havey, M. J. "Onion and Other Cultivated Alliums." In *Evolution of Crop Plants*, edited by J. Smartt and N. W. Simmonds, 2d ed., pp. 344–350. New York: Wiley, 1995.

Janssen, P. L. T. M., et al. "Effects of the Flavonoids Quercetin and Apigenin on Hemostasis in Healthy Volunteers: Results from an in Vitro and a Dietary Supplement Study." *American Journal of Clinical Nutrition* 67 (1998): 255–262.

Jones, Henry A., and Louis K. Mann. *Onions and Their Allies*. New York: Interscience Publishers, 1963.

Lawson, L. D. "Garlic: A Review of Its Medicinal Effects and Indicated Active Compounds." In *Phytomedicines of Europe*, edited by L. D. Lawson and R. Bauer, 176–209. American Chemical Society Symposium Series, no. 691. Washington, D.C.: American Chemical Society, 1998.

Pooler, M. R., and P. W. Simon. "True Seed Production in Garlic." *Sexual Plant Reproduction* 7 (1994): 282–286.

Randle, W. M., et al. "Quantifying Onion Flavor Compounds Responding to Sulfur Fertility: Sulfur Increases Levels of Alk(en)yl-cysteine Sulfoxides and Biosynthetic Intermedi-

ates." *Journal of the American Society for Horticultural Science* 120 (1995): 1075–1081.

Rubatzky, Vincent E., and Mas Yamaguchi. *World Vegetables*. 2d ed. New York: Chapman and Hall, 1997.

Sloan, A. E. "The Top Ten Functional Food Trends." *Food Technology* 54 (2000): 1–17.

Thomas, D. J., and K. L. Parkin. "Quantification of Alk(en)yl-L-Cysteine Sulfoxides and Related Amino Acids in Alliums by High-Performance Liquid Chromatography." *Journal of Agricultural and Food Chemistry* 42 (1994): 1632–1638.

Wall, M. M., and J. N. Corgan. "Relationship between Pyruvate Analysis and Flavor Perception for Onion Pungency Determination." *HortScience* 27 (1992): 1029–1030.

Irwin L. Goldman

ORGANIC AGRICULTURE. Organic agriculture originated as a response to a growing awareness that the health of the land is linked to the health and future of the people. It is a holistic and philosophical approach to agriculture, which has as its goals the protection and conservation of the land for future generations, the production of high-quality food, the return to many traditional agricultural methods, and the harmonious balance with a complex series of ecosystems. Land, water, plants, animals, and people are all seen as interlinked and interdependent.

Definition

The final rule of the United States Department of Agriculture (USDA), which implements the Organic Foods Production Act of 1990, describes organic production as one which will "respond to site-specific conditions by integrating cultural, biological and mechanical practices that foster cycling of resources, promote ecological balance and conserve biodiversity." Organic agriculture promotes linkages and connections between land and water, plants and people. Soil fertility is enhanced through the use of composted waste to be generated at the farm site and recycled into it, multiple crops and rotations, a belief in the beneficial results of encouraging biodiversity through numerous species, and no use of synthetic fertilizers or pesticides. Further, stringent inspections, record keeping, and certifications are required to verify and maintain the organic status of the land and the food produced.

The terms "alternative," "sustainable," and "ecological" agriculture are also sometimes used, in place of organic, although not everyone believes that these terms are interchangeable. The European Union protects three terms: "organic," "ecological," and "biological" and abbreviations like "bio" and "eco" in all European Union languages. This is to prevent their use in a misleading or false manner. In the United States, the definition of organic agriculture by the National Organic Standards

Board is "an ecological production management system that promotes and enhances biodiversity, biological cycles and soil biological activity. It is based on the minimal use of off-farm inputs and on management practices that restore, maintain, and enhance ecological harmony."

Today, organic agriculture is practiced in almost every country in the world, and the amount of certified organic land is growing as well. The total area is more than 42 million acres worldwide. The bulk of the organic land (45 percent) is in Oceania; Europe has 25 percent; North America, almost 8 percent; and Latin America, 22 percent. The emphasis in organic agriculture is on sustainability, local resources, and the stewardship of the environment, as well as expanding its global impact beyond food supply and into ecological health. Economically, the International Trade Center estimates the world retail market for organic food and beverages increased from $10 billion in 1997 to $17.5 billion in 2000. Revenue distribution by 2001 is estimated to be at 46 percent in Europe and 37 percent in the United States.

History

At the beginning of the twentieth century, 39 percent of the United States population lived on farms, compared with less than 2 percent in 1990. Large land holdings were designed as federal lands to protect the natural environment and provide public access. Food quality, adequacy of supply, and public health were concerns. Issues with food quality led to the Pure Food and Drug Act of 1906. Extensive research was carried out to make plants disease resistant, and to improve yield. In the 1920s Rudolf Steiner, an extremely charismatic and complex individual, gave a series of eight lectures about agriculture that were the foundation of biodynamics, a concept in which all life forms and the land are in balance and combine with agriculture to address the health of the land with a spiritual dimension. By the 1930s hybrid seed corn had became common, and the devastation of the dust storms destroyed millions of acres of farmland in the Plains states. Two world wars had decimated farms and farmlands in much of Europe. Food supply for present and future populations was becoming a global concern. The vitality of the soil was seen by many as the key to a healthy future population.

Sir Albert Howard of England was one of the visionary leaders, if not the founder, of the organic agricultural movement in Europe. Philosophically, he linked the health of the land to the health of the people. Howard believed that agriculture as mainly practiced, with chemical fertilizers and a single crop, was out of balance with the environment and that many traditional agricultural practices should be revived. His major concern was for the health of the soil, which he felt could be maintained by a diversity of plant and animal crops, recycling of waste to enrich the soil, minimal depth in plowing, natural pest control, and smaller labor-intensive farms, emulating traditional methods.

Rows of parsnips, carrots, beets, and spinach are shown in these organic vegetable plots at Ryton, near Coventry, England. © MICHAEL BOYS/CORBIS.

By the 1940s, chemical fertilizers and pesticide and insecticide use had increased. However, a USDA report from the same time warned that insecticides were present in food and advocated the use of naturally occurring products as insecticides. Some believed that conservation practices like cover crops, crop rotation, strip planting, and contouring of the planting were critical to preserve the soil both by keeping it in place and by maintaining its fertility. At the same time, conventional farming was stressing yields, mechanization, and modern practices. In 1949, official guidance was issued from the U.S. government on how to appraise the toxicity of chemicals in foods.

In America, J. I. Rodale had founded *Organic Gardening Magazine* and the Soil and Health Foundation (now the Rodale Institute). Many credit him from the mid-1940s onward with promoting and supporting organic agriculture in America. He went on to create numerous publications and with his research and publishing delivered his core message of "healthy soil = healthy food = healthy people."

In 1959, the cranberry crop in the United States was recalled due to the presence of a cancer-causing chemical used to kill weeds. In 1962, Rachel Carson's work

Silent Spring had a massive impact: Many Americans, for the first time, saw the link between the loss of plant and animal populations and the use of pesticides. By that time organic farming was well established as an alternative approach. Further environmental activism in the 1970s made many aware of organic agriculture and organic foods.

Alice Waters opened her restaurant Chez Panisse in Berkeley in 1971 and has been a promoter and champion of quality ingredients, supporting growers who farm organically. Her influence in turn promoted and sustained many other organic growers. The fame and growing impact of Chez Panisse have affected chefs and the public alike. Numerous chefs today provide details about ingredients on their menu, and many base their entire approach to food on organic products.

Likewise, vegetarians have long focused on the quality of the ingredients in their diet. John and Karen Hess in their landmark book *The Taste of America* decried the quality of food in America in the 1970s, stating that "[t]he health food and organic movements and the counterculture generally, have made some small but enormously promising steps toward reviving the taste of our food. . . . They are our hope" (p. 298). Organic agriculture has slowly grown, spurred by various scares but hampered by the counterculture label. Reports and findings in the 1990s with regard to the effect of pesticides and chemicals in food on humans, particularly children (for example, the use of alar on apples), drove the increasing demand for organically produced food, which in turn spurred the growth of organic farms.

Application of Principles

Although many people associate organic agriculture primarily with fruits and vegetables, organic agricultural practices are applied effectively to all crops and animals. All crops—grains, citrus, nuts, fruits, herbs, vegetables, oilseeds like flax and sunflower, beans, cotton, grasses for pastureland—can reinforce a basic organic tenet: grow a variety of crops in a rotation system. Many people prefer organic agriculture because of its systemic approach that ties food production to ecology, and connects land, people, plants, and animals to a common goal, a healthy vital environment for all. Food produced organically is thought to be more flavorful, have higher nutritional values, be safer to eat, and be ecologically sound. Each food safety crisis, environmental scare, and dietary concern has increased the steadily growing pool of organic farmers and consumers.

The founders of the organic agricultural movement—Rodale, Balfour, and Howard, to name a few—passionately shared the belief that the health and vitality of the soil were key to the future of the land and food production. A fundamental principle of organic agriculture is that no synthetic fertilizers or pesticides are permitted. Complex ecosystems that encourage a rich diversity of plants, animals, and insects are considered

necessary for a viable and living soil. Composting, worms and beneficial insects in the environment, recycled farm wastes, use of manures, composts, ash, and crop residues contribute to the vitality of the soil, which in turn leads to healthy plants and animals. Further, organic agriculture addresses the broader environmental issues of pesticide and fertilizer residues, run-offs, and concentrations, which affect, not just the health of the organic farm system, but the ecosystems around it. The concept of balance between nature and human actions and stewardship of the land is integral to organic agriculture; in fact, it cannot be maintained otherwise. The inspection process leading to organic certification usually requires a minimum of three years in the United States (two years in the United Kingdom) to allow all traces of past land use practices to disappear. The first usable harvest follows the third year, assuming all other criteria are met for organic certification. This sizable commitment of resources is economically difficult and is one reason that many countries, although not the United States, have subsidies to help farmers certify their land for organic production.

Many feel strongly that organic foods, which are grown without synthetic pesticides, eliminate the concern for ingesting the residues or additives.

Organic Foods

Most consumers believe, and some studies have shown, that there are more nutrients and flavor in organic products. Generally, organic products are more costly than foods grown by conventional agriculture. They are more labor intensive and must meet much stricter regulation, and therefore the cost of organic foods reflects the cost of production. Organic agricultural practices, which utilize local resources and eliminate outside needs as much as possible, fit developing countries' needs very well as well as countries with food supply issues, for example, Cuba.

Cuba is considered one of the success stories of organic agriculture. Heavily dependent upon the Soviets for food and agricultural support, the collapse of the former USSR in 1989 left Cuba desperate for food. Overnight, supplies of synthetic fertilizers and pesticides and mechanized equipment all disappeared. Urban spaces were turned into gardens, plot sizes decreased, and organic practices were followed, as there was no alternative. The results have been dramatic, both in creating a new career for many and dramatically changing both the diet of the population and the appearance of Cuba. Now many people have access to fresh organic foods and unused land is turned to food production. Over one-half million tons of food were grown in Havana alone in 1998.

Before the 1990 Organic Foods Production Act, Title XXI of the Food, Agriculture, Conservation, and Trade Act of 1990, many state and other organizations certified organic production. The 1990 rules, published in December of 2000 after a decade in development, review, and revisions, set national standards for certification of agricultural products as organic. Certification for all but the smallest growers and compliance for all agricultural products sold under these standards must be completed by late 2002. Certain practices and types of substances, like synthetic fertilizers and pesticides, are prohibited. The use of the word "organic" is now nationally regulated. In the United States, a raw or processed product labeled "100 percent organic" must contain only organic ingredients, although it can contain water and salt; if labeled "organic" it must be at least 95 percent organic and if labeled "made with organic ingredients" it must have at least 70 percent organic ingredients. Both the "100 percent organic" and "organic" designations can use an approved "USDA Organic" seal and penalties can be levied if there is any deliberate misrepresentation.

Land under Organic Cultivation
In 1997, 1.3 million acres in forty-nine states were certified organic, and although this number had more than doubled in the 1990s, certified organic land still represents just 0.2 percent of all cultivated land (828 million acres). These totals include crop, range, and pasture lands. All indicators are that the amount of certified organic land is increasing rapidly, however. For example, in California, certified organic acreage increased by 38 percent between 1995 and 1997 and in Washington it increased by 150 percent between 1997 and 1999. The highest production crops that are certified organic are corn and wheat, although thirty-five states are producing a variety of certified organic grains. Tomatoes, lettuce, and carrots are the primary organic vegetables, with about 48,227 acres in organic vegetable production (in 1997); grapes produced on 39 percent of the acreage and apples on 18 percent of the certified organic farm land account for about 2 percent of the certified land that is devoted to producing these crops. Organic herbs are grown in thirty-two states; three states have certified specific land for harvesting wild herbs.

Prior to this national legislation for organic certification, organic land certification was given by over 40 organizations, which included twelve state programs. For example, California grew almost half of all certified organic vegetables in 1997; vegetable farming in Vermont, which has been promoting organics for 30 years, was 24 percent organic. Many states have started to develop incentives for organic conversion.

Sales
Most organic farms are about one-third the size of the conventional farm and average about 140 acres. Organic vegetables are generally grown on even smaller holdings, with the majority less than 10 acres in size. They are frequently marketed directly to the consumer primarily through farmers' markets and restaurant chefs, accounting for 3 percent of total organic sales. A very popular form of direct marketing is subscription farming, some-

times known as CSA, an innovative way of connecting the consumer directly with the farm and crop. In 1998, there were 2,746 farmers' markets operating in the United States. Natural food stores, long a source for all organic products, recorded sales of $4 billion in 1999, and an annual sales growth rate of at least 20 percent. Total retail sales of all organic products are estimated at $7.8 billion in 2000, and $833 million of fresh organic fruits and vegetables were sold in natural food stores in 1999.

Organic Agriculture Worldwide
On a global level, in Europe, Japan, the United States, and the United Kindom, retail organic food and beverage sales accounted for about 2 percent of the total, about $13 billion in 1998, with an anticipated annual growth rate of 20 percent.

In 2001, Canada reported of 246,923 farms, 2,230 produced certified organic products, and 614 of these, or 27.5 percent, produced fruits, vegetables, or greenhouse products. Nearly fifteen hundred farms, or 64.7 percent, reported organic field crops. In Canada, the formation of the Land Fellowship in Ontario in the 1950s provided the foundation of the organic farming movement. As in the United States, these early visionaries were joined in the 1970s by a host of individuals and organizations whose concerns for the environmental health of the planet made an immediate linkage to the principles of organic agriculture. Numerous organizations, like the Canadian Organic Advisory Board, which is composed of volunteers, promote and support organic agriculture in a variety of ways throughout the provinces. Canada's National Standard for Organic Agriculture is a voluntary standard for organic production, whose principles and practices focus on protection of environmental biodiversity, a comprehensive and systematic use of organic practices for the production of foods, and a verification process to ensure the standards are met.

Sir Albert Howard is not the only founder of the early organic movement in the United Kingdom to have a global impact. Lord Walter Northbourne is credited with creating the phrase "organic farming" in his 1940 book *Look to the Land*, and Lady Evelyn Balfour, whose book *The Living Soil* was based on years of comparative farming data, inspired many to support the principles of organic agriculture put forward by Howard. Lady Balfour was also involved in the founding of the Soil Association in the United Kingdom in 1946. The Soil Association remains an active advocacy group for organic standards. Throughout the United Kingdom, there is a wide range of organizations, government ministries, colleges, and research centers focused on research, education, advocacy, and sustaining organic agricultural practices. The first organic standards were published by the Soil Association. The group performs the majority of the inspections, although several other approved inspection groups also perform certification inspections.

In the United Kingdom there were 2,865 licensed organic farmers in production, or in conversion, in 2000, a dramatic increase from the 828 listed in 1997. In late 1999, 2 percent of all agricultural land (a little over 1 million acres) was farmed organically (fully organic or in conversion). Organic vegetable production value for 1999 was $28.8 million in the United Kingdom. Nearly half of the consumers interviewed said they bought organic produce for the taste.

The Food and Agricultural Organization of the United Nations (FAO) has published the *Codex Alimentarius* to establish global food standards and guidelines for organically produced foods. The FAO states:

> Foods should only refer to organic production methods if they come from an organic farm system employing management practices which seek to nurture ecosystems which achieve sustainable productivity and provide weed, pest and disease control though a diverse mix of mutually dependent life forms, recycling plant and animal residues, crop selection and rotation, water management, tillage, and cultivation. Soil fertility is maintained and enhanced by a system which optimizes soil biological activity and the physical and mineral nature of the soil as the means to provide a balanced nutrient supply for plant and animal life as well as to conserve soil resources. Production should be sustainable with the recycling of plant nutrients as an essential part of the fertilizing strategy. Pest and disease management is attained by means of the encouragement of a balanced host/predator relationship, augmentation of beneficial insect populations, biological and cultural control and mechanical removal of pests and affected plant parts.

In Europe, the European Union countries have a total of 10 million acres held in 145,113 organic farms, which represent about 2 percent of farms and about 3 percent of the farming acreage. This figure represents a rapid rate of growth, about 25 percent over the last ten years in European Union member countries. For example, as of 2001, France had over 10,000 organic farms, an increase of 12 percent from the previous year. Ongoing research in organic agriculture is being conducted in most countries, and some have adopted educational programs that support the organic farmers as well as the consumers. Uniformity of standards and dissemination of research are critical to the future of organic agriculture. The International Federation of Organic Agriculture Movements (IFOAM) was founded in 1972 to coordinate research and represent organic agriculture worldwide in forums for policy and law. Currently, IFOAM is working in 100 countries with more than 690 member organizations. Perhaps most important, it sets, maintains, and revises the IFOAM Basic Standards of Organic Agriculture and Food Processing, which are translated into eighteen languages and ensure the quality of and equal application of the organic certification through the IFOAM Accreditation Programme.

See also **Agriculture, Origins of; Agronomy; Canada; Codex Alimentarius; Crop Improvement; Ecology and Food; Environment; Farmers' Markets; Food Politics: United States; Food Production, History of; Green Revolution; Organic Farming and Gardening; Organic Food; Pesticides; Tillage; Toxins, Unnatural, and Food Safety.**

BIBLIOGRAPHY

Altieri, Miguel. *Agroecology: The Science of Sustainable Agriculture.* Boulder, Colo.: Westview, 1995.

Balfour, Evelyn. *The Living Soil.* London: Faber and Faber, 1943.

Barton, Gregory. "Sir Albert Howard and the Forestry Roots of the Organic Farming Movement." *Agricultural History,* 75, no 2 (2001): 168–187.

Carson, Rachel. *Silent Spring.* New York: Houghton Mifflin, 1962.

Codex Alimentarius Commission and the FAO/WHO Food Standards Programme. Codex Alimentarius: *Organically Produced Foods.* Rome: FAO/WHO, 2001.

Department for Environment, Food, and Rural Affairs (DEFRA). *2000 Statistics on the Organic Sector.* London, 2001.

EarthPledge Foundation. *Sustainable Cuisine White Papers.* New York: 1999.

FIBL (Research Institute of Organic Agriculture). *Organic Farming in Europe.* Provisional Statistics 2001. Available at Organic-Europe, www.organic-europe.net/europe_eu/statistics.asp.

Funes, Fernando, Luis Garcia, and Martin Bourque, eds. *Sustainable Agriculture and Resistance: Transforming Food Production in Cuba.* Oakland, Calif.: Food First, 2002.

Gates, Jane Potter. "Tracing the Evolution of Organic/Sustainable Agriculture: A Selected and Annotated Bibliography." *Bibliographies and Literature of Agriculture* 72. Beltsville, Md.: Agricultural Research Service, U.S. Department of Agriculture, 1988.

Greene, Catherine. *U.S. Organic Agriculture.* Washington, D.C.: USDA, 2001.

Greene, Catherine. "U.S. Organic Farming Emerges in the 1990s: Adoption of Certified Systems." *Agricultural Information Bulletin* 770. Washington, D.C.: USDA, 2001.

Greene, Catherine, Carolyn Dimitri, and Nessa Richman. "Organic Marketing Features Fresh Foods and Direct Exchange." *Food Review* 24, no. 1 (2001): 31–37.

Hess, John, and Karen Hess. *The Taste of America.* New York: Penguin, 1977.

House of Commons Select Committee on Agriculture. *Organic Farming*: Second Report. London: Parliament, The Stationery Office, 2001.

Howard, Albert. *An Agricultural Testament.* Oxford: Oxford University Press, 1943.

Leopold, Aldo. *A Sand County Almanac and Sketches Here and There,* New York: Oxford University Press, 1949.

MacRae, Rod. *A History of Sustainable Agriculture, Ecological Agricultural Projects.* Quebec: McGill University, 1990.

National Research Council. *Alternative Agriculture.* Washington, D.C.: National Academy Press, 1989.

Northbourne, Walter. *Look to the Land.* London: Dent, 1940.

Rodale, Jerome. *Pay Dirt: Farming and Gardening with Composts.* New York: Devin-Adair, 1945.

USDA. *Soils and Men.* The Yearbook of Agriculture. Washington, D.C.: USGPO, 1938.

USDA. *Technology on the Farm: A Special Report by an Interbureau Committee and Bureau of Agricultural Economics of the U.S. Department of Agriculture.* Washington, D.C.: 1940.

Yussefi, Minou, and Helga Willer. *Organic Agriculture Worldwide 2002.* Biofach in collaboration with International Federation of Organic Agriculture Movements (IFOAM), SOEL, Foundation for Ecology and Agriculture, Germany.

Daphne L. Derven

ORGANIC FARMING AND GARDENING.

Organic farming is the practice of growing crops and livestock without applying any synthetic products such as inorganic fertilizers, growth hormones, genetically modified organisms, or pesticides. In contrast, the modern practice of growing crops that relies largely on the use of synthetic (human-made) products is termed "conventional" agriculture. Organic farming not only consists of using a different set of production tools to grow crops, but its philosophical approach to farming also differs from that used by "conventional" farmers. In general, organic farmers intend to establish a production system that works with nature instead of one that dominates nature. For instance, organic farmers strive to maximize natural nutrient cycles that mimic those found in natural ecosystems. Similarly, organic farmers strive to exploit natural pest control mechanisms, such as biological controls, which are also typical of natural ecosystems. In contrast, conventional growers rely on capital- and energy-intensive production methods, such as those that use inorganic fertilizers and pesticides, to overcome problems of poor soil fertility or to manage the outbreak of damaging pests and diseases.

History

The organic farming movement was born in the twentieth century as a response to the concerns of some agricultural ecologists that so-called conventional farming practices were causing environmental harm, and that in the long term were basically unsustainable. Concerns that organic farming practitioners have with conventional farming include contamination of ground waters with fertilizers and pesticides, loss of genetic crop diversity, eutrophication of aquatic habitats, and depletion of soil fertility. Organic farming proponents used production techniques that built upon those long used by traditional farmers prior to the discovery of agricultural chemicals. In fact, even today, millions of small farmers in the developing world continue to follow chemical-free production techniques. Most of these subsistence farmers, located in tropical areas, follow chemical-free practices by default, because they lack the capital or access to relatively

DEFINITIONS

Eutrophication. Oxygen depletion in aquatic habitats due to excessive nutrient leaching (especially phosphorus) from agricultural runoff, resulting in the death of aquatic biota.

Community supported agriculture (or CSA; also termed subscription farming). Members of the community purchase "shares" from local growers, "investing" in the current production season, and thereby sharing in both the risk and bounty of agriculture. Produce from the farm is distributed to members on a weekly basis during the harvest season.

Soil quality. In general terms soil quality refers to a combined number of physical and biological soil attributes that result in optimal crop growth. The particular attributes that affect soil quality may vary across locations and by the crop being grown. Some traits that promote soil quality include high organic matter content, good texture, no compaction, good drainage, optimal temperature, and a deep soil profile.

Natural enemies, or beneficials. The typical farm is a host to a wide number and diversity of macro- and microorganisms living both above and below ground. Only a very small percentage of these organisms is considered harmful to crop growth—and thus categorized as a pest. Organisms in the soil or in the plant canopy that feed on, or that in some way antagonize, crop pests are called natural enemies or "beneficial" organisms.

Organic certification guidelines. Written guidelines have been established for growing crops organically in many parts of the world. Farms that follow these guidelines can become certified, which allows farmers to label their products as organic in the marketplace. Federal organic standards in the United States will facilitate the global expansion and consumer awareness of this growing eco-industry.

expensive synthetic products. In the developed world, organic farming increased rapidly in popularity in Europe, Japan, Oceania, and the United States, beginning in the second half of the twentieth century. Even though organic farms still represent less than 5 percent of all the agricultural acreage, their popularity continues to increase in both developed and developing countries. Despite the fact that the acreage under organic farming is rapidly increasing, to date the demand for organic produce has actually outpaced the available supply. Because of the real

CULTURAL PRACTICES TYPICAL OF ORGANIC FARMING

- Increased soil organic matter through organic amendment applications
- Rotations
- Use of cover crops and green manures to break pest and disease cycles and to improve soil fertility
- Increased vegetational diversity
- Enhanced biological control
- Alternative marketing techniques such as Community Supported Agriculture or direct marketing to health-food stores.
- Use of organic fertilizers and organic pesticides approved by the Federal Organic Standards list of approved products.

or perceived safety of organic produce, the appeal and demand for organic products are expected to continue to increase exponentially in the foreseeable future.

Organic farmers normally undergo a rigorous on-farm certification process before they can label their products as organic. This process, created to protect the consumer, simply certifies the production process, but the organic label itself makes no claims as to the safety or chemical composition of the labeled product. The recently established federal organic standards in the United States, and similar standards already established worldwide, will further facilitate the expansion and trade of organic products on a global basis.

Production Practices

One of the fundamental principles of organic farming is the goal to maintain and improve soil quality. Proponents believe that having a healthy soil is the basis for having a sound crop production system. According to this perspective, crops grown on healthy soils will grow faster, will better tolerate or resist pests and diseases, will have better quality, and will result in adequate yields, year after year. Important tactics to improve soil quality include increasing the organic matter content of the soil, crop rotations, and growing a diversity of crops on the farm. Organic matter is added to the soil by applying composts, using organic mulches, or by growing cover crops as part of the crop rotation program. If the soil suffers from a nutrient imbalance or lacks a particular nutrient, this can be rectified by applying accepted natural materials such as lime, rock phosphate, or sulfur. A healthy soil is also believed to result in crops that better resist or outgrow

pest invasions. Other important cultural practices used to minimize pest attack include crop rotations, field sanitation, planting resistant varieties or cultivars, crop diversification, and the conservation of natural enemies. When pest outbreaks occur, as a last resort, organic farmers may apply naturally occurring pesticides (such as sulfur), use botanicals, release beneficials purchased from a commercial supplier, or use other tactics approved by the organic certification guidelines.

Historically, organic farmers have received little support from established research universities, as the overall research focus to date has been to increase yields of conventionally grown crops. However, as the demand for organic products continues to increase worldwide, more and more research resources are gradually being devoted toward improving organic systems. Thus, in the foreseeable future, research will improve our knowledge of how organic systems function, revealing new alternative methods to maintain long-term fertility of the soil, and ways to manage important pests and diseases.

Risks and Benefits of Organic Farming

Farmers throughout the world have adopted organic farming mainly because of a concern about the environment, to protect the health of the family farm and its hired labor, and with the goal of marketing crops that are free of pesticide residues or genetically modified products. However, the label of an organically certified crop only makes claims about the production process, and not about the quality or nutritional composition of the crop being sold. While organic produce sold in the marketplace is, for the most part, considered safe for human consumption, critics point out that organic produce may pose a health risk due to the possible presence of biological contaminants (such as *E. coli*), or toxic botanical pesticides. Other real or perceived problems with organic farming include a higher cost of production, lower relative yields, lower quality due to a greater incidence of blemishes in the produce caused by insects and diseases, and the general lack of technical information currently available to manage large-scale organic production systems to supply a large consumer base with high-quality produce on a year-round basis.

Future Trends and Opportunities

The organic farming industry is currently undergoing a fast transformation from a relatively small niche market, into a part of the mainstream global produce production and distribution system. As the demand for organic produce continues to increase at about 20 percent annually, the supply cannot currently keep up with the growing demand. As the size of the organic industry grows and as the international markets develop, the industry will grow in sophistication from a production and marketing standpoint to meet the quality and service standards expected by consumers. Thus, the organic industry will need the support of universities and government agencies to continue to develop the technological know-how and marketing infrastructure needed to establish a dynamic and competitive world-class organic produce industry.

See also **Adulteration of Food; Biodiversity; Biotechnology; Crop Improvement; Farmers' Markets; Genetic Engineering; Green Revolution; High-Technology Farming; Organic Agriculture; Organic Food; Sustainable Agriculture.**

BIBLIOGRAPHY

Bradley, Fern Marshall, and Barbara W. Ellis, eds. *Rodale's All-New Encyclopedia of Organic Gardening: The Indispensable Resource for Every Gardener.* Emmaus, Pa.: Rodale Press, 1997.

Gliessman, S. R., ed. *Agroecosystem Sustainability: Developing Practical Strategies.* Boca Raton, Fla: CRC Press, 2001.

Howard, A. *The Soil and Health: A Study of Organic Agriculture.* New York: Schocken Books, 1947.

Lampkin, N. *Organic Farming.* Ipswich, U.K.: Farming Press, 1990.

Oelhaf, R. C. *Organic Agriculture: Economic and Ecological Comparisons with Conventional Methods.* New York: John Wiley, 1978.

Powers, L. F., and R. McSorley. *Ecological Principles of Agriculture.* Albany, N.Y.: Delmar, 2000.

Rodale, J. I., ed. *The Encyclopedia of Organic Gardening.* Emmaus, Pa.: Rodale Books Inc., 1959.

Sooby, J. *State of the States: Organic Farming Systems Research at Land Grant Institutions 2000–2001.* Santa Cruz, Calif.: Organic Farming Research Foundation, 2001.

Stonehouse, B., ed. *Biological Husbandry: A Scientific Approach to Organic Farming.* London: Butterworths, 1981.

Hector Valenzuela

ORGANIC FOOD. Organic food refers to crops or livestock that are grown on the farm without the application of synthetic fertilizers or pesticides, and without using genetically modified organisms. In contrast, the type of agriculture followed by most farmers, which does include the use of synthetic pesticides and fertilizers, is termed "conventional" agriculture. In 2002, with a value in the United States of over $4 billion, organic foods still represent only a small segment of the entire food industry. However, since the early 1980s the organic food industry has increased considerably both in the acreage devoted to grow organic products and in its popularity with the general public.

Consumer surveys indicate that the public is concerned about the safety of the produce that they purchase in stores due to possible pesticide contamination. The media has also highlighted some environmental concerns that exist with "conventional" farming. These environmental concerns include pollution of aquatic habitats and aquifers by synthetic fertilizers and pesticides; agricultural labor and consumer exposure to pesticides; the short-term approach to "conventional" farming, which often results

in unproductive unfertile soils a few years after intensive use of the land; the loss of biological diversity by replacing natural landscapes with extensive monocultures (the practice of growing the same crop, on the same location, year after year); the potential threats to native habitats and wild species from contamination by genetically modified organisms; and the displacement of the family farm by large plantations or corporate-style farming operations. The list of real or perceived health and environmental problems that exist with conventional farming, has in part, contributed to the increased popularity among the general public of organically produced food.

During the 1990s the U.S. organic food industry grew at a fast pace of over 20 percent annually. Because the supply has not been able to keep up with the high demand, organic food normally commands a premium price, compared to conventional food. Thus, organic farming is an attractive proposition for both established and new farmers concerned about human health and about the environment, and also because of the premium price obtained from selling organic produce in several countries.

History of the Organic Movement

The organic farming movement was born in the early twentieth century as a response to the concern that some agricultural ecologists had with conventional agriculture. Early critics of conventional agriculture and organic farming proponents included agricultural ecologists such as Sir Albert Howard in both England and India, and Scott Nearing and J. I. Rodale in the United States. For conventional agriculture, they claimed, short-term profits took a precedence over the environment, resulting in rapid degradation of fertile agricultural lands. From their perspective, the excessive reliance on external inputs such as fertilizers and pesticides, and continuous monocultures, antagonized the natural nutrient cycles and pest suppression mechanisms that exist in natural ecosystems. They proposed and developed production systems that precluded the use of synthetic external inputs, and substituted them with alternative production methods, only allowing the use of naturally available amendments such as composted animal manures, botanical pesticides, and the use of green manures (a cover crop, such as clover, that protects the soil from erosion and is subsequently turned under to amend the soil). Early organic production techniques were actually built upon production practices that were originally used by subsistence farmers throughout the world before the discovery of synthetic fertilizers and pesticides. These early farmers, over millennia, developed farming systems that worked closely with nature, resulting in a finely tuned system that periodically "regenerated" itself from an ecological standpoint, and thus ensured that the land would remain healthy and productive indefinitely. From the early twentieth century, organic farmers have continued to promote those well-tested techniques used originally by subsistence farmers,

This cereal was produced organically in England and has been certified as organic on the side of the box shown here. © IAN HARWOOD; ECOSCENE/CORBIS.

and have continued to modify and perfect them, and to introduce new innovative techniques as they learn more through research and experience.

From a production standpoint, the heart of organic farming is considered to be a healthy soil. Organic farmers consider the soil to be a living entity that needs to be cared for and nurtured. Furthermore, they claim, many of the ailments that today's farmers encounter in the field, in terms of nutritional problems or pest damage on their crops, is nothing but a symptom of an unhealthy soil. Modern research has actually substantiated that all aspects of the production system of the farm are interrelated. Some studies have found links between soil quality and pest, weed, or disease outbreaks. Key tactics used by organic farmers to improve soil quality include incorporation of organic amendments such as composts; the use of organic mulches, which also serve to smother weed growth and retain moisture; and the use of cover crops or green manures, which are incorporated into the soil after reaching a particular stage of growth. If the soil suffers from a nutrient imbalance or lacks a particular nutrient, this can be rectified by applying accepted natural materials such as lime, rock phosphate, or sulfur. Today, organic farmers can monitor the quality of their soils, not only by observing how well their crops are growing, but also by having their soils analyzed by certified diagnostic chemical laboratories.

Crop losses from pest attack can be one of the primary production problems for a farmer. Organic farmers believe that a healthy soil rich in organic matter will

result in a balanced system that allows crops to better resist or outgrow pest invasions. The farmer's goal, concerning management of pests in the organic farm, is to establish a balanced system, in which pests and diseases are kept in check through natural pest suppression mechanisms, including the activity of natural enemies. Natural enemies are macro- or microorganisms that act as predators or parasites to reduce pest populations. Populations of natural enemies can be promoted in the farm through crop diversification, including intercropping, and by growing a diversity of crops concurrently on the farm. Other important cultural practices used to minimize pest attack include crop rotations, field sanitation, and planting resistant varieties. When pest outbreaks occur, as a last resort, organic farmers may apply naturally occurring pesticides (such as sulfur) and botanicals, release beneficials purchased from a commercial supplier, or use other tactics approved by organic certification guidelines.

The Organic Certification Process

Because the organic food industry is relatively small and new, it is important that consumers become aware of its claims, limitations, and potential benefits. In order to better protect the consumer, organic certification programs were created in many parts of the world to develop a label for organic food. An organic certification label makes a claim as to the production process used to grow a crop, but the label makes no claims concerning either the quality or the chemical composition of the product itself. Thus, an organic label does not claim that a particular product is more nutritious, pesticide-free, or tastier—it only indicates that the product was grown following a defined set of organic practices as certified by an accredited state, federal, or international certifying agency.

As the organic food industry grows in size, popularity, and value, its products are increasingly traded across national borders and continents, as it joins the global food trade market. To further the national and international expansion of this industry, and the ability of local growers to export organic products, the United States published a set of federal organic production standards in early 2001. The new federal organic standards will cover the entire country, and replace the guidelines previously used by independent or state agencies in various parts of the country. Because a similar area-wide certification program also exists in Europe and in other regions, it will become easier in the future to trade organic products across borders. In the end, the certification process results in an organic label in every item sold as organic, and this label assures the consumer that this product was produced following a strict set of standards that are uniform across the United States, and similar to those followed in other parts of the world.

The process to certify a farm as organic is a rather rigorous task that involves a lot of planning, good management, and record-keeping. Farmers rely on published organic certification guidelines to find out what practices are acceptable and what products are allowed for use on the farm. For land to be certified as organic, no synthetic fertilizers or pesticides can be applied to it for three years prior to certification. Part of the application process involves a detailed plan provided by the farmer that describes the entire operation, with a focus on what organic techniques will be used to produce and market crops in the farm. If the original fertility of the soil is deficient, the plans detail what will be done to rectify this problem. The certification process also includes taking soil samples to evaluate soil fertility and to detect the possible presence of any unacceptable pesticides in the soil. To ensure that the farm remains in compliance, organic inspectors will visit the farm annually. The record-keeping maintained by the farm helps the inspector to double-check that the farm operations are being conducted as indicated in the original farm plans.

Risks and Benefits of Organic Foods
Currently, organic products are sold at premium prices in an ever-increasing number of stores, and increasingly compete for shelf space with conventionally grown produce in supermarkets. Reasons for the premium prices obtained for organic products include that they are grown without pesticides and thus may be more expensive to produce because of the added labor; because they are grown in a way that does minimal harm to the environment; because no genetically modified organisms are used in the production process; because of a perception that they are better tasting; and also because the produce may have been grown locally and the consumer wishes to support small family farms. Because conventionally grown products are often bred to withstand shipping and to withstand a long shelf life after harvest, often at the expense of flavor, consumers often prefer to purchase tastier varieties, grown locally under organic conditions. However, consumers should be aware that exceptions may occur, and that in some instances conventionally grown products may actually be more nutritious, tastier, and grown in ways that minimized damage to the environment. Also, in some instances some organic farms may not be managed correctly, resulting in environmental problems such as excess erosion. Botanical pesticides, even though they are "natural," should also be evaluated for their risk to humans, wildlife, and the environment. Similarly, improper handling of organic produce after harvest may result in product contamination and in food-borne illnesses. Thus, it is important that the consumer becomes educated about both the benefits and possible risks of purchasing either conventional or organic products, so that better decisions can be made about what products to buy, and whether it pays to invest in products with a premium price.

Current Trends for Organic Foods
Because of its popularity, the organic industry grew at a fast pace since the mid-1980s. Throughout the 1990s in the United States, the organic industry grew by 20 per-

cent annually. Similar trends were observed in regions where affluent and educated consumers support environmentally sound production programs, small family farms, locally grown produce, and products free of pesticide residues or bioengineered materials. Thus the organic industry has also grown in Europe, Japan, New Zealand, and Australia, sometimes at a faster pace than in the United States. However, questions exist as to the future expansion of the industry. Even though many conventional farmers are interested in converting to organic production, this process becomes more difficult as the area under production increases. As the area of production increases significantly, from farming only a few acres, into farming hundreds of acres, problems of soil fertility or pest outbreaks become more difficult to manage with organic techniques. This lack of appropriate technology is explained in part because in the past little formal research was conducted by universities to support organic farmers. During the twentieth century, most agricultural researchers were busy supporting an agricultural system that relied on the use of expensive synthetic chemicals. Thus, considerable research support will be necessary in the future to develop production techniques that will allow for the successful production of organic crops on a wider scale than is possible today. Considerable consumer support will also be necessary to facilitate the expansion of the organic industry. Better informed consumers may learn to accept products with minor blemishes, realizing that the minor defects do not affect taste or nutrition and that these products were grown without the use of toxic chemicals. Educated consumers may also be willing to pay a premium price for organic products, knowing that a large organic industry translates in the long term into a healthier environment with cleaner lakes and rivers and potable aquifers.

If the organic farming movement is to expand the area under cultivation and into other countries, the industry will have to grow in sophistication, to establish a seamless delivery system from the farm to the dinner table. The organic industry also will need to better educate the public about what organic farming is, and what it is not. The newly released national organic standards in the United States, and equivalent certification programs in Europe and elsewhere, will facilitate this process. Because the certification standards clearly delineate the entire production system, the public will be better assured of what they are purchasing when they see an organic label. Misconceptions about organic products will have to be overcome to build public trust in the industry. For example, proponents often claim that organic products are tastier and more nutritious than conventional products. While some isolated studies have indicated that in some cases organic food was more nutritious (more vitamins, etc.), this cannot be generalized to all crops and locations. On the other hand, contrary to some public perceptions, organic produce is not often infected with microbial contaminants, and the risk of food-borne illnesses from organic produce is minimal.

Thus, from the consumer's standpoint, there are several important reasons to purchase organic products. These include supporting the production of farm products that are grown in a manner that minimizes negative impacts on the environment; advocating a system that protects the health of the agricultural workers by minimizing their exposure to toxic chemicals; supporting a system that helps to maintain a rich wildlife in rural areas; and standing for an agricultural system that provides a fair price for the food that is purchased, thus allowing small organic farmers to lead independent, productive lives. A number of innovative marketing techniques bring urban consumers into closer contact with the land. One example of this trend is called Community Supported Agriculture (CSA), or subscription farming. With CSA, community members purchase "shares" of an organic farm—and thus help the farmer to purchase needed inputs prior to the production season. By doing this, the community shares the risk of crop losses that farmers face every season. As part of the program, the CSA farm distributes to its members products from the farm on a weekly basis, providing a bounty of fruits, vegetables, and often dairy products. The urban family members also visit the farm, sometimes to help with the harvest, once or more during the growing season. This type of marketing program helps bridge the wide gap that exists between urban and rural areas, and both parties benefit from this innovative arrangement. The urban families, especially children, learn about where their food comes from, allowing them to become better consumers, and to understand the impacts of agriculture on the environment. In turn, this symbiotic association allows the CSA farmer to become more savvy about the likes and dislikes of the urban consumer, allowing the farmer to modify and improve the farm's menu of products year after year.

See also **Adulteration of Food; Artificial Foods; Biodiversity; Biotechnology; Crop Improvement; Farmers' Markets; Genetic Engineering; Green Revolution; High-Technology Farming; Natural Foods; Organic Agriculture; Organic Farming and Gardening; Sustainable Agriculture.**

BIBLIOGRAPHY

Bradley, Fern Marshall, and Barbara W. Ellis, eds. *Rodale's All-New Encyclopedia of Organic Gardening: The Indispensable Resource for Every Gardener*. Emmaus, Pa.: Rodale Press, 1997.

Gliessman, S. R., ed. *Agroecosystem Sustainability: Developing Practical Strategies*. Boca Raton, Fla.: CRC Press, 2001.

Howard, A. *The Soil and Health: A Study of Organic Agriculture*. New York: Schocken Books, 1947.

Lampkin, N. *Organic Farming*. Ipswich, U.K.: Farming Press, 1990.

Lampkin, N. H., and S. Padel. *The Economics of Organic Farming: An International Perspective*. Wallingford, U.K.: CAB International, 1994.

Oelhaf, R. C. *Organic Agriculture: Economic and Ecological Comparisons with Conventional Methods*. New York: John Wiley, 1978.

Powers, L. F., and R. McSorley. *Ecological Principles of Agriculture*. Albany, N.Y.: Delmar, 2000.

Rodale, J. I., ed. *The Encyclopedia of Organic Gardening*. Emmaus, Pa.: Rodale Books Inc., 1959.

Sooby, J. *State of the States: Organic Farming Systems Research at Land Grant Institutions 2000–2001*. Santa Cruz, Calif.: Organic Farming Research Foundation, 2001.

Stonehouse, B., ed. *Biological Husbandry: A Scientific Approach to Organic Farming*. London: Butterworths, 1981.

Hector Valenzuela

ORGANIZATIONS. *See* **Government Agencies; International Agencies.**

P

PACIFIC OCEAN SOCIETIES. Oceania, the collective name for islands in the Pacific Ocean, consists of high volcanic islands, atolls, and two larger continental islands. On the volcanic and continental islands, the topography, climatic range, and rich soil allow a range of foods to be grown. On atolls, in contrast, the poor soil, shortage of fresh water, and exposure to salt spray restrict the plants that will grow. Fiji thus has a wider inventory of foods than the atolls of the Marshall Islands and Tuamotus. Increasing population size also places stresses on local plant foods.

The islands of the Pacific Ocean are surrounded by seas that cover half the surface of the globe. They have been settled over the last three thousand years by people who sailed east from Southeast Asia, carrying the planting material for taro, yam, and breadfruit, and possibly coconut. Later westward voyages from South America carried other plant stock, such as sweet potato, cassava, and Xanthosoma taro, that added to the biodiversity. The settlers on the various islands gradually developed autonomous groupings and discrete identities and languages, along with different food preferences. These Pacific island societies became subject to colonial control from the early nineteenth century until the 1960s, when each society sought independence on its own terms. Coconut and sugar cane became plantation crops, while coffee, cocoa, and other plants were introduced. With the development of a cash economy, imported foods such as rice, flour, and canned meat have played an increasing role in people's diets.

Staple Foods

Root and tree crops are the starch staples of Pacific Ocean societies. These roots and edible fruits are usually eaten with fish, or, if none is available, then a piece of coconut. Several varieties of the root crops and tree starches have been developed in situ, so that Hawaiians had seventy-two different types of Colocasia taro that they used for food. Sago is another starchy tree crop that is widely used throughout New Guinea. The coconut tree provides nuts, the meat of which is a major accompaniment to any of these starches. Coconut juice is a pure beverage, and other parts of the tree are used in food preparation and other products. Rice imported from countries is a recent

and ubiquitous addition to the diet (Malolo et al., 1999; Pollock, 1992).

All these plants only reproduce vegetatively, so they had to be transported by people who knew their value. Over time many varieties have been selected for size of the root or fruits, extended seasonal availability, and reduced acridity. Taste has become more varied as fermented roots and fruits are either processed directly, or added to the fresh pulp, and then cooked. Cassava, sweet potato, and Xanthosoma taro (Xanthosoma chamissonis) have been added to the inventory, brought from the Americas. While widely accepted for household use, they have lesser status for ritual and ceremonial occasions. Taro and yam remain the major status foods for both household and ritual occasions (Pollock, 2002).

Diet and Nutrition

These starchy foods make up the bulk of the diet, because "they make us feel full" (Leota, in Pollock and Dixon, 1997:72–75); in local languages they are termed "real food" (Fijian *kakana dina*). About 80 percent of daily intake comes from one or a combination of these starches (including rice) (Malolo et al., 1999). But the starchy food must be eaten with an accompaniment for people to say they have "eaten." That accompaniment may be a piece of coconut or fish, or shellfish, and is vital to the feeling of satisfaction from eating. Outsiders may term these two components a "meal," though that is a concept introduced from the West (Pollock, 2000).

Local starchy foods are high in energy, and they provide some protein, minerals, vitamins, and dietary fiber (Malolo et al., 1999, p. 11). The nutrient content of the foods generally consumed by peoples of the Pacific islands is considered good (Dignan et al., 1994). Some Colocasia taro varieties can have 7 grams of protein per 100 grams, while Xanthosoma taro has a high Vitamin C content. Cassava is high in energy/calories but low in protein so is best consumed along with other root crops. The major source of fat in the diet comes from coconut and fish, though fried doughnuts and chicken are recent delicacies that are eagerly consumed when available, mainly in towns.

The traditional diet was high in fiber but low in salt, fat and sugars. However, the introduced foods, such as

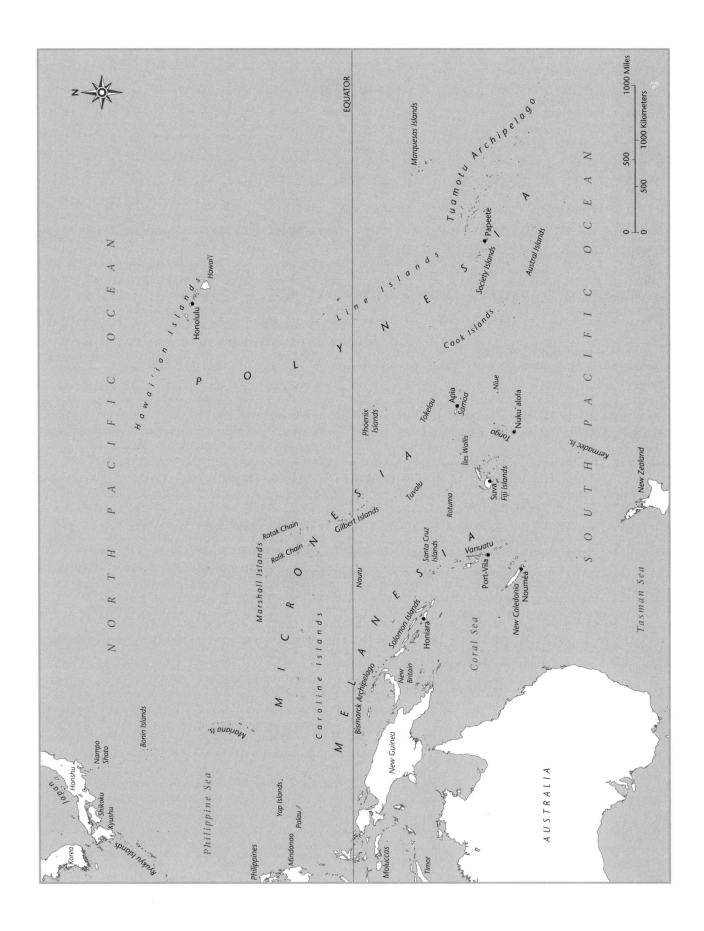

fried chicken, turkey tails, and soft drinks, have increased the amount of fat, salt, and sugar in the diet and are thus considered to be major contributors to health problems, notably diabetes, hypertension, and obesity (Coyne, 1984). The Pacific Islands Nutrition newsletter, which is distributed in all the island communities, stresses the links between diet, health, and lifestyle and suggests how diet can be improved (i.e., no. 43, March 2000).

Production of local starchy foods is diminishing as land is diverted to cash crops. Farmers can get a high price for their taros or yams when sold in the local market and in urban centers, but the returns from export crops such as sugar and ginger are better. Competition with low-priced imported foods, such as rice and flour, is a concern to nutritionists, since these imported starches have less nutritional value than the local starches. Local campaigns, such as that run by the Fiji Food and Nutrition Committee, have highlighted the attributes of local foods with an "Eat More Local Foods" slogan.

Food Preparation and Eating Habits
The traditional manner of eating once a day, or perhaps only three or four times a week, has changed with Western ideology and practices. Early visitors to the Pacific islands decried the large amounts of food they saw being consumed at feasts, terming it "gourmandizing" or "gluttony." They taught the people to regulate their food intake, that is, to eat at least once a day (Pollock, 2000). Today people eat two or three times a day.

That earlier pattern of irregular eating was well suited to the seasonal nature of the root and tree crops as well as to the organization of daily life. People ate what was available, and then waited until the next occasion when the roots and fruits had been harvested and cooked in the earth oven. But that pattern of gluttony and abstinence was deemed uncivilized by the early missionaries. The regularity of meals is one contributing factor to the obesity that is being recorded today (Pollock, 1995).

Cooking of the root and tree starches is essential to render them edible. The earth oven was the most ubiquitous form of cooking, but it has been largely replaced by quicker forms of cooking, such as frying and boiling. In the earth oven, the peeled starches together with fish, or pig for a feast, were placed on hot coals and covered for a couple of hours, so the food was steamed. Much of the cooking in Polynesia was young men's work, with the women peeling the roots and fruits for the men to cook in the earth oven. Today women cook in the kitchen, using quicker processes, while the earth oven is used mainly for communitywide ceremonial feasts. The earth oven is more economical in the use of wood fuel, but the newer forms of cooking are a problem for those Pacific communities without access to electricity.

Fermented foods were in part a means of storing any excess but also a means of adding a distinct taste to the rather bland root and tree foods. At the end of the main

Men and boys in American Samoa prepare earth ovens for a large feast. © JACK FIELDS/CORBIS.

breadfruit season, the Marshallese (and other Pacific peoples) devised a system of placing the ripe breadfruit in a pit in the sand lined with leaves, where it fermented for a few months. The resulting paste, which is said to resemble cheese, could then be prepared either on its own, or mixed with some fresh breadfruit and baked as a loaf. These pits were a valuable means of storage for times when the breadfruit trees were decimated by hurricanes, or the taro pits were inundated by a tidal wave. In Hawaii, poi was an important product of fermented taro that was highly valued when eaten with fish. Food researchers have commercialized poi, as it has properties that make it suitable for sick babies, the elderly, and those suffering from grain crop allergies.

Feasts
Feasts, an integral part of Pacific island life, are marked by a proliferation of foods, many prepared in more elaborate ways than the daily meal. These foods are generally referred to as "puddings" though they are unlikely to contain sugar. Whole fish, turtle, pork, and suckling pig (particularly in Tonga) form the centerpiece. Foods not eaten by those present at the feast are carried home to be shared with other household members. Traditionally, such feasts were the means of honoring a chief or important visitors. They still highlight important events, such as the coming of age of a Tongan princess. The feast is often part of a wider social display that is likely to include dancing, sports such as *krikiti* (cricket) in Samoa, and music.

Problems of Food Security
Sharing food is a hallmark of Pacific Ocean societies and continues to be a major way of fostering a feeling of food security. Food has been and still is exchanged on a daily basis between households and communities. Brothers and sisters send food to their mother and father. Well-being is assessed in terms of types of food available, abundance,

and generosity toward extended family members and others. Such exchanges have contributed to the diversification of foodstuffs. They have evened out disparities so that no family should be shamed by failing to have enough to provide for others.

Imported food from outside the Pacific islands has increased markedly in the twentieth and twenty-first centuries. It adds further variety but only for those with the cash to buy those foods. Reliance on rice as a cheap everyday food is blamed for many of the nutritional and health problems now appearing for the first time in Pacific Ocean societies. Food poverty is a major concern noted in the Fiji Poverty Study (1996). Worst off are urban family households with only one income, which may have to feed some twelve or fifteen people. At the state level, governments have been trying to reduce the high proportion of food imports, which ranges between 12 and 35 percent of total imports. Support for local food producers is essential if the islands are to resolve the food crisis.

Food security is the key concern for the future. The gap between the food-poor and those with adequate food is increasing. Rice and tea or bread and tea may be all a family can provide on a daily basis if they have no land and little money. Weaning infants on sweet tea mixed in rice gives them a poor start in life. The problems of food security thus range from overeating to undereating: some island peoples consume too much fatty food and pop drinks, while many struggle to feed the growing numbers in their households.

Household food security has thus become a major concern for island peoples who until the 1960s had established a regime, both social and material, that met their needs. Today's needs are more complex and require complex solutions.

See also **Cassava; Fruit: Tropical and Subtropical; Southeast Asia: Indonesia, Malaysia, and the Philippines; Tubers.**

BIBLIOGRAPHY

Coyne, T. "The Effect of Urbanisation and Western Diet on the Health of Pacific Island Populations." *South Pacific Commission Technical Paper*, no. 186. Nouméa, New Caledonia: South Pacific Commission, 1994.

Dignan, C. A., et al. *The Pacific Islands Food Composition Tables.* Palmerston North, N.Z.: New Zealand Institute for Crop and Food Research, 1994.

Leota, Jackie Ann. "Samoan Choices." In Nancy J. Pollock and Debbie Dixon, *Understanding Food Decisions in New Zealand.* Wellington, N.Z.: Department of Social Welfare, 1997.

Malolo, Mele, et al. *The Staples We Eat: Pacific Foods.* Nouméa, New Caledonia: Secretariat of the Pacific Community, 1999.

Pollock, Nancy J. "Breadfruit Fermentation." *Journal de la Société des Océanistes* 40 (79) (1984):151-164.

Pollock, Nancy J., and Igor de Garine, eds. *Introduction to Social Aspects of Obesity.* New York: Gordon and Breach, 1995.

Pollock, Nancy J. "Meals and Their Social Dimension." In *Revista d'Etnologia de Catalunya, Spain*. Edited by Amado Fuertes, 2000.

Pollock, Nancy J. *These Roots Remain: Food Habits in Islands of the Central and Eastern Pacific Since Western Contact.* Laie, Hawaii: Institute for Polynesian Studies, 1992.

Pollock, Nancy J. "Vegeculture as Food Security for Pacific Communities." *Vegeculture in Eastern Asia and Oceania.* Edited by Shuji Yoshida and Peter Matthews. Japan Centre for Area Studies Symposium Series. Japan Centre for Area Studies, National Museum of Ethnology. Osaka, Japan: 2002, pp. 277–292.

Pollock, Nancy J., and Debbie Dixon. *Understanding Food Decisions in New Zealand.* Wellington, N.Z.: Department of Social Welfare, 1997.

Nancy J. Pollock

PACKAGING AND CANNING, HISTORY OF.

In preindustrial society, packaging of food was far from being unknown. It was used for food storage at home and for transport from the production place, the farm, or workshop to the local or regional market. Examples are the transport of cereals or flour in bags, tea in wooden boxes or tinplate canisters, and oils in jars. At the household level, people salted meat and pickled vegetables and preserved them in jars. In groceries at the end of the nineteenth century, most commodities were still unpacked and sold in bulk. Products such as tea, coffee, sugar, flour, or dried fruits were weighed out in front of the customer and wrapped in paper or put into a bag. In major cities in the 1880s, the milkman came around with a dipper and can to deliver milk, which was often dirty.

Origin of Modern Packaging and Canning
Early methods of sealing jars included waxed paper, leather, or skin, followed by cork stoppers and wax sealers. The beginning of modern food technology started with the experiments of the French confectioner Nicolas Appert (1750–1841). In 1795, the French government offered a prize of 12,000 francs to anyone who could find a way to preserve food because Napoléon Bonaparte needed to provide the military with a safe food supply. (The requirements of providing adequate food supplies for armies and navies have been of great significance in the history of modern packaging and food preservation.) After fourteen years of experimentation, Appert developed a method for preserving foods by heating. The food, meat, or vegetables, was first cooked in open kettles and placed in glass jars. After removing as much air as possible, the jars were carefully sealed with corks wired in place and then submersed in boiling water.

Appert chose glass for the container because he believed that it was air that caused the spoilage—glass is a material least penetrated by air. It is of importance to note that, in Appert's time, it was not known that microorganisms caused food to spoil. The processes in-

The introduction of the kitchen range brought about a revolution in home canning and preserving. The Mudge Stovetop Canner (shown here) was introduced in the early 1900s as a tool for sealing jars. Glass jars were placed inside the tight-fitting metal containers. Boiling water in the base caused steam, which built up pressure and thus sealed the jars. ROUGHWOOD COLLECTION. PHOTO CHEW & COMPANY.

volved in food spoilage were not understood until the second half of the nineteenth century as a result of the work of scientists such as Louis Pasteur (1822–1895) on microorganisms (Thorne, 1986).

In 1810 Appert published his prize-winning essay on food preservation and the French emperor Napoléon awarded the 12,000-franc prize to him. Within a year, an English version appeared in London, and the new method of preserving food in glass spread quickly to other countries.

Canning

Two individuals in England are given credit for applying and improving Appert's invention, Bryan Donkin and Peter Durand. Bryan Donkin, an associate of John Hall's at his Dartford Iron Works, realized in 1811 that iron containers could be used instead of the fragile glass, and in 1812 the factory began to produce canned food such as meat. In 1810, Peter Durand patented the use of metal containers, which were easier to make and harder to break than glass jars. (The glass jars used by Appert frequently broke.) He covered iron cans, which were prone to rust, with a thin plating of tin (which is not adversely affected by water), and invented the "tin can." By 1813,

Durand was selling canned meat to the Royal Navy. The British admiralty bought these foods as part of the medical stores for distribution to sick men as well as to supply expeditions.

By 1819 canning had arrived in the United States, but no one wanted canned food until the Civil War started. In 1821, the William Underwood Company in Boston introduced commercial canning in the United States. For a long time, people regarded canned foods with suspicion, and for good reasons. In the middle of the nineteenth century, the foods produced by the canning industry were as likely to spoil as not because of inadequate heating techniques (Morris, 1958). Then, beginning in 1868, first in the United States and later in Europe, handmade cans were replaced by machine-cut types. The new technology made it possible for giant meat-canning firms like P. D. Armour to emerge in Chicago and Cincinnati. The product, however, was packed in big, thick, clumsy red cans and was not very appetizing.

The American Gail Borden was a pioneer in food canning. In 1856 he successfully produced sweetened condensed milk in cans and was granted a patent on the process. With financial support, the New York Condensed Milk Company was established in 1857. The demand for condensed milk was at first limited, but during the American Civil War (1861–1865) it was introduced on a large scale. The Civil War contributed significantly to the popularization of canned foods in general (Clark, 1977). The army had to be fed and the government contracted with firms to supply food. Under difficult circumstances, people learned that canned foods such as condensed milk can be tasty and nourishing. The invention of practical can openers at the end of the nineteenth century made cans easier to open, making them even more convenient for consumers.

For many years, however, the flavor of most canned food left much to be desired. On the other hand, it should be realized that products such as canned peas and salmon were usually sold to people living on the American prairies or in the urban slums in Great Britain, most of whom had never eaten the fresh product. In addition, losses due to spoilage caused by microorganisms remained high. It was not until the end of the nineteenth century that research carried out at Massachusetts Institute of Technology made a substantial contribution to improving the keeping quality, nutritional value, and taste of food products preserved in cans and glass.

In the early twentieth century, the heavy cans were replaced by those made of lighter materials, and manufacturers could stress that their products were hygienically processed and, therefore, safer to eat than the traditionally unpackaged products that had been sold in bulk. As food technology advanced, numerous chemical additives were developed to control or speed up food processing and to increase the keeping quality of canned foods.

Originally, the nutritional value of food preserved by canning was not high, mainly due to the length of time required by the heating techniques. From the 1920s onward, however, the nutritional value of canned foods gradually approached that of the fresh product, thanks to modern food technology. Finally, in the 1960s, Reynolds and Alcoa companies succeeded in making all-aluminium cans out of one piece of metal, thereby solving the problem of the weight of the cans; only the lid needed to be attached (Clark, 1977). At the same time, the invention of the rip-off closure and the pop-top lid on aluminium cans made them even more convenient, and made can openers unnecessary. For consumers, the choice between fresh or canned food became largely a question of taste, convenience, and preference.

Glass
Despite its fragility and high production costs, glass had an advantage over cans: glass is chemically inert. In a metal can, iron, tin, and even lead may interact with the water of the preserved food due to chemical or galvanic reactions (although that problem had been solved when iron was replaced by lighter material). The problem of lead contamination had been removed in 1904 when the

production system of the Sanitary Can Company in New York made soldering of the can unnecessary. Glass became a relatively cheap and convenient form of packaging in1903 when Michael J. Owen in Britain invented a semiautomatic machine for producing both jars and bottles. In the nineteenth century a major problem with glass containers had been finding a way to close a relatively expensive container without making the bottle or jar useless after it had been opened (Lief, 1965). Glass bottles could be closed with a cork, but closing bottles and jars that had wide mouths remained a problem.

Numerous ingenious inventions and innovations sought convenient ways to open and close glass containers (and cans as well). The breakthrough came with the invention of the zinc cap for the shoulder-seal jar. The most significant inventions were the Mason Jar in 1858 (named for its inventor, John Landis Mason), a glass jar with a thread at the neck that could be closed by screwing on a metal cap, and the Crown Cap for bottles, invented by William Painter in 1898.

In rural households in Europe from the 1890s until about the 1950s, food preservation in jars of glass and bottles by means of Appert techniques was common (Shephard, 2000), and small portable canning machines made it possible to use the new food preservation techniques in the 1930s and 1940s. As the technology of food preservation improved, however, homemade food preservation by means of salting and pickling in pots and jars of glass gradually decreased. With the invention of the home freezer, it largely disappeared.

Food Wrapping, Paper, Cartons, and Plastic
Paper and cardboard cartons emerged at the end of the nineteenth century as material for wrapping and packaging food. For a long time the price of materials for food packaging—tinplate, glass, and, to a lesser extent, paper—remained high and was often more costly than the food itself. Technological innovations made it possible to produce packaging material cheaply. Paper became important for wrapping food when it could be produced from wood pulp, but paper and cardboard cartons were not yet suitable for packaging fluids. In the 1880s in the United States, paper and cartons could be made impermeable to fat and fluid by coating them with a thin film of paraffin.

In the 1930s, cellophane became an important material for food packaging, but it was gradually replaced by the expanding possibilities of polyethylene and other forms of plastic (Borgstrom, 1967). Another breakthrough was the invention of the Tetra Pak in Sweden in 1952, which increased the capabilities of carton containers for packaging milk, fruit drinks, and other liquids. The carton container coated with polyethylene became a serious threat to the market for glass and cans.

In the 1940s, food packaging entered the era of fully disposable packaging. The convenience of the microwave was further enhanced in the 1980s with the development of special packaging materials. The demand for ready-to-eat fresh vegetables and fruits stimulated the development of Modified Atmosphere Packaging (MAP).

Labels and Brand Names

Closely associated with the history of food packaging is the development of food labels and brands (Opie, 1987). In the first half of the nineteenth century, food manufacturers realized that their products would sell better if a brand name was attached to them, a name with prestige that potential customers could easily recognize. Initially, labels with information about the contents were put on glass containers or cans. Gradually, the label and the packaging as a whole became a means for promoting the food product. In most industrialized countries, legislation regulates the information that must be provided on packaging for consumers' protection.

Since the beginning of the nineteenth century, food packaging has been closely associated with industrialization and urbanization. Originally, food packaging in glass and cans was primarily meant to preserve food, but convenience became the most significant aspect of food packaging in the twentieth century. The retail revolution, when supermarket chains supplanted family-owned grocery stores, made food packaging an indispensable part of urban food culture. On the other hand, it created problems of waste disposal, a much-discussed concern of critical consumers.

See also **Food Safety; Marketing of Food; Microorganisms; Military Rations; Preserving; Storage of Food**.

BIBLIOGRAPHY

Borgstrom, George. "Food Processing and Packaging." In *Technology in Western Civilization*, edited by Melvin Kranzberg and Caroll W. Pursell, vol. 2, pp. 386–402. New York: Oxford University Press, 1967.

Clark, Hylma M. *The Tin Can Book: The Can as Collectible Art, Advertising Art, and High Art*. New York: New American Library, 1977.

Lief, Alfred. *A Close-Up of Closures: History and Progress*. New York: Glass Container Manufacturers Institute, 1965.

Morris, T. N. "Management and Preservation of Food." In *A History of Technology*, edited by C. Singer et al., vol. 5, pp. 26–52. Oxford: Clarendon, 1958.

Opie, Robert. *The Art of the Label: Designs of the Times*. Secaucus, N.J.: Chartwell, 1987.

Shephard, Sue. *Pickled, Potted, and Canned: The Story of Food Preserving*. London: Headline, 2000.

Thorne, Stuart. *The History of Food Preservation*. Kirby Lonsdale, Cumbria, England: Parthenon, 1986.

Adel P. den Hartog

PACKAGING AND CANNING, MODERN.

Food packaging is an important part of food processing operations and food preservation. "Packaging" ensures safe product delivery to the ultimate consumer in a sound condition and at a minimum cost (Paine and Paine, 1983). In the last quarter of the twentieth century, many important developments in both materials and packaging systems led to the reduction of packaging costs and the development of novel and minimally processed foods.

Packaging serves a number of different functions including preservation, containment, and convenience. Preservation is one of its major roles: packaging protects the contents against environmental, physical, and mechanical hazards (oxygen, water/moisture, light, contamination from microorganisms, rodents, and insects, physical damage, chemical attack, etc.) during storage and distribution. Containment is another important function: packaging contains the food and keeps it secure until it is used. Packaging is also a means of providing useful information to the consumer; communication is its third important function. It provides a way of identifying the contents; attractive or eye-catching packaging helps to sell the product; and it provides a means of fulfilling any regulatory requirements concerning labeling of foods. In addition, food packages provide convenience: they unitize or group products together in useful amounts, have features like easy opening, dispensing, resealing after use, and so on. Finally, a successful, effective food package should fulfill many other requirements. It should have good machinability (that is, it should be easily filled, closed, and processed at high speeds); it should be aesthetically pleasing, recyclable or reusable, nontoxic, tamper-resistant (or tamper-evident); it should have a functional size and shape, be disposed of easily, have low cost, and be compatible with the food it contains.

There are three levels of packaging: primary, secondary, and tertiary. A primary package is in direct contact with the product. Usually, primary packages provide the major protective barrier. A secondary package usually contains several primary packages, and provides the strength for stacking in the warehouse. Like the secondary, a tertiary package contains a number of secondary packages. Its function is to hold together the secondary packages during distribution.

Due to the large variety of food products, a great deal of packaging materials, container types, packaging systems, and techniques exist. The selection and development of a package depend on the nature of the food, the desired shelf life of the product, the storage conditions, and the cost. It is a difficult task and requires in-depth knowledge of the food product and its deterioration mechanisms, transportation hazards, market and distribution requirements, and, finally, the properties and characteristics of all available packaging materials, machines, and systems.

Paperboard

Paper, and some combinations of paper-based packaging material, represents the most economical form of packaging. About 50 percent of all paperboard packaging is used to form corrugated boxes, and another 25 percent goes into fiberboard cartons. Paperboard packaging provides absolutely no oxygen or moisture protection for the product, but it does provide rigidity, mechanical support, and light barrier properties. Fiberboard cartons are popular forms of packaging materials: they are economical, collapsible, and printable; they provide versatility and excellent mechanical handling; they can have dispensing and/or resealing features, windows for product observation, and they can be used in multipacks. Another type of paperboard packaging, the corrugated box, is the most common type of shipping container. Paperboard is also used for the manufacture of composite cans and aseptic cartons, which consist of combinations of thin layers of aluminum foil, paperboard, plastic, adhesive, and coatings. The layers are either wound around a mandrel (composite can) or layered in a sheet (aseptic carton).

Glass

Glass containers are generally classified into two groups: bottles with narrow necks and jars with wide necks. Glass is chemically inert, it provides nearly absolute protection from oxygen, moisture, microorganisms, rodents, and insects, and, if colored properly, can filter out harmful UV light. However, glass has two negative properties: its heavy weight and fragility. Consumers prefer plastic packages to glass containers because plastic is lightweight, convenient, and not fragile. As a result, plastic packaging has replaced glass containers for many products and continues to do so. For example, glass containers for packaging milk, fruit juices, cooking oils, mayonnaise, soda drinks, and salad dressings have been replaced by plastic ones. Recently, the development of high-temperature resistant plastics led to the partial replacement of glass containers for jelly, ketchup, and spaghetti sauces. As plastic technology advances, other products usually packaged in glass containers will also be packed in plastic.

Metal

Metal containers, specifically those called "tin cans," have been widely used in the past and are still used for the production of commercially sterilized food products. The development of the metal can and the sterilization process are closely related. The series of operations that are part of the sterilization process is commonly called "canning." In canning sterilization processes, the product is sealed in a metal container and then treated thermally in order to destroy all pathogenic and spoilage microorganisms. This sequence of operations does not allow recontamination of the product after thermal treatment, and, as a result, it remains shelf-stable for a long period of time.

The use of metal containers has many advantages: they can be sealed hermetically; they provide excellent protection from gases, moisture, microorganisms, rodents, and insects; they are stackable, tamper-proof, and relatively inexpensive; and, in general, they can be thermally processed. On the other hand, the quality of the final product in cans is generally low; there are some safety issues (cut fingers); the containers are heavy, easily damaged, and not microwavable; and they usually do not open easily.

The most common type of metal container is the three-piece can, which consists of two ends and one body. One of the ends is applied by the can manufacturer and the other by the food packer. Most steel-based, three-piece can bodies are welded together, but they can also be secured mechanically. Aluminum cans cannot be welded economically. As a result, most aluminum cans are two-piece containers. Most metal containers are thermally processed. A series of ridges, known as "cluster beads," are embossed in the sidewall of the can to improve its strength and prevent collapse or paneling when pressure differential is encountered during the thermal process.

Two-piece metal containers consist of a can body and one end applied by the food packer. Two-piece cans are rapidly replacing three-piece cans due to their aesthetic appeal and their lower cost.

The portion of the can formed by rolling the curled edge of the end and the can body together, forming a hermetic seal, is called a "double seam." The double seam is a critical part of any can because it is the weakest point of the can. Each component of the double seam (Figure 1), particularly the overlap, must have the correct dimension and conform to strict guidelines to ensure a tight seal. A thermoplastic sealing compound attached to the cover melts during the formation of the double seam, fills the spaces in the seam, and results in a hermetic seal.

Most metal containers use the "tinplate" as their basic construction material. The tinplate is composed of a thick layer of steel with tin added on either side. The tin layers protect the steel from being corroded by the prod-

FIGURE 1

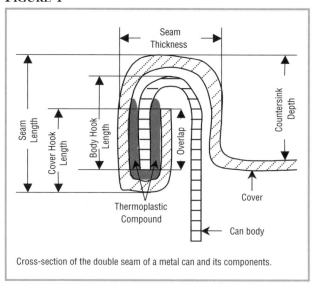

Cross-section of the double seam of a metal can and its components.

TABLE 1

Plastic materials used for food packaging and some of their properties

Properties – characteristics	Materials					
	PE	PP	PET	PS	PVC	Composite materials
Barrier:						
Moisture	Excellent	Excellent	Good	Poor	Medium	Excellent
Oxygen	Poor	Poor	Good	Poor	Poor	Excellent
Thermal stability and sealing	Excellent sealant; non-retortable	Retortable; good sealant	Hot Fill up to 185°F; crystallized form retortable (CPET)	Heat barrier (styrofoam)	Good sealing strength; microwaveable	Easy to seal or double seam
Mechanical	Good puncture resistance; can be made stiff	Good for films, stiff, brittle at low temperatures	Excellent resistance to mechanical abuse	Brittle form (HIPS)	Stiff and rigid when unplasticized	Not convection ovenable; retortable; need to protect from moisture
Chemical	Flavor scalping	Blooms; oil and grease resistant		Oil and grease resistant		
Optical	Cloudy appearance w/o colorant	Cloudy	High clarity	Good clarity	Good clarity	
Cost	Very low	Low	Moderate	Low	Low	High
Recyclability	Recyclable	Recyclable	Easy to recycle	Recyclable	Recyclable	Not recyclable

uct and by atmospheric moisture. Beyond the tin layers, there are coatings that also help to protect the metal from corrosion.

Decreasing tin resources and the resulting increase in the price of tin led to the development of tin-free steel (TFS). Tin-free steel plates use phosphates, chromium, aluminum, or nickel as protective coatings.

Aluminum cans are also coated for protection against corrosion. They are mostly used for carbonated beverages (beer and soda) because the high internal pressure helps the thin, soft metal container hold its shape and withstand mechanical damage.

Plastics

Plastics are long-chain polymers that can be melted, formed into a desired shape, and solidified during cooling. The general advantages of using plastic materials in food packaging include consumer acceptance and preference, excellent safety characteristics (nonfragility), less weight than other materials, good moisture and gas barrier properties, good puncture resistance, low heat conductivity, good sealant properties, recyclability, and microwavability. On the other hand, potential disadvantages include flavor scalping and migration issues. ("Flavor scalping" refers to absorption of the product's flavor compounds by the packaging material, and, conversely, "migration" is the transfer of compounds from the package to the product.)

There are many different plastics available for food packaging. The most important plastics in terms of volume are: (1) low density polyethylene (LDPE); (2) high density polyethylene (HDPE); (3) polypropylene (PP); (4) polyethylene teraphthalate (PET); (5) polystyrene (PS); (6) polyvinyl chloride (PVC); and (7) composite multilayer structures. The properties of the different plastics are presented in Table 1.

In addition to these plastics, other types are also used as food packaging materials, but they are not as popular due to their high cost. As a result, they are used only when their properties are required for the package. These plastics include: polyvinylidene chloride (PVDC), an excellent gas and water vapor barrier material; ethylene vinyl alcohol (EVOH), with excellent gas barrier properties; and some acrylics and nylons.

Laminates

When two or more plastic films are combined together, either with an adhesive or by co-extrusion, they form a laminate. The purpose of laminating materials is to combine the best properties of each film into a single packaging structure. The combination of different films into a laminate can provide a stronger seal, better mechanical properties, machinability, barrier properties for moisture, gas, odor, and light, graphics quality, and, in general, improved characteristics and appearance at a relatively low cost. Some disadvantages of the laminates include their low line speeds and environmental issues, since they are not recyclable.

When very low gas and moisture transmission through the package is desired, the use of an aluminum foil-laminated film is required. However, sometimes, when the foil in the laminate is very thin, it becomes susceptible to flex-cracking and pin-holing, which reduce significantly its barrier properties. A solution to this problem is the use of the metallization process. Vacuum metallization is the deposition of a thin metal layer on a polymeric material under vacuum. Metallized films are not as susceptible to flex-cracking or pin-holing, which gives them a distinct advantage over foil-laminated films. The most common metallized film is oriented polypropylene, which is used widely by the snacks industry, particularly for pretzels and potato chips.

Plastics and their laminations are used to make a variety of packages: bottles, cups, trays, tubs, pouches, bags, films/flexible packages, and composite structures. The large variety of plastics with a wide range of properties, and technological innovations in plastic manufacture, are the main reasons that plastics and their laminations are used increasingly for food packaging. At the same time, these technological innovations have led to the development of many novel and minimally processed products.

Microwavable Packaging

A major area of packaging development is in the microwavable products category. Consumer demands for convenient foods that need minimum time for preparation are satisfied by the use of plastics and their combination with other packaging materials that allow the product to be rapidly heated in a microwave oven. As a result, many shelf-stable, refrigerated, and frozen microwavable products are available in markets.

Another popular application in this category is the metallization of plastics and the development of susceptor technology for microwavable products (susceptors are metallized portions in packages that reflect microwaves). In the microwave, the metallized area creates localized hot spots to enhance heating, and, in some cases, to assist with browning. Examples of susceptor packaging include microwave popcorn, frozen dinners, and frozen pizza.

Modified Atmosphere Packaging

Another recent packaging development involving plastic films is modified atmosphere packaging (MAP). This method involves the alteration of the composition of the air in the package. This can be done by mechanically removing the air and obtaining vacuum, by flushing the package with another gas or mixture of gases, or naturally by the respiring product in the package (Floros, 1990). The modification of the atmosphere has a desired effect on the quality and shelf life of the product. Thus, modified atmosphere packaging can be considered an integral part of the processing operation. The composition of the modified atmosphere depends on the nature of the product and the desired outcome. The barrier properties of plastics play an important role in obtaining the desired result. The gases used for atmosphere modification include oxygen, carbon dioxide, nitrogen, carbon monoxide, sulfur dioxide, ethanol, and argon. The purpose for

using each gas varies. Research regarding the use of ozone, chlorine dioxide, and other gases with antimicrobial properties indicates that the use of such gases in modified-atmosphere packaging increases the safety of the products.

The market for fresh-cut and minimally processed produce has grown tremendously over the past ten to fifteen years, and this is the result of the development and availability of plastic materials, packaging systems, and technologies, such as modified atmosphere packaging, that extend the shelf life of these products. Active packaging is a special type of modified atmosphere packaging. It involves the addition of an active substance inside the package that will cause a certain modification during storage. The substances used may be oxygen absorbents, moisture absorbents/regulators, antimicrobial agents, or other compounds with specific properties. An evolving technology is the incorporation of active substances into the packaging material itself (Floros, Dock, and Han, 1997).

Aseptic Packaging

One of the major applications of laminates is in aseptic packaging. The major difference between aseptic packaging and traditional methods of food packaging is that the product and the packaging material are continuously sterilized separately. Then, under aseptic conditions that prevent recontamination of the product, the sterile package is filled with the sterile and cooled product and hermetically sealed to produce a shelf-stable final product with extended shelf life and no need for refrigerated storage. This technique has allowed for substantial improvements in the quality of the final product, mainly due to the much milder heat treatment that the product undergoes compared to the traditional thermal process (Floros, 1993).

A popular aseptic package is the "brick pak," a type of aseptic carton. Its composite structure usually contains both paper and aluminum foil. Paper is a mechanically stable, stiff, and groovable material with good heat resistance. It also provides good light protection and a printable surface. On the other hand, aluminum foil is an excellent gas, water, and light barrier (particularly when laminated between two plastic layers) and it is thermally stable. The combination of these properties has made paper/foil/plastic laminations popular in aseptic packaging. Aseptic cartons are used extensively for products such as fruit juices, milk, and other drinks.

Many changes in the packaging of food took place in the last quarter of the twentieth century, producing a wide variety of materials and technologies. The steady accumulation of research developments indicates that food packaging will continue to evolve and respond to the increased needs and demands of consumers.

See also **Fast Food**; **Food Safety**; **Frozen Food**; **Microorganisms**; **Microwave Oven**; **Military Rations**; **Storage of Food**.

BIBLIOGRAPHY

Floros, John D. "Controlled and Modified Atmospheres in Food Packaging and Storage." *Chemical Engineering Progress* 86, no. 6 (1990): 25–32.

Floros, John D. "Aseptic Packaging Technology." In *Principles of Aseptic Processing and Packaging*, edited by James V. Chambers and Phillip E. Nelson, 2d ed., pp. 115–148. Washington, D.C.: Food Processors Institute, 1993.

Floros, John D., Lotte L. Dock, and Jung H. Han. "Active Packaging Technologies and Applications." *Food, Cosmetics, & Drug Packaging* 30 (1997): 10–17.

Food and Agriculture Organization of the United Nations. *Guidelines for Can Manufacturers and Food Canners: Prevention of Metal Contamination of Canned Foods.* Rome, Italy: Food and Agriculture Organization of the United Nations, 1986.

Gnanasekharan, Vivek, and John D. Floros. "Shelf Life Prediction of Packaged Foods." In *Shelf Life of Foods and Beverages: Chemical, Biological, and Physical Aspects.* Edited by George Charalambous, pp. 1081–1118. New York: Elsevier, 1993.

Paine, Frank A., and Heather Y. Paine. *A Handbook of Food Packaging.* Glasgow, Scotland: Leonard Hill, 1983.

Potter, Norman N., and Joseph H. Hotchkiss. *Food Science.* Reprint, Gaithersburg, Md.: Aspen, 1998.

Robertson, Gordon L. *Food Packaging: Principles and Practice.* New York: Marcel Dekker, 1993.

John D. Floros
Konstantinos I. Matsos

PAINTING. *See* **Art, Food in.**

PAKISTAN. *See* **Asia, Central; India.**

PALEONUTRITION, METHODS OF. There are several kinds of data that inform us about what our ancestors ate. Reviewed in this entry are the data from studies of living primates, archaeology, paleontology, and living hunter-gatherer societies.

Primate Studies

The living primates include prosimians, New World monkeys, Old World monkeys, Asian and African apes, and people. Fossil evidence indicates that all primates evolved from insectivore-like mammals that lived some seventy-five million years ago. Primate ancestors may have been those insectivores that moved into the flowering trees of these tropical forests to exploit insects, and then the flowers, fruits, gums, and nectars of those trees. The large number of essential nutrients required in the human diet (forty to fifty essential nutrients) is likely a consequence of the tropical primate diet. Tropical forests are characterized by having a high diversity of species, but a low density of any given species. With a wide variety of food resources, especially fruit, foliage, and insects, ancestral primates were able to obtain many vitamins, minerals, protein, carbohydrates, and fats from their diet. It is metabolically expensive, in terms of energy consumption, for an organism to manufacture its own nutrients (a process called autotrophism). Through mutation and selection, those early primates that reduced autotrophism, and shifted to a dependency on dietary intake to meet their nutrient needs would have gained an energetic advantage, one that could be put to use, for instance, to increase reproduction.

The human primate is unusual in that seeds, grasses, roots, and vertebrate meat are major components of both its modern and ancient diet. Grasses and roots are the category of plant food most often missing from the diet of other primates. Seeds, grasses, and roots have their nutrients protected by cellulose membranes that must be mechanically broken. This can be done by mastication (chewing), or by using technology. Humans, and our hominid ancestors dating back to Australopithecus, possess the anatomy (e.g., small canines, flattened molars, and enlarged pterygoid muscles—those that move the lower jaw from side to side) that allows for a type of chewing called rotary grinding, which can break cellulose. Humans, and our ancestors of the genus *Homo*, are also dependent on technology (e.g., tools or fire) for food processing. Technology is also required for hunting at a level that makes vertebrate meat a regular part of the diet. For this reason, meat from vertebrates, either hunted or scavenged is not reported as a major component for any nonhuman primate species, although some baboons and chimpanzees regularly hunt mammalian prey.

Archaeology and Paleontology

Archaeological methods focus on the recovery and identification of food remains, of tools and other artifacts used for the acquisition and processing of food, on the analysis of food contained within coprolites (fossilized feces), on the reconstruction of ancient habitats, and on the analysis of hominid fossils. Paleontological data are derived from the kinds and percentages of fossil remains found at a site. Each type of evidence contributes some knowledge, but each has serious limitations. The association of hominid fossil remains with the skeletal remains of other fossil vertebrates may result from geologic forces, such as rivers carrying dead carcasses to a central location or a volcanic eruption burying simultaneously a community of animals, rather than hominid food gathering behavior.

In *The Descent of Man* (1871), Charles Darwin proposed that hunting large game provided much of the selection pressure for human evolution. That view persisted through the 1960s, but more recent data, based on fossil and archaeological remains and the study of living hunting and gathering people, such as the !Kung and Australian Aborigines, show that gathering and processing of plant foods is the main activity of tropical foragers.

Moreover, women in living foraging societies provide most of the calories consumed by these people. These observations turned "man the hunter" into "woman the gatherer."

Additional evidence is based on analyses of bone and stone tool material associated with early hominids. Scanning electron microscope images of mammalian long bones dating to 1.7 million years ago show that cut marks produced by stone tools were incised above those made by carnivore teeth and the teeth of known scavengers, such as porcupines. If one assumes that the order of markings reflects the order of use by hunters and scavengers, the hominids were the last to have at the bones, even after porcupines. Early hominids may have been collecting bones for their marrow and brain tissue rather than for any meat still remaining on the surface of the bone. Marrow and brain are high in fat and protein, but few carnivores have the morphology necessary to break open large long bones. The invention of stone tools, first manufactured by hominids about 2.2 million years ago, may have been a dietary adaptation for extracting marrow. Hominids may also have scavenged for larger pieces of meat, perhaps stealing meat from leopards. Leopards carry their kills up into trees and consume their prey over several days. J. A. Cavallo believes that human ancestors may have scavenged these arboreal caches of meat.

Despite the evidence for scavenging animal carcasses and, perhaps, preying on leopards, the bulk of the hominid diet has almost always been from plants. The stone tools of the early hominids may also have been used to process hard to chew plant foods, such as seeds. Studies of the finer details of early hominid dental structure and tooth wear using the scanning electron microscope and tooth wear experiments found that the diet of the early hominids, including Australopithecus and *Homo habilis*, was largely herbivorous, including softer plant foods (leaves, fruits) as well as the tougher seeds and tubers. Given all the evidence now available, perhaps it is safest to say that the gathering of plants, insects, bird's eggs, and other relatively immobile foods and the scavenging of marrow from carnivore kills typified early hominid food behavior.

Homo erectus added fire to its repertoire of technology. Fire, which may have been used as early as 1.4 million years ago and was certainly controlled by 750,000 years B.P., provided warmth, light, protection, and a new way to process foods. Where and how cooking was invented is a matter for speculation. Cooking, by roasting or boiling, increases the nutritional benefit of many vegetable foods by helping to break down the cellulose of those foods that is indigestible to people. Fire may be used to open large seeds that resist even stone tools. Cooking, especially drying or smoking, helps to preserve foods for storage. Fire may also be used to get foods, especially by driving game towards a convenient killing site. All of these uses of fire did not appear simultaneously, and many appear to be the invention of *Homo sapiens* rather than *Homo*

erectus. What is certain is that the controlled use of fire was a significant addition to hominid technology with profound consequences for nutritional status.

Coprolites are fossilized feces. Such "hard evidence" might seem to provide unequivocal verification of dietary habits, but coprolites are subject to misinterpretation. First, the coprolite must be identified unambiguously as being from a hominid. Second, coprolites can only verify that a particular substance was eaten. That substance may or may not have been a food item itself, it may have been ingested coincidentally along with a food, such as a seed or insect clinging to an animal or plant. Third, only indigestible substances will be found in feces and those substances must be suitable candidates for fossilization to be preserved in a coprolite. Thus, coprolite analysis may provide a very biased picture of the true dietary intake. Even so, considerable information has been obtained about the diet of prehistoric humans and limited information about the diet of hominid species ancestral to modern people. The animal affinity of desiccated coprolites can be determined by placing the specimen in a trisodium phosphate solution for seventy-two hours. Human coprolites turn the solution an opaque dark brown or black color and no other species produces this effect. Other characteristics of human feces are inclusions of charcoal and the presence of undigested animal parts from a wide variety of species. Charcoal comes from cooking food over a wood fire. Since people cook their food and other animals do not, the presence of charcoal in feces is indirect evidence for a unique human behavior. People also have an eclectic diet compared with most other mammals, so undigested parts from a wide variety of species is another indicator of the human affinities of a coprolite.

More than a thousand paleoindian coprolites from the American Southwest have been identified and analyzed. One group of specimens was collected from Texas sites that date from 800 B.C.E. to 500 C.E., representing the temporary camps of hunting and gathering peoples. By comparing the pollen content of the coprolites with that found in the adjacent soils it was determined that the people had consumed high quantities of flowers. Because the physical characteristics of flower pollens are unique to each species it was possible to determine that flowers of agave, sotol, yucca, prickly pear cactus, gilia, and leadtree were popular foods. Also found were remains of wild onion bulbs, bark, grasshoppers, fish, small reptiles, and snails. Although not the current cuisine of Texas, this diet is typically human in its diversity of species. The flower pollen even provides a time frame for the occupation of the sites, spring and early summer.

The oldest verified coprolites of a hominid species are from the *Homo erectus* site of Terra Amata located on the French Mediterranean. These coprolites may be as old as 300,000 B.P. and they are heavily mineralized. They have only a slight reaction to trisodium phosphate rehydration. The specimens contain sand grains, charcoal, and mollusk shell fragments. The sand and shell are expected since Terra Amata is a beach front site, and the charcoal helps establish that foods were cooked before consumption (perhaps evidence for a prehistoric clam bake).

Trace element and stable isotope analysis. A general picture of the relative amounts of plant and animal food in the diet may be available from chemical analyses of stable isotopes and trace elements in skeletal remains. For example, the more $\delta 13C$ (a form of the element carbon) in a skeleton the more C4 plants in the diet. C4 plants include the domesticated grains maize, millet, and sugarcane, while C3 plants include virtually all those growing wild in temperate regions. The amount of the stable nitrogen isotope $\delta 15N$ in skeletons indicates an animal's place within the food web. The amount of $\delta 15N$ is higher as more animal protein is included in the diet. Figure 1 illustrates the relationship of these stable isotopes to diet in several mammalian species. This method is most useful when analyzing human skeletons during the transition to agriculture, that is, during the past ten thousand years. A greater dependence on agricultural crops shows up in human skeletons as more C4 plants ($\delta 13C$) and, generally, less animal protein ($\delta 15N$). Agricultural societies are often stratified socially into higher and lower social classes. Higher classes often have greater access to animal protein. Thus, within agricultural societies the upper classes may have more $\delta 15N$ in their skeletons. This allows archeologists to use stable isotopes as markers of social status.

There are exceptions to the usual $\delta 15N$ indicator of social status. In 1995 Douglas Ubelaker and coworkers analyzed the skeletons from high and low status graves at the archeological site called La Florida in Ecuador. The site dates from 100 to 450 C.E. There were no differences in the levels of protein ($\delta 15N$) in these skeletons, but there is a statistically significant difference in the C4 levels between the two groups. The high status group had higher levels of C4. The only C4 plant—the only domesticated plant—that ancient people of highland Ecuador consumed in quantity, was maize. The researchers explain that the extra maize consumed by the elites was in the form of an expensive and politically restricted food called beer. Elites controlled the production and consumption of beer. Maize beer was produced by the chief's household and was doled out to the commoners at feasts in return for their labor. Chiefs also paid tribute to each other in the form of beer and offered copious amounts of beer at royal funerals. Chiefs were buried with many ceramic vessels, and at La Florida 70.5 percent of these were devoted to the brewing and serving of maize beer.

Studies of Living Hunters and Gatherers

All but one-tenth of 1 percent of humans derive their food from some form of agriculture. However, from the time of the Australopithecus until about ten thousand years ago, a period that covers 99 percent of human evolution, all hominids lived in bands and produced food by foraging—the gathering, scavenging, and hunting of wild foods. Most human physical traits, and many behavioral propensities, evolved during the time that hominids lived as hunters and gatherers. This includes current human dietary requirements, adaptations for food acquisition and processing, and biocultural responses to food. Studies of the few remaining cultures of hunting and gathering peoples offer an indirect view of that ancient style of life, now nearly extinct.

Foragers are a diverse group geographically and culturally, ranging from the arctic Inuit and Eskimo, to the tropical forest Ache (Paraguay), to the dry scrub San (Africa), and the desert Australian Aborigines. Yet, the research shows some consistencies in behavior and diet. The diversity of food resources utilized is high among gathering and hunting peoples compared with agriculturists. The !Kung San of southern Africa, for instance, eat 105 species of plants and 144 species of animals (Lee, 1984). The Australian North Queensland Aborigines exploit 240 species of plants and 120 species of animals. The Ache forage on fewer species, about 90 types of plants and animals. Even the Dogrib, residing in the subarctic of Canada, gather 10 species of plants and 33 species of animals (Hayden, 1981). That is a small food base for hunters and gatherers, but still a large number relative to agriculturalists who, on a world-wide basis, subsist largely on four species of plants (wheat, rice, potatoes, and maize) and two species of animals (cattle and hogs).

A second common feature is that gathered foods (plants, insects, bird's eggs, turtles, etc.) are the primary subsistence base in most foraging societies. Lee compared fifty-eight forager groups and found that the primary subsistence source was gathering for twenty-nine, fishing for eighteen, and hunting for eleven. Often, the use of many species for subsistence is correlated with the high diversity, low density, or seasonality of food items in the environment. In habitats where low density is combined with the wide dispersal of foods, foragers must be mobile and live in small groups. A small mobile social group is a third typical feature of forager societies. Average group size ranges from nine to fifty-five and average densities range from one to two hundred people per hundred square miles. Mobility ranges from daily movement from camp to camp to seasonal sedentariness at one camp, such as a winter lodge or a summer camp.

A fourth common feature is that all foragers depend on technology to procure, process, and store food. Technology ranges from simple to complex, both in amount and sophistication. Savanna and desert foragers, such as !Kung and Australian Aborigines, use a digging stick to get at roots and tubers that are hidden from view or not possible to extract using hands alone. The digging stick seems simple, but that tool more than doubles the calories available to the people who use it as compared with nonhuman primates living in similar habitats. Bow and arrow are used by some groups to hunt large game. At the other extreme of material culture are the Inuit and Eskimo, who possess dozens of pieces of equipment for hunting or fishing, including hooks, spears, sleds, knives, and specialized clothing. The relative complexity of Inuit and Eskimo material culture is required to extract food from a harsh environment.

Food preparation techniques include cooking (such as boiling, steaming, roasting, and frying), soaking, grinding and grating, pounding, drying, fermenting, and putrefying (as in "aged" meat). Many human foods are poisonous prior to preparation by one or more of these techniques. Such toxic raw foods include acorns and horse chestnuts, eaten by many North American Indian foragers and manioc, a root crop, which is a dietary staple of many African societies. The toxins in all these foods are removed by leaching, that is, by boiling them in water and then allowing the food to dry prior to consumption. Rhubarb and cashews, eaten by some people in modern industrial societies, are also toxic until cooked by boiling or roasting. Finally, food storage by drying, caching, and, where possible, freezing or salting is common to many forager groups. It is essential to point out here that dependence on technology for food procurement, the processing of food, and food storage are all behaviors unique to the human species and found universally in all known human cultures.

Sharing and the division of labor comprise a fifth characteristic of foragers. All known living hunters and gatherers share some food, even small game and vegetables in many cultures, and have some division of labor indicating that this is a universal human nutritional adaptation. Sharing and division of labor may best be viewed as behaviors that, first, reduce the effects of unpredictability and variance in food supply, and, second, increase reproductive fitness—that is to say, they increase the healthy development of the individual and his or her likelihood to reproduce. By dividing the social band into working groups based on sex and age, more of the necessary subsistence tasks may be accomplished in a shorter period of time. In tropical and temperate regions, adults may gather plant foods, honey, insects and other small animal foods, and hunt larger animal prey. Children may remain at the camp in an age-graded play group, with older children caring for younger children, or may accompany their parents so as to learn foraging techniques. In extreme environments children may provide significant amounts of foraged food, as they do in Hadza society.

Summary
The human diet is unusual because of our high intakes of grasses, seeds, and grains and, for some people, high intakes of meat. No other primate has this mixture of foods in its diet. The interaction between the biological history and the sociocultural behavior of people accounts for our diet. The human place in nature as primates explains our broad requirements of essential nutrients. Fos-

sil and archaeological evidence help to account for the development of the types of foods eaten and the technology needed for food acquisition, preparation, and storage. The study of living hunting and gathering peoples compliments and supports these other sources of evidence. Five features of food, behavior, and demography are typically found in hunting and gathering societies: a high diversity of food types; greater dependence on gathering rather than hunting; small mobile social groups; dependence on technology for acquiring and processing foods; and division of labor and sharing (a sixth feature, stable population size with high infant and childhood mortality balancing fertility, is not discussed here, but see Bogin, 2001). Taken together, the sources of knowledge reviewed here provide the basis for understanding human paleonutrition and the biocultural nature of contemporary human nutrition.

See also **Agriculture, Origins of; American Indians; Animals: Primate Diets; Anthropology and Food; Australian Aborigines; Food Archaeology; Inuit; Maize; Prehistoric Societies.**

BIBLIOGRAPHY

Blumenschine, R. J., and J. A. Cavallo. "Scavenging and Human Evolution." *Scientific American* 267 (1992): 90–96.

Bogin, B. *The Growth of Humanity*. New York: Wiley-Liss, 2001.

Bryant, V. M. Jr., and G. Williams-Dean. "The Coprolites of Man." *Scientific American* 232 (1975): 100–109.

Cartmill, M. "Rethinking Primate Origins." *Science* 184 (1974): 436–443.

Hayden, R. S. O. "An Order of Omnivores: Nonhuman Primate Diets in the Wild." In *Omnivorous Primates*, edited by R. S. O. Hayden and G. Teleki, pp. 191–214. New York: Columbia University Press, 1981.

Lee, R. B., and R. Daly. *The Cambridge Encyclopedia of Hunters and Gatherers*. Cambridge, U.K.: Cambridge University Press, 1984.

Schoeninger, M. J. "Stable Isotope Studies in Human Evolution." *Evolutionary Anthropology* 4 (1995): 83–98.

Schoeninger, M. J., et al. "Meat-eating by the Fourth Ape." In *Meat-eating and Human Evolution*, edited by C. B. Stanford and H. T. Bunn, pp. 179–198. Oxford: Oxford University Press, 2001.

Ubelaker, D. H., M. A. Katzenberg, and L. G. Doyon. "Status and Diet in Precontact Highland Ecuador." *American Journal of Physical Anthropology* 97 (1995): 403–411.

Wrangham, R. W., et al. "The Raw and the Stolen." *Current Anthropology* 40 (1999): 567–595.

Zihlman, A. L. "Women as Shapers of Human Adaptation." In *Women the Gatherer*, edited by F. Dahlberg, pp. 75–120. New Haven, Conn.: Yale University Press, 1981.

Barry Bogin

PANTRY AND LARDER. In modern parlance, pantry and larder are used interchangeably to designate a place where food is stored. Historically, the two were once separate areas with very narrowly defined functions. During the Middle Ages, food was purchased in bulk; therefore, storage rooms were required for different types of food.

The larder was originally a cool room or cellar for storing meats, especially meats put down in large barrels or crocks of lard—hence the name. It was once common practice to partially cook meats and sausages, and then cover them with rendered lard until needed. Dried or smoked meats were generally stored in a loft or garret away from dampness. This division of function led to the evolution of the terms wet larder (cool room or cellar) and dry larder. The wet larder was used not only for meats stored in lard, but also as a holding room for uncooked meat, game, and vegetables. The dry larder would contain such things as dried fruit, grain chests, and even some types of hard-rind cheeses. Large loaves of rye bread were often buried in the grain chests for long-term keeping.

The term "pantry," and related words like "pantryman" and *pannier*, derive ultimately from Latin *panis* (bread). The core idea was a closet or cupboard where bread was stored, as in Old French *paneterie*, the term that passed into medieval English as *panetrie*. In aristocratic medieval households, the pantry was a standing cupboard where the bread was kept for the table. The finer sorts of cupboards were often elaborately carved since they stood in the room where dining took place.

The pantler was the servant in charge of the bread and was the individual who actually sliced it for the table. This position attracted a degree of prestige since bread was such a critical part of the medieval meal. For this reason, in households belonging to the high nobility, the pantler was often a member of the lesser nobility. By the eighteenth century this function was more or less subsumed in hotels and large commercial establishments by the pantryman, a paid position whose main function was to oversee the supplying and resupplying of bread and provisions.

During the Middle Ages, two sorts of bread came from the pantry. The best bread was the *manchet* or dinner roll (normally round) made of the finest wheat flour. This bread was held in the hand and used like a utensil for dipping or scooping, since medieval diners ate with their fingers. The other sort of bread was the trencher bread, a coarse bread usually made from a combination of wheat and rye flours. Trencher bread was sliced and trimmed of crust to make a disposable plate on which the diner placed food, since dishes were only used as serving pieces during this period. Trenchers were changed frequently during a meal because they became soggy; thus it was the pantler's duty to remain vigilant and keep the table well supplied with trenchers.

By the seventeenth century, the function of the pantry had been expanded to include not only a bread storage cupboard, but also a closet or small room in which

The interior of a larder as depicted in a 1668 illustration by Wenceslaus Hollar for an edition of *Aesop's Fables*. Note the storage of pies and roasts for reserving at a later time. Rats in the foreground are enjoying a meal of their own. COURTESY OF TOM JAINE. ROUGHWOOD COLLECTION.

all sorts of food could be stored together. It was a cold room in that it was unheated and often ventilated with air from outside. Normally this closet stood near the kitchen, and it was common practice to put there roasts of meat, pies, and other items of uneaten food so that they could be reserved the next day. It became the butler's duty in large households to keep tabs on what was in the pantry, and this gave rise to the idea of a more specialized butler's pantry in the nineteenth century. This was a small room normally situated between the kitchen and dining room where fine silver, glassware, and china were stored. Aside from extensive cupboards and shelves, it also featured a sink. It was here that the butler, or his assistant, could undertake the final preparations for many dishes, such as decanting wine, heating a chafing dish, garnishing a roast on its way to table, or preparing fruit for dessert. A subsidiary pantry called the housemaid's pantry also evolved out of this. It was here that the head maid stored her tools. Butler's pantries were a common feature in upper-class American households on the East Coast well into the 1940s. Today, the term "pantry" has devolved into a much less specialized concept. The refrigerator and deep freezer have replaced the old larders

L. Schumacher's handbook for the "perfect" steward and pantry cook was published in Hamburg, Germany, in 1914. It includes many recipes for salads and mixed drinks and was intended for use on passenger ships between Germany and the United States. ROUGHWOOD COLLECTION.

of the past, and the breadbox has replaced the pantry. In general, pantry and larder are now applied to any unheated storage room where food is kept, especially packaged foods, canned goods, and pickles.

See also **Food Pantries; Gardening and Kitchen Gardens; Preserving; Storage of Food.**

BIBLIOGRAPHY

Brooke, S. *Hearth and Home: A Short History of Domestic Equipment in England.* London: Mills and Boon, 1973.

Keeley, C. J. H. *Bungalows and Modern Homes.* London: Batsford, 1928.

Labarge, M. W. *A Baronial Household of the Thirteenth Century.* Brighton: Harvester Press, 1980.

Mead, W. E. *The English Medieval Feast.* London: Allen and Unwin, 1967.

Sambrook, P. A., and Peter Brears, eds. *The Country House Kitchen, 1650–1950.* Stroud, England: Alan Sutton Publishing and The National Trust, 1996.

William Woys Weaver

PARKINSON, JAMES WOOD. James Wood Parkinson (1818–1895) was one of the most influential American cooks of the nineteenth century. Trained by professional chefs from England, Italy, France, and Germany, his role was one of mentor to the profession rather than that of a popular cookbook author like Eliza Leslie or Sarah Josepha Hale. The core of his culinary education, however, came from his Scottish-born mother, Eleanor Wood, and his English-born father, George Parkinson, both confectioners by trade.

In 1818, Parkinson's parents purchased the Pennsylvania Arms, a Philadelphia tavern, with the intention of going into inn keeping. However, his parents' flair for confectionery soon established the family's reputation for ice cream, and it was the Parkinson family which made Philadelphia ice cream famous throughout the nineteenth century. During a banquet for the Marquis de Lafayette in 1824, the Parkinsons introduced vanilla ice cream featuring tiny flecks of the beans, thereby establishing a perfume essence as a signature flavor for a luxury desert.

By the mid-1840s, with financial backing from General George Cadwallader, the young Parkinson had established himself as a restaurateur in a lavishly furnished Philadelphia mansion located at 180 Chestnut Street. Complete with a rose garden for outdoor dining as well a delicatessen featuring imported foods from all over the world (including five types of French liver patés), Parkinson's Salon was generally considered not only one of the finest restaurants in America, but equal to those of Paris and Vienna.

James Parkinson was a master at marketing and something of an inventive genius when it came to recipes. In 1841, his delicatessen was the first in the country to feature Santa Claus at Christmas in order to draw children into a wonderland of French confections and imported toys. In 1850, he introduced his Champagne *frappé à la glace* which is now considered to be the original recipe on which the non-alcoholic ice cream soda was based. Parkinson's fame was firmly established in 1851 when he accepted a challenge from the Delmonico brothers to prepare a dinner that would would be more outstanding than one given earlier by Delmonico's. Parkinson's "Thousand Dollar Dinner" became a legend that helped launch the era of grand banquets in nineteenth century America. The menu survives and features such novelties as early eighteenth century wines, truffled poultry braised in Champagne, and a rare Tokay from the imperial wine cellars in Vienna frozen as sorbet.

Parkinson's influence continued even after he retired from the restaurant business during the 1860s. When the

Parkinson's restaurant at 180 Chestnut Street in Philadelphia was once a private mansion. There was a separate entrance for the confectionery store (on the right). Wood engraving from *Gleason's Pictorial* (May 1853). ROUGHWOOD COLLECTION.

Grand Duke Alexis of Russia visited the United States during the winter of 1871–1872 and declared that there was no true American cuisine, James Parkinson responded with his culinary manifesto *American Dishes at the Centennial*. In a call to arms for the nation's cooks, Parkinson extolled the rich variety of American ingredients and said that it was this body of regional foods that should serve as a basis for our national cuisine. It was his hope that these ingredients would be showcased at the U.S. Centennial in 1876. Unfortunately, due to Centennial politics, Parkinson was never invited to put his vision into practice, yet even today this theme is one of the underlying forces in modern American cookery.

Parkinson's manifesto also launched his career as trade editor for the *Confectioners' Journal*, a position he held from 1874 until his death in 1895. During this period he published hundreds of articles on specific topics such as "The Raspberry: Its Peculiarities and Uses," "Gelatin," or "Colored Sugars for Decoration." His material not only contains information not readily available in cookbooks of the period, but also a wide selection of rare recipes from leading cooks and confectioners.

See also **Candy and Confections**; **Delmonico Family**; **Ice Cream**; **Leslie, Eliza**.

BIBLIOGRAPHY

Confectioners' Journal. Philadelphia, 1874–1895.

"Famous Old Caterer Dead," *Philadelphia Times* (16 May 1895).

Hines, Mary Anne, Gordon Marshall, and William Woys Weaver. *The Larder Invaded*. Philadelphia: Library Company of Philadelphia, 1986, pp. 61–62

Kynett, Harold. *For Better or For Worse*. Privately printed, 1949, pp. 97–98.

Parkinson, Eleanor, *The Complete Confectioner*. Philadelphia: Lea and Blanchard, 1844.

Parkinson, James W. *American Dishes at the Centennial*. Philadelphia: King & Baird, 1874.

"Parkinson, Provider for Epicures," *Philadelphia Ledger*, December 1, 1907.

Valentine, R. B. "Les Bon Vivants," *Confectioners' Journal* (Jan. 1880), 16–17.

William Woys Weaver

PASSOVER. Passover celebrates the Exodus of the Israelites from Egypt in the second millennium B.C.E. as narrated in the Bible (Exod. 1–15). According to the Jewish calendar, the holiday begins on the evening of the fourteenth of Nisan, which falls in late March or early April. Passover is observed for seven days in Israel and eight days elsewhere. On the first one or two evenings of the holiday, Jews are required to recite the Exodus story (Exod. 13:8) at a family feast called the seder and to eat matzo, an unleavened flat bread. They are prohibited from eating foods containing leaven (*hametz*) during the entire holiday.

History of Passover
The eating of a sacrificial animal, together with unleavened bread and bitter herbs, was central to Passover observance until the destruction of the Second Temple in 70 C.E. However, the paschal sacrifice and eating unleavened bread actually predate the Exodus, even in the Exodus account itself (Exod. 12:8), and are associated with two distinct holidays: Pesach, a pastoral holiday during which animals were sacrificed and eaten, probably as a propitiatory measure to protect the flocks; and Hag Ha'Matzoth, an agricultural festival associated with the beginning of the barley harvest, during which unleavened bread was eaten. The Bible distinguishes these two holidays (Lev. 23:5–6; Num. 28:16–17) and, in Exodus 12, juxtaposes them. The Samaritans still observe them as two separate events. Unleavened bread was also an ordinary bread made in haste. Sarah served it to guests (Gen. 18:6), and Lot offered it to the angels (Gen. 19:3). It is thought that eventually these two spring festivals were observed together and were later identified with the commemoration of a historical event, the Exodus, which also occurred in the spring.

According to the biblical account of the Exodus, God visited ten plagues on the Egyptians to persuade them to release the Israelites from bondage. Before the last plague, during which the firstborn in each household would be slaughtered, God told Moses to tell the Israelites to slaughter an unblemished yearling lamb or kid and smear the blood on their two door posts and lintel so their homes would be passed over and their firstborn spared. The Israelites, as instructed, roasted and ate the animals just before leaving Egypt but were in such a hurry that their bread had no time to rise (Exod. 12:1–28). Also symbolizing the food eaten by slaves and the poor, matzo is known as the bread of affliction or poverty (Deut. 16:3).

Passover became one of three pilgrimage festivals during which Israelites traveled to Jerusalem to make offerings, including the sacrifice of animals, at the Temple. They consumed parts of the roasted animal at a family feast. After the destruction of the Second Temple, animals could no longer be sacrificed, but the practice was remembered through symbols, such as the roasted shank bone placed on the seder table.

After the destruction of the second Temple in 70 C.E. and the wide dispersal of the Jews, Passover was gradually codified, and many local variations developed. The laws concerning Passover are in the Bible (Exod. 12–15), Tractate Pesahim of the Mishnah and Toseftah (compilations of the Oral Law completed in about 200 C.E.), Talmud, and later works. The *Shulhan Arukh*, written by Joseph Caro (1488–1575), with glosses by Rabbi Moses ben Israel Isserles (1530–1572), is the basis for modern religious practice.

Haggadah

The story of the Exodus is recounted from the Haggadah, which means 'narrative' in Hebrew, at the seder, during which participants eat foods symbolizing the Exodus from Egypt. The traditional Haggadah, which contains passages from the Bible and the rabbinic literature, blessings, prayers, and songs, is based on a compilation that began to be assembled in the Second Temple period. With several core elements in place by 200 C.E., the Haggadah continued to evolve, as did the seder, whose form is set out in the Haggadah.

The diverse Jewish communities of the Diaspora have created thousands of distinctive Haggadahs and modified them to reflect such concerns as egalitarianism (removing masculinist language), feminism (emphasizing the role of women in the Exodus story and in Jewish history), environmentalism (adding pollution and other dangers to the list of plagues), oppression (expressing solidarity with African Americans, Soviet Jews, Tibetans, Palestinians), social justice (adding poverty, homelessness, and AIDS to the list of plagues), humanism (stressing the theme of freedom rather than divine intervention), personal liberation (freedom from addictions), and remembering the Holocaust. These texts have encouraged the creation of new kinds of seders, whether adaptations of the seders held on the first two nights of Passover or a special third seder, as well as new and newly

interpreted symbolic foods and cuisines. For example, Tibetan food is served at interfaith and international seders for a free Tibet, whether on American university campuses or in Dharamshala, India, home of the Dali Lama in exile.

Seder

The seder is organized around seven symbolic foods. They include three matzoth (two in some communities); four glasses of wine; a roasted bone (*zeroa*) symbolizing the Paschal animal sacrificed at the Temple; a green vegetable for spring; bitter herbs (*maror*) for the bitterness of slavery and for the ancient practice of eating hyssop with the Paschal offering; a roasted egg symbolizing a festival sacrifice once made at the Temple; and a mixture of fruit, nuts, spices, and wine or vinegar (*haroset*) for the mortar used by the enslaved Israelites.

Ashkenazim (Jews who derive from Germany and central and eastern Europe) present these foods on a special seder plate. Some Sephardim (Jews who derive from the Iberian Peninsula and the places they settled after the Expulsion in 1492) place these foods in a basket. Yemenite Jews set little bowls on a table covered with leafy green vegetables. In the late twentieth century, vegetarians replaced the bone with a roasted beet, or "Paschal yam," to symbolize the blood of the Paschal lamb. Among the many new Passover traditions is an orange on the seder plate, a practice introduced in the early 1980s by Susannah Heschel as a gesture of solidarity with those who have been marginalized within the Jewish community, including lesbians, gay men, and widows.

The seder, which means 'order' in Hebrew, proceeds through a set sequence of fifteen elements. These include blessings on the wine, the matzoth, and other symbolic foods; blessings and ceremonial washing of the hands; recitation of the Haggadah; eating the festive meal; the *afikoman* (half of the second of two or three matzoth); grace before and after the meal; and concluding songs and poems.

Many customs vary. Toward the end of the seder, Ashkenazim set aside a special goblet of wine for the Prophet Elijah and open the door to allow him to enter. The arrival of the Prophet Elijah is believed to herald the coming of the Messiah. A feminist innovation is the addition of Miriam's goblet, which is filled with water because Miriam, the older sister of Moses, is called a prophetess in the Exodus account and is associated with a miraculous well (Exod. 15:20). According to Erich Brauer (*The Jews of Kurdistan*, 1993, first published in 1947), with the mention of each of the ten plagues, Jews from Ushnu dip a finger in wine and shake a drop into an empty eggshell, to which they add some arrack, tobacco, and bitter herbs. Then "one of the men takes the egg and in silence throws it on the doorstep of one known to hate the Jews, returns in silence, and washes his face and hands before taking any further part in the Seder" (Brauer, 1993, p. 288). During the song "Dayenu," in which the refrain "that would have been enough" follows a verse describing how God executed justice, some Sephardi, Afghani, and Persian Jews beat each other gently with scallions to symbolize the lashes of Egyptian taskmasters.

Haroset

Haroset is eaten at points nine *(maror)* and ten *(koreh)* in the seder sequence, after which the meal proper commences. Many of the ingredients in *haroset*, which vary from one community to another, have symbolic significance. The spices stand for the straw that was mixed into the mortar, red wine refers to the plague of blood, sweetness signifies hope, apples are mentioned in the Song of Songs (8:5), and various fruits (figs, dates, raisins) are associated with Bible lands. Ashkenazim favor apples, nuts, cinnamon, and red wine. Yemenite Jews, who refer to *haroset* as *dukeh*, a Talmudic term that only they use, combine dates, raisins, dried figs, roasted sesame seeds, pomegranate, almonds, walnuts, black pepper, cumin, cinnamon, ginger, cardamom, and a little wine vinegar. The Lopes family in Jamaica makes a paste of dates and sultanas soaked in orange juice and adds grated citron rind, port wine, and shredded coconut. The paste is shaped into little bricks and dusted with cinnamon (Michel, 1999).

Afikoman

The *afikoman*, a reminder of the Paschal sacrifice, is the last morsel consumed at the seder. The word *afikoman* derives from the Greek *epikomion* ('dessert') and *epikomioi* ('revelry'), which are associated with the final phases of the Greek symposium. While the seder resembles the Greek symposium in other ways, most importantly Socratic dialogue and learned discussion in the context of a festive meal (the symposium generally followed the meal), the rabbis stressed the differences between them because the symposium was associated with excessive drinking and licentious behavior. Many similarities between the seder and symposium (drinking wine, reclining, song) were characteristic of ancient banquets rather than unique to either of them, but these and other common practices (for example, dipping appetizers in a condiment) acquired special meaning in the Passover seder.

Ashkenazim hide the *afikoman* and reward a child for finding it at the end of the meal. While neither Sephardic nor Yemenite Jews hide the *afikoman*, they do reenact the Exodus, consistent with the obligation stated in the Haggadah that one is obliged to see oneself as if one had personally left Egypt. Syrian Jews do this by wrapping the *afikoman* in a special embroidered napkin cover, throwing it over their shoulders, reciting Exodus 12:34, and then asking and answering the following questions in Arabic: Where are you coming from? (Egypt) Where are you going to? (Jerusalem) (Dobrinsky, 1986, p. 256). In some Mediterranean and Central Asian Jewish communities, a piece of the *afikoman* is saved as a protection against misfortune. It is also a Sephardic custom, when breaking the

Manuscript illumination from the fifteenth century showing a couple celebrating the Passover seder. © ARCHIVO ICONOGRAFICO, S. A./CORBIS.

afikoman during the seder, to do so in a way that forms a letter of symbolic significance.

Matzo

Although matzo is required only during the seder, it is customary to eat matzo throughout the holiday. To mark the distinction, many Jews use guarded *(shmurah)* matzo for the seder and regular matzo on the remaining days, while others eat *shmurah* matzo throughout the holiday. To ensure that the grain never comes into contact with any water or trace of leaven, *shmurah* matzo is guarded from the moment the wheat is harvested until the matzo leaves the oven, whereas regular matzo (matzo *peshutah*) is made from wheat that has been supervised only from the point of milling. Of concern is the practice of tempering grain by moistening it with water before milling. The flour for *shmurah* matzo is mixed with *mayim shelanu*, water that has been drawn from a natural source after sunset and left to stand overnight in a cool place.

All matzo, to be kosher for Passover, must be made from dough mixed, kneaded, rolled, perforated, and baked at a high temperature within eighteen minutes. A rabbi supervises the process and checks that the matzoth are properly backed, with no bubbles, folds, or soft spots. Between each batch of matzoth, tables and tools are scrupulously cleaned to ensure that no traces of dough adhere to them. In Yemen, Jews used to bake matzoth during Passover in order to have fresh soft matzoth throughout the holiday. Baked directly on the walls of a clay oven, these matzoth were somewhat like pita. Yemenites served thick matzoth at the seder, as did medieval Jewish communities, and thin ones during the rest of the holiday.

A traditional rich matzo (matzo ashirah) is made with white grape juice or eggs rather than with water. Only those who have difficulty digesting regular matzo, including the sick, elderly, or young children, may eat this kind of matzo during Passover. The Talmud and later sources debate the permissibility of decorating matzoth, whether by pressing them into molds or perforating them to make patterns, because the extra time devoted to this process might cause the dough to ferment. Illustrated Haggadahs show, however, that matzoth were indeed ornamented. In 1942, matzoth in the shape of V, for victory, were baked in the United States.

Rolled by hand, shmurah matzoth are round, in contrast with the square matzoth made by machines introduced during the 1850s in Austria. Machine-made matzoth were controversial for several reasons. First, round matzoth were stamped out of sheets of dough. Because the scraps were reused, there was a delay between mixing and baking the dough, prompting concern that the dough would start to rise. Second, to fulfill the religious obligation of eating matzo during the seder, matzo must be made intentionally for that purpose. Whether or not the intentional starting of the machine is sufficient to meet this requirement has been debated, and steps have been taken to increase human involvement in the machine process.

In time, square matzoth made by machine came to be widely accepted, so much so that matzo companies, such as Manischewitz, established in Cincinnati in 1888, made every effort to diversify their matzo products and to create a market for them all year round. Since the 1930s, their cookbooks have provided recipes for how to use their matzo products in everything from tamales to strawberry shortcake. In the late twentieth century, Manischewitz added an apple cinnamon matzo to its product line. Chocolate-covered matzo has become popular.

The claim that Jews added a victim's blood to the matzo or drank the blood at the seder is a late addition to the long history of blood libels accusing Jews of kidnapping and killing a Christian, usually a child. Blood libels have led to the execution of accused Jews and the massacre of Jewish communities. In 2002 in Saudi Arabia, a blood libel accused Jews of using the blood of non-Jewish teenagers in their Purim pastries.

Hametz

Whereas one is only obligated to eat matzo at the seder, hametz is prohibited during all eight days of Passover. Hametz refers to any of the five species of grain mentioned in the Bible (wheat, rye, oats, spelt, barley) that have come into contact with water after being harvested and allowed to ferment. These grains and anything that has come into contact with them or has been made from them cannot be eaten or be in one's possession during the holiday. Preparation for Passover entails a scrupulous cleaning of the home to remove every last trace of hametz, the "sale" to a non-Jew of any remaining hametz in one's possession (and repurchase following the holiday), the use of dishes and utensils dedicated exclusively to Passover or specially prepared for that purpose, and consumption of food that is kosher for Passover.

To prevent any possibility of violating the prohibition, "fences" have been created around these rules. Many Ashkenazim do not eat kitniyot (legumes, grains, and beans, including lentils, rice, corn, peas, millet, buckwheat, and anything made from them or their derivatives, such as oil, sweeteners, or grain alcohol). Sephardim generally eat fresh beans, and some groups eat rice. Most Hasidim do not eat gebrokts (matzo, whether whole, broken, or ground into meal, that has been mixed with water). Italian Jews do not consume milk during Passover, while Ethiopian Jews abstain from consuming fermented milk products. Many Jews do not conform to these restrictions, while some observe kashruth (Jewish dietary laws) during Passover but not during the rest of the year.

Cuisine

Passover dietary restrictions and requirements have prompted distinctive culinary responses. Signature dishes of the seder meal itself vary according to Jewish communities. While many are also served on the Sabbath and other holidays, some are specific to Passover.

Ashkenazim serve clear chicken broth with dumplings (kneydlakh) made from matzo meal and noodles made of egg and potato starch or matzo meal, gefilte fish (poached balls of ground fish), roasted fowl, stewed carrots, and nut tortes made without flour. Because of the limited availability of fresh fruits and vegetables in eastern Europe during late March and early April, carrots, beets, radishes, potatoes, and other root vegetables are important. Rosl, prepared weeks in advance by allowing raw beets covered with water to ferment, is the basis for a hot or cold borscht consumed during the week. Delicacies include beet or black radish preserves, khremslakh (pancakes made from matzo meal), sponge cakes, macaroons, and ingberlakh (candies made with grated carrot or small pieces of matzo and honey, nuts, and ginger).

Sephardim prepare haminados, eggs in their shells braised in water with red onion skins, vinegar, and saffron. Favorite Passover dishes among Moroccan Jews include dried fava bean soup with fresh coriander and stewed lamb with white truffles, which are harvested in February. Greek Jews feature artichokes with lemon, fish in rhubarb sauce, stuffed spinach leaves, leek croquettes, various dishes calling for lamb and lamb offal, and a baklava made with matzo. East European Jews traditionally made their own raisin wine for Passover, while Greek and Turkish Jews made *raki*, a liqueur derived from raisins through a process of distillation. Purchased wine must not only be kosher, which involves many strict religious regulations, but also kosher for Passover.

As if to demonstrate that Passover dietary restrictions are no impediment to innovation and variety, the kosher food industry has developed an astonishing array of Passover products. The historian Jenna Weissman Joselit, in "The Call of the Matzoh," notes that by 1900 Bloomingdales and Macy's featured Passover groceries, wine, and other holiday necessities (Joselit, 1994, p. 221). The most widely observed of the Jewish holidays, Passover occupies only 3 percent of the calendar, but generally accounts for 40 (and in some areas up to 60) percent of kosher food sales in the United States annually. This makes kosher for Passover products an estimated $2 billion industry. According to *Kosher Today*, a trade publication of the kosher food industry, more than six hundred new Passover products were introduced in 2001 alone, which gave consumers up to four thousand items from which to choose. However, in a world where almost everything is becoming kosher for Passover, from pizza to noodles, Passover may lose some of its culinary distinctiveness.

Public Seder

Whereas the seder is traditionally a family event, public and organizational seders arose even before the twentieth century in Europe, the United States, and elsewhere to meet the needs of Jewish soldiers away from home (for example, during the American Civil War and today in Israel); Jews confined in hospitals, nursing homes, and prisons; and the destitute. During the twentieth-century, the kibbutz, a collective agricultural settlement in Palestine and then in Israel, created its own Haggadahs and seders, consistent with the socialist and even atheistic tendencies of its founders and the practice of eating together in large public dining halls. During the Holocaust, Jews in Bergen-Belsen, separated from their families, organized to observe the holiday as best they could. Unable to obtain matzo, they determined that *hametz* was permitted and created a special prayer to say over it.

Even before World War I, seaside resorts in the United States attracted Jewish visitors who preferred to avoid the elaborate preparations for Passover and observe the holiday away from home. According to *Kosher Today*, over seventy-five thousand people participated in Passover programs in hotels during 2000 in the United States, and the Passover getaway business, which has grown in size and variety, hoped to fill thirty thousand rooms in 2002. In Israel, many orthodox families spend all eight days of the holiday at a hotel or kibbutz pension to avoid the considerable effort of preparing for Passover. Communal seders are also held in Europe. The first communal seder in Beijing took place in 1998. Caterers organize seders in banquet halls, and restaurants offer seders, in part as a response to the dispersal of families. Wolfgang Puck, at the prompting of his Jewish wife, began to host Passover seders at Spago, his Los Angeles restaurant, in 1985. The menu features such delicacies as roasted white Alaskan salmon (Panitz, 1999). Peter Hoffman, who has been hosting seders at his Mediterranean-style restaurant Savoy since 1994, created a seder inspired by Marrano traditions. Other restaurants may simply include matzo on the menu.

Third Seder

Whereas only one seder is required in Israel (and among some Reform Jews) and two seders in the Diaspora, a Lubavitcher tradition holds that the Baal Shem Tov, the eighteenth-century founder of Hasidism, a pietist movement, instituted a Messiah's Feast, mirroring the seder with matzo and wine, on the afternoon of the eighth day of Passover. During the 1920s, Zionist groups and members of the Jewish Labor movement organized third seders, although radical secular Haggadahs, which stressed human agency over divine intervention, were printed as early as the 1880s. In 2002 the Workmen's Circle, which is associated with the Jewish Labor movement, celebrated fifty years of its annual Third Seder, recently renamed A Cultural Seder. Their special Yiddish Haggadah, which makes no mention of God, focuses on liberation struggles and Yiddish cultural achievements. In the late twentieth century, they incorporated elements of the traditional seder for those who only observe this one seder. Other groups, prompted by such crises as Israeli soldiers missing in action and AIDS, also have created a third seder.

The Christian Seder

There is disagreement as to whether the Last Supper took place during the evening of the fourteenth of Nissan, after the Paschal sacrifice, in the form of a Passover meal (synoptic Gospels), or on the afternoon of the preceding day as an ordinary meal (Gospel of John). Consistent with the former, some Christians reenact the Last Supper as a seder, usually on Holy Thursday, based on practices thought to have been followed at the time of Christ. The Christian seder typically includes lamb, unleavened bread, bitter herbs, *haroset*, *karpas* (raw vegetables), and wine; washing of hands and feet; reclining at the table; recitation of appropriate blessings and passages from Exodus, and singing of Psalms. As Gillian Feeley-Harnik explains in *The Lord's Table: Eucharist and Passover in Early Christianity* (1981), the Last Supper, as a sacrificial meal, "most closely resembles the passover, but every critical element in the passover is reversed: the time, the place, the community, the sacrifice, and ultimately the significance of the meal" (Feeley-Harnik, 1981, p. 19).

Mimouna

In some communities, a special meal ushers out the holiday or otherwise marks the return to everyday life. Moroccan Jews celebrate the Mimouna after sundown on the last day of Passover and on the following day with a great variety of post-Passover foods, music, and dance. The earliest record of the holiday dates from the eighteenth century. While the etymology of Mimouna remains unclear, some find a connection with *maimouna* (Arabic, meaning 'wealth', 'good fortune'), *emunah* (Hebrew, meaning 'faith'), and *mammon* (Hebrew-Aramaic, meaning 'riches', 'prosperity'). Some link the timing of the Mimouna with the anniversary of the death of the revered Rabbi Maimon, father of Moses Maimonides, who moved from Cordoba to Fez in 1159/1160. Moroccan Jews believe the holiday originated in Fez.

The evening holiday is traditionally celebrated at home, with doors open to relatives and friends. Ears of wheat and flowers are placed on the table and around the room. A lavish table is set with a white cloth, and depending on the community, symbolic foods may include flour, yeast, wine, five coins, five beans, five dates, five eggs, sweets, nuts, fruits, milk, buttermilk, butter, a live fish, and *mofleta*, the first leavened food eaten after Passover. Mofleta is a yeast-risen pancake fried in a skillet, spread with butter and honey, and rolled. In Morocco, where Jews "sold" their *hametz* to their Muslim neighbors before Passover, the Muslims brought the wheat, flowers, dairy products, and other foods to the Jews during the afternoon of the last day of Passover. After Passover, Muslims returned the *hametz* and were rewarded, in addition to receiving a piece a matzo, believed to bring good fortune. The day following Passover is a time for family excursions and picnics. During the Mimouna, a time of courtship, young people dressed in their finery, and betrothed couples exchanged gifts. With the immigration of North African Jews to Israel, other Maghrebi and Levantine Jews also celebrate the Mimouna, which has become a large public event.

See also **Bible, Food in the; Christianity; Fasting and Abstinence; Feasts, Festivals, and Fasts; Islam; Judaism; Last Supper; Middle East; Religion and Food; United States: Ethnic Cuisines.**

BIBLIOGRAPHY

Bokser, Baruch M. *The Origins of the Seder: The Passover Rite and Early Rabbinic Judaism.* Berkeley, Calif.: University of California Press, 1984.

Bradshaw, Paul F., and Lawrence A. Hoffman, eds. *Passover and Easter: The Symbolic Structuring of Sacred Seasons.* Two Liturgical Traditions series, vol. 6. Notre Dame, Ind.: University of Notre Dame Press, 1999.

Brauer, Erich. *The Jews of Kurdistan.* Edited by Raphael Patai. Detroit, Mich.: Wayne State University Press, 1993.

Dobrinsky, Herbert C. *A Treasury of Sephardic Laws and Customs: The Ritual Practices of Syrian, Moroccan, Judeo-Spanish, and Spanish and Portuguese Jews of North America.* Hoboken, N.J., and New York: Yeshiva University Press, 1986.

Feeley-Harnik, Gillian. *The Lord's Table: Eucharist and Passover in Early Christianity.* Philadelphia: University of Pennsylvania Press, 1981.

Fredman, Ruth Gruber. *The Passover Seder: Afikoman in Exile.* Philadelphia: University of Pennsylvania Press, 1981.

Goodman, Philip. *The Passover Anthology.* Philadelphia: Jewish Publication Society of America, 1961.

Joselit, Jenna Weissman. "The Call of the Matzoh." In *The Wonders of America: Reinventing Jewish Culture, 1880–1950,* pp. 219–263. New York: Hill and Wang, 1994.

Michel, Joan. "The Mortar the Merrier." *Jewish Week* (New York) (1999).

Panitz, Beth. "A New Tradition: Dining Out for Passover." *Restaurants USA* (1999).

Segal, Judah Benzion. *The Hebrew Passover, from the Earliest Times to A.D. 70.* London Oriental Series, vol. 12. London, New York: Oxford University Press, 1963.

Schauss, Hayyim (Shoys, Hayim). *Guide to Jewish Holy Days: History and Observance.* New York: Schocken Books, 1962.

Shuldiner, David P. "The "Third" Seder of Passover: Liberating a Ritual of Liberation." In *Of Moses and Marx: Folk Ideology and Folk History in the Jewish Labor Movement,* pp. 119–140. Westport, Conn.: Bergin and Garvey, 1999.

Stavroulakis, Nicholas. *Cookbook of the Jews of Greece.* Port Jefferson, N.Y.: Cadmus Press, 1986.

Weinreich, Beatrice S. "The Americanization of Passover." In *Studies in Biblical and Jewish Folklore,* edited by Raphael Patai, Francis Lee Utley, and Dov Noy, pp. 329–366. Bloomington, Ind.: Indiana University Press, 1960.

Barbara Kirshenblatt-Gimblett

PASTA. Ground grain of the wheat plant (genus *Triticum*; family *Gramineae* or grass), native to Eurasia, forms the fundamental component of commercial "pasta," the generic term for what the U.S. Federal Standards of Identity call "macaroni products." Italian commercial dried pasta combines durum wheat (*Triticum durum*, hard wheat, or semolina, its coarsely ground endosperm) and water into a large number of shapes and sizes. Soft or common wheat (*Triticum vulgare*) is used for homemade or "fresh" pasta (which often contains egg, and sometimes oil and salt), as well as for bread and pastries. These are the two most important wheat grains in the Mediterranean diet.

Pasta is a versatile, nutritious, economical, thus democratic, and increasingly international food. In past times, it was fried and sweetened with honey, or tossed with *garum* (fish paste) by the ancient Romans. Or it might have been boiled, or baked in rich pies, called *timballi*, that defied Renaissance sumptuary laws. Today, pasta is usually boiled to a slightly chewy, resistant consistency (*al dente*), and dressed with a variety of sauces, eaten in soup, or baked. The oldest, most traditional Italian condiment from the thirteenth to the nineteenth centuries consisted of butter and cheese (and sugar, cinnamon, and other spices); pasta was also boiled in meat broths. Only since the 1830s was it combined with the now familiar tomato sauce. In the course of its history, pasta has been both a luxury, and only recently (in the nineteenth century), a popular food.

As late as the 1960s, the people of northern Italy normally ate risotto, polenta, and egg pasta—just as, in terms of fats, butter versus oil divided the cooler North from the warm South. The leveling of traditional foodways has made pasta a truly national food. However, this Italian first course (*primo*) has been adapted to main dish, side dish, salad, and even dessert in its diverse cultural naturalizations.

History: Dough Versus Pasta

It is vital to distinguish between two classes of pasta in order to make sense of its history. The most ancient form of pasta is flattened dough (Italian *sfoglia*) from which many fresh pasta forms (with and without egg) have evolved. Cereal-derived foods, based on whole, crushed, or finely ground grains, have been common to the Mediterranean for several millennia, taking the primitive form of mush (for example, Roman *puls*). Dough might be kneaded and shaped, and then fried, roasted, baked, or boiled. When it was flattened into a thin sheet and cut into strips, then boiled, a proto-pasta was created. This final step in the process appears to have created the archetypical category known today as "pasta."

Because a flour dough base is common to both pasta and bread, the histories of these foods have been merged and blurred. Although pasta may seem a simpler food, bread has held a more central place in the Mediterranean and Italian diet and worldview. Were historians to agree upon a common categorization of pasta, based on ingredients and cooking method (boiling in liquid), it might facilitate a clearer distinction between pasta and other forms of dough-based foods.

Terminology

Dough for boiling evolved into a variety of shapes. The original form appears to have been string-shaped, thread-shaped, worm-shaped, or ribbon-shaped—that is, long and thin, flat or round, as the earliest terms attest. For example, Latin *lásanum* (earthenware pot, from Greek *lásanon*, three-footed pot) blended with *láganum* (a long strip of thin, rolled dough), whence *lasagne*, a plural form in standard Italian. Still today, in Neapolitan or Calabrian dialect, a rolling pin is known as a *laganatura*. Other terms include Latin *tracta* (a long piece of dough, literally, 'drawn out'), Arabic *itrija* (string-shaped dough, whence southern Italian *trii* or *tria*, and Spanish *aletria*), Italian *vermicelli*, and later, *spaghetti*, *tagliatelle*, and *fettuccine*. Other early forms of pasta were created from small bits of rolled dough (Latin *lixulae*, Italian *gnocco* 'knuckle') or stuffed dough (*ravioli*). Standard Italian *maccherone* and dialectal Italian *maccarone* (source of English "macaroni"), an early synonym of *gnocco*, is said to derive from the Indo-European verbal root *mak-* ('to knead with force', whence Italian *ammaccare* 'to crush', e.g., *macco* fava bean

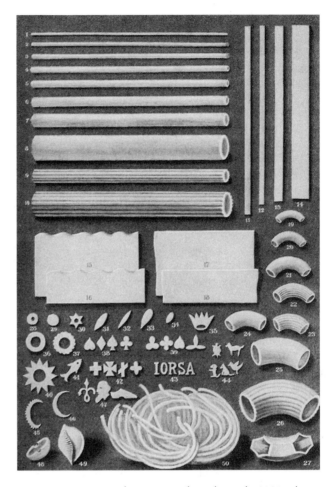

An American pasta advertisement from the early 1920s showing all the shapes of pasta and macaroni available at that time. ROUGHWOOD COLLECTION.

purée); if so, it testifies to the force required to knead and shape durum wheat dough.

But even the earliest Italian terms for pasta present wide regional variation. Indeed, Italian pasta history has been vexed, enlivened, and bedeviled by profound lexical specificity. One outwardly identical term may designate different things, historically and geographically. For instance, *maccarone*, from its first citation in the twelfth century, has referred to short dry pasta (twelfth century and twentieth century), long dry pasta (southern Italy, eighteenth through the twentieth centuries), long fresh pasta (regional Italian), *gnocchi* (fourteenth through the seventeenth centuries), and even ravioli. And it is not clear whether *lasagne* (*lágana*), widely used by the thirteenth century, were not more like fritters (compare today's Carnival sweets, *cenci*, *bugie*, *chiacchiere*) than boiled dough.

Pasta means 'paste, dough, batter' in Italian. An earlier, now obsolete, term was "alimentary paste," a loan translation from Italian *pasta alimentare*. Today, a lexical shift makes "pasta" the generic term for which all others stand as subsets, and "macaroni" (Italian *maccarone/*

maccheroni) now refers to hollow, short dry pasta, with a few exceptions surviving as regional homemade specialties in southern Italy.

Origins: East or West

Spontaneously invented forms of pasta existed simultaneously in various parts of the world—East and West—a clear case of polygenesis. Even a cursory look at this basic starch in the food systems of China and Italy, for instance, makes this parallel development obvious. While certain similarities may be surprising (noodles = *tagliatelle*; wonton = ravioli), the differences are no less so. Pasta is eaten by a variety of peoples but in significantly different ways.

The innovative leap—and the part of pasta's history that is more closely associated with Italy—is the revolution that *dry* pasta entailed, in conservation, economy, and diffusion. This process was established by the twelfth century in the Sicilian-Arab world. Thus, only in Italy (and a few parts of Asia) did pasta become so central to diet and cuisine, and such a diversified food. Further, Italy must be credited with pasta's global diffusion.

Historical landmark versus legend. A few landmarks mark fixed points in an otherwise fluctuating ocean of pasta history. Alongside such documentation, however, exists a substantial body of pasta mythology, the most notable involving the vexed question of Marco Polo's supposed introduction of Chinese noodles to Italy, likely attributable not to the *Milione* itself (which, however, mentions noodles made from the sago palm tree, enjoyed by Polo in Fanfur, likely Sumatra), but to the October 1929 issue of *The Macaroni Journal* (of the American Association of Pasta Makers), featuring "The Saga of Catay." This legend tells of the encounter of a sailor named "Spaghetti" with a Chinese maiden preparing a strange dish of boiled strands of dough, and of how he divulges this secret to the West. The story evidently sought to create a plausible link between the presence of noodles in China's more ancient civilization (documented during the Shang dynasty, 1700–1100 B.C.E.), and the predominantly Italian identity of pasta in the modern world.

Polygenesis is not a concept that is easily grasped or generally appealing. Italians had been making, consuming, even exporting pasta before Polo's return in 1292, as the earliest document, a Genovese testament predating Polo's return by at least twelve years, clearly attests. Internal evidence further suggests that Polo considered the sago variety a type of pasta, which presupposes the existence of, and familiarity with, pasta as a food. Other data confirms the parallel development of this food in the West.

Etruscan and Roman. The Etruscan tomb "La Tomba dei Rilievi," in Cerveteri, fourth century B.C.E., provides iconographic evidence: a woman in the act of rolling out dough, accompanied by familiar implements (for example, rolling pin, sack of flour, water container, knife), al-

though it is not clear how the flattened dough might have been prepared. Horace (*Satires* VI, book l) mentions the comfort of his simple dish of chickpeas, leeks, and *lágana*, whence Salentine *ciceri e tria*, still eaten today; Cicero also speaks of these long strips of thin, rolled dough made with water and flour. Apicius, in *De re coquinaria* (book IV, chapter 2), describes *lágana* fried in oil and tossed with pepper and (that all-purpose Roman condiment) *garum*—a dish of which Petronius's character, parvenu host Trimalchio (in the *Satyricon*), was particularly fond—and *tractae* (evidently dried durum pasta) for thickening broth. He also elaborates on a rich, layered *lágana* dish involving meats, fish, sauce, and spices.

Sicilian-Arab geographer. The first clear Italian reference to dried—hence preservable—pasta, and to a pasta industry, comes from Arab Sicily. In 1138, a Moroccan geographer, Abu Abdullah Muhemmed ibn Idris (known as Idrisi in Sicilian), was commissioned by Roger II, the Norman king of Sicily, to survey his kingdom. In his 1154 codex, he describes the vast fields, many mills, and farms at Tràbia (30 kilometers from Palermo), where a string-like pasta (referred to by its Arabic name, *itrija*) was produced and exported in "shiploads" to Calabria, and to other parts of the Muslim and Christian worlds. The pasta was evidently dry, and a large-scale operation is being described. Although no generic term, hence no notion of pasta, existed in Arab gastronomy at this time, Arabs knew of this dried convenience food—particularly useful for long caravan rides, and later to seafaring Genovese and Sicilian sailors. Beginning in the twelfth century, in fact, Genovese merchants became agents of Sicilian pasta's northward diffusion. By the fourteenth century, they began producing and selling *vermicelli* and other pasta "di Genova"—so that Genoa became, after Sicily, one of the earliest production centers in Italy.

Genovese barrel of maccheroni. In the bequest of a soldier, Ponzio Bastone, written by notary Ugolino Scarpa (2 February 1279), a *bariscella plena de macaronis*, a small barrel of dried pasta, is listed. This earliest attestation of the term *macaroni* is important for three reasons: it suggests the value of the food product (for example, worthy of being listed in a will); that it was indeed dry pasta (for example, conserved in a barrel); and that it was, by this date, known as a generic term (as pasta is today).

Gastronomic utopias: Cuccagna. In the mythic land of plenty, known to the Italians as *il paese di Cuccagna*, and in medieval Europe as Cockaigne, there was a very peculiar mountain. The Italian version of the myth was first described by Boccaccio (*Decameron*, VIII, 3, Calandrino, a fool's tale). In this gastronomic utopia, which he calls Bengodi, a cauldron sits on top of a Parmigiano-cheese mountain and continuously spews forth *maccheroni* and ravioli that roll down the mountain's side, land in a rich capon broth, and are free for the taking by the poltroons. Such macaroni, however, were evidently synonymous with *gnocchi*, chestnut-sized or larger balls of flour dough (not potato), often pictured as served on a skewer. This shape accounts for the ease with which they could roll down the *Cuccagna* mountain.

The Maccheronic Muse

Since pasta has inspired myth, legend, literature, art, film, and graphic design, its history ought take into account historical data as much as its presence in cultural history, for it has a long oral as well as written tradition. Its creation myths have involved the noblest of gods in the Roman pantheon, emperors, and magicians; pasta miracles have promoted worthy candidates to sainthood (for example, St. William the Hermit turned dirt-filled ravioli into a delicious dish); folk narratives often feature magic (pasta) pots; traveler's tales tell of marvelous and strange pasta dishes (for example, Marco Polo); and street theater masks—and actual Neapolitans—have made a public spectacle of pasta. The maccheronic muse has also inspired carnivalesque literature, theater, song, odes, proverbs, and more.

Pasta gave its name to a linguistic/literary phenomenon known as Maccheronic poetry, peaking in the fifteenth century. It was a pastiche of Latin and vernacular Italian, frequently producing a comic effect by borrowing a vernacular term that reflected the rustics, who, in turn, were referred to by the gross and simple food they ate, *maccherone* or *gnocco* (noodle-head), and who spoke no Latin, the language of culture. The most notable example of this tradition is the Maccheronic poet, Teofilo Folengo (alias Merlin Cocai), author of the mock-heroic epic *Baldus*, in which pasta-maker muses reside on Mount Cockaigne, and whose genius is attributed to the consumption of *maccheroni* and *lasagne*.

Eighteenth-Century Naples as Pasta Capital

Naples began to import pasta from Sicily at the end of the fifteenth century, but it was not until the eighteenth century that Neapolitans earned the title of *mangiamaccheroni* (macaroni-eaters)—a title earlier borne by Sicilians. Naples became the emblematic capital of pasta, and the city's representative was the *commedia dell'arte* character, half-starved Pulcinella, who on stage was always eating or talking about macaroni. By 1785 there were 280 pasta shops in Naples. Pasta became a street food and its most devoted consumers were street people—*lazzaroni*—as seen in myriad popular prints of the time, where they are characteristically portrayed holding the long strands, dressed with Romano cheese, with their fingers, and at arms length sliding them, often unchewed, down the gullet. Indeed, so unique was this spectacle that it became a must-see tourist attraction, and gentlemen on the grand tour often ordered up a plate of pasta for a *lazzarone*, just to see it performed.

Immigrants and Pasta

Neapolitans and other southern Italians were critical to pasta's diffusion throughout the world. For it was as much immigration—and the majority of immigrants were, in fact, Neapolitan and southern—as technological advances and transatlantic trade, that brought pasta to the world's attention. Along with the wave of late-nineteenth-century immigrants came shiploads of spaghetti in blue wrap (for example, Napoli Bella and Vesuvio brands), olive oil, and condensed tomato paste. Americans first considered these inedible foreign foods and tried to reform the newcomers' diet, but spaghetti won out and eventually became American, not merely ethnic, fare. Italian immigrants were to introduce many other cultures to pasta wherever they settled.

Although Thomas Jefferson, much interested in macaroni and pasta technology, brought cases of the foodstuff to America in 1786 (and later had a pasta machine shipped to him from Campania), it was not until 1848 that it began to be produced commercially in America. The World War I years and the interruption of pasta imports from overseas gave rise to an expanded pasta industry in the United States, as many Italian-American pasta importers became manufacturers, through small family operations, many of which still exist. Prohibition may have given pasta a boost as well, since it seemed a logical accompaniment to speakeasy wine. In the expanding pasta industry of the 1930s, pasta ceased to be merely Italian and became an American food.

Pasta as Emblem

Ethnic stereotyping frequently makes reference to food. Italians have long been associated with pasta, and Italians from different regions represent themselves by the type of pasta they eat. In England, from approximately 1750 to 1850, a "macaroni" referred to a foppish Englishman, a dandy, who affected foreign (Italian) style by overdressing, wearing a preposterous wig, and perhaps eating foreign foods (for example, *Yankee Doodle Dandy* who "stuck a feather in his hat and called it macaroni" and the London gentlemen's club, The Macaroni Club). On the negative side, a cultured Italian might have referred to a simpleton or country bumpkin as a *gnocco*, *maccarone*, or *spaghetto*. Sicilians—later Neapolitans—were derogatorily labeled *mangiamaccheroni* (macaroni-eaters) by Italians farther north. Americans have referred to Italians as "Spaghetti Benders." And Marinetti's Futurist Manifesto did not help matters when it declared war on traditional foods, especially pasta, a food which, the avant-garde insisted, promoted moral and physical laxity. The ideal, evidently, was the Germanic meat-eater, a virile warrior race. Italians ignored the Futurists' cultural violence. Instead, Mussolini waged a battle on wheat (*battaglia del grano*) in an attempt to make Italy wheat-sufficient. The vastly increased wheat acreage had the effect of shifting the epicenter of production northward (pasta producers included Agnesi in Oneglia, Buitoni in San Sepolcro, Barilla in Parma), thereby ending the dominance of Naples by the 1940s.

Many legendary Italian pasta-eaters have helped raise the image of this food: Rossini, Caruso, Sophia Loren. Pasta iconography, old and new, traces its presence in cultural history, from early popular prints of *Cuccagna* or of Neapolitan pasta-eaters, to pasta advertisements, packaging, and film (for example, Charlie Chaplin in *City Lights*, Disney's *The Lady and the Tramp*, and in Italy, Totò, Sophia Loren)—all of which molded pasta's image for millions.

Commercial Pasta: From Artisan Guilds to Multinationals

From the fourteenth to the sixteenth centuries, pasta became well established all over Italy. Pasta makers became so numerous that they formed corporations and guilds, largely to protect their interests against competing guilds (for example, bakers). These guilds were in Florence (*lasagnari*), 1337; Genoa, 1574; Savona (*fidelari*), 1577; Naples (*vermicellari, pastai*), 1579; Palermo, 1665; Rome, 1642.

It is in the passage to dried pasta that the quantum historic leap is achieved and pasta commerce begins, the earliest record of which goes back to medieval Arabs and Sicilians. In more recent times, increasingly efficient technology relating to the basic phases in pasta production—kneading, pressing, extruding, cutting, and drying—together with improved distribution networks and power sources (electricity), have led to an enormous increase in production and consumption. Indeed, by the mid-twentieth century, commercial pasta had truly become a universal food for all classes.

Large-scale pasta production first flourished in coastal areas (Palermo, Genoa, later Naples) where plenty of sun, and alternating warm and cool sea breezes allowed for outdoor drying—the most critical part of the process—and also made shipping easy. Like laundry, spaghetti was hung to dry on outdoor lines and became part of the Neapolitan folkloric milieu. Pasta brands from Gragnano and Torre Annunziata, where warm Vesuvian air and cool sea breezes created perfect drying conditions, became renowned. Once artificial drying technology was devised, however, manufacturing was freed from such climatic considerations.

Other technological milestones included mechanical kneaders, continuous feed presses, even refinements of the fork. Cesare Spadaccini of Naples invented the first mechanical kneader to replace feet (although this was not developed), as well as a four-prong shortened fork to make spaghetti twirling easier and its consumption possible at the Neapolitan court of Ferdinand II (circa 1840). But it was a spate of mostly nineteenth-century inventions that revolutionized the industry: for example, Féreol Sandragné's prototype of the "continuous" feed machine, and the "Marsigliese," a mechanical sieve that could sort crushed grain.

Early artisans' guilds and small family-run businesses have largely given way to multinational giants who count pasta manufacturing among their diversified holdings and enjoy large market shares of a lucrative, expanding global market. Some of these companies are the following: Borden (largest pasta producer in the United States, sole U.S. distributor for De Cecco since 1988, and head of an empire of small, regional companies); Philip Morris (parent company of General Foods, acquired Kraft in 1988); Nestlé (acquired Buitoni in 1988); Hershey's; Campbell's; and Lipton.

Wheat

Sicily and southern Italy—ancient Rome's, then Italy's, breadbasket—was an early source of durum wheat for Italian pasta, which, since 1967, has been the only legally mandated grain allowed for this food. While Italians came to produce and consume the world's largest quantities of pasta outside Asia (over fifty pounds per capita in 1988), Italy's capacity to produce wheat was easily overwhelmed. In the nineteenth century, other sources were added. Genovese merchants imported the best Kubanka wheat (up to 19 percent protein), grown in the fertile black earth of Taganrog, Crimea, on the Black Sea. But famines, revolution, and genocide had destroyed this mythic Russian wheat by the 1920s and 1930s, apparently forever. North American wheat from Manitoba and North Dakota filled the vacuum. American durum wheat production—which, in turn, boosted the American pasta industry—was largely due to the efforts of one man. Mark Carleton, an agronomist for the U.S. Department of Agriculture and an expert in plant pathology, went to Russia in 1898 looking for rust-resistant wheat and, upon returning, converted farmers, milling companies, chemists, and hotel and restaurant cooks to accept durum wheat.

Pasta Typology: Cutting the Linguistic Dough

Estimates of the number of pasta shapes range from 600 to 1000. Pasta atlases are only recently beginning to appear. The sheer volume of regional, traditional, and also industrial and historical types—although only a fraction of them remain in common use—makes this task a daunting one. Some of the earliest terms refer to length and thinness, for example: Arabic *itrija* and *sev* or *seviyan* (from Hindi *sevika* 'thread'), Italian *vermicelli* ('small worms', originally, finger-length), and later, Italian *spaghetti* (from *spago* 'string'). Other terms refer to the dough and to shaping techniques that involve cutting (Italian *tagliatelle*, from *tagliare* 'to cut'), rolling, or stamping. Greatest variation occurs in commercial, not homemade pasta, for the obvious reason that industrial dies have made such innovations possible.

A raviolo by other names. The language of pasta (as of music) is Italian. Much of its rich lexicon is attributable to the richness of the Italian language itself. There are suffixes, given in their plural forms here, that can reduce its dimensions (-*elli*, -*etti*, -*ini*, -*otti*, as in *ravioli/ravioletti* and *tortelli/tortellini*), or increase its dimensions (-*oni*, as in *ravioloni*, *tortelloni*), or subtly grade it by increasing width (*tagliolini* > *fettuccine* > *tagliatelle* > *pappardelle* > *lasagne*). There is also rich regional variation. For example, the case for filled pasta (of which Emilia-Romagna is the heartland) is known as *casoncelli* (*cansonsei*) in Bergamo, *tortelli* in Emilia-Romagna, *agnolotti* in Piedmont, *pansoti* in Liguria, *cappelletti* or *ravioli* in central Italy. As for the most common homemade ribbon-shaped egg pasta, *tagliatelle* are also known (with slight variation in size) as *fettuccine*, *lasagnette*, *trenette*.

Still today, a marked distinction exists between egg-based fresh pasta, a special, often festive food, and dried commercial pasta, daily fare. But Italians also divide pasta as follows: pasta in clear broth (*pastina in brodo*); pasta in heartier vegetable soup (*minestra*, whence *minestrone*); dried pasta drained and served with a sauce (*pasta asciutta*); and baked pasta (*pasta al forno*: for example, *lasagne*, *timballo*, *pasticcio*).

Pasta typologies might further be ordered according to varying criteria: method or place of preparation (home, restaurant, factory); grain type (soft, durum, whole, alternative); calendrical occurrences (festive versus penitent pasta, for example, with and without meat sauce or eggs); Italian versus non-Italian or emigrant pasta (for example, Italian-American spaghetti and meatballs); and finally, pasta morphology. Pasta can even be classified according to consumer profile, age, cultural background, and health concerns. For instance, adult pasta differs from children's varieties: there is Italian nursery food, *pastina in brodo* (tiny pasta in clear broth); American macaroni and cheese and canned dinosaur or alphabet pasta; and pasta on toast for the British. Special pastas have been developed for the wheat intolerant; and gourmet pastas are aimed at the high-end market. Homemade pasta can be further classified according to the instrument used: rolling pin versus pasta maker or small press (for example, a *torchietto* for extruding *bigoli* in the Veneto); a "comb" or *pettine* (for example, for *garganelli* in Romagna); a zither-like instrument, known as a *chitarra* (guitar), over which thin dough is stretched and rolled to produce thin strands (for example, for *tonnarelli*, resembling square spaghetti, in the Abruzzo); a long metal rod or *ferro* (for long *maccheroni* in Calabria, Puglia, Sicily).

Then there is morphology—long versus short, smooth versus ribbed, hollow versus filled, straight versus fluted. The myriad shapes draw on many semantic areas—human, natural, and even divine. There are helixes, tubes, shells, pearls, nests, worms, butterflies, snails, birds, stars, moons, waves, threads, ribbons, bowties, even "priest-stranglers" (*strozza-* or *strangolapreti*). Paternosters and avemarias (resembling rosary beads), and other shapes inspired by politics (*garibaldini*, *mafalde*, *tripoline*, *assabesi*, *abissini*), are no longer made. But innovation continues, even though some shapes prove to be mere fads (for example, radiators, UFOs).

Matching pasta to sauce, determining pasta to sauce ratio, and knowing the correct cooking time are subtle areas of pasta connoisseurship, traditional for Italians but learned by others (although traditional canons are shifting even in Italy). In a fifteenth-century cookbook, *De honesta voluptate ac valetudine* (Of honest pleasure and well-being), Bartolomeo Sacchi (pseudonym Plàtina) cautioned that pasta should be cooked "for as long as it takes to say three paternosters"—a short amount of time, even for fresh pasta.

Trends
Pasta trends take place within wider social and nutritional contexts. There has been a move toward whole foods and alternative grains such as corn, buckwheat, and spelt. Innovative ingredients—some restaurant-driven—include colored pasta (tomato, herb, beet, mushroom, shrimp, even chocolate) and novelty-stuffed pasta (seafood, artichoke, dried tomato). There has also been a trend toward fusion cuisines, for example, blending East and West. New health guidelines advise lower fat, higher fiber, increased vegetarianism, less processing. The American trend toward greater convenience favors ready-cooked, frozen, microwaveable, and cold-serve pastas, although the Slow Food movement is beginning to counter this trend in the new millennium. Americans are becoming more sophisticated in regard to better quality products, taste, nutritional value, authenticity, seasonality, and the artisan tradition.

Nutritional Value: Fat or Skinny?
Pasta's fortunes have fluctuated over its long history: it has been considered both a luxury food (in the sixteenth century, Neapolitan authorities prohibited its consumption in times of famine or scarcity of wheat) and a vernacular staple. Commonly perceived as a poor man's food at the beginning of the twentieth century, pasta began, with the support of nutritionists extolling the virtues of the Mediterranean diet in the 1970s, to experience a rehabilitation. New nutrition guidelines (and the food chart reformulated in the 1990s) recommend less protein, less saturated animal fat, more fiber, and more complex carbohydrates. Pasta, therefore, is now recognized to be a healthy food. It is also a highly versatile, immediately satisfying food, recommended for athletes ("carbo-loading" sustains energy before strenuous sports) and even for refined palates.

Vegetables, lean meats, or fish, combined with good quality (even enriched or whole wheat) pasta, makes an excellent, balanced meal. Components of pasta include moisture (water), energy, protein, fat, carbohydrates, and ash. According to the U.S. Department of Agriculture bulletin (1981), nutrient values for one cup of spaghetti (two ounces uncooked) are approximately seven to fourteen grams of protein, thirty-nine grams of carbohydrates, and when enriched, it provides calcium, phosphorus, iron, potassium, thiamin, riboflavin, and niacin.

The caloric value of one cup of cooked pasta is approximately 190 calories (if *al dente*) and 155 (if tender).

See also **China; Italy; Noodle in Asia; Noodle in Northern Europe; Wheat.**

BIBLIOGRAPHY

Agnesi, Eva. *E tempo di pasta* [It's pasta time] (includes writings of Vincenzo Agnesi). Rome: Museo Nazionale delle Paste Alimentari, 1998.

Alberini, Massimo. Introduction to *Pasta & Pizza*, by Anna Martini. Milan: Mondadori, 1974.

Alberini, Massimo. *Maccheroni e spaghetti: Storia, letteratura, aneddoti, 1244–1994* [Macaroni and spaghetti: history, literature, anecdotes]. Casale Monferrato (AL): Piemme, 1994.

Alberini, Massimo. *Storia della cucina italiana* [History of Italian cuisine]. Casale Monferrato (AL): Piemme.

"Contre Marco Polo: Une histoire comparée des pâtes alimentaires" [Against Marco Polo: a comparative history of pasta] *Médiévales* 16–17 (1989): 27–100.

Cùnsolo, Felice. *Il libro dei maccheroni* [The macaroni book]. Milan: Mondadori, 1979.

Davidson, Alan. "Pasta." In *The Oxford Companion to Food*, edited by Alan Davidson, pp. 580–584. Oxford: Oxford University Press, 1999.

Del Conte, Anna. *Portrait of Pasta*. New York: Paddington Press, 1976.

Del Giudice, Luisa. "Mountains of Cheese and Rivers of Wine: *Paesi di Cuccagna* and other Gastronomic Utopias." In *Imagined States: National Identity, Utopia, and Longing in Oral Cultures*, edited by Luisa Del Giudice and Gerald Porter. Logan: Utah State University Press, 2001.

Hazan, Giuliano. *The Classic Pasta Cookbook*. Sydney, Australia: RD Press, 1993.

Lawson, Nigella. *Il museo immaginario della pasta* [The imaginary museum of pasta]. Turin, Italy: Allemandi, 1995.

Medagliani, Eugenio. *Pastario, ovvero, Atlante delle paste alimentari italiane: Primo tentativo di catalogazione delle paste alimentari italiane* [Pastarium, or the Italian pasta atlas: A first attempt toward an Italian pasta catalogue]. 3d ed. Lodi, Italy: Bibliotheca Culinaria, 1997.

Montanari, Massimo. "Macaroni Eaters." In *The Culture of Food*, translated from *La fame e l'abbondanza*, pp. 140–148. Oxford: Blackwell, 1994.

Morelli, Alfredo. *In principio era la sfoglia: Storia della pasta* [In the beginning there was sfoglia: the history of pasta]. Pinerolo, Italy: Chiriotti Editori, 1991.

Prezzolini, Giuseppe. *A History of Spaghetti Eating and Cooking for: Spaghetti Dinner*. New York: Abelard-Schuman, 1955.

Prezzolini, Giuseppe. *Maccheroni & C.* 2d edition. Milan, Italy: Longanesi, 1957.

Rizzi, Silvio, and Tan Lee Leng. *The Pasta Bible*. New York: Penguin Studio, 1996.

U.S. Department of Agriculture, Nutrition Monitoring Division. *Composition of Foods: Cereal Grains and Pasta: Raw, Processed, Prepared*. Washington, D.C.: U.S. Government Printing Office: 1989.

The U.S. Pasta Market: A Business Information Report. Commack, N.Y.: Business Trend Analysts, 1991.

Valli, Carlo. *Pasta nostra quotidiana: Viaggio intorno alla pasta* [Our daily pasta: journeying around pasta]. Padua, Italy: MEB, 1991.

Luisa Del Giudice

PASTEUR, LOUIS.

Coupling true scientific genius with a talent for dramatic self-promotion, Louis Pasteur (1822–1895) rose from humble beginnings as the son of a tanner in a small French village to international fame before his death.

Pasteur was trained as a chemist, and his earliest work on the crystals of tartaric acid, a naturally occurring by-product of wine production, caught the attention of several established chemists, who promoted his career and helped him secure an appointment as professor of chemistry at the University of Strasbourg.

Arriving in Strasbourg in January of 1849, he met Marie Laurent, daughter of the university's rector. With characteristic decisiveness, Pasteur proposed marriage within a few weeks, and in May of that year he and Marie were married. He chose well: For the rest of his life, Marie Pasteur supported and assisted him in his work; often they spent their evenings together, with Pasteur dictating notes or letters to his wife.

The Pasteurs moved in 1854 to the university at Lille, a thriving industrial area of France. Pasteur encouraged the practical application of science to the industries around him. His efforts on behalf of a local manufacturer who made alcohol from sugar beets were his first serious study of fermentation.

Moving on to Paris, he assumed positions at his old college, the Ecole Normale Supérieure, and later at the Sorbonne as well. He was not provided with a research laboratory, so he set one up at his own expense in a cramped unused space. This included a compartment under the stairs so small that he had to crawl in on his hands and knees to check his cultures.

In 1863, Emperor Napoleon III asked Pasteur to assist France in combating various "diseases" of wine that often caused exported French wine to go bad before it reached its destination. Pasteur believed that the yeasts observed in wine were the cause of fermentation, a fact that was not understood by much of the scientific community. These living yeasts appeared so mysteriously that many chemists believed they were generated spontaneously. Pasteur devised ingenious experiments to demonstrate that the yeasts came from the atmosphere. His belief in germs as causative agents that could infect a new medium on contact was sustained in his later work with animal and human diseases.

Pasteur also observed that other microbes besides the wine yeasts were present whenever the wines soured. In fact, he and his assistants soon learned to predict the taste of a wine according to which microbes they spotted in it with their microscopes. Pasteur urged the winemakers to provide conditions conducive to the growth of wine yeast and not to that of other microbes. He suggested a prolonged gentle heating, which discouraged undesirable microbes without altering the taste of the wine. A jury of wine experts conducted a taste test at Pasteur's request to establish that the taste was unaffected by the heating. This technique, which is today regularly applied to all kinds of foodstuffs, especially milk, quickly came to be called "pasteurization." Pasteur took out a patent on this process, but he soon allowed it to pass into the public domain. Though less dramatic than his later work with diseases, pasteurization is perhaps Pasteur's greatest contribution to the safety of food throughout the world. Pasteur was not the first to preserve foods by heating and protecting them from contamination, but he extended the practice to a variety of foodstuffs and offered a theoretical basis for its success.

Pasteur also advised vinegar makers, as well as the French beer industry. He hoped to make French beer superior to German as a gesture of revenge for the Franco-Prussian War of 1870. He taught hygienic practices to France's silk industry and, less easily, to the medical profession. The germ theory was then successfully applied to the development of vaccines for anthrax and other animal diseases, and finally to prevent the development of the dread rabies in human beings.

Pasteur achieved all this by dint of persistent hard work. His was not a balanced life. His labors, his ambition, and his aggressiveness in promoting his theories and reputation may all have been culprits in his severe stroke at age forty-five, which paralyzed his left side and left him with a limp. However, he continued to work for another two decades before his increasingly frail health gradually slowed him down.

Despite stirring up a good deal of controversy, Pasteur was given many honors in his lifetime. He received scientific prizes and awards and was elected to the French Academy of Sciences, the Academy of Medicine, and finally the august Académie Française. In 1888, the private Pasteur Institute was established in Paris, funded by contributions large and small from all over the world. Pasteur's seventieth birthday was the occasion for a national jubilee, and at his death he was given a state funeral in Paris before his body was interred in a grand tomb at the Pasteur Institute.

Even before his death, Pasteur was regarded, especially in France, almost as a secular saint. His earliest biographies were hagiographic, in keeping with the preference of the late nineteenth and early twentieth centuries for heroes of mythic proportions. The current age, on the other hand, needs to debunk, demythologize, and deconstruct the legends of the past. Accordingly, a modern reassessment of Pasteur has been in progress since the late twentieth century, aided by material from Pasteur's private laboratory notebooks, which have been available to scholars only since 1971. In the end, when all the evidence is gathered and reconsidered, the popular view of him may be altered, but Pasteur will remain a human being whose unceasing effort, scientific imagination, and inspired intuition unquestionably improved the food we eat and the world we live in.

See also **Fermentation; France: Tradition and Change in French Cuisine; Microorganisms; Food Safety; Wine from Classical Times to the Nineteenth Century.**

BIBLIOGRAPHY

Debré, Patrice. *Louis Pasteur*. Paris: Flammarion, 1994.

De Kruif, Paul. *The Microbe Hunters*. New York: Harcourt, Brace, 1926. Two chapters on Pasteur.

Dubos, René J. *Louis Pasteur: Free Lance of Science*. Boston: Little Brown, 1950.

Duclaux, Émile. *Pasteur: The History of a Mind*. Translated by Erwin F. Smith and Florence Hedges. Philadelphia; London: W. B. Saunders, 1920. Duclaux was Pasteur's assistant and his successor at the Pasteur Institute.

Geison, Gerald L. *The Private Science of Louis Pasteur*. Princeton, N.J.: Princeton University Press, 1995.

Loir, Adrien. *A l'ombre de Pasteur*. Paris: Le Mouvement Sanitaire, 1938. Loir was Pasteur's nephew and lab assistant.

Vallery-Radot, Pasteur. *Pasteur inconnu*. Paris: Flammarion, 1954. The author is Pasteur's grandson.

Vallery-Radot, René. *La Vie de Pasteur*. 2 vols. Paris: Hachette et cie, 1900.

Vallery-Radot, René. *M. Pasteur, histoire d'un savant par un ignorant*. Paris: J. Hetzel, 1883. A short work written by Pasteur's son-in-law and corrected by Pasteur himself.

Alice Arndt

PASTRY. Pastry is flour mixed with shortening and flavoring ingredients to produce a coherent mass, used for pies and other dishes in North American, European, and Middle Eastern cuisines. Basic additions are fat, a little salt, and water. Pastry-making, *pâtisserie* in French, has developed as a special branch of cookery. Specialized products of the pastry cook or pâtissier include delicate flour and sugar confections (cakes, cookies, waffles, meringues, frostings, glazes, and fillings) combined in small pastries for snacks, taken with tea or coffee or after meals. By extension, the word pastry is sometimes used collectively to indicate sweet, flour-based items for dessert.

Defining pastry types is difficult, as there are numerous variations. Three basic ones are short-crust or pie pastry, puff pastry, and flaky or rough puff. Short-crust pastry is one part fat (butter, lard, or commercial pastry fat) to two of flour by weight. The fat is cut or rubbed into the flour until the mixture resembles breadcrumbs, a little ice water is added, and the mass is pressed together with minimal working to make a dough. French *pâte brisée* is similar, but uses a little more fat and is mixed with egg. Variations include sweetened *pâte sucrée* and *pâte sablée* (very rich, similar to cookie dough). Short pastries are crumbly when cooked and used for many pies and tarts.

Puff pastry or *pâte feuilletée fine*, is an elaborate, layered pastry with a tender melting texture and excellent flavor. Equal proportions of butter to flour by weight are used. About a fifth of the butter is cut into the flour, and water is added to make a dough. This is allowed to rest in a cool place, and then rolled out; the remaining butter is then placed as a block in the center of the sheet of dough, which is folded over it. It is rerolled and folded in three, a process known as a "turn." Four turns are made with rests between, giving a dough with thin, even layers of fat between leaves of dough; air pockets also get trapped in the layers. Well-made puff pastry has up to 240 layers, and expands up to eight times its original

Vienna still reigns as the capital of fine pastries. These pastries, ornamented with strawberries and kiwi fruit, were displayed in the window of Janele's Bakery in Vienna, one of the well-known pastry shops in the city. © WOLFGANG KAEHLER/CORBIS.

thickness during baking. It is used for napoleons, cornets (cone-shaped pastries often filled with whipped cream or ice cream), and other fine pastries, sweet or savory, in the French tradition. Yeast-leavened doughs are turned with butter in the same way to make croissants and Danish pastries.

Flaky or rough puff pastries, French *demi-feuilletées*, are less well-defined. They usually have fat-to-flour ratios that are higher than that of short-crust but lower than that of puff pastry. They are made with the general method used for making puff pastry, but the butter may be spread over the dough in one batch or incorporated in three fractions, one each time the dough is turned. Quick versions are made by cutting the fat into pea-sized lumps, adding water to make a dough, and then giving it three or four turns. The dough has a light and layered effect but does not rise as high as puff pastry. It is also used in similar ways, especially with meat dishes such as beef Wellington.

Many other pastry recipes exist. *Choux* pastry uses a very different method. Water and butter are heated together; the result is mixed with flour, and eggs are beaten into the mass. The paste produced is soft and supple, and is piped to make cream puffs, chocolate éclairs, and other shapes, or flavored with cheese for the French *gougère*. English cookery includes hot-water crust: water and lard heated to the boiling point and mixed with flour, giving a malleable, strong paste that is raised while hot to make tall pies of pork or game; and suet crust, made of flour, beef suet, and water, and used for suet puddings and dumplings.

In Central Europe, the Middle East, and North Africa, strudel and phyllo pastries are made from a dough of flour, a little butter or oil, and water, which is worked to form an elastic mass that is stretched into a paperthin sheet. When the pastry is ready for use in baking, its surface is brushed with melted butter. Strudel pastry is rolled around fillings such as apples or poppy seeds, while phyllo is often cut into sheets and stacked in layers with nuts to make sweet dishes, or with spinach and cheese for savory ones.

Indian cookery involves pastry made from flour with a little ghee (clarified butter) or oil. This is used to enclose savory fillings for *samosas* (turnovers), and is deep-fried, providing the crispness that baking gives to pastries from the European traditions. Some types are cooked alone and drenched in sugar syrup to give sweet pastries. Chinese cookery also includes a few plain short-crust–type pastry recipes, notably that used for moon cakes, filled pastries traditionally eaten to celebrate the Moon (or Mid-Autumn) Festival.

Protein content of the flour is important: too much, and the pastry is tough and shrinks; too little, and it is very mealy. A medium protein content is best. Development of gluten (the protein complex that gives texture to bread) is inhibited by cutting in the fat, a process which

The pastry shop became a social institution by the end of the nineteenth century. This painting of the Gloppe Pastry Shop by Jean Beraud in the Musée Carnavalet, Paris, provides a vignette of the dainty snacking once associated with these elegantly appointed establishments. © ARCHIVO ICONO-GRAFICO, S. A./CORBIS.

coats the flour particles, preventing the water from reaching the proteins. In flaky and puff pastries, turning encourages limited gluten development in horizontal sheets for the characteristic texture.

Fat choice is also important. Butter gives a good flavor but produces a less short texture than lard, which gives a flaky texture. Lard has a coarse crystal structure that coats the flour particles more effectively and is one hundred percent fat, unlike butter, which contains a little water. Some cooks consider a mixture of lard and butter to give the best balance of flavor and texture. Margarine and specially tailored vegetable fats are often substituted on grounds of cost, nutrition, or ethics. Oils give very crumbly pastry. Keeping pastry cool during working is also important, otherwise the fat becomes oily and the texture suffers.

During baking, the water in pastry vaporizes and allows crisp flakes of dough to form. In puff pastry, water vapor and air trapped between the layers expand and force them apart, making the pastry rise; a similar effect produces the characteristically hollow texture of *choux* pastry.

The history of pastry has been little explored. Pastry of a sort was known to both Greek and Roman civilizations, but it was oil-based, and limited in its applications. Late medieval references to pastry do not make it clear what type is being referred to. In the seventeenth century, the work of La Varenne (originally published in 1651) and others shows that several types of pastry were recognized. Methods for puff pastry had developed, as had pastes rich with butter, cream, or eggs, used for little tarts and pies. These were intended to be eaten, unlike the coarse puff paste made for great pies, which was plain, made from brown rye flour with only a little fat. It protected game and meat fillings from intense heat during cooking, and acted as a container that excluded air and preserved the contents afterwards. By the nineteenth century, pastry making was a complex art, recorded by chefs such as Jules Gouffé who moved between the great houses of Europe, learning and codifying techniques from different places. Pastry had also developed as a traditional product in certain areas, such as Cornwall in England, where Cornish pasties, semicircular turnovers filled with meat and vegetables, had become a traditional food for miners.

The ingredients of pastry make it an energy-dense food, and the use of fats such as butter and lard gives it a high cholesterol content, but it is so important and convenient as an edible container that it seems likely to remain popular. Many types of sweet pastry that were developed were intended to be treats, not everyday food; it is only the abundant wheat and fat production of modern agriculture that has made them so accessible.

See also **Baking**; **Butter**; **Candy and Confections**; **Pasta**; **Pie**; **Wheat: Wheat as a Food.**

BIBLIOGRAPHY

Beck, Simone, and Julia Child. *Mastering the Art of French Cooking*, vol. 2. London: Penguin Books, 1970

Davidson, Alan. "Pastry." In *The Oxford Companion to Food*, edited by Alan Davidson, pp. 585–587. New York: Oxford University Press, 1999.

Gouffé, Jules. *The Royal Cookery Book [Le Livre de cuisine].* Translated from the French and adapted by Alphonse Gouffé. London: Sampson Low Son and Marston, 1868.

La Varenne, François Pierre. *The French Cook.* With an introduction by Philip and Mary Hyman. Lewes, U.K.: Southover Press, 2001.

McGee, Harold. *On Food and Cooking.* New York: Scribners, 1984.

Laura Mason

PEANUT BUTTER. Peanuts (*Arachis hypogaea*), also widely called "groundnuts," originated between southern Bolivia and northern Argentina. In pre-Columbian times, they were found throughout Brazil, Peru, Mexico, and the Caribbean. Early in the sixteenth century, European explorers transported them to Africa and Asia. From the beginning, peanuts were ground into paste and used as a flavoring in soups, stews, and other dishes.

Through the slave trade, peanuts were introduced into the British North American colonies. Slaves grew peanuts in their gardens and introduced them into mainstream cookery. Hand-ground peanuts appeared as an ingredient in American recipes by the 1830s.

John Harvey Kellogg

Ground peanuts were a minor product until popularized by John Harvey Kellogg, the vegetarian director of the Seventh-Day Adventist Sanitarium in Battle Creek, Michigan. In 1894 he created a process to make "nut butters," which were intended as a substitute for cow's butter and cream. Peanuts were the least expensive "nuts" available, and the product made from grinding them was promptly called peanut butter. It was served to members of America's elite who visited the sanitarium, and vegetarians began selling it in small batches. Kellogg's new culinary treat spread throughout the United States and, subsequently, the world. Kellogg decided not to patent the process for making peanut butter, but he did create the Sanitas Nut Food Company to sell his nut butters.

Peanut butter quickly became a fad among health food manufacturers in America. Vegetarians adopted it almost immediately, and recipes for making it appeared in vegetarian cookbooks beginning in 1899. Vegetarians employed peanut butter for many purposes, but particularly for making mock meats or meat substitutes that purportedly imitated the appearance and taste of such diverse products as chicken, veal cutlets, tenderloin steak, oysters, and meat loaf.

Mainstream Peanut Butter

Peanut butter quickly spread into the culinary mainstream and was employed as an ingredient in salad, fudge, biscuits, muffins, cookies, and breads. A major early use of peanut butter was for making sandwiches, which were initially flavored with a variety of ingredients, such as mayonnaise, cayenne, paprika, nasturtiums, cheese, watercress, meat, Worcestershire sauce, and cream cheese. Recipes for peanut butter sandwiches proliferated throughout the early twentieth century. The first known reference to combining jelly with peanut butter was published in 1901. During the early 1900s, peanut butter was considered a delicacy and, as such, it was served at New York's finest tearooms.

Commerce and Industry

Initially, peanut butter was made by grinding a few nuts at a time in a mortar and pestle. As this was a slow and difficult process, it was unlikely that peanut butter would ever have become a major culinary product. It was at this point that technological innovation intervened, and converted a food fad into an industry. Commercial peanut butter made its debut in 1896. Before the development of special grinders, the peanuts were ground in adapted meat grinders. The peanut butter was manufactured in small quantities by individuals and sold from house to house; then small factories sprang up, and peanut butter became a familiar article on grocers' shelves. The first recorded peanut butter trademark was granted to the Atlantic Peanut Refinery in Philadelphia in December 1898. The recipe consisted only of ground peanuts with salt added. By 1899, an estimated two million pounds of peanut butter were manufactured in the United States. The largest producers were located in the South and the West. By 1929, there was hardly a city that did not have one or more peanut butter factories, and its consumption during the next five or six years equaled that of all preceding years combined.

Peanut butter sandwiches moved down the class structure as the price of peanut butter declined. After the invention of sliced bread in the 1920s, children could make their own sandwiches without using a sharp knife. The combination of these two factors helped make peanut butter sandwiches one of the top children's meals in America. Beginning in the 1920s, manufacturers lobbied school cafeterias to buy inexpensive peanut butter. Its flavor was liked by children, and minimum time and equipment were required to prepare it. However, peanut allergies among children have recently been on the rise, and peanuts and peanut products have been banned from some schools.

Today, three major peanut butter manufacturers dominate the market: Skippy, created by Joseph L. Rosefield of Alameda, California (first produced in 1932); Peter Pan peanut butter, manufactured by the E. K. Pond Company (Pond, a subsidiary of Swift & Co., began making peanut butter in 1926); and Procter & Gamble's Jif

56

(first produced in 1958), whose plant in Lexington, Kentucky, is the largest peanut-butter-producing facility in the world.

Peanut Butter as an American Icon

Peanut butter was initially considered a health and vegetarian food, but it quickly became a major mainstream staple, a mass-produced commodity sold in almost every grocery store in America. It was employed on virtually every type of food from soups, salads, sauces, and main courses to desserts and snacks of every description. Few other products in American culinary history have achieved such influence in so many ways in such a short period of time, and peanut butter has remained a staple food in America ever since.

Peanut butter has been employed in a number of other commercial products—cakes, confections, cereals, and many snack foods—the most successful being in the manufacture of chocolate bars. In 1928 H. B. Reese Candy Company produced a chocolate-covered peanut butter cup, which subsequently became known as "Reese's Peanut Butter Cup." Two years later, Frank and Ethel Mars introduced the "Snickers Bar," a combination of peanut butter nougat, peanuts, and caramel encased in milk chocolate. Snickers quickly became America's most popular candy bar, a position it has held ever since. Chocolate and peanut butter are combined in some of America's best-selling chocolate bars, including Snickers and Reese's Peanut Butter Cup.

Peanut butter cookbooks have been regularly published since William Kaufman's "I Love Peanut Butter" Cookbook was published in 1975. The Adult Peanut Butter Lovers' Fan Club currently counts over sixty thousand members. Today, Americans consume annually about 857 million pounds of peanut butter, or 3.36 pounds per person. It can be found in 83 percent of American households. Peanut butter is also consumed in Saudi Arabia, Canada, Japan, Korea, and Western Europe.

See also **Kellogg, John Harvey**; **Legumes**; **Nuts**; **Oil**; **Snacks**.

BIBLIOGRAPHY

Frank, Dorothy. The Peanut Cookbook. New York: Clarkson Potter, 1976.

Hoffman, Mable. The Peanut Butter Cookbook. New York: HP-Books, 1996.

Holmes, Leila B. Plain Georgia Cookin': 100 Peanut Recipes. Thomasville, Ga.: Barnes Printing, 1977.

Kaufman, William. The "I Love Peanut Butter" Cookbook. Garden City, N.Y.: Doubleday, 1965.

Kolpas, Norman. The Big Little Peanut Butter Cookbook. Chicago: NTC/Contemporary Books, 1990.

Smith, Andrew F. "Peanut Butter: A Vegetarian Food that Went Awry." Petits Propos Culinaires 65 (September 2000): 60–72.

Smith, Andrew F. Peanuts: The Illustrious History of the Goober Pea. Urbana: University of Illinois Press, 2002.

Woodroof, Jasper Guy, ed. Peanuts: Production, Processing, Products. 3d ed. Westport, Conn.: AVI Publishing, 1984.

Zisman, Larry, and Honey Zisman. The Great American Peanut Butter Book. New York: St. Martin's, 1985.

Andrew F. Smith

PEANUTS. *See* **Legumes; Nuts; Oil; Peanut Butter.**

PEAS. Peas are among the oldest cultivated vegetables and once served as a dietary cornerstone for the early agrarian societies of Europe and the Middle East. The English word for pea derives from Latin pisum, a term that now serves as the name of the genus to which peas belong. Pea is thus used in English in two senses: as a descriptor for other pea-like vegetables, such as cowpeas, chickpeas, pigeon peas, and winged peas; and as the specific name for Pisum sativum, the peas employed by humans as food or for such agricultural uses as fodder and green manures.

Genetic Origins

All true peas belong to the same species, but are divided out into three distinct groups or subspecies. This means that even though peas are self-fertile, they readily hybridize in nature and as a result, there a numerous crosses that often blur the differences between the subspecies. This discussion will focus exclusively on the three subspecies and their historical uses as a source of food.

The genetic origin of peas is thought to be southwest Asia, somewhere in the vicinity of Afghanistan. The ancestral pea is now extinct, although its immediate descendants, the wild pea (Pisum sativum, spp. elatius and spp. humile) survive in the Middle East. This is a vining plant with tiny flowers (often crimson or rose) that rambles over rocks or climbs on low bushes for support. Like modern peas, it has tendrils that allow it to use the limbs of nearby plants so that the pods are raised up and out of reach of rodents and other small animals. Stone Age sites in Greece and coastal Turkey dating from about 5700 B.C. have yielded carbonized remains of the elatius subspecies, whereas sites from the same period more inland in present Israel and especially the Tigris Valley, have produced remains of the subspecies humile. The general conclusion is that wild peas were recognized for their food value at an early date and were gathered both as a fresh vegetable in June (when the seeds are green and sweet) and as a dry seed for use during the rest of the year.

Wild peas later appear in the remains of Swiss lake dwellings (about 3000 B.C.E.), so it is evident that they were carried out of their native habitat into Europe and maintained either as a cultivated plant or as a managed plant in the wild. Since the pea formed a dietary triumvirate with lentils and such ancient grains as emmer,

Advertisement for the Wordsley Wonder, a marrowfat pea introduced in 1888 by Webb & Sons of Stourbridge, England. Where Americans have developed a passion for tomatoes, the English have taken their passion for peas even farther. Between 1700 and 1900, the English developed over a thousand varieties of peas, and perfected methods of growing them in large fields, as seen in the background of this woodcut. ROUGHWOOD COLLECTION.

einkorn, and barley, it is likely that peas traveled as a useful weed along with the migration of early grains. Archaeological evidence suggests that wild peas were commonly found in areas planted with grain and that the entire plants were harvested, hung up and dried, then threshed as needed. Wild peas were mashed and cooked alone or with grains to make porridges, or they were ground into flour and mixed with other flours to make flat breads. Pea flour was also used as a medicine, especially in the treatment of wounds.

Cultivated Peas

The next step in the evolution of the pea was the appearance of the field pea, which is written botanically as *Pisum sativum*, spp. *arvense*. This is a form of pea that evolved artificially through human intervention and supplied early agricultural societies from China to Ireland with one of the most important staple foods down to the eighteenth century. Pease pottage was a common dish in the Middle Ages, and in India, *vatana* (dal made from peas) is still an important element of everyday diet. In

the southern portion of the United States, people commonly refer to cowpeas as field peas, but the practical point is clear: this is not a plant grown in kitchen gardens; it is an American substitute form for the true field peas of Europe. Field peas, like wild peas, were harvested on the vine and dried in the barn. The peas were threshed as needed and the straw given as fodder to the livestock.

There are many heirloom varieties of field peas surviving today, although they are grown mostly as fodder or as a green manure (plowed under to enrich the soil). In the Middle Ages they were food for man and beast, and it is this type of pea that was introduced into China from India during the T'ang Dynasty. Pea soup even appears in early Buddhist texts as a healthful, albeit simple dish consistent with a monastic lifestyle.

Regardless of where they are cultivated, all field peas share certain common features that separate them from the so-called garden peas which later became more important. The vines are generally shorter and stronger than those of wild peas, the plants are more compact, and through natural mutation and careful selection over time, they normally yield a higher number of pods often with large seeds. However, to the casual viewer, the most distinctive feature is the flower, which is multicolored. Some of the most beautiful flowers in this species appear on field peas. Furthermore, the dry seeds are normally speckled. The tiny, speckled Jämtlands Grä Förder Ärt of Sweden, and the tan-seeded Groch Pomorski (Pomeranian Pea) of medieval Poland are two surviving examples of this type.

Field peas are often referred to in horticultural literature as gray peas, a term that seems to have evolved in the low countries owing to the color of the seed and the flour they yield. During the late Middle Ages, Capuchin monks in Holland and northern Germany devoted considerable energy to the improvement of field peas for agricultural purposes. This has resulted in a group of large-seeded gray peas referred to as Capuchin, especially those from the Netherlands where the breeding of new pea varieties became a national pastime by the early 1600s. One of the classic peas from this group and one which dates from the 1500s is the handsome blue pod Capucijner, a soup pea growing on six-foot (two m) vines.

Garden Peas

Dwarfism is a recessive gene in peas, and every so often short plants will appear in the field. This dwarfism was noted by Dutch growers in the seventeenth century and manipulated through careful selection to produce a variety of so-called bush types. Holland Capucijners with two-foot vines, and the delicious raisin Capucijners (which actually do look like dried raisins) represent a further evolution of this old category of pea. While they are technically field peas, these bush varieties were also adapted to kitchen gardens and therefore moved up a notch in culinary status. This brings us to the true garden pea, which is genetically different from its cousins in the field.

The garden pea is written botanically as *Pisum sativum*, spp. *sativum* and is readily recognized by its white flowers. The white flower suggests albinoism, especially since the flowers of wild peas are not naturally white. Genetic mutation is further supported by the fact that the seeds are generally very light in color, from near-white to yellow, and when dry are either smooth or wrinkled. Horticulturists now group garden peas by these seed textures since the two types yield peas with different culinary characteristics. Both types, however, contain more sugar than field peas when green, and it was this unusual sweetness that probably first caught the attention of observant gardeners in the Mediterranean some two thousand years ago.

The common white flowering garden pea was known to the ancient Greeks and Romans, but its precise place of origin and date of appearance is unknown. It appears to have been treated as an aristocratic vegetable, hence its mention by Apicius and other classical authors. It was raised in the gardens of the great Roman estates for the luxury of the nobility, but it was not food for the masses: field peas were their sustenance. Garden peas continued to be grown during the Middle Ages, again as food for the aristocracy and church princes. It is not until the horticultural revolution of the 1600s that we find this pea moving into middle-class gardens. The Dutch took the lead in developing new varieties like the tender mangetouts (snap or sugar peas) and the dwarf *petit pois*, but it was the French court of Louis XIV that made green peas fashionable. During the reign of William and Mary, Dutch horticultural enthusiasm caught on in England, and England has remained the center of pea development ever since.

The English have developed elaborate horticultural categories for classifying peas, but doubtless their marrowfats stand out as a singular contribution to this class of vegetable. Marrowfats are peas that are sweet and buttery when cooked green, although they are rarely sold that way in England. Their dry seeds are somewhat chalky in appearance and reduce to a creamy texture when used in soups. Most commonly they are canned, and as a canned product, they became a standard feature of English cookery by the late Victorian period. The very best varieties were developed by Thomas Andrew Knight (1759–1838), a genteel horticulturist who was responsible for a wide range of improved fruits and vegetables. Many of Knight's peas were used by later breeders like Thomas Laxton and Alan MacLean to create some of the Victorian varieties that are still popular today, among them Laxton's Fillbasket (1872) and MacLean's Paradise Marrow (also known as Champion of Paris) introduced in the 1850s.

On the other side of the English Channel, the Paris seed house of Vilmorin introduced some of the most popular pea varieties in nineteenth-century Europe, especially several French varieties that are now much sought after by Paris chefs. These would include Gloire de Quimper, a dwarf bush pea of the *petit pois* type similar to American Wonder, the scimitar-podded Serpette d'Auvergne from the 1830s, and the Pois Géant sans Parchemin (Giant Sugar Pea), which has bicolor flowers, a tell-tale sign of its field pea ancestry.

Through trade contacts with the Dutch and Portuguese, the Chinese and Japanese were introduced to mangetouts (sugar peas) in the seventeenth century. Since then, they have developed numerous new varieties of tender-podded peas popularly referred to in present-day seed catalogs as snow peas or Chinese peas. The sprouts and young pods are commonly employed in stir-fries and should not be confused with commercial American snap peas. Snap peas are large sweet peas with a crisp, edible pod. This name is somewhat misleading since many peas, like the Sickle Pea of the eighteenth century, can be eaten whole like a snap pea when picked very young. Snap peas are really nothing more than an improvement of the old melting marrows or melting sugar peas, as they were called in the 1800s.

Many of the more recently developed varieties, like the Slim Pea, or the odd Parsley Pea with its bushy tendrils, have evolved to reflect very specific shifts in contemporary diet. In the case of the Slim Pea, it makes an ideal freezing pea for small gardens owning to its diminutive vines, not to mention that the name implies weight loss and low calories (peas are very high in calories). Peas were among the first vegetables marketed as frozen food in the 1920s, and today there is increasing commercial interest in varieties that can be frozen and then cooked in the microwave oven. The Parsley Pea represents a much different mentality, since it is a pea that appeals to organic gardeners and followers of macrobiotic or vegetarian diets. Its peas and pods are edible and its tendrils may be cooked and transformed into faux seaweed salad for a meal with the ascetic appointments of Taoist simplicity.

PEAS THE FRENCH WAY

Shell your Peas, and pass a quarter of a Pound of Butter, gold Colour, with a Spoonful of Flour; then put in a Quart of Peas, four Onions cut small, and two Cabbages cut as small as the Onions; then put in half a Pint of Gravy, season with Pepper, Salt, and Cloves. Stove this well an Hour, then put in half a Spoonful of fine Sugar, and fry some Artichokes to lay round the Side of the Dish; serve it with a forced Lettuce in the Middle.

SOURCE: *Adam's Luxury, and Eve's Cookery* (London, 1744).

See also **British Isles: England; Frozen Food; India; Legumes; Low Countries; Mediterranean Diet; Porridge; Tillage.**

BIBLIOGRAPHY

Hedrick, U. P., ed. *The Vegetables of New York: Peas of New York.* Albany: State of New York, Education Dept., 1928.

Körber-Grohne, Udelgard. *Nutzpflanzen in Deutschland.* Stuttgart: Konrad Theiss Verlag, 1988.

Miller, Naomi F., and Kathryn L. Gleason, eds. *The Archaeology of Garden and Field.* Philadelphia: University of Pennsylvania Press, 1994.

Vilmorin-Andrieux, M. M. *The Vegetable Garden* (London, 1885).

Weaver, William Woys. *Heirloom Vegetable Gardening: A Master Gardener's Guide to Planting, Growing, Seed Saving, and Cultural History.* New York: Henry Holt and Co., 1997.

William Woys Weaver

PEPPER. *For pepper (spice), see* **Herbs and Spices;** *for peppers, see* **Chili Peppers.**

PESTICIDES. A pesticide is any agent used to kill or control a pest. Pests include insects, weeds, and diseases, such as fungi. In addition, mice, rats, birds, and algae may become pests at some time. When pests damage plants or property, people often use pesticides to control them. The term "pesticide" can apply to insecticides, herbicides, fungicides, antimicrobials, growth regulators, defoliants, and desiccants, most of which are applied to food or food plants before or after harvest. Common pesticides are encountered every day—in pet flea collars, kitchen disinfectants, cockroach baits, swimming pool chemicals, and mosquito repellents. Pesticide products contain both active and inert ingredients, and both must be specified on the label.

Pesticide Controversy

Modern farmers use pesticides to help them to grow almost all of the world's food. In general, pesticides have been a quick, effective, and inexpensive method of control for pests that attack most of the world's food crops. Pesticides are credited with helping to save millions of lives by controlling diseases, such as malaria and yellow fever, which are spread by insects. However, most pesticides present some risk of harm to humans, animals, or the environment because they are designed to kill living organisms.

Sulfur, herbal extracts, tobacco, soaps, oil, arsenic, pyrethrum, and lime have been used as pesticides for many centuries, but the widespread use of synthetic pesticides is a relatively recent phenomenon. Dichlorodiphenyltrichloroethane, or DDT, is probably the best known early pesticide. DDT was created in 1873, but it was not until the late 1930s that Swiss researcher Paul Müller discovered that the compound was effective in killing insects. Müller won the Nobel Prize in Physiology and Medicine in 1948 for his work. DDT was an inexpensive and effective solution to many insect problems, and it virtually eliminated malaria from parts of the world. After World War II, DDT became a common agricultural pesticide. In the 1950s, the United States was producing 220 million pounds of DDT per year.

Insect resistance to the substance developed quickly. DDT residues were found in human milk and fatty tissues, and in wildlife food chains. In 1962 writer and ecologist Rachel Carson wrote *Silent Spring* to warn the public about the long-term effects of misusing pesticides. Carson challenged the practices of agricultural scientists and the government, and called for a change in the way humankind viewed the natural world. Carson testified before Congress in 1963, calling for new policies to protect human health and the environment. While no longer used in the United States, DDT use continues in other parts of the world. Many tropical countries still use DDT to control malaria.

All pesticides (natural and synthetic) have the potential to cause harm during their manufacture or refinement, at the time of application to crops, as residues that persist on food, and in the disruption of the natural balance that exists between pests and their natural enemies. For example, traces of the natural insecticide "rotenone" may be found on vegetables after cooking. Atrazine, a weed-killer commonly used on corn and soybeans, suburban lawns, and utility rights-of-way, has contaminated groundwater where those crops are grown. Insecticides like DDE and dieldrin, which are related to DDT, were banned in the United States in the 1970s, but still show up in the U.S. food supply. Persistent residues of these chemicals travel long distances in global air and water currents. These insecticides are still produced and used in many countries. Recent studies have linked pesticides with acute poisonings, cancer, brain damage, reproductive harm, and many childhood illnesses and learning problems, leading concerned citizens to feel that pesticides should be banned.

Organic Agriculture

Some agricultural experts predict that the quality and quantity of our food supply would be lessened if pesticides were eliminated. However, practitioners of organic agriculture (organic farmers use no synthetic agricultural chemicals and instead rely on management practices such as crop rotation, disease-resistant varieties, and natural enemies to control crop pests) claim that food quality and yield are equally productive under organic management. Fortunately for conventional and organic farmers, the number of safer, reduced-risk options for pest control is increasing. For example, there were approximately seven hundred new, biological pesticide products registered by 1999. Biological pesticides are certain types of pesticides derived from such natural materials as animals, plants, bacteria, and minerals.

Garlic, mint, and baking soda all have pesticide-like properties and are considered biological pesticides. Biological pesticides include the common cabbage worm killer *Bacillus thuringiensis*, which produces a protein that helps to kill specific worm pests. Some of the new reduced-risk pesticides, while synthesized in a laboratory, are considered safer because they do not kill beneficial insects (such as lady beetles and lacewings), or they break down quickly to inactive products. In 1977 U.S. president Jimmy Carter issued a Presidential Decree that mandated the use of integrated pest management (IPM)—a comprehensive approach to pest control that uses a combination of less toxic means to reduce the status of pests to tolerant levels, while maintaining a quality environment. Together, the new reduced-risk pesticides and IPM practices have helped to lessen the amount of pesticides that are used on food and other crops. Levels of pesticide residues on IPM produce have been reported as higher than those of organically grown food, but lower than those in conventionally grown produce.

Pesticides and Their Regulation
In the United States, pesticides are regulated by the Environmental Protection Agency (EPA). EPA regulates the sale, distribution, and use of pesticides and has the authority to suspend or cancel the registration of a pesticide if information shows that continued use would pose unreasonable risks. In 1996 the Food Quality Protection Act (FQPA) was signed into law, giving EPA more effective power. Among its many benefits, the FQPA established a new health-based safety standard for pesticide residues in food; included special provisions for infants and children; required periodic tolerance reevaluations; incorporated provisions for endocrine testing; and allowed for enhanced enforcement of pesticide residue standards.

Scientists predict that, in the future, pesticides will continue to play a role in pest management of food crops, partly because reduced-risk pesticides have become less harmful to the environment, and less toxic to people and wildlife. Societal concerns, scientific advances, and regulatory pressures continue to drive some of the more hazardous pesticides from the marketplace. In addition, consumer interest in safe and healthy food will create more demand for organically grown products.

See also **Herbicides; Organic Agriculture; Organic Farming and Gardening; Food Safety; Toxins, Unnatural, and Food Safety.**

BIBLIOGRAPHY
Cruising chemistry. An introduction to the chemistry of the world around you. "DDT: An Introduction." University of California, San Diego. Available at http://www.chem.duke.edu/jds/cruise_chem/pest/pest1.html.

Entomology at Rutgers. Agricultural Entomology and Pest Management course. Entomology 370–350—Spring 2001, Dr. George Hamilton. Available at http://aesop.rutgers.edu/hamilton/agent.htm.

"The Future Role of Pesticides in U.S. Agriculture." 2000. Committee on the Future Role of Pesticides in U.S. Agriculture, Board on Agriculture and Natural Resources and Board on Environmental Studies and Toxicology, Commission on Life. Available at http://books.nap.edu/books/0309065267/html/17.html.

Lear, Linda. *The Rachel Carson Website*. Available at http://www.rachelcarson.org/.

Natural Resources Defense Council. Available at http://www.nrdc.org/health/pesticides/default.asp.

Paul Hermann Müller—Biography. Nobel e-Museum. The Nobel Foundation. The Official Web Site of The Nobel Foundation. Available at http://www.nobel.se/medicine/laureates/1948/muller-bio.html.

Pesticide Action Network Pesticide Database. Available at http://docs.pesticideinfo.org/documentation3/ref_general3.html.

Pesticide Action Network Toxicity Ratings. Available at http://docs.pesticideinfo.org/documentation3/ref_toxicity2.html.

Pesticide Data Program. USDA Agricultural Marketing Service Science and Technology Programs. Progress Report 2001. Available at http://www.ams.usda.gov/science/pdp/progress.htm#skipusers).

U.S. EPA Office of Pesticide Programs. *Biopesticides*. Available at http://www.epa.gov/pesticides/citizens/biopesticides.htm.

U.S. EPA Office of Pesticide Programs. *Highlights of the Food Quality Protection Act of 1996*. Available at http://www.epa.gov/opppsps1/fqpa/fqpahigh.htm.

U.S. EPA Office of Pesticide Programs. *What the Pesticide Residue Limits Are on Food*. Available at http://www.epa.gov/pesticides/food/viewtols.htm.

Patricia S. Michalak

PETRONIUS. In the surviving manuscript, the authorship of the Latin picaresque novel *Satyrica* is credited to "Petronius Arbiter." Most scholars believe (although conclusive evidence is lacking) that this is Gaius (or Titus) Petronius, who served the Roman emperor Nero as *Arbiter Elegantiae* (judge of elegance, or director of entertainment). He fell from the emperor's favor and was ordered to commit suicide in A.D. 66. The historian Tacitus describes the courtier's death in his *Annals* (book 18, sections 18–19).

The *Satyrica* is a novel of low life in Roman Italy, centering on the narrator Encolpius and his boyfriend Giton. The author may seem to celebrate—he certainly does not condemn—his characters' amoral lifestyle: they are usually penniless and often involved in disreputable sexual adventures.

In medieval Europe the *Satyrica* was a secret classic. No complete copy survived to modern times; we have only fragments. The longest surviving episode (sections

26–78), important for food history, is known as *Cena Tri-malchionis*, or 'Trimalchio's dinner'. This immensely rich former slave regales his guests (including Encolpius) with food and conversation intended to display urbanity but more truly betraying empty pretentiousness. The main course is a roast pig, served as if still whole. In fact it had been gutted normally, and afterward stuffed with cooked sausages, which look like (and are made from) intestines: a clever, but tasteless, presentational trick. The wine is labeled "opimian, one hundred years old," but at the date of the fictional dinner any surviving Italian wines of the famous opimian vintage were 180 years old and almost undrinkable: such contradictions are meant to reveal the host's ignorance of gastronomy. Almost every item in the menu has some satirical undertone. Cleverly balancing between naive astonishment and cynical disdain, the narrator tells us a lot about gastronomy and dining customs under the early empire. Featured among the hors d'oeuvres at Trimalchio's dinner, dormice (roasted, dipped in honey and rolled in poppy seeds) will forever remain typical of Roman cuisine.

See also **Rome and the Roman Empire.**

BIBLIOGRAPHY

Courtney, Edward. *A Companion to Petronius.* Oxford: Oxford University Press, 2001.

Petronius. *The Satyricon.* Translated by William Arrowsmith. Ann Arbor: University of Michigan Press, 1959.

Petronius. *Satyrica.* Translated by R. Bracht Branham and Daniel Kinney. London: Dent, 1996; Berkeley: University of California Press, 1997.

Tacitus. *The Annals of Imperial Rome.* Translated by Michael Grant. Harmondsworth and Baltimore: Penguin, 1956.

Andrew Dalby

PHILIPPINES. *See* **Southeast Asia.**

PHOSPHORUS AND CALCIUM. Phosphorus and calcium are essential macronutrients in the human diet. Most of the phosphorus in the human body is found in association with calcium (as the mineral complex hydroxyapatite) in bones and teeth, where it is essential to structure. This form of phosphorus, along with phosphorylated sugars and proteins, is termed *inorganic phosphorus*. Organic phosphorus occurs primarily in the form of phospholipids.

Phosphorus absorption in the human body is proportional to the dietary intake, unlike calcium, where absorption is inversely related to the logarithm of intake. Absorption of phosphorus is facilitated by vitamin D. Phosphorus levels in urine are also directly related to dietary intake.

Important regulatory functions of phosphorus in the human body include maintaining the pH of body fluids,

TABLE 1

Amounts of calcium and phosphorus in 100 grams (3.5 oz.) of selected foods, and the ratio of these two elements

Food	Calcium (mg/100 g)	Phosphorus (mg/100 g)	Ca:P Ratio
Dairy Products			
Buttermilk	116	89	1.30
Cheese, camembert	387	347	1.12
Cheese, cottage, low fat	69	151	0.46
Cheese, processed	720	511	1.41
Cheese, ricotta, whole milk	207	158	1.31
Cheese, Swiss	959	607	1.58
Milk, canned sweetened condensed	284	253	1.12
Milk, nonfat	123	101	1.22
Milk, nonfat canned evaporated	290	195	1.49
Milk, whole	119	93	1.28
Yogurt, low fat	199	157	1.27
Yogurt, whole milk	121	95	1.27
Vegetables			
Broccoli	47	66	0.71
Carrots	27	44	0.61
Corn	5	63	0.08
Cornmeal	350	623	0.56
Kale	138	28	4.93
Lettuce, iceberg	19	20	0.95
Okra	96	46	2.09
Parsley	140	60	2.33
Peas, green	24	90	0.27
Rhubarb	145	8	18.13
Spinach	100	50	2.00
Turnips	152	34	4.47
Meat			
Chicken	20	229	0.09
Crab	101	260	0.39
Duck	12	203	0.06
Oyster	62	159	0.39
Sardine	382	490	0.78
Turkey	25	213	0.12
Cereals			
Barley	19	221	0.09
Couscous	24	170	0.14
Oat bran	59	734	0.08
Rice, brown	10	83	0.12
Rice, white	28	115	0.24
Wheat flour, white	338	619	0.55
Legumes and nuts			
Lentils	19	180	0.11
Lima beans	21	74	0.28
Macadamia nuts	71	198	0.36
Peanuts	88	519	0.17
Pecans	71	279	0.25
Soybeans	145	245	0.59
Miscellaneous			
Chocolate, semisweet	32	132	0.24
Egg, whole	48	178	0.27
Kiwifruit	26	39	0.67

SOURCE: Adapted from the Nutrient Data Laboratory, United States Department of Agriculture, Beltsville, MD (http://www.nal.usda.gov/fnic/foodcomp/)

the cellular osmotic pressure, and the energy transfer system in cells. Phosphorus is also an important component of DNA and RNA. Phosphorus deficiencies are rare and have been linked to anorexia, rickets, and skeletal and muscular abnormalities.

The amount of calcium consumed is not always related to the amount retained by the body. Availability of calcium for absorption is referred to as bioavailability, and is improved by factors such as the presence of phosphorus, vitamin D, and the extent to which the calcium mineral salt is ionized to form the divalent Ca^{2+} ion. Cellulose and hemicellulose fibers decrease absorption of calcium in the intestine. Sodium and caffeine both increase urinary calcium. Caffeine also causes an increase of calcium secretion into the human gut. Unabsorbed fats interfere with calcium absorption by forming a fatty acid–calcium soap complex, which is subsequently excreted. The bioavailability of calcium ranges from 5 to 70 percent for most foods, depending upon the type of mineral from which it is derived, the food product, and the presence of inhibitory substances. Oxalate and phytate both inhibit calcium absorption. A diet deficient in calcium may increase the risk of rickets, hypertension, osteoporosis, and scurvy. Vitamin D stimulates the absorption of calcium and phosphorus into bones. Osteoporosis is one consequence of low calcium intake during the younger years of bone mineralization. There are conflicting opinions on the efficacy of increasing the intake of calcium for older people who are already suffering from osteoporosis.

About 1.5 percent of the weight of an average person is made up of bones, which contain 99 percent of the body's calcium. Approximately 0.05 percent of the calcium in bones is exchanged daily by a process of solubilization and precipitation. In addition to its structural function, calcium in its ionized form allows blood clotting to take place. Calcium also regulates muscle contraction and relaxation.

Calcium is often found in association with phosphorus, forming the mineral calcium phosphate. This mineral is less soluble at higher temperatures (unlike most other minerals), resulting in "boiler-scale," a white precipitate on surfaces that come into contact with hot mineralized water. Table 1 presents a selection of foods containing phosphorus and calcium and gives the ratio of calcium to phosphorus in each; this is one important indicator of bioavailability. A low calcium to phosphorus ratio is associated with bone loss over time.

Milk is a very good source of dietary calcium. Calcium in milk is found primarily in the mineral calcium phosphate, which is approximately 30 percent bioavailable. It is possible that the high level of insoluble calcium phosphate in milk could cause calcification of the mammary gland, but casein milk proteins solubilize the mineral calcium phosphate. Calcium phosphate and proteins are responsible for much of the high buffering capacity of milk, which is a resistance to change in pH after the addition of acid or base. This allows milk to absorb a large amount of acid, such as that found in the human gut, providing some relief from acid reflux. Milk also contains a large amount of lactose. This precludes the use of milk as a source of dietary calcium and phosphorus for people suffering from lactose intolerance, an inability to metabolize lactose. For these people, other dairy products such as matured cheese and yogurt can be used to provide dietary calcium. Both of these dairy products are low in lactose. More information on calcium phosphate and lactose in milk can be found in Table 1 under Dairy Products.

Calcium in used in food to increase the gel formation of polysaccharides such as alginate and pectin, which can be used to increase the firmness of canned vegetables. Calcium also increases the firmness of milk gels and the rate of milk clotting, such as what occurs in cheese manufacture, by promoting aggregation of casein milk proteins. Phosphorus is present in emulsifiers used to produce the smooth texture required for processed cheese. It is also used to increase moisture retention in comminuted meats, as a leavening agent, as a pH buffering agent, and to acidify beverages. Phosphorus-containing agents such as phytate, oxalate, and phosphate act as chelating agents by binding calcium strongly.

The recommended dietary allowance for calcium is 210 mg/day (from birth to six months), 270 mg/day (aged seven to twelve months), 500 mg/day (aged one to three years), 800 mg/day (aged four to eight years), 1,300 mg/day (aged nine to eighteen years) and 1000 mg/day above eighteen years of age. The recommended dietary allowance for phosphorus is 100 mg/day (from birth to six months), 275 mg/day (aged seven to twelve months), 460 mg/day (aged one to three years), 500 mg/day (aged four to eight years), 1,250 mg/day (aged nine to eighteen years) and 700 mg/day above eighteen years of age.

See also **Body Composition; Composition of Food; Dairy Products; Dietary Assessment; Dietary Guidelines; Digestion; Enteral and Parenteral Nutrition; Lactation; Milk, Human; Nutrient Bioavailability; Nutrients.**

BIBLIOGRAPHY

Fennema, O. R., ed. *Food Chemistry*. New York: M. Dekker, 1966.

Hunt, Sara M., and James L. Groff. *Advanced Nutrition and Human Metabolism*. St. Paul, Minn.: West, 1990.

David W. Everett

PHYSICAL ACTIVITY AND NUTRITION.

Regular physical activity and proper nutrition are critical for optimal health. Both have been linked to reducing the risk of a large number of common chronic diseases. In most cases, it is difficult to separate the roles

---

BENEFITS OF REGULAR PHYSICAL ACTIVITY

- Decreases the risk of premature death
- Decreases the risk of dying prematurely from coronary heart disease
- Decreases the risk of Type II diabetes mellitus
- Decreases the risk of hypertension
- Helps reduce blood pressure in people with hypertension
- Decreases the risk of colon cancer
- Decreases feelings of depression and anxiety
- Helps control body weight
- Helps build and maintain healthy bones, muscles, and joints
- Improves strength in older adults and decreases their risk of falling
- Promotes psychological well-being

---

these two factors play in decreasing disease risk. The importance of both of these factors is highlighted by the United States government in the *2000 Dietary Guidelines for Americans* published by the U.S. Department of Health and Human Services and the U.S. Department of Agriculture. The guidelines' recommendations include aiming for a healthy weight; being physically active each day; following the food guide pyramid; eating a variety of grains, fruits, and vegetables each day; choosing a diet low in saturated fat and cholesterol and moderate in total fat; consuming less sugar and salt; drinking alcohol only in moderation, if at all; and keeping food safe to eat. These suggestions can greatly reduce disease risk. The role of physical activity in particular is a primary focus in the article that follows.

Benefits of Physical Activity

The 1996 Surgeon General's report, *Physical Activity and Health*, summarized many of the advantages obtained through participation in regular physical activity. It should be noted that these benefits can be acquired through a broad variety of activities; thus, the terms "exercise" and "physical activity" should not be limited solely to describing activities that are specifically designed to enhance fitness. Activities considered beneficial to health include structured exercise (e.g., walking, running, cycling, weight lifting, etc.), participation in sports, leisure-time and recreational pursuits, occupational duties, and other forms of movement.

Jeremy Morris and colleagues (1953) were among the earliest researchers to suggest that physical activity confers benefits to health. In their study, the rate of coro-

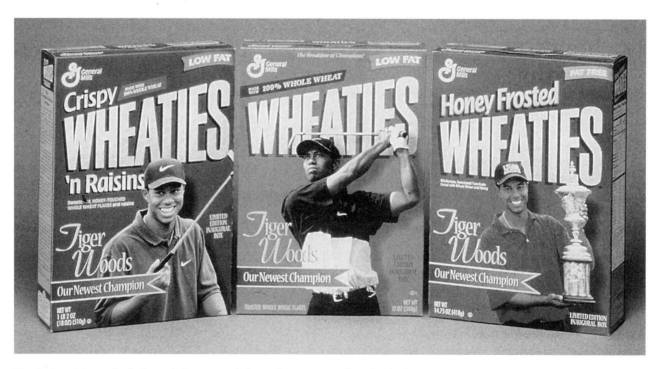

Physical activity and a balanced diet are underlying themes in modern food advertising. This breakfast cereal uses golfing hero Tiger Woods to draw a connection between the food product and winning a sport. It could be argued that the easy pace of golf should not be equated with a full physical workout. © AP/WIDE WORLD PHOTOS.

64

AMERICAN COLLEGE OF SPORTS MEDICINE GUIDELINES FOR FITNESS

Cardiorespiratory Fitness and Body Composition
1. Frequency of training: 3–5 days per week.
2. Intensity of training: 55/65 percent–90 percent of maximum heart rate. The lower intensity values (55–65 percent) are most applicable to individuals who are quite unfit.
3. Duration of training: 20–60 minutes of continuous or intermittent (minimum of 10-minute bouts accumulated throughout the day) aerobic activity. Duration is dependent on the intensity of the activity; thus, lower-intensity activity should be conducted over a longer period of time (30 minutes or more), and, conversely, individuals training at higher levels of intensity should train at least 20 minutes or longer.
4. Mode of activity: Any activity that uses large muscle groups, that can be maintained continuously, and that is rhythmical and aerobic in nature, e.g., walking-hiking, running-jogging, cycling-bicycling, cross-country skiing, aerobic dance or group exercise, rope skipping, rowing, stair climbing, swimming, skating, and various endurance game activities or some combination thereof.

Muscular Strength and Endurance, Body Composition, and Flexibility
1. Resistance training: Resistance training should be an integral part of an adult fitness program and should be of a sufficient intensity to enhance strength and muscular endurance, and to maintain fat-free mass. Resistance training should be progressive in nature and individualized, and should provide a stimulus to all the major muscle groups. One set of 8–10 exercises that conditions the major muscle groups 2–3 days per week is recommended. Multiple-set regimens may provide greater benefits if time allows. Most persons should complete 8–12 repetitions of each exercise; however, for older and more frail persons (approximately 50 to 60 years of age and above), 10–15 repetitions may be more appropriate.
2. Flexibility training: Flexibility exercises should be incorporated into the overall fitness program sufficient to develop and maintain range of motion. These exercises should stretch the major muscle groups and be performed a minimum of 2–3 days per week.

nary events (i.e., angina pectoris, thrombosis, death) for double-decker bus and tram conductors in London was compared to that of their more sedentary driving counterparts. Conductors had an overall lower incidence of coronary events and mortality than drivers, and the authors suggested that the greater level of physical activity that results from conducting versus driving might be the explanation. Many other investigators have since confirmed the notion that being more active reduces risk of heart disease and premature death, as well as many other common health problems.

Many of the health benefits of exercise are probably indirect, through control of body weight; however, physical activity alone also appears to be helpful. A recent review of the literature by Stephen Blair and Suzanne Brodney (1999) concluded that the current understanding of the importance of exercise to health suggests that physical activity reduces health risks that are usually associated with overweight and obesity, even in those who remain obese. Furthermore, they concluded that inactivity and low cardiorespiratory fitness increase the risk of premature death so that the risk is equal to being overweight or obese. Thus, physical activity is essential for optimal health regardless of body weight.

The reasons for the apparent health benefits of physical activity with regard to multiple disease conditions have been addressed by many studies. Although all of the mechanisms are not yet completely understood, several physiological effects of exercise have been observed and may be responsible. It is likely that improved cardiac and musculoskeletal function account for many of the benefits. Additionally, physical activity alters metabolic and hormonal processes that may modify disease risk, and activity also appears to be involved in improving immune function.

Physical Activity Guidelines
Quantifying the optimal level of physical activity required to reduce the risk of disease has proven difficult. However, leading organizations have provided recommendations for minimal levels of activity. Exercise guidelines from the American College of Sports Medicine (1998) for cardiorespiratory fitness, muscular strength and endurance, flexibility, and body composition are provided in the sidebar "American College Sports Medicine Guidelines for Fitness." Additionally, the Surgeon General's report (1996) recommends that people of all ages include a minimum of thirty minutes of physical activity of moderate intensity (such as brisk walking) on most, if not all, days of the week. Furthermore, two objectives of Healthy People 2010 (2000), a set of health objectives developed by the United States Department of Health and

Human Services, are, first, to increase the proportion of adolescents who engage in vigorous physical activity that promotes cardiorespiratory fitness three or more days per week for twenty or more minutes per occasion, and, second, to increase the proportion of adults who engage regularly, preferably daily, in moderate physical activity for at least thirty minutes per day.

Although numerous positive effects of physical activity exist, participation in strenuous exercise and work is not completely without risk in all circumstances. Primary risks include musculoskeletal injuries and cardiovascular events such as heart attacks. To avoid musculoskeletal injuries, it is most commonly recommended when beginning a physical activity program that the participant gradually increase the duration and intensity of the routine. Although physical exertion can result in a cardiovascular event, this is a rare occurrence in the healthy population. However, the Surgeon General's report (1996) suggests that adults with chronic diseases, such as heart disease, diabetes, or obesity, consult a physician before starting a program of physical activity, as should men over forty years of age and women over fifty years of age who plan to start a "vigorous" exercise program.

Conclusions

Many beneficial effects of diet and exercise are known; however, the interactive effects of the two are less understood. The relative importance of these lifestyle choices on various risk factors for chronic diseases is not clear. In some cases, physical activity and proper nutrition effects may be additive. In other cases, a synergistic effect of the two may exist. Additionally, it is also possible that for some risk factors, high levels of physical activity may even negate the adverse effects that a poor diet typically has on more sedentary individuals. For example, regular strenuous exercise appears to abolish the cholesterol-raising effects of a diet high in saturated fat. Clearly, the interaction between physical activity and nutrition relative to health benefits deserves considerable investigation now and in the future, so that we may optimally manage risk for chronic diseases.

See also **Assessment of Nutritional Status; Dietary Assessment; Dietary Guidelines; Dietary Systems; Dietetics; Fats; Food Politics: U.S.; Health and Disease; Malnutrition; Nutrients; Nutrition; Nutritionists; Obesity.**

BIBLIOGRAPHY

Blair, Steven N., and Suzanne Brodney. "Effects of Physical Activity and Obesity on Morbidity and Mortality: Current Evidence and Research Issues." *Medicine and Science in Sports and Exercise* 31 (1999): S646–S662.

Healthy People 2010. U.S. Department of Health and Human Services, Washington, D.C., 2000.

Morris, J. N., J. A. Heady, P. A. B. Raffle, C. G. Roberts, and J. W. Parks. "Coronary Heart Disease and Physical Activity of Work." *The Lancet* 2 (1953): 1053–1057, 1111–1120.

Physical Activity and Health: A Report of the Surgeon General. U.S. Department of Health and Human Services, Washington, D.C., 1996.

Pollock, Michael L., Glenn A. Gaesser, James D. Butcher, et al. "ACSM Position Stand on the Recommended Quantity and Quality of Exercise for Developing and Maintaining Cardiorespiratory and Muscular Fitness, and Flexibility in Adults." *Medicine and Science in Sports and Exercise* 30 (1998): 975–991.

Mark Kern

PICA. *See* **Geophagy.**

PICNIC. There is no reliable etymology for the word *picnic*, with the original use of the word lagging about three hundred years behind the first descriptions of *alfresco* (open air) dining. From about 1340 until the very early 1800s, there are three contextual descriptions of picnics, whether or not the word is actually used: a pleasure party at which a meal was eaten outdoors; a hunt assembly; and an indoor social gathering or dinner party. An outdoor meal in a garden is described in Italian literature by Giovanni Boccaccio in a poem that dates from about 1340. Sixty years later a similar event occurs in one of Geoffrey Chaucer's *Canterbury Tales*. It seems certain that the *assemblée*, or meal served during the hunt that is described and illustrated in the hunt manual of Jacques du Fouilloux's *La Vénerie* (Hunting) (1560) and George Turberville's *The Noble Arte of Venerie* (1575), are picnics in all but name. By 1692, the concept of the *alfresco* meal shifted, and when cited in Gilles Ménage's *Dictionnaire du Etymologique de la Langue Françoise* (Etymological dictionary of the French language) *piquenique* is assumed to be of unknown origin, but means *un repas où chacun paye son écot* (a meal where each pays his share). By 1750, Ménage's editors suggest that *piquenique* may be of Spanish origin and that it appeared in 1664 in a French translation of works by Francisco Quevedo. Oliver Cromwell, Lord Protector of Great Britain, had a dinner served on the grounds of Hyde Park in 1654. Samuel Pepys, the English diarist, ate many meals while boating on the Thames or sitting on its banks. These are picnics in all but name, but they are only recorded as a dinner alfresco.

The *Oxford English Dictionary* says that the word "picnic" originally referred to fashionable social entertainment in which each person contributed a share of the provisions, and says that the first recorded use of "picnic" in English appears in 1748 in a letter from Lord Chesterfield to his son, in the sense of an assembly or social gathering. It seems that the word was used in this sense widely in Germany, as Chesterfield's son was in Berlin at the time. A subsequent mention occurs in a letter from Lady M. Coke to Lady Stafford in 1763 from Hanover. Gustaf Palmfelt, a Swede, in a 1738 translation into Swedish used "picnick" (in the sense of an assembly); Swedish continues to use "picnick" and suggests that it is of French or English origin. *Larousse Gastronomique* (2002) states that 'picnic' is a contraction of *pique* (to pick), *piquante* (sharp or pungent), and *nique* (of small value). This suggestion seems commonsensical, but it is guesswork based on the technique of word formation by clipping words together to form a new word.

In the arts and literature, picnics tend to be more concerned with place, action, and figurative meanings and less concerned with food, if it is mentioned at all. Oliver Goldsmith, whom Georgina Battiscombe (*English Picnics*, 1949) credits with describing the first picnic in English literature in *The Vicar of Wakefield* (1766) provides these bare bones: "Our family dined in the field, and we sat, or rather, reclined round a temperate repast, our cloth spread upon the hay." Battiscombe insists that a picnic must be a meal eaten outdoors to which diners bring something to eat, even if there is no sharing. She suggests that before the Romantics made nature fashionable "no one connected the idea of pleasure with the notion of a meal eaten anywhere but under a roof" (p. 4).

In London, the so-called Picnic Society (1802) was a short-lived elite social club organized for entertainment. But a decade later "picnic" is used only in the sense of a meal eaten outdoors. Occasionally, it was used in the sense of an anthology, as in Charles Dickens's *The Pic-Nic Papers, by Various Hands* (1841), or as a term of disapprobation as in a person accused of picnickery and nicknackery, or being frivolous.

Germans use *picnick* in the sense of holding a meeting, as in the phrase *ein Picknick halten*. The verb is *picknicken*, which literally means holding a picnic as you would hold a meeting or a party. Italians use *scampagnata* (holiday in the country), or *colazione sull'erba* (luncheon on the grass). Spaniards use *comida al aire libre* (luncheon on the grass), or *comida campestre* (eat in the country). Spanish dictionaries seem unaware that Ménage thinks the word may be of Spanish origin. Koreans use both the Chinese *so pong* (a little meal in the country) and "picnic." Their favorite picnic time occurs when the cherry trees are in bloom. The Japanese have a long history of depicting meals taken outdoors, often celebrating *hanami*, the cherry blossom season, or another seasonal event. In 1862, "picnic" was translated as *shokuji* (meal), and in the twentieth century, the Japanese adopted the loanword *pikunikku*.

Food Writers on Picnics

Cookbooks are excellent resources for picnic menus and recollections. Jean Anthelme Brillat-Savarin delights in the hunt assembly ("Halts of a Shooting-Party"), which he does not call a picnic: "At the appointed hour we see arrive light carriages and prancing horses, loaded with the fair, all feathers and flowers. . . . Seated on the green turf they eat, the corks fly; they gossip, laugh, and are merry in perfect freedom, for the universe is their drawing-room, and the sun their lamp" (*Physiologie du goût*,

AN EGYPTIAN PICNIC

Claudia Roden's "A Middle Eastern Affair" in *Everything Tastes Better Outdoors* (1985) tells that her favorite picnic spot was in the dunes of Agami in Alexandria, where she was raised as a child. She explains that in the Middle East eating out is a way of life: "There are even official occasions for picnic. Among these are the *mulids,* when people flock to the principal scenes of religious festivals, public gardens, shrines, tombs of saints, and burial grounds. Thousands gather sometimes for days and nights, sleeping under tents . . . . The most important of the national picnics in Egypt is not a religious occasion. It is *Shem en Nessem,* which celebrates the arrival of spring. Town dwellers go out in the country or in boats, generally northward, eating out in fields or on the riverbank, smelling the air, which is thought to be particularly beneficial on the day" (pp. 167–168). Picnic foods include *blehat samak* (Fish rissoles), *qras samak* (Arab fish cake with burghul,) brains Moroccan style, sanbusak (pies filled with meat and pine nuts), meat ajja (an omelet) kukye gusht (an Iranian omelet) *kibbeh naye* (raw lamb and cracked wheat paste), *bazargan* (burghul salad), *tabbouleh* (cracked wheat salad), stuffed vegetables, stuffed onion, leeks, zucchini, lemon chicken, *lahma bil karaz* (meatballs with cherries), *salq bi loubia* (spinach with black-eyed beans), lentil tomato salad, and *loubia bi zeit* (green beans in olive oil).

pp. 152–153). Mrs. Isabella Beeton's recommendations for a picnic for forty persons are for formal entertaining carried outdoors in some location where an elaborate feast could be organized and served by servants.

Elizabeth David, a known lover of picnics, says that

Picnic addicts seem to be roughly divided between those who frankly make elaborate preparations and leave nothing to chance, and those others whose organization is no less complicated but who are more deceitful and pretend that everything will be obtained on the spot and cooked over a woodcutter's fire conveniently at hand (*Summer Cooking*, p. 208).

James Beard suggests that a picnic requires that you travel somewhere to eat. He is certain that

Wherever it is done, picnicking can be one of the supreme pleasures of outdoor life. At its most elegant, it calls for the accompaniment of the best linens and crystal and china; at its simplest it needs only a bottle of wine and items purchased from the local delicatessen as one passes through town. I recall a recent

Grapes are one of the oldest and most universally popular picnic fruits, and no tasteful American picnic is complete without wine and cheese—or the ever-popular cold fried chicken. © ARTHUR ROTHSTEIN/CORBIS.

picnic in France where we bought *rilletes de Tours* (in Tours), and elsewhere some excellent *salade museau*, good bread, ripe tomatoes and cheese. A bottle of local wine and glasses and plates from the Monoprix helped to make this picnic in a heather field near Le Mans a particularly memorable one (*Menus for Entertaining*, p. 272).

Claudia Roden, aficionado of picnics and outdoor eating, describes English picnics, Revival Week picnics, a Middle Eastern Affair, a Japanese Picnic, and a Picnic in the Himalayas. Roden confesses,

> The pleasures of outdoor food are those that nature has to offer, as ephemeral as they are intense. A bird will sing his song and fly away, leaves will flutter and jostle the sunlight for a brief second—sky, flowers, and scents have each their small parts to play in the perfect happiness of those enchanted moments. They serve, as Jean Jacques Rousseau said, to "liberate the soul" (*Everything Tastes Better Outdoors*, p. 4).

See also **Beard, James; Beeton, Isabella Mary; Brillat-Savarin, Anthelme.**

BIBLIOGRAPHY

Battiscombe, Georgina. *English Picnics*. London: Harvill Press, 1949.

Beard, James. *Menus for Entertaining* [1965]. New York: Marlowe and Company, 1985.

Brillat-Savarin, Jean Anthelme. "Meditation XV," *Physiologie du gout* [The Physiology of Taste: Meditations on Transcendental Gastronomy] [1825]. Translated by Charles Monselet. New York: Liveright, 1948.

Craigie, Carter W. "The Vocabulary of the Picnic." *MidWestern Language and Folklore Newsletter*, 1978: 2–6.

Crookenden, Kate, Caroline Worlledge, and Margaret Willes, compilers. *The National Trust Book of Picnics*. London: The National Trust, 1988.

Cunningham, Marion, ed. *The Fanny Farmer Cookbook*. 13th edition. New York: Alfred A. Knopf, 2000.

David, Elizabeth. *Summer Cooking* [1955]. London and New York: Penguin Books, 1965.

Eyre, Karen, and Mirielle Galinou. *Picnic*. London. Museum of London, 1988.

Hemingway, Joan, and Connie Maricich. *The Picnic Gourmet*. New York: Random House, 1977.

Hern, Mary Ellen. "Picnicking in the Northeastern United States 1840–1900," *Winterthur Portfolio*, 24 (2–3) 1989: 139–152.

Roden, Claudia. *Everything Tastes Better Outdoors*. New York: Alfred A. Knopf, 1985.

Walter Levy

PIE. The word *pie* derives from a related word *piece*, as expressed in medieval Latin *petia* or *pecia*. Both terms can be traced to Gaulish *peth* (Lambert 1997), which appears as *pighe* in Irish and Scottish. The core meaning of the word both in Celtic and in later medieval Latin was twofold: a morsel which could be eaten with the fingers and which also contained some type of filling—in short, a pastry envelope.

Pocket Pies

The Gaulish origin of our English word does not imply that the Celts invented the pie concept; it merely underscores the fact that this culinary idea is one of great age and wide distribution, with many counterparts in the Near East and Asia. It also reaffirms the growing realization among food historians that many modern concepts, such as *bouillon-blanc* (early medieval *bugillo albo*) derive from non-Roman European cultures, although they are transmitted to us through Medieval Latin.

In keeping with this, the original "pie" at least as it was known to continental Celts, consisted of a square, triangular, or more commonly a circular piece of dough folded over a filling and pressed together to form a half-moon or pocket. This concept was carried over into medieval cookery, and linguistic evidence suggests that these pies were large, since diminutive adjectives or endings were needed to describe small ones. In medieval everyday cookery such pies probably served as a substitute for roast meat since they could employ meat leftovers or such foraged poverty fillings as elderberries or sorrel. Furthermore, they could be baked down hearth in a kettle set on a tripod over hot coals, with some of the coals scattered over the kettle lid. The ease with which such fare could be prepared in very simple medieval kitchens may explain why the pie became so firmly integrated into the traditional cookery of the British Isles. However, in medieval court cookery, handheld pies formed an adjunct to other dishes brought to the table, and very often contained exotic ingredients or flavors intended to contrast with carefully orchestrated sauces, dips, and roasted meats.

The identifying pocket shape, which is highly convenient in societies where food is eaten with the fingers, may be found in many traditional grain-based cookeries where flour is compounded with oils or fats in a variety of ways. This age-old concept survives in the form of Spanish *empanadas*, in English turnovers, in Greek *kolokotes*, and in a vast number of other similarly shaped foods now prepared in both the Old and New worlds—even in the modern pop tart invented for toasters.

One thread common to all forms of traditional pocket pies is that the crust was usually short (with a high fat content). Because of this, the pie was normally associated with festive or special occasion cookery, and thus forbidden by the Christian church for consumption on lean days or on days of fasting. This restriction varied regionally since ecclesiastical enforcement was at best uneven.

Restrictions were profoundly altered during the Protestant Reformation, which did away with fast days. Thus the pie became a status symbol, which in time assumed far more importance in English cookery than it did on the Continent. This cultural emphasis was transferred to North America through English colonization. Furthermore, by the time the pie reached American shores in the seventeenth century, it had already undergone several transformations in England, so that there was not one, but five types of pastry called pie: pocket pies, two-crusted pies, one-crusted pies, standing pies, and potpies. All these forms evolved distinctive English identities during the late Middle Ages and were slow to change, since they became tied up with concepts of English national identity.

Even into the nineteenth century, the pocket pie in its most ancient meaning lingered on alongside the newer forms in both demotic speech and literature, especially in cookery books of a highly colloquial nature. The unifying principle was that they were considered finger food during a period of English cookery predating the introduction of forks—quite literally something broken or cut into pieces. Indeed, this idea of eating with the hands has persisted for a very long time and is still preserved in such American creations as the Pennsylvania Dutch shoofly pie, a breakfast cake baked in a pie shell and meant to be sliced, held in the hand, and dipped into strong coffee.

This marriage of very different types of pies under the umbrella of one term is further linguistic evidence that the turnover shape was indeed the oldest type and

DRIED PUMPKIN PIE

In the age before canned pumpkin puree, home cooks had only two choices: fresh pumpkin from the winter pantry, or dried pumpkin. The internal reference to a brick bakeoven suggests that the setting for the following recipe is a well-off farm somewhere in the Middle States, where bread baking was still done in an outdoor bake house.—Ed.

Dry the pumpkin after the following manner: — Boil it a good while, then spread it upon plates, or drop a spoonful at a time upon buttered paper, which is laid on tins, forming cakes, as it were, and set the tins into a brick oven after you have removed your baking; it dries in this way, without getting dusty.

In making the pies, take for one pie three cakes of pumpkin, and three eggs; sugar to your taste; soften the pumpkin in warm milk; strain through a colander; spice with cinnamon, and bake in a deep dish. This is an excellent pie, and preferred by some persons to the fresh pumpkin.

When well dried, the pumpkin will keep more than a year.

SOURCE: *Breakfast, Dinner, and Tea* (New York, 1883), p. 176.

that the English language did not have a wide range of indigenous terminologies to accommodate the newer forms. It is also evidence that the transition from one form to the next was sometimes gradual, especially in the countryside. Food historians generally concur that there is a definite genealogical link between the ancient pie and its modern two-crust descendant, although there is no firm agreement as to how this transition took place. There are several possible avenues of evolution. The shallow dish or saucer pie and the deep dish or potpie offer two theoretical possibilities.

The Saucer Pie

A turnover or large pocket pie that is baked in a saucer-like dish were known colloquially as saucer pies (Coolidge, 1875; Weaver, 1990) and consisted of one, sometimes two, turnovers baked in a small redware saucer and served in it. Milk could be poured over the pie, which was mashed and thus eaten like porridge. The next stage in the evolutionary line is achieved when the pastry dough is spread over the saucer and the dish rim is used for sealing the upper crust. The pie then moves from half-moon or pocket shape to circular. It can still be lifted from the dish and eaten out of hand, but the new shape now requires the use of a knife to cut it.

MUGGETY PIE

The following is a traditional British pie of a highly regional type made with an unusual sort of mincemeat: sheep's pluck, otherwise known as sheep's heart.—Ed.

> Prepare a sheep's pluck by soaking in water and thoroughly cleaning. Boil for several hours, and when cooked, put through mincing machine; then add a few currants, season well, and flavour with parsley or spice. Mix well together, put into a pie dish, cover with good short crust, and bake three-quarters hour.

SOURCE: Edith Martin, *Cornish Recipes* (Truro, England, 1937), 38.

An alternative form, which persisted into the nineteenth century (Leslie, 1857), was the saucer pie with only a thick upper crust. The baked pie was then turned out into a bowl with the top crust down so that it could be broken up and eaten with the fingers or so that milk could be poured over it for eating communally with a spoon. In either case, the underlying concept is one of expansion: the small handheld pie evolves into something of larger size for communal consumption.

The Potpie

The deep-dish or potpie form evolved parallel to this and appears to have very old antecedents in military and seafaring diets. It was a pragmatic adaptation imposed by limited equipment, in this case the employment of an iron kettle or cauldron over charcoal or over an open fire. The interior of the pot was lined with dough and the pot filled with ingredients including small pieces of dough often referred to as dumplings, then sealed on the top with a pastry lid. The pie was more or less stewed until thick inside its pastry cocoon, rather than baked, but like the one-crusted saucer pies, it too was turned out with its pastry parts and eaten communally with a spoon or piece of bread. The fish chowders of the North Sea Celts were prepared in this manner. Early American peach potpie conforms to this premedieval type, although the ingredients give it a thoroughly New World twist. If the potpie is taken one step further and prepared in a shallow dish, it is transformed into the sort of common two-crusted pie we know today. This is yet another possible line of evolution.

The potpie was especially popular on the American frontier, and the lore surrounding that historical role is rich. It continues to be a popular one-pot meal with many Americans even to this day, but it has evolved into a type of baked stew served with or without a largely ornamental top crust and has little resemblance to the rustic ancestral form once prepared in a large iron pot.

Two-Crusted Pies

In the context of English cookery, both types of two-crusted pies appear to have gained in popularity during the Reformation. They gradually moved from Sunday fare in the eighteenth century, to almost daily fare for farmers during the nineteenth. In both England and America, lard was the universal shortening ingredient for the crust. Butter was only used by the well-to-do. One of the most common types of round, two-crusted pies was also the cheapest: pies made with apple fillings, either from fresh apples or from dried apples soaked in hot water or cider. The apple pie was such standard fare in British and American farmhouse cookery that it became a symbol for the cookery as a whole.

Pies Derived from Tarts

The two other types of pie in Anglo-American cookery derive from quite divergent origins. The first is the shallow pie without top crust (or ornamented with a latticework crust). These are often referred to as tarts in old English cookery books, and in fact derive from flat cakes covered with a filling. This category of pie includes fruit tarts and baked puddings, the most famous of the latter being American pumpkin pie (technically a custardlike pudding). It also appears in the blurring of distinctions inherent in such Americanisms as "pizza pie," a linguistic attempt to make a traditional Mediterranean flatbread conform to older Anglo-American notions of pielike things. The pizza is, after all, cut up into pieces and eaten out of hand.

The Raised Pie

The fifth type of pie is the raised or standing pie. This type of pie reached its zenith during the Middle Ages, when it served as an *entremet* or showpiece for banquet entertainments. In this case, emphasis was not so much on the taste as on the spectacle it created when brought to table, for there are many well-documented instances where pies were constructed to resemble castles, or built to encase whole roasted animals, or which popped open to reveal musicians, or served as a temporary prison for the four-and-twenty blackbirds mentioned in an old children's rhyme. The crust of such pies was incidental as food, and normally consisted of coarse flour mixed with hot water until it could be molded like clay. It baked hard and was given to the hounds or to the poor.

The game and fish pies of the Victorian era baked in copper or tin molds are lineal descendants of this old culinary tradition. In fact, several English china manufacturers created serving pieces imitating the color and shapes of elaborate game pies. These ceramic substitutes dispensed with the trouble and unpredictability of crusts assembled by poorly trained cooks, and of course they could be used over and over as needed. Like elaborately crusted pies made of real pastry, the expensive china ones also served as the focal point for festive occasions, such as Christmas, a hunt luncheon, or a wedding.

However, the standing pie of greatest importance in English cookery appears to have been mincemeat, and the elaborate construction of the crust was no less important than the spiciness of the filling inside. The Reformation did away with sumptuary restrictions; thus mincemeat could be consumed all through the winter. In fact, it became a fixture in winter cookery both in Britain and America. Diaries from the eighteenth and nineteenth centuries often mention baking large numbers of mincemeat pies for storage in a cold pantry and then consuming them as breakfast, dinner and supper fare. Ground beef, suet, chopped apples, and dried fruit (commonly raisins) formed the core ingredients and doubtless provided high-energy food for hardworking farmers. This common man's mincemeat pie devolved from the elaborate standing crust of a manorial Christmas feast to the sort of old two-crusted affair tracing its origin back to the pocket pie. Indeed, pocket pies filled with mincemeat also served farmers as snacks in the field, their convenience and practicality ensuring the survival of the form into this century under the dialect name of pasty (also called fried pie), especially in eastern mining towns and in the American upper Midwest. Pasty is also a term used for the leek-and-potato pies of Cornwall in England.

The Pie as a Styled Centerpiece

There has been a noticeable evolution down through the centuries in the presentation of pies as culinary centerpieces to the formal dessert course. Part of this is due to the ever-changing role the pie has played as a symbol of wellbeing and status. In fact, the treatment of the pie probably mirrors larger shifts in social values about food, indeed even the philosophical aspirations of the beholders.

The medieval standing pie, with its elaborate detail, gilding, and highly artificial appearance doubtless reflected a sense of suppressing nature through art. The choice of ornamental themes definitely appealed to medieval idealism and a fascination with romantic anachronisms—such as the popular tale of the fish-woman Mélusine. This boisterous artificiality is certainly carried down into Renaissance and Baroque cookery, but by the same token, it is obvious from period paintings and prints that pie bakers were also masters of crust design. Even small pies were meant to be studied up close, and therefore they were covered with neat, tight patterns as crisply executed as sculpture. The farmhouse pie was never quite that elaborate, but it was a centerpiece and a measure of the housewife's cooking abilities. So her crusts were no less neat, even if only ornamented with a careful rim and the so-called "bird-track" patterns commonly seen in nineteenth-century prints. This preoccupation with fine detail was important to a world in which everything was made by hand: the more artificial, the more sculpted, the more it stood out as a thing of beauty.

Industrialization changed this attitude dramatically. The craftsmanship of pie baking was replaced by the industrial pie sold frozen in tin pans, the crusts pressed out

METHODIST MINCEMEAT

Why eat mincemeat? It is a symbol of Christmas luxury, and therefore deeply embedded in religious sensibilities, at least in the English-speaking world. Rather than reject it on grounds of high church decadence, the object of some Protestant groups became to reform it, that is, to bring it in line with their shifting religious values. This reform was undertaken on two fronts, although they overlapped considerably. One was to eliminate alcohol, the other to abjure the "carnal kitchen"—the consumption of meat. Temperance and vegetarianism come together in the following working-class version of Christmas luxury purified of sin.—Ed.

Yield: one 9-inch pie or 12 tartlets
Short crust
1 large lemon
8 tablespoons unsalted butter
½ cup brown sugar
1½ cups dried currants
3 large apples
⅓ cup lemon juice
2 teaspoons ground cinnamon
¼ teaspoon ground clove
1 teaspoon freshly grated nutmeg
½ cup chopped candied citron

Line the pie pan or tartlet pans with short crust. Remove the pithy membranes from the lemon and cut the rind into quarters. Place the rind on a saucepan and cover with boiling water. Simmer 20 to 30 minutes, or until the rind is tender. Strain, reserve the lemon rind, and discard the bitter water. Chop the rind very fine in a food processor.

Preheat the oven to 350°F (210°C). Melt the butter in a deep stewing pan, add the sugar and currants and cover. Stew the currants until they are plumped. Pare, core, and chop the apples, and add them to the currants together with the chopped lemon rind, the lemon juice, and the spices. Cook for 15 minutes, then add the citron and remove from the stove.

When the filling is cool enough to work with, fill the pie shells and cover each with a top crust. Bake in the preheated oven for approximately 25 to 30 minutes; the tartlets will bake in about 20 minutes.

SOURCE: William Woys Weaver, *The Christmas Cook* (New York, 1990), p. 42. Adapted from a recipe in the *Methodist Christian Advocate and Journal* (New York), 16 November 1827.

by machine. Therefore, in the early twenty-first century, the rustic look is in. Large, crudely executed patterns, clumsy rims, crusts indeed much too thick for the pies

CLASSIC LEMON MERINGUE PIE

Recipe of Cecilia Rubio, Perris, California, and 1987 national winner of the Crisco American Pie Celebration contest.

Yield: one 9-inch pie
one 9-inch pie crust pre-baked and cooled.
Filling:
1½ cups sugar
¼ cup cornstarch
3 tablespoons all-purpose flour
¼ teaspoon salt
1½ cups hot water
3 egg yolks, beaten
2 tablespoons butter or margarine
1½ teaspoons grated lemon peel
⅓ cup plus 1 tablespoon fresh lemon juice

Meringue:
½ cup sugar, divided
1 tablespoon cornstarch
½ cup cold water
4 egg whites
¾ teaspoon vanilla

Preheat the oven to 350°F (210°C). Assemble the filling by combining the sugar, cornstarch, flour, and salt in a medium saucepan. Add the hot water, stirring constantly. Cook and stir over a medium heat until the mixture comes to a boil and thickens. Reduce the heat to low. Cook and stir constantly for 8 minutes, then remove from the heat. Slowly add about 1/3 of the hot mixture to the egg yolks and mix well. Return this to the saucepan and bring to a boil over a medium heat. Reduce the heat to low and cook 4 minutes, stirring constantly. Remove from the heat and add the butter and lemon peel. Add the lemon juice slowly so that it does not curdle the mixture, then spoon the mixture into the pre-baked pie crust.

To prepare the meringue, combine 2 tablespoons of sugar with the cornstarch and cold water in a small saucepan. Stir until the cornstarch is fully dissolved, then cook and stir over a medium heat until the mixture is clear. Set aside to cool.

Combine the egg whites and vanilla in a large bowl. Beat until soft peaks form, then beat in the remaining sugar, adding it 1 tablespoon at a time. Combine the meringue with the cornstarch mixture and beat until it forms stiff peaks. Spread this over the filling so that it completely covers the pie and seals it at the edges.

Bake in the preheated oven for 12 to 15 minutes or until the meringue becomes golden. Cool to room temperature before serving.

---

they cover, nonetheless convey the immediate impression that they are handmade and therefore of greater intrinsic value than the commercial article. To the master pie baker of the past, these modern-day creations would appear as though flopped on the table by a child, but it is this very naïveté, this "country look" that modern food journals find so appealing as cover art subjects. That the pie is a perennial showpiece for the covers of magazines and cookbooks speaks volumes about its power as a food symbol.

The Pie as Symbol: Motherhood and Apple Pie

It is no exaggeration to suggest that the pie is perhaps one of the ultimate icons of American cookery. This idea is not new. In an 1874 issue of the *Household* the editor made this comment:

> If we have a national dish . . . we suppose its name is Pie. The line between winter and spring is accurately defined in the minds of half the housewives in the country as the time when there is nothing to make pies of. Dried apples are used up, prunes are too expensive, and rhubarb has not yet made its appearance.

The pie became a symbol of American cookery because of its huge diversity and easy adaptability to seasonal dietary changes. There are pies for festive occasions: cranberry, mincemeat, and oyster pies for Christmas; pumpkin pies for Thanksgiving. There are pies for life cycle events, such as the funeral pie (otherwise known as raisin pie) among the Pennsylvania Dutch. And there are a great number of pies closely identified with regional cookeries, such as Boston cream pie in New England; pecan, sweet potato, and Key lime pies in the South; tuna pie (made with cactus pears) in the Southwest; and vinegar and molasses pies in the Midwest. Both of the latter pies were also known as harvest pies since they were served to field hands during haying and other harvest periods.

The harvest was one of the most evocative subjects for American art and literature in the preindustrial era, and images of pies are woven into that rich tapestry of food iconography. Industrialization did not destroy the pie's symbolic value, but rather transformed it into new images like pie à la mode (literally "pie in the latest style"), which married a scoop of vanilla ice cream to a slice of pie. This symbol of working class indulgence soon became an icon for diner and soda fountain fare. Likewise, the numerous meringue covered pies, originally referred to by the baking trade as pies in the "hotel style" (a

A late medieval baker prepares raised pies for the oven. The pies are filled with meats or fruit, or both. Fifteenth-century Italian fresco in the Castile di Issogne (Aosta Valley) in Northern Italy. © ARCHIVO ICONOGRAFICO, S.A./CORBIS.

metaphor for luxury food), achieved their greatest popularity as standard fare at diners and truck stops during the Great Depression. Homemade meringue pies were also featured desserts for church suppers, not to mention worthy material for pie baking contests.

The voluptuousness of a well-made meringue pie was not lost on Hollywood, since the culinary perfection it stood for could be converted into high comedy by means of the outbursts of pie throwing which occur in many old black and white films. We do not see apple pie (a symbol of patriotism) or mincemeat pie (a symbol of Christmas) thrown into peoples' faces. But meringue clinging to the cheeks of a wide-eyed blonde-haired woman elicited laughter, real and perhaps also somewhat nervous, because in the context of those times the image was unquestionably lewd.

See also **Baking; Cake and Pancake; Candy and Confections; Pastry; Pizza.**

BIBLIOGRAPHY

Armstrong, Sara, ed. *Best Recipes: Crisco Pies for All Seasons.* Lincolnwood, Ill.: Crisco, 1992.

Coolidge, Susan. "The Fortunes of a Saucer-Pie." *St. Nicholas* (November 1875): 42–44.

Lambert, Pierre-Yves. *La langue gauloise* [The Gaulish language]. Paris: Editions Errance, 1997.

Kirkland, John. *The Bakers' ABC.* London: Gresham, 1927.

Leslie, Eliza. *Miss Leslie's New Cook Book.* Philadelphia: T. B. Peterson, 1857.

Weaver, William Woys. *The Christmas Cook.* New York: HarperPerennial, 1990.

Wilson, C. Anne. *Food and Drink in Britain.* New York: Barnes and Noble, 1974.

Whitehead, Jessup. *The Hotel Book of Fine Pastries.* Chicago: National Hotel Reporter, 1881.

William Woys Weaver

PIG. Human beings eat more meat of the pig than any other domesticated livestock on earth, even with pig being a food forbidden to more than one billion followers of Islam or Judaism. This lowly beast, whose intelligence and cleanliness has been underestimated for centuries, is a prolific animal that quickly converts a variety of feeds to a mild-flavored meat. One of the first domesticated animals, the pig appears in oriental and Greco-Roman mythology as well as in the Torah, the Bible, and the Qur'an. Despite its utility as a source of food, leather, and pharmaceuticals, the word, pig, is an insult or gentle rebuke in many cultures. While the pig itself may not have grown more controversial, its modern, industrialized husbandry draws criticism from an array of opponents.

The Omnivorous Pig
The pig, *Sus scrofa domestica*, is a subspecies of *Sus scrofa*, the Eurasian wild boar. It is in the order of mammals, Artiodactyla, which means even-toed and hoofed. That order includes ruminant livestock such as cattle. Bacteria in the rumen help these animals digest cellulose in grasses. *Sus scrofa* is a member of the Family Suidae, or swine. These animals do not ruminate and cannot digest grasses. They are omnivores. In the wild, their diet is fungi, leaves, roots, bulbs, tubers, fruit, snails, earthworms, small vertebrates, eggs, and carrion. The Suidae family includes African bush pigs and African warthogs.

There are some three hundred breeds of domestic pigs. Most are endangered. In the United States, only eight breeds are widely used for commercial production: the Berkshire, Chester White, Hampshire, Duroc, Yorkshire, Landrace, Poland China, and Spots. The Meishan breed, developed in China two thousand years ago, was imported to the United States in 1989 for research and to add genetic diversity.

In common usage, most people make no distinction between a pig and swine, but the precise meaning of pig is "a young swine." The experienced swine breeder Kelly Klober notes that "what really separates the pros from the tenderfeet is how the word 'pig' is used. To be country correct, it is the term for a very young pig. A hog is a swine that weighs over 120 pounds" (Klober, p. 24). A mature female swine is a sow. A mature male is a boar. Barrows are castrated male pigs raised for slaughter. Gilts are immature females. Both are sold as "market hogs" at five to seven months of age and at weights of between 220 to 260 pounds. Mature hogs can grow much larger. Boars have topped one ton.

Use of the meat of the pig, known as pork, is also not without controversy. Until the early twentieth century, the hog was bred for fat, or lard, just as much as for meat. Later in that century, the saturated fats found in many types of meat were targeted as contributors to coronary heart disease. Breeding and changes in the way hogs are fed has made modern swine 30 to 50 percent leaner than in 1950. At the beginning of the twentieth century, the lard-type hog, nicknamed "cob rollers," was so fat that its stubby legs were barely visible.

Pushing the Chicken Fat Barrier
The leanest cuts of pork can approach the fat content of skinless chicken breast. According to U.S. Department of Agriculture (USDA) nutrition data cited by the National Pork Board, an industry group, a three-ounce roasted pork tenderloin has 4.1 grams of total fat, more than the 3.1 grams in a comparable portion of roasted, skinless chicken breast, but much less than the 9.3 grams in a chicken thigh.

Lean cuts of pork are also richer in some essential vitamins and minerals than other meats. Another USDA database lists broiled fresh pork as having .923 milligrams of thiamin, or vitamin B1, in a 100 gram serving (about 3.5 ounces). That amount is more than half of the recommended daily consumption of thiamin and ten times the amount of thiamin found in a comparable cut of beef and even more than the amount in chicken breast (0.070 mg). The body uses thiamin to metabolize carbohydrates, protein, and fat.

The Pig's Fatty Underbelly
For all of modern pork's improved qualities, the pig is still a source of less desirable calories. As much as two-thirds of each slaughtered hog is used for processed meats—hams, sausages, and bacon. These meat products can be much higher in fat and salt than the amounts considered healthy by the medical profession.

The Center for Science in the Public Interest in the United States characterizes bacon, hot dogs, and sausage, all of which can contain pork, as among the most unhealthy foods available, recommending that consumers buy bacon and sausage that has no more than 45 percent of its calories from fat and no more than 480 milligrams of sodium per serving. In a recent survey of products sold in grocery stores, typical pork bacon (which comes from a pig's belly) had a whopping 9 percent of its calories in the form of fat. Only certain brands of turkey bacon were truly "low fat." The pork bacon was lower than turkey bacon in sodium, however, with only 170 milligrams.

Lean or fat, the swine family is an old one, geologically and in the archeological records of early human agriculture and civilization. The swine family has inhabited the earth since about forty-five million years ago, when the horrific seven-foot-high entelodont roamed central Asia and North America. Like modern pigs, entelodonts had cloven hooves and were omnivores. Their scarred fossils show evidence of fierce battles. They had much smaller brains and may not have had the social herding characteristics of modern swine. They died out twenty-five million years ago and were succeeded by smaller direct ancestors of the wild boar and modern pig.

The Javan warty pig (*Sus verrucosus*) will win no prizes for good looks or sweet temper, but it is important for preserving the biodiversity of the species. It is found only on the island of Java in Indonesia. PHOTO COURTESY OF BIOS.

Older Than the Cow

The pig is one of the first domesticated animals: its remains in some archeological excavations have been found to date earlier than the bones of cattle. Agricultural settlements raised pigs in the Middle East at least nine to ten thousand years ago. In Jericho, one of the world's most ancient cities, archeologists unearthed domesticated pig bones in soil layers predating 7000 B.C.E. Archeological excavations in the East Indies and Southeastern Asia show evidence of domesticated swine at about the same time. The East Asian pig arrived in China around 5000 B.C.E. Some of the first written recipes for pork are from China, where the pig has been an integral part of agriculture for thousands of years, feeding on garden waste and table scraps in pens next to farm huts. Recent archeological evidence suggests that Neolithic farmers rapidly spread agriculture, and pigs, along the Mediterranean shore of Europe before 5500 B.C.E.

The pig appears again in the writing and art of first recorded history. Pork was a popular food in early dynasties of Egypt. The ancient Greeks ate pigs. The Romans were masters of smoking and salting pork. From the time of medieval Europe through colonial North America, pigs were allowed to forage for acorns, nuts, and other foods in the forest in a semi-wild state. In the fall, they would be rounded up, slaughtered, butchered, and preserved by smoking, salting, and curing. In the United States, the pig was the most popular source of meat through the nineteenth century. The westward migration of American settlers into what would become the Corn Belt in America's Midwestern states was the perfect marriage of an Old World livestock with the grain of native Americans. The diet of swine shifted ever more from woodland forage and scraps to corn. Not until the 1950s did beef surpass pork as the most popular meat in

America. Increased beef consumption coincided with the rise of industrialized cattle feedlots and post-World War II affluence. With suburbanization came the popularity of backyard grilling of steaks and hamburgers.

Many of the breeds of swine raised in North America came from England, as their names, Hampshire, Yorkshire and Berkshire, suggest. Some of these English breeds are at least four hundred years old, according to both historical records and DNA studies.

Prolific and Efficient Meat Producers

The Spanish, too, brought hogs with them to the New World. The explorer, Hernando de Soto landed in what is now Tampa Bay, Florida, in 1539 with thirteen hogs. Three years later, the swine herd had grown to seven hundred.

This ability to multiply rapidly is a quality that endears the pig to some of the poorest farmers on earth as well as the most modern swine production complexes. A sow produces almost three litters of pigs a year, although 2.25 litters per year is more realistic on smaller, traditional farms. From each litter eight or more pigs usually survive. Sows on large commercial farms can produce nearly twenty-six pigs per year.

Not only are pigs prolific, they grow fast on modest amounts of feed. A pig easily gains a pound for every three to five pounds of feed it eats, reaching more than two hundred pounds in six months. In some intensive industrial swine farms, where pigs are confined in a small space with little to do but eat, feed efficiency has approached one pound of meat for every two pounds of feed—about the same as poultry. Pigs are much more efficient at converting grain to meat than cattle or sheep.

PET PIGS OF NEW GUINEA

Perhaps nowhere on earth is the pig so honored and well treated as in the highlands of Papua New Guinea—at least until it is eaten.

The great anthropologist Margaret Mead visited the Stone Age tribes of New Guinea and noticed that pigs there acted like dogs. "They assume all of the characteristics of dogs—hang their heads under rebuke, snuggle up to regain favor, and so on," she wrote in *Letters from the Field: 1925–1972.*

In this still primitive island nation south of the equator and north of Australia, the women of highland tribes rear pigs and treat them as well as their own children. They will even nurse a pig if it is orphaned. Women, children—and pigs—eat and sleep in huts that are separate from those of the men. The pigs are named, hand-fed, groomed, and fussed over if they become sick. Not until they are large are the pigs kept in a separate pen in the hut.

Eventually, though, the men slaughter some of these pigs in a ritualized sacrifice. Then the pigs become a feast for the tribal village. Pork and sweet potatoes cooked on hot stones add flavor to weddings, funerals, festivals, and other special events.

To Westerners, this may seem like bizarre, almost schizophrenic behavior. But within the context of New Guinea's tribal cultures, it is a bit more logical.

Pigs have great economic, political, and even mystical importance in New Guinea. They are symbols of wealth. They are used to buy a bride, for example. Pigs are sacrificed to appease ancestral spirits. Some tribes consider them humanlike—and humans, piglike.

Eating one's best friend does not seem so strange in New Guinea, where only a few decades ago cannibalism was practiced. And breast-feeding pigs is just a low-tech version of U.S. sheep ranchers bottle-feeding orphaned lambs. Valuable animals often receive loving care in many livestock-rearing cultures.

Even today, decades after Margaret Mead lived in New Guinea in the 1930s, the tribes there prize their pigs. At the turn of the twenty-first century, Jeff Tyler traveled to New Guinea for *The Savvy Traveler,* a public radio travel program and Web site in the United States.

Tyler joined a group of American and Australian tourists who visited a mountain village where a sow was ritually slaughtered. Village men, covered with black and ceremonial paint, clubbed the sow and cooked her for their guests.

Tribal warfare still continues in New Guinea. A local guide tells Tyler, "There is a reason for tribal warfares. The main reason is we fight for land. We fight for woman. And we fight for pigs."

Until the late twentieth century, pigs were weaned from their sow from about thirty-five to fifty-six days after they were born. From a birth weight of about three pounds, they would reach a weaning weight of about forty to fifty pounds by fifty-six days. After a short period of receiving a rich "starter feed" of grains, milk products, and perhaps medication, the pigs were ready to sell to another farmer who specialized in "finishing," or feeding hogs to market weights. Sometimes the farmer whose sows produced the pigs would keep the pigs and move them to another barn or pen to feed them to market weight in a method of production called "farrow to finish." (Farrowing refers to the action of a sow giving birth.) Farrow-to-finish production was typical of small- and medium-size "family farms" in North America. On some farms, farrowing took place in small huts big enough for one sow, placed in a pasture of alfalfa or other digestible forage. After 1950, farrowing more commonly took place in specialized buildings or modified barns.

The farmers who specialized in farrowing would cross several breeds of swine in order to produce stronger,

healthier pigs that grow faster. This benefit from cross-breeding was called hybrid vigor. Farmers who specialized in feeding pigs for slaughter began to separate them by sex, so that the males and females could be given different feeding rations tailored to the nutritional needs of each sex.

Commercial Complexity

In large commercial farms, swine production is even more complex, having moved beyond the traditional one-site or two-site production system. On these farms, pigs are weaned at much earlier ages, sometimes when only ten to fourteen days old. This technique, called medicated early weaning, was developed in Britain in the 1980s by veterinary medicine professor Tom Alexander at the University of Cambridge. Alexander discovered that very early weaning could prevent a sow from passing certain swine diseases to the next generation of piglets. Weaned pigs are moved to separate nursery buildings, at enough distance to lessen the chance of infection by wind-born disease agents. The pigs are usually held in the nursery for seven weeks. before they are moved to another set of buildings for the "finisher-production" stage, where they reach slaughter weights.

In large pig farms, pigs are kept in small groups that remain isolated from older pigs. By avoiding the mixing of pigs after they are weaned, the risk of spreading diseases is lowered. Each week, while one group of pigs is moved from the site where they were born to a nursery building, another group is moved from a nursery to a finishing building, and yet another is moved out of a finishing building to the slaughter plant. After each group is moved, the building is washed and disinfected. To make this system work like a well-oiled machine, the farm or hog producing company must have 12,000 to 24,000 sows. This system can produce more than 600,000 market hogs a year.

Industrialized Production Spreads across the Globe

This multisite system of production has existed along with the more traditional ones, in which farmers raised only a few hundred or a few thousand pigs for slaughter. But at the start of the new millennium, multisite production was rapidly taking over the industry. In Corn Belt hog-producing states, individual families that ran grain farms still fed hogs, but only in the second and third stages of multisite production. The families no longer owned the pigs. Instead, they raised them for large companies, much as local entrepreneurs run franchise outlets for fast-food chains. The pigs were owned, from birth through slaughter, by large companies, including packers. The parent animals in this system are complex proprietary mixtures of breeds owned by a handful of multinational companies. By the late 1990s, more than half of U.S. production was in some stage of this "vertical integration," meaning that each step in hog raising is owned or controlled by one company. The multisite pig production system was becoming global, existing not only in the United States and Britain, but also in Canada, Mexico, Brazil, Chile, Spain, Germany, Poland, Italy, China, and France.

Many of these countries are also the top producers and consumers of pigs. China is the leader, producing 43.2 million metric tons of pork in 2002, more than half of the global production of 85.2 million tons. The European Union was a distant second, with 17.8 million tons. The United States ranked third, producing 8.7 million metric tons of pork. China's livestock practices supply the main reason the world eats much more pork than other meats. Of the world annual beef production of about fifty million tons, China raises only 5.8 million tons of beef.

Pigs Led to Slaughter

Just as pig farming has changed, so has the slaughter of hogs and the curing of pork. Hogs are trucked to packing plants where they are unloaded, held in pens to fast, and then slaughtered, most commonly by stunning with a high-voltage electrical shock. Then the carcass is hung by the hind legs from an elevated conveyor line, bled, and cut apart. The treatment of hogs before slaughter is both an economic issue as well as one of humane treatment. If the animals are frightened and stressed for a long period of time, lactic acid builds up in the muscles, affecting meat quality. Some breeds of pigs are more susceptible to stress than others and can produce pale, watery fresh meat. The swine industry has dealt with the problem two ways. First, it has bred hogs to exclude lines that produce poor quality meat when stressed. Second, the packing industry is changing slaughter methods to treat hogs more humanely, which also reduces stress.

Colorado State University animal scientist Temple Grandin has devoted her life to making the last few minutes of cattle and hogs as pleasant as possible. As a result of her studies of how animals react to new environments, both farmers and slaughter plants are starting to move pigs through curved chutes onto trucks, and out of trucks into the packing plant to prevent pigs from witnessing what lies at the end of the line. Pigs are instinctively frightened when forced into a confined space. In Denmark, slaughter plants are experimenting with stunning hogs with carbon dioxide gas, which may be less stressful than electrical shock.

Refrigeration is the modern method of preserving pork, even for most ham and bacon, which is injected with brine, smoke flavoring, and, usually, sodium nitrite to give the meat a pink color and to protect against the growth of toxins responsible for botulism.

The Art of Curing and Cooking Pork

Traditional methods of air curing, which may date to pre-Roman times, are still used in China, Europe, and the American South. Hams are made by covering the meat, usually from the upper rear leg or hip but sometimes from the shoulder, with salt, sometimes sugar, and flavorings for several days in a cooler. The meat is then smoked at room temperatures in a smokehouse for about ten days and allowed to cure for at least six months. Before cooking, traditional air-cured hams should be soaked in cold water to remove excess salt.

Exactly why so much of the pig is cured and made into bacon and ham, while less beef and lamb is consumed as dried or smoked products may be a question for archeologists, not historians. One theory about the popularity of cured pork, offered by the National Pork Board, is that pork is a mild meat that, having less flavor than some meats, readily takes on added flavors.

Fresh pork faces another obstacle when compared to flavorful cured meats. As it became leaner in the late twentieth century, the potential to make fresh pork less palatable by overcooking increased. With less fat in the meat, overcooking can make pork taste very dry. The habit of overcooking stems from consumer fears that rare pork risks exposure to the parasite that causes trichinosis.

The parasite has been virtually eliminated from pork in most developed countries. To be safe, food experts recommend cooking pork until internal meat temperatures reach 170 degrees Fahrenheit, or piercing to the center of a cut of cooked pork. If the juices run clear, the meat is done, and no further cooking is needed.

Fighting the Flavor Drought

Dry pork is just one factor causing a growing reaction against raising pigs in the industrial system. As North Americans and Europeans consume more natural and organic vegetables, grains, and dairy products, a market is developing for natural and organic meats raised on smaller farms, sometimes with methods that animal welfare organizations consider more humane.

In the United States, one company, Niman Ranch of San Francisco, California, hires farmers to raise pigs without antibiotics or growth hormones for sale to natural foods stores and upscale restaurants. These farmers raise pigs in pastures or on straw bedding in barns and sheds and periodically submit samples of meat to a taste panel to make sure that it is not too lean to be palatable. They use swine breeds that are not quite as lean as the crossbred hogs in large multisite hog businesses. After tasting this type of pork, *New York Times* food writer Marian Burros reviewed it as "so delicious it needed no seasoning beyond salt and pepper.... [The] meat was superior heirloom pork, suffused with a bright clean flavor, with none of the unpleasant aftertaste that pork often has" (September 1999).

Dry pork is less of a problem in China, where much of the pig meat consumed in that country still comes from small farms and traditional breeds that are not as lean as those from Europe. The western provinces of China, known for spicy Szechwan dishes, also produce a type of ham, Yunnan or Xuanwei ham, that is exported to Southeast Asia and Europe. Mu Shu pork, consumed in the northern provinces near Beijing, is a dish that is popular in the United States as well. This rural Chinese dish is a mixture of sautéed pork and diced vegetables that is wrapped in small, steamed pancakes and dipped in a sauce. Unlike in the West, where pork is eaten by itself, in China most recipes use it sparingly, cut into small pieces and mixed with other ingredients. Blending flavors of many foods, an important principle of Chinese cuisine, has stretched supplies of pork and other meats in times of scarcity. The preciousness of pork may also be why no part of a pig is wasted in China. Even the head of the pig continues to be served by some pushcart vendors and urban restaurants.

Fear and Loathing of Pigs

As beloved as pork is in many cultures, the pig is despised in the traditions of others. Many theories exist to explain why Islam and Judaism consider the meat of pigs unclean. To some followers of these faiths, the abhorrent nature of pigs is obvious. The animals often wallow in mud and

look dirty. But pigs, unable to sweat, wallow in mud as an efficient way to stay cool. Nevertheless, their breeding conditions may have created a social stigma. Animal scientists M. Eugene Ensminger and R. O. Parker point out that because "close confinement was invariably accompanied by the foul odors of the pig sty . . . early keepers of swine were often regarded with contempt" (Ensminger and Parker, p. 1).

Anthropologist Marvin argues that the pig's downfall in the Middle East was economic. Pigs are costly to raise in the climate of the Middle East. They are more difficult to herd than the sheep and goats favored by the desert nomads who quickly adopted Islam. And there is evidence that over the past ten thousand years, the environment in the Middle East grew less hospitable for animals originally adapted to foraging in forests.

Harris contends that for Jews, "the food laws of Leviticus were mostly codifications of traditional food prejudices and avoidances" (Harris, 1985, p. 79). A book of the Torah, Leviticus was written in 450 B.C.E., long after swine herding and consumption had lost prestige in many other ancient near eastern cultures as well as in ancient Israel. He finds even more support for his theory in China, where pork-disdaining Islam failed to penetrate far. There, the pig complemented an agrarian ecology, eating stems, leaves and scraps from many vegetable crops, and in turn, being eaten.

Archeological digs in the Middle East give evidence that the pig was once worshipped as well as eaten. In early stages of Phoenician, Egyptian, and Babylonian civilizations, people freely ate pork. But as those civilizations matured, pork fell from favor. When the Greek historian Herodotus visited Egypt before 430 B.C.E., he saw that "the pig is regarded among them as an unclean animal so much so that if a man in passing accidentally touches a pig, he instantly hurries into the river and plunges in with all his clothes on" (quoted in Harris, 1985, p. 83).

The anthropologist Carlton Coon attributes the demise of pigs in this region of the world to deforestation and population increases. At the beginning of the Neolithic period, pigs could root in oak and beech forests. As human population density increased, Coon argues, the forests were cleared to make room for more farms, especially olive groves, and in times of famine and scarcity, pigs competed with humans for life-giving grain.

Pigs Provide More Than Meat

In the future, the economic relationship to cultural and religious taboos may be tested if pigs become more than a source of meat and go on to save more lives. Besides providing pigskin leather and byproducts with industrial uses, pigs are already a source of pharmaceuticals, such as insulin. Since 1971, pig heart valves have been used to replace damaged human heart valves. Pig valves are treated and contain no living cells, preventing rejection by the human immune system. Soon, genetic manipula-

SPAM

Spam might be described as the Woody Allen of the meat world. Like the American film actor, this small 12-ounce can of pork is a commercial success thriving on self-deprecation. In enticement, the rectangular block of pink processed meat sliding from the can onto a platter cannot contend with a juicy steak or a real ham. Consumer advocates cite it as an example of a high-fat food. The Oxford English Dictionary defines the adjective, spammy, as "consisting or tasting chiefly of 'bland' luncheon meat. . . mediocre, unexciting."

Spam drew widespread ridicule in the 1970s in a comedy skit on British television's *Monty Python's Flying Circus* when a Spam-pushing waitress was drowned out by a group of Vikings singing "Spam, spam, spam, spam. Lovely Spam! Wonderful Spam!" More recently, this trademarked brand of canned meat received a dubious tribute in the adoption of the term "spam" to denote unwanted e-mail, or unsolicited electronic mail messages. The association of the term with a food product may, in fact, have been overwhelmed by its new slang definition.

Even so, Hormel Foods Corporation, the maker and inventor of the original Spam, has profited on the sale of some five billion cans of the stuff, marketed in roughly one hundred countries, since its introduction in 1937 as "Hormel Spiced Ham." The Austin, Minnesota–based food company, founded in 1891 as Geo. A. Hormel & Company, pioneered the production and sale of canned hams in the 1920s. A New York actor, Kenneth Daigneau, won a naming contest by calling it Spam.

Spam is made from ham, pork shoulder meat, and a secret mix of spices. World War II turned this depression-era canned luncheon meat into a global product. Spam helped keep Russian troops from starving. It cheered the British palate. And it drew ribbing from U.S. forces in the South Pacific, where they named one encampment "Spamville." After the war, U.S. president Dwight Eisenhower admitted that he, too, ate his "share of Spam along with millions of other soldiers" (Hormel website).

In recent years, Hormel reports selling one hundred million cans of Spam annually in the United States, and another forty-two million overseas. Hawaiians are the top per capita consumers of Spam in the United States, at more than four cans per consumer a year. South Korea and the United Kingdom are the top overseas buyers of Spam.

In 2001 Hormel opened a 16,500 square-foot SPAM Museum in Austin, Minn. The following summer, it planned a media event with television stars; Barbara Billingsley, who played June Cleaver on the series *Leave It to Beaver,* was invited to present her favorite Spam recipe, "Overnight SPAM & Broccoli Cheese Strata."

Spam's notoriety has achieved recognition. An original Spam can is in the Smithsonian Institution's National Museum of American History in Washington, D.C. Spam inspired a book of haiku poetry, *Spam-Ku: Tranquil Reflections on Luncheon Loaf.* Meanwhile, the company valiantly fights misuse of the word "spam" for what it calls "unsolicited commercial email (UCE)." Hormel's "official SPAM Home page. The one in good taste," gives company policy: "We do not object to use of this slang term to describe UCE, although we do object to the use of our product image in association with that term." Hormel also prefers that the name of its trademarked food be capitalized as SPAM, while "spam" as junk e-mail should be lowercase.

The company seems to recognize that its original Spam is high in fat. With 140 of a serving's 170 calories coming from fat, those eating half of a can would have nearly exceeded the recommended daily intake for saturated fat and sodium. In response to these concerns, Hormel began offering SPAM Oven Roasted Turkey, SPAM Smoke Flavored, SPAM Lite, and SPAM Less Sodium with "the same great taste."

BIBLIOGRAPHY

Cho, John Nagamichi, comp. *SPAM-Ku: Tranquil Reflections on Luncheon Loaf.* New York: HarperPerennial, 1998.

Hormel website. "The Role of SPAM in World War II." Available at http://www.hormel.com.

Wyman, Carolyn. *SPAM: A Biography.* San Diego, Calif.: Harcourt Brace, 1999.

tion may allow transplants of whole, living organs from pigs to humans. Pigs offer an advantage over other animalsby closely matching those of humans.

Many scientific barriers remain, but in early 2002 two rival biotechnology companies announced a major step toward xenotransplantation (the transplanting of an-

imal organs into humans). Both had cloned pigs that are missing a gene that causes an immune reaction in humans. The offending gene sets off production of an enzyme that makes a sugar that human bodies recognize as foreign. Pig organ transplants without the gene may be less likely to be rejected.

Trade card (circa 1883) showing a prizewinning Chester White boar named "Kennett." This breed of hog was raised primarily for lard, which explains why there is so much fat on the animal. ROUGHWOOD COLLECTION.

Even in cultures that do not view pigs as unclean, xenotransplantation has vocal opponents, including animal rights activists and others who worry that this technology may introduce new viruses from pigs to humans.

The Pig in Myth
It remains to be seen whether pigs will physically become parts of humans. Symbolically, they have been transplanted into human culture for centuries, in medieval Europe, modern China, and ancient Mesopotamia. Pigs first symbolized deities, and later, human weaknesses and strengths.

In China, the pig is one of twelve animals symbolizing a year in a twelve-year lunar calendar. According to Chinese mythology, all animals were invited to race for this honor. A year was assigned to the first twelve winners, as each one finished. The pig came in twelfth. Just as westerners who believe in astrology tie personality traits to signs of the Zodiac, the Chinese attribute personality traits to the year in which they were born. Those born in the Year of the Pig (also called Year of the Boar) are said to be easygoing, sincere, tolerant, and honest. They are also considered naïve. Naïveté was linked to pigs in Homer's *Odyssey*, when Ulysses' men were turned to pigs by the sorceress Circe. While the men themselves were naïve, their behavior even before their conversion was almost piglike. They were attracted by Circe's sweet voice and lulled to complacency by her rich meal. Homer seems to use this tale to impart a sensuality to pigs, as well as a pig-likeness to the mariners. The pig was sacred to Aphrodite and an important image in Celtic mythology.

A vision of a sacred white sow was part of the legend of the founding of Rome. In Christian Europe, the sensuality of pigs came to take on a harder edge, an association with gluttony, perhaps because Jesus is depicted as casting demons into swine. The strong personality of the squealing, ever-present pig became a convenient device for the writers and fable makers of Europe in the eleventh through thirteenth centuries. Moralized fables called bestiaries made use of pigs to symbolize the Seven Deadly Sins, not just gluttony, but also pride, covetousness, lust, envy, anger, and sloth.

Pigs are recognized as intelligent, exhibiting a range of emotions and behaviors in real life just as in fables and mythology. For centuries, farmers have found herding and catching pigs difficult. This intelligence makes pigs a priority for animal rights organizations that challenge the methods of confining pigs in intensive industrial production, in which pigs are kept on concrete floors with slats that allow for the collection and flushing of manure into earthen lagoons or metal holding tanks.

Modern confinement appears clean compared to hogs wallowing in outdoor pens. The use of metal crates to restrict sow movement is humane, say the system's defenders, because it prevents newborn pigs from accidentally being crushed by a heavy sow. The U.S. National Pork Board's position on animal welfare is that "because the welfare of their animals directly affects their livelihood, pork producers work to ensure their animals are treated humanely. Anything else would be self-defeating." Some farmers are, in fact, beginning to revise their methods.

Attempts to Treat Pigs More Humanely
At the urging of farmers in Sweden, that nation in 1986 banned the routine use of antibiotics in raising animals for food. In 1988, it required that all animals used for food be allowed to behave naturally. Small metal stalls that restrict the movement of sows about to give birth were banned. Minimum space requirements for sows and boars were established for hog buildings. If pigs were housed inside, straw bedding was required, to absorb manure, to keep pigs clean and dry, and to give pigs a place to root, a natural behavior. In the United States, the Animal Welfare Institute, founded in 1951, has worked with farmers to set up voluntary use of Swedish pig-raising methods.

Straw bedding must periodically be moved onto farm fields to keep pig buildings clean. This requires labor that larger intensive farms may not have. Large farms flush manure with water into lagoons or tanks. That manure is also spread onto farmland as fertilizer. But critics charge that current environmental standards in the United States do not require the manure to be spread over a wide enough area and allow it to eventually build up excessive amounts of nutrients in soils that can wash into streams or contaminate groundwater. Spills of manure have already caused fish kills and stream pollution in Midwestern states. In 1999 a large hog-producing company in Missouri, Premium Standard Farms, agreed to pay $25 million to settle a lawsuit accusing it of violating the state's Clean Water Act.

Clearing the Air?

Untreated pig manure stored in open-air lagoons or tanks just plain stinks to neighbors and rural residents. In part because of complaints from rural voters, the Iowa legislature passed a law in 2002 that will require manure from confined hogs to be spread over more land. In a state with five times as many pigs as people (nearly fifteen million), the Department of Natural Resources is also developing a scoring system that considers community and environmental needs before the department approves construction of any more large hog buildings. Yet the law gives local governments no control of hog farm growth, critics say.

Adding low levels of antibiotics to pig feed may be the most serious environmental challenge from large-scale confined livestock. Feeding antibiotics has fostered antibiotic-resistant bacteria in livestock, including pigs. These antibiotic-resistant bacteria can be transferred from animals to people. Resistance genes may also transfer from one bacteria type to another more dangerous one such as salmonella.

In 1999, the Center for Science in the Public Interest, the Union of Concerned Scientists and several environmental groups petitioned the U.S. Food and Drug Administration to rescind the approval of agricultural use of antibiotics when their use endangers human health. Other groups supporting that view include the World Health Organization, the Centers for Disease Control and Prevention, and the American Public Health Association. Some of these antibiotics have been banned from feed in Europe.

Hygiene, humane farming, and health benefits and threats are among the many controversies surrounding the controversial pig, an animal that is likely to continue to feed the minds and stomachs of billions of humans as it has already for thousands of years.

See also **Cattle; China; Folklore, Food in; Food Safety; Goat; Judaism; Livestock Production; Mammals; Meat; Middle East; Packaging and Canning; Sheep.**

BIBLIOGRAPHY

Brennan, Jennifer. *The Cuisines of Asia.* New York: St. Martins/Marek, 1984.

Dohner, Janet Vorwald. *The Encyclopedia of Historic and Endangered Livestock Breeds.* New Haven, Conn.: Yale University Press, 2002.

Ensminger, M. Eugene, and R. O. Parker. *Swine Science.* 5th ed. Danville, Ill.: Interstate Printers, 1984.

Harris, D. L. *Multi-site Pig Production.* Ames: Iowa State University Press, 2000.

Harris, Marvin. *Good to Eat: Riddles of Food and Culture.* New York: Simon and Schuster, 1985.

Klober, Kelly. *A Guide to Raising Pigs.* Pownal, Vt.: Storey Publishing, 1997.

Rath, Sara. *The Complete Pig: An Entertaining History of Pigs.* Stillwater, Minn.: Voyageur Press, 2000.

U.S. Department of Agriculture, Agricultual Research Service. 2001. USDA Nutrient Database for Standard Reference, Release 14. Nutrient Data Laboratory Home Page, available at http://www.nal.usda.gov/fnic/foodcomp.

Dan Looker

PIZZA. Although it is one of the world's simplest and most popular foods, pizza is oddly difficult to define. Centuries of evolution have transformed it from the patties made of mashed grains that were its earliest antecedents into a dish that, though related to those early grain cakes, is almost unrecognizable as their descendant. Most significant is the change in the primary ingredient, from various coarse grains to a solely wheat-based dough, and eventually to a dish made almost exclusively with white flour.

However, though pizza has taken many forms, and its composition, toppings, seasonings, methods of preparation, and the equipment used to make it have altered radically over the years, it has usually been a flatbread baked at high temperatures.

Early History of Pizza

For millennia, pizza, a food of various origins and multiple styles, has played an important role in the diet of those who inhabited the land now called Italy. Neolithic nomads, the Etruscans from the North, and the Greeks from southern regions were the three earliest societies to develop pizza prototypes, for example, *focaccia.* Each group made small adaptations that changed the original product into a slightly more refined dish.

As early as the Stone Age, Neolithic hunter-gatherer tribal groups foraged throughout what would become Italy for wild grains, among them wheat varieties such as emmer and einkorn, as well as barley. Commonly first soaked or boiled, these grains were mashed into pastes and cooked on hot stones over open fires.

Later, around 1000 B.C.E., the Etruscans, a people of uncertain origin, introduced their flatbread to Northern Italy. Like the Neolithic tribes before them, the Etruscans pounded their grains. However, unlike their predecessors, the Etruscans baked their mash on stones and buried the stones in the ashes, creating smoky tasting bread. They further elaborated on the primitive Neolithic flatbread by seasoning the mash with oil and herbs after baking it. Though little more than rough slabs of cooked grain, these Etruscan flatbreads, among the earliest forms of this type of food documented, were often used as dough "plates" in lieu of dishes.

The Greeks, who had superior baking skills and technology, further advanced and elaborated on pizza during their 600-year (730–130 B.C.E.) occupation of the southern areas of the Italian peninsula. Like their predecessors, they produced a grain-based mash, but instead of placing the toppings on the cooked breads, they placed

DERIVATION OF THE TERM "PIZZA"

The word "pizza" simply means "pie" and is a Southern Italian derivative of the Roman term *picea,* both a bread itself and the ash-blackened underside of the Roman bread called *placenta.* Some say this term eventually evolved into "piza," then "pizza." Similarly, another flat bread, *pitta,* thought by some to have been introduced to southern Italy during the sixth-century Byzantine conquest, may also have influenced the modern day pronunciation of "pizza."

them on the raw dough prior to baking, perhaps to ensure a more highly flavored dish. *Plakuntos,* for example, flat, round breads, were made with various simple toppings, among them oil, garlic, onion, and herbs. Additional Greek contributions included the use of ovens, instead of open fires, and the development of kneading, which produced a more digestible bread. Evelyne Sloman highlights early excerpts from Plato's *Republic* that refer to meals created from barley flour kneaded and cooked into "cakes" with olives and cheese (Sloman, 1984, p. 5).

Although it is not firmly established, many also credit the Greeks with improving on the knowledge of leavening agents that came down to them from the Egyptians, and then introducing yeast into their own flatbreads. The Greeks also added a raised rim to the outside of their dough circles, to stabilize their dough "plates," making them easier to hold, and, perhaps, even helping to keep the toppings in place.

Much later, the Romans combined the Etruscan and Greek techniques to create the pizza antecedent most like the pizza known today. They valued the intense heat the Etruscans achieved by baking their flatbreads below the fire, and they appreciated the Greek idea of preseasoning the dough. They also modified the Greek *plakuntos.* Known to them by the Latin term *placenta,* their adapted bread, though still round, was topped with cheese and baked on a wood-burning hearth. *Laganum,* a light, thin wafer bread, was also cooked on the hearth.

If the Greeks and Etruscans were primarily responsible for creating the prototypes of what was to become pizza, and the ancient Romans were responsible for improving it, it was largely the Neapolitans who brought it fame. Probably not coincidentally, the Neapolitans were responsible for the addition of the ingredient most commonly associated with pizza today—the tomato.

No one is sure of the precise reason, but it took well over two centuries from the time the New World tomato was introduced to the continent of Europe during the Columbian food exchange for Neapolitans, and various other inhabitants of the peninsula, to begin consuming tomatoes in quantity.

There are several theories about why adoption of a fruit that has almost come to symbolize Italian cuisine took so long. One argues that it was because tomatoes were believed to be poisonous, another that the earliest tomatoes were inferior and, therefore, eaten only in modest amounts until quality improved enough to make the fruit genuinely popular. In the area of Naples, for example, a key moment appears to have come in the middle of the eighteenth century with the development of a pleasing, large, and sweet tomato. The fruit quickly became the mainstay of Neapolitan pizza toppings.

It was also around this time, during the era of Bourbon King Ferdinando I and Queen Maria Carolina, whose empire included Naples, that one of the earliest pizza legends took root. In one version of the story, the queen (Marie Antoinette's sister and the daughter of Empress Maria Teresa of Austria) is said to have been described by the king as having "common tastes," apparently a quality thought to explain her love of pizza, a dish of the people. It is, however, a measure of the confounding nature of pizza lore that in a variant of the story, it is the king who relishes pizza and the refined queen who does not understand his passion.

Whichever of their majesties was the real enthusiast, the object of desire was probably flavored with lard (a less expensive alternative to oil), tomatoes, salt, and sometimes tiny eels, anchovies, or sardines. Over time, craving for this pie became so great that either the king, to gratify his wife's yearning, or the queen, to gratify the king's hunger, had a pizza oven built at the Capodimonte palace, so they could make the dish at home, an act that brought the pie even more attention. Pizza became the fashion, and other nobles followed suit, building pizza ovens where they lived.

However, it was not until 1889, a time when yet another ingredient is purported to have become part of the equation, that pizza began its march toward wide celebrity. It was then that inspiration is said to have struck Raffaele Esposito, a noted Neapolitan *pizzaiolo* (pizza chef), who decided to pay homage to Queen Margherita and King Umberto I of Savoia, the ruling house of Italy, by adding mozzarella to the traditional tomato and basil pie. The combination of red, white, and green suggested the colors of the Italian flag and saluted the United Kingdom of Italy, a gesture that for patriotic reasons is said to have made the pie a favorite of the queen.

Though most stories of origin give Esposito credit for adding cheese and thereby inventing the tri-color pizza, still known as Pizza Margherita, others deny it, believing that mozzarella had been used earlier. There is no doubt, however, that Esposito popularized the "made for each other" combination of cheese, dough, and tomato that produced a dish even more delicious than before, thereby setting the modest pie on a course to fame that he could never have imagined.

In Italy today, pizza exists in a number of regional styles, of which two of the most famous are the Neapolitan and the Roman. Both schools knead the dough, but *pizza alla Napoletana* is round, has a high border, takes diverse toppings, and is generally sold in pizzerias, while *pizza alla Romana*, also called *pizza bianca*, is more or less rectangular, often as much as a meter long, topped only with oil and salt, and sold by weight, primarily in bakeries and groceries, according to the size of the piece requested. Many other regions of Italy—Sicily, for example—also have distinctive versions of pizza. However, the popularity of the dish has meant that the styles are not always confined to the geographical areas in which they were created. Neapolitan-style pizza, for example, can be found in many places in Italy, as can *Pizza alla Romana*.

The Birth of the Pizzeria

From the beginning, pizza was rarely prepared at home because few people had the skill to stretch the dough properly or the money to build a wood-fired oven in which to bake it. Consequently, it was almost always bought from small stalls or from pizza sellers carrying their aromatic wares through the crowded Neapolitan streets. Some more elaborate open-air pizza stands offered slightly more upscale options, along with makeshift seating, but it was not until 1830 that the first documented pizzeria, that is, an inexpensive gathering place specializing in pizza and equipped with wood burning stoves, began doing business in Naples. It was called Port'Alba. Still in operation, its opening marked the birth of a style of eating establishment now known around the world.

The notion of a pizzeria as a fast-paced, economical restaurant has continued. In fact, the institution of the pizzeria is as critical to its vast global appeal as the food itself is.

The Development of Pizza as an American Icon

Although pizza is not exclusively Italian in origin, there is no question that from a cultural standpoint, it is an iconic food of Italy. Italians "own" this delicacy. Nevertheless, pizza in the United States may also be considered an icon food, perhaps even more so than in the land of its birth. The dish has become an American institution—embracing food-on-the-run, corporate enterprise, and American ingenuity, and it may fairly be said to be as representative of American foodways, food customs, and food choices as it is of Italian ones.

Pizza arrived in the United States in the latter half of the nineteenth century, along with a wave of largely southern Italian immigrants. Soon many of those immigrants were making their livelihood operating bakeries and groceries where they sold pizza alongside produce and staple ingredients.

The first real American pizzeria, opened in New York City in 1905 by Gennaro Lombardi, was located in

Pizza has evolved from a relatively simple peasant dish into a vast array of preparations, including "gourmet" and vegetarian interpretations. © GERALD ZANETTI/CORBIS.

Manhattan, at 53⅓ Spring Street. As with other early pizzerias, the clientele was composed predominantly of southern Italian immigrants, who wanted to eat their own dishes in a familiar and homey atmosphere. However, after World War II, when GIs returned from Italy well acquainted with pizza and other Italian foods, they forged a new and growing market for those foods.

As is the case with so many other traditional Italian foods, pizza underwent significant changes in the United States. Thanks to the American postwar emphasis on excess and increased portion size, as well, possibly, as the desire of poor Italian immigrants to eat more copiously than they had been able to do at home, the delicate Neapolitan pizza was transformed. Formerly lightly embellished with tomatoes and other toppings, it was increasingly laden with an abundance of meats and cheese, sometimes creating slices weighing close to a pound.

Other differences developed in the United States, too. The pie acquired regional American styles, New York, Chicago, California, and New Haven the best known among them. New York pizza is cheesy and gooey, with a high, dense border and medium-thick crust; it can be bought by the slice or whole. California style has a very thin crust, adorned with an array of toppings unlikely to be found in Italy, ranging from goat cheese to tandoori chicken, to *moo shu pork* or bacon with pineapples. Chicago style is "deep dish," prepared in a pan, and based on a thick-crust pizza. New Haven style is somewhat similar to New York pizza, but is known especially for its white clams.

In addition to the regional pizzas available in the United States, ethnic variations exist. Because the costs of opening a pizzeria are relatively low compared with those of opening a more formal restaurant, the business of pizzerias has long attracted immigrants. In addition,

PREPARATION OF THE PIZZA

Pizza preparation is simple, with few rules dictating a sublime product. The dough is made only with flour, natural yeast or brewer's yeast, salt and water. Dough is then kneaded either by hand or mixer, and the dough is punched down and shaped by hand.

Although most pizza is served as a round pie, a folded over variation, known as a calzone (or pants leg, so called because of the calzone's resemblance to the loose trousers once worn by Neapolitan men), is also popular. Originally from Naples, as is pizza itself, this style of turnover appears elsewhere as a *mezza-luna* (half moon) or *panzerotti* (stomachs). Additionally, there are double-crusted, or stuffed, pizzas filled with all sorts of meats, fish, vegetables, and cheeses. They are referred to by the same name as flat pizzas, but some argue that such famous examples as pizza *rustica* and pizza *pasqualina* come out of a different tradition entirely, one that dates back to the pies of Medieval times. In addition, there is a rolled variety of pizza called *bonata,* known to Americans as *stromboli.*

While standard toppings—among them, sausage, ricotta cheese, peppers, mushrooms, and meatballs—vary from region to region and city to city, the dough remains quite similar. Although any flour may be used, prized pizza is prepared using the high-gluten variety that produces strong dough that rises easily. Such flour, along with yeast, water, salt, and olive oil, creates the perfect dough.

Equipment

- Commercial pizza oven—may be wood, coal, gas, or electric, but ideally should achieve a temperature of at least 700°F. Pizza stone or quarry tiles (to supply intense heat) simulate a pizza oven's temperature for home use.
- Pans—pizzas are either first baked in round pans to secure the shape or baked directly on the stones or oven floor.
- Pizza peel or paddle—an elongated wooden or metal paddle used to place the pizzas in and remove them from deep ovens.

because pizza seems to be a blank slate inviting adaptation, Arabs, Chileans, Israelis, Greeks, Indians, and a diversity of other pizzeria owners often serve ethnicized versions next to traditional Italian pies. Depending on ownership, the menu may offer curried double-crust pizza, or pizza topped with feta cheese, or falafel. (It should also be noted that the same process occurs abroad.

Pizza flourishes in Tokyo, Shanghai, Tel Aviv, Moscow, and other cities around the world. Though still associated with Italy or, perhaps, even the United States, the pizza itself often bears minimal resemblance to the original dish.)

Once a handcrafted art form, pizza in America (and often elsewhere) is now mass-produced by an overabundance of pizza chains that incorporate the technological advances featured in the monthly print-and-on-line trade journal *Pizza Today.* In 1951, just ten years after the Minneapolis-based members of the Totino family founded one of the first Midwestern pizzerias, that family initiated the frozen pizza business. In 1953, 100,000 stores were offering refrigerated or frozen pizza (Trager, 1966, p. 544), and at least 15,000 pizzerias similar to the Totino original were operating in the United States. Shakey's opened in 1954, Pizza Hut in 1958, Little Caesar's in 1959, and Domino's in 1960. In 1973, perhaps cashing in on the American attraction to anything French, Stouffer's introduced frozen French bread pizza.

In 1982, the California chef Wolfgang Puck joined the California food revolution and introduced his super thin–crusted, "designer" pizzas, featuring among other choices, a smoked salmon variety. This marked the beginning of the "anything goes" upscale and innovative pizza, completely characteristic of quintessentially American iconic foodways.

See also **Bread; Icon Foods; Italy; Take-out Food; United States: Ethnic Cuisines.**

BIBLIOGRAPHY

Anderson, Burton. *Treasures of the Italian Table.* New York: William Morrow, 1994.

Behr, Ed. "Pizza in Naples." *The Art of Eating* 22 (Spring 1992): 1–14.

Del Conte, Anna. *The Gastronomy of Italy.* New York: Prentice Hall, 1987.

Field, Carol. *The Italian Baker.* New York: Harper and Row, 1995.

Piras, Claudia, and Eugenio Medigliani, eds. *Culinaria Italy.* Cologne, Germany: Könemann-Verlagsgesellschaft, 2000.

Romer, Elizabeth. *Italian Pizza and Hearth Breads.* New York: Clarkson Potter, 1987.

Rosengarten, David. "Pizza Now in New York City: The New Reality." *Rosengarten Report* 1, no. 7 (January 7, 2002): 15–19.

Schwartz, Arthur. *Naples at Table.* New York: Harper Collins, 1998.

Sloman, Evelyne. *The Pizza Book: Everything There Is to Know about the World's Greatest Pie.* New York: Times Books, 1984.

Trager, James. *The Food Chronology: A Food Lover's Compendium of Events and Anecdotes from Prehistory to the Present.* New York: Henry Holt, 1995.

Jennifer Berg
Cara De Silva

PLACES OF CONSUMPTION. A discussion of places of consumption should begin where food has been consumed since the beginning of humankind, in the home. In the twenty-first century in most countries the home remains the primary location for eating. That is not to say that the nature of the food eaten in the home has remained constant or that the preparation of the food has not changed. Even the formality and regularity of dining in the home was altered in the twentieth century.

During the nineteenth century and the early twentieth century in the United States, dining at home was usually regular (breakfast, lunch, and dinner) and occurred at the kitchen table or in the dining room. Food was often seasonal. The heaviest meal (dinner) was at noon or, if the breadwinner worked outside the home, in the evening. If the lighter meal occurred at night, it was called supper. The fare did not include a great deal of variety.

The improvement in the means of transporting food and people as well as the advancements in preservation markedly increased the places of consumption and the types of food consumed in much of the world. With modern transportation and refrigeration in mind, this overview examines places where people eat, starting with the contemporary home, moving to the world of work, touching upon the varying modes of travel and places where people play, and concluding with the increasingly vast array of dining-out possibilities.

The Home
The sit-down meal three times a day at set times is disappearing. Although such mealtimes happen, they are becoming a rarity in technologically advanced societies, where mothers and fathers work and children come and go more freely. The family eats when there is time and often not together. Dress is casual. People eat at the

The interior of a typical nineteenth-century Viennese restaurant by artist Karl Josef Richard Zajicek. © Archivo Iconografico, S.A./ CORBIS.

kitchen counter, in a breakfast nook, in front of a television, in bed, on the porch, on a patio, on a lanai, or in the yard. The dining table has become a catchall that is only cleared for company. Food is seldom prepared from "scratch." More often than not the food is semiprepared in the cupboard, the refrigerator, or the freezer. Ready-to-eat meals are found in supermarkets and delicatessens.

The mainstay of the diet in the United States and most other countries of the world, is the sandwich, which competes with the rice ball in Asia. It can be prepared quickly and can be eaten in any room or while walking. Traditionally, bread forms the basis of the meal, but the tortilla wrap is making inroads. Fillings vary, and the most common in the United States are peanut butter and jelly, tuna, meat slices, and cheese. Each of these fillings alone may form the basis of the sandwich, or each may be combined with one another, other fillings, vegetables, and condiments.

Take-out meals may be purchased from most restaurants, and ethnic foods, such as Chinese, Thai, and Mexican, are especially popular in the United States. Pizza is a favorite either ordered and delivered or frozen ready to heat and eat. Barbecues are frequent in sunny climates and are not unusual in colder ones, where the cook must bundle up to prepare the main course.

Entertaining at home is usually informal. The dining table, kitchen counter, or cooking island may serve as a buffet table. While complete meals may be served, "heavy" hors d'oeuvres are not uncommon because guests can consume their meals standing. If dinner guests are seated for a traditional meal, the number invited is usually limited to one or two couples. This is not the case for family gatherings, when substantial meals are served and guests find seating either at a large table or throughout the house.

In sum, whether preparing food for the family or for guests, contemporary home cooking utilizes the many available shortcuts to delicious cuisine. It should be noted that worldwide the less advanced the society, the more traditional the meals at home.

The Workplace

For most of the workers of the world, lunch is the meal most frequently consumed at work. Traditionally it was brought to work in a paper sack or a lunch pail. Among blue-collar and white-collar workers the principle source of nourishment was the sandwich. In Asian countries the rice ball was most common. While this custom continues to some extent in the twenty-first century among blue-collar workers, white-collar workers generally purchase their lunches either in the workplace or nearby.

White-collar workers usually work in office buildings with many other personnel. Frequently the company that employs them provides a cafeteria or food machines for their convenience. A lunchroom is usually available with hot and cold running water, a refrigerator, and a mi-

crowave. Executives often have their own dining room, which comes with a dress code, a view, a higher cost, and presumably better food. Until the late twentieth century it was expected that food would be consumed away from the desk. This custom has been relaxed, and many office employees are allowed and encouraged to eat while working through their lunch hours.

Office workers have food choices outside their buildings. Many restaurants cater to the lunch crowd and offer quick service and specials. In areas where the work population is not so large and the location is more remote, lunch trucks service the workers. As in the office building, dress for the most part is working attire. Many blue-collar workers may bring their lunches because, particularly with construction workers, sites vary and the nature of the work produces a real appetite. Factories usually provide cafeterias, and lunch trucks are regular fixtures.

In the United States coffee is considered a necessity at any place of work. The coffee break is usually for fifteen minutes midmorning and midafternoon, even if the food consumed is tea, soda, or a snack. In a traditional office coffee was consumed in a break room. By the late twentieth century it was most likely enjoyed at a desk. Whether fresh-brewed or freeze-dried, coffee is provided when possible, often twenty-four hours a day. If that is impossible, most workers bring their own in appropriately insulated containers. While work sites around the world have similar customs, some substitute tea, and the younger generation prefers soft drinks.

Some work sites are so remote or removed from modern technology that food consumption requires high-tech preparation. The U.S. military frequently runs into this situation when its troops are in the field. The dried food of the past has been replaced by meals ready to eat (MRE). Whether eaten in a jungle or a desert, the MRE has generally received a positive response. Astronauts also dine in outer space on compacted and nonperishable food. Interestingly, advances made for consumption in these unusual sites have found their way into the modern home as convenience foods.

Some workers earn their living by driving, and they find restaurants along the highways as well as in the towns and cities they drive through. Although truck drivers can eat in their trucks, many of them want to get out of their drivers' seats and park their long, cumbersome vehicles. Consequently a place of consumption was created just for them, the truck stop. Known for its large portions, filling food, and affordable prices, the truck stop services truckers and other travelers interested in a casual yet substantial meal.

Many jobs are combined with travel, and the next section overlaps travel for work with travel for leisure. Like consumption at home, consumption at work reflects modern society. Even the more primitive cultures have access to some type of refrigeration and dehydration, making for a more varied working diet.

Traveling

The earliest form of travel was by foot. The fare was simple, was carried in a knapsack, and was eaten on the trail. Hiking is no longer a necessity, but it is a popular activity throughout the world. The variety of edibles contained in the backpack would astound early travelers. Trail mix, a popular edible designed for eating while walking, has appeared on grocery shelves for general consumption. Overnight camping can be high tech and effortless, but many hikers prefer cooking over an open fire for taste, smell, and aesthetics.

The modern automobile comes equipped with holders designed to facilitate consumption. Many workers carry a travel mug containing their hot or cold beverage of choice in the car for consumption on the way to work. Those who choose not to brew at home find convenient drive-ins featuring breakfasts and hot beverages. This continues through the day and evening as drive-ins and restaurants compete for automobile or roadside diners. Travelers by car have a food treat not afforded other modes, the roadside fruit and vegetable stand. Travelers may stop at the side of the road and enjoy the fruit or juice of the region. Eating in the car has become so common that Americans have developed a slogan, "Friends don't let friends eat and drive." The campaign is not likely to be effective because around the world the automobile is an exceedingly popular place of consumption.

Travel by air has prompted two places of consumption, the airport and the airplane. Airplane travelers expect food on long flights, although expectations are not high, even in first class. Perhaps because of the reputation of airplane fare, many passengers eat before boarding or buy food at the airport to eat in flight. Airports often feature regional cuisine that offers the traveler one last chance to enjoy a local dish, albeit an expensive one.

One of the lures to travel by train was the dining car. Trains around the world offered white tablecloths and the appearance of fine dining. While a few specialty routes offered fine fare and required passengers to dress accordingly, on most twenty-first century trains clothing is casual, and food is adequate. It is usually the view passing the window that makes dining on the train memorable. Like the airport, the train station offers food for immediate consumption or for the trip. Prices are more reasonable than at most airports. The food is varied, and in some locations, such as Union Station in Washington, D.C., and Grand Central Station in New York City, the station is a destination for dining, not just travel.

Travel by water also provides eating opportunities. Whether by ferry or luxury liner, food is available en route. Ferries usually offer drinks and snacks. Hot beverages are especially appreciated in colder climates. Luxury liners offer fine cuisine with appropriate attire and manners. Most cruise ships offer opportunities for more casual dining too. Passengers wishing an informal trip by water choose a freighter, often by its reputation for providing tasty food. In the Western world, yachts and small boats come with small kitchens. Eastern vessels may lack the kitchen but carry a small charcoal grill onboard. Traveling by sea seems to stimulate the appetite, even on the brief dinner cruise.

Whether traveling by foot, air, train, or boat, the modern traveler expects food and gets it. Of the four the traveler by boat is probably the best fed. Each mode may offer a splendid vista to gaze upon while consuming food. Of all the food consumers, travelers have the most exotic places of consumption.

Playing

All work and no play is an old adage. Since the beginning of recorded history, the consumption of food has been an important component of play. This section features the variety of places where people eat and play, starting with some of the older pastimes still popular in the twenty-first century.

Fairs began as an annual event to celebrate the foods, crafts, entertainment, athletic prowess, and livestock of a given locale. Fairs have expanded to encompass states, countries, and the world. Food, such as candied apples and cotton candy, and the smells of barnyards and sawdust floors are unforgettable memories of many fairgoers. Fairs are not dress-up occasions in part because they are usually outdoor events held in temporary structures and tents.

The circus and later the carnival grew out of the fair. Both were situated out of doors and provided food for participants, notably popcorn, peanuts in the shell, and caramel corn. Today, there are fewer carnivals, and circuses have moved indoors. They have largely been replaced by television and theme parks. One outgrowth of the circus that seems here to stay and is found worldwide is the food circus, a grouping of food stalls featuring foods from around the world that can be enjoyed indoors and outdoors from Seattle to Singapore.

Athletic prowess has been celebrated by itself, as the long history of the Olympic Games testifies. Sports stadiums and arenas are traditional sites for food consumption. Baseball celebrates its memorable edibles—peanuts and cracker jack—in song. These staples have expanded to include hot dogs with mustard and sauerkraut and regional favorites such as tacos in the West and saimin in Hawaii. Other team competitions, such as football and soccer, include a variety of hearty snacks, regional treats, and lots of beer. The tailgate party precedes football games across the United States. With a distinctive regional flavor, food is often prepared adjacent to the car in the parking lot over hot coals and is shared with other sports enthusiasts. The lazy tailgater can find tailgate fare to go in the city.

The younger set also enjoys eating at the sites of their baseball, football, or soccer games. They do not provide the food, their parents do. More often than not the parents arrange a potluck. That way each family contributes,

Dining in shaded pavilions by cool pools of water has been a recurring theme in the history of Middle Eastern eating habits. This inviting enclosure is located at the Palace of Nerenjestan in Iran. © CORBIS.

and all share in the bounty. Athletic events seem to increase appetites and expand the places of consumption.

The street vendor has always existed around the world, in industrialized and developing countries. The food on each cart is limited, regional, and usually cooked at the site, and in underdeveloped countries it is often of questionable sanitation. For the brave the taste is delicious, but the suffering afterward may be keen. Tourist destinations, such as temples, museums, and historic sites, often offer an edible specialty of the area. It may have begun with priests and monks preparing food for the weary travelers. However, modern tourists expect to be able to purchase a drink or a snack upon reaching their destinations. If there is a specialty item to eat, some find it as exciting as the monument.

Natural beauty attracts visitors. Mountains, ocean beaches, deserts, lakes, and nature's curiosities draw crowds. With the crowds, opportunities to eat appear. When the sites are made into national or state parks,

some aesthetic control is established. If not, places of consumption can be unattractive to the eye and to the palate as well as a distraction from the beautiful scenery.

The movie theater has carried on the popcorn tradition. Popcorn and soda are musts for most moviegoers. Twenty-first century theaters, like cars, provide holders for drinks. Theaters must be swept after performances to remove the litter caused by moviegoers eating in the dark.

Walt Disney created the theme park, and with its advent came new places of consumption. Within the theme park are restaurants, fast-food facilities, and vendors. As theme parks developed into adventure parks, the places of consumption continued to grow.

Many enjoy an opera, concert, or play. Unlike their neighbors at the movies or athletic events, they cannot eat during the production. They are offered an intermission, when wine, beer, or snacks may be purchased, but they must not be taken back into the theater or concert hall.

For many throughout the world, shopping is an enjoyable leisure-time activity, of which food is an important part. Shopping malls are replete with food to be eaten seated or while walking. Shopping centers offer family-style restaurants and fast food. Department stores often devote a floor to eating establishments. While grocery stores may offer free promotional samples, large wholesale food chains offer so many samples that customers can and do make a meal of the shopping expedition. Little doubt exists that eating and playing go hand in hand around the world.

Dining Out

The consumption of food in the home is more traditional in less-advanced societies, but highly technological societies have a vast array of dining-out opportunities and increasingly take advantage of them. This section introduces the myriad possibilities. The discussion is arranged from the most formal dining to the least and concludes with some special sites where food is consumed.

The finest dining, measured by expense and formality, usually occurs in large cities around the world. Such locations have dress codes that require men to wear suits or sport coats and ties. Women are monitored as well but, because of the nature of female attire, not as closely. In the most exclusive establishments, one must be appropriately attired to dine. Expensive but less-exclusive places offer men a "house" sport coat or tie. The emphasis on fine clothing is matched by the dress of and attention provided by the entire house staff, the quality of the china and tableware, the reputation of the chef, and most importantly the cuisine.

To afford the ultimate in exclusivity, private dining clubs are located around the world in major cities. Traditionally these were for men only. While this is no longer the case in the United States due to sexual discrimination laws, it remains a phenomenon elsewhere around the world. Private dining clubs are often affiliated with a leisure pastime, such as tennis, golf, or yachting. Patrons of these clubs usually have dining areas where they may eat in the attire of the sport. However, on special evenings the dress code can be formal. In private clubs the places of consumption are attractive to the eye, are furnished with style, and offer a view if possible. Interestingly, the restaurant with the finest view seldom serves the finest food. Nonetheless fine dining usually means the finest money can buy.

The moderately priced restaurant is found worldwide. In the United States it is often a franchise with set menus and standardized ingredients. Whether serving families or corporately owned businesses, medium-priced restaurants are found wherever people congregate or travel. They offer food of the region and food from locations far away. In the United States the foods of China, Mexico, Italy, Thailand, and Vietnam abound. In fact, Chinese food or something resembling it is available throughout the world.

Dress codes are not restricted to fine dining establishments. Medium-priced restaurants in beach locations often require a shirt and footwear other than rubber sandals. Shorts may be banned for both sexes. These restaurant owners obviously believe that the attire of the patrons is part of the ambiance of their places of business.

Outdoor dining is not as commonplace in the United States as it is in Europe and many countries in Asia. These establishments, called cafés, are generally located along city streets and offer dining inside and out. Coffee is always on the menu, and a cup of it alone can offer the patron an hour or two of street watching.

Specialty coffee shops serving latte, espresso, and cappuccino are popular places of consumption world wide. Students study in them, senior citizens visit in them, and professionals dash in and out for a caffeine hit. The cost of both the coffee and the food sold therein is anything but cheap.

Around the world, bars and pubs (the word "tavern" is disappearing) are places to drink, to eat, and to congregate with friends. For many the neighborhood bar is a home away from home. While classic food items like pigs' feet and hard-boiled eggs may still be offered, hearty sandwiches and salty snacks are the norm. Visiting the sports bar with its wide-screen television is almost as good as going to the game itself. Some would argue that it is better.

In the technologically advanced twenty-first century people are in a hurry. Food is often eaten on the run. As a result, fast food eateries have flourished, especially in the United States, in every city, town, and village and along most highways. They are apt to be franchised with standard fare. Patrons may eat inside in clean, colorful, sparse, and plastic surroundings or, more the norm, may take their food home, to another site, or consume it in the car. The items most frequently offered include hamburgers, hot dogs, fried chicken, and a standardized version of Mexican food.

The drive-in restaurant appeared in the 1950s in the United States and afforded Americans a place to be waited on and to eat in the car. This novelty, just like the drive-in movie, has worn off and almost disappeared. It has been replaced by the drive-thru. The drive-thru offers fast food and is most often found in conjunction with a fast-food restaurant. However, depending on the part of the country, it may offer specialty items. In the Pacific Northwest, for example, the drive-thru latte abounds.

Caterers allow people to consume food in many locations where food is not prepared. Some examples are botanical gardens, meeting halls, aquariums, and outdoor sites. Many occasions, such as birthdays, anniversaries, showers, graduations, weddings, awards banquets, and even funerals, are celebrated with food. While they may be held in restaurants, many are catered in a variety of locales.

Whether dining in an automobile, a bar, or a bed, people around the world consume food several times a day. They appear to be limited in location only by their imaginations and the availability of food. Seldom does either limitation present a barrier to the consumer in the twenty-first century.

See also **Fast Food; Restaurants; Serving of Food.**

BIBLIOGRAPHY

Bober, Phyllis Pray. *Art, Culture, and Cuisine: Ancient and Medieval Gastronomy.* Chicago: University of Chicago Press, 1999.

Chang, K. C., ed. *Food in Chinese Culture: Anthropological and Historical Perspectives.* New Haven: Yale University Press, 1977.

David, Elizabeth. *Harvest of the Cold Months: The Social History of Ice and Ices.* New York: Viking Penguin, 1994.

Fisher, M. F. K. *The Gastronomical Me.* New York: Duell, Sloan, and Pearce, 1943.

Jacob, H. E. *Six Thousand Years of Bread: Its Holy and Unholy History.* Garden City, N.Y.: Doubleday, Doran, 1944.

Laudan, Rachel. *The Food of Paradise: Exploring Hawaii's Culinary Heritage.* Honolulu: University of Hawaii Press, 1996.

Nabhan, Gary Paul. *Coming Home to Eat: The Pleasures and Politics of Local Foods.* New York: Norton, 2001.

Root, Waverly. *Food: An Authoritative and Visual History and Dictionary of the Foods of the World.* New York: Simon and Schuster, 1980.

Schlosser, Eric. *Fast Food Nation: The Dark Side of the All American Meal.* Boston: Houghton Mifflin, 2001.

Sheffer, Nelli, and Mimi Sheraton. *Food Markets of the World.* New York: Abrams, 1997.

Sokolov, Raymond. *Why We Eat What We Eat: How the Encounter between the New World and the Old Changed the Way Everyone on the Planet Eats.* New York: Summit, 1991.

Tannahill, Reay. *Food in History.* 2d ed. New York: Crown, 1989.

Visser, Margaret. *The Rituals of Dinner: The Origins, Evolution, Eccentricities and Meaning of Table Manners.* New York: Grove Weidenfeld, 1991.

Doric Little

PLATINA. A noted humanist of the Italian Renaissance, Platina, born Bartolomeo Sacchi (1421–1481), is distinguished for culinary historians as the author of the first work on cookery ever printed: *De honesta voluptate et valetudine*, first in Rome c. 1470, without printer or date, then in Venice in 1475. Translation of the Latin title helps to define a central premise of the revolution in thought that broke with medieval traditions in fifteenth-century Italy. "On honest [meaning 'legitimate'] pleasure and good health" speaks of Platina's allegiance to new understanding and validation of the philosophy of Epicurus brought about from the 1430s by Lorenzo Valla, recognizing that rather than hedonism, it celebrated the creator's love for humans in sensory endowments if these were enhanced through self-control and moderation.

In addition to an Epicurean orientation, Platina underscored his devotion to another Greek philosopher, Pythagoras, by signing the *i* in his name as the Pythagorean *Y*, symbolizing the divided path at which one must choose virtue over its alternative; the conceit appears also in the funerary inscription he designed for himself and his brother (Rome, S. Maria Maggiore). From Sacchi's birthplace at Piadena near Cremona came his classicized name Platina, chosen in conformity with practice among fellow members of a premier Roman sodality of humanist scholars under the leadership of Pomponius Laetus, Platina's friend and neighbor on the Quirinal, near the ruins of the Baths of Constantine. Reformist ideas gained from early Church fathers and from pagan antiquity that invested the self-styled "academy" of the Pomponians added to Platina's problems in the curia of Pope Paul II. He was among those imprisoned and tried in 1468 for heresy, but shared in their return to favor under Sixtus IV from 1471. By 1475 Platina had been appointed chief administrator of the Vatican Library.

His treatise on cookery and good health seems to have been written and circulated in manuscript by 1465, following a summer spent with his patron, formerly his pupil in Mantua, the young Cardinal Francesco Gonzaga, as guests of the contemporary "Lucullus" of Rome Ludovico Scarampi Mezzarota, Cardinal Trevisan. The final six books of Platina's study are Latin translations of recipes acknowledged as those of his friend, Maestro Martino of Como, head chef to Trevisan. Added to Platina's advisories on principled well-being, essays on natural history, and Galenic medical lore inspired by humanist research in the writings of the ancient Roman agricultural writers, Pliny the elder, and Apicius (whom he calls "Caelius"), these final books or chapters enhanced the reputation of the work.

Platina/Martino remained in print until well into the seventeenth century, seeing Italian editions (often retranslating Martino's vernacular text) in 1487 and 1494, a French translation in Lyons by 1505, and one in German by 1542, plus at least fourteen Latin editions. Abetted by pirated editions of Martino (whose manuscripts were not edited until modern times) such as Epulario (Venice 1516, said to be by one Roselli and very influential in translation for Tudor England) and another by Clement VII's chef, Maestro Giovane, *Opera dignissima (et) utile per chi si diletta di cucinare* (A both elegant and practical guide to cooking; Milan, c. 1530), *De honesta voluptate* may be called the thinking man's guide to Renaissance foodways, as opposed to representatives of a courtly tradition.

See also **Apicius; Chef, The; Cookbooks; Epicurus; Italy; Pythagoras; Renaissance Banquet.**

BIBLIOGRAPHY

Beck, Leonard N. "Praise Is Due Bartolomeo Platina: A Note on the Librarian-Author of the First Cookbook," *Quarterly Journal of the Library of Congress*, 32 (1975), 238–253.

Campano, A. and P. Medioli Masotto, eds. *Bartolomeo Sacchi il Platina (Piadena 1421–Roma 1481)* Cremona, Italy: Atti del Convegno internazionale di Studi per il Centenario, November 1981; Padua, 1986.

Milham, Mary Ella. "Platina. *On Right Pleasure and Good Health.*" In *Medieval and Renaissance Texts and Studies*, vol. 168. Tempe, Ariz., 1998.

Riley, Gillian. "Platina, Martino, and Their Circle," In *Proceedings of the Oxford Symposium on Food and Cookery 1995: Cooks and Other People*. Totnes, Devon, 1996.

Vehling, Joseph D. *Platina and the Rebirth of Man*. Chicago: W. M. Hill, 1941.

Phyllis Bober

PLEASURE AND FOOD. The pleasure of food is the sensation of well-being that derives from the fulfillment of a natural instinct. Two essential elements are involved in food pleasure, the emotional and psychological tension created by the initial impulse or desire and the subsequent consummation of that inner need. Thus eating pleasure clearly corresponds with the two basic requirements of life, replication and sustenance.

Along the thresholds of pleasure, two distinct worlds intersect, the internal and the external. Pleasure from within is derived from a desire to satisfy the basic necessity of existence, while pleasure from without corresponds with the means of achieving that satisfaction. Both worlds are connected by the senses. Eating pleasure acquires enormous existential importance when confronted by the problem of the sensation or experience of living. This category of pleasure belongs to an area of the senses that is most basic and primal to the concept of happiness. In classical Greco-Roman culture it was consummated in the Greek *symposion*, where primal pleasure was linked to a Platonic communication of ideas—in other words, the intersection of physical pleasure with spiritual pleasure. The biblical Book of Ecclesiastes also arrives at this conclusion, where the pleasure of feasting and the pleasure of friendship are found to be the only human alternatives to the vanity of existence.

The superiority of eating pleasure over all other forms of pleasure is obvious, for it is related to needs that are more long-term and vital, embracing the entire life span, from feeding at the mother's breast to the final moment of existence. In human beings the pleasant necessity of eating is renewed daily, and because it is ineludible, it also transcends any moral code. On the other hand, since the human animal is omnivorous, the sensory stimulation must be infinitely varied to accede to this kind of pleasurable experience. This same rationale collaborates with hedonism so fantasy can develop its maximum potential. From this comes the popular expression of "creating a need from pleasure," which, when reworded in a more precise manner, ought to become "creating pleasure out of necessity." Is this necessity a requirement for pleasure? Pleasure is one of the rewards for eating.

In the initial approach to the pleasure of food, the first signal comes in the impulse or need to eat. Later the bodily senses direct the person to a means for satisfying this impulse. Finally, distension is created in the act of eating itself. Yet culturally this simple phenomenon becomes more complex than that, since the stimulation deriving from food directly intervenes in the need to eat to the point of provoking it. Consequently the pleasure of eating has evolved into an art, the art of food consumption, with the goal to contain, draw out, and direct in a more focused and concentrated manner the primal necessity of nourishment. Unquestionably the need for satiety and for satisfying the senses plays a role in the pleasure of eating. Human and cultural contexts also add to this. Out of these conflicting sensations evolved the perceived ties between the pleasure of eating and the source of the food (such as climate and geography) as well as diverse cultural ideas defining it.

Pleasure and Culture
Contrary to popular belief, the determining factor in the importance of food pleasure is not derived from the taste of foods produced in a given place but from their cultural contexts or definitions. For example, it is not the intense flavor of a homegrown orange that pleases, rather the idea that it is homegrown, which is a cultural value. Taste is chemical and biological; food pleasure is perceptional. Although pleasure derived from the act of eating is beyond question, its importance also competes with other forms of pleasure or other forms of interest current in a given social context. The availability of time, the relationship to other forms of pleasure, its ritualistic value, and its connection to health all help to define the hedonistic role.

Using Western civilization as a point of reference, the excess amount of food available creates a problem in selecting and determining the line of preparation a person should follow with any given choice, which is one reason for the proliferation of cookbooks. All of this may increase the pleasure of creativity in the kitchen but not the actual act of eating. Cultures in which the sources of nutrition are more limited exhibit a realization that consumption must take place as soon as time and circumstance will permit. Indeed in primitive cultures hunting, gathering, and eating all day long was a necessity. Thus in those cultures all the potential for pleasure was concentrated in the act of daily nourishment, even if it was just one meal from a common pot.

In non-Western societies the act of eating is sometimes occasional because of the sporadic nature of food gathering as well as the difficulty of conserving food in areas of high temperature and humidity. When the sources of food become secure and predictable, the food itself propitiates the ritualization of meals at fixed times. Mediterranean culture is paradigmatic in this regard, since daily, family-oriented meals take place at set times. These times are referred to as "sacred" because changing the fixed pattern would cause an imbalance within family relationships and personal well-being. The intimate relationship between pleasure and necessity makes it difficult to know to what extent pleasure affects such eating habits, since it is normal for pleasure to accommodate itself to all nutritional possibilities.

Appreciating the determinate element in pleasure requires an analysis of all gratuitous and extraordinary factors that intervene in the refinement and culinary expression of food. Unusual or complex methods of preparation not justified by any other reason, the inclusion of spices and additives that are purely hedonistic, extraordinary ingredients, and the presence of stimulating beverages, such as wine and liquor, are all elements clearly associated with food pleasure.

Cultural Differences
The islands of Asia, especially Japan, have developed the visual elaboration of food to an art form. In continental cultures the importance of taste acquires greater emphasis. In the cultures of coastal regions with a mild climate, spices and herbs magnify the aroma of food. In the industrialized West closely managed food production and fixed times of consumption have altered pleasure with precooked or packaged meals. While this promotes growth for the food industry on a mass-market level, the elements of pleasure derived from the time devoted to preparation and consumption are diminished. Some examples of these elements are visual, as in Japanese dishes that resemble ikebana; intense flavor, as in the excessive heat in many tropical cookeries; the rich aromas of Mediterranean home cookery; and the infinite varieties of elaborate desserts available in all cultures. Yet food pleasure is mutable, and an inherent contradiction derives

The pleasures of tippling, heavy flirting, and good food are brought together in this memorable scene of a Twelfth Night feast painted about 1656 by Dutch artist Jacob Jordaens. © ARCHIVO ICONOGRAFICO, S.A./CORBIS.

from the fact that even microwave popcorn eaten in front of the television is pleasurable.

Each individual has his or her own pleasure values for food and alcohol, which for some is an actual addiction, such as chocolate, and for others a natural dimension of the extended food experience. The latter evolves into such things as wine as an aperitif before the meal, wine to embellish consommés, fish and meats, sparkling wines for celebrations, and sweet wines for dessert. Arguably wine is not necessary for food pleasure, for this is easily demonstrated in cultures that prohibit alcohol. The point, however, is that its pleasures are cultural, and where alcohol is perceived as part of the eating pleasure, it is employed to enhance it.

The evening meal has become by definition the most hedonistic, although the motives that give rise to this type of food pleasure may be quite diverse, such as business gatherings, a sentimental or romantic rendezvous, or celebrations and anniversaries. The classical symposium of the ancient Greeks has been preempted by restaurants and hotels, especially those meals of a ritualistic nature. An example is wedding banquets, which are common and are becoming more and more similar the world over. To this can be added specific religious life-cycle observances, such as baptisms, communions, circumcisions, funerals, and the like. In the more industrialized countries the pleasures of food and eating have been banished to the position of last, behind such factors as dieting for better health or weight loss, fear of contaminants, and minimal time in preparation and consumption. Much of this has been defined by the various artificial "styles" of consumption created by the food-packaging industry in such labels as "home style" and "Oriental style."

The Ritualized Pleasures of Food

Ritualized pleasure may be defined as the pleasure derived from the time designated for eating over the course of the day, and it varies greatly from one culture to the next. In Europe it is defined by breakfast, dinner, and supper, to which some cultures also add optional meals in between. Two of these would be the light aperitif and the late afternoon break or snack. Both follow purely hedonistic impulses, both are defined by economic status, and both are limited by such considerations as care of children, the sick, the elderly, or workers who may require more nourishment due to hard labor. The aperitif has a more social and hedonistic quality since alcoholic beverages play an important role.

The Pleasure of Beverages as Food

The problems alcoholic beverages pose derive from their double roles as mood-altering drugs and as hedonistic elements of food consumption. To begin with, the higher the alcoholic content, the more likely the beverage will be employed as a pleasurable drug rather than as an adjunct to food. Wine, with its infinite variations of aromas, tones, textures, and alcoholic content, is the beverage most used for pleasure at the table. Without a doubt it is also the beverage endowed with the most hedonistic associations, not to mention its intimate relationship with Judeo-Christian culture and Greco-Roman culture.

Liquors have a double origin in that they are often derivatives of other beverages of lesser alcoholic content, such as beer and wine. One of the major contributions of human ingenuity to the search for pleasure was the discovery that alcohol could be extracted from seemingly unlikely substances. Such is the case with liquors from cacti, milk, honey, seeds, or indeed any nutrient containing carbohydrates susceptible to alcoholic fermentation. These types of beverages with higher alcoholic content are the most distant from pleasures of the table because they are most like drugs, and many were in fact first employed as medicines. Wine alone is intimately associated with gastronomic culture.

Pleasure for Pleasure's Sake

It has been said that the human being is the only animal capable of detaching itself from the pleasures of the natural instincts that sustain life. In the case of food, since it is connected to a vital necessity, expectation induces excitement. Pleasure, separated from necessity, is aimed more at taste than smell, more to the scarcity and cost of the food item, and more to the capacity for satiety, including the dimension of danger.

The history of elegant and refined food is written with rare and costly materials, which become the criteria for cultural values. The Romans prepared dishes appreciated because of their rarity, such as peacock eyes, which later seemed absurd and repugnant. Some foods that were once scarce and thus greatly valued subsequently were later viewed as vulgar because they were everywhere accessible. This commonness lessened the pleasure of their consumption due to the loss of their exotic and sumptuous qualities.

Finally, the ultimate forms of food pleasure come to the element of extreme danger. Mushrooms have always posed a great risk due to the possibility of poisoning, especially in earlier periods. This fear has not detracted from their gastronomic interest, rather, the risk has made them all the more attractive. Risk has achieved an even higher level of refinement in the consumption of fugu, a Japanese fish that poses sudden death due to the presence of dangerous toxins its the entrails. A dish composed of this particular species of fish and prepared by a specially certified chef is a luxurious delicacy in Japan, a pleasurable mockery of fear that can be experienced in the intense tingling the fish causes to the lips and mouth. Here the delicate meal passes beyond the boundaries of mere satisfaction. It is no longer food; it is a victory over death.

See also **Acceptance and Rejection; Appetite; Eating: Anatomy and Physiology of Eating; Luxury; Sensation and the Senses; Sex and Food**.

BIBLIOGRAPHY

Bernhard, Thomas. *The Cheap-Eaters*. London: Quartet Books, 1990.

Brillat-Savarin, Jean Anthelme. *The Physiology of Taste*, translated by M. F. K. Fisher. New York: Harcourt Brace, 1949.

Derenne, Jean-Philippe. *L'amateur de cuisine* [The lover of food]. Paris: Harcourt Brace, 1949, 1996.

Logue, A. W. *The Psychology of Eating and Drinking*. New York: Freeman, 1986.

Schivelbusch, Wolfgang. *Tastes of Paradise*. New York: Pantheon, 1992.

Schwabe, Calvin W. *Unmentionable Cuisine*. Charlottesville: University Press of Virginia, 1985.

Tiger, Lionel. *The Pursuit of Pleasure*. Boston: Little, Brown, 1992.

Weinstein, Jeff. *Learning to Eat*. Los Angeles: Sun and Moon Press, 1988.

Alicia Ríos

Translated from the Spanish by Enrique Balladares-Castellón

POACHING. The "moist heat" technique of poaching was very much a part of the recorded recipes of the ancient world. In one of the earliest cookbooks, the Roman Apicius's *De re Coquinaria*, recipes for delicacies like *Isicia Plena* (Dumplings of Pheasant) show that stiff forcemeat dumplings were poached in water seasoned with garum. And certain other savory and sweet recipes, like *Aliter Patina Versatilis* (A Nut Custard), instructed cooks to pour custard into molds to be placed into pans partially filled with hot water. After the invention of the printing press and the appearance of the first printed cookbook, *Le viandier* (1490), by the Frenchman Taillevent, the various aspects of poaching found a broader audience. However, it was not until the seventeenth century and the ever-increasing management of fire that poaching as a culinary technique gained in popularity. In 1651, with the printing of original cookbooks in addition to the collected works of the past, recipes began to integrate a repertory of techniques, basic mixtures, and raw materials. Lightly cooking certain ingredients in a small amount of liquid was not only part of a process of making a certain dish, but it also opened the possibility of refining the dish with savory sauces.

When Charles Ranhofer, chef of the famous New York establishment Delmonico's, published *The Epicurean* in 1893, various poached egg, seafood, and chicken dishes were featured as sophisticated menu offerings. Ten years later in his monumental cookbook *Ma Cuisine*, Georges-Auguste Escoffier listed 141 variations for *oeufs pochés* along with fifteen more recipes for cold preparations including *en gelée* and *chaud froid* dishes. And when Prosper Montagné published *Larousse Gastronomique* in 1938, he provided the formulas for several poached egg dishes beginning with *oeufs Aladin* (poached eggs on a mound of saffron risotto, garnished with sweet peppers, and napped with tomato sauce) and ending with *oeufs à la zingara* (poached eggs placed on oval fried croutons covered with thin slices of ham, and coated with Zingara sauce, a tomato-flavored demi-glace with a julienne of ham, tongue, and mushrooms). The same sophistication in the utilization of poached fish and poultry could be seen in recipes for *filets de soles à la normande* and *suprêmes de volaille*. And with the advent of nouvelle cuisine and especially *cuisine minceur* (calorie-defused dishes developed by the French chef Michel Guerard) in the 1960s, poaching various ingredients in flavorful liquids and substituting innovative vegetable and herb purées for sauces canonized the technique of poaching as a healthy trend.

In comparing the various examples of "moist heat" cooking, the amount of liquid, the timing, and the temperature are distinguishing factors. In poaching, the item to be cooked is generally submerged entirely in liquid, except in shallow poaching, when the item is only partially submerged in liquid and loosely covered with parchment paper. Timing is critical and depends on the size, density, and ripeness of the item to be cooked. The temperature for poaching registers between 160° and 180°F (71–82°C), and should always be maintained lower than a simmer (185°F [85°C]) to guarantee tenderness.

Although plain water or salt and vinegar-infused water is used in poaching, the liquids more frequently utilized in this cooking method are usually more flavorful. Stock, court bouillon, vegetable juice, vermouth, and various aromatics, such as herbs, spices, and citrus zest, contribute to the taste of the item cooked and also serve as the basis for a congenial sauce to nap the prepared poached fish, poultry, vegetable, fruit, or meat.

Unlike boiling, which requires only water, a pottery or metal pot, and heat to perform, poaching has acquired through the years a distinctive *batterie de cuisine*. An ob-

long covered pan called a poacher with handles at both ends and a convenient rack for lifting the prepared item from the pan greatly facilitates cooking a large fish. Egg poachers feature an insert with a specified number of round or oval, often perforated, cups to submerge eggs in a pan of water. Also used are metal rings that contain the entire egg when it is slipped into the water. A specific kind of shallow skillet with sloping sides called a *sauteuse* is used for poaching smaller items. And to insure even cooking and avoid curdling, various custards, timbales, and terrines are poached in their containers in a bain-marie, or water bath.

Poached Eggs

Instructions for poaching eggs are varied, many, and often contradictory. Some directions, for instance, recommend adding salt or vinegar to the poaching water; some call for breaking eggs into a saucer before lowering into the water; others for boiling eggs in the shell for ten seconds before breaking and poaching in water; still others for creating a whirlpool in the center of the pan and dropping each egg into it individually; and others for removing eggs and trimming them to the desired oval shape before serving.

The use of salt is debatable, although some chefs suggest that it speeds up the cooking process. Vinegar and acids, like lemon juice and wine, denature the proteins in egg whites and should be added to the poaching water. Breaking the egg into and as close to the poaching water as possible is the direct approach, but some cooks prefer the perforated cup method. Without exception, however, recipes for poached eggs advocate the use of the freshest eggs possible because the yolk membrane will still be strong, and the egg white will cling firmly to the yolk in a mass and not trail off in feathers. The older the egg, the looser the white becomes. Timing in poaching depends on the size and grade (Grade AA is preferable) of the egg, and the temperature of the poaching liquid. Some cooks suggest immersing in lightly boiling water and then, when the whites begin to set, reducing the water temperature to 175°F (79°C) or covering the pan and removing it from the heat. Cooking for too long a period of time, or with too hot a temperature, toughens the proteins. So attention to cooking time and water temperature is necessary, especially if the eggs are to be stored in fresh cold water for use later.

Recipes for poached eggs appear in almost every cookbook either as comforting food *pour un malade*, a display of the skill and inventiveness of the cook, or a staple of the breakfast/brunch buffet. Many distinctive dishes also are garnished with a poached egg, including the traditional veal cutlet dish Wiener schnitzel; the famous curly endive and lardon salad of Lyon, France; the American breakfast steak; and corned beef hash. In 1861, the Englishwoman Isabella Beeton suggested serving poached eggs on toasted bread or on slices of ham or bacon in her *Book of Household Management*. A hundred years later, avoiding what she called "that sodden toast," in *French Country Cooking* (1959), Elizabeth David recommended serving a poached egg on a purée of split peas, corn, or mushrooms, with fried bread on the side. And she included a traditional recipe for *oeufs Benedictine*, in which poached eggs are placed on a bed of creamed salt cod in individual flat dishes and napped with Hollandaise sauce. In *Simple French Food* (1975), an avid American practitioner of French cooking, Richard Olney, recommends preparing poached eggs and placing them in artichoke bottoms, topped with Mornay (cheese) sauce and surrounded by a julienne of lightly blanched vegetables (p. 101).

In the United States, serving poached eggs on a piece of toast covered with a slice of ham and napped with Hollandaise sauce translated into an American idiom when it was named after a Wall Street stockbroker (the term appeared in print for the first time in 1928). Lemuel Benedict reputedly used poached eggs, toast, and bacon sauced in Hollandaise as a cure for the extravagances of the "night before." In time Oscar Tschirky, maître d'hôtel of the Waldorf-Astoria hotel in New York, refined the dish by substituting toasted English muffins and ham for the toast and bacon, and by adding shaved truffles. Eggs Benedict was also served at Delmonico's restaurant in New York. The dish has not gone out of favor, but has been enhanced by many variations on the basic theme of a poached egg, toast, ham, and sauce blanche.

From the breakfast and brunch table to the buffet, chefs have devised multiple variations of *oeufs-en-gelée*, or cold poached eggs in jelly. Time-consuming but easy to make, jellied consommé or aspic is systematically added to a mold holding a poached egg and various garnishes until the mold is filled. After the final setting of the jelly, it is unmolded, and served.

Poached Seafood

Poaching is an ideal way to cook a large fish because no fat is used. The skin can be easily removed, and the delicate flavor and texture of the fish is preserved. The cooking process begins in cold liquid, usually a court bouillon (vegetable broth and wine) and is maintained at 176°F (80°C). If a fish poacher is too large, small whole fish, fillets, and steaks are usually wrapped in cheesecloth for easy removal and poached in any pan large enough to hold sufficient liquid to cover the fish. Some cookbooks also suggest poaching delicate fillets in melted butter in an enclosed casserole, but rather than poaching, the French call this technique *poêler*.

Because the poaching liquid is both flavorful and acidic, reduction and emulsified sauces can be made to nap the fish, however, the glories of French cuisine have been more traditionally displayed in the repertory of elaborate sauces—Blanche, Bordelaise, Diplomat, Dauphin, and Hollandaise—frequently prescribed for fish.

Delicate shellfish like scallops, oysters, and shrimp can also be poached in wine, aromatics, or in their own liquor. And seafood mousses in various-sized porcelain molds are always poached either on top of the stove or in the oven in a pan half-filled with water at 176°F (80°C).

Poached Meats and Poultry

Almost any tender cut of meat or poultry can be poached, and this technique offers an alternative to meats whose exteriors are browned and caramelized in the cooking process. Sweetbreads, eye of the round, small legs of lamb, duck and chicken breasts, and even beef tenderloins can be poached in stock, with or without vegetables, in a comparatively short time, and either served hot with a variety of sauces or served cold encased in a flavorful jelly or *chaud-froid* preparation. (*Chaud-froid*, literally "hot-cold," is a seasoned white or brown sauce to which gelatin is added; it is then spooned over fish or meat and glazed with aspic.) *Boeuf à la ficelle* is a classic variation on the traditional pot-au-feu, in which the beef tenderloin is tied with a string for easy removal from the poaching pan and served with vegetables and a reduction of the cooking stock. Formulas for finishing poached chicken breasts are as varied as the sauce repertoire for fish fillets, and again feature main course entrees as well as cold preparations.

A galantine is a dish made from the ground meat or forcemeat of poultry or meat that is stuffed into the skin of the chicken or duck of which it is made. Frequently the forcemeat is garnished with small cubes of ham, tongue, truffles, or pistachios. It is usually shaped into a cylindrical shape, wrapped in cheesecloth, tied with string, and poached in 176°F (80°C) liquid until an internal temperature of 160°F (77°C) is reached. When cool, the galantine is usually coated with aspic or a *chaud-froid* preparation.

Timbales, Terrines, and Quenelles

A large timbale (Arabic *thabal*, drum) is basically a preparation of forcemeat, meat, fish, or fruit baked with eggs and seasonings in a crust in a round mold with high sides. Small timbales are single servings of custards with forcemeat, shellfish, fish, puréed vegetables and fruits made in glass or porcelain round molds instead of a crust and poached in a water bath of 176°F (80°C) in a warm oven. Nouvelle cuisine, especially, espoused a variety of flavorful puréed vegetable timbales which captured the essence of the flavor of the main ingredient.

Whether a terrine is made with well-seasoned goose, duck, rabbit, venison, pork, or liver combined with forcemeat or delicate shellfish, fish, and vegetable mousse, the rectangular mold in which it is baked in the oven should be standing in a water bath whose temperature does not rise above 176°F (80°C). It is the gentle poaching that distinguishes the terrine from the pâté, which is baked in a crust in a hot oven.

Quenelles, on the other hand, are meat or fish forcemeat dumplings that are bound with eggs, either piped or shaped into their distinctive oval shape with two spoons, and poached in lightly salted water. Small shaped quenelles are often used as elements in various garnishes, such as *financière* and Toulouse. Larger quenelles, usually containing truffles, are used to embellish sizeable whole fish and other entrée presentations.

Poached Fruits

Although many nutritionists maintain that eating fruits raw provides the most vitamins, many out-of-season fruits or slightly under-ripe fruits can benefit from light cooking or poaching in a sugar syrup variously flavored with a cinnamon stick, cloves, orange, lemon zest, or vanilla. Cooking with the proper proportions of water and sugar firms the fruit, and when the fruit is lightly cooked and removed from the liquid, the fruit syrup can be reduced and thickened. At that point, fruit liquors, brandy, or rum can be added to the fruit sauce to reduce the sweetness and add more flavor. Fruits prepared this way make for simple but elegant desserts; however, poached fruits can also be glazed and served on meringues or cookies, or in custards or fruit tarts and compotes as in the classic Peach Melba and Pears Belle Hélène.

As a cooking technique that is almost ten thousand years old, poaching has always had a certain culinary cachet. Associated more often with feasting than with famine, the process of gently cooking delicate marrows, fish, shellfish, eggs, fruits, and certain kinds of poultry and meats in savory liquids has always lent finesse to various dishes, while, at the same time, exhibiting the skill of the cook.

See also **Beeton, Isabella Mary**; **Boiling**; **Chef, The**; **Delmonico Family**; **Eggs**; **Escoffier, Georges-Auguste**; **Fish**; **France**; **Gelatin**; **Health Foods**; **Sauces**; **Soup**; **Taillevent**; **Utensils, Cooking**.

BIBLIOGRAPHY

Child, Julia. *The Way to Cook*. New York: Knopf, 1989.

Corriher, Shirley O. *Cookwise: The Hows and Whys of Successful Cooking*. New York: William Morrow, 1997.

Culinary Institute of America. *The New Professional Chef*. Edited by Linda Glick Conway. New York: Van Nostrand Reinhold, 1991.

David, Elizabeth. *French Country Cooking*. New York: Knopf, 1980.

Ehlert, Friedrich W., et al. *Pates and Terrines*. New York: Hearst Books, 1984.

Montagné, Prosper. *Larousse gastronomique: The Encyclopedia of Food, Wine, and Cookery*. Edited by Charlotte Turgeon and Nina Froud. New York: Crown, 1961. First English edition.

Montagné, Prosper. *Larousse gastronomique: The New American Edition of the World's Greatest Culinary Encyclopedia*. Edited by Jennifer Harvey Lang. New York: Crown, 1988. Second English edition.

Montagné, Prosper. *Larousse gastronomique: The World's Greatest Culinary Encyclopedia*. Edited by Jennifer Harvey Lang. New York: Clarkson Potter, 2001. Third English edition.

Olney, Richard. *Simple French Food*. New York: Atheneum, 1975.

Ranhofer, Charles. *The Epicurean*. Reprint of 1893 Edition. New York: Dover, 1971.

Wheaton, Barbara Ketcham. *Savoring the Past: The French Kitchen from 1300 to 1789*. Philadelphia: University of Pennsylvania Press, 1983.

Joan Reardon

POISONING. Throughout history and across cultures food and drink have been used to deliver lethal poison. Since a person's demise from a slow-acting poison mimics so many natural diseases, and there is typically a time lapse between administration and expiration, this method made it almost impossible in early times to prove homicide. With the advent of chemical analyses for poisons (rudimentary arsenic tests were introduced in the 1840s) and autopsy, poisoning in the early twenty-first century, if suspected, is readily detected.

Poisoning in History

Since at least Greek and Roman times, there is historical documentation of poisonings. During the reign of Artaxerxes II of Persia (405–359 B.C.E.), it was said that his queen, Parsysatis, poisoned her daughter-in-law, Satira, by serving slices of fowl carved with a knife that had been coated on one side with venom. This allowed the queen to dine with Satira—Parsysatis reserving for herself the uncontaminated slices.

When selecting food or wine to serve as vehicles for poison, poisoners prefer a substance that will mask the bitter taste of the poison. Consequently, sweet foods were often selected. Wine had the advantage of preventing the victim from being on guard. Tea, coffee, hot chocolate, tarts (sweet and savory), jams, puddings, fruit pies, pastries, steak and kidney pie, chocolates, corned beef, porridge, and rice have all been used in poisonings.

According to medieval literature, many prelates, sovereigns, and pretenders or heirs to the throne were victims of poisoning plots. The murderers were most often from the victim's inner circle. In 1152, for example, Hugues d'Amboise was poisoned by a coterie of his knights at a banquet given by his brother. The historical heyday for poisonings was Renaissance Italy (1400–1700). So many deaths occurred that Romans hardly believed that any man of prominence or wealth had died a natural death. The legendary Borgia family, specifically Lucretia, gained a wide reputation for poisonings, especially of cardinals. Cantarella, a slow-acting poison, was said to have been dropped into food or drink, even sacramental wine. These murders were supposedly undertaken on behalf of Lucretia's father, Pope Alexander VI, who as head of the Roman Catholic Church was heir to the cardinals' estates. As these allegations were repeated, they became part of the historical record. More recently, they been revealed to be outright myth.

There are other instances in which an assumed poisoning has profound historical implications. When the exiled Napoleon Bonaparte died in 1821, his demise was at first attributed to stomach cancer, but examination of his hair has found the presence of arsenic. In the 1960s, the U.S. Central Intelligence Agency (CIA) devised a number of food- and drink-based poisons for assassination, including a lethal milkshake intended for Cuban leader Fidel Castro. Ultimately, the spy agency abandoned this, as the delivery system was too unreliable; it was thought to be much easier to get a target to inhale poisonous gas. In his 1962 autobiography, the late King Hussein I of Jordan relates his uncovering of a Syrian Intelligence plot to bribe his cook to poison his food. The tip-off: The untimely deaths of the palace cats, victims of the assassin's experiments.

Poisoning in Fiction

Poisonings have become the stuff of myth and legend, and a staple of mystery writers. The premeditation of the crime—acquisition of poison, calculation of lethal dosage, decision about which food or drink to use, preparation of the concoction, and making the victim consume it—adds to the insidiousness of the murder. In the fairy tale *Snow White*, a story that has survived for centuries in all European countries and languages, the wicked queen offers Snow White a poisoned apple that will induce a deathlike coma. The duel scene in Shakespeare's *Hamlet* features a poisoned cup of wine intended for the prince but mistakenly and fatally drunk by his mother, Queen Gertrude. In the 1941 American play "Arsenic and Old Lace," two seemingly innocent sisters in their sixties poison twelve men (a thirteenth as the curtain falls) with their homemade, arsenic-laced elderberry wine. In the 1996 literary mystery bestseller *The Debt to Pleasure* by John Lancaster, gourmet murderer Tarquin Winot suffers a brief setback when his intended victim turns down one of Winot's famous mushroom (Death Cap) omelets, saying he is allergic to eggs. After arguing that migraine is a small price to pay for gustatory pleasure, Winot recoups and whips up mushrooms on toast. In this poisoning, the food is not simply a disguise for poison, but the poison itself.

Gender and Poisoning

Although poisonings are committed by both men and women, they have been stereotyped as a female crime. In 1584, English writer Reginald Scot claimed women had invented poisoning and were "addicted" to the method. Nineteenth-century European writers, including criminologists, always profiled the poisoner as female. As recently as 1961, criminologist Otto Pollak claimed in *The Criminality of Women* that poison was the murder method of choice of most female offenders. Women's social roles as wives, meal-preparers, and caretakers, he argued, afford them unique opportunities to commit poisonings.

ROYAL TASTERS

During the Middle Ages and Renaissance, fear of poisoning was so great that royalty required that their food and drink to be tasted in their presence before they would eat. The tasting—a complex ceremony—usually fell to the food-preparers and servers. For Charles the Bold, Duke of Burgundy from 1467 to 1477, for example, the kitchen steward first tasted all food under the watchful eyes of the house steward. Then, as each dish was uncovered before the duke, a sample was given to official plate-bearer for tasting. The butler was the last servant to taste the dishes.

Wine required its own ritual. The royal cupbearer poured the libation into not only the duke's glass but into a tumbler as well. The glass was immediately covered, and water was added to the tumbler, which was drunk by the cupbearer's assistant. Only then would the wineglass be placed in front of the duke.

Tasting practices were largely abandoned in the mid-sixteenth century, although the ceremony was retained until the seventeenth century. Tasting is still practiced in the early twenty-first century in some Middle Eastern countries and Thailand.

In some form, tasting rituals have been with us since hunter-gatherer days when it was by trial and error that our ancestors learned to distinguish toxic from nontoxic plants. In the 1990s, research on taste has identified a subset of people known as supertasters, most often female, who have the genetic ability to sense tastes more intensely. They are so supersensitive to bitter tastes (a characteristic of poison) that the flavor actually causes them pain.

Throughout the literature, there are numerous examples of poisonings associated not only with women but also with their adultery, magic, and witchcraft. The near hysteria that swept nineteenth-century Victorian England, generated by tabloid reports of trials of forty women for putting arsenic in their husbands' food, was misplaced paranoia. When death records were examined, it was found that spousal murder of all kinds had risen dramatically between 1830 and 1900, with about one thousand people being found guilty. More than 90 percent of these murders were committed by men, the result of beatings and stabbings; only twenty cases were poisonings of wives by husbands.

In the twentieth century, concerns about poisoning of both food and water came to focus on bioterrorism.

In a celebrated case in 1984 in The Dalles, Oregon, members of a religious cult inserted salmonella bacteria in salad-bar foods, provoking 751 cases of infection. The purpose (this was only a trial run) was to keep voters away from the polls in an election several weeks hence where a land-use issue involving the cult's property could have an unfavorable outcome. Intentional criminal poisoning was not suspected at first; it was proved a year later. A paper written on the case was not published until 1997 out of fear of stimulating "copy-cat" incidents. Two other cases in Asia in 1996 include a mass poisoning with cyanide inserted into a curry stew at a festival in Japan, killing four people and, in India, the contamination of rice at a canteen with datura, a poisonous weed of the nightshade family, causing fifty-two fatalities. In the wake of the terrorist attacks in New York and Washington in 2001, the possibility of intentional poisoning of the food and/or water supply is being taken very seriously, particularly where botulinum toxin, the most deadly chemical known, is concerned. Where heads of state and other dignitaries are concerned, this has translated into extensive background checks on food preparers, servers, and suppliers as well as x-raying of liquor and produce received by restaurants and close surveillance in the kitchen.

BIBLIOGRAPHY

Chelminski, Rudolph. "Did Napoleon Die at the Hands of a Secret Assassin?" *Smithsonian* 13, no. 1 (1982): 76–82, 84–85.

Durant, Will. *The Renaissance: A History of Civilization in Italy from 1304–1576 A.D.* New York: Simon and Schuster, 1953.

Farrell, Michael. *Poisons and Poisoners: An Encyclopedia of Homicidal Poisonings.* London: Hale, 1992.

Hussein I, King. *Uneasy Lies the Head: The Autobiography of His Majesty King Hussein I of the Hashemite Kingdom of Jordan.* New York: Geis, 1962.

Lancaster, John. *The Debt to Pleasure: A Novel.* New York: Holt, 1996.

Marks, John D. *The Search for the "Manchurian Candidate": The CIA and Mind Control.* New York: Times Books, 1978.

Pollak, Otto. *The Criminality of Women.* New York: A. S. Barnes, 1961.

Robb, G. "Circe in Crinoline: Domestic Poisonings in Victorian England." *Journal of Family History* 22, no. 2 (1997): 176–190.

Serventi, Silvano. "The Taste Test." *Slow* (1999): 10–17.

Linda Murray Berzok

POLAND. *See* **Central Europe.**

POLITICAL ECONOMY OF FOOD. In the eighteenth and nineteenth centuries the term "political economy" referred to concerns classified under the discipline of economics. In the twentieth century Marxist and Social Democratic critics of the emergent discipline, who believed it was blind to systematic social inequalities, primarily used the term. In the twenty-first century inequality, both national and international, continued as the hallmark of any work identified with the tradition of political economy.

Three kinds of work typically are classified under the rubric of political economy of food. The most widely recognized is political economy of hunger, especially the work of the Nobel laureate Amartya Sen. A second group concentrates on food fights between great powers, such as the conflicts between Japan and the United States over rice imports into Japan. The third group focuses on the development of underdevelopment, that is, processes by which poor nations are kept poor.

Political Economy of Famines

Sen and his associates developed a richly empirical research agenda showing that famines occur not because of too many mouths to feed but because the poor cannot access food. Famines in the late twentieth century occurred in sparsely populated regions, such as sub-Saharan Africa, not in densely populated China, India, or Bangladesh. Although populations continued to grow dramatically in India and Bangladesh, those nations last experienced famines in 1947 and 1974 respectively, the dates they became independent. This implies that where political will exists famines can be averted by following "famine codes." Developed in British India in the 1880s, famine codes are both early warning systems and suggested countermeasures, such as wage employment in public works. Famine codes are only effective in the presence of a relatively coherent public administration and transportation and communication infrastructures. Ethiopia, Somalia, and Afghanistan lacked these elements. The last catastrophic famine in China, which probably killed about 20 million people between 1959 and 1961, occurred in the context of a disintegrating communication system within the Chinese Communist Party.

Why repeated famines in sub-Saharan Africa? The immediate problems of eastern sub-Saharan Africa are civil war and the dispersal of the rural population, which is 18 persons per square kilometer (8 for Somalia), compared to 228 for India, 681 for Bangladesh, and 104 for Nigeria. In a dispersed population the transportation system is underdeveloped and cannot support relief efforts. Dispersed settlements also provide little scope for building efficiencies in terms of the social division of labor and market development. Furthermore in much of this part of Africa the primary form of agriculture is slash-and-burn cultivation, which is a fragile system of sustenance in the first place. Yet such an extensive approach is essential to survival on land of some of the poorest quality anywhere in the world. On the African continent 60 percent of the area has a high expectation of drought, and only 30 percent of the land is suited to rain-fed production of millet, sorghum, and maize (Drèze et al., 1995).

Much of the potentially good land is exposed to endemic sleeping sickness that affects both livestock and humans.

Most people starve because they are either unemployed or the price of the agricultural commodity they sell is so low they cannot afford enough food in exchange. If the latter is the cause, as in most of sub-Saharan Africa, producing more cheap food in the first world for export to the poor nations drives down prices further and creates more misery.

Food Fights

Geopolitics have been central to the highly visible food fights between the affluent nations of the European Union, the United States, and Japan. In the 1940s the United States and the European nations assumed that agriculture would be relatively protected for reasons of reconstruction following World War II. But once Western European farmers revived, the U.S. government defended its share of the domestic agricultural market with the 1952 Defense Production Act, which banned the importation of anything from Danish cheese to Turkish sultana raisins (Friedmann, 1993). By 1975, when the European community had become a net exporter of wheat, the transatlantic trade conflict had become significantly hotter. In 1992 the Common Agricultural Policy of the European Union introduced support for domestic oilseed production and brought the transatlantic cousins to the brink of a trade war. Subsequently the most visible fights centered on hormone-injected beef and bananas.

Similarly during the military occupation of Japan, the United States sought to create a social base for the democratic system it was seeking to impose. The United States allowed Japanese protection of farm incomes both for the sake of recovery and in the interest of strengthening Japanese democracy. However, once the Japanese economy was independent it inevitably generated a conflict with the United States over markets and farm subsidies. This time instead of centering on wheat, maize, dairy products, and soybeans as with Europe, the conflict concerned rice, citrus, beef, and soybeans. Eventually the parties compromised on Japanese national sufficiency in rice and dependence on the United States for soybeans, nonrice grains, and beef. Protected rice remained an irritant in U.S.–Japanese relations in the twenty-first century.

Development of Underdevelopment

Political economists of underdevelopment concentrate on a segment of the international trade in food products that is distorted to benefit first world nations. Their basic argument is that free trade in food products never has existed. The U.S. government, among the most ideologically committed proponents of free trade, paid American farmers $71.5 billion in agricultural subsidies between 1996 and 2000. While pressuring third world nations to remove subsidies to their farmers, the first world nations heavily subsidize their capital-intensive agricultural systems. International trade in agricultural produce is shaped not by comparative advantage but by comparative access to subsidies (Watkins, 1996). Highly subsidized first world agricultural surpluses have created a serious disincentive for poor farmers in the developing world.

Furthermore it is argued that these unfair trade practices serve the interests of large corporations in the first world, such as General Foods, as illustrated by the case of instant coffee, the penultimate product of a commodity chain that begins with green coffee beans. Coffee is grown mostly in third world countries and is consumed in the first world. Most value-added parts of roasting, grinding, and packaging are done in first world countries. At the end of World War II the market was dominated by first world corporations, but major producers of green coffee, such as Brazil, sought "forward integration," from coffee to instant coffee, to appropriate more value-added parts of the chain. Brazilian prices were about 20 percent lower, and the quality of the powder was higher (Talbot, 1997, p. 124). General Foods opposed Brazilian imports that cut into the company's profits. The corporation lobbied hard for Article 44 of the Coffee Agreement, which compelled Brazil to impose an export tax on instant coffee and to sell 560,000 bags of green coffee beans per year to its competitors in the United States without the export tax. Receiving almost one-half of this coffee, which it converted to instant coffee, General Foods developed a further advantage over its Brazilian competitors by way of marketing and distribution networks.

In the larger pattern Mike Davis (2001) showed how colonial governments created the third world at the end of the nineteenth century through agricultural policies in the course of subsistence crises in 1876–1879, 1889–1891, and 1896–1902. These three crises were triggered by El Niño events, but capitalism had destroyed traditional networks of support, such as patron-client relations and their associated notions of customary charity, which resulted in the deaths of about 30 million people in the third world and generated conditions of chronic poverty. For example, Europe and India had relatively equal standards of living in 1800, but by 1900, Europe's standard of living was about twenty-one times higher than that of India, by economist Romesh Chunder Dutt's estimation based on the quality of housing, clothing, and diets (Davis, 2001, p. 292). By the end of the nineteenth century the processes of underdevelopment were firmly in place.

See also **Food as a Weapon of War**; **Food Security**; **Food Supply, Food Shortages**.

BIBLIOGRAPHY

Davis, Mike. *Late Victorian Holocausts: El Niño Famines and the Making of the Third World*. London: Verso, 2001.

Drèze, Jean, Amartya Sen, and Athar Hussain, eds. *The Political Economy of Hunger: Selected Essays*. Oxford: Clarendon Press, 1995.

Friedmann, Harriet. "The Political Economy of Food: A Global Crisis." *New Left Review* 197 (January 1993): 29–57.

Talbot, John M. "The Struggle for Control of a Commodity Chain: Instant Coffee from Latin America." *Latin America Research Review* 32, no. 2 (Spring 1997): 117–136.

Watkins, Kevin. "Free Trade and Farm Fallacies: From the Uruguay Round to the World Food Summit." *Ecologist* 26, no. 6 (November–December 1996): 244–256.

Krishnendu Ray

POLYNESIA. *See* **Pacific Ocean Societies.**

POPCORN.   Popcorn was an early variety of maize, whose range in pre-Columbian times extended from the American Southwest to Chile. It was introduced into New England about 1800 and almost immediately became popular. Its main advantage was that, when heated, it exploded. While this trait is not unique, popcorn expands to a much greater extent than other varieties of maize and other seeds. This explosion fascinated children, and popcorn became increasingly associated with children and children's holidays, such as Halloween, Thanksgiving, Easter, and particularly Christmas, when it was given to children and employed as tree decorations. Popcorn was also used in children's confections such as popcorn balls, which were sold at circuses, baseball games, and fairs. Cracker Jack, a popcorn, peanut, and molasses combination, became the most famous confection in the world by the early twentieth century.

Movie Popcorn

Until the 1930s, popcorn was not sold in movie theaters. To some owners, vending all concessions was an unnecessary nuisance because profits were negligible compared with the trouble and expense of cleaning up spilled popcorn and scattered boxes and sacks. Theater owners shifted their perspectives dramatically during the Depression, when popcorn's profit margin of almost 80 percent generated more income than did the box office sales.

During World War II, sugar and chocolate were rationed, and popcorn was the obvious alternative. Popcorn sales soared. By 1945, almost half of the popcorn grown in America was consumed in theaters. By 1949, surveys showed that 86 percent of the movie theaters in the United States sold popcorn, which six out of every ten patrons bought.

When television took America by storm in the 1950s, movie popcorn sales declined. Despite initial misgivings, however, the advent of television gave popcorn producers a boost unparalleled in their history. Americans who bought popcorn in movie theaters also wanted popcorn when watching television. The first product for the home market, "TV Time" popcorn, was unsuccessful. However, it triggered a convenience revolution in popcorn. Frederick Mennen experimented with an aluminum package to which he attached a wire handle. (Electric

Popcorn has become an icon food largely through its association with the cinema. It was one of the first foods to be served in movie theatres and remains one of the most popular of all foods eaten in theatres. © CORBIS.

poppers were manufactured shortly after the turn of the twentieth century. They did not become big sellers until major retail stores began offering them in their catalogs.) In October 1959 the newly created Mennen Food Products Company launched "Jiffy Pop." It was marketed as a fun food that youngsters could easily prepare and parents could conveniently tidy up, and a national advertising campaign made it an immediate sensation. In 1960 Jiffy Pop sales exploded. American Home Products acquired Jiffy Pop, which continued to sell well throughout the 1960s and into the 1970s.

Microwave Popcorn

Percy Spencer of Raytheon discovered the heating properties of microwaves when he leaned in front of the microwave tube with a candy bar in his pocket—it promptly melted. He then popped corn using the microwave tube. Spencer's discovery led to the birth of microwave ovens. Spencer's first patent application for heating food with microwaves was submitted in 1945. However, the cost of the early microwave ovens was simply too high to justify buying one to pop corn.

During the 1960s, two major events turned the microwave oven industry around. The first was the invention of a compact, low-cost magnetron. The second was the invention of the self–stable microwave popcorn, "Micro-Pop," which had a multilayered film package that kept moisture in and oxygen out. Today, the majority of popcorn consumed in America is popped in a microwave oven—its second major use in the United States.

Orville Redenbacher

Before the 1950s, popcorn was sold at the regional level, rather than on a nationwide basis. It was considered a generic item, and quality was not a key factor in selling the product. It was promoted as an economical snack. High poppability of all the kernels in a package was the main claim advertised to consumers. Orville Redenbacher and Charles Bowman singlehandedly introduced the concept of "gourmet" popping corn, proving that consumers would pay more for a product that popped up "bigger, fluffier, and more tender." At first, Redenbacher literally sold Red Bow out of the trunk of his car. He and Brown visited Gerson, Howe and Johnson, a public relations firm located in Chicago, who convinced them to change the name from Red Bow to "Orville Redenbacher's Gourmet Popping Corn." As the price was higher than that of other popcorn, the agency argued that consumers needed to be convinced that Redenbacher's popcorn was of a better quality than its competitors. With virtually no advertising, they had achieved their success through word-of-mouth promotion. But Redenbacher and Bowman could not market their product nationally without additional assistance. In 1973 they teamed up with Blue Plate Foods, a subsidiary of Hunt-Wesson Foods based in Fullerton, California, to market their gourmet popcorn nationally. This connection permitted national advertising and a widespread distribution system. Appearing on numerous television shows as part of a massive advertising campaign, Redenbacher became a television personality. He made hundreds of personal presentations a year and appeared in scores of television commercials. Redenbacher was one of America's most unlikely television stars. His bow tie, dark-framed spectacles, and Midwestern accent convinced many that he was just an old country hick. Consumers easily recognized the glass jar and simple label adorned with Redenbacher's folksy image. It lent the product owned by a corporate giant a homey, small-town aura.

Popcorn represents less than 0.02 percent of the entire maize crop. Of all the types of maize, however, none is more commonly recognized than popcorn. Americans eat popcorn in movie theaters, amusement parks, and sports arenas, and around campfires. As a snack food, we feast on ready-to-eat savory and candied popcorn confections. American intake of popcorn in all forms has more than doubled during the past two decades, and consumption abroad has expanded at an even faster pace. As trivial as popcorn may appear when compared to the to-tal maize crop, Americans annually devour 11 billion popped quarts, an average of about forty-four quarts per person. By volume, popcorn is America's favorite snack food. And, partly aided by the spread of American popular culture overseas—including the export of American films—popcorn consumption has also increased in Europe and Asia.

See also **Art, Food in: Film and Television; Fast Food; Halloween; Maize; Snacks.**

BIBLIOGRAPHY

The American Pop Corn Story and Recipe Collection. Sioux City, Iowa: American Pop Corn Company, n.d. History of one of America's oldest popcorn producers.

Sherman, Len. *Popcorn King: How Orville Redenbacher and his Popcorn Charmed America.* Arlington, Tex.: Summit, 1996. Biography of Orville Redenbacher.

Smith, Andrew F. *Popped Culture: A Social History of Popcorn in America.* Columbia: University of South Carolina Press, 1999. General history of popcorn in America.

Andrew F. Smith

POPULATION AND DEMOGRAPHICS.

Every place in the world has a population, human or otherwise. Big or small, old or young, growing or declining, every population changes over time and space. Human populations inhabit countries, cities, suburbs, and rural areas. In some places populations are dense, in others sparse. In some places there are more young people, in others more old people. Men dominate in some places, women in others. All of these factors constantly change over time. The study of all the statistics that describe how populations change over time and space is termed "demography." Demographic data includes, among other things, the size of a population, its density, spatial distribution, age, and gender.

Population Distribution

The distribution of the world's population is spatially uneven. Deserts contain very few people, for example, and cities contain many. Different countries, too, have very different populations. For example, consider the contrast between China and the United States. With a population of over one billion, China contains 21 percent of the world's population, whereas the United States, with a population of 283 million, has less than 5 percent. The number of people per unit area of land—the population density—also varies among countries. In a small country like the United Kingdom (population 59 million), the density is 628 people per square mile. In comparison, a large country like the United States has a population density of 76 people per square mile, despite its larger population. Within countries, population densities vary significantly. São Paulo, Brazil, for example, has a density of around 17,000 people per square mile, whereas

Amazonia has one of the lowest population densities in the world.

Since birth and death rates change over time, and since people migrate from one place to another, the world's population distribution is always changing. Countries where birth rates are greater than death rates will, in the future, gain a greater share of the world's population, as compared to countries where birth rates are similar to or less than death rates. Cross-country migration is another important factor contributing to changes in population distribution. In the early twenty-first century, some 150 million people, or 2.5 percent of the world's population, migrated either temporarily or permanently away from their countries of origin. For example, due to high rates of immigration (mainly from Latin America), the foreign-born population of the United States increased from 9.6 million in 1970 to 24.4 million in 1998. People also move within countries from rural to urban areas in a process known as urbanization. In less developed countries, for example, urbanization takes place at a rapid rate: just 18 percent of people lived in urban areas in 1950, compared to 40 percent in 2002. This number was expected to reach 56 percent by 2030.

Populations are likewise characterized by age and gender distributions. Some countries have an overwhelmingly young population, most notably those in Latin America and Africa, while others have aging populations, such as the more industrialized countries of North America and Europe. Different populations also have different sex structures. Urban societies, for example, have more males than females, a higher proportion of young adults, and a greater life expectancy.

World Population Growth

On a worldwide scale, population increases when births outnumber deaths. Although experts disagree on how exactly the world's population has grown over time, it is clear that for most of human history population growth proceeded at a very slow rate. Estimates suggest that in 40,000 B.C.E. the world's population was approximately 1.5 million, and it increased to 700 million by 1750. A falling death rate and a steady birth rate resulted in a marked increase of population to 1.6 billion in 1900. After this, in what is often termed the "population explosion," the world's population took an unprecedented move upward. In a mere sixty years the population almost doubled to 3 billion. Forty years later, in 2000, it had doubled again to over 6 billion. The reason for this growth was a rapidly falling death rate, a trend usually attributed to an increase in the world's food supply and a reduction in the rates of disease. Birth rates also fell, partially as a result of the spread of contraceptive practices, thus slowing the potential growth rate. The continuing decline of the birth rate means that the rate of population growth, though still rapid, has been slowing down. In 2002 the birth rate stood at around 1 percent, or 80 million more people per year.

Population and Food Supply

To some, the growth of the world's population has been the cause of much alarm. Even though greater food availability is part of the explanation for the ever-increasing population, at one time it seemed unthinkable that the world could support so many people. The relationship between population growth and the human food supply has, in fact, been the subject of a heated debate for hundreds of years. On one side are the so-called neo-Malthusians, named for the English clergyman Thomas Malthus. In 1798 Malthus wrote the "Essay on the Principle of Population," in which he argued that population has a tendency to increase geometrically (or more appropriately stated, exponentially), but food production increases arithmetically. Thus, population will eventually outstrip food supply, the result being many deaths from starvation. Neo-Malthusians tend not to share Malthus's analysis in its entirety; they simply share his belief that it is possible to have too many people in the world. The world, in other words, can become "overpopulated" if the number of people exceeds a carrying capacity determined by food availability and environmental resources.

Modern-day neo-Malthusians—such as Lester R. Brown, Paul Ehrlich, Joel Cohen, Donella H. Meadows, Thomas F. Homer-Dixon, David Pimentel, and Norman Myers—believe that population growth is a cause of famine and environmental destruction. Growth, they argue, has limits. Generally speaking, they claim that the increased demand for food arising from population growth reduces agricultural resources per person, degrades the environmental conditions in which agriculture is practiced (via soil erosion and deforestation), and exacerbates macro-environmental change (such as global warming and the depletion of the ozone layer). These changes result in a decline of food production per person and, consequently, specific populations (especially those in poor countries) experience increased death rates from malnutrition. In his book *The Population Bomb*, Paul Ehrlich predicted that by the 1980s the world would see massive famines as a result of food shortages stemming from overpopulation. The much-discussed 1972 Club of Rome report "Limits to Growth" concluded that the world could not support economic and population growth indefinitely. Environmentalist Lester Brown argued in numerous texts, most notably 1994's *Full House*, that the demand for food leads to the adoption of more intensive agriculture, which degrades environmental resources and leads to a slowdown of food output. In *Environment, Scarcity, and Violence*, Thomas F. Homer-Dixon maintained that environmental resources are being degraded by rapid population growth, a situation he believed would lead to conflict and insurrection, particularly in the developing world.

On the other side of the population growth debate are those who are more optimistic about the growth of the world's population. Although they possess a wide variety of views, the so-called optimists look at the situation differently. Broadly speaking, they reject the concept of overpopulation and the notion that earth has a certain carrying capacity determined by food supply and environmental limits. Rather, the optimists believe that population and resources can be manipulated by humans through ingenuity and innovation and are therefore relative.

Some of Malthus's critics are termed "cornucopians" because they believe population pressure induces technological and institutional changes that can raise food output per person. Ester Boserup argued in *The Conditions for Agricultural Growth* that population growth stimulates improved methods of agricultural production—via crop rotation, fertilizers, and so on—thereby increasing food supply. The economist Julian L. Simon was another prominent cornucopian. In *The Ultimate Resource*, he reasoned that the demand for food influences the choice of agricultural technique and leads to adoptions of innovations in market agriculture. Simon also argued that a larger population also stimulates food availability, first by expanding the pool of inventive thinkers, thereby in-

creasing the propensity for technological change, and second by making effective food distribution systems more cost-effective. An example of technological change often put forward to disprove Malthus's thesis is the development of high-yielding varieties of crops such as rice. Bred as part of the "Green Revolution" in the 1960s, these kinds of crops arguably enabled India and other countries to feed themselves, thereby counteracting fears of calamitous starvation.

Other thinkers do not concur with Malthus simply because they believe that political and economic conditions, not population growth, determine famine and environmental destruction. An early critic of Malthus was the political economist and philosopher Karl Marx. In works like *Capital* (volume one), written in the 1860s, Marx accused Malthus of excusing the social conditions of his time, conditions that Marx believed were the real cause of poverty and hunger. The need to accumulate profit, Marx said, inherently means that at certain times there is a "relative surplus population," a labor force that is largely superfluous to the needs of industry. Thus,

FIGURE 1

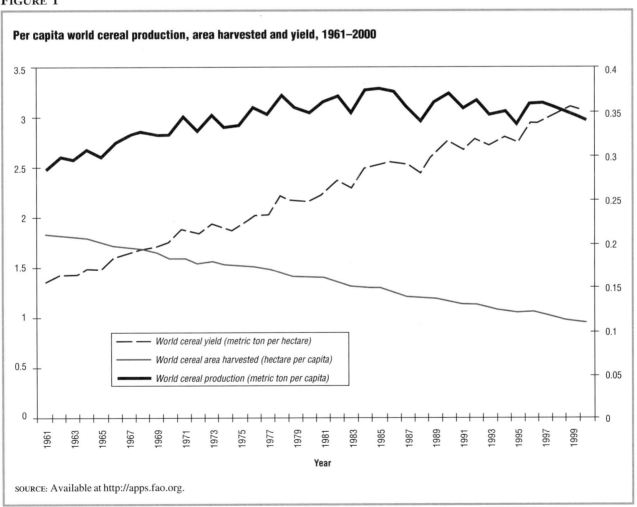

Per capita world cereal production, area harvested and yield, 1961–2000

- - - World cereal yield (metric ton per hectare)
—— World cereal area harvested (hectare per capita)
━━━ World cereal production (metric ton per capita)

SOURCE: Available at http://apps.fao.org.

there is a class of people who periodically are unable to earn enough to afford a means of subsistence. In this way Marx asserts that it is the economic system, not population growth, that creates a population in which too many people do not have enough to eat. Economics professor and Nobel Laureate Amartya Sen has also argued that poverty and famine cannot be blamed on overpopulation. Though he accepts that population growth can place undue pressure on the environment and the lives of women, in *Poverty and Famines* he argues that famine results from a collapse in people's ability to purchase or otherwise acquire food, not from a shortage of food. Another critic is advocate Frances Moore Lappé and her colleagues. In *World Hunger: Twelve Myths*, she noted that there is no correlation between population density and hunger, and that population growth is not the root cause of hunger but is itself a consequence of social inequality. The solution, she said, is to distribute more equally the world's resources.

Trends in Population and Food Production

Throughout history, the world's food supply has grown faster than the world's population, as illustrated by the increase in the amount of cereals produced per capita. Figure 1 gives an example from recent history, indicat-

ing that cereal production has outstripped population growth since 1960 as a result of increasing yields. The area harvested per capita has actually declined.

Given this trend, it appears that neo-Malthusians have been overly pessimistic about the growing population. Most neo-Malthusians now accept that changing methods of food production have stimulated yield in a way not predicted by Malthus, but they claim the real problems have only just started. As evidence, they point to the declining rate of per-capita cereal production since 1985 (Figure 1) and the stark contrasts in food supply at the regional level (Figure 2). For example, cereal production is 0.125 metric tons per person in sub-Saharan Africa and has been declining over the past few decades. In South Asia, the per-capita rate of cereal production is higher, and the trend has been moving steadily upward. The developed world, as exemplified by the United States, produces far more cereals per capita (1.21 metric tons), but the amount has fallen since 1985.

Long-range future projections by the United Nations suggest the world's population will continue to grow, reaching 7.67 billion in 2020, and eventually 11 to 12 billion or higher by the end of the twenty-first century. Over 95 percent of growth will occur in the devel-

FIGURE 2

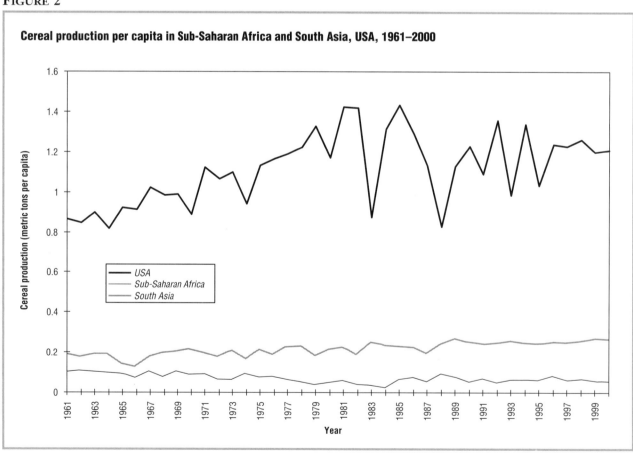

Cereal production per capita in Sub-Saharan Africa and South Asia, USA, 1961–2000

oping world, and the largest absolute and relative population increases will occur in Asia and Africa, respectively. Much of this growth will be in cities. The developing world's urban population is projected to double from the 1995 level of 1.7 billion to 3.4 billion in 2020.

This ever-growing population means an increased demand for food. Estimates of how much will be needed depend on the weight given to demographic factors, such as population growth, and nondemographic factors, like changing per-capita consumption. In an estimate by Tim Dyson in 1996, population growth alone will stimulate cereal demand by 728 million tons from 1990 to 2020; if nondemographic factors are accounted for, demand will be over 1 billion tons in total. Simulations by the International Food Policy Research Institute (IFPRI) predict that the world's population will demand 690 million tons more of cereal in 2020 compared with 1995. Eighty-five percent of the added demand will come from developing countries. The increasingly urbanized nature of the population means that the demand for meat will increase by 115 million tons.

The question of whether the food supply will keep up with the growing population is also the subject of a debate that has grown on local, regional, national scales. Concerns are greatest about developing countries. IFPRI predicts that food supply will not keep up with food demand in these countries. Yet IFPRI also points out that if cereal imports from the developed world doubled from 1995 levels to 2020, demands would be met. On the regional scale, sub-Saharan Africa has been the subject of significant attention. Issues such as drought and land degradation, warfare, and HIV/AIDS are all predicted to have an impact on the current trend toward declining per-capita food production. At the national scale there have been particularly marked debates about China. In *Who Will Feed China?* Lester R. Brown predicted that factors such as declining land availability and the degradation of water supplies will result in a shortfall of cereal production relative to population growth.

More recently, the debate has moved toward the community and household scale, the level at which people access and consume food. At this scale, however big or small the population, people are only able to eat enough food if they can access it. In order to do that, they need the means to grow food for themselves or, more likely, the money to buy it.

See also **Cereal Grains and Pseudo-Cereals; Food Politics: United States; FAO (Food and Agriculture Organization); Food Supply and the Global Food Market; Food Supply, Food Shortages; Geography; Government Agencies; Political Economy.**

BIBLIOGRAPHY

Boserup, Ester. *The Conditions for Agricultural Growth.* Chicago: Aldine, 1965.

Brown, Lester R. *Who Will Feed China? A Wake-up Call for a Small Planet.* New York: Norton, 1995.

Brown, Lester R., and Hal Kane. *Full House: Reassessing the Earth's Population Carrying Capacity.* New York: Norton, 1994.

Dyson, Tim. *Population and Food: Global Trends and Future Prospects.* London: Routledge, 1996.

Ehrlich, Paul. *The Population Bomb.* New York: Ballantine Books, 1968.

Homer-Dixon, Thomas F. *Environment, Scarcity, and Violence.* Princeton, N.J.: Princeton University Press, 1999.

Lappé, France Moore, Joseph Collins, and Peter Rosset. *World Hunger: Twelve Myths.* 2d ed. New York: Grove Press, 1998.

Malthus, Thomas R. *Population: The First Essay.* Ann Arbor, Mich.: University of Michigan Press, 1959.

Marx, Karl. *Capital,* vol. 1. New York: Viking, 1977.

Meadows, Donella H., Dennis Meadows, Jorgen Rangers, and William W. Behrens III. *The Limits to Growth.* New York: Universe Books, 1972.

Pinstrup-Andersen, Per, Rajul Pandya-Lorch, and Mark W. Rosengrant. *World Food Prospects: Critical Issues for the Early Twenty-First Century.* Washington, D.C.: International Food Policy Research Institute, 1999.

Sen, Amartya. *Poverty and Famines: An Essay on Entitlement and Deprivation.* New York: Oxford University Press, 1981.

Simon, Julian L. *The Ultimate Resource.* Princeton, N.J.: Princeton University Press, 1981.

Corinna Hawkes

PORK. *See* **Mammals; Meat; Pig.**

PORRIDGE. Porridge is generally defined as a dish made by stirring oatmeal or rolled oats into boiling water and simmering the mixture gently until it is cooked. It is usually eaten hot; often, though not invariably, for breakfast. Meal or flour from other cereals may be used, in which case the dish is so designated; the cooking liquid may be water or milk or a mixture of both.

Porridge is considered an essentially Scottish foodstuff—it was hailed by Robert Burns, Scotland's national poet, as 'The halesome parritch, chief o' Scotia's food'— even though oats are grown in many regions of the world. The words "porridge," "parritch," and variants are allied to the word "pottage," indicating the practice of cooking ingredients together in a pot and thickening it with cereals, though "pottage" itself came to mean soup or broth. They may also be linked to *porray*, which is derived from *porrum*, the Latin word for leek—an age-old pottage vegetable. The Scottish *purry* was a mixture of oatmeal and kail.

Cooking and Serving

Traditions surround the making and eating of porridge. Stirring should always be done clockwise (for luck) with

Pewter porringer (*écuelle*) with lid. France, circa 1740. The rustic porringer, which throughout the Middle Ages provided hearty sustenance for kings and peasants alike, reached its zenith of elaborate detail in eighteenth-century France. ROUGH-WOOD COLLECTION. PHOTO CHEW & COMPANY.

DEVELOPMENTS

In 1877 the Quaker Oats Company of the United States developed rolled oats or oatflakes by steaming and rolling the coarsest grade of oatmeal—the so-called pinhead oatmeal, which is the whole grain halved. This innovation simplified the preparation of porridge and all oat-based dishes.

The muesli of today, regarded as a health food, is generally formulated with oats as its principal ingredient, with the addition of other cereal flakes, dried fruits, and nuts. It requires no cooking and has grown more sophisticated over time, but it is still recognizably a derivative of the Scottish porridge.

a *spirtle* or *theevil*, a wooden stick tapering to a rounded point, for stirring, and a carved head. In Scots, porridge was always referred to in the plural and was customarily eaten while standing, but the reasons for this latter custom are obscure. Some aver it was due to the proverb: "A staunin' sack fills the fu'est" (A standing sack fills the fullest), while others consider folk ate standing up lest an enemy catch them unawares.

Once cooked, the porridge was ladled into porringers (bowls) with a separate bowl of milk, buttermilk,

MAKING PORRIDGE BY THE TRADITIONAL SCOTTISH METHOD

For each person allow about a handful of oatmeal to half an (imperial) pint of water and a small teaspoonful of salt. Bring the water to the boil and add the oatmeal in a slow but steady stream, stirring briskly. Once it has returned to the boil simmer gently until cooked, about 20 to 25 minutes. Add the salt near the end of the cooking time.

Quantities are necessarily inexact as meals vary, as do the tastes of those eating the end product. Rolled oats require less cooking, so follow the manufacturer's instructions; the microwave, too, shortens the cooking time.

or thin cream close by. Each spoonful of porridge was dipped into the cold liquid and then eaten. Some sprinkled sugar over the porridge, and others preferred honey, treacle or syrup, or a knob of butter—the men might replace the milk with ale or small beer. Porridge was sometimes poured into a drawer in the kitchen dresser to be sliced when cold, either for eating out in the fields or for reheating in the evening.

The basic mixture allowed for numerous permutations, all with their own nomenclature according to locality. Brose was made by pouring boiling water over oatmeal, butter, and salt: with meat stock it became fat brose, while the addition of a green vegetable gave kail brose. Hasty Pudding was a form of porridge enriched and sweetened. Gruel was made by boiling the liquid that oats had soaked in, flavoring it with assorted ingredients and allowing it to cool to a jellylike substance. To make *sowans*, oat husks were soaked until sour, at which point the mixture was sieved and the husks thrown out. The liquid was a pleasant drink and the starchy sediment underneath was boiled and eaten either hot or cold, with milk, cream, or beer again served separately.

Oatmeal augmented every type of dish and some drinks, too, while assorted oatcakes and bannocks baked on a girdle (a flat iron plate hanging over the fire) took the place of yeasted bread.

Porridge is highly nutritious because oatmeal contains protein, carbohydrate, fats, and soluble fiber, all the B vitamins, vitamin E, calcium, and iron. The lack of vitamins A, C, and D is redressed when it is combined with milk or vegetables. Research has revealed that porridge might aid in the prevention of coronary heart disease as well as in the treatment of hypertension and certain diabetic conditions.

A Scottish Staple

The consumption of porridge, together with other oat-based products, is considered an essential benchmark of Scottish nationality. In the geographical and climatic conditions of Scotland, both oats and barley provided a more reliable harvest than did wheat, but oats did not predominate until the eighteenth century. Thereafter, they played an increasing role in the diet, particularly in rural areas where oatmeal often formed the basis of every meal: "Oatmeal, with milk, which they cook in different ways, is their constant food, three times a day, throughout the year, Sunday and holidays included," observed J. Donaldson in 1794 regarding the farm laborers in the Carse of Gowie, a fertile area along the River Tay's north bank. Places in England and Wales with similar conditions saw a parallel dependence on oatmeal. Emigrants from the United Kingdom, but most especially the Scots, took their traditional habits with them, including their food preferences, and oatmeal was subsequently exported to many far-flung corners of the globe.

See also **British Isles**; **Cereal Grains and Pseudo-Cereals**; **Middle Ages, European**.

BIBLIOGRAPHY

Barker, T. C., J. C. McKenzie, and John Yudkin, eds. *Our Changing Fare: Two Hundred Years of British Food Habits.* London: Macgibbon and Kee, 1966.

Donaldson, Gordon. *The Scots Overseas.* London: Hale, 1966.

Donaldson, James. *General View of the Agriculture of the Carse of Gowrie in the County of Perth.* London: Macrae, 1794.

Fenton, Alexander. *Scottish Country Life.* Edinburgh: Donald, 1976.

Hope, Annette. *The Caledonian Feast.* Edinburgh: Mainstream, 1987.

Lythe, S. G. E., and J. Butt. *An Economic History of Scotland, 1100–1939.* Glasgow and London: Blackie, 1975.

Mason, Laura, and Catherine Brown. *Traditional Foods of Britain: An Inventory.* Totnes, U.K.: Prospect, 1999.

McNeill, F. Marian. *The Scots Kitchen: Its Traditions and Lore with Old-Time Recipes.* London and Glasgow: Blackie, 1929.

Steven, Maisie. *The Good Scots Diet: What Happened to It?* Aberdeen: Aberdeen University Press, 1985.

Una A. Robertson

PORRIDGE, POTTAGE, GRUEL. In Great Britain, porridge is synonymous with hot oatmeal gruel, a common breakfast food that also has become an icon of Scottish cookery or at least an icon of presumed Scottish origin. Food packaging and mass-market advertising have helped create this mythology, but in fact porridge is a universal dish that cuts across many cultures and geographic boundaries. Furthermore, oats are not a defining feature. They do not even play a role in the origin of the word "porridge."

The old children's rhyme moves closer to the real meaning of porridge: "Peas porridge hot, peas porridge cold, peas porridge in the pot nine days old." The key ingredient here is not oatmeal but peas, and not fresh peas but rather dried peas cracked into grits. The dried pea probably was not the only ingredient in peas porridge, because porridge, the original porridge, was a vegetable preparation, not a dish based on cereal grains (as in the case of gruel). The etymology of porridge has not been neatly worked out because the chain of evolution has a number of missing links, but this much is clear: porridge shares a common ancestry with words like "pottage," "porringer," "puree," and "potage," the latter the French word for soup. This word family also includes *potager*, the hearth where vegetable soups were boiled, and by extension the kitchen garden, in which those ingredients were grown.

The presumed underlying link for all of these concepts is the Latin word *porrum* or *porrus*, a leek. It appears in the Middle English word *porree*, a term used for leek porridge. It would seem, from etymological evidence, that originally porridge was a preparation made from leeks (or green onions resembling leeks) and secondarily from other ingredients in the kitchen garden. In home cookery this type of porridge may have been relatively coarse, with the ingredients chopped or pounded, then stewed until tender. In court cookery, where more attention was paid to delicate textures, leek porridge was most probably served as a smooth purée thickened with bread—many medieval recipe collections contain directions for making just this sort of dish. It finds its counterpart in the modern-day Spanish preparations known as *porra*, which are made by pounding the ingredients in a mortar until they form a thick pulp. They are eaten like gazpacho, scooped up with a piece of bread rather than with a spoon.

A parallel theme in all of these dishes is the fact that they are thickened in some fashion. The most elegant medieval preparations were thickened with white bread, yet presumably lower down on the economic ladder poorer cooks used whatever coarse thickeners were on hand. Dark bread was one alternative. Animal blood, especially the blood of fowl or hogs, was certainly employed during the butchering season. Combining pounded vegetables with meal or grits was also one common solution. In southern Europe barley, emmer wheat (*farro* in Italian), or millet appear to have been the thickeners of choice among the peasants. In northern Europe oats, barley, and rye were commonly employed, depending on what was most abundant in a particular region. The great variation in the use of thickeners may have given rise to the idea of national "styles" of porridge, when in fact national identities as understood in the twenty-first century are of recent origin. While the British may be inclined to call prepackaged oatmeal gruel a porridge, historical evidence suggests that if indeed it was once a porridge, it has been stripped of all key vegetable ingredients, most importantly the leeks.

William Woys Weaver

PORTUGAL. *See* **Iberian Peninsula.**

POTASSIUM. *See* **Electrolytes; Minerals.**

POTATO. The potato is a tuber—a short, thick, underground stem with stored starches and sugars—of the potato plant. It was given its botanical name, *Solanum tuberosum*, in 1596 by the Swiss botanist Gaspard Bauhin, and belongs to the Solanaceae family, the nightshades, which includes eggplant, peppers, and the tomato. (The sweet potato is not a potato; it belongs to the morning glory family.) Growing wild as early as 13,000 years ago on the Chilean coast of South America, potatoes were first cultivated by farmers in the Andes Mountains nearly seven thousand years ago.

Nutritionally, the potato supplies complex carbohydrates—essential for energy—and a very low amount (about 10 percent) of protein. One serving (a 5.3-ounce medium potato) provides: 45 percent of Recommended Daily Intake (RDI) for vitamin C (most of it in the millimeters-thick layer immediately under the skin), 21 percent of potassium, 3 grams of fiber, essentially no fat, and only 100 calories. It is rich in the minerals iron and magnesium and supplies all the vital nutrients except calcium and vitamins A and D.

Potatoes are the vegetable eaten most frequently in the United States, and the one ordered most when Americans eat out. In 2001, the average American ate 41 pounds of potatoes. In 1996, the annual per capita consumption increased with age among those over eighteen: between eighteen and thirty-four, 74.3 pounds; thirty-five to forty-four, 80.6; forty-five to fifty-four, 87.4; fifty-five to sixty-four, 88.9; and, for those sixty-five and older, 109 pounds. Interestingly, consumption again peaked among those between thirteen and seventeen (83.2 pounds) and six to twelve (85.5 pounds), who presumably consume most of their potatoes as french fries, chips, and novelty forms.

The United States ranks fourth in world potato production, with an estimated 1.26 million acres planted in 2001. Russia is the largest producer. With a world harvest of 291 million tons grown in more than 100 countries, potatoes are second only to rice as a world food crop.

South American Origins

The potato was domesticated high in the Andes Mountains in South America by 3000 B.C.E., but it was not until the Incan civilization (ca. 100–1530 C.E.) that the tuber's true agricultural potential was realized. The climatic challenges of growing crops in the heights of the Andes are formidable. Radical swings in temperature, from highs of 62°F (17°C) to lows below freezing (most nights of the year), occur even within a twenty-four-hour period, and constantly disrupt the potato plant's physio-

logical processes. Yet, potatoes are ideally suited to these conditions; the plant grows in even the poorest soils, and the hardiest species can survive at an altitude of 15,000 feet.

The Inca devised agricultural innovations that maximized the potato crop. The introduction of terracing enabled steep slopes to be planted. A system of canals efficiently distributed water from higher in the mountains to each terrace level. In the absence of plows and oxen, a wooden foot plow called a *taclla* was invented that is still used in the Andes today. A representation of this tool is found in a Spanish woodcut from the late sixteenth or early seventeenth century (but the tool is presumed to predate that). The Inca wisely prized agricultural diversity, growing 3,000 varieties of potatoes in various sizes, textures, and colors. Their goal was to develop a different kind of potato for every type of soil, sun, and moisture condition. Thus, the rulers could secure a high yield of potatoes—enough to feed thousands of members of the expanding empire—from disproportionately small plots of land.

The Inca also serendipitously discovered how to freeze-dry potatoes. At night, the cold of the Andes froze the tubers. (Raw potatoes are 80 percent water.) During the day, however, they thawed in the warmth of the sun. As they defrosted, laborers stamped on them to press out all the moisture. After several days of alternating freezing and defrosting, the potatoes were dehydrated and transformed into a lightweight, transportable substance known as *chuno*. Stored in sealed, permanently frozen underground storehouses, the freeze-dried potatoes kept for five or six years. When needed for sustenance during the lean months, the *chuno* could be reconstituted by soaking in water, then being cooked or ground into meal, with no loss of nutritional value. *Chuno* was so precious to the Inca that it was used as currency and collected as tribute. It was also believed that potatoes have healing properties. Raw slices were placed on broken bones, aching heads, and rubbed on bodies to cure skin diseases, and slices were carried to prevent rheumatism

From South America to Europe

When the Spanish arrived in South America around 1537, they were not impressed by the potato. The strange tubers, misshapen and bitter, were about the size of peanuts, and bore little resemblance to potatoes we know today. The Spanish mistook them for a kind of truffle, calling them *tartuffo*. The Inca routinely consumed the choice, large tubers, and planted only the rejects, thereby propagating progressively inferior tubers.

Gradually, the Spanish realized that potatoes were perfect food for sailors on ships returning from Peru. The tubers traveled well, were cheap, nutritious, required little preparation, and prevented scurvy. Returning to Spain by way of sub-Saharan Africa, the Spanish introduced potatoes there in 1538. Leftovers from shipboard food found their way to Spain in the 1550s but, in most areas,

HEIRLOOM POTATOES: THE PURSUIT OF OLD-TIME FLAVOR

While the discussion over genetic diversity in crop potatoes has polarized the agricultural community today in much the same manner as the finger-pointing during the 1850s over the causes of the 1840s potato blight, market forces are quietly building new niches for time-tested heirloom varieties. Limited choices in the supermarket and hybrid potatoes without much character or flavor have sent frustrated chefs and small growers in search of the old standbys that once made home cooking so memorable. Interest began with the "fifty-somethings," the not-quite-antique varieties like the Pimpernel (1953) developed in Holland and the French yellow-fleshed fingerling called Roseval (1950). Both are good producers with very distinctive cooking qualities.

Those criteria have become important again, especially since heirloom potatoes are different from heirlooms passed down via seeds. Heirloom plants are generally defined as open-pollinated varieties that have been handed down over several generations, with particular emphasis on varieties dating from before the 1940s. Because potatoes are increased by planting pieces of tubers, they are genetic clones of their parents. That is why heirloom potatoes actually taste like the past. Potato classics like pink-skinned Early Rose (1867), developed by Albert Bresee of Vermont, and creamy 1840s Peach Blow from New Jersey sell out as quickly as growers can supply them. What better potato was ever invented for mashed potatoes, gnocchi, or dumplings than the aptly named Snowflake (1874)? Steam it, and it turns to fluffy snow.

The growing affection for heirloom potatoes is not just a grass-roots trend in the United States and Canada. Arche Noah, a private seed organization in Austria, has been building up an heirloom potato collection for many years, and the recently organized Association Kokopelli in France is establishing chapters in most of the leading countries in the European Union. Kokopelli is comparable to a horticultural Slow Food movement, and doubtless one food network will soon be influencing the other. Purple-skinned treasures like Violette du Lac Bret, a rich-flavored blue potato from Canton Vaud, Switzerland, and its cousin Vitelotte noir (1815) of France are finding their way onto the leading restaurant tables in those countries, just as La Ratte d'Ardéche (1872) has now become the salad potato most favored by Paris chefs.

In the British Isles, waxy yellow Duke of York, developed in Scotland in 1891, still reigns as the classic salad potato of choice. Lilac-skinned Arran Victory, developed in 1918 by Donald Mackelvie of Lamlash, Isle of Arran, Scotland; and Archibald Findlay's Catriona (1920), splashed with patches of blue on the skin, are considered by connoisseurs to be among the finest-tasting potatoes ever developed. Their flavors are complex, with hints of walnuts or hazelnuts, or, as some enthusiasts claim, Scotland's answer to truffles.

William Woys Weaver

The potato market in Elmer, New Jersey, 1907. Note the complete absence of motor vehicles. ROUGHWOOD COLLECTION.

they did not grow well and were not popular. Still, as early as 1570, potatoes could be purchased in markets in Seville, and, by 1573, they were being fed to hospital patients in other parts of Spain.

Through the first half of the seventeenth century, potatoes were eaten primarily by the poor and soldiers in Spain. In 1653, however, the historian Bernabé Cobo made a laudatory reference to the culinary properties of *chuno*, describing how Spanish women were able to grind the substance into more white flour than could be obtained from wheat, and from which they made sponge cakes and pastries with almonds and sugar.

Not until 1760 did Spanish plant breeders start to improve the potato. Eventually, it was found that potatoes grew well in the mountainous Pyrenees and along the Atlantic coast, where they were popular among Basque fishermen during their voyages to the Grand Banks of Newfoundland.

The Potato Diaspora

From Spain, potatoes spread to all parts of Europe. Spanish ships carried the vegetable to Italy around 1560, making that country the first after Spain to eat potatoes on an appreciable scale. Potatoes also traveled along the "Spanish road" that connected Spain's imperial provinces in northern Italy with the Low Countries.

By 1600, the potato had entered Austria, Belgium, Holland, France, Switzerland, England, Germany, and, most likely, Portugal and Ireland. Some historians claim that it was Basque fishermen who first brought potatoes to Ireland, when they came ashore to dry their catches on their return voyages from Newfoundland. Others maintain it was Sir Walter Raleigh who planted the first potatoes on his estate in Ireland. The potato was introduced in India, possibly as early as 1615, and had reached the most remote parts of China by 1643. Beginning about 1730, the Scottish Highlands adopted potatoes as completely as Ireland had.

Fear of Potatoes

It is not unusual for new foods to be met with skepticism and fear, especially those arriving from a strange, faraway continent where they are consumed by "uncivilized" non-Christian peoples. The potato, however, had a tougher battle for acceptance than many other foodstuffs introduced from the Americas. Aside from its odd, unaesthetic appearance and initially bitter taste, the tuber was feared for a variety of reasons. Since it was not mentioned in the Bible, it was often associated with the devil. As a consequence, in the north of Ireland and in Scotland, Protestants flatly refused to plant them. In Catholic Ireland, to be on the safe side, peasants sprinkled their seed potatoes with holy water and planted them on Good Friday.

Another source of prejudice against the potato was its membership in the nightshade family, which includes a number of poisonous members: deadly nightshade (bel-

ladonna, which is poisonous), mandrake (known as a soporific and fertility drug), tobacco, and henbane (poison). Some of these substances have traditionally been associated in various cultures with magic and witchcraft. In many folk beliefs there is a grain of truth. Solanine, contained in the tubers and common to all plants in the nightshade family, is indeed a poison. Unlike modern potatoes, which contain only a nonharmful trace amount, tubers of the sixteenth and seventeenth centuries had much higher levels, not enough to cause death, but sometimes a rash appeared. That led to its association with the deadliest disease of the time, leprosy. So great was the fear that, when Frederick the Great of Prussia ordered his people to plant potatoes in 1744, they pulled them up. Frederick was forced to post soldiers to guard the crops. Ten years later, in 1754, the king of Sweden also ordered his subjects to grow potatoes. Yet, when famine struck Kolberg in 1774, wagonloads of potatoes sent by Frederick were rejected.

All over Europe, it was believed that the potato plant would bring disease. In the seventeenth century, the parliaments of Franche Compté and adjacent Burgundy actually prohibited its cultivation. In the early nineteenth century, Ludwig Feuerbach and other German radicals believed that "potato blood" was weakening the people and delaying the anticipated revolution. In Sicily, potatoes were used like voodoo dolls: the name of an enemy was attached to a tuber and buried in the belief that this would ensure his or her death. Even as late as 1928 in America, Celestine Eustis, the author of *Cooking in Old Creole Days*, advised readers to throw out the water in which potatoes had been boiled because it was poisonous.

At the same time potatoes were feared and reviled, and being grown only in the gardens of botanists, there was also a developing literature in sixteenth-century European herbal books asserting that potatoes had some therapeutic effects. Among the diverse claims were enhanced sexual desire, fertility, and longevity, and cures for diarrhea, tuberculosis, and impotence.

The Potato in Time of War

Europeans quickly discovered that the potato afforded them a military advantage; it was ideally suited to combat starvation caused by war. During the Dutch Wars (1567–1609), for example, Spanish soldiers crossed the Alps on foot from Italy, marching north through Franche Compté, Alsace, and the Rhinelands. Villagers along the route quickly discovered that tubers carried by the soldiers could be planted, hidden underground, and dug as needed, unlike grain. Nearly every military venture after about 1560, including World War II, resulted in more acreage being planted in potatoes.

When French, Austrian, and Russian armies invaded Prussia during the Seven Years War (1756–1763), peasants escaped starvation by eating potatoes. As a result, the Austrian, Russian, and French governments all persuaded their own peasants to grow potatoes. In 1778, the

War of the Bavarian Succession was called "the potato war" because most of the action consisted of destroying the enemy's food supplies.

In Russia, crop failure in 1838–1839 convinced people in central and northern parts of the country to raise potatoes. In the course of the nineteenth century, potatoes displaced bread as the principal food for poorer classes from Belgium to Russia. They were cheaper than bread, required less preparation, and were just as nutritious.

Potatoes in England
Potatoes appeared in the British Isles in the 1590s. The historical record is unclear about which of two famous explorers introduced them, Sir Francis Drake or Sir Walter Raleigh. Regardless, the first English potatoes did not, contrary to popular myth, originate in Virginia. This mistaken notion gained credence because the first tubers destined for England passed through Virginia after having been taken aboard in South America.

The tubers were not immediately embraced in Great Britain, remaining a garden crop grown by botanists until 1780. The English, traditionally not fond of vegetables, based most of their meals on meat, and the potato carried a social stigma as the food of savages and peasants. The earliest potato crops in England were produced to feed sailors. By 1700, a stew called *lobscouse*, consisting of potatoes, meat, onions, and strong seasonings, was recorded in Lancashire. When hardtack was added as an accompaniment, lobscouse became the standard dish of choice for shipboard crews. Yet, the tuber was so despised during the reign of George III (reigned 1760–1820) that it took years of botanical experiments before the English conceded that potatoes might be acceptable as cattle feed.

In the 1700s, northwest England began to produce an abundance of potatoes, as many as 13.5 tons per acre. Cultivation occurred, too, in Cornwall and outside London, where industry was beginning. In many ways, the potato fueled the Industrial Revolution; it was good, cheap food for another lowly multitude—workers. This trend was also generated by the simultaneous decline in bread production. In 1832, the Bread Acts were rewritten so potato flour could be used without losing the right to call the product "bread." By 1836, two million people who used to subsist on wheat flour—one-seventh of the population—were living chiefly on potatoes. By 1850, Londoners were consuming 3,000 tons of potatoes a week. Baked potatoes played a special role in London working-class life—they were sold by street vendors both to eat and to use as hand warmers.

The perennial British working-class favorite, fish and chips, reached the streets as two separate dishes, with fish coming at least thirty years before chips. Neither was fried in deep fat until the 1860s. By 1888, there were between 10,000 and 12,000 fish-and-chips shops in the United Kingdom serving the duo wrapped in newspaper and sprinkled liberally with vinegar.

Meanwhile, the elite consumed potatoes in very different forms—disguised as other foods. Unadulterated, naked potatoes were not considered appropriate food for the upper classes, and Queen Victoria's chef carved the tubers into shapes like olives and pears, or buried them entirely in purées and soups. By 1914, however, people in England said they would rather pass up greens, butter, and nearly all their precious meat before they would give up potatoes—quite a change of heart. It was the English who coined the word "spud" for potato, a slang expression that originally referred to a potato-digging spade.

The Great Irish Potato Famine
Ireland was the first country in Europe to accept the potato as a field crop, in the seventeenth century, and to embrace it as a staple in the eighteenth. To the poverty-stricken peasantry, this tuber was a safeguard against unemployment, overpopulation, crop failure, and starvation. Landless laborers rented tiny plots that they sowed with potatoes. One acre could feed a family of six, averaging ten pounds of potatoes per person a day. Potatoes did not replace meat immediately, but other staples like oats, beans, barley, herring, and bread gradually disappeared from the table. Over time, the diet shifted to one of boiled potatoes supplemented by milk, which supplied calcium and vitamins A and D, making the meal nutritionally complete.

As early as 1740, the potato saved Ireland from famine. Between 1780 and 1841, when the potato achieved its dominance, the population doubled in Ireland. According to historic sources, it cannot be said with certainty that the potato was responsible, but surely it played a role. By 1845, about 40 percent of the Irish population was dependent on the tubers raised on 65,000 farms of not more than one acre each. Potatoes were also used to feed pigs.

In 1845, blight struck potato fields throughout Europe, but those most devastatingly affected by the fungus *Phytophthora infestans* were in Ireland. The assumption is that the blight was carried back by ship from North America on a diseased tuber. Livid purple patches appeared, covering whole potato plants—roots, tubers, and foliage—after which they turned brown and rotted. Whole fields went under in a matter of hours, destroying 40 percent of the crop. Yet, few deaths occurred because many people slaughtered their pigs, which normally ate a third of the crop. In 1846, the blight redoubled, killing 90 percent of the potatoes and preventing a new crop from being sown. The fungus was not as virulent in 1847, but reappeared in full force in 1848–1849. About five to six months later, famine set in, and diseases including typhus, dysentery, relapsing fever, respiratory infections, and cholera were not far behind. Ultimately, two million people died, one-quarter of the entire population. One million immigrated to the United States.

How the Potato Twice Changed World History

The historian William H. McNeill (1999) believes that potatoes twice made a critical difference in world history: first, in South America, where the vegetable provided the principal energy source for the Inca and their Spanish successors. There would have been no great Incan civilization, McNeill contends, without *chuno*. Not only was it collected as taxes from the peasant-farmers, it was also disbursed from storehouses to pay labor gangs for building roads, waging war, and erecting great monuments. Once the Spaniards arrived and conquered the Inca, *chuno* is what fed thousands of conscript miners, forced by the conquistadors to work the silver mines in Bolivia. This tremendous influx of silver contributed to worldwide monetary inflation, and enabled Spain to build a powerful naval fleet.

The second way in which the potato changed world history was in northern Europe. The extraordinary strength of the industrial, political, and military changes between 1750 and 1950 could not have taken place without an enormously expanded food supply from potatoes, which served to feed a rapidly growing population, McNeill argues. Germany could not have become the leading industrial and military power of Europe after 1848, and Russia could not have assumed so threatening a stance on Germany's eastern border after 1891. Both events helped set the stage for two world wars.

The Potato Becomes Haute Cuisine

The French were no more enamored of the potato at first than any other Europeans. Legrand d'Aussy, in his 1782 *Histoire de la vie privée des Français* (History of the private life of the French) wrote that the pasty, indigestible tuber should be eliminated from aristocratic households and left to the poor. Also in 1783, a Parisian gourmet expressed outrage that the potato had achieved a certain cachet in the capital. The nineteenth-century French gastronome and author of the esteemed *La physiologie du goût* (The physiology of taste, first published in 1825), Brillat-Savarin agreed that the tasteless potato was good only as a defense against famine.

As in other European countries, the peasantry took to potatoes much more quickly because it could be used in their diet like turnips. Around 1620 (during the reign of Louis XII), the Abbey of Remiremont accepted payments in potatoes. As early as 1673, the tubers were being cultivated on a large scale in Lorraine. By the first half of the eighteenth century, the potato was well established in France, even if it was only among the peasants. By the middle of the century, potatoes began to be grown in the Pyrenees and Dauphiné, both very mountainous areas. By 1780, potatoes were the chief food of the Pyrenean highlands. By 1840, the potato was well established in French cuisine, making its way in through the soup pot, where it added bulk and absorbed flavors.

The person most credited with winning acceptance for the potato in France was eighteenth-century army pharmacist Antoine Parmentier. As a prisoner in Germany during the Seven Years War (1756–1763), he was forced to eat potatoes almost exclusively and became convinced of their virtues. He set about analyzing their chemistry. Then he won a competition sponsored by the Academy of Besançon to identify foods that could stem mass hunger after the famine of 1770. To counter the fear of anything in the nightshade family (more intense in France than in England), in 1771 the Faculté de Paris published a paper stating emphatically that the potato was innocuous. After yet another famine, Parmentier himself wrote in 1789 that, although the tuber was a nightshade, it was not soporific. To further convince the populace of the potato's appeal, he had the tubers planted on the worst possible land on the outskirts of Paris. During the day, the field was guarded by soldiers who left at night. The peasants, intrigued by such an important crop, went into the field and stole potatoes to plant in their own gardens, which is exactly what Parmentier wanted to happen.

Realizing that acceptance of the potato needed to begin at the top, Parmentier is said to have convinced Louis XVI to encourage planting and eating the tuber by throwing all-potato banquets. Even Marie Antoinette was said to wear potato flowers in her hair at court. Although these colorful stories may be apocryphal, between 1770 and 1840 potatoes became widely cultivated in northern parts of the country. When famine struck in 1788 because the grain crop failed, potatoes were available.

In 1793, during the "Reign of Terror," the French people celebrated potatoes as their republican salvation. Even the royal Tuileries gardens were symbolically converted into a potato field. Realizing the political strength potatoes could provide, the Republic published ten thousand copies of a pamphlet on cultivation. A year later, a cookbook, *La cuisinière républicaine*, presented twenty recipes. The annual potato crop burgeoned from 59,640,000 bushels in 1815 to 332,280,000 by 1840. By 1843, France produced almost half a million bushels of potatoes, possibly the largest crop on the continent and in all of Europe.

Potatoes gradually acquired a place in haute cuisine. Collinet, the chef for King Louis Phillippe (reigned 1830–1848), accidentally created the famous *pommes soufflées* (puffed potatoes) when he plunged fried potatoes into extremely hot oil to reheat them when the king was late for dinner. Much to the chef's surprise, the potatoes puffed. *Pommes frites* (what we call french fries) appeared on city streets in the north of France around 1870. The Larousse *Gastronomique*, the encyclopedia of French cuisine, first published in 1938, contains dozens of classic French recipes for potatoes.

The Potato in America

While potatoes migrated from South America to Europe, they failed to travel out of South America to North America or even to Central America and Mexico. In fact, Mexico did not have potatoes before the eighteenth century.

It took about two hundred years—after the tubers made their way to Europe—before they were introduced into North America. This may have happened as early as 1613 in Bermuda, and on the mainland in 1621. The first North American colonial potato growing dates from 1719, when Irish immigrants, escaping starvation from the famine, introduced the potato to New Hampshire.

Americans did not subject the potato to class distinctions, so its popularity grew rapidly. In 1806 the American Gardener's Calendar included only one variety of potato; by 1848, almost one hundred kinds were exhibited at the Massachusetts Horticultural Society fair. By 1860, American output of potatoes was calculated at 100 million bushels, 90 percent produced by the northern states, with New York the single largest producer, followed by Pennsylvania, Ohio, and Maine.

A major step forward in potato cultivation was made in 1872 when the botanist Luther Burbank discovered that the Early Rose potato produced a seed ball, and was able to breed plants with larger tubers whose yield sometimes doubled or tripled that of its parent. The resulting progeny became known as the Burbank potato, which a few decades later mutated into the Idaho (or Russet).

For nineteenth-century farming life, the potato was a real boon for the same reason it became popular elsewhere as a cheap, nutritious, convenient way to feed farmhands and families. The potato, however, was not kept down on the farm; in 1876, some American hotels offered five different potato dishes for breakfast. During the Alaskan Klondike gold rush (1897–1898), potatoes were at times almost worth their weight in gold, so valued for their vitamin C that desperate miners traded gold for them.

In October 1995, the potato became the first vegetable to be grown in space. NASA and the University of Wisconsin created the technology with the goal of feeding astronauts on long space voyages, and, eventually, feeding future space colonies.

Cultivating Potatoes

Potatoes are most often grown in cooler climates in moist, acidic soil (pH slightly less than 6). They must be able to gather sufficient water from the soil to form the starchy tubers that range anywhere from three to twenty in number on any one plant, depending on variety, weather, and conditions. In the United States, most potatoes are produced in Idaho, followed by Washington, Oregon, Maine, North Dakota, California, Minnesota, and Wisconsin. Six varieties account for 80 percent of the crop yield.

Although potatoes are perennials, they are treated as annuals since the edible part of the plant that contains the buds is dug up each year. Farmers grow particular tubers as seed potatoes (not intended to be eaten) for propagating new crops. These potatoes are cut into what are called "sets," small pieces, with at least one eye or leaf bud on the surface, with some of the flesh of the potato still attached to supply the initial energy for the plant. The sets are planted with the eyes facing upward; new plants sprout from the eyes.

The potato plant produces leaves and flowers that can be white, purple, lilac, or violet, depending on variety. If fertilization of the flower is successful, a small green fruit ball is produced containing fifty to two hundred seeds, known as true seed. These can be planted for the next year's crop rather than using seed potatoes. The leaves supply abundant food for the plant's growth, and the generated surplus moves down into the underground tuber for storage. Potatoes can be left in the ground for four to six weeks. They are harvested when all of the leaves and tops of the plants have withered. A potato that is harvested young, usually in the spring or early summer, and sent directly to market instead of being stored, is known as a new potato.

Before potatoes can be sold or shipped, they must be sorted for size and quality. This process is called "grading" and special implements are used. These can be as simple as a wooden slat with a bag on the end for acceptable potatoes, or a more complicated conveyor-belt system that moves potatoes toward the bag at the end as inspection is performed.

Potatoes produce the steroidal alkaloid solanine, which seems to protect the tubers and foliage from some predators and insects. Still, potatoes are vulnerable to such pests as the Colorado potato beetle, red slugs, and blister beetles, and are still attacked by blight. Since 1990, fungicide-resistant strains of blight have struck fields in various parts of North America.

Culinary Preparation of Potatoes

Potatoes figure prominently in many of the world's cuisines, particularly in the Americas, in Europe, and in countries colonized by Europeans: *pommes de terre soufflées* and *pommes Anna* in France; hot potato salad, noodles, dumplings, pancakes, and bread in Germany; as a base for soups and puddings and stuffing for pierogi in Russia and Poland; colcannon—a mixture of potatoes and kale, turnips, or cabbage—and cobbledy, potatoes mashed with milk, butter, salt, pepper, and onions in Ireland; as an ingredient in the Spanish omelette; in the latkes and knishes of Jewish food; for the sauce *skordalia* in Greece; in *raclette* and *roesti* in Switzerland; for gnocchi in Italy; stuffed potatoes and savory *causa*, mashed potato cake, in Peru; for *lefse*, thin potato pancakes in Norway; in fish and chips, mashed potatoes, shepherd's pie, and Cornish pasties in England; potato casserole in Finland (*Imellettyperunasoselaatikka*), a dish that undergoes a malting process wherein the starch of the potatoes breaks down to form a simple sugar; french fries, potato chips, and stuffed potatoes in the United States.

Potatoes can be used in every course of a meal, even dessert. They can be fried, boiled, steamed, braised, roasted, sliced, diced, chopped, and mashed. A large part of their versatility is their neutral taste, which provides a palatable backdrop for almost all other foods. For dessert, potatoes can be used with or without chocolate in cakes, pies, doughnuts, cookies, and candies. Since potatoes contain no gluten, adding some mashed potato to dough makes it particularly tender.

For cooking, potatoes are classified according to starch content—high, medium, or low—which affects the way they cook and the resulting texture. High-starch potatoes (Russets and Idahos), also known as mealy or floury, are the first choice for baking and frying. The use of the microwave to bake potatoes has considerably shortened what used to be a lengthy process. The large starch granules swell up and separate, making for a light and fluffy texture. Medium-starch potatoes (white all-purpose and yellow-fleshed, including Yukon Golds) have a creamy texture and become soft but do not disintegrate when cooked. Low-starch potatoes (round red and white boiling potatoes), also known as waxy potatoes, are the first choice for boiling, steaming, and roasting. They contain more of the starch known as amylopectin, with granules that stay close and dense even after cooking.

Once purchased, potatoes need to be stored in a dark, but dry, place to ensure they do not turn green or sprout. Generally, store-bought potatoes have been sprayed with a chemical that inhibits sprouting. Even a little warmth and light, however, may provoke the eyes to use the stored energy in the tuber for growing.

The substance that sometimes appears as a greenish cast under the skin and in the eyes of the potato is the alkaloid solanine, the natural pesticide that protects the plant as it grows. All potatoes contain trace amounts (1–5 mg). Its appearance on store-bought potatoes means they have been "light-struck," exposed either to natural or artificial light. According to Federal Food and Drug Administration guidelines, levels higher than 20 mg per 100 g of potato make the vegetable unfit to eat. Consequences of solanine toxicity range from minor upset stomach to serious illness. To avoid this, proper storage and cutting away all traces of green on the potato are necessary.

Relation to Human Biology

Potatoes contain anthoxanthins, pigments that produce the white color and act as antioxidants, believed to have some cancer-preventing activity. Specifically, unfried potatoes are among those vegetables containing the highest levels of the antioxidant glutathione. When compared to bell peppers, carrots, and onions, potatoes have the greatest overall antioxidant activity. Only broccoli is higher.

French fries and potato chips, however, may pose a cancer risk. Separate studies by the national food agencies of Sweden, Britain, and Norway have reported high levels of acrylamide, a carcinogen in rats and probably one in humans, in potato products fried at high temper-

atures. Until there is more evidence, the World Health Organization and the United Nations Food and Agriculture Organization have not been able to determine whether consumers should cut back on their intake of fried potato foods, particularly chips.

Eating unfried potatoes contributes to the minimum goal of five servings of fruits and vegetables a day, recommended by the U.S. Department of Agriculture's (USDA) Food Guide Pyramid and designed to provide optimum good health.

Symbolism of the Potato

In the United States, the potato has found its way into pop culture. A "couch potato" is a sedentary person; "hot potato" indicates a volatile issue or topic; "small potatoes" refers to something that is not a big deal; a "meat and potatoes" person is someone who eats only the basics. Calling someone a "potato head" is not a compliment because it means someone who is dense. A familiar children's rhyme begins, "One potato, two potato, three potato, four." The children's toy Mr. Potato Head®, introduced by Hasbro in 1952, and Mrs. Potato Head®, in 1953, came packaged with plastic eyes, ears, nose, mouth, feet, and hats to insert into a real potato supplied by the buyer. In 1960, the kit also came with a potato-shaped plastic body. The image has been licensed worldwide for a variety of popular uses including T-shirts, clocks, and Halloween masks.

Since its earliest appearance in Europe, the potato has been associated with the poor and the working class. When the Spanish first stumbled on the potato in Peru, they looked down on it as slave food. The exotic sweet potato was brought from Haiti to Europe as soon as it was discovered by Columbus, but it took the conquistadors more than thirty years to bring potatoes to Spain, and then they came as food for sailors. For a long time, the potato continued to be regarded as food fit only for the poor and as animal fodder, useful only in the event of starvation.

In America, where the potato did not have a class barrier to break down, its association with fat and grease—deep frying—has reinstated some of its lowly image. A headline a few years ago in the *New York Times* read, "The Rich Get Richer and the Poor Get French Fries." The irony is that, by cooking it in fat, the 99.9 percent fat-free fresh potato is transformed into a high-fat snack.

Commercialization of Potatoes

An early reference to commercial potato growing dates from 1762, when the tubers became a field crop in Salem, Massachusetts. In the following year, Connecticut valley potatoes were listed as an export, but the buyers were West Indian planters, looking for cheap food for slaves. By 1848, about half a dozen varieties of potatoes were being grown commercially, the same number grown in the twenty-first century.

Processing of potatoes began not long after they began to be grown commercially. In the 1870s and 1880s in both France and America, manufacturers began making equipment for deep frying, which made commercial production of fried potatoes and french fries a reality. Mass production depended on the availability of cheap oils that appeared right after the Civil War. In 2002 in the United States, nearly half of the potato harvest ends up being fried.

Unfortunately, processing takes much of the taste out of potatoes, and undermines their quality as growers shift to varieties demanded by processors rather than those that are best fresh. Potato products are made from potatoes that have been reduced to powder in one of two ways. The first is simple cooking, drying, and grinding, which preserves the solids in more or less their original proportions. This is how potato flour is made. Derivatives of potato flour include instant mashed potatoes, frozen potato products, and potato chips.

The second method involves extracting starch from potatoes by a washing process. This is how potato starch is made, which is commercially packaged to be used as a thickener and to make cakes, biscuits, puddings, pies, and sauces for Jewish Passover to fulfill the religious requirement that no flour be used in their preparation.

The first large-scale production of dehydrated potatoes began in 1942, when the potato processor John Richard "Jack" Simplot, already the nation's largest shipper of fresh potatoes, won a government contract to supply dried potatoes to the armed forces during World War II. By 1945, he had supplied about 33 million pounds of dehydrated potatoes to the military. French's Instant Potato was introduced by the R. T. French Company in 1946. Frozen potatoes came later, at first simply precut for french fries. By 1962, frozen, dehydrated, and canned potatoes accounted for 25 percent of U.S. potato consumption. By 1966, per capita consumption had risen to 44.2 pounds a year, up from 6.3 in 1950.

The Potato Chip

In 1853, that quintessentially American product, the potato chip, was invented serendipitously. Annoyed when Commodore Cornelius Vanderbilt (the railroad magnate) sent back his fried potatoes because they were too thick, George Crum, the chef at the Half Moon Hotel in Saratoga Springs, New York, thought he would teach him a lesson. Crum sliced some potatoes paper thin, deep-fried, and salted them. Vanderbilt loved them.

Potato chips began to be commercially manufactured as early as 1915, when Van de Kamp's Saratoga Chips, a storefront operation, opened in Los Angeles. In 1921, Wise Potato Chips were introduced in Berwick, Pennsylvania, by Earl Wise, a local grocer. Finding himself overstocked with old potatoes, Wise peeled and sliced them, and then followed his mother's recipe for making chips and put them in brown paper bags. In the early 1930s, he switched to the more practical cellophane bags. By 1942, Wise had opened a 40,000-square-foot plant.

In 1969, General Mills introduced Chipos, and Procter & Gamble brought out Pringles, both made from cooked, mashed, dehydrated potatoes that were then reconstituted into dough and cut to uniform size (rather than made from sliced potatoes fried in oil). These new "chips" were packaged in break-proof, oxygen-free containers to prolong their shelf life. The Potato Chip Institute sued to prevent the products from being sold as chips, but lost. The Food and Drug Administration ruled that chip products not made from fresh potatoes must be labeled "potato chips made from dried potatoes." By the time the ruling was to have taken effect in 1977, fabricated chips had already lost their appeal.

In 2001 in the United States, nearly $2.7 billion worth of bags were sold, according to Information Resources, a market research firm. A survey by the Department of Agriculture found that the average American snacker eats 33 pounds of chips per year.

Issues in the Twenty-first Century

To combat the threat of pest damage and fungicide-resistant blight, scientists have experimented with breeding blight-resistant germ plasm and biotechnology that involves placing a gene into an already existing variety to improve its resistance to disease, insects, or stress. For example, resistance to the Colorado potato beetle has been placed into the Russet Burbank potato by inserting genetic material from the bacterium *Bacillus thuringiensis* into the plant. This causes a protein to be manufactured that disrupts the digestive system of the beetle when it feeds on the leaves. The Shepody variety of potato has been improved to make it more resistant to viruses, one of the major causes of declassification of seed in the potato industry. The gene prevents replication of a virus after it has been introduced by aphids. Monsanto's NewLeaf potato is the first genetically engineered potato, designed to protect it from the Colorado potato beetle. It was approved in the United States in 1995, and subsequently in Canada, Mexico, and Japan. The NewLeaf Plus, the next generation from Monsanto, resists both the beetle and the potato leaf roll virus.

Biotechnology is not without controversy. Some critics point out that it gives corporations like Monsanto a profitable monopoly on the seed since it must be replanted each year. Others are concerned that the long-term effects are not known. A major concern is that there is no requirement to label genetically engineered products. There are even larger questions about whether biotechnology offers a reasonable way to feed the world's hungry; most experts maintain that the amount of food is sufficient and it is distribution that is the crucial issue.

Genetic Diversity

Many observers believe that the solutions to the agricultural issues lie in plant breeding and preserving the genetic diversity of potatoes. By planting a larger number of varieties, farmers guard against damage of blight or insects that might destroy one variety but not another. There is some reason to believe that, if Ireland had planted its fields with a diverse crop, the toll from the famine would not have happened.

Today, only half a dozen varieties constitute the vast majority of the nation's crop. In the final decade of the twentieth century, there was a resurgence of interest in potato varietals and their preservation and development. Of particular interest are heirloom potatoes, those developed over centuries for which the seeds have been handed down from one generation to the next.

To protect the genetic diversity of the potato, and to make it available for systematic manipulation, the International Potato Center in Lima, Peru, under the auspices of the Consultative Group on International Agricultural Research, has collected about 5,000 samples of native cultivars from nine countries in Latin America, representing about 3,500 genotypes. Every aspect of the potato and its place in the environment and human society is studied. Recent projects have included an effort to develop tropical varieties for Africa, Hong Kong, and the Philippines.

See also **Biotechnology; Central Europe; Columbian Exchange; Distribution of Food; Fast Food; French Fries; Genetic Engineering; Germany, Austria, Switzerland; Hamburger; Ireland; Scurvy; Snacks; Sweet Potato; Vegetables.**

BIBLIOGRAPHY

Bernand, Carmen. *The Incas: People of the Sun,* translated from the French by Paul G. Bahn. New York: Abrams, 1994.

Clarkson, Leslie A., and E. Margaret Crawford. *Feast and Famine: Food and Nutrition in Ireland, 1500–1920.* Oxford: Oxford University Press, 2001.

Correll, Donovan Stewart. *The Potato and Its Wild Relatives;* Renner, Tex.: Texas Research Foundation, 1962. Section on Tuberarium of the Genus *Solanum.*

Crosby, Alfred W. *The Columbian Exchange: Biological and Cultural Consequences of 1492.* Westport, Conn.: Greenwood, 1972.

Davies, Nigel. *The Incas.* Niwot, Colo.: University Press of Colorado, 1995.

Dean, Bill B. *Managing the Potato Production System.* New York: Food Products, 1994.

Dodge, Bertha S. *Potatoes and People.* Boston: Little, Brown, 1970.

Finamore, Roy. *One Potato, Two Potato.* New York: Houghton Mifflin, 2001.

Hawkes, John Gregory. *The Potato: Evolution, Biodiversity, and Genetic Resources.* Washington, D.C.: Smithsonian Institution, 1990.

Kissane, Noel. *The Irish Famine: A Documentary History.* Dublin: National Library of Ireland, 1995.

Lisinska, Grazyna. *Potato Science and Technology.* London and New York: Elsevier, 1989.

McNeill, William H. "How the Potato Changed the World's History." *Social Research* 66, no. 1 (Spring 1999): 67–83.

Meltzer, Milton. *The Amazing Potato: A Story in Which the Incas, Conquistadors, Marie Antoinette, Thomas Jefferson, Wars, Famines, Immigrants, and French Fries All Play a Part.* New York: HarperCollins, 1992.

Salaman, Redcliffe N. *The History and Social Influence of the Potato.* Rev. ed., edited by J. G. Hawkes. Cambridge: Cambridge University Press, 1985.

Sokolov, Raymond. "The Peripatetic Potato." *Natural History* 99, no. 3 (1990): 86–91.

Terry, Theodore Brainard. *The ABC of Potato Culture.* 2d ed., rev. Medina, Ohio: A. I. Root, 1911.

Viola, Herman J., and Carolyn Margolis, eds. *Seeds of Change: A Quincentennial Commemoration.* Washington, D.C.: Smithsonian Institution, 1991.

Weatherford, Jack M. *Indian Givers: How the Indians of the Americas Transformed the World.* New York: Fawcett Columbine, 1988.

Zuckerman, Larry. *The Potato: How the Humble Spud Rescued the Western World.* Boston and London: Faber & Faber, 1998.

Linda Murray Berzok

POTLATCH. "Potlatch" is anglicized from the Nootka (Nuu-chah-nulth) word *patshatl,* which means "giving." The Nootka term came to be used in Chinook jargon, a Northwest Coast of North America lingua franca, in the 1860s with the beginning of Euro-Canadian settlement. Potlatch denotes a ceremonial feast and gift giving held in winter, usually marking a rite of passage, such as a funeral, wedding, or elevation to a noble title. Late nineteenth-century Kwakiutl (Kwakwaka'wakw) potlatches described by Franz Boas displayed oratorical boasting and overwhelming quantities of gifts and food, asserting the aristocratic host's wealth and high rank. Neighboring noble houses vied for even more generous potlatches, escalating the competition for status. For example, in 1803, a Nuu-chah-nulth chief gave away 200 muskets, 200 yards of cloth, 100 mirrors, and gunpowder; in 1921, a Kwakiutl chief gave away thousands of dollars worth of purchased goods, including gas-powered boats and boat engines, sewing machines, pool tables, and gramophones. Canada's 1884 Potlatch Law (rescinded in 1951) outlawed these feasts but succeeded only in repressing them, not in exterminating them.

From the point of view of Northwest Coast people, potlatches sustained the reciprocal relationships among noble houses, including their dependent families. In the northern part of the region "houses" or lineages (often called clans in English) were grouped into pairs, such as Ravens and Wolves, that were expected to alternate as host and guest, thus ensuring a balanced series of feasts and gifts. In the central part of the region guests came from neighboring villages, and marriages between villages gave persons noble titles in both parents' lineages,

116

creating a more fluid social order. Throughout the Northwest Coast the emphasis was on visibly recognizing rank by the seating order and the amount of the gift. Anthropologists suggest that late nineteenth-century potlatch extravagances reflected an increase in consumer goods from Euro-Canadian towns and traders that also brought severe decreases in Indian populations from disease epidemics and political instability.

The Danish ethnologist Kaj Birket-Smith, who worked in Southeast Alaska, hypothesized that ancient contacts around the Pacific spread the institution of "feasts of merit" and publicly marked an investiture in higher status. He pointed out similarities between potlatches and such feasts in Southeast Asia and Polynesia. Through trade across the interior mountains, the potlatch may be related to "giveaways," held at powwows among Plains First Nations, that stem from the requirement that leaders must be generous. Giveaways are customary at memorial feasts and on such occasions as a child dancing in a powwow for the first time or a person earning a college degree. In both Northwest Coast potlatches and Plains giveaways, new blankets are the standard gift. Especially honored guests are given embroidered robes or star-pattern quilts, lesser acquaintances smaller items, and visitors who have earned the friendship of the hosts may be recognized with gifts of embroidered jackets or other clothing emblematic of the hosts' style. All guest share in feasting, the gift of food. Potlatches and giveaways share the ethos that giving a gift honors both giver and recipient.

Food at a potlatch must be abundant. Ideally the guests should not be able to finish what is served but should take the surplus home. "Traditional" foods are served, though what is traditional has been modified over time as introduced foods have become standard in the community. Salmon, dried for winter use, has been the prized and usually abundant principal food. Other dishes include berries, seaweed, and meat of mountain goats, elk, moose, bears, seals, small mammals, and halibut, all smoked or dried. Traditionally eulachon, a smelt abundant in early spring, were caught in large quantities and processed into a rich oil used as a sauce at every meal. Potlatches were noteworthy for the lavish outpouring of eulachon "grease," to the point of ladling gallons into hearth fires until the flames roared to the roof. A description of Tsimshian feasts notes, "The foods that were most valued were those that were scarce, available only seasonally, required intensive labor (and entailed organization by a person of rank), 'imported items' (including European foods as they became available), grease, and anything preserved in grease" (Halpin and Seguin, 1990, p. 271).

Dances, both ritual and social, are integral to Northwest Coast potlatches. Elaborately costumed and ingeniously propped dance-dramas, especially those involving a wild cannibal who roared and apparently bit people before the wise elders tamed him, horrified Christian missionaries. When the Canadian government banned potlatches, First Nations protested that the dancing at potlatches was simply "winter amusement," like Euro-Canadians' balls and theatrical entertainments. Furthermore they protested that potlatch feasting provided quality food to their elderly and poor. Most government agents looked away when potlatches were held, recognizing that the First Nations had banned killing slaves and burning houses in favor of conspicuous consumption. By the early twenty-first century potlatches in many Northwest Coast First Nations communities celebrated appropriate occasions without the earlier ostentatious rivalry. Accommodating contemporary employment, twenty-first century potlatches last for a weekend rather than for weeks and are held in community halls. Core practices and foods continue, fostering First Nation identities through public displays of ancient titles, heritage arts, and regional foods.

See also **American Indians.**

BIBLIOGRAPHY

Birket-Smith, Kaj. *Studies in Circumpacific Culture Relations.* Vol. 1: *Potlatch and Feasts of Merit.* Copenhagen: Munksgaard, 1967.

Codere, Helen. "The Amiable Side of Kwakiutl Life: The Potlatch and the Play Potlatch." *American Anthropologist* 28 (1956): 334–351.

Drucker, Philip, and Robert F. Heizer. *To Make My Name Good: A Reexamination of the Southern Kwakiutl Potlatch.* Berkeley: University of California Press, 1967.

Halpin, Marjorie M., and Margaret Seguin. "Tsimshian Peoples: Southern Tsimshian, Coast Tsimshian, Nishga, and Gitksan." In *Handbook of North American Indians,* edited by William C. Sturtevant et al. Volume 7: *Northwest Coast,* edited by Wayne Suttles, pp. 267–284. Washington, D.C.: Smithsonian Institution, 1990.

Simeone, William E. *Rifles, Blankets, and Beads: Identity, History, and the Northern Athapaskan Potlatch.* Norman: University of Oklahoma Press, 1995.

Alice Kehoe

POULTRY. Poultry are domesticated birds raised for food: chickens (including Cornish game hens and poussins), turkeys, ducks, and geese, plus minor species such as squab (young pigeons) and ostrich. Game birds such as quail and Canada geese can also be prepared in much the same ways, although their meat is tougher than that of birds raised on farms. Chickens and ducks are among the most widely distributed food animals in the world and are part of nearly every major cuisine.

Poultry were the last major group of food animals to be domesticated. Humans likely began by raiding the nests of wild birds to steal their eggs, just as nonhuman predators do. Eventually the birds themselves were caught and kept in confinement, or, when thoroughly domesticated, allowed to range around the farmstead or village to find their own food.

PEKING DUCK

An elaborate method of preparing, cooking, and serving duck was developed by cooks in China's capital city and is known as Peking Duck. The cook will inflate the duck's carcass by blowing air between the skin and the body, blanch the duck in hot water, coat it with malt sugar, and pour boiling water into the cavity. The bird is then hung in a special vertical oven and roasted over a wood fire, preferably using the wood of fruit trees. The result is a bird with a taut golden skin and moist tender meat. Often only the skin is eaten at table, and the meat is sent back to the kitchen to make into other dishes. Or the meat can be cut into thin slices and rolled up in thin pancakes. Elaborate ceremony often attends the slicing of the bird.

Chicken, in particular, has had an increase in popularity in the United States in recent years; according to the U.S. Department of Agriculture, sales climbed from 39 pounds per capita in 1970 to 77 pounds per capita in 2000. The surge in chicken's popularity is attributable partly to its low fat content as compared to beef. Three-and-one-half ounces (one hundred grams) of roasted chicken breast with its skin removed has only 120 calories and 1.5 grams of fat, while the same serving of cooked sirloin steak has 170 calories and 6 grams of fat.

Also propelling chicken toward the center of the nation's plate is its versatility and convenience. Chicken is convenient to prepare and less likely to be ruined by overcooking than the competition. Chicken has become a kitchen favorite for cooks who are both pressed for time and somewhat inexpert at cooking.

Cost is also a major factor in the rise of poultry's popularity. In constant dollars, the wholesale price of a whole chicken dropped 50 percent from 1978 to 2000, while the price of skinless, boneless breast dropped 70 percent.

In contrast to chicken and turkey, duck, goose, squab, and other minor species are expensive and are served mainly on special occasions in the home or in high-end restaurants or restaurants specializing in ethnic cuisine. Peking duck is a mainstay of Chinese cookery, for example.

Chickens

The most prevalent of the domestic fowl worldwide, the chicken is descended from the Red Jungle Fowl, a bird whose native territory stretches from east India to Malaysia. It is not clear exactly where the bird was first domesticated, but it has been raised by humans throughout its range since ancient times. Polynesian explorers took the chicken across the Pacific as far as Hawaii. Chickens were exported from India to China as early as the fourteenth century B.C.E. and spread to the Near East via the trade routes, and thence to Egypt, Greece, and Rome. Domestic fowl are not mentioned in the Old Testament, but the ancient Egyptians kept fowl and developed large ovens capable of incubating thousands of eggs, indicating that they had large flocks. The Greeks had chickens by the fourth century B.C.E., and many a family in ancient Athens kept a hen to produce eggs. The Romans took up the bird and carried it throughout their empire and beyond; the Germanic and Celtic tribes north of the Roman frontier had chickens before the Christian era. Both Greeks and Romans gave chickens a prominent place in their cuisine and recorded elaborate recipes for cooking them. Poultry shops were so well-established in England by the fourteenth century that their proprietors prevailed upon the authorities to prohibit country people from bringing poultry into the city to sell in the streets in competition with them. Medieval and Renaissance banquets featured chickens along with other fowl: Pope Pius V (d. 1572) gave a banquet that included chicken pie—two chickens to each pie—and spit-roasted quails and pigeons.

A hen in her prime will produce from 100 to 250 eggs per year, a remarkable output for the size of the animal, so the chicken has always been kept more for its egg-laying capability than for its value as meat. Since a hen will lay eggs whether they are fertilized or not, and a single male bird can adequately service a large number of females to ensure reproduction of the flock, most of the male birds are superfluous to an egg-laying flock. They are, however, easily castrated when young, and the resulting birds, known as capons, grow fat and tender. From ancient times until quite recently, capons were the best choice for roasting, with older hens sent to the stew pot. Young male birds, known as cockerels, although smaller than capons, were also available for roasting or other forms of cooking.

Production of birds for their meat has traditionally been a sideline to the egg-laying business. Not until the 1920s were large flocks of chickens raised specifically for their meat, which are called broilers or fryers (the terms are interchangeable). Today about 97 percent of the chicken found in a U.S. supermarket consists of broiler-fryers, with most of the balance consisting of stewing hens (older birds) and a few Cornish game hens. The capon, once a prized dish, is now rare.

The chicken has a short generation span, since the female reaches sexual maturity in about a year. Consequently, the development of different breeds can occur rapidly. Poultry keepers bred birds for desirable characteristics, which traditionally included prolific egg production. The Leghorn is the longtime champion of layers. More recent breeding has emphasized abundant

FIGURE 1

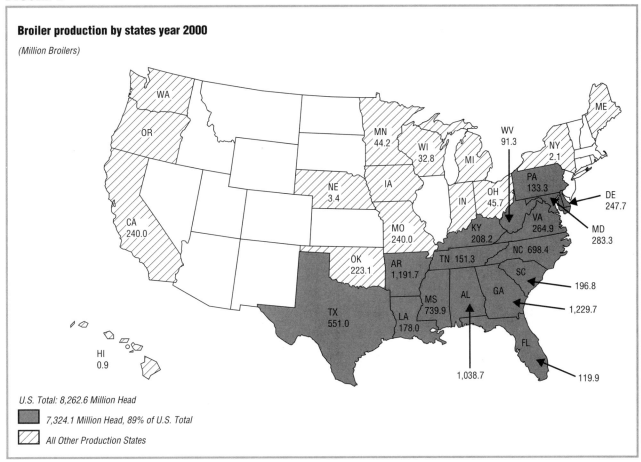

Broiler production by states year 2000

(Million Broilers)

WA

OR

MN 44.2

WI 32.8

MI

ME

NY 2.1

WV 91.3

PA 133.3

DE 247.7

NE 3.4

IA

OH 45.7

IN

VA 264.9

MD 283.3

CA 240.0

MO 240.0

KY 208.2

NC 698.4

OK 223.1

AR 1,191.7

TN 151.3

SC 196.8

TX 551.0

MS 739.9

AL

GA 1,229.7

LA 178.0

FL 119.9

HI 0.9

1,038.7

U.S. Total: 8,262.6 Million Head

7,324.1 Million Head, 89% of U.S. Total

All Other Production States

meat production. Specialized breeding companies cross different breeds to attain the right mix of desirable characteristics.

Turkeys

The wild turkey (*Meleagris gallopavo*) is native to the Americas and inhabited northern Mexico and what is now the eastern United States when Columbus arrived. All of the domesticated turkey breeds descended from this hardy bird, which was domesticated by the Aztecs and other Native Americans. Montezuma himself dined on turkeys, ducks, quails, and other birds, according to a Spanish eyewitness. Early in the sixteenth century, the Spaniards took the bird home, where it began a rapid spread through Europe. People were accustomed to eating large birds—swans and peacocks had graced noble tables since ancient times—and the turkey provided an abundance of meat. In this respect, the turkey was very different from the chicken, since the turkey has been prized chiefly as a source of meat rather than eggs.

The name given the bird by Europeans reflected mass confusion about its origins and perhaps a similarity to another bird, the guinea fowl, which had recently been reintroduced into Europe after an absence dating to the fall of Rome. The guinea fowl was called an "India chicken" by many, apparently because it reached Europe from the east and was thought to have originated in India, although in fact it is from Africa. When the turkey showed up, it looked like a bigger version of the same bird and was dubbed the "bird of India" in nearly every language: "coq d'Inde," cock of India (later *dinde*), in French, "indianische Henn" in German, and variations on the same in other European languages. Eventually the turkey took sole possession of the "India" name and the guinea fowl was renamed after the Gulf of Guinea in west Africa. The only major exception was England, where the bird was called the "turkie cock" (or hen). This may reflect a belief that the bird came from Turkey, since many exotic products, edible and otherwise, had passed through the eastern Mediterranean on their way to western Europe. A more specific theory is based on the fact that English trade to that region was dominated by the Company of Merchant Adventurers Trading to the Levant, popularly known as the Turkey Merchants. Officers of the company reportedly stopped in Spain and picked up some of the birds on their way back to England, and the bird was named after them.

TABLE 1

Production of poultry meat and eggs, leading nations, 2001

In metric tons

Nation	Poultry meat	Chicken meat	Turkey meat	Duck meat	Goose meat	Primary eggs*
WORLD	70,358,813	60,258,645	5,085,889	2,936,687	2,058,969	56,594,078
United States	16,747,600	14,210,000	2,485,000	52,600	Neg.	5,080,000
China	13,286,850	9,401,030	1,990	2,009,980	1,873,850	23,354,520
European Union (15)	8,852,099	6,632,852	1,860,960	343,112	14,075	5,303,441
Brazil	6,394,850	6,222,700	165,000	7,150	Neg.	1,582,700
France	2,077,100	1,100,000	735,000	235,000	6,000	1,047,000
Mexico	1,945,038	1,897,546	27,242	20,250	Neg.	1,881,645
United Kingdom	1,561,700	1,257,500	256,000	45,800	2,400	644,751
Thailand	1,366,500	1,260,000	Neg.	105,000	1,500	810,000
Japan	1,180,012	1,180,000	12	Neg.	Neg.	2,526,000
Italy	1,156,000	816,000	340,000	Neg.	Neg.	707,000
Canada	1,092,300	943,000	141,000	7,400	900	362,800
Spain	1,034,000	1,012,000	22,000	Neg.	Neg.	563,700

*Table eggs of all species, including chicken, duck, and goose.

Neg.: Negligible production

The production of poultry meat and eggs constitutes a large industry worldwide. Nearly every country produces chicken meat and eggs; turkey is popular largely in Europe, North America, and Brazil; duck meat production is found largely in China and Europe; and goose meat is largely Chinese. The United States is the leading producer of poultry products, particularly chicken (14 million metric tons produced in 2001) and turkey (two and a half million tons), in both of which it leads the world. China is second in chicken production with about nine million tons, and dominates the world in goose meat and duck meat production. In fact, 91 percent of all the goose meat produced in the world, and 68 percent of the duck meat, is produced in China.

Other major countries in chicken meat production include Brazil, France, Mexico, the United Kingdom, and Thailand, while the leading turkey producers after the United States are France, Germany, Italy, the United Kingdom, Brazil, Canada, and Hungary. France and Thailand are the leading duck meat producers after China, followed by Viet Nam, the United States, Malaysia, the Republic of Korea and the United Kingdom. The goose meat industry is very small outside China, with the biggest countries being Hungary, Egypt, Madagascar, and Poland.

China produces more than 23 million metric tons of eggs, or more than forty percent of the world's supply, which includes goose and duck eggs as well as chicken eggs. The United States is next with five million tons, followed by Japan with two-and-a-half million tons and Russia, India, and Mexico with about two million tons each. Japan is the leading consumer of eggs on a per capita basis, with China in second place. In the United States, per capita egg consumption has dropped in recent years, largely in response to concern about the cholesterol content of eggs.

SOURCE: United Nations Food and Agriculture Organization Statistical Databases; U.S. Department of Agriculture Foreign Agriculture Service.

Whatever the reason for its odd name, the turkey seems to have taken Europe by storm. It arrived in Spain around 1524, was mentioned by Rabelais in 1548, and was served at a royal wedding feast in France in 1570. In England, the bird was established even sooner, being mentioned in the sumptuary laws of 1541. Turkeys could be raised by peasants and by the turn of the seventeenth century were being husbanded throughout Europe. The Pilgrims recognized the local turkeys when they settled in Massachusetts and learned that the Native American name for the bird was amazingly close to their own. The natives called it a "furkee."

Ducks and Geese

Ducks and geese are distributed worldwide and were trapped and domesticated by humans in antiquity for both eggs—especially duck eggs—and their meat. Ducks were probably domesticated before geese, and both were certainly domesticated in most of the world long before chickens. Ducks were raised in China two thousand years B.C.E. The Incas of Peru kept ducks, and the Spanish brought home what became known as the Muscovy duck (continuing the tradition of naming birds for lands far from their own).

Ancient peoples in Europe and Asia tamed mallard ducks, which were the foundation of most breeds of domestic duck, such as the Pekin (or Peking) of China, the Aylesbury of England, and the Rouen of France. Most ducks consumed are slaughtered at a young age and thus termed ducklings; mature ducks are tough and are used mainly in processed products.

In the United States, modern production began when a clipper ship brought three Pekin ducks and a drake from China in 1873. All of today's Pekins are direct descendents of these pioneers. Strains of the Pekin were used to produce the Long Island Duckling, which became the most desirable breed. Production of these birds in the United States eventually moved largely to the Midwest, but only birds actually raised on Long Island for at least seven days and processed there may be labeled "Long Island Duckling." Birds that are otherwise essentially identical, but raised in Indiana or other states, are labeled "White Pekin Duckling."

Regardless of where it is raised, the White Pekin is a tender and juicy bird and is the most popular choice for the table. The Muscovy has a stronger flavor than the White Pekin. The White Pekin and the Muscovy have been crossed to produce the Moulard, which is raised mainly for the sake of its liver for *foie gras*. (*Foie gras* is a delicacy consisting of duck or goose liver that has been enlarged to many times its normal size by excessive feeding of the birds. In Europe, where goose is preferred, the bird is "crammed" with feed through a funnel put down its throat. [See photo on page 127.] In the United States, ducks are encouraged to overeat but are not crammed.) The familiar, green-headed Mallard is both raised on farms and hunted in its wild state. It is smaller and tougher than the White Pekin and tends to be quite greasy. Ducks are considered "red-meat" birds, and the breast meat when fully cooked will be pink, which in chickens and turkeys would be a sign of undercooking.

Geese have been domesticated since ancient times in many parts of the world, but the Greylag goose of Europe, which is still found in the wild, is the ancestor of most of the domesticated breeds in existence today. The all-white Emden and the all-gray Toulouse are the two most popular breeds in the United States today; many African and White Chinese are also raised. The Chinese goose is descended from the swan goose of Asia rather than from the Greylag.

Goose production is a small industry in the United States, representing only two-tenths of 1 percent of poultry production, and might virtually disappear were it not for the fact that geese also produce down, which is much in demand for its insulating properties. Down is used in ski jackets, comforters, pillows, sleeping bags, and other cold-weather gear.

Both Greeks and Egyptians kept geese and crammed them with grain to fatten them and enlarge their livers. The Romans apparently adopted geese from the Gauls; Pliny wrote of flocks of geese being driven to Rome from what is now Picardy. The goose was the most prized domestic fowl in Europe for hundreds of years after the heyday of Rome, and the Gauls and their descendents, the French, became the acknowledged masters of the art of creating *foie gras* by force-feeding the birds. The goose became a holiday bird in much of Europe and is considered an alternative to the turkey in the United States. The meat is all dark and has the consistency of roast beef when properly cooked.

Squab

Squabs are young pigeons that have never flown, usually slaughtered at four weeks old. If a squab is slaughtered much after four weeks or after it has begun to fly, the muscles will have hardened and the meat will not be as tender as when the bird was in the nest.

Pigeons are widely spread around the world and have been raised for their meat since antiquity. Pigeon keeping was widespread in ancient Egypt; by the first century B.C.E., dovecotes with one thousand nesting places were common. The design of the dovecotes, using earthen jars as nesting places, survived into modern times. Twenty thousand pigeons were served as a feast given by an Assyrian king in the ninth century B.C.E. Pigeons were popular in ancient Greece, Rome, and during medieval times.

Squab is considered a delicacy around the world today. In the United States, squabs are available mainly through specialty food shops or in ethnic and high-end restaurants.

Production and Life Cycle

All the major forms of poultry are produced in similar although not identical systems. The model in the United States is the highly efficient broiler chicken sector, which produces the vast majority of the poultry products consumed by Americans. Turkeys and other forms of poultry are raised under conditions that are similar to those of chickens.

The chicken industry was localized, with entrepreneurs buying surplus chickens from egg operations and backyard flocks for the city markets, until early in the twentieth century, when more organized, long-distance shipping of live poultry commenced. New York and other cities received rail cars of live birds that were distributed to butcher shops or slaughtered and dressed at processing plants for distribution. In the 1920s, farmers discovered that large flocks of chickens could be raised specifically for their value as meat. These farmers needed regular batches of chicks, supplied by large-scale hatcheries, and feed, which they got from commercial feed mills. The hatcheries and mills typically had better access to capital and marketing channels than farmers, and they formed the core of the all-purpose companies that dominate the business today. In the mature industry, a single company typically handles the entire life cycle of a bird, including hatching, feed formulation and production, processing, and marketing. This business model is known as "vertical integration," and there are about fifty such companies in existence in the United States (as of 2001). Breeding of the animals for desirable characteristics is handled by either the integrated company itself or by one of a several specialized breeding companies. Once hatched, the birds are typically taken to privately owned farms, where they are raised to market weight by farmers working under contract to the company.

Production of turkeys is somewhat less centralized than the chicken business, although the turkey industry has been moving in the direction of greater integration. The duck industry is very similar to the chicken model. Most of the squabs in the country are processed and marketed by a cooperative. The goose industry is small and integrated.

Life Cycle

The life cycle of a broiler begins with a specialized breeding flocks, where roosters and hens produce fertile eggs that are collected every day and taken to a hatchery, where thousands of eggs are kept in each incubator under carefully controlled conditions of temperature and

Guinea fowl from a detail of a mosaic floor in the house of Eustolios, Kourion, Cyprus, circa 300 C.E. PHOTO WILLIAM WOYS WEAVER.

humidity. The chicks hatch out on the twenty-first day and are taken to the farm where they will be raised for six to seven weeks. The typical growout facility is a barn-like, one-story structure about forty feet wide and four hundred feet long, which contains about twenty thousand birds. The trend in recent years has been to even larger houses holding up to thirty-three thousand birds. The birds have the run of the building, as cages are not used in broiler production.

Feed is made largely from corn and soybeans with the addition of animal fats for energy, animal protein, amino acids, minerals, and vitamins. Chickens eat almost continuously, pausing to digest each meal before going back to the feeder for more.

When the birds reach market weight of about five and a half pounds, they are collected and taken to the processing plant where they are stunned, killed, defeathered, eviscerated, inspected for wholesomeness by personnel of the U.S. Department of Agriculture, chilled, and either packed for shipment or, more typically, sent to another plant to be cut into pieces, deboned, and processed into a wide variety of products. The finished weight of a whole bird is usually about three and a half pounds, with birds destined for the fast-food market being typically smaller than birds being sold at retail.

Marketing

Poultry companies market their products through supermarket chains, restaurant chains, and independent distributors. The process is highly organized and efficient. Unlike red meat, in which an in-store butcher handles

the final cutup, poultry is usually packaged at the plant and shipped to stores ready for sale, with computerized scales at the processing plant weighing the packages and applying the price set by the retailer.

Approximately half the chicken consumed in the country is sold through supermarkets and other retail outlets while half is sold through fast food and other restaurants, cafeteria, and other food service outlets.

Poultry Health

Chickens and other poultry are subject to a wide variety of diseases whether they are kept indoors or not. They are normally vaccinated against certain diseases while they are still in the egg and then again as chicks. One of the most prevalent problems is colonization of the chicken's gut by microscopic, parasitic animals known as coccidia. Most producers, even "organic" or "free range" ones, add chemical compounds to the chicken feed to control coccidia. Poultry flocks are monitored by the farmer and by company representatives for signs of other diseases, which, if they begin to claim more than a certain number of victims, will be treated with antibiotics administered through the feed or water. Some antibiotics, when used in the feed at low levels over a period of time, also result in measurable increases in the bird's weight. The exact mechanism for this "growth promotion" is not known, but poultry experts believe that the antibiotics eliminate organisms in the chicken's gut that would otherwise compete for nutrition. The practice of using antibiotics for purposes other than treating disease is somewhat controversial, and some experts in human health object to it on the grounds that low-level use of antibiotics, some of which are also used in human medicine, can promote the rise of bacteria that are resistant to the drugs. These can be passed to humans either on food products or by entering the environment and could create infections in humans that could be resistant to antibiotic therapy. The National Research Council has found that "there is a link" between the use of antibiotics in food animals and antibiotic resistant infections in humans and recommended further study.

Hormones

Federal law prohibits producers of chickens and other poultry from giving artificial or added hormones to their animals. Producers are allowed to give only those pharmaceuticals or additives that are on the Food and Drug Administration's approved list, and there are no hormones on the list for chickens or other poultry raised for their meat. It would be impractical to give hormones anyway, since they cannot be given in the feed and have to be repeatedly injected as the animal grows, virtually an impossibility in a flock of twenty thousand birds or more.

Alternative Production and Processing Systems

Some have criticized the mainstream industry for its style of mass production, confinement of the animals, and use of antibiotics. The "free range" style of production is intended to address these concerns. In a "free range" system, the birds have access to a pen outside the growout house. Some producers provide a pen as large as the growout house itself, while others provide a much smaller fenced area. The pen gives the chickens the opportunity for exercise, sunlight, and fresh air. Chickens will not necessarily take advantage of the opportunity, however, if the food and water are located only inside the house. Many "free-range" birds thus do little actual ranging.

Since chickens will peck at anything in search of food, a small pen can be quickly denuded of vegetation. Some small-scale producers address this problem by confining the chickens in a covered, portable pen that is moved each day to a different plot of grass; this is called "pastured poultry." Few if any producers will actually turn chickens loose to fend for themselves, although some turkey producers will do so in an area in which forage is available, such as an orchard, in which the turkeys can feed on fallen fruit. "Free range" chickens generally cost considerably more than standard chickens, and they represent only a small portion of total production—probably less than 1 percent.

"Organic" production is another attempt to differentiate the product from those of large-scale producers. The term was used for years on a wide variety of food products without a consistent nationwide definition. The U.S. Department of Agriculture promulgated regulations in 2000, to take effect in 2002, which prohibit the use of the term "organic" unless the production and processing of the product is consistent with the regulation. A qualifying product can carry a "USDA Organic" label. Poultry labeled "organic" must be raised on feed made from organically grown grain that cannot contain animal by-products; cannot be given antibiotics or anti-parasiticals; and must be given access to the outdoors, among other requirements.

Kosher Processing and Specialized Labeling

"Free range" and "gourmet" chickens are processed in a manner that is essentially identical to standard chickens and are killed by high-speed mechanical devices. Kosher chickens, however, are slaughtered manually by rabbis, not by machine, and are soaked in salt water to draw out the remaining blood to meet the requirements of Jewish law. As a result, Kosher chickens are generally more expensive than standard birds.

In France, the national ministry of agriculture and fisheries operates a program called the "Label Rouge," or "Red Label," which is intended to recognize higher-quality products. Products bearing the red label must employ more traditional methods of production than more standardized products. France offers the red label to qualifying producers of chicken, guinea fowl, turkey, capons, duck, and geese, as well as other animals.

Symbolism

Poultry has long figured in human symbolism and legend. Geese supposedly saved ancient Rome from a surprise attack in the fourth century B.C.E. by cackling loudly when the invaders tried to sneak up on the Capitol. Pigeons were offered as sacrifices by the Hebrews of the Bible. The sixteenth-century Flemish artist Pieter Bruegel the Elder—a great fan of fantastic-looking animals—used the turkey as a symbol of envy in his series of paintings on the seven deadly sins. But the domestic fowl most often used as a symbol is the ordinary chicken.

In ancient Greece, chickens were offered in sacrifice to the god of medicine, Aesculapius, to protect against disease, to thank the god for recovery, or to prepare for imminent death. Aristotle conducted the first known systematic study of embryology by opening hen's eggs at each day of incubation. Less scientific ancients used the birds for magic, sorcery, and divination.

The chicken has always been one of the most familiar domesticated animals since almost any family could afford to keep a hen, and chickens were kept in the city as well as the countryside. Humans therefore had abundant opportunity to observe the chicken at close range. They could hardly help but notice the insatiable sexual appetite of the male bird, which can copulate up to thirty times a day in his prime. The traditional term for the rooster—the cock—was given in slang to the male sexual organ, and the upright, strutting posture of the male, and his domineering behavior toward the females, seemed to symbolize traditional male supremacy.

The rooster's habit of crowing loudly at dawn has made it for centuries the symbol of awakening. The most famous example is the prediction by Jesus of Nazareth that his chief apostle, Simon Peter, would deny knowing him three times before the cock crowed twice. When Peter heard the crowing and realized the prediction had come true, "he went out and wept bitterly." The rooster's role as a herald has continued to this day. A rooster figures prominently in a tapestry hanging in the United Nations headquarters in New York that commemorates the Chernobyl nuclear power plant disaster, presumably as a symbol of the world's need to awaken to the danger of uncontrolled technology.

Food Safety

Chickens, turkeys, and other types of poultry are produced on farms and processed in clean but not sterile plants, so their meat can carry microorganisms that potentially harmful to humans. For example, approximately 10 percent of raw chickens carry *Salmonella*, which can cause illness and even death in humans. Improved processing technology and stricter government regulations have improved the situation considerably in recent years, but consumers should always handle raw meat and poultry with care.

To ensure that poultry products are safe to eat and to avoid contaminating other foods with the bacteria that may be carried on raw poultry, the cook should keep four basic points in mind:

1. **Clean:** Keep working surfaces clean. Wash cutting boards after cutting raw poultry and before using them for other foods, such as vegetables. Wash the hands before touching other foods. Wash utensils in hot, soapy water.

2. **Cook:** Cook foods to the recommend temperature. Proper cooking deactivates bacteria and renders the food safe to eat.

3. **Chill:** Bacteria such as *Salmonella* do not grow well at cold temperatures, so prompt refrigeration at 40°F or below will help control the growth of bacteria on raw foods. After poultry is cooked, in order to control the growth of molds, yeasts, and spoilage organisms, it should not be left out at room temperature for more than two hours. *Listeria* is an exception to the rule, however, since it will grow at refrigerator temperatures. *Listeria* is sometimes found on products that were cooked at the plant, such as hot dogs and lunch meat. Vulnerable individuals—chiefly pregnant women, small children, the elderly, and immuno-compromised people—should reheat such foods until they are steaming hot before consuming them to eliminate the risk of *Listeria* contamination.

4. **Avoid cross-contamination:** Poultry juice can contain millions of bacterial cells. Prevent poultry juice from dripping onto other foods by overwrapping the packages if necessary in plastic wrap.

Selection

Poultry comes in a dizzying array of forms ranging from a package of chicken wings weighing two ounces each to whole turkey weighing twenty pounds or more. The consumer can buy products based on specific meal plans or based on cost consideration, for example, stocking up on boneless chicken breast when it is on sale. In determining quantities, keep in mind that the edible yield from boneless products is far greater than from bone-in; in fact, while boneless chicken costs considerably more than bone-in, the price difference almost disappears when the bones are excluded. On the other hand, much of the weight of ducks and geese consists of fat that will drain off when the bird is cooked. As a rule of thumb, four ounces of skinless, boneless chicken will serve one adult, while a whole chicken will serve approximately one person per pound. For a whole turkey, figure on one pound per person. A whole duck or goose, which has less meat, bigger bones, and more fat than turkey, will serve three persons, or four if there are enough side dishes, while one squab is an individual serving.

Classes of Chickens

Chickens are classified primarily by the size, weight, and age of the bird when processed. Chickens are produced to meet specific requirements of the customer, which can be a retail outlet, fast food chain, or institutional buyer, among others. The weights given here are "ready to cook," that is, eviscerated or "dressed."

Broiler—Chicken raised for meat products; of either sex; usually six to seven weeks old; often labeled "tender young chicken."

Poussin—Less than twenty-four days of age and about one pound or less.

Cornish Game Hen—Less than thirty days of age and about two pounds.

Fast-food Size Broiler—two pounds four ounces to three pounds two ounces, (mostly two pounds six ounces to two pounds fourteen ounces), usually cut-up, without necks and giblets, may have tail and leaf fat removed, and less than forty-two days of age.

3's and Up—three to four and three-quarter pounds, usually with neck and giblets for retail grocery; whole, cut-up, parts, and forty to forty-five days of age. Typical retail size.

Broiler Roaster—five to six pounds, hens usually fifty-five days of age.

Broilers for Deboning—five to six pounds, males usually forty-seven to fifty-six days of age. Deboned for nuggets, patties, strips, and similar boneless products.

Heavy Young Broiler Roaster—six to eight pounds, sold fresh or frozen through retail grocery, both whole and parts, less than ten weeks of age. Typical "roaster."

Capon—Castrated male broilers weighing seven to nine pounds, and about fourteen to fifteen weeks of age. Considered to be very flavorful.

Stewing Hen or Heavy Hen—breeder hens that are no longer commercially productive for laying hatching eggs, usually five to five-and-one-half pounds, about fifteen months of age, used for cooked, diced, or pulled meat. Sometimes sold whole at retail for use in homemade soup. While tougher than younger birds, the stewing hen has developed a deeper flavor.

Turkey

The male bird, or "tom," tends to be bigger than the hen, although there is no noticeable difference between the two in the quality of their meat. Almost all the turkeys in the supermarket are young turkeys, slaughtered at about fourteen weeks of age for hens and eighteen weeks for toms.

Turkey breast is even leaner than chicken and is very widely used in sandwich meat and other delicatessen-type products, as well as sold fresh in the meat case. Turkey dark meat is also widely used in hot dogs, bologna, and other processed meat products. Whole birds are available year round but are especially popular as the main course at Thanksgiving and Christmas. Turkey parts are increasingly popular both year round and at the holidays: whole or half breasts, tenderloins, and legs.

Storage

Poultry is generally sold with a "sell-by" date on the package, which, for chicken, is typically ten to fourteen days from processing. Poultry should be cooked or frozen within a few days of purchase to maintain its quality. Fresh poultry should be kept in its original wrapping and stored in the coldest part of the refrigerator. If the package is leaking fluid, it should be overwrapped with plastic or aluminum foil.

Frozen poultry will keep six months or more in the freezer set at 0°F. Frozen whole birds or parts can be defrosted in the refrigerator, which can take twenty-four hours or more, or in cold water, which should be kept running or changed every 30 minutes. A whole turkey should be defrosted in water because defrosting in the refrigerator takes too long. Whole chickens and all types of parts can be defrosted in the microwave, but a very low power setting should be used and caution exercised to ensure that the product does not begin to cook during the defrosting.

A Note on Doneness.

Poultry parts reach the desired state of doneness at different internal temperatures. Boneless chicken breast cooked on an outdoor grill can be cooked without reaching 150°F (even though 160°F is usually given as the minimum temperature that breast meat should reach). Yet drumsticks, because of their dark meat and higher fat content, will not be done until they register 180°F. Bones conduct heat, so when taking the temperature of a part or a whole bird, do not let the thermometer rest against a bone.

Generally, boneless white meat such as chicken or turkey breast should be cooked to 160°F, bone-in parts usually need to reach 170°F; and dark meat should hit 180°F.

Poultry will usually be safe to eat before it is done. Any food is safe to eat at 160°F because bacteria are destroyed at temperatures over 140°F. One exception: it is impossible to make spoiled food safe to eat by heating it because spoilage organisms create toxins; even if the bacteria are destroyed, the toxins remain. Spoiled food cannot be fixed by cooking and must be discarded.

Methods of Preparation: Chicken

As befits its reputation as the most versatile of meats, chicken can be prepared in a host of different ways. Here are the principal methods of preparation and the chicken products most appropriate for them.

Roasting. A whole roast chicken is a magnificent sight, browned to perfection and rich in the promise of tender, juicy meat. Because of its small size relative, say, to a turkey, roasting a chicken takes only a couple of hours

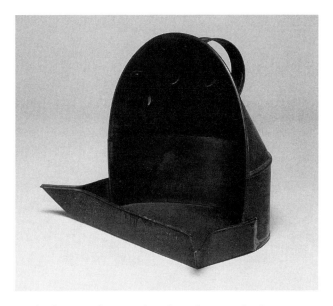

Tin bird roaster for open hearth cooking. England, ca. 1860. Small birds such as squab were suspended from hooks inside the bonnet. ROUGHWOOD COLLECTION. PHOTO CHEW & COMPANY.

and is perfect for a Sunday afternoon dinner. Be sure to remove the giblets (heart and liver) from the cavity if present and discard unless you intend to make gravy with them. The chicken may be stuffed with any type of bread-based stuffing, although this increases cooking time. Some experts recommend cooking the stuffing in a sauce on the stove. To ensure even cooking and present a tidy appearance in the finished product, it is best to truss the chicken, that is, to use kitchen string or other clean white string to ties its legs over the cavity and secure its wings to the body.

Preheat the oven to 325°F and place the chicken on a rack in a roasting pan or a deep baking dish. Use of the rack will keep the chicken from sitting in its own grease.

Roast for about an hour, basting occasionally with the pan juices. The chicken is done when the internal temperature reaches 180°F on a thermometer inserted deep into the thigh without touching bone. Let stand 20 minutes to allow the juices to settle before carving.

Baking. Roasting and baking are essentially the same thing, the difference merely being that a whole chicken is roasted while parts are baked. Any poultry part can be baked, but the method is most appropriate for legs, thigh, and drumsticks. Preheat the oven to 400°F, place the chicken part in a lightly oiled roasting pan or in a deep baking dish, and place in the oven for 40 to 45 minutes. Use of a rack will help keep dark meat parts from picking up too much melted fat; it is not necessary for breast meat.

Broiling. In broiling, meats are placed several inches under the heat. This works well for all chicken parts, but especially for boneless or bone-in breasts. Preheat the broiler and broil the breasts for approximately 15 minutes per side. Bone-in breasts are placed six to eight inches from the heat; boneless breast lie flat and can be placed closer. Cook the rib side of bone-in breasts, or the rough side of boneless breasts, first, and then finish with the skin side of skin-on breasts or the smooth side of skinless, boneless breasts.

Sauté. Boneless parts such as breast or thigh can be cooked in a pan on top of the stove in a little liquid, which can be chicken stock, wine, butter, olive oil, or some combination. The trick is to brown the chicken on both sides before reducing the heat to cook it through. Boneless breast cooked in butter and olive oil and seasoned with lemon and rosemary is a delicious dish. It can be made even more delicate by slicing the breast portion in two with the knife held parallel to the counter, resulting in two breast fillets. A thin piece of breast will cook in just a few minutes on each side.

Fried. Fried chicken is a mainstay of southern cooking, although Southerners clearly did not invent it; a cookbook published in England in the eighteenth century included a recipe for fried chicken that could be used today. Fried chicken has fallen somewhat into disfavor, along with many other types of fried foods, due to its fat content and reputation for clogging arteries. However, the best fried chicken is not greasy and does not have exceptionally high added fat. The key seems to be to keep the frying oil very hot so that the skin of the chicken is sealed quickly, thus keeping the liquid fat out of the meat. Oil tends to lose its frying ability with use, so either start with plenty or keep heating up new batches of oil. Drumsticks and wings are the parts traditionally considered most suited to frying, but breasts and thighs will do just as well.

Southern cooks often recommend soaking the raw chicken in buttermilk and refrigerating for several hours. Then let the excess milk drain off, dredge the chicken parts in seasoned flour, and dunk into hot oil in a deep pan or heavy skillet. Many a cook has found the skillet lid a handy shield against spattering grease. Keep the oil at about 350°F until all the parts are added, then reduce the temperature to around 320°F and cook 10 to 12 minutes per side or until the juices run clear. (Five minutes per side for boneless breast.) The chicken is done when it turns golden brown. Drain on paper towels to get rid of as much grease as possible.

When frying wings, split them at the joints and discard the outermost and least meaty part, which is known as the "flapper." The meaty first joint is known as the "drummette." Wing portions make excellent appetizers.

Soups and stews. The stewpot was traditionally the destination of older and tougher birds that needed long, slow cooking to make them tender enough to eat. Old, tough birds are hard to find these days, although the chicken companies will sometimes market played-out hens in the dead of winter precisely for this purpose. Newer soup recipes, such as those based on Asian dishes, are light and delicate and perfectly suited to the young and tender birds that dominate the market.

Grilled. Chicken has ridden the wave of popularity of both outdoor and indoor grilling in recent years. Dark meat in particular, such as legs and thighs, stand up well to the intense heat of grilling because of its higher fat content and the presence of collagen, which melts and keeps the meat moist. Breasts should be marinated to keep them moist during grilling and will cook in no more than 15 minutes per side. Boneless breast will cook in about 6 minutes per side. Strong favors such as vinegar and soy sauce can be used with chicken bound for the grill. The grill itself should be brushed or rubbed with oil to keep white meat from sticking to it. If barbecue sauce is used, save it until you have turned the chicken skin side up.

Turkey

Norman Rockwell knew his business when he chose a roast turkey as the symbol of abundance in his painting called *Freedom from Want*. There is nothing more American than the Thanksgiving turkey.

Roasting. Roasting a turkey can be a trying experience, especially one that tips the scales in excess of twenty pounds. It is hard to get the dark meat cooked through without overcooking the breast. One approach is to eliminate the dark meat entirely and buy a turkey breast (or two if the whole family is coming). The all-white meat breast is easily cooked according to the package directions, usually in a 350°F oven. If there are dark meat fans in the crowd or if cooking anything less than a whole bird seems somehow un-American, then satisfactory results can be obtained by roasting the bird at 325°F for 10 to 12 minutes per pound, shielding the breast with aluminum foil for the first hour, and continuing to cook until a meat thermometer registers 180°F when inserted into the deepest part of the thigh without touching bone. If the bird is stuffed, the stuffing must reach 160°F to ensure safety. Basting the breast with melted butter can help it stay moist. Another trick is to lay raw strips of bacon over the breast, letting the bacon release its fat to the breast as it crisps. Many turkey processors provide "self-basting" birds, which are injected at the plant with oil to maintain their moistness. If you do not have a thermometer, the pop-up thermometers inserted at the plant are generally reliable. Or you can wiggle the legs and wings to see if they move freely, or insert a knife or fork into he bird to see if the juices run clear. Let the bird sit for 20 minutes after coming out of the over before trying to carve it. And give yourself plenty of time—an eighteen-pound bird that goes into the oven after breakfast will not be ready until early to mid-afternoon.

Turkeys are sold both fresh and frozen. It is a matter of opinion whether one tastes better than the other.

One thing is certain, however—a fresh turkey will not have to be defrosted, which can be a difficult and time-consuming process. Just keep a fresh bird in the refrigerator until you are preheating the oven, when you can take it out, rinse it off, remove the neck and giblets from the cavity, and pat it dry. A frozen turkey should be placed in a clean sink or large pan and defrosted under cold running water. It takes several hours to defrost a large, solidly frozen turkey.

Grill. Turkey thighs and drumsticks can be grilled just like chicken parts. So can turkey cutlets, which are slices of skinless, boneless turkey breast. Turkey breast is the lowest in fat of all the cuts of poultry, however, so breast meat should be marinated or brushed with oil before being subjected to the heat of grilling.

Sauté. Cutlets sliced very thinly are called turkey scaloppini, and they lend themselves very well to being sautéed in a pan and finished with a flavorful sauce.

Other turkey products. Turkey is a major factor in the delicatessen counter, with turkey rolls providing lunch meat and the dark meat used very extensively in frankfurters and other already-cooked products. Since breast meat is tends to be quite dry, processors form breast meat into rolls and inject them with a saline solutions to keep the meat moist and easily carved. Ground turkey is a popular substitute for ground beef in many recipes due to its lower fat content, and turkey is turning up in sausages and other products as processors continue to try to get away from relying on holiday sales to carry them through the year.

Squab

Squab can be roasted, broiled or grilled. The bird weighs only about one pound and will cook quickly whichever method is used. The key is to cook the bird only until the breast meat is medium-rare, with the juices till running pink and the meat still juicy and pinkish. Broiled squab should be turned once and will cook in 15 to 20 minutes. If grilling squab, start with the skin side down to melt the fat under the skin. If grilling is desired, it is best to buy boneless squab and also discard the wings so that the bird will lie flat on the grill. Boneless squab can also be sauteed in a pan.

Cornish Game Hens and Poussins

Cornish game hens and poussins are simply small chickens. They are generally intended to be served whole, or, at most, split in two (although these birds, like other chickens, are marketed in larger sizes then they used to be). They can be roasted at 350°F for 25 to 40 minutes, depending on size. They can also be broiled with the backbone removed so the split bird lies flat on the broiling pan.

Duck

Duck is all dark meat; the breast tastes more like turkey drumstick than it does like chicken breast. Smoked duck,

Poultry farmer in Alsace force-feeding a goose in order to fatten the liver for paté. This feeding method is not legal in the United States. Photo circa 1900. ROUGHWOOD COLLECTION.

when sliced, is easily mistaken for roast beef. The challenge in cooking duck is that the bird has quite a lot of fat and it is difficult to end up with meat that is moist but not greasy from the melting fat and skin that is crisp and flavorful instead of rubbery. High heat would help get rid of the fat while crisping the skin, but the fat melts quickly and begins to smoke. The cook can find the kitchen full of smoke and can even have a fire in the oven if the rendering process is not controlled.

Two methods are generally successful in rendering the fat while crisping the skin. The first involves medium heat while the second involves steam as well as dry heat.

Roasting. Prick the skin with the tip of a paring knife, being careful to pierce the fat layer without breaking the skin. This will help drain off the fat during cooking. Roast the bird in a 350°F oven, breast side up on a rack in a roasting pan, for one hour and fifteen minutes. Drain the fat out of the roasting pan and roast for 40 additional minutes at 350°F and then 15 minutes at 500°F to crisp the skin.

Twice-cooked. Chinese cooks use a different method to get rid of the fat and produce a crisp skin. With skin pricked as in the basic roasting directions, the duck is placed on a rack in a roasting pan with half an inch of boiling water in the bottom. The pan is covered and placed over heat to keep the water simmering for about an hour, until the skin pulls away from the wing joints, exposing the meat. The bird is then cooled to room temperature, brushed with soy sauce or other seasonings, and roasted in a 400°F oven for 30 to 40 minutes, or until crisp. For an even crisper skin, rub the raw bird with salt and allow it to dry in the air in the refrigerator for several hours before cooking.

Broiled. Duck parts can also be broiled, although the fat released by the parts can smoke and even catch fire. Remove as much visible fat as possible before placing the parts in a broiling pan four inches from the preheated broiler. Broil 30 to 45 minutes or until golden brown. Drain off fat as it accumulates or sprinkle the melted fat with salt to reduce the chance of fire.

Goose

Goose is typically purchased and cooked whole. The meat is even darker than duck and, when cooked, resembles fully cooked roast beef. The goose is also even fattier than the duck, since it has an even thicker layer of fat under the skin. Dry heat works better than steam to render the fat and produce a crisp skin.

Prick the skin all over with the point of a paring knife, being careful not to pierce the skin. Roast for one and a half hours, breast side down, in a 325°F oven. Remove from the oven and pour off the grease. Return to the oven and roast for another one and a quarter to one and a half hours until the skin has puffed up around the breastbone. Turn the oven up to 400°F, remove the goose from the oven and transfer, with rack, to a clean pan and roast for another 15 minutes until the skin is crisp. Let stand 30 minutes before carving.

Ostrich and Emu

Ostrich and emu are birds originally from southern Africa and Australia, respectively. The ostrich is the largest bird species and can reach eight feet in height. The emu is the second biggest bird species and tops out around six feet. Ostriches were formerly raised for their feathers, which were greatly prized for use in women's hats. When long feathers went out of fashion, the industry collapsed. It has revived in recent years, however, because of an interest in ostrich meat, which has very little fat or cholesterol. Both birds have deep red meat which reminds many people of venison. The meat can be sauteed or grilled

and should be cooked only to medium-rare, since overcooking leaves the meat tough and dry.

See also **China: Beijing (Peking) Cuisine; Seabirds and Their Eggs.**

BIBLIOGRAPHY

Beilenson, Evelyn L., ed. *Early American Cooking: Recipes from America's Historic Sites.* White Plains, N.Y.: Peter Pauper Press, 1985.

Belk, Sarah. *Around the Southern Table.* New York: Simon & Schuster, 1991.

Boer, Nicholas. "Chefs Say Well-Fed Free-Range Chickens Are a Beautiful Thing." *The Contra Costa Times* (Contra Costa, Calif.), 23 May 2001.

Clifton, Claire, and Colin Spencer, eds. *The Faber Book of Foods.* London: Faber and Faber, 1993.

Corriher, Shirley O. *CookWise: The Hows and Whys of Successful Cooking.* New York: William Morrow and Co., 1997.

Davidson, Alan. *The Oxford Companion to Food.* New York: Oxford University Press, 1999.

Editors of *Cook's Illustrated. The Cook's Illustrated Complete Book of Poultry.* New York: Clarkson N. Potter, Inc., 1999.

Flandrin, Jean-Louis, Massimo Montanari, and Albert Sonnenfeld, eds. *Food: A Culinary History from Antiquity to the Present.* New York: Penguin Books, 1999.

Grizmek, Bernhard, ed. *Grizmek's Animal Life Encyclopedia.* New York: Van Nostrand Reinhold Co., 1972.

National Research Council. *Use of Drugs in Food Animals: Benefits and Risks.* Washington, D.C.: National Academy of Sciences Press, 1999.

North, Mack O., and Donald D. Bell. *Commercial Chicken Production Manual.* New York: Van Nostrand Reinhold, 1990.

North American Meat Processors Association. *The Poultry Buyers Guide.* Reston, Va.: North American Meat Processors Association, 1999.

Rombauer, Irma S., Marion Rombauer Becker, and Ethan Becker. *The Joy of Cooking.* New York: Simon & Schuster, 1997.

Smith, Page, and Charles Daniel. *The Chicken Book.* Athens, Ga.: The University of Georgia Press, 2000.

Tannahill, Reay. *Food in History.* New York: Crown Publishers, 1989.

Toussaint-Samat, Maguelonne. *History of Food.* Cambridge, Mass.: Blackwell Publishers, 1992.

Richard L. Lobb

POVERTY. About 31.1 million, or 11.3 percent, of Americans were poor in 2000. "Poor," as used here, means living below the poverty threshold, a dollar amount determined by the United States Bureau of the Census by taking a family's total income before taxes and then adjusting for the size of the family and the number of related children under eighteen years of age. In 2000, the poverty threshold ranged from $8,259 for an individual sixty-five and older to $33,291 for a family of nine or more individuals, including eight or more related children under eighteen. The poverty threshold for a family of two adults and two related children was $17,463. Individuals sixty-five and older, blacks and Hispanics, people in families with no workers, households headed by women, and people living inside central cities suffered disproportionately higher rates of poverty compared with other Americans.

The federal poverty threshold originated in the 1950s and is based today on the cost of the Thrifty Food Plan, a minimal-cost food plan determined to be nutritionally adequate according to national dietary guidelines, its cost multiplied by a factor of three (based on the assumption that nutritionally adequate food will cost one-third of a family's income) to account for other living expenses. Although it is updated annually according to the Consumer Price Index for inflation, a chief criticism of the poverty threshold is that food expenses have accounted for less than 15 percent of average income since 1965 (10.2 percent in 2000), making the multiplier too small, while other living expenses (such as housing, health care, transportation, and child care) have increased dramatically, especially for the poor.

Quantitative descriptions of the food and nutrient intakes of poor Americans can be found in analyses of national surveys that collect dietary and sociodemographic data from representative samples of the U.S. population. Analysis of the 1994–1996 Continuing Survey of Food Intakes by Individuals (CSFII) showed that poor Americans, defined as adults aged twenty years and older with incomes below 131 percent of the poverty threshold, tended to consume fewer servings of grains, fruits, vegetables, and dairy foods, but more servings of meats and meat alternates and more added sugars, compared with adults with higher incomes. Fewer servings of grains, fruits, vegetables, and dairy foods, and lower energy and nutrient intakes were found for men and women with less than a high-school education, a proxy measure for poverty, compared with men and women who had completed high school and beyond.

Analyses of a number of national surveys conducted between 1977 and 1996 show that dietary intakes of low-income adults have changed over time. For example, overall dietary quality improved among low-income white and Hispanic women, primarily due to reductions in total and saturated-fat and cholesterol intakes. However, fruit and vegetable intakes remained below the recommended amounts, as did those of key nutrients such as calcium, iron, and folic acid.

Poverty, Food Insufficiency, Food Insecurity, and Hunger

Poverty is inextricably linked with food insufficiency (not having enough to eat some or all of the time), food insecurity (uncertainty about or inability to acquire nutritionally adequate foods in socially acceptable ways), and hunger (the physical consequence of not having enough

to eat). According to data from the Third National Health and Nutrition Examination Survey (NHANES III), food insufficiency affected 4.1 percent of U.S. households, or between 9 and 12 million individuals. Data from the September 2000 Current Population Survey Food Security Supplement showed the prevalence of food insecurity to be 10.5 percent, and the prevalence of hunger to be 3.1 percent, affecting 11 million and 3.3 million Americans, respectively. Numerous studies of national survey data have shown lower intakes of several nutrients among men, women, and children who experience food insufficiency or food insecurity. Analysis of food intakes and serum nutrients of adults from food-insufficient families has also shown lower intakes of fruits, vegetables, and dairy products, and lower concentrations of serum albumin, serum carotenoids, and serum vitamins A and E. Additional analyses of food-insufficient adults and children reveal a higher prevalence of overweight and obesity, poor health status, and iron deficiency.

Results from qualitative analyses of dietary data, in the form of ethnographic research studies, complement findings from quantitative studies and confirm differences in food choices between poor and nonpoor Americans. Poor Americans tend to consume more starches, fats, and sugars but less of foods associated with good health, like fruits and vegetables, high-fiber grains, and low-fat dairy items. Although specific food choices may differ by ethnicity or geographic location, commonalities in eating patterns exist among poor Americans. Food intakes can vary quite dramatically in the course of a month, with greater quantities and more varied foods purchased immediately after a pay period or allotment of food assistance (such as food stamps) and very limited quantities, of little variety, purchased as funds run out. Also, food intakes are not equal within households. A common occurrence is for the wife or mother of the family to reduce her intake in order to feed her children. Communal dining may also be impossible when income limits available cookware or dining facilities, or sporadic work schedules keep all members of a family from being together at one time. Feelings of deprivation, often rooted in childhood, may lead to buying nonnutritious foods (such as soda and snack foods) that are also attractive because inexpensive. Although studies show that, in theory, consuming a minimal-cost diet in accordance with the latest dietary guidelines is possible, poor Americans are more likely to purchase foods from small, nearby stores that charge an average of 10 percent more than large supermarkets farther from home.

Food Assistance in the United States

Many poor Americans are eligible for federal food-assistance programs like the Food Stamp Program, the National School Lunch and School Breakfast Program, and the Special Supplemental Nutrition Program for Women, Infants, and Children (WIC). In addition to or as a substitute for government assistance, many poor

Americans also receive charitable assistance from food pantries and soup kitchens. In 2000, 50.4 percent of Americans identified as food-insecure received assistance from one of the three federal food-assistance programs, 16.7 percent received food from a food pantry, and 2.5 percent had family members who ate at a soup kitchen. Although participation in these programs and services may reduce food insecurity, the dietary quality of participants' food may not be better than that of nonparticipants. Given societal pressures to join the dominant culture and eat the most advertised, least expensive, most accessible foods—healthful or not—the challenge is how to improve the diets of all Americans, especially the poor.

See also **Class, Social; Cost of Food; Food Pantries; Food Riots; Food Stamps; Homelessness; Nutrition Transition: Worldwide Diet Change; Population and Demographics; Rationing; Sociology; Soup Kitchens; WIC (Women, Infants, and Children's) Program.**

BIBLIOGRAPHY

Alaimo, K., R. R. Briefel, E. A. Frongillo, and C. M. Olson. "Food Insufficiency Exists in the United States: Results from the Third National Health and Nutrition Examination Survey (NHANES III)." *American Journal of Public Health* 88 (1998): 419–426.

Andrews, M., L. S. Kantor, M. Lino, and D. Ripplinger. "Using USDA's Thrifty Food Plan to Assess Food Availability and Affordability." *Food Review* 24 (2001): 45–53.

Center for Nutrition Policy and Promotion. *The Thrifty Food Plan, 1999.* CNPP-7A. Available at http://www.usda.gov/cnpp/FoodPlans/TFP99/Index.htm.

Dalaker J. "Poverty in the United States: 2000." U.S. Census Bureau, *Current Population Reports*, Series P60-214. Washington, D.C.: U.S. Government Printing Office, September 2001.

Dixon, L. B., M. A. Winkleby, and K. L. Radimer. "Dietary Intakes and Serum Nutrients Differ between Adults from Food-Insufficient and Food-Sufficient Families: Third National Health and Nutrition Examination Survey, 1988–1994." *Journal of Nutrition* 131 (2001): 1232–1246.

Fitchen, J. M. "Hunger, Malnutrition, and Poverty in the Contemporary United States: Some Observations on Their Social and Cultural Context." *Journal of Food and Foodways* 2 (1988): 309–333.

Kaufman, P. R., J. M. MacDonald, S. M. Lutz, and D. M. Smallwood. "Do the Poor Pay More for Food? Item Selection and Price Differences Affect Low-Income Household Food Costs." Washington, D.C.: U.S. Government Printing Office, November 1997.

Kumanyika, S., and S. M. Krebs-Smith. "Preventive Nutrition Issues in Ethnic and Socioeconomic Groups in the United States." In *Primary and Secondary Preventive Nutrition*, edited by A. Bendich and R. J. Deckelbaum. Totowa, N.J.: Humana Press, 2001.

Nord, M., K. Nader, L. Tiehen, M. Andrews, G. Bickel, and S. Carlson. *Household Food Security in the United States, 2000.* Washington, D.C.: U.S. Government Printing Office, September 2000.

Sharpe, D. L., and M. Abdel-Ghany. "Identifying the Poor and Their Consumption Patterns." *Family Economics and Nutrition Review* 12 (1999): 15–25.

Siega-Riz, A. M., and B. M. Popkin. "Dietary Trends among Low Socioeconomic Status Women of Childbearing Age in the United States from 1977 to 1996: A Comparison among Ethnic Groups." *Journal of the American Medical Women's Association* 56 (2001): 44–48.

United States Department of Agriculture, Economic Research Service. *Food Consumption per Capita Data System.* Available at http://www.ers.usda.gov/data/foodconsumption/datasystem.asp.

L. Beth Dixon

PRE-COLUMBIAN AMERICAS. *See* Inca Empire; Mexico and Central America, Pre-Columbian.

PREHISTORIC SOCIETIES.

This entry includes two subentries:
Stone Age Nutrition: The Original Human Diet
Food Producers

STONE AGE NUTRITION: THE ORIGINAL HUMAN DIET

Aside from casual interest, there is a reason to appreciate the nutrition that fueled nearly all of human evolution. An increasing number of investigators believe the dietary patterns of our ancestors may constitute a guide to proper nutrition in the present. Early twenty-first-century dietary recommendations run a broad gamut, from the ultra-low-fat Pritikin program, most recently championed by Dean Ornish, to the 30:30:40 (protein:fat:carbohydrate) Zone diet of Barry Sears, to the low-carb, high-fat-and-protein Atkins diet. These popular authors are not the only ones whose recommendations vary widely, however. Academic nutritionists writing in prestigious medical journals advocate a similarly broad range of nutritional regimens, from the low-fat East Asian eating pattern to the much more fat-liberal Mediterranean approach. These conflicting recommendations, especially when they originate in respected professional publications, tend to confuse and dismay health-conscious readers who frequently learn of dietary findings through simplistic and often sensationalized media accounts. Sometimes completely contradictory nutritional findings are announced just a few years apart. For example, beta-carotene appeared to reduce cancer risk in initial studies; then it seemed to increase risk in a later investigation. Dietary fiber was first thought to reduce colon cancer susceptibility, and then it was found to have no such effect. Sodium consumption has been linked to high blood pressure in many studies but not in numerous others. High-fat diets cause coronary heart disease, but consider the "French paradox": the French consume at least as much saturated fat as do Americans, but they have considerably fewer heart attacks and other manifestations of coronary artery disease.

In light of such inconsistencies, it is not surprising that dietary recommendations vary. A logical, straightforward, and understandable starting point from which to develop research protocols and upon which generally accepted recommendations may ultimately be based is highly desirable. The ancestral human diet might provide such a foundation. Even though the Stone Age occurred in the very distant past, eminent paleoanthropologists, geneticists, biologists, and evolutionary theorists believe that human genes have changed hardly at all in the interim. Although many refer to modern times as the "Space Age," genetically speaking, human beings are still Stone Agers. One can argue that the genetic determinants of our current biology were selected not for contemporary circumstances, but for the conditions of life as experienced in the remote past. There are two potential corollaries to this argument. First, that the afflictions of affluence (chronic degenerative diseases such as diabetes, many cancers, atherosclerosis [including coronary heart disease], hypertension, osteoporosis, and obesity) are prompted by dissonance between human genes and the lives of certain groups of people. Second, that the impact of these diseases, which are the major causes of illness and mortality in affluent nations, might be greatly reduced or, in some cases, eliminated altogether by reinstating essential features of the ancestral lifestyle, including relevant nutritional practices, into current existence.

Early humans, who appeared about 50,000 years ago, were hunter-gatherers (or foragers) and were similar in most respects to hunter-gatherer groups studied during the twentieth century. However, there were important differences between these groups. Modern hunter-gatherers have been increasingly restricted to infertile areas that are poorly suited to farming and where the availability of animals for hunting, especially large game, has been much reduced. Also, modern foragers generally have some contact with nearby agriculturists, which affects their culture to some extent. Hunter-gatherer groups that came under observation in the twentieth century were commonly used as models for the prehistoric and pre-agricultural peoples of 25,000 years ago. The modern hunter-gatherer groups were the best available surrogates for prehistoric peoples, but researchers also needed to consider the altered circumstances of otherwise similar people living many thousands of years apart.

Ancestral Foods: Plants

The vegetable foods available to prehistoric foragers grew naturally, without cultivation, and included nuts, leafy vegetables, beans, fruits, flowers, gums, fungi, stems, and other similar items. These had been primate staples for tens of millions of years, but at some point along the ho-

minid (human-like) evolutionary track, the digging stick came into use. This simple implement widened dietary breadth by providing access to roots, bulbs, and tubers, which were plentiful but previously inaccessible sources of food energy. The nutrient values of such foods vary naturally, but if one pools the several hundred representative vegetable foods that hunter-gatherers utilized during the twentieth century and then compared their averaged nutrient content with the mean values of vegetable foods commonly consumed in Western nations, several noteworthy differences emerge. For example, wild-plant foods provide less energy per unit weight. A 3.5-ounce (100 gram) portion of the fruits and vegetables that our ancestors ate would yield, on average, only about one-third the calories that 3.5 ounces of contemporary vegetable food provide. This is primarily because so much of our current plant-food intake is derived from high-energy cereal grains—rice, corn, wheat, and the like. Stone Age humans knew that grains were a potential food source. However, given the technology available to them, the work required to process wild cereals into digestible form was generally excessive compared with the work needed to gather and process other types of wild plants. Foragers generally viewed grains as emergency goods to be used during times of shortage. It was only "late" in the human career, perhaps thirty thousand years ago in Australia and between ten an fifteen thousand years ago elsewhere (for example, the Near East), that evidence of routine cereal-grain use became common.

Another difference between the vegetable foods of the hunter-gatherers and those of Western nations is illustrated as follows. The nutrient content of wild-plant foods is high, especially when one considers the ratio of nutrients to calories. While there is, of course, considerable individual variation among these foods, a mixed grocery bag of the fruits and vegetables available to ancestral humans would provide substantially more vitamins, minerals, and fiber than would a comparably representative collection of contemporary plant foods. In many cases, vitamins and some minerals are artificially added to current foods, making them "enriched." This enrichment process is less successful for adding fiber and is not yet feasible for phytochemicals, which are plant constituents that influence the body's metabolic reactions. Phytochemicals can be considered semi-vitamins, but their total number (at least dozens, perhaps hundreds) is unknown and their mode of action is poorly understood. However, the importance of phytochemicals for optimal health is becoming increasingly well established. Ancestral human biology became genetically adapted to the phytochemicals provided by fruits and vegetables over hundreds to thousands of millennia. The phytochemicals of modern-day cereal grains, in contrast, are relative newcomers to the human metabolism. It is perhaps for this reason that fruit and vegetable intake appears to reduce cancer susceptibility and consumption of cereal grain products has little or no such effect.

Lastly, the plant foods available to ancestral humans afforded a fairly balanced ratio of essential polyunsaturated fatty acids. Like essential amino acids, the body does not synthesize these fatty acids—humans must obtain them from their diet. Polyunsaturated fatty acids are necessary for cell membrane fabrication, especially in the brain, and they are also the basic molecules from which eicosanoids, a large class of important locally acting hormones, are made. Essential fatty acids are divided into two families: omega 6's and omega 3's. Both types are required in mammalian physiology, but they produce opposing biochemical effects, so roughly equal amounts in the diet are desirable. Their effects on blood clotting provide a good example. If there is too much omega 6 in a person's system, their blood clots too easily, which increases the likelihood of coronary thrombosis (heart attack). An overabundance of omega 3 in a person's system reduces blood clotting excessively and increases the risk of cerebral hemorrhage (one kind of stroke). Roughly equal dietary intake of each type of these polyunsaturated fatty acids avoids both undesirable consequences. Unfortunately, in recent decades the use of safflower, corn, sunflower, and cottonseed for spreads and cooking oils has distorted the ratio. These materials contain fifty to one hundred times more omega 6 than omega 3 and, overall, Americans now consume ten to fifteen times more omega 6's than omega 3's.

Ancestral Foods: Animals

The wild game that human ancestors ate differed in important ways from the commercial meats available in the twenty-first century. In the first place, modern commercial meat is fatter. Whether one compares the whole carcass or the most popular cuts (for example, flank, loin, shank, etc.), commercial meat has up to four times more fat than game. For example, 3.5 ounces of regular hamburger provides 268 kilocalories, whereas the same amount of venison yields 126 kilocalories. Even when all visible fat is removed from a T-bone steak, the resulting separable lean portion contains 30 percent more energy than game. These energy differences reflect the greater fat content of commercial meat.

Not only is there more total fat in commercial meat, but the chemical composition of the fat in this meat also varies from that in game animals. In general, fat from commercial meat has a higher proportion of saturated fatty acids (the kind that tend to raise serum cholesterol levels) than does the fat from game. Saturated fatty acids containing either fourteen or sixteen carbon atoms have a special propensity for raising serum cholesterol. Game fat typically has less than one-fifth the content of these substances when compared to an equal amount of fat from commercial meat. Another chemical difference between these two types of meat involves the essential polyunsaturated fatty acids discussed earlier. These fats are present in nearly equal amounts in wild-animal adipose tissue, as compared to the uneven ratios in most commercial meat. Grain feeding appears to be responsible for this difference: the essential fatty acid composition of animals whose feed is based on corn becomes skewed, as their systems contain a far greater amount of omega 6 than omega 3 fatty acids.

Other Considerations

Several categories of foods that are regularly consumed at present were uncommonly used or wholly unavailable for ancestral humans. These "new" foods confer some advantages, but, in several cases, there are important negatives as well.

Grains. Today cereal grains are "superfoods." This term is not a characterization of their nutrient properties, but rather it is recognition that in many parts of the world, members of the grain family may provide from one-third to two-thirds or more of the population's daily caloric intake. The consumption of rice in the Far East, corn in Mesoamerica, and sorghum in parts of central Africa are examples. Such a dependence on one or a few plant foods contrasts with the more broad-spectrum subsistence pattern of hunter-gatherers, who commonly utilize one hundred or more types of food plants during the year. With limited exceptions, which probably did not apply in the remote past, no one of these approaches the "superfood" status accorded cereals today.

It was mentioned earlier that ancestral humans used grains infrequently. Hand milling grains to render them digestible was such hard work that it was not desirable to use grains unless other foods were in short supply. The situation changed when pre-agricultural populations reached a point where a nomadic life was no longer feasible. This shift came about when several groups of people started to migrate towards the same areas. When people were required to settle more or less permanently in a given area, grain consumption became a viable option because other types of plant and animal food became increasingly difficult to obtain. It became apparent shortly that raising grains like wheat or barley could increase the total food energy available from a given geographical area. When people began to farm regularly, population growth accelerated to rates greatly exceeding those before the advent of agriculture. On the other hand, individual health seems to have deteriorated. People became shorter in stature, and skeletal evidence of nutritional stress and infection became more frequent. Average life expectancy also appears to have declined, so the adoption of agriculture may not have been the societal boon it is often considered. In fact, Pulitzer Prize winner Jared Diamond has called it "the worst mistake in the history of the human race" (*Discover* [May 1987]: 64–66).

Dairy foods. For most humans, dairy foods are important constituents of each day's diet, but for free-range non-human mammals, a mother's milk is the only "dairy product" ever consumed. After weaning, milk was not available for any primates, including humans, until the domestication of cows, goats, camels, and the like. However, dairy foods have been an important component of official nutritional recommendations, at least in Western nations, since the first of these foods were introduced. Nevertheless, human ancestors, including behaviorally modern humans during four-fifths of their existence, thrived and evolved without any dairy foods whatsoever after they ceased breast-feeding.

Alcohol. In the United States, alcohol provides from 3 to 5 percent of the average adult's daily caloric intake. It is not clear when the production of alcoholic beverages first developed, but most anthropologists doubt that wine, beer, mead, and especially distilled spirits were manufactured before agriculture. No hunter-gatherer groups studied in the twentieth century made such drinks.

Separated fats. The fats that ancestral human consumed were generally obtained as integral components of whole foods; both animal and vegetable fats came part and parcel with the other nutrients intrinsic to the original source. In contrast, separated fats are staples for contemporary humans. Olive oil, butter, margarine, vegetable oils, lard, and the like are all vital ingredients for today's cooks. Such separated fats enhance our cuisine, but because fat provides about nine calories per gram (versus about 4 calories per gram for protein and carbohydrate), the availability of fat in this form makes it possible to increase the energy density of our food in ways our ancestors could not.

Refined flour and sugar. Like separated fats, refined flours and sugars allow us to create foods with unnaturally high energy density. Essentially, they are nearly pure energy—empty calories with few or no associated vitamins, minerals, or fiber. Although there are essential amino acids and essential fatty acids (required building blocks our bodies need to make necessary structural elements and required hormones), there are no essential simple carbohydrates like those available from refined flour and sugar. Such carbohydrates are a convenient and efficient source of energy, but they provide little if any nutritional benefit over and above their caloric content. Fortified flours have additional nutrients that food manufacturers consider desirable. Our ancestors obtained their carbohydrate together with the nutrients that nature provided.

Processed and prepared foods. Humans are the only free-living creatures that consume foods whose natural origins are obscure. Individuals unfamiliar with our culture would be unable to identify the ultimate sources of bread, pasta, sausage, cheese, and similar items that have been staples for millennia. Less traditional artificially fabricated foods became immensely popular during the twentieth century, to the point that for some people these foods, often laced with gratuitous sodium, fat, and sugar, made up most of their daily intake. The list of ingredients on the wrapper of almost any prepared-food package provides one of the most telling commentaries on the differences between contemporary nutrition and that of pre-agricultural human ancestors.

Artificial constituents. Organic food proponents would quickly point out that there are still other important differences between the naturally occurring plants and animals of twenty thousand years ago and most of those available to today's grocery shopper. Pesticides, hormones, fertilizers, antibiotics, dyes, and other additives are widely used in contemporary food production but were not, of course, considerations in the remote past when humans ate exclusively "organic" food. The pros and cons of these modern innovations are debatable, but there is no question that such innovations are "unnatural," and that humans evolved for millions of years before encountering the adulterated foods that most of us eat at present.

Overall Dietary Patterns

There was no one universal pre-agricultural diet. Our ancestors ate foods that were available locally and focused on those that returned the most food energy for the least expenditure of physical energy—a general rule for all biological organisms. Two important factors affecting diet choices were latitude and rainfall. In the savanna-like environment of northeast Africa, which according to the "out of Africa" theory is thought to have been the epicenter of human evolution, both game and vegetable foods were plentiful. Gathering plant foods in such an environment was an integral aspect of the food quest for both males and females before human ancestors and those of chimpanzees diverged and for an uncertain length of time thereafter. At some point, most likely during the later stages of Australopithicine evolution, scavenging is thought to have become a significant component of hominid subsistence. It is not known whether this was an exclusively male function or whether females participated as well. Because potential competitors for animal remains included hyenas and similarly dangerous beasts, as well as the original predators, scavenging was a little less hazardous than hunting, the main difference being the degree of technological expertise required. Later, most likely for the past 500,000 years and almost certainly since the appearance of behaviorally modern humans about fifty thousand years ago, obtaining food probably resembled the pattern observed among modern foragers: a division of labor according to gender, with men hunting and women gathering.

Where large animals such as mammoths, red deer (similar to elk), horses, megamarsupials (some as large as rhinoceroses), and eland were relatively abundant, hunting them made sense in terms of energy expended. More food energy could be obtained from one such carcass than from many smaller animals, and the physical energy expended by the hunters in such a process is substantially less compared to hunting small animals. Where large animals had become scarce, a variety of sophisticated techniques, including trapping and net hunting, were used to increase the efficiency of obtaining small game. Weirs and nets were used along rivers where fish migrated seasonally (for example, salmon runs). Stone Agers sometimes lived year-round in such locations, abandoning a nomadic life, establishing relatively large communities, and developing an early form of social stratification with elites—as opposed to nomadic hunter-gatherers who were almost always egalitarian.

Gathering was not confined to plant foods: women often brought home shellfish, eggs, small mammals, frogs, turtles, and the like. This process could be physically demanding. Women occasionally walked several miles, dug through hard ground (with a digging stick) to obtain roots or tubers, then walked back to camp carrying twenty to thirty pounds of foodstuff.

The relative contributions of hunting and gathering to a forager economy have been the subject of debate. The respective importance of these tasks almost certainly varied according to season and was surely affected by latitude. In the mammoth steppe of central Siberia, which was surprisingly well populated during the late Paleolithic era of ten to thirty thousand years ago, abundant wild grasses supported great herds of large game, especially mammoths, so hunting flourished. However, edible plant food for humans was scarce. In this region, hunting must have greatly exceeded gathering as a means of acquiring subsistence.

On the other hand, in northeast Africa, both game animals and wild plant foods were plentiful, and in such areas hunting and gathering were of almost equal importance. Early studies of foraging groups inhabiting regions of this sort suggested that about two-thirds of food was obtained by gathering. However, later analyses suggested that hunting actually made a somewhat greater contribution than gathering. The newer interpretation fit well with "optimal foraging theory," an anthropological law that formalizes the common-sense observation that humans, like all other biological organisms, arrange their subsistence activities to maximize return relative to effort expended. When animals are plentiful and hunting techniques are well developed, as seems to have been the case for the past 100,000 years (and probably longer), the average returns from hunting exceed those from gathering. Nevertheless, gathering remained very important because even skillful hunters can experience unsuccessful periods of a sometimes of uncomfortable duration. The practical botanical knowledge of foragers is so great that the women's success rate in finding plant food in fruitful regions approached 100 percent; many times tsi-tsi beans, baobab fruit, water lily roots, and the like would have been our ancestors' only menu choices for dinner.

Macronutrient Ratios

Overall subsistence patterns in East Africa are of particular interest. If the "out of Africa" theory is correct, which seems increasingly likely, what was eaten routinely in this region affected genetic adaptation in the direct ancestors of all living humans, while what was consumed elsewhere, even as late as fifty or sixty thousand years ago, had little or no direct bearing on the contemporary human gene pool. The reconstructed nutritional patterns in this area, beginning perhaps 200,000 years ago, are quite useful to those interested in the original "natural" human diet.

With behavioral modernity came increasingly rapid cultural change, which has, to an ever-greater extent, outpaced genetic evolutionary adaptation. Because of this cultural change, subsequent dietary innovations, including the routine use of grains by everyone and of dairy foods by adults, as well as the Mediterranean, East Asian, and vegetarian approaches to healthy eating have emerged. However, these trends have appeared too recently to have had a marked effect on our genetic makeup. If there is a basic nutritional pattern to which humans are genetically adapted, the constituents provided by foods consumed in East Africa 100,000 years ago arguably define its nature.

During that time, energy intake would have been higher than at present—probably about three thousand kilocalories per day for males and perhaps 2,750 kilocalories for females. Because humans at that time lacked motorized equipment, draft animals, and the most simple machines, caloric expenditure at this level was obligatory. In fact, it is likely that up until the early twentieth century energy expenditure and intake requirements remained substantially above those typical at present.

About 55 percent of nutrients would have come from animal and fish sources, while about 45 percent, on average, would have been of vegetable origin. Total caloric intake was likely partitioned about 25–30 percent from protein, 30–35 percent from carbohydrates, and 40–45 percent from fat. These estimates differ from the contemporary American pattern and also from current orthodox recommendations:

Prehistoric societies

	East African hunter-gatherers*	Contemporary U.S.A.	Current recommendations
Protein	25-30%	15%	15%
Carbohydrate	30-35%	48%	55%
Fat	40-45%	34%	30%
Alcohol	–	3%	–

*Surrogates for our earliest truly human ancestors

The differences are striking and, at first glance, suggest that the Paleolithic diet was unhealthy. A little further analysis, however, is comforting for health-conscious paleoenthusiasts.

Fats

Our ancestors ate more fat than modern humans. Muscle meat from game animals is very lean, but Stone Agers ate everything edible, such as marrow, brain, organ meat, and fat deposits from the thoracic and abdominal cavities, not just muscle as we tend to consume today. Optimal foraging means using the whole carcass. Many different parts of farm animals, such as tripe, chitlins, tongue, sweetbreads, brain, gizzard, etc., were considered standard fare only a few generations ago, and in a few places they still are. However, in contrast to fat from today's cattle, sheep, and pigs, the carcass fat of wild animals has relatively little serum cholesterol-raising effect. Most game fat is of the cholesterol-neutral monounsaturated variety, a substantial proportion is polyunsaturated, and much less is the saturated, cholesterol-raising type. Also, ancestral foods contained little or none of the cholesterol-raising *trans* fatty acids that commercial hydrogenation adds to current diets. That the hunter-gatherer diets are heart-healthy is corroborated by the finding that the serum cholesterol levels of such people from around the world average below 130 mg/dl as opposed to a bit over 200 mg/dl for Americans. Although the available evidence is not ideal (for example, no coronary angiograms and few autopsies), coronary heart disease is virtually unknown among hunter-gatherers, as far clinical data can show. An additional factor that enhanced the heart-healthy nature of Paleolithic diets was the nearly equal proportions of omega 6 and omega 3 essential polyunsaturated fatty acids in those diets. The great preponderance of omega 6's in contemporary Western diets is believed to be a factor contributing to the cardiovascular disease epidemic in countries with such eating patterns.

Carbohydrates

Ancestral humans ate fewer carbohydrates than is typical for contemporary humans, the major difference being the near total absence of cereal grains from pre-agricultural diets. However, the amount of fruits and vegetables consumed in areas resembling east Africa substantially exceeded amounts consumed in any part of the world and was more than double the typical fruit-and-vegetable consumption in western and northern Europe. Contemporary carbohydrates comprise refined flours and simple sugars, which are quickly absorbed and capable of inducing rapid rises in pancreatic insulin secretion. Stone Agers loved honey, but its availability was usually limited and seasonal (as indicated by their relatively cavity-free dental remains). A large proportion of ancestral carbohydrates was in the complex form that had a less adverse effect on insulin secretion.

Protein

As far as nutritionists and exercise physiologists can ascertain, the levels of protein our ancestors consumed are not necessary for health, even for weight trainers and other high-performance athletes. On the other hand, earlier studies that attributed negative health effects to excessive dietary proteins now seem suspect. Initial reports suggested that high protein intake might cause renal failure, colon cancer, and/or elevated blood cholesterol levels. However, more recent investigations have reversed or at least significantly modified scientific opinion about their relationships. High-protein, low-carbohydrate diets have, in some cases, been shown to be beneficial. High-protein diets do aggravate kidney failure once it is established, but they do not appear to initiate the process. Autopsy studies of traditional Inuit (Eskimos) whose protein intake was extremely high did not reveal any extra incidences of kidney disease. It was once thought that high-protein diets were associated with colon cancer. There is a connection here, but this is primarily because Westerns diets that contain a lot of meat provide excess saturated fat along with protein, and it is the saturated fat, not the protein, which seems to foster the development of colonic neoplasms. Diets rich in meat were once thought to raise serum cholesterol levels, but here again, associated saturated fat is the culprit. High-protein diets that contain little saturated fat actually lower serum cholesterol levels, an investigative result that might have been predicted based on findings among hunter-gatherers studied during the last century.

Micronutrients

Americans and many others in affluent nations spend enormous amounts of money on vitamins (and, to a lesser extent, minerals) presumably in the hope that consuming such micronutrients will minimize the adverse effects of an otherwise unhealthy diet and lifestyle. Nutritionists usually decry this practice, arguing that micronutrient intake above and beyond recommended daily allowance (RDA) levels is unnecessary, and that a balanced diet provides all the vitamins and minerals one needs.

From a Paleolithic perspective, there is some virtue to both these views. Nutritionists follow Stone Age practice when they argue that it is better to obtain micronutrients from real foods rather than from capsules. However, ancestral micronutrient intake exceeded RDA levels in nearly every case (sodium and, in some areas, iodine were the exceptions). The greater total caloric intake necessitated by a physically vigorous lifestyle together with a micronutrient:energy ratio much higher for ancestral foods than for those commonly consumed at present means Stone Agers typically obtained from 1.5 to 5 times the RDA levels of vitamins and minerals each day. However, they did not obtain anything near the recommendations of megavitamin enthusiasts, which can be 10 to 100 times the RDA in some instances.

Words like lycopene, anthocyanin, lutein, sulforaphane, isothiocyanate, and indole have begun to appear regularly in popular articles on nutrition. These substances and many others with equally unfamiliar names are phytochemicals, which, as noted earlier, are vitamin-like molecules that affect our metabolism and biochemistry. Phytochemicals in fruits and vegetables seem much more vital to human health than those from cereal grains, presumably because our metabolism became adapted to the former over many millions of years as opposed to the few thousand years during which human biochemistry has routinely interacted with phytochemicals from cereals. There has been little research on the phytochemical content of uncultivated fruits and vegetables, but it is likely that the phytochemical load in such foods would have paralleled their high content of known vitamins and minerals. Based on this supposition, in addition to the fact that Stone Agers in most areas consumed abundant quantities of fresh fruits and vegetables, it is probable that ancestral phytochemical intake exceeded that of the present.

Only 10 percent of the sodium consumed in Western nations is intrinsic to the foods people eat. The remainder is added during processing, preparation, and at the table. For human ancestors, as for all other free-living terrestrial mammals, potassium intake exceeded sodium intake, a circumstance almost certainly relevant to blood-pressure regulation and to maintenance of cell-membrane electrical potential. After salt became commercially available, and especially after it became inexpensive, our diets have inverted the potassium–sodium relationship that characterized human and pre-human evolution, perhaps from the appearance of multi-cellular organisms over 500 million years ago.

Fiber

Since Denis P. Burkitt's research first drew public attention to the value of fiber in human diets, official recommendations for fiber intake have centered on about 0.07 ounces (20 grams) per day. However, our nearest non-human primate relatives, chimpanzees, consume about 7 ounces (200 grams) of fiber per day. The fiber intake of ancestral humans would have been strongly influenced by the proportion of fruits and vegetables in their subsistence base because dietary fiber comes exclusively from plant foods. Stone Agers living at high latitudes, where edible vegetation was scarce, would have consumed even less fiber than modern humans. However, in east Africa, where modern human metabolism evolved, Paleolithic fiber intake is estimated to have been between 1.77 and 3.53 ounces (between 50 and 100 grams) per day.

There are two main fiber types, both of which are necessary for optimal human physiological function. Most plant foods provide some of each, but the proportions vary. Whole wheat and brown (unpolished) rice contain predominantly insoluble fiber, which is good for intestinal tract function. Oats, corn, and most fruits and vegetables provide a high proportion of soluble fiber, which is valuable for regulating cholesterol absorption after meals. Modern, refined grain-centered diets generally have too little fiber, but, in addition, they have a disproportionate amount of insoluble fiber. Pre-agricultural diets featuring more fruits and vegetables than at present provided a better balanced insoluble-to-soluble fiber ratio.

Conclusion

The uncultivated plant foods and wild game that nourished ancestral humans and their pre-human predecessors were those to which our genetic makeup became adapted. Increasingly rapid cultural innovations during the past few thousand years have transformed our nutrition such that Cro-Magnons might not recognize many constituents of a typical meal. However, genetic evolution during the same period has been glacially slow; thus human beings' genetically determined biology remains adapted for the literally natural and organic foods of the remote past. This dissonance between human genes and human lives has critical implications for human health.

See also **Agriculture, Origins of; Anthropology and Food; Food Archaeology; Nutritional Anthropology; Paleonutrition, Methods of.**

BIBLIOGRAPHY

ATBC Cancer Prevention Study Group. "The Effects of Vitamin E and Beta Carotene on the Incidence of Lung Cancer and Other Cancers in Male Smokers." *New England Journal of Medicine* 330 (1994): 1029–1035.

Brand Miller, Janette C., and Susanne H. A. Holt. "Australian Aboriginal Plant Foods: A Consideration of Their Nutritional Composition and Health Implications." *Nutrition Research Review* ll (1998): 5–23.

Cohen, Mark Nathan. *Health and the Rise of Civilization.* New Haven: Yale University Press, 1989.

Cohen, Mark Nathan, and George J. Armelagos, eds. *Paleopathology at the Origins of Agriculture.* New York: Academic Press, 1984.

Cordain, Loren, et al. "Plant-Animal Subsistence Ratios and Macronutrient Energy Estimations in Worldwide Hunter-Gatherer Diets." *American Journal of Clinical Nutrition* 71 (2000): 682–692.

Cordain, Loren, S. Boyd Eaton, Janette Brand Miller, and Kim Hill. "The Paradoxical Nature of Hunter-Gatherer Diets: Meat-Based Yet Non-Atherogenic." *European Journal of Clinical Nutrition* 56, suppl. 1 (2002): S1–S11.

Eaton, S. Boyd, and Melvin Konner. "Paleolithic Nutrition: A Consideration of Its Nature and Current Implication." *New England Journal of Medicine* 312 (1985): 283–289.

Eaton, S. Boyd, et al. "An Evolutionary Perspective Enhances Understanding of Human Nutritional Requirements." *Journal of Nutrition* 126 (1996): 1732–1740.

Eaton, S. Boyd, and Loren Cordain. "Evolutionary Aspects of Diet: Old Genes, New Fuels." *World Review of Nutrition and Dietetics* 81 (1997): 26–37.

Eaton, S. Boyd, and Stanley B. Eaton III. "Hunter-Gatherers and Human Health." In *The Cambridge Encyclopedia of Hunters and Gatherers,* edited by Richard B. Lee and Richard Daly. Cambridge, U.K.: Cambridge University Press, 1999.

Eaton, S. Boyd, and Stanley B. Eaton III. "The Evolutionary Context of Chronic Degenerative Diseases." In *Evolution in Health and Disease,* edited by Stephen C. Stearns. Oxford and New York: Oxford University Press, 1999.

Eaton, S. Boyd, Stanley B. Eaton III, and Melvin J. Konner. "Paleolithic Nutrition Revisited." In *Evolutionary Medicine*, edited by Wenda R. Trevathan, E. O. (Neal) Smith, and James J. McKenna. New York and Oxford: Oxford University Press, 1999.

Fuchs C. S., et al. "Dietary Fiber and the Risk of Colorectal Cancer and Adenoma in Women." *New England Journal of Medicine* 340 (1999): 169–76.

Howe, G. R., et al. "Dietary Intake of Fiber and Decreased Rate of Cancers of the Colon and Rectum: Evidence from the Combined Analyses of 13 Case-Control Studies." *Journal of the National Cancer Institute* 84 (1992): 1887–1896.

Klein, Richard G. *The Human Career. Human Biological and Cultural Origins.* 2d ed. Chicago: University of Chicago Press, 1999.

Larsen, Clark Spencer. "Dietary Reconstruction and Nutritional Assessment of Past Peoples: The Bioanthropological Record." In *The Cambridge World History of Food*, edited by Kenneth F. Kiple and Kriemhild Coneè Ornelas, vol. 1. Cambridge, U.K.: Cambridge University Press, 2000.

Lee, Richard B. "What Hunters Do for a Living, or How to Make Out on Scarce Resources." In *Man the Hunter*, edited by Richard B. Lee and Irven De Vore. Chicago: Aldine, 1968.

Menkes, M. S., et al. "Serum Beta-Carotene, Vitamins A and E, Selenium, and the Risk of Lung Cancer. *New England Journal of Medicine* 315 (1986): 1250–1254.

Milton, Katherine. "Diet and Primate Evolution." *Scientific American* 269 (August 1993): 86–93.

Sinclair, Andrew. "Was the Hunter-Gatherer Diet Prothromboic?" In *Essential Fatty Acids and Eicosanoids*, edited by Andrew Sinclair and R. Gibson. Champaign, Ill.: American Oil Chemists Society, 1992.

Stringer, Christopher B., and Robin McKie. *African Exodus: The Origins of Modern Humanity.* New York: Holt, 1996.

Taubes, Gary. "The (Political) Science of Salt." *Science* 281 (1998): 898–907.

S. Boyd Eaton

FOOD PRODUCERS

The more than six billion humans living on earth at the beginning of the twenty-first century were almost exclusively dependent upon a narrow range of domesticated foods produced on some thirty-eight percent of the world's total land surface. More than three quarters of our annual global harvest is cereal-based, the bulk of which is composed of as few as four species. Although humans and their ancestors have inhabited the earth for several million years, food production is relatively recent, spanning the Holocene epoch or last ten to eleven millennia. The two thousand or more species of plants and animals that humans domesticated during this relatively brief period represent only a tiny fraction of the earth's biota, and with some recent exceptions of minor exotic or luxury foods, most of the important dietary items were domesticated relatively early on.

From the beginning of the Holocene, plants and animals have been selectively bred to provide food and medicine, clothing and companionship, draft and transportation, tools and weapons, and fertilizer. Domestication can increase the efficiency and reliability of food procurement, which can further facilitate an increase in human population size and density. While some hunter-gatherers are highly sedentary and many farmers somewhat mobile, food production often provides the necessary foundation that enables larger populations to live in fixed settlements for longer periods of time.

Domestication
Domestication is not a discovery but a process by which humans modify plants and animals by selectively encouraging certain characteristics that they want. In time, the domestication process can so genetically alter a population that it is no longer capable of flourishing in the wild. This dependency is usually bidirectional as humans and domesticates become reliant upon each other for survival. The process of domestication can be deliberate or unintentional as humans select for specific qualities of interest. Certain plants and animals are somewhat pre-adapted to domestication. Seed plants, for example, often thrive as weeds that colonize sunny clearings exposed by human occupation. Over time, subtle and important changes in the original population structure can be encouraged by inadvertently dropping or intentionally planting selected seeds in and around these open areas.

What characteristics do humans select? Domesticated plants mature simultaneously and lack the botanical ability to self disperse, attributes which are controlled by and for human consumers. Rapidly germinating plants that produce seeds with greater initial reserves and thin-coats are desired. Self-pollinating plants that readily adapt to the conditions of human settlement are also favored. Preferred animals include: fast growing herbivores that can be economically raised and consumed; docile taxa that can be bred in captivity; and herding species with a natural dominance hierarchy that humans can readily commandeer. Characteristically, many of the earliest domesticated plants were locally exploited and rapidly growing self pollinators that produced high yields of readily storable edible seeds. Early domesticated animals included locally available generalists that were placid, gregarious, and amenable to confinement.

The Geography of Early Domestication
Where and when were certain plants and animals initially domesticated? The Swiss botanist and geographer Alphonse De Candolle (1779-1841) was the first to document the geographical origins of cultivated plants, a subject that was greatly elaborated by the Russian botanist and geneticist Nikolai Vavilov (1887-1943?), who suggested that the area of origin for a domesticate was likely centered in regions where it is presently most diverse. Currently, with the aid of genetics and molecular techniques, archaeologists, biologists, and geographers attempt to delineate the area in which a plant or animal may have been first domesticated by defining the present

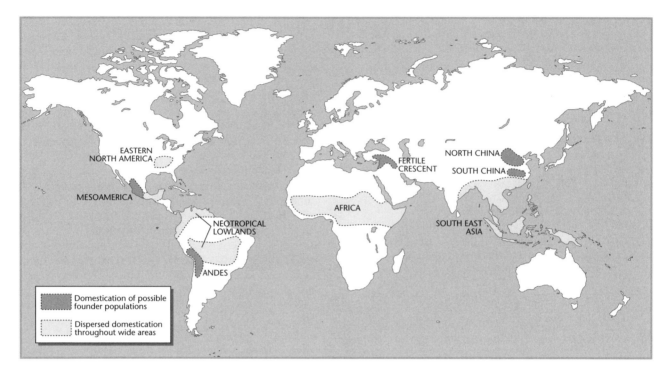

Independent areas of early prehistoric food production.

geographical distribution of its known wild progenitor and studying its subsequent development therein.

The early history of food production is an interdisciplinary undertaking which combines the techniques and methods of archaeology, botany, and zoology. Primary data are often recovered using specialized techniques and methods like flotation devices and pollen corers, and include preserved seeds, pollen, starch grains, phytoliths or mineral impressions of plant cell walls, bones, teeth, horns, and hair. Inferences are also drawn from tools, agricultural infrastructure, cultural implements, artistic portrayals, and written accounts. We can estimate how old our primary evidence is by radiometrically dating associated materials or the preserved organics themselves. Nevertheless, the entire endeavor hinges on the vagaries of sampling, luck of preservation, and intensive fieldwork. As a result, we understand the early origins of food production better in some areas than we do in others.

Much of the earliest evidence for food production comes from sites in arid areas. This may be simply because our primary data preserve better in these settings; however, the bulk of our major contemporary crops appear to have originated in regions with protracted dry seasons. We can identify some relatively circumscribed regions in which a core founder population of local plants and/or animals was originally domesticated. In other areas, the pattern of domestication was likely more diffuse. We can also recognize regions into which all or a few of the founder domesticates were introduced, after which local species were domesticated. Often it is difficult to

know precisely whether or not the introduction was through indigenous adoption or direct population invasion from outside. Currently, we can recognize some five to nine early areas of independent food production, from where domesticates, people and their domesticates, and/or the idea of domestication may have spread to other regions.

West Asia

We find our earliest and so far best evidence in a 2000 km arc of southwest Asia, bounded to the north by higher forested terrain and to the south by desert. This Fertile Crescent stretches from the eastern shores of the Mediterranean north of the Negev desert, around present day Syria and Turkey, and into the plains of the Tigris and Euphrates where it is bordered in the east by the Zagros mountains of present day Iran. Here, climatic amelioration at the end of the Pleistocene created local conditions suitable for large stands of wild grasses with abundant forage for various grazing herbivores. This topographically and floristically diverse region was rich in large-seeded and self-pollinating annuals adapted to seasonal rainfall and protracted dry seasons. It also supported a diverse population of mammals which, apart from the dog (*Canis familiaris*), included the world's earliest domesticated animals.

Around 10,000 B.P. (before the present) we find evidence for domesticated barley, first as a two-rowed (*Hordeum vulgare ditichum*) and somewhat later as a six-rowed (*H. v. hexastichum*) variety, along with emmer

(*Triticum turgidum dicoccum*) and einkorn (*T. monococum*) wheats. Possibly after 9000 B.P., sheep (*Ovis aires*) and goat (*Capra hircus*) were domesticated in the north and east respectively, with the subsequent additions of domesticated pig (*Sus scrofa*) and cattle (*Bos taurus*) from present day Turkey. At roughly the same time, the early menu was supplemented with domesticated pulses, especially lentil (*Lens culinaris*), pea (*Pisum sativum*), chickpea (*Cicer arietinum*), and bitter vetch (*Vicia ervilia*), along with flax (*Linum usitatissimum*) for oil and fiber. The protein rich cereals provide an excellent source of carbohydrates but lack an essential amino acid for the manufacture of animal protein. This is provided by the pulses, which can also fix nitrogen into soils when planted alongside cereal crops. Flax was used for textiles and oil, while animals provided a reliable protein source, and were eventually used for dairying, clothing, traction, and transport. Together, this balanced package formed an important founder population of domesticates that variably spread into other world regions.

Archaeological evidence tracks the rapid diffusion of Neolithic food production to the African and European shores of the Mediterranean by 8000 B.P., and a little later into Italy, Greece, and the Balkans. Farming spread quickly throughout temperate Europe after 7000 B.P., reaching Scandinavia and England by around 5000 B.P. We also see the appearance of southwest Asian food production in the Nile Valley by 6500 B.P., and farther abroad into Ethiopia and the Indus Valley. Western domesticates reach China by 3300 B.P.

In most cases, we don't know whether these patterns represent foreign food producers who migrated into new regions, local populations that adopted farming due to external stimulus, or a mix of both. We do know that many important cultivars were subsequently domesticated. A list of some of the more popular and their possible region of origin includes: faba bean (*Vicia faba*), olive (*Olea europaea*), grape (*Vitis vinifera*), fig (*Ficus carica*), and date (*Phoenix dactylifera*) in the Near East and Fertile Crescent; bread wheat (*Triticum aestivum*), rye (*Secale*), hemp (*Cannabis sativa*), lettuce (*Lactuca sativa*), and horse (*Equus caballus*) in western Asia; dromedary camel (*Camelus dromdarius*), and coffee (*Coffea arabica*) in Arabia; Old World cotton (*Gossypium*) in the Indian subcontinent; oat (*Avena sativa*), and poppy (*Papaver somniferum*) in Europe and the Mediterranean; and, donkey (*Equus asinus*) in Egypt.

East Asia

An early center of cereal based food production is found along the Huang Ho (Yellow) River in northern China. Transitionally located between semi-arid uplands to the west and forested plains to the east, prehistoric farmers cultivated foxtail (*Setaria italica*) and broomcorn (*Paniscum miliaceum*) millet by at least 7500 B.P. Although the area was likely warmer and wetter at the time, both plants are somewhat drought resistant. Shortly thereafter, diet was supplemented by domesticated chicken (*Gallus gallus domesticus*) and pig. Although pigs were possibly present in southern China a thousand years earlier, either claim can support an ancient introduction from western Asia or independent domestication. Some later domesticates from north China include soybean (*Glycine max*), hemp (*Cannabis*), popular tree fruits like Chinese pear (*Pyrus pyrifolia*), peach (*Prunus persica*), apricot (*P. armeniaca*), varieties of apples (*Malus domestica*), species of cherry (*Prunus* spp.), and silk worm (*Bombyx mori*), along with many local derelict cultivars that survive today as weeds.

To the south, wet rice agriculture developed by 8000 B.P. along the Chang Jiang (Yangtze) River. Early evidence comes from the middle and lower reaches of this wet and marshy region, where varieties of long-grained (*Oryza sativa* var. *indica*) and short-grained (var. *japonica*) rice may have been domesticated at a time when temperatures were warmer than today. Some two thousand years after possible pig domestication in south China, water buffalo (*Bubalus bubalus*) is recorded south of the Chang Jiang delta, along with bottle gourd (*Lagenaria siceraria*) and cultivated aquatic plants including water caltrop (*Trapa* spp.) and fox nut (*Euryale ferox*). Other notable domesticates from south China include water chestnut (*Eleocharis tuberosa*), Asian arrowroot (*Sagittaria sinensis*), red bean (*Vigna angularis*), and duck (*Anas platyrhynchos*).

Although domesticated rice is found in India and Southeast Asia as early as 5000 B.P., east Asian domesticates dispersed less quickly into Europe and western Asia. Rice was unknown to much of the West before Hellenistic times, and many domesticates were only introduced through merchant voyaging in the past five to six hundred years. It is unknown whether or to what extent the introduction of rice agriculture into Southeast Asia supplanted an indigenous domestication of root and tree crops, which included yam (*Dioscorea* spp.), bananas and plantains (*Musa* spp.), citrus (*Citrus* spp.), mango (*Mangifera indica*), breadfruit (*Artocarpus* spp.), and various spices. Tantalizing evidence hints at the possibility of early agriculture in Papua New Guinea around 9000 B.P. Many plants were domesticated in the Pacific islands, including sugarcane (*Saccharum officinarum*), coconut (*Cocos nucifera*), taros (*Alocasia, Cyrtosperma, Colocasia*), sago (*Metroxylon*), kava (*Piper methysticum*), and numerous spices. We can trace a relatively early spread of southeast Asian food production into nearby islands, beginning in Taiwan as early as 7000 B.P. and subsequently spreading to Borneo by 4500 B.P. Subsequent colonization into Polynesia between 3500 and 2500 B.P. introduced fowl, dogs, pigs, and various root and tree crops.

Africa

Before west Asian farming arrived in the Nile Valley, the Sahara was inhabited by nomadic pastoral groups that herded indigenous domesticated cattle along with sheep or goat introduced from the Mediterranean. The southern boundary of this early "pastoral neolithic" was controlled by tsetse fly infestation in the forests and savannas of sub-Saharan Africa, where nagana disease wasted domestic livestock. Early evidence for indigenous African plant domestication in savanna and Sahel regions south of the Sahara include native grains like sorghum (*Sorghum bicolor*) around 4000 B.P. in Niger, pearl millet (*Pennisetum glaucum*) after 3000 B.P. in Mauritania, and African rice (*Oryza glaberrima*) after 2000 B.P. in Mali. Other important African domesticates with possible savanna origins include cowpea (*Vigna ungulata*) and African yams (*Dioscorea* spp.). Finger millet (*Eleusine coracana*) and tef (*Eragrostis tef*) were locally domesticated in the highlands of eastern Africa, as were ensete (*Musa ensete*), noog oil (*Guizotia abyssinica*), and narcotic chat (*Catha edulis*).

Forest zones contributed oil palm (*Elaeis guineensis*), kola nut (*Cola nitada*), and guinea fowl (*Numida meleagris*) in the west, and okra (*Hibiscus esculentus*) and robusta coffee (*Coffea canephora*) in equatorial Africa. The somewhat misnamed Arabian variety (*C. arabica*) actually originated in mountain forests of southern Ethiopia and Sudan. Desertic regions contributed cantaloup (*Cucumis melo*), watermelon (*Citrullus lanatus*) possibly after 3000 B.P. in Mauritania, and perhaps date (*Phoenix dactylifera*). The house cat (*Felis catus*) may have been domesticated in Egypt, where we also see early evidence for bottle gourd around 5500 B.P. Archaeologists have traced the later diffusion of pastoral groups into southern Africa as they reached the Cape coast by the time of Christ.

North America

Early evidence for a nutritionally balanced founder population of domesticated squash, beans, and maize is found in Mesoamerica. Orange pumpkin squashes (*Cucurbita pepo*), that today include acorn and zucchini varieties, appear around 10,000 B.P. in Mexico. Ancient farmers may have selected squash for their seeds rather than pulp, later adding winter (*C. moschata*), cushaw (*C. argyrosperma*), and fig leaf cultivars (*C. ficifolia*). The chayote (*Sechium edule*) was more recently added, while ancient evidence for the bottle gourd suggests that it may have rafted across the Atlantic from Africa. The common bean (*Phaseolus vulgaris*) was independently domesticated twice, once in Mexico as early as 6000 B.P., and later joined by members of the same genus including tepary (*P. acutifolius*), runner bean (*P. coccineus*), and botil (*P. polyanthus*). Maize (*Zea mays*) was likely domesticated from a wild teosinte in southwestern Mexico. Direct dating of maize remains suggests its earliest appearance around 5500 B.P., after which it spread rapidly throughout the hemisphere. The common chile pepper (*Capsicum annum*) is also found very early in Mesoamerica. Later domesticates of note include grain amaranths (*Amaranthus* spp.), tomatillo (*Physalis philadelphica*), tree crops like cacao (*Theobroma cacao*) and sapote (*Pouteria sapota*), hairy cotton (*Gossypium hirsutum*), various species of Agave for hennequen and sisal fiber, as well as fermented drink, and a domesticated bird, the turkey (*Meleagris gallopavo*).

Maize appears in the American Southwest by 3500 B.P., but becomes a major staple with squash and beans much later. By 2000 B.P. maize eventually enters the southeast, where independently domesticated squash (*Cucurbita pepo*), sunflower (*Helianthus annuas*), marsh elder (*Iva annua macrocarpa*), and goosefoot (*Chenopodium berlandieri*) were all already under cultivation, possibly by 4500 B.P. Some 2000 years later, erect knotweed (*Polygonum erectum*), maygrass (*Phalaris caroliniana*), and little barley (*Hordeum pusillum*) assume greater dietary significance, but only after roughly 1000 B.P. does maize-centered agriculture dominate eastern North America.

South America

An early complex of domesticates that may have developed by 5000 B.P. in highland areas from south-central Peru to Bolivia, eventually dispersed throughout the ancient Andean world by the time conquering Spaniards arrived. Included were quinoa (*Chenopodium quinoa*), kaniwa (*C. pallidicaule*), and kiwicha (*Amaranthus caudatus*), all high altitude pseudocereals that provide flour for baking, soups, and beverages. Indigenous tuber crops like oca (*Oxalis tuberosa*), mashua (*Tropaeolum tuberosum*), ullucu (*Ullucus tuberosus*), and potato (*Solanum tuberosum*) are also adapted to the cold conditions of high elevation.

The only native New World mammalian domesticates, llama (*Lama glama*), alpaca (*L. pacos*), and cuy or guinea pig (*Cavia aparea porcellus*) round out the highland package. Direct dating of archaeological specimens indicates that domesticated South American common (*Phaseolus vulgaris*) and lima (*P. lunatus*) beans were added somewhat later, possibly at slightly lower elevations in the southern highlands. Other Andean domesticates included roots like maca (*Lepidium meyenii*), and arracacha (*Arracacia xanthorrhiza*), and tree crops as pepino (*Solanum muricatun*) and tree tomato (*Cyphomandra betacea*).

Phytolith evidence could suggest the appearance of maize around 7000 B.P. in northern neotropical lowlands; however, others argue a more recent introduction around 4000 B.P. in accordance with Mesoamerican data. Early lowland contexts also reveal domesticated jack beans (*Canavalia plagiosperma*), cotton (*Gossypium barbadense*), and the root crops achira (*Canna edulis*), leren (*Calathea allouia*), and arrowroot (*Maranta arundinacea*). Phytolith evidence also supports early use of bottle gourd and squash; indigenous domesticated squash include the hubbard (*Cucurbita maxima*) originally from Argentina, and possibly the relict *C. ecuadorensis* of southwestern Ecuador. Many domesticates come from areas of the lowland neotropics, including: manioc (*Manihot esculenta*), cocoyam (*Xanthosoma* spp.), yam (*Dioscorea trifida*), sweet potato (*Ipomoea batata*), peanuts (*Arachis hypogaea*), capsicum peppers (*Capsicum* spp.), various drug and medicinal plants, tree and palm crops like cashew (*Anacardium occidentale*), avocado (*Persea americana*), guava (*Psidium guajava*), and peach palm (*Bactris gasipaes*), and the muscovy duck (*Cairina moschata*).

Why Domesticate?

Ancient agriculturalists customarily attributed their origins to an act of divine intervention. As scientists began to seek alternative explanations for the beginnings of food production, they persisted in the teleological assumption that domestication was initially a discovery. Cultural innovation took place especially in areas where resources were concentrated, either naturally or as unintended consequence of human behavior. It is, however, reasonable to assume that humans everywhere possessed, from earliest times, a sophisticated understanding of the plants and animals that surrounded them. This is easily confirmed in the detailed knowledge of hunter-gatherers who, moreover, actually spend less time procuring food than their agricultural brethren. Bioarchaeological study of skeletal assemblages also indicates that early agriculturalists may have suffered poorer health than hunter-gatherers. So, why bother to produce food? Causation came to be viewed as a response to stress or disequilibrium; humans began to produce food in order to keep up with unceasing population growth and/or as an adaptation to their changing environment. Some view the adoption of food production as the product of rational economic decisions in which optimizing foragers weighed costs against benefit. Others seek social origins for early agricultural, suggesting that early cultigens were originally prestige items used in specific, highly politicized contexts.

Whatever the ultimate cause, it appears that food production antedated the appearance of sedentary village life. It likely took place in settings where populations were neither internally nor externally threatened, and evolved out of a lengthy mutualistic association between plants, animals, and humans. The distinction between domesticator and domesticated is simply a matter of perspective, as food and food producers eventually launched a trajectory that would irreversibly change the way we live.

See also **Agriculture, Origins of; American Indians: Prehistoric Indians and Historical Overview; Food Archaeology.**

BIBLIOGRAPHY

Clutton-Brock, Juliet. *A Natural History of Domesticated Mammals*. 2d ed. Cambridge, U.K.: Cambridge University Press, 1999.

Diamond, Jared. *Guns, Germs, and Steel. The Fates of Human Societies*. New York: Norton., 1999.

Harlan, Jack R. *The Living Fields: Our Agricultural Heritage*. Cambridge, U.K.: Cambridge University Press, 1995.

Kiple, Kenneth F., and Kriemhild Conceè Ornelas, eds. *The Cambridge World History of Food*. Cambridge, U.K.: Cambridge University Press, 2000.

Mason, Ian L., ed. *Evolution of Domesticated Animals*. London: Longman, 1984.

Piperno, Dolores R., and Deborah M. Pearsall. *The Origins of Agriculture in the Lowland Neotropics*. San Diego: Academic Press, 1998.

Price, T. Douglas, and Anne Birgitte Gebauer, eds. *Last Hunters-First Farmers*: New Perspectives on the Prehistoric Transition to Agriculture series. Santa Fe: School of American Research Press, 1995.

Purseglove, J. W. *Tropical Crops. Dicotyledons*. London: Longman, 1968.

Purseglove, J. W. *Tropical Crops. Monocotyledons*. London: Longman, 1972.

Sauer, Jonathan D. *Historical Geography of Crop Plants: A Select Roster*. Boca Raton, Fla.: CRC Press, 1993.

Smith, Bruce D. *The Emergence of Agriculture*. New York: Scientific American Library, 1995.

Zohary, Daniel, and Maria Hopf. *Domestication of Plants in the Old World*. 3d. ed.. Oxford: Oxford University Press, 2000.

Peter W. Stahl

PREPARATION OF FOOD. Food preparation has been a constant chore since the first human beings picked up cutting and mashing stones. In return, this effort to make food edible, preserve it, and transform its character has sustained an ever-increasing population. Many techniques, including grinding, sifting, drying, salting, sealing, fermenting, and applying heat, are extremely ancient. Few fundamentally new techniques have been introduced in the past two centuries, among them microwaving. The main long-term change has been the shifting of tasks from the domestic hearth to centralized factories.

The processes of food preparation might be divided according to their primary science, whether physical (such as extracting nuts from their shells), chemical (adding salt), or biological (brewing beer). Perhaps more helpfully, they might be categorized according to their intended purpose. Some foods are toxic until prepared properly. Others are scarcely edible until softened. Preparation can bring together nutritional variety. It can add intriguing flavors. Food preparation can also have negative impacts, especially on nutrients.

Viewed socially, food preparation has typically been female work, requiring hours of often hard and repetitive effort. Over history, it has gradually been shifted out of the home and typically made a male concern. Butchery, milling, baking, and brewing are among the oldest extradomestic industries, conducted by specialists for thousands of years. These and most other tasks have been more scientifically and centrally managed over the past two centuries.

Preparation is a core human activity that can be examined from the perspectives of many biochemical, nutritional, technical, cultural, social, historical, and economic sciences. Many aspects of food preparation are treated in greater detail elsewhere in this work. This entry outlines its purposes, its history and social position, and provides snapshots of people at work, from an an-

Large-scale food preparation requires large-scale solutions. In the traditional culture of Cyprus, entire villages are invited to wedding feasts, which necessitates moveable ovens, since all of the food is baked in earthenware pots. The blending of tradition and modern technology is evident in this catering invention, which will feed about six thousand people. PHOTO ILYA LOYSHA.

cient Roman peasant making a *moretum* (suggestive of an Italian pesto) to global corporations preparing hamburgers.

Defining "Preparation"
In *Cooking, Cuisine, and Class*, social anthropologist Jack Goody distinguishes five basic phases in the process of "providing and transforming food": namely, production (growing on the farm), distribution (market activities, including storage), preparation (cooking in the kitchen), consumption (eating at the table), and disposal (clearing up) (p. 37). While such a production chain might seem straightforward, it can be misleading. Traditionally at least, food preparation included preservation and storage. Preparation thus came immediately after food "production" in the sense of hunting, gardening, and farming.

It is even harder to define where preparation ends, giving way to such possible next steps as "consumption," "cooking," "serving," or "eating." Just the word "consumption" has two basic meanings. It can be eating, in which case preparation includes the fullest possible range of food handling. Consumption can also mean purchasing in the modern market, which possibly leaves some

cooking to be done in the domestic kitchen. "Cooking" introduces further complications, because this can mean the transformation of food with heat (the usual dictionary definition) or something more all-encompassing.

These definitional problems arise because food preparation is viewed as a transformation of a plant or animal into food to the neglect of some basic social considerations, in particular, distribution. Central institutions, markets, and meals can distribute food at any point between "raw" and "cooked." For example, the breaking down of an animal carcass into small cuts of meat almost seems to come before "preparation" (because the nutritional change is marginal), but its social implications are crucial, for the best serves have typically gone to the most powerful people. Restaurants distribute food not even as semiprepared products but as finished meals. Accordingly, restaurant preparation (often called just "the prep") is done before the customer arrives—the food is taken from its packages, neatly chopped, and perhaps partly cooked. When the cooks turn their attention to "service," they concentrate on last-minute stove work and assembly, which might be translated as "serving out in the kitchen."

142

The appearance of "preparation" thus largely depends on which stage of its distribution the food is being prepared for. For the purposes of this discussion, "preparation" comes early in the raw–cooked continuum. It is closer to the farm, whereas cooking is found nearer the table. Preparation's transformations are oriented toward nutrition and palatability rather than more purely social and cultural aspects, such as presentation and serving.

Basic Techniques

Food preparation techniques range from chopping up through fermentation and emulsifying to pressure-cooking, vacuum packing, and homogenizing. One way to understand them is to examine immediate purposes, which can be categorized as separating out edible foods; removing toxins; softening and otherwise making ingredients more edible and digestible; distributing foods; storing them; and making them into new compositions.

Separation. The immediate need for preparing food is the separation of edible from inedible parts. This includes simple shelling, peeling, husking, and sifting. Sometimes such hazards as small stones need removing. The separation of cream may involve machinery, but the tools and techniques are generally not complicated. Some steps in meat butchery come under this heading.

Detoxification. Some foods have to be made safe to eat. Among important examples is the root, cassava, which forms prussic acid that can be dispelled by soaking and cooking. The green color appearing near the skin of potatoes is simply cut off. Expert cutting is also required with the notorious Japanese delicacy, the *fugu* or puffer fish. Communities have traditionally been amazingly adept at dealing with local dangers, because learning to recognize and treat hazardous species must have necessitated long, life-threatening trial and error.

Making edible and digestible. The next major purpose of preparation is making food more easily chewed and digested. This can achieved by a range of techniques, such as grinding, pounding, soaking, and cooking in the sense of heating, which includes boiling, roasting, baking, steaming, shallow and deep frying, and microwaving.

In the case of wheat, for example, the heads of grain must be threshed to break them up, then winnowed to separate the wheat from the chaff. After that, it is probably ground into flour, which can again be separated and perhaps soaked or turned into a paste. The flour mixture can then be poured on a plate and fried, shaped into a loaf to be fried, baked or roasted, or pulled, extruded, or rolled out as noodles or pasta, when it is commonly boiled.

Distribution. Food is transported in the arms, bark containers, pots on the head, baskets, panniers on donkeys, ships, trains, and refrigerated trucks, all of which involve various kinds of preparation. Food is also physically divided up, especially with the use of knives and cleavers, and the central social role of knives is outlined by Michael Symons in an essay in historical sociology called "Cutting Up Cultures."

The butchery of meat can be viewed as distribution; for example, everything is used of a pig "but the squeal." A small festival occurs during the division of a household pig into numerous parts, washing the intestines for sausage casings, preserving legs with salting and drying as ham, making pancakes from the blood, and so on. Commercial pig distribution is known in France as charcuterie.

Storage. Some foods such as grains and roots are more readily storable without preparation. They might just need to be kept in a cool, dry, airy place or left buried, and protected from pests. Others can be prepared to greatly extend their storage life. Preservation methods include drying, salting, pickling, sealing, cooking (heating), smoking, candying, fermenting, and freezing. These mainly rely on making a hostile environment for microorganisms that produce decay. For example, sealing keeps air away by placing the food perhaps under oil, in a tight container or under a vacuum. Through the changes introduced by fermentation, milk can be kept as cheese, soybeans turned into soy sauce, grain and fruit made into beer and wine.

Composition. Some preparation techniques amalgamate more than one ingredient into a composition: what might aptly be called a new preparation. A variety of foods might be simmered together to make the family of sauces, stews, and soups. The use of yeasts in dough makes breads rise. A sophisticated technique is emulsification (effectively, the mixing of oil in water), which is employed to make a range of sauces, such as hollandaise.

History

In social terms, food preparation has largely been done by women. Among the numerous tasks, women have carried the water. They have tended the fire, fetched firewood, and found a light. They have ground and pounded with stones. Spanish gastronomic author Alicia Ríos spoke of the mortar and pestle as an everyday contrivance at the Oxford Symposium on Food and Cookery in 1988. She extolled the "rhythmic drumming of pestles pounding in mortars, coming from the kitchens of city tower blocks and quiet village houses. The familiar sound is the hint of aromas to come." The pestle originally made grains edible, its crushing action replicating the human jawbone. As a second main task, "a variety of sometimes opposing elements are mixed together," achieving an "integration." For Ríos, "the use of the mortar is universal," although she accepted that a "question mark hangs over the continued survival of this instrument which is at the same time practical, magical and symbolical."

If the first social generalization is that food preparation has largely been done by women, then the second is that this labor has through history been taken over by industry, shifting the work to the public, male-controlled sphere. That is, the homely pounding and "integration" that Rios found all around her have, for many others, disappeared behind factory walls.

The basic methods of food preparation are extremely ancient. Some techniques, such as podding and peeling, are shared with other animals. The use of tools suggests distinctively human behavior, the pestles augmenting the jawbones and various cutting implements extending the claws and teeth. The earliest social groups are thought to have been essentially opportunistic omnivores, who could scavenge in a range of habitats. Food preparation further increased the available species through detoxifying and softening, in which fire eventually played a crucial role.

When people adopted the settled, agrarian way of life around 10,000 years ago, they constructed shelters for food that became shelters for themselves as well, for the secret of the agrarian mode of production was food storage. Initially, this meant collecting and then growing basic foods, such as seeds, roots, and tubers that had intrinsic keeping qualities. Early settled societies also kept otherwise perishable foods through drying, sealing under oil, fermenting to make cheese, and so on. The keeping qualities of foods often make them less humanly digestible, too. Accordingly, the settled, food-stockpiling way of life required a range of basic preparation techniques to "pre-chew" and "pre-digest."

The settled mode was also marked by increased division of food preparation among specialists. Men had long hunted, cut up, and roasted meat, leading some anthropologists to characterize roasting as "male" as opposed to "female" boiling. Other tasks then went to artisans, including millers (using human, animal, water, and wind power and eventually engines), bakers, and brewers. Most of these were male tasks, although taverns were often run by women.

Pre-industrial food preparation was often done within close domestic groups, villages, temples, and palaces. But this compactness of production, distribution, preparation, and consumption broke down. Salt was among the earliest traded commodities. Spices were light and considered desirable enough to carry over vast distances. Such trade might have originally been between chiefs and kings, but markets opened up, and an increasing range of prepared foods exchanged.

As an illustration of women's domestic manufacture for medieval markets, Swedish rural historian Janken Myrdal has described the spread of the plunge churn for butter making. Butter fat had long been separated by shaking milk in a skin, pot, or wooden vessel. By about 1,000 years ago, the plunge churn had taken over across a wide area of Europe and Asia. Myrdal found much the same plunge churn, a cylinder usually of wood and up to about 3.3 feet high, from Ireland to Tibet. The plunging of the milk of cream with a staff above a cross or disk

causes the fat to coagulate. Since the plunge churn requires a relatively large amount of liquid, Myrdal suggests that its introduction must have accompanied a widespread stimulus to commercial production. At least in Europe, this probably came from the entrenched feudal social structure, with tenants having to pay rents and taxes, which they did in a luxury food, butter.

The trade routes eventually brought the so-called New and Old Worlds together. Ocean voyages depended on salted and pickled foods, along with ship's biscuits. These became some of the earliest industrial food products. Bottling or canning was developed by Nicolas Appert in France at the close of the eighteenth century, aimed initially at seafarers, the armed forces, and other mobile populations.

The effects of refrigeration have long been applied through the use of cool, dry spaces. In China, ice was employed in transport at least by the seventeenth century, because Frederick W. Mote observes in *Food in Chinese Culture*, edited by K. C. Chang, that "refrigerated shipping also seems to have been taken for granted in Ming times, long before we hear of such a development in Europe" (p. 215). During the nineteenth century, ice was carried across oceans from New England lakes, and railway networks adopted ice for food transport. In 1850 an Australian, James Harrison, designed the first practical ice-making machine.

"Roller" flour mills were used from the 1870s, quicker and easier than grinding between flat stones, as well as producing whiter flour. Breakfast cereals were developed in United States to meet needs of vegetarian groups, notably Seventh Day Adventists. From that time, artisanal businesses that had grown into regional ones became national and finally global corporations. Capital had been invested first in agriculture and from the mid-nineteenth century in food preservation and distribution. The third major step reorganized the final cooking of food in the second half of the twentieth century.

Food Quality

The need to supply the rapidly expanding cities of the early nineteenth century made more room for food adulteration. Various writers sought to draw public attention to this practice, Frederick Accum causing the greatest stir with a *Treatise on the Adulterations of Food and Culinary Poisons* in 1820. The considerable work then done by Dr. Hassall and others to improve the honesty of food preparation in the 1850s is also described by Jack Drummond and Anne Wilbraham in the *Englishman's Food*.

The rush to industrialize food preparation could not be stopped, however. Writing under the initials "M. M." in 1851, Mary Allen Meredith complained in her article "Gastronomy and Civilisation" in *Fraser's Magazine* (no. 264) that "[w]e have let the beer of the people disappear, and have grown ashamed of roast beef. . . . Draught ale has vanished, and all the bottled compounds that go by that name are but unwholesome concoctions of drugs and camomile. We have brought chemistry into our kitchens, not as a handmaid but as a poisoner."

Nineteenth-century gourmets sometimes hailed bottled fruits out of season, and believed that some mass-prepared items such as packet spaghetti (or *pastasciutta*) could maintain high quality; other oddities such as jellies and sweet corn in cans gained nostalgic appeal. However, these were exceptions, and in the early twenty-first century the balance of gastronomic opinion is against factory preparation. The food processing industries that so effectively supplied armies and, increasingly, urban populations generally degraded quality. The main trouble seems to be the drive to reduce costs. Highly processed foods are then brought back to life, so to speak, through cosmetic means, supplemented by vivacious marketing.

A writer specializing in Jewish cooking, Evelyn Rose, told the Oxford Symposium of Food and Cookery in 1987 about her experiences in recreating "homemade" flavor for a commercial supplier of kosher products, Rakusen's Ltd., in Leeds, England. She worked with the firm on canned soups since they presented relatively minor processing challenges. Any use of additives put canned soups "into a different category" from homemade ones, she found. For example, "modified starch" thickeners gave a glutinous texture and diluted flavor, and flavor enhancers left a synthetic taste. Accordingly, to thicken Rose's Tuscan bean soup, they puréed half the solids. To stop her Dutch pea soup from becoming the color of "mud," they used new technology and top quality split peas. To ensure chunks of vegetables were neither so large as to be unsightly nor so small as to melt away, she specified precise dimensions. While the homemade flavor was "universally acknowledged," she reported that the soups had to be sold at the same "luxury" price of game soup and lobster soup.

With the transfer of food preparation from households and local artisans to commercial factories, using increasingly complex processes, the ordinary person lost skills and knowledge. This was accompanied by an enormous inrush of information of other kinds. On one hand, this was dietary, with increasingly obese and otherwise unhealthy populations concerned about the quantity of fat and sugar, especially in so-called junk foods. On the other hand, the lack of real knowledge was replaced by commercial image making.

The resulting consumer confusion can be illustrated by the scandal when Snow Brand milk poisoned more than 16,000 people in Japan in the summer of 2000. The cause was publicly revealed to be contaminated nonfat dry milk (NFDM). This drew widespread attention to the fact that much "milk" was not raw (fresh) milk but powdered milk, which gave manufacturers much more flexibility in their operations, bulking out supplies in the off-season and adjusting the chemical balance of special milks. Ironically, the contaminated NFDM in Japan went into just those types of milk preferred by "health con-

Food is often prepared at the table, as in the case of this curious old implement called Passmore's Patent Conjurer made by Thomas Passmore of Philadelphia, circa 1797. Constructed of sheet iron and wrought iron, the conjurer permitted small articles of food such as oysters or lamb chops to be cooked over oil lamps in the manner of a pressure cooker. ROUGHWOOD COLLECTION. PHOTO CHEW & COMPANY.

scious" people who had been persuaded to purchase calcium-enriched, lowfat milk and yogurt drinks.

An Early Account of Food Preparation

The Latin poem *Moretum* is perhaps the oldest surviving detailed account of a person preparing food. Scholars used to think it was written by Virgil, but now credit an unknown successor between 8 and 25 B.C.E. The poem, which has been translated and introduced by classicist E. J. Kenney, describes the preparation of a basic meal in order to convey the hand-to-mouth grind of peasant life.

On a winter's morning, while still dark, the rustic cultivator, Simulus, gropes for the hearth and eventually coaxes the embers into fire. He fetches some grain from a "miserable heap" in a cupboard. His right hand turns the grinding stone rapidly, with the left feeding it, until he reverses arms from weariness. Singing an uncouth country song, he sieves the meal, the black siftings staying on the upper surface, the unmixed flour sinking through the holes. He piles it on a smooth board, pours on water warmed by the flame, and works the mixture until it becomes cohesive, occasionally sprinkling with salt. He smooths the kneaded dough into regular rounds, marking each with the characteristic eight segments of a Roman loaf. He inserts it into a swept part of the hearth, covers it with crocks (pieces of broken pottery), and heaps fire on top.

So that bread alone should not displease his palate, Simulus finds an accompaniment. He has only a round cheese pierced through the middle with a string. So our "far-seeing hero" contrives another resource, the poet tells us. He has a kitchen garden next to his hovel, where he leads water from nearby streams to his cabbages, beet, sorrel, and other plants. However, these are for selling at the local market. For his own use, he chooses garlic, parsley, bushy rue, and coriander.

Simulus sits again beside the bright fire and, with mortar and pestle, mashes the herbs, along with salt, the hard cheese, a little olive oil, and vinegar. Round and round goes his right hand, the original ingredients gradually losing their own properties and becoming one (or, in the poet's Latin, *e pluribus unus*). Often the sharp smell goes right up his nostrils, so that he passes judgment on his dinner, while with the back of his hand he wipes his streaming eyes. He mixes and thoroughly remixes the mass. Finally, he wipes it out into a single ball, to produce a perfect *moretum*. With bread and *moretum*, he can leave to do the plowing, "with the fear of hunger banished, and free from care for that day."

Simulus is an unusual domestic cook in being a man (perhaps the poet wanted a man to do women's work to emphasize the lowliness of the scene). He appears to cook merely for himself (although he might live with an African woman, mentioned in the poem). He uses no obvious cooking pot. Otherwise, much else is universal. So much cooking throughout the world for perhaps 10,000 years has been done with a small fire, storage bin, water jug, stones for milling grain, and mortar and pestle for preparing herbs and spices.

Commentators have called the *moretum* a "country salad" and "herbed cheese." However, the closest equivalent known to many these days is probably the Italian sauce of basil, parmesan cheese, pine nuts, and olive oil called pesto. His is a typical agrarian meal of two parts. The basic element is the staple, such as rice, potatoes, or cereals, which make the bread here. This is accompanied by a tastier, nutritional complement, which has commonly been something like the *moretum* prepared from vegetables and perhaps a little protein.

Wealthier people employed cooks to serve elaborations of such a meal. The foods have been more numerous, and more luxurious. Rather than a sauce accompanying the staple, it might have accompanied meat. Sauces not unlike the *moretum* are called the "trademark of the Roman chef" by classical scholar Jon Solomon (p. 115). Of the nearly five hundred entries in the Roman cookery book of Apicius, *De re coquinaria* (The Art of Cooking), he finds that nearly four hundred are devoted to the preparation of a sauce. They begin with the pulverizing of herbs and spices in a mortar. Fruits and nuts are then added, and finally, liquid such as water, honey,

oil, milk, mustard, or *liquamen* (a fermented fish sauce also known as garum). This mixture is often boiled over a fire, and sometimes thickened with wheat starch, egg, rice, and so on. For example, the dozen different sauces for lamb (or kid) include a simple bread and oil sauce, a sweet milk and date sauce, and a vinegar and plum sauce.

Medieval Recipes

In some of the oldest recipes in English, numerous sentences instruct the cook to take one or more ingredients, using such archaic words as "tak," "nym," and "recipe" (giving the name for culinary prescriptions). Once cooks have "taken," the same medieval recipes call on them to "grind," "dyce," "shred," "mince," "bray" (crush with mortar and pestle), "quarter", "quare" (cut into squares), "swyng" (swinge or beat), "alye" (mix), and "medle" (mix). Heat is then used to "frye," "parboile," "boyle," and "seeth in gode broth" (seethe or boil in a good broth). The recipes conclude with "serve it forth" or, which means the same, "messe it forth." In summary, cooks "take" and, having "meddled" (mixed), they "send."

Babylonian Dishes

Babylonian scribes impressed the oldest surviving recipes onto three clay tablets in cuneiform 3,700 years ago. The tablets, which their French translator Jean Bottéro describes in an essay entitled, "The Most Ancient Recipes of All," reveal a cuisine of striking refinement for such an early period.

The best-preserved tablet takes just seventy-five lines to give twenty-five recipes. One name, "Assyrian stew," suggests it has come from the northern part of the country and another, "Elamite stew," ascribes it to neighboring people. Most headings, however, indicate various bouillons of such meats as deer, gazelle, kid, lamb, pigeon, and perhaps rat. The instructions typically start with the meat of the title with other meat added, then water and fat, along with condiments and often thickeners. Here is an example:

> Lamb bouillon. You need other meat too. Place in water. Add fat, salt as you wish, crumbed cereal cake, onion and *samidu* [not yet translated], coriander, cumin, leek and garlic. Serve. (Bottéro, p. 251)

The compressed style suggests aides-mémoirs for professional chefs. The other readable tablet devotes 250 lines to just 7 recipes for various kinds of birds, both domestic and game. The recipes indicate many steps, numerous utensils, complex combinations, and sometimes as many as ten different seasonings.

From a tantalizing glimpse of a vast gastronomic literature around 4,000 years old, it seems that the ancient Babylonians took great care in balancing flavors in complete dishes. They did not just throw birds on the fire, but followed complicated recipes calling for as many as ten seasonings. Historian Jean Bottéro acknowledges that this was the cuisine of rich people, who had the "skilled personnel, requisite cooking vessels and stoves, and money for expensive provisions" (p. 254). While the recipes were probably prescriptions for some kind of ritual, he presumes that domestic cooks turned out tasty and imaginative dishes, even if not quite so complex or varied.

The LoDagaa

The ordinary meal of the LoDagaa people in West Africa consisted of one dish, "a single but filling dish," which was much the same from day to day. The preparations were observed by anthropologist Jack Goody and summarized in his wider study of *Cooking, Cuisine, and Class* in 1982 (especially pp. 69–78). He reports that the dish came in two parts, which he calls "porridge," made from guinea corn or millet, and accompanying "soup," usually made from ground nuts or leaves of one type or another.

The preparation of meals, largely done by the women, took a long time because produce had to be transformed all the way from its original state. In the case of guinea-corn or millet, the grain had to be removed from the head, husked, and winnowed. The grinding was especially hard, and the women would lighten their work by singing songs and chatting. Other laborious tasks were the processing of shea nuts to make oil and the turning of cassava into a safe food (the prussic acid formed in cassava dissolves readily in water and is driven off by heat).

One advantage of the cassava root is that it can be kept in the ground. Women also laid out the fruits of the okra, pepper, and soup leaves on the roofs to dry before being packed away in pots and baskets for the empty season. The LoDagaa sometimes stored grain in its malted form for brewing beer later.

The women could now use matches for lighting the fire, although men might still make fire using a stone, a piece of iron, and kapok for rituals. "Like yeast, fire was one of those marvels passed down from hand to hand, the embodiment of communal living, difficult to start, easy to keep going, especially if one has kin and neighbours on whom to rely," Goody writes (p. 70). The usual hearth consisted of three stones, on which the pots balanced. Virtually all the food was boiled. Fish and meat were occasionally smoked for preservation above the fire. Some frying was done, although more often in market for delicacies such as bean cakes. Corn cobs might be roasted, but roasting was more typical of meat and carried out by men. Baking was done in the new bread ovens in market towns.

Beer could be purchased in any of the LoDagaa markets. In fact, the evening markets seemed only to exist for beer and cooked food. Beer was also brewed daily at someone's house. Women spread their days over their six-day week, so that today Brumo would brew, tomorrow Popla, and so forth. The men would often go to buy a pot, partly for the company.

Goody found that a conspicuous new feature of many African villages was the grinding mill, established by some enterprising trader and powered by a diesel motor. "Here women queue up to have their grain ground into flour, preferring to try and earn a little extra money in the market or by brewing beer, rather than undertake the heavy work of grinding by hand" (p. 69).

Numerous anthropologists have made similar field observations as those of Jack Goody. They have found tribal women devoting much of their day to fetching water, pounding roots, grinding grain, maintaining a fire, boiling a staple and its slightly more varied accompaniment, and perhaps using fermentation, as when brewing beer. Anthropologists have often noticed some tasks being done by specialists, such as bakers and tavern keepers, and the very presence of outside observers also suggests that agribusiness and related food industries will soon bring an even more centralized mode of preparation.

Fast Food

According to one picture, the modern preparation of food is conducted by sophisticated corporations that employ advanced technologies to supply plentiful, healthy, tasty, and often "fast" food without tedious labor. According to an alternative version, high-pressure marketing promotes junk food that makes everyone fat, resulting from the heartless unloading of unskilled and dangerous work on youthful racial minorities.

Corporate historian John F. Love says in *McDonald's: Behind the Arches* that the fast-food firm showered the "lowly hamburger, french fry, and milk shake with more attention, more study, and more research than anyone had dreamed of doing" (p. 120). But quality would appear to have lost out to other considerations. The main effort went into making the food easily handled and cheap. For example, all McDonald's ground beef was frozen after 1968 (p. 130).

When McDonald's System, Inc., was formed, french fries account for fewer than 5 percent of all potatoes sold in the United States, Love reports. By the mid-1980s, they accounted for more than 25 percent (p. 121). To maintain consistency, potato processors added sugar in one season and leached it out in another. This is one of the many findings described by investigative journalist Eric Schlosser in *Fast Food Nation* (p. 131). Fast-food chains abandoned skilled bakers in favor of automated factories, replaced farmers with scientifically managed batteries of chickens and feed lots of cattle, and coped with the uncertainties of chefs by doing away with them. For example, the firm of IBP (Iowa Beef Packers) led the revolution in meatpacking in the United States, by centralizing the slaughterhouses, by using cheap, often immigrant labor and, in Schlosser's words, "by crushing labor unions and championing the ruthless efficiency of the market" (p. 164).

Armed with gas chromatographs and mass spectrometers, chemists synthesized a vast number of food flavors by the mid-1960s. They manufactured the taste of Pop Tarts, Bac-Os, Tab, Tang, Filet-O-Fish sandwiches, and thousands of other new foods, according to Schlosser. When he toured the laboratories and pilot kitchens of International Flavors and Fragrances (IFF) in Dayton, N.J., he found a snack and savory laboratory responsible for the flavor of potato chips, corn chips, breads, crackers, breakfast cereals, and pet food. The confectionery laboratory devised the flavor for ice cream, cookies, candies, toothpastes, mouthwashes, and antacids. In one pilot kitchen, Schlosser saw a pizza oven, a grill, a milk-shake machine, and a french fryer "identical to those I'd seen behind the counter at countless fast food restaurants" (pp. 120–131).

Schlosser writes that "more than half of all American adults and about one-quarter of all American children are now obese or overweight. Those proportions have soared during the last few decades, along with the consumption of fast food. . . . The rate of obesity among American children is twice as high as it was in the late 1970s" (p. 240). One factor is the increasing size of fast-food servings. During the late 1950s the typical soft drink order in a fast-food restaurant contained about 8 ounces; now a "child" order of Coke at McDonald's is 12 ounces; a "large" Coke is 32 ounces.

"Every day in the United States, roughly 200,000 people are sickened by a foodborne disease, 900 are hospitalized, and 14 die. According to the Centers for Disease Control and Prevention (CDC), more than a quarter of the American population suffers a bout of food poisoning each year," Schlosser reports. "Although the rise in food-borne illnesses has been caused by many complex factors, much of the increase can be attributed to recent changes in how American food is produced. . . . [T]he nation's industrialized and centralized system of food processing has created a whole new sort of outbreak" (p. 195). The "rise of huge feedlots, slaughterhouses, and hamburger grinders seems to have provided the means" for the deadly *E. coli* 0157:H7 pathogen to become widely dispersed (p. 196).

See also **Baking; Beer: Production and Social Use; Boiling; Broiling; Cooking; Crushing; Distribution of Food; Fast Food; Frying; Grilling; Hamburger; Marinating and Marinades; Recipe; Roasting; Storage of Food; Women and Food.**

BIBLIOGRAPHY

Alegre, Edilberto N. "Cooking as Language." In *Sarap: Essays on Philippine Food.* Edited by Doreen G. Fernandez and Edilberto N. Alegre. Audana (Intramuros), Manila: Mr. and Ms. Publishing Company, 1988.

Bourdain, Anthony. *Kitchen Confidential: Adventures in the Culinary Under-belly.* New York: HarperCollins, 2000.

Chang, K. C. *Food in Chinese Culture: Anthropological and Historical Perspectives.* New Haven, Conn.: Yale University Press, 1977.

Drummond, J. C., and Anne Wilbraham. *The Englishman's Food: A History of Five Centuries of English Diet.* Revised by Dorothy Hollingsworth. London: Jonathan Cape, 1957. Classic survey of the industrialization of eating. Originally published in 1939.

Fine, Gary Alan. *Kitchens: The Culture of Restaurant Work.* Berkeley, Calif.: University of California Press, 1996.

Goody, Jack. *Cooking, Cuisine and Class: A Study in Comparative Sociology.* Cambridge, U.K.: Cambridge University Press, 1982.

Kenney, E. J. *The Ploughman's Lunch: Moretum, A Poem Ascribed to Virgil.* Bristol (England): Bristol Classical Press, 1984. Kenney's translation is reprinted in Alan Davidson, ed., *On Fasting and Feasting: A Personal Collection of Favourite Writings on Food and Eating* (London: Macdonald Orbis), 1988.

Love, John F. *McDonald's: Behind the Arches.* New York: Bantam, 1986.

McGee, Harold. *On Food and Cooking: Science and Lore in the Kitchen.* New York: Scribners, 1984.

Myrdal, Janken. "The Plunge Churn from Ireland to Tibet." In *Food and Drink and Travelling Accessories: Essays in Honour of Gösta Berg,* edited by Alexander Fenton and Janken Myrdal, pp. 111–137. Edinburgh: John Donald, 1988.

Ríos, Alicia. "The Pestle and the Mortar." In *Oxford Symposium on Food and Cookery 1988: The Cooking Pot, Proceedings,* edited by Tom Jaine, pp. 125–135. London: Prospect Books, 1989.

Rose, Evelyn. "Replicating the Taste of Home Made Soup in a Canned Product." In *Oxford Symposium on Food and Cookery 1987: Taste, Proceedings,* edited Tom Jaine, pp. 180–182. London: Prospect Books, 1988.

Schlosser, Eric. *Fast Food Nation: What the All-American Meal Is Doing to the World.* London: Allen Lane, 2001. Also published as *Fast Food Nation: The Dark Side of the All-American Meal.* New York: Houghton Mifflin, 2001.

Solomon, Jon. "The Apician Sauce: *Ius Apicianum.*" In *Food in Antiquity,* edited by John Wilkins, David Harvey, and Mike Dobson, pp. 115–131. Exeter: University of Exeter, 1995.

Symons, Michael. "Cutting Up Cultures." *Journal of Historical Sociology* 15, no. 4, 2002.

Symons, Michael. *A History of Cooks and Cooking.* Urbana and Chicago: University of Illinois Press, 2000. Originally *Pudding That Took a Thousand Cooks: The Story of Cooking in Civilisation and Daily Life.* Harmondsworth, England: Viking, 1998.

Michael Symons

PRESENTATION OF FOOD. The presentation of food often refers to its visual composition on the plate, in a state of readiness to be eaten. Modern color photography has promulgated enticing artworks that have come to be the signatures of stylish cooks. All manner of theater is employed in the careful display of food to consumers, appealing to all senses, not just sight, and appearing not just at meals, but throughout the entire marketplace for food.

Plate Presentation

Cooks often pay close attention to plate presentation, choosing ingredients and techniques to suit a desired effect, following a standard arrangement and wiping away drips. Some foods are included mainly to set off others, such as a parsley garnish, and such elements as shells are not to be consumed at all. Checking the food's appearance, which is the cook's last task, becomes the eater's first. Diners are often transfixed by the food when it arrives at the table, as if taking in the whole meal. Yet even the most impressive sculpture collapses at the strike of a knife, fork, or spoon, so that plate presentation is evanescent.

Vision is crucial in identifying ingredients, their quality, and the techniques used, and even has a bearing on the perception of flavor. A dish not displayed traditionally may "not taste the same," and an unfamiliar color, such as blue, may be off-putting.

Japanese diners recognize the importance of eye appeal, to the extent of photographing their meals at restaurants around the world. Their cooks display fanned slices, neat parcels, sculpted vegetables, and noodles placed in soups. Cut fish displayed without sauces contributes to a clean look. Chefs might "spend the day considering the aesthetics of arranging three sardines," according to Richard Hosking in *A Dictionary of Japanese Food* (p. 209). *Moritsuke* (food arrangement) follows seven basic patterns, including *sugimori* (strips and slices of food in a slanting pile), *kasanemori* (overlapping slices), *tawaramori* (blocks or rounds placed horizontally in a pyramid), and so on. Illustrating invention within a highly regulated framework, the *shojin ryori* cookery tradition arranges food like a seasonal landscape—perhaps blue mountains in summer, red in autumn, brown in winter, and flowery in spring. The resulting scene is so abstract that it may appear as one or two objects on a plate to the untutored eye.

As Japanese cooks and diners also appreciate, food is framed by the plate, which might be a beautiful object in its own right, and by the table setting; by other foods, including drinks; by decorations, such as flowers; and by a garden outlook or streetscape.

By contrast, some gourmands in the European tradition worry that an overemphasis on appearance downplays food's other qualities, notably taste and flavor. These cooks may contend that the visual aspect is food's most superficial and that the eyes are quickly contradicted by the tongue.

Atmosphere and Setting

Even before seeing the food, diners might be enticed by menu descriptions. Cooks sell their efforts through sizzling sounds and enticing aromas, so that food is presented at the right temperature and dish covers removed to release captured smells. A charming dining room is comfortably warm and filled with the right music (which might be only the clink and chatter of dining itself). Pre-

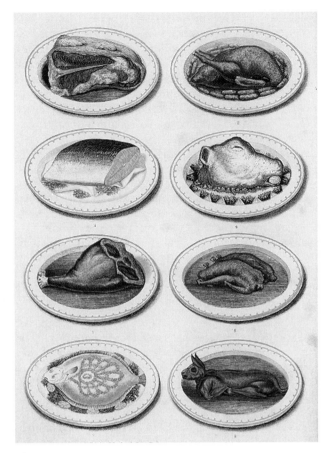

The appearance of food on the table has changed greatly over time to reflect shifts in custom and tastes. In this plate from *Cassell's Household Guide* (London, circa 1878), various meat and fish dishes are displayed according to proper Victorian presentation—with heads attached. Garnishing is minimal because this style of food is intended for home cookery rather than for hotel fare. All of the meats except the calf's head are served in lakes of gravy. ROUGHWOOD COLLECTION.

sentation is also social, and servers participate through such means as well-spoken descriptions, the use of elaborate platters, and carving at the table. Food is also generally enhanced by a convivial circle; many good meals are enveloped in conversation.

Much effort goes into presentation away from the table, too. Market stall-holders stack food showily, shopkeepers arrange eye-catching window displays, and confectioners design luxurious-looking chocolate boxes. Hot bread, roasting chestnuts, and coffee sell themselves through aroma.

Food Fabrication and Marketing

The modern industry fabricates foods from non-traditional ingredients and additives to look like a familiar product (margarine masquerading as butter; emulsifiers, thickeners, and artificial flavors masquerading as ice cream, and so on). Teams of brand managers, flavorists, marketing specialists, graphic designers, and others devise new products, whose acceptance hinges on presentation. Advertising programs, promotions through free samples, discounts and prizes, and point-of-sale materials and packaging provide the final sales pitch. Marketing relies on supermarket shelf exposure, which is boosted by multiple sizes and flavors, and on food's photogenic qualities, which are geared to be so mouth-watering as to induce sales.

Purpose of Presentation

The drive toward balancing colors and textures in front of the eater, experienced in all cuisines at least rudimentarily, has a nutritional basis: providing a healthy variety. Responding to contemporary dietary trends, cooks may include, for instance, green and orange colors in their presentations. Another source of the cooks' aesthetic impulse is the mixture and distribution of ingredients according to a routine or pattern. This repetition can lead to a pared-back elegance.

Cooks who want to show off ingredients find that presentation encourages inspection. Alternatively, in search of amusement, cooks may make foods look like something else, such as a fish made out of vegetables. Cunning cooks can contrive the look of expensive, forbidden, or unobtainable ingredients, and war-time rationing has encouraged such subterfuge. The profit motive comes in here, too, with growers and manufacturers employing many scientific means—from growth hormones to artificial flavors—to improve the appearance especially of cheaper and more readily handled products. Presentation can hide food's origins; some vegetarians contend that meat-eaters only find meat palatable when it no longer resembles "dead animal."

In *The Civilizing Process* (1939), German sociologist Norbert Elias argues that the increasing complexities of society are accompanied by more self-restrained, courteous, and sophisticated culture, including refined food presentation. Demonstrating social power with extravagant displays is captured in American sociologist Thorstein Veblen's phrase "conspicuous consumption" (*The Theory of the Leisure Class*, 1899). Presentation can also symbolize a seasonal festival or other occasion, as in the historical development of the white, possibly tiered, and carefully decorated cake as the nuptial centerpiece. Cakes were first used for weddings in the seventeenth century and became the familiar gleaming structure in the nineteenth.

Food is styled to look good in photographs for mass-circulation newspapers, magazines, and cookery books. Many cooks also follow an artistic impulse beyond mainstream lifestyle publications, seeking to avoid last year's accents and playing a competitive game through fashion. Because the pressures to achieve elegance, pretense, camouflage, and artistic expression can spoil the final effect, critics have long demanded that presentation be simplified and that food should look more "real."

Ancient Lavishness

Elaborate presentation has its roots in ancient times. The Greek epicure Athenaeus describes lavish feasts, not uncommon in third century B.C.E. Macedonia, at which as many as twenty guests were crowned in gold tiaras and presented with silver cups to keep. Mountains of food were pressed upon them, accompanied by musicians, dancing girls, and drinking. A large pig was then carried in, its belly disclosing numerous birds and fishes. After more drinking, guests were served a piping-hot kid, with another silver platter to keep, as well as spoons of gold, and ivory bread baskets. Naked women tumbled among swords and blew fire from their mouths before crystal platters arrived with baked fish.

Such excesses were also frowned upon. Some of the mightiest medieval minds, including St. Thomas Aquinas, considered *gula*, or gluttony, the foremost of the seven deadly sins, and Chaucer's Parson inveighed characteristically against the "apparelling," or dressing up, of food, which included pastry and aspic designs, marzipan armorial quarterings, meat dishes such as Cockentrice (the front half of a chicken sewed to the back half of a suckling pig, and vice versa), and "musician" pies that contained live instrumentalists.

Most famously, at seventeenth-century Versailles, under the "Sun King" Louis XIV, court life consisted of vast dinners enlivened by musicians and fireworks and the arts of conversation and good manners. The king, as the head of the household, lived in semi-public ("in state"), a crowd watching as he arose (*lever*), went to bed (*coucher*), and had meals in between. Parisians and provincials would come to admire Louis XV's fine bearing and elegance, and his deft striking off of the top of a boiled egg with the back of his fork.

Adapting the royal family's grandeur, the ambitious French chef Marie Antonin Carême published in *Le pâtissier pittoresque* (1815), one of the earliest of his several books, more than a hundred depictions of *pièces montées*, elaborate architectural pastry follies.

At table during the London "season" early in the nineteenth century, conversation was prevented by a "huge centre-piece of plate and flowers." It was "strange that people should be invited, to be hidden from one another," wrote the English advocate of a simpler "Art of Dining," Thomas Walker, in his weekly newspaper, *The Original* (2 September 1835; 1928, p. 11), noting that fashionable tables required "excessive breadth" to hold the cumbrous ornaments and lights, the dessert with side-dishes. He opposed fussy cooking, especially "a very inconvenient love of garnish and flowers, either natural or cut in turnips and carrots, and stuck on dishes, so as greatly to impede carving and helping. . . . But there is a still worse practice, and that is pouring sauce over certain dishes to prevent them from looking too plain, as parsley and butter, or white sauce over boiled chicken" (1928, p. 14).

Perhaps all the singing, dancing, fabulous table displays, glamorous surroundings, and networks of diners and servants meant that presentation had overwhelmed the food. However, lavishness lent importance to the entire social and cultural event, a point recognized by the Parisian restaurant of the late eighteenth century, which attracted customers with mirrors, upholstery, and elegant service. Here individuals could order anything from a list at any time and even for a table of one, thereby narrowing the focus to what appeared immediately in front of them and giving rise to the modern fixation on the plate. In *The Invention of the Restaurant*, Rebecca Spang finds "a world in which eating was not a biological imperative but an artistic passion, and in which food came not from farm or field but from ornately decorated boutiques." The new gastronomic writers hailed "the grand restaurant's ability to stimulate and satisfy any desire" (pp. 150–151).

Modernism
Fashionable food presentation moved toward a simplifying modernism during the twentieth century. Worshiping "the geometric splendor of speed," the Italian branch of the Futurist movement under Filippo Tommaso Marinetti turned food into art in the 1930s. The Futurists advocated "optimism at the table," accompanied by "experimentation with new, apparently absurd mixtures." Believing that "form and color are just as important as taste," they struggled against "puddles of sauce, disordered heaps of food, and above all, against flabby, antivirile pastasciutta" in an appeal to Italians to abandon pasta that captured headlines around the world (Marinetti, pp. 21, 36, 38, 67, 133).

French semiotician (scholar of signs) Roland Barthes ridiculed "ornamental cookery" in one of his *Mythologies* essays written between 1954 and 1956. The color photographs in *Elle* magazine sold a "dream of smartness" to the working class, he wrote. Shown from a high angle, at once near and inaccessible, the food could be consumed "simply by looking" by people who could dream of partridges but not afford them. Any actual food was "no more than an indeterminate bed-rock" beneath "sedimentary layers" of smooth "coatings and alibis." For the "primary nature of foodstuffs, the brutality of meat or the abruptness of seafood" was buried beneath sauces, creams, icing and jellies. These coverings were the blank page for a "fairy-land reality" of chiseled mushrooms, carved lemons, shavings of truffle, and arabesques of *glacé* fruit.

French restaurant cooking returned triumphantly to the basics with nouvelle cuisine in the mid-1970s. The waiters were less likely to serve from silver platters ("flats"); instead, cooks positioned the food carefully in the kitchen and on plates about one-third larger, accentuating the lighter portions. The food was more geometrically laid out, relying on the natural colors of the primary ingredients with sauces underneath rather than on top. This less laborious food required more genius, and so was often copied badly. But the trend spread quickly, largely because of its striking, somewhat Japanese look, originally photographed from above but increasingly from the side to benefit its often elevated constructions.

Food for the Camera
Food that is cooked for the camera is captured by specialized photographers attuned to the fashion demands of art directors for billboards, television advertisements, magazines, and cookbooks. The focus, color, shine, and unreality of food photo spreads have earned the epithet "gastro-porn." Because posed food will wilt, shrink, go soggy, dry out, and lose its gloss under the lights, "food stylists" are just outside the shot, coaxing food into pleasing shapes with tweezers, syringes, sprayers, and dry-ice. They employ refillable butane blowtorches and paint strippers to help with "cheese melts" and browning. The stylists employ hairspray and jars of Aqua Gel to make realistic-looking water droplets or to thicken sauces. Since the food is to be seen and not eaten, mashed potato might masquerade as ice cream.

Dishes, such as one-pot stews, that do not photograph well may have their recipes excised. Cuisines, such as those of India, may be considered unfashionable, because they have typically been arranged in several dishes, any one of which might look somewhat nondescript.

In turn, cooks can become overly inspired by brilliant photography. But they should be careful not to make food seem too good to eat, as if it were some untouchable work of art, as the German sociologist Georg Simmel warned in his 1910 essay on the meal. Good presentation can contribute greatly to, but should not be allowed to distract from, either conviviality or the appreciation of the food's natural roots.

See also **Advertising of Food; Art, Food in: Film and Television; Chef, The; Cookbooks; France: Tradition and Change in French Cuisine; Japan: Traditional Japanese Cuisine; Luxury; Marketing of Food; Restaurants; Sensation and the Senses; Serving of Food; Styling of Food; Waiters and Waitresses.**

BIBLIOGRAPHY

Athenaeus. *The Deipnosophists.* 7 vols. Translated by Charles Burton Gulick. Cambridge, Mass.: Harvard University Press, 1927–1941.

Barthes, Roland. *Mythologies.* New York: Hill and Wang, 1972.

Charsley, Simon R. *Wedding Cakes and Cultural History.* London: Routledge, 1992.

Cosman, Madeleine Pelner. *Fabulous Feasts: Medieval Cookery and Ceremony.* New York: Braziller, 1976.

Elias, Norbert. *The Civilising Process.* 2 vols. Translated by Edmund Jephcott. Oxford: Blackwell, 1978 and 1982. Originally published in 1939.

Hosking, Richard. *A Dictionary of Japanese Food: Ingredients and Culture.* Rutland, Vt.: Tuttle, 1996.

Marinetti, Filippo Tommaso. *The Futurist Cookbook.* Translated by Suzanne Brill. San Francisco: Bedford Arts, 1989.

Simmel, Georg. "The Sociology of the Meal." Translated by Michael Symons. *Food and Foodways* 5, no. 4 (1944): 345–350. Originally published in 1910.

Spang, Rebecca L. *The Invention of the Restaurant: Paris and Modern Gastronomic Culture.* Cambridge, Mass.: Harvard University Press, 2000.

Symons, Michael. *A History of Cooks and Cooking.* Urbana and Chicago: University of Illinois Press, 2000.

Walker, Thomas. *The Original.* London: Renshaw, 1838. Originally published in 1835. Selections have also been published as *The Art of Dining.* London: Cayme Press, 1928.

Yoneda, Soei. *Good Food from a Japanese Temple.* Tokyo: Kodansha International, 1982.

Michael Symons

PRESERVING.

Food preservation conserves food for future use. Most of the basic processes have been employed throughout the world for millennia. The primary methods of salting, canning, drying, pickling, smoking, salting, fermenting, cold storage, and freezing all provide an extreme environment in order to stabilize the food for later use. Although most of these methods are used both commercially and in the home, the basic techniques are the same.

Early Methods of Preservation
The idea of preserving food for future consumption was probably first practiced by storing it in a secure place. Original practices mirrored natural processes, such as cold storage, freezing, drying, and even fermentation, which can naturally occur in fruit. Food preservation is evidenced in the archaeological record and in early written records, which indicate the use of salt, snow, smoke, pickling, drying, and fermenting. Ancient Mesopotamia, Egypt, Greece, and Rome all practiced many of these methods of food preservation. Evidence from a Chinese tomb dating prior to 2,000 years ago gives instructions on inscribed bamboo for salting, drying, and pickling. Sixteenth-century records from the observations by the European conquerors of the Maya indicate the use of smoking to preserve peppers and other foods. Methods of preservation like sun drying, smoking, and salting might have been used very early on to preserve the most perishable types of food, such as fish.

Salt, naturally occurring in deposits or as evaporated seawater, could have been dissolved in water as a brine, or in combination with other processes, like drying and smoking, could have preserved many foods. Some foods were not edible in their natural state, like certain tubers or olives, and would have required brining. Grains in particular, once harvested, were probably kept for consumption throughout the year and as protection against the failure of a future harvest. Storage in a dry and cool environment would have prevented molds and sprouting of grains. Fermentation of grain to make beer and of grapes to yield wine can preserve a large and perishable crop.

Early food preservation included simple "banking" in pits, which were dug in the ground and lined with various substances like wood, straw, and leaves to create a barrier between the soil and the food. Caves and storage vessels that were buried or sunk into the ground were also used to create a secure storage environment for the food. Food could be stored in skins, baskets, pottery vessels, or special structures built for certain commodities like grain. Liquids required a much more specialized container, and large supplies of certain commodities, like olive oil, beer, and wine, while difficult to transport, were valuable trade items, and required secure seals to protect the quality of the contents.

Pests, insects, damage from weather or moisture, molds, fungus, decomposition, or a combination of these factors lower the quality of or even destroy the food, and these factors had to be taken into account. Whether the food preserved is being held to guard against future crop or harvest failures, for trade or barter for other commodities, or to divy out certain foodstuffs as part of the yearly diet, the quality of the food preserved had significant impact upon the future quality of life.

Canning
Canning refers to a technique used both commercially and in the home to preserve food in sealed containers. In the early twenty-first century, metal cans are used commercially and glass jars are used in the home. The concept of preserving foods by cooking them and then sealing them in a container is ancient. Olive oil, lard, wax, pitch, clay, and skin have all been used to seal vessels containing food, but are not very reliable. In the late eighteenth century, France offered a monetary award for a method that could be used to preserve food for soldiers. After years of experimentation, Nicholas Appert successfully used sealed glass jars, whose contents had been thoroughly cooked in a water bath, to create portable and potable food. He was awarded the prize in 1809 for his work and went on to publish his findings in "L'art de conserver pendant plusieurs années toutes les substances animales et vegetales" (The art of preserving all kinds of animal and vegetable substances for several years). In 1810, Englishman Peter Durand received a patent for the same process but included tin containers as well as glass.

Tin containers had been used for food storage previously, but it was the combination of the water bath and the sealed container that was so successful. Initially made by hand, tin-plated cans sealed with lead solder were used. By 1819 the Arctic explorer William Edward Parry had included canned foods with the expedition supplies, but the discovery in the 1980s of some of the bodies of those lost on John Franklin's last Arctic expedition in 1847 and their analysis in the 1980s and 1990s indicates that they were suffering from lead poisoning from the lead seals in food cans. Food cans manufactured in the United States have not used lead solder since the mid-1990s, but canned food products from other countries could contain lead solder.

In the United States, various individuals worked on streamlining tin can production, improving the methods of canning various foods, like corn, tomatoes, and lobster. During the mid-nineteenth century in the United States, both commercial canning and home canning expanded, driven by the demand for product by the westward expansion of settlers. The armies of the Civil War used canned goods. Another significant milestone was canned condensed milk, which provided canned milk that was safe to drink, and was developed by Gail Borden in the mid-nineteenth century.

As more foods became available in cans, home cooks "canned" in glass a wide variety of products using basically the same techniques. In both commercial and home canning critical factors were sufficient temperature, sterile containers, and an effective seal. John Mason patented a glass jar with a screw cap to seal it in 1858; numerous patents followed for a reliable and effective seal. The consequences could be illness and even death from bacteria that could grow inside the container, generally the naturally occurring botulism bacteria (*Clostridium botulinum*). Invented in the early twentieth century, the new and most common jar closure used today has two parts that separate the jar cover from the threaded ring. Commercial canned goods created a dependable and transportable food, and are used extensively by consumers all over the world. Canned soup, tuna, juice, corn, tomatoes, and condensed milk are some of the most popular canned foods. In the United States, the cooperative agriculture extension service of the USDA is a source of accurate and inexpensive advice on all types of home preserving. Home canning has diminished in the United States as families moved away from their source of food, but in a 1996 survey, 56 percent of all U.S. households said they had canned in the past, of whom 28 percent had canned within the last two years. Although pressure canners are considered safer, many still use the conventional water bath for home processing.

Drying

Drying occurs naturally with food left in the sun, or on the vine, like beans, or grapes. Some foods, like apples and tomatoes, are generally cut into smaller pieces for drying, a practice which allows the moisture to uniformly evaporate. Herbs are frequently dried whole and on the stem. Low humidity, heat, and air circulation are important so that mold does not occur. Meats and fish can be dried to the point of extreme desiccation, resulting in a product usually called jerky. Drying racks, screens, bags, strings, and bunches can be dried outdoors or in a warm dry spot indoors. Ovens or specialized equipment like dehydrators can be used to create the low temperatures necessary. Once dried, foods can keep for up to a year in a cool and dry environment. Dried foods are sometimes additionally smoked or salted.

Dry storage is usually used for grains, whole vegetables, and fruits like potatoes, onions, carrots, apples, pears

Ceramic preserve jar depicting General George Washington, Pennsylvania, circa 1870. PHILADELPHIA MUSEUM OF ART, BAUGH-BAKER FUND.

and turnips, herbs, and chilies. By keeping the food whole, at certain temperatures, with low humidity, in the dark, and pest free, supplies can last for months, or years. While dry storage is sometimes in separate structures, dried food can also be stored in root cellars and cold rooms below ground or partially below ground.

Fermentation

Fermenting produces beverages like wine and beer and foods like cheese and bread. Fermentation can occur naturally and with naturally occurring yeasts, or lactic acids. Early records in the Sumerian language indicate the manufacture of both beer and bread. Ancient wine making uses yeast and bacteria to transform raw material into the fermented beverage. Fermentation is the result of enzyme activity, naturally occurring proteins present in the food, or can be introduced into it. Sauerkraut and fermented vegetables, like the Korean dish *kimchi*, are produced with lactic acids. The cabbage, vegetable, or mixture is salted and placed in a container where it will ferment, creating an acid environment that will preserve it. This fermentation process is called pickling, just as the use of vinegar and the use of brine are also called pickling.

Vegetables can be very difficult to preserve without processing, but a wide variety of vegetables can be preserved by the addition of salt, after which the juices then drain from the vegetables and ferment. Certain sausages, vegetables, yogurts, and cheeses are all preserved by fermentation. Louis Pasteur's wide-ranging research, which included studying the fermentation process in wine and beer making, led to pasteurization and also to the theory that bacteria existed. The presence of harmful bacteria explained why food preservation had to follow very strict aseptic guidelines, or the food could become spoiled, inedible, or at its worst deadly.

The origins of yogurts and cheese are frequently explained as the result of milk being stored in a skin and warmed, which caused the milk to ferment, and separate into solids and liquids, or curds and whey. Through the use of lactic acid, salt, and heat, and by draining the liquids, cheese is created. By draining, application of pressure to remove the moisture, and by aging cheese can be held for years. Butter can also be preserved with salt. The quantity of salt necessary to preserve butter was such that early instructions required that the butter be washed before use. Unsalted butter is more perishable and has a different flavor.

Cold Storage

Cold storage or refrigeration slows down decomposition of food. Initially, cold storage used natural snow and ice usually kept below ground and covered with straw, or branches. Snow was usually compressed to slow melting. In much of the ancient world, snow and ice were harvested, stored, usually in pits, and used in the summer.

Melting and storage were continuing problems. Much time and effort were devoted to solving these problems over the centuries, but it was in the nineteenth century that many technological advances occurred. In 1803, a Maryland farmer patented an insulated icebox using layers of insulation with charcoal dust. Icehouses were generally below ground structures, although circular brick ones were also used, and filled with layers of ice. In 1827, a more efficient horse-drawn ice cutter was invented for cutting natural ice off lakes and rivers. By the 1840s refrigerator railroad cars were in use in the United States. Around that same time various advances were made in artificially creating ice and refrigeration. John Gorrie, a physician in Florida, received a patent for ice manufacture in 1851. The technology existed, but the product was too expensive compared to natural ice. However, after the blockade of the South and the Civil War, artificial icehouses began to open. For example, the steam-operated Louisiana Ice Manufacturing Company opened in 1868, selling ice for $1.75 for a hundred pounds. By the 1880s ice plants were located throughout the United States, but natural ice was still sold as well. In the twentieth century, ice became universally accessible. In 1913, the first home refrigerator became available and by the 1940s, 56 percent of all U.S. kitchens had electric refrigerators.

Freezing

Freezing food originally took advantage of natural freezing, or below freezing temperatures, but artificially freezing food is an ancient practice as well. Frozen foods are quite stable, although flavor and texture may change. Experiments in compression and condensation led to mechanized ice production, and improved efficiency eventually dropped the price of artificial ice, so it was competitive with natural ice. Home machinery initially stored the ice needed to cool the food. Today, automatic ice and frozen food storage are present in most homes. Clarence Birdseye is generally credited with creating the commercial market in frozen foods, based on his experience with fish in the Arctic. After some years of experimentation mainly with fish, he had perfected his process by 1924, and coupled with advances in freezer cases in stores, frozen foods became widely available.

Freeze-drying is thought to have originated in Peru where the potato has been cultivated for about nine thousand years. At high altitudes, the potato harvest was spread on the ground and exposed to extreme cold and then pressure was applied to remove all moisture. Like other dried products, water is used to reconstitute the dried potato. Freeze-dried coffee was developed in the 1930s, and the United States space program used freeze-dried foods because of their light weight and stability for the astronauts' meals.

Irradiated Food

Irradiated food is exposed to radiation from gamma rays or electron beams or X-rays to kill bacteria, insects, and parasites and reduce spoilage. NASA irradiates food used by its astronauts. Irradiation of food began in 1963, and in addition to the United States, a variety of countries use irradiation for food, including Russia, France, China, and South Africa. Currently, some fruits, vegetables, spices, and meats are irradiated and must be marked with an international symbol called a radura and sometimes a statement such as "irradiated to destroy harmful microbes."

Pickling

Like many of the terms used in food preservation, the term "pickling" can mean several things. It can be used for preserving vegetables, fish, or meat with an acetic acid, or a vinegar. It can also be used to refer to a salt solution, or brine. Generally, it is used to describe the use of vinegar, spices, and salt to preserve vegetables, herbs, and fruits.

Salt is used as a dry packing material or dissolved in water as brine. In both cases it removes liquid from the meat, fish, plant, or dairy product, and prevents decay. To salt for preservation is to use salt to remove the moisture from the fish, meat, or vegetable. The brining method uses salt that has been dissolved in water. The salt is sometimes mixed with sugar and spices. Fish may be hung to dry afterwards, and can then be smoked. Salted codfish is still popular and widely available in spite of pressure on the diminishing population in the Atlantic Ocean. Cuts of meat can remain in the dry cure for a period of time based on weight, usually about twenty-five days, and then are frequently smoked.

Brining is a similar process, with water, salt, sugar, and spices as usual parts of the brine. In brining, it is very important that the meat stays below the surface of the liquid. Time in the brine is related to weight, and the brine must be checked regularly to ensure that it is stable. Temperature fluctuations or insufficient salt can result in the loss of the ability of the brine to preserve the food, and decomposition can begin. The first evidence of this is usually the formation of a mold or "scum" on the surface. Early directions all indicate that the barrels or containers should be checked daily for this reason. Vegetables can also be preserved in brine, or with a dry salt coating. Anchovies, butter, capers, lemons, and herbs, even eggs are also commonly preserved with salt. Salt is also used to produce extremely concentrated and highly flavored sauces, particularly of soy, and/or fish, which have been in use since antiquity and were extremely important for flavor. The Romans had *garum* and other sauces, and the Chinese had soy sauce, for example. These condiments have modern counterparts in soy sauce, hot pepper sauce, fish sauces, and Worcestershire sauce. The purpose of all of these concentrated sauces, ancient and modern, is to carry an extremely dense flavor and saltiness into foods. Sweet flavors, in preserved fruits, were intensified by the combination of sugar and concentration through cooking.

Smoking

Smoking is frequently used in combination with salting. For example, the ancient Mayans preserved chilis, as well as fish and meat, by smoking; in his treatise "On Farming," Cato describes salting and smoking a ham. Smoking takes two basic forms, hot and cold. In cold smoking, the purpose is to impart flavor, not to cook the food, whereas in hot smoking, the appropriate temperature for the fish or meat is necessary to "cook" it.

Sweeteners

Early sweeteners included honey and syrups made from grapes, figs, or dates. Sugar made from cane was costly, but it became more available by the sixteenth century when the sugar plantations that were planted in the Caribbean and South America became major producers. Beet sugar was also in production by the nineteenth century. In preserving with sugar, fruit and a sweetener are cooked together until thickened and then packed into containers. Sometimes are included pieces of the fruit, and other times the mixture is strained and just the resulting liquid is kept. Whole fruits can also be cooked in syrup, until they have completely absorbed the sugar, and then left whole and eaten as a confection.

Our sense of taste identifies flavors as sweet, sour, salty, bitter and some say, *umami* (or savory). The major

preservation techniques utilize these very flavors, creating the core of our palate.

See also **Beer; Birdseye, Clarence; Cheese; Fermentation; Fermented Beverages Other than Wine or Beer; Fish, Salted; Fish, Smoked; Food Safety; Frozen Food; Jam, Jellies, and Preserves; Meat, Salted; Meat, Smoked; Microorganisms; Packaging and Canning, History of; Pasteur, Louis; Soy; Storage of Food; Wine.**

BIBLIOGRAPHY

Ashbrook, Frank. *Butchering, Processing, and Preservation of Meat.* New York: Van Norstrand Reinhold, 1955.

Bailey, L. H. *Encyclopedia of American Agriculture.* Vol. 2. New York: Macmillan, 1907.

Baumgartner, J. G. *Canned Foods: An Introduction to Their Microbiology.* London: Churchill, 1943.

Brothwell, Don, and Patricia Brothwell. *Food in Antiquity: A Survey of the Diet of Early Peoples.* Maryland: Johns Hopkins University Press, 1998.

Cato, Marcus Porcius. *De Agricula* [On farming]. Translated by Andrew Dalby. Blackawton, U.K.: Prospect, 1998.

Chang, K. C., ed. *Food in Chinese Culture: Anthropological and Historical Perspectives.* New Haven: Yale University Press, 1977.

Coe, Sophie. *America's First Cuisines.* Austin: University of Texas Press, 1994.

Collins, James. *The Story of Canned Foods.* New York: Dutton, 1924.

David, Elizabeth. *Harvest of the Cold Months: The Social History of Ice and Ices.* London: Viking, 1995.

Dawson, Thomas. *The Good Huswifes Jewell.* 2 vols. Norwood, N.J.: Johnson, 1977. Originally appeared between 1596 and 1597.

Erlandson, Keith. *Home Smoking and Curing.* London: Ebury, 1989.

Feeney, Robert. *Polar Journeys: The Role of Food and Nutrition in Early Exploration.* Fairbanks: University of Alaska Press, 1997.

Flandrin, Jean-Louis, and Massimo Montanari. *Food: A Culinary History.* Translated by Albert Sonnenfeld. New York: Columbia University Press, 1999.

Foster, E. M. *Historical Overview of Key Issues in Food Safety.* 3, no. 4. Special issue. *Emerging Infectious Disease.* Atlanta, Ga.: National Center for Infectious Diseases, Centers for Disease Control and Prevention, Oct.–Nov. 1997.

Frenzen, Paul, et al. *Consumer Acceptance of Irradiated Meat and Poultry Products.* Agricultural Information Bulletin 757. Washington, D.C.: USDA, 2000.

Grierson, Bill. "Food Safety through the Ages." *Priorities for Health* 9, no. 3. New York: American Council on Science and Health, New York, 1997.

Kurlansky, Mark. *Salt: A World History.* London: Cape, 2002.

Laszlo, Pierre. *Salt Grain of Life.* New York: Columbia University Press, 2001.

Riddervold, Astri, and Andreas Ropeid. *Food Conservation: Ethnological Studies.* London: Prospect, 1988.

Riley, F. R. *The Role of the Traditional Mediterranean Diet in the Development of Minoan Crete: Archaeological, Nutritional, and Biochemical Evidence.* British Archaeological Reports S810. Oxford, 1999.

Shephard, Sue. *Pickled, Potted, and Canned: How the Art and Science of Food Preserving Changed the World.* New York: Simon and Schuster, 2000.

Thorne, Stuart. *The History of Food Preservation.* Cumbria, U.K.: Parthenon, 1986.

Toussaint-Samat, Maguelonne. *History of Food.* Translated by Anthea Bell. Cambridge, Mass.: Blackwell, 1992.

Tressler, Donald, and Clifford Evers. *The Freezing Preservation of Food.* New York: Avi, 1943.

Von Loesecke, Harry. *Outlines of Food Technology.* New York: Reinhold, 1942.

Wilkins, John, David Harvey, and Mike Dobson, eds., *Food in Antiquity.* Exeter, U.K.: University of Exeter Press, 1999.

Wilson, C. Anne, ed. *Waste Not, Want Not: Food Preservation from Early Times to the Present.* Edinburgh: Edinburgh University Press, 1991.

Daphne L. Derven

PROFESSIONALIZATION. Professionalization in food preparation, food media, food styling, restaurant training, and food production assures the consumer that professionals incorporate current educational and practical experience in foods, and possess unique knowledge and skills that solve particular problems facing the food industry. The food professional's goal is to take a body of abstract knowledge and effectively convert it into comprehensible terms for the public. Through the ages, specific knowledge about food was passed first from families, through guilds, and then to professional associations.

In the third century B.C.E., Rome's citizens handed grain to professional bakers (a practice that continued through the thirteenth century), yet bread baking also continued to be done at home. Before the second century B.C.E., Greek observer Athenaeus reported seventy-two kinds of bread in Greece. Rome's culinary advantage was based on outlying regions with efficient trade and transportation; it benefited from pickles from Spain, lemons from Libya, and peaches from Persia. In Rome a good cook was considered an artist, manipulating out-of-season foods. Yet after the appearance of the cookbook of Marcus Gavius Apicius, a first-century Roman epicure, no European cookbooks were issued until the thirteenth century. Historian Michael Symons associates this lapse with the influence of Plato, who warned against taking an interest in cooks. But by the twentieth century, Western scholars had become food specialists writing for public consumption.

Apicius's emphasis on the over-dramatization of the act of eating is what professionals are continually in danger of reproducing. Romans cooked for the eye, not the palate. In the fourteenth and fifteenth centuries, an emer-

gence of food-related trades was represented by guilds that secured exclusive rights to prepare and sell food products previously managed by journeymen. The French Revolution of the eighteenth century gave birth to the modern restaurant, transferring the art of cooking from courts to the middle and working classes, which signaled the death of the guilds. Modern-day restaurants have become, according to food historian W. K. H. Bode, "dormitories for the food manufacturing industry" that "sell their wares under long-established and well respected culinary language which have taken chefs . . . much toil" (Bode, pp. 233, 237). Modern man eats better, but he knows less about the preparation and presentation of food.

During the 1800s and 1900s, increases in population and food production stimulated the world economy with automated technology and mass-production marketing. Georges-Auguste Escoffier's introduction of the brigade system in kitchens broke down the craft barrier and gave rise to the appearance of assembly lines. Cooks became highly specialized, and cooking was corporatized. In eighteenth-century Britain, James Boswell, the literary biographer, defined man as a "cooking animal," noting that it is not tool making, but cooking that separates humans from nature. In pre-Christian Rome, sixth-century Italy, seventeenth-century Europe, and the present millennium, Western consumers did not worry about regional or seasonal limitations because with affluence and a good chef one could have what one wanted all year around.

The influence of cooks on society includes the areas of arts and technology. Before 4000 B.C.E., food was gathered by cooks; later, it was distributed by cooks; and in the last century, cooks organized foods, their efforts garnering professional recognition. Professional cooks were born from home cooks, a tradition that has been replaced with science and technology, a manipulation of foods. The advances that man has devised have changed the shape and taste of food consumed. Taste buds are no longer educated to distinguish the purity of foods.

Over time, food professionals have practiced by creating a recipe, consuming time and money, and refining it for specialized consumption. In the evolution to saturating foods with sauces and producing presentations merely for display, many food professionals disregarded primitive tastes based on indigenous products and cooking equipment made of local wood, fiber, and clay. Artisan work, craft in all phases of food preparation, fell more and more to cultivated specialists, who closely guarded their craft. As specialists begin to exert their knowledge more broadly, professionals may no longer dominate the foreground. The more knowledge is shared, the larger the impact on the profession that was founded on formalized techniques and apprenticeships.

Specialists who share their skills contribute to decisions on dietary needs by emphasizing less, but better-quality, healthy, safe, ecologically sound foods that exhibit global concern and may re-awaken consumers' faith. Professionals "revisiting" food through the specialist "eye" learn from the past, and from global, urban, and rural foods.

Some philosophers contend that thinking of food as a movement changes its significance. The recognition by other professions of the significance of making food can dispel ignorance and disrespect of food and enable research into such subjects as bioterrorism in the food supply. Our identity with food is transformed at the speed of technology, and food specialists, by sharing skills and information, help manage this transformation that shapes our history and forms our future.

See also **Apicius; Chef, The; Cookbooks; Escoffier, Georges-Auguste; Restaurants.**

BIBLIOGRAPHY

Bode, W. K. H. *European Gastronomy.* London: St. Edmundsbury, 1994.

Caplow, Theodore. *The Sociology of Work.* New York: McGraw Hill, 1964.

Davidson, James N. *Courtesans and Fishcakes: The Consuming Passion of Classical Cuisine.* New York: St. Martin's, 1997.

Etzioni, Amitai, ed. *The Semi-Professions and Their Organization.* New York: Free Press, 1969.

Giacosa, Ilaria Gozzini. *A Taste of Rome.* Translated by Anna Herklotz. Chicago: University of Chicago Press, 1992.

Pavalko, Ronald, M. *Sociology of Occupations and Professions.* 2d ed. Itasca, Ill.: F. E. Peacock, 1971.

Pillsbury, Richard. *No Foreign Food: The American Diet in Time and Place.* Boulder, Colo.: Westview Press, 1998.

Root, Waverly, and Richard De Rochemont. *Eating in America.* New Jersey: Ecco Press, 1995.

Schlosser, Eric. *Fast Food Nation: The Dark Side of the All-American Meal.* New York: Houghton Mifflin, 2001.

Senauer, Ben, Elaine Asp, and Jean Kinsey. *Food Trends and the Changing Consumer.* St. Paul, Minn.: Eagan Press, 1991.

Sonnenfeld, Albert. *Food: A Culinary History from Antiquity to Present.* New York: Columbia University Press, 1999.

Spang, Rebecca L. *The Invention of the Restaurant: Paris and Modern Gastronomic Culture.* Cambridge, Mass.: Harvard University Press, 2000.

Symons, Michael. *A History of Cooks and Cooking.* Urbana: University of Illinois Press, 2000.

Toussaint-Samat, Maguelonne. *History of Food.* Translated by Anthea Bell. Cambridge, Mass.: Blackwell, 1992.

Susan Sykes Hendee
Loring Davena Boglioli

PROTEINS AND AMINO ACIDS.

The average human body, weighing 65 kilograms, contains about 11 kilograms of protein, 40 kilograms of water, and 9 kilograms of fat. The protein provides the "machinery" of the body, including not only the voluntary muscles and the heart muscles, but also the walls of the gut and the blood vessels, as well as the enzymes, the skin, and the hair. The word "protein" is used to describe a group of different compounds with varying properties—soluble, insoluble, and so on. Originally they were classed together because, unlike fats and carbohydrates, proteins also contain nitrogen in addition to carbon, hydrogen, and oxygen. Now, we know that they are all composed of chains of "amino acids" linked together like enormous necklaces of thousands of individual beads. To continue the analogy, there are twenty different varieties of "bead" (or amino acid). The chemists' shorthand representation of the common formula for each amino acid is "$H_2N.CHR.COOH$," where "$—H_2N$" is the basic amino group, "$COOH$" is the organic acid group, and "R" the general symbol for whatever additional group is present for that particular "bead." Amino acids can form chains by reaction between the amino group of one molecule and the acidic group of another to give:

$$—HN.CHR1.COO—HN.CHR2.COO—$$

The body makes its own proteins and obtains amino acids from the digestion of the proteins in the foods that we eat. These large protein molecules cannot be absorbed through the gut walls into the bloodstream, but a series of digestive enzymes (which are proteins themselves, having these special digestive functions) break down the chains of amino acids into the individual amino acids, which are then absorbed. A small proportion of protein may remain undigested, especially with the more fibrous plant foods such as bran, where the cellulosic cell walls are not easily broken down in the tissues, but, for most mixed human diets, one can assume at least 90 percent protein digestibility.

The final nutrients that we obtain from our foods are thus amino acids rather than proteins, and we build our own protein "necklaces" up from the pool of free amino acids circulating in our body. This pool is also derived in part from body proteins that are continually being broken down and resynthesized. Our bodies are in a dynamic state and are constantly turning over.

Each protein in our body has a specific function and is made up of a predetermined succession of amino acids that, when the protein is being synthesized, are added one by one to the chain. If a particular amino acid is missing from the site of synthesis, the process stops. Of the different varieties of amino acids, some are termed "essential," which means that our bodies are unable to synthesize them by modification of another molecule. Four amino acids in this category are lysine, methionine, threonine, and tryptophan. Others, the "nonessential" amino acids, can be made in the body from other nitrogenous compounds.

Protein Functions

Obviously, a growing body needs dietary protein in order to increase its own body tissues. This is particularly clear in species where the young grow quickly, such as calves and particularly piglets, and it is interesting that the dams' milk in these species is considerably higher in protein than is human breast milk, the natural food that meets the needs of much more slowly growing human infants. It is also obvious that older children need protein for their continued growth and that pregnant and lactating women need it to provide for the growing fetus and then for the suckling infant. The protein needs of other adults are not so obvious, except for the slow but continuous growth of hair and fingernails, the replacement of rubbed-off skin, and other minor losses. However, adults require much greater amounts of protein than would be expected to replace these losses—something like 50 g/day.

It is true that living tissue is in a dynamic state, with protein being continually broken down to its constituent amino acids and resynthesized, but this should not increase requirements because the amino acids are fully available for reuse. However, there are enzymes in the liver whose function is to break down an excess of circulating amino acids. These enzymes allow the elimination of nitrogen in the form of urea and the utilization of the carbon-containing side-chains of the amino acids as energy sources for the tissues. It appears that what we might call the "idling rate" of these enzymes sets the requirement for amino acids to replace those lost in this way. In the course of evolution there has presumably been no advantage, in general, in selecting for individuals with lower "idling levels" because protein intake was not a limiting factor. However, evolutionary selection may explain the apparently lower protein requirements of natives in an area of Oceania with a traditionally low-protein diet.

At one time it was thought that the muscular contractions required in any kind of physical work consumed protein, as if the muscle used itself up or was its own fuel. We now know that this is not the case, and that carbohydrate and fat are the normal sources of the energy required for physical work. The erroneous belief that physical work uses up protein has, in the past, been of some practical import since it meant that traditional working-class families would give a large proportion of what meat was available to the "breadwinner" father because of his greater physical labor, so that little remained for the others even when the wife was pregnant and her requirement for more concentrated sources of nutrients was actually more critical.

Protein Levels in Foods

From the preceding discussion, it is obvious that meat from other animal species is a rich source of protein. The only qualification is that fat can seriously dilute the concentration of protein available. Lean muscle has a 3:1 ratio of water to protein, whereas fats are laid down without associated water. Thus, a cut of meat with 20 percent fat will also have only 20 percent of protein (that is, 1/4 of 80 percent). Further, since fat provides 9 Calories of en-

ergy per gram and protein only approximately 4, it follows that 9/13, or approximately 70 percent, of the energy provided by the meat will be coming from animal fat. (Note that the dietitian's Calorie, spelled with a large "C," is one thousand times the standard "calorie" and is the heat needed to raise 1 kilogram of water by 1°C).

The working parts of plants, principally enzymes, also consist of proteins; and seeds always include protein that will be required for the synthesis of new tissues when the seed germinates. In general, the concentration of protein is lower than that in animal tissues because the structural components consist of fibrous carbohydrates and, for seeds or root stores, large amounts of starch and sugars are usually also present as a reserve of energy.

There are several different ways of comparing the relative richness of different foods in protein. The simplest way would be a straight comparison of the percentage of protein in each food. Thus, whole milk contains just over 3 percent while white bread contains 8 percent or a little over, that is, more than twice as much. Yet the dietitian's practice when considering adult-type menus is to compute the quantity provided by a typical "serving." Thus, for milk the standard serving is 1 "cup" (245 grams), which provides 8 grams of protein. If we take two slices (50 grams) as the standard serving for white bread, this provides only 4 grams of protein, that is, less. So, there is a contradiction. Milk, of course, is nearly 90 percent water. Dried whole milk contains 27 percent protein and dried bread only 13 percent. This is perhaps a fairer comparison since one would consume more water with a meal if one were not drinking fluid milk, and it leads to one finally regarding milk as being the richer source of protein.

Common refined cereals (white flour, white rice, and de-germed cornmeal) all contain about 10 g protein per 100 g dry matter, with wheat providing a little more and rice a little less, as do potatoes. Lean fish and meat have up to 60 percent protein in their dry matter and skim milk has 40 percent. Among plant products, the legume crops (peas and beans) have the highest values, commonly 20 to 25 percent of dry matter. Legumes that are rich in fat (the so-called oil-seeds) can be processed to remove the oil, and the residues have even higher protein values. Extracted soybean meal has 45 percent protein and materials of this type have been used to make vegetarian substitutes for meat.

One would expect that the wealthier countries, with their greater use of animal products of high protein concentration, would have overall diets of higher protein content, but this is not always the case. Wealthier population groups also consume higher levels of fat and sugar, much of them in fast foods and "cola-type" drinks. These dilute the protein concentration of the diet to the levels of those poorer countries whose diet is based on cereals with less in the way of supplementary foods of either high or low protein content.

A particular problem exists where a poor community has plantains and/or cassava (manioc) as its staple foods. These have only about 2 to 4 percent of their dry matter in the form of protein, that is, values much lower than the corresponding value for grains. In addition, these foods are so bulky that young children being reared on them are commonly unable to consume enough to meet even their energy needs. They are thus at constant risk of both protein and energy deficiencies and should be given more concentrated foods.

Protein Quality

As mentioned above, if a human diet were to be totally deficient in one essential amino acid, a child would immediately cease to grow and even an adult would go into decline. In practice this never happens. Even though one can extract from some plants an individual protein that is of this kind (for example, the gluten present in wheat), the total mixture of proteins in any natural food contains some of each of the amino acids, though not usually in the exact ratio in which the human body will use them. This is not a problem so long as the essential amino acid is present at the lowest level that is adequate to meet the body's need for it. The remaining amino acids will conversely be present in excess, and, as explained in the previous discussion, mechanisms exist to metabolize these amino acids to provide an additional source of energy.

Providing fast-growing young rats with wheat flour as their sole source of protein in a diet that is otherwise well balanced, will result in relatively slow growth; rats fed on the same diet supplemented with a small quantity of the amino acid lysine will grow considerably faster. Under these experimental conditions, the protein of wheat flour is said to have a low "biological value" and its "limiting amino acid" to be lysine.

Mixtures of foods that have different limiting amino acids can supplement each other. Thus, if one protein source, such as a grain, is limited by its lysine content, but has methionine in excess, and another protein source, such as a legume, has a good level of lysine but is short of methionine, a mixture of the two will have a better balance than either alone. This phenomenon can be clearly demonstrated in experiments where young growing rats, for example, are fed a mixture of wheat flour, primarily deficient in lysine, and navy beans, primarily deficient in methionine. Young rats grow faster when they are fed with both wheat flour and navy beans, as opposed to being fed with either protein source separately, but still not as well as when they are fed with well balanced egg protein because the mixture is still partially deficient in a third amino acid, threonine.

There has been a great deal of research and controversy about how serious partial deficiencies of individual amino acids are in human diets. In poor communities in North Africa wheat has been the traditional staple food, with only small quantities of supplementary foods. When synthetic lysine became available at a reasonable cost, a trial was carried out to determine if fortification of the traditional diet with lysine at the time the grain was milled would result in improved vigor in people and in improved health among children. However, there was no evidence of any benefit. Nor was any benefit seen in comparable trials in Thailand.

It is clear that the young rat can be a misleading model for humans. A child grows much more slowly to its adult size then a small animal and, at its fastest rate of growth, adds no more than 3 grams of protein to its tissues in a day—a very small amount in relation to its protein intake, which would normally be ten times as great even with a diet containing no more than 10 PCal%. A more common problem than diet based on grain that is deficient in an essential amino acid, is the fact that people do not eat enough to cover their energy needs—in adults, because of poverty in most cases; and in young children in the developing world because their food is too bulky for them to be able to consume all they need. In such cases adults can lose muscle power and general vigor and small children can develop kwashiorkor, a potentially fatal disease that appears to be a combined deficiency of energy and protein, because what protein is ingested has to be used as additional fuel.

Vegetarian Diets

It is clear from what has been written already that vegetarians can have an adequate intake of protein, particularly if they are willing to consume milk and eggs which provide good supplements to the protein of grains, and do not require animals to be killed. Vegans, who eliminate all animal products from their diets, commonly ensure that, in addition to consuming grains, they have a good intake of legumes as a supplementary source of proteins relatively rich in lysine. The legumes may not always be essential, but the supplementation provides a useful safety margin. The long-term problem for vegans is that they will become deficient in vitamin B_{12}, unless they take a special vitamin supplement, because this vitamin occurs naturally only in animal tissues or from the fermentation of certain bacteria.

Protein Requirements.

The recommended daily dietary allowance for an adult of average build is 0.8 grams of protein per kilogram of body weight, equivalent to 0.36 grams of protein per pound of body weight, regardless of sex. Since "average" men and women in the United States are assumed to weigh about 170 and 130 pounds, respectively, these standards give us an intake of 61 grams protein for the average man and 47 grams of protein for the woman, with a further addition of 15 grams of protein per day for women during pregnancy and lactation. These standards were designed to be adequate for diets containing protein of average quality and to contain some margin of safety. Virtually all American diets contain more than this amount of protein.

Despite children's need for growth, their requirement for protein as a proportion of their total food is lower than that of adults, because their energy expenditures in relation to their size are greater than those of adults, and their growth is so gradual. However, if a child's appetite is very poor and/or the diet is very bulky, the diet can become protein deficient because some of the small amount of protein consumed will be used as an energy source.

See also **Assessment of Nutritional Status; Caloric Intake; Calorie; Disease; Lactation; Malnutrition; Nutrients; Nutrition.**

BIBLIOGRAPHY

Carpenter, Kenneth J. *Protein and Energy. A Study of Changing Ideas in Nutrition.* New York: Cambridge University Press, 1994.

World Health Organization. *Energy and Protein Requirements.* Technical Report Series No. 724. Geneva: World Health Organization, 1981.

Kenneth John Carpenter

PROVERBS AND RIDDLES.

Proverbs and riddles are pithy verbal expressions handed down over the course of many generations. Both forms are grounded in the familiar, but in opposite ways. While proverbs tend to re-familiarize the familiar, riddles tend to de-familiarize the familiar. More specifically, proverbs function like mini-allegories by embodying an abstract truism in concrete imagery drawn from familiar experience; the truism is thus reified and made "extra-familiar." For example, in the sixteenth century, the abstract truism "change occurs gradually" was reified in a vivid proverb that invoked a familiar domestic situation: "Little by little the cat eats the bacon." In contrast, riddles cause their reader to see an ordinary object in a new and extraordinary light. For example, the riddle "A little white house without door or window" prompts the reader to re-apprehend the thing implied by the riddle: "an egg." In the moment that this solution is guessed or given, the egg is perceived not merely as something to fry or hatch, but as a home or shelter, an analogue to the reader's own house. Because riddles and proverbs alike are grounded in the familiar (albeit in different ways), food and culinary situations supply the raw material of many of them.

Food Proverbs

The study of proverbs is called paremiology. Some paremiologists distinguish proverbs from maxims, saws, sententiae, and other kinds of folk sayings, but in practice these distinctions are hard to maintain. In this article, the term "proverb" is employed in its widest sense.

Over the centuries, food proverbs have enjoyed and suffered the same vagaries of popularity as proverbs in general. In ancient times, proverbs were much esteemed, as evidenced by the Old Testament Book of Proverbs, which includes many food-based maxims such as "Eat thou not the bread of him that hath an evil eye, neither desire thou his dainty meats" (23:6). Aristotle, too, is reputed to have written a work on proverbs, now lost. During the Middle Ages, sermons and other didactic works popularized hundreds of proverbs, such as "He must have a long spoon that shall eat with the devil," first recorded in 1395. During the sixteenth century, numerous ancient Greek and Latin proverbs were revived thanks to the Dutch humanist Erasmus, who published a collection of three thousand proverbs derived from classical literature, including "You are decorating a cooking pot" (meaning "You are doing needless work") and "When offered turtle-meat, either eat or don't eat" (meaning "Make up your mind, one way or another"). The popularity of proverbs among learned authors increased through the seventeenth century, but then began to decline in the eighteenth century, when they came to be seen as evidence of vulgarity rather than erudition. In 1741, for example, Lord Chesterfield belittled "common proverbs" because they were "proofs of having kept bad and low company. For example, if, instead of saying that tastes are different . . . you should let off a proverb, and say 'that what is one man's meat is another man's poison' . . . everybody would be persuaded that you had never kept company with anybody above footmen and housemaids." (461)

Proverbs about food reflect, naturally, the gastronomic and culinary norms of the culture in which they arise. For example, the proverb "from eggs to apples," meaning "from beginning to end," originated in ancient Rome, where it was customary to begin a meal with eggs and end it with apples. In China, proverbs abound that mention rice or tea, including "Talk doesn't cook rice" and "Better to be deprived of food for three days than tea for one." In Azerbaijan, many proverbs refer to yogurt and halva, including "He who burns his mouth on milk will blow on yogurt when eating it" and "Your mouth won't get sweet just by saying 'halva.'" In Germany, where wine-making is common, one encounters the proverb "Big and empty, like the Heidelberg tun," an allusion to a wine cask renowned for its 58,000-gallon capacity. In England, the prevalence of proverbs involving eggs attests to the long-standing importance of that foodstuff in that nation's diet; *A Dictionary of the Proverbs in England in the Sixteenth and Seventeenth Centuries* cites twenty-seven egg proverbs. Some of those egg proverbs are still current, such as "Don't put all your eggs in one basket" and "As sure as eggs be eggs." Others are less familiar, such as "Better an egg in peace than an ox in war," "It is hard to shave an egg," and "Who means to have the egg must endure the cackling of the hen." Other food proverbs survive only by virtue of their being used in Shakespeare, such as "to take eggs for money," meaning "to exchange something valuable for something worthless." Still others have been obsolete for centuries, such as "to come in with five eggs," meaning "to interrupt with an idle story," while others have been rendered obsolete by changing social conditions, such as inflation: "as dear as two eggs a penny."

On the other hand, some proverbs persist even when they cease to make literal sense. The proverbial phrase "to bet dollars to doughnuts" is still current even though the rising cost of doughnuts has diminished the original disparity of the wager. Likewise, the proverbial phrase "to eat humble pie," meaning "to be forced into apologizing in a humiliating manner" remains current even though it has been largely forgotten that "humble pie" was originally "umble pie," and that the umbles were the innards of a deer, often cooked into a kind of meat pastry. The proverbial phrase "to dine with Duke Humphrey," meaning "to go hungry," is still heard occasionally, even though the origin of that expression has been lost even to paremiologists.

Like proverbs in general, many food proverbs have changed their form over time. The early-sixteenth-century proverb "Many things fall between the cup and the mouth" evolved, by the mid-nineteenth century, into the more familiar "There's many a slip 'twixt cup and lip." The use of rhyme in the latter proverb is one of several literary devices that characterize many proverbs, including food proverbs. These literary devices make proverbs easier to remember, and also signify their special ratified status, rather like placing a frame around a picture. Other literary devices include alliteration (as in the fifteenth-century proverb "the more crust, the less crumb"), parallelism (as in the fourteenth-century proverb "the nearer the bone, the sweeter the flesh"), and antimetabole (as in the sixteenth-century proverb "while one wastes drink, the drink wastes him").

Proverbs, including food proverbs, continue to be invented up to this day, though perhaps not at the rate they were centuries ago. One recent addition, often heard in the more northern parts of the United States and Canada, is the ironic maxim "Don't eat yellow snow."

Food Riddles

While proverbs re-familiarize the familiar, and riddles de-familiarize the familiar, the distinction between the two forms is sometimes unclear. For example, the seventeenth-century proverb "An egg will be in three bellies in twenty-four hours" has the declaratory form of many proverbs, but in substance it is much like a riddle: the three bellies are the belly of the hen that lays it, of the oven that bakes it, and of the human who eats it. Other proverbs can easily be converted into riddles by suppressing, rather than declaring, the familiar element: the sixteenth-century proverb referred to above—"while one wastes drink, the drink wastes him"—becomes a riddle when expressed in this form: "As you waste it, it wastes you." Aristotle noted that riddles are also closely allied to metaphors: "Metaphors imply riddles, and therefore a good riddle can furnish a good metaphor" (*Rhetoric* book 3, chapter 2). Put another way, many riddles are merely

MISCELLANEOUS FOOD PROVERBS

Hunger is the best sauce.
He is an evyll coke that can not lycke his owne lyppes.
Don't cry over spilt milk.
The proof of the pudding is in the eating.
Butter wouldn't melt in his mouth.

incomplete metaphors: one half of the identity relationship is deliberately elided. For example, this Filipino riddle—"A trunk of a king; if opened it cannot be shut"—becomes a metaphor once the missing element is re-inserted: "An egg is a trunk of a king; if opened it cannot be shut."

Also like proverbs, riddles are ancient in origin. In the ancient Greek legend of Oedipus, the Sphinx terrorized the people of Thebes when they could not solve its riddle. In the Old Testament, Samson successfully antagonized the Philistines by challenging them to solve this riddle: "Out of the eater came forth meat, and out of the strong came forth sweetness" (Judg. 14:14). The solution to the riddle was a lion, Samson having previously encountered a lion carcass that bees had filled with honey. Ninety-one ancient riddles are also preserved in the Exeter Book, a late-tenth-century manuscript collection of Anglo-Saxon literature. Of these ninety-one riddles, ten are food- or drink-related, including this one, whose bawdy double-entendres de-familiarize the everyday thing implied by the riddle:

> I am a wondrous creature: to women a thing of joyful expectation, to close-lying companions serviceable. I harm no city-dweller excepting my slayer alone. My stem is erect and tall—I stand up in bed—and whiskery somewhere down below. Sometimes a countryman's quite comely daughter will venture, bumptious girl, to get a grip on me. She assaults my red self and seizes my head and clenches me in a cramped place. She will soon feel the effect of her encounter with me, this curl-locked woman who squeezes me. Her eye will be wet.

The solution to this ribald riddle is "onion."

Inventing new riddles continues to be a popular activity among some authors and educators. In the nineteenth century Lewis Carroll devised riddles, including a long and elaborate food-related one, for *Through the Looking Glass*. In the twentieth century, J. R. R. Tolkien created many riddles for *The Hobbit*, including this one: "A box without hinges, key, or lid. Yet golden treasure inside is hid." The solution is familiar: "an egg."

See also **Art, Food in; Folklore, Food in; Magic; Metaphor, Food as; Myth and Legend, Food in; Religion and Food; Symbol, Food as.**

BIBLIOGRAPHY

Baz, Petros D. *A Dictionary of Proverbs, with a Collection of Maxims, Phrases, Passages, Poems, and Anecdotes from Ancient and Modern Literature*. New York: Philosophical Library, 1963.

De Proverbio: Electronic Publisher of Proverb Studies and Collections. Available at http://www.deproverbio.com.

Dobrée, Bonamy. *The Letters of Philip Dormer Stanhope, 4th Earl of Chesterfield*. Volume 2. London: Eyre and Spottiswoods, 1932.

The Exeter Book Riddles. Translated by Kevin Crossley-Holland. Harmondsworth, England: Penguin Books, 1979.

Mieder, Wolfgang. *A Dictionary of American Proverbs*. New York: Oxford University Press, 1992.

Tilley, Morris Palmer. *A Dictionary of the Proverbs in England in the Sixteenth and Seventeenth Centuries*. Ann Arbor: University of Michigan Press, 1950.

Whiting, Bartlett Jere. *Early American Proverbs and Proverbial Phrases*. Cambridge, Mass.: Harvard University Press, Belknap Press, 1977.

Whiting, Bartlett Jere. *Proverbs, Sentences, and Proverbial Phrases; from English Writings Mainly before 1500*. Cambridge, Mass.: Harvard University Press, Belknap Press, 1977.

Wilson, Frank Percy. *The Oxford Dictionary of English Proverbs*. Oxford: Clarendon Press, 1970.

Mark Morton

PUDDING. *See* **Custard and Pudding.**

PULSE CROPS. *See* **Legumes.**

PYTHAGORAS. Pythagoras (c. 580–c. 580 B.C.E.) was a Greek mathematician, philosopher, and mystic. He wrote nothing himself, so his ideas survive through the writings of others, including Aristotle. Many people are familiar with him as the mathematician who formulated the Pythagorean theorem in geometry that relates the lengths of the sides in a right triangle. Others know him as a mystic and the first person known to be motivated by moral and philosophical concerns to adopt a vegetarian diet.

The schools and societies Pythagoras founded in the southern Italian area of Magna Graecia flourished for a while, and they developed and spread many of his concepts, which were later adopted and expanded by others. These concepts include bodily humors (evident in modern descriptions of melancholic and phlegmatic personalities), a tripartite soul, reincarnation, and the numerical ratios that determine the concordant intervals of the musical scales. Permeating all of his thoughts was the idea that all things are numbers. Numbers (individuals, groups, and series) were imbued with mystical properties that were carefully guarded and only shared among initiates to the Pythagorean schools founded by him or his disciples.

Pythagoras and his followers practiced one of the first recorded diets known as vegetarianism. He advocated a diet devoid of the flesh of slaughtered animals partially because he felt food influenced the distribution of the bodily humors and thereby the health of the individual and partially because it would prevent the killing of a reincarnated individual and its transmigrated soul. Up until the late nineteenth century non–meat eaters were generally known as "Pythagoreans."

Pythagoras is also alleged to have admonished his disciples to abstain from eating beans. Ancient and medieval writers ingeniously ascribed this pronouncement to the belief that beans contained or transmitted souls. The Greek phrase supporting this gastronomic recommendation, however, could also be construed to imply that his followers should avoid politics. Black and white beans were used as counters in voting in Magna Graecia. The school Pythagoras founded there became actively involved in the populist political views that gained ascendancy in the town of Kroton, where he lived for many years. Later an opposing aristocratic party gained control of the city and banished him and his followers for their political views and activism. Pythagoras died in exile. His supposed warning to "abstain from beans" is therefore thought to have meant "avoid politics." Alternatively he may have realized that eating undercooked broad (fave) beans (Vica faba vulgaris), a common food of the Mediterranean region, produced a severe hemolytic anemia (favism) in some people. Interestingly the same mutant gene that makes people sensitive to favism also increases their resistance to the malarial parasite, possibly accounting for the widespread presence of the mutant gene in regions with endemic malaria.

See also **Greece, Ancient; Vegetarianism.**

BIBLIOGRAPHY

Bamford, Christopher, ed. *Homage to Pythagoras*. Hudson, N.Y.: Lindisfarne Press, 1994.

Gorman, Peter. *Pythagoras*. London: Routledge and Kegan Paul, 1979.

Spencer, Colin. *The Heretic's Feast: A History of Vegetarianism*. London: Fourth Estate, 1993.

Walters, Kerry S., and Lisa Portmess, eds. *Ethical Vegetarianism: From Pythagoras to Peter Singer*. Albany: State University of New York Press, 1999.

Mikal E. Saltveit

R

RABELAIS, FRANÇOIS. Little is known with complete accuracy about the life of Rabelais (1483 or 1494?–1553). Born in or near Chinon, France, where his father was a lawyer, he entered the priesthood as a novice of the Franciscan order. Here he was able to study languages, literature, and the sciences. Abandoning holy orders, Rabelais traveled to Montpellier, where he obtained a degree in medicine and became a physician at Lyons Hospital and a professor of medicine. It is here that he began writing the series of satirical books for which he is best remembered today. The four books (the fifth is of doubtful authenticity) tell the bawdy, rollicking tales of the giants *Gargantua* and *Pantagruel*. Often difficult to read, and frequently misunderstood as works of gross indecency, the stories are strewn with references to eating, food, and drink that help paint a vivid picture of Renaissance life. But it is in the use of food as part of satirical allegory that Rabelais is at his most inspired. Food imagery helps create a cloak of laughter to thinly conceal his pointed comments on important contemporary issues of the day.

One example of the vivid food imagery founds in Rabelais' works occurs in the fourth book of *Gargantua and Pantagruel* when, in the course of an epic voyage, his heroic characters, Pantagruel and the ship's company, go ashore on the Wild Island, ancient abode of the Chitterlings. Here they encounter sausage-people who are locked in an irreconcilable war with their enemy Quaresmeprenant (Shrovetide). Learning that Chitterlings are preparing to ambush the heroes, Friar John orders the construction of a giant sow, similar in principle to the Greeks' Trojan horse, and mans it with a company of noble and valiant cooks ready to do battle in a "culinary war." In the midst of battle, the cooks spill forth and rout the Chitterlings, handing victory to Pantagruel.

Exemplifying the difficulty people have with the interpretation, this episode has been viewed as either a representation of the battle between Carnival and Lent; as a satire on Church and State, specifically on the German-

"Chitterlings are Chitterlings, always duplicitous and treacherous."

Book 4, Chapter 36

François Rabelais, a medical doctor and master of languages, was one of the most learned men of his time. In his exaggerated and irrepressible *Gargantua and Pantagruel*, he attacked the monks' ideal of self-denial with detailed depictions of eating—thousands of cattle must be slaughtered to satisfy the giants' appetites—and of bodily functions. Although he is assumed to have been a great lover of food and drink, as Balzac observed, Rabelais "was a sober man who drank nothing but water." PORTRAIT COURTESY OF THE LIBRARY OF CONGRESS.

speaking Protestants and the Council of Trent; and as a moral message supporting moderation.

Rabelais remains often misunderstood. But his books continue to inspire as literary masterpieces of satire, full of wit and wisdom, and displaying both a genuine humanist love of life and a quest for truth.

See also **Art, Food in: Literature**; **Christianity: Western Christianity**; **France**; **Metaphor, Food as**.

BIBLIOGRAPHY

Barzun, Jacques. *From Dawn to Decadence*, pp. 128–133. New York: HarperCollins, 2000.

The Complete Works of François Rabelais. Translated by Donald M. Frame. Berkeley: University of California Press, 1999.

Plattard, Jean. *The Life of François Rabelais.* New York: Knopf, 1931.

Rabelais, François. *The Histories of Gargantua and Pantagruel.* Translated by J. M. Cohen. London: Penguin Books, 1955.

Screech, M. A. *Rabelais.* Ithaca: Cornell University Press, 1979.

Colin Sheringham

RAMADAN. Ramadan, the major fast of the Islamic year, falls in the ninth lunar month. Traditionally, Ramadan commences and ends with the sighting of the new moon, though now a standard calendar is more commonly used.

The month-long fast involves abstinence from food, liquids, smoking, and sexual intercourse between the hours of sunrise and sunset, but at night the holiday has turned into a feast in many Arab countries, each of which has its favorite special Ramadan foods and recipes. Moreover, fasting must be undertaken with spiritual intent (*niyyah*), and this intent must be renewed each day before dawn. Mean-spirited words, and thoughts and deeds

Cooks frying cakes for Ramadan in Karachi, Pakistan. COURTESY AP/WIDE WORLD PHOTOS.

such as slander, lying, and covetousness negate the value of fasting. The fast commences each day at dawn, immediately prior to which an early morning meal, *suhoor*, should be eaten. It usually includes a special bread called *mushtah* and a sweet cream-filled pastry called *kilaj*, which are served only during Ramadan. During the day no food or drink may be taken, which can be a severe test when Ramadan falls during the hot summer season. The day's fast is broken with a small meal, *iftar*, taken as soon as possible after sunset. Traditionally, this is dates and water in remembrance of Muhammed, who always broke his fast by first eating dates, followed by lentil soup and salad. A larger, often quite elaborate meal may be eaten later at a mosque or shared with visiting friends and family. There are no particular rules governing what should be served for the main course. Sweets are very popular during Ramadan.

Although the fast is obligatory for all sane adult Muslims in good health, a number of exemptions are allowed. These are seen as proof of Allah's wish not to place too onerous a burden on His people.

1. Children are not required to fast until they reach the Age of Responsibility (twelve years for girls; fifteen years for boys). Children from the ages of six to eight may fast for half the day, gradually increasing the duration until old enough to fully observe the fast.

2. The elderly and the chronically ill whose health may be compromised by fasting may substitute the feeding of one poor person for each day of fasting missed.

3. Pregnant and nursing women, women in post-childbirth confinement, and menstruating women may postpone the fast and make up the days later.

4. Those who are sick, traveling, or engaged in hard labor may make up missed fast days later.

Unintentional breaking of the fast is not punished, and Muslims are enjoined to break their fast if there is a threat to health. Other types of infractions require restitution. This is of two kinds: *Qada*, which involves making up missed days, and *Kaffarah*, which additionally exacts a penalty from the transgressor.

Fasting in a religious context is often undertaken for reasons of self-denial, penance, or mourning. In contrast, the Ramadan fast is a festive occasion of gratitude and thanksgiving to God. It has also acquired moral, social, and physical virtues. Observance of the fast is commonly seen as a way of receiving pardon for past sins; it creates empathy with the plight of the hungry, and it teaches self-control and endurance of deprivation.

Following Ramadan there is a three-day festival of prayer and feasting known as 'Al Id-Fitr. Special sweet dishes are prepared, giving the festival its other name of Sweet Id. Muslims give thanks to Allah for enabling them to perform their duty of fasting, and there is much visiting and exchange of gifts, including food, with family and friends. Charitable giving is also encouraged.

See also **Africa: North Africa; Fasting and Abstinence: Islam; Islam; Middle East.**

BIBLIOGRAPHY

Maulana, Muhammad Ali. *The Religion of Islam: A Comprehensive Discussion of the Sources, Principles and Practices of Islam.* 6th ed. Lahore: Ahmadiyya Anjumun Isha'at Islam, 1990.

Wagtendonk, K. *Fasting in the Koran.* Leiden: E. J. Brill, 1968.

Welch, Alford T. "Islam." In *A New Handbook of Living Religions*, edited by John R. Hinnells. Cambridge, Mass.: Blackwell, 1997.

Paul Fieldhouse

Food rationing often occurs during times of national crisis, as in England during World War II. These English housewives are queuing up at a meat shop that sells horse meat which is, according to the sign near the door, "Passed as Fit for Human Consumption." © AP/WIDE WORLD PHOTOS.

RATIONING. Food rationing is a program by which governments or private organizations oversee the allotment of food to citizens, usually during times of war or scarcity. By ensuring that all people get enough to eat or at least have a chance to purchase highly desired foods, mandatory rationing of food helps maintain citizens' physical health and psychic well-being. In doing so, it helps secure public allegiance and compliance, factors critical to institutional welfare during wartime or in the midst of a food crisis. In addition to ensuring an equitable distribution of scarce resources, rationing accompanied by price controls is designed to combat fierce inflation that often occurs with heightened demand and inadequate supply. Items distributed through such systems are often referred to as rations. Goods bought and sold illicitly outside of rationing and price control programs are said to be on the black market. Rationing is arguably a more democratic system of distributing food and other scarce resources. Theoretically, its most distinct function may be that of leveling economic and class inequality. Those on the lower end of the economic spectrum, for example, and those without the luxury of time to wait in long lines or to scout out caches of available goods, are allowed an equal chance to purchase high-status foods.

Rationing has also been used for more complicated or nefarious reasons. At one point, food allowances given to indigenous peoples in Australia and the United States, among other places, functioned as a form of social control. For Australian Aborigines, food rations were used as a tool to draw people to certain areas; their removal was intended as a form of punishment. Adolf Hitler, convinced that the German public had turned against the Weimar Republic because of food shortages, employed rationing in the 1930s to avoid domestic food emergencies. Occasionally, rationing has been implemented to ensure the unequal distribution of food, as when World War II concentration camp inmates voluntarily rationed food according to age and physical state (in the hope that this would allow the most able-bodied to survive). In early-twentieth-century China, rationing was controlled by elite "team leaders" who were allowed to distribute food and other goods according to personal discretion, which in turn afforded them power and control over local peasants. Most often, however, rationing has been employed to allow a relatively equal dispersal of food among citizens (with some reduction in allotment to infants and young children, and occasionally the very elderly). In Great Britain, World War II rationing is credited with improving the health of many by allowing the economically disadvantaged access to a stable, nutritious food supply. Currently, food rationing is most frequently implemented in countries that are the targets of international sanctions, including Cuba and Iraq.

Food rationing has been practiced in virtually every society of record, from antiquity to the present, in countries all over the globe, including Argentina, Australia, Bangladesh, Canada, Chile, China, Cuba, France, Germany, Great Britain, India, Iran, Iraq, Israel, Japan, Mexico, the Netherlands, Pakistan, Russia, and the United States. Rationing was practically universal during World War II, and continued for several years afterward in many parts of the world, including industrialized countries, which traditionally have had a more stable food supply than developing countries, whose governments have tended to implement food rationing more frequently out of necessity.

Foods deemed critical to ration can be either staples or luxuries. Staple foods—those vital to basic survival and the central elements in a cuisine—often vary according to culture, region, and tradition, and may include rice, flour, bread, milk, meat, cooking oil, canned goods, and salt. Highly desirable, psychologically important items such as cheese, butter, sugar, coffee, tea, and tobacco are arguably as important as staples to ensuring public contentment and cooperation, and thus are regarded as essential to ration. Such nonfood items as shoes, clothing, gasoline, heating oil, and tires are typically rationed in times of scarcity as well.

Food rationing tends to be implemented through two methods, the coupon system or the point system. During World War II, for example, sugar and coffee were rationed in the United States according to the coupon method, under which consumers would relinquish a coupon to purchase an allotted amount every few weeks. For rationing meat, butter, and canned goods, the government introduced the more complicated point system. Each month the federal Office of Price Administration (OPA) issued each person five blue and six red stamps worth ten points each, a total of fifty blue points for processed foods and sixty red points for meat, fats, and some dairy products. Each item—canned pineapple or pork chops, for instance—was assigned a point value determined by both availability and consumer demand. The point values were periodically reevaluated; for instance, the OPA lowered the point value of canned peaches to encourage increased consumption following a 1943 bumper crop of the fruit. The point system maintained government control over rationing but at the same time allowed the consumer a reasonable amount of control over the family's diet. With such a system, a consumer could choose to spend some of the family's points on more highly desired and scarcer items with high point values, such as beefsteak, knowing that fewer points would be left that month to buy other meats and fats. The system had its flaws, but consumers in general consistently supported it, and some even campaigned to continue rationing through the postwar years in order to allow more food to be distributed to war-ravaged and famine-stricken countries overseas.

The success of rationing in any country is highly dependent on efficient and effective administration and on unyielding honesty of and cooperation among government officials, farmers and food processors, wholesalers, grocers, and consumers. Rationing can break down at any level and through a variety of means: theft of ration books and favoritism in their distribution; lowering or misrepresenting the quality of products produced (shrinking the size of bread loaves; adding inferior grain); selling goods for higher prices or without collecting ration points; hoarding food; or bribery. While rationing has been deemed ineffective in many places, as in the Soviet Union during its early period, it is remarkable that, given its potential to break down at any point, the system has succeeded so much of the time. For the city of Lyons, France, in the Great Winter of 1709, food rationing along with other forms of public relief successfully averted widespread famine. Israel in its early years of statehood relied heavily on rationing to equitably apportion meager supplies of food.

Politics of Rationing

Because voluntary compliance is crucial to the success of rationing, concerted propaganda campaigns, even in openly democratic countries, are designed to urge people to feel personally invested in complying with rationing. Food is politicized, whether consumed in public or in private spaces. With wartime rationing, the grocery store, the kitchen, and the family meal—where food is purchased, prepared, and consumed—become public spheres as rhetorically important as the battlefield. Farmers with pitchforks and gardeners with trowels are likened to soldiers bearing rifles. Women, as traditional food procurers and preparers, become akin to soldiers at the battlefront. Wasting or hoarding food is characterized as aiding the enemy. Sacrificing food in order to send more to the military, or growing one's own food so that commercially prepared food is more available to distribute to citizens under enemy rule, is seen as performing one's patriotic duty.

Food rationing can become a positive site for communal expression of democratic obligation. Preventing waste, avoiding black markets, producing food, and abiding by rationing, however trivial they may have seemed, allowed American citizens during World War II to contribute to, and feel a part of, the war effort daily and communally. By sacrificing some of their abundant food supply to send more to the military and to those in desperate need, people could exhibit their patriotism and support of the war. Rationing not only ensured a sufficient, if at times unexciting, diet but also helped instill a sense of public commitment to the war, community involvement, and patriotism. These same sentiments have prevailed in other countries and times as well.

Despite its potential for positive meanings and uses, the implementation and eventual dismantling of rationing can be highly political. Food producers and processors may exert extreme pressure to lift rationing, arguing that consumer demand for goods should be unfettered. Those opposed to centralized food distribution see rationing as placing too much power in hands of government. Government officials benefiting from the program in any number of ways may be reluctant to disassemble the system. While some consumers have regarded food rationing as too restrictive and anticapitalistic, most, in times of crisis, have considered it as the (albeit imperfect) guarantor of their entitlement to a stable food supply.

See also **Food as a Weapon of War; Food Pantries; Food Riots; Food Security; Food Supply, Food Shortages; Government Agencies, U.S.; International Agencies; Military Rations; Political Economy.**

BIBLIOGRAPHY

Benjamin, Medea, and Joseph Collins. "Is Rationing Socialist? Cuba' Food Distribution System." *Food Policy* 10 (Nov. 1985): 327–336.

Bentley, Amy. *Eating for Victory: Food Rationing and the Politics of Domesticity.* Urbana: University of Illinois Press, 1998.

Chowdhury, Nuimuddin. "Where the Poor Come Last: The Case of Modified Rationing in Bangladesh." *Bangladesh Development Studies* 16 (1988): 27–54.

Osokina, H. A. "Soviet Workers and Rationing Norms, 1928–1935: Real or Illusory Privilege?" *Soviet and Post-Soviet Review* 19, no. 1–3 (1992): 53–69.

Rowse, Tim. *White Flour, White Power: From Rations to Citizenship in Central Australia.* Cambridge: Cambridge University Press, 1998.

Zweiniger-Bargielowska, Ina. "Bread Rationing in Britain, July 1946–July 1948." *Twentieth Century British History* 4, no. 1 (1993): 57–85.

Amy Bentley

RECIPE. A recipe is a set of instructions or advice for preparing food. The English word comes from the Latin imperative *recipe* for "take," because recipes typically used to start, "Take one pound of flour. . . ."

The modern recipe often follows this format: (1) a title or a brief announcement of what is to be achieved; (2) a list of necessary food ingredients and sometimes special equipment; (3) the method, which spells out the steps to achieve the finished dish or component; and (4) serving instructions. A recipe can also include explanatory notes, which might give advice about ingredients, including possible substitutions; tips on method; snippets of historical and cultural background; and an acknowledgment of the source of the recipe. Particularly in collections, a recipe might come with comparative data, such as difficulty rating, total time necessary, and likely cost of ingredients.

An effective recipe requires maximum accuracy, minimum ambiguity, and an appropriate level of detail for its audience. Omitting one step or ingredient can be catastrophic, and imprecision can leave the cook frustrated. Barbara Gibbs Ostmann and Jane L. Baker help authors, particularly Americans, in *The Recipe Writer's Handbook* (2001).

The form of a recipe has been broadly consistent for thousands of years, although older recipes usually provide less detail because cooks had command of the techniques, which tended to be less demanding. The ancient Greek cookery writer Philoxenus of Leucas wrote, "For [seafoods] the casserole is not bad, though I think the frying-pan better." Elsewhere he advised, "The wriggling polyp, if it be rather large, is much better boiled than baked, if you beat it until it is tender" (Athenaeus, vol. 1, 1927, pp. 21, 23). If these are typical, they help explain why the vast gastronomic compilation *The Deipnosophists* (Philosophers of dinner) made by Athenaeus about 1,800 years ago includes so few recognizable recipes. Philoxenus's advice presumably helped with novel foods in the flourishing Greek marketplace.

Another common purpose for a recipe is as an aide-mémoire (memory prompt) for occasional or complicated procedures, and a cook's shorthand can be difficult for others to decipher. A recipe can be prescriptive, particularly in religious and medical uses. It can provide an ethnographic record, and gourmets have brought notes back from their travels since ancient times. A recipe can play an important part in culinary reproduction, as when a delighted guest takes home a copy. It might be a teaching device, as in the great compilations of household management. It might promote a chef, restaurant, cooking school, or commercial product, such as a proprietary ingredient or a generic food like beef. A recipe can even become literature in its own right and be read for pleasure.

While a recipe is a powerful aid, it never replaces actual experience. Without some knowledge, the maker of a beurre blanc sauce could never be confident of having succeeded. No two cooks ever produce identical results from the same recipe. Julia Child and her colleagues Simone Beck and Louisette Bertholle required lengthy detail to introduce solid technique to many Americans with *Mastering the Art of French Cooking* in 1961. While recipes seem to promise the whole world of cooking, there is pressure to rely on a standard repertoire of techniques. Successful recipe writers are advised to restrict themselves to readily available ingredients. Recipe-based cooking favors smart-seeming compositions over untouched foods, however excellent.

An Ancient Invention

Written recipes are presumably as old as literacy, which emerged to control food supplies in the earliest civilizations. Recorded instructions had the advantages of wide and accurate transmission and archival retrieval. The power of naming, discussing, and borrowing was reserved to the tiny literate elite for thousands of years, contributing to the separation of high cooking, investigated by the social anthropologist Jack Goody in *Cooking, Cuisine, and Class* (1982). In general, traditional societies did without recipes in the sense of formal accounts, usually written, of food preparation. A girl watched and helped her mother with familiar routines, and an apprentice was shown trade secrets.

The oldest surviving recipes are probably those impressed into three clay tablets 3,700 years ago somewhere in what is now Iraq. Held in the Yale University cuneiform collection and previously mistaken for pharmaceutical formulas, the recipes would have been recorded by Babylonian scribes on behalf of the male cooks of a temple or palace. Their translator, Jean Bottéro, said the best-preserved tablet fits twenty-five recipes into just seventy-five lines. The recipes list the chief ingredients, the basic steps, and the name, which is derived from the chief ingredient or appearance when served. The only other readable tablet devotes 250 lines to seven recipes for various kinds of birds, both domestic and game. The recipes indicate many steps, numerous utensils, and complex combinations.

Some of the earliest Chinese recipes, at least 2,500 years old, are contained in the sprawling text *Li Chi*, which originated in the Chou dynasty. Reprinted by K. C. Chang in a chapter in *Food in Chinese Culture* (1977),

HOW TO READ AN OLD (HANDWRITTEN) RECIPE

Old manuscript recipes are frequently difficult to interpret because they were often written as personal memory aids for the cooks, and for their eyes only. Added to this is the difficulty of archaic language and the fact that writers spelled words as they pronounced them, as in the case of the following recipes from the cookbook of Francis Boothby, dated 1660. (Francis was either the wife or daughter of Sir Thomas Boothby of Essex, England.) Her recipes can be adjusted to modern English in the following manner.

33. Sace [Sauce] for a Shoulder of Mutton
     A few oysters, some sweet herbs, an onion, a pint of white wine, a little beaten [ground] nutmeg, and large [whole] mace. A lemon peel [grated zest]. If you have no oysters, a few capers instead, and the gravy of the mutton.
     [The oysters were pickled in brine, which is why capers can be substituted.]

34. A White Pote [A White Pot: Baked Custard]
     Take a pint and a half of cream, a quarter of a pound of sugar, a little rosewater, a few dates slit, some reasons [raisins] of the sun, 6 or 7 eggs, large mace [whole mace], a slice of pippin [tart cooking apple] or lemon, sippets wett in sack [slices of toast softened in white wine]. Put them in your dish. So bake it.

35. Sace [Sauce] for a Pickerell [pickerel is a fish]
     Take some claret wine [any red Bordeaux wine], thicken it with grated bread. [Add] a sprig of rosemary, a little beaten [ground] cloves, and synamon [cinnamon], some sugar, [then] set it on the fire, let it boil a little [boil up until it thickens]. So serve it.

William Woys Weaver

The oldest surviving collection in the West is the *De re coquinaria* (Art of cooking), which was attributed to a Roman gourmet called Apicius and was compiled around the year 400 C.E. More of than half of the nearly five hundred entries are devoted to the preparation of sauces. Recipes flourished during other periods of gastronomic ferment, such as the Arab culinary excitement after the advent of the Abbasid dynasty in the eighth century and Chinese cookery with the Sung period from the tenth century.

In medieval English manuscripts, numerous sentences begin "Tak wyte wyn" (Take white wine) and "Tak partrichys rostyd" (Take roasted partridges). Others instruct "Nym water" and "Nym swete mylk," using the archaic "nim" (or "nym"), which means "take." Yet others start "Recipe brede gratyd, & eggis" (Take grated bread and eggs), borrowing the Latin verb *recipere* (to take). Medieval recipes generally did not include measurements and times, providing a challenge for modern interpreters, who often are divided over how spicy the original dishes tasted.

The proliferation of recipes in Europe was boosted by the advent of the printing press (using the principle

A page from the manuscript cookery book of Frances Boothby, dated 1660. Frances Boothby was either the wife or the daughter of Sir Thomas Boothby of County Essex, England. ROUGH-WOOD COLLECTION.

they instruct: "For the (Soup) Balls, they took equal quantities of beef, mutton and pork, and cut them small. Then they took grains of rice, which they mixed with the finely cut meat, two parts of rice to one of meat, and formed cakes or balls, which they fried" (Chang, 1977, pp. 51–52).

Europe's oldest recipe collections were written at the end of the fifth century B.C.E. by Greeks in southern Italy, and the first of these was probably *The Art of Cookery* by Mithaikos of Syracuse. Athenaeus has handed down only one recognizable recipe, which says, "Clean the insides of a ribbon-fish after cutting off the head, wash and cut into slices, and pour cheese and oil over them" (Athenaeus, vol. 3, 1929, p. 465).

HOW TO WRITE A RECIPE

The elements of effective recipe writing vary according to the recipe's intended purpose and audience. For example, a personal reminder by a working cook will be very different from a travel writer's evocation of the flavor of an exotic dish. Yet some requirements are relatively constant, including the need for accuracy, completeness, and lack of ambiguity. Like a rotten apple, just one missing ingredient, mistaken measurement, or misleading instruction can spoil the whole recipe, and one faulty recipe can spoil a whole collection. Seeking to maintain a reputation for reliability, many publishers provide authors and editors with recipe style guides, and expect recipes to be tested in test kitchens.

Food businesses and industry associations that use recipes for marketing purposes also go to great lengths to ensure that the writing is effective. Such marketers want newspaper cookery writers and others to relay the recipes, which they will do more readily if they have confidence in the source.

The (U.S.) National Cattlemen's Beef Association keeps its recipe style guide up-to-date, and revised it in accordance with the the results of research (Gatten & Company, Chicago, 1992) regarding consumer preferences in recipe formats. This study found that consumers primarily desired "ease of preparation." Recipes should not merely "eliminate guesswork," but also appear easy, something accomplished by a simple format and style.

Based on this research, the recipe style guide of the Beef Association's test kitchens includes these recommendations:

- Use a straightforward descriptive name for the finished dish, rather than a name that is fun or creative.
- Indicate preparation and cooking times at the beginning.
- List ingredients separately at the top of the recipe.
- List the main ingredient (such as meat) first.
- Group other ingredients according to the part of the recipe for which they are needed.
- Choose readily available ingredients or substitutions.
- Try to give more than one measure for each ingredient, for example, "4 cups cooked shell macaroni (8 ounces, uncooked)."
- Avoid abbreviated measures, for example, "teaspoon" rather than "tsp."
- Specify the equipment and utensils when possible.
- List the preparation steps with numbers or bullet-points, since this makes the recipe look simpler.
- Do not "divide" an ingredient (for example, "mix half the flour"); provide a precise measurement for each use.
- Do not write "one teaspoon each of sugar, cinnamon, and nutmeg"; repeat the measurements for each ingredient.
- Provide preheating directions.
- Make the recipe easier to read by using large print.
- Provide a photograph of the finished dish.

Michael Symons

---

of grape and oil presses) around 1440. The relatively ready availability of recipes facilitated social emulation and gastronomic discussion and broke the nexus of master-apprentice. Early modern cooks may have been reticent to publish arcane information, but the dearth of French publication ended in the 1650s. As Barbara Ketcham Wheaton suggests in *Savoring the Past* (1983), "Perhaps the balance shifted, and secrecy became less valuable than fame" (Wheaton, 1983, p. 113).

Several modern features were established around the middle of the nineteenth century. Until then the more usual English word was "receipt," from the feminine past particle of the same Latin verb, *recipere*. "Recipe" had predominantly been used for medical prescriptions (leading to the abbreviation R or Rx), with which culinary prescriptions had overlapped. It has been suggested that "recipe" eventually won out because it appeared more learnedly Latin.

In the early 1800s the title was often still of the descriptive form, announcing what would be achieved; for example, Priscilla Hazehurst explains in the *Family Friend* (c. 1810), how "To make a Bride Cake" (p. 76), "To preserve Damsons another way" (p. 107), "To disguise a Leg of Veal" (p. 147), "To boil Artichokes" (p. 161). The concern was to treat individual foods properly rather than to transform them into a higher order of creation, that is, into named "dishes" (or "made dishes," as they were called).

The most important change early in the nineteenth century was toward numerical rigidity. Instructions such as "do it till it is done" can be unsettling. However, traditional cooks knew when "it is done" better than they knew "twenty-five minutes." Abstract time measurement and punctuality only became ingrained in industrial, urban society. The preoccupation with precise recipes belongs to "rationalization," the shift from hands-on,

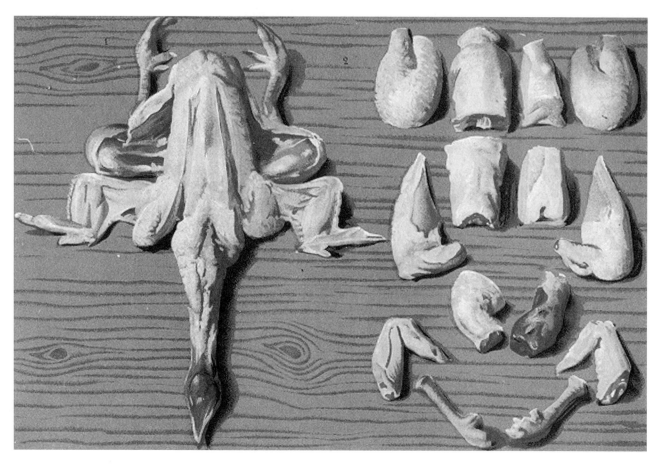

This plate from Jules Gouffé's *Royal Cookery Book* (London, 1868) shows the proper method for cutting up a chicken into serving-size pieces. This is an example of how a written recipe could never convey in words the carving process that is obvious at a glance from the picture. ROUGH-WOOD COLLECTION.

traditional methods to calculation, measurement, and control.

In 1817 the English author William Kitchiner claimed that his book *Apicius Redivivus; or, The Cook's Oracle* introduced scientific precision. Writing for the "rational Epicure" (Kitchiner, 1821, p. xi), he rejected obscure expressions like "a little bit of this—a handful of that." His recipes were the "results of experiments carefully made, and accurately and circumstantially related" (Kitchiner, 1821, pp. 30–31). The time requisite for dressing was stated and the quantities set down in number, weight, and measure. "This precision has never before been attempted in Cookery books," he boasted, not entirely accurately (Kitchiner, 1821, p. 31). Even then, an English cookery book did not require many measurements. The bulk of Kitchiner's recipes explained each of the main methods, which for him were boiling, baking, roasting, deep frying, and broiling. The few recipes for accompanying sauces specified quantities. The category of "Broths, gravies, and soups" also occasioned some pre-

cision. This left merely the final one-eighth of the book to cover expressly "Made Dishes, &c.," prescribing the likes of Haricot of Beef, Broiled Rump Steak with Onion Gravy, and Bread and Butter Pudding. As many cooks can confirm, recipe measurements have remained imprecise and inconsistent. American writers tend to use volume rather than weight, so measures of even sugar and flour are given in "cups." "Teaspoon" and "tablespoon" are hangovers from a less-finicky era. Many recipes contain vague statements such as "low heat."

With mass literacy and the mass production of cookery books from the mid-nineteenth century, enormous treatises extended to a thousand pages and by the early twentieth century exceeded two thousand pages. Meanwhile cooks exchanged innumerable recipes on scraps of paper and in exercise books.

Since the late nineteenth century, recipes have been a widespread marketing device, intruding into domestic culture on behalf of new products from gelatine to electric stoves. Incalculable numbers of recipes arrive on packaging; supermarket leaflets; in newspapers, magazines, and books; and on the Internet. Customers are invited to "send a self-addressed envelope for a free copy of our recipe booklet." With much at stake, food manufacturers and marketing bodies rely on highly experienced writers and "test kitchens" to generate promotional recipes that are readily understood and immediately successful. In turn, many cookery writers in newspapers and elsewhere rely on these recipes.

Recipes as History

Old recipes provide clues as to how others dined, but their relationship with actual practices is far from straightforward. The existence of a recipe might even be misleading, because the need for an aide-mémoire suggests rarity; common procedures did not need spelling out. Printed texts have often represented a sometimes idiosyncratic or idealized version of reality. For such reasons, culinary historians have shown an interest in personal recipe manuscripts. Relatively little concerted effort has yet gone into recording actual foodways before they are lost, however.

As recipes shifted in identification from seemingly ageless traditions to individual creativity, plagiarism became an issue. Eighteenth-century authors commonly protested their own originality against others' piracy. Reviewing his predecessors, Kitchiner declared that "cutting and pasting seem to have been much oftener employed than the Pen and Ink" (Kitchiner, 1821, p. 24). Eliza Acton was honest enough to boast in *Modern Cookery* in the mid-nineteenth century that she relayed "carefully tested recipes," and she appended the occasional notation "Author's Receipt" and "Author's Original Receipt" rather than see "strangers coolly taking the credit and the profits of my toil" (Acton, 1868, p. ix).

Contributors to the cookery history journal *Petits propos culinaires* have meticulously tracked down and exposed particular eighteenth-century plagiarists, such as Vincent La Chapelle, who stole from François Massialot's *Le [nouveau] C[c]uisinier roïal [roya]l et bourgeois* (1691); Hannah Glasse, who purloined extensively; and John Farley, who lifted from Glasse and Elizabeth Raffald. Yet meticulous sleuthing, such as Fiona Lucraft's in "The London Art of Plagiarism" on Farley "the fraudster," can be seen as a misplaced preoccupation with property rights in an unashamedly collective form, in which everyone borrows from everyone. A recipe might almost be the better for not being original, for having proved itself. In the converse of plagiarism, cookery authors acknowledge a source and then provide a "modernized, adapted" travesty.

Recipes remain essentially in the public domain. Belonging to no one, they are free and innocent. Or they would be, except for recipes as commercial promotions, which are quickly joining the scarcely traceable pool.

See also **Apicius**; **Cookbooks**; **Preparation of Food**.

BIBLIOGRAPHY

Acton, Eliza. *Modern Cookery, for Private Families [etc]*. Rev. ed. London: Longmans, Green, Reader, and Dyer, 1868. Originally published in 1845 and revised 1855.

Apicius. *The Roman Cookery Book: A Critical Translation of "The Art of Cooking" by Apicius*. Translated and edited by Barbara Flower and Elisabeth Rosenbaum. London: Harrap, 1958.

Athenaeus. *The Deipnosophists*. 7 vols. Translated by Charles Burton Gulick. Cambridge, Mass.: Harvard University Press, 1927–1941.

Beck, Simone, Louisette Bertholle, and Julia Child. *Mastering the Art of French Cooking*. New York: Knopf, 1961.

Bottéro, Jean. "The Most Ancient Recipes of All." In *Food in Antiquity*, edited by John Wilkins, David Harvey, and Mike Dobson, pp. 248–255. Exeter, U.K.: University of Exeter, 1995.

Chang, K. C., ed. *Food in Chinese Culture: Anthropological and Historical Perspectives*. New Haven, Conn.: Yale University, 1977.

Goody, Jack. *Cooking, Cuisine, and Class: A Study in Comparative Sociology*. Cambridge, U.K.: Cambridge University Press, 1982.

Kitchiner, William. *The Cook's Oracle: Containing Recipes for Plain Cookery [etc.]*. 3d ed. London: A. Constable, 1821. Originally published as *Apicius Redivivus; or, the Cook's Oracle*, 1817.

Mennell, Stephen. "Plagiarism and Originality—Diffusionism in the Study of the History of Cookery." *Petits Propos Culinaires* 68 (November 2001): 29–38.

Ostmann, Barbara Gibbs, and Jane L. Baker. *The Recipe Writer's Handbook*. Rev. and expanded. New York: John Wiley, 2001.

Wheaton, Barbara Ketcham. *Savoring the Past: The French Kitchen and Table from 1300 to 1789*. Philadelphia: University of Pennsylvania Press, 1983.

Michael Symons

RELIGION AND FOOD. There are almost as many ways to define religion as there are religions, but scholars basically tend to think about it in two ways. Some concentrate on religion's functions in societies while others focus on grasping its mysterious, universal essence. This essay will examine how food factors into these ways of understanding religion. The connections between religion and food vary widely and are often quite complex. There are, however, several common connections between religion and food that scholars have begun to document in recent decades.

Function

In the functionalist view, religion provides meaning, identity, and structure within what Geertz has called "cultural systems." Religion reflects the human desire for order, but it provides order because people believe it has its origins in the divine. Food often figures prominently in functional interpretations of religion. Lévi-Strauss described food as a type of language that helps human beings express their basic perceptions of reality. He observed that rules about eating cooked and raw foods in some cultures are dictated by sacred stories (myths) and prohibitions (taboos). These rules reflect underlying notions about differences between nature and culture.

Mary Douglas has shown how food communicates ideas about holiness that provide identity and order. The ancient Hebrew dietary laws functioned as controls on identity in a context in which incursion by other tribes and their gods was a frightening possibility. To be holy, in this context, is to be wholly separate. Israelites were "clean" because they remained within the bounds of God's covenantal order, not mixing with outsiders, their gods, or their ways. This separation was reinforced by dietary restrictions such as the prohibition against eating pork. Pigs are "dirty" because their physical characteristics are abnormal according to the way in which the ancient Israelites understood types of animals (i.e., they have cleft hooves and do not ruminate, unlike the edible animals otherwise similar to them like cattle and sheep). A pure and separate people does not make an animal that is not clearly like other grazing animals part of itself by consuming it. Purity of food and body help to strengthen the boundaries of Israelite society and religion. The laws of kashruth have continued to be among the distinguishing marks of Jewish identity and lifestyle through the centuries.

Functionalist understandings are especially helpful for exploring the relationships between religion and food in particular contexts like ancient Israel. They also illumine the connections between religion, food, and other culturally constructed systems such as gender norms. Scholars have shown how Graeco-Roman table etiquette affected the development of women's roles in early Christianity and may help to explain the tension around women's leadership in early Christianity (Corley). Focusing on gender and food expands our understandings of the scope of religion. Feminist scholars have shown that women may be religious experts through their control of food in societies where previous scholarship has focused on the male exclusivity of sacred knowledge. Among the Thai Buddhists that Van Esterik studied, it is the women whose feeding of monks and deities primarily determines attainment of merit and thus shapes the eternal destiny of their people both dead and living. Bynum's study of medieval Christian mysticism shows that women exercised control and spiritual power through refusing to eat or eating only in a spiritual manner.

Religious food rules may also be codes for class distinctions. The Hindu caste system, for example, is communicated primarily in terms of who can cook for and who can eat with whom. Religious purity is attached to the maintenance of social boundaries. Brahmans, the highest caste, maintain their purity by avoiding foods touched by those of lower castes. Yet Brahman-prepared food is permitted to all. In ancient sacred myth, Brahman created the world by cooking it in sacrifice, thus performing a priestly act. A Brahman's privileged status in society still is still enforced by his role as priest. He stands between the gods and rest of the world. As the ancient texts declare, the world cooked by the Brahman is to fulfill its duties to him (Malamoud).

Essence
Here, religion primarily refers to the human encounter with an irreducible sacred such as a god. Scholars such as Mircea Eliade map this experience through universally recognizable types of orientation (sacred time and sacred space), narrative (myth), and activity (ritual). Religion in this view essentially concerns the otherworldly expressed and responded to through patterns, which often involve food.

Those patterns are still important for describing and understanding religion, even if their universality has been questioned. As Jonathan Z. Smith puts it, they serve the observer as "maps," but should not be confused with the vast diversity of "territories" known to believers. They are more like recipes written by a food professional based on traditional dishes that community cooks make from scratch by heart. Sacred time, sacred space, ritual, and myth as categories only give the general flavor of a religion.

Sacred space and time. Sacred space often focuses on food and table setting. The most holy point of some Christian churches is the altar where the sacred meal of Christ's body takes place. In others, a pulpit might replace the altar; however, it is from that point that Christians are fed God's word. In Hindu temples, devotees are often separated from images of the deities by a rail from which they offer food to the gods and receive it in turn. Sacred space is the place where the divine and human communicate, very often over a meal.

Domestic eating spaces can be sacralized as well. Hindu and Buddhist homes may have shrines that are miniature temples for deities who are fed daily. Chinese kitchens contain a shrine to the stove god. In Sicily and Sicilian communities in the United States, families construct elaborate altars of food to celebrate St. Joseph's Day. During *Sukkoth*, tent-like dwellings outside their homes remind Jews of their nomadic ancestors as they celebrate the harvest's bounty.

Sacred time is also often delineated by food. In many religions, time is marked by periods of eating and abstention. Fasting during Ramadan is one of the five pillars of Islam, and the cycle of eating and abstaining from food marks its days. These are holy times, where one's relationship to food expresses one's connection to holiness through a balance of disciplined avoidance of carnal pleasures and partaking in Allah's bounty. Both feasting and fasting, in different ways, are concerned with submission to Allah.

Ritual, myth, and symbol. Eating in sacred space and at sacred times is a primary mode of ritual activity. Ritual unites believers with the holy as they carry out patterned activities that parallel those of gods or ancestors. The Passover meal commemorates and reconnects Jews with the ancient Israelite ancestors through the bitter herbs, the sacrificed lamb, and the quickly made unleavened bread. "You shall observe this rite as an ordinance for you and for your sons forever," Exodus 12 admonishes the Israelites about this practice. "Do this in remembrance of me" is evoked each time Christians reenact Christ's last supper with his disciples. By commemorating Christ's last meal, repeating his words and gestures, Christians re-create the sacred time of Christ and his disciples and eat with him again as they eat in community as his body. Or, Christians believe that they actually eat Christ's sacrificed body in the form of the bread host and in so doing are incorporated into it "to live forever" with God. It is first of all feeding the deity, rather than feeding on the deity, that sanctifies Hindus who present foods to the gods for their consumption. The gods then return the leftovers as sacred *prasadam* for devotees to eat.

Sacred boundaries of time and space and ritual activities are narrated in sacred stories or myths. For the believer, mythic truth is truer than fact; it is the way the gods did it. In the Christian Eucharist, the priest begins with the words of sacred myth: ". . . the Lord Jesus the same night in which he was betrayed took bread: And when he had given thanks, he brake it, and said, Take, eat: this is my body, which is broken for you: this do in remembrance of me." (1 Corinthians 11) Following the mythic pattern correctly in ritual is of utmost importance since it is a recreation of cosmic order; however, religious communities often disagree about details of performance as well as interpretation. Rituals generally represent beginnings that come out of chaos or involve a change of state. Food, as something that changes state or that can create new identity in communal consumption, is often the centerpiece of ritual controversy. A familiar example is the debate over the real or symbolic presence of Christ in the Eucharist that became the most divisive theological issue of the Christian reformations of the sixteenth century.

The preparation and consumption of food are common in myth. As in the Hindu scriptures already discussed, creation and food are often related in myths of origins. In the Abrahamic religions (Judaism, Christianity, and Islam), the origin of sin takes place in a forbidden act of eating. And it is eating the sacrifice of the Passover lamb or "Christ, Lamb of God," that restores their relationship with God for Jews and Christians respectively. For Muslims, God rescues their progenitor Ishmael from thirst by a miraculous spring in the desert. Muslims fulfilling the hajj reenact Hagar and Ishmael's

Food plays a significant ritual role in all of the world's religions as well as in the religions of the past. This bronze Celtic bucket discovered near Aylesford, England, was used to hold the ashes of a cremated noble. Around it were placed various foods the deceased was to partake of in the afterworld. The bucket is in the collection of the British Museum, London. © WERNER FORMAN/CORBIS.

quest for water as part of the pilgrimage into sacred time and space.

When myths no longer function to order human activity, when they cease to speak of the holy, they are myths in the more common sense of the term. Myths are, however, quite resilient, especially ones involving food. An underground Christian sect in Japan that survived the suppression of Christianity in the seventeenth century accommodated its situation by celebrating sacred meals with fish and rice wine rather than unavailable bread and wine (Whelan). When the buffalo were erased from the North American landscape, the Oglala Sioux accommodated by treating the cattle forced on them by the United States government as if they were buffalo, hunting them ritualistically. This not only preserved their myths, ritual hunts, and feasts, but also quickly changed their dietary preferences. Whereas they had previously avoided beef as unsavory, it quickly became an accepted food staple (Powers and Powers).

Japanese Christians and the Oglala were able to adapt and survive through shifts of symbolism. Symbols are the building blocks of myth. Food symbols are among the most powerful because they connect the reality of life in a place to the holy in tangible and vital ways. Ghee, clarified butter from the sacred cow, feeds deities and humans in India. Survival in Japan depended on rice and rice was already sacred in indigenous religious traditions there. The Christian minority initially took bread and wine as identity markers that differentiated it from the dominant culture; but when survival was threatened, they christianized an older symbol, rice wine. While food seems to be a universal sacred symbol, meanings can vary broadly. The cow so sacred to Hindus that it must not be killed, is the "spotted buffalo" sacralized in its killing and consumption by the Oglala.

Symbols are also powerful because they communicate the holy through what they are. Wine and bread remind believers of Christ's blood and flesh by their physical properties. Christianity has debated whether the Eucharistic meal is a perpetual sacrifice, is like a sacrifice, or recalls a final sacrifice. Some early Christian vegetarians interpreted Christ's death as the end of all sacrifice, including the slaying of animals for human consumption. They marked their sacred meals with water, rather than the blood-like wine. Medieval theology, however, reinforced the sacrificial understanding of the Eucharist; a bleeding host was a common element in medieval devotional stories told to emphasize the sacrifice of Christ's flesh in every ritual meal performance.

Some scholars hold that sacrifice, which literally means "to make holy," is at the root of religion. Much mythic vocabulary associates death and food in the service of life. Many religious groups deal with the death-giving-life paradox by sanctioning killing as a gift to the gods, of which humans may share and become holy themselves. Others, like the Jain of India, deal with the reality of suffering by trying to avoid it. For them, eating from plants not killed in the process of harvest and totally avoiding meat are major forms of achieving a meritorious existence. Buddhist monks avoid getting mired down in the world of suffering by refusing to kill animals for food. They may, however, eat whatever is provided for them by householders as long as they remain detached from the desire for it.

Sacred rituals reintegrate believers with each other as well as the gods; this is often accomplished in commensality. Eating the same foods, often from common vessels, draws boundaries around community, making it holy and like family. Early Christians adapted the kin-based Jewish Passover to bond spiritual brothers and sisters. Food exchanges or ceremonial meals are common in marriage rituals. The ancient Jewish wedding was essentially a meal that brought together husband, wife, and their kin. Hindu marriages still involve elaborate exchanges of food. Extension of the community through eating is not always a hospitable occasion. Again, death is often involved in a shared sacrifice. For the ancient Aztecs, eating from the bodies of human victims was a

way of incorporating their strength as well as feeding with the gods (Carrasco).

Rituals often extend outside the bounds of community through food. The Christian Eucharist concludes by sending believers who have been fed "into the world in peace" to help sanctify it. Making the world holy is often accomplished by the extension of community through charitable feeding. Devotees of Lord Krishna, for example, are famous for their temple feeding programs. By feeding the outsider, they serve Krishna by extending his presence through food that has been sanctified by him (Singer). Muslims are required to practice charity and often do so by giving food to non-Muslims. *Bakra Eid* commemorates the sacrifice of Ishmael and is a day on which Muslims worldwide bind community through sacrificing at the same time. But the community is extended in this event, in which sacrificed meat may be portioned out not only among family and the poor, but also to non-Muslim neighbors (Murphy).

Food, Religious Performance, and the Body

Religious peoples are more likely than scholars to appeal to essential experiences of holiness when they articulate religious foodways. That is, when they consciously articulate them at all. Helpful here is the work of Katherine Bell and Ronald Grimes, who emphasize the performative character of religious behavior. This is particularly important for understanding the relationships between religion and food. Most people harvest, kill, eat, cook, serve, hunger for, or otherwise encounter food and holiness primarily through physical action and sensation, rather than through belief and interpretation. The power of foods to evoke strong memories and feelings, essential to the efficacy of religious ritual, is related to the sensory experience of food. Food rituals recall not just abstract ideas, but smells or tastes that bring back another time or place. Passover offers Jews the opportunity to reconnect viscerally with their ancestors through tastes of what their lives were like on the Seder plate.

It is important to underline this embodied nature of the connection between religion and food. Because religious experience via food is a physical experience, it can vary widely even while following the same ritual practices. This does not make ritual less powerful; rather, it helps to bring it alive for devotees. Paradoxically, religious expression is all the more real, meaningful, and transcendent because it is new each time even if it is as old as the world. Each time a religious act involving food is performed, it is experienced by the body in the moment of receiving, smelling, and tasting, and this strengthens feelings and beliefs about the presence of holiness in the activity.

Because of the ambiguities in some traditions associated with the body, food and eating can be powerfully complex signs of both the profane and the sacred. The "perfect ones" in dualistic groups like the ancient

Manichees and medieval Cathars starved themselves to death in rejection of the body and all things earthly. Fear of the female body particularly has driven the ascetic impulse in several religious cultures to sanctify the renunciation of food. Some early Christian writers associated female fasting with rejecting the sexual body, holding that the fasting body made virgins "more attractive" to Christ, their bridegroom (Shaw, 250–252). Lelwica and Griffith have noted parallels between traditional female holiness and dieting among contemporary American women.

Food, Meaning, and the Secular World

While it is a common observation that religious tradition and belief have shaped diet and foodways in the past, modern observers tend to focus on the waning of religious influences on eating. Reformed Judaism, which does not require adherence to the dietary laws, is an example often cited. The persistence of irrational dietary traditions, as among the strictly kosher Hasidim, is viewed as a rejection of modernity.

Even people with a disenchanted, scientific worldview may unconsciously act according to sacred meanings. Ordinary profane experiences of eating may be meaningful bases for memory, reflection, and orientation and can be recognized as such to the extent that they are patterned on hidden sacred structures. Indeed, what constitutes a meal is often based on unconscious associations with primordial meals. Meals can return even the most secular person to another time and place. The language often used to describe such experiences is the religious vocabulary of symbol, myth, and ritual. American Thanksgiving, a secular holiday that celebrates consumerism as much as anything else, still centers on a meal modeled on sacral elements: sacrificial fowl and harvest fruits. What remains of its semireligious origins is perhaps a quick prayer and traditional dishes (some of rather recent origin). As anyone who has tried to vary a Thanksgiving menu knows from familial reaction, the sacred survives in turkey, stuffing, and mashed potatoes.

Furthermore, postmodernity has seen many conscious attempts at re-enchantment through foodways by those exhibiting what Eliade called "nostalgia for origins." Elizabeth Ehrlich's recent memoir of her progression from being a secular Jew to keeping the kosher kitchen of her foremothers is a good example.

Summary

Examining connections between food and religion helps to illumine how religion functions in cultures, and why religious experiences are powerful for believers. It can also underline the fact that food feeds many hungers. Scholars have only just begun to examine the myriad ways in which this is true for religious peoples. It is safe to say that most scholars of religion would agree that religions provide humans with meaning-making structures that often involve food. These structures reveal the essence of the sacred through eating, sacrificing, preparing, or serving food to believers. They may serve as paradigms for all ordinary foodways as well. This domestication of sacred foodways in turn helps to perpetuate the process of meaning-making that is the function of religious practice and belief. Believers may or may not reflect on the importance of food for their religious identity. Knowledge of food's centrality for meaning-making is not limited for believers to theological abstraction. To use Ronald Grimes's phrase, it is more often felt "deeply into the bone" through the rites of preparation and consumption that help to order life every day as well as to mark special occasions. Brillat-Savarin's "Tell me what you eat and I'll tell you who you are" translates in the words of one woman recently interviewed after cooking a family meal, "Food is Judaism for me. I don't think about it. It's who I am."

See also **Buddhism**; **Christianity**; **Fasting and Abstinence**; **Feasts, Festivals and Fasts**; **Gender and Food**; **Hinduism**; **Islam**; **Judaism**; **Last Supper**; **Sin and Food**; **Women and Food**.

BIBLIOGRAPHY

Bell, Catherine. *Ritual Theory, Ritual Practice.* New York: Oxford University Press, 1992.

Bell, Rudolph M. *Holy Anorexia.* Chicago: University of Chicago Press, 1985.

Bynum, Carolyn Walker. *Holy Feast and Holy Fast: The Religious Significance of Food to Medieval Women.* Berkeley: University of California Press, 1987.

Carrasco, David L. *City of Sacrifice: The Aztec Empire and the Role of Violence in Civilization.* Boston: Beacon Press, 1999.

Corley, Kathleen E. *Private Women, Public Meals: Social Conflict in the Synoptic Tradition.* Peabody, Mass.: Hendrickson Publishers, 1993.

Cumbo, Enrico Carlson. "*La Festa del Pane:* Food, Devotion and Ethnic Identity: The Feast of San Francesco di Paola, Toronto." Available at http://www.materialreligion.org/journal/festa.html.

Douglas, Mary. "Deciphering a Meal." In *Myth, Symbol and Culture,* edited by Clifford Geertz, et al., pp. 61–81. New York: Norton, 1971.

Douglas, Mary. *Purity and Danger: An Analysis of Concepts of Pollution and Taboo.* London: Routledge, 1966.

Ehrlich, Elizabeth. *Miriam's Kitchen: A Memoir.* New York: Viking, 1997.

Eliade, Mircea. *The Sacred and the Profane: The Nature of Religion.* Translated by William R. Trask. London: Harcourt, Brace, and Jovanovich, 1959.

Feeley-Harnik, Gillian. *The Lord's Table: The Meaning of Food in Early Judaism and Christianity.* Washington: Smithsonian Institution Press, 1994.

Geertz, Clifford. *The Interpretation of Cultures.* New York: Basic Books, 1973.

Griffith, R. Marie. "Don't Eat That: The Erotics of Abstinence in American Christianity." *Gastronomica,* 1, 4 (Fall, 2001): 36-47.

Grimes, Ronald L. *Deeply into the Bone: Re-inventing Rites of Passage.* Berkeley: University of California Press, 2000.

The Journal of the American Academy of Religion 63.3 (1995). Food and religion is the theme of this volume, which contains several pertinent essays.

Khare, R. S., ed. *The Eternal Food: Gastronomic Ideas and Experiences of Hindus and Buddhists.* Albany: State University of New York Press, 1992.

Latham, James E. "Food." In *The Encyclopedia of Religion*, edited by Mircea Eliade, Volume 5, pp. 387–393. New York: Macmillan, 1986.

Lelwica, Michelle M. *Starving for Salvation: The Spiritual Dimensions of Eating Problems Among American Girls and Women.* New York: Oxford University Press, 1999.

Lévi-Strauss, Claude. *The Raw and the Cooked: Introduction to a Science of Mythology.* Volume I. London: Jonathan Cape, 1970.

Leylerle, Blake. "Clement of Alexandria on the Importance of Table Etiquette." *Journal of Early Christian Studies* 3 (1995): 123–141.

McGowan, Andrew. *Ascetic Eucharists: Food and Drink in Early Christian Ritual Meals.* New York: Oxford University Press, 1999.

Malamoud, Charles. *Cooking the World: Ritual and Thought in Ancient India.* Translated by David White. New York: Oxford University Press, 1996.

Murphy, Christopher P. H. "Piety and Honor: The Meaning of Muslim Feasts in Old Delhi." In *Food, Society and Culture: Aspects in South Asian Food Systems*, edited by R. S. Khare and M.S.A. Rao, pp. 85–119. Durham: Carolina Academic Press, 1986.

Powers, William K., and Marla M. N. Powers, "Metaphysical Aspects of an Oglala Food System." In *Food in the Social Order: Studies of Food and Festivities in Three American Communities*, edited by Mary Douglas, pp. 40–96. Russell Sage Foundation, 1984.

Roden, Claudia. *The Book of Jewish Food: An Odyssey from Samarkind to New York.* New York: Knopf, 1996.

Sack, Daniel. *Whitebread Protestants: Food and Religion in American Culture.* New York: St. Martin's Press, 2000.

Shaw, Teresa M. *The Burden of the Flesh: Fasting and Sexuality in Early Christianity.* Minneapolis: Fortress Press, 1998.

Singer, Eliot A. "Conversion Through Foodways Enculturation: The Meaning of Eating in an American Hindu Sect." *Ethnic and Regional Foodways in the United States*, edited by Linda Keller Brown and Kay Mussell, pp. 195–214. Knoxville: University of Tennessee Press, 1984.

Smith, Jonathan Z. *Map is Not Territory: Studies in the History of Religions.* Leiden: Brill, 1978.

Smith, Jonathan Z. *To Take Place: Toward Theory in Ritual.* Chicago: University of Chicago Press, 1987.

Van Esterik, Penny. "Feeding Their Faith: Recipe Knowledge Among Thai Buddhist Women." In *Food and Gender: Identity and Power*, edited by Carol M. Counihan and Steven L. Kaplan, pp. 81–97. Newark, N.J.: Harwood Academic Press, 1998.

Whelan, Christal. *Otaiya: Japan's Hidden Christians.* Documentary Film. 1997. Available from Documentary Educational Resources.

Corrie E. Norman

RENAISSANCE BANQUETS. The banquet, as a particular form of festivity, flourished in Renaissance Europe from the mid-fourteenth century to the early seventeenth century. It began as a specifically secular celebration; in medieval times the "feast" (French *fête*, Italian *festa*) referred primarily to religious celebrations, special days in the church calendar—Easter, Christmas, saints' days—although it also denoted a sumptuous meal. As a lavish, ceremonial meal in honor of an individual or exceptional occasion, such as a wedding, the new banquet observed no such periodicity, and in its conspicuous consumption tended toward a blatant demonstration of wealth and power. It was distinguished not only by its extravagance and ostentatious scale but also by its theatricality and use of symbolism.

In the sixteenth century a banquet could also refer to the less ostentatious—though no less lavish, in relative terms—annual ceremonial dinners of *confréries* or guilds, groups of men linked through their craft or their parish. Usually held on a relevant saint's day, these were not only a ritual celebration but also a demonstration of goodwill.

Origins and Etymology

Elaborate, extravagant, ceremonial meals had been offered before the adoption of the word "banquet." Descriptions of the dinners in honor of Pope Clement VI in the mid-fourteenth century, which included a centerpiece of a fountain spurting forth five different types of wine, show that lavish entertainment was nothing new. Nevertheless, the "banquet" must have differed in some way if a new word had to be brought into the language.

Initially, it appears, the banquet was a lavish meal presented in a different style, with various dishes set out on a long table, as would be a buffet today. Both the term and the event had their origins in fourteenth-century Italy. The Italian word *banchetto* derives from *banco*, 'a long bench or table'. "*Insieme disinano e cenano con banchetti molto abondevoli di varii cibi e bonissimi vini*," wrote the Italian Matteo Bandello in the early sixteenth century ("Together they dine and sup, the tables displaying a great abundance of diverse dishes and excellent wines").

The French term *banquet*, which entered common usage around the middle of the fifteenth century, and the Spanish *banquete* (documented early sixteenth century) were both borrowed from the Italian; in England the word "banketti," derived directly from the Italian, predated the French term *banquet*, adopted early in the sixteenth century. By this time the form of the banquet had evolved considerably, according to the accounts of Christoforo di Messisbugo, and included theatrical and musical performances.

In his capacity as steward at the court of the dukes of Este, Messisbugo orchestrated many banquets and in his book, *Banchetti: Compositioni di vivande et apparecchio generale* (1549), he describes, in unparalleled detail, the

176

management and staging of these lavish, formal, ceremonial feasts, from the setting of the tables with several tablecloths and ornamental figures of sugar or marzipan to the accompanying music and the dances performed during the course of the meal.

In sixteenth-century England the banquet evolved in two different directions. As well as an opulent and stage-managed feast, it became an elaboration of what had previously been the final course of a grand dinner, the dessert, an array of sweetmeats often served in purpose-built banqueting houses in the parks of great houses, or in an outside arbor or summerhouse.

Banquet Food
One of the most striking features of banquet food was the presence of sugar, for both visual and symbolic effect, the lavish use of this expensive ingredient underlining the host's magnificence. The banquet menus appended to the printed edition of the *Viandier* of Taillevent (c. 1315–1395) in the last decade of the fifteenth century suggest an extravagant and incongruous application of sugar to roast quail, chicken and pigeon. (Originally compiled in the fourteenth century and attributed to the royal chef Taillevent, *Le Viandier* represents one of the few records of the cuisine of medieval northern France. The late-fifteenth-century printed edition contains additional material not included in the early manuscripts.) The chapter titled "Banqueting and made dishes with other conceits and secrets" in Gervase Markham's *The English Hus-wife* (1615) is composed of recipes for essentially sweet dishes such as fruit tarts, marmalades, preserves, marzipan, and jelly.

Sugar was used in dishes such as jellies, blancmange, and quince paste, and on dishes such as fritters and pies (Italian *torte*). It was an essential ingredient in the candied nuts and spices offered at the end of the meal, in jewel-like glazed fruits often hung on miniature trees of silver, and in decorative marzipan figures and in sculpted sugar table ornaments. For a banquet given by don Ercole, son of the duke of Ferrara, to a group of nobles including his father, Messisbugo ordered a sugar model of Hercules and the lion, colored and gilded, to decorate the table; with the final course of *confetti* came more sugar models representing Hercules defeating the bull, together with Venus, Cupid, Eve, and other mythical figures.

Because the banquet was itself an exceptional meal, banquet food had to be out of the ordinary (out-of-season asparagus, gilded and silvered calves' heads). This typically translated as the most prestigious, most expensive ingredients—meats such as veal and capons—prepared in the most elaborate, spicy ways so as to emphasize the art and skill of the cooks (which, in turn, reflected glory back on the reputation of the family). It also meant many services, each usually composed of several dishes, although it was not expected that everyone would eat something from every service—dishes were to be admired as much as consumed. The banquet offered by Gaston

LA CONDAMNATION DE BANQUET

In the late fifteenth-century French morality play *La Condamnation de banquet*, banquet was an additional meal, differentiated from *dîner* and *souper* by the absence of servants; an array of food was set out on the table and guests helped themselves. It was also differentiated from the other two meals by the refined, elaborate dishes on offer, including a selection of sweet tarts, custards, fruits and nuts together with sweetened spiced wine.

Since the purpose of this play was probably to demonstrate the price of overindulgence, it should not be assumed that in fifteenth-century France the banquet was a supplementary evening meal, following the two standard meals of *dîner*, around midday, and *souper* in the early evening. In the play, the three meals are personified; after enjoying the hospitality of Dîner and Souper, the happy group of revellers—rejoicing in such names as Gourmandise, Friandise, Bonne Compagnie (Good Company), Passe-Temps (Leisure)—are led on, by Banquet, to a banquet. Here, however, they find they have been double-crossed as a horde of maladies (Gout, Colic, Jaundice, Quinsy) attack them. Those guests who escape bring a case before Dame Experience who finds Banquet, and to a lesser extent, Souper, guilty of corrupting the guests. Banquet is executed, and Souper is ordered to keep a respectable distance from Dîner. It is clear that the banquet was seen as promoting a pleasure-seeking lifestyle which, given the importance of the sin of Gluttony, would hardly have met with church approval.

IV, count of Foix, in honor of the ambassadors of Hungary in 1458 was comprised of seven services punctuated by four entremets; some of Messisbugo's menus ran to ten services, each composed of six or more dishes.

Especially when elements of performance were included, banquets could last many hours, and often led into a ball. At don Ercole's dinner, after all the courses and all the performances, the guests danced until daybreak, "*fino al giorno chiaro*" (until the light of day).

Entremets
Designed to appeal to all the senses, banquets increasingly incorporated musical and theatrical elements. The entremets, the between-courses divertissements, were spectacles incorporating elements of surprise and trickery to amaze and impress the guests. Often elaborated to honor the occasion or the guest of honor, they were additional elements inserted in the structure of the meal.

In the fourteenth and fifteenth centuries, entremets were often the product of the kitchen, elaborated under the charge of the head cook, although they might well have involved carpenters and costume makers as well. The cooks' contributions included pastry castles, pies filled with live birds, gilded roast chickens and sucking pigs and fire-breathing roast swans and peacocks, re-dressed in their plumage. Almost invariably, music in some form accompanied the presentation of these entremets.

By the sixteenth century the entremets had undergone a transformation, with the culinary and theatrical elements separated. The between-course entertainment consisted almost entirely of performance—music, mime, dance, and acrobatics—leaving cooks free to devote all their skills to culinary artistry and visual display.

The banquet for don Ercole, for example, began with the performance of a comedy by Ariosto, after which guests moved to another room where they were entertained with music while tables were being set with silver candelabra, silver salt cellars, and intricately folded serviettes, or napkins. On their return they washed their hands in perfumed water before the dishes of the first service were presented, to the accompaniment of music and song.

Messisbugo specified precisely the vocal and instrumental complements to each of the services, continuing through the interval between services, as well as the performance of a group of Venetian jesters.

Banquet Symbolism

Since the raison d'être of a banquet was to honor an occasion such as a marriage involving powerful and wealthy families, or the visit of a noble guest, or the arrival or departure of a prince (when it was often associated with the dramatic ritual of a procession), then it was necessary to highlight this purpose, typically through the entremets and table decorations. The sugar sculptures of Hercules at don Ercole's banquet were a clear reference to his strength and power, just as the recurring theme of a castle symbolized might and authority.

If the role of the banquet were to promote or strengthen strategic alliances (and marriages could easily fall into this category), the entremets might be designed to flatter the guests of honor. Thus at the dinner offered the Hungarian ambassadors the entremets presented paid homage to the guests and their mission. The first, a large castle atop a rocky peak, was decorated with the banners

---

BANQUET OF THE PHEASANT

Because of their political significance, banquets often attracted the attention of chroniclers. One of the best known is the Banquet of the Pheasant, held at Lille in February 1454, which was thoroughly documented by Olivier de la Marche, who helped organize the event for Philip the Fair, Duke of Burgundy. The ostensible purpose of this banquet was to inspire knights to join a crusade to recapture Constantinople, recently taken by the Turks.

The chronicler says little about the food and wine, but a great deal about the visual effects. The banquet took place in a large room, decorated with tapestries depicting the life of Hercules, in which were three tables, each displaying a series of entremets. On the first was a delicately constructed church, a model of a naked young boy pissing rosewater, a ship laden complete with cargo and sailors, and a fountain, fashioned partly of glass, and surrounded by trees, fruit, and flowers of glass. On the second table was a large *pasté* (a pastry case) in which were twenty-eight musicians, while from another castle jets of orange-flower water sprayed into the moat and the figure of a man atop a barrel in a vineyard invited guests to help themselves. On the third table was a forest with wild animals, moving as if they were alive, ac-

cording to Olivier de la Marche. On a tall dresser were displayed platters of gold and silver, together with crystal jugs decorated with gold and precious stones. Near the wall were two high pillars, one supporting the figure of a woman whose right breast gushed spiced wine, and the other a lion, guarding the woman.

After admiring these, the guests were seated and a series of musical and other diversions followed, culminating in the presentation of a white-clad lady, representing the church, who pleaded to be rescued, her speech incorporating the motto of the Crusades, *Dieu le veut* (God wills it; or, God's will be done). At the end of her lament a live pheasant, richly ornamented with gold and jewels, and the duke (who, noted our diarist, knew exactly his purpose in organizing this banquet) made his vow to save Christianity, whereupon other nobles followed his example. After yet more music and spectacle, the dancing began, hippocras and candied spices were served, and guests enjoyed themselves until two or three in the morning.

SOURCE: *Mémoires de Messire Olivier de la Marche. Collection complètes des mémoires relatifs à l'histoire de France.* Edited by Claude B. Petitot. Paris: Foucault, 1820.

AN ITALIAN RENAISSANCE WEDDING BANQUET

Banquet celebrating the marriage of the Marquis Gian Giacomo Trivulzio with Beatrice d'Avalos d'Aragona, Milan, 1488.

1. Rosewater-scented water for the hands
   Pastries of pinenuts and sugar
   Other cakes made with almonds and sugar, similar to marzipan
2. Asparagus (to the amazement of the guests, since it was enormous and out of season)
3. Tiny sausages and meatballs
4. Roast grey partridge and sauce
5. Whole calves' heads, gilded and silvered
6. Capons and pigeons, accompanied by sausages, hams and wild boar, plus delicate "potages"
7. Whole roast sheep, with a sour cherry sauce
8. A great variety of roast birds—turtledoves, partridges, pheasants, quail, figpeckers—accompanied by olives as a condiment
9. Chickens with sugar and rosewater
10. Whole roast sucking pig, with an accompanying "brouet"
11. Roast peacock, with various accompaniments
12. A sweetened, sage-flavored custard
13. Quinces cooked with sugar, cinnamon, pinenuts, and artichokes
14. Various preserves, made with sugar and honey
15. Ten different "torte," and an abundance of candied spices

SOURCE: Mario Bendiscioli and Adriano Gallia. *Documenti di storia medioevale, 400–1492.* Milan: Mursia, 1970, pp. 267–268.

and coat-of-arms of the king of Hungary and the visiting nobles while the second, a fire-breathing tiger, bore the royal coat-of-arms on its collar.

Banquets also served to demonstrate, on a grand scale, the generosity of the host and, obliquely, his wealth and influence. Commenting on the growing popularity of banquets in northern France in the second half of the fifteenth century, Olivier de la Marche notes that their splendor accrued as each noble who gave a banquet wished to outclass the previous one. Their political importance meant that an element of social obligation was also involved; Messisbugo records the banquets don Ercole gave as well as those at which he was a guest.

Sumptuous, wealth-displaying spectacles involving food and performance continued into the seventeenth century. Vatel, a French counterpart to Messisbugo, was responsible for the organization of one such event in 1661 at the chateau of Vaux-le-Vicomte, to which the young Louis XIV was invited. Later at Versailles, Louis himself entertained on an even grander scale but by this time the term *banquet* seems to have referred simply to formal dinners, the Versailles extravaganzas being known as *fêtes*.

See also **Medieval Banquet; Taillevent.**

BIBLIOGRAPHY

Bober, Phyllis Pray. *Art, Culture, and Cuisine.* Chicago: University of Chicago Press, 1999.

Jeanneret, Michel. *A Feast of Words: Banquets and Table Talk in the Renaissance.* Translated by Jeremy Whitely and Emma Hughes. Cambridge, U.K.: Polity Press, 1991.

Messisbugo, Christoforo di. *Banchetti: Compositioni di vivande et apparecchio generale.* Ferrara, Italy, 1549.

Montanari, Massimo. *The Culture of Food.* Translated by Carl Ipsen. Oxford, U.K., and Cambridge, Mass.: Blackwell, 1994.

Strong, Roy. *Splendour at Court: Renaissance Spectacle and Illusion.* London: Weidenfeld and Nicholson, 1973. Detail of theatrical aspects of festivities, mostly late Renaissance.

Wilson, C. Anne, ed. *'Banquetting Stuffe': The Fare and Social Background of the Tudor and Stuart Banquet.* Edinburgh: Edinburgh University Press, 1986.

Barbara Santich

RESTAURANTS. Throughout much of recorded history, eating away from home and in a public place has been experienced as a burden rather than a pleasure. The emergence of restaurant going as an enjoyable, leisure time activity and of restaurants as spaces clearly distinct from cafés, taverns, inns, or brothels is a comparatively recent development. In the West, restaurant culture is no more than 250 years old (and, in many localities, it is much younger). In southeastern China, restaurants were already part of urban culture in the thirteenth century; Marco Polo was astonished by the lavish eating establishments he found in Hangzhou, where regional cuisines such as Szechwan and Honan were readily available. Yet if some cultures have a centuries-long history of public, commercial, gastronomy, many others do not. In many parts of the world, businesses clearly identifiable as restaurants have developed only in the past fifty years. They are the products of post-1945 developments in travel and trade, such as the emergence of global tourism and the spread of multinational corporations.

Europe: Ancient, Medieval, and Early Modern

There were no restaurants in Europe or North America until the mid-eighteenth century, but food was often eaten away from home. In a time when people had neither running water nor refrigeration nor gas nor electricity, and when journeying between cities was a matter of weeks rather than hours, people often ate away from their places of residence. Yet, they did not rely on restaurants. Travelers expected either to carry their own food or to depend on private hospitality; public eating establishments were viewed largely with suspicion and disgust. Since antiquity, numerous writers have accused innkeepers of fraudulent trade practices and unsanitary preparations: the classical medical authority, Galen, claimed that the innkeepers of Rome substituted human meat for pork! In a less spectacular vein, countless patrons over the past two millennia have complained of being served vinegar mixed with water rather than the wine for which they had paid. Affluent travelers therefore preferred to stay with friends along the way or to purchase raw ingredients and have meals prepared by the servants who accompanied them. This was the case even when traveling great distances, such as from London to Scotland during the Middle Ages. In the eighteenth and nineteenth centuries, the existence of many recipes for traveling sauces and portable soups attests to the continued disrepute of public eateries.

Throughout antiquity and the medieval period, shops or stalls selling hot food therefore catered not to the gastronomically adventurous but to the urban poor, whose rudimentary living arrangements made food preparation nearly impossible. In the southern Italian city of Pompeii (destroyed by volcano in 79 C.E.), taverns and *popinae* (foodselling establishments) clustered around the baths and gladiators' dormitories but were not to be found in the more prosperous parts of the city. Members of the Roman elite preferred to recline on couches while eating, but most food-retailing establishments were furnished only with tables and chairs. Ceremonial meals of many sorts played a significant role in the political and social life of Greece and Rome, but these were always held in private residences. Moreover, women were prohibited from these exclusively male events. In these and other ways, the food culture of Mediterranean antiquity was very different from that of the West today, in which restaurants play such a major role.

During the Middle Ages, the large numbers of religious pilgrims who traveled across Europe and into the Near East sought food and shelter in monasteries and in the hostels and hospices run by religious orders. In some areas, inns and taverns provided commercial hospitality but such establishments were rare outside of cities. Nor did even the most reputable inns fully escape stigma and suspicion. Taverns and alehouses were also common in much of western Europe, but these drinking places served only a few foods to soak up the alcohol. The association of public sociability with riotous drinking meant that these were also largely male institutions, at least in theory and imagery. In the seventeenth and eighteenth centuries, they were increasingly avoided by social and cultural elites of both sexes.

Well into the 1800s, inns and cookshops primarily served meals at a single large table, known in English as an "ordinary" and in French as a *table d'hôte* (literally, "host's table"). These shared meals provided travelers with the opportunity (not always desired) to meet each other, but they were better suited to the regular habits of local patrons than to the erratic schedules and varied preferences of passing voyagers. Service was "French style," that is, all the different dishes were placed on the table at once and customers were expected to help themselves to whatever was in front of them. This arrangement worked well for any assertive patrons seated near the roast at the middle of the table, but it could be frustrating for shy or foreign-language-speaking guests positioned with the condiments at the far corners. Given that the food was all placed on the table simultaneously, it was also inconvenient for travelers who arrived fifteen minutes after the meal had begun.

The First Restaurants

Scholars agree that the first self-styled "restaurateurs" opened for business in Paris during the 1760s, but there is some disagreement as to the significance of these establishments. For many years, a man named Boulanger has been credited with having been the first to have sold a wide variety of choice dishes and to have served them at small, oilcloth-covered tables in his shop on the rue des Poulies. Since the early nineteenth century, it has also been usual to cite the tale of Boulanger's dispute with the city of Paris's guild of cook-caterers (*traiteurs*) over the precise status of his signature dish, sheep's feet in sauce. Lore and legend says that in 1765 the cook-caterers tried to shut down Boulanger's shop because the dish infringed their legal monopoly on the sale of all *ragoûts* (dishes cooked in a sauce). Some authors claim that the cook-caterers won their lawsuit and others say they lost, but all use this story to support the broader contention that restaurants were largely impossible until the French Revolution of 1789.

The Boulanger story has been repeated and embellished until it has become one of the most familiar items in the culinary-history, but its sources are largely apocryphal. First briefly noted by P. J. B. Le Grand d'Aussy in his 1782 *Histoire de la vie privée des françois* (History of the private life of the French), an early, encyclopedic venture in writing the history of food and eating, Boulanger's adventures were a popular subject with nineteenth-century antiquarian scholars keen to show how much Paris had changed since the Revolution. However, this account of the origins of restaurant going assumes that the desire to "eat out" has been largely constant throughout history and needed only the cookery talents of one man and the legal changes of one Revolution to take the form familiar today. It cannot explain how the restaurateurs of the 1760s overcame centuries of prejudice against "public cooks" and tells us little of the real importance of this new form of service. Recent scholarship, therefore, places the development of restaurant culture within broader social and historical contexts. It looks for changes not only in what was being cooked and by whom, but in the entire social and cultural framework. The first self-defined restaurateurs built on Enlightenment ideas about science and sentiment; in doing so, they created a cultural institution distinct from the eating-houses and inns of earlier periods.

Restaurateurs in mid-eighteenth-century Paris took their name from the "restorative bouillons" in which they specialized. Made by sweating large quantities of veal, game, and poultry over high heat, these bouillons were concentrated meat broths deemed beneficial for those who were too weakened by illness or exertion to eat an entire solid meal. As they were also costly to prepare, it is hardly surprising that these bouillons were most often recommended to members of the urban elite (both male and female). Within the fashionable culture of the day, the inability or reluctance to eat a full meal was a sign of emotional and intellectual, as well as physical, sensitivity. The first restaurateurs did not cater to customers who were hungry and hurried; rather they provided a milieu in which people could make public show of their private sensibility. Opulent furnishings, mirrored walls, and porcelain consommé dishes all ensured an environment distinctly different from the hurly-burly of the tavern or inn.

In the long run, the most important innovation of the 1760s and 1770s was in the form of service. Restorative bouillons had vanished from most restaurant menus by the 1820s but the basic features of restaurant service remained. These included seating groups of patrons at their own tables, serving meals at unspecified times, and providing a menu from which customers made their own choices. All these elements created the impression that restaurants provided individual and personalized service. Restaurants were public places, insofar as they had neither membership fees nor admission requirements, but they were public places where people went for privacy. Many Paris restaurants, such as the Maison Dorée and the Cadran Bleu, were especially distinguished by their private rooms (*cabinets particuliers*) that were ideally suited to romantic trysts and other secretive meetings.

Restaurants in Nineteenth-Century Paris

Though they first emerged in the eighteenth century, restaurants are most commonly identified as institutions of nineteenth-century Parisian life. It is often said that they were instrumental in democratizing formerly aristocratic privileges: the one-time chefs of princes and dukes found themselves unemployed after their titled patrons fled France during the Revolution. A few early nineteenth-century restaurateurs made much of their aristocratic connections, but most restaurateurs had no such ties and were more closely linked to the other retail food trades. Antoine Beauvilliers, former pastry chef to the king's brother, did open a well-known restaurant, but he did so before the Revolution and much of his fame came from the cookbook, *L'art du cuisinier* (The cook's art) that he published in 1814.

Poster advertising the Grand-Café Zürcherhof in Zurich, Switzerland. Large establishments such as this, with the added amenities of a billiard academy and theater, became popular in many parts of Europe at the turn of the twentieth century. Art Nouveaux lithograph by P. Krawutschke, 1908. ROUGHWOOD COLLECTION.

One important development of this period was the distinction of two types of service: *prix fixe* (fixed price) and *à la carte* (from the menu). In the former, the customer ordered from a restricted number of items but was guaranteed to have a two- or three-course complete meal for the price specified. With service *à la carte*, the diner had the freedom to order anything listed on the menu but may have been surprised at the size of the final bill. In the 1820s and 1830s, these were two separate types of establishments (the latter usually being more prestigious), but today it is not uncommon to find both forms of service available in a single restaurant. Indeed, since the 1970s, a shift has occurred, such that a comparatively brief menu, restricted to locally available, seasonal ingredients, is now often seen as the mark of an upscale restaurant, while the lengthy menu parading hundreds of items is looked at with derision.

Based on early nineteenth-century texts, a short listing of the most famous first restaurants would have to include the following: Véry's (at the peak of their fame, the Véry brothers ran two prominent restaurants, one in the Palais Royal and the other in the Tuileries Gardens); the Rocher de Cancale on the rue Montorgeuil (famous both for oysters and for the epicurean singing societies that met in its private rooms); the Trois Frères Provençaux (three business partners who introduced some of the cookery of southern France to the capital—they were especially known for their *brandade*, a dish of puréed salt cod, traditionally eaten on Good Friday); Méot's and Robert's (two well-known establishments of the late 1790s); the Café Hardy (despite its name, a restaurant noted for its grilled meats); and LeGacque's (home to a famous eating club, the Wednesday Society). Many restaurants of a slightly later period play a significant role in the realist novels of the 1830s and 1840s, especially those of Honoré de Balzac. At the end of the century, restaurant and café scenes featured prominently in the works of some Impressionist artists.

Two businesses currently in operation often make claims to be the oldest restaurant in Paris. These are the Tour d'Argent, housed in a sixteenth-century inn, and the Café Procope, a famous meeting place for eighteenth-century intellectuals. Since neither actually started as a restaurant *per se*, some may dispute their right to this title. Other old restaurants still in operation include the Véfour in the Palais Royal (converted from café to restaurant in 1817) and LeDoyen's on the Champs Elysées.

The Spread of the French Model

The use of French names for restaurants in many parts of the world indicates the nineteenth-century predominance of the Paris model. Two of the first restaurants in Sydney, Australia were named after two of the most famous ones in Paris, the Trois Frères Provençaux and the Café-Restaurant de Paris. Another famous Paris restaurant name, Véry's, was replicated in central London, where Verrey's was a Regent Street fixture from the 1850s to the 1920s. In Mexico City, the Tivoli and Maison Dorée restaurants borrowed their names and their menus from the French capital.

By the first decades of the nineteenth century, restaurants may have been fixtures in the Paris landscape but they were still uncommon in the French provinces and even more rare elsewhere. As late as the 1850s, American and British visitors to Paris remarked on how strange and marvelous it was to be offered the choice of dozens of different dishes and to eat those dishes in an ornate dining room surrounded by groups of both men and women. Many of London's exclusive gentlemen's clubs were famous for their chefs (Louis Eustache Ude at Crockford's Club and Alexis Soyer at the Reform Club are just two examples) but these clubs, restricted to members only and forbidden to women, were not the same as restaurants. An important British institution, gentlemen's clubs were copied in the colonies, especially India, where the Bengal Club (Calcutta) was founded in 1827. For members of the Victorian middle class, domestic comfort played a central part in defining their own national, social, and gender identities. Many Britons therefore looked askance at restaurants as offering proof that the French had no real home lives and, hence, no sense of family.

Hotel Restaurants and "International" Cuisine

The luxurious hotels of the late nineteenth century played an important part in introducing restaurant culture to the British and North American upper classes. These sumptuous hotels with their grand entrance lobbies and ornate dining rooms were made possible, in part, by the greatly expanded travel habits that developed with the railroad and the steamship. The French model remained preeminent in hotel restaurants for several reasons, including that country's long established reputation for luxury goods and Paris's international appeal. The standardization of a *haute cuisine* (high cookery) that came to be identified with "French" food and the rise of hotel training programs may also have played a role. Georges-Auguste Escoffier, a chef who worked closely with the hotel entrepreneur, César Ritz, is often credited with having rationalized restaurant kitchen work in a fashion that made it easier to teach and replicate. His cookbooks and menus were often copied and his way of organizing kitchen work became standard practice.

Until the nouvelle cuisine and fusion foods of the last third of the twentieth century, Escoffier's version of "international cuisine" dominated the hotel restaurants and so-called "fine dining" establishments of much of the world. This cuisine was international insofar as it was served to diners in grand hotels around the globe, but the recipes, ingredients, and seasonings were western European in inspiration. In many parts of the world, the introduction of this so-called "international" cookery and Western-style restaurant service went hand in hand. Organizations such as the Japanese Travel Bureau (a joint venture between government and private railroad, steamship, and hotel companies, founded 1912) actively encouraged the establishment of "European restaurants" where Western travelers would find forks and knives, printed menus, and meals served in several courses. Teahouses (frequented only by male customers) and Japanese restaurants (*ryōri-ya*) were already widespread, but concern to show Japan as a "civilized" (i.e., Western) country led to new businesses that were furnished with tables and chairs, served large quantities of meat, and severed all ties to prostitution. During the following decades, and especially with the Allied occupation after World War II, businesses and government alike were keen to promote an image of Japan as a country that foreigners would find both reassuringly comfortable and pleasantly exotic. This demand was met by restaurants in which service duplicated that to be found in Paris, Chicago, or

New York, but where the dining room was decorated with chrysanthemums, bamboo, and cherry blossoms and the menu might include a few notionally Japanese dishes.

Early Restaurants in the United States

As was true of Europe, colonial North America had taverns and boarding houses, but no restaurants. Coffee houses and oyster houses began appearing in the late eighteenth century, but the word "restaurant" was not commonly used until the 1830s or 1840s. Delmonico's, which opened in Manhattan in 1831 and occupied several different locales until it finally closed during Prohibition, is often cited as the first American restaurant but this is far from certain. Nonetheless, whether it was the first or the fifty-first, Delmonico's became a model throughout the nineteenth century. In 1868, the first railway restaurant car in the United States was named "Delmonico's" even though it operated on the Chicago-Alton line, half a continent away from New York. Charles Ranhofer, chef at Delmonico's from 1863 to 1895, helped spread the restaurant's fame in the pages of his enormous cookbook, *The Epicurean*, which also included anecdotal stories about the famous patrons he had met and the great meals he had cooked.

Scenes of adulterous dalliances and tipsy festivities, restaurants such as these were as infamous for scandal as they were famous for food (lobsters and champagne were the usual fare). Central to one stereotype of New York nightlife, they were largely irrelevant to many of the city's inhabitants. It should not be forgotten, however, that the lavish scale of turn-of-the-century restaurants and hotels depended on the existence of a largely immigrant underclass from which staff members were drawn. Indeed, the East Coast restaurant and hotel labor market at this time was effectively segregated by ethnicity and gender. Eastern and southern European women worked as maids, and African-American women were employed as chambermaids in the grandest hotels, while most waiters were men of French or Italian descent. Although the food served was French in name or inspiration, most of the chefs were German; French men worked as waiters or as specialized cooks, such as pastry chefs.

Mass Market Restaurants in the United States

The grand hotel restaurants of the late nineteenth century were fixtures in major cities, but they fed only a small percentage of the American population. Unlike earlier taverns or oyster houses, the lobster palaces and cabarets welcomed both men and women but this gave them an air of promiscuity that worried cultural conservatives, religious leaders, and prohibition activists. Levenstein has argued that Prohibition, by dissolving the association of eating out with alcohol consumption, did much to make eating away from home acceptable for single women and members of all social classes. It is certain that the 1920s witnessed both the closing of many of the most luxurious barrooms and the opening of numerous luncheonettes and tearooms. (It remains unclear, however, whether Prohibition caused these changes or whether Prohibition and luncheonettes were both responses to other, more fundamental, changes in American society.)

By the 1930s, the U.S. Bureau of the Census counted 200,000 food-retailing outlets, including 124,000 restaurants and over 45,000 lunch counters. The latter category included drugstore soda fountains, sandwich shops, and diners as well as hot-dog stands and box-lunch companies. It is interesting to note that the Census Bureau included automats and self-service cafeterias under the heading of restaurants.

According to Richard Pillsbury, the postwar period did not see an immediate boom in the number of restaurants, but it did witness the transformation of American culture that was crucial to their eventual growth. Changes in family life, increased urbanization, the omnipresence of the automobile, and the affluence of the middle classes all contributed to making restaurant meals a regular part of life for many Americans. Drive-in restaurants made it possible to "eat out" within the comfort of one's very own automobile. Yet variation by region and by socioeconomic class should not be overlooked. Nor should it be forgotten that eating places in the South were often segregated, and that interracial "dine ins" played a significant part in the Civil Rights movement of the 1960s.

In the last quarter of the nineteenth century, Fred Harvey developed one of the first restaurant chains, in cooperation with the Atchison, Topeka, and Santa Fe Railroad. Along the route, he built and operated seventeen Harvey Houses, which were recognizable by their décor and by the waitresses' identical uniforms. The menus were coordinated, however, to guarantee that the restaurants' pleasing familiarity did not extend to the food served, and the traveler was guaranteed of never being served the same fare two meals in a row. This show of variety under an umbrella of uniformity has been the hallmark of restaurant chains ever since.

Prior to World War II, chain restaurants were comparatively novel, accounting for only 15 percent of all restaurant business. (In contrast, chain grocery stores in the 1930s were already responsible for nearly half of all grocery sales.) Howard Johnson's, initially a New England ice cream chain, expanded along the highways of the 1930s and 1940s much as Harvey House had along the railroads.

In the late twentieth century, franchised businesses have accounted for much of the U.S. restaurant industry's expansion. In 1994, nearly 60 percent of the total 406,000 U.S. restaurants were chain units and 200,720 restaurants belonged to chains that included over 200 units. Many of these were fast-food establishments such as McDonald's, Burger King, or Kentucky Fried Chicken, but many others were full-service restaurants such as the Outback Steakhouse, the Olive Garden, Bennigan's, or Denny's. The success of these chains suggests that customers value familiarity. Eating out has become routinized.

Ethnic Restaurants

So-called "ethnic" restaurants may seem a logical outgrowth of the waves of immigration to the United States in the late nineteenth and early twentieth centuries, to Australia in the same period, and to Great Britain in the period since World War II. In part, they are, for economic marginalization and racism have often caused recently arrived immigrants to concentrate in businesses requiring comparatively small capital investment, such as catering. Moreover, recruitment of new workers for these enterprises is usually done informally, through family and community connections, and further concentrates the members of an ethnic group in a few businesses. Since most restaurant employees do not actually speak to the customers, it is seen as an ideal line of work for recent immigrants who feel uncertain about their linguistic abilities.

Yet it should not be imagined that these restaurants have simply been transplanted from the immigrants' home country. Nineteenth-century Greece had few, if any, restaurants (and the inns were as disreputable as they had been two thousand years before), but late-nineteenth-century Greek immigrants to the United States quickly became concentrated in the restaurant industry.

The food served in ethnic restaurants often constitutes a distinct cuisine. In all cultures and contexts, there are some foods that are almost exclusively eaten in restaurants and others that never are. (For example, one would have to read a great many U.S. restaurant menus before finding those two staples of the American diet, peanut-butter-and-jelly sandwiches and popcorn.) If we consider Indian restaurants in the United Kingdom, we find that by the 1990s, they employed more people (roughly 70,000) than the shipbuilding and steel industries combined. Many of these were staffed by immigrants from the province of Sylhet in the northeastern corner of Bangladesh, but the food served had its roots in other parts of the subcontinent. Ingredients and cooking methods from the northwestern region of Punjab dominate "Indian" restaurant food in much the same way that one version of "French" cooking was once the norm in Western restaurants. This may be because the 1947 partition caused many Punjabis to migrate to Delhi and other cities where they started running food stalls. When the Indian government established catering colleges in the 1960s to train employees for the tourist industry, the instructors came from these Punjabi families. Since they taught north Indian cooking, this was what the students learned, regardless of the students' own ethnic or regional background.

Working in Restaurants

Restaurants combine characteristics of both production and service industries. Since William Foote Whyte's clas-

sic study, *Human Relations in the Restaurant Industry* (1948), social scientists have recognized that this combination leads to a conflict of interests between kitchen and dining-room employees. While the waitstaff must be constantly attentive to the demands and desires of the customers, the kitchen workers have their own distinct priorities. If a few famous chefs such as Paul Bocuse, Joel Robuchon, or Alice Waters seem to set the standards to which gourmets aspire, many other chefs and kitchen employees see themselves as ordinary, working-class, people, who have little in common with their middle-class and upper-middle-class patrons (see Fine, 1996).

Labor historians have long puzzled over the very low rates of unionization in restaurant work. One explanation is that the industry has largely institutionalized a system of informal rewards that would be lost with formal contracts: tipping encourages competition among members of the wait staff, rather than solidarity. Furthermore, waiting tables is commonly casual work rather than a lifelong career. Finally, the antagonistic, often combative, relation between kitchen and dining-room employees means that no single union has ever had much success in reaching both groups of workers.

It may be difficult to imagine that the first restaurant kitchens were fueled by coal or wood, but so they were. Smoke-filled, sooty, and with little in the way of refrigeration, the restaurant kitchens of the early nineteenth century would appall any health inspector today. The Belle Epoque restaurant boom in Australia and elsewhere was made possible by the increasing ease of railroad transportation and the availability of refrigeration techniques, while it was made further profitable by the expansion of advertising. The steakhouses so popular in the Anglophone world of the 1950s and 1960s (such as the Steak & Ale chain in the United States or the Berni Inns of Great Britain and Japan) served Argentinean beef and a limited number of simple side dishes, all easily prepared by semiskilled labor. Today, much of the inexpensive food consumed in restaurants, like the convenience food prepared at home, is made possible by the introduction of microwave technology. Any account of the spread and standardization of the industry should also consider the growth of restaurant-supply firms.

Restaurant Guides and Reviews

A. B. L. Grimod de La Reynière (1758–1837) is generally credited with having invented the restaurant review. His yearly *Almanach des gourmands* (Gourmands' almanac), published in the first decade of the nineteenth century, pointed its readers to the finest restaurants, pastry cooks, and gourmet shops of Napoleonic Paris. A bestseller in its day, it also set the precedent for later ventures in restaurant reviewing. The advent of rail and automobile travel expanded the market for restaurant guides. The Michelin tire company published its first hotel/restaurant guide to France in 1900 and awarded its first stars in 1926. Since then, airlines and automobile manufacturers have often ventured into the guidebook/cookbook business, though none have had the enduring importance of the Michelin guides and their rankings. Governments keen to promote tourism have also entered the business of publishing guidebooks and encouraging the hospitality industry.

In the mid-twentieth century, a somewhat different form of restaurant guide emerged, written neither by a lone gastronome nor by a faceless corporation. Duncan Hines (*Adventures in Good Eating*) in the United States and Raymond Postgate (*Good Food Guide*) in the United Kingdom both promised to publish recommendations sent by their readers. Postgate did this much more than Hines, but both contributed to the idea that members of the ordinary eating public might have their opinions heard. In the early twenty-first century, thousands of amateur reviewers made their opinions known on their own websites.

Why People Do Not Go to Restaurants

The idea of voluntarily going out to eat sits uneasily with the teachings of many religions. People who obey Jewish, Moslem, Jain, or Hindu dietary laws may find it no easier to eat in a Michelin three-star restaurant than in a stockyard or petshop. Both Jewish and Moslem law prescribes how livestock should be slaughtered. Unless an eatery is run by a known member of the community, observant patrons may not be willing to eat the meat served there. Brahmans, members of the highest Hindu caste, are forbidden to eat or drink anything prepared by a member of another caste. In addition, only other Brahmans are supposed to see them eating. Many Orthodox Hindus of all castes are highly reluctant to consume food (or even drink water) prepared and brought by unknown hands, even when traveling long distances. Jains are so profoundly vegetarian that they refuse to eat food prepared by someone who is not, even if the meal includes no animal products. None of these dietary laws can be obeyed in a restaurant where the cook remains unknown to the diner. In such a context, a restaurant meal can be only an ordeal.

As mentioned above, British middle-class culture, with its emphasis on domesticity, was slow to adopt the custom of eating out. In the late 1800s, the famous grill-room, Simpsons in the Strand, tried to attend to cultural norms by offering separate dining rooms for men and women. Lower down the social scale, working-class Britons in the early twentieth century might sometimes rely on takeout from local fish-and-chip businesses, but the association of restaurants with upper-class Francophilia meant that they, too, were unlikely to go out to eat. In many respects, then, it was not until the 1950s and 1960s that restaurant culture became a significant part of British life.

Why People Go to Restaurants

In many parts of the world, certain specialty foods are rarely, if ever, prepared at home and the chance to eat

Many large department stores feature restaurants where shoppers may take lunch or dinner. The restaurant at Harrods, Knightsbridge, London is both a fashionable eatery and retail shop for gourmet food products. © BO ZAUNDERS/CORBIS.

them may be one incentive for eating out. For example, local businesses limited to the time-consuming and messy business of preparing tripe are common in France, Greece, and Portugal. In Japan, only licensed chefs in specialist restaurants are allowed to prepare the highly poisonous blowfish (fugu). In China, snakes are never eaten at home but they are nonetheless considered a great delicacy when served by restaurants that specialize in them.

It may seem paradoxical, but food is rarely the only reason that people go out to eat. The evidence of the past several centuries indicates that restaurants may serve many different functions. Even within a single dining room, some customers may be celebrating a wedding anniversary and others may be cheating on their spouses. By entertaining guests or meeting friends in a restaurant, people can shield their domestic lives from others; in France today, only the very closest friends are ever invited into the home. In moments of domestic conflict, eating in the comparatively public space of a restaurant may be a way to reestablish the outward forms and appearances of civility.

As publicly accessible places in which patrons are seated at their own tables and eat their own meals, restaurants seem to provide a window into other people's private lives. The elaborately mirrored dining rooms of many nineteenth-century restaurants made it especially easy to observe one's fellow patrons without staring at them directly. Diners could preserve the illusion of their own privacy, even as they peered into that of others. Since the 1980s, there has been a brief trend toward very large and loud restaurants where the crowded atmosphere may further blur the distinction between private and public. There has also, however, been a renewed interest in intimate private dining rooms far from the eyes of star-struck strangers and the ears of curious waiters.

The various "ethnic" restaurants found in American cities in the 1930s were distinguished more by their furnishings and music than by their cuisine. Today's cult of culinary authenticity may scoff at the notion that red lacquer walls and a Pekingese under the table suffice to make a restaurant "Chinese," but it is important to recognize that many supposedly national cuisines have been produced by the demands of restaurant culture.

See also **Chef, The**; **Delmonico Family**; **Escoffier, Georges-Auguste**; **Fusion Cuisine**; **Grimod de La Reynière**; **Kitchens, Restaurant**; **Nouvelle Cuisine**; **Places of Consumption**; **Waiters and Waitresses**.

BIBLIOGRAPHY

Davidson, Alan, ed. *The Oxford Companion to Food*. Oxford: Oxford University Press, 1999.

Erenberg, Lewis A. *Steppin' Out: New York Nightlife and the Transformation of American Culture*. Chicago: University of Chicago Press, 1984.

Fine, Gary Alan. *Kitchens: The Culture of Restaurant Work*. Berkeley: University of California Press, 1996.

Gabaccia, Donna. *We are What We Eat: Ethnic Food and the Making of Americans*. Cambridge, Mass.: Harvard University Press, 1998.

Levenstein, Harvey. *Revolution at the Table: The Transformation of the American Diet*. Oxford: Oxford University Press, 1988.

Mennell, Stephen. *All Manners of Food: Eating and Taste in England and France from the Middle Ages to the Present*. Oxford: Basil Blackwell, 1985.

Pillsbury, Richard. *From Boarding House to Bistro: The American Restaurant Then and Now*. Boston: Unwin Hyman, 1990.

Spang, Rebecca L. "All the World's a Restaurant: On the Gastronomics of Tourism and Travel." In *Food in Global History*, edited by Raymond Grew. Boulder, Colo.: Westview, 1999.

Spang, Rebecca L. *The Invention of the Restaurant: Paris and Modern Gastronomic Culture*. Cambridge, Mass.: Harvard University Press, 2000.

Trubek, Amy. *Haute Cuisine*. Philadelphia: University of Pennsylvania Press, 2000.

Walker, Harlan, ed. *Public Eating* (Oxford Symposium on Food and Cookery, 1991). Totnes, Devon, U.K.: Prospect Books, 1992.

Whyte, William Foote. *Human Relations in the Restaurant Industry*. New York: McGraw-Hill, 1948.

Rebecca L. Spang

RETAILING OF FOOD. In agricultural societies all over the world, food marketing took place in central marketplaces in towns and cities. In larger cities, specialized merchants operated temporary stalls and permanent warehouse/stores alongside farmers who brought produce and animals directly to market. The Greek agora is an example of such a marketplace. The ruins of Pompeii provide examples of merchant's streetfront stores.

Expanding industrialization in the late nineteenth century ushered in mass consumerism in the United States and Europe. New forms of food purveying transformed the structure of the food business, the nature of retail ownership, and the social relations of food shopping. Innovations in food shopping that developed in the late nineteenth and early twentieth centuries spread throughout the world with varied significance and direction.

Victorian Food Halls, Public Markets, and Local Family-Owned Stores

Mass production created both new commodities and a new professional-managerial consumer class in the late nineteenth century. Grand emporia, called "department stores," developed in response to this new type of customer. Centrally located, these palaces of consumerism used elegant, monumental ambience to display commodities. Early department stores usually incorporated food halls in which high-end customers were introduced to new products at separate stations in sanitized settings. Samples and demonstrations of new products were offered.

At the same time, large public markets continued to purvey fresh produce and meat brought directly from the country to central markets where they were purchased by the working classes, servants to the middle classes, and the small-scale vendors of raw and cooked foods who served dispersed communities.

Corporate Chains and Supermarkets

During World War I and the interwar years, the inflation of food prices made the high cost of living a major political issue. In the 1920s and 1930s new forms of food stores were invented in the United States to rationalize costs. This occurred in a two-step process, with centralized chain stores followed by the new self-service supermarkets. The Atlantic and Pacific Tea Company (A&P) was the largest of the early chain stores. Expanding from a chain of tea stores to encompass all food products, A&P was concentrated mostly in the Northeast. Other pioneering chains were Safeway in the West and Krogers in the Midwest. Chains achieved economies of scale through buying in bulk and a higher volume of sales. A&P also relied on its own production of house brands to cut wholesale costs.

The first chains in the United States retained the same spatial/social organization as family-owned counterparts. Clerks still presented wares over the counter and helped make selections, gave product information, often bargained over price, and arranged for such services as credit and delivery. This changed with the advent of self-service marketing. Michael Cullen, an employee of Krogers, opened his first self-service King Kullen store in New York in 1930 when Kroger executives rejected his new concept. Recognizing that larger stores were necessary to achieve profitable sales volumes, self-service emerged as an adaptation to size. Cullen's stores were ten times larger in square footage than chain stores. As James Mayo reports (p. 117), the term "supermarket" came into use in the 1930s and was defined by a threshold sales volume, parking lots, and self-service.

FOOD HALLS IN JAPAN

In Japan, where efficient public transit has forestalled reliance on cars, supermarkets are less developed, and small family-owned stores and chain-owned convenience stores near neighborhood public transit are heavily used. In addition, department stores located at major transit junctions devote much space to food halls. These food halls provide offerings ranging from perishable produce and sushi to a broad selection of cooked dishes representing traditional Japanese, other Asian, and European cuisines. Hawkers use traditional calls to attract customers to their stands, reproducing the ambience of the old urban marketplace for middle-class housewives and office workers within this modern, sanitized site of overconsumption.

Window display of a high-class London fruiterer, 1918. All of the produce shown in the window is sourced by country of origin and name of fruit variety. ROUGHWOOD COLLECTION.

Showcasing the product is an important aspect in retailing food. Here forty-eight flavors of ice cream are displayed behind fancy chocolates (under the glass). PHOTO FROM THE 1940s COURTESY OF H. WILLIAM ISALY AND BRIAN BUTKO.

In self-service stores, goods were displayed to allow the consumer to make autonomous choices based on fixed prices. Also referred to as "cash and carry" stores, they did not provide the conveniences, such as credit or delivery, that formerly bound merchant to customer. Instead they provided an often desirable anonymity and private decision-making. The grocery cart was developed in 1937 and expanded the possibilities for bulk shopping. Increasing automobile and refrigerator ownership enabled infrequent bulk shopping to replace frequent or daily shopping..

These enterprises were important sites in the development of a mass market of middle-class consumers. The United States, unlike Europe, lacked a history of aristocracy and strong class distinctions in taste. Media advertising used specials and brand imaging to shape consumer desire for standardized, reliable mass-produced foods and to foster trust in corporate chains.

In contrast, Europe retained clearly marked class distinctions in taste and consumption. An active food co-op movement was at the center of debates about food prices. Traditional wholesalers and their shopkeeper allies had considerable political clout. They promoted the benefits

of artisan production over mass production in food processing. Independent grocers and wholesalers fought successfully for protectionist legislation to thwart chain-store development and the food co-op movement. According to Victoria de Grazia in her article, "Changing Consumption Regimes in Europe" (pp. 71–74), this protest occurred particularly in Germany, France, Austria, and Italy, in contrast to Great Britain and Sweden.

Post–World War II Global Trends

Supermarkets became the dominant sites for food shopping in the United States during the post-World War II era of abundance. As technology was fetishized to symbolize modernity, supermarket architecture and design became strikingly modern, emphasizing service by machines rather than people. Innovations in shelving, lighting, open refrigerator cases, and newly designed promotional displays highlighted the abundance of products and encouraged impulse shopping. Furthermore, as mass ownership of automobiles enabled the sprawl of suburban settlements, new stores in developing suburbs were less densely distributed and much larger in size, drawing customers from long distances.

In the postwar era in Europe, traditional state-protected food distribution was rapidly transformed. Self-service stores in Germany increased in number from 39 in 1951 to 17,132 in 1960 and 35,000 in 1965. At the same time in France, the "hyperstore" was invented, joining food with other consumer goods in even larger stores. Promodes, a provincial Normandy food wholesaler, merged with two rival family firms in the 1960s and within a decade developed a multinational retail network.

ETHNIC MARKET SUCCESSION

In Philadelphia, a multiblock area called the "Italian Market" served originally as a site where Italian immigrants could purchase fresh seasonal produce grown by Italian truck gardeners in southern New Jersey, as well as imported cheese and oil. Butchers slaughtered pigs in the fall and made sausages for Christmas Eve celebrations and the long winter. In spring, paschal lambs were available. Today, the area is still identified on tourist maps as the Italian Market. Yet aside from the remaining cheese and sausage purveyors and a few venerable restaurants, most vendors and consumers are Vietnamese who are now dominant in this area and have special ethnic food needs.

THE SUPERMARKET IN DEVELOPING COUNTRIES

Supermarkets require private transportation for bulk purchases. In developing nations, chains such as Carulla in Colombia develop as soon as automobile suburbs emerge. Aspiring middle-class people without cars often pool their resources to use transportation such as unlicensed taxis and buses to take them shopping in these outlets.

Another major French chain, Carrefour, opened its first North American hyperstore in Montreal in 1973, and by 1989, there were eighteen European-style hyperstores in the United States. Today many supermarket chains are truly global in ownership and in the commodities that are purveyed. In 1979, A&P itself was bought by Tengelmann, a German-owned multinational. At the same time, U.S. corporations such as Pathmark have created "superstores" that sell more than food.

Post-Industrial Reaction and Counterreaction

Today, many consumers see drawbacks in corporate food distribution. Centralized stocking practices are far removed from local customer needs as they rely more on corporate relations with food manufacturers and formulas for profit margins. In spite of the illusion of unlimited choice, variety in packaging and a parade of "new" products that are minor variations of existing ones, provide a limited veneer of novelty. Long-distance produce, cultivated for preservation and not for taste, is limited in its variety. Moreover, supermarket shelves are dominated by the products of a few large conglomerates whose power facilitates shelf preference and agreements to exclude competing products.

As corporations cut back on labor costs, workers are fewer and less knowledgeable. Meats once handled by skilled butchers are now packaged in the processing plant. As service declines, work is transferred to the customer. Huge stores mean a longer time spent walking down the aisles and waiting on checkout lines. Surveillance cameras limit one's privacy.

However, for certain urban populations, small stores remain central. Post-industrial capitalist elites who aestheticize food and leisurely eating, as those in the Italian-initiated "Slow Food" movement and their global counterparts, eschew mass-produced foods and long-distance produce. They are served by artisan bakeries, homemade-pasta shops, and local farmers markets. In-creasing numbers of global immigrants are served by small shops that have ethnic foods and merchants who speak their languages. In addition, poor people in inner cities avoided by chains are dependent on small high-priced stores.

Seeking a broad customer base, corporate chains are continually responding to new demands. As people become more and more pressed for time, dispersed convenience stores allow quick purchases by people on the run. Prepared-food offerings and salad bars have expanded in supermarkets. Chains of upscale markets, such as the Whole Foods network in the United States, have developed to address high-end consumer desire for fresh quality produce and gourmet take-out foods. At the other extreme are chains of huge stores like Costco and Walmart, which sell mass quantities at near wholesale prices. Some chains try to resocialize the impersonal space of food stores by providing eating spaces, sponsoring singles nights for young professionals, and reaching out to local communities through promotions for local schools.

See also **Farmers' Markets**; **Food Politics: United States**; **Marketing of Food**.

BIBLIOGRAPHY

De Grazia, Victoria. "Changing Consumption Regimes in Europe, 1930-1970: Comparative Perspectives on the Distribution Problem." In *Getting and Spending: European and American Consumer Societies in the Twentieth Century*, edited by Susan Strasser, Charles McGovern, and Matthias Judt, pp. 59–84. New York: Cambridge University Press, 1998.

Deutsch, Tracey. "Untangling Alliances: Social Tensions Surrounding Independent Grocery Stores and the Rise of Mass Retailing." In *Food Nations: Selling Taste in Consumer Societies*, edited by Warren Belasco and Phillip Scranton. New York: Routledge, 2001.

Goode, Judith. "Encounters over the Counter: Workers, Bosses, and Customers on a Changing Shopping Strip." In *Newcomers in the Workplace: Immigrants and the Restructuring of the U.S. Economy*, edited by Louise Lamphere, Alex Stepick, and Guillermo Grenier, pp. 251–280. Philadelphia: Temple University Press, 1994.

Mayo, James M. "The American Grocery Store: The Business Evolution of an Architectural Space." *Contributions to American History* no. 150. Westbury, Conn.: Greenwood Press, 1993.

Strasser, Susan, Charles McGovern, and Matthias Judt, eds. *Getting and Spending: European and American Consumer Societies in the Twentieth Century*. New York: Cambridge University Press, 1998.

Tedlow, Richard. *New and Improved: The Story of Mass Marketing in America*. Cambridge, Mass.: Harvard Business School Press, 1996.

Judith Goode

RIBOFLAVIN. *See* **Vitamins**.

RICE.

This entry includes three subentries:
The Natural History of Rice
Rice as a Food
Rice as a Superfood

THE NATURAL HISTORY OF RICE

Rice has fed more people than any other crop has for thousands of years. The ancient Indian name for rice, *Dhanya*, means "sustenance for the human race." Especially in much of Asia, life without rice has been unthinkable. Rice feeds more than half of the world population, but most rice is consumed within ten miles of where it is produced.

Rice is the second largest crop in planting acreage after wheat. Global rice production was 596.5 million tons from 155 million hectares (ha) in 1999. The major rice growing regions are found in more than a hundred countries in Asia, Latin America, and Africa. But major rice exporting countries only include Thailand, the United States, Vietnam, Pakistan, and India. About 85 percent of total rice production is for human consumption. Rice provides 23 percent of the global human per capita energy and 16 percent of the per capita protein (IRRI, 1997). In Asia, where people typically eat rice two or three times a day, 250 million rice farms (the average rice land per farm is less than 1 ha) produce more than 90 percent of the world's rice. For example, Myanmar consumes 195 kg of rice per capita per year, whereas the average annual rice consumptions in Europe and America are 3 kg and 7 kg, respectively. The three most populous nations, China, India, and Indonesia, are rice-based countries, which together have 2.5 billion people (about half of the current world population).

Rice can be processed into rice bran oil, wine, rice cakes, and other foods. Rice flour can be used as the main component of face powders and infant formula or for polishing expensive jewelry. Rice bran oil can be used in cooking, making soap, and as an ingredient in insecticides. Silica-rich rice husks can be used as raw materials for construction materials such as insulation, as a conditioner for commercial fertilizers, as an ingredient in hand soaps and furfural (a chemical used in synthetic resin manufacture), as mulch, as an abrasive, as a fuel, or as an ingredient to make thermoplastics (Yekani Amonollah: United States Patent: 6,172,144). Rice straw has been used for livestock feed, bedding for livestock, straw mushroom production (in China and Thailand), and in industries for arts and crafts. In early times, rice straw was also used for thatching roofs in Asia, and to make ropes, mats, paper, baskets, and bags. Now rice straw is mostly used for animal feed or as field manure.

Rice Biology

Classification. Rice has 120,000 varieties, the richest gene bank in the plant kingdom. There has been great progress in rice genome sequencing projects recently by using both *Indica* (9311) and *Japonica* (Nipponbare) varieties. This will greatly enhance rice improvements in the near future. From the taxonomy of rice, Asian rice belongs to the grass (Gramineae) family and genus *Oryza*. Wheat, corn, and barley also belong to the grass family. *Oryza* has twenty-three species, which can be classified into four groups. The *O. ridleyi* complex and *O. meyeriana* complex contain species in lowland swamp forests and upland hillside forests, respectively. The *O. officinalis* complex consists of perennial species throughout the tropics. The *O. sativa* complex includes two cultigens and the wild relative of these two cultigens. Only two *Oryza* species, the tetraploid *O. schlechteri* and the diploid *O. brachyantha*, are different from these four groups. Based on another classification method for *Oryza* species, the common wild rice or so-called *O. perennis* complex includes Asian wild rice (*O. rufipogon*), African wild rice (*O. longistaminata* or *O. barthii*), and Oceanian wild rice (*O. meriodinalis*) (Chang, 1976). *O. rufipogon* is the wild relative of *O. sativa* and a noxious weed in rice-growing countries. This wild rice has the characteristic of easy shedding to facilitate easy dispersal and easy crossing with the Asian cultivars, which results in the degradation of the variety and contamination of red-grained plants. The wild rice (or Indian rice or water oats) of North America (*Zizania palustris* or *Z. aquatica L.*, 2n = 30) belongs to a different genera and even a different tribe of the grass family. It was traditionally harvested by native Americans in the Great Lakes region, and now is commercially produced in Minnesota, Wisconsin, northern California, and Manitoba, Canada. It has nutty and rich flavor and boasts a pleasant chewiness. It is high in protein and B vitamins but low in fat.

Rice has only two cultivated species, *Oryza sativa* Linn. (the Asian cultivated species) and *Oryza glaberrima* Steud. (the West African cultivated species). *O. sativa* is by far the more widely utilized of the two. By contrast, *O. glaberrima* has much less diversity because of a relatively short cultivation history and a narrower dispersal than *O. sativa*. The main differences in botanical morphology between these two cultivated species are the ligule size and glume pubescence. Most of *O. glaberrima* varieties have fewer hairs, short ligules, and fewer or no branches, and also have red-hulled grains on the shattering panicle. They are generally more resistant to flood, alkaline soils, and blast than *O. sativa* varieties. Another difference is that *O. glaberrima* is strictly annual, whereas *O. sativa* is potentially a perennial. It is generally thought that there are two major subspecies in *O. sativa*: *indica* (or *hsien*) and *japonica* (sometimes called *sinica* or *keng*). *Japonica* is generally short, less leafy, and has a strong culm and short grains. *Japonica* varieties are grown in temperate areas such as northern China, Japan, Korea, Spain, Australia, and California. When cooked, *japonica* rice is sticky. *Indica* rice generally has long, slender, and fluffy grains, many tillers, and is tall, leafy, and tolerant of

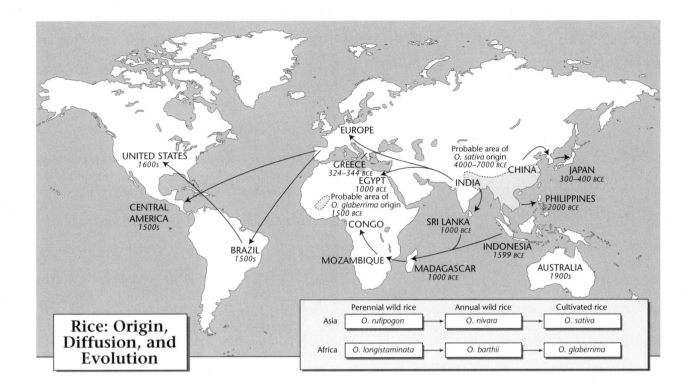

Rice: Origin, Diffusion, and Evolution

	Perennial wild rice	Annual wild rice	Cultivated rice
Asia	O. rufipogon	O. nivara	O. sativa
Africa	O. longistaminata	O. barthii	O. glaberrima

drought. It does not stick when cooked. *Indica* rice is usually grown in hot (tropical or subtropical) climates such as in India, Thailand, Vietnam, and Southern China. The so-called *javanica* can be classified as a tropical *japonica* and is mostly grown in Indonesia and the United States. *Javanica* was originally grown in equatorial areas with abundant water and is generally vulnerable to drought.

Morphology. Rice has the following three main developmental phases: the vegetative phase (from germination to panicle initiation), the reproductive phase (from panicle initiation to flowering), and the ripening phase (from flowering to maturity). A typical rice plant during reproductive and ripening stages has the following organs: roots, a main stem and a number of tillers (or side shoots), leaves, panicles, flowers (or florets) when flowering, and grains when maturing. The edible part of a rice plant is in the rice grain, which includes glumes, endosperm, and embryo. Some varieties have awns at the tip of the grain. More detail about rice morphology can be found in literature by Chang and Bardenas (1965) and by Grist (1986).

Rice has a fibrous root system, that is, it has temporary seminal roots or embryonic roots, then secondary adventitious roots. The fibrous roots only last for a short time after seed germination. An alternative is the classification of rice roots based on the spatial pattern as crown roots (including mat roots) below the soil and nodal roots above the soil. The function of rice roots is to absorb water. It is estimated that it takes 5,000 liters of water to produce 1 kg of irrigated rice. Owing to the great consumption of water in rice production, future rice cultivation will face the looming water deficiency in some countries.

Plant height can range from approximately 0.4 m to more than 6 m (in floating rice) depending on the rice variety or environmental conditions. The rice culm is round, hollow, jointed, and hairless. A maturing rice plant has a main stem and a number of tillers depending on the variety and cultural conditions. Each stem has a certain number of nodes (generally ranging from 13 to 16 nodes) and internodes under a certain environmental condition for a rice variety.

Rice leaves are rather flat. The first rudimentary leaf or prophyllum is at the base of a tiller and, with only a two-keeled bract, has no blade. The uppermost leaf immediately below the panicle is called the flag leaf. The leaf blade and leaf sheath are attached at the node, where there is an auricle (a pair of claw-like appendages encircling the stem), and the ligule (a thin, upright papery and triangular structure) immediately above the auricle. When young, the major difference between rice and a common grassy weed (*Echinochloa* spp.) is the presence of auricles and ligules.

Rice has a terminate panicle having the following structures: the base, axis, primary, secondary, and sometimes tertiary branches, pedicel, rudimentary glumes, and spikelets. Each panicle generally bears from 50 to 300 flowers or spikelets.

The rice panicle is a perfect and determinate inflorescence. A rice spikelet has two sterile lemmas, the

Horses threshing rice in the Italian Veneto. From a copper engraving in Gian Battista Spolverini's *La coltivazione del riso* (The Cultivation of Rice) printed at Verona in 1758. ROUGHWOOD COLLECTION.

rachilla and the floret. A rice floret includes six stamens and a pistil having stigmas, styles, and ovary, enclosed by the lemma and palea, sometimes with an awn. Even though rice is pollinated by wind, the natural crossing rate is low (less than 3–4%) because of the floral characteristics. The stigma (a plumose structure) functions to catch pollen for fertilization. This function is important for the out-crossing rate in hybrid rice seed production.

The rice grain generally refers to rough rice or paddy consisting of brown rice (or caryopsis) and the hull. Brown rice consists of the endosperm, embryo, and several thin layers of differentiated tissues—the pericarp (the ovary wall), the seed coat, and the nucellus. The seed coat consists of six layers of cells, with the aleurone layer the innermost. The rice embryo is small and contains the embryonic leaves (plumule) enclosed by a sheath (coleoptile), embryonic primary root (radicle) ensheathed by the coleorhiza, and the joining part (mesocotyl). Rice endosperm consists mostly of starch granules in a proteinaceous matrix, together with sugar, fats, crude fiber, and inorganic matter. Hull weight is about 20 percent of the total grain weight. The hull of a typical *indica* rice variety has the palea, lemmas, and richilla, but the hull of *japonica* rice usually only includes rudimentary glumes and perhaps a portion of the pedicel. The lemma is usually tough, archmenlike, sometimes awned, and bigger than the palea. Generally, pigmentation in rice does not cause any problems except for the pigmented apiculus or hull, which may stain the endosperm during parboiling, thus affecting the marketing value. Grain ripening stages (15–65 days) can be subdivided into milky, dough, yellow-ripe, and maturity stages based on the texture and color of the growing grains.

Nutrition. According to the U.S.A. Rice Federation (May 2002), half-cup servings of white rice and brown rice contain 103 calories and 108 calories of energy, respectively. The composition of typical brown rice, milled rice, rice bran, and germ or embryo are indicated in Table 1. Although the nutritional value varies with different varieties, soil fertility, fertilizers applied, and other environmental conditions, the following trends still exist by comparison with other cereals: lower fat content after the removal of the bran, lower protein content (about 7–10 percent), and higher digestibility of proteins. Fresh harvested rice grains contain about 80 percent carbohydrates, including starch, glucose, sucrose, dextrin, fructose, galactose, and raffinose. Polished rice grains have an insufficient supply of iron, considerable Vitamin E content, rich pantothenic acid, pyridoxine of Vitamin B complex, low riboflavin content, negligible vitamin A and D content, and an unfavorable calcium to phosphorus ratio.

Milling, rinsing before cooking, and boiling reduce the nutritional value of rice. For example, milling removes about 80 percent of thiamine from brown rice, thus causing beriberi and other dietary deficiencies. However, most rice consumers still prefer well-milled rice since brown rice has an unfavorable chewier texture and flavor.

Protein: Crude protein content in rice can be measured using micro-Kjeldahl analysis and other methods. In addition to varietal differences, protein content is affected by environmental conditions, such as soil and nitrogen fertilizer application. Protein is mainly distributed in the bran and periphery of the endosperm. The central part of the rice grain only contains a small proportion of rice's protein. Rice protein has all essential amino acids, in rather a well-balanced proportion, for the human body. Though the amount of protein is not high, the quality of rice protein is one of the highest. Rice protein has a biological value of 86, compared to 75 to 90 of the biological value in fish fillet protein. Rice is unique in the richness of alkali-soluble proteins or glutelin (about 70 percent), whereas the other cereals are rich in alcohol-soluble proteins or prolamin (rice has only about 3 percent prolamin in its gross protein content). The other components of rice proteins include 4 to 9 percent water-soluble proteins or albumins and about 10 percent salt-soluble proteins or glubulins. Rice proteins are rich in arginine and contain tryptophan and histidine, but are poor in lysine and threonine. However, by comparison with other cereals, rice protein is one of the most nutritious because it contains about 4 to 5 percent lysine (higher than that in wheat, corn, or sorghum). Efforts have been made to improve protein content through conventional breeding, but so far, it has not been successful. Rice varieties with high protein contents tend to have worse flavor, are less tender, less cohesive when cooked in the same amount of water, and longer cooking times are needed because of lower water absorption.

Carbohydrate: More than ninety percent of the energy in rice comes from carbohydrates. Rice contains both simple and complex carbohydrates. Simple carbohydrates or sugars include glucose, fructose, lactose, and sucrose.

Complex carbohydrates in rice are starch and fibers. As for fiber, one-half cup cooked brown rice and the same volume of cooked white rice have 1.6 grams and 0.3 grams of dietary fiber, respectively. About 85 percent of the rice grain weight is starch. Amylose is the linear fraction of the rice starch, and is negatively correlated with the cohesiveness, tenderness, color, and the gloss of the cooked rice. The rice starch has to be gelatinized during cooking or else rice is too firm to be eaten comfortably. Glutinous or waxy rice, sometimes referred to as "sweet" or "mochi," contains 1 to 2 percent amylose, has white and opaque kernels, and often is used for such ethnic foods as mochi cake and crackers, desserts, puffed rice, and parboiled rice flakes. The nonglutinous rice varieties can also be classified as low-amylose (8–20 percent), intermediate (21–25 percent), and high-amylose (>25 percent) types. Generally *Japonica* has low amylose content and the amylose content of *indica* varies widely. Environmental conditions can greatly influence amylose content as much as 6 percent for the same variety in the different seasons. Intermediate amylose content is preferred by the major world rice market. For high-amylose rice varieties, a gel consistency test can complement the amylose test by separating these varieties into three categories: hard gel consistency for very flaky rice (<40mm for the length of gel), medium gel consistency for flaky rice (41–60 mm), and soft gel consistency for soft rice (>60 mm).

Fat: Rice contains a trace of fats (0.9 and 0.2 g of fats in a half-cup of cooked brown rice and a half-cup of cooked white rice, respectively). Rice is a health food because it does not contain any cholesterol, but it does contain linoleic acid, accounting for 30 percent of the total rice fats that cannot be converted from carbohydrates, proteins, or other fats.

Vitamins: Rice contains several kinds of vitamins (Table 1). Thiamine (vitamin B_1) has positive health effects for the brain and heart, but unfortunately it cannot be stored in a human body and must be supplied in the daily diet. One half-cup of cooked brown rice and a half-cup of cooked white rice contain 7 percent and 6 percent of the U.S. Daily Value (D.V.) for thiamine, respectively. Riboflavin (vitamin B_2) is important for energy production and the health of skin and eyes. Rice has a very small amount of riboflavin, about 1 percent of the D.V. in one half-cup of cooked brown rice. Niacin (vitamin B_3) is essential for healthy skin, digestive, and nervous systems. One half-cup of cooked brown rice and the same amount of cooked white rice have 8 percent and 6 percent of the D.V. for niacin, respectively. Pyridoxine (vitamin B_6) indirectly helps to control amino acids in the body. A shortage of pyridoxine has negative effects on the central nervous system. The folate or folic acid is important for the manufacture of DNA and hemoglobin. Rice also has traces of vitamin E that protects vitamin A and essential fatty acids from oxidation. Recently, scientists in Switzerland and Germany developed "Golden Rice™" through genetic engineering and substantially increased vitamin A content in rice (Ye et al., 2000).

Minerals: Iron is important in humans for oxidation and other enzymatic reactions. One half-cup serving of cooked brown rice and one-half-cup serving of cooked white rice have 8 percent and 7 percent of the D.V. for iron, respectively. Phosphorus is critical for healthy bones and teeth and other metabolisms. Phosphorus in rice can be best absorbed when supplemented with milk or vegetables. One half-cup of cooked brown rice and a half-cup of cooked white rice have 8 percent and 3 percent of

TABLE 1

Nutrients in rice

Nutrient	Brown rice	Milled rice	Rice bran	Rice embryo	Polished rice
Percentage of total					
Protein (%N x 5.95)	7.1–8.3	6.3–7.1	11.3–14.9	14.1–20.6	11.2–12.4
Crude fat	1.6–2.8	0.3–0.5	15.0–19.7	16.6–20.5	10.1–12.4
Crude fiber	0.6–1.0	0.2–0.5	7.0–11.4	2.4–3.5	2.3–3.2
Crude ash	1.0–1.5	0.3–0.8	6.6–9.9	4.8–8.7	5.2–7.3
Available carbohydrates	72.9–75.9	76.7–78.4	34.1–52.3	34.2–41.4	51.1–55.0
Starch	66.4	77.6	13.8	2.1	41.5–47.6
Free sugar	0.7–1.3	0.22–0.45	5.5–6.9	8.0–12	
Micrograms per gram					
Vitamin A	0.1	Trace	4.2	0.3	0.95
Thiamine	2.1–4.5	Trace–1.8	10–28	45–76	16–30
Riboflavin	0.4–0.9	0.1–0.4	1.7–3.4	2.7–5.0	1.4–3.4
Niacin	44–62	8–26	241–590	15–99	228–385
Pyridoxine	1.6–11.2	0.4–6.2	10–32	15–16	10–31
Pantothenic acid	6.6–18.6	3.4–7.7	28–71	3–13	26–92
Biotin	0.06–0.13	0.005–0.07	0.16–0.47	0.26–0.58	0.14–0.66
Folic acid	0.20–0.60	0.06–0.16	0.50–1.46	0.9–4.3	0.4–1.90
Vitamin B_{12}	0.0005	0.0016	0.005	0.0105	0.003
Vitamin E (tocopherols)	13	Trace	149	87	63

193

the D.V. for phosphorus, respectively. Rice also has traces of calcium, potassium, and sodium.

Rice grain quality. The aroma of rice can be detected in rice leaf tissue, rice kernel, and cooked rice. It was reported that 2-acetyl-1-pyrroline was a major aroma component in aromatic rice. There is an excellent description about the evaluation of rice grain quality in a book chapter by Webb (1985). Grain quality is determined by the appearance (milling quality), texture and ease of cooking (cooking quality), flavor and smell (eating quality), nutritive characteristics, cleanness, and purity. For parboiled rice, light-hulled (straw-colored) rice is preferred and bran color should have uniform light color. Rice can be classified, based on the grain length on the traditional U.S. market, as follows: extra long (>7.50 mm), long (6.61–7.50 mm), medium (5.51–6.60 mm), and short (<5.50 mm). Rice also has the following classification based on the grain shape (measured as length/width ratio): slender (>3.0), medium (2.1–3.0), bold (1.1–2.0), and round (<1.1)

Endosperm is preferred to be bright, clear and translucent by the market, with the exception of waxy rice having an opaque endosperm. Excessive chalkiness is undesirable because chalkiness greatly affects the milling yield and milling quality. Chalkiness can be categorized as white belly, white core, and white back depending on the location of the chalkiness on the rice endosperm. Chalkiness is influenced both by the variety and by environmental factors such as weather conditions when harvesting, and by different agronomic or field managements.

Milling quality is determined by the following factors: size and shape of the grain, ripeness, drying method, age, moisture content, and the method of storage. High head rice and high milled rice are critical for the commercial success of a rice variety. To determine the milling quality, the rough rice percentage is measured after removing the foreign materials (dockages). After removing hulls and most of the bran layers and germs, total milling yield and head (or whole-grain) rice yield can be measured. Total milling yield includes the whole (head) rice and broken rice yield from total unclean rough rice.

The economic value of rice depends on its cooking and processing quality, which can be measured in terms of major methods: amylose content, alkali spreading value, gelatinization temperature, gel consistency, and protein content. Sometimes, parboiling-canning stability and specific brewing cookability with malt diastase need to be measured for specific purposes. The gelatinization temperature is the temperature at which 90 percent of the starches in the rice have gelatinized or turned liquid and lost their crystalline structure. Gelatinization temperature can be evaluated by measuring alkali spreading value (ASV). Gel consistency is used to differentiate among the high-amylose rice varieties with different amylograph pasting viscosities. The major factors affecting gel consistency are fat (lipid) content and degree of milling.

History

Origin and diffusion. Origin and diffusion of rice are still unsettled issues (Huke and Huke, 1990). Asian cultivated rice originated in the region from south China to the Ganges in South and Southeast Asia, including the river valleys and deltas of the Brahmaputra of northern India, the Irrawaddy of Burma, the Mekong of Vietnam, and the Yangtze of China. Based on the number of wild rice species and the evidence of rice glumes in the burnt clay from the late Neolithic period, Ting (1949) concluded that rice might have originated in South China and then spread northwards. Copeland (1924), Chang (1975) and some Japanese rice scientists asserted that rice might have originated from South or Southeast Asia, including India, China, Thailand, and Indonesia. Thermoluminescence and carbon-14 tests of the pottery shards with the imprints of rice grains in Thailand indicate that rice could be dated back to at least 4000 B.C.E. (IRRI, 1997). The three oldest pieces of archaeological evidence for rice origin are from Maharaga of India (6500–4500 B.C.E.), Non-Nok-Tha of Thailand (about 6000 B.C.E.), and Pen-tou-shan of China (7150–6250 B.C.E.) (Abrol and Gadgil, 1999; Chang, 1998). Great diversity of rice and linguistic evidence support the argument for Southeast Asia as the origin of rice cultivation. It was believed that the early spread of rice was from southern China or northern Vietnam to the Philippines about 2000 B.C.E., and then to Indonesia about 1599 B.C.E. by Deutero-Malayans. Most likely, the techniques of rice cultivation radiated outward from the Yangtze delta of China towards Korea and then Japan. Japan became known as *Mizumono kuni* (the Land of Luxurious Rice Crop) about 300–400 B.C.E., but rice did not become the staple Korean dish until the 1930s. Sri Lanka had rice as a crop as early as 1000 B.C.E. Rice was introduced to Greece and the neighboring Mediterranean c. 344–324 B.C.E., and then gradually to Europe and Africa (IRRI, 1997). There have been debates about the introduction of Asian rice into Africa. *O. sativa* was believed to have been introduced to Africa primarily from Malayo-Polynesia a few centuries B.C.E. or from Sri Lanka and Indonesia. It was postulated that at different times *O. sativa* was introduced to Egypt from India, to Madagascar from Indonesia as early as 1000 B.C.E., to Mozambique and East Africa from Madagascar, and finally to West Africa by Portuguese spice traders between the fifteenth and seventeenth centuries, or by traders or Muslim missionaries in the ninth or tenth centuries. Lu and Chang (1980) argued that Asian rice entered into the Congo from Mozambique in the nineteenth century. The other possibilities for the introduction of rice into Europe are from Persia, central Asia, or directly from China. Later the Portuguese brought rice to Brazil, and the Spanish introduced rice to Central and South America. The Malays brought rice to Madagascar. The United States might have been first introduced to rice from the Malagasy Republic, Europe, or the Far East. It was often cited that a storm-battered ship from Madagascar had brought rice seeds "Golde

Seede Rice" to South Carolina in 1694. Not until 1888 did the first large-scale growing of rice plants occur in Louisiana and Texas, although rice was introduced to Virginia as early as 1609. Later the Gulf Coast grew rice because of the popularization of mechanical farming. The current major rice-producing states in the United States include Arkansas, California, Louisiana, Texas, Mississippi, and Missouri. Rice was first commercialized in Australia in 1924, even though in as early as 1892 experimental planting of rice took place in New South Wales.

It was believed that *O. glaberrima* originated in the central Niger river delta of Mali about 1500 B.C.E. (Portères, 1956). Two secondary centers of diversity are located to the southwest near the Guinean coast. *O. glaberrima* has two ecotypes, deepwater and upland, and is now only grown in the flooded area of the Niger and Sokoto River basins. *O. glaberrima* in some parts of the Africa was gradually replaced by *O. sativa*. The ongoing rice improvement project of the West Africa Rice Development Assocation is also targeting these regions by substituting new varieties for *O. glaberrima* through *glaberrima-sativa* interspecific crossing.

Domestication. Chang (2000) made exhaustive descriptions on the evolution and early spread through several routes for rice, especially Asian rice. In his review the pattern for rice evolution was suggested as from perennial wild to annual wild and then to cultivated. Therefore, the evolution for *O. sativa* is *O. rufipogon* to *O. nivara* to *O. sativa* in Asia. In parallel, the evolution for *O. glaberrima* is *O. longistaminata* to *O. barthii* and then to *O. glaberrima* in Africa. It is believed that rice originated in the marsh areas and spread toward the dry lands and hills. The domestication of rice, including such cultural practices as puddling and transplanting, might have first taken place in China. The ancient Chinese cultural practices for rice then shifted to Southeast Asia and other parts of the world (De Data, 1987). Only in the twentieth century did systematic rice improvement start. For example, IRRI scientists Peter R. Jennings, Te-Tze Chang, and Henry M. Beachell developed the semi-dwarf variety "IR8" in 1966, which initiated the "Green Revolution" (Lang, 1996). China also successfully developed hybrid rice in 1973. These achievements have greatly increased the rice yield so as to feed the increasing world population, especially in Asia.

Oka (1988) indicated that domestication of rice involves decreased seed dormancy, increased seed shattering and selfing rate, and other adaptive characteristics. Wild rice usually has one month or more of seed dormancy resulting in nonsynchronous germination. This is an adaptive characteristic to increase the probability of regenerating success under changing environments. Seed maturity on a panicle also does not synchronize and the flowering for wild rice can last more than one month instead. Grain dormancy protects rice grains from sprouting on panicles because of frequent raining during

These Vietnamese rice paddies are not only used for growing rice, they are sometimes flooded for fish farming, and ducks can be raised in the paddies while the rice is young. PHOTO COURTESY OF THE NATIONAL ARCHIVES AND RECORDS ADMINISTRATION.

ripening. Generally, *Japonica* has little dormancy, but *Indica* has some degree of dormancy. The tropical *Indica* in particular has quite strong dormancy. But grain dormancy is affected by the weather. For the same variety, sunny and dry weather will make the grain less dormant than humid weather. It was deduced that the substance(s) for grain dormancy exist mainly in the flowering glumes and the hull (palea and lemma) because dormancy was broken by simply removing the hull from the seed. Grain dormancy can be broken by chemicals, such as fungicides or diluted nitric acid, or by heat treatment (50° C for four to six days or even longer).

Grain shattering is affected by the strength of the spikelet attachment to its pedicel. The requirements for the resistance to grain shattering vary with the environmental and cultural conditions in the modern rice cultivation. Regions with strong winds at rice maturity require non-shattering varieties. Intermediate-shattering types should be grown for mechanical harvesting using a combine. If harvested by hand harvest and threshing, the intermediate type with resistance to shattering is preferred. In Asian rice, *Japonica* is highly resistant to shattering, but most *Indica* varieties have intermediate resistance to shattering. Wild rice has easy shedding or shattering and thus easy dispersal. Also, some wild rice has awns on the tip of the grain. Some rice varieties are either fully awned or partially awned among spikelets on the same panicle. This characteristic might be favorable for dispersal through water. The cross-pollinated feature of wild rice (similar to that of wild barley) might be favorable for rice evolution.

Hybrids. Before the 1970s, rice breeders extensively studied the utilization of rice heterosis after they realized the great potential of using heterosis to improve crops such as corn. Generally speaking, hybrid rice has more than 15 to 20 percent yield advantage over the best conventional rice varieties in China, Bangladesh, Brazil, Colombia, Ecuador, India, Indonesia, Malaysia, Myanmar, the Philippines, Sri Lanka, and Vietnam. Unfortunately, no large-scale planting of hybrid rice was successful until China developed a three-line (cytoplasmic male sterile line, male sterile maintainer line, and restorer line) system hybrid rice in 1973 and commercialized this technology in 1976. This was because of the very small reproductive organs and difficulty in finding or developing a cytoplasmic male sterile line in rice. China has greatly increased its rice production by the utilization of hybrid rice technology and therefore has been able to feed its rapidly growing population in the last quarter of the twentieth century. Now China is trying to increase the rice yield by employing the two-line system hybrid rice (male sterile line and restorer line) and intersubspecific heterosis (i.e., the heterosis between *Indica* and *Japonica*) utilization. By following China's success, other countries, including India, Vietnam, Myanmar, and Bangladesh, are currently learning to use the hybrid rice technology to boost the rice yield. FAO is also providing financial support to activities of networks on hybrid rice such as the International Task Force for Hybrid Rice and the Working Group on Hybrid Rice in Latin America and the Caribbean (GRUTHA). Outside China, the planting acreages under hybrid rice in Vietnam, India, and Bangladesh in 1998 were 250,000 ha, 120,000 ha, and 20,000 ha, respectively.

Production and Processing

Distribution. Generally speaking, the rice paddy is adaptable to regions that have sufficient rainfall, high temperature, and prolonged solar radiation. Rice has evolved into four major ecosystems based on different ecological or environmental conditions: irrigated (53 percent of the total rice crop area, exemplified by China), rain-fed lowland (23 percent), deepwater (11 percent), and upland (13 percent, exemplified by Latin America). Rice is cultivated on all continents except Antarctica. Recent estimates list 112 rice-growing countries, including all the countries in Asia and most of the countries of West and North Africa, some countries of East and Central Africa, most of the South and Central America countries, and Australia (De Datta, 1987). Geographically, current rice cultivation regions range from latitudes 53° N in Moho, China, to latitudes 35° S in central Argentina and New South Wales, Australia, from sea level in Bangladesh to an altitude of 3,000 m in Nepal. Asia produced 90.6 percent of the total rice production in 1999; Latin America, 4 percent; Africa, 3 percent; Europe, 0.5 percent; Australia, 0.2 percent; and the United States, 1.6 percent. The ten countries with the largest rice production in 1999 were China, India, Indonesia, Bangladesh, Vietnam, Thailand, Myanmar, Brazil, Japan, and the Philippines, in descending order. Outside Asia, rice is consumed as a staple food in Guyana, Guinea, Liberia, Sierra Leone,

and Madagascar. Based on the above geographical distribution of rice, currently there are three major international rice research centers from Consultative Group on International Agricultural Research (CGIAR), including the International Rice Research Institute (IRRI) in the Philippines, Centro Internacional de Agricultura Tropical (CIAT) in Columbia, and West Africa Rice Development Association (WARDA) in the Ivory Coast.

Cultivation. Rice can be grown in many ecosystems from upland to deepwater conditions. For the irrigating system, fields are plowed with a wooden plow, and then a harrow drawn by a docile and reliable water buffalo in most Asian countries. Some Asian countries, such as India and China, are still practicing transplanting the rice seedlings to suit for the double cropping or multiple cropping systems. Developed countries in Europe and America, such as the United States, employ direct seeding cultivation without transplanting, to avoid the cost of expensive labor and to take advantage of the advances in the mechanization of rice production. There are two methods for direct seeding: (1) dry seeding before sprouting, followed by a flow of water in Louisiana and Texas, and (2) wet seeding by low-flying aircraft in California and Arkansas because rice is unique, among cereals, in being able to germinate when submerged in water. In rice cultivation, the most serious pests include stem borers and leaf hoppers. The most dangerous diseases are rice blast, bacterial blight, sheath blight, and seedling blight. These pests and diseases can be controlled at the proper stage by chemicals or other measures. Now more efforts are being focused on breeding for resistant rice varieties through conventional approaches or through modern biotechnology, such as Bt. rice. The most persistent weeds in rice cultivation are barnyard grass (*Echinochloa spp.*), water hyacinth (*Eichhornia crassipes*), *Eleocharis acidularis*, *Typha* spp., and red rice. These weeds can be controlled by cultural approaches or by herbicides.

Harvesting and post-harvest operations. Rice is considered to be a photoperiod or daylength sensitive crop, although there are daylength-insensitive rice varieties. Short photoperiods or daylengths (less than 11 hours) will shorten its growth duration, which ranges from 90 to 160 days or even longer depending on the photoperiod sensitivity, the basic vegetative phase, and the temperature sensitivity. The approximate duration from flowering to maturity is thirty days. Photoperiod-insensitive rice varieties, such as most of the current rice varieties in tropical Latin America, are increasingly preferred because of their greater adaptability to a wide region and the flexibility in planting dates. But in some rice-growing regions, the strong photoperiod sensitivity of rice is used to grow rice in the rainy season; it is then harvested after the rainy season and before the dry season water shortage. The maturity of rice is also influenced by air temperature, planting methods, and nitrogen fertilization. The best time for mechanical harvesting is when panicles become yellow but the stem and leaves still have green color. At that time the moisture contents of grains should be 20 to 25 percent. By visual inspection in the field, rice can be harvested when the kernels on the upper part of the panicle are fully ripe and the ones in the lower part reach a hard-dough stage. For some rice-growing regions with some extra time beyond one rice-growing region, ratooning of the first rice crop is possible by using the varieties with high ratooning ability for maximizing the annual rice yields without too much investment. Currently, harvesting can be done with a combine in the more developed countries. However, most Asian and African countries are still harvesting rice by hand sickles, scythes, or knives, because of scarcity of capital, availability of inexpensive labor, and the topographical limits, such as small rice fields, mountainous fields, or deep-water areas. A rice combine threshes the harvested paddy after cutting. Hand threshing or threshing by animals or simple foot- or gasoline-powered threshing machines is still being used in some countries.

Storage. Before storage, the moisture content of rice grains should be reduced to below 14 percent. The most convenient method is sun drying if the weather permits—drying rice grains in the open air and under strong sunshine for one to two days. But the sun drying method can produce "sun checks," which reduce the head rice and increase the rice bran percentage; this method also requires intensive labor. Therefore, artificial drying such as batch dryers in Japan and the hot air dryers in the United States became an alternative to sun drying. The artificial drying can avoid rapid dehydration, which causes reduced head rice. The cleaning of rice grains is important to remove foreign seed and trash before storage. There are three major cleaning methods: air cleaning by using a hand winnower, mechanical cleaning by using sieves, and gravity cleaning. In rice mills, all impurities, odds and ends such as stones, and pieces of soil and straw must be removed by a screening or riddling process and a fan. Further removal of nails or bits of iron can be done with a magnet. Since aging through storage increases water absorption and paste viscosity and reduces solids dissolved in cooking water, cooked fresh rice tastes worse than rice with six to twelve months of storage because rice grains cooked immediately after harvesting tend to disintegrate and to be more cohesive. The curing process can be completed through keeping the rice in heaps of straw for several days or through domestic curing methods. However, long storage time should be avoided, especially for undermilled rice. Cooked rice, after several months of storage, becomes less sticky and more flaky. In addition to moisture, metabolisms of grain tissues, microorganisms, insects, and mites also causes storage losses.

Milling. Milling in the rice industry can refer either to the overall operations that include cleaning, hulling, pearling, polishing, and grading; or simply to one operation, removal of the rice bran or outer layers. Typically, the pericarp accounts for 1 to 2 percent of the weight of the whole rice caryopsis, seed coat and aleurone 5 percent, embryo 2 to 3 percent, and endosperm 89 to 91 percent (Wadsworth, 1994). The edible part of rice grain is enclosed in the glumes, which need to be first separated by hulling. The most primitive implement for hulling is the system with wood mortar and pestle or a treadle or watermill. These hulling methods are still used in some of rice growing regions in Asia and Africa. Now mechanical hulling or milling is popular in most of the rice growing countries. The hulled rice grains are then winnowed in order to remove the chaff and bran. Rice with the hulls removed but the bran left on is called "brown rice." "Milled rice" refers to the rice after removing all hulls, bran layers, and germ. After hulling, the removal of germs or outer coats—the so-called polishing —is necessary by using mechanical hulling or milling for better appearance to meet the market's need, with sacrifice of the flavor and healthy constituents in rice grains. Rice is generally marked either as polished rice or as coated rice with talc and glucose. Rice grains after polishing contain portions of broken grains that have to be separated and sorted to meet market standards. This separation can be accomplished by passing through a series of sieves or cellular cylinders or trieurs. Some discolored rice grains can be removed by electric sorting.

Enrichment. For restoration of vitamins and minerals lost during milling, the enrichment of rice is important for better nutrition. There are two major approaches: powder enrichment and coated kernel enrichment. For preblended powder enrichment, mixes include thiamine, riboflavin, niacin or niacinamide, and ferric orthophosphate (white iron), ferrous sulfate (yellow iron), or reduced iron. This is an easy and less expensive approach for enrichment of rice. But the disadvantages of the powder enrichment are that the nutrients are easily washed off by rinsing, less stability of vitamins and minerals, and their reaction with the food components. An alternative approach is the coated kernel enrichment. This method integrates the powder-blended enrichment with the insoluble food-grade coating. This coating is broken down and the enriched vitamins and minerals are released when the coating reacts with the acid environment of the stomach. This method has the advantage of more efficient use of the enriched vitamins and minerals.

Global and contemporary issues

In the first quarter of the twenty-first century, another 1.2 billion new rice consumers will be added in Asia. Currently, less than 5 percent of world rice production is traded internationally. Therefore, rice production in Asia must be increased by one third from today's 320 million tons to 420 million tons, even though rice land is decreasing.

For future rice production, there are also the following challenges: (1) genetic erosion because of the popular adoption of the high-yielding varieties (for example, *javanica* rice germplasm suffered significant losses in Java and Bali, Indonesia); (2) water pollution by chemical pesticides, herbicides, and air pollution; (3) less cultural management afforded to rice because more rice farmers, especially the young farmers, are moving to work in industry and metropolitan areas, particularly in such countries as China and Japan; and (4) decreasing water resources and increasing land salinity. Global warming might make this trend even more significant.

See also **Africa; China; India; Japan; Korea; Southeast Asia.**

BIBLIOGRAPHY

Abrol, Yash P., and Sulochana Gadgil, eds. *Rice: In a Variable Climate.* New Delhi: APC Publications. 1999.

Chang, Te-Tzu, and Eliseo A. Bardenas. "The Morphology and Varietal Characteristics of the Rice Plant." *Technical Bulletin* (Manila, Philippines: International Rice Research Institute) no. 4 (December 1965).

Chang, Te-Tzu. "The Origin, Evolution, Cultivation, Dissemination, and Diversification of Asian and African Rices." *Euphytica* 25 (1976): 435–441.

Chang, Te-Tzu. "The Rice Cultures." Paper presented at Discussion Meeting on the Early History of Agriculture, sponsored by the Royal Society and British Academy, London, April 1976.

Chang, Te-Tze. "II.A.7. Rice." In *The Cambridge World History of Food*, vol. 1, edited by Kenneth F. Kiple and Kriemhild Coneè Ornelas. Cambridge University Press, 2000.

Copeland, Edwin Bingham. *Rice.* London: Macmillan, 1924.

De Datta, S. K. *Principles and Practices of Rice Production.* Malabar, Fla.: Robert E. Krieger, 1987.

Grist, D. H. *Rice*, 6th ed. London and New York: Longmans, 1986.

Huke, R. E., and E. H. Huke. *Rice: Then and Now.* Manila, Philippines, International Rice Research Institute, 1990.

International Rice Research Institute. *Rice Almanac*, 2d ed. Manila, Philippines: International Rice Research Institute, 1997.

Lang, James. *Feeding a Hungry Planet: Rice, Research, and Development in Asia and Latin America.* Chapel Hill: The University of North Carolina Press, 1996.

Lu, J. J., and T. T. Chang. "Rice in its Temporal and Spatial Perspectives." In *Rice: Production and Utilization*, edited by B. S. Luh. Westport, Conn.: AVI Publishing, 1980.

Oka, H. I. *Origin of Cultivated Rice.* Japan Scientific Societies Press. New York: Elsevier, 1988.

Portères, R. "Taxonomie agrobotanique des riz cultives: *O. sativa* Lin. et *O. glaberrima* Steudel: I–IV." *Journal d'Agriculture Tropicale et de Botanique Appliquée* no. 3 (1956): 341–384, 541–580, 627–700, 821–856.

Ting, Y. "The Origin of Rice Cultivation in China." *Agron. Bull. Sun Yatsen Univer. Ser III.* No. 7 (1949): 18.

Wadsworth, James I. "Degree of Milling." In *Rice Science and Technology*, edited by Wayne E. Marshall and James I. Wadsworth. New York: M. Dekker, 1994.

Webb, B. D. "Criteria of Rice Quality in the United States." In *Rice Chemistry and Technology*, 2d ed., edited by Bienvenido O. Juliano. St. Paul, Minn.: American Association of Cereal Chemists, 1985.

Ye, X. D., et al. "Engineering the Provitamin A (Beta-Carotene) Biosynthetic Pathway into (Carotenoid-free) Rice Endosperm." *Science* 287 (2000): 303–305.

Jiming Li

RICE AS A FOOD

There are some countries with high annual rice consumption per capita (up to 130–180 kg, equal to 55–80 percent of total caloric source) such as Bangladesh, Cambodia, Indonesia, Laos, Myanmar, Thailand, and Vietnam (Chang 2000). Even in most parts of Africa, rice is a secondary staple food next to cassava, yams, corn, and millet. However, in the following African countries rice is consumed as a staple food: Liberia, Sierra Leone, Guinea, Ivory Coast, Ghana, Madagascar, and part of Nigeria. By comparison with the rice production and consumption in Asian countries, Latin America is often overlooked. However, annual rice consumption in the following countries exceeds more than 32 kg per capita: Brazil, Columbia, Ecuador, and the Dominican Republic.

Rice is the best cereal crop in terms of food energy per production area and is consumed in various forms, including plain rice, noodles, puffed rice, breakfast cereals, cakes, fermented sweet rice, snack foods, beer, wine and vinegar. Rice starch is used as a thickener in baby foods, sauces, and desserts or can be made into sweet syrup. However, most consumption of rice is as cooked rice served simultaneously with vegetable, poultry, beef, seafood, and other dishes. Rice as a comfort food is economical, delicious, nutritious, versatile, easy to prepare, and bland enough to pair with other foods. Rice is convenient to store on shelves in cupboards and pantries.

Preparation and Consumption

Rice consumption falls into the following three categories: direct food use, processed foods, and brewer's use. Detailed methods and recipes for rice food preparations were described by Bor S. Luh (1991), Sri Owen (1993), Jeffrey Alford and Naomi Duguid (1998), and Bor S. Luh (1999).

Direct food use. Rice is easy to prepare, has a soft texture for the human palate and stomach, and has the ability to absorb flavors while retaining its texture. Therefore, rice has gained popularity as "the pasta of the 1990s" in the West. Both the short-grain *japonica* and the long-grain *indica* rice include non-glutinous and glutinous types. Non-glutinous rice is somewhat transparent and is less sticky than glutinous rice when cooked. There are some rice varieties with an attractive aroma, such as basmati. Parboiled rice was originally produced in Asia, but the parboiled rice produced in the United States now, such as by the company Uncle Ben's, is of high quality. Arborio rice has large tan grains with central white dots

198

and, because of its creamy, chewy texture, can be used to make risotto.

American wild rice is a coarse grass (not a true rice by taxonomy), and now has become more and more popular in the United States and Canada. It is grown in shallow waters and has medium to long grains and a nutty flavor.

Rice is cooked by heating (either boiling or steaming) soaked rice for full gelatinization of the kernels and evaporation of excess water. Generally there are three rice cooking methods: large-amount-of-water method, absorption method, and steaming method. The lot-of-water technique is good for arborio, basmati, or parboiled rice, but not for Thai jasmine or japonica rice with low amylose content, which should be cooked by steaming. Rice cooking methods also include rinsing, boiling, baking, roasting, frying, and pressure-cooking. It is customary to wash rice before cooking to remove dust, husks, insects, and other impurities. American-grown rice does not require washing or rinsing before cooking because these "cleaning" processes further remove nutrients, including vitamins and minerals that were added before packaging by fortification or enrichment.

Juliano (1985) indicated that rice cooking methods vary with different countries. Either uncooked rice or fully cooked rice combines well with other protein-rich foods such as meat, poultry, fish, cheese, and eggs because rice is bland in flavor and carries the flavor of the mixed ingredients. People in the Middle East lightly fry rice before boiling. Americans often add salt, butter, or margarine to soaked rice. People in China, Korea, and Japan add extra water to cook rice into porridge (thick gruel) or congee (thin soup). Rice can be cooked with curries (in India and Malaysia) or sauce (in the Philippines) or combinations of various ingredients, including pork, shrimp, chicken, and vegetables (in China) (Boesch 1967). Steamed rice is preferred in some countries because more vitamins and minerals are retained. Rice can be steamed in a bamboo steamer or, currently, in an electric metal steamer. Steamed rice can be served plain or mixed with other ingredients. Mixed steamed rice also varies among countries. For example, Malaysians steam glutinous rice with mixed meat in a bamboo joint over a fire. Cambodian *kralan* is steamed rice mixed with grated coconut and beans. Iranians steam rice with oil or with butter, and sometimes with yogurt, while rice is cooked with water and oil in Brazil, Chile, Ecuador, Germany, Mexico, and Peru. Some countries, such as France, Korea, Burma, Thailand, Japan, and the Philippines, add rice to cold water for cooking. Presoaking is a common practice in India. Detailed descriptions of recipes from different countries for cooked rice are provided by Virmani (1991). Rice can be kept as long as five days in the refrigerator. The leftover rice is good for stir-frying into egg fried rice with chopped carrots and the like. Rice can also be cooked with certain amounts of water and meat, seafood, vegetables, or other additions in clay pots or high-pressure metal pots to make thin or thick congee (or *juk*) or gruel (*okayu*, in Japanese).

Parboiled rice: Parboiling is popular in India, Sri Lanka, Pakistan, Brazil, the United States, and Italy. Parboiling changes rice starch from the crystalline form to an amorphous form by a series of procedures including cleaning, grading, soaking, steeping, steaming, drying, tempering, milling, color sorting, and finally packaging. It involves the treatment of grains in cold water and then hot water with low pressure. The treated rice can be dried by the steam or sun. Problems of off-color and off-flavor that resulted from conventional parboiling procedures have been overcome by various inventions, such as the H. R. Conversion and Malek Processes (D. H. Grist, 1986). Major advantages of parboiling over ordinary milling include easier dehulling; less breakage in milling; higher retention of nutrients after milling, washing, and cooking; and better resistance to insect and fungus infestation, which makes it possible to store the rice for longer periods of time. Also, parboiled rice gelatinizes the starch and makes better consistency, greater hardness, and better vitreousness of the kernel. The main disadvantages of parboiling include greater rancidity during storage, longer cooking time, greater difficulty in milling, and additional cost (De Datta, 1987).

Rice-flour products: Rice flour does not contain gluten and therefore its dough cannot retain gases during baking as wheat flour does. Therefore, rice flour is widely used in making baby foods, breakfast cereals, unbaked biscuits, snack foods, pancakes, and waffles. For example, a composite baking flour, made by adding 10 percent rice flour to wheat flour, is used to make pastry products in Italy.

Rice-flour products are exemplified by the following foods: *yuan zi* (or *tang yuan*) is a popular food in China. It is made from glutinous rice flour and water by adding sweet or savory fillings to the rice dough. The quality of *yuan zi* preparation depends on the amylopectin content, the flour particle size, and the recipe for the fillings. (The higher the amylopectin content, the softer and more sticky the rice flour becomes when the same amount of water is added.) *Yuan zi* is fried with vegetable oil or thoroughly cooked in boiling water and served with sugar or other condiments.

Rice bread is a good substitute for other gluten-containing cereal flour, as some people are allergic to these flours. The medium- and short-grain rice varieties are preferable to the long-grain type for making rice bread. Formulation is important in making rice bread by adjusting the levels of sucrose, yeast, water, nonfat dry milk, and other additives.

Processed foods. *Rice noodles:* Rice noodles are called *mi fen* in Chinese, *sen mee* in Thai, and *harusame* in Japanese. *Mi fen* is often produced from non-glutinous rice by soaking, grinding, steaming, kneading, and drying. If dehydrated, it can be stored up to two years. In Thailand,

199

mung bean is added to rice to make a special rice noodle called *fung-shu* (or *tong-fun*) that is more resistant to texture changes during reconstitution. In Asia, rice noodles are consumed in soups or as snacks. *Mi fen* is served with water, meat or chicken, green vegetables, soy sauce, and other ingredients.

Rice snacks: Rice snacks have an attractive taste, flavor, texture, and aroma. They are often made from glutinous rice because of its sticky characteristics and easy expansion into a porous texture. However, non-glutinous rice also can be used for making some rice snacks.

The rice cracker is a typical rice snack. The Japanese soft rice cracker made from glutinous rice is called *arare* or *okaki* in comparison with the less popular and tougher *senbei* (the rice cracker made from non-glutinous rice). The production process involves washing, grinding, steaming, kneading, cooling, pounding, drying, baking, seasoning, cutting, and packing. The production of rice crackers is now developed as a continual process that takes place within 3–4 hours. To add flavors and color to rice crackers, the following ingredients are often added: seaweed, sesame, red peppers, sugar, food pigments, and spices. Moreover, high-quality, refined oil should be used for oil-fried crackers.

Rice fries can even compete with the French fries made from potatoes because rice fries have a crisp exterior crust and fluffy interior. To make rice fries, rice should be fully cooked with butter, salt, and other seasonings.

Rice cakes: Rice cakes are popular in China, Japan, and other Asian countries. They can be made either from glutinous or non-glutinous rice by soaking and steaming. Before steaming, various ingredients can be added for more flavor, such as sugar, salt, monosodium glutamate, crushed radish, crushed mung bean (for *lu du gao*, a special cake in China), and crushed taro.

Glutinous or waxy rice is very sticky when cooked and is mainly consumed in northern Burma, northern Thailand, Laos, and Vietnam. It is often used to make rice cakes. However, fermented rice cakes, such as *fakau* in China and *bibingka* in the Philippines, can also be made from non-glutinous rice.

Puffed rice cakes are popular in China and the United States because they are rich in taste, low in calories, and free from cholesterol. To make puffed rice cakes, some minor ingredients, such as sesame seed, millet, and salt, should be added to brown rice.

The Chinese rice cake *zong zi*, the same as *chimaki* in Japan, is made from glutinous rice and soda ash, wrapped in bamboo leaves to form a tetrahedron, bound with string, and served with honey or sugar. There are two main categories of *zong zi*: *chien zong* and *rou zong*. The difference between *chien zong* and *rou zong* is that pork or ham and other ingredients are added to *rou zong* to enrich the flavor and nutritional value. Other ingredients include mushrooms, soy sauce, monosodium glu-

tamate, sugar, black pepper, sherry wine, fried garlic, cooking oil, and shrimp meat.

Neng gao or *nian gao* (*mochi* in Japanese) is also a special rice cake for the celebration of the Chinese Lunar New Year. It is produced either from glutinous rice or from nonglutinous rice. The main production procedures involve soaking, steaming, kneading, and packing. For better taste and flavor, *neng gao* is sometimes sweetened with sugar or enriched with lard and cinnamon flour.

In Japan, sushi is a rice cake or roll or cube topped with raw fish or other delicacies and served with wasabi (Japanese horseradish). Fresh raw fish used in sushi include tuna, bonito, shrimp, squid, and shellfish. Vegetables such as cucumber and seasoning gourd also can be put in the middle of the rolls, which are then wrapped with seaweed (*nori*). Sushi usually is served with rice vinegar and soy sauce (*shoyu*).

There are many other types of rice cakes made in Asia. For example, *biko*, *cuchinta* (or *kutsinta*), *puto*, *suman*, and other rice cakes are made in the Philippines.

Rice puddings: Rice can be made into creamy puddings by mixing cooked rice with milk and sugar. Indian consumers sweeten rice pudding with palm sugar. Rice puddings were served to the rich during the time of the ancient Romans. Now, rice pudding has become a popular dish for children. A delicious Chinese pudding is the Eight Jewel Rice Pudding, prepared from eight different kinds of fruit and steamed glutinous rice with honey.

Quick-cooking rice: The preparation and cooking of conventional rice take about one hour. Now, quick-cooking rice product is popular in developed countries, such as Japan, the United States, and other Western countries. Completely precooked rice requires no further cooking. However, quick-cooking rice often requires five to fifteen minutes for cooking. To produce quick-cooking rice, rice should be precooked by gelatinizing the rice starch in water and/or steam and then dried. Quick-cooking rice mainly is produced by the soak-boil-steam-dry, freeze-thaw-drying, expansion–pre-gelatinization, and gun puffing methods.

Canned and frozen rice: For convenience of consumption, canned and frozen rice are produced in Japan, Korea, the United States, and other countries. After precooking, canned rice is sold by wet pack and dry pack. The preparation of frozen cooked rice includes soaking, draining, steaming, boiling, and freezing. To serve the frozen cooked rice, microwave heating is a common practice. Frozen rice also can be made into freeze-dried rice by sublimation under high vacuum. This rice has a long storage life of one to two years.

Rice breakfast cereals: Some rice breakfast cereals require cooking before eating, while others can be eaten directly. They commonly are fortified with minerals and heat-stable vitamins, such as niacin, riboflavin, and pyridoxine. The ready-to-eat breakfast cereals include oven-puffed, gun-puffed, extruded, and shredded rice. Oven-puffed rice is made from short-grain rice with sugar and salt by cooking, drying, tempering, enriching, and packaging. Gun puffing is a traditional method and is still practiced in some Asian countries, such as China. The procedure consists of heating, cooking with high pressure in a sealed chamber or gun, and suddenly releasing the high pressure. Because of the lack of continuity in processing, gun puffing is less popular in developed countries. Instead, making extruded rice has high and continuous production rates, great versatility in product shape, and ease of controlling product density. The production of extruded rice can be accomplished by extruding superheated and pressurized doughs. Shredded rice is produced by washing, cooking, drying, tempering, shredding, fortifying, and packing.

Baby foods: Rice has highly digestible energy, net protein utilization, and low crude fiber content. Therefore, it is suitable for baby food. Although baby foods can be in the form of rice flour or granulated rice, precooked infant rice cereal is the most common use of rice for baby food. The key to making this type of cereal is ensuring the ease of reconstitution with milk or formula without forming lumps. The starch is converted from crystalline to amorphous form by the addition of amylase, which breaks down starch into dextrin and oligosaccharides. Ingredients in this baby food include rice flour, rice polishings, sugar, dibasic calcium phosphate, glycerol monostearate (emulsifier), rice oil, thiamine, riboflavin, and niacin or niacinamide. Sometimes, fruit is added to these precooked rice cereals.

Rice-bran products: Rice bran can be sprinkled on a dinner salad or used as a major ingredient of ready-to-eat cereals, baked products, pasta, and other foods. Like oat bran, rice bran has high-quality protein, laxative properties, and dietary fiber components. Rice bran can lower serum cholesterol in humans and reduce the risk of cardiovascular disease and colon cancer. The bran also contains most of the vitamins in the rice kernel, including 78 percent of its thiamine, 47 percent of its riboflavin, and 67 percent of its niacin. The major carbohydrates in the rice bran are cellulose, hemicelluloses (or pentosans), and starch.

Rice bran has hydrolytic rancidity after milling. Therefore, the following treatments are necessary before it is processed as a food: indigenous lipase inactivation by parboiling, or moisture-added or dry extrusion, or other alternative methods.

Rice bran has 16–32 percent oil, including palmitic, oleic, linoleic, and other fatty acids. Therefore, rice bran can be processed into rice oil of the highest quality in terms of cooking quality, shelf life, and fatty acid composition. Oil extraction can be carried out with a variety of solvents using a hydraulic press or specially designed extractors before refining by dewaxing, degumming, neutralization, bleaching, winterization, and deodorization.

Women processing rice at a cooperative in Mozambique. © ADRIAN ARBIB/CORBIS.

After these steps, rice bran oil has greater stability than any other vegetable oil. Rice oil also can be used in cosmetics and paints.

Brewer's use. Rice alcohols include rice beer and rice wine, which is usually served at weddings and other annual rituals. Rice wine is distilled spirits having about 20 percent alcohol content. China has a long history of making rice wine, such as *wang tsiu* ("*Shao Shing* rice wine"). Nepal also has a slightly sweet rice wine called *nigar*. Other rice wines include *tapuy* in the Philippines, *mukhuli* in Korea, *lao rong* in Thailand, and *moonshine* rice wine and *ba-xi de* (a glutinous rice wine) in Vietnam.

In China, *tian jiu niang* is a popular mixture of rice grains, alcohol, lactic acid, and sugar. It is made from steamed glutinous rice. *Jiu qu*, containing *Rhizopus, Mucor, Monilia, Aspergillus*, and in some cases, yeast or bacteria, is used to ferment the steamed rice.

Sake is a brewed alcoholic beverage having 14–16 percent alcohol content. The production of sake began in third century Japan. Sake is made from highly-polished rice, water, *koje*, and sake's yeast. *Koje* are microbes similar to those used in the production of cheese, *shoyu* (soy sauce), and miso (soy bean paste). *Sakamai* or *shinpakumai* rice should be selected for sake production for better quality because of its high starch content and its large and soft grain. Another important ingredient is the spring water, which leads to rich flavor.

The processes to make sake can be summarized as the following: (1) saccharification: conversion of the starch in cooked rice into glucose with *koje* or *koji*; (2) fermentation: conversion of the rice sugar into alcohol by sake's yeast. Fermentation for 20–25 days (three or four times longer than the fermentation in normal wine production) produces a balanced taste and fresh flavor from a wide variety of amino acids and low alcohol content (8–15 percent); and (3) further steps including filtration, setting, heating, aging, and bottling. Sake should be preserved in a cool and dark place without any exposure to light and open air.

Nutritive, Health-related, and Psychopharmacological Value

Rice ranks high among the most nutritious foods available because brown rice provides high levels of fiber, complex carbohydrates, certain B vitamins, vitamin E, lysine, calcium, iron, and phosphorus. Furthermore, many fewer people are allergic to rice than to wheat or other cereals. Rice can be included in a weight-loss diet because it has no cholesterol, a trace of fat, and about 160 calories per cooked cup.

Recent studies have indicated that rice hull or bran contains antioxidants such as isovitexin (a C-glycosyl flavonoid), and it has been demonstrated that rice bran oil can lower both the total and the low-density lipoprotein cholesterol in non-human primates (Nicolosi et al., 1990). Some health problems, such as beriberi (thiamin deficiency), growth retardation, marasmus, and vitamin A deficiency, can result from consumption of only white rice, from which a portion of the proteins and most of the fat, vitamins, and minerals are removed. Rice bran (*tiki-tiki*) is used to cure beriberi in the Philippines.

Since rice is low in sodium and fat and free of cholesterol, it can help relieve mental depression. Rice starch can substitute for glucose in an oral rehydration solution for infants suffering from diarrhea caused by a spleen-pancreas deficiency (Juliano 1985). Rice oil is believed to reduce the likelihood of ischemic heart disease.

Although not scientifically proven, rice is believed to have medicinal uses. Powdered rice is used to treat certain skin ailments, and boiled rice "greens" are used as an eye lotion in Malaysia. A thick paste made from rice grains and water is used in India for massage for curing arthritic pain. The Chinese believe that rice can increase appetite and cure indigestion. Rice water (a decoction of rice) is prescribed as an ointment for skin inflammation. Glutinous rice is believed to strengthen the kidneys, spleen-pancreas, and stomach because of its easier digestion compared to regular rice. The Chinese also believe that rice mixed with honey butter and water can build energy and blood and counter emaciation and other disorders (Wood 1999).

BIBLIOGRAPHY

Alford, Jeffrey, and Naomi Duguid. *Seductions of Rice: A Cookbook*. New York: Artisan, 1998.

Boesch, Mark J. *The World of Rice*. New York: Dutton, 1967.

Chang, Te-Tze. "7. Rice." In *The Cambridge World History of Food*, edited by Kenneth F. Kiple and Kriemhild Coneè Ornelas, vol. 1. Cambridge: Cambridge University Press, 2000.

De Datta, S. K. *Principles and Practices of Rice Production*. Malabar, Fla: Krieger, 1987.

Grist, D. H. *Rice*. 6th ed. London and New York: Longmans, 1986.

Juliano, B. O., ed. "Polysaccharides, Proteins, and Lipids of Rice." In *Rice: Chemistry and Technology*, edited by D. F. Houston. St. Paul, Minn.: American Association of Cereal Chemists,1985

Luh, Bor S. "Rice products." In *Asian Foods: Science and Technology*, edited by Catharina Y. W. Ang, KeShun Liu, and Yao-Wen Huang. Lancaster, Pa.: Technomic, 1999.

Luh, Bor S., ed. *Rice*, Volume II. *Utilization*. 2d ed. New York: Van Nostrand Reinhold, 1991.

Owen, Sri. *The Rice Book*. New York: St. Martin's Press, 1993.

Sukphisit, Suthon. "Cool Cuisine," *Bangkok Post*. Bangkok, Thailand, April 15, 1998.

Virmani, Inderjeet K. *Home Chefs of the World (Rice and Rice-based Recipes)*. Manila, Philippines: International Rice Research Institute, 1991.

Wongtip, Wisetpong. "Elegant Complexity." *The Nation*, Bangkok, Thailand, 26 April 1998.

Wood, Rebecca Theurer. *The New Whole Foods Encyclopedia*. New York: Penguin Books, 1999.

Jiming Li

RICE AS A SUPERFOOD

Widely adapted to diverse environments, rice is an important part of culture, traditions, and subsistence in some countries, especially those in Asia. There is a wealth of literature on the rituals and traditions of rice consumption throughout the world (Virmani, 1991; Piper, 1993; Newman, 1999).

Languages and Symbolism

In Asian languages, daily or important events are expressed in terms of rice. In many Asian countries, such as Thailand (*tarn kao*), Bali (*ngajengang*), Laos PDR, and Bangladeshi, the phrase for eating rice is synonymous with eating food (Williams, 1996). More directly, Chinese and Japanese people refer to breakfast, lunch, and dinner, as morning rice, afternoon rice or noon rice, and evening rice, respectively. Chinese say, in addition to "Happy New Year," "May your rice never burn!" at the beginning of the Chinese Lunar New Year. A common daily greeting in China, Thailand, and Bangladesh is "Have you eaten rice today?" instead of "How are you?". A Japanese proverb says "a meal without rice is no meal," just as the Chinese think that if their friends who are invited to dinner do not eat rice, they have eaten nothing. Rice is so important in Malagasy that the Malagasy word for rice is used as a unit of measurement for time and distance, and in expressions, proverbs, and riddles. Malagasy people refer to "friendship" as rice and water, and to "perfection" as rice with milk mixed with honey.

Rice generally is a positive symbol. In ancient Japan, rice was considered most important next to the emperor. Any wasting of rice was not allowed. In the Japanese feudal period, the chiefs were ranked based on their rice yield. In some Asian countries, such as the Philippines, rice cakes are used as ceremonial foods because they mean long life, happiness, abundance, prosperity, and good fortune. Koreans also believe that a baby will become rich if the child chooses rice from among all the objects put on the table in a "choosing" ceremony.

Rice has other meanings. In Chinese culture, death is symbolized by sticking chopsticks into a mound of rice. Chopsticks are placed on the rice bowl at one end as a memorial of the dead at festivals or important family gatherings. In addition, rice grain symbolizes devotion, affection, generosity, and respect in Nepal, and it is symbolic of a man's body to Thai villagers.

Cultural Preferences

Preferences for rice vary from culture to culture, and from person to person. Most of the major rice-consuming countries eat plain or mixed rice prepared from regular or parboiled rice. Korean rice consumers prefer new rice because of its fresh taste and white color. Laotians prefer the sticky, short-grain varieties and often cook them plainly. In Pakistan, a large quantity of rice is consumed typically as biryani, which is cooked in a meat sauce with other ingredients. In Thailand, *khao tom* (a soft soupy rice gruel) is served as breakfast with other dishes, but the most popular rice dishes include garlic rice, saffron rice, rice colored with coconut milk, and fried rice with meat and tomato ketchup or fish paste. In the Middle East, sautéed rice with vegetables, fruits, and nuts is popular. People in Central Asia consume rice as a festival food and eat rice prepared as rice pilaf. For example, Iranians eat boiled long-grain rice with grilled meat and soup or tea. Most African people also eat plain boiled rice with soup, meat, and seafood. But in some regions in Vietnam, mixing rice with several other dishes is socially unacceptable. India has the following common preparations for rice meals: plain boiled rice, *khichri* (rice cooked with mung beans), *pullao* (fried rice), and *kheer* (rice pudding). Parboiled rice is also important in India. In the Philippines, rice is served at each meal in the form of steamed rice with meat or seafood. In Indonesia, rice is eaten all the time, either as a main dish or as a side dish with other vegetables, fruits, or meat. Many Indonesian consumers eat red rice and unpolished rice. *Ketuput liontong* (rice rolled and steamed in banana leaves), *nasi goreng* (fried rice sprinkled with saffron or turmeric), and *nasi tumpeng* (a cone of white rice garnished with red, black, and yellow food) are specialty rice foods in Indonesia. Rice can be prepared or served in banana or palm leaves in Malaysia. In Japan, non-glutinous rice is used

in daily meals, together with pickles. Pot rice, prepared with rice, soy sauce, fish sauce, and sometimes seafood, meat, or vegetables and mushrooms, has become a popular rice food in Japan. In Korea, the daily meal consists of steamed rice and vegetables, fish, meat, soup, and *kimchi*. A popular Korean dish is *pah jook* (a combination of rice and beans). Pakistanis generally eat aromatic rice, either plain or cooked with meat.

Cultural preferences for different rice varieties also exist. Rice consumers in Peru prefer long-grain and non-glutinous rice prepared with oil, garlic, and salt. Brazilians like soft, non-glutinous, and aromatic rice prepared in various ways. In Australia, rice consumption reflects an increase in the influence of Asian culture, and people generally prefer long-grain rice despite domestic production of short-grain *japonica* rice.

Rice is served as other forms of foods. Vietnamese usually steam soft rice with extra water and make rice noodles or pancakes. For their breakfast, they usually eat a large bowl of noodle soup, sometimes with sticky rice gruel. In the south of India, the common rice foods include steamed rice muffins and rice pancakes for breakfast. In Myanmar, favorite dishes include *mohinga* (rice noodles served with fish, eggs, and other ingredients), rice cooked with coconut milk, and rice with hot and sweet vegetable soup. *Nasi dagang* is a traditional Malaysian food made from unpolished glutinous rice with coconut milk and other ingredients. In Thailand, rice is also consumed as rice balls, rice cakes, rice pudding, and rice noodles.

Rice is sometimes indirectly consumed. In the Middle East, rice is used as a stuffing in other foods. Iraqis prefer short-grain rice in the form of plain boiled rice or rice stuffed in peppers or in chicken or turkey. In ancient Japan the rice wine sake was consumed primarily in the imperial court, larger temples, and shrines. Today, it is served at traditional ceremonies in Japan. In South and North America, rice is a supplemental food in Mexico, Peru, and Brazil. Rice is consumed as rice noodles, fried rice, rice cakes, and rice pudding (in Mexico). European people prefer rice cakes and rice puddings made from long-grain and aromatic rice.

Cooked rice can be served and eaten in different ways. Bowls and chopsticks are used for eating rice and other foods in China and Japan. But flat plates, spoons, and forks are used in Thailand instead. In India, rice is served on a banana leaf, a plate, or a metal tray, and eaten with the hands.

Rituals

There are many rituals for each stage in the production of rice. When opening a water channel, holy water from central lakes is sprinkled onto the field and the priests from the mountain temple make blessings. After sowing the seeds, a dance feast is held in Borneo, in which masks are worn to frighten away the rice evil spirits. Rice seed development is considered as if it were a pregnancy. Therefore, there are birth rituals in which people sing to the baby rice. Harvest is celebrated with dances as a Thai tradition. During rice harvest in Bangladesh, *pithas* (a popular dish) are made from new rice flour. The Iban farmers of Malaysia will whisper an apology or make amends with a special ritual for any rice grain wasted.

Customary Beliefs

The origin of rice is believed by Malaysian people to be associated with the sky (Sri Owen, 1993). It is believed in some countries that rice is holy and therefore should be well treated, protected, and honored. For example, men are usually not allowed to carry rice to the granary and cook it. Women also should show deference to rice. They should enter the rice granary at night or noon when rice spirits are sleeping, and be properly dressed without making noises by talking or chewing. Their breasts should be covered and they should enter the granary with right foot first. In China and Singapore, a good job is symbolized by an iron rice bowl, and a broken rice bowl means "out of a job." It also is considered bad luck to upset a rice bowl.

Festivals and Holidays

Rice is an important ritual food to celebrate the New Year. To celebrate the Japanese New Year, *Oshogatsu*, *mochi* (a glutinous rice cake) is prepared by toasting over a fire (a similar tradition to the current practice in central China) and served to begin the year on the "right foot." A special spiced rice wine, *toso*, is used for the celebration of the New Year. The New Year ends with special rice porridge. Similarly, to celebrate the Chinese New Year, *nieu koay* (a sweet and sticky rice cake) is offered to the deities in Malaysia, and *Tet* (the Lunar New Year) is celebrated with glutinous rice cakes in Vietnam. *Nien gao* (glutinous rice cakes of different shapes and colors), sounding like "going high" in Chinese, is served in China for the celebration of the Chinese Lunar New Year as a good luck symbol. To celebrate the Lunar New Year in Thailand, sticky rice cakes are prepared with mortar and pestle and cooked in the fire until a golden brown color is obtained.

Rice plays an important role in other festivals or ceremonies. In Sri Lanka, for the first day of every month and for festivals, *karibath* is served with milk and curries. On May 15 every year, the small town of Lucban in Quezon Province, the Philippines, celebrates the *Pahiyas* (precious offerings) Festival by decorating the outside of the houses with *pahiyas* made of rice flour paste. For the Chinese *Duan Wu* (Dragon Boat) Festival on the fifth of the fifth lunar month, *zong zi* (triangular and leaf-wrapped rice cakes) is prepared and dropped into the river or sea for appeasing the soul of an ancient minister, *Qu Yuan*, before the boat races. *Zong zi* is often eaten before the family-union feasts for celebration of the *Duan Wu* festival. In the Philippines, *pagdidiwata* (a thanksgiving festival) is celebrated by sharing rice wine with spirits. Rice

is involved in other ceremonies or festivals in India, including naming ceremonies (*namkaran*) and birthday celebrations. Rice also is important in India during the *Bhai Dhooj* (sister-brother day), *Diwali* (festival of light), *Makar Sakranti* (January 13), and *Pongal* festivals.

In Thailand, the Royal Plowing Ceremony has been a great event in front of the Grand Palace in Bangkok for more than 700 years. In the ceremony, the *Phraya Raek Na* (Lord of the Festival) performs a rite to predict the weather during the coming season, plows the field with a pair of ceremonial bulls, and scatters the rice seeds into the field with the help of the four *Nang Thepis* (consecrated women). People will rush to the field to pick up the sacred rice grain to take home. In the past, the traditional dance *Rabam Mae Posop* was performed to honor the rice goddess. Cambodia also has a similar royal plowing ceremony to mark the beginning of the rice-growing season.

Social Behavior

Rice (scented rice, colored rice, or rice alcohol) also can be served to family and friends to cement relationships or to enhance status. These ceremonies include the following situations: at marriage, at births, before building a house, before a major hunt, and before the start of a new season.

Rice is popularly used in wedding ceremonies because it is the symbol of life and fertility. In Indian wedding ceremonies, a handful of rice is tied to the corner of the sari of the bride when newlyweds take their vows. Upon arrival at the groom's house, she will step on a pan full of rice and the rice spilled out of the pan will be kept by the family for remembrance. In India, Sumatra, the United Kingdom, and some parts of the United States, rice grains are showered on the newly wedded couple for good luck and a fruitful marriage. It is suggested that this tradition might originate from China (Boesch, 1967). In wedding ceremonies in Myanmar, colored rice grains are showered on relatives and friends, as well as on the newlyweds, for good wishes. During Japanese weddings, the newly wedded bride and groom are required to take three sips of sake from each other's cup. Rice grains or rice flour are served during wedding ceremonies. In *pokok nasi* (a wedding ceremonial offering in Malaysia), glutinous rice is used as bedding for the artificial tree made of boiled eggs, leaves, and stems. In Bangladesh, *biryani*, a spicy dish consisting of rice and goat's meat, is served at wedding receptions in the urban areas. Special rice cakes called *nakshi pithas* also are prepared for wedding ceremonies. In the later part of wedding ceremonies in Sumatra, the newlyweds will "pull chicken from yellow rice" by custom.

Rice is an essential ingredient of offerings at birth celebrations. In Perak, Malaysia, rice is traditionally used to present the newborn to the spirit of the river by making offerings (rice packets, betel, and eggs) at the river side; rice dust and parched and yellow rice are sprinkled and scattered on the water. In Korea, *Yakbap*, glutinous rice steamed with nuts and honey, is served on festive occasions, such as birthdays and New Year's. Rice cakes or rice meals and *bobju*-wine (a rice wine) are served during wedding ceremonies and the celebration of births. The sharing of rice cakes among one hundred people symbolizes good luck and long life for the baby.

Rice can be found in other significant events. Special sweet and mild sake is used to celebrate *Hinamatsuri* (the Japanese Girl's Day). Rice paste is involved in purification ceremonies in Malaysia and other countries.

Spiritual Beliefs

There are many origin myths and much folklore about rice (Sri Owen, 1993). It is believed that there are many gods or goddesses related to rice. The gods or goddesses gave rice to humans and taught them how to grow rice. Religious use of rice takes place in India, China, Thailand, Indonesia, Sri Lanka, and Malaysia. In Asia, the rice spirit is female and often a mother figure. Cambodian rural villagers believe that *Yiey Tep* (a female guardian spirit) stays in the rice field. Therefore, they offer food (often sweet rice porridge) at the corners of rice fields (Solieng Mak, 1998). The Chinese believe that, in order to save hungry people, the goddess Guan Yin squeezed her breast so hard that her milk and blood went into the rice grains. That is why we have both white and red rice. In the northern Himalayas, the goddess *Pavarti* is believed to be the first to have grown rice. Indians worship rice as *Lakshmi*, the Hindu goddess of wealth. For Indians in Malaysia, rice flour is used to decorate the entrances of houses to welcome Lord Krishna and the goddess *Lakshmi* at *Deepavali* (the Festival of Lights). Indonesian people perform rituals to honor the goddess *Dewi Sri*. The "first fruits ritual" occurs before the harvest, in which rice dolls symbolizing *Dewi Sri* and her partners are made and placed in the rice granary or at home to ensure a bumper harvest. The Balinese honor *Dewi Sri* by offering dyed rice paste at celebrations. The *jaja*, which is made from colored rice paste of different shapes and prepared in different ways, is used for decorating offerings of fruits and flowers at merry or solemn Balinese ceremonies or festivals. At many other festivals, cooked and colored rice cakes are offered, decorated with flowers and palm leaves. The Balinese believe that *Indra* (Lord of the Heavens) taught men how to grow rice and rice is the soul of man. When the Balinese plant the first rice seedlings in the field, a special planting pattern is followed for the first nine seedlings after offerings are made to *Dewi Sri* (the goddess of rice). Multicolored cones of cooked rice are used for recalling the *nawa sanga* (rose of the winds) (Piper, 1993). In Japan, it is said that the sun goddess *Amatereshu-Omi-Kami* first grew rice in the field of heaven, and Prince Ninigi brought it for human culture. Japanese classic records also indicated that rice came from the eyes of the food goddess *Ohegetsu-hime*. The goddess for rice is *Bok Sri* in Java. The union of *Bok Sri* with *Djaka Sudana* (the male rice spirit) is celebrated by people working in the nearby fields. In Thailand, the rice goddess or rice mother, *Mae Posop*, is worshiped and believed to bring good harvest. Therefore, no men, loud noises, or talk of death or demons are permitted before harvest since *Mae Posop* is shy and easily frightened; miscarriage of her pregnancy during harvest time might occur. *Khao Chae* in Thailand also originated from the celebration of the first day in the lunar calendar when the Mon people offered *Kao Songkran* (*Songkran* rice), later *Khao Chae* modified with ease to be soaked (*chae*) in water, to the female guardian spirit of the New Year. The Rungao people in Vietnam believe that the shadow on the moon is the goddess heaping rice.

Other religious beliefs include the following: *Pulang Gana* is the spirit for rice growth in the beliefs of the Iban people. In Nepal, *tika*, the holy mark made from rice grains and yogurt, is put on the forehead of youngsters by elders for blessings during religious occasions. Similarly, at the *Durga Pcoja* festival, rice sprouts are offered to youngsters as good blessings from the goddess *Durga*.

People believe that rice spirits are involved in rice production. For the Iban, *padi pun* (the sacred rice) is protected by prohibitions, acts of respect, and deference. For example, it is not handled by men and never sold to others. It is harvested last after harvesting other rice without any break in the path of harvesting. Sometimes, the bamboo pole is used as a bridge to the gap between harvesting locations with singing, prayers, and offerings so that the spirits from all harvested rice eventually come to the *padi pun*. When the Iban people harvest rice, they use a concealed knife in order not to offend or scare away the rice soul. The Brou people in Cambodia have a similar tradition when clearing the forests for growing rice. They show their respect to the local *arak* (minor spirits having a particular location) with offerings and ceremonial articles such as a knife, axe, banana shoot, and chick legs on which chicken blood is poured. When harvesting, beer and chicken are placed in the rice field as thanks. Both Iban and Brou people pray for an increase in the quantity of rice in the granary.

BIBLIOGRAPHY

Mak, Solieng. "Rainfed Lowland Rice and Agricultural Change in Cambodia." Ph.D. dissertation, 1998.

Newman, Jaqueline M. "Cultural Aspects of Asian Dietary Habits." In *Asian Foods : Science and Technology*, edited by Catharina Y. W. Ang, KeShun Liu, and Yao-Wen Huang. Lancaster, Pa.: Technomic, 1999.

Piper, Jacqueline M. *Rice in South-East Asia: Cultures and Landscapes*. Kuala Lumpur and New York: Oxford University Press, 1993.

Sri Owen. *The Rice Book*. New York: St. Martin's Press, 1993.

Virmani, Inderjeet K. *Home Chefs of the World (Rice and Rice-based Recipes)*. Manila, Philippines: International Rice Research Institute, 1991.

Williams, W. W. "From Asia's Good Earth: Rice, Society, and Science." *United Airlines Hemispheres*, 1996.

Jiming Li

RICKETS. *See* **Vitamins.**

ROASTING. Roasting is a dry-heat method of cooking whereby meat or poultry is cooked on a spit over a fire or in a pan in an oven. Roasting began in prehistoric time when the first human stuck a piece of meat on a stick and held it over a fire. Spit-roasting fowl and game was common in ancient societies. In the Middle Ages, hunting was a prime occupation of the noble classes, and the game was usually roasted on a spit. Suckling pigs were also candidates for the spit. Beef, however, was not; it was considered "vulgar" because cattle did not have to be hunted. Not until the seventeenth century did roast beef became widely accepted in Europe.

Roasting, perhaps because it requires prodigious amounts of fuel and large pieces of meat, has always been considered the most prestigious form of cooking. The world's largest and oldest gastronomic society, the Confrérie de la Chaîne des Rôtisseurs (The Brotherhood of the Chain of the Roasters), was founded in Paris in 1248 by masters in the art of roasting geese (called "rotisseurs"). The object of the Guild was to perpetuate the standards of quality befitting the royal table under Louis IX, King of France. The king loved his roast for the same reason people still love roasted meat: roasting develops and improves the flavor, color, and aroma of food. Properly roasted meat is tender, delicious, appetizing, and easier to digest than meat cooked by other methods.

The roasting method is one of the simplest ways to cook fine cuts of prime beef, lamb, pork, and veal, but, as any culinary student can tell you, simplicity in the field of culinary arts can be tricky. In cooking, as in all of the arts, simplicity is the sign of perfection. Roasting is often the method of choice because it yields a tender pink interior and crisp browned exterior through prolonged oven cooking. Before beginning the oven-cooking phase of the roasting process, the meat must be trimmed, tied, seasoned, and, if possible, seared.

A roast begins as a piece of meat either on the bone or with the bone removed. A roast can range in size from a small pork loin, boned and rolled, that can feed four, to a beef round on the bone that can serve up to one hundred people. Such large, or primal, cuts are usually cooked by the roasting or rotisserie method. As a verb, "to roast" means to oven-cook food in an uncovered pan, over indirect heat. A "rotisserie," the noun, cooks food by slowly rotating it over direct heat.

A rotisserie contains a spit fitted with a pair of prongs that slides along its length. Food (usually meat) is impaled on the spit and the prongs are screwed tightly into place to hold the food securely. Roasting and rotisserie cooking produce the best results with reasonably tender pieces of meat or poultry. Tougher pieces of meat usually require moist cooking methods such as braising or pot-roasting. When time allows, less tender but larger, fatty meat joints can also be cooked rotisserie style to achieve the same results as tenderer cuts.

The standard temperature for cooking roasts is 350°F, but the ideal temperature (or set point) can vary plus or minus 50°F, depending on the cut. Technically, the lower the heat of the oven, the better the final roasted product will be. At a lower temperature, the meat takes longer to cook but produces more flavor, retains more moisture, and shrinks less. In the process, the crispy outer character associated with the classic roast is somewhat diminished. When roasting meat at a temperature below 200°F, most professionals rely on Altra-Sham® cooking technology, a method that combines a constant, precise low temperature with relatively high humidity. At these same low temperatures, other wood-fired heat source methods of roasting—barbecuing, pit-roasting, and smoking—also produce desirable results.

Barbecuing is a roasting method of cooking. Food is covered and slowly cooked in an open pit or on a spit, using hot coals or hardwood as a heat source. The food is basted, usually with a highly seasoned sauce (with a vinegar or sweet tomato base) to keep it moist. North Carolina and Kansas City are two of the most famous U.S. spots for barbecue.

TABLE 1

Roasting times and temperatures (temperature in degrees Fahrenheit)

Food	Oven temperature	Roasting time	Doneness and temperature
Beef: Whole tenderloin (4 lbs.)	400	35–45 minutes	Rare 120–130; medium rare 130–140
Top loin (4½ lbs.)	425 for 15 minutes, then 350	1¼–1½ hrs.	Rare 120–130; medium rare 130–140
Prime Rib(5-rib, 12-lb. roast)	325	5-rib (11–13 lbs.): 2¼–2¾ hrs. 3-rib (7–8½ lbs.): 1½–1¾ hrs.	Rare, 120–130; medium rare 130–140
Leg of lamb (8 lbs.)	350	1hr.–1½ hrs.	Rare 120–130; medium rare 130; medium 140
Pork loin boneless (4 lbs.)	350	2¼–2½ hrs.	Cook to 160
Chicken (4–7 lbs.)	400	1 hr.–1¾ hrs.	Cook to 175 in thigh
Turkey (10–25 lbs.)	325	10–12 minutes per lb. unstuffed; 12–15 minutes per lb. stuffed	Cook to 175–180 in thigh

This roasting apparatus for chicken was devised in England in the early nineteenth century for use in hotels. This scene dates from about 1850. The rotisserie turns as the cook turns the crank. The reed screen on the left suggests that this was extremely hot work. ROUGHWOOD COLLECTION.

When meat is cooked slowly in a large hole in the ground, it is pit-roasted (more precisely, "pit-braised"). A hardwood fire is built in a pit and the wood is allowed to burn until the pit is partly filled with burning coals. The coals are then completely sealed with gravel and sand. Sometimes the meat is wrapped in fresh leaves, especially whole carcasses like pig, lamb, and goat. The wrapped meat is placed on the sand and then completely covered with earth, which holds in the heat and steam. Cooking times can vary from five to ten hours, depending on the size and thickness of the meat and how fast the coals are burning.

Smoke-roasting, also called hot smoke-roasting, is generally considered a restaurant application. Specialized ovens that apply constant heat and variable smoke intensity from a built-in smoker compartment are used to produce hot-smoked food. This application of heat and wood smoke are ideal for roasting meat, poultry, and fish because the food cooks at a low temperature under static conditions and there are no drying drafts of air moving through the smoker. The result is a tender, moist roast with consistent smoke flavor.

Once the internal temperature for a roast has been determined, the cook prepares the roast itself. The typical procedure for the roasting method is to place the prepared meat (trimmed, seasoned, and seared) into the oven in a roasting pan on a roasting rack. A roasting rack is required for a successful roast because it holds the roast above the pan in which it is roasting. This prevents the meat from cooking in its drippings and allows adequate air circulation for even cooking and browning.

Meat is roasted until a meat thermometer (inserted in the roast) indicates that its ideal internal temperature has been reached. The ideal temperature depends on the type of animal, the type of roast (bone-in or tied), and the cut of meat. There are many ways to tie a roast using either hand-trussing or butcher-wrapping. Roasts are tied for two reasons: to keep the roast in an aesthetically pleasing round shape or to hold stuffing inside of it. After the meat has rested, usually about fifteen minutes, the string can be removed from the exterior of the roast.

During the process of cooking, as meat achieves its ideal internal temperature, many chemical changes occur

HOW TO ROAST

Roast beef, pork, and poultry are among the most satisfying and impressive dishes the home cook can create, especially for family meals and festive occasions. Roasting is most successful when used with foods with some moisture or fat content. Drier cuts should have some fat added to keep them moist in cooking.

Essential to the appeal of roasting is the fact that it produces a tasty, crunchy crust on the surface of the food. Commonly known as browning, this phenomenon is known to food science as the Maillard reaction, after Louis Camille Maillard, the French chemist who first described the process in 1912. In a Maillard reaction, the heat of cooking causes protein components and natural sugars in the food to break down, combine in complex ways, and produce a brown pigment (technically called "melanoidin"), and the result is a crust that usually tastes rather sweet. The process can be magnified by the cook with the addition of more sugar, such as the glucose in corn syrup, or protein, such as butter.

Meat that is to be roasted should be allowed to sit at room temperature for an hour or two, depending on the size of the roast, in order to let the interior lose its refrigerator chill. (This step is not as important with poultry because the center of a chicken or turkey is hollow, whereas a meat roast is solid.) Allowing a meat roast to sit out for a time should not present a food safety hazard unless the kitchen is very warm; for added safety, the cook might sear the meat to kill any surface bacteria.

There are several ways the cook can be sure to produce a delicious, juicy roast. The roasting pan should not be covered. A covered pan traps the moisture escaping from the meat and surrounds the meat with steam, producing a mushy rather than crisp exterior and a flabby taste. In order to avoid losing the natural juices of the meat, the meat should not be pierced with a fork nor should it be salted before or during cooking. The one exception to the rule against piercing the meat is that a meat thermometer can be used to check for doneness. (See accompanying table for recommended temperatures.) Insert the thermometer before the roast goes into the oven and leave it in during cooking. Measure the temperature in the center of the roast, not touching bone (since bone conducts heat better than muscle and will give a higher reading). Be sure to remove the roast when it reaches a point ten to fifteen degrees below the target temperature since the temperature will continue to rise after the roast is removed from the oven. Allow the roast to "rest" for fifteen to twenty-five minutes (depending on size) after removing it from the oven because heat causes the proteins of the meat to coagulate and give up their

juice; if the meat is carved as soon as it is out of the oven, the juice will rush out, leaving much of the meat rather dry. If the roast is allowed to rest, the meat relaxes and much of the moisture is reabsorbed, allowing for juicy sliced meat.

Meat classified as "Prime" by the U.S. Department of Agriculture has more flecks of fat in the muscle than the next-best grade, "Choice." Even leaner and tougher is "Select." Prime meat is hard to find in most supermarkets since it is more expensive and generally sold to the restaurant trade. Choice cuts will roast well, but Select cuts should be cooked with a moist-heat method.

Many different foods are suitable for roasting. Meat made from the rib, short loin, and sirloin cuts make the best beef roasts since they are the tenderest parts of the animal and do well in the dry heat of the oven. Beef cuts ideal for roasting include the tenderloin, standing rib, rolled (boneless) rib, rib-eye, strip loin, sirloin, beef round, and eye of round. Cuts that are both tender and relatively small, such as the tenderloin or rib-eye, can be cooked at high temperatures (400°F) to achieve a well-browned exterior and juicy, tender interior. Larger cuts, such as "prime rib" (standing rib roast) need a lower temperature (250°F to 350°F) to prevent the exterior from overcooking before the interior reaches the desired state of doneness.

Various cuts from pork loin are suitable for roasting, including the tenderloin, top loin roast, crown roast, and rib roast. The whole ham or portion (shank or butt) is a classic roasted dish.

Leg of lamb is considered by some connoisseurs to be the most magnificent cut of meat available for roasting. It can be roasted on the bone; if the leg is deboned, it can be rolled for roasting.

Whole chickens and turkeys are easily roasted, the only challenge being to keep the white meat of a large bird moist until the dark meat, which cooks more slowly, is done. Poultry parts, such as legs or breasts, that are cooked in the oven are said to be "baked," while the whole bird is "roasted." Duck and goose can also be roasted, although the fat content, especially with goose, is considerably higher than that of chicken or turkey and the cook will likely find a large amount of grease in the pan.

In the vegetable world, the most commonly roasted items are the potato and sweet potato. In a reversal of the terminology used for poultry, a whole potato is said to be "baked" while potatoes cut up and put in a dish are said to be "roasted."

Richard L. Lobb

that affect its appearance, taste, and texture, including shrinkage, browning, and flavor development. The first effect of roasting is that muscle proteins shrink and moisture is lost. As meat is heated, the muscle proteins coagulate and shrink, squeezing out water. The longer meat is cooked, the more water is forced out. This is why "dry" and "overcooked" have become synonymous. The loss of juices through drip, evaporation, and cooking time, along with the intramuscular fat or marbling content, determine the meat's juiciness, amount of shrinkage, and, thus, the final cooked weight or portion yield. An accurate internal meat thermometer is an essential piece of equipment for roasting because overcooking produces meat with so little remaining moisture that it is dry and tough.

Heat also affects the internal pigmentation of meat and changes its color. In beef, for example, the red color of uncooked beef changes to light pink, then to brownish-gray as the internal temperature increases from 125°F to 165°F. During long, slow cooking, most connective tissue softens, and collagen (fibrous protein) gelatinizes. Heat also causes fat to melt, and slightly browning fat develops flavor.

It is a myth that searing meat seals in the juices during roasting. Searing or browning the outer, lean surface of meat, usually at a fairly high temperature, does develop flavor and color as a result of Maillard reactions. It is an important step in several dry-cooking methods, including roasting, in order to produce a tasty outcome. When roasting meat, sear it to a good brown color to improve appearance and flavor, remembering that overcooked lean meat will be dry, and therefore not as good to eat as properly cooked lean meat, which is succulent and juicy. Two solutions are available to the cook. One is to bard meat with fat (cover it with strips of fat, usually pork fatback), an outdated practice but one still taught in cooking schools, or to add a fat cap or caul fat wrapping to lean meat. The rule of thumb is to use caul fat on fowl and bard lean roasts before roasting.

See also **Barbecue; Broasting; Broiling; Cattle; Cooking; Frying; Game; Goat; Grilling; Mammals; Meat; Meat, Smoked; Pig; Preparation of Food; Sauces.**

BIBLIOGRAPHY

Corriher, Shirley. *CookWise: The Hows and Whys of Successful Cooking.* New York: Morrow, 1997.

Flandrin, Jean-Louis, and Massimo Montanari, eds. *Food: A Culinary History from Antiquity to the Present.* Translated by Clarissa Botsford. New York: Columbia University Press, 1999.

Lee, Frank A. *Basic Food Chemistry.* 2d ed. Westport, Conn.: AVI, 1983.

McGee, Harold. *On Food and Cooking: The Science and Lore of the Kitchen.* New York: Simon and Schuster, 1997.

Meiselman, Herbert L., ed. *Dimensions of the Meal: The Science, Culture, Business, and Art of Eating.* Gaithersburg, Md.: Aspen, 2000.

Montanari, Massimo. "Peasants, Warriors, Priests: Images of Society and Styles of Diet." In *Food: A Culinary History from Antiquity to the Present,* edited by Jean-Louis Flandrin and Massimo Montanari, pp. 178–185. New York: Columbia University Press, 1999.

Paston-Williams, Sara. *The Art of Dining: A History of Cooking and Eating.* London: National Trust, 1993.

Pépin, Jacques. *La Méthode: An Illustrated Guide to the Fundamental Techniques of Cooking.* New York: Times Books, 1979.

Villas, James. *American Taste: A Celebration of Gastronomy Coast-to-Coast.* New York: Lyons and Burford, 1996.

Francis McFadden

ROME AND THE ROMAN EMPIRE. Roman gastronomy, or gluttony, impresses all who read the Latin and Greek literature composed under the great Mediterranean empire of the first four centuries C.E. Feasting was a central feature of Roman society. The cuisine of Rome, much influenced by ancient Greece and the Near East, is the direct ancestor of the national cuisines of most of western Europe.

Ancient texts form one of the source materials for reconstructing Roman food behavior. These texts include scientific and technical writings (such as the earliest surviving recipe book, *Apicius,* probably compiled in the fourth century C.E.) as well as lively depictions of food, wine, and banquets in classical Latin prose and poetry. Archaeology is is an equally important source of information on this topic. Notable in this context are the finds at Pompeii, the Italian city buried in 79 C.E. by the disastrous eruption of Mount Vesuvius.

Historical Outline

Rome was said to have been founded by Romulus and Remus in 753 B.C.E. on the banks of the Tiber in central Italy. It was a country town whose power gradually grew until it was the center of a world empire. In the third and second centuries B.C.E., Rome fought and defeated the Carthaginians of north Africa, a victory that opened the way to Roman domination of the whole western Mediterranean; in the second and first centuries B.C.E., successive victories in Greece, Anatolia (Turkey), Syria, and Egypt extended Rome's power and wealth eastward.

The rule of the first Roman emperor, Augustus (27 B.C.E.–14 C.E.), marks the beginning of a four-hundred-year period, unique in history, during which a single political power governed the whole Mediterranean. Travel and trade were relatively free throughout the region and there was intensive cultural interaction. Travel was slow, however: it was a five-month voyage from the Pillars of Hercules (Straits of Gibraltar) to Antioch at the eastern end of the Mediterranean. Only foods that were dried, pickled, or salted, and only special wines (see below), would withstand the rigors of such a journey.

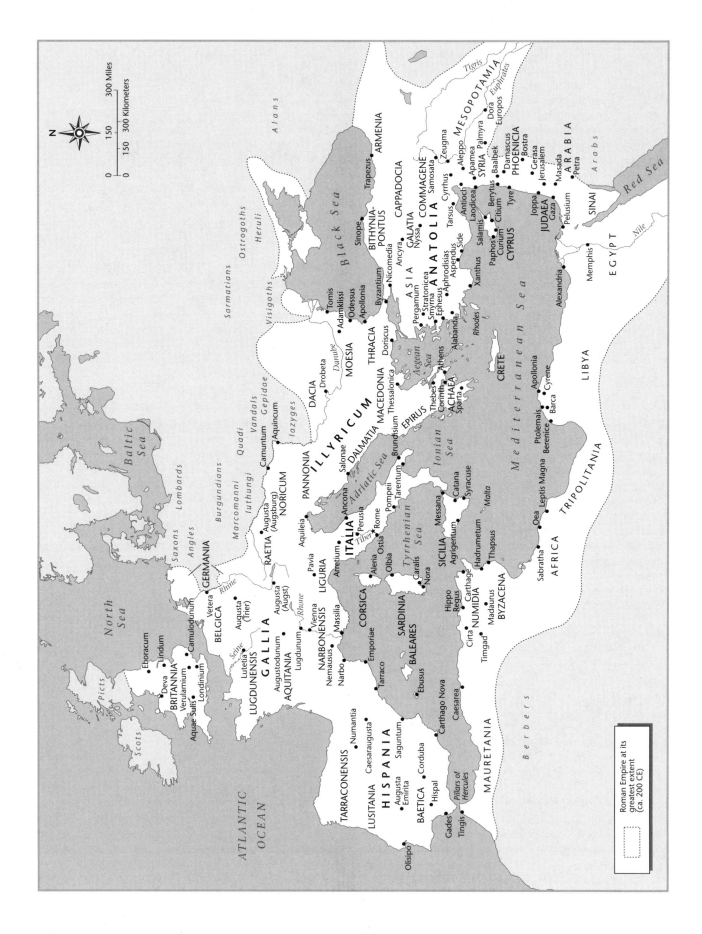

300 Miles

150   300 Kilometers

0   150   300

Tigris

Euphrates

MESOPOTAMIA

Alans

Ostrogoths

Heruli

ARMENIA

Trapezus

Dora
Europos

Palmyra

Zeugma

SYRIA

Aleppo

Apamea

Samosata

COMMAGENE

Cyrrhus

Antioch

Laodicea

CAPPADOCIA

Damascus

Baalbek

Bostra

PHOENICIA

Gerasa

Masada

ARABIA

Jerusalem

Petra

Black Sea

Sinope

BITHYNIA-
PONTUS

Nicomedia

Byzantium

Ancyra

GALATIA
Nyssa

Tarsus

Berytus

Citium

Tyre

Joppa

Gaza

JUDAEA

SINAI

Red Sea

Arabs

Sarmatians

Visigoths

Vandals

Gepidae

Iazyges

CYPRUS

Paphos
Curium

Salamis

Apendus

ASIA

ANATOLIA

Pergamum

Stratonicea

Smyrna

Side

Aspendus

Ephesus

Aphrodisias

Alabanda

Rhodes

Xanthus

Alexandria

Memphis

Nile

EGYPT

Tomis

Adamklissi

Odessus

Apollonia

THRACIA

Doriscus

*Aegean
Sea*

Athens

ACHAEA

Corinth

Sparta

Thebes

Mediterranean Sea

CRETE

LIBYA

Drobeta

DACIA

MOESIA

ILLYRICUM

MACEDONIA

Thessalonica

EPIRUS

DALMATIA

Salonae

Brundisium

*Ionian
Sea*

Apollonia
Cyrene

Barca

Ptolemais
Berenice

TRIPOLITANIA

Danube

*Baltic
Sea*

Lombards

Burgundians

Marcomanni

Iuthungi

Quadi

Carnuntum

Aquincum

Augusta
(Augsburg)

NORICUM

PANNONIA

RAETIA

Aquileia

Ancona

Perusia

ITALIA

Rome

Ostia

Pompeii

*Tyrrhenian
Sea*

Catana

Messana

Syracuse

SICILIA

Agrigentum

Malta

Leptis Magna

Oea

Sabratha

AFRICA

Thapsus

Hadrumetum

BYZACENA

Madaurus

Timgad

Carthage

NUMIDIA

Cirta

MAURETANIA

Berbers

Saxons

Angles

GERMANIA

Rhine

BELGICA

Augusta
(Trier)

Vetera

Augustodunum

Augusta
(Augst)

LUGDUNENSIS

GALLIA

LIGURIA

Lugdunum

Rhone

Vienna

Pavia

Arretium

Aleria

Olbia

Caralis

Nora

CORSICA

SARDINIA

Adriatic Sea

Tarentum

NARBONENSIS

AQUITANIA

Massilia

Nemausus

Narbo

Emporiae

BALEARES

Ebusus

*Pillars of
Hercules*

Caesarea

Carthago Nova

Tingis

Gades

Hippo
Regius

Madaurus

Tarraco

*North
Sea*

Eboracum

Lindum

Camulodunum

Deva

Verulamium

Londinium

BRITANNIA

Aquae Sulis

Picts

Scots

Lutetia

Seine

TARRACONENSIS

Numantia

Caesaraugusta

Saguntum

HISPANIA

Corduba

BAETICA

Augusta
Emerita

Hispal

LUSITANIA

Olisipo

ATLANTIC
OCEAN

Roman Empire at its
greatest extent
(ca. 200 CE)

Crises in the third and fourth centuries C.E. led to the division of the empire into two parts, which had quite different fates. The Eastern Roman Empire was directly continued in the Byzantine Empire. The Western Roman Empire collapsed, finally disappearing in 476 C.E. However, the "barbarian" kingdoms that took its place inherited Roman dietary ideas and developed a way of life that had many Roman features.

Even before those eastern conquests, Romans had become rich enough to spend their wealth enthusiastically on imported luxuries. Lavish banquets became fashionable, and the price of slave cooks rose steeply. Moralists inveighed against these developments, but they did so in vain. Meanwhile, other changes had affected the Roman diet. The acquisition of new territories provided the opportunity for experimentation in agriculture and food production. Romanization in the provinces encouraged people to demand that what was available in the capital should also be available more widely, especially to Roman legionaries and provincial administrators. The province of Britain, whose conquest began in 43 C.E., provides an example: vines, peaches, walnuts, celery, coriander (cilantro), carrots, and several other important foods were first transplanted to that province in Roman times. Wine, olive oil, olives, figs, lentils, chickpeas, and rice were among the commodities that Roman traders first exported to Britain in response to the popularity of Roman fashions in that region.

Many special features of Roman administrative and economic life left their marks on the food and cuisine of the vast region that was once the Roman Empire. Great frontier armies, whose zones of recruitment ensured movement and mixture of populations, required the delivery of reliable, standardized supplies on well-built roads. Inscriptions show that periodic markets existed: they were held every eight days in Italian towns, twice a month in North Africa, and three times a month in Asia Minor.

The Literature of Food

The oldest Latin prose text, written about 175 B.C.E., is *De Agri Cultura* (On farming) by the statesman Cato. This work focuses on the two great cash crops of Italy—wine and olive oil—and also includes recipes for cakes and flavored and medicinal wines suitable for farmhouse production. The tradition of Roman agricultural texts culminated in Columella's detailed manual *On Agriculture*, written about 50 C.E. Columella provides much information on food throughout the manual, as well as a long section (Book 12) full of recipes for household preserves and other food products. Written at about the same date, the Latin encyclopaedia *Historia Naturalis* (Natural history) by Pliny the Elder contains eight books (12–19) on plants and their uses, with special attention to fruits and vegetables. Book 14 is devoted entirely to grapes and wine. Although Latin was the native language of Rome, many medical and scientific texts of the Roman Empire were written in Greek: examples are a dietary manual, *On the Properties of Foods*, by the imperial physician Galen (129–199 C.E.), and a medical and dietary textbook by one of his successors, Oribasius (c. 325–400 C.E.). These dietary manuals list foods in great detail, which allowed the reader to work out suitable diets. The manuals also make allowances for seasonal factors and each individual's constitution, lifestyle, and current state of health, in accordance with ancient medical theories. (For English translations of all the texts named in this paragraph see the bibliography.)

Poetry and literary prose give a different perspective on food from that of the technical texts. The personal poetry from the period of Augustus is full of insights on food and dining among the elite, demonstrating the growth of gastronomy and the ways in which food articulated social relations. Authors of this period include Propertius, Horace, and Ovid. Written about one hundred years after the time of Augustus, the picaresque novel *Satyrica* by Petronius mocks the luxurious lifestyle of the new rich. The series of biographies of emperors by the imperial archivist Suetonius (*Lives of the Twelve Caesars*, written about 115 C.E.) provides a glimpse into palace lifestyles, in which feasts sometimes turned into Roman orgies. Lives of poorer people are depicted in the fictional *Metamorphoses* (often translated under the title *The Golden Ass*) by Apuleius (born 125 C.E.), and later in the biographies of Christian hermits and saints.

It was common in Roman writing to despise complicated dishes designed for show rather than for taste. Yet, in practice, Romans reveled in the spices and deli-

Interior of the bakery of Sotericus at Pompeii, Italy. © MIMMO JODICE/CORBIS.

cacies of the whole ancient world: the pepper of south India and even the cloves of the Spice Islands were prized luxuries. In the recipes of Apicius, the flavor of the main ingredient is often enhanced with ten or fifteen spices and herbs. Rich households must have spent much money and slave labor on the finding of rare ingredients and the elaboration of showpiece dishes. The parrot wrasse (a type of fish) and the dormouse fetched high prices not because of their flavor but because of the way they looked on the table. Peacocks, and peahens' eggs, were in demand among gourmets for their rarity more than their quality.

It was also a commonplace to boast of the freshness and simplicity of the farm produce that one was offering to one's guests. There is a tradition of poetic "invitations to dinner" that demonstrate changes in style as well as individual responses to food fashion, extending from about 50 B.C.E. to 110 C.E.: authors of this genre include Catullus (*Poems* 13), Horace (*Epistles* 1.5; *Odes* 3.29, 4.12), Martial (*Epigrams* 5.78, 10.48, 11.52), Juvenal (*Satires* 11), and Pliny the Younger (*Letters* 1.15).

Staple Foods and Major Flavorings

Rome's status as an overgrown city-state was signaled in one of the special privileges enjoyed by inhabitants of the city: the free bread ration. Interruptions in the wheat supply led to riots. Rome's annexation of Egypt, after Cleopatra's suicide in 30 B.C.E., ensured the continuity of the supply. Thereafter, huge grain ships left Alexandria regularly throughout the sailing season, bringing wheat to Ostia at the mouth of the Tiber. It was on such a ship that St. Paul reached Italy after having been shipwrecked on Malta. Roman bakers baked leavened bread, both white and wholemeal. Small-scale baking required a dome-shaped baking-crock (*testum* and *clibanus*). Archaeologists often find fragments of these. A commercial bakery, complete with fossilized loaves, has been excavated at Pompeii.

The traditional staple food of early Italy had been not wheat bread but *puls* (porridge made from emmer wheat). The staple diet of the Roman provinces varied considerably, depending on climate and local custom. Barley, although widely considered a respectable, even desirable, staple food in ancient Greece and Italy, was viewed by Roman soldiers as punishment rations. This increased the demand for wheat wherever Roman armies were stationed.

Always in use in the Roman kitchen were olive oil, fish sauce, and wine. All three were manufactured and distributed on a large scale. *Garum* was the major source of dietary salt: scarcely any *Apicius* recipes call for pure salt. Grape syrup was also much used in flavoring, as were honey and dates. Many recipes begin with the instruction, "Pound pepper and lovage," a reminder that both exotic spices and local herbs were appreciated (lovage, native to Liguria in northern Italy, is a bitter culinary herb resembling parsley). Other commonly used flavor-ings were onion, mustard, dill, fennel, rue, savory, thyme, mint, pine kernels, caraway, cumin, ginger, and *asafoetida*, the central Asian substitute for the *silphium* that the Greeks had appreciated so much.

Pliny the Elder and Galen—both of whom were wine enthusiasts, judging from their writings—provide full information on the wines that Romans drank with their meals. Italy had many fine wines to boast of. The famous Caecuban vineyards in Latium (modern Lazio) succumbed to urbanization, but Falernian wine, from hillsides in northern Campania, maintained its reputation throughout the empire. In the world's oldest recorded tradition of wine vintage years, fine wines were labelled with the name of one of the consuls elected for the year. The Opimian vintage (121 B.C.E.) was legendary: Opimian wines were served, already 160 years old, at a banquet given for the emperor Caligula in 39 C.E. Horace addressed an amusing poem to a jar of wine: "born, as I was, when Manlius was consul," (that year was 65 B.C.E.). It was in Roman times that the wine-growing regions of Spain and southern Gaul (France) first came to real economic importance. Long-distance transport of wines was less risky if they were "cooked" and sweetened with honey or grape syrup; it was in this form that Greek wines were enjoyed in Rome. Roman territory eventually extended northward far beyond the latitude at which grapes ripen to full sweetness. In these regions, including northern Gaul and Britain, Roman legionaries developed a taste for local beer, which was usually brewed from malted barley.

Food in Roman Society

City dwellers in imperial Rome, many of whom lived in apartment blocks, had little opportunity to cook: cooking required an open fire, often an unacceptable risk. However, street food was always available to the city dweller. Street stalls and cookshops sold cakes and sweets, mulled wine, hot sausages, hot chickpea soup, and porridge. "In the tavern all are equally free," wrote Juvenal (born 67 C.E.) with an undertone of disapproval. He continues, "all drink from a common cup, the couch is barred to no man, the table is no closer to one than it is to another," (*Satires* 8.177-8). The philosopher Seneca the Younger (died 65 C.E.) gives us the sounds of the busy street just outside his apartment window: "pancake-sellers and a sausage-vendor and a confectioner and all the proprietors of cookshops selling their wares, each in his distinctive accent" (*Letters to Lucilius*, 56).

Poor countryfolk had to depend largely on food from their own fields and gardens, supplemented by herbs and fruits gathered from the wild. Meat and fish were uncommon in their diets. For a sense of the flavors of a Roman peasant diet, see the poem "Moretum" (c. first century B.C.E.).

For the peasant population of the ancient countryside, food preparation was a shared task, but in general it was the special responsibility of women. Large households had kitchens staffed with slaves, the skilled cook himself often being an expensive and carefully-chosen acquisition.

Romans tended to eat little during the first part of the day: a breakfast (*ientaculum*) was a snack that many did not trouble to take at all, and only the greedy wanted a heavy lunch (*prandium*). There was no better preparation for a full evening meal, (*cena*) the one big meal of the day, than a couple of hours at the baths. These were fashionable meeting places, ideal locations for informal business discussions. One could easily spend a whole evening there, for food and wine were available at bars and restaurants.

Typical larger Roman houses had a special dining room, the *triclinium*. Three couches arranged in a U-shape, each large enough for three diners, surrounded a central table. A house with a big enough garden might have had a garden dining area, as well, which was shaded by vines and creepers, with three stone couches sloping gently upwards to the middle (cushions and pillows made these comfortable). The open side of the square was for waiters to come and go.

Servants took off guests' sandals as they reclined and brought water to wash their hands. A sequence of dishes began with the appetizer or hors d'oeuvre (*gustus*), followed by an aperitif such as honeyed wine (*mulsum*) or spiced wine (*conditum*). The appetizers were generally more varied and more costly than the main course, though not as bulky. At one religious dinner attended by Julius Caesar, sixteen hors d'oeuvres awaited the priestly celebrants. The appetizers ranged from sea urchin and clams to slices of venison and wild boar.

The main courses were accompanied by bread and wine. Diners ate with their hands, with the occasional help of a knife. Waiters were constantly coming and going, bringing new courses, clearing away dishes, and supplying perfumed water for finger-rinsing. Music and dance from hired performers, usually slaves, often accompanied the drinking, which tended to continue long after the meal itself was over. The emperor Augustus preferred to entertain his guests by employing traditional storytellers.

A napkin, which lay in front of the diners as they reclined, might serve as a knapsack to take home the little gifts (*apophoreta*) with which a host would regale his friends as they departed. Similar gifts were given to dependents not lucky enough to be invited to a real dinner. Martial (c. 100 C.E.) wrote a collection of short poems intended to accompany such gifts. They are the most obvious sign that hospitality helped to articulate the patron/client relations that permeated Roman society. The Greek satirist Lucian (second century C.E.) wrote a convincing sketch of daily life in a rich Roman household and addressed it to a friend who had been offered a post as private tutor. Placed at the lowest table, Lucian warned, the friend would be sneered at by slaves and

would taste little of the fine cuisine except the mallow leaves that garnished the serving dishes (*On Salaried Posts in Great Houses*, 26).

Among upper-class Romans, unlike Greeks, the sexes were not segregated at meals. It was said that Roman women once sat demurely at the feet of their husbands' dining couches, but by imperial times the women also reclined. It was said, too, that in the old days women did not drink wine, and that the kiss a Roman husband gave his wife when returning home was a way of assuring himself that this rule had been kept.

See also **Ancient Kitchen, The; Ancient Mediterranean Religions; Apicius; Feasts, Festivals, and Fasts; Greece, Ancient; Greece and Crete; Italy; Luxury; Petronius; Wine in the Ancient World.**

BIBLIOGRAPHY

The standard modern survey of Roman food and the most detailed study of Roman wine are both in French: André, Jacques. *L'alimentation et la cuisine à Rome* [Food and cuisine in Rome]. 2d ed. (Paris: Les Belles Lettres, 1981. Tchernia, André. *Le Vin de l'Italie romaine* [The wine of Roman Italy]. (Rome: Ecole Française de Rome, 1986). Plenty of useful information in English will be found in: Alcock, Joan P. *Food in Roman Britain*. (Brimscombe Port, Gloucestershire, U.K.: Tempus, 2001); Fleming, Stuart J. *Vinum: the Story of Roman Wine*. (Glen Mills, Pa.: Art Flair, 2001); Garnsey, Peter. *Food and Society in Classical Antiquity*. (Cambridge: Cambridge University Press, 1999); Slater, William J., ed. *Dining in a Classical Context*. (Ann Arbor: University of Michigan Press, 1991); White, K. D. *Roman Farming*. (London and New York: Thames and Hudson, 1970); Wilkins, John, David Harvey, and Mike Dobson, eds. *Food in Antiquity*. (Exeter, U.K.: Exeter University Press, 1995).

Modern translations of most of the Roman literary texts cited in this article are easily found in libraries. For examples of Christian biographies see Russell, Norman, trans. *The Lives of the Desert Fathers*. (Oxford: Mowbray; Kalamazoo, Mich.: Cistercian Publications, 1981). The following is a list of specialized Roman sources on food that are available in English: Dalby, Andrew, trans. Cato, *On farming*. (Totnes, Devon, U.K.: Prospect Books, 1998); Ash, Harrison Boyd, E. S. Forster, and Edward H. Heffner, trans. Columella, *On Agriculture*. 3 vols. (Cambridge, Mass.: Harvard University Press, 1941–1955); Rackham, H., et al., trans. Pliny, *Natural History*. 10 vols. (Cambridge, Mass.: Harvard University Press, 1938–1963); Grant, Mark. *Galen on Food and Diet*. (London and New York: Routledge, 2000); Grant, Mark. *Dieting for an Emperor: A Translation of Books 1 and 4 of Oribasius' Medical Compilations*. (Leiden: Brill, 1997).

For Roman recipes with modern adaptations see: Grant, Mark. *Roman Cookery: Ancient Recipes for Modern Kitchens*. (London: Serif, 1999); Dalby, Andrew, and Sally Grainger. *The Classical Cookbook*. (Los Angeles: J. Paul Getty Museum; London: British Museum Press, 1996. See also under Apicius).

For information on the spice trade see: Miller, J. Innes. *The Spice Trade of the Roman Empire*. (Oxford: Clarendon Press, 1969); Dalby, Andrew. *Dangerous Tastes: the Story of Spices*. (London: British Museum Press; Berkeley: University of California Press, 2000). For works on country people and their food see: Frayn, Joan M. *Subsistence Farming in Roman Italy*. (London: Centaur Press, 1979); Kenny. E. J., ed. *Moretum: the Ploughman's Lunch*,

A Poem Ascribed to Virgil (Bristol: Bristol Classical Press, 1986). For information on markets see: Frayn, Joan M. *Markets and Fairs in Roman Italy*. (Oxford: Clarendon Press, 1993); de Ligt, L. *Fairs and Markets in the Roman Empire*. (Amsterdam: Gieben, 1993).

Emily Gowers, in *The Loaded Table* (Oxford: Oxford University Press, 1993) explores the hidden meanings of food in Latin poetry: she makes a special study of the poetic invitations to dinner. Andrew Dalby's *Empire of Pleasures: Luxury and Indulgence in the Roman Empire* (London and New York: Routledge, 2000) is a survey of the empire's foods and other luxuries, showing their use in constructing Roman imperial identity. The best outline of Roman daily life, dated in some ways, but well documented and not superseded, is: Carcopino, Jérôme. *Daily Life in Ancient Rome*. (New Haven: Yale University Press, 1940; London: Routledge, 1941).

Andrew Dalby

RUSSIA. Russian food is typically hearty in taste, with mustard, horseradish, and dill among the predominant flavorings. The cuisine is distinguished by the many fermented and preserved foods that are necessitated by the short growing season of the Russian North. Cabbage (sauerkraut) and cucumbers (pickles) are enjoyed greatly, as are a wide range of salted fish, vegetables, and meats. Fish and produce are also frequently dried or brined for lengthy storage. Foraged foods, especially mushrooms, are important to both Russian diet and culture. Although the Russians have never excelled at making hard cheeses, they prepare an expert array of fresh dairy products, such as creamy curd cheese (*tvorog*) and various cultured yogurt-like preparations (*riazhenka, prostokvasha*), in addition to excellent sour cream (*smetana*). Honey is the traditional Russian sweetener and is used as the basis for drinks, fruit preserves, and desserts. Early condiments (known as *vzvar*, from the word "to boil") consisted of onions or beets cooked slowly in honey until rich and sweet.

Russian cuisine is known for its extensive repertoire of soups. The national soup (*shchi*) is made from cabbage, either salted (sauerkraut) or fresh, in which case it is known as "lazy" *shchi*. The beet soup (*borshch*) commonly associated with Russian cuisine is actually native to Ukraine, to the south of Russia; it became popular abroad following Jewish emigration from that region. Soup is traditionally served at the midday meal and is accompanied by an assortment of small pies, croutons, or dumplings. The Russian diet tends to be high in carbohydrates, with a vast array of breads, notably dark sour rye, and grains, especially buckwheat (*grechnevaya kasha*).

The national cuisine is further distinguished by wonderful pies filled with myriad combinations of meat, fish, or vegetables. Prepared in all shapes and sizes, pies are both festive and a practical way to use up leftovers. The most elegant pie is, perhaps, the *kulebyaka*, a multilayered fish pie with thin pancakes (*blinchiki*), kasha, and salmon (including the spinal marrow or *viziga*) that was adopted into French cuisine as *coulibiac*.

Diet of the Early Slavs

Early Slavic agriculture was largely grain based. Hearty crops like rye, oats, barley, buckwheat, spelt, and millet provided the mainstay of the diet, most often in the form of gruel or baked into cakes made of meal sweetened with honey and flavored with berry juice. Although wheat was cultivated in the South, it remained of secondary importance. From the Scythians, a Eurasian tribe that roamed the steppes of southern Russian from the eighth to the fourth centuries B.C.E., the early Slavs learned how to make leavened breads, using primarily sourdough. Grains were supplemented by legumes (*gorokh*), an important source of protein. Freshwater fish and wildfowl, both of which were abundant, provided additional sources of protein. Vegetable and nut oils (especially hempseed and linseed), foraged mushrooms and berries, and orchard fruits such as cherries, pears, plums, and apples supplemented the largely carbohydrate diet. Also critical were cultivated vegetables, including turnips, beets, radishes, onions, garlic, cabbage, and cucumbers. Turnips were an important staple until the widespread (and enforced) cultivation of the potato in the nineteenth century. Given the geographical limitations on agriculture, much of the population lived in a state between hunger and starvation, and up through the twentieth century Russia experienced frequent famines.

The earliest domestic livestock included cows, pigs, sheep, and goats; chicken, ducks, geese; turkey was introduced somewhat later. Butter was traditionally prepared from cow's milk by heating sour cream, rather than by churning it from sweet cream, a method the Russians learned only in the eighteenth century from the Finns.

By the twelfth century the Russians were already boiling down salt from water from the White Sea, but salt remained an expensive commodity that only the wealthy could afford. Even those who could afford salt used it sparingly. A seventeenth-century German visitor Adam Olearius, complained that "in Moscow, they use coarse salt fish, which sometimes stinks because they are thrifty with the salt. Nevertheless, they like to eat it." In general, the affluent had a plentiful assortment of fish, meat, fruits, vegetables, and grains, a diet that contrasted greatly with the meager rations of most of the population, who subsisted on little more than oatmeal gruel (*tolokno*) and rye bread. Although the soil around Moscow and in the south of Russia yielded excellent produce, the growing season was short, and most people did not have access to a variety of foods.

Cooking Methods

Apart from the methods used for preserving food, boiling and baking were the most common ways of preparing foods (frying and grilling were also practiced). By 1600 rich and poor alike were cooking food in the Russ-

ian masonry stove (*pech'*), which was massive enough to take up nearly one-quarter of a peasant cottage. This stove defined the living space, demarcating the female and male spheres of the room into the cooking area (female) to the left of the hearth, and the icon-dominated "beautiful corner" (male) to the right. The earliest stoves had no flue, causing smoke to issue directly into the cottage; more prosperous families replaced these "black" stoves with more refined "white" stoves fitted with chimney pipes. Russian peasants generally believed that the stove held mystical powers, with a house spirit (*domovoi*) residing beneath or behind it.

Food could be prepared in many different ways on the stove—boiled, baked, steamed, roasted, and braised. Many of Russia's most typical dishes reflected the specific properties of the stove, which blazed and was very hot after firing and then gradually diminished in the intensity of its heat. Breads and pies were baked when the oven was still very hot, either right in the fire's ashes or immediately after they had been scraped out. Once the temperature began to fall, grain dishes could cook in the diminishing heat, which ensured that porridges were crusty on top and creamy within. As the oven's heat continued to subside, the stove was ideal for the braised vegetables and slow-cooked stews that represent the best of Russian cooking. Dairy products were cultured in any residual oven heat.

Whether the medieval Russian diet was varied or sparse, the cooking methods for rich and poor were nearly analogous. Although Tsar Peter the Great introduced the cooktop (*plita*) from Holland in the eighteenth century, and metal stoves became common in urban dwellings in the nineteenth century, the Russian stove remained in use in the countryside well into the twentieth century.

Influence of the Russian Orthodox Church

In 988 Grand Prince Vladimir of Kievan Russia adopted Christianity for his people. Many of the existing pagan celebrations, such as those marking the seasonal solstices, were transformed into religious holidays like Christmas and Easter. The Orthodox Church had a profound influence on the Russian diet, dividing the year into feast days (*skoromnyi*) and fast days (*postnyi*). The latter accounted for approximately 180 days of the year. The fast periods largely coincided with times in the agricultural year when food supplies were running low. Most Russians took fasting seriously, strictly following the proscriptions against meat and dairy products. In addition to meatless Wednesdays and Fridays, the Russians also observed extended fasts, the most important of which were the Great Lenten Fast (forty days, plus one week, Passion Week, which precedes Easter), the Christmas or Filippov Fast (the six weeks preceding Christmas), the Fast of Saints Peter and Paul (beginning in late May or June and lasting from one to six weeks, depending on when Easter fell); and the Fast of the Dormition (two weeks in August). On the most stringent fast days (Lent and the Dormition Fast), even fish and vegetable oil were forbidden. Generally, the poorer the household, the more devoutly it fasted, since meat and dairy products were at best scarce even on non–fast days. For the wealthy, fasting did not necessarily mean deprivation. A mid-seventeenth-century state dinner given on a fast day for the English ambassador Carlisle offered no fewer than five hundred dishes, not one of which was made with meat products. Throughout the nineteenth century, cookbooks offered suggestions for both feast day and fast day meals. In addition to recipes for fish and vegetarian dishes, the cookbooks provided information on substituting nut oils and almond milk for dairy products in cooking and baking.

Holidays and Ritual Foods

Numerous feast days compensated for the stringent fasts. Feasts were held in celebration of weddings, funerals, and the name days of saints, which the Russians observed instead of birthdays. Many religious holidays were also considered feast days. Just before the rigorous Lenten fast came Butter Week (*Maslenitsa*), similar to Mardi Gras, except that it lasted a full week. Although no meat was allowed, the Russians consumed excessive amounts of dairy products, most often in the form of blinies. These traditional yeast-raised pancakes, made with buckwheat or wheat flour, are porous enough to soak up plenty of melted butter. Topped with caviar, smoked fish, pickled herring, or sometimes jam, the bliny can be traced back to pagan times, when the early Slavs baked round pancakes in the image of the sun to welcome its return at winter's end.

Easter is the most important holiday in the Russian Orthodox year. Throughout Easter week a table is kept laden with food. The two most traditional foods are *kulich*, a tall loaf of bread enriched with eggs, butter, sugar, and candied fruits, glazed with confectioners' sugar, and often topped with a rose; and *paskha*, fresh farmer's cheese mixed with cream and butter and molded into a pyramid shape. Raisins or nuts are used to decorate it with the letters XB for "Christ is Risen."

Virtually every festive occasion calls for a special bread. Pies, such as an elaborate chicken pie layered with vegetables (*kurnik*), are served at weddings; a sweet, pretzel-shaped loaf (*krendel'*) is traditional for name days; and animal-shaped buns are distributed to Christmas revelers. These buns, as well as the lark-shaped breads baked to celebrate the return of the birds in spring, predate the Christian era. Other breads, such as one baked in the shape of a ladder for the holiday of the Ascension, have Christian roots. *Kut'ia*, which is a dish of wheat berries sweetened with honey and flavored with dried fruits or nuts, is traditionally served at funeral repasts.

The Tradition of Hospitality

The Russian word for hospitality (*khlebosol'stvo*) derives from the words for bread (*khleb*) and salt (*sol'*). Taken together, they mean a regalement with that which is most basic to life, and that which is a luxury. A large, round loaf milled from the finest flour (*karavai*) was traditionally presented as a symbol of hospitality or was offered to newlyweds as a housewarming gift. The loaf often had an indentation in the top crust to hold a small dish of salt. The act of honoring guests lies at the heart of the Russian national identity. As counseled by the *Domostroi*, a sixteenth-century manual that teaches household management and piety, guests are sacred; by receiving them well, you also serve God. One should offer guests are the very best food available. The Russians took this advice to heart: even the poorest households did not turn strangers away.

The sharing of bread was ritualized in the practice of "begging for crusts," which occurred whenever food shortages threatened the peasantry. Unlike simple begging, which was looked down upon, "begging for crusts" was accepted as part of the natural order: each peasant family knew that the situation could be reversed, and next time they might be the ones in need of food after a bad harvest.

In medieval Russia hospitality to foreigners was expressed through the institution of the *podacha*, a ritualized presentation of food. Privileged guests at the tsar's palace were given confectionery items to bring home at the end of each feast; the amount given was determined by the person's rank. Anyone unable to attend the festivities might have the *podacha* delivered to his residence by couriers, who would parade through the streets of Moscow in a display of the tsar's power and largesse.

Today, the hissing *samovar* or tea urn is the acknowledged symbol of Russian hospitality, ready to serve unexpected guests at a moment's notice. However, this tradition is relatively recent, as use of the samovar became widespread only in the second half of the nineteenth century.

Alcohol Consumption

The *Primary Chronicle*, Russia's earliest historical record, relates that Grand Prince Vladimir proclaimed "Drinking is the joy of Rus'" when he chose Christianity over Islam, which forbids the consumption of alcohol. From the earliest times the Russians enjoyed alcoholic beverages, especially mead, a fermented honey wine flavored with berries and herbs; *kvas*, a mildly alcoholic beverage made from fermented bread or grain; *berezovitsa*, lightly fermented birch juice; and beer. Distilled spirits, in the form of vodka, appeared only in the fifteenth century, introduced from Poland and the Baltic region. Vodka was originally used for medicinal purposes, but it gradually displaced the older beverages in popularity, and by the seventeenth century spirits were already causing social problems. Because the high taxes on vodka filled the state coffers, the government was not eager to curtail use of the substance (a few privileged noblemen were given the right to produce vodka, but the government basically had a monopoly on its production). In the late nineteenth century the famous chemist Dmitri Mendeleev set the optimal alcoholic content of vodka at 40 percent spirits diluted with distilled water. Commercial producers capitalized on Mendeleev's pronouncement, and Russia has been known ever since for its excellent vodka.

Tsar Ivan the Terrible established the first taverns (*kabaki*) in the sixteenth century by for the sole benefit of his elite guards. Since then the government has vacillated between strict and lax approaches to vodka consumption, at times encouraging it to build up the state treasury and ease public unrest, at other times curtailing access to the drink. Tsar Peter the Great was known to ply his guests with drink in order to find out what was really going on at court, and he himself engaged in drinking binges that lasted for days at a time. More recently, in the Soviet era, two Communist leaders, Yuri Andropov and Mikhail Gorbachev, attempted to control access to vodka. Their ill-fated attempts caused widespread discontent, as well as severe shortages of sugar, which people purchased in bulk to produce moonshine.

Eastern Influence on Russian Cuisine

In 945 Russia, though still not unified, initiated trade with Constantinople, the seat of the Byzantine Empire. In exchange for honey and furs, the Russians received rice, spices, and wines. In 1237 the Mongols invaded the Russian principalities, and for nearly two hundred years Russia had to pay tribute to the Golden Horde. The occupation was not without culinary benefits. The Mongols reopened the ancient trade routes between China and the West, which had become too dangerous due to frequent tribal wars. Foods introduced along these routes included noodles and cultured milk products such as *koumiss*, the fermented mare's milk drunk by Turkic nomads.

With Russia's conquest of the Volga region in the mid-sixteenth century, the Russians were able to trade for spices like pepper, saffron, cinnamon, and ginger, as well as rhubarb, which became an extremely lucrative export crop. Also from the Volga region came sweet watermelons from Astrakhan, at the mouth of the Volga, and increased access to sturgeon, sterlet, and caviar from the Caspian Sea.

Tsar Ivan IV (the Terrible; 1530–1584) led a series of Eastern campaigns to subjugate the khanates of Kazan, Astrakhan, and Tatar Bashkiria; in 1582 he also annexed Siberia. This eastward expansion introduced the Russians to *pel'meni*, wonton-like pockets of boiled dough filled with ground meat and onions. The Russians serve these dumplings either with vinegar and mustard or with butter and sour cream. Pel'meni are frequently made in large quantities at the beginning of winter and kept frozen outdoors in a bag, ready for boiling into a quick meal. Exotic fresh and dried fruits were also introduced from the East, and raisins and dried apricots have held a prominent place in Russian cuisine ever since.

Tea also arrived in Russia by way of Siberia. As early as 1567 emissaries from Ivan IV had spoken of this strange brew, but it wasn't until 1638 that tea found its way to the royal court. The signing of the Treaty of Nerchinsk in 1689 established regular trade between Russia and China. From then on tea became a valuable commodity, although until the nineteenth century tea drinking was largely confined to Moscow's urban population.

With the expansion of the Russian Empire into the Caucasus and central Asia, beginning in the late eighteenth century and continuing under Soviet rule, dishes from Eastern cuisines entered into the Russian repertoire. From Georgia came grilled meats (*shashlyki*), flattened chicken cooked under a brick (*tabaka*), and herbed kidney beans (*lobio*); from Armenia came flat bread (*lavash*); from Azerbaijan, ground lamb kebabs (*lyulya-kebab*); from Tatar Crimea, fried meat pies (*chebureki*); from Uzbekistan, rice pilaf (*plov*) and dumplings (*manty*); and from Kyrgyzstan, lamb and noodle stew (*lagman*).

The Era of Muscovy

During the era of Muscovy (from the fourteenth to early eighteenth centuries) the disparity between rich and poor became firmly established, resulting in two very different cuisines. The poor ate little more than bread, gruel, and soup made from vegetables and grains. The wealthy, on the other hand, ate so lavishly that foreign visitors like the French envoy Foy de la Neuville, on a 1689 visit, declared them gluttons. Foreigners generally considered the Russians uncivilized, not only due to their prodigious appetites, but also due to the pleasure they so openly expressed from their meals via belching and other bodily sounds.

The wealthy indulged in feasts that lasted for hours. Pickled or salted beef, ham, suckling pig, elk, boar, lamb, and rabbit all appeared on the table. Swan was considered the most luxurious of birds, although the wealthy also enjoyed crane, heron, black grouse, hazel hen, partridge, lark, goose, duck, and chicken. Veal was rarely consumed, and the Russian Orthodox Church forbade eating doves, since the birds symbolized the Holy Spirit. Hot and cold soups, noodle dishes, roasts, and sauces were seasoned with onion, garlic, pepper, saffron, and sometimes savory. The combination of sweet and sour so typical of medieval foods throughout Europe was especially compatible with Russian tastes. Rich, dark swan meat was often served with vinegar or a combination of sour milk, pickles, and prunes.

The tsar's table was furnished year-round with fish from distant waters, transported whole or in pieces, fresh or salted, or brined in barrels. Sturgeon and sterlet were brought live in tanks from the Caspian Sea to Moscow; whitefish came from Lake Ladoga; and several varieties of salmon were sent overland from the Kolsk Peninsula in the far North. Pike, bream, perch, pike-perch, and many other sorts of excellent fish were caught in the rivers and ponds around Moscow.

CAVIAR

The Russians were the first to develop a caviar industry based on the several varieties of sturgeon that they fished, and the world's best caviar still comes from the Caspian Sea. The thirteenth-century court of Grand Prince Yaroslav of Novgorod had a special sturgeon master to oversee the procurement, preparation, and serving of sturgeon. The roe was particularly relished. (Although Russians consider sturgeon roe the finest, they also enjoy the eggs from such fish as burbot, white salmon, pike, carp, and grayling, although technically this roe is not considered caviar.)

Making caviar is extremely labor-intensive, as the fish eggs are both fragile and perishable. The roe must be extracted by hand, then kept cold during processing (generally at 28°–32°F [−2°–0°C]) to keep it fresh. Salt is added to lower the temperature at which the eggs will freeze, as well as to help preserve them. The best fresh caviar, which contains roughly 4 percent salt, is known as *malosol* ("little salt" in Russian). Today, for exports to Europe, the Russians also add a small amount of borax to the roe, which works as a preservative and reduces the need for salt. Borax gives the eggs a slightly sweeter taste and makes them a bit oilier. Russia omits the borax for caviar imported into the United States, which prohibits the sale of borax-treated eggs.

The flavor and quality of caviar depend on the type of sturgeon it is taken from. The most common types, in decreasing order of size, are beluga, osetra, and sevruga. Beluga sturgeon can weigh over two thousand pounds; its roe is a pearly gray and has a very subtle flavor. Many Russians prefer the strong flavor of *payusnaya* or pressed caviar, made from eggs that have been broken in processing or from very mature eggs pressed into a concentrate the consistency of thick jam.

Caviar was standard fare for the wealthy on the numerous fast days dictated by the Russian Orthodox Church, when meat and dairy products were proscribed. Medieval Russians often left the roe in the egg sac. They seasoned it with salt and pepper, then dusted it with flour and fried it, serving an onion, cranberry, or saffron sauce on the side. Sometimes they offered the cooked caviar cold, cut into slices and flavored with an herb vinegar or mustard sauce. For the Muscovite dish *kal'ia*, pressed caviar was cut into thin rounds, then placed in an earthenware pot with chopped onion, pepper, pickles, pickle brine, and water. This mixture was steamed in the Russian stove, with additional pepper added upon serving. Nineteenth-century culinary fashion called for slicing pressed caviar and serving it in a napkin as "serviette caviar." Elena Molokhovets, Russia's Mrs. Beeton, suggested a more practical use for pressed caviar. In her classic cookbook, *A Gift to Young Housewives*, she explains how to clarify bouillon with pressed caviar, using one-quarter pound of the caviar in place of two egg whites.

By the mid-nineteenth century the finest sturgeon caviar had become rare enough that it was generally served unadorned. Astrakhan caviar, with its large, gray grains, was considered the ultimate roe. It was served on toast points or mounded in a pyramid and decorated with lemon wedges with croutons on the side. Late-nineteenth-century cookbooks sometimes cautioned against buying caviar with a greenish tinge, which was caused by treatment with a dye containing copper salts.

All varieties of sturgeon are endangered, due to environmental pollution and poaching (there is a thriving black market in caviar in southern Russia). The political and economic chaos that afflicted Russia after the collapse of the Soviet Union caused many foreign purveyors to turn to Iran for the highest quality caviar. Now, in order to keep up with world demand for the roe, scientists are experimenting with farm-raised sturgeon, particularly in the Caspian waters belonging to Kazakhstan.

Eighteenth-Century Reforms

The reforms carried out by Peter I (the Great; 1672–1725) affected virtually every aspect of Russian life. Upper-class women, who had previously lived in seclusion, were allowed into male company and could eat at the same table as men. Peter introduced napkins from Holland (until his reign, tables had been covered with short cloths, the edges of which were used to wipe the hands and mouth while eating). Since large joints of meat were carved and served in small pieces at table, several people would generally share forks and knives among them, but Peter encouraged the use of individual two-pronged forks.

In the kitchen, the most significant development for Russian cuisine was the introduction of the Dutch range, which, contrary to the traditional Russian stove, relied on a cooktop more than on oven chambers. This change necessitated more labor-intensive cooking methods as well as new utensils. Saucepans, for instance, replaced the customary earthenware pots.

Peter was eager to acquaint Russians with new foodstuffs and culinary methods that he had learned on his extensive travels. From Holland he imported not only hothouse vegetables and fruits (pineapples became a particular Russian passion), but also aged cheeses, which the

Russians did not know how to make. He sought grape varietals that could thrive in southern Russia and placed the two-centuries-old Astrakhan winery under the supervision of a French vintner to increase its quality and production.

In 1712 the imperial court moved from Moscow to Saint Petersburg. The design of the commercial center (*Gostinyi dvor*) incorporated a canal right in the building so that boats could unload their wares on site. Petersburg's significant foreign population influenced the city's eating habits, and foods such as waffles and artichokes found welcome reception. Furthermore, the young Russian men whom Peter had sent abroad to further their education returned with new tastes. Seeking more variety in their diet, they began to import exotic foods. When Peter hired a Saxon as his private chef, the nobility soon followed suit. Thus Russia's first foreign chefs came primarily from Saxony, Bavaria, and Austria.

Because the founding of Saint Petersburg had caused trade to decline at the far northern port of Archangel on the White Sea, in 1721 Peter issued an *ukaze* ordering his people to eat ocean fish. Previously the Russians had used only freshwater fish from rivers and lakes, and many were suspicious of such strange species as cod, whiting, and mackerel.

French Influence on Russian Cuisine

The culinary changes wrought during Peter's thirty-six-year reign were so great that by the time his daughter Elizabeth seized the throne in 1741, lemons and oranges were no longer a luxury, and English beer was in greater vogue than traditional Russian brews. As the century progressed, more and more European influences came to bear on traditional Russian methods. The vocabulary introduced into Russian over the course of the eighteenth century reveals influences from the Dutch, German, English, and ultimately French cuisines. By the close of the eighteenth century, food in the homes of the wealthy was unabashedly French, and Russia's most affluent families employed French chefs, whose style supplanted the Germanic influences of Peter's era.

With so much foreign influence, Russian cuisine lost its simple national character and became increasingly complex. By the end of century, meat was cut into small pieces that demanded complicated handling, as opposed to the large joints of meat that had been roasted or braised in the great Russian stove, or grilled on a spit. As the nineteenth century drew near, many French dining habits were firmly entrenched in Russia, although sometimes with a Russian twist. One practice that came into vogue among the aristocracy was the open table, at which any nobleman, invited or not, was welcome to dine. The conservative prince Mikhail Shcherbatov, in his treatise *On the Corruption of Morals in Russia*, complained that the nobility's excessive socializing at table led to moral deterioration. He was troubled that the nobility gave so little thought to the relationship between the food served and the religious obligations underlying it. Even so, Peter the Great's reforms and the subsequent refinements to the table broadened and polished Russian cuisine. Adapting western trends to their own needs and tastes, the Russians ultimately made their table quite sophisticated.

Table Service and Meal Times

The Russian peasantry ate their meager fare from a communal bowl, with each individual wielding his or her own spoon. The wealthy, however, sat down to a vastly different table, which was also distinct from its European counterparts. By the seventeenth century society meals throughout Europe were served in the style known as *service à la française*, which meant that for each course, all of the foods were set out on the table, ranked according to size and symmetrically arranged. The Russians ate in a manner that came to be known as *service à la russe* (it eventually replaced the French style of service in Europe in the late nineteenth century). Here the table was not previously laid with the foods for each course. Instead, each dish was brought individually to the table and presented with fanfare before being removed to the kitchen or sideboard for carving. Each diner received a portioned serving, which ensured that the food was still hot and at the peak of freshness. Furthermore, diners were not limited to the foods located within reach. The drawback of service *à la russe* was that it entailed a large and well-trained staff.

Under Peter the Great, the multicourse banquets typical of the Muscovite era began to evolve into the sequence of four courses that is familiar today. Peter's war with Sweden and his travels in Holland resulted in the introduction of the lavish *zakuska* (hors d'oeuvres) table that has become the hallmark of Russian cuisine. Adapted from the Swedish smorgasbord, an array of salted and smoked foods, including caviar, salmon, sturgeon, herring, pickles, and ham, is offered before the main course. Open-faced sandwiches with meat or cheese reflect a direct borrowing from Dutch practice. After the *zakuski*, soup is served, then a main course, followed by dessert.

Meal times were rather flexible. The wealthy, having no immediate tasks to attend to, often slept late and did not have breakfast until mid-morning. The main meal of the day (*obed*) took place at around 2:00 P.M., followed by a late-afternoon collation or tea, then supper between 8:00 and 10:00 P.M. Peasant families had more structured mealtimes. Breakfast (*zavtrak*) was typically eaten at 5:00 or 6:00 A.M., followed by the so-called second breakfast (*vtoroi zavtrak*) at around 10:00 A.M., providing a break from the day's labors. Dinner was eaten any time between 12:00 and 2:00 P.M., with a midday snack (*poldnik*) at 4:00 or 5:00 P.M. Supper (*uzhin*) was generally served at 8:00 P.M., and, after tea drinking became an established custom in the late nineteenth century, tea (*chai*) often followed. For those who could afford a variety of foods, the Russian breakfast was a hearty affair, complete with porridge (often buckwheat or semolina), smoked or pickled fish, and eggs or pancakes. The main meal of the day was still not considered complete without a soup course before the entrée.

Revolutionary Changes

The indulgent lifestyle of the aristocracy and gentry came to an abrupt end with the Revolution of 1917 and the subsequent establishment of the Soviet Union. The new Bolshevik government undertook a radical transformation of social life, promoting as one of their platforms the liberation of women from kitchen drudgery. To this end, vast communal dining facilities ("factory kitchens") were set up. However, because the food was bad, and most families did not like the impersonal cafeteria style of these facilities, the experiment ultimately failed. What did take hold, however, were communal kitchens in urban houses that had been requisitioned by the government. The great influx of people into the cities following the Revolution of 1917 caused a housing shortage that led to the creation of communal apartments, with sometimes as many as a dozen families sharing a kitchen. Communal kitchens, some of which still exist, contributed to the disintegration of family life and created social tensions.

The political and economic turmoil of the Civil War (1917–1922), coupled with drought in the Volga region, caused a severe famine between 1921 and 1922, in which nearly half a million people died. But this loss of life is small in comparison to the many millions who perished during Joseph Stalin's enforced collectivization of agriculture, which he carried out between 1929 and 1934, especially in Ukraine. Under this policy, private farms were destroyed and agriculture organized into state-run collective farms (*kolkhozy*). Collectivization proved disastrous for Soviet agriculture, as it was inefficient and discouraged personal initiative. The Soviet Union was forced to import much of its grain from the United States and Canada and frequently suffered from food deficits.

The Soviet Era

The Soviet Union was never a fully egalitarian society. Most of the populace subsisted on a monotonous diet of poor-quality food, but the government and cultural elite had access to special stores and goods, so they were able to eat well. Although the government ensured that no one went hungry (all factory workers, for instance, received a free lunch at state expense), the average diet was not especially nutritious, as it was low in fresh fruits and vegetables.

The Soviet period was marked by extraordinary hardship. Following collectivization and the political purges of the late 1930s, the Russians endured World War II, also known as the Great Patriotic War. During the Siege of Leningrad (1941–1944), which lasted for nearly nine hundred days, roughly one million people died of starvation. At the most critical point in the siege, the bread ration for factory workers was only 250 grams (8.8 ounces) a day, 125 grams (4.4 ounces) for all others,

with no other food available. Leningraders resorted to eating whatever they could scavenge from the city or find in their apartments, including tooth powder, Vaseline, glycerine, cologne, wallpaper paste scraped from the walls, flour dust collected from cracks in the kitchen floorboards, and spattered grease that was licked from the kitchen walls.

Although life stabilized after the war, the Soviet era was generally characterized by a low standard of living. Shopping was especially difficult, with long lines even for basic foodstuffs. There was very little variety. When so-called deficit items did suddenly appear, shoppers had to stand in line for hours. The vocabulary reflected this reality: products were "obtained" (*dostat'*) rather than "bought" (*kupit'*). Because of the hierarchy of food distribution, country dwellers flooded daily into Moscow, increasing the crowds and further limiting availability.

The state food stores had very little to offer, but decent foodstuffs could be purchased at the farmers' markets, where entrepreneurs from Georgia, Armenia, and central Asia sold lemons, melons, and high-quality meat and produce, often at steep prices. To survive, most Soviet citizens became adept at working the unofficial barter economy, and they knew how to take advantage of the black market. Restaurants were few; those that existed frequently offered only one item from their menu and subjected diners to surly service. Therefore most Russians ate at home. The Soviet-era kitchen table became the site of the most important social interactions, where information was exchanged, poetry recited, politics argued, friendships expressed. Despite the food shortages, the difficulty of shopping, and the cramped living space, Russians still took pride in being generous toward their guests, and the tradition of hospitality endured.

Post-Soviet Russia

The Soviet Union was officially disbanded at the end of 1991. The following year saw the introduction of stringent market reforms, which brought economic hardship to the general population. With a safety net no longer in place, beggars appeared on the streets. The countryside, in particular, suffered from insufficient food. Russia's economic problems were exacerbated by the crash of 1998, when the ruble lost two-thirds of its value. Still, the Russians are a resourceful people, and in the early twenty-first century the economy was back on its feet.

The collapse of the Soviet state initially brought a rash of investors to Russia, and numerous fast-food chains, such as McDonald's, gained a foothold. In response to so many Western imports, a feeling of national pride gradually emerged, and domestic chains like Russkoye Bistro began to compete with the foreign establishments. Homegrown products again appeared on the market when the economic turmoil of the 1990s caused many foreign firms to leave. Once the economy stabilized, many restaurants opened that offered expensive and elegant pre-Revolutionary fare, nostalgic country-style cooking, and ethnic cuisine. After seventy years of isolation under Soviet rule, the populace was eager to experiment with new tastes.

With the appearance of self-service grocery stores, shopping was simplified, and it was no longer necessary to stand in line for food. However, one might question whether shrink-wrapped tomatoes imported from the Canary Islands represent progress when locally grown produce can be bought at the market or at curbside kiosks. The slick grocery stores with their aisles of imported goods and the expensive restaurants were status symbols for the wealthy class of New Russians who had money to spare: the majority could not afford them. These New Russians also bought food magazines (unheard of during the Soviet era) and cookbooks: both the French Cordon Bleu cooking course and the *Hare Krishna Book of Vegetarian Cooking* were translated into Russian. Young Russians became increasingly aware of diet and nutrition, the down side being that eating disorders began to appear.

Meanwhile, average Russians could only admire the glossy publications and the wide variety of foods, which were beyond their means. Police in a number of cities have had to put Operation Harvest into effect to protect the potato fields—which were now private property—from hungry poachers. Significantly, the consumerism of the moneyed class was balanced by a return to spiritual values, as many Russians once again expressed their identity through the foods they choose either to eat or forego.

See also **Asia, Central; Central Europe; Christianity: Eastern Orthodox Christianity; Food as a Weapon of War; France; Siberia.**

BIBLIOGRAPHY

Baron, Samuel H., ed. and trans. *The Travels of Olearius in Seventeenth-Century Russia.* Stanford, Calif.: Stanford University Press, 1967.

Chamberlain, Lesley. *The Food and Cooking of Russia.* London: Allen Lane, 1982.

de la Neuville, Foy. *A Curious and New Account of Muscovy in the Year 1689.* Edited and introduced by Lindsey Hughes. Translated from the French by J. A. Cutshall. London: School of Slavonic and East European Studies, University of London, 1994.

Glants, Musya, and Joyce Toomre, eds. *Food in Russian History and Culture.* Bloomington, Ind.: Indiana University Press, 1997.

Goldstein, Darra. *A Taste of Russia: A Cookbook of Russian Hospitality*, 2d ed. Montpelier, Vt.: Russian Life Books, 1999.

Goldstein, Darra. "Gastronomic Reforms under Peter the Great: Towards a Cultural History of Russian Food." *Jahrbücher für Geschichte Osteuropas* 48 (2000): 481–510.

Herlihy, Patricia. *The Alcoholic Empire: Vodka and Politics in Late Imperial Russia.* New York: Oxford University Press, 2002.

Kliuchevskii, V. O. *Istoriia russkogo byta: Chteniia v shkole i doma* [History of Russian daily life: Readings at school and at home]. Moscow, 1867. Reprint, Moscow: Vash Vybor TsIRZ, 1995.

Kovalev, V. M. and N. P. Mogil'nyi. *Russkaia kukhnia: Traditsii i obychai* [Russian cuisine: Traditions and customs]. Moscow: Sovetskaia Rossiia, 1990.

Kostomarov, N. I. *Domashniaia zhizn' i nravy velikorusskogo naroda: utvar', odezhda, pishcha i pit'e, zdorov'e i bolezni, nravy, obriady, priem gostei* [Domestic life and morals of the great Russians...]. Moscow, 1887. Reprint, Moscow, 1993.

Lotman, Iu. M., and E. A. Pogosian. *Velikosvetskie obedy* [High Society Dinners]. St. Petersburg: Pushkinskii fond, 1996.

Petit, Alphonse. *La Gastronomie en Russie.* Paris: Chez l'Auteur, 1860.

Pokhlebkin, V. V. *Natsional'nye kukhni nashikh narodov* [National cuisines of our peoples]. Moscow: Pishchevaia Promyshlennost', 1978.

Pouncy, Carolyn, ed. and trans. *The "Domostroi": Rules for Russian Households in the Time of Ivan the Terrible.* Ithaca, N.Y.: Cornell University Press, 1994.

Pryzhov, I. T. *Istoriia kabakov v Rossii v sviazi s istoriei russkago naroda* [History of taverns in Russia in connection with the history of the Russian people]. 1863. Reprint, Moscow: Book Chamber International, 1991.

Smith, R. E. F., and David Christian. *Bread and Salt: A Social and Economic History of Food and Drink in Russia.* Cambridge: Cambridge University Press, 1984.

Tereshchenko, A. V. *Byt russkogo naroda* [Daily life of the Russian people]. Vol. 3. Sankt-Peterburg: Ministerstvo vnutrennykh del, 1848.

Toomre, Joyce, trans. and introduction. *Classic Russian Cooking: Elena Molokhovets' A Gift to Young Housewives.* Bloomington, Ind.: Indiana University Press, 1992.

Wasson, Valentina Pavlovna, and R. Gordon Wasson. *Mushrooms, Russia and History.* New York: Pantheon Books, 1957.

Darra Goldstein

RYE. *See* **Cereal Grains and Pseudo-Cereals.**

S

SACRIFICE. Sacrifice is the ritualistic and reverential slaughter, cooking, and distribution of meat. Conventional accounts of sacrifice stress the colorful and religious aspects of slaying an animal for the benefit of the participants' relationships with the gods. This understanding leads to the generalized use of the word "sacrifice" to mean giving up something—including other foods—in anticipation of more valuable rewards.

From the viewpoint of a cultural outsider, sacrifice may seem a brutal or incomprehensible practice. Yet historically, sacrifice has been a common practice in many tribal and agrarian societies, as have food offerings, in a more general sense. Sacrifices serve various functions: the ancient Chinese text *Li chi* describes ceremonies that summon spirits from above to restore social harmony. Maintaining environmental balance is also a common sacrificial motive. Sacrifices are important in the doctrines of Hindus, Jews, Christians, and Muslims: they enable participants to share a table with their deity, give thanks, atone for sins, or appease angry forces. For example, Muslims believe that the animal slaughtered at the Id al-Adha (Festival of Sacrifice) at the conclusion of their pilgrimage to Mecca will carry them to Paradise.

Social scientists have explained that dramatic rituals encourage group solidarity. The act of coming together to present gifts helps to bind members of a group together as well as any blood oath can. According to Scottish anthropologist W. Robertson Smith in *The Religion of the Semites* (1889), sacrifice originated in a meal shared between people and their god. French sociologist Émile Durkheim and his associates asserted that sacrifice constantly renews group consciousness of the sacred and that the all-powerful god which society worships is itself.

Ceremony promotes social cohesion, but such theories are incomplete because they do not explain why cohesion important in the first place. As stated earlier, the underlying action of a sacrifice is the coming together for the slaughter and distribution of meat. This core social action is elaborated on cultural and religious levels. The animal is not lost but is allocated to the group according to precise rules. In groups that perform sacrifices, animals are valuable enough food to warrant special attention, typically at a festival, and often the animals are large enough to warrant wider dispersal than within an immediate household. This dispersal typically takes place at some central place such as a temple.

Early Jewish celebrations of Passover traditionally required the sacrifice of one lamb for each household or for distribution among several small households; the lamb was then eaten with unleavened bread and bitter herbs (Exodus 12:1–28). This ritual is a seasonal festival that, on one level, recalls the nomadic origins of the Hebrews, who would annually gather to celebrate increased flocks. On another level, however, Passover recalls the escape from Egypt after Moses had cursed the Egyptians to suffer the death of their first-born males. To avoid this curse, the Hebrews placed on their door posts a sign made from the blood of sacrificial lambs.

Gods have traditionally played key roles in food distribution. Each temple-state in ancient Mesopotamia had its own deities who lived in the ziggurat and who were fed offerings from the surrounding farms. This tribute not only supported the temple bureaucracy and artisans but also fed the poor of the region. In other places, this type of food redistribution also took place in kingdoms that were under the leadership of warrior rulers. For example, the ancient leader King Solomon oversaw the apportioning of 22,000 oxen and 120,000 sheep at the dedication of his temple. These sacrifices served as a vast round of public meals, which were shared by "all Israel . . . a great assembly" from distant places. These meals also lasted for quite some time, as Solomon dismissed the crowd on the eighth day (1 Kings 8:62–66).

The role of the *mageiros* in ancient Greece also illustrates the social centrality of sacrifice. This same word was used for priest, cook, and butcher (which might bewilder the modern mind). Nevertheless, the common link among these individuals was that each of them was responsible for the cutting up of meat, the priest wielding his cleaver (or *machaira*) ritualistically, the butcher commercially, and the cook artistically.

Aztec priests gained notoriety for sacrificing human victims. In *The Sacred Cow and Abominable Pig*, the anthropologist Marvin Harris argues that such "warfare cannibalism" occurs when captives have greater value as meat than as slaves (pp. 199—234). Yet many claims of human sacrifice are often suspect, as they can be misrepresentations of others as "less civilized." For example, some people in the ancient world mistook Christians for cannibals because they spoke of their savior as a sacrificial lamb and of their eucharistic bread and wine as his flesh and blood.

Because the acquisition and distribution of meat are so fundamental in society, they have been surrounded by many different relationships, rituals, and meanings. The allocation can become so formalized, the portion of food "lost" to the gods so large, and sacramental feelings so profound that the process may no longer resemble sharing. In addition, many accounts have overemphasized religious meanings at the expense of focusing on the sacrificial process of cooking offerings. However, a gastronomic interpretation of sacrifices need not diminish the importance of the ties among people, natural forces, and gods that sacrifices represent. On the contrary, taking the sharing of food under serious consideration arguably grounds the religious aspects of sacrifice and increases their relevance.

In much of the world, the act of slaughtering meat has been removed from plain view to the city outskirts. It has shifted from the butcher's shop to behind a supermarket wall. The final carving of joints now tends to be kept to the kitchen, and the image of cattle is separate from that of hamburgers. Greater sympathy with ceremonial sacrifice may help reconnect meat-eaters with their metabolic universe. A keener sense of the sacred when eating meat might help counterbalance tendencies toward instant gratification, conspicuous consumption, viewing animals as commodities, and the increasingly unbalanced distribution of the world's resources. If animal-devouring gourmets do not entirely embrace such religious impulses as atonement, propitiation, divine commensalism, and thanksgiving, they might nevertheless remember that to "immolate"—from the Latin for 'sacrifice'—is to sprinkle with a condiment.

Arguing for a more materialist reverence that brings the sacred back into the kitchen, Episcopal priest Robert Farrar Capon advises cooks to remember that they inhabit "bloody ground and holy ground at once." In his recipe book and "culinary reflection," *The Supper of the Lamb*, he confronts the dilemma of the "bloody, unobliging reciprocity in which life lives by death, but still insists that death is robbery" (pp. 45–52).

See also **Anthropology and Food; Aversion to Food; Christianity; Disgust; Fasting and Abstinence; Feasts, Festivals, and Fasts; Hinduism; Islam; Judaism; Meat; Pig; Religion and Food; Sheep; Sin and Food; Taboos.**

BIBLIOGRAPHY

Capon, Robert Farrar. *The Supper of the Lamb: A Culinary Reflection.* Garden City, N.Y.: Doubleday, 1969.

Detienne, Marcel, and Jean-Pierre Vernant. *The Cuisine of Sacrifice among the Greeks.* Chicago: University of Chicago Press, 1989.

Harris, Marvin. *The Sacred Cow and the Abominable Pig: Riddles of Food and Culture.* New York: Touchstone, 1987. Originally entitled *Good to Eat*, 1985.

Symons, Michael. "Cutting Up Cultures." *Journal of Historical Sociology* 15, no. 4 (December 2002).

Symons, Michael. "The Kitchen of the Gods." *Australian Religion Studies Review* 11, no. 2 (Spring 1998): 114–125.

Michael Symons

SAFFRON. *See* **Herbs and Spices.**

SALAD. Although the ancient Greeks and Romans did not use the word "salad," they enjoyed a variety of dishes with raw vegetables dressed with vinegar, oil, and herbs. Pliny the Elder in *Natural History*, for instance, reported that salads (*acetaria*) were composed of those garden products that "needed no fire for cooking and saved fuel, and which were a resource to store and always ready" (*Natural History*, XIX, 58). They were easy to digest and were not calculated to overload the senses or stimulate the appetite.

The medical practitioners Hippocrates and Galen believed that raw vegetables easily slipped through the system and did not create obstructions for what followed, therefore they should be served first. Others reported that the vinegar in the dressing destroyed the taste of the wine, therefore they should be served last. This debate has continued ever since.

The cookery writer Marcus Apicius of the first century C.E. offered several salad recipes, some of which were unusual. His recipe for "bread salad" covers the bottom of a large salad bowl with bread, then adds layers of sliced chicken, more bread, sweetbreads, shredded cheese, pine nuts or almonds, cucumber slices, finely chopped onions, then finishes with another layer of bread. A dressing made of celery seed, pennyroyal, mint, ginger, coriander, raisins, honey, vinegar, olive oil, and white wine is poured over the salad. Another dressing Apicius used on lettuce was a cheese sauce that included pepper, lovage, dried mint, pine nuts, raisins, dates, sweet cheese, honey, vinegar, *garum* (fish sauce), oil, wine, and other ingredients. Other Roman salads were similar to present-day ones, such as lettuce and cucumbers or raw endive dressed with *garum*, olive oil, chopped onion, and vinegar or a dressing of honey, vinegar, and olive oil. Roman salad dressings eventually became more complex. Apicius gave a recipe for one containing ginger, rue, dates, pepper, honey, cumin, and vinegar. With the fall of Rome, salads were less important in western Europe, although raw vegetables and fruit were eaten on fast days and as medicinal correctives.

Many medical professionals did not approve of fresh fruits and uncooked vegetables. Both were considered "cold" in the humoral system of medicine. To counter this coldness, salads were seasoned with salt and olive oil, which were thought to be "hot," thus counteracting the coldness of the raw fruits and vegetables. However, this health concern continued into the nineteenth century.

The Emergence of *Salade*

The term *salade* derived from the Vulgar Roman *herba salata*, literally 'salted herb'. It remained a feature of Byzantine cookery and reentered the European menu via medieval Spain and Renaissance Italy. At first "salad" referred to various kinds of greens pickled in vinegar or salt. The word *salade* later referred to fresh-cooked greens or raw vegetables prepared in the Roman manner.

Under the category of herbs and vegetables, Platina's *De Honesta Voluptate et Valetudine* (1470) included salads, such as raw lettuce seasoned with a vinaigrette composed of olive oil, vinegar, and salt; boiled endive, borage, or bugloss with a vinaigrette seasoned with calamint and mint parsley; purslane with a vinaigrette seasoned with onions; boiled mallow placed in a dish like asparagus and seasoned with a vinaigrette; pimpernel seasoned with a vinaigrette; sorrel served as a first course with bread seasoned with a vinaigrette; and asparagus served in wine. Platina also offered a salad (*pantodapum*) composed of lettuce, borage, mint, calamint, fennel, parsley, wild thyme, marjoram, chervil, sow-thistle, and other herbs seasoned with a vinaigrette and served in a large dish. Common Italian salads of the twenty-first century include *insalata condita*, a green salad; *insalata caprese*, composed of sliced tomato and mozzarella with fresh basil dressed with olive oil; *insalata russa*, composed of cooked vegetables; and *insalata di mare*, a seafood salad.

French *Salade*

The French cookery manuscript *La Viandier* from the fourteenth century includes a recipe titled *"Poree de Cresson,"* a leek stew, which mutated into a vegetable stew of a soupy consistency. *La Viandier* recommends serving boiled watercress and chard with oil, cheese, meat broth, and salt. In the following century the French sprinkled raw vegetables with oil and vinegar in the Roman manner. François Rabelais (1490–1553) mentioned a long list of *salades*, including ones with cress, hops, wild cress, asparagus, and chervil. In the next century Louis XIV (1638–1715) had a weakness for salads. According to the French culinary historian Maguelonne Toussaint-Samat, in *History of Food* (1992), Louis XIV "ate a prodigious quantity of salad all the year round." Hygienic precepts of the time held that salads were "moistening and refreshing, liberate the stomach, promote sleep and appetite, temper the ardors of Venus and quench the thirst" (Toussaint-Samat, 1992, pp. 695–696).

Prejudice against raw vegetables and fruit continued, and green salads were not commonly served on the tables of the upper class until the late eighteenth century. Jean-Anthelme Brillat-Savarin, in *The Physiology of Taste* (1986) felt obliged to recommend salads "to all who have

Modern restaurant salads have evolved into studies in the deliberate arrangement of raw plants of different colors and textures. Since the food must be arranged by hand, some food critics have decried this as unnecessary and overly fussy, yet the eye appeal cannot be denied. © Aaron Rezney/CORBIS.

confidence in me: salad refreshes without weakening, and comforts without irritating; and I have a habit of saying that it makes me younger."

Common French salads include *salades simples*, plain salad composed of raw salads and cooked salads composed of vegetables; *salade andalouse*, cooked rice seasoned with vinegar, salt, and paprika; *salade de légumes*, a vegetable salad seasoned with oil, vinegar, salt, and pepper; *Rossini salade*, truffles dressed with vinegar, lemon juice, salt, and pepper; *salade parisienne*, vegetable salad with lobster or crayfish and truffles dressed with mayonnaise; and *salade Niçoise*, composed of diced potatoes, hard-boiled eggs, French beans, olives, capers, tomatoes, and anchovies dressed with olive oil, vinegar, salt, and pepper. French salads are frequently seasoned with a vinaigrette of oil, vinegar, mustard, salt, and pepper. Anchovies, cream, bacon fat, garlic, lemon juice, egg yolks, paprika, and tomato juice are sometimes added to the vinaigrette.

English *Salet* or Salad

In the late fourteenth century the English *salade* or *salet* (also *sallet*) was frequently composed of leafy vegetables served as an accompaniment to cooked meats or poultry. *The Forme of Cury* (c. 1390) includes a recipe that calls for parsley, sage, garlic, chives, onions, leeks, borage, mint, cress, fennel, rue, rosemary, and purslane. Other

The construction of the perfect salad was done with great flourish in the nineteenth century; aside from carving meat, it was one of the few food preparation activities allowed to men at table. This much-copied image first appeared in *Salad for the Social* (New York, 1856) by American essayist Frederick Saunders (1807–1902). ROUGHWOOD COLLECTION.

salad recipes included flowers, and later fruits, such as oranges and lemons, were added at least in a decorative role. John Gerard's *Herball* (1597) offered many serving suggestions. As new vegetables, such as sweet potatoes from the Caribbean and red beets from Europe, entered England, they were added to the list of salad ingredients. At first salads were simple compositions, such as sliced lemons with sugar. But these became increasingly complex and could be assembled from many herbs, fruits, nuts, spices, and flowers. In the late seventeenth century the grand *sallet* had multiple ingredients, including borage, capers, carrots, cowslips, currants, marigold, primrose, purslane, violets, and sugar and were dressed with oil and vinegar.

John Evelyn's *Acetaria* (1699; 1982) was the first salad book published in the English language. Evelyn defined *sallet* as "a particular Composition of certain *Crude* and fresh herbs, such as usually are, or may safely be eaten with some *Acetous* Juice, Oyl, Salt, &c. to give them a grateful Gust and Vehicle." He included roots, stalks, leaves, and flower buds but excluded fruit, although the juice and the grated rind of oranges and lemons were listed among the herbs. Evelyn's salads have no meat. His recipe for salad dressing says, "Take of clear, and perfectly good *Oyl-Olive*, three Parts; of sharpest *Vinegar* . . . *Limon*, or Juice of *Orange*, one Part; and therein let steep some Slices of *Horse-Radish*, with a little *Salt*" (Evelyn, 1982, pp. 121–122). But Evelyn banned garlic, although he admitted that Spaniards and Italians used it "with almost everything."

By the early nineteenth century the art of salad making in the French style had been introduced to England by émigrés who fled to London during the French Revolution. By the mid-nineteenth century salads and their dressings were taken seriously in England. Mrs. Beeton's *Book of Household Management* (1859–1860) includes the first known recipe titled "fruit salad."

American Salad

Americans had little interest in green salads and most other salads before the Civil War. Some exceptions did exist. German immigrants brought with them hot potato salad, usually made with bacon, onion, and vinegar. The Shakers made fruit salads, which might not include any greens at all. The medical establishment considered raw fruits and vegetables unhealthy and the cause of illness. However, by the mid-nineteenth century the medical profession reversed its earlier opposition to eating raw fruits and vegetables and promoted salads as healthful. Poultry and cooked vegetable salads occasionally graced the American table.

During the 1880s salads joined the culinary experiences of all Americans. The first known American cookbook solely dedicated to salad making was Emma Ewing's *Salad and Salad Making* (1883). At that time molded salads, composed with gelatin or aspic and sugar or sweet fruits, were invented. Salads included such greens as watercress, dandelions, sorrel, chicory, escarole, chives, kohlrabi, and celeriac. Although tomatoes had been used as or in salads for decades, the ubiquitous lettuce and tomato salad first appeared in the United States in the late nineteenth century, when it became one of the more common salads in cookbooks. It was popularized by Fannie Merritt Farmer's *Boston Cooking School Cook Book* (1896). Another common dish was the perfection salad, which was composed of shredded cabbage, diced celery, minced onions, canned pimento, and chopped olives held together with gelatin, vinegar, lemon juice, sugar, and Worcestershire sauce.

European-style salads were served to the upper class in restaurants in large cities. In New York, for instance, Delmonico's Restaurant specialized in the then novel green salads dressed with vinegar and olive oil. Oscar Tschirky, initially a chef with Delmonico's, moved to the Waldorf Astoria, where he invented the Waldorf salad, a combination of lettuce, apple, and celery dressed with mayonnaise. Walnuts were added in the 1920s. The salads were popular, but the salad dressings were also. The New York restaurateur George Rector noted in *À la Rectors* (1933) that a new salad dressing could become "the talk of the town" and could attract customers away from other restaurants. By the end of the century, salads had found a place in many middle-class homes and restaurants. In *The American Salad Book* (1899) Maximilian De Loup reported that Americans preferred them to "heavy bulky materials," and he believed green salads were the wave of the future.

Beginning in the late nineteenth century, salads were promoted by manufacturers of salad dressings and oils.

Until the passage of the Pure Food and Drug Act in 1906, vinegar and olive oil were frequently adulterated with acetic acid and cottonseed, peanut, rapeseed, and poppy seed oils. To promote their products in the twentieth century, companies composed booklets of recipes for salads dressed with commercial dressings. Early commercial manufacturers of salad dressings included Best Foods, E. R. Durkee & Company, R. T. French Company, H. J. Heinz Company, Richard Hellman, Jell-O Company, Kraft-Phoenix Cheese Corporation, and Tildesley & Company, and those manufacturing oil included Mazola and Wesson Oil. By the 1920s, bottled mayonnaise and salad dressings were commonly used in households across the United States.

Salads flourished where the raw ingredients were easily available, particularly in Florida and California. Francis Harris's *Florida Salads* (1914) was revised and reprinted several times during the early twentieth century. However, California was considered the "land of salads" and salad dressings. Green Goddess Dressing, introduced by the Palace Hotel in San Francisco in the early 1920s, was purportedly inspired by the British actor George Arliss, then performing in the play by that name. In 1926 Robert Cobb, owner of the Brown Derby restaurant in Los Angeles, introduced Cobb salad, which consists of avocado, tomato, watercress, lettuce, bacon, chicken, Roquefort cheese, and a hard-boiled egg arranged in a striped pattern in a flat bowl and topped with French dressing. So pervasive was the California influence on food that the chef's salad became a meal in itself throughout the United States.

Salads arrived in the United States from other countries, continents, and cultures. German potato salad, a cold or hot side dish made with potatoes, mayonnaise, and seasonings, became popular in mainstream America in the second half of the nineteenth century. In the twentieth century Caesar Cardini, an Italian immigrant who opened several restaurants in Tijuana, Mexico, created the Caesar salad with romaine lettuce, garlic, olive oil, croutons, Parmesan cheese, Worcestershire sauce, and often anchovies. The Caesar salad became popular with Hollywood movie people who frequented Tijuana, and it quickly spread to Los Angeles and other cities. Italian immigrants helped popularize the lettuce and tomato salad and introduced cold pasta salads of tortellini, mayonnaise, and dill.

In the late twentieth century, health food advocates championed salads, which were greatly advanced by the invention of the salad bar purportedly by the Chicago restaurateurs Rich Melman and Jerry Orzoff, whose R. J. Grunts featured a long counter of greens, seasonings, vegetables, and condiments. Many restaurants and delis throughout the United States quickly adopted and expanded this concept.

Salad dressings range from simple to elaborate. Three common dressings of the early twenty-first century are vinaigrette, commonly called Italian dressing in the United States, composed of three parts oil to one part vinegar; Thousand Island, a mayonnaise-based dressing flavored with chopped tomatoes, peppers, and other ingredients that is presumably named for the small islands in the St. Lawrence River between the United States and Canada; and Roquefort or, more accurately, blue cheese dressing.

See also **Apicius**; **Brillat-Savarin, Anthelme**; **Fruit**; **Lettuce**; **Oil**; **Vegetables**.

BIBLIOGRAPHY

Adam, Hans Karl. *Salate und Gemüüse, lecker und gesund*. München: BLV Verlagsgesellschaft, 1973.

Brillat-Savarin, Jean-Anthelme. *The Physiology of Taste; or, Meditations on Transcendental Gastronomy*, translated by M. K. F. Fisher. San Francisco: North Point Press, 1986. (Reprint, originally published in New York: Knopf, 1978, 1949. Brillat-Savarin's *Physiologie du goût* originally published in 1826.)

De Loup, Maximilian. *The American Salad Book*. New York: Knapp, 1899.

Evelyn, John. *Acetaria*. London: B. Tooke, 1699. Reprint, London: Prospect Books, 1982, pp. 4–5. Originally published in 1699 as *Acetaria: A Discourse of Shallets*.

Ewing, Emma. *Salad and Salad Making*. Chicago and New York: Fairbanks, Palmer, 1883.

Harris, Frances Barber. *Florida Salads: A Collection of Wholesome, Well Balanced, Easily Digested Salad Recipes That Will Appeal to the Most Fastidious*. Rev. and enlarged ed. Boston: Bruce Humphries, 1926. Originally published in 1914.

Heath, Ambrose. *Vegetable Dishes and Salads for Every Day of the Year, Collected for the British Growers Council*. London: Faber and Faber, 1938.

Kegler, Henri. *Fancy Salads of the Big Hotels*. New York: Hotel Industry, 1923.

Murrey, Thomas J. *Fifty Salads*. New York: Frederick A. Stokes, 1889.

Ninety-nine Salads and How to Make Them, with Rules for Dressing and Sauce. San Francisco: Shreve, 1897.

Printz, Stacey. *The Best Fifty Salad Dressings*. San Leandro, Calif.: Bristol Publishing, 1998.

Rector, George. *Á la Rectors*. Fairbanks, Alaska: Palmer & Co., 1933.

The Salad and Cooking Oil Market. New York: Packaged Facts, 1991.

Shapiro, Laura. *Perfection Salad: Women and Cooking at the Turn of the Century*. New York: Henry Holt, 1986.

Stucchi, Lorenza. *Le Insalate*. Milan: Fratelli Fabbri, 1973.

Toussaint-Samat, Maguelonne. *A History of Food*, translated by Anthea Bell. Cambridge, Mass.: Blackwell, 1992.

Andrew F. Smith

SALMON. *See* **Fish: Sea Fish.**

SALT. Because salt is indispensable to life, acts as a food preservative, and uniquely flavors foods, humans have been preoccupied with it since the beginning of recorded history. The desire to obtain salt politically or militarily has influenced the histories of countries in Asia, Africa, Europe, South America, and the Middle East. Indeed, salt was used as a form of currency and had greater value than gold in some ancient societies. Even religious and magical significance has been attributed to this mineral.

In chemistry, the term "salt" generally refers to any compound that results from the interaction of an acid and a base. In the fields of geology and agriculture, the term "salt" is used as a synonym for the word "mineral." Although numerous salts are essential to human health (for example, potassium chloride, sodium hydroxide), in the following paragraphs the term "salt" will refer specifically to the inorganic, white crystalline substance that is known as sodium chloride (abbreviated NaCl), unless otherwise noted. It is also known as table salt, rock salt, sea salt, and saline. The reader should be aware that some paragraphs below refer to sodium chloride, whereas others refer to sodium, the mineral/ion/electrolyte.

When sodium chloride enters the body, it dissociates almost completely into its constituent particles, the ions sodium and chloride. Sodium chloride is soluble in water and glycerin. Sodium is the most plentiful ion in blood. As electrically charged particles, positively charged sodium (Na^+) and negatively charged chloride (Cl^-) are classified as electrolytes because they conduct electricity when dissolved in water.

Dietary Salt

Sodium exists in many foods that are commonly consumed in Western diets including processed sandwich meats, cheese, canned vegetables, pickled foods, salty snacks, and soft drinks. Other sources of sodium are not as well recognized: condiments, sauces, baking soda, baking powder, and bread. In restaurant foods, fast-food meals, and Chinese cuisine the sodium levels can be very high. Only about 10 percent of the sodium in Western diets is due to discretionary salt added at the table.

The sodium content of plants and vegetables depends on numerous factors. These include plant maturity, genetics, agricultural practices, soil salinity, soil fertility, soil pH, the rate at which water percolates through soil, as well as meteorological factors such as rainfall, cloud cover, and sunlight.

For most Americans today, eating preserved and processed foods has become a way of life. Sodium chloride is the most common food additive. Approximately 75 percent of sodium in Western diets originates from processed foods. Because salts of all kinds, including sodium chloride, are very stable, it is virtually impossible to remove sodium from foods that have been canned in glass or metal containers. In fact, the addition of sodium may occur during home meal preparation as well as commercial processes. For example, it is possible that a veg-

etable contains only 2 mg of sodium per 100 g on the vine but may contain 2 to 310 times that amount after canning. Processes such as adding a salt solution to prevent discoloration of vegetables (that is, brining), or the use of sodium salts as processing aids, also result in the addition of sodium to the final product.

Salt in Food Processing

In the late nineteenth and early twentieth centuries, before modern processing techniques existed, food preservation consisted primarily of heat sterilization used in combination with the addition of salts and spices. Salt was used to suppress the growth of unwanted bacteria. Today, sodium is added to processed foods in several forms. Sodium nitrate and sodium nitrite are added to meats as preservatives. Sodium citrate monobasic is added as a pH buffering agent. Both sodium fumarate and malic acid sodium salt are added to foods as buffering agents and flavor enhancers. These salts are used in concert with numerous other food additives in the United States (for example, antioxidants, stabilizers, colors, sweeteners, enzymes, and emulsifiers), under the direction of the U.S. Food and Drug Administration.

Fergus Clydesdale, a professor at the University of Massachusetts at Amherst, explained in 1988 that the loss of sodium during processing is solely due to leaching (that is, extraction, rinsing, or filtration). Canning, boiling, steaming, blanching, and cooking are the processes most likely to cause leaching of sodium and other salts. However, the extent to which these electrolytes are lost varies with the food product, type of processing, and properties of each ion. The amount of water used in a given commercial process also affects mineral losses. Steaming, for example, uses less water than boiling. Further, the total processing time may affect sodium losses from foods. Brief procedures will likely extract less salt than lengthy ones.

Various other salts (for example, potassium chloride, magnesium chloride, sodium nitrate, sodium benzoate, and sodium acetate) are added to foods during commercial processing. They serve to cure meats, provide or intensify the flavor of numerous products, decrease caking of dry products, stabilize pH (that is, when used with jams, gelatins, baked goods, pasteurized cheese), fortify nutrients, and enhance texture. Sodium nitrite, for example, reacts with meat pigments to develop a characteristic pink color. In bread and baked goods, salt serves a variety of functions including the control of the rate of fermentation in yeast-leavened products. Fermented vegetables such as sauerkraut require salt for flavor and to extract water and other nutrients from the plant tissue to form brine, in which desirable organisms flourish and undesirable ones are subdued. The firmness and color of fruits and vegetables are preserved by the calcium salt of lactic acid. In cheese products, salt is added to the curd or applied to the cheese surface to remove whey and to slow the production of acid. Sorbic acid and its salts are antimicrobial agents that work to suppress the growth of bacteria; molds in cheese, sausages, fruits, jellies, bread and cakes; and yeasts in salad dressings, tomato products, syrups, candies, and chocolate syrup.

Biological and Physiological Considerations

The various minerals in the human body serve to maintain acid-base balance, blood volume, and cell membrane permeability, and provide the constituents of bones and teeth. Sodium chloride is important in maintaining the proper concentration of body fluids (that is, osmolality), expediting fluid movement between cells, enhancing glucose absorption, and allowing proper conduction of impulses along nerve and muscle tissues.

Body fluids are distinguished as either intracellular (that is, existing inside muscle and organs) or extracellular (that is, circulating blood plus the interstitial fluid that lies between cells). To accomplish their functions, body tissues maintain intracellular and extracellular ions in different concentrations. This requires considerable energy, approximately one-third of all resting metabolism, and is accomplished by molecules that are embedded in cell membranes throughout the body; these large protein molecules are known as pumps because their action causes an unequal distribution of an ion on the inside and outside of a membrane. In blood, the concentrations for some ions (for example, potassium and calcium) are maintained within narrow limits. Table 1 illustrates these concepts for sodium, chloride, potassium (K^+), and magnesium (Mg^{2+}). Chloride is the most common negative ion that combines with sodium in the extracellular fluid. Sodium and chloride account for more than 80 percent of all particles in the extracellular fluid. Potassium, magnesium, and phosphate are the most abundant intracellular ions. Potassium speeds energy metabolism and is involved in the synthesis of proteins and a storage form of carbohydrate (that is, glycogen). Magnesium allows the body's chemical reactions and biochemical pathways to function efficiently. Approximately 60 percent of the body's magnesium exists in the skeleton, in combination with calcium and phosphorus; in fact, 99 percent of all calcium exists in bones and teeth. The remaining magnesium is present in red blood cells and muscle, supporting the transport and storage of oxygen.

The concentrations of ions in sweat and urine, which constitute the major avenues of loss, may vary markedly between individuals. This large range exists in sweat and urine because diet, acute exercise, chronic physical training, and heat acclimatization alter the loss of these ions—especially sodium and chloride—at the sweat glands and kidneys.

Sodium Metabolism

Sodium is so intimately related to other intracellular ions, extracellular ions, and water that it is difficult to consider the factors that regulate its metabolism independently. Nevertheless, the following text is limited to the regulation of sodium retention and excretion.

TABLE 1

Sodium, chloride, potassium, and magnesium ion concentrations (mmol/L) in intracellular fluid and in four extracellular fluids

Source	Sodium	Chloride	Potassium	Magnesium
Intracellular fluid	8	150	31	10
Extracellular fluids				
Sweat	15–53	4–8	2–5	15–70
Urine	32–224	43–60	8–10	39–218
Blood plasma	96–110	3–6	1–2	135–145
Saliva	11–45	11–23	0.1–0.4	10–75

At rest, the kidneys filter circulating blood at the rate of 1.0 to 1.5 L/min, causing the kidneys to generate approximately 180 L of fluid during a 24-hour period. Because the average urine volume of normal adults totals 1.3 L/day, almost all of the renal filtrate is reabsorbed and returned to the bloodstream. The amount of sodium excreted into the urine depends upon the body's need for sodium. If excess sodium is consumed without water, the kidney excretes urine with a high concentration of sodium. If dietary sodium is restricted, the kidneys are capable of producing a dilute urine that maintains the concentration of sodium in body fluids at a normal level.

Whole-body sodium balance is maintained over a wide range of dietary and environmental conditions, primarily due to the action of the hormone aldosterone on the kidneys. When dietary sodium is high, urinary sodium increases to excrete the excess. When dietary sodium is low, aldosterone reduces the loss of sodium in urine appropriately. Thus, a sodium deficiency is rare, even among individuals who consume very low-sodium diets (see below). The body may experience a sodium deficiency when sweat losses are large and persistent, or when illness (for example, chronic diarrhea, renal disease) results in inadequate sodium retention by the kidneys. Following major changes in dietary sodium levels, concentrations of the following hormones also adapt, suggesting that they minimize perturbations of extracellular fluid-ion balance: renin, angiotensin II, atrial natriuretic peptide, and nitric oxide. The latter compound plays a pivotal role in blood pressure maintenance by regulating sodium and water excretion at the kidneys. Despite our knowledge of these facts, scientists cannot explain the exact mechanism by which the brain assesses whole-body sodium status.

A predictable sequence of events occurs when a normal individual limits the intake of sodium (for example, 230 mg daily). During the initial days of salt restriction, urinary sodium levels progressively decrease until about the fifth day, when the 24-hour losses become small (for example, 115 mg or less). This individual ordinarily loses 1 or 2 kg of body weight, which is attributable to the loss of sodium and an appropriate volume of water. Initially, the reduced body water comes almost exclusively from the extracellular fluid; as time passes, the intracellular fluid compartment also shrinks. For the next few days, urinary sodium concentration remains low, and the body continues to maximize salt conservation until a reduced whole-body sodium equilibrium is established. Sweat sodium levels decrease in a manner similar to urine during dietary restriction; both are due to the action of the hormone aldosterone.

Toxicity

As is true for virtually all nutrients and compounds, salt can be detrimental or lethal in large quantities. Direct contact with sodium chloride can cause skin irritation, and heating it to high temperatures emits a vapor that irritates the eyes. When heated to the point of decomposition, it emits toxic chloride and disodium oxide (Na_2O) fumes. When consumed in large amounts, sodium chloride can cause stomach irritation. In addition, laboratory experiments have shown the following dose-response effects: 50 mg/24 hr, skin irritation in rabbits; 100 mg/24 hr, moderate eye irritation in rabbits; 125 ml/L, inhibition of DNA synthesis in isolated human cells; 27 mg/kg body weight, abortion of a human fetus; and 3,000 mg/kg body weight, lethal oral dose for 50 percent of the animals tested. Potassium chloride causes physiological responses at the following doses: 500 mg/24 hr, mild eye irritation in rabbits; 125 g/L, lung cell death in hamsters; 2,600 mg/kg body weight, lethal oral dose for 50 percent of the animals tested. Calcium chloride is lethal for 50 percent of the animals tested at a dose of 1,000 mg/kg body weight, when administered orally, and at an intraperitoneal dose of 264 mg/kg body weight. Studies have shown that magnesium chloride is lethal for 50 percent of rats tested at an oral dose of 2,800 mg/kg body weight.

The preservatives known as sulfites (see Sodium and Hypertension, below) can produce deleterious side effects, when consumed in large quantities. Investigations involving laboratory animals have shown that sulfites may inhibit some of the body's biochemical reactions and retard whole-body growth in infants; cause gastrointestinal distress; and induce reversible anemia, nutrient deficiency (for example, thiamine), and gene mutations. A lethal oral dose of sodium bisulfite (50 percent of the animals tested) was 498 mg/kg body weight in rats and 300 mg/kg body weight in mice.

Monosodium glutamate (MSG) is added to foods by chefs to potentiate various flavors. This effect is greatest in meat- and vegetable-based soups, sauces, gravies, and spice blends. The levels of MSG in foods range from approximately 0.3 percent in spinach and tomatoes to about 10 percent in parmesan cheese and 20 percent in dehydrated soup mixes. Some consumers also mix additional MSG into foods in the form of sauces. This may be strongly influenced by cultural food preferences. In Korea and Taiwan, for example, the average adult consumes six to ten times more MSG each day than the average person in the United States. Because sodium is a part of the molecular structure of MSG, it becomes available as free, metabolically active sodium. Therefore, individuals who consume restricted-sodium diets (see Sodium and Hypertension, below) should monitor both the natural levels of MSG in foods as well as the amount that is intentionally added. Monosodium glutamate also produces unwanted side effects in some individuals, including warmth, tingling, tightness, headache, swelling of the liver, and a feeling of pressure in the upper body or face. This phenomenon is often associated with consumption of Chinese food because of its high MSG content. The toxicity of MSG has been studied extensively and it is relatively low, compared to other salts. It has been estimated, for example, that an average adult, weighing 70 kilograms, would have to consume more than 3 pounds of MSG at one time to experience a toxic effect. This does not mean, however, that detrimental effects are nonexistent. A large quantity of MSG has been associated with convulsions, vomiting, and nerve cell damage in research animals, although there are great differences between species. Studies have shown that MSG is lethal, for 50 percent of rats tested, when consumed as an oral dose of 17,300 mg/kg body weight. Thus, when consumed in typical amounts, MSG does not appear to induce illness or toxicity. Because the scope of this article does not allow detailed considerations of the toxicities of other salts, the reader may refer to the book *Food Additive Toxicology* for further information.

Sodium and Hypertension

Because the kidneys regulate the volume of circulating blood, they are intimately involved in the genesis of high blood pressure (that is, hypertension). This disease often involves excessive retention of extracellular fluid, especially in the bloodstream. For unknown reasons, resistance to blood flow through the kidneys is increased two- to fourfold. And, unfortunately, even though blood pressure may be reduced by prescription medications, the kidneys do not excrete normal amounts of salt and water in urine. This scant urine output causes water and sodium retention until blood pressure rises again to an elevated level. Treatment for this fluid and electrolyte retention often involves diuretics, which increase hourly water and salt losses in urine markedly. Considering these facts, a multiple-stage scientific hypothesis has evolved. This concept proposes that a high dietary sodium intake (1) overloads the kidneys' capacity to excrete sodium and results in fluid retention, (2) increases endocrine gland secretion (that is, natriuretic hormone), (3) inhibits cell membrane function, (4) increases the sodium concentration inside cells and calcium levels in the smooth muscles that encircle blood vessels, which (5) subsequently increases the resistance to blood flow and blood pressure. Interestingly, some research indicates that hypertension may be dependent on the coexistence of sodium and chloride in the diet. Consumption of chloride salts (for example, potassium chloride and calcium chloride) is associated with hypertension, in a way similar to that of sodium.

Forty-three million Americans live with persistently high blood pressure, defined as readings of 140/90 mm Hg or above; this represents 24 percent of the adult population of the United States. This makes it one of today's most prevalent disease conditions. High blood pressure increases the risk of stroke, heart disease, and kidney failure. Individuals with a family history of hypertension, the elderly, middle-aged men, and middle-aged black women are at greatest risk. Yet, everyone is vulnerable because blood pressure typically rises with age.

It is important to acknowledge that heredity plays a critical role in hypertension and that this complex disease is affected by many different genes. Present wisdom states that, without these genes, a person will not develop high blood pressure. Such individuals, whose blood pressure increases with increasing sodium consumption, are salt-sensitive. This explains why there are great differences in human responses to sodium chloride.

Several factors play a role in reducing high blood pressure. In hypertensive adults, for example, a single aerobic exercise session (45 minutes) reduces blood pressure for 12 to 24 hours. A healthy diet (high in fruits, vegetables, low-fat dairy products; low in saturated and total fat) also reduces blood pressure. But salt has received the most attention. There is a large body of evidence, and consensus within the scientific community, that dietary sodium chloride is a risk factor for high blood pressure, independent of other risk factors such as alcohol and obesity. During the last 25 years, numerous professional organizations and advocacy groups have supported reductions of sodium in commercially processed foods, including the American Academy of Pediatrics, American College of Cardiology, Food Research Action Center, American College of Preventive Medicine, American Health Foundation, National Alliance of Senior Citizens, and National Urban Coalition.

In countries where dietary sodium is low, high blood pressure is rare. According to clinical investigations, when hypertensive adults reduce salt consumption their blood pressure usually decreases, although not always to a normal level. Additional evidence suggests that a high-salt diet aggravates other illnesses including asthma, gastric cancer, kidney stones, and osteoporosis. Therefore, consuming a low-salt diet will, for many people, reduce their risk of developing or aggravating a chronic illness such as cardiovascular stroke.

Individuals who are placed on sodium-restricted diets often consume other salts in place of sodium chloride. This increases the daily potassium intake because salt substitutes usually contain a high percentage of potassium chloride. This dietary strategy offers potential health benefits in the form of lowered blood pressure and reduced risk of stroke. For some individuals, however,

TWO LOW-SODIUM RECIPES

The April 1985 issue of *FDA Consumer* magazine provided two recipes as examples of low-sodium meal items that are easy to prepare. The first describes baked dinner rolls and yields 100 servings: 3¼ ounces active dry yeast, 2 quarts water, 7¼ pounds all-purpose flour, 1⅓ cups sugar, 1 tablespoon salt. Normally, a recipe of this size would utilize 4 tablespoons of salt, resulting in a sodium content of 295 mg in each roll. By reducing the amount of salt by 25 percent, each roll contains only 73 mg of sodium.

The second recipe describes low-sodium sausage patties and yields 16 servings. Mix 1 pound ground beef with 1 tablespoon lemon juice, ¼ cup dry bread crumbs, ¼ teaspoon sage, ¼ teaspoon ginger, 1 teaspoon garlic powder, 1 teaspoon onion power, and ½ teaspoon liquid smoke. Dissolve 1 low-sodium bouillon cube in water and add this solution to the ground beef mixture. Mix thoroughly and let stand for 15 minutes. Form sixteen 1-ounce patties. Brush skillet with vegetable oil and cook the patties for seven to eight minutes on each side, or modify the time as desired. The use of low-sodium bouillon is the key to sodium reduction in this recipe.

the use of a potassium-containing salt substitute can cause illness or death. Individuals with a disease, those taking medications, and the elderly should be advised that these salt substitutes ought to be used only to enhance taste, and not for cooking purposes. Sulfites also should be considered. These compounds preserve food by retarding deterioration, rancidity, or discoloration and thus are categorized as antioxidants. At least three sulfites are commonly used as food additives: sodium sulfite (Na_2SO_3), sodium metabisulfite ($Na_2S_2O_5$), and sodium bisulfite ($NaHSO_3$). Because these preservatives contain sodium that becomes free and metabolically active in cells, each contributes to the diet's total sodium load.

Unfortunately, reducing the salt content of foods, to restrict sodium consumption, affects the quality and properties of foods. In the meatpacking industry, for example, reducing sodium chloride extremely results in inferior meat cohesion and water retention, and reduces shelf life. These and other unwanted effects explain why commercial food processors usually do not reduce the sodium chloride levels in their products voluntarily.

Managing Dietary Sodium

Compared to the average daily intake in the United States, ranging from 2,300 to 6,900 mg/day, the minimum physiological need for sodium (40 to 300 mg/day) and the intake necessary for good health (500 mg/day) are very small. In fact, the amount of sodium in fresh vegetables alone may be enough to meet an adult's basal requirement. Eight simple procedures make reducing salt intake effective. First, cook with only small amounts of added salt. Second, add little or no salt to food at the dinner table. Third, limit your intake of salty foods such as potato chips, salted nuts, pretzels, popcorn, soy sauce, steak sauce, garlic sauce, pickled foods, and cured meats. Fourth, request that the chef omit salt from your restaurant meal. Fifth, educate yourself about foods that contain large qualities of sodium and seek low-sodium brands when shopping for crackers, pasta sauce, canned vegetables, bread, and other commercial products. Sixth, develop a taste for the unsalted flavor of foods. The taste preference for salty foods can be altered with patience. Seventh, evaluate your diet by reading food labels carefully to determine the sodium content. This can be especially helpful in the aisles of a supermarket because you cannot eat what you do not purchase. Eighth, make a mental list of foods that you will avoid because they contain too much sodium. Here are a few examples, presented in units of milligrams per 100 g of food: fried crisp bacon, 2,400; baking soda, 9,000; beef bouillon cube, 24,000; bologna, 1,300; celery salt, 28,000; cured ham, 1,100; dill pickle, 1,400; frankfurters, 1,100; salt pork, 1,800; green pickled olives, 2,400; and processed cheese, 1,500.

Careful selection of low-sodium food items also will prove to be useful. Table 2 provides a comparison of the sodium content of several vegetables, in fresh and canned forms. Obviously, individuals who desire to reduce their total dietary sodium levels should substitute fresh vegetables for canned varieties, whenever possible. The exception to this recommendation lies in vegetables that lose sodium during processing, due to leaching. This provides the added benefit of ensuring that other dietary nutrients are not lost during commercial packaging (that is, leaching, boiling, blanching).

Another excellent way to lower sodium intake is to alter food preparation practices in the home. Many spices, herbs, and other flavorings do not contribute significant amounts of sodium but may be used to improve the flavor of low-sodium meals. These include allspice, basil, bay leaf, chives, cinnamon, cloves, curry, dill, garlic, ginger, leeks, lemon juice, mint, mustard, nutmeg, orange extract, oregano, paprika, parsley, pepper, peppermint, pimento, poppy seed, saccharin, saffron, sage, sesame, brown and white sugar, tarragon, vanilla extract, and wine.

In determining the amount of sodium that a person consumes, groundwater is often ignored. However, the sodium content of public and private aquifers in the United States varies greatly from one location to another. Although most sources of water include less than 20 mg of sodium per liter, a minor input to daily sodium, certain areas of Arizona, Texas, and Illinois report 325 to

TABLE 2

Sodium content (milligrams per cup) of vegetables: Fresh versus canned

	Fresh, raw	Canned
Asparagus	4	285
Beets	57	36
Carrots	31	280
Green beans	8	536
Green peas	2	236
Lima beans	1	310
Sweet potatoes	24	48
Tomatoes	2	18
Tomato juice	2	230

432 mg of sodium per liter of groundwater. Considering the fact that the average adult consumes more than 2 L of fluid each day, this could mean that some Americans receive over 1 g of sodium per day from tap water alone. If a water softener is used to reduce hardness from a local water supply (for example, remove the mineral calcium carbonate), sodium content can be magnified.

Individuals on low-salt diets also should be concerned about the adequacy of other nutrients. It has been estimated that 40 percent of all low-sodium diets lack other essential nutrients, especially protein, the B vitamins, riboflavin, and calcium. These deficiencies result from the removal of food items that contain sodium.

Salt Restriction and Sodium Deficiencies
As noted above, the basal physiologic need for sodium is 40 to 300 mg/day and the amount recommended for good health is 500 mg/day. Field studies, conducted between 1931 and 1962, confirmed that adults can eat low-sodium diets and remain healthy. Interestingly, some of these populations lived in tropical climates, where sweat losses were great, including the vigorous Masai warriors of Africa who consume less than 1,955 mg of sodium per day, the inhabitants of tropical Nigeria who ingest less than 2,760 mg of sodium per 24-hour period, and Galilean naturalists who ingest only 736 mg of sodium per day.

It is difficult to deplete the body of sodium. The action of the hormone aldosterone on the kidneys, and the relatively large per capita daily intake of sodium in Western diets relative to basal physiological needs, are quite adequate to maintain whole-body sodium levels. Thus, sodium deficiencies are rare, but may be experienced in three extraordinary situations. The first involves dietary salt restriction as therapy for disease (for example, hypertension or congestive heart failure). The possibility that sodium depletion may occur in these illnesses does not contraindicate the use of a low-sodium diet when suitable, but it is important that the patient be monitored carefully. Frequent measures of serum sodium concentration are desirable during the first few weeks of a salt-restricted diet. A decline in serum sodium level should prompt a reevaluation. The second circumstance involves diseases of the kidneys or endocrine glands that alter normal sodium balance, such as Addison's disease or diabetes insipidus. The third situation, involving hot environments, is considered in the following section.

Hot Environments Exaggerate Salt Losses

Exercise or labor in cool environments increases the sweat loss and water intake, but the psychological drive to drink and fluid-electrolyte hormones regulate total body water within +0.2 percent (+150 g) of the normal body weight each day. Blood plasma volume is regulated within + 0.7 percent (+ 25 g) on consecutive days.

During mild-to-moderate intensity exercise in a hot environment, voluntary water intake does not keep pace with water losses. Most humans produce 0.8 to 1.3 L of sweat per hour, but replace only one-third to three-fourths of this amount by drinking. Thus, if exercise in a hot environment is prolonged and strenuous, a 3 to 5 percent body weight loss can occur. This is significant because, at these levels, both endurance and strength decline.

Table 1 demonstrates that sweat contains sodium, chloride, and other minerals. In fact, sweat contains more than forty distinct organic compounds. Regarding the sodium chloride content, considerable interindividual differences exist among healthy adults. Physically fit athletes who are heat-acclimatized (that is, adapted to exercise in a hot environment) usually lose 400 to 800 mg of sodium chloride per liter of sweat. In contrast, the sweat of unfit, nonacclimatized adults contains from 1,000 to 3,000 mg of sodium chloride per liter. This difference occurs because physical training and heat acclimatization reduce the concentration of salt in sweat.

Salt Balance during Exercise and Labor

Table 3 provides estimates of the amount of fluid and salt lost in sweat, during different activities that are conducted in hot environments. Obviously, water and sodium chloride losses increase in proportion to the duration and the intensity of exercise. As a point of reference, Table 4 describes selected nutrients that are consumed by an adult in the United States. The intake of sodium chloride averages 4,600 to 12,700 mg, and water consumption averages 2.5 L/day. Comparing these two tables, it becomes obvious that 30 minutes of mild gardening produces a small fluid and sodium loss that can be replaced by a normal diet. An ultramarathon, requiring 20 to 30 hours to complete, involves extraordinary salt (14,400 to 70,000 mg NaCl) and water (18.0 to 35.0 L) losses that far exceed normal 24-hour food consumption. Clearly, constant fluid-electrolyte intake is required, during and after an ultramarathon, to replace lost nutrients.

Three fluid-electrolyte disorders involve sodium (that is, heat exhaustion, heat cramps, and exercise-related hy-

ponatremia) and have become the most common illnesses among athletes and laborers in hot environments. Heat exhaustion, an inability to continue exercise in the heat, is primarily a fluid depletion disorder in which either large sodium, water, or mixed sodium-water losses occur during exercise-heat exposure. Heat cramps occur most often in the abdominal wall and large muscles of the extremities and are due to whole-body sodium depletion. Treatment for these two heat illnesses involves replacing the sodium chloride and water that was lost in sweat and urine. Exertional hyponatremia involves a reduced serum sodium concentration (<130 mEq/L) and represents a marked dilution of the extracellular fluid. This disorder, unlike the previous two, involves overhydration. Athletes

TABLE 3

The amount of water and sodium chloride lost in sweat during labor or during exercise in hot environments

Event, Duration, Personal Characteristics	Total Water Loss (L)	Sodium Loss (mg)[a]
Mild gardening, 30 min, sedentary adult	0.3–0.5	240–2,000
Strenuous work, 60 min, experienced laborer	0.8–1.5	640–4,500
10-km run, 40 min, healthy adult	0.5–1.0	400–4,000
Leisure hike, 2 hr with rest, heat-acclimatized adult	2.0	1,600–6,000
Intense cycling, 2–4 hr, physically-fit cyclist	3.0–8.0	2,400–24,000
Ultramarathon, 20–30 hr, highly trained runner[b]	18.0–35.0	14,400–70,000

[a]Loss in sweat and urine; these calculations assume a range of 800–4,000 mg sodium chloride per liter of sweat; physical training and heat acclimatization increase a person's sweat rate but decrease the sodium content of sweat and urine.
[b]Running pace is slow and includes walking.

SOURCE: Average Consumption of Selected Minerals and Sodium Chloride in the United States (mg/day). National Research Council, 1989.

TABLE 4

Consumption of selected nutrients in the United States (mg per day), as published by the National Research Council in 1989.

Mineral	Amount consumed (mg/day)[a]
Sodium chloride	4,600–12,700
Sodium	1,800–5,000
Potassium	2,500–3,400
Magnesium	207–329
Calcium	530–1,179

[a]The water intake of a 70-kg adult is approximately 2.5 L/day, in solid foods and fluid.

Salt jar made at the Schofield Pottery, Penrith, Cumberland, England, circa 1930. This traditional form, dating to at least the 1600s, was intended for use near the open hearth, where it hung from a hook. ROUGHWOOD COLLECTION. PHOTO CHEW & COMPANY.

or laborers, who consume and retain a large volume of pure water (for example, 10 L in 5 hr), may experience a life-threatening series of physiological changes that signal water intoxication. The most serious effects are coma, fluid in the lungs (pulmonary edema), and brain swelling (cerebral edema).

Replacing Salt Losses due to Exercise

Individuals who exercise for more than two hours, and who are not hypertensive, should increase their salt intake slightly (see Table 3). Similarly, if a weight loss of 3 percent or more is due to fluid losses during work or exercise, a minor sodium deficit should be expected. The simplest means to replace these deficits after exercise involve adding salt to your meals and selecting saltier foods. Canned soup, for example, contains 1,950 to 2,450 mg of sodium chloride; canned tomato juice contains 1,525 mg. Fluid-electrolyte replacement beverages contain 150 to 300 mg, and 1 percent low-fat milk contains 300 mg sodium chloride It also is wise to eat more fruits, such as bananas and watermelon, to replace lost potassium.

See also **Assessment of Nutritional Status; Body Composition; Electrolytes; Fish, Salted; Meat, Salted; Microbiology; Minerals; Nutrition; Sodium; Thirst.**

BIBLIOGRAPHY

Appel, Lawrence J., Thomas J. Moore, Eva Obarzanek, William M. Vollmer, Laura P. Svetkey, Frank M. Sacks, George A. Bray, Thomas M. Vogt, Jeffrey A. Cutler, Marlene M. Windhauser, Lin Pao-Hwa, and Njeri Karanja. "A Clinical Trial of the Effects of Dietary Patterns on Blood Pressure." *New England Journal of Medicine* 336 (1997): 1117–1124.

Buskirk, Elsworth, and William B. Farquhar. "Sodium in Exercise and Sport." In *Macroelements, Water, and Electrolytes,* edited by Judy A. Driskell and Ira Wolinsky, pp. 109–136. Boca Raton, Fla.: CRC Press, 1999.

Clydesdale, Fergus M. "Minerals: Their Chemistry and Fate in Food." In *Trace Minerals in Foods,* edited by Kenneth T. Smith, pp. 57–94. New York: Marcel Dekker, 1988.

Dahl, L. K. "Salt and Hypertension." *American Journal of Clinical Nutrition* 25 (1972): 234–244.

Denton, Derek. "Salt in History: Symbolic, Social, and Physiological Aspects." In *The Hunger for Salt,* pp. 76–90. Berlin: Springer-Verlag, 1982.

Freeman, Thomas M., and Owen W. Gregg. *Sodium Intake—Dietary Concerns.* St. Paul, Minn.: American Association of Cereal Chemists, 1982.

Greeley, Alexandra. *A Pinch of Controversy Shakes Up Dietary Salt.* Health and Human Services Publication HE20.4010/A:SA3/3. Rockville, Md.: Food and Drug Administration, 1997.

Hubbard, Roger W., and Lawrence E. Armstrong. "The Heat Illnesses: Biochemical, Ultrastructural, and Fluid-Electrolyte Considerations." In *Human Performance Physiology and Environmental Medicine at Terrestrial Extremes,* edited by Kent B. Pandolf, Michael N. Sawka, and Richard R. Gonzalez, pp. 305–360. Indianapolis: Benchmark Press, 1988.

Maga, Joseph A., and Anthony T. Tu. *Food Additive Toxicology.* New York: M. Dekker, 1995.

Miller, Roger W. *Low-Sodium Menus Pass School Tests.* Health and Human Services Publication 85-2204. Rockville, Md.: Food and Drug Administration, 1985.

National Research Council. Food and Nutrition Board. *Sodium-Restricted Diets. The Rationale, Complications, and Practical Aspects of Their Use.* Publication No. 325. Washington, D.C.: National Research Council, 1954.

National Research Council. *Recommended Dietary Allowances,* 10th ed. Washington, D.C.: National Academy Press, 1989.

Sofos, John N., and S. Raharjo. "Salts." In *Food Additive Toxicology,* edited by Joseph A. Maga and Anthony T. Tu, pp. 235–268. New York: M. Dekker, 1995.

Taylor, Reginald J. *Food Additives.* Chichester, England: John Wiley & Sons, 1980.

Taylor-Tolbert, Nadine S., Donald R. Dengel, Michael D. Brown, Steve D. Cole, Richard E. Pratley, Robert E. Ferrell, and James M. Hagberg. "Ambulatory Blood Pressure After Acute Exercise in Older Men with Essential Hypertension." *American Journal of Hypertension* 13 (2000): 44–51.

United Nations Food and Agriculture Organization. *Specifications for Identity and Purity of Certain Food Additives.* Rome: United Nations, 1986.

United States House of Representatives. *Sodium in Food and High Blood Pressure*. Committee on Science and Technology Document No. 84-015O. Washington, D.C.: U.S. Government Printing Office, 1981.

Lawrence E. Armstrong

SANDWICH.   The bread-enclosed convenience food known as the "sandwich" is attributed to John Montagu, fourth earl of Sandwich (1718–1792), a British statesman and notorious profligate and gambler, who is said to be the inventor of this type of food so that he would not have to leave his gaming table to take supper. In fact, Montagu was not the inventor of the sandwich; rather, during his excursions in the Eastern Mediterranean, he saw filled pita breads and small canapés and sandwiches served by the Greeks and Turks during their mezes, and copied the concept for its obvious convenience. There is no doubt, however, that the Earl of Sandwich made this type of light repast popular among England's gentry, and in this way, his title has been associated with the sandwich ever since. The concept is supremely simple: delicate finger food is served between two slices of bread in a culinary practice of ancient origins among the Greeks and other Mediterranean peoples.

Literary references to sandwiches begin to appear in English during the 1760s, not only in connection with their presumed Englishness, but also under the assumption that they are a food consumed primarily by the masculine sex during late night drinking parties. This connotation does not change until the sandwich moves into general society as a supper food for late night balls and similar events toward the end of the eighteenth century.

That sandwich, the creation of caterers, is amply described by Louis Eustache Ude, an illustrious cook who finished his career as chef de cuisine of the Crockford Club in London, in his *French Cook* (1818). Ude took particular care to outline a proper supper and the critical execution of the superior sorts of English sandwich that originally gave the food its high status. He explained that bread for sandwiches filled with salads must be specially baked in molds so that the texture is dense, though the crust not dry, to avoid sogginess once the sandwiches are stacked on a silver tray, as they should not bend when held in the hand. Breads for other sandwiches should be baked long and round like a tube so that the slices are even and thus fit neatly together without lumpiness or air spaces between. Furthermore, all crusts on sandwich breads should be rasped so that they acquire the texture of chamois. His sandwiches for two or three hundred persons included fillet of guinea fowl with cold béchamel sauce ("make them towards nine o'clock to serve up at twelve"), fillet of pheasant poached in a fumet, fillet of sole à la Ravigotte, salad sandwiches made of small lettuces and cresses ("cut the salad off which protrudes . . . observe much neatness in the preparing of these sandwiches and do not confide them to any of the kitchen

John Montague (1718–1792), the Earl of Sandwich, whose title is now the name of a popular food. From an eighteenth-century engraving. © CORBIS.

maids.") And finally, anchovy sandwiches: "the pieces of anchovy should not touch each other, as they might then be too salt, unless when eaten to assist wine drinking."

Charlotte Mason was one of the first English cookbook authors to provide a recipe for sandwiches, which she published quite appropriately along side other supper dishes like Welsh rarebit and salmagundi (an elaborate ornamental salad): "Put some very thin slices of beef between thin slices of bread and butter; cut the ends off neatly, lay them in a dish. Veal and ham cut thin may be served in the same manner." Her homey recipe is quite different from the sort of grand fare sent up by the likes of Ude, but far more typical of what happened to the sandwich in the hands of Victorian home cooks.

During the nineteenth century, as midday dinner moved later and later into the day, the need for a hot supper declined, only to be replaced with light dishes made of cold leftovers, ingredients for which the sandwich proved preeminently suitable. Thus the sandwich became a fixture of intimate evening suppers, teas, and picnics, and popular fare for taverns and inns. This latter genre of sandwich has given rise to multitudes of working class creations, such as the butty and sarny of Britain, and the bacon-lettuce-and-tomato sandwich of the American diner. In the home, however, for such meals as English high tea, or the late-night Quaker "tea" parties of nineteenth-century Philadelphia, sandwiches were not usually premade, but rather, sliced bread was provided, enabling diners to assemble a sandwich from the various tidbits laid out for the meal.

Cookbook author Eliza Leslie was one of the earliest American writers to publish sandwich recipes in the United States. Her *Directions for Cookery* (1837) contained a recipe for what has become a ubiquitous American institution: the ham sandwich. Her sandwich consisted of thinly sliced bread spread with butter and mustard (French mustard flavored with tarragon), and sliced or finely chopped ham, with no other embellishments. "You may either roll them up, or lay them flat on plates. They are used at supper, or at luncheon." The fact that they needed explanation at all may be taken as a sign of their uncommonness outside of urban centers, since the sandwich of the 1830s was still more or less a creature of upper-class cookery; Leslie's use of French mustard gives further evidence of that fact.

During the early years of the railroad, sandwiches proved an ideal form of fast food, especially since they could be sold at train stations when everyone got off to buy snacks. With the appearance of the dining car, the sandwich became a travel-related institution, and it remains so as the typical meal served as lunch on airplanes. During the late nineteenth and early twentieth centuries the sandwich came into its own, especially as a response to the Temperance Movement. Taverns and saloons offered free sandwiches with drinks in order to attract customers, which led to the development of many distinctive sandwiches that have endured. In the United States, these include the club sandwich, a multi-layered affair designed to combine two or three types of sandwich into one, a meal in itself, which earned its name through its popularity with businessmen in private dining clubs.

Among working-class men, the submarine loaf became a popular vehicle for hearty sandwiches made with various fillings. This long, narrow Viennese loaf first appeared in the early 1880s as a marketing gimmick in connection with the Gilbert and Sullivan operetta "H. M. S. Pinafore," which features a ditty with sexual innuendos about submarines. The sandwiches made with this type of bread bear different names in different parts of the country: subs, grinders, poor boys, torpedoes, and hoagies, all featuring very localized types of ingredients. For example, the Philadelphia hoagie (derived from "hokey-pokey man," the sandwich vendor), contains the essentials of a southern Italian antipasto, including cold cuts, Italian cheeses, peppers, olive oil, and oregano. New England gave birth to the lobster roll: cold, cooked lobster served with mayonnaise in a small toasted submarine loaf (which evolved into hot dog rolls). A hot counterpart to this, the so-called beefsteak sandwich, was first popular in the nineteenth century as fried chipped beef and onions served over toast. Once married to the submarine loaf, it further evolved with the addition of cheese and various hot pepper sauces.

Luncheonettes of the 1920s served grilled cheese sandwiches and the Cuban sandwich, which resembles a hoagie pressed between two hot irons so that it is slightly flattened and hot when eaten. In spite of its association with Havana, this sandwich was created in New York and New Jersey. The most famous of the American hot sandwiches, however, is the Reuben, which was introduced at Reuben's Restaurant in New York City (there was also a branch in Miami, Florida). The restaurant was essentially a Jewish-owned sandwich shop that offered a wide range of creations named after famous personalities of the 1930s and 1940s: Danny Kaye, Hedda Hopper, Judy Garland, Ozzie Nelson, to name just a few. The Reuben Special, the hot grilled sandwich of fame, contained turkey, Virginia ham, Swiss cheese, cole slaw, and Russian salad dressing. The substitution of pastrami and sauerkraut came later, as a courtesy to kosher Jewish customers, who could not eat ham or a mixture of meat and cheese. Reuben also sold steak sandwiches for $2.00 (the most expensive sandwich on the menu), a specialty called Chicken Reubenola, and hamburgers on a roll.

The hamburger, at one time simply a meat patty eaten with bread and gravy, has, in the hands of McDonalds and similar global food chains, become the ultimate industrialized food eaten throughout the world, as well as a dubious symbol of American culture in far-off places. While the Earl of Sandwich might not recognize his finger food thus transmogrified and chef Ude might be appalled by the sloppiness of its presentation, neither could find fault with the hamburger's convenience or its cross-gender, cross-cultural, cross-generational appeal.

See also **Bread; Fast Food; Hamburger; Leslie, Eliza; Lunch; Picnic; Take-out Food.**

BIBLIOGRAPHY

Battiscombe, Georgina. *English Picnics.* London: Country Book Club, 1951.

Leslie, Eliza. *Miss Leslie's Directions for Cooking: An Unabridged Reprint of the 1851 Classic.* Mineola, N.Y.: Dover, 1999.

Mason, Charlotte. *The Lady's Assistant for Regulating and Supplying the Table . . .* London: J. Walter, 1773.

Montagu, John, fourth earl of Sandwich. *A voyage performed by the late Earl of Sandwich round the Mediterranean in the years 1738 and 1739.* London: Printed for T. Cadell Jr. and W. Davies, 1799.

Ude, Louis Eustache. *The French Cook.* London: John Ebers, 1818.

Wilson, C. Anne. *Luncheon, Nuncheon, and Other Meals: Eating with the Victorians.* Seventh Symposium on Food History. Dover, N.H.: Alan Sutton, 1994.

William Woys Weaver

SAUCES. Sauces are food preparations with a fluid consistency, often with nutritional richness and a relatively pronounced taste, that are used to complement other foods. Although they typically stand out as a special development of cookery, their social and historical importance tends to be underrecognized.

Sauces may be divided into two broad categories. First, they can be essentially nutritious partners to a staple, such as the sauces eaten with pasta, corn chips, rice, and so on. Historically, this group arrived with settled society, when communities relied on perhaps only one cereal (such as barley, wheat, rice, or maize) or tuber (potato, taro, yam, or cassava). These foods could be cultivated in bulk and stored from one crop to the next. However, they were starchy foods that were nutritionally incomplete, requiring the addition of vegetables, legumes, meat and other animal products, often cooked separately as a sauce.

A second category primarily imparts flavor and is often served separately on, or in addition to, meat and vegetables rather than the staple cereal or tuber. These sauces range from relishes, such as tomato ketchup, which are often preserved, to subtle compositions often based on stocks and egg emulsifications and slightly sticky to form a coating. Because they are so refined and velvety, sauces became the pride of French cooking. Just as the first category of sauces catered to the culinary needs of civilization, the second brought to dining a certain luxury and high standard of taste.

Sauces are not normally eaten by themselves, generally require some sort of preparation (a raw ingredient, such as poured cream, is not conventionally considered a sauce), often have a homogenous look and texture, and are usually soft or runny in consistency. However, the boundaries are blurred, variations are many, and language is imprecise.

Some sauces merge with soups and stews, which differ in that it is possible to eat either alone. On the other side of the spectrum, some sauces merge with relishes and condiments. A fluid state is normal, although many pounded compositions are considered sauces (e.g., Italian *pesto* consisting of basil, Parmesan, garlic, and olive oil), and chopped ingredients often act like sauces. For example, pizza toppings are virtually identical to pasta sauces. Although sauces are usually placed on top of other foods, they can also bind other ingredients or function as fillings, encased in buns, pastry packets, sheets of pasta, rice balls, and so on. While the range includes sweet toppings (such as chocolate sauce), soft, sweet pastry fillings are more likely to be called creams or crèmes. Runny custard (*crème anglaise*) can be a sauce, but usually not a set custard or ice cream. Nonetheless, one's definition of the "sauce" category should be flexible, especially for sauces that fill the two roles already described, namely, as a nutritional complement to a staple, or a taste complement to a nutritional complement.

Reasons for Sauces

The role of sauces may be hedonistic; they are clearly designed to be pleasurable. A more disparaging view is that sauces simply exist to make people overeat, and such an assumption lies behind the familiar saying, "hunger is the best sauce" (perhaps first used by Cervantes in *Don Quixote*). Yet another line of argument suggests that certain sauces are used repeatedly within a cuisine to mark a food as familiar and generally "safe," so that cultural knowledge replaces the eaters' own instincts.

In a more specialized sense, sauces may put the salt back into cooked food from which it was leached. The modern words "sauce," "salsa," and so on derive from the Latin word *sal* for 'salt', which highlights the fact that many sauces have frequently been too salty, often as a result of added ingredients that have been preserved with salt.

Apart from any of this, sauces' historical origin was as a nutritional accompaniment to complex carbohydrates. The ancient Mesopotamian, Egyptian, and Chinese civilizations, and subsequent ones, were based on basic agricultural products, the progenitors of wheat and barley, and so on. In all cases, these staples were complemented by what might, broadly, be termed "sauces." Accordingly, the Chinese speak of supplementing *fan* with *ts'ai*, that is, supplementing cereal and starchy dishes (porridge, steamed rice, dumplings, pancakes, noodles) with vegetables, meat, or fish. The two have to be in balance, although more *fan* might be prepared for everyday meals and more *ts'ai* for feasts. Many of the *ts'ai* preparations are recognizable sauces, served in separate dishes or contained within the staple, such as pork buns.

An Indian meal is focused on a bowl of rice (in the south) or bread (in the north), surrounded by small bowls of vegetables, extra ingredients such as lentils, and possibly meats. These are typically cooked with a careful blend of spices and herbs to make what is called a *masala*, and the best known is *garam masala* from the north. Particularly in southern India, where a more liquid stew better accompanies a larger portion of rice, a wet *masala* is made by adding yogurt, coconut milk, and other liquids. English "curry"—which is based on *Tamil kari*, a sauce in which meat, fish, or vegetables are stewed —often results from the addition of a dry powder by the same name, but this is a mere caricature of the richer, more flavorful Indian curry sauces, which vary depending on the cook's social status, religion, and geographical location.

Foods to accompany staples have often been preserved. Among the various cheeses, dried fruits, pickles, and other relishes that fall in this category, many are readily classified as sauces. Fermented fish sauce, known as *garum* or *liquamen* to the ancient Romans, appears in Asian variants, such as Vietnamese *nuoc mam*. Soy sauce is a similar product (made from fermented soya beans), and Worcestershire sauce is a commercially successful English variant. Bottled sauces have become important, too, notably any kind of tomato sauce.

Bain-Marie or water bath for keeping prepared sauces hot. From a wood engraving, circa 1880. Roughwood Collection.

Some of the sauces just mentioned are used more for their spicy or pungent flavor, rather than any nutritional value. Such flavorings can be considered a second category of sauces, often refined from the original more nutritious versions.

Kinds of Sauces

The primary sauces are pounded, stewed, stock-based, starch-thickened, emulsified, preserved, or sweet (which includes custards, syrups, and fruit purées).

Pounded. The mortar and pestle have been successfully used to produce an enormous variety of pastes across the globe, including the Italian *pesto* and Indian *masala* already mentioned. Purées, such as tomato sauce, are rubbed through a sieve or finely chopped in a food processor.

Stewed. Cooking meat, vegetables, legumes, and/or herbs in a pot with water or other liquid can produce soups, stews, and also sauces. An important example is the Italian accompaniment to *pastasciutta*, the meat *ragù* or *sugo*, known elsewhere as *bolognese* sauce. The *mole* sauces from Mexico are cooked mixtures of many ingredients, including chili and chocolate in the famous *mole poblano* used with turkey.

Stock-based. The roasting or baking pan may be deglazed (residues scraped up with liquid and then reduced) to provide gravy. Much more important, the *fonds* ("foundation") of French cooking is stock, which requires meat, bones, and vegetables to be simmered gently to extract flavor (often after browning the ingredients by baking or frying). Stock can be reduced and then reduced again. Jean-Anthelme Brillat-Savarin wrote in the *Physiology of Taste*, appearing in 1825, that Bertrand, the steward of the Prince of Soubise, used fifty hams for one supper, but only one ham appeared on the table, the rest being essential for his *sauce espagnole*, white sauces, and so forth (1949, p. 54). The secret is the large quantity of gelatin produced when collagen in animal connective tissue is heated in water. Gelatin is a wonderful thickening agent owing to its peculiar, long molecular structure.

Starch-thickened. Starch in wheat and corn flours is useful because of its behavior in hot water. Put starch into cold water and the granules slowly sink, but hot water disrupts the long starch molecules so that the granules become amorphous networks of starch and water intermingled. A little flour can thicken a great deal of liquid. Eighteenth-century England was accused of having "sixty different religious sects, but only one sauce" (attributed to both Voltaire, 1694–1778, and Francesco Caraccioli, 1752–1799)—this was the ever-present "melted butter," which was butter and (usually) water, thickened with flour.

Emulsified. Some sauces acquire their velvety consistency as emulsions, which are suspensions of one liquid in another with which it does not ordinarily mix, notably oil in water. The simplest is a dressing of oil and vinegar (dilute acetic acid) called vinaigrette. In hollandaise, mayonnaise, and their variations, the heated butter and oil are suspended with the help of egg yolk as an emulsifier.

Preserved. Vegetables and fruits are cooked and then immersed in vinegar and spices to make pickles and chutneys. Fish sauces are fermented, and soy sauce comes from fermenting soya beans. Bottled sauces have become important, too, notably tomato.

Sweet. Custards are sweet, moist, tender gels of egg protein. A creamy rather than solid custard is made by stirring continuously during heating to prevent the proteins from bonding into a solid mass. Sugar syrup is sugar dissolved in water with heating to arrive at the desired coloring.

The French Triumph

One of the great French chefs of the twentieth century, Fernand Point, proclaimed the secret of his cuisine as follows: "Butter! Give me butter! Always more butter!" Much of it went into sauces, which, for him, were the mark of a good cook. Among the players in the kitchen, according to Point, "the saucier is a soloist." He also wrote in *Ma Gastronomie* (1969) that the making of béarnaise sauce is a virtuoso performance: "What is it? An egg yolk, some shallots, some tarragon. . . . Well, believe me, it takes years of practice for a perfect result. Lift the eyes for a moment, and your sauce is unusable."

Beginner, or even moderately experienced, cooks have difficulty not only preparing grand French sauces, but also differentiating the vast array of sauces, often with distinguished-sounding names, such as *périgueux*, *financière*, and *grandveneur*. Some chefs have attempted to identify the basic sauces (*sauces grandes* or *sauces mères*, meaning "great" or "mother" sauces), which, with various additions, become compound sauces (*sauces composées*). *Soubise* sauce has onions, Robert mustard, and *madeira*, the fortified wine of the same name. The "mother" sauces generate brown sauces (*sauces brunes*), derived from meat stock, and white sauces (*sauces blanches*), derived from *béchamel* sauce (milk thickened with flour). Nonetheless, both stock and flour have thickened many sauces, and the browning of their original ingredients helps determine color, as when roux (equal quantities of butter and flour) is browned to a required extent. For a third family tree, hollandaise is the primary egg and butter sauce; béarnaise is its popular offspring. Then, there are cold sauces based on mayonnaise (yolks and oil).

An often-cited delineation of sauces is that of the renowned chef Auguste Escoffier, who wrote in his *Guide Culinaire* (1903), of five leading sauces: *espagnole* (brown stock, brown roux, and tomatoes), *velouté* (white stock, yellow roux), *béchamel* (milk, white roux), *tomate* (tomato), and *hollandaise* (butter, eggs, vinegar or lemon juice).

The nouvelle cuisine of the 1970s gave new life to sauces: by favoring "lighter" (less thick and flour-enriched) renditions, by rediscovering more rustic versions such as *beurre blanc* (butter, vinegar, shallots), and by featuring colorful purées, using one of the few important twentieth-century contributions to good cooking, the food processor. Though nouvelle chefs were also more likely to place the sauces underneath the food rather than on top of it, the goals remained the same. The first aim is a slightly sticky consistency that will coat other foods even when they are picked up with a fork. Thickening is achieved by the gelatin in stock, starch in the roux, reduction (evaporation), cream, egg emulsification, sugar syrup, and so on. The second aim is an intriguing flavor. Third, the sauce should look glossy, which usually means a long and careful clarification.

Jean-François Revel recounts in *Culture and Cuisine* (1982) that French chefs took flavor to a new level in the eighteenth century. They replaced "old-style cuisine of superimposition and mixture" (i.e., crude additions of flavors) with the "new cuisine of permeation and essences" (subtle combinations). He bases this view on the foreword to François Marin's *Les Dons de Comus* [which means the Gifts of Comus, the Roman god of feasts], published in 1739. The author (thought to be two Jesuit priests) explained that the science of cooking was to mix and blend foods to make a harmonious whole, not dominated by any one ingredient.

English gastronomic writer Launcelot Sturgeon sought to relay his enthusiasm for the art that "binds the whole fabric of society" in two chapters, "On the Physical and Political Consequences of Sauces" and "On the Importance of Forming Good Connexions [Connections]," in his *Essays, Moral, Philosophical, and Stomachical,* originally published in 1822. He spoke of two primary indications of "the connexion [connection] of sauces," namely, the harmony of the sauces and the social harmony they produced. Sauces, which are ingredients combined in "exquisite concord," draw people together around a table, connecting them "by ties which no one ever wishes to dissolve."

Modern chemistry took Sturgeon's work one step further by showing how molecules tie sauces together. Culinary investigator Harold McGee details starch-thickening, emulsification, and other methods in *On Food and Cooking* (1984).

See also **Condiments; Cooking; Nouvelle Cuisine; Preparation of Food; Serving of Food**.

BIBLIOGRAPHY

Brillat-Savarin, Jean Anthelme. *The Physiology of Taste: Or, Meditations in Transcendental Gastronomy.* Translated by M. F. K. Fisher. New York: Heritage Press, 1949. Originally *La Physiologie du goût,* Paris, 1829.

Escoffier, Auguste. *The Complete Guide to the Art of Modern Cookery.* Translated by H L. Cracknell and R. J. Kaufman. London: Heinemann, 1979. Originally published as *Le Guide Culinaire,* 1903.

McGee, Harold. *On Food and Cooking: Science and Lore in the Kitchen.* New York: Scribners, 1984.

Point, Fernand. *Ma Gastronomie.* Paris: Flammarion, 1969.

Revel, Jean-François. *Culture and Cuisine: A Journey through the History of Food.* Translated by Helen R. Lane. New York: Doubleday, 1982. Originally published as *Un festin en paroles,* 1979.

Sokolov, Raymond A. *The Saucier's Apprentice: A Modern Guide to Classic French Sauces for the Home.* New York: Knopf, 1976.

Sturgeon, Launcelot. *Essays, Moral, Philosophical, and Stomachical, on the Important Science of Good Living,* 2nd ed. London: G & W.B. Whittaker, 1823. Originally 1822.

Symons, Michael. *A History of Cooks and Cooking.* Champaign: University of Illinois Press, 2000. Chapter 6 is devoted to sauces.

Michael Symons

SAUSAGE. Essentially, sausages are just seasoned forcemeat. In cuisines around the world, however, countless variations have been played on this simple theme. Sausages were probably first invented as a means of preserving blood, offal, and small scraps of meat in convenient edible containers—the stomachs and intestines of the slaughtered animal. The earliest known reference to sausage dates to Greece in the eighth or ninth century B.C.E. It appears in Homer's *Odyssey* (XX: 24-27), where Odysseus, lying in his bed, is seen

> rolling from side to side
> as a cook turns a sausage, big with blood
> and fat, at a scorching blaze, without a pause,
> to broil it quick

They are also found in Apicius's *De re coquinaria* (Rome, first century C.E.), a cookbook that was clearly intended for diners with discriminating palates. While sausages may have begun in frugality, they had already evolved into delicacies worthy of a gourmet's attentions.

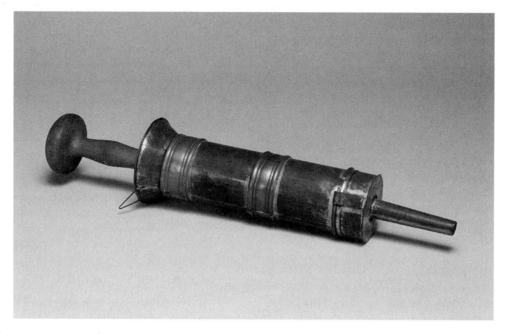

Sausage stuffer. Berks County, Pennsylvania, circa 1860. Wood handle, tin and copper. Ground meat was pressed through the tube into a gut, which was then twisted to make sausages. ROUGH-WOOD COLLECTION. PHOTO CHEW & COMPANY.

In form, sausages may be patties of freshly chopped and seasoned meat or they may be stuffed in casings, dried, fermented, smoked, or produced using any combination of these techniques. The meats can be ground exceedingly fine (*weisswurst*) or simply cut into large chunks (headcheese). Some are eaten cooked, using any of the traditional methods for cooking meats, while some are so heavily cured and smoked that they can safely be eaten raw (*salame crudo*).

Pork is the meat most commonly used to produce sausages, although almost any sort of protein will do (sausages have even been made from gluten and soy proteins) providing they contain enough fat to maintain a juicy product. Beef, chicken, duck, lamb, seafood, and veal have all been used in sausages. Game, such as venison or rabbit, tends to be very lean, so pork fat or beef suet are usually added. Typically, a sausage forcemeat contains 20 to 30 percent—and sometimes as much as 50 percent—fat by weight. Fats chosen must be flavorful and not too soft, so that they don't melt out too quickly during cooking. Depending on cooking method, much of the fat may be removed before the sausage comes to the table.

All sausages contain salt (indeed, the word "sausage" is descended from the Latin *salsus*, meaning 'salted'). Salt serves three purposes. It acts to preserve perishable meats, killing some bacteria through osmotic pressure. In addition, salt dissolves some globular protein from the meats, which then acts as a binding matrix for the bits of meat when the sausage is cooked. The globular protein is released when the meats are ground or kneaded (the

sausagemaker can see when this has occurred because the forcemeat becomes sticky). Salt, of course, also provides flavor, and it reinforces the flavors of other seasonings, especially in foods that are served cold.

Seasonings vary according to the cuisine producing the sausage. Black pepper is almost universal; in fact, the simplest fresh Italian sausages contain nothing but pork, salt, and pepper (Italian sausages made in the United States almost always add fennel seeds and red pepper). Garlic is a key ingredient in sausages of many countries, including Germany, Hungary, France, Poland, Portugal, Spain, and the United States. Chili pepper, in forms ranging from dried flakes to cayenne to paprika, appears in sausages around the world (although its use in sausages is limited in northern cuisines that typically avoid hot pepper). Fresh breakfast-type sausages usually contain sage, and often marjoram. Cloves, cinnamon, and nutmeg are sometimes used, especially in black (blood) sausages. Chinese sweet sausages (*lop cheong*) are flavored with sugar, soy sauce and five spice powder (a mixture usually consisting of ground cassia, cloves, fennel seeds, star anise, and Szechuan pepper).

Natural casings include sheep casings (breakfast links, chipolata), hog casings (Italian sausage, bratwurst), hog bungs (liverwurst), caul fat (*crépinettes*), beef middles (salami), and beef rounds (mortadella). Haggis, the Scottish national dish, is nothing more than a large sausage made of seasoned sheep organ meats and oats, stuffed in the sheep's stomach. Synthetic casings, made of cellulose, collagen, or plastic, can be made in any size, and are used for spreadable pâtélike preparations (braunschweiger), salamis and other cold cuts, and skinless frankfurters. Dolmas, grape leaves stuffed with a mixture of seasoned lamb and rice, can even be considered a form of sausage.

Sausages are often dried by hanging, in cool circulating air, to preserve them as well as enhance their flavor and texture. Once they are fully dried, they can be kept unrefrigerated for weeks. Before they are dry, however, they can spoil, so a curing salt—such as Prague powder, a mixture of salt and sodium nitrite—is used to prevent the development of the bacteria (*Clostridium botulinum*) that cause botulism. The nitrite has an additional advantage; it prevents the cooked meat from turning gray (the characteristic pink color of cured hams results from the nitrite in the cure). Nitrites, used in recommended quantities, do not cause the development of carcinogenic nitrosamines that were formerly found in cooked meats containing nitrates (saltpeter). Some dried sausages are also fermented, either with naturally occurring organisms or through the addition of a starter (lactobacillus) to the forcemeat. These bacteria produce lactic acid, which preserves the meat while providing a tangy flavor. *Sopressata* and some kinds of chorizo are fermented, but quick recipes for fresh chorizo substitute a little vinegar for the lactic acid that would have developed through fermentation.

Smoking adds flavor to sausages. It acts as a preservative, both by adding a number of phenolic compounds found in smoke, and by forming a tough coating on the outside of the sausage. This impervious layer is known as the pellicle.

Sausages continue to appear in recipes around the world, even after the development of other means of preserving meats. In many peasant cultures, the largely vegetarian diet is enhanced by small quantities of sausage. In modern diets sausages make up for their high fat and sodium content by contributing more flavor and variety than their size would suggest. Thus sausages satisfy sophisticated palates with lower quantities of food.

See also **Apicius; Meat; Meat, Salted; Meat, Smoked; Pig; Preserving.**

BIBLIOGRAPHY

Aidells, Bruce. *Bruce Aidells's Complete Sausage Book: Recipes from America's Premier Sausage Maker*. Berkeley, Calif.: Ten Speed Press, 2000.

Apicius. *De re coquinaria* [On cookery]. Translated by John Edwards. Point Roberts, Wash.: Hartley and Marks, 1984.

Davidson, Alan. *The Oxford Companion to Food*. Oxford: Oxford University Press, 1999.

Grigson, Jane. *Charcuterie and French Pork Cookery*. London: Michael Joseph, 1967.

Hippisley-Coxe, Antony, and Araminta Hippisley-Coxe. *The Great Book of Sausages*. Woodstock, N.Y.: Overlook Press, 1992.

Kinsella, John. *Professional Charcuterie: Sausage Making, Curing, Terrines, and Pâtés*. New York: Wiley, 1996.

Kinsman, Donald M. *Principal Characteristics of Sausages of the World, Listed by Country of Origin*. Boston: American Press, 1983.

McGee, Harold. *On Food and Cooking: The Science and Lore of the Kitchen*. New York: Scribners, 1984.

Merinoff, Linda. *The Savory Sausage: A Culinary Tour around the World*. New York: Poseidon, 1987.

Wise, Victoria. *American Charcuterie: Recipes from Pig-by-the-Tail*. New York: Viking, 1986.

Gary Allen

SCANDINAVIA. *See* **Nordic Countries.**

Window display of local sausages and radishes in the Liebold Butcher Shop, Bamberg, Germany. Germany is renowned for its large variety of sausages and meat products. © DAVE G. HOUSER/CORBIS.

SCHOOL MEALS. Operating primarily in industrialized countries, such as England, Japan, and the United States, school meals programs have become an integral part of the school day. If efforts by the United Nations and the United States are successful, up to 20 million children in developing countries will be able to participate in a similar program for the first time beginning in the early years of the twenty-first century.

Typically started on a local level, school feeding programs emerged as recognition grew of the link between malnourishment and academic performance. Numerous cities in Europe and the United States, including London, Milan, New York, Paris, and Zurich, established feeding programs by the early twentieth century. Over time, the local programs evolved into statewide and nationwide programs. In 1946 the United States established its National School Lunch Program (NSLP), after finding that many men were rejected for military service during World War II due to malnutrition. The lunch program has grown from serving daily 4.6 million children in 1947 to more than 26 million by the end of the twentieth century. In the 1960s the feeding program was expanded to include a school breakfast program and a summer feeding program primarily targeted to low-income children. In the United States school meals programs are required to offer free and reduced-price meals to children from low-income families. About half of the children participating in the NSLP receive free lunches.

Until 1996, U.S. school meals were required to comply with a meal pattern designed to meet, on average, one-third or one-fourth of the U.S. Recommended Dietary Allowances (RDA) for essential nutrients for the lunch or breakfast programs, respectively. The meal pattern for lunch consisted of one serving of meat or meat alternate, two or more servings of vegetables or fruits, a serving of bread or bread alternate, and a serving of fluid milk. Until 1974 lunches were also required to include a teaspoon of butter. Children's diets were found to be high in calories, fat, cholesterol, and sodium, and the number of children who were overweight had more than doubled between 1960 and 1990. In 1995 the United States Department of Agriculture updated its nutritional standards to reflect current scientific knowledge about disease prevention and health promotion. For instance, it is now standard to require that school meals contain no more than 30 percent calories from fat and 10 percent from saturated fat. Earlier in the decade a nationwide study of school meals had found that school lunch and breakfast programs met the RDA requirements, but were well above the nutritional guidelines for fat, saturated fat, cholesterol, and sodium. As a result, both school lunch and breakfast programs, for the first time, had to conform to the 1990 Dietary Guidelines for Americans. States are responsible for ensuring that schools are compliant. Since then most of the nation's 96,000 schools have substantially reduced their fat and saturated fat levels, and increased their levels of carbohydrates.

At times, the dual mission of providing nutritious school meals and encouraging the consumption of domestically grown commodities has created a tension between nutrition advocates and farm groups. The distribution of government commodities was often viewed by the nutrition and health communities as a barrier to providing healthy meals. This conflict has diminished with the new nutrition standards and policy changes in commodity purchases that include increased purchases of fresh produce and lower fat items. Unresolved issues seen by nutrition advocates include the presence of junk food vending machines in schools and the growing number of private food service companies replacing or competing with the government's school meals programs.

See also **Dietary Guidelines; Food Stamps; Government Agencies, U.S.; Malnutrition; Nutrition; Obesity; WIC (Women, Infants, and Children's) Program**.

BIBLIOGRAPHY

Gunderson, Gordon W. *The National School Lunch Program: Background and Development.* Washington, D.C.: U.S. Department of Agriculture.

School Nutrition Dietary Assessment Study II. Washington, D.C.: Food and Nutrition Services, U.S. Department of Agriculture, 2001.

Patricia McGrath Morris

SCOTLAND. *See* **British Isles.**

SCURVY. A corruption of the earlier word "scorby," scurvy is the name given to the disease that is the consequence of a prolonged deprivation of vitamin C. The minimum daily requirement to prevent the disease is approximately 7 mg, but it takes several weeks of depletion of body reserves before the problem becomes evident. There are many descriptions of the disease as it appeared among sailors engaged in the long voyages that began to be undertaken from the end of the fifteenth century. After ten or more weeks at sea, men began to experience general pain and stiffness, while their lower body became covered with large purple spots. In addition their gums would swell and grow over their teeth, which became loose; and old wounds would reopen. Finally, sufferers would die suddenly, "in the middle of a sentence," to the astonishment of their mates. This is now explained as the consequence of impaired protein synthesis, with connective tissues weakening, so that the wall of a major artery would finally burst. It soon was discovered that the disease could be prevented, and even cured, by sailors consuming fresh fruit and vegetables. Long sea voyages were only indirectly responsible, by preventing crews from living on anything but foods that could be stored for long periods, like salt meat, dried peas, and flour that could be cooked into bread and puddings. The same disease appeared on land when fresh food was unavailable for long periods, as in the California gold rush, for example. The first "antiscorbutic" (i.e., antiscurvy) foods to be prized by sailors were oranges and lemons, but they would become moldy on long voyages, and juices preserved with brandy or rum were more stable alternatives that also proved to be more palatable. Sailors in the British navy were required, from early in the nineteenth century, to take a portion of lime juice in their daily ration of rum; men from other navies called them "limeys" as a term of abuse, implying that "real men" did not need to drink fruit juice. Another tradition among sailors on long whaling expeditions was to take a large store of potatoes. These are not very rich in the vitamin but contain enough to prevent the disease if one is eaten freshly cooked every day.

In the early twenty-first century the disease still appears occasionally in adults, typically as "widowers' scurvy," among men who have never learned to cook and,

This patient in an 1842 drawing shows all of the major signs of Vitamin C deficiency, including the sores on the arms. © VI-SUAL IMAGE PRESENTATIONS.

when left to fend for themselves, subsist on things like breakfast cereals and sandwiches made from bread and cheese or ham. It also has appeared in people living on very restricted "fad" diets, such as a Zen macrobiotic diet of brown rice sprinkled with sesame seeds.

With the recognition of the importance of bacteria in causing diseases, at the end of the nineteenth century, it became a practice in some cities to sterilize cows' milk by autoclaving it. Children's deaths from "summer diarrhea" were reduced greatly as a result of this practice. However, this processing also resulted in the destruction of most of the vitamin C in the milk and, when it was fed to infants with only a cereal supplement, scurvy became a common problem. The addition of orange juice to the infants' diets provided a simple solution. With modern technology, milk can be freed from pathogens and potatoes can be dried under milder conditions, so that vitamin C is preserved; alternatively, the synthetic vitamin can be added to restore vitamin C levels in foods.

See also **Beriberi; Niacin Deficiency (Pellagra); Nutrient Bioavailability; Nutrients; Nutrition; Vitamin C; Vitamins.**

BIBLIOGRAPHY

Carpenter, Kenneth J. *The History of Scurvy and Vitamin C.* Cambridge, U.K., and New York: Cambridge University Press, 1986.

Hess, A. F. *Scurvy Past and Present.* Philadelphia: Lippincott, 1920.

Kenneth John Carpenter

SEABIRDS AND THEIR EGGS. Seabirds and their eggs played an important part in the coastal economies and life patterns of many areas of the North Atlantic fringes of Europe into the twentieth century. In the struggle for survival in peripheral socioeconomic settings, the harvesting of seabirds and their eggs was a means of providing seasonal fresh foods and of augmenting the supply of preserved foodstuffs for winter and spring. The exploitation of these natural resources was an activity that required adaptation to the environment, ingenuity, courage, and a taste for foodstuffs often considered unpalatable by inland dwellers.

Seabird fowling and egg collection were undertaken by men while women were normally involved in the preparation and processing of the birds and eggs for household food or sale. Since seabirds exist primarily on the sea but come to rocks, cliffs or grassy sea-slopes, to breed and roost, they and their eggs were normally taken from these habitats by scaling up or down the rocks, cliffs or slopes. Bird-catching was a complex activity and a wide range of catching methods were employed depending on the roosting habits of the birds. Among the most common along the North Atlantic region were catching or seizing by hand, using snares consisting of a single noose or jaw attached to the end of a fowling rod, arranging multiple nooses on the ground, and using nets of various kinds, to trap the birds.

Seabird fowling and egg collecting varied in intensity along the north Atlantic region from Iceland in the north to Ireland in the south. The harvesting of seabirds on the Faroe Islands was described by Kenneth Williamson in 1948 and more recently by Arne Nørrevang (1977). John R. Baldwin has compared the fowling equipment, techniques and allied terminology of the Faroes with the centuries-old practice of seabird fowling on islands off the northwestern and northern coasts of Scotland, an activity that has attracted attention for several centuries. Sir Donald Munro mentions Sula Sgeir in that context in 1549, and Martin Martin in *A Description of the Western Islands of Scotland* (c. 1695), tells that the inhabitants of the isle of St. Kilda (abandoned since 1930) killed and preserved an enormous quantity of seabirds and preserved seabirds' eggs in peat ash, which gave then an astringent taste. St. Kilda was, in fact, unique in Scotland for its organized farming of the fowling cliffs. The year's cycle has been described as "killing of gannets and some shearwaters in April, collecting eggs of puffins and catching fulmars in May, snaring puffins in July, catching fulmars and

Finlay MacQueen snaring puffins on the isle of St. Kilda, west of the Outer Hebrides, Scotland. COURTESY OF R. L. ATKINSON, SCHOOL OF SCOTTISH STUDIES PHOTOGRAPHIC COLLECTION, EDINBURGH.

gannets in August and catching young gannets in September" (Fenton, 1987, p. 170).

These activities on St. Kilda were a response to an extreme environment. Elsewhere in Scotland wild birds and their eggs were welcome seasonal supplements to the diet, rather than being a major focus of economic activity. May was the time for harvesting the eggs of gulls, fulmars, puffins, razor-bills, guillemots and so on. Guillemot and gannet flesh was eaten. A limited cull of the young of the gannet (Gaelic: *guga*) still takes place on Suileisgeir (Gaelic: *Sula Sgeir*, "gannet reef"), a small barren island with craggy cliffs covered in guano, lying forty miles northwest of Lewis. This centuries-old tradition is carried on by the community of Ness, at the northernmost tip of the Island of Lewis, also in the Outer Hebrides. It is the only surviving gannet hunt in the British Isles.

Gannet hunting on Suileisgeir was regulated by the First Bird Protection Act of 1869, which gave the men of Ness a special dispensation to take gannet chicks. Nowadays, annual licences to take 2,000 such birds, starting only from the first week in September, when the birds are about three months old, are necessary. A crew of ten men spend two weeks on the rock catching and prepar-

ing the birds. All equipment, food supplies, including fresh water, and salt to dress the birds, must be ferried to the rock.

The method of catching has changed little over the centuries, and men still go down the steep cliff-faces on ropes to trap the birds. They are caught using a long fowling rod with an iron jaw fixed at the end, which is put around the bird's neck and pulled closed by a rope to trap the bird. The manner of processing has also changed little over time. They are plucked, and the down is removed by singeing over a peat flame, which apparently confers its unique flavor on the flesh. The ribcage and entrails are removed, and cuts made in the four pockets of meat at the wings and legs are packed with salt. The finished birds are then carefully laid in a wheel-like formation, lair upon lair, in order to retain the pickle drawn from the flesh by the salt so that it will not become hard and salty.

The birds are sold on the quay on return and are much in demand. They are scrubbed clean with washing soda, placed in a pot, covered with boiling water and boiled for twenty minutes. The water is then changed and the bird is boiled for a further twenty minutes. This procedure is repeated a third time. In this way the salt content in the bird is reduced. The flesh has the texture of meat with a salty and fishy flavour. It is, indeed, an acquired taste.

The role of the gannet chick as a food in the Ness community has changed greatly in the course of the twentieth century. No longer necessary as a welcome variation in diet, it has become somewhat of a delicacy which embodies a sense of identity for the people of Ness.

Seabird fowling and egg collecting were also seasonal activities along parts of the Atlantic coast of Ireland, from Rathlin island in the northeast where the cliffs and sea-slopes were apportioned in strips, and individual men in search of eggs and birds would lower themselves on ropes attached to iron spikes in the cliff edge, westwards to the great cliffs in southwest Donegal, northwest county Mayo, around the Conamara coast, in the Aran Islands in Galway Bay, and in county Clare on the towering Cliffs of Moher, in some cases into the twentieth century.

Further south on the islands and coastlands of county Kerry, seabirds, their eggs and feathers, were important in the food-provision strategies and local market economy of the Blasket Islands and contiguous mainland from at least the eighteenth century. The most westerly of the Blasket Island group, a towering rock appropriately named Tiarach "westerly isle" was the seabirds' haunt par excellence especially of the puffin population, whose eggs and chicks were exploited for food.

On the Great Blasket Island the eggs of the oyster catcher, guillemot, razor-bill, puffin and seagull were eaten. The flesh of guillemot, razor-bill and to some extent that of the Manx shearwater, cormorant and storm petrel were eaten, fresh, or preserved by salting for later use. Salted seabird were also sold on the mainland. The young of the puffin was considered the "chicken of the sea" and was much sought after. Because of its fat content it was roasted in a pot or grilled on a tongs laid over live cinders to allow some of the fat to escape. The storm petrel, a very small bird, was similarly cooked to discharge its fat. Regarded as a delicacy, and an acquired taste, it appears to have been swallowed whole rather than chewed.

By the early twentieth century seabird-fowling was no longer an organized, specific food-provision strategy on the Great Blasket Island due in some measure to the expansion and demands of the fishing industry during the summer months, but also to changing tastes, reflected, too, in the cessation of the hunting of seals for food.

Gannet hunting, for the flesh and feathers of the young chicks, was still practiced commercially on the Little Skellig, a great towering sea-crag lying in the Atlantic to the south of the Blasket Islands, and the second largest gannetry worldwide, in the course of the nineteenth century. By the end of that century, however, this activity was no longer viable, and the rock was too distant and the sea too rough for local light rowing-craft to reach. And the very strong and fishy taste of these birds was no longer desired.

BIBLIOGRAPHY

Baldwin, John R. "Sea Bird Fowling in Scotland and Faroe," *Folk Life* 12 (1994): 60–103.

Evans, E. Estyn. *Irish Folk Ways*. London: Routledge, 1957.

Fenton, Alexander. *Country Life in Scotland: Our Rural Past*. Edinburgh: John Donald, 1987.

Fenton, Alexander. *The Northern Isles: Orkney and Shetland*. Edinburgh: John Donald. 1978. New edition. East Linton, Scotland: The Tuckwell Press, 1997.

Flower, Robin. *The Western Isle or the Great Blasket*. Oxford: Oxford University Press, 1944.

Harman, Mary. *An Isle Called Hirte: A History and Culture of St. Kilda to 1930*. Waternish, Isle of Skye: Maclean Press 1997.

Lysaght, Patricia. "Food-Provision Strategies on the Great Blasket Island: Sea-bird Fowling." In *Food from Nature: Attitudes, Strategies and Culinary Practices*, edited by Patricia Lysaght, pp. 333–363. Uppsala: Royal Gustavus Adolphus Academy, 2000.

Mac Conghail, Muiris. *The Blaskets: People and Literature*. Dublin: Country House, 1994.

Munro, R.W., ed. *Munro's Western Isles of Scotland and Genealogies of the Clans 1549*. Edinburgh: Oliver and Boyd, 1961.

Nørrevang, Arne. *Fuglefangsten på Færøerne*. København: Rhodos, 1977.

Synge, John M. *The Aran Islands*. Dublin: Maunsel, 1906. Edited with an introduction and notes by Tim Robinson. London: Penguin 1992.

Talbot, Rhona. "Guga: Its Place in the Ness Community of Lewis." In *Food from Nature: Attitudes, Strategies and Culinary Practices*, edited by Patricia Lysaght, pp. 320-332. Uppsala: Royal Gustavus Adolphus Academy, 2000.

Sigurdardóttir, Frída Á. *Medan nóttin lidur*. Reykjavik: Forlagid 1990. (Translation: *Night Watch*. London: Mare's Nest. 1995.)

Waddell, John, Jeffrey W. O'Connell, and Anne Korff. *The Book of Aran*. Kinvara, Co. Clare: Tír Eolas Press 1994.

Williamson, Kenneth. *The Atlantic Islands*. London: Collins 1948.

Patricia Lysaght

SEEDS, STORAGE OF. Seeds are by far the single most essential cultivated source of food, with wheat, rice, corn, soybean, barley, millet, and sorghum providing the vast majority of food for humans and their domesticated animals. While root and tuber crops, such as potatoes, yams, sweet potatoes, and cassava, are important sources of food in certain regions, they come in a distant second behind seeds. Besides serving as food, seeds also give rise to the next generation of crops. In general, annual crops are grown from seed (for example, grains, legumes, and vegetables), while perennial crops rely on vegetative propagation. Seeds are therefore stored not only to ensure a stable source of food, but also to provide the propagules from which additional crops can be grown.

Importance of Seeds

Modern agriculture is based on the establishment and growth of uniform stands of crops. Plant density should be uniform throughout a field, as should the plant age and stage of development. Uniform propagules and growing conditions are necessary to assure crop uniformity. Propagules are either produced sexually (as in seeds), or asexually (through cutting, graphing, budding, and division, etc.). Even vegetatively produced crops (such as tree fruits) use seed to produce rootstocks and in breeding programs. Seeds are composed of an embryo, stored food, and a protective covering. They fulfill a number of functions besides being the product of sexual reproduction. Seeds assist in the replication of individuals in a population, aid in dispersal of the species into new areas, and provide protection for the delicate embryo. The food sequestered in the seed to nourish the germinating embryo and growing seedling is the source of our food, while the embryo is the source of a new plant.

Seeds Stored for Food

By far the greatest bulk of stored seeds are used as food. Huge silos store wheat, corn rice, soybeans, and other grain, and legume crops prior to their being processed into flour, bread, corn meal, cornstarch, and the myriad other products we consume daily. Seed-derived vegetable protein can be mixed with colors and flavors and then extruded under moist heat and high pressure to produce various shaped and sized products that can be used in place of meat. Oils can be extracted from seeds, and sweeteners can be produced from the starch in seeds through enzyme digestion. Storage conditions for these seeds are designed to minimize loss of food value resulting from seed respiration and metabolism, and contamination or loss due to the growth of mold and insects, while at the same time retaining desired processing qualities. Low degrees of moisture and temperature are the two most important factors in storage of seeds for food. Both of these factors reduce seed respiration and the growth of pests.

Seeds Stored for Propagation

If seeds are not stored in a manner that maintains their vigor and viability, there will be no food for the next season. Seed vigor and viability is primarily based on generic factors, so differences occur among species, and in varieties within a species. The conditions under which seeds were produced can also affect seed longevity. Temperature, rainfall, humidity, nutrition, and diseases during seed production all influence seed viability, as does seed maturity when harvested. Mature seeds remain viable longer than immature seeds. Seed vigor usually decreases with time in storage; exceptions are seeds in which the embryo must develop or mature before they are ready to germinate (as with elm).

There are three general categories of seeds based on their desiccation tolerance and the time they remain viable in storage. Most annual and biennial crops, and horticultural crops produce orthodox, or desiccant-tolerant, seeds that can easily be stored for many years in a dry, cool storage environment. These crops include grains, legumes, vegetables, floral crops, and temperate fruit trees. By contrast, recalcitrant, or desiccant-intolerant, seeds are difficult to store and usually remain viable for only a few weeks or months before they are killed by desiccation. Desiccant-intolerant seeds do not enter dormancy after maturing. Their continued respiration and physiological activity leads to rapid deterioration. They must be planted while still fresh, or stored moist at low temperatures. Even if properly stored, they can only be kept for short periods of time before they succumb to fungal or bacterial rots, or exhaust their food reserves. They include tropical perennials (such as avocado, mango, and coconut) and some temperate deciduous trees (such as chestnut, buckeye, maple, and oak). Between these two extremes are the intermediate seeds that can be stored for a few years if maintained under proper conditions of temperature and humidity. They include tropical and subtropical perennials (for example, coffee, citrus, macadamia, and papaya), and some tree nuts (such as hazelnut, hickory, pecan, and walnut).

In order to maintain seed quality in storage, the relative humidity of the air (in percentage relative humidity, or RH) and the temperature of the seeds (in degrees Fahrenheit) should total, as a general rule, less than 100. This means that the relative humidity around seeds stored at room temperature (about 72°F) should be less than 28 percent, while it should be less than 63 percent for seeds stored in a household refrigerator (about 37°F). Storage life of orthodox seeds is doubled for every 10°F drop in temperature, or every 1 percent drop in seed moisture content. Seeds are hydroscopic, meaning they will absorb or lose water from the atmosphere until they come into equilibrium. At the same relative humidity, seeds containing mainly carbohydrates will contain more water than do oil-containing seeds. At a relative humidity of between 20 and 70 percent, the seed-moisture content of a carbohydrate containing wheat seeds is around 30 percent more than that of oil-containing soybean seeds at the same relative humidity. So the relative humidity around stored seeds must be adjusted to produce the same level of moisture in seeds of different composition.

Whether plants were selected for domestication because they produced seeds that stored well, or whether plants were bred to produce seeds that stored well as they were domesticated, the seeds of most cultivated plants are orthodox and can be stored for a few years at near ambient conditions of moisture and temperature. The vigor and viability of most seeds of cultivated annuals can be maintained for two to five years under favorable storage conditions of 30 to 60 percent RH (8 to 14 percent seed-moisture content) and 40 to 60°F. Difficult-to-store seeds can be kept for extended periods at very low temperatures. This technique of cryopreservation can maintain

Seed storage warehouse of Philadelphia seedsman Robert Buist. From an 1891 wholesale seed catalog, ROUGHWOOD COLLECTION.

recalcitrant seed for decades at liquid nitrogen temperatures (−320°F; −196°C). However, the vigor of seeds stored at even these low temperatures declines over time. The continued maintenance of specific seed lines requires that they periodically be removed from storage and used to produce a new crop of seeds. Seed storage facilities, therefore, need not only modern storage equipment, but also the land, personnel, and expertise to periodically grow the stored seeds under conditions that maintain their genetic purity.

High vigor is characterized by the seed's ability to germinate and for the embryo to grow under stressful conditions that can include compacted soil, pathogens, salinity, and cold or hot temperatures. Seeds with higher vigor possess greater storage potential and can be stored for longer periods before the seed becomes nonviable. Both vigor and viability decline gradually during the early stages of seed storage; they parallel one another initially, with vigor ultimately declining in advance of viability. Later in storage, there is a sharp decline in both, until the seed only produces a weak seedling that quickly succumbs to environmental or pathogenic stresses.

Seeds that are planted in a field should have been sorted to produce a group of seeds that will germinate and grow at the same rate to produce uniform plants. Cracked, deformed, and small seeds should be eliminated in this winnowing process. In addition to selecting robust seeds, various preplanting treatments can increase

seed viability and ensure uniform seedling establishment. Seeds' viability can be increased by partially germinating them under optimal conditions before planting. Holding seeds in an aerated aqueous solution for a week or so and then immediately planting them or drying and planting them later can also increase viability. The osmotic strength of the solution allows the seeds to take up water but not to germinate. Another method is to enclose each seed in a porous clay coating that contains fertilizers or fungicides to assist the seedling during early stages of growth.

Preparation of Seeds for Storage

Seeds should be harvested after maturing on the plant, separated from the fruit or protective plant parts in which they developed, and cleaned. Desiccant-tolerant seeds can be slowly air dried over a few days at low relative humidity and then sealed in moisture-tight containers before being placed in a refrigerator. If the seeds are sufficiently dry, they can be stored in the freezer section. Desiccant-intolerant seeds must be stored moist and need to be planted as soon as possible.

Stored Seeds Preserve Genetic Resources

Before the advent of scientific plant breeding, farmers would keep seed from the previous harvest to plant for the next season. From this process, numerous land races of the major crops developed that were specifically adapted to the conditions of their environment, such as climate, cultural practices, diseases, pests, soils, weeds. The availability of commercially produced seed with improved quality characteristics, pest resistance, and yields have supplanted many of these local varieties, and many have disappeared. Older crop and heirloom varieties of many horticultural and ornamental plants have also been lost because no one kept their seeds. Recognizing that such seeds may contain traits and genes (for example, pest resistance) whose introduction could improve modern varieties, private and governmental groups have developed seed banks and germplasm repositories to collect and preserve seeds and other propagules for long periods of time. These facilities include the National Seed Storage Laboratory in Fort Collins, Colorado; the Seed Savers Exchange in Decorah, Iowa; and the National Genetic Resources Program (NGRP), authorized in 1990 by the U.S. Congress. The Plant Sciences Institute (PSI), part of the National Germplasm Resources Laboratory (NGRL), is located at the Beltsville Agricultural Research Center, Agricultural Research Service, U.S. Department of Agriculture.

See also **Barley**; **Biodiversity**; **Crop Improvement**; **Maize**; **Rice**; **Soy**; **Storage of Food**; **Vegetables**; **Wheat**.

BIBLIOGRAPHY

Agarwal ,V. K., and J. B. Sinclair. *Principles of Seed Pathology.* 2d ed. Boca Raton, Fla.: Lewis, 1997.

Ashworth, Suzanne. *Seed to Seed: Seed Saving Techniques for the Vegetable Gardener.* 2d ed., rev. Decorah, Iowa: Seed Savers, 2002.

Basra, Asmarjit S., ed. *Seed Quality: Basic Mechanisms and Agricultural Implications.* New York: Food Products Press, 1995.

Copeland, Lawrence O., and Miller B. McDonald. *Principles of Seed Science and Technology.* 4th ed. Boston: Kluwer, 2001.

Doijode, S. D. *Seed Storage of Horticultural Crops.* New York: Haworth, 2001.

Kelly, A. Fenwick. *Seed Production of Agricultural Crops.* New York: Wiley, 1988.

Whealy, Kent, ed. *Garden Seed Inventory: An Inventory of Seed Catalogs Listing All Non-hybrid Vegetable Seeds Available in the United States and Canada.* 5th ed. Decorah, Iowa: Seed Savers Exchange,1999.

Mikal E. Saltveit

SENSATION AND THE SENSES.

Striving for variety and intensity in sensory experiences may be a fundamental human characteristic, likely reflecting our evolutionary history as both foragers of foods and omnivores. The enduring popularity of high-speed activities such as roller coaster rides or extreme sports, as well as films or computer games with impressive visual and sound effects, points to sensation seeking as still being an important aspect of many people's lives. Yet, in terms of the *range* of sensations they evoke, these experiences might be con-

sidered trivial by comparison with those delivered every day by foods and beverages. Particularly in the chemical senses (the collective term for smell, taste, and pungency), food consumption provides a continuous stream of sensory information to be processed and evaluated. Far from being mundane, even eating an apple provides an enormously varied set of sensations that begins even prior to the first bite.

Appearances and Expectations

When it comes to assigning priority to sensory information, humans are visual animals. Given uncertainty or conflict in the sensory information we receive, we tend to rely most on what we see. This is the basis of ventriloquism illusions. It is perhaps surprising, though, that a visual bias is so important with foods, where we might think that odors and tastes should predominate. Nevertheless, initial judgments of foods and beverages very often rely on appearances. In fact, our ability to identify even common flavors is typically very poor, so vision may sometimes be a more reliable source of information. Thus, foods that are miscolored—for example, a lime drink colored red—are often identified on the basis of the color rather than the flavor.

As well as being appreciated in their own right, visual aspects of foods provide important clues as to other sensory qualities, creating expectations about what we are soon to consume. We learn to associate the appearance of a food with its other sensory qualities, and the impact of these associations is perhaps most obvious in the effects of food colors. Whether an apple is red or green, for example, will lead us to expect a certain degree of ripeness and, often, quite specific levels of sweetness and acidity. Surface textures and color brightness can also provide clues to internal textural properties such as hardness. Because of such associations, colors can also influence *what* we perceive. Adding red coloring to a sweet solution increases the perceived sweetness, while the addition of any color to a solution containing an odor increases how intense we perceive that odor to be.

Expectations about a food's sensory properties can also be created in advance of consumption by information about a food, for example, on labels. These have the ability to influence a product's acceptability. Serious mismatches between what we expect a product to taste like and its actual sensory properties can be an important determinant of whether the food is ever consumed again. Like color, information can also be powerful enough to influence perceptions. For instance, labeling a product as high in fat has been shown to lead to higher ratings of "fattiness" and lower ratings of flavor intensity, relative to the same product with a low-fat label. The mechanism appears to be that, when mismatches between prior expectations and the reality of the product are relatively minor, "assimilation" takes place. That is, perceptions and preferences can be "brought into line" with product claims. These effects are an excellent reminder that, ultimately, perception is a cognitive process that receives information both from the sensory impact of food ingredients and from other sources of information about the food.

Odor Perception

While the odor of a food can also generate expectations for other sensory properties, its most valuable role is to help us to identify foods. Olfaction provides us with more information about what we consume than perhaps any other sense. Most important, whether as part of a flavor in the mouth or as an aroma that we sniff, odors reliably inform us whether we have experienced a food before. To a great extent, this assists us in making a decision to consume or not.

Olfaction has been called a dual sense. Both at a distance from the food, and when the food is in the mouth, our sense of smell acts as a detector of volatile (i.e., gaseous) chemical compounds. The mixture of compounds that we perceive as apple odor reach the olfactory receptors in the patch of tissue known as the olfactory epithelium, a mucus membrane at the top and back of the complex maze of passages found within the nose. The physiological processes that such odors initiate in the receptors are not completely understood. We do know, however, that the small odor molecules bind to receptor proteins present on the cilia, hair-like extensions of olfactory nerve cells that protrude from the epithelium. This binding initiates complex sequences of biochemical changes leading to depolarization, and firing, of the olfactory cell. This electrical signal travels via the olfactory nerve to the olfactory bulb in the brain.

How we recognize such neural signals as specific odors is perhaps *the* crucial question in the science of olfaction, particularly if we consider just how many odorants humans are capable of detecting. In stark contrast to the relatively small number of different taste qualities (see below), we can certainly perceive thousands, if not tens of thousands, of distinct odor qualities. Moreover, there does not seem to be any underlying organizing principle that we can use to classify these qualities. Historically, various schemes have been proposed for categorizing odors. Linnaeus, for example, classified odors as "aromatic," "fragrant," "musky," "garlicky," "goaty," "repulsive," and "nauseating." This and many other classification systems suffer from the use of categories that are either too general ("fragrant") or clearly related to the acceptability of the odor, rather than its sensory properties ("repulsive," "nauseating").

In practice, odors are often classified into categories that make sense to their users, whether they are winemakers, flavorists, or perfumers, as well as having practical applications. While they often have an internal logic and consistency—fruit odors may be grouped together, for instance—such classifications relate primarily to the object producing the odor, to a lesser extent to the odor

chemistry, and not at all to how the brain codes the odor information. The molecular properties of the odorant must be responsible a priori for odor quality, but any laws that could allow us to reliably predict a particular quality from those properties are not as yet apparent. Instances of dissociations between structure and quality make this a challenging task. The compounds D-carvone and L-carvone have the same structure, differing only in that they are optical isomers (effectively, molecular mirror images) of one another, yet one smells of spearmint and the other of caraway.

A milestone in our understanding of the mechanism of odor perception came in 1991, when Linda Buck and Richard Axel of Columbia University identified a family of genes that encode olfactory receptor proteins. It is thought that this family, now believed to include more than 1,000 genes or around 3 percent of our total genome, is able to generate an equally large number of receptors. It is unlikely, though, that we have a unique receptor for each odorant since this would seem to be an inefficient way of coding. The most promising hypothesis regarding olfactory coding suggests that patterns of activity across different receptors, perhaps each expressed by a different member of the gene family, form the basis of odor qualities. Olfactory coding is thought to be also partly mediated by organization of the olfactory epithelium into four different zones, each zone containing receptors expressed by different genes. A given odor will likely activate receptors in more than one zone, creating a spatial, as well as a receptor-specific, code.

Any complete theory of odor perception must explain how what we perceive as apple odor is the product not just of a single apple-like compound, but of the mixture of the compounds 2-methylbutyl acetate, butanol, and hexyl acetate (amongst many others), none of which smells uniquely of apple. The odors of the majority of the foods and beverages that we consume consist of mixtures of the odors of many separate compounds. For example, hundreds of different compounds, each with their own distinct odor, combine to make coffee and chocolate odors. What we perceive, though, is a single unique quality. A major question in our attempts to understand how the brain processes odors is how this information is combined. There does seem to be some sort of limit to the number of individual odors that we can combine and still detect. Beyond a mixture of three or four different odor qualities, we are unable to say which of a set of individual odors the mixture contains, even if we are very familiar with those components. At the same time, however (and seemingly paradoxically), complex odors can contain "notes" in addition to having an overall quality, although these notes cannot be related to the odors of the specific chemical compounds in the mixture. One of the challenges for food scientists in industry is to be able to identify which of the multitude of chemical compounds within a food are essential for producing its characteristic odor and flavor.

HOW MANY TASTES?

The conventional wisdom in both the scientific community and among the general public is that taste is composed of a set of discrete qualities, almost like separate senses. Sweet, sour, salty, and bitter have formed the core of our understanding of taste since Aristotle. While other tastes have been proposed from time to time—astringent, pungent, fatty, insipid, alkaline, to name some—these four qualities have almost always been recognized as fundamental.

Outside of the laboratory, however, we seldom experience so-called pure tastes. Fruits are often simultaneously sweet, bitter, and sour, and savory dishes may be salty, sweet, sour, and high in *umami*. Similarly, many chemicals that produce tastes are not "pure" examples. Potassium chloride is both bitter and salty. To what extent do we perceive these mixtures as sets of basic qualities, and to what extent as unique tastes themselves? Are such compounds steps along a continuum of tastes (as orange exists along a continuum of colors from yellow to red), rather than having discrete and separate qualities? These questions challenge the orthodoxy of a set of discrete basic tastes.

The recent evidence that the taste of glutamate appears to constitute a fifth basic taste, *umami*, is somewhat embarrassing for those who strongly argued for four primary qualities. If five, then why not six, or seven? In fact, there is evidence to support the notion of a taste associated with fatty acids and of the quality metallic as an independent taste. A case can be made for the survival value of such tastes: fats are important sources of energy, while the salts of metals such as iron, copper, and zinc are both metabolically necessary and toxic at high levels. Arguments have also been mounted for recognition of the tastes of other amino acids and starch as basic qualities.

Beyond such challenges to the concept of four (five) basic tastes, it has been argued that the whole notion of basic tastes is flawed. Robert Erickson and Susan Schiffman, both of Duke University, have proposed that the paradigm of a limited number of basic tastes has impeded our understanding of this sensory system. In the early part of the twentieth century, Hans Henning proposed that the four basic tastes could be represented at the points of a tetrahedron. Did Henning mean to convey that there were no intervening qualities on the tetrahedron's surface or were the basic tastes merely distinct points on

continua? This influential attempt to classify tastes has been interpreted both ways, but Erickson and Schiffman argue that the evidence favors the latter interpretation. They point out that there are no strong physiological reasons to accept only four basic tastes. There appear to be more than four transduction (receptor) mechanisms for taste; not only are there not four distinct types of taste neurons in the brain, but taste cells are broadly sensitive to many qualities.

What do we really perceive?

Erickson and Schiffman have suggested that the acceptance of the idea of a limited number of basic qualities prejudices our understanding of taste. In other words, if you accept that sweet, sour, salty, and bitter are the only tastes we can detect, then all taste sensations will be *a priori* classified into one of these categories. In one study, they asked subjects to indicate which of a variety of taste compounds, some of them mixtures of basic tastes, were singular tastes or mixtures of tastes. Many of the mixtures were viewed as a single taste, sometimes one that was distinct from the four basic tastes. Spatial mapping of the quality of a selection of tastants, based on ratings of the similarity of each pair (more similar tastants are mapped closer together, and so on), also did not conform to a pattern that could be represented by four basic qualities.

Similarly, Michael O'Mahony and colleagues at the University of California, Davis, asked subjects to sort a number of tastants into groups based on taste quality, but without using the traditional category names. Their subjects not only came up with more than four categories, but also used more than four self-generated labels to describe the different qualities. When asked to use only the four traditional qualities, these subjects were forced to label different groups using the same word, suggesting that restricting labels to the four terms was inadequate to describe the range of taste experiences.

Despite all these potential problems with the doctrine of basic tastes, there is widespread acceptance of sweet, sour, salty, bitter and, increasingly, *umami* as fundamental taste qualities, although perhaps not the only qualities. Certainly, for the foreseeable future, the existence of distinct, basic tastes will continue to be the key assumption behind research aimed at elucidating the fundamental mechanisms of taste perception.

Flavor: Sensory Qualities in the Mouth

It is only after we have taken a bite that the characteristic apple flavor, consisting of odors and tastes, emerges. After entering the mouth, the same odor compounds that

we detected previously, now released and concentrated by the combined actions of heating and chewing, reach the olfactory receptors via the nasopharyngeal passage at the back of the mouth, a process known as retronasal perception. The reason we commonly refer to characteristic food qualities as tastes—apple taste, coffee taste, and so on—is that we are not conscious of this alternate route for the sense of smell. In fact, these "tastes" are mainly odors.

Odor and taste perceptions are so well integrated in flavors that there are seldom any obvious signs as to where one sense ends and the other begins. This gives rise to the illusion that retronasal olfactory qualities are perceived in the mouth. Our language both reflects and encourages this confusion, in that we use the terms "taste" and "flavor" interchangeably. Simply holding the nose while a food or drink is in the mouth is sufficient, however, to demonstrate just how large a contribution the sense of smell makes to flavor. The complaint of loss of taste during a head cold is also a consequence of this misunderstanding. In fact, taste is largely unaffected, and it is the sense of smell that suffers.

At the same time as the odor volatiles in our apple are released during chewing, acids and sugars stimulate taste receptors in the mouth, producing perceptions of sourness and sweetness. For a sense that is so crucial to both our survival and our enjoyment of life, it is remarkable that taste is so poorly appreciated. Perhaps this is because, after subtracting odor qualities (and other sensations such as pungency and various aspects of "mouthfeel"—see below) from the overall flavor of a food or beverage, we are left with a rather small group of sensory qualities—traditionally, sweetness, saltiness, sourness, and bitterness. This limited set of qualities is clearly inadequate to describe much of the sensory complexity of any cuisine. Compared to the rich, perhaps limitless, inventory of odors that contribute to the flavors in even an average diet, the sense of taste initially seems remarkably unimpressive. Yet, in forming the essence of any flavor, taste supplies information that is crucial to our survival and well-being.

Basic Tastes

Taste is usually considered to be an *analytic* sense, composed of a key set of unique, indivisible qualities. In contrast to the *synthetic* sense of smell in which combinations of odors can produce a new quality entirely distinct from the components, tastes do not combine to form new qualities. Combining salt, sugar, and lemon juice may result in changes in the intensity of the tastes involved (different tastes typically suppress one another in mixtures), but it will only produce a mixture with the qualities of saltiness, sweetness, and sourness. As a result, these taste qualities, together with bitterness, are commonly talked about in terms of a set of *basic tastes*. It should be noted that this classification system is not without controversy but is adopted here, as it is the premise of most scientific literature on taste.

Taste Perception

To be perceived as a taste, a chemical compound or food ingredient has to be soluble (for example, in water or saliva) in order to reach the taste receptors. These are located within 3,000 or so taste buds, which are themselves located within structures on the tongue called *papillae* (although there are also small numbers of taste buds in other parts of the mouth). The most numerous of these structures, the *fungiform papillae*, are apparent as tiny bumps on the tongue's front upper surface. The *circumvallate papillae*, larger structures arranged in a chevron pattern, are located further back on the tongue, while the *foliate papillae* occupy the tongue's sides. Contrary to popular belief, taste buds are not specialized according to tongue location—we are capable of perceiving all tastes at any tongue location where taste buds are present (although our sensitivity to detecting different tastes does vary somewhat across different locations). The commonly seen tongue map, showing salty and sweet perception at the front of the tongue, sour at the side, and bitter at the back, results from a prolonged misinterpretation of the outcomes of studies published in 1901 by the German psychologist D. P. Hanig. In fact, lack of anatomical specialization for the different qualities is a characteristic of the taste system.

How a dissolved chemical compound becomes converted into a perception of, for example, sweetness or sourness, is increasingly understood. A large number of taste cells occupy every taste bud, extending their finger-like microvilli towards the pore through which the tastant compound will enter. For each taste quality, the microvilli of a cell contain different receptor mechanisms, which are responsive to the chemical structure of the tastant. Sodium and some other ions (potassium, calcium, and lithium) interact directly with channels on the membrane of the microvilli, entering the cell and producing biochemical changes that result in a nerve response interpreted by the brain as saltiness; the hydrogen ion (H^+) in acids is similarly responsible for sourness. Bitterness and sweetness are thought to bind to specific receptor proteins on the surface of the microvillar membrane, and it is this binding that initiates the biochemical changes within the cell.

Unlike sourness and saltiness, sweetness and bitterness can be produced by substances belonging to a wide variety of chemical classes: not only sugars, but some proteins and amino acids are sweet. Other amino acids are bitter, as are alkaloids and some salts. This diversity appears to be reflected in multiple receptors for each of these qualities, although whether we perceive different types of sweetness and bitterness is currently under debate. Once the neural signals reach the brainstem, carried by the VIIth (chorda tympani), IXth (glossopharyngeal) and, to a lesser extent, the Xth (vagus) cranial nerves, there is still no direct relationship between quality and anatomy. Taste cells in the brain respond best to some qualities ("salt best" or "sweet best," for example) but will in general respond somewhat to each of the basic qualities. This has led to the view that taste is coded (identified) in the brain through a pattern of responses across many taste cells.

In addition to the four well-known qualities, there is now considerable evidence for the existence of another basic taste, known as *umami* (pronounced oo-ma-me). This Japanese word, translated approximately as "savory deliciousness," refers to the quality of foods containing significant amounts of naturally occurring glutamate (a derivative of glutamic acid, an amino acid), its sodium salt, monosodium glutamate (MSG), or 5'-ribonucleotides. *Umami* quality is perhaps most evident in the taste associated with rich sauce or soup bases made from stocks, mushrooms, or tomatoes. Adding Parmesan cheese to pasta provides another means of increasing the *umami* quality of the dish, as do many of the manufactured sauces throughout the world, for example, soy sauce. The status of *umami* as a unique taste derives not just from this quality being perceived as distinct from the other four basic tastes, but also from evidence for the existence of both glutamate receptors within the tongue's taste cells, and cells within the brain which respond preferentially to the *umami* taste. Very recent evidence has also pointed to the existence of taste receptors that respond broadly to many of the other amino acids (twenty in total) that make up proteins.

The Hedonic Properties of Tastes

A limited set of basic tastes suggests that each of the qualities must be significant in some way. Why have we evolved to be sensitive to these qualities specifically? The answer lies in our hedonic responses to tastes. If our imprecise use of the word "taste" reflects our confusion about the different qualities that make up flavors, then perhaps in compensation, our language also provides clues as to the role that taste plays. In addition to describing food qualities, we also talk about tastes as a way of indicating good or bad aesthetic judgment, and we say that someone is bitter, or sweet, or has a sour face. Our use of taste qualities to describe such positive or negative emotions or qualities unwittingly reflects the underlying structure of the taste experience itself. In providing a hedonic basis to food and beverage flavors, taste functions as a built-in arbiter of what is good and bad in those things that we consume. As Brillat-Savarin noted in his gastronomical meditations (*The Physiology of Taste*, 1825), taste can be reduced "in the last analysis, in the two expressions, agreeable or disagreeable."

In contrast to our preferences for odors, which are molded by exposure and reinforcement from an early age, hedonic responses to pure tastes are remarkably fixed. Distinct hedonic responses to sweetness and bitterness are present at birth, and are essentially the same as those we experience as adults. Both in terms of amounts ingested, and also in terms of their ability to elicit characteristic facial expressions, sweetness is highly liked and bitterness rejected in human neonates. Sourness also seems to be disliked. A preference for saltiness, on the other hand, develops in the first few post-natal months. While MSG in solution is not well accepted by neonates (or, indeed, adults), soups to which it is added are preferred. These hedonic responses to pure tastes also seem to be relatively independent of culture or diet. Comparisons across cultures whose diets are very different, for example, Japan, Taiwan, and Australia, have found highly similar patterns of likes and dislikes for pure tastes.

The significance of taste hedonics. Whether as a genetic predisposition, or as a result of *in utero* influences, the origin of relatively fixed hedonic responses to pure tastes appears to lie in an adaptive capacity to respond appropriately to the nutritional implications of these qualities. Taste palatability, and ultimately the palatability of foods, seems to reflect either provision of energy, an individual nutritional need, or a warning of the presence of a potential toxin.

Sweetness is thought to signal the presence of energy in the form of calories provided by sugars and other carbohydrates, which are crucial to survival. Sweetness is thus a positive quality, reflected in its universally high palatability. This palatability is mediated by opioid (morphine-like) biochemical receptor systems in the brain, which are thought to be the biochemical basis for reward. This explains why sweetness can sometimes act like an analgesic, reducing crying in infants, for example.

Saltiness acts as a survival cue, by signaling the presence of the sodium ion (Na), necessary for maintaining the body's fluid balance. A liking for salt, while present at all times, grows substantially if we are deprived of it below what is physiologically necessary. Although there are many claims that cravings for various foods and nutrients exist, that for salt is the only one that is well-documented in humans.

The strong dislike that we naturally have to bitterness is thought to be a protective mechanism. Many plants manufacture toxins as a defense against predators, and very many of these toxins are bitter. Not surprisingly, then, we tend to be extremely sensitive to bitterness. However, as a result, we often reject levels of bitterness that are not in fact toxic to humans—witness the common fate of the poor brussels sprout. The significance of our dislike for high levels of sourness is not as clear-cut. It may be a signal for unripeness/spoilage in foods, or the fact that concentrated, and thus extremely sour, acids can cause tissue damage.

Because glutamic acid is an amino acid present in proteins that we consume, it has been suggested that the *umami* taste of glutamate acts as a signal for the presence of protein, thus promoting consumption. However, preference for *umami* actually seems to be strongest when protein intake is within normal limits. Alternatively, since dietary glutamate is involved in crucial metabolic processes and may possibly be used as an energy source within the gut, it may be that our preference for additional glutamate in foods reflects the importance of these functions.

TASTE AND SMELL DISORDERS

The loss of our ability to smell or taste is perhaps not as immediately debilitating as the loss of the senses of vision or hearing, but such disorders can nevertheless have a profound impact on people's lives. The enjoyment of foods, beverages, perfumes, and nature, and our ability to avoid spoiled foods and environmental toxins, depend upon the proper functioning of these systems. Chemosensory disorders are also relatively common. As a conservative estimate, up to one percent of the population have some degree of smell or taste loss or disturbance. Given that alterations in the flavor of foods are the most immediate consequence of smell loss, it is not surprising that problems with "taste" are the most common chemosensory complaint.

In fact, complete loss of the ability to taste is rare mainly because, as a sensing apparatus, taste is highly redundant. Unilateral damage to the cranial nerves carrying taste information can eliminate sensitivity to taste on half of the tongue, but appears to produce few noticeable changes in our ability to appreciate tastes. Likewise, taste is able to survive even severe trauma to the tongue. *Aguesia* (total inability to taste), when it does occur through illness or accident, is reported to have devastating consequences in terms of food acceptability, food intake, and, consequently, physical and mental health. *Dysguesias,* or distortions of taste sensations, are, however, not uncommon. These, and partial taste losses (*hypoguesias*), can result from disorders of oral health, dental procedures, and some commonly prescribed medications (including antibiotics, antidepressants, antihypertensives, psychiatric drugs, analgesics, and chemotherapy agents). Neurological disorders such as Alzheimer's disease, renal and liver disease, diabetes, and viral infections have all been reported to be associated with taste losses or distortions.

The list of diseases associated with partial (*hyposmia*) or complete (*anosmia*) smell loss, or smell distortion (*dysosmia*) is even more extensive. Significant losses are reported in renal and liver disease, HIV infections, thyroid illness, epilepsy, Alzheimer's, and Parkinson's diseases. Most commonly, though, smell losses are associated with both acute and chronic diseases of the upper respiratory tract (including colds and influenza), nasal sinus disease, and allergies. Five percent of victims of head trauma also have some degree of smell loss. In cases of severe head trauma, smell loss is often complete and irreversible, resulting from a shearing of the olfactory nerve fibers at the point where they enter the brain through the base of the skull.

Olfactory functioning is also susceptible to environmental toxins, making smell loss an occupational health issue. A variety of compounds used in manufacturing and other work environments, including metal dusts such as those of cadmium and nickel, solvents (acetone), and irritant gases (formaldehyde) have been implicated as causes of smell loss, particularly with long-term exposure. Cigarette smoking is known to produce chronic decreases in olfactory sensitivity, although this tends to recover once smoking is given up.

Diseases that affect smell and taste tend to be more prevalent as we age, as does the taking of medications that can produce deficits. Beyond these causes, however, we can also look forward to a "natural decline" in our ability to detect and identify smell and taste qualities, and a lessening of their impact. Using a 40-item "scratch and sniff" odor identification test, Richard Doty and colleagues at the University of Pennsylvania Medical Center showed that in both men and women, odor identification is reasonably stable until we reach our eighth decade. From this point on, the decline is fairly pronounced, corresponding to some extent to declines in vision and hearing during these years. Odors, and consequently flavors, are also less intense as we age, and our ability to detect subtle changes in intensity is reduced.

The sense of taste tends to survive aging somewhat better than our ability to smell. The threshold level at which tastes are detected increases, and taste intensity decreases, although not substantially, and not equally for all taste qualities—bitterness perception is particularly diminished. The ability to distinguish between different concentrations of tastants is also affected. Such losses, while not dramatic, can still have significant consequences. The levels of sweetness and saltiness that are considered by elderly people to be optimum in foods are generally higher, and food that is not adjusted accordingly may be considered bland.

One notable consequence of both smell and taste losses due to aging is that eating enjoyment is reduced. Particularly in institutionalized or hospitalized elderly people, this may exacerbate problems of anorexia and poor nutrition.

These seemingly distinct adaptive processes reflect an underlying principle on which the hedonic properties of tastes are based. Animal studies have suggested that the palatability of any taste compound, and the responsiveness of taste cells in the brainstem, is strongly related to its toxicity. At one end of the spectrum are highly toxic

MEASURING THE SENSORY QUALITIES OF FOODS

To produce foods that meet consumer needs, food manufacturers need to know the relative contributions of the various sensory qualities—tastes, odors, and textures—to the flavor of foods. Arguably, until this is known, it is difficult if not impossible to understand the consumer's responses to the product. Such information can be used to guide product development and ensure a quality product by allowing measurement of the effects of different production methods, changes in ingredients, and storage.

The process of describing and measuring the sensory qualities of foods and beverages is known as descriptive analysis (DA). To perform DA, small panels of typically ten or twelve individuals receive extensive training, often over a period of many months. During this time, the panelists learn to be consistent in their use of specific labels to describe sensory qualities. Such intensive training is necessary because of our generally poor ability to identify odors and flavors. Even with common food flavors, correct identification can be as low as 50 percent. Despite being able to say that an odor or flavor is highly familiar, we are often at a loss to identify the correct name. This has been labeled the "tip of the nose" phenomenon. In addition, to describe texture qualities, an entire vocabulary must be learned and applied appropriately. Fortunately, our ability to attach names to sensory qualities improves with feedback and practice. Importantly, too, training allows "concept alignment"—essentially an agreement as to the meaning of sensory descriptors and what constitutes examples of the concept. For example, the panel might need to agree that the term "lemon odor" refers to the odor of fresh lemon juice but not that of lemonade.

Providing labels for sensory qualities actually improves our ability to "see" those qualities in the midst of a complex food or beverage. To a novice wine drinker, a glass of sauvignon blanc tastes like white wine; with

experience, however, we learn that this wine variety often has odor "notes" reminiscent of asparagus or cut grass. Providing examples of these notes allows panelists to perceive these qualities within the wine. As a result, they are increasingly better able to detect that note each time they encounter this wine variety—in effect, panelists end up perceiving a collection of sensory qualities, whereas before they could only identify the taste as that of white wine.

Quantifying the intensity of those qualities that are identified is a key aspect of DA, allowing us to measure differences between products in a scientific manner. Training improves our ability to measure sensory qualities using rating scales. Measurements made with rating scales are always relative—they do not quantify an absolute quantity unlike, for example, measuring the concentration of a chemical compound. But they can nevertheless be used reliably with training. Moreover, there are no alternatives. No instrument yet devised can reflect the complexity of human perception.

When developing these skills, trained panelists become less and less like consumers of the product. In fact, the aim is to have them approach the product in an entirely analytical way, which means ignoring any likes and dislikes and responding as though they were an instrument.

Once a panel is trained for a specific food, they are able to produce a flavor profile for a selection, or sometimes all, of the product's sensory qualities. In effect, this becomes the "sensory recipe" for that product. While flavor profiles say nothing about whether or not a product is liked, knowing the flavor profile of foods that are highly preferred can provide valuable information to guide future product development and predict the effects of variations in the sensory qualities.

compounds, which are rejected as unpalatable by both humans and many animals primarily due to bitterness; at the other end are highly nutritive substances with low toxicity that are well accepted, mainly because they are sweet. This neural and behavioral organization has led to the hypothesis that preferences for tastes are the method by which our bodies maintain their own physiological well-being. This makes considerable sense if our gustatory system is viewed as being at the interface between the external and internal environments. In this regard, we can view taste as being a "gatekeeper" whose function is to ensure that ingested substances maximize our sur-

vival. At least in this functional way, it is appropriate to talk about tastes as a continuum and to view sweetness and bitterness as opposites.

Consistent with the "gatekeeper" idea, regions of the brain responsible for processing information about tastes also receive neural information from the gut, and there is ample evidence of mutual interactions between taste perceptions and internal metabolic processes. Thus, metabolic states can modulate the palatability of tastes. The craving for salt when deprived of it has already been mentioned—but how does the body let us know it wants

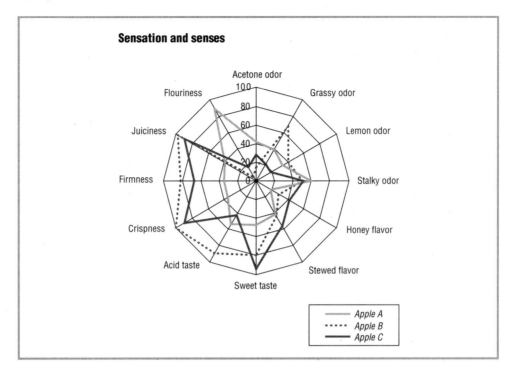

A "spider-web" graph used to show the mean ratings given by a descriptive analysis panel for a variety of odor, taste, and texture attributes in three apple varieties. This provides a sensory profile of these apples, allowing study of their similarities and differences. Distance from the center of the web represents increasing intensity of each sensory attribute, so that Apple B has the strongest *grassy* odor, followed by Apple A, with Apple C being the least intense for this quality. GRAPH COURTESY OF SHANE WALKER AND HORT RESEARCH, NEW ZEALAND

more salt? Studies in rodents have shown that "salt-best" taste cells in the brain actually decrease their responsiveness to salt following salt deprivation. Interestingly, however, this is accompanied by increases in the responsiveness of "sweet-best" cells to salt. This suggests that salt has become more pleasant, which would act to promote salt consumption to restore normal salt levels. In humans, too, the preferred level of salt in foods increases following salt depletion, and the rated desirability of salty foods goes up. This effect has also been shown for amino acids in cases of malnourished children and the elderly, in studies in which the addition of an otherwise unpalatable amino acid mixture increased the consumption of a soup. Similarly, animals fed a diet deficient in just one essential amino acid such as lysine will recognize its presence in foods, consuming them preferentially. Just the reverse seems to happen as a response to repletion. Sweetness becomes less pleasant following consumption of glucose, a phenomenon that is accompanied by decreased activity in "sweet-best" taste cells in the brain. Conversely, tastes are also able to influence metabolic processes, even prior to the nutrients' absorption by the gut. These so-called cephalic phase responses include increases in salivation and secretion of gastric enzymes and insulin, changes that prepare one for receiving the nutrients and energy provided by foods.

Chemesthesis: The Perception of Pungency

If the acidity in our apple is high enough, we might also perceive a degree of "bite" or "sharpness" due to activation of the free nerve endings of the Vth (trigeminal) cranial nerve. This nerve, which sends branches into the eyes, the nose, the mouth, and especially the tongue, transmits information regarding a wide range of tactile sensations, plus warmth, cooling, and even pain (think *very* hot curry). These sensations, often called pungency in the context of foods, are important to our appreciation of flavor in many foods and beverages. A cola drink without the fizz; the glass of wine without its sharpness; and onion, mustard, and horseradish without their bite or ability to induce tears have lost much of their defining quality. Whenever we talk about tactile sensations—stinging, biting, burning, numbing, tingling, or cooling—we are referring to pungent or chemesthetic qualities.

Trigeminally mediated sensations also very often contribute to the odors that we perceive in our environment. The eye-opening qualities of ammonia and many solvents derive from their ability to stimulate the trigeminal nerve as well as olfactory receptors. Not all such sensations are unpleasant. The cooling effects of peppermint, producing the pleasant illusion that our nasal passages have suddenly opened, are similarly mediated.

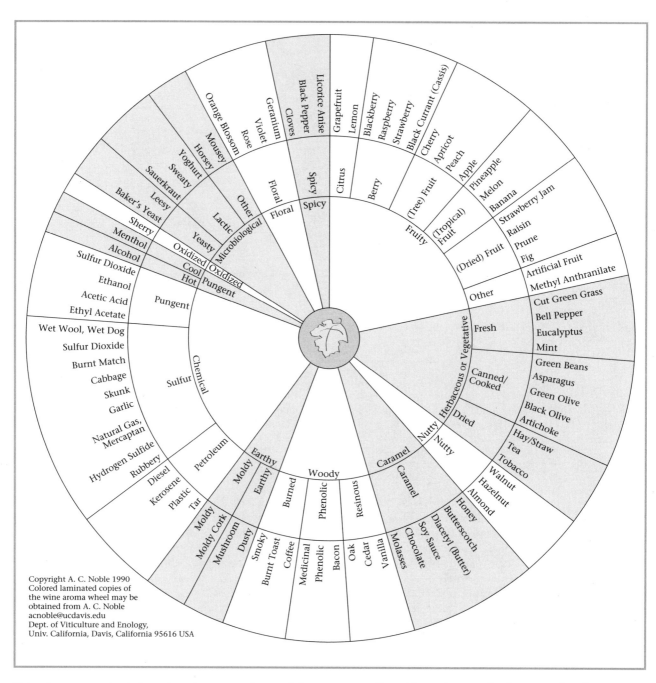

This wine aroma wheel shows how taste, sensation, and the senses are affected by various smells, flavors, and such taste components as saltiness, bitterness, and sweetness. For example, start from the center with fruity. Taste a wine and then narrow the fruitiness to berry or citrus (or both), then taste again to judge what flavor sensations are appropriate in the outer wheel. COURTESY A. C. NOBLE.

The trigeminal nerve also transmits information about temperature. It is not surprising then that chemically mediated chemesthetic qualities are modified by heating and cooling. The most obvious example of this is the ability of cool water to instantly eliminate chili-induced burning; conversely, this same burning is greater if the food is also (temperature) hot.

While pungent qualities are important sensory components of foods throughout the world, pungency is often associated primarily with cultures such as those of Korea, Vietnam, Thailand, and Mexico, whose cuisines use a lot of chili. These cuisines provide much greater flavor impact than typical Western diets, and their recent popularity in Western countries may reflect not just increased availability, but a striving for new, intense culinary sensations. Even so, many people have reservations about hot (spicy) food. This is not surprising given that pain, oral or otherwise, is a clear signal to warn that damage has occurred or is imminent. The main heat-producing compound in chilies is capsaicin, a powerful irritant. However, despite common anxieties, there is no evidence that it damages otherwise healthy stomach linings or kills taste buds.

Even regular hot-food eaters complain, though, that if a food is *too* hot, appreciation of other aspects of flavor are spoiled or overwhelmed. On the face of it, it seems evident that such a strong sensation should overwhelm a weaker one. We are used to suppression of flavor and taste qualities by other flavors and tastes—for example, reducing the sourness of lemon juice by adding sweetness. Yet, the research evidence for this occurring with "heat" is fairly weak. When capsaicin (even at levels equivalent to a very spicy meal) is combined with tastes or odors in mixtures, only sweetness is reliably reduced.

The failure to find stronger effects of burning sensations is certainly contrary to popular belief and, perhaps, experience. Wine commentators, grappling with the question of what to drink with spicy food, commonly invoke the idea that hot foods overwhelm "subtle" wine flavors. However, it may be that burning sensations are simply a more prominent or memorable sensory experience since they persist long after the tastes and flavors have disappeared. Evaluating the intensity of something, we typically make comparisons ("sweet compared to what?"). Especially if the level of pungency is higher than an individual finds pleasant, this phenomenon might simply reflect the fact that the burn is intense and the flavor is not a "real" reduction of flavor intensity.

Texture and Mouthfeel

Problems with texture are a common reason for rejecting foods. It is unlikely that we will finish an apple if it is either mushy or rock-hard. Our perception of many texture qualities relies on information from mechanoreceptors in the tongue, gums, and palate (also part of the trigeminal nerve) that detect the shape of food particles, together with pressure sensors in the jaw and gums. These sensors give feedback on how much force to exert in chewing, information that forms the basis for hardness perception. Compared to some other senses, hearing is perhaps of lesser importance in food appreciation. Nevertheless, the sound of the crunch when we bite into an apple allows us to fully appreciate its freshness and ripeness, and forms an integral part of our perception of its texture.

Sometimes in the past considered a taste, the property of astringency is now generally accepted as a set of *mouthfeel* sensations. Characteristic of foods and beverages containing tannins, including some fruits, nuts, tea, and cranberry juice, astringency consists of sensations of drying, puckering, and roughness felt on the mucous lining of the mouth. These sensations result when the tannins cause the lubricating proteins in saliva to precipitate out. Although it sounds largely unpleasant, astringency is a good example of how responses to sensory qualities are often highly dependent on context. While one of the reasons that we might not eat a green banana is that it tends to leave the mouth feeling like a sandpit, drinkers of red wine value these sensations, at least to some extent. When a wine is described as "dry," the sensation is due to a significant extent to astringency.

Other textural sensations are produced by the water (for example, juiciness) or fat content of foods. Fat, in particular, is a key component of many of those foods that are highly liked, including red meat, desserts, cakes, chocolate, and dairy foods. Fat not only produces a sought-after texture, it is also an important carrier for flavor. Fat-reduced foods have often failed to be accepted because they were generally low in both flavor and textural properties such as creaminess. In addition to the desirable properties that fats create, liking for fat may actually be innate, because of its ability to provide energy (in a similar way to sweetness). This possibility is supported by recent evidence to suggest that fatty acids may have their own receptor—in other words, our bodies adapt to be able to detect fat. Given these considerations, it is not surprising that many people report that it is the sensory properties of low-fat foods that are responsible for poor compliance to dietary advice.

Sensory Integration: What Are We *Really* Perceiving?

Despite the contribution from all of these senses, what we ultimately perceive—as opposed to the sensations we've experienced—is *an apple*. In his seminal *The Senses Considered as Perceptual Systems* (1966), the psychologist J. J. Gibson proposed that the purpose of perception was to seek out objects in our environment, particularly those objects that are biologically important. Nowhere is this more evident than in our perception of food qualities. Although we know implicitly that, while eating, a variety of signals are impinging on our gustatory, olfactory, tactile, visual, and auditory systems, this type of analysis does not come naturally. Thankfully, what we perceive when we sit down to dinner are "objects"—a steak and a glass of red wine—rather than a collection of distinct sensory signals. Moreover, likes and dislikes naturally spring from this synthetic mode of perception since we are responding to objects that we have learned to recognize as foods and that are therefore important to survival. Initial, "gut" responses to foods are almost always hedonic, and this naturally precedes accepting or rejecting the food.

The perception of food qualities reflects the integration of information from multiple sources. This is seen in the convergence of inputs from different sensory modalities in the brain. Edmund Rolls of Oxford University has described convergence of taste and odor information in what may be the physiological basis of flavor

TASTE PERCEPTION: ARE WE ALL THE SAME?

"Now, anatomy teaches that all tongues are not equally provided with these papillae, and that one tongue may possess three times as many as another . . . the empire of taste also has its blind and deaf subjects." —Brillat-Savarin, *The Physiology of Taste* (1825)

Black coffee and beer are not only amongst the most commonly consumed beverages in many countries, they are also amongst the most commonly rejected by first-time users—primarily due to their bitterness. Clearly, preferences for initially disliked foods and beverages can develop. Repeated consumption itself tends to lead to increased liking. But why do some people more easily develop a liking for beer than others, and why, for some, does it remain unpalatable because of the bitterness? Research has begun to focus on individual differences in taste sensitivity as an explanation. While there have been some previous attempts to classify responses to tastes—for example, into those whose liking for sweetness tends to increase (sweet likers), versus those whose degree of liking flattens out or decreases (non-likers), with increasing concentrations of sweeteners—such classifications are poor predictors of food likes and dislikes. Recently, however, there has been a growing body of research that has investigated individual differences in taste sensitivity, the results of which have raised the possibility that these variations may be important influences on food preferences.

In 1931, A. L. Fox, an industrial chemist with the DuPont Company, reported the discovery that some people appeared to be "blind" to the bitterness of a compound, phenylthiocarbamide, or PTC. Subsequent research confirmed that this difference between individuals had a genetic basis, and it was initially thought that non-tasters might lack a receptor for PTC and other thiourea compounds. For several decades following Fox's discovery, the main focus of research was on this genetic basis, and how this might vary across different population groups.

In the 1970s, however, this phenomenon began to interest taste scientists, in particular, Linda Bartoshuk from Yale University. Since then, our understanding of such genetic variations in taste sensitivity has grown considerably. Using a compound chemically related to PTC, 6-n-propylthiouracil (PROP), Bartoshuk and colleagues have demonstrated that each of us belongs to one of three groups—non-tasters, medium-tasters, or super-tasters—each varying in their response to PROP. Non-tasters, around 20–25 percent of the population (at least in Western cultures), find PROP tasteless, or very weakly bitter. Medium-tasters (approximately 50 percent) find PROP mildly to moderately bitter, while super-tasters (20–25 percent) find this compound almost traumatically bitter.

---

perception. He identified neurons in the olfactory area of the monkey cortex that responded specifically to qualities that occur together in flavors, for example, the sweetness of glucose and fruit odors. However, these neurons did not respond to incongruous combinations, such as saltiness and these same odors. Such neurons may actually start off responding only to odors and learn to respond to sensory combinations during repeated pairing of particular tastes and odors when they occur together as a flavor. Multimodal neurons in other sensory systems are thought to enhance the detection of, and reduce ambiguity associated with, external stimuli. In the case of odors and tastes, these neurons could help to resolve any ambiguity regarding the wisdom of consuming particular foods. Perceiving whole flavors, rather than distinct sensory signals, can be seen, therefore, as a survival strategy.

Interactions within Flavors

The brain's integration of food qualities makes it difficult to discuss the different sensory systems in isolation from one another since these systems tend to interact. The way in which sensory properties like color can influence odors and tastes was mentioned earlier. Because sensory properties are perceived as aspects of the same

"object," we repeatedly associate the occurrence of one property with that of another.

In addition to setting up expectations for other sensory qualities to follow, learned associations between different qualities in foods can actually determine the qualities that we perceive. One of the most interesting examples is the ability of odors to rapidly form associations with other sensory qualities, especially tastes. In what appears to be the perceptual equivalent of the neurons described by Rolls, novel odors that are repeatedly experienced combined with a sour taste start to smell "sour"; those combined with sweetness start to smell "sweet." These effects are borne out in everyday experience. When asked to describe the odor of vanilla or caramel or raspberry, we will commonly use the word "sweet." This seems to be more than simply the fact that the odor recalls a food that was sweet since such odors can influence the intensity of that taste. Strawberry odor when placed together with tastes in solution can both enhance the sweetness of sucrose and reduce the sourness of citric acid, just as the addition of "real" sugar would.

Thus, our final perceptions receive input not just from a variety of sensory systems, but also from our mem-

Such findings would merely be of academic interest if it were not for the fact that, as observed so long ago by Brillat-Savarin, there is also considerable variation between individuals in the number of fungiform papillae on the tongue. In fact, different degrees of sensitivity to PROP are highly correlated with such variations in the density of fungiform papillae. Since individual papillae are not specialized for specific tastes, it is not surprising that those sensitive to PROP also tend to be sensitive to other bitter compounds, including caffeine and quinine, and also to the sweetness of sucrose, the sourness of citric acid, and the saltiness of common salt. The artificial sweetener, saccharin, is perceived as both sweeter and more bitter by PROP tasters than by non-tasters. Bartoshuk has suggested that, effectively, the different taster groups inhabit different taste worlds.

Although these are not taste qualities, PROP taster groups also vary in their perception of the texture of fats and the pungency of alcohol and chili. This is because fibers of the trigeminal nerve in the mouth, responsible for transmitting information on the majority of tactile and irritant qualities that we perceive in foods, tend to be anatomically associated with taste cells. So, the more taste cells that an individual has, the more trigeminal fibers they also possess.

These differences in taste *perception* influence how much tastes are liked, which ultimately produces different patterns of food preferences. For example, coffee, spicy, and sharp-tasting foods such as some cheeses are liked more by non-tasters than tasters. Liking for cruciferous vegetables such as broccoli, cabbage, and brussels sprouts also appears to be related to variations in perception of their bitterness, and hence they are less likely to be consumed by PROP medium- and super-tasters than by non-tasters.

These relationships, apparent in both young children and adults, may turn out to be crucial in our understanding of food choice as it relates to disease risk. Increased consumption of cruciferous vegetables and reduced consumption of fats have both been linked to reduced risks for certain cancers. While the links between diet and diseases such as cancers and cardiovascular disease are increasingly being demonstrated, the notion that taste sensitivity could also predict risk has only recently been suggested, and may represent an important step in our understanding of susceptibility to dietary-related diseases. Sensory factors have frequently been implicated in the difficulties that we face in switching to healthier foods, e.g., lower-fat foods. These recent findings suggest that how successfully we are able to switch from a food containing a high level of sugar, salt, or fat to a version that is more consistent with health requirements may also be partly determined by genetic variations in taste sensitivity.

ory of past associations. In practical terms, it means that our perception of a quality like sweetness within foods will often include a contribution from a sweet odor and a sweet taste. Such phenomena also help us to appreciate that the sensory properties that foods possess derive not just from perception of their chemical constituents, but also from complex cognitive processes. Understanding these processes—even for the humble apple—requires inputs from a variety of scientific disciplines, most notably psychology, food science, neurophysiology, and molecular biology.

See also **Brillat-Savarin, Anthelme; Eating: Anatomy and Physiology of Eating; Wine.**

BIBLIOGRAPHY

Bartoshuk, Linda M. "History of Taste Research." In *Handbook of Perception: Tasting and Smelling.* Edited by Edward C. Carterette and Morton P. Friedman. Volume VI A. New York: Academic Press, 1978.

Bartoshuk, Linda M. "Bitter Taste of Saccharin Related to the Genetic Ability to Taste the Bitter Substance of 6-n-Propylthiouracil." *Science* 205 (1979): 934–935.

Bartoshuk, Linda M. "The Biological Basis of Food Perception and Acceptance." *Food Quality and Preference* 4 (1993): 21–32.

Bartoshuk, Linda M., Valerie B. Duffy, and Inglis J. Miller. "PTC/PROP Tasting: Anatomy, Psychophysics, and Sex Effects." *Physiology & Behavior* 56 (1994): 1165–1171.

Beauchamp, Gary K. "The Human Preference for Excess Salt." *American Scientist* 75 (1987): 27–33.

Breslin, Paul A. S. "Human Gustation." In *The Neurobiology of Taste and Smell*. Edited by Thomas E. Finger, Wayne L. Silver, and Diego Restrepo. 2nd ed. New York: Wiley-Liss, 2000.

Brillat-Savarin, Jean-Anthelme. *The Physiology of Taste.* Translated by Anne Drayton. London: Penguin, 1994.

Buck, Linda, and Richard Axel. "A Novel Multigene Family May Encode Odorant Receptors: A Molecular Basis for Odor Recognition." *Cell* 65 (1991): 175–187.

Cain, William S. "Educating Your Nose." *Psychology Today* 15 (1981): 48–56.

Chaudhari, Nirupa, Ana Marie Landin, and Stephen D. A. Roper. "A Metabotropic Glutamate Receptor Variant Functions as a Taste Receptor." *Nature Neuroscience* 3 (2000): 113–119.

Christensen, Carol M. "Effects of Color on Aroma, Flavor, and Texture Judgments of Foods." *Journal of Food Science* 48 (1983): 787–790.

Clydesdale, Fergus M. "Color as a Factor in Food Choice." *Critical Reviews in Food Science and Nutrition* 33 (1993): 83–101.

Deems, Daniel A., Richard L. Doty, et al. "Smell and Taste Disorders, A Study of 750 Patients from the University of Pennsylvania Smell and Taste Center." *Archives of Otolaryngology Head and Neck Surgery* 117 (1991): 519–528.

Deliza, Rosires, and Halliday J. H. MacFie. "The Generation of Sensory Expectation by External Cues and Its Effect on Sensory Perception and Hedonic Ratings: A Review." *Journal of Sensory Studies* 11 (1996): 103–128.

Delwiche, Jeannine. "Are There 'Basic' Tastes?" *Trends in Food Science & Technology* 7 (1996): 411–415.

Drewnowski, Adam, and Cheryl L. Rock. "The Influence of Genetic Taste Markers on Food Acceptance." *American Journal of Clinical Nutrition* 62 (1995): 506–511.

Erickson, Robert P. "The Evolution of Neural Coding Ideas in the Chemical Senses." *Physiology & Behavior* 69 (2000): 3–16.

Frank, Robert A., Nicolette J. van der Klaauw, and Hendrick N. J. Schifferstein. "Both Perceptual and Conceptual Factors Influence Taste-Odor and Taste-Taste Interactions." *Perception & Psychophysics* 54 (1993): 343–354.

Friedman, Mark I., Michael G. Tordoff, and Morley R. Kare, eds. *Chemical Senses.* Vol 4. *Appetite and Nutrition.* New York: M. Dekker, 1991.

Fuke, Shinya, and Tetsuji Shimizu. "Sensory and Preference Aspects of Umami." *Trends in Food Science & Technology* 4 (1993): 246–251.

Ganchrow, Judith R. "Ontogeny of Human Taste Perception." In *Handbook of Olfaction and Gustation.* Edited by Richard L. Doty. New York: M. Dekker, 1995.

Getchell, Tom V., Linda M. Bartoshuk, et al., eds. *Smell and Taste in Health and Disease.* New York: Raven Press, 1991.

Gibson, John J. *The Senses Considered as Perceptual Systems.* Boston: Houghton Mifflin, 1966.

Guo, Sun-Wei, and Danielle R. Reed. "The Genetics of Phenylthiocarbamide Perception." *Annals of Human Biology* (2000): 1–31.

Kawamura, Yojiro, and Morley R. Kare, eds. *Umami: A Basic Taste.* New York: M. Dekker, 1987.

Laing, David G., William S. Cain, Robert L. McBride, and Barry W. Ache, eds. *Perception of Complex Smells and Tastes.* Sydney: Academic Press, 1989.

Lawless, Harry T. "Flavor." In *Handbook of Perception and Cognition,* Vol. 16, *Cognitive Ecology.* Edited by Edward C. Carterrette and Morton P. Friedman. San Diego: Academic Press, 1996.

Lawless, Harry T., and Barbara P. Klein, eds. *Sensory Science Theory and Applications in Foods.* New York: M. Dekker, 1991.

McBride, Robert L., and Halliday J. H. MacFie, eds. *Psychological Basis of Sensory Evaluation.* New York: Elsevier Science Publishing, 1990.

McBurney, Donald H., and Janneane F. Gent "On the Nature of Taste Qualities." *Psychological Bulletin* 86 (1979): 151–167.

McLaughlin, Susan, and Robert F. Margolskee. "The Sense of Taste." *American Scientist* 82 (1994): 538–545.

Mombaerts, Peter. "How Smell Develops." *Nature Neuroscience* 4 (2001): 1192–1198.

Noble, Anne C. "Analysis of Wine Sensory Properties." In *Wine Analysis.* Edited by H. F. Linskens and J. F. Jackson. Berlin: Springer-Verlag, 1988.

Oakley, Bruce. "Basic Taste Physiology: Human Perspectives." In *Clinical Measurement of Taste and Smell.* Edited by Herbert L. Meiselman and Richard S. Rivlin. New York: Macmillan, 1986.

Prescott, John. "Flavor as a Psychological Construct: Implications for Perceiving and Measuring the Sensory Qualities of Foods." *Food Quality & Preference* 10 (1999): 349–356.

Prescott, John, and Richard J. Stevenson. "Pungency in Food Perception and Preference." *Food Reviews International* 11 (1995): 665–698.

Prescott, John, David Laing, et al. "Hedonic Responses to Taste Solutions: A Cross-Cultural Study of Japanese and Australians." *Chemical Senses* 17 (1992): 801–809.

Rawson, Nancy E. "Human Olfaction." In *The Neurobiology of Taste and Smell.* Edited by Thomas E. Finger, Wayne L. Silver, and Diego Restrepo. New York: Wiley-Liss, 2000.

Rolls, Edmund T. "Taste and Olfactory Processing in the Brain and Its Relation to the Control of Eating." *Critical Reviews in Neurobiology* 11 (1997): 263–287.

Rozin, Paul. "Taste-Smell Confusions' and the Duality of the Olfactory Sense." *Perception & Psychophysics* 31 (1982): 397–401.

Schiffman, Susan S. "Perception of Taste and Smell in Elderly Persons." *Critical Reviews in Food Science and Nutrition* 33 (1993): 17–26.

Schiffman, Susan S., and Robert P. Erickson. "A Psychophysical Model for Gustatory Quality." *Physiology & Behavior* 7 (1971): 617–633.

Schiffman, Susan S. and Carol A. Gatlin. "Clinical Physiology of Taste and Smell." *Annual Review of Nutrition* 13 (1993): 405–436.

Scott, Tom R. "Taste, Feeding, and Pleasure." In *Progress in Psychobiology and Physiological Psychology.* Edited by Alan N. Epstein and Adrian R. Morrison. New York: Academic Press, 1992.

Smith, David V., and Robert F. Margolskee. "Making Sense of Taste." *Scientific American* 284 (March 2001): 32–39.

Stein, Barry E., and M. Alex Meredith. *The Merging of the Senses.* Cambridge, Mass.: MIT Press, 1993.

Steiner, Jacob E., Dieter Glaser, et al. "Comparative Expression of Hedonic Impact: Affective Reactions to Taste by Human Infants and Other Primates." *Neuroscience & Biobehavioral Reviews,* 25 (2001): 53–74.

Stone, Herbert, and Joel L. Sidel. *Sensory Evaluation Practices.* 2nd ed. Orlando, Fla.: Academic Press, 1993.

Zellner, Debra A., and Lori A. Whitten. "The Effect of Color Intensity and Appropriateness on Color-Induced Odor Enhancement." *American Journal of Psychology* 112 (1999): 585–604.

                                                    John Prescott

SERVING OF FOOD.

The step between cooking and eating is far from insignificant. With sophisticated production and preparation, the serving of food involves important role divisions, etiquette, and cultural forms.

Such are the intricate social and cultural pressures that being served at an unfamiliar table or even just the arrival of an unfamiliar food can make diners uncomfortable. Families can fight over shares—the social struggle for resources in microcosm. But the serving of food is also a site of courtesy and generosity. Domestic hospitality depends on serving graciously, taking care of guests first, and offering second helpings. Professional waiters commit complicated orders to memory, return smoothly without mix-ups, perhaps conduct elaborate serving rituals, and note before anyone else any missing components.

Types of Service

One logistical variable is the proximity of the cooking. This can be immediately in front of the diners so that the cook, host, or diners serve, at an adjacent kitchen as in restaurant waiter service, or at a distant factory when packaged snack foods are trucked to coin-activated machines. Serving can be done from staging posts, whether the immediate table, sideboard, dumb-waiter, trolley (as in the Hong Kong *yum cha*) or picnic basket. Diners sitting regally along only one side of a table enable service from the front; served from behind, dishes are conventionally offered from the left and taken from the right.

The number of diners changes the picture: from a handful of people around a campfire to thousands in dining halls, to vast street banquets, which have sometimes been served using bicycles.

Another key variable is the ratio of servers to diners. A ratio of one-to-one or even higher has enabled magnificent displays, vast tableaux, from which attendants could retrieve helpings on command. One waiter for ten diners or more can readily take orders and carry individual plates already made up in the kitchen. Even lower labor levels are needed for a cafeteria or hotel buffet, where diners help themselves and face the indignities of queuing.

The food itself is the most important variable. Dishes might require dressing, lifting, pouring, spooning, slicing or, most impressively, carving. In agrarian societies, eaters have helped themselves, or been served, from a common bowl or pot, but many meals involve two or more containers. The boxed Japanese meal called a *bentō* should display at least ten pretty items ready for the

STYLES OF SERVING

à la carte: 'by the card'. The diner orders the progression of dishes beforehand from a menu or bill of fare typically showing the price of each item.
service à la française: 'service in the French manner'. Each course magnificently arrayed like a buffet, from which the diner or servant selects.
service à la russe: 'service in the Russian manner'. One dish at a time, either served at the table or already plated in the kitchen.
table d'hôte: 'host's table'. A common meal served at a fixed price, typical of an inn.

choosing. Sometimes diners have no choice, which is the case with table d'hôte (sharing the "host's table" typical of an inn), but a selection is often served. Chinese diners select food from the table and perhaps from a lazy Susan (central revolving stand). This can magnify into whole tables or "services" of food, which might even be changed through the meal as in the grand French style, service *à la française*.

The alternative, service *à la russe*, brings a series of dishes through the meal, perhaps carved in the dining room but often plated in the kitchen for each person, and is particularly associated with French-style restaurants. The food tends to be hotter and the meal to last longer. Individual choice is restored in restaurants with à la carte, that is, selections made previously from a menu or bill of fare.

The nineteenth-century debate about service *à la française* and service *à la russe* is not arcane, but reflects the broad historical trend from simultaneous serving to successive presentation, and from mass displays to individualized plates. The distinction is blurred, though, since many meals have been served sequentially, and the grand French spread (*le grand couvert*) already had several courses. Each plate in the modern Western style will probably carry several items.

Server and Served

The sharing of food in meals gives serving its social significance. Meals also enable the sharing of roles, or division of labor, each person contributing what they can. Herein lies a paradox, for the very act of sharing food introduces a split between server and served.

Servers can take pride: Italian waiting can be highly skilled and as entertaining as any opera, French service so suave as to be hardly noticed, and the proverbially "resting" New York actors can demonstrate people skills.

There were several methods of serving food in the nineteenth century, the newest style being service *à la russe* (Russian style) shown here. This is the serving style employed by most modern restaurants, whereby the food is cut up into serving portions in the kitchen rather than at the table. Wood engraving from Alphonse Gouffé's *Royal Cookery Book* (London, 1868), copy of Charles Delmonico. Roughwood Collection.

In a civilized society, people might take turns being served and serving. Jesus said he came "not to be served but to serve" (Mark 10:45 and Matthew 20:28). The Greek *diakonia* could mean "service" in a general sense, but Jesus meant the specific serving at table, his mission centered on table-fellowship.

However, serving has generally retained low status. "Beulah, peel me a grape," ordered American actor-writer Mae West in her movie *I'm No Angel* (1933). The words "serve," "service," and "servant" derive from the Latin *servus* for 'slave'.

When people began keeping livestock and other stored wealth, they introduced the concept of private property. Given that men made themselves the owners of the new sources of foodstuffs, this phase marked the "world-historic defeat of the female sex," continues German social philosopher Friedrich Engels in the *Origin of the Family, Private Property and the State* (chapter 2, "The Family") in 1884. The "woman was degraded, enthralled, the slave of the man's lust, a mere instrument for breeding children." She also cooked and served.

Women have often served men first—and larger shares than warranted by different body sizes and energy requirements—even at the expense of their own health. In *Cooking, Cuisine, and Class* (1982), British anthropologist Jack Goody notes that women of the Gonja of Ghana distributed larger portions of cooked meat to men's bowls. Even when the meat went into a common soup, he found that educated women held back, though the men "jokingly claim that if women do not help themselves beforehand, they are fools" (p. 68). The differential distribution of food between sexes shows up in modern societies, as Nickie Charles and Marion Kerr illustrate in *Women, Food and Families* (1988).

Friedrich Engels also argued (chapter 9, "Barbarism and Civilization") that the increase in production with agrarian civilizations increased the demand for labor, which was furnished by captives of war made into slaves. The Roman propertied classes numbered their household slaves in dozens, sometimes hundreds, and they ran the meals. A crowd, typically male and properly attired, carried in the meal's three to six courses. A contemporary observed that "all night long they have to stand around, hungry and dumb." Real prestige belonged to the wine waiters—who were expected to be "young, smooth-shaven (but long-haired), and sexually attractive," writes John H. D'Arms in "Slaves at Roman *convivia*" (1991).

To believe the satire of a nouveau riche banquet at the height of Nero's Rome, described in the *Satyricon* of Petronius, the "boys" might make dozens of entrances, pouring out snow-cooled water, sprinkling the room with colored sawdust, carrying round bread, towels and hot water, anointing the diners' feet, singing, clapping, and dancing. Elaborate carving was already well established, and Petronius describes a man slashing at a great platter of plump fowls, sows' udders, a hare and fish, with his hands moving in time to the orchestra, "like a charioteer battling to the sound of organ music." At the same feast, a whole boiled calf is demolished by a carver playing the warrior Ajax in a scene from Homer, sharing the pieces on the point of his sword among the surprised guests.

Slaves routinely had access to leftovers, but any concessions to conviviality have to be set against the fundamental powerlessness. Suetonius, a biographer of the Caesars, relates how Emperor Tiberius once publicly reprimanded the lecherous old spendthrift Cestius Gallus, while privately accepting his dinner invitation as long as the waitresses were naked. Humiliation and punishment (including murder) contrasted with the convivial setting. Again according to Suetonius, a slave stole a strip of silver from a couch at a public dinner, so Emperor Caligula had the executioners lop off the slave's hands, hang them around his neck, and take him on a tour of the tables.

Being a house rather than field slave could bring privileges in the American South. As Eugene D. Genovese notes in *Roll, Jordan, Roll* (1975), "servants trained and polished for elegant performance as butlers, cooks, and dining-room attendants were hard to obtain and not easily spared" (p. 329). But the household staff could also have less free time, have to snatch meals when they found a moment, miss out on plantation singing and feasting, and were continually reminded of their deprivation.

Courtly Service
The recipes in the courtly English book dated around 1390, *The Forme of Cury* [Cookery], begin "Take . . ." and usually conclude "serve it forth" or "*messe* it forth." The word *mess* has referred to a portion of food, a liquid food, a made dish, and a course of foods, all of which had been "messed" forth—from the Latin *mittere*, 'to send'. Those sitting together at a banquet and sharing from the same dish were called a *mess*.

The officers in grand medieval households, where regular diners numbered in the hundreds and even thousands, included the ewerer who carried washing water and towel, the cupbearer who fetched wine, the butler who supervised butts of wine and ale, and the surveyor who controlled the surveying board to which the cook directed the platters. The carver's was still an exalted domestic station, with intricate rules to "break" that deer, "display" that crane, *alay* that pheasant, *tranche* (slice) that sturgeon, and so forth. Madeleine Pelner Cosman writes in *Fabulous Feasts* (1976) that the titles, responsibilities, and implements of food service could be carried by noblemen and sons of gentlemen. Serving could prove a means for political and professional advancement; Cardinal Morton predicted that the young Sir Thomas More, who was waiting on him, would prove a marvelous man (p. 26).

The disappearance of public carving in stylish European culture was accompanied towards the end of the nineteenth century by the switch from service *à la française* (each course or "service" arrayed like a buffet) to service *à la russe* (one dish at a time). With the cook often "plating up" behind the kitchen door, the mealtime distribution of food was moving to the back room and from the hierarchical to the individualistic. This reflected the shift in power from the aristocracy to the business class, and their more private meals.

This rationalization of food serving was supported by Thomas Walker, the London essayist of "aristology" (the art of dining). Devoting much of his 1835 weekly newspaper, *The Original*, to what he calls "attendance," Walker protested against the "cumbrous" ceremony of service *à la française*. Servants would take each dish on a circuit, and the wines move "languidly round two or three times." He favored service *à la russe*. "I like the familiar and satisfactory style both of cooking and of eating, with the dish actually before me on *mensa firma*, the solid table—not a kickshaw poked from behind, and dancing in the air between me and my lady neighbour's most inconvenient sleeve, without time to think whether I like what is offered." A small party of eight should assemble, and every dish be "served in succession, with its proper accompaniments, and between each dish there should be a short interval, to be filled up with conversation and wine, so as to prolong the repast as much as possible, . . . time would be given to the cook, and to the attendants."

Self-Service
If not enforced by marriage or slavery, household servants have been tied through affective, material and financial dependence. The smaller households late in the nineteenth century had just one or perhaps two live-in domestics, a cook and a maid. However, the employers confronted a "servant problem," because many young women preferred more public work as shopgirls. This helped stimulate the feminist dream of "kitchen-less" homes reliant on central facilities.

If the keynote of the nineteenth century was the reduction in servants, that of the twentieth was the effort to displace serving entirely. The "service industries" took over more roles of a servant with less labor. The factory took over more finished food preparation. Costs might also be reduced by "self-service." In the cafeteria, a line of customers might choose items, place them on a tray, and carry them to the cashier. Oddly, this was like a return to service *à la française*, without assistance.

McDonald's has become emblematic of casual, deskilled, and formulaic service. In 1948, at the drive-in restaurant of the McDonald brothers, Dick and Mac, at San Bernardino, about fifty miles east of Los Angeles, twenty young women waiters called "carhops" served up to 125 cars from the twenty-five item menu, featuring beef and ribs cooked in a barbecue pit fuelled with hickory chips. But the brothers faced increasing competition and labor and advertising costs, so they sacked their carhops, slashed the menu, halved the price of a hamburger to an unheard-of 15 cents, abandoned china and flatware in favor of paper bags, wrappers and cups, organized industrial kitchen equipment, and adopted rigid operating procedures to "eliminate the principal obstacle to fast-food service—the human element," corporate historian John F. Love observes in *McDonald's: Behind the Arches* (1986, pp. 11–18). The brothers put an "industry that prided itself on extremely personalized procedures" on the assembly line. Under subsequent owners, McDonald's introduced the world to the inane-sounding, "Have a nice day."

Having meals in company requires the serving of food, but this can become exploitative and inequitable. One answer is a "help yourself" culture of individualized service, but generosity is maintained when people take turns as server and served.

See also **Class, Social; Kitchens, Restaurant; Places of Consumption; Restaurants; Waiters and Waitresses.**

BIBLIOGRAPHY

Cosman, Madeleine Pelner. *Fabulous Feasts: Medieval Cookery and Ceremony.* New York: Braziller, 1976.

Charles, Nickie and Marion Kerr. *Women, Food, and Families.* Manchester, U.K.: Manchester University Press, 1988.

D'Arms, John H. "Slaves at Roman *convivia.*" In *Dining in a Classical Context,* edited by William J. Slater, pp. 171–183. Ann Arbor: University of Michigan Press, 1991.

Engels, Friedrich. *The Origin of the Family, Private Property and the State.* Moscow: Progress, 1948. Originally published in 1884.

Genovese, Eugene D. *Roll, Jordan, Roll: The World the Slaves Made.* New York: Pantheon, 1974.

Goody, Jack. *Cooking, Cuisine, and Class: A Study in Comparative Sociology.* Cambridge, U.K.: Cambridge University Press, 1982.

Hieatt, Constance, and Sharon Butler. *Curye on Inglysch.: English Culinary Manuscripts of the Fourteenth Century (including The Forme of Cury[e] [Cookery]).* London: Oxford University Press, 1985.

Love, John F. *McDonald's: Behind the Arches.* New York: Bantam, 1986.

Petronius, *The Satyricon,* and Seneca, *The Apocolocyntosis.* Translated by J. P. Sullivan. Harmondsworth, U.K.: Penguin, 1977.

Suetonius [Gaius Suetonius Tranquillus]. *The Twelve Caesars.* Translated by Robert Graves. Rev. ed. Harmondsworth, U.K.: Penguin, 1979.

Symons, Michael. *A History of Cooks and Cooking.* Urbana and Chicago University Press of Illinois Press, 2000. Originally published as *The Pudding That Took a Thousand Cooks: The Story of Cooking in Civilisation and Daily Life,* 1998.

Symons, Michael, "Did Jesus Cook?" In *Food, Power and Community: Essays in the History of Food and Drink,* edited by Robert Dare, pp. 16–28. Kent Town, South Australia: Wakefield, 1999. Discusses the Greek *diakonia* for "service."

Walker, Thomas. *The Original.* London: Renshaw, 1838. Originally 1835. Selections have also been republished as *The Art of Dining,* London: Cayme Press, 1928.

Michael Symons

SEX AND FOOD.

Food and sex are inextricably linked. Feeding insures survival of the individual while sexual activity insures survival of the species. Beyond biology, making love and eating share psychological attributes as two of life's greatest pleasures, both capable of providing a sense of nurturing, comfort, and being loved as well as instant gratification. Paradoxically, the two drives can also be the source of much psychological conflict, guilt, and shame. They generate anxiety in many cultures, partly because these are traits we share in common with animals.

Speaking of Food and Sex

The language we use to describe sex and food is very similar. In *The Rituals of Dinner* (p. 18), food anthropologist Margaret Visser describes a meal as a ritual in which "desires are aroused and fulfilled." We speak of fat, in particular, with sexual connotation—words like "juicy," "tender," "satisfying," "greasy," "soft," "great mouthfeel." In popular culture, the semantic commonality and double entendres are even more pronounced. A T-shirt sold in New Orleans, for example, displays a picture of a Louisiana oyster with the words "Eat me raw" (Schell, p. 203). The pages of women's magazines are largely filled with articles on food or sex with a typical headline reading "The Next Best Thing to Sex is . . . Chocolate." Advertising plays on sensuality in promoting acquisition of food products. Häagen-Dazs premier ice cream, for example, has run a campaign based on the tagline "Too much pleasure?" Best-sellers using food as a theme, including such sensual novels as *Chocolat* by Joanne Harris and *The Mistress of Spices* by Chitra Banergee Divakaruni, as well as memoirs with erotic elements such as *Aphrodite: A Memoir of the Senses* by Isabel Allende and *Comfort Me with Apples* by Ruth Reichl vie with self-help books about sex for top billing. In 1972, physician and sex expert Alex Comfort published his classic sex manual *The Joy of Sex,* a play on the title of the classic cookbook *The Joy of Cooking.* His approach of prescribing "recipes" for good sex was criticized.

Life's Greatest Pleasures or Pain?

Sigmund Freud blamed sexuality and the need to master and socialize sexual impulses as the root cause of psychological angst. These feelings, he reported, began at birth. He described sexual response in nursing infants, tracing the arc of sexual arousal and fulfillment, flushing of the skin, and sleep following the satisfaction of feeding. More recently, food psychologist Paul Rozin of the

University of Pennsylvania theorized in *Social Research* (p. 9) that Freud would have had a stronger case making eating the culprit in the clash between biology and society. The feeding drive, he argued, is more frequent, urgent, and crucial to everyday life and human evolution than sexuality.

A love affair that ends can provoke great pain. Similarly, in some cultures, eating too much and gaining weight can undermine self-worth and compromise chances of finding a sexual partner. Much overeating is conducted in secret, just as sex often takes place behind closed doors. It is interesting that some people, not necessarily overeaters, suffer from a social phobia in which there is a fear of being watched or humiliated while eating a meal. This phobia provokes such overwhelming anxiety that it is impossible to enjoy the pleasure of going to a restaurant. Both sex and food are associated with physical as well as psychological danger—namely the morbidity and mortality consequences of obesity, food-borne illnesses and bioterrorism as well as the risk of contracting sexually transmitted diseases (STDs) and autoimmune deficiency syndrome (AIDS).

Sexual and Feeding Appetite

To some extent, appetite for both sex and food increases with variety. Some fad diets succeed temporarily because they reduce the number of permitted foods, a restriction that presumably suppresses appetite. It is interesting to note that as variety and availability of foods, particularly imports, has increased in the United States over the past one hundred years, so has obesity. Among males, at least, a new or novel sexual partner can stimulate a sexually spent male to copulate again. This novelty effect, also known as the Coolidge effect, is not true for females, according to the newsletter of the Human Behavior and Evolution Society. Sexual appetite may be suppressed in a long-term monogamous relationship with a familiar partner.

Across Cultures

Anthropologists have long studied how sex and food intersect in less developed cultures. Among the Langkawai, a Malay island culture, kinship is defined by "incorporation," the process of neutralizing differences between people by taking in ("incorporating") some of their "foreign" substance, food or sexual fluids, through the rituals of feasting and marriage. Both acts serve to convert the Other, someone unrelated in this case, into kin, and therefore nonthreatening. In the Hua society of New Guinea, there is an implicit association between feeding and sexual intercourse in which one partner "feeds" the other. Both acts are believed to achieve the transfer of *nu*, the vital essence.

Food Sharing: Key to Intimacy

Sharing food is a way of establishing closeness. There are profound differences among cultures in this practice. Re-

Cover logo for a men's magazine called *Hot Dog* (Cleveland, Ohio, 1925). The hot dog, a food icon, is transformed into a metaphor of sexual innuendo. ROUGHWOOD COLLECTION.

search has focused on heterosexuals, but there is no reason to think that the same principles would not apply to homosexual couples. In France, sharing of restaurant food between a man and a woman takes on a sexualized characteristic. It is a common flirtatious practice to eat out of each other's plates. In this playful exchange, each partner may be testing how far the other is willing to go toward greater sexual intimacy.

Research conducted by Miller, Rozin, and Fiske has found that, in the United States, at least, college students perceive variations in food sharing as revealing the level of intimacy. The students viewed videotapes of opposite-sex couples sharing food in one of three ways: (1) simple sharing, such as passing a dish; (2) feeding the partner from his or her plate by hand or utensil; or (3) offering food from which one has already taken a bite or lick. The observers were asked to assess which couples, were involved in a sexual relationship. Those who practiced "simple sharing" were perceived as nonsexual friends; the couples who either fed each other or exchanged already sampled food were perceived as sexually involved. Across cultures, offering and accepting food that has already been eaten or licked (like an ice cream cone), meaning that it is potentially "contaminated" by saliva and germs, is often perceived as limited to people who are intimately related. There is a survival rationale—the saliva of someone one does not know is more likely to contain dangerous foreign germs.

Courtship feeding among couples is common, ranging from the proverbial Valentine's Day gift of a box of chocolates, to the dinner date as a prelude to sexual activity, to preparation of dinner or food gifts for a potential lover. Food here serves as foreplay. A sensual experience in the eating sphere is expected to lead to one in the sexual sphere.

Gender Differences

In most cultures men and women generally occupy prescribed gender roles in the arenas of both food and sex. The women's movement aside, females are still most often expected to be the "cooks," the presenters of enticing tidbits which may be themselves, while men are the consumers. In homosexual relationships, one partner may self-select to assume the more traditional female role. Beginning in the early twentieth century and well into the 1960s, many U.S. cookbooks offered women culinary and sexual/marital advice side by side. In 1962, food writer Mimi Sheraton suggested in *The Seducer's Cookbook* that a woman use her culinary wiles to lure a man into the bedroom. In 2001, British television cook Nigella Lawson was still perpetuating gender stereotypes in her book *How to Be a Domestic Goddess*. At the same time, the media have discovered the macho sex appeal of many male chefs such as Ming Tsai, Marcus Samuelsson, and Anthony Bourdain, who may well be alluring to both sexes.

Women in many cultures are still encouraged to deny their hunger and desire both for food and sex. In various cultures at different points in time, slender bodies have been idealized in an apparent attempt to restrain women's sexual desire. Historian Carol Groneman notes that in eighteenth-century France, nymphomania was thought to be caused by, among other things, eating rich food and/or too much chocolate. Paradoxically, while being told to restrain their desires, women are at the same time expected by most cultures to provide food and sexual pleasure for others. This contradiction has been blamed by some feminists for the preponderance of low sexual desire and eating disorders among women.

That women at least are judged both morally and sexually on the basis of what they eat was demonstrated in a unique experiment at Arizona State University in 1995. Subjects were asked their opinions of the morals of two fictional twenty-one-year-old women of the same height and weight, based on their diets. The first "Jennifer" ate fruit, salad, homemade whole wheat bread, chicken, and potatoes. The second favored steak, hamburgers, French fries, doughnuts, and double-fudge ice cream sundaes. The Jennifer who ate the lean, healthy diet was perceived as moral, feminine, attractive and sexually monogamous. The second was labeled immoral, inconsiderate, unconcerned, and sexually promiscuous.

Sexy Foods

Particular foods—often high in fat and sugar, like chocolate—have come to be specifically associated with sexuality. In nineteenth-century Glasgow, Scotland, when ice cream was introduced by Italian entrepreneurs, it was blamed for loosening the sexual mores of the young. The fact that this rich treat was served in a new kind of public eating establishment, a café, patronized by unchaperoned adolescents, was part of the threat. However, Francis McKee in his paper "Ice Cream and Immorality" designated the ice cream itself, with its overtones of the forbidden and of sexuality, as at the root of the fear. Other foods are considered erotic because of their physical resemblance to sexual organs. Shellfish such as mussels and clams are said to look like female genitalia. Sausages, hotdogs, and corn on the cob are often the subject of jokes based on their phallic appearance.

Rules for Sex and Food

The lure of unrestrained enjoyment of food and sexuality for their own sakes has evoked a long history of cultural tension. Societies that fail to limit the expression of these biological drives are often considered doomed. The fall of Rome is typically depicted as a consequence of excess—too much sex, food, and wine consumed at the nightly orgies of the wealthy. Few cultures tolerate such freedom of expression. Consequently, taboos, moralizing, and laws are imposed to control and "civilize" the drives. Christianity has identified gluttony and lust as two of the classic "seven deadly sins." The number-one food proscription, across cultures, is the taboo against cannibalism. The equivalent in the sexual sphere is the incest taboo. It has been noted that the first has been more successful than the second.

Urging people to strive for slimness for health and aesthetic reasons has the effect of curbing the sensual pleasure of eating. So does the frequent emphasis on the health risks of certain foods. Attitudes vary widely from one culture to another. In a study of the attitudes toward food in four cultures—Japan, Flemish Belgium, France, and the United States—Rozin found that the French had the least concern about health consequences of high-fat food and placed the greatest premium on food's ability to enhance the quality of life. The moralization of food and lack of interest in its pleasure-enhancing effects is more typical of Western cultures, specifically Great Britain and the United States. Rozin has also noted that it is ironic that in America, where food is plentiful, the major maladaptive response is overconcern about health risks, with no thought given to the benefits lost in terms of quality of life.

See also **Anorexia, Bulimia; Appetite; Gender and Food; Metaphor, Food as; Obesity; Pleasure and Food; Women and Food.**

BIBLIOGRAPHY

Bloch, Maurice. "Commensality and Poisoning." *Social Research* 66, 1 (1999): 133–149.

Carsten, Janet. *The Heat of the Hearth, the Process of Kinship in a Malay Fishing Community.* Oxford: Clarendon Press, 1997.

Groneman, Carol. *Nymphomania: A History.* New York: Norton, 2000.

Liss-Levinson, Nechama. "Disorders of Desire: Women, Sex and Food." *Women and Therapy* 7 (1988): 121–129.

McKee, Francis. "Ice Cream and Immorality." *Oxford Symposium on Food and Cookery*, Proceedings, 1996, edited by Harlan Walker, pp. 199–205. Devon, U.K.: Prospect, 1997.

Meadow, Rosalyn M., and Lillie Weiss. *Women's Conflicts about Eating and Sexuality: The Relationships between Food and Sex.* New York: Haworth, 1992.

Meigs, Anna. *Food, Sex and Pollution: A New Guinea Religion.* New Brunswick, N.J.: Rutgers University Press, 1984.

Miller, Lisa, Paul Rozin, and Alan Page Fiske. "Food Sharing and Feeding Another Person Suggest Intimacy; Two Studies of American College Students." *European Journal of Social Psychology* 28 (1998): 423–436.

Nemeroff, Carol J., and Richard I. Stein. "Moral Overtones of Food: Judgments of Others Based on What They Eat." *Personality and Social Psychology Bulletin*, 21 (1995): 480–490.

Neuhaus, Jessamyn. "The Joy of Sex Instruction: Women and Cooking in Marital Sex Manuals, 1920–1963." In *Kitchen Culture in America: Popular Representations of Food, Gender, and Race*, edited by Sherrie A. Inness. Philadelphia: University of Pennsylvania Press, 2001.

Rozin, Paul. "Food is Fundamental, Frightening, and Far-Reaching." *Social Research* 66, 1 (1999): 9–30.

Rozin, Paul. "Sweetness, Sexuality, Sin, Safety, and Socialization: Some Speculations." In *Sweetness*, edited by John Dobbing. London: Springer, 1987.

Rozin, Paul. "Attitudes to Food and the Role of Food in Life in the U.S.A., Japan, Flemish Belgium and France: Possible Implications for the Diet-Health Debate." *Appetite* 33 (1999): 163–180.

Rozin, Paul. "Disorders of Food Selection: The Compromise of Pleasure." *Annals of the New York Academy of Sciences* 575 (1989): 376–385.

Schell, Heather. "Gendered Feasts: A Feminist Reflects on Dining in New Orleans." In *Pilaf, Pozole and Pad Tha: American Women and Ethnic Food*, edited by Sherrie A. Inness. Amherst: University of Massachusetts Press, 2001.

Visser, Margaret. *The Rituals of Dinner: The Origins, Evolution, Eccentricties and Meaning of Table Manners.* New York: Grove Weidenfeld, 1991.

Wiederman, Michael W. "Women, Sex and Food: A Review of Research on Eating Disorders and Sexuality." *The Journal of Sex Research* 33, 4 (1996):301–111.

Linda Murray Berzok

SHEEP. If the dog is humankind's best friend, then sheep are its most ancient provider. Sheep may be the first domesticated ruminant, tamed by nomadic people in the Middle East and Asia 11,000 years ago, perhaps even before agriculture gave rise to civilization. Thousands of years before sheep appear in the writings of Abrahamic faiths, they were slaughtered for religious rituals. Neolithic farmers, who raised them for meat, herded them into Europe. Wool breeds appeared at least 8,000 years ago, in plenty of time to supply the looms of ancient Egypt and Babylon. Vikings carried sheep to Iceland. The Spanish brought them to the Americas. Today, sheep are found from the Arctic region to Australia and in the tropics from Africa to the Caribbean. Yet the world's billion sheep are a modest source of meat. Humans eat ten times as much pork as lamb and mutton. Sheep is not a forbidden food, though. It is eaten readily by Hindus, Muslims, Jews, and Christians. And thanks to its global acceptance, lamb can be a gourmand's delight. Its earthy flavors blend well with the spicy seasonings of Spanish *asadar*, Chinese red-cooked lamb, or just the smoke of an open-pit barbecue.

Origins

Sheep, the species *Ovis aries*, are descended from the mouflon, an endangered wild sheep native to Asia Minor and Cyprus. The mouflon has a reddish-brown hair coat with an undercoat that is shed seasonally. Europe also has a mouflon that prefers rocky slopes of mountains and may have escaped from flocks of primitive domesticated sheep. Wild and domestic sheep and goats belong to the subfamily Caprini, which evolved ten to twenty million years ago in the mountains of Central Asia. They are in the order of mammals Artiodactyla, which means even-toed, hoofed. That order includes ruminant livestock such as cattle. Bacteria in the rumen help these animals digest cellulose in grasses. With more than two hundred domestic breeds, sheep may have the largest number of breeds that are in active commercial production.

In the United States, most sheep are eaten as lamb, animals that are less than a year old. Worldwide, much lamb, especially "spring lamb" slaughtered at three to seven months of age, is not grain fed. (In the United States, most lamb is grain fed, which gives it a milder flavor.) Lambs sold for meat usually weigh between 70 and 100 pounds, accounting for the relatively low rate of world lamb consumption as compared with other livestock. A mature market hog, for instance, is more than twice as heavy, and pigs are much more prolific. Adult female sheep, or ewes, weigh about 150 to 200 pounds while mature males, or rams, weigh about 250 to 350 pounds. Mutton, the meat of mature sheep, is more popular in Britain and Europe than in the United States.

Methods of Consumption

In the developed world, sheep are processed and slaughtered in much the same way as cattle and hogs, in assembly-line, refrigerated packing plants. But in the tropics and deserts where they are still herded by nomadic people, they offer the advantage of being small enough to be consumed in a day, eliminating the need for refrigeration.

As with other meats, lamb's fat content varies with cooking methods and the cut of lamb chosen. Lamb loin chops, which correspond to pork loin chops and New York Strip steak in beef, are slightly leaner than either the beef or pork cuts, with 9.73 grams of fat in a 100-gram cooked serving trimmed to 1/4 inch fat and broiled, according to U.S. Department of Agriculture nutritional data. With 2 milligrams of iron, lamb has twice as much iron as pork, and nearly as much as the 2.47 milligrams in beef. Lamb is also a good source of phosphorus and zinc.

A comparison by the American Sheep Industry Association, a trade group, shows a 3-ounce portion of lean cooked lamb leg has 7 grams of fat, equal to that in beef round, less than fresh pork ham or chicken dark meat (both with 8 grams of fat), but more than the 4 grams of fat in chicken light meat.

The consumer group, the Center for Science in the Public Interest in Washington, D.C., lists lamb souvlaki at Greek restaurants as a relatively healthy food that compares favorably with other forms of red meat, at 310 calories and 11 grams of fat.

In a few less developed areas of the world, sheep are kept mainly for milk, or blood. A well-known vestige of sheep milking in the developed world is Roquefort cheese, made in France. Sheep's milk has almost twice as much fat as cow's milk (6.7 percent), but is denser in other nutrients as well, including calcium.

The main nonnutritional product of sheep is wool. Wool is one of the few fibers that will maintain body heat when wet. Wool also makes durable, fire-resistant rugs and carpets. Other widely used sheep products include skins and pelts for coats and rugs. Sheep lanolin, the purified grease that is washed from wool, is found in many cosmetics, salves, and ointments.

Nomadic Livestock with a Rich History

Archeologists have found evidence of sheep domestication from about 11,000 years ago, in northeastern Iran. Sheep bones nearly as old have been found in Palestine. A small statue of a woolly sheep from about 6,000 B.C.E. that was found in Iraq shows that the development of wool breeds is also ancient. By 6,000 years ago, Egyptians and Babylonians were weaving spun wool into fabric.

Sheep appear in early religious and mythological writing and history. In Ancient Egypt, the ram was the symbol of several gods. In Greek mythology Jason pursued the Golden Fleece. The Abraham of the Bible and Torah sacrificed a ram instead of his son. Long before agriculture gave rise to civilization, human hunting cultures seemed to have worshiped animals. The 30,000-year-old paintings of animals at the Chauvet Cave in France include the ibex, a wild relative of goats. Perhaps because sheep were domesticated early, their slaughter became ritualized in religious ceremonies.

Sheep breeds have outlasted civilizations. The Merino, which has come to dominate high-quality wool production today in Australia, the world's top wool exporter, may date to the reign of the Roman Emperor Claudius in the first century C.E. Many in the sheep industry believe that the breed was developed then in what is now Spain when breeders crossed the Roman Tarentine breed with the Laodician sheep of Asia Minor. When the Romans reached Britain, other sheep breeds were already there. The Romans built Britain's first woolen mill in Winchester in about 50 C.E. In the centuries that followed the fall of the Roman Empire, both Britain and Spain dominated wool production. In Spain, selling Merino sheep without the permission of the king was a crime punishable by death.

Spanish monarchs did allow explorers to bring Merinos to the New World. The Navajo sheep in the United States and the Criollo of Latin America are their descendants. When slaves were brought to the Americas, African sheep breeds adapted to hot climates came with them. These breeds have a coat of shorter hair and do not produce wool. The West African Dwarf type of sheep gave rise to several tropical American breeds, including the Barbados Blackbelly. The Tunis breed of North Africa was two thousand years old when George Washington imported some to rebuild his own sheep flock after his presidency.

Sheep have long been herded by nomads in Central Asia. The portable dwellings, or yurts, of Mongolia are made of wool felt. In the fourth century B.C.E., the Chinese called the hinterlands of central Asia "the land of felt."

In contrast to tropical sheep, primitive sheep breeds from northern Europe have long outer wool coats of up to 15 inches in length as well as a soft inner coat. The Icelandic sheep, brought to Iceland by the Vikings in 874 C.E., are the purest breed of this type.

Modern sheep production began in the eighteenth and nineteenth centuries with two important developments. One is that the Spanish monopoly ended when Napoléon invaded Spain, making Merino sheep widely accessible. The other was the development of meatier breeds of wooled sheep in Britain in the eighteenth century by Robert Bakewell, an English agriculturalist who revolutionized the breeding of sheep and cattle through selection and inbreeding. At a time when wool prices were depressed, Bakewell began to select Leicester sheep that were heavier and stockier. This helped feed Britain's Industrial Revolution. Sheep were not herded long distances in Britain as they were in Spain, so the British Isles developed many more local breeds. Other breeders followed Bakewell's example of choosing breeds that have a dual purpose. In the United States, dual purpose and wooled breeds that excel in meat production are preferred in the eastern half of the country. The finer wool breeds are preferred for the western range because they are easier to herd.

Pansy, Vicky, and Lady Scott, prize black-top Spanish merino ewes bred in 1887. From the *National Stockman and Farmer* (February 7, 1889). ROUGHWOOD COLLECTION.

Though adaptable and hardy, sheep are more difficult to raise in the humid tropics. They are scarce in Southeast Asia and the islands of the South Pacific and even northern tropical Australia.

Effects of Domestication
Domestication has changed sheep so much that they are almost helpless in the wild, according to animal scientists M. E. Ensminger and R. O. Parker, who in *Sheep and Goat Science* note that "domesticated sheep of all breeds are universally timid and defenseless and the least intelligent and least teachable of all the domestic four-footed animal. . . . Unlike other farm animals, they are unable to return to a wild life" (p. 4).

The Merino are among the most easily herded sheep. For centuries in Spain they were driven to northern pastures in the spring and back south in the fall. This resulted in selection for ease of herding. More primitive breeds remain more independent. Sheep farmers in Iceland often lose a few of their Icelandic sheep when driving them from summer mountain pastures to lowlands. One unusual type of sheep in Hawaii, the Feral Hawaiian, mostly of Merino stock, has confounded the experts by actually going wild. It was introduced in 1791 when Captain George Vancouver visited the islands.

Trends in Sheep Production
Britain and Spain once dominated sheep production and trade. In the early twenty-first century, dominance has shifted to former British colonies of the Southern Hemisphere. Australia ranks first in wool exports. Second-ranked New Zealand is a big exporter of carpet wool, mainly from its Romney breed, a native of English lowlands. Both nations are also top exporters of lamb. At the end of the twentieth century, Australia had 115.8 million head of sheep, slightly behind the world's largest flock, 131 million head in China (where they are mainly for domestic use). New Zealand was third with 45 million sheep, followed by South Africa and Turkey. China is a leading importer of wool for its mills.

By contrast, the United States produced only about 7 million sheep and lambs in 2001, a sharp decline from the beginning of the twentieth century, when the United States had nearly ten times as many sheep—61 million head. U.S. wool production has fallen from 260 million pounds to 49 million in a century.

American agricultural practices and the rise of industrial fibers—plastic—contributed to this decline. The industry survived in Great Britain, partly due to European Union subsidies. In the United States, government subsidies rewarded eastern U.S. crop farmers who grew corn and soybeans instead of those raising small marginal flocks. Corn and soybeans then flowed to large, mechanized complexes for hog and poultry, which convert grain to protein faster than can sheep. In the western range land, the federal government dropped wool subsidies in 1996 only to reinstate them in 2002 in an attempt to help a struggling industry. Only about 1 percent of the meat

The French prepare a number of dishes using parts of sheep not commonly eaten in the United States. This salad of lamb brains was prepared at the Restaurant Guy Savoy in Paris. © OWEN FRANKEN/CORBIS.

consumed by Americans was lamb. By 2000 per capita lamb consumption in the United States was less than 1 pound per year, compared to an estimated 221 pounds per year of all red meats and poultry. Growing popularity of ethnic foods, along with immigration from Mediterranean nations that relish lamb, ensured a remaining niche market for this meat. But outside of large cities, many consumers had to hunt in grocery store meat cases for a package or two of lamb chops or perhaps a single leg of lamb.

Reasons for the decline in U.S. sheep production seem to be both economic and cultural. Competition from plastic fibers, including polyester fleece, which has some of the desirable properties of wool, has hurt demand for a key product from sheep. A booming economy in the late twentieth century contributed to the already tough task of finding workers willing to take on the solitary task of herding sheep on the western range.

American taste for lamb may have been hurt by bad experiences of American servicemen and women during World War II, who sometimes ate old mutton from Australia and New Zealand and mistook it for lamb. But the main factor is undoubtedly economic. With a small market for U.S. wool, and therefore lamb, the meat has become an exotic, more expensive specialty food. A similar decline has taken place in Canada.

North America has also faced stiff competition from New Zealand and from the Australians, who rival the Spaniards as finicky producers of fine wool, developing several strains of Merino breeds best adapted to their climate. Both Australia and New Zealand offer longer grazing seasons than the northern United States and Canada, giving those nations another advantage. New Zealand farmers can graze their sheep from eight to twelve months of the year and are world leaders in developing microchip-controlled electric fences to allow the most efficient use of pastures. A flock is moved into a small paddock where the sheep graze all of the available forage before moving into another small field. New Zealanders can raise twenty-five sheep on a hectare of land (2.47 acres) with this method.

Unlike American and European farmers, Australia's and New Zealand's sheep producers receive no large government subsidies, which keeps their farm economies lean, preventing artificial inflation of land prices that boost costs. As the twenty-first century began, both nations had an exporting advantage of lower-valued currencies compared to the American dollar.

Even so, the returns in 2002 on sheep production in Australia lagged behind those enjoyed by U.S. grain farmers, and in New Zealand, where there are a dozen sheep for every person, the sheep population has declined from a peak of 70.3 million in 1982 to about 45 million, "due to declining profits compared to other types of farming," explains a wool products website, Sheep World.

The biggest challenge to sheep may still be plastic. Australian researchers are looking for new ways to turn wool into a fabric without weaving—a response to a 10 percent annual growth in "nonwovens," synthetic fabrics used in car seats, home draperies, and disposable wipes. Ironically, felt, the original nonwoven material, was made from sheep's fleece before spinning and weaving were invented. If the wool industry can compete successfully with the plastics industry, the availability of lamb as a food might increase.

A Case for Saving Sheep

From a gastronomic perspective alone, it would be a shame if sheep became extinct. Chefs Bruce Aidells and Denis Kelly argue in *The Complete Meat Cookbook* that lamb's flavor "makes this animal a favorite in cuisines all over the world. . . . No meat marries better with the pungent flavors of garlic, mustard, rosemary, thyme, oregano, savory and fennel, to name just a few" (p. 427). Among the world's most notable lamb dishes are Moroccan lemon *tagine*; kabobs (called souvlaki in Greece; *sis kebabi* in Turkey); and baked leg of lamb *asadar* from Spain (in Spain a whole lamb is roasted in a wood-fired brick oven).

Do-it-yourself gourmands should be aware of pitfalls. To avoid lamb's hard fat, which some people find disagreeable when it becomes cold, trim as much fat as is possible from lamb before cooking and be sure to keep lamb dishes hot at the table.

Other practical reasons for saving sheep include environmental ones. Although sheep were associated with some of the first human environmental degradation—soil erosion associated with overgrazing—properly managed, sheep can improve grasslands and range land. They will eat weedy plants that cattle ignore, including sagebrush, leafy spurge, and tansy ragwort. Some ranchers and wheat farmers consider them more effective at controlling plant pests than herbicides.

One serious problem that could instantly make sheep an unwanted food source is bovine spongiform encephalopathy, or BSE. Sheep may have been the indirect source of this dreaded affliction, known as mad cow disease. The incurable disease literally turns a cow's brain spongy, causing a progressive dementia that kills the animal. In Britain, rendered sheep, goat, and cattle not fit for human use were added to cattle feed to boost the protein content. Some scientists believe that a related disease in sheep, scrapie, somehow crossed the "species barrier" when the rendered sheep were fed to cattle in the 1980s. Scrapie, a rare but very old disease of sheep, has never been known to infect humans, but BSE apparently has killed Britons who ate infected beef. This family of diseases, which also includes chronic wasting disease in deer and elk, is poorly understood. The infectious agent is a prion, a type of protein that has no genetic material, like a virus or bacteria. Prions are extremely resistant to heat and antiseptics and can survive in soil for years. Yet certain types of sheep seem to have a greater genetic disposition to scrapie than others.

European and British health officials are concerned that sheep in that part of the world may also have been infected with BSE, rather than normal scrapie. If so, it would have the potential to make European lamb unsafe to eat. Even though scrapie itself is not deadly to humans, the possible confusion of BSE in sheep with scrapie has led the United States to start a scrapie eradication program in domestic sheep. New Zealand and Australia are believed to be free of the scrapie as well as BSE.

Finally, the loss of sheep and lambs to competition from plastic fabrics and more industrialized meats would be a blow to the collective memory of human history and tradition. The Bible has more references to lambs and sheep than to any other animal. The blood of the lamb protected Jews during the first Passover. Muslims break the month-long fast of Ramadan with a meal of lamb and rice. And to Christians, the lamb is the symbol of Christ sacrificed on the cross.

As a result of the efforts of rare breed preservationists, hobbyists, and home wool spinners, it is unlikely that sheep will ever become completely extinct, even if their long-term commercial success faces challenges.

See also **Australia and New Zealand; Christianity; Dairy Products; Food Safety; Greece and Crete; Herding; Islam; Judaism; Lamb Stew; Livestock Production; Mammals; Meat; Religion and Food.**

BIBLIOGRAPHY

Aidells, Bruce, and Denis Kelly. *The Complete Meat Cookbook.* New York: Houghton Mifflin, 1998.

Dohner, Janet Vorwald. *The Encyclopedia of Historic and Endangered Livestock and Poultry Breeds.* New Haven, Conn.: Yale University Press, 2001.

Ensminger, M. E., and R. O. Parker. *Sheep & Goat Science.* Animal Agriculture Series. 5th ed. Danville, Ill.: Interstate Printers, 1986.

Gatenby, Ruth M. *Sheep Production in the Tropics and Sub-Tropics.* New York: Longman, 1986.

Harris, Marvin. *Good to Eat: Riddles of Food and Culture.* New York: Simon and Schuster, 1985.

Sheep World Web site. Available at http://www.sheepworld .co.nz.SheepFarming.htm.

Simmons, Paula. *Raising Sheep the Modern Way.* Pownal, Vt.: Storey, 1989.

United States Department of Agriculture. Nutrient Database for Standard Reference Release 14. 2001. Available at http://www.nal.usda.gov/fnic/foodcomp/Data/SR14/ reports/sr14page.htm.

Dan Looker

SHELLFISH. *See* **Crustaceans and Shellfish.**

SHERBET AND SORBET. Sherbet and sorbet are both frozen desserts. Sorbet is flavored syrup with a slushy texture; it is sometimes called a water ice, and contains no dairy ingredients. Sherbet describes a similar product, but contains milk. One definition, by the International Dairy Foods Association, states that sherbet should contain 1–2 percent of milk fat in the final product. Despite this, the word sherbet is sometimes colloquially applied to sorbets. Related recipes, such as ice milk, frappés, and granita (a grainy water ice of Italian origin) lead to further confusion.

In other countries, the definition of sorbet remains consistent, but that of sherbet varies considerably. In British English it means a class of children's candies, powders which give a fizzy sensation on the tongue, sweetened and flavored with lemon or other fruit. In the Middle East, sherbet is a chilled soft drink. The constants in these different foods are sugar, a sweet-sour flavor combination, and the idea (if not the actuality) of cool refreshment.

A complicated history of linguistic and culinary borrowing lies behind these definitions. Modern writers have despaired of untangling the subject. Liddel and Weir comment that it is almost impossible to define the word sherbet, because of a shifting background of common usage, local customs, and legislation.

Sorbets and sherbets in North America both start with sugar syrup. This may be specially made, but sugar and water are also naturally present in ingredients such as fruit juice, wine or milk and individual recipes allow for this. Flavors other than fruit are provided by infusing flowers, herbs, or spices in the base syrup. If too much sugar is present, the sorbet will not freeze properly. Large-scale producers, and those seriously interested in making sorbets by craft methods, measure the syrup concentration. The optimum is between 17–20° on the Baumé scale. Sorbets containing alcohol use a lower density of 14–17° Baumé. Although excellent sorbets are made using only sugar, water, and flavoring, some recipes require egg whites or gelatin. These act as stabilizers, especially in sorbets which melt quickly, or when fruits with a high pectin content (which affects texture) are used. Occasionally, egg whites are added as meringue, for instance in champagne sorbets.

Freezing by churning produces the smoothest texture, although at home a still-freezing method can be used. As the temperature gets lower, ice crystals begin to form, kept small and evenly distributed by churning or periodic beating. The ice consists of pure water, so in the liquid fraction of the sorbet, the sugar content becomes increasingly concentrated. Sugar lowers the freezing point of water, and prevents the mixture becoming completely solid. Alcohol also freezes at a lower temperature than water, which is why sorbets containing wine need a less dense syrup to achieve the same slushy texture.

In sherbet recipes, milk provides some water for the basic mixture. It also adds small amounts of lactose, protein, and fat, giving a slightly different texture and a creamier flavor. However, sherbet is usually a very low-fat product. Sherbets and sorbets feel colder in the mouth than ordinary ice cream. This is partly because of the lack of fat (which helps to make ordinary ice creams smoother on the tongue), and partly because of their high sugar content, which makes the mixture both freeze and melt at lower temperatures.

A granita has an even lower syrup density (9–10° Baumé), and is always still-frozen, allowing relatively large ice crystals to form in the mixture. Minimal stirring keeps these evenly distributed and of a regular size, giving a characteristic grainy texture.

How do the iced desserts of North America relate to the sherbet candies and drinks to the east of the Atlantic? A clue lies in the derivation of the words sherbet and sorbet. Ultimately they can be traced back to a medieval Arabic root *sharâb*. This originally meant a sweetened drink (the word syrup shares a similar derivation), but was later applied to beverages containing alcohol. It gave eighteenth-century English the term *shrub* for an alcoholic punch. A slightly altered Arabic form, *shabât*, emerged to denote sweetened, nonalcoholic drinks. This passed into Turkish as *sherbet*, a word which diffused into European languages. However, the Turkish pronunciation only seems to have survived in English. Southern European languages dropped the *h*, following the Italian form which emerged as *sorbetto* (Spanish, *sorbete*; French, *sorbet*).

The sherbet mixtures of Arabia, Turkey, and Persia have always been flavored syrups that are diluted with water and served chilled, a welcome refreshment in hot weather. In the past, ice or snow was stored in winter for summer use with these drinks. Sometimes the syrup was boiled to the point at which it formed a solid candy. A version of this is still to be found in Turkey under the name *gul sekeri* (literally "rose sugar," although it is actually flavored with cinnamon). Popular flavors include lemon, pomegranate, flowers such as rose or violet, and herbs such as liquorice or mint. The importance of sherbet in the Middle East is apparent from evocative descriptions given by Roden (1970) and Shaida (1992).

In seventeenth-century Italy, *sorbetto* came to mean a flavored syrup frozen to a point at which the texture was obviously iced but not hard. In the past, these cooling ices were considered medicinal. In Italy, *sorbetti* were given to people suffering from fevers and malaria, a custom also recorded in Persia. It was the iced aspect of these drinks that became important for sorbets. Although they seem to have remained liquid throughout the eighteenth century, in nineteenth-century in France, sorbets became chilled confections with a texture somewhere between a drink and a modern water ice, sometimes with added alcohol. As the century progressed, sorbets were served colder and colder, and at some point they became solid enough to be eaten with a spoon. The culinary ascendancy of the French during the nineteenth century must

Turkish sorbet vendor as depicted in Friedrich Unger's *Conditorei des Orients* (Confectionery of the Orient), published in 1838. Unger was royal confectioner to King Otto of Greece. COURTESY OF THE BAYERISCHE STAATSBIBLIOTHEK, MUNICH.

have led to the adoption of sorbet as a standard term in restaurant cookery, giving it a relatively fixed definition.

In English, the word "sherbet" retained the sense of a sweet drink throughout the centuries. It was made from fresh lemons, or perhaps mixed from chunks of flavored sugar candy which were already being imported in the seventeenth century. The drink aspect continued to be important throughout the eighteenth century. In London in the 1820s, a street seller of sherbet and soft drinks devised a powder of sugar, bicarbonate of soda, tartaric acid, and lemon flavoring. When mixed with water, this made a sweetened lemon flavored "sherbet" which effervesced as the soda and acid reacted to give off bubbles of carbon dioxide. By the early twentieth century, sherbet and lemonade powder had become synonymous, and candy manufacturers began to incorporate it into their products. Sherbet in Britain is now seen purely as this particular type of candy—cheap, usually lemon flavored, and always effervescent. Sorbet has retained the sense of a water ice.

In North America, sherbet developed down the iced dessert route. The sultry summer climate of the eastern United States, together with the commercial exploitation of lake ice stored for summer use, must have stimulated demand for such refreshments. During the mid-nineteenth century, sherbet and sorbet seem to have been synonymous, both words indicating frozen syrup, often served with wine or another alcoholic drink poured over. The habit for serving them between courses at dinner is also recorded. How sherbet came to acquire the meaning of an iced dessert which included milk is obscure. Recipes past and present do not make matters any clearer. Household recipes from the early twentieth century use the word to describe anything from a coarse crystal water ice (similar to a granita) through a standard sorbet, to mixtures containing milk. Later sherbet recipes sometimes contain buttermilk or milk and cream.

By the mid-twentieth century, ice-cream companies were producing sherbets flavored with lemon, lime, orange, or raspberry. Orange sherbet seems to be the one which stands out in childhood memories. In the 1980s and 1990s, there was a renewed interest in sorbets. The idea of serving them between courses in restaurants enjoyed a revival, but most compelling was the fact that they offer a dessert with no fat or dairy produce involved. Flavors have gone beyond the traditional lemon, lime or champagne into vanilla or chocolate, perhaps so that the products compete more overtly with conventional ice-creams. Sherbet, on the other hand, seems to have slipped into a slightly old-fashioned, declassé niche. Neither product offers a serious challenge to premium quality ice creams in the affections of the American public.

Nutritionally, sherbets and sorbets do offer low-fat alternatives to ice creams. Their principal contribution to the diet is energy, and their syrup bases give them a relatively high sugar content and higher calorie count than dieters might suspect. The milk in sherbet makes a small, but not a significant contribution of protein, fat, vitamins, and minerals. Fruit-based sorbets and sherbets, provided the fruit has not been heated or processed for a long time, contain a little ascorbic acid (vitamin C), but large quantities would have to be consumed to make them a significant source. The role of these items in the diet is principally one of a pleasant refreshment and light dessert.

See also **Candy and Confections**; **Dairy Products**; **Ice Cream**; **Syrups**.

BIBLIOGRAPHY

David, Elizabeth. *Harvest of the Cold Months.* London: Penguin Books, 1996.

Davidson, Alan. *The Oxford Companion to Food.* New York: Oxford University Press, 1999.

Liddel, Caroline, and Robin Weir. *Ices: The Definitive Guide.* London: Grub Street, 1995.

McGee, Harold. *On Food and Cooking.* New York: Scribners, 1984.

Mason, Laura. *Sugar Plums and Sherbet.* Totnes, Devon, U.K.: Prospect Books, 1998.

Roden, Claudia. *A Book of Middle Eastern Food.* London: Penguin Books, 1970.

Shaida, Margaret. *The Legendary Cuisine of Persia.* Henley-on-Thames, U.K.: Lieuse Publications, 1992.

Laura Mason

SHROVE TUESDAY. The day immediately preceding Ash Wednesday, the beginning of Lent in the Christian churches of the West, is known in English as Shrove Tuesday. It occurs between 2 February and 9 March, depending on the date of Easter. The day takes its name from "shriving"—the pre-Lenten confession and absolution of the faithful as a preparation for Lent that was common in the European Middle Ages. Feasting on foods initially prohibited during Lent, such as meat, eggs, and milk products, was integral to Shrove Tuesday observance. The German term *Fastnacht* and the Dutch *Vastenavond* (eve of the fast) refer to the Lenten fast about to begin, while the French *mardi gras*, the Italian *martedì grasso*, and the Portuguese *terça-feira gorda*, all meaning "Fat Tuesday," refer to the feasting on foods rich in fat prior to the austerity of Lent. The Spanish term *martes de carnaval* (Carnival Tuesday) possibly reflects the formerly rigorous Lenten abstinence from meat commencing on Ash Wednesday and lasting through the forty days of Lent. The word "carnival" is thought to derive from Medieval Latin *carnem levare*, which means 'to take away or remove meat'.

The historical origin of carnival celebrations is obscure. The word "Lent" derived from Anglo-Saxon *lencten*, denoting the spring season. It may be, therefore, that carnival had its roots in an ancient spring festival or pagan agricultural rite marking the transition between winter and summer. Aspects of such ancient festivals are thought to be reflected in modern carnival celebrations connecting the change in nature with social and biological renewal. Thus, temporary social transformation, masking, processions, erotic dances, eating, and drinking still characterize carnival celebrations in much of Europe. The ludic element—the public, communal revelry—remains in the fore in carnival celebrations in the United States, especially in the New Orleans Mardi Gras, and in Brazil in the famous Rio de Janeiro Carnival.

In Britain this three-day period of ludic license was called Shrovetide. Various sports were common, especially games of football. One form of cruel sport prevalent at Shrovetide was pelting cocks and wagering, and this was still practiced in areas of English settlement in Ireland in the late eighteenth and early nineteenth centuries.

CARNIVAL

As a point of closure for Christmas and Twelfth Night abundance, and a ritual sending off of the old year, Carnival evolved into a late-winter feast day of special importance to the Roman Catholic world.

The underlying theme to Mardi Gras or Carnival is that the days immediately preceding Lent were traditionally set aside for conspicuous feasting. In a medieval context, conspicuous consumption was a show of wealth, since it signaled that the lean days of winter to come were not an inconvenience imposed by financial or by religious considerations.

Since animal flesh was forbidden during the strict fast days of Lent, Shrovetide also became a period when weddings were once popular. This interesting fact is substantiated by medieval wedding records and makes economic sense, if we consider that June (a popular wedding month today) fell in the middle of harvest or planting according to the old calendar. This calendrical sensitivity placed the birth of the child in November, when there was nothing left to do in the fields. Thus Carnival also had an important influence on very basic human lifecycles far and beyond the actual month of celebration. It was also a time of general revelry in village and city alike, with processions of elaborately costumed and masked figures, dancers, and noise makers. It was in essence, a "feast of fools," a time when the usual rules of everyday behavior could be relaxed, even to the extent that such tabooed behavior as cross-dressing could make its appearance in parades with general approval.

European scholarship has meticulously analyzed the masking and de-masking of participants in the traditional Mardi Gras Carnival. On the one side there is a definite affinity to masks representing demons and animals, totemism disguising the living from the spirits of the dead, who were thought to be abroad on this eve of Lenten austerities. On the other hand, the serving of nourishing, satisfying fat foods at Shrovetide expresses the basic idea in European folk culture that one should, in Harvey Cox's words in *The Feast of Fools*, indulge in conscious excess. In some European regions it was customary to eat seven or even nine different kinds of food on Shrove Tuesday. These included butter and milk, roast pork, fish, peas, and millet. Feasting was sometimes interrupted by "wise" individuals, as evidence of aiding fertility. Fish were folkloric prognosticators of wealth to come—so many scales or eggs, so much the profit. The same benefit was claimed for millet—the more tiny millet grains eaten on Shrove Tuesday, the more coins one could hope for in the future.

The pre-Lenten feasting was thought to betoken an abundant harvest in the coming summer. Because Shrovetide cakes were products of a church festival, they acquired virtues beyond the nutritional. Crumbs were fed to the chicken on Shrove Tuesday so that they would produce more eggs and be protected from predators. Leftovers were also scattered for the angels, foxes, hawks, and martens, undoubtedly with mixed messages to the recipients to ward off danger. Even the Shrovetide lard was used in folk medicine as a wound salve, and ploughshares and wagons were symbolically greased with it before they were first used in the spring farm work.

However, one of the greatest legacies of Shrove Tuesday is the urban carnival which took place in large cities like Rome, Paris, Cologne, Munich, and Basel. They assumed the form of huge processions, with rites of crowning a prince and princess (or king and queen). Similar feast day parades are found throughout the Americas, but especially in Mexico and South America. The most famous of these is the great Carnival parade in Rio de Janeiro, Brazil, an event for which the city prepares throughout the entire year. Much older Carnival traditions can be found in the mountain villages of the Black Forest and in the Austrian Tyrol, where carvers of wooden masks are still working a traditional art form that predates Christianity.

At the time of the Reformation, Protestant countries for the most part gave up traditional Carnival rites connected with the official ecclesiastical celebration. Mumming and masking were in particular dropped, or shifted to Christmas, New Year's Day, and Twelfth Night (Epiphany). This residual mumming was once popular in colonial North America, and survives today as the New Year's Day Mummers Parade in Philadelphia.

Don Yoder

Shrovetide was also a period of dietary license, and foods forbidden in Lent were consumed in abundance. Eggs and milk were at one time forbidden in Lent and therefore any supplies had to be used up before Ash Wednesday. On Shrove Monday, in parts of England, meat and eggs were eaten, or gifts of pancakes, flour, eggs, or money to provide Shrove Tuesday fare were collected by children or adults, who often recited a "shroving" verse. Refusal to contribute could result in shard- or stone-throwing, or loud knocking with clubs on doors.

Shrove Tuesday was also known as "Pancake Day" in England. After the Reformation, the Shriving Bell, which had hitherto called parishioners to be shriven, signaled the

Tossing the pancake. An engraving from Mr. and Mrs. Samuel Carter Hall's *Ireland: Its Scenery, Character &c.* (London, 1841). PUBLISHED WITH PERMISSION OF THE FOLKLORE SOCIETY, LONDON.

commencement of revelry and pancake-making. In parts of Wales children formerly collected pancake ingredients, while in the Isle of Man, pancake-making has apparently replaced the older custom of serving oatmeal and gravy for midday dinner and meat and pancakes in the evening.

In Scotland, beef was eaten on Shrove Tuesday (also called "Fastern's E'en") to ensure household prosperity. Oatmeal bannocks enriched with eggs and milk were baked, and, together with the beef broth, were used in marriage divination by the inclusion of a ring to betoken marriage, or other items to indicate the rank or occupation of the future marriage partner. The identity of the beloved might be revealed in dreams induced by placing a bannock under the pillow.

In Ireland, Shrove Tuesday (i.e., pre-Lenten) weddings were formerly popular, a custom seemingly connected to the canonical prohibition on the solemn celebration of the sacrament of matrimony during Lent, and pranks might be played on those still unwed at that time. Shrove Tuesday was especially a household festival, when "nobody should be without meat" (Danaher, p. 42). Pancakes—often including a ring to signify early marriage—were eaten, and pancake-tossing as a form of marriage divination was still practiced in the nineteenth

century in areas of strong English settlement in Ireland from late medieval times.

Relaxation of the austere Lenten regulations meant that it was unnecessary to use up supplies of milk, eggs, and butter on the eve of Lent. Yet pancakes retain their festive connection to Shrove Tuesday. Homemade or commercially produced pancakes remain popular on Shrove or "Pancake" Tuesday in Great Britain. The traditional pancake greaze at Westminster School in London still takes place on Shrove Tuesday: the cook tries to toss a pancake over the pancake bar, and the boy who succeeds in getting the most cake in the ensuing "greaze" or scrimmage is declared the winner.

In Ireland also, pancakes sprinkled with castor sugar and served with a slice of lemon are much enjoyed as a Shrove Tuesday treat and are also a treat, though increasingly with multicultural dimensions, in British and Irish communities in North America, Australia, and New Zealand.

In many parts of Europe, a variety of pastries rich in milk, butter, and eggs and cooked in hot fat are eaten during carnival celebrations. In Slovenian and Croatian Istria, for example, they are termed *fritoli* and *kroötule*, while in Sardinia, these doughnut-like pastries are called *zeppole*. They are similar in texture to the small rectangular pastry called *Funkenküchle*, popular during carnival festivities in western Austria, parts of South Tyrol, several areas in Switzerland, and certain regions of southern and western Germany. This latter pastry is made of flour, salt, sugar, and cream, cooked in hot fat, and sprinkled with cinnamon and sugar. It is eaten around a large fire lit on the first Sunday of Lent (*alte Fastnacht*, old eve of fast) since the introduction of the Gregorian calendar in 1582. *Fastnachtkuchen* are still popular among the Pennsylvania Dutch. These were originally rectangular or diamond-shaped, but today many are made round like doughnuts.

See also **Fasting and Abstinence: Christianity; Feasts, Festivals, and Fasts; Holidays; Religion and Food.**

BIBLIOGRAPHY

Atzori, Mario, Luisa Orrú, Paolo Piquereddu, and M. Margherita Satta, eds. *Il Carnevale in Sardegna.* Cagliari, Sardinia: 2d Editrice Mediterranea, 1989.

Bahktin, Mikhail. *Rabelais and His World.* Translated by Helene Iswolsky. Cambridge, Mass.: MIT Press, 1968.

Banks, M. Macleod. "Shrove Tuesday." In *British Calendar Customs. Scotland*, vol. 1, pp. 2–29. London: William Glaisher for The Folklore Society, 1937.

Beitl, Richard. *Wörterbuch der Deutschen Volkskunde. Zweite Auflage.* Stuttgart: Alfred Kroner Verlag, 1955.

Biluš, Ivanka, Brkan, B., Ćorić, Rodè, C. *Croatia at Table: The Aromas and Tastes of Croatian Cuisine.* Zagreb: Alfa, 1977.

Cox, Harvey. *The Feast of Fools: A Theological Essay on Festivity and Fantasy.* New York: Harper and Row, 1970.

Danaher, Kevin. *The Year in Ireland*. Cork, Ireland: The Mercier Press, 1977.

Drewes, Maria. *Tiroler Küche*. Innsbruck-Wien: Tyrolia-Verlag, 2000.

Eco, Umberto, V. V. Ivanov, and Monica Rector. *Carnival!* Edited by Thomas A. Sebeok with Marcia E. Erickson. Berlin, New York, and Amsterdam: Mouton, 1984.

Gaignebet, Claude. *Le carnaval*. Paris: Payot, 1974.

Grimm, Jacob, and Wilhelm Grimm. *Deutsches Wörterbuch. Dritter Band*. Leipzig: Verlag von S. Hirzel, 1862, pp. 1354–1355.

Jones, T. Gwynn. *Welsh Folklore and Folk Custom*. London: Methuen, 1930.

Kinser, Samuel. "Carnival." In *Medieval Folklore. An Encyclopedia of Myths, Legends, Tales, Beliefs and Customs*, edited by Carl Lindahl, John McNamara, John Lidnow, vol. 1, pp. 134–139. Santa Barbara, Ca.: ABC-Clio, 2000.

LaFlaur, Mark. "Mardi Gras (Shrove Tuesday)." In *Festivals and Holidays*, pp. 210–217. New York: Macmillan Library Reference, 1999.

Livingstone, E. A., ed. *The Oxford Dictionary of the Christian Church*, 3d ed. Oxford: Oxford University Press, 1977.

McNeill, F. Marian. "Fastern's E'en." In *The Silver Bough: A Calendar of Scottish National Festivals*, vol. 2, pp. 39–45. Glasgow: William MacLellan, 1959.

Pucer, Tina Novak. "Food Culture in Istria." In *Food and Celebration: From Fasting to Feasting*, edited by Patricia Lysaght, pp. 45–52. Ljubljana: Založba, 2002.

Shoemaker, Alfred L. *Eastertide in Pennsylvania: A Folk-Cultural Study*. Foreword by Don Yoder. Mechanicsburg, Pa.: Stackpole Books, 2000.

Wright, A. R. "Movable Festivals." In *British Calendar Customs. England*, edited by T. E. Lones, vol. 1, pp. 1–31. London: William Glaisher for the Folklore Society, 1936.

Patricia Lysaght

SIBERIA

SIBERIA. Siberia occupies a huge territory with a wide variety of climatic conditions and geographic landscapes. Apart from the Russian-speaking Siberians, about one-twentieth of the population consists of aboriginal groups. To better understand the food and meal traditions of the Siberian people, it is necessary to review the geography, climate, and the history of this region.

Geography and Climate

Siberia occupies about 5.2 million square miles, which roughly corresponds to about 9 percent of Earth's dry land mass. It is bounded by the Ural Mountains in the west and by the Pacific Ocean in the east. To the south lies central Asia, Mongolia, and China, and to the north the Arctic Ocean. For many people Siberia is synonymous with an intensely cold climate, but this image is only partially correct. The climate of most of Siberia is continental, which means there are large temperature differences between summer and winter. The Siberian win-

Detail of *pel'meni* showing the dumplings and various spices added to the broth in which they are boiled. On the right, *smetana* (sour cream), traditionally served with Siberian *pel'meni*. PHOTO BY ILYA VIKTOROVICH LOYSHA COURTESY OF STOLICHNAYA RUSSIAN VODKA.

ter is indeed long and cold, yet summers are fairly warm—warm enough to allow for the cultivation of watermelons in western and southern Siberia. Although there is relatively little precipitation in eastern Siberia, and the winter frost penetrates quite deep, the climate becomes milder and warmer towards the west and south. Due to heavy rainfall, the region is drained by numerous rivers and dotted with lakes filled with a variety of fish.

The Siberian northern coastal region along the Arctic Ocean is occupied by a wide strip of arctic tundra, which is inhabited by an enormous population of reindeer. South of this is a vast area of evergreen pine forest, which gradually changes to fertile *chernozem* (black earth) steppes. The far southeastern part of Siberia, near Manchuria and the Pacific Ocean, consists of subtropical forests.

Siberian People and History

Much of Siberia (excluding the far north) was united for the first time under the rule of the Mongolian leader Genghis Khan in the beginning of the thirteenth century. Since the Mongolian Empire included China, Persia, and central Asia and stretched as far as Europe, many new culinary ideas from far-off places were introduced. *Pelmeni* and *chaj* (tea) are perhaps the most long-lasting remnants of that period.

Siberian history of the past four centuries has many parallels with the colonization of the Americas. Colonization of Siberia by tsarist Russia began in the 1580s and ended in 1860 with the founding of Vladivostok on the coast of the Sea of Japan. Most of the population of present-day Siberia consists of a mixture of different immigrant ethnicities and people of various aboriginal backgrounds. Siberians of mixed race and ethnic background

refer to themselves as Chaldons and view themselves as an ethnic identity separate from Russian.

Siberia was colonized and settled by a variety of European ethnic groups rather than just by the Russians. During the seventeenth century, settlers included Russians, Komi peoples, Lithuanians, Ukrainians, and Byelorussians, and small numbers of Germans, Greeks, and even a few baptized Tartars and Turks. Later on, there were waves of other immigrants, some of whom were exiled forcibly. These included Swedish prisoners of war, German and other European technical specialists, Polish, Lithuanian, Byelorussian, Ukrainian, and Jewish exiles from rebellious Polish territories, as well as settlers who came from the central regions of Russia, Ukraine, and Byelorussia after the abolishment of serfdom in 1861. Colonization was especially intensive during the construction of the Trans-Siberian railway (1891–1905). The population of Siberia reached almost ten million people by 1914.

Since the political exiles who came to Siberia in the nineteenth century were generally well educated, many of them became involved in the improvement of truck farming, grain growing, the cultivation of oil-yielding crops (such as hemp), and the introduction of new vegetables and modern methods of cultivation. Each of the immigrant groups brought something of their own cookery to the big Siberian stewpot, thus enriching what is now called Siberian cuisine. For example, Korean spicy carrot salads, stuffed fish baked in the oven, and stewed sour cabbage and pork became Siberian national dishes.

Prior to Russian colonization of Siberia, local ethnic groups of various origins populated the region, including Turkic, Finnic, Mongolic, and other tribes. Some of these peoples intermarried with Europeans and some ethnic groups remained discrete, but in any case, colonists adopted many local food traditions through mixed marriages or through daily contact.

Cookery of the Chaldony

Due to the huge size of the country, almost limitless natural resources, a surplus of free land, and the absence of serfdom, life in the wilderness of Siberia was always more free, happier, and more prosperous than life in European Russia. It was easy to protect one's freedom in Siberia—

when faced with bureaucratic oppression, one could simply leave and settle in remote places or deeper forests. Because of this freedom and abundant local and foreign food products, Chaldon cuisine originated as a rich mixture of European and aboriginal traditions.

Before the Bolshevik Revolution, the Chaldon people produced basic food products on their own farms. These foods included dairy products, meat, vegetables, eggs, breads and other cereal products, vegetable oils, as well as mushrooms, wild berries, pine nuts, fish, and game. Although every family possessed hunting guns and traps, game was not central to the Siberian diet. Food was stewed, boiled, or baked in a Russian oven or fried in oil or drawn butter.

Breads and other cereal and legume products.
Chaldon farmers grew rye, barley, oats, buckwheat, millet, peas, and beans. Wheat was raised in the southern regions, such as Altay. Wheat flour of very high quality, which was used for cookies and cakes, was usually bought at market fairs in large cities.

Every village family and many city households made their own rye, barley, and wheat breads in a round or *kalatch* (padlock-shaped) form; some families had wooden bread molds. Bread flour was mixed with milk and homemade hop yeast and was left standing over night. In the morning, when the bread dough was finished, eggs, *postnoya maslo* (Lenten oil), and milk were often added to the bread. Wealthy families might have used pine-nut oil instead—such bread had a unique flavor and could be kept longer than usual. During times of food shortages, some people baked a green emergency bread made from flour and a large proportion of ground dried nettle leaves.

Kasha.
Kasha is the Russian word for gruel or porridge. It is used to describe any kind of boiled cereals, peas, beans, other seeds, or even potatoes and vegetables. Kasha can be made sweet or salty, and it can contain almost any kind of additions, like meat, milk, nuts, fresh or dry fruits, and even pumpkin. Kasha can be made from a mixture of different seeds and/or other components that are boiled or baked in an oven. It is eaten hot or cold, as a main dish or as a garnish, plain or with the addition of fruit jams, or diluted with fresh milk if buckwheat is used.

During the first part of the twentieth century, Siberians made many different kashas from barley, millet, or oats. Peas, string beans, and fava beans were also used. Rice was uncommon and used only on special occasions—unlike all other Orthodox Christians who use wheat for *kut'ya* (a funeral dish), the Chaldons make *kut'ya* from rice and raisins.

Pirogi, pirozhki, and bliny.
Leavened dough was widely used for *pirogi* (large pies) and *pirozhki* (small pies). Pirozhki could be fried or baked and stuffed with potatoes, carrots, green onion and eggs, liver, minced meat, fish, or fresh or dried berries (black currant, raspberry, bird cherry, haws) mixed with malt. The Siberian analogue of pizza was a round, flat pie called *shangi*, which was topped with cottage cheese and sour cream and then baked. Another round pie, called *beliash*, was stuffed with meat, closed up, and fried. *Beliash* can be traced to a Tartar heritage, since in Kazan tartar cookery there was a meat pie called *belish*. The traditional large holiday pie of Chaldons, often called *kurnik*, was made with fish or chicken.

There are also sweet holiday open-faced berry-pies (usually made with black currant).

Many different recipes exist for *bliny* (large thin pancakes) and *oladyi* (smaller pancakes of thicker dough usually oval in shape). These could be made of wheat or rye, leaven or unleavened, and some buckwheat flour, milk, and eggs. Oil and honey could also be added. Once they were made, *bliny* could be stuffed with caviar and eaten cold, or filled with cottage cheese or meat and then baked in the oven or fried. Usually people had a separate frying pan or two for pancakes, and only a pigeon wing was used to grease the pan.

Other types of baked pastries included *pechen'ya* (cookies), *prianik* (a type of honey-cake), *sooshka* (ring-shaped pretzels, small *kalatch* dipped into boiling water before baking); *smetannyya kalatchiki* (baked pies of unleavened dough based on sour cream), and *kulich* (Easter cake with raisins or other dry fruits).

Oils and fats.
Unlike that of European Russia, Siberian cookery involved many fried dishes. The reason for this is simple: Chaldons had a lot of vegetable oil. The most common oils were hemp-seed and linseed oils; rarer were sunflower and poppy-seed oils. The most expensive oil was pine-nut oil, produced only in forest areas. Since Siberians had many cows, they produced large quantities of butter, which was even exported to Europe. The Chaldony, however, preferred drawn butter for frying foods. The use of fish oil was adopted from local fishermen tribes. It was very rarely used in European Russia, but in the north of Siberia it served as a substitute for vegetable oils. For example, in northern Siberia, pies were fried in tench oil.

Meat.
At the beginning of the twentieth century, meat was one of the main features of the Siberian menu. It was always on the table, excluding, of course, fasting days preceding the big Christian holidays, as well as Wednesday and Friday of every week.

The most important meats were beef, lamb, chicken, and goose. Meat-and-cabbage soup, called *shchi*, was usually cooked on a daily basis. Borscht, the red-beet meat soup, was popular among settlers from southern Russia. Due to the convenience of Russian ovens, boiling or stewing was the most common way of cooking meat.

According to the old custom only three-year-old bulls, "that had enough time to put on weight," were slaughtered for meat. *Kolbasa* (sausages) were traditionally made of beef; only at the end of the nineteenth century did Chaldon cooks learn recipes for pork *kolbasa* from newly arrived European immigrants. Horse meat was also used for sausages and was cooked in a variety of ways in the areas where Russian Siberians were in close contact with horse-breeding aboriginals. The Chaldony applied the same logic to reindeer venison in the areas of reindeer-raising tribes and to *maral* (Siberian deer) venison in the Altay Mountains of southern Siberia.

One of the most popular traditional foods in Siberia was aspic or meat jelly, called *kholodets*. It came from the legs and ears of cows and pigs that are boiled for a long time over a low heat. The meat was then cut off the bones, chopped into very fine pieces, and covered with its broth. Usually onion, garlic, and black pepper were added, as well as carrots and other root vegetables. Especially delicate was the *kholodets* made of duck, goose, or chicken feet, which required the most laborious preparation. *Kholodets* was usually served with very hot Russian mustard or horseradish sauce, often as a cold meal accompanied by vodka.

Kotlety, an oval-shaped rissole made from a mixture of minced beef and pork (with additions of onion, garlic, and white bread soaked in milk), was adopted from German settlers, as were *rybny* and *kurinny kotlety*, made from minced fish or chicken.

Pel'meni. *Pel'meni* was a very distinctive Siberian stuffed pasta dish traditionally cooked during winter. In form, *pel'meni* was a thin round (about 2–3 inches in diameter) of soft pasta dough folded over a minced meat filling to make a semicircle, with the two arms (the corners) twisted around and stuck together. One could find hundreds of *pel'meni* filling recipes involving chicken, game birds, elk, fish, reindeer, mushrooms, and many vegetarian variations; some restaurants even used meat from a brown bear as a local delicacy. However, the filling was made traditionally of two (beef and pork) or three (with the addition of lamb) types of meat, along with onion, salt, and ground black pepper.

In some villages, Chaldony made thousands of *pel'meni* during the first cold winter weeks, freezing them in the *seni* (unheated hallway) and storing them in sacks for consumption as fast-cooking food throughout the winter. *Pel'meni* were not cooked over steam, as many similar central Asian dishes were; rather they were boiled in water. In the past, *pel'meni* was the food normally given to travellers, especially to the *yamschik* (winter coachmen) who conveyed goods and passengers by *sani* (sleds) over huge distances of Siberia. The name *pel'meni* originates from the Komi language: *pel'*, meaning 'ear', and *nian'*, meaning 'bread'. In turn, the origin of Komi's *pel'nian* recipe can be traced to thirteenth-century China. When the Russian colonization of Siberia began at the end of the sixteenth century, Perm', the land of Komi, was used as the base for expansion. Not only did all Russian expeditions to Siberia go through Perm', where Russians learned about *pel'meni*, but also about 30 percent of the colonists were recruited from the Komi people. As a result, *pel'meni* spread throughout the huge colony and became a Siberian national dish.

Fish. Fish is a plentiful and favorite food of native Siberians. It is used for *ouha* (fish soup), pies, frying, and for pickling. Siberians love baked stuffed fish (usually pike); some scholars consider that it was adopted from Jewish cuisine, but differences in the recipe show that it is an indigenous local dish. *Eekra* (caviar) in Siberian cookery is not just a delicacy but also an everyday food. Siberians also make flat round caviar cakes—usually these cakes are just pure fried caviar, sometimes with the addition of chopped onion, black pepper, and a little flour. Fresh sterlet, sturgeon, salmon, or pike caviar is served slightly salted and mixed with fresh chopped onions.

From Siberian aborigines the Chaldony adopted such simple but extremely tasty food as fish *stroganina* or *chush*—thin chips cut from a large boneless piece of fresh frozen fish. *Chush* is a kind of simple but delicious accompaniment for vodka, usually eaten straight or with salt and black pepper, sometimes with chopped onion and vinegar.

Milk and egg dishes. Households of Siberian old-timers usually had many milk cows. *Tvorog* (cottage cheese) and *smetana* (sour cream) were mixed together to make a popular breakfast dish (a kind of thick yogurt) that was often eaten with honey or berry jams. In the areas near Turkic tribes, dried cottage cheese cakes were popular, and in Altay, cottage cheese cakes were smoked. *Tvorog* is the base for the dough of the popular Siberian *syrniki* (thick flat cottage cheese pancakes); it is made by combining *tvorog*, flour, milk, and eggs. *Paskha* (literally Easter, or in this case, traditional Russian Easter cake) is also based on cottage cheese mixed with eggs, raisins, honey, and candied fruits. Sour cream is used as a base for sauces and almost always as a soup dressing for *shchi*, borsch, mushroom soup, *okroshka*, and other soups, as well as a base for sweet cake creams.

Mushrooms and other wild plants. Mushrooms are an important source of proteins and are an essential raw material in Siberian cuisine: they are used in Siberian cooking much more often than in Europe. Many a Siberian family can collect up to 700–1,100 pounds of various wild mushrooms over a typical season (June to the end of September) just for the family's use. Agaric mushrooms are used for pickling with such ingredients as brine, dill, horseradish, and garlic, and, sometimes, oriental spices like black pepper, bay leaf, and cloves are added. Only saffron milk cap, chanterelle, and sometimes Armillaria (honey mushrooms) are fried on their own or stewed with potatoes. Armillaria can also be dried together with all spongy mushrooms: cep, brown cap boletus, orange-cap boletus, mossiness mushroom, *Boletus luteus*. In addition to drying for later use for winter mushroom soup or frying, spongy mushrooms are fried or stewed with pota-

Pel'meni are generally served with a variety of other foods, including special homemade bread, fish roe, sour cream, and of course, vodka. PHOTO BY ILYA VIKTOROVICH LOYSHA COURTESY OF STOLICHNAYA RUSSIAN VODKA.

toes, added to kashas, baked with eggs, and used in various mushroom soups.

Festive food. Patron saints' days, the so-called *guliaschi den'* (idle day) when nobody works, were planned well in advance. People made vodka and beer days ahead of time. Lots of guests from the neighborhood were invited into homes, and groups of people went from place to place visiting different houses. Every house had to prepare ample food, as in every house people were eating, drinking, singing, and dancing. Such holidays were only meant for married couples; young people were not entitled to take part in the feast.

For such feasts people always made pancakes, honeycakes, cookies, and various pastries. Meat- and fish-jelly and fish pie were some standards among a great number of other dishes. Before the guests approached the table, they would offer their good wishes to the hosts: "Bread on the table and salt on the table. Let it always be this way for you." After the meal and the merriment, parting guests would say: "Our Lord, save the hosts; give them good health, concord and ransom."

A Chaldon funeral repast consisted of a minimum of twelve dishes. The first items on the menu were the *kut'ya* (boiled-rice funereal dish), then *bliny*, boiled eggs sliced

in half, and *okroshka* (cold soup) with meat. Chicken and meat soups, mushrooms, corned beef, aspic, meat and chicken, boiled meatballs, and kashas followed. The last dish was fruit compote or berry kissel along with small pies or a big sweet pie. Strong drinks were not served.

For the funeral repast usually all people who knew the deceased were invited. Then ninth day, fortieth day, and one year funeral repasts followed. For the ninth day repast, just relatives and those who were helping at the funeral and funeral party were in attendance; for the forty days meal, all who came for the ninth day and those who dug the grave attended. All who came to the funeral were invited to the one year repast.

The table at a wedding celebration was especially rich: the party was three days long and cost a lot of money. A tale from the Tomsk province tells of a wedding party where everything was ready and in place, but the bride's previous boyfriend stole her away. As much money and effort had been spent in preparation for the party; the empty-handed bridegroom decided to marry another girl, saying: "Since everything is ready why should I throw out so much food?"

Maslenitsa (Shrovetide) was the last week before Lent. Traditional foods for this time included *bliny*, fish, and caviar. The best food, including lots of meat, was prepared for *Paskha* (Easter). Traditionally painted eggs, *kulich*, and *Paskha* (the Easter cake) were also served. Christmas merrymaking took place over the course of three to four days. Pork gammons, chickens, and turkeys were cooked, as well as lots of pies with various fillings.

General Changes and Foreign Foods

In spite of political changes and the pressure of permanent shortages during the eighty years of Soviet rule, Siberians have preserved a large portion of their traditional culinary identity. A new, entrepreneurial approach is underway to market the foods of the region both for local consumption and for export. In the beginning of the twentieth century, European, especially French, influence was evident only in the cuisine of the upper classes and in restaurant cooking. It has now extended to the food customs of ordinary people, and some other influences have appeared as well. In cities, central Asian foods such as *shurpa* (meat and vegetable soup), *bishbarmak* (noodle and meat soup), *shahslyk* (small pieces of marinated meat grilled on sticks), *manty* (pasta stuffed with meat and onion, then steamed), and *plov* (rice pilaf and meat) are now quite popular. Many markets sell Korean prepared salads, and the basic Korean hot carrot salad is so popular that many Siberian families now own a special grater to cut carrots to make their own version of this salad at home. Young fern shoots that are salted, dried, or fresh became popular in the Altay region after locals started stocking it in the 1980s for orders from Japan. Perhaps of all the foreign influences now affecting the cuisine of Siberia, the foods of Japan and Korea are becoming the most widely accepted.

Siberia's Aboriginal Peoples

Historically all of the territory in Siberia can be divided into two large cultural (and economic) parts: the South—a region of ancient stockbreeding and agriculture, and the North—territories that have been populated by hunting, fishing, and reindeer-raising tribes. An overview of the cooking of the two major Siberian aboriginal ethnic groups, the Yakout (Saha) in eastern Siberia and the Khant of Finnic origin in western Siberia, may provide some idea of aboriginal Siberian cooking.

Yakout (Saha) People

Yakouts are of Turkish origin and number about 380,000 people. They follow the Christian Orthodox religion, but with some remnants of shamanism. Their country, Saha (Yakoutia), has one of the most severe climates in Siberia; it lies in the far northeastern part of Siberia and occupies an area of about 1.1 million square miles (which is about twelve times the size of Great Britain).

Between the tenth and fifteenth centuries C.E., the Mongols forced Yakout tribes out of their homeland in the steppes of south Siberia. There is clear linguistic proof of the Yakouts' southern origin: their language has

such words as *khoy* (ram) and *khakhay* (tiger), even though in their country both do not exist. The environment of Yakoutia is forest, steppes on the sandy frozen meadows, and thermokarst lakes (arctic lakes formed when water holds heat that thaws the permafrost below). People live mainly in the areas of river meadows.

Yakouts are surrounded by various fishing, hunting, and reindeer-raising tribes. While the Yakout people have lived in this inclement climate over the centuries, they have not changed their traditional lifestyle of southern horse- and cattle-breeding nomads. Yakout horse, an extremely hearty breed, is the base of the traditional Yakout economy and their traditional cuisine. Yakout food is very rich in fats, including many milk, cream, and sour-milk products, and meat. Yakout people do not eat mushrooms.

Milk products. The traditional Yakout breakfast is *kuerchah*—a kind of sweet Western-style yogurt that is made of fresh cream and red whortleberries (very sour fruit) whipped into a homogeneous paste. *Kuerchah* is also frozen to make little round cakes, which in some cases include sugar. Another Yakout breakfast dish is a cake of dried cottage cheese.

Meat. The main meat for Yakouts is horseflesh, or more specifically, the meat of one-year-old colts. The horses graze all year on open pasture, in winter digging the food from under the snow, but the ones that are raised for meat are given extra food.

Thus for a year, a Yakout family of six people eats one and a half carcasses of horseflesh, a half carcass of beef, and three to four pigs. Reindeer venison is not eaten as it is considered unfit for consumption. Soviet collective farms bred reindeer, sheep, and even camels; but these meats were never popular.

The best *khan* (blood and milk pudding or sausage) is made from cow's milk and horseflesh (beef can be used but it is not as good). For spices, wild onion, garlic, and black pepper are added. These sausages are kept fresh-frozen, and boiled just before consumption.

Soups and bread. The most characteristic and popular is the beef intestines and flour soup. A fish soup is made with crucian (a kind of carp). From the beginning of Russian colonization in the seventeenth century, wheat and rye were introduced to Yakoutia and have been grown successfully ever since. Traditional Yakout bread is an unleavened flat cake. Modern Yakouts eat also "Russian" yeast-raised bread and make thick pancakes rather than the wide variety of pies known to the other Siberians. As a dainty treat, traditional bread is cut into squares and mixed with cream made of milk and butter, then it is frozen.

Vegetables. In modern times, Yakouts plant vegetables in greenhouses, but traditionally the Yakout people collected and preserved wild vegetables. Every spring they collected a lot of wild green onions that grew along the river Lena; these fresh onions were added to all dishes and were kept salted for year-round use. Wild garlic and some other plants were also collected. In springtime children eat the soft cones of larch trees, as these cones have a pleasant tart taste and contain a high quantity of vitamin C.

Beverages. The Yakouts drink *Chay* (tea) with cream or milk all day long. *Mors,* a fruit drink made of red whortleberries, is consumed instead of water. There are also many sour-milk drinks, like milk whey and herbs (tansy, thyme, wormwood), which is drunk on hot summer days as a cooling and tonic drink. For an alcoholic drink, fermented mare's milk is preferred: it provides the basis of such drinks as *koumiss* (which includes herbs such as wormwood) and *araghy.*

Festive food. *Salamat,* a ritual dish, is a type of rich buttery flour porridge. *Salamat* is served at weddings, housewarmings, funerals, and at many other important events. Since Yakouts are Russian Orthodox, funerals and funeral repasts are performed according to Russian Orthodox traditions. However, there is one important difference: all the personal possessions of the deceased have to be burned, only the most intimate belongings are put on top of the coffin, and what can not be burned is disposed of in the garbage.

Khant People

Until the 1930s, the Khant people were called Ostiak. Their dietary laws are very much influenced by their religion and taboos, and mystery and legend govern many of the Khant people's actions, including eating habits. For example, people of the beaver clan cannot eat beaver, and people of the elk clan cannot eat elk. Elk meat cannot be cut with a knife or even salted.

The bear is a relative to all Khants and is considered the guardian of world order, arbitrator, and the judge. Especially sacred is the front part of the bear: no woman is allowed to touch it. Dogs must not have any access to a bear's bones, and bear bones are not cut or broken. The Khant people believe that if they follow all of these rules, then a consumed bear will regain his flesh and walk again in the forest. Boiling crucian in the same cauldron as other fish is also prohibited, because crucian is fish for the dead who live in the underworld. All things white are holy and belong to their god, and therefore cannot be eaten, such as swans, ermine, and albino deer.

The cooking custom involving the burbot (a freshwater fish of the cod family) is also illustrative of the Khant people's reliance on tradition and mystery. Once burbot is caught, a Khant fisherman takes the fish's liver out through its mouth. If he succeeds in getting out all the liver, the rest of the flesh is eaten as well. But if the liver is cut and only a part of it is removed, the fish has to be released to the two sides of the world: the lower side (North) and upper side (South). The extracted liver is grilled on wooden sticks at the side of a bonfire. But the wood of the bonfire must be of the kind that is pleasing to the god. Willow wood is used for burbot liver cooking.

The whole cuisine of the Khant people is based on the products of fishing and hunting. Fish are so important that even the bread of the Khants is made with the addition of fish powder, and the main source of fat in their cooking is fish oil. Khants drink *chai* (tea) and eat dry wild berries for sweets.

See also **Asia, Central; Central Europe; China; Horse; Japan; Russia.**

BIBLIOGRAPHY

Bolshaya Sovetskaya Enciclopedia [Large Soviet Encyclopaedia]. 3d ed., volume 17. Moskva: Sovetskaya Encyclopaedia, 1976.

Bushkov, R. A., and F. G. Mazitova. *Kazanskoy kuchni tsvet* [Flower of Kazan' cooking]. Kazan': Tatarskoye Knizhnoye Izdatel'stvo, 1995.

Cherepnin, V. L. *Pischeviya rastenia Sibiri* [The food plants of Siberia]. Novosibirsk, Izdatel'stvo "Nauka" sibirskoye otdelenie, 1987

Enciclopedischeskiy Slovar' Granat [Granat's Encyclopaedia], vol. 43, article on Siberia. Moskva: Tovarischestvo, Br. A. I. I. Granat I Ko, 1917.

Enciclopedicheskiy Setovar' Brokgauza i Efrona [Brockhaus and Efron Encyclopaedia], vol. 29, article on Siberia–St. Petersburg: Izdatel'skoe Obschestvo F. A. Brokgauz–I. A. Efron, 1898.

Litavar, V. V., and G. L. Kaydanov. *Kak postroit' Pech, Kamin, Baniu* [How to build a stove, a fireplace, or a bathhouse]. Minsk, Byelorussia: Uradjay Publications, 1990.

Maynicheva, A. J. *Osobennosti kul'tury zhizneobespechenia nemtsev v usloviyah inoetnichnogo okruzhenia – Upper Ob', pervaya tret' XXv* [Characteristics of the life support of Germans in the foreign ethnic environment]. Available at http://www.Zaimka.ru/culture/maynich4.shtml.

Maynicheva, A. J. *Pitaniye Russkih Krest'yan Verhnego Priob'ya. Konets XIX–pervaya tret' XXvv* [Food of Russian Farmers of Upper Ob'. End of XIX–First Third of XX Century]. Available at http://www.zaimka.ru/culture/maynich1.shtml.

"Obozrevaya Okrestnosti" *Priamurskie Vedomosti Vladivostok* 25 (August 2000).

Russkaya Kuhnia [Russian Cuisine]. Moskva: EKSMO, 1997, p. 7.

Rodinson, Maxime, A. J. Arberry, and Charles Perry. *Medieval Arab Cookery.* Totnes, U.K.: Prospect Books 2001.

Roumiantseva, Elena, and Dmitry Zhogolev. *Kitayskaya kuhnia* [Chinese cuisine]. Moskva: Mir knigi, 2000.

Russkie [Russians] – Moscow: Izdatelstvo "Nauka," Rossiyskaya Akademia Nauk [Russia's Academy of Science], 1999

Scheglov, I. V. *Chronologichesky perechen' vazhneishikh dannykh iz istorii Sibiri 1032–1882* [Chronological index of the most important facts of the Siberian history 1032–1882]. Sourgout, AIIK: Severny Dom, 1993.

Tikhonovich, Anatoly. *Starinnaya Sibirskaya Kukhnia* [Old Siberian cuisine]. Toms: Izdatel'stvo Tom'lad, 1992.

Ilya V. Loysha

SILVERWARE.

"Silverware" often refers generically to any flatware used for eating by most people in the Western world, and some parts of Asia and Africa—knives, forks, and spoons—whether it is made of silver, stainless steel, or a silver-plated base metal. Flatware, especially that used by most people when they eat informally, is usually made of stainless steel, not silver. "Silverware" also refers to dishes used for serving food and some decorative objects such as candlesticks.

In its narrowest sense, "silverware," which includes eating utensils, serving dishes, and decorative items, is made either of sterling silver—925 parts silver to 75 parts another metal, perhaps copper—or has layers of silver plated over another metal, often nickel silver. The more layers, the better the quality, and buyers are cautioned that flatware will be more durable and worth having if it is at least triple plate. Some manufacturers put extra silver on pieces at the point of most wear, for example, on the back of the bowl of a spoon, where it rests on the table.

Of the three pieces of cutlery used by most often by Westerners for eating, the knife was the first utensil. Because early humans were hunters and scavengers and ate meat when they could get it, knives—made of flint or obsidian—were necessary both for cutting meat away from the bone of a kill and for cutting it into manageable pieces for carrying it back to the campsite and for eating. Gradually, as metallurgy developed, knives were made of bronze, iron, and, finally, steel.

From the earliest times until well into the Middle Ages, knives were used for hunting and personal protection, and men always carried them. Because no utensils were provided with meals at the inns and taverns at that time, travelers used their own knives, which they also kept on the table in case they were attacked. Later, inns began to supply knives with the food they served.

Early spoons, used for eating liquids, were made of wood. Shells with attached wooden handles were also used fashioned as spoons. Metal spoons, when they began to be used, were made from the same metal used to make knives of the era. Forks were used in Roman kitchens, with smaller versions being used to carve meat at the side of the table. It is said that a Byzantine princess introduced table forks into Venice in the eleventh century, and their use as eating utensils spread across Italy. Eating with forks did not become fashionable, however, until the seventeenth century. The fact that forks had only two tines at first may account for the delay in adopting them as eating utensils because they were awkward to use. Thomas Coryate, an English traveler, is credited with introducing forks to England in 1608 after a visit to Italy. He wrote that forks were usually made of steel or iron, but that the nobility ate with silver forks. As the use of forks became popular, people began to carry their own forks in special cases when they dined at friends' homes.

CHRISTENING SPOONS

Wealthy Romans customarily presented a silver spoon to a newborn child. To be "born with a silver spoon in its mouth" meant that the child had many advantages from birth. When the Roman Empire adopted Christianity in 312 C.E., Romans continued to give silver spoons to newborns. To indicate that the child had been baptized, the Chi-Rho, or XP, the Greek symbol for Christ, was engraved on the bowl of the spoon. The Corinium spoon was found in Roman ruins in England, near what is now Cirencester, called Corinium during the Roman occupation of Britain. Sterling silver replicas of the christening spoon were sold in the 1970s by Leonard Jones Ltd. of Cirencester.

Since the Romans, silver has been used to make utensils, but only royalty or the very wealthy could afford it until the end of the nineteenth century. Indeed, the ability to own and control precious metals has always been the prerogative of nobility and the wealthy merchant classes. During the Ottoman Empire, for example, only the Sultans ate from gold dishes, while the women of the harem had silver dishes for dining.

In the eighteenth century, silver eating utensils and serving pieces were popular in Europe and America for those who could afford them. Gorham Manufacturing Company began making table silver in the United States in 1831. Each piece was hand-forged, and two men could produce two dozen pieces a day. In eighteenth-century American society, silverware was identified with women of the moneyed classes. At that time, women could not legally own land or other property, so the scope of their lives was limited to home and family. For this reason, silverware was significant as a woman's contribution to the financial part of a marriage, and it was often purchased for her one piece at a time and kept in what was called a "hope chest," along with other household goods such as linens and quilts. Because it was bought with a woman's taste in mind, most silverware was designed for women. Silver flatware, along with other household goods, has traditionally been monogrammed with the bride's initials.

During the latter part of the nineteenth and early part of the twentieth centuries, wealthy families had servants who prepared and served elaborate dinners that required the use of many different pieces of silverware. There was a great amount of flatware and hollowware made from silver, and some of those servants were responsible for keeping all of it polished. It was a task that kept them busy. Complete sets of silver flatware came with specialized versions of the standard utensils: luncheon knives and forks, smaller than those used for dinner; place spoons (later called "soup spoons" in the United States and "dessert spoons" in Europe, but still listed as place spoons by manufacturers), which are larger than teaspoons; and salad forks and dessert forks, often the same fork used interchangeably. Specialty items of flatware included: iced drink spoons and fish cocktail forks, both long-handled and still available in flatware sets; butter spreaders, short knives that fit on bread plates in individual place settings (also still available); chocolate spoons for hot chocolate; ramekin forks (smaller than salad forks, to fit into small dishes—called ramekins—used to bake individual servings of food); tea forks and knives, about the size of luncheon silverware; sifting spoons with pierced bowls, to be used in sifting sugar over food; fruit knives; and demitasse, or coffee, spoons.

There was even special flatware made for children: pap spoons, which were small spoons with slightly elongated handles for feeding infants; small versions of forks and spoons for children old enough to feed themselves; and pushers, each piece with a plough-like blade attached at a right angle to the handle, used to push food onto a fork or spoon.

People in European countries also enjoyed silver flatware, but used different pieces specialized to accommodate Continental eating habits, for example, marrow spoons. These are long, narrow scoops, suitable for digging flavorful marrow out of meat bones. Special fish knives and forks are also used extensively. The fish knife has a broad flat blade, which makes lifting the flesh from the bones easy, and the fork tines are usually not as sharp as those of other forks. The flatware made to serve fish is similar, but larger. Fish sets are still used in European homes and restaurants, especially in Germany, Scandinavia, and Britain.

Serving pieces used in Europe, the United States, and Canada include tomato servers (or slices), which are flat, circular, slotted pieces; tongs, ranging from large ones for serving salad or asparagus to very small ones for sugar cubes; cheese scoops, used to serve from large chunks of cheeses; dressing or stuffing spoons (called "hash spoons" in Ireland and Scotland), large, long-handled spoons suitable for digging stuffing from the insides of turkeys; ladles; and strainer spoons (like sifter spoons), used secularly to strain seeds from fruit punch bowls and ecclesiastically to strain impurities from the communion wine. Potato forks, wide, with six tines, were made in Liverpool, London, and Dublin. There were spoons for serving candy, nuts, and ice cream. Specialty forks were made to serve sardines, macaroni, and poached eggs. There were grape shears, cracker scoops, butter picks, nut picks, and lobster picks. Pie and cake servers and serrated cake knives are still being made. (A cake knife can be engraved with the names of a bride and groom and given to them for a wedding gift.) Berry serving spoons have broad, deep bowls, and lemon forks are short, with three tines, wide

apart. The most common serving pieces are tablespoons, some with holes for straining vegetables served in their cooking liquid, and meat forks.

Flatware has also been made of silver combined with various other materials such as gold, porcelain, wood, or enameled metals other than silver. Inspiration from other cultures influenced styles of silver produced in the United States. Textile designs and other forms of art from Russia, Persia, India, China, Japan, and England were imitated to develop designs for silver pieces. Mokume, a wood-grained metal from Japan, was also copied in silver.

Like flatware, silver hollowware has been used for centuries and made for many purposes. There are containers for every conceivable food. Bowls of all sizes and shapes have been made of silver, along with water pitchers, tea and coffee serving sets, sauce boats, cups, goblets, tankards, salt dishes, salt-and-pepper shakers, bread trays and baskets. Containers for cooking or keeping foods hot have been made of silver: chafing dishes, coffee serving sets, and samovars, the Russian urns in which tea is made. Silver vases, candlesticks, and other decorative objects have all been used on dining tables to enhance the place settings and make the meal a special occasion for families and guests.

By the end of the nineteenth century, the United States led the world in manufacturing silverware and purchasing it as well. In the 1890s, as the price of silver bullion kept decreasing and competition among manufacturers increased, silver became sufficiently inexpensive that lower-middle-class consumers could afford to own it.

Like other Continental nations, Scandinavians used silver for fine dining and held it in high regard. Georg Jensen Solvsmedie, a firm in Copenhagen, Denmark, began manufacturing tableware in 1904. Jensen's modern, clean designs were a change from the rococo and neoclassic designs of the nineteenth century, and, by 1938, the United States was the largest market for Danish sterling silverware. At the beginning of the twenty-first century, there was still a Georg Jensen showroom in New York City.

SILVER SERVICE

In Britain, a formal type of restaurant service is called "silver service." Foods are brought to the table in silver-plated serving dishes and platters and are placed on the diners' plates by the serving staff.

Silver and gold ice cream spoons in the Burgundian style, Germany, circa 1880. The large spoon in the center was meant for serving. ROUGHWOOD COLLECTION. PHOTO CHEW & COMPANY.

The purchase and use of silverware, however, have been steadily declining since World War II, perhaps because families are unwilling to spend money on it and have neither the time nor the servants to care for it. Furthermore, many European families lost their silverware during wars and so had none to pass on to the next generation. It is also true that meals have become less formal, and stainless steel flatware and hollowware better-looking and more acceptable, not to mention less expensive, than silver as the twentieth century ended. However, sterling silver is still for sale and is still being collected and enjoyed by those who can afford it.

See also **Cutlery; Etiquette and Eating Habits; Kitchen Gadgets.**

BIBLIOGRAPHY

Cullen, Noel C. *Life beyond the Line: A Front-of-the-House Companion for Culinarians.* Upper Saddle River, N. J.: Prentice-Hall, 2001.

Dolan, Maryanne. *1830s–1990s American Sterling Silver Flatware: A Collector's Identification and Value Guide.* Florence, Ala.: Books Americana, 1993.

Hagan, Tere. *Sterling Flatware: An Identification and Value Guide.* Rev. 2d ed. Tempe, Ariz.: TAMM, 1994.

Newman, Harold. *An Illustrated Dictionary of Silverware.* London: Thames & Hudson, 2000.

Tiffany & Company. *Tiffany Table Settings.* New York: Crowell, 1960.

Trager, James. *The Food Chronology: A Food Lover's Compendium of Events and Anecdotes from Prehistory to the Present.* New York: Holt, 1995.

Venable, Charles L. *Silver in America, 1840–1940: A Century of Splendor.* New York: Abrams, 1995.

Mary Kelsey

SIN AND FOOD. "Rich as Sin," "My Sin," "Sin Pie"—all are recipe names found in community (and church!) cookbooks in the United States today. Initially these may entice the prospective cook or eater with the implied promise of an exceptionally delicious indulgence, so delicious in fact, that it ought to be too good for humans. Behind these sweet temptations, however, is a somber history. Because these foods are too sweet, too rich, too good, humans who eat them go too far. People have long associated food with sin. Although a complex concept that varies throughout human cultures, sin is at its most basic a violation of the boundary between the sacred and the profane. In most religious traditions, food, literally and symbolically, is a vehicle for transgressing limits. As an ancient Babylonian psalmist confessed, "The food that belongs to god, I have eaten." This is one side of a powerful paradox. Food has divine origins as other recipes for "Heavenly Hash," "Angel Food," and quite literally, "Ambrosia" (food of the gods) attest. It is the means by which life is sustained and through which mortals may commune with the divine and each other. To take food in ways that violate divine intentions, however, can have grave consequences.

In early religions, sin is usually an offense against the cosmic order of things rather than personal disobedience of a god's command. It is the violation of a prohibition, or taboo, that leads to defilement. To be in right relationship with the cosmos is to be pure or in one's appropriate state vis-à-vis the cosmos. Religions often have rules about food consumption and preparation that symbolize order on many levels. The Hua of Papua New Guinea, for example, have a complex system of food-related taboos. One should not eat the food of another with whom conflict may exist, as the vital essence transferred in eating may have negative affects. Pregnant women should not eat hard yams lest they induce a hard labor. Young men must avoid foods prepared in certain ways by menstruating women lest they be weakened by them. In each case, the idea of ordered relationships that perpetuate life is reinforced.

The major Eastern traditions, Hinduism and Buddhism, also conceptualize transgression as a violation of order or karma. In the Hindu caste system, offenses are relative to one's assigned station in life. A Brahman of the highest caste can be rendered impure by eating food touched by a lower caste Hindu. Even Brahman women render food impure if they touch it during menstruation, a time of ritual impurity. Among the major offenses in Hinduism are two general food-related ones. Killing or eating a cow, which is sacred, is forbidden. Drinking intoxicants is also forbidden because it arouses human sensibilities to levels for which they are not intended. Violating either of these proscriptions will lead to a lower state of existence in the next life. In Buddhism, one of the three roots of evil is *lobha*, which has a range of meanings including "craving." Craving foods, being attached to this existence through them, affects one's karma negatively. Eating must be done dispassionately lest it lead one out of the bounds of discipline. Conversely, the disciplined consumption of rice and tea have become means to enlightenment in some Buddhist traditions. Some gurus have advanced to such a high spiritual state that they are able to go without eating for long periods, having lost the need for feeding. In their perfectly balanced existence, they are self-replenishing.

Western religious traditions have defined sin primarily as willful disobedience of God's commandments and the resulting immoral actions. The sense of disorder and taboo remain, however. In Judaism and Islam, dietary codes help to define proper relationship to God. Jews must not eat foods that are *terefah* (unfit). Many foods are unfit because they are hybrids that defy order

themselves. Shellfish are *terefah* because they do not have fins like other fish. To eat such foods is to become impure, separate from God and God's people. Muslims must avoid *haram* (unlawful) foods. Jewish and Muslim dietary laws overlap somewhat, most notably in the prohibition against consuming pork. Disciplined eating and periods of abstaining from food aid Muslims in their quest to submit themselves to Allah's will.

The connection between cosmic defilement and offending God also remains in Christianity. Some early Christians, as evidenced most clearly in the epistles of St. Paul, followed classical notions of food as healthy for the body and a licit pleasure to be enjoyed in moderation. For St. Paul, eating meat had nothing to do with one's spiritual state. Others maintained the Jewish dietary laws or other forms of dietary restriction such as vegetarianism. While the Pauline position won out in normative Christianity, and Christian sects that advocated special diets were often suspected of heresy, the notion that food had nothing to do with one's relationship to God did not pass into Christianity unchallenged. Gradually, eating became associated with desire that cannot be curbed and seen as an illicit pleasure that distracted from godly matters. And it became connected to that other unruly human urge, sexuality. Some church leaders advocated fasting, especially for women, as a means of curbing sexual desire. Thus celibacy and abstaining from food became hallmarks of Christian purity. Original sin, as St. Augustine came to define it, further connected food, sexuality, disobedience, and disorderliness. Because the first parents, Adam and Eve, ate fruit God had forbidden, every human inherits their lack of control through lust. For St. Augustine, it was the uncontrollable desire for the pleasure of eating, even more than sex, that was most difficult for him to control. So although the paradigm for communion with God in Christianity is a sacred feast, eating has become suspect in the Christian tradition as something mired in the profane and attached to human weakness. This takes many forms. Somewhat like the Eastern gurus, medieval Christian mystics gave up earthly food and fed only on Christ's body.

Though the "sinful" recipes in church cookbooks are taken lightly by the communities that enjoy them in fellowship meals, a growing movement among evangelical women in the United States encourages them to abandon their sinful cravings for food and strive to be, in the words of Christian dieter Patricia Kreml, "Slim for Him."

Food is often the central focus of another side of sinning, the failure to consider the needs of others as well as one's own. Greed, closely associated with gluttony and lust, is railed against in all of the world's major religious traditions. *Lobha* means 'greed' as well as 'craving', implying the close connection between transgression against the divine and the community. *Taqwa* (piety), a chief Muslim value, involves the proper fear of Allah and purity of intention, mind, and body. But charity and hospitality toward others are also necessary to *taqwa*. During

Ramadan, a fasting period in which Muslims strive with particular rigor to submit to God, giving food to the poor is also required. Attitudes toward another's feeding reflect one's relationship with the divine. St. Augustine illustrated the human condition in a story about an infant wailing loudly while his brother fed at their mother's breast: "But it can hardly be innocence, when the source of milk is flowing . . . abundantly, not to endure a share going to one's blood-brother, who is in profound need, dependent for life . . . on that food." (*Confessions*, I, vi).

The association between food and sin runs deeply through human cultures, perhaps because eating so clearly involves penetration of boundaries. It is the gift of God that comes from the earth, the sustainer of life through slaughter and harvest, substance that becomes self; and binder of one to another, child to mother, human to divine. Such transformation is mysterious business, not without risks. As anyone who has overindulged at a fellowship meal well knows, too much of a good thing can make food of the gods into devil's food.

See also **Buddhism**; **Christianity**; **Cookbooks, Community**; **Fasting and Abstinence**; **Feasts, Festivals and Fasts**; **Hinduism**; **Islam**; **Religion and Food**; **Women and Food**.

BIBLIOGRAPHY

Augustine, Saint. *Confessions.* Translated by Henry Chadwick. New York: Oxford University Press, 1991.

Griffith, R. Marie. "Don't Eat That: The Erotics of Abstinence in American Christianity." *Gastronomica* 1, 4 (Fall 2001): 36–47.

Grimm, Veronika E. *From Feasting to Fasting: The Evolution of a Sin.* New York: Routledge, 1996.

Kreml, Patricia Banta. *Slim for Him.* Plainfield, N.J.: Logos International, 1978.

LaCocque, André. "Sin." In *The Encyclopedia of Religion*, edited by Mircea Eliade, vol. 13, 325–331. New York: Macmillan, 1987.

Langdon, Stephen. *Babylonian Penitential Psalms.* Paris: P. Geuthner, 1927.

Meigs, Anna. "Food as Cultural Construction." In *Food and Culture: A Reader*, edited by Carole Counihan and Penny Van Esterik, 95–106. New York: Routledge, 1997. (Previously published in *Food and Foodways* 2 [1988], 341–359.)

Murphy, Christopher P. H. "Piety and Honor: The Meaning of Muslim Feasts in Old Delhi." In *Food, Society and Culture*, edited by R. S. Khare and M. S. A. Rao, 85–119. Durham: Carolina Academic Press, 1986.

Corrie E. Norman

SLOW FOOD. Slow Food Arcigola, founded in 1989 by Carlo Petrini and known simply as Slow Food, is an international movement headquartered in Bra, Piedmont, Italy, and organized around small, local chapters. Formed in 1986 in opposition to an attempt by McDonald's to place its golden arches in the Piazza di Spagna area of Rome, Slow Food's mission is to cultivate public appreciation for locally produced foods, wines, and authentic tastes. Pleasure and conviviality at the table are brought into harmony with humane, wholesome conditions of production. The movement encourages opposition to fast food and the fast life to improve the quality of life. While aiming to educate the public's palate, it advocates biodiversity in foods; local food and artisanal production; conservation of traditional foods and foodways and the environments that produce them; and measures to make traditional foods economically viable.

At the beginning of the twenty-first century the Slow Food movement counted sixty-five thousand members in forty-five countries on five continents. Chapters, called *convivia* internationally, numbered 560 worldwide, 340 of which were in Italy, where they are called *condotte*. The group's activities include public education forums, such as guided taste workshops, school programs, and conventions; and publications, such as guides to wines, cheeses, restaurants, food and wine cultures and their histories, and tourism. Slow Food is committed to philanthropy, including *Le Tavole Fraterne* or Friendship Tables; financing solidarity projects; and international charity programs, including sponsoring a soup kitchen in an Amazonian indigenous hospital and a school cafeteria in Sarajevo and rebuilding a cooperative cheese factory in Umbria, Italy, that was damaged in the 1997 earthquake. Through the Ark of Taste projects, begun in 1996, the movement advocates identifying and safeguarding endangered food "treasures," for example, charcuterie, cheeses, grains, vegetables, and local breeds; small, quality food products, such as *lardo di Colonnata*—lard packed in salt and herbs, served in thin slices on bread—and Protected Designation of Origin (DOP) cheeses; and agricultural and food heritage sites, such as, cafés, pastry shops, inns, and restaurants. The Slow Food presidia have focused on these areas to guarantee their economic and commercial futures, to protect the land from degradation, and to create new job opportunities. Small, quality food producers need protection against the industrial food complexes that control ever larger market shares and large-scale distribution. The industrial complexes often influence laws that threaten the very existence of traditional producers.

In the tradition of avant-garde manifestos, *The Slow Food Manifesto* (Paris, 1989) states, "We work towards the rediscovery of the richness and aromas of local cuisines by opposing the leveling effect of the Fast Life . . . which has changed our lives and threatens the environment and landscape." The movement's apt symbol therefore is the snail—small, cosmopolitan, prudent, and slow. The manifesto warns against being "too impatient to smell and taste" and "too greedy to remember what [we] have just devoured." Opposing fast cheap food and the values and systems of globalized food production, Slow Food can be firmly placed in the biocultural ecology movement. The mission statement of Slow Food USA reads:

Recognizing that the enjoyment of wholesome food is essential to the pursuit of happiness, Slow Food USA is an educational organization dedicated to the stewardship of the land and ecologically sound food production; to the revival of the kitchen and the table as centers of pleasure, culture and community; to the invigoration and proliferation of regional, seasonal culinary traditions; and to living a slower and more harmonious rhythm of life.

The success of its agenda and the growth of its membership—attributable to the rise of an ecological consciousness among educated, affluent consumers, that fosters a concern with the quality of foods and their sources—have encouraged Slow Food to expand its publications, such as the *Slow* journal, published in Italian, French, English, and German; and to open offices in Switzerland (1995), Germany, (1998), New York (2000), and to make plans for an office in Paris. The group's highly successful international taste fair, *Il Salone del Gusto*, first held in Turin, Italy, in 1996, is a review of quality food and wine. With the theme of biodiversity, the fair between 5 and 9 November 1998 attracted 126,000 visitors and featured 300 stalls displaying Italian and foreign artisanal food in three halls devoted to charcuterie and cheeses; gastronomy; and pastry, cakes, chocolate, and coffee. Participants experienced tastings, conferences, seminars, and cooking and tasting courses.

The biennial Slow Food cheese fair was first held in September 1997 in Bra, Italy. The 1998 cheese fair was organized as a market devoted to the 127 European DOP cheeses. The Slow Food movement has also organized *Excellentia* for people to experience various wines; *La Settimana del Gusto*, a week of low-cost menus in restaurants throughout Italy to encourage those under age twenty-six to participate in quality food experiences; and *Il Gioco del Piacere*, biennial blind wine tastings attended by over fifteen thousand people.

See also **Artificial Foods**; **Fast Food**; **Natural Foods**.

BIBLIOGRAPHY

Slow Food Editore, established in 1989, has produced about sixty publications, largely in Italian, devoted to the pleasures of wine, food, and conviviality. Among its best-known publications are the quarterlies *Slow* and *Slowine; Osterie d'Italia* [Taverns of Italy], a guide to traditional eating establishments; *Vini d'Italia* [Wines of Italy], a comprehensive guide to Italian wines with Gambero Rosso; and *L'arca*, the review of the Slow Food presidia project. Slow Food also publishes monographs on cheeses, beers, wines, and oils. Among them are *Formaggi d'Europa* [Cheeses of Europe], which includes the 127 European DOP cheeses; the taste manuals *Dire, fare e gustare* [Saying, doing, and tasting]; and Giacomo Leopardi, *Il piacere del vino* [The pleasure of wine]; Italian regional recipe books, such as Anna Gosetti della Salda, *Le ricette regionali Italiane* [Regional Italian recipes]; books on food history, such as *Il gusto dell'agro* [Savoring the sour], a history of vinegar; tourism books, such as *Venezia: Draghi, santi e capesante* [Venice: Dragons, saints, and scallops]; and reprints of classics, such as Silvano Serventi, *Il cuoco Piemontese* [The Piedmontese cook] (Bra, Italy: Slow Food, 1995), an

eighteenth-century text on Piedmontese cuisine. The Slow Food Web site is available at http://www.slowfood.com.

Luisa Del Giudice

SNACKS. Throughout human history, the frequency and content of meals has varied. From ancient times, light foods or leftovers were consumed between meals. These tended to be natural, sweet foods that required little or no preparation, such as grapes, figs, or apples. In nineteenth-century America, interest in snack foods shifted from natural foods to prepared commercial foods, with a high salt and sugar content. It is these processed foods that are considered snack foods in the early twenty-first century.

Salty Snacks

America's first commercial snack foods were peanuts and popcorn, which were cheap, tasty, filling, and eminently portable. Peanut and popcorn vendors sold their products on the streets, circuses, and fairs, and later at sporting events. One successful peanut vendor was Amedeo Obici, an Italian-born immigrant living in Wilkes-Barre, Pennsylvania. In 1906, he, along with another Italian immigrant, formed the Planters' Peanut Company. They constantly improved their products and packaging. To promote their products, the company adopted "Mr. Peanut" in 1917—a logo has appeared subsequently on almost every Planters package. Both popcorn and peanuts were marketed to children and were connected with children's holidays. These characteristics have become standard for snack foods.

Homemade pretzels were probably sold for centuries before they were first commercially produced in 1861. Pretzels did not become an important national snack until the 1930s, when a machine was invented to automate production. Recipes for potato chips appeared in the early nineteenth century. Under the name "Saratoga chips," they were popularized by George Crum, the chef of the Moon's Lake Lodge in Saratoga, New York. First manufactured by John E. Marshall of Boston in the 1890s, potato chips were sold in barrels but quickly became stale after a barrel was opened. Potato chips did not become popular until the 1920s, when Laura Scudder asked employees to iron two pieces of wax paper to form a bag. This set off a packaging revolution that permitted chips to be sold airtight bags. Corn chips were originally a Mexican snack—cut-up, fried, or dried tortillas. The first-known commercial corn chips were the *friotes*, which were made from fried *masa* (corn flour) in San Antonio. Elmer Doolin purportedly bought a bag of *friotes* and then bought the recipe for one hundred dollars. In 1932, Doolin began manufacturing them under the name Fritos. His renamed product was a success, and his sales expanded as far as St. Louis, Missouri. In 1945, Doolin met potato chip manufacturer, Herman W. Lay, who agreed to distribute Fritos, which became popular

SOME POPULAR SNACKS

Animal Crackers: Invented in 1871 by Pennsylvanian David F. Stauffer.

Baby Ruth: Introduced in 1920 by the Curtiss Candy Company of Chicago, this candy is filled with peanuts covered with nougat and a chocolate covering.

Butterfinger: Introduced by the Curtiss Candy Company in 1923.

Candy canes: Developed in Europe and arrived in the United States via German immigrants. Produced commercially in the 1920s, they became popular in the 1950s.

Cheetos: Invented by the Frito-Lay company in 1948.

Chocolat Delicieux à Manger: Produced by J. S. Fry around 1847, it is thought to be the first handmade chocolate candy bar.

Cotton candy or floss: Made by spinning colored sugar causing it to puff into cotton-like strands, became popular at circuses and fairs before 1900.

Eskimo Pie: Originally called the I-scream bar, it was created by Chris Nelson in Onawa, Iowa, in 1920.

Fig Newton: Invented by Charles M. Roser of Ohio, who sold recipe to what became NABISCO, which first sold them commercially in 1891.

Fortune cookies: An American invention started during the early 20th century, probably in San Francisco. They were first commercially manufactured about 1920.

Hershey Chocolate Bar: Introduced by Milton S. Hershey about 1900. It is the world's first manufactured chocolate candy bar.

Jelly beans: Probable descendent of Turkish Delight. French confectioners developed the process of "panning" necessary to make jelly beans. In America, jelly beans were a penny candy sold by weight. They were not associated with Easter until the 1930s.

Junior Mints: Originally produced by James O. Welch Company, the chocolate covered peppermint now a part of NABISCO Confections, Inc.

Life Savers: Developed in 1912 by Clarence A. Crane of Cleveland, Ohio. These round, white peppermints have holes in the middle that resemble life preservers on a boat, hence their name.

Kit Kat: A chocolate-covered wafer produced by the Rowntree and Company's Chocolate Crisp, it was renamed the Kit Kat in 1937.

Lollipops and Suckers: Unclear origin; a machine for making lollipops was developed by Russian immigrant Samuel Born in 1916 in San Francisco, but Wisconsin's Racine Confectioners Machinery Co. claims to have done so in 1908.

M & M's: Introduced in 1940. The company's goal was to create a candy that did not melt, and the idea was said to have originated during the Spanish Civil War, when soldiers ate chocolates covered with a thin layer of sugar candy that prevented the chocolate from melting in the heat. M&M's quickly became the best-selling confection in the world, but the original version did not contain peanuts. Mars introduced M&M Peanut Chocolate Candies in 1954, and they have been a good seller ever since.

Milky Way: Introduced by Mars, Inc., in 1923.

Mounds: Coconut and chocolate confection was released in 1922 by Peter Paul Halajia of Naugatuck, Connecticut.

Mr. Goodbar: Introduced by Hershey, it was a chocolate-peanut based confection released in 1925.

NECCO wafers: Hard cylinder-shaped candies released by NECCO (an acronym for the New England Confection Company), first appearing in 1912.

Nestlé's Crunch: Released in 1938 by Nestlé, it is a combination of milk chocolate and crisped rice.

Oh, Henry!: Introduced by George H. Williamson of Chicago in 1920, it was originally a log-shaped bar with a fudge center surrounded by a caramel and peanut layer and coated in pure milk chocolate.

Payday: Manufactured by the Pratt and Langhoff Candy Company in 1932.

Pez: Invented in 1927 by Eduard Haas III, of Vienna, Austria, the hard candy is named for the German word for "peppermint." Pez dispensers were invented in 1948.

Potato chips: Recipes were published early in the nineteenth century, and were first manufactured in 1890s by John E. Marshall of Boston. Potato chips did not become popular until the 1930s, after a packaging revolution permitted the chips to remain fresh.

Reese's Peanut Butter Cup: Introduced by the H. B. Reese Candy Company, the chocolate-covered peanut butter candy was first manufactured in 1928.

Snickers Bar: Created by Mars, Inc., in 1930, the candy bar, composed of a combination of peanut butter nougat, peanuts, and caramel encased in milk chocolate, was first marketed in 1930.

3 Musketeers: Created by Mars, Inc., in 1932, the candy bar consisted of three levels of chocolate coating and was named after the novel by Alexander Dumas.

Toblerone: Invented by the Swiss Theodor Tobler and Emil Baumann, the chocolate-covered almond nougat candy bar was first manufactured in 1908.

Tootsie Roll: Introduced in 1896 by New Yorker Leo Hirschfield, this round, chewy candy was named after his daughter who was nicknamed "Tootsie."

Twinkies: Invented by a Chicago bakery manager named Jimmy Dewar, the cream-filled sponge cake was first marketed in 1930.

nationwide, and the two companies merged. The Frito-Lay Company introduced Cheetos in 1948, and continued to grow by introducing new snacks and acquire other snack food companies. Owned by PepsiCo. today, Frito-Lay is the largest snack food conglomerate in the world. Many other chip-based snacks have been developed. Some more famous ones include nachos (1943), a snack purportedly developed in Eagle Pass, Texas, and Doritos, first marketed by Frito-Lay (1966).

Sweet Snacks

Peanuts and popcorn combined to create America's first successful commercial sweet confection. Frederick W. Rueckheim, an immigrant from Germany, combined peanuts, popcorn, and molasses to create Cracker Jack. By 1923 the Cracker Jack Company sold more than 138 million boxes annually. However, sweet snacks had been sold well before Cracker Jack. They fall into four major categories: hard candy, baked goods, chocolate candy, and frozen sweets

Candies have been produced in Asia for thousands of years. Homemade candies, such as lemon drops, jujubes, and peppermints, were produced in Europe by the late eighteenth century. Penny candies were frequently sold in grocery stores. During the nineteenth and twentieth centuries, thousands of candies have been manufactured, including saltwater taffy (1883), first manufactured commercially in Atlantic City, New Jersey, and Life Savers (1912), manufactured by Clarence Crane of Cleveland, Ohio.

The second broad category of sweet snacks are baked goods. Small baked cakes and pastries with sugar had been produced since the late Middle Ages in Europe and likely originated in Arab lands, particularly Baghdad. "Cookies," an American word derived from Dutch, initially referred to sugar cookies flavored with spices. The word was subsequently extended to include other kinds, such as wafers, snaps, and macaroons. Initially, cookies were handmade and were sold in grocery stores. They were first manufactured in the United States in the late nineteenth century. Animal Crackers (1871) and Fig Newtons (1892) were among the first commercially manufactured cookies. Numerous commercial varieties have been manufactured since, such as OREO's, a chocolate sandwich cookie, and gingersnaps. Several chains that bake fresh cookies have emerged in the last quarter of the twentieth century, including Famous Amos' in 1976 and Mrs. Field's Cookies in 1977. Many other baked goods were also converted into commercial snacks. Hostess Cup Cakes were first manufactured in 1919. Twinkies were invented by a Chicago bakery manager named Jimmy Dewar in 1930, and were later acquired by Hostess.

Chocolate Candy

The third broad category is chocolate-based candy. In 1847 Joseph Storrs Fry, a British Quaker, invented a process of combining cocoa powder, sugar, and melted

Hot dogs make a perfect urban snack food since they are sold on the street, easy to handle, and easy to eat. © PATRICK GIARDINO/CORBIS.

cocoa butter that produced a thin paste which could be shaped in a mold. The handmade Chocolat Delicieux à Manger is considered to be the first chocolate bar. J. S. Fry and Company became the largest manufacturer of chocolate in the world. In Switzerland, Henri Nestlé developed the process of making milk chocolate in 1867. Another Swiss chocolate manufacturer, Daniel Peter, used Nestlé's chocolate to make a milk chocolate bar in 1879. A third Swiss, Theodor Tobler, marketed in 1908 his Toblerone, consisting of a triangular chocolate bar with almond-and-honey nougat. Other chocolate-making companies emerged, such as Lindt of Switzerland (1845) and Belgium's Godiva Chocolates (1926).

In the United States, chocolate candy and caramels became important by the 1870s. These were expensive in part because they were all handmade. Boxed chocolates were manufactured by the 1840s. Early chocolate confection makers included the Walter Baker Chocolate Company and Walter M. Lowney Company, both headquartered in Boston. The Whitman Sampler became a national boxed chocolate by 1907. Retail candy stores have developed, including See's Candy (1921) and Fanny Farmer (1919).

The first American to manufacture chocolate bars was Milton Hershey, who in 1903, began to build what would become the world's largest chocolate manufacturing plant in Derry Church (later renamed Hershey), Pennsylvania. Hershey's Chocolate Bars were the first of thousands of chocolate bars to roll off the assembly line, followed by Hershey's Chocolate Kisses in 1907. Hershey produced many new products including Mr. Goodbar, composed of chocolate and peanuts, and the Krackel, composed of chocolate and rice.

Hershey's success encouraged others to produce chocolate bars. Otto Y. Schnering of Chicago founded the Curtiss Candy Company, which released the Baby Ruth candy bar in 1920. Curtiss later introduced the

Butterfinger. George H. Williamson, a salesman for a candy broker in Chicago, opened a candy store and launched the Oh Henry! candy bar in 1920. In the same year, Frank and Ethel Mars of Minneapolis started up Mars, Inc. Three years later they produced the Milky Way candy bar, followed in 1930 by the Snickers Bar, which quickly became America's most popular candy bar—an honor it still holds today. This was followed by M&M's in 1940.

Frozen Sweets

Ices and ice cream have been produced for centuries. Ice cream parlors probably originated in Italy and France and have sold their goods since at least the late eighteenth century. The three major snack products have all been American inventions: the ice cream cone, ice cream bar, and popsicle. The ice cream cone was invented during the late nineteenth century and was popularized at the St. Louis World's Fair. The cone made it possible to consume ice cream without the need of a spoon and cup. Ice cream parlors have continued to thrive and major chains, such as Carvel's (1934), which serves soft-serve ice cream, and Baskin-Robbins (1948), have become very well known.

Handheld ice cream bars quickly became an important snack food in America. The Eskimo Pie originated in Iowa in 1920. In the same year Harry Burt invented the chocolate-covered vanilla ice cream bar on a stick in Youngstown, Ohio. Ice cream bars became popular during the following decades. The popsicle, frozen flavored water, was first commercially manufactured in the United States during the 1920s.

Snack Food in the Early Twenty-First Century

Many snacks are heavy on calories, fat, and salt. The term "junk food" was popularized in 1972 by Michael Jacobson of the Center for Science in the Public Interest. The concern with empty calories has continued, and of particular concern has been the targeting of youth by snack food companies. As a response to junk food charges, a natural snack food industry developed during the 1970s. This included such snacks as gorp, composed of various combinations of raisins, peanuts and other natural foods, used by hikers and now available commercially in most grocery stores.

The commercial snack food industry is a major component of America's economy. When the total statistics of commercial candy, baked snacks, chocolates, and frozen snacks are combined, the industry sells annually in excess of $75 billion of products in the United States alone.

See also **Candy and Confections; Chocolate; Ice Cream; Marketing of Food; Popcorn.**

BIBLIOGRAPHY

Brenner, Joël Glenn. *The Emperors of Chocolate; Inside the Secret World of Hershey and Mars.* New York: Broadway Books, 2000.

Broekel, Ray. *The Great America Candy Bar Book.* Boston: Houghton Mifflin, 1982.

Brown, Cora, Rose Brown, and Bob Brown. *10,000 Snacks; a Cookbook of Canapés, Savories, Relishes, Hors D'Oeuvres, Sandwiches, and Appetizers for before after and between Meals.* Garden City, N.Y.: Halcyon House, 1948.

Damerow, Gail. *Ice Cream! The Whole Scoop.* Macomb, Ill.: Glenbridge, 1991.

Dickson, Paul. *The Great American Ice Cream Book.* New York: Atheneum, 1972.

Matz, Samuel A. *Snack Food Technology.* 3d ed. New York: Van Nostrand Reinhold, 1993.

Rubin, Charles J., et al. *Junk Food.* New York: Dell, 1980.

Smith, Andrew F. *Popped Culture: A Social History of Popcorn in America.* Columbia: University of South Carolina Press, 1999.

Smith, Andrew F. *Peanuts: The Illustrious History of the Goober Pea.* Urbana: University of Illinois Press, 2002.

Snack Food Association. *Fifty Years: A Foundation for the Future.* Alexandria, Va.: Snack Food Association, 1987.

Andrew F. Smith

SNAILS. *See* **Mollusks.**

SOCIOLOGY. Sociology involves the study of how people relate to each other, as well as how the institutions of society affect behavior and attitudes. For most of the past hundred and fifty years, sociologists have focused mainly on social institutions and structures. It was only around the middle of the twentieth century that they turned their attention to the important roles that technologies (including food production and processing) play in society. Other disciplines (particularly anthropology) have a much longer history of research into food and culture.

Food and food habits have been only implicitly assumed in sociological literature until just recently. Food studies have been an integral part of both rural sociology and medical sociology. For rural sociologists, food has been central in studies of agricultural and technological change. Food has also been a main focus in the studies of farms, community living, social change, and consumer issues. In fact, rural sociologists began to study food production in the 1930s through research on the adoption and diffusion of innovations (new technologies).

For medical sociologists, food and nutrition are now recognized as an important factor in the study of health and wellness. Sociologists examine how our nutritional habits are based on cultural identity, gender, race and ethnicity, and social class. Although food is a fundamental concern for human life, sociologists are now just establishing a sociology of food by identifying how lifestyles, social class, gender, and ethnicity influence food selection and consumption. In fact, much of the market research that food companies conduct is in fact a form of sociological research (e.g., focus groups, surveys, and interviews).

The sociological study of food is important in understanding social change, the state, and consumer society. For example, positive social change has come about as a result of epidemiological and sociological studies of the importance of sanitation. Sociological studies based on food exportation, importation, and food agricultures have examined how states develop. In addition, research into the inequality of distribution and access to food comprises another way that sociologists can expose to explain class, race, and gender differences, as well as forms of political domination. Food is also important in explaining consumerism, cultural assimilation, modernization, and how beliefs and rituals change.

Sociologists have always been interested in social inequality and stratification (i.e., through analysis of gender, ethnic, and class differences.) For example, some foods are associated with women and some with men. Women eat less food overall, and they are usually light foods or foods that can be nibbled, such as salad or fish. Men tend to eat more food, and prefer foods associated with strength, such as red meat. Food habits also vary significantly with age. For example, soft or strained foods are appropriate for very young children who have no teeth, as well as for the elderly (for the same reason). As people age, they also become more concerned about the role of diet in their overall health.

Food also represents distinctive cultures; for example, pasta is associated with Italian culture, or curry with Indian culture. Cultures evolve to suit the local environment. For instance, spicy foods are more popular in the warmer climates. Class distinctions in foods abound. In the early 1900s in Great Britain, people in the upper classes ate more meat than those of the middle or lower classes. However, by the middle of the century, all people ate about the same amount of meat, as advances in food technology put meat in the range of everyone. Economically disadvantaged groups are sometimes forced to eat what is cheap, and these foods may not be as nutritious as higher-priced foods. Disadvantaged groups then are more vulnerable to health problems, such as heart disease or obesity.

It has been said that "We are what we eat." Food becomes part of our self-identity. From a very young age, an individual is socialized into his or her adult eating habits. A person eats what his family eats when he is young—these habits do not tend to change that much with age. In Western cultures, young children are taught that the insects they find are not to be eaten. In other cultures, however, young children are taught that certain insects are edible and they become part of the diet. Foods are part of the rituals we use to accept new members into our group, to celebrate milestones, and to express religious or political beliefs. For example, a new neighbor might be presented with a basket of food or a homemade pie as a welcome gift.

Celebrations, such as birthdays and anniversaries, usually involve some kind of cake or other sweet food. National holidays usually include foods associated with the country. For example, Americans celebrate Independence Day with backyard barbecues (including hamburgers and hot dogs, potato chips and watermelon). Thanksgiving is closely associated with turkey. Religious holidays also use symbolic foods, such as ham at Christmas for Christians. Some religions have specific taboos on food. For instance, Jewish people do not eat pork, while Hindus do not eat beef, and Seventh-Day Adventists do not eat meat at all. Many religions also endorse fasting as part of their rituals.

Sociologists have shown how the level of development within a country influences food habits and preferences. Industrialized countries consume and waste more food than developing countries. Americans may waste up to 25 percent of their food. Waste results from poor storage and processing, as well as from unused leftovers and spoiled foodstuffs that are never used. There is less consumer waste in developing countries. However, this practice is increasing as more countries adopt Western ideas and values concerning food.

Almost every culture has some form of food taboo. In fact, there is only one taboo that is universal, and that is the restriction on eating human flesh. This was not always the case, however. Early people, such as the South American Indians, would grind up the bones of their ancestors into a communal pot, to share their strength and wisdom with all tribal members. Some taboos restrict certain kinds of foods to certain meals. For example, Americans eat cereal for breakfast, but not for dinner. Food taboos may be based on cleanliness standards, but taboos may also be used to change entire food systems. Sometimes it is easier to restrict foods on religious beliefs, than to convince people rationally to change their eating habits. Emotions also play a major role in decisions about what people eat and why. Sociological research and theory are therefore important for understanding how to increase human health through better diet and nutrition.

See also **Anthropology and Food; Feasts, Festivals, and Fasts; Food Politics: United States; Icon Foods; Political Economy; Population and Demographics; Religion and Food; Taboos; United States: Ethnic Cuisines.**

BIBLIOGRAPHY

Beardsworth, Alan, and Terresa Keil. *Sociology On The Menu.* New York: Routledge, 1997.

Gabaccia, Donna. *We Are What We Eat.* Cambridge, Mass.: Harvard University Press, 1998.

McIntosh, Alex, *Sociologies of Food and Nutrition.* New York: Plenum Press, 1996.

Thomas Jefferson Hoban IV

SODIUM. Sodium is normally present in food and in the body in its ionic (charged) form rather than as metallic sodium. Sodium is a positively charged ion or cation (Na^+), and it forms salts with a variety of negatively charged ions (anions). Table salt or sodium chloride (NaCl) is an example of a sodium salt. In solution, NaCl dissociates into its ions, Na^+ and Cl^-. Other sodium salts include those of both inorganic (e.g., nitrite or bicarbonate) and organic anions (e.g., citrate or glutamate) in aqueous solution, these salts also dissociate into Na^+ and the respective anion.

Types and Amounts of Common Foods that Contain the Recommended Levels of Sodium

Only small amounts of salt or sodium occur naturally in foods, but sodium salts are added to foods during food processing or during preparation as well as at the table. Most sodium is added to foods as sodium chloride (ordinary table salt), but small amounts of other salts such as sodium bicarbonate (baking soda and baking powder), monosodium glutamate, sodium sulfide, sodium nitrate, and sodium citrate are also added. Studies in a British population found that 75 percent of sodium intake came from salts added during manufacturing and processing, 15 percent from table salt added during cooking and at the table, and only 10 percent from natural foods (Sanchez-Castillo et al., 1987). Most sources of drinking water are low in sodium. However, the use of home water softening systems may greatly increase the sodium content of water; the system should be installed so that water for cooking and drinking bypasses the water softening system.

The estimated minimum safe daily intake of sodium for an adult (0.5 grams) can be obtained from ¼ teaspoon of salt, ¼ of a large dill pickle, ⅕ can of condensed tomato soup, one frankfurter, or fifteen potato chips. The effect of salt added in processing is noted by the calculation that, whereas one would need to consume 333 cups of fresh green peas (with no salt added during cooking or at the table) in order to consume 0.5 grams of sodium, the estimated minimum safe daily intake of sodium is provided by only 1.4 cups of canned or 2.9 cups of frozen green peas.

Whereas the estimated minimum safe intake for an adult is 0.5 g/day of sodium (1.3 g/day of sodium chloride), average Americans consume between 2 and 5 g/day of sodium (between 5 and 13 g/day of sodium chloride) (National Research Council, 1989). Sodium chloride, or salt, intake varies widely among cultures and among individuals. In Japan, where consumption of salt-preserved fish and the use of salt for seasoning are customary, salt intake is high, ranging from 14 to 20 g/day (Kono et al., 1983). On the other hand, the unacculturated Yanomamo Indians, who inhabit the tropical rain forest of northern Brazil and southern Venezuela, do not use salt in their diet and have an estimated sodium chloride intake of less than 0.3 g/day (Oliver et al., 1975). In the United States,

BRIEF OUTLINE OF THE HISTORY OF SALT

Common salt is the chemical compound NaCl. Salt makes up nearly 80 percent of the dissolved material in seawater and is also widely distributed in solid deposits. It is found in many evaporative deposits, where it crystallizes out of evaporating brine lakes, and in ancient bedrock, where large extinct salt lakes and seas evaporated millions of years ago. Salt was in general use long before history began to be recorded. Salt has been used widely for the curing, seasoning, and preserving of foods.

individuals who consume diets high in processed foods tend to have high sodium chloride intakes, whereas vegetarians consuming unprocessed food may ingest less than 1 g/day of salt. Individuals with salt intakes less than 0.5 g/day do not normally exhibit chronic deficiencies, but appear to be able to regulate sodium chloride retention adequately.

Recommended Intake of Sodium

The daily minimum requirement of sodium for an adult is the amount needed to replace the obligatory loss of sodium. The minimum obligatory loss of sodium by an adult in the absence of profuse sweating or gastrointestinal or renal disease has been estimated to be approximately 115 mg/day, which is due to loss of about 23 mg/day in the urine and feces and of 46 to 92 mg/day through the skin (National Research Council, 1989). Because of large variations in the degrees of physical activity and in environmental conditions, the estimated level of safe minimum intake for a 70-kg adult was set at 500 mg/day of sodium (equivalent to 1,300 mg/day of sodium chloride) by the National Research Council (1989). Although there is no established optimal range of intake of sodium chloride, it is recommended that daily salt intake should not exceed 6 grams because of the association of high intake with hypertension (National Research Council, 1989). The *Dietary Guidelines for Americans*, published in 2000, include a recommendation to choose and prepare foods with less salt.

Individuals who wish to lower their sodium or salt intakes should use less salt at the table and during cooking, avoid salty foods such as potato chips, soy sauce, pickled foods, and cured meat, and avoid processed foods such as canned pasta sauces, canned vegetables, canned soups, crackers, bologna, and sausages. Individuals should also become aware of and avoid "hidden" sources of sodium such as softened water, products made with baking soda, and foods containing additives in the form of sodium salts.

The need for sodium chloride is increased during pregnancy and lactation, with the estimated safe minimum intake being increased by 69 mg/day and 135 mg/day, respectively, for women during pregnancy and lactation. The estimated minimum requirement for sodium is 120 mg/day for infants between birth and 5 months of age and 200 mg/day for infants 6 to 11 months of age (National Research Council, 1989); these intakes are easily met by human milk or infant formulas. The estimated minimum requirements of sodium for children range from 225 mg/day at one year of age to 500 mg/day at 10 to 18 years of age.

General Overview of Role of Sodium in Normal Physiology

Total body sodium has been estimated at 100 grams (4.3 moles) for a 70-kg adult. In general, the cytoplasm of cells is relatively rich in potassium (K+) and poor in sodium (Na+) and chloride (Cl−) ions. The concentrations of sodium (and potassium and chloride) ions in cells and the circulating fluids are held remarkably constant, and small deviations from normal levels in humans are associated with malfunction or disease. Na^+, K^+, and Cl^- are referred to as electrolytes because of their role in the generation of gradients and electrical potential differences across cell membranes. Sodium and sodium gradients across cell membranes play several important roles in the body. First, sodium gradients are important in many transport processes. Sodium tends to enter cells down its electrochemical gradient (toward the intracellular compartment that has a lower Na^+ concentration and a more negative charge compared to the extracellular fluid compartment). This provides a secondary driving force for absorption of Cl^- in the same direction as Na^+ movement or for the secretion of K^+ or hydrogen ions (H^+) in the opposite direction in exchange for Na^+. The sodium gradient is also used to drive the coupled transport of Na^+ and glucose, galactose, and amino acids by certain carrier proteins in cell membranes; because as Na^+ enters down its electrochemical gradient, uptake of glucose/galactose or amino acids can occur against their concentration gradient. Second, sodium ions, along with potassium ions, play important roles in generating resting membrane potentials and in generating action potentials in nerve and muscle cells. Nerve and muscle cell membranes contain gated channels through which Na^+ or K^+ can flow. In the resting state, these cell membranes are highly impermeable to Na^+ and permeable to K^+ (i.e., Na^+ channels are closed and K^+ channels are open). These gated channels open or close in response to chemical messengers or to the traveling current (applied voltage). Action potentials are generated in nerve and muscle due to opening of Na^+ channels followed by their closing and the re-opening of K^+ channels.

A third important function of sodium is its osmotic role as a major determinant of extracellular fluid volume. The volume of the extracellular fluid compartment is determined primarily by the total amount of osmotic particles present. Because Na^+, along with Cl^-, is the major determinant of osmolarity of extracellular fluid, disturbances in Na^+ balance will change the volume of the extracellular fluid compartment. Finally, because Na^+ is a fixed cation, it also plays a role in acid-base balance in the body. An excess of fixed cations (versus fixed anions) requires an increase in the concentration of bicarbonate ions.

Consequences of Deficiency or Excessive Intake Levels

Sodium balance in the body is well controlled via regulation of Na^+ excretion by the kidneys. The kidneys respond to a deficiency of Na^+ in the diet by decreasing its excretion, and they respond to an excess of Na^+ by increasing its excretion in the urine. Physiological regulatory mechanisms for conservation of Na^+ seem to be better developed in humans than mechanisms for excretion of Na^+, and pathological states characterized by inappropriate retention of Na^+ are more common than those characterized by Na^+ deficiency.

Retention of Na^+ occurs when Na^+ intake exceeds the renal excretory capacity. This can occur with rapid ingestion of large amounts of salt (for example, ingestion of seawater) or with too-rapid intravenous infusion of saline. Hypernatremia (abnormally high plasma concentration of Na^+) and hypervolemia (abnormally increased volume of blood), resulting in acute hypertension, usually occur in these situations, and the Na^+ regulatory mechanisms will cause natriuresis (urinary excretion of Na^+) and water retention.

The body may be depleted of Na^+ under extreme conditions of heavy and persistent sweating or when conditions such as trauma, chronic vomiting or diarrhea, or renal disease produce an inability to retain Na^+. Sodium depletion produces hyponatremia (abnormally low plasma concentration of Na^+) and hypovolemia (abnormally decreased volume of blood) which place the individual at risk of shock. Medical treatment includes replacement of Na^+ and water to restore the circulatory volume. If the loss of Na^+ is not due to renal disease, mechanisms to conserve Na^+ and water are activated. Loss of Na^+ can also be caused by the administration of diuretics, which inhibit Na^+ and Cl^- reabsorption, or by untreated diabetes mellitus, which causes diuresis.

Regulatory Processes that Govern the Uptake and Excretion of Sodium

The kidneys are the main site of regulation of Na^+ balance. The intestines play a relatively minor role. Under normal circumstances, about 99 percent of dietary Na^+ and Cl^- are absorbed, and the remainder is excreted in the feces. Absorption of Na^+ and Cl^- occurs along the entire length of the intestines; 90 to 95 percent is absorbed in the small intestine and the rest in the colon. Intestinal absorption of Na$^+$ and Cl$^-$ is subject to regulation by the nervous system, hormones, and paracrine agonists released from neurons in the enteric nervous system in the wall of the intestines. The most important of these factors is aldosterone, a steroid hormone produced and secreted by the zona glomerulosa cells of the adrenal cortex. Aldosterone stimulates absorption of Na$^+$ and secretion of K$^+$, mainly by the colon and, to a lesser extent, by the ileum.

The kidneys respond to a deficiency of Na$^+$ in the diet by decreasing its excretion, and they respond to an excess by increasing its excretion in the urine. Urinary loss of Na$^+$ is controlled by varying the rate of Na$^+$ reabsorption from the filtrate by renal tubular cells. Individuals consuming diets that are low in Na$^+$ efficiently reabsorb Na$^+$ from the renal filtrate and have low rates of excretion of Na$^+$. When there is an excess of Na$^+$ from high dietary intake, little Na$^+$ is reabsorbed by renal tubular cells, resulting in the excretion of the excess Na$^+$ in the urine. As much as 13 g/day of Na$^+$ can be excreted in the urine.

The most important regulator of renal excretion of Na$^+$ and Cl$^-$ is the renin-angiotensin-aldosterone system (Laragh, 1985). Sensors in the nephrons of the kidney respond to changes in Na$^+$ load by influencing the synthesis and secretion of renin (Levens et al., 1981). A decrease in renal perfusion or Na$^+$ load will increase the release of renin. In the circulation, renin acts to initiate the formation of active angiotensin II from angiotensinogen, a protein produced by the liver. Angiotensin II conserves body Na$^+$ by stimulating Na$^+$ reabsorption by the renal tubules and indirectly via stimulating secretion of aldosterone. Secretion of aldosterone by the adrenal cortex is stimulated by a low plasma Na$^+$ concentration and by angiotensin II. Aldosterone stimulates cells of the renal tubules to reabsorb Na$^+$.

Because of the close association of Na$^+$ and Cl$^-$ concentrations with effective circulating volume, Na$^+$ (and Cl$^-$) retention results in proportionate water retention, and Na$^+$ (and Cl$^-$) loss results in proportionate water loss. Expansion or contraction of the extracellular volume affects the activation of vascular pressure receptors, as well as the release of natriuretic peptides by certain tissues, and result in changes, mediated largely by antidiuretic hormone (ADH), in renal excretion of Na$^+$, Cl$^-$, and water. A deficiency of sodium chloride and hypovolemia have also been shown to produce an increase in appetite for salt, which will increase sodium chloride intake.

Evidence that Sodium Intake May Be Related to Risk of Hypertension

Both epidemiological and experimental studies implicate habitual high dietary salt intake in the development of hypertension (Weinberger, 1996). Primary hypertension, or abnormally high blood pressure, is a significant risk factor for cardiovascular disease, stroke, and renal failure in industrialized societies. Diets that are high in fat, high in sodium, low in potassium, low in calcium, and low in magnesium may contribute to the development of hypertension (Reusser and McCarron, 1994).

Although epidemiological and experimental evidence suggest a positive correlation between habitual high-salt consumption and hypertension, controversy remains regarding the importance of sodium salts in the regulation of blood pressure and the mechanisms by which salt influences blood pressure. This is not surprising, because the response of blood pressure depends on an interplay of various factors, such as genetic susceptibility, body mass, cardiovascular factors, regulatory mechanisms mediated through the neural and hormonal systems, and renal function.

A large comprehensive study on the role of sodium in hypertension was carried out in fifty-two geographically separate centers in thirty-two countries by the INTERSALT Cooperative Research Group (Stamler, 1997). Four centers included in the study had median values for Na$^+$ excretion that were under 1.3 g/day. Subjects in these four unacculturated centers had low blood pressure, rare or absent hypertension, and no age-related rise in blood pressure as occurred in populations in the other forty-eight centers in which mean values for Na$^+$ excretion were between 2.4 and 5.6 grams Na$^+$ per day. Although blood pressure and sodium intake appeared to be associated when all fifty-two centers were included, the correlation between systolic blood pressure and excretion of sodium was not significant when the four centers with the lowest median values of sodium excretion were excluded from the analysis.

Intervention studies of dietary salt restriction to lower blood pressure have produced mixed results. This may be explained by the facts that not all hypertensive patients are salt-sensitive and that many cases of hypertension are due to other causes. Nevertheless, various clinical trials indicate some beneficial effects of dietary restriction of sodium on blood pressure (Cutler et al., 1997; Reusser and McCarron, 1994) with response being greater in older patients, patients with the highest degree of restriction, and in nonoverweight, mildly hypertensive patients.

Researchers are currently attempting to identify the genetic basis of salt-sensitive hypertension and to identify polymorphisms associated with salt-sensitive hypertensive individuals. More than thirty different gene variations could be responsible for essential hypertension, and hypertension is considered to have a complex genetic basis. Further insight into the basis of hypertension may help to determine individuals for whom lowering salt intake would be beneficial and to facilitate the prescription of appropriate drugs.

See also **Dietary Guidelines; Fast Food; Fish, Salted; Health and Disease; Meat, Salted; Preserving; Salt.**

BIBLIOGRAPHY

Church, Charles F., and Helen N. Church. *Food Values of Portions Commonly Used: Bowes and Church.* Philadelphia: J. B. Lippincott, 1970.

Cutler, Jeffrey A., Dean Follmann, and P. Scott Allender. "Randomized Trials of Sodium Reduction: An Overview." *American Journal of Clinical Nutrition* 65 (1997, Supp.): 643S–651S.

Kono, Suminori, Masato Ikeda, and Michiharu Ogata. "Salt and Geographical Mortality of Gastric Cancer and Stroke in Japan." *Journal of Epidemiology and Community Health* 37 (1983): 43–46.

Laragh, John H. "Atrial Natriuretic Hormone, the Renin-Aldosterone Axis, and Blood Pressure—Electrolyte Homeostasis." *New England Journal of Medicine* 313 (1985): 1330–1340.

Levens, Nigel R., Michael J. Peach, and Robert M. Carey. "Role of Intrarenal Renin-Angiotensin System in the Control of Renal Function." *Circulation Research* 48 (1981):157–167.

National Research Council. *Recommended Dietary Allowances.* 10th ed. Washington, D.C.: National Academy Press, 1989, pp. 247–261.

Oliver, Walter J., Erik L. Cohen, and James V. Neel. "Blood Pressure, Sodium Intake and Sodium-Related Hormones in the Yanomamo Indians, a 'No-Salt' Culture." *Circulation* 52 (1975): 146–151.

Reusser, Molly E., and David A. McCarron. "Micronutrient Effects on Blood Pressure Regulation." *Nutrition Reviews* 52 (1994): 367–375.

Sanchez-Castillo, C. P., S. Warrender, T. P. Whitehead, and W. P. James. "An Assessment of the Sources of Dietary Salt in a British Population." *Clinical Science* 72 (1987): 95–102.

Sheng, Hwai-Ping. "Sodium, Chloride, and Potassium." In *Biochemical and Physiological Aspects of Human Nutrition*, edited by Martha H. Stipanuk, pp. 686–710. Philadelphia: W. B. Saunders Co., 2000.

Stamler, Jeremiah. "The INTERSALT Study: Background, Methods, Findings, and Implications." *American Journal of Clinical Nutrition* 65 (1997, Supp.): 626S–642S.

United States Department of Agriculture. *Nutrition and Your Health: Dietary Guidelines for Americans.* 5th ed.. Washington, D.C.: U. S. Government Printing Office, 2000.

Weinberger, Myron H. "Salt Sensitivity of Blood Pressure in Humans." *Hypertension* 27 (1996): 481–490.

Martha H. Stipanuk

SORBET. *See* **Sherbet and Sorbet.**

SOUL FOOD. *See* **United States: African American Foodways.**

SOUP. A soup is a broth that is infused with flavor. It may be thin and crystal clear like a consommé, voluptuously smooth and creamy like a creamed soup, or so chunky with meat, fish, grains, and/or vegetables that it

Soups play an important role in traditional cookeries all over the world, especially in medical dietetics. Shown here is garlic soup from Nepal. While such preparations may soothe and comfort, the act of heating garlic destroys its antimicrobial properties. © Macduff Everton/CORBIS.

is just this side of a stew. A soup may be the first of several courses, intended just to whet the appetite; it may be one of many dishes served at the same time; or it may be a hearty meal in a bowl. The bottom line is that in order to be a soup, it must be enough of a liquid preparation that eventually one gets around to sipping it, or eating it with a spoon.

Soup is an important mainstay in the everyday diet of most cultures. It was probably one of the earliest cooked preparations because it could be made with just about anything (including leftovers from the day before) and could be extended greatly simply by adding more liquid. Where food is scarce, soup is a staple: The moral of the "Stone Soup" fable is that soup can be made from nothing at all but stones, water, and generosity.

Although classic French cuisine developed as a result of the availability of many types of food and involves many courses, it has also given soup a place of singular

ORIGINS OF SOUP

While soup is firmly imbedded in most cookeries of the world, the historical situation was somewhat different. Light soups were more generally viewed as adjuncts to medicine, easily digestible preparations employed in feeding the sick, the elderly, or small children. In Africa the stock from boiled greens served this purpose. In ancient China turtle stock was viewed as a potent restorative for the feeble or sick. During the Middle Ages the *iusculum consummatum* was administered in the same manner. Its modern descendant is beef consommé, but in the eighteenth century a concoction of this general class of clear soups was known as a "restaurant" and became fashionable in Paris as a health food. Soon the health food itself lent its name to the place where it was eaten: thus the soup house became the restaurant. During the late 1700s the restaurant quickly evolved from a soup house to an establishment where full meals could be purchased.

English includes several words that provide clues regarding the older meanings of this largely liquid form of food: "soup," "supper," "sip," and "sops," to name four. The Middle English word *soupen* meant to drink in sips, which is how most soups were consumed by the sick and the elderly. The Old French word *souper,* obviously a parallel term, meant to take an evening meal. In this context the evening meal was presumed to be light, and soup was in fact one way to create a *rechouffé* from the remains of midday dinner. However, the *soupe* itself was

the piece of bread placed in the bowl into which broth was poured. In English this piece of bread was once referred to as the sops, and it was universal practice down to the nineteenth century for country people to put bread in soup before eating it. More fashionable recipes called for toast or even chopped bread fried in butter (croutons), but the essential concept was the same: the moist bread thickened the soup. This custom lingers on in only the most traditional types of recipes, such as French onion soup, where toast or croutons help keep the melted cheese from sinking before the soup reaches the table.

The addition of bread to soup was viewed as inelegant by the end of the eighteenth century—"farmish," to use the term of the nineteenth-century American cookbook writer Eliza Leslie. Other types of thickeners, especially roux (flour fried in lard or butter) grew in popularity, but so did purees. Puréed cooked vegetables, such as parsnips, turnips, or potatoes (or all three), often appear in Victorian recipes as more healthful substitutes for roux. Roux is largely banned from haute cuisine, and soups are thickened with a wide array of ingredients. Plastic squeeze bottles with tiny nozzles allow cooks to ornament soups with colorful swirls of coulis or intense-tasting herbal sauces. In spite of the emphasis on garnish and appearance, the universal appeal of soup is not its appearance but how it comforts the body.

William Woys Weaver

---

importance. According to the eighteenth-century French gastronome Grimod de la Reynière (1758–1838), "It [soup] is to dinner what a portico or a peristyle is to a building; that is to say, it is not only the first part of it, but it must be devised in such a manner as to set the tone of the whole banquet, in the same way as the overture of an opera announces the subject of the work." In other words, soup should inspire, set the stage, for the rest of the meal.

Classic French cuisine divides soups into two broad categories: clear soups and thick soups. These classifications are made on the basis of a Western, and specifically French, way of thinking about food that is essentially one of theme and variation. All soups in the "clear" category are prepared using a fundamental technique; variations on and additions to this technique create derivative soups. Once the cook has mastered the basic technique, he or she can make all derivations. One should not assume that other cultures think about food in the same way—in fact, the opposite can be assumed. But since soups from non-

Western cultures fall well within this kind of classification system, it nonetheless seems a reasonable way to approach the topic. Such a system can also be adjusted to embrace ethnic as well as Western cuisines by redefining the categories this way: broth-based soups and thick soups.

Broth-Based Soups

Broth-based soups are soups made by simmering flavorful ingredients (meats, poultry, seafood, legumes, vegetables, herbs and/or spices) in water or stock to make a thin broth. The broth may then be garnished and seasoned in a variety of ways at the whim of the cook (e.g., with fresh meats and vegetables, herbs, grains or pastas), so that although the broth of such a soup is thin, the soup itself may also be hearty. Stocks are a kind of soup as well: water is simmered with bones, vegetables, and other flavoring agents such as herbs, to infuse the water with their flavor. (In the case of the Japanese stock, *dashi,* the vegetable is seaweed and the flavoring agent dried tuna.)

Unlike soups, stocks are not intended to be eaten on their own. They are a base or ingredient from which to build something more complex—a sauce, a stew, or a soup.

The most famous broth-based soup in the world must be chicken soup, made by cooking chicken in stock or water. Once the chicken is cooked, it may be boned and returned to the soup or eaten separately; then vegetables, rice, noodles, or matzoh balls are added to the soup, depending on the preference of the cook. If the chicken is cooked whole in stock with vegetables, and the resulting broth is served as a first-course soup, followed by the chicken and vegetables, it is called a *poule au pot* —which means "chicken in a pot" and is a meal in itself. If egg and lemon are whisked into the simmering broth until the egg "strings," and then rice is stirred in, it is the Greek *avgolemono.* Wonton soup (a soup traditionally served at the end of a Chinese meal although a formal dinner may include more than one soup) is made by poaching wontons in a ginger-scented chicken broth; when the broth is seasoned with fragrant lemongrass, kaffir lime leaves (the mildly lemon-tasting and highly fragrant leaves of the kaffir lime), and galangal (a root that tastes something like lavender) and enriched with coconut milk, it becomes the Thai soup *tome kha gai.* An Indonesian chicken soup may be flavored with lemongrass too, saffron or turmeric, and a cooked paste of shallots, garlic, kemiri nuts (a local nut that resembles a macadamia nut), shrimp paste, ginger, and coriander seeds. And if the broth is flavored with a purée of onion, garlic, and tomato, then garnished with crisp, fried strips of fresh tortilla and grated cheese, it becomes the Mexican *sopa de tortilla.*

There are just as many soups based on a beef broth, which may be made from the bones alone, or from an inexpensive cut of beef such as short ribs (which are usually served with the soup) or shin (usually discarded after cooking). French onion soup is one such soup, in which the broth is simmered with well-browned onions until it is sweetened and enriched with their flavor, then poured over thick slices of bread, and covered with a layer of broiled cheese. Onion soup belongs to a genre of bread soups—also broth-based soups—in which broth is poured over bread; the starch from the bread thickens the soup and makes a meal out of it. Bread soups are typically poor man's food and are likely to be made with water rather than stock. In *Catalan Cuisine,* Colman Andrews mentions a vegetable bread soup made with onions, garlic, sweet pepper, and tomato cooked in a liberal amount of olive oil, and poured over bread. *Ribollita* is another traditional bread soup, from Tuscany, chunky with cabbage and vegetables.

Vietnamese *pho bac* is a noodle soup based on a rich beef broth, spiced with ginger, anise, cinnamon, and chilies and seasoned with fish sauce (a pungent, salty liquid made from fermented anchovy) that is poured over thin slices of raw beef, rice noodles, sliced onion, bean sprouts, and fresh chilies, and garnished with fresh mint and cilantro. According to Nicole Routhier, *pho* is a traditional breakfast soup. (Throughout much of Southeast Asia, soup may be eaten at any meal and is served along with all main-course dishes.) Korean cooks make a beef soup with browned short ribs, flavored with toasted sesame seeds, soy sauce, garlic, ginger, and scallion; the ribs are then eaten with the soup. Russian borscht and goulash from Hungary are two Eastern European vegetable and meat soups made with beef broth (or probably with water and vegetables alone during lean times). For Japanese *shabu-shabu,* thin slices of beef, onion, cabbage, daikon, and mushrooms are dropped into a pot of simmering water flavored with a piece of kelp, then eaten with a variety of condiments; the flavorful broth— sometimes extended with noodles—is drunk at the end of the meal.

Thin vegetarian soups, like French pistou, are made the same way, by poaching vegetables in simmering water. Then the flavor of the broth is augmented by a purée of basil, garlic, Parmesan cheese, olive oil, and sometimes tomato. South Indian vegetarian cuisine includes a genre of fiery hot soups called *rasams* in which the flavor of the

Soup is also an icon food in some cultures. American alphabet soup assumes a patriotic shape in this clever serving of tomato soup. © TECMAP CORPORATION; ERIC CURRY/CORBIS.

Aside from military rations, canned soup was expensive for most people during the nineteenth century. Shown here is an 1893 advertisement for French-style tomato and mock turtle soups illustrating both the fancy labeling and the tissue wrapping (on the right) which went around the cans to preserve the labels from damage. ROUGHWOOD COLLECTION.

broth is derived largely from spices and then balanced with tomato, lemon, lime, and/or tamarind to add a sour taste. Although *rasams* may be served during the meal, they are also traditionally offered to guests as they enter the house, as a beverage, like tea, in anticipation of the meal to follow.

Seafood soups are almost a category unto themselves because they encompass such a tremendous variety of tastes, textures, and techniques. A simple Western-style seafood soup is made by simmering aromatic vegetables and herbs (and perhaps a bit of cured and/or smoked pork) with water or fish stock, and poaching fish and/or shellfish in the resultant broth. In *Japanese Cooking*, Shizuo Tsuji lists a soup made by poaching shrimp and seaweed in *dashi* seasoned with soy sauce. (Tsuji notes that such "clear" soups are traditionally served at the Japanese table at the beginning of the meal, after the appetizer; more luxurious banquets may include a second soup midway through the meal.) Some thin shellfish soups are made by opening the shellfish in simmering wine, water, or broth, perhaps flavored with aromatic herbs and vegetables. Broth-based seafood soups also include hearty concoctions made with a variety of different types of fish and shellfish poached in a broth. The seafood may be served in the broth, or separately, as in a bouillabaisse.

If chicken soup is the most famous broth-based soup, then one of the most elegant (at least in Western culture) must be the consommé. A consommé is made with a stock that is "clarified," which means that the stock is returned to the stove, several egg whites are whisked in, and the whole concoction is brought slowly to a simmer. As the mixture heats, the egg white coagulates into a gray-colored "raft" on top of the stock that traps and filters out the impurities that make the stock cloudy. When the raft is skimmed off, the stock has, almost magically, become perfectly transparent. Finely chopped fresh meat and vegetables are usually added during the clarification process since the egg white seems to rob the stock of flavor along with the impurities. Consommés may be served as is, or embellished with any number of garnishes including, at the simplest level, tiny chopped vegetables or herbs, or more complex preparations such as tiny quenelles—tender, oval-shaped dumplings of chopped fish, poultry, or meat, bound with egg—or royales, tiny, delicate cut-up shapes from a baked egg custard. A consommé may be served hot, chilled, or as an aspic.

Thick Soups

Thick soups are soups in which the liquid is thickened—what cooks call "bound"—in one of a variety of ways: by the addition of flour, cream, and/or egg, or by the action of puréeing. Classic French cuisine of the nineteenth and early twentieth centuries was particularly rich in this type of soup, although puréed soups were certainly common in France much earlier than that: The medieval cookbooks *Le Viandier and Le Menagier de Paris* include several recipes for puréed soups. An example of a very simple thick soup, achieved by puréeing alone, is a potato-leek soup made by simmering sliced potato and leek in water or chicken broth and then puréeing the mixture—the starch in the potato causes the soup to thicken. Any vegetable soup can be made this way; alternatively, rice, tapioca, pasta, and legumes will also provide thickening when cooked and puréed with the soup.

During the French Revolution, chefs who had made their living cooking for the aristocracy and royalty fled their homeland to other parts of Europe (particularly England) and America, bringing classical French cooking with them. By the late nineteenth century, French chefs were running the kitchens of fine American restaurants, particularly in New York City and Philadelphia, and wealthy Americans were dining in lavish French style. Creamed soups, characterized by a silky smooth texture, made of purées bound with flour and often further enriched with cream and/or egg, belong to this era of luxurious eating. (In 1917 Louis Diat, the French-born chef at the Ritz Carlton hotel in New York City, turned his mother's home-style, puréed leek and potato soup into a new soup, vichyssoise, by puréeing it very finely, enriching it with cream and milk, and then chilling it.) Bisques are a type of intensely flavored creamed soup, typically made with crustaceans such as lobster or crayfish, but also with vegetables, as in tomato bisque. The ingredients are cooked in a broth, then puréed (shell and all, for the seafood, to extract the considerable flavor of the shells), carefully strained, and next creamed. Traditional recipes used bread or rice to thicken the bisque, but that technique is no longer commonly employed.

Finally, chowders and gumbos are another variety of thick, distinctly American, soups. Chowders are soups made with milk or cream; they theoretically contain a starchy vegetable such as corn or potato. Gumbos are regional American soups from Louisiana, thickened either with a very dark roux—a mixture of flour and fat that is cooked to a deep brown color—okra, or file powder (made from dried sassafras leaves).

See also **Chicken Soup**; **Cuisine, Evolution of**; **France**; **Grimod de la Reynière**; **Stew**; **Taillevent**; **United States**, *subentries on* **Cajun Cooking** *and* **New England**; **Vegetables**.

BIBLIOGRAPHY

Andrews, Colman. *Catalan Cuisine*. New York: Atheneum, 1988.

Bayless, Rick. *Authentic Mexican*. New York: William Morrow, 1987.

Beard, James. *James Beard's American Cookery*. Boston: Little, Brown, 1972.

Brennan, Jennifer. *The Original Thai Cookbook*. New York: GD/Perigree Books (Putnam), 1981.

Escoffier, Auguste. *The Escoffier Cook Book*. New York: Crown, 1969.

Kafka, Barbara. *Soup*. New York: Artisan, 1998.

Law, Ruth. *The Southeast Asia Cookbook*. New York: Donald I. Fine, 1990.

McDermott, Nancie. *Real Thai*. San Francisco: Chronicle Books, 1992.

Montagné, Prosper. *Larousse gastronomique: The Encyclopedia of Food, Wine, and Cookery*. Edited by Charlotte Turgeon and Nina Froud. New York: Crown, 1961. First English edition.

Montagné, Prosper. *Larousse gastronomique: The New American Edition of the World's Greatest Culinary Encyclopedia*. Edited by Jennifer Harvey Lang. New York: Crown, 1988. Second English edition.

Montagné, Prosper. *Larousse gastronomique: The World's Greatest Culinary Encyclopedia*. Edited by Jennifer Harvey Lang. New York: Clarkson Potter, 2001. Third English edition.

Padmanabhan, Chandra. *Dakshin*. San Francisco: Thorsons, 1992.

Peterson, James. *Splendid Soups*. New York: Wiley, 2001.

Routhier, Nicole. *The Foods of Vietnam*. New York: Stewart, Tabori & Chang, 1989.

Trager, James. *The Food Chronology*. New York: Henry Holt, 1995.

Tropp, Barbara. *The Modern Art of Chinese Cooking*. New York: William Morrow, 1982.

Tsuji, Shizuo. *Japanese Cooking*. Tokyo: Kodansha International, 1980.

Willan, Anne. *La Varenne pratique*. New York: Crown, 1989.

Stephanie Lyness

SOUP KITCHENS. Soup kitchens have been providing nourishment to the poor and hungry since at least the eighteenth century. Though no longer serving solely a fare of soup and bread, they remain an important com-

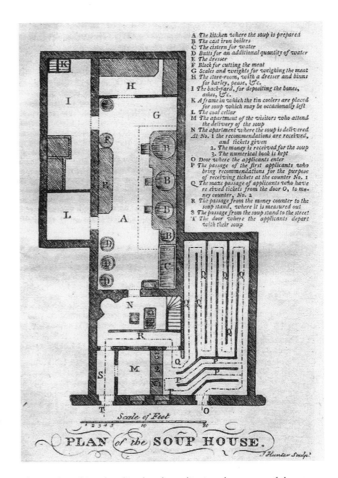

The Duke of Portland's plan for relieving the stress of the poor, published at Chester, England, in 1799. This is one of the earliest designs for a soup house, or soup kitchen as it is now called. Applicants for food enter at "O" on the plan and stand in line until they reach the money counter at "R." They exit the kitchen at "T." ROUGHWOOD COLLECTION.

ponent of private food relief three centuries later. Patterned after soup societies in Europe, soup kitchens had their genesis in the work of Count Rumford who sought to create a low-cost, nutritionally sound diet for the Bavarian military. He found that the cheapest, most savory, and nourishing food was a soup composed of pearl barley, peas, potatoes, cuttings of fine wheaten bread, vinegar, salt, and water in certain proportions. (He also made a culinary discovery: the crouton.)

Rumford's soups became famous throughout Europe. Originally they were used to feed the military but soon soup houses were established throughout Europe, England and the United States to feed the poor. In London, as many as sixty thousand people were fed daily from Rumford's soup kitchens. The Humane Society of New York City founded one of the earliest soup kitchens in the United States in 1802. Typical of soup kitchens in its day, the Society printed soup tickets that both public and private organizations purchased and distributed to the poor.

I'm spending my nights at the flop-house,
I'm spending my days on the street,
I'm looking for work, and I find none,
I wish I had something to eat.
Soup, soup, they give me a bowl
of soup, soup, soup. They give
me a bowl of soup.

Depression-era song (1930s)

Soup kitchens lost their popularity by the 1820s as civic leaders and charity reformers began to believe that indiscriminate handouts encouraged pauperism by destroying self-reliance. New emphasis was placed on reforming the moral character of the poor rather than on feeding them or providing other material needs. As a result only a small number of soup kitchens continued, often only on a temporary basis during unusually harsh economic times. One notable exception to this trend was the Salvation Army's food depots or soup kitchens, which remained in continuous operation after the organization was established in England in the late 1800s.

It was not until the Great Depression that there was resurgence in soup kitchens. Along with breadlines, soup kitchens became a daily part of the life of millions during the 1930s. They were immortalized in numerous poems, songs, and stories. Their heyday, however, waned as government income support and food assistance programs were established. In the early 1980s, when numerous reports of increased hunger surfaced, soup kitchens once again opened in large numbers.

Soup kitchens have become an integral part of a larger, ongoing, emergency food and hunger network. Known as emergency food relief (EFR) programs, soup kitchens and food pantries dominate the private sectors effort to feed the hungry. Soup kitchens usually prepare and serve meals on-site to individuals and families, while food pantries provide a package of several days worth of food for home preparation. It is estimated that between twelve and twenty-one million people each year rely on soup kitchens and food pantries. Second Harvest, the largest private food distribution program, is a national network of two hundred regional food banks providing food to more than 94,000 local soup kitchens, food pantries, and other food programs throughout the United States.

The modern soup kitchen meals are typically free and unlike public food assistance programs often do not have income or other eligibility requirements. The majority of soup kitchens are affiliated with larger nonprofit organizations, most often that of churches, which usually supply the facility and equipment, financial resources, food and volunteers to staff the operation. Additional resources, most often in the form of food, are obtained from the local food bank, government commodity distribution programs, community retail outlets, and community food drives. Many soup kitchens extend their assistance beyond feeding to include such services as information and referral to other social assistance programs.

Soup kitchens are usually opened on weekdays, typically serving lunch or dinner, but rarely both. They serve a diverse group of people, including homeless, unemployed, working poor, public assistance recipients, elderly, and people with health problems and disabilities. People often rely on these programs as a daily source of nourishment for many months, even sometimes several years. The limited information concerning the nutritional status of people relying of soup kitchens indicates that many frequently experience hunger despite their use of soup kitchens. Often the soup kitchen meal is their only daily meal.

Unlike in the past, soup kitchens serve a variety of meals often consisting of sandwiches or such casserole dishes as stews, tuna noodle casserole, macaroni and cheese and pasta with tomato sauce. Beverages most often served are coffee, tea and fruit drinks. If fruit or vegetables are offered, they are most often canned and rarely is fresh produce served. Desserts are often served and typically comprise cakes, cookies, donuts and pies. The scarce research on the nutritional quality of soup kitchens

PROFILE OF COUNT RUMFORD

Count Rumford, who was responsible for popularizing soup kitchens, is also credited with the invention of the cooking range, double boiler, and drip coffee pot, among other items now commonplace in the kitchen. Born Benjamin Thompson in Woburn, Massachusetts in 1753, he was a loyalist during the American Revolution and immigrated to Europe after independence. Leopold of Bavaria commissioned him to build an efficient and disciplined Bavarian Army. As part of his effort, Thompson discovered that by enclosing a cook fireplace it could cook food faster and more evenly. This invention became known as the kitchen range. He also invented cooking pots and pans to prepare large quantity meals. Prior to these inventions, each soldier was allotted a certain amount of food that he had to cook over a small fire for himself. For his work, the Bavarian government gave Thompson the title Count Rumford.

SALVATION ARMY'S SOUP KETTLE

The soup kettle tended by a volunteer ringing a bell is a well-known symbol of the Salvation Army visible at Christmas time. Legend credits the origin of this practice to an incident in December 1894. Survivors of a shipwreck near San Francisco had been taken to a nearby Salvation Army post. Seeing that the soup was almost gone, a volunteer took the huge black soup kettle from the kitchen and affixed a sign to it that read: "Keep this kettle boiling." She then placed the kettle and sign on a street corner and stood by it ringing a bell to attract people. Within a short time passers-by tossed in enough money to buy plenty of food for the victims of the shipwreck. Ever since, Army volunteers have rung bells and stood by kettles.

meals indicates that the vitamin and mineral content of meals varies widely among kitchens and that several nutrients may be consistently below recommended guidelines. The nutrients most often found lacking are calcium, vitamin D, vitamin B_6 and vitamin B_{12}. In addition, riboflavin and iron may be inadequate for women of childbearing age. Foods from the dairy group and in particular milk, all excellent sources of vitamin D, calcium, and riboflavin, are rarely served in soup kitchens. Dark green leafy vegetables, such as spinach or kale, rich in folate and vitamin B_6, are rarely served. And a full portion of meat, an excellent source of iron and vitamin B_{12}, is rarely served. Meats are most often served in small portions in casseroles. Meals may also be high in fat and sodium as they serve highly processed and canned foods.

Throughout their history soup kitchens and other emergency feeding programs have frequently been met with opposition. In the early years, critics claimed that soup kitchens encouraged pauperism and contributed to the moral decay of individuals. Contemporary critics claim that, at best, soup kitchens provide a short-term band-aid remedy to hunger but do not get at the root causes of hunger such as poverty, low wages, and affordable housing. Many soup kitchen supporters concede that their approach may offer only a short-term response to hunger, but they argue it plays a vital role in trying to meet immediate food needs of the poor.

See also **Class, Social; Food Stamps; Poverty; School Meals; Soup; WIC (Women, Infants, and Children's) Program.**

BIBLIOGRAPHY

Carrillo, Teresita E., Judith A. Gilbride, and Mabel M. Chan. "Soup Kitchen Meals: An Observation and Nutrient Analysis." *Journal of the American Dietetic Association*, vol. 90, no. 7 (July 1990): 989–992.

Second Harvest. *Hunger:The Faces and Facts*. Chicago: Second Harvest, 1998.

Morris, Patricia McGrath. "An Evaluation of the Nutritional Quality of Meals Served in Soup Kitchens in New York State and an Examination of the Factors that Determine Quality." Master's Thesis, Cornell University, 1988.

Patricia McGrath Morris

SOUTH, THE (UNITED STATES). See **United States.**

SOUTH AMERICA. South America is a continent composed of twelve countries and one French colony. The Spanish-speaking countries are: Argentina, Bolivia, Chile, Colombia, Ecuador, Paraguay, Peru, and Venezuela. (Portuguese-speaking Brazil is treated separately in this encyclopedia.) The former colonies of Guyana and Suriname use English and Dutch, respectively, as their official languages, although many in their populations speak indigenous languages. The same can be said for the French colony of Guiana, the home of the cayenne pepper, where French is the official language. The geography of South America is even more varied than that of North America, with long coastlines, lowlands, highlands and mountains, and tropical rain forests. The climate varies from tropical, lying as the continent does across the Equator, to alpine in the high Andes, the backbone of the continent.

The cookery of South America reflects this rich diversity of culture and geography. The indigenous cookeries of pre-Columbian South America have gradually merged with imported cuisines from Europe and Asia. While the Spanish and Portuguese conquistadors introduced their own culinary traditions to the native peoples of South America, indigenous ingredients changed the cuisines of the Old World. The South American contributions included chocolate, vanilla, maize (corn), hot peppers (called *ají* in South America), guavas, sweet potatoes, manioc (cassava), tomatoes, potatoes, avocados, beans, squash (particularly the ancestor of zucchini), peanuts, quinine, and papayas, as well as turkeys.

Maize plays a key role in the cuisine of South America, and it is genetically different from the maize now grown in the Old World, manifested most obviously in its characteristically large kernels. The potato is another vegetable indigenous to South America that has played an important role in cooking worldwide. There are also many vegetables in South America largely unknown beyond the continent, including *ahipa, arracacha, maca, yacon, olluco,* and *oca.*

The demographics of South America are critical for understanding the diversity of its cuisines. In countries

Caribbean Sea

Paraguaná Peninsula

ATLANTIC OCEAN

Barranquilla
Cartagena
Maracaibo
Valencia
Caracas

Medellin

VENEZUELA

GUYANA

Georgetown
Paramaraibo
Cayenne

SURINAME

FRENCH GUIANA

Cali
Bogotá

Orinoco

COLOMBIA

Ilha de Marajó

EQUATOR

Pichincha
Quito
Cotopaxi

Belém

São Luis

ECUADOR
Guayaquil

Manaus

Fortaleza

Amazon

Natal

Trujillo

Andes

BRAZIL

Recife
Maceió

PERU

Lima
Machu Picchu

Salvador

Lake Titicaca
Arequipa
La Paz
Tiahuanaco

BOLIVIA

Sucre

Santa Cruz

Brasília

Goiânia

Belo Horizonte

CHILE

PARAGUAY

Chaco

Paraguay

Paraná

Rio de Janeiro
São Paulo

TROPIC OF CAPRICORN

Curitiba

Asunción

Paraná

PACIFIC OCEAN

Porto Alegre

Córdoba
Rosario

URUGUAY

ARGENTINA

Andes

Santiago

Buenos Aires

Montevideo

Pampas

Rio de la Plata

Mar del Plata

ATLANTIC OCEAN

Patagonia

Golfo de San Jorge

N

Falkland Islands

★ Capital city
● Other city
▲ Peak
∴ Ruin

Strait of Magellan

South Georgia

0   300   600 Miles
0   300   600 Kilometers

Tierra del Fuego

like Bolivia, Ecuador, and Peru, the indigenous populations predominate, and their foods and foodways are the most important cuisines. In contrast, Argentina's cookery was heavily influenced by a large European immigration dominated by Spaniards and Italians. Throughout South America, there is also an African influence due to the slave trade, which has added to the culinary mix.

Venezuela

Venezuela was discovered in 1498 by Columbus when he found the mouth of the Orinoco River. In 1499 the Venezuelan coast was explored by Alonzo de Ojeda and Amerigo Vespucci. Vespucci, coming upon an island in the Gulf of Maracaibo, called it Venezuela because, according to legend, the native villages were built above the water on stilts. Venezuela rises from lowlands to highlands with coffee plantations ascending to the white-capped Andean peaks. It has a mild climate due to its proximity to the Caribbean. Caracas, Venezuela's capital, is the cultural, commercial, and industrial hub.

Local dishes. Venezuelan cuisine relies heavily on maize. The two most important preparations are *hallacas* and *arepas*. *Hallacas*—traditionally eaten during holidays, especially Christmas—are boiled dumplings wrapped in banana leaves, but there are innumerable variations, depending on region and family tradition. *Hallacas* are made with a dough made of maize flour mixed with water, which is then filled with meat, vegetables, and spices. *Arepas* are versatile flatbreads, also made of maize flour, that can be baked, grilled, fried, or steamed and served either sweet or savory.

Black beans, called *caviar criollo*, are a Venezuelan favorite. They are served with *arepas* and are also part of the national dish, *pabellón caraqueño*. A hearty dish, it is said to resemble the national flag (*pabellón*), because of the colors of the beef, beans, rice, and plantains in it.

The most popular fish in Venezuela is *pargo*, a red snapper found in semitropical waters, which is a member of the family Lutjanidae. Imported salt cod, brought to the region by the conquistadors, is also important in the cuisine. A favorite dish throughout South America is chicken with rice, but in Venezuela cooks add olives, raisins, and capers to the rice.

Arequipe, milk pudding (milk cooked with sugar until very thick), is a favorite dessert in Venezuela, as it is throughout South America. It has different names in different places, but is perhaps best known in the United States as *dulce de leche*.

The traditional beverages of Venezuela are *chicha*, made of fermented maize, and *masato*.

Colombia

Colombia has two coastlines, one on the Pacific and the other on the Caribbean, that provide the country with a large choice of seafood. Colombia rises from the Pacific coast through a series of plateaus to the capital, Bogotá. Colombian cooks have a wide range of foods to choose from, including bananas and plantains, papayas, sugarcane, avocados, potatoes (especially in the Andes), and such tropical root vegetables as the sweet potato, taro, cassava (manioc), and *arracacha*. Apricots, pears, grapes, apples, and peaches all grow in Colombia as well.

Local dishes. In Colombia, coconut milk is used with great imagination in cooking fish, for example, herring simmered in coconut milk. One very popular soup is *sancocho de pescado*, a fish stew consisting of a variety of ingredients such as plantains, manioc (cassava), herbs, and coconut milk. Stews, usually served with rice, are the preferred way to cook meat, usually beef, especially with vegetables and fruits. Another traditional dish is *gallineta en barro*, an unplucked guinea fowl marinated in spices and lime juice and wrapped in an envelope of clay. It is then buried in hot coals and baked for approximately two hours. When the clay shell is broken, the skin is clean and golden brown and the meat is tender and flavorful.

During colonial times, sugarcane was introduced in Cartagena, one of the most important port cities in the Spanish empire. Due to its wealth as a mercantile city, Cartagena became a center of luxury cookery in which sugar figured as the main ingredient. Modern Colombia has inherited this rich confectionery tradition.

Ecuador

Ecuador, as the name implies, straddles the equator, which can be reached from the capital, Quito, in about half an hour. Home to two ranges of the Andes, Ecuador is quite mountainous, although the hot and humid Pacific coast lies to the west of the Andes and the rain forest falls largely to the east. Quito (elevation ten thousand feet) is known all over the world for its architectural beauty and cultural refinement. Unfortunately, for outsiders the elevation can cause discomfort. The city lies within a short distance of the extinct volcano, Pichincha. On clear days, a ring of eight volcanoes can be seen from Quito, among them the fabled Chimborazo and Cotopaxi.

Local dishes. Ecuador has two cuisines: a highland cuisine of the Andes and a lowland cuisine of the coast. Potatoes, indigenous to the Andes, play a central role in Ecuadorian highland cooking, and its magnificent vegetables and fruits are used liberally in recipes. *Locro*, a thick potato and cheese soup, is sometimes served with avocado slices. Another popular soup, *sopa de maní*, is made from peanuts. Peanuts also figure in *salsa de maní*, a dip consisting of unsweetened peanut butter, hot peppers (*ají*), achiote (annatto), tomatoes, lime juice, garlic, and onions. The paste is also used to flavor meats and vegetables.

Fish is plentiful and most commonly prepared as seviche. One popular seviche from the coastal city of Guayaquil consists of shrimp, *ají*, and vegetables marinated in lime juice. Once the shrimp are ready to serve, they are garnished with toasted corn kernels (*cancha*), which add an interesting texture and flavor. Stews are popular in the highlands. The spicy and flavorful pork stew, *seco de chanco*, is colored with achiote oil and cooked with beer.

Although the people of Ecuador mainly eat fruit as dessert, a richly flavored pumpkin (or winter squash) cake is very popular.

Bolivia

Bolivia, a high landlocked country in central South America, is bordered by Argentina, Brazil, and Peru. The famous Lake Titicaca, between Bolivia and Peru, lies at 12,500 feet. Legend has it that an island in the lake is the ancestral home of the Incas. Near the lake's southeastern end are the ruins of Tiahuanaco, a pre-Incan city. After the conquest, Bolivia became part of Peru and was known as El Alto Peru, highland Peru. With independence, the name was changed to Bolivia to honor the liberator, Simón Bolívar.

Local dishes. Bolivians like their food hot, and *ajíes* (hot peppers) are widely used. In addition to familiar grains like wheat and corn, quinoa, an indigenous grain that the Incas called "sacred mother grain," is still commonly consumed. The Spanish prohibited the cultivation of quinoa, but it never entirely lost its appeal to the native population. It is hardy and well suited to poor conditions, such as cold weather and high altitudes. Beef and pork, introduced by the Spaniards, are important foods, as are farm-raised guinea pigs (*cuys*), a native dish popular in Bolivia and Peru. In the native culture of Bolivia, the potato played such a significant role that it was used for predicting the future, among other things. In fact, Bolivians categorized potatoes as male or female, depending on their shape, and were used accordingly in their cuisine.

In Bolivia, many food traditions remain from pre-Columbian times. One of the relics of the Inca empire is *chicha*, a popular alcoholic drink made from fermented maize.

Argentina

The second largest nation in South America, Argentina extends from the subtropics to Tierra del Fuego. Although now a separate country, Argentina was once part of the Viceroyalty of the Río de la Plata (River Plate) with Uruguay. The pampas are primarily cattle country and famous for ranching and farming, but this fertile land also produces good crops and fine wine.

Local dishes. Finger foods are very popular and are served in cafés, called *whiskerias*, that evolved from tea shops. Empanadas, stuffed pies, are popular throughout South America, and in Argentina they come in various sizes and are eaten as hors d'oeuvres, for light lunches, or with cocktails. One popular filling combines meat and fruit.

Meat is grilled or prepared in stews (*carbonadas*). The Argentines are fond of combining meat and fruit in their stews, but the most famous meat dish is *churrasco* (barbecue), beef, with large salt crystals embedded in it for flavor, is marinated in spices and lime juice and grilled on spits over an open fire. *Viscacha*, a large wild rabbit or hare, is also appreciated on the pampas. Although the focus is on meat in Argentina, excellent fish are harvested from the waters off the coast and prepared in all the usual ways, including seviche and *escabeche* (pickled fish).

Dulce de leche (milk pudding) is particularly popular in Argentina and throughout neighboring Chile and Uruguay.

Maté, also called *yerba maté*, a popular tea in Argentina, is made from the dried leaves of the evergreen, *Ilex paraguariensis*, which is indigenous to South America. The name comes from the Inca word for the calabash that was used as a container. *Maté* can be served either hot or cold.

Chile

A long, narrow country stretching down between the Andes and the Pacific Ocean, Chile is noted for its copper mines as well as for its wines. The cold Humboldt Current gives Chile the most unusual seafood in the world, including the *erizo de mar* (sea urchin) and *locos* (abalone). The middle third of the country, where table and wine grapes and other fruits and vegetables are raised, enjoys a temperate climate and is very fertile. Seafood and vegetables and fruits are more important in the diet than meat because of the relative lack of land for grazing. Because the seasons in the Southern Hemisphere are the reverse of those in the Northern Hemisphere, so-called winter fruits—apples, pears, and grapes—are exported to North America.

Local dishes. Empanadas, often served with the local wine, are popular. Chileans like soups, and, since their fruits and vegetables are plentiful and particularly good, and are enjoyed raw or cooked, many are used for soup—cabbage, for example, and tomatoes. Fish and shellfish are plentiful along the coast and are cooked every conceivable way. One of the finest fish is *congrio*, the conger eel, unique to Chilean waters. Chicken and guinea pig, both raised at home, are family fare. Meat is not so popular, though Chilean meatballs, made with veal rather than beef, are very special.

The fertile soil produces beautiful fruits, which make admirable desserts. *Pisco*, a powerful brandy made from grapes, is served both as an aperitif and as an after-dinner drink.

Uruguay

A wedge of a nation tucked between Brazil and Argentina on the Atlantic coast, Uruguay is one of the smallest countries in South America and, after Ecuador, the most densely populated. The climate is generally warm, with

Roasting meat on an open fire in the province of Buenos Aires, Argentina. This is the classic Argentine beef *churrasco* in its most rustic form. © HUBERT STADLER/CORBIS.

an even distribution of rainfall throughout the seasons. Rolling grasslands of black, potash-rich soil make raising cattle and sheep the lifeblood of the nation's economy, and roads are edged with fenced driveways for livestock. The capital, Montevideo, is home to a large percentage of Uruguay's population. Much of its industry is centered on processing wool, meat, and hides.

Local dishes. Like other South Americans, Uruguayans favor soups and stews. The Atlantic supplies some seafood, and the River Plate (Río de la Plata) is a source of freshwater fish and large frogs, both often used for soup. Meat remains paramount, however. Beef and lamb are grilled as well as braised. *Albóndigas*, fishballs or meatballs, are very popular, particularly when served with a barbecue sauce enriched with wine. *Humitas*, a seasoned corn puree, is sometimes steamed in corn husks, like tamales.

Fresh fruit is abundant and popular for dessert, especially *feijoa* (also called "pineapple guava"), an egg-shaped fruit with a wonderful perfume.

Gin Fizz (pronounced "jeen feez"), as made in Montevideo, has been described as the great glory of Uruguayan drinks. The secret probably lies in the delicate flavor of the local lemons and limes.

Paraguay

A small landlocked country, bordered by Bolivia, Brazil, and Argentina, Paraguay is known as much for its arts and culture as for its food. Asunción, the capital and by far the largest city in Paraguay, is also the cultural center of the country. The landscape is quite diverse, with lush grasslands, rolling hills, and dense forests, as well as the Chaco prairie in the west. Cattle raising and the industries associated with it are economically significant. Guaraní, the local Indian language, and Spanish are the primary languages of the country, although most Paraguayans learn Guaraní before Spanish.

Local dishes. In Paraguay, manioc (cassava), the staple food, is consumed at least twice a day, but maize is also important in the diet. Soups and stews, whether vegetable-, beef-, or fish-based, are quite popular. *So'o-yosopy* (*sopa de carne* or beef soup) is more of a stew than a soup; it is so robust that little more is needed than a light dessert to make a complete meal. It is usually accompanied with *sopa paraguaya*, which is not a soup at all but a cheese cornbread that is also served with grilled meats. Very good fish are harvested from the Paraguay River, particularly *dorado*, a firm-fleshed white fish.

Bananas are widely used in Paraguay, fresh and cooked in desserts. *Tereré* is a refreshing tea mixed with cold water and aromatic herbs such as mint, traditionally drunk during the midmorning or early afternoon break for relief from the heat. *Maté* (also *yerba maté*), which has a great deal of caffeine, is pleasantly stimulating and traditionally drunk in the morning.

Peru

The Andes, which rise from sea level on the Pacific coast to 22,500 feet, dominate this country. Peru was once the center of the Inca Empire, which extended more than

Vendors selling potatoes in the market at Saquisilí, Ecuador. Ecuador is home to some of the oldest potato varieties in the New World. © CARL & ANN PURCELL/CORBIS.

ica. Besides grilled meats, Peruvian city folk are fond of *chicharrones*, pork rinds fried in lard, sold by street vendors.

In addition to potatoes and the local large-kernel maize, Peruvians cultivate many other vegetables, including a number of special hot peppers (*ajíes*), which they use in soups and stews, often serving them alone as well. Although Peruvians like sweets—homemade puddings and cakes, store-bought pastries, and convent sweets (although that tradition is dying out in Peru)—they are generally prepared and eaten outside the home, as they are in Europe. Dessert at the end of a meal is more likely to be fresh fruit. *Pisco*, the potent Peruvian brandy, is enjoyed straight or in a *pisco* sour.

See also **American Indians: Prehistoric Indians and Historical Overview; Brazil; Caribbean; Central America; Coffee; Columbian Exchange; Fruit; Iberian Peninsula; Inca Empire; Maize; Mexico; Mexico and Central America, Pre-Columbian; Vegetables.**

BIBLIOGRAPHY

Aguilar de la Cruz, Isolina. *Comidas Típicas del Cusco.* Lima: Papeles y Anexos, 1994.

Arnold, Denise Y., and Juan de Dios Yapita, eds. *Madre Melliza y Sus Crías = Ispall Mama Wawampi: Antología de la Papa.* La Paz, Bolivia: Hisbol/Ediciónes, 1996.

Consultor Culinario, por Pascal. Montevideo, Uruguay: A. Barreiro y Ramos, 1917.

Cox, Beverly, and Martin Jacobs. *Spirit of the Earth: Native Cooking from Latin America.* New York: Stewart, Tabori and Chang, 2001.

Hermann, Michael, and Joachim Heller. *Andean Roots and Tubers.* Rome: International Plant Genetic Resources Institute, 1997.

Fonde Vallecaucana. *Cocina Vallecaucana.* Cali, Colombia: Imprenta Deptal, 1960.

Foppiani, Luis. *Moderno Manual de Cocina Criolla.* Lima: Editorial "Fenix," 1950.

Llano Restrepo, María Clara, and Marcela Campuzano Cifuentes. *Chicha: Una Bebida Fermentada Atraves de la Historia.* Bogotá, Colombia: Instituto Colombiano de Antropología, 1994.

Muchnik, Jacobo. *Especialidades de la Cocina Criolla.* Buenos Aires: Bibliotheca de Mucho Gusto, 1958.

Páez de Salamé, Beatriz. *Hallacas: Aromas de una Tradición.* Caracas, Venezuela: Derrelieve, 1995.

Paz Lagarrigue A., María. *Recetas de las Rengifo.* Santiago, Chile: Editorial del Pacífico, 1961.

Pazos Barrera, Julio. *Cocinemos lo Nuestro.* Quito, Ecuador: Corporación Editora Nacional, 1991.

Rosay, E. *Nuevo Manual de la Cocina Peruana.* Lima: Librería Francesa Cientifíca, 1926.

Un Libro de Cocina. Montevideo, Uruguay: E. Miguez, 1933.

Vélez de Sánchez, Maraya. *Postres y Pastelería de la Cocina Europea y Americana.* Paris: Cabaut, 1928.

Villegas, Benjamin. *The Taste of Colombia.* Bogotá, Colombia: Villegas Editores, 1997.

2,500 miles along the Pacific coast of South America. The capital, Lima, is on the coast. Most of the people of the empire were Quechuas. Although the term "Inca" is commonly used to describe the people of the empire, "Inca" originally referred only to the emperor. The Incas terraced and irrigated a difficult terrain, and built roads to link the parts of the empire, enabling farmers to come to town with their produce. The architecture of the Incas is known for its great size and skillful construction. Machu Picchu, one of their most famous cities, stands on a heavily forested mountaintop in the Andes. The Incas were also well known for their administrative skills.

The Incas cultivated thousands of varieties of potatoes many thousands of years ago, and figured out ways to preserve them at high altitudes, either by drying or freeze-drying. The Quechuas also raised quinoa, a hardy plant that thrives where corn cannot grow. The Quechuas had few animals except for the cameloids (the llama and the alpaca) and the *cuy* (guinea pig). The *cuy* is an excellent food animal, and the llama provides wool, leather, fat, and dung for fertilizer, fuel, and building material, as well as meat. Llama meat is made into ham, and *charqui*, or dried llama meat, has remained popular among the native population.

Local dishes. Peru has a real food culture. Peruvians like to eat at home and on the street. For example, in Lima the best place to buy *anticuchos* (skewered beef heart) is from stalls outside the *plaza de toros*, built in the 1700s. At home, they make an excellent hors d'oeuvre. Fish and shellfish are enormously popular on the coast and are prepared in myriad ways, including seviche. Along the shore, *cebicherias* serve fresh seviche night and day. Fowl have been known since pre-Columbian days, and the Quechuas knew how to freeze-dry duck. Turkey is very popular, especially for special occasions. The Europeans brought their domestic animals with them, and these have had enormous impact in Peru and elsewhere in South Amer-

Wilson del Solar, Luisa. *Mi Cocina*. Valparaiso, Chile: Imprente Victoria, 1959.

Elisabeth Lambert Ortiz
With contributions by Enrique Balladares-Castellón

SOUTHEAST ASIA.

This entry includes three subentries:
Indonesia, Malaysia, and the Philippines
Thailand
Vietnam

INDONESIA, MALAYSIA, AND THE PHILIPPINES

Since cuisines are born on the land and grow within its climate, contours, topography, and geography, Indonesia, Malaysia, and the Philippines have bred sister cuisines that find similarities as well in Thailand, Vietnam, Laos, Cambodia, and Brunei Darussalam. It is thus possible to speak of Southeast Asian cuisine even while acknowledging the regional differences that come from history, society, and culture.

Indonesia, for example, with its fifteen thousand islands, covers a large portion of Southeast Asia, and in the early twenty-first century its population (209.4 million) ranked fourth among the world's most populous nations. Although the islands vary greatly in size, climate, and soil and thus in cuisine, it is possible to speak of pan-Indonesian culinary traditions, to set them in their regional contexts, and to invite comparisons with their neighbors.

Malaysia is contiguous to Singapore on one side and to Brunei on the other. Its land, weather, and geographical features are similar to those of the rest of Southeast Asia. However, its population (23 million) is composed of Malay Muslims, Peranakan or Straits Chinese with roots in South China, and Indians, mainly from South India, so it developed three principal cuisines, Malay, Indian, and Chinese. The country's leaders emphasize its multicultural nature and consider all three cuisines equally national.

The Philippines (population 75.8 million), with seven thousand islands, many of them small, has the longest discontinuous coastline in the world. With its tropical weather, plains and mountains, and wealth of water sources, it developed a culinary pattern similar to those of Indonesia and Malaysia. History and the colonial experience, Spanish for almost four hundred years and American for forty years, mediated and transformed its basic Asian cuisine.

Indonesia, Malaysia, and the Philippines therefore demonstrate cuisines that grew on virtually the same soil and in analogous weather conditions but which developed individual, regional characteristics through the actions of history and society on the countries' cultures. Certain similarities and commonalities stand out, however, even before the differences.

Rice

Meals in all three countries assume the presence of rice, without which the repast is not a meal but a snack,

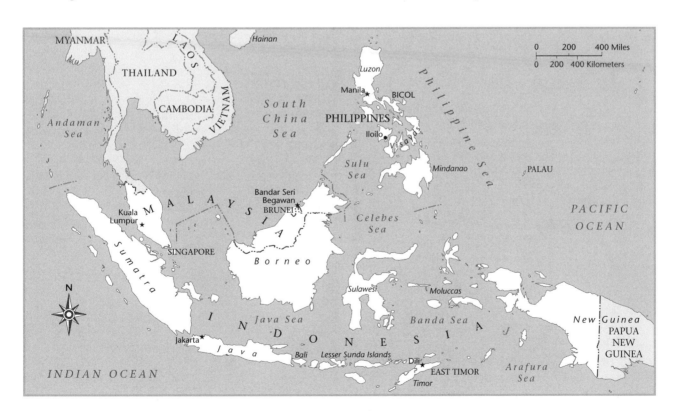

309

pangtawid gutom, just to bridge hungers, Filipinos say. To the native varieties modern research, for example, that conducted by the International Rice Research Institute (IRRI) in the Philippines, has added high-yield, pest-resistant strains. But Asians treasure traditional strains for their fragrance, particular characteristics, and lore.

Deep from mythic history come the rice stories. The Bagobo people of Mindanao talk of the hero Lumabat, who wished to explore the sky with his sister Mebuyan. She refused, sitting firmly in a rice mortar, which sank into the earth with her as she scattered handfuls of rice. She has stayed underground since then. In a Javanese story Tisnawati, daughter of the supreme god Batara Guru, falls in love with a mortal, Jakasudana, of whom her father disapproves. The father punishes her disobedience by turning her into a rice stalk, but then, in pity, he transforms Jakasudana as well. Their marriage is reenacted by the Javanese harvest ritual in Malaysia.

The cooking of rice proceeds in similar ways. It is washed, cooked in water (steamed, boiled, or parboiled), and made the background and taste-shaper of Southeast Asian meals. Because of its mildness, rice invites contrasting tastes, the hot curries of Malaysia, for example, the chili-hot *sambals* of Indonesia, or the salty preserved fish (*tuyo, daing*) of the Philippines. It can be fried, as in Indonesian *nasi goreng* and the morning-after garlic-flavored Philippine breakfast rice (*sinangag*). Malaysians cook rice in coconut milk for the favorite breakfast dish *laksa* and cook thick coconut milk with fragrant herbs until it becomes oil to make *nasi ulam*, which the writer Sri Owen calls a Malaysian version of the British-Indian kedgeree.

All throughout the region, of course, rice is the basis of cakes and other snacks. Glutinous rice cooked in coconut milk with sugar or salt, sparked by ginger, appears everywhere, bare in bamboo baskets; layered, varishaped, or colored; wrapped ingeniously in coconut fronds, banana leaves, or other leaves; and in fresh and artful native packaging designs. *Kue bugis* are Indonesian steamed-rice cakes filled with sweetened grated coconut and cooked in banana leaves. Malaysia has *kui wajek*, a pudding of glutinous rice, coconut milk, palm sugar, and knotted pandanus (screw pine) leaves and tapeh, fermented glutinous rice with sugar.

The word *suman* is used in the Philippines for many kinds of steamed, leaf-wrapped glutinous rice rolls eaten with grated coconut and sugar and sometimes with ripe mangoes. *Bibingka* is a flat, golden rice cake cooked with coals above and below, and *puto* refers to innumerable steamed cakes of rice flour, some small and round, others platter-sized or cylindrical. A traditional Christmas food is *puto bumbong*, a violet-colored rice (*pirurutong*) steamed upright in bamboo tubes.

Rice is also cooked soft as a porridge, congee, snack, or breakfast food. Filipinos, who inherited rice directly from Chinese traders and migrants, serve it with condiments, such as minced vegetables, shredded meat, chopped nuts, and century egg slices; plain, especially for children and the sick; or cooked with fish, chicken (*arroz caldo* or rice soup), or tripe (*goto*) and served sprinkled with browned garlic, green onions, fish sauce, and lime juice. In a dish learned from Mexico, rice is also cooked with chocolate (*champurrado*) and served with bits of salted fish or dried venison.

Malaysian *kai cheok* is a rice porridge with shredded chicken meat, crisp-fried shallots, a little oil, pepper, shredded ginger, spring onions, and light soy sauce. Indonesia has a chilled rice soup made from soft-cooked rice with fresh coconut milk and small slices of sweet papaya that is served for breakfast or as a cool summer refresher.

The main dishes range through the region's favored flavors, including the Indonesian *sambal goreng udang* of prawns or shrimp and rice; the Hainanese chicken rice of Singapore and Malaysia with its soup, rice steamed in broth, and sauces hot and otherwise; and the Philippine *bringhe* of glutinous rice, coconut milk, chicken, and Spanish chorizo. Rice as staff of life—food for principal meals and for snacks, food for rituals and celebrations, food that shapes tastes and dietary patterns—certainly is a common denominator in Southeast Asia.

The Coconut

The "tree of life" is shared by Southeast Asia and the Pacific Rim. From Hawaii and Tahiti and all through mainland and island Southeast Asia, coconuts are grated, often on beautiful graters of folk design, and squeezed in water for the "first milk" or cream then again for the thinner milk, for which there are specific uses in dishes.

The milk is thick when used in *rendang*, the Minangkabau dish of buffalo meat or beef cooked long and spicy with shallots, garlic, ginger, turmeric, chilies, and *laos*. The dish can keep for months because the milk turns to oil in the course of cooking. The Malaysian *kambing korma* or lamb curry is mutton or lamb cooked in spices and thick coconut milk. The Javanese *pepes ikan*, on the other hand, is fish wrapped in banana leaves with herbs, spices, and desiccated coconut soaked in warm water for five minutes (not squeezed). The Philippine Bicol region is known for many dishes of meat (beef, chicken, pork), fish, shrimp, and vegetables (*santol* pulp, young jackfruit, chilies) cooked in coconut milk that is thick or thin or both.

Young coconut is also used. In Laguna province in Luzon it is cut in strips and sautéed like noodles or steamed with river shrimp in coconut water. In Iloilo Province in the Visayas it is cooked with chicken into a soup called *binacol*. Young and mature coconuts, including the "sport" coconut, called in Filipino *makapuno*, full, because it is flesh filled, make possible a stellar parade of candies and sweets, including the Philippine *bukayo* (coconut candy) and sweet *makapuno* (syrup, lime rind); the doughnut-like Malaysian *kuih keria* of sago, rice, and

SPICES OF SOUTHEAST ASIA

The range, subtlety, intensity, melding, and reinvention of flavors are made possible by the spice table shared by almost all of Southeast Asia. Among the spices are:

English	Malaysian	Indonesian	Filipino
garlic	*bawang puteh*	*bawang-putih*	*bawang*
ginger	*haliya*	*acuga, jahe*	*luya*
galingale	*lengkuas*	*laos*	*langkawas*
chili	*chilli-api, chabai*	*lombok kecil*	*siling labuyo*
lemon grass	*serai*	*seri*	*tanglad*
Kaffir lime	*limau purut*	*jeruk purut*	
curry leaves	*daun kari*		
mint	*pohok*	*janggat*	*yerba buena*
basil, holy	*sellaseh kemangi*	*kemangen*	*sulasi*
basil, sweet	*selaseh putih*	*selasih*	*balanoi*
coriander			
leaf cilantro	*ketumbar*	*katumber*	*wan soy*
coriander seed		*ketumbar*	*kulantro*
turmeric		*kunyit*	*dilao*
star anise		*bunga lawang*	*sangke*
cloves		*cengkeh*	*clavo*
cinnamon		*kayu manis padang*	
cumin		*jintan puteh*	*jinten*
pepper		*merica*	*paminta*
parsley	*shelwri*	*patraseli, seledri*	*parsli*
mustard seed	*biji savi*		*mustasa*
nutmeg		*pala*	
tamarind	*asam*	*asam Java*	*sampalok*

grated coconut; and the Indonesian *serikaya* (coconut custard) and *onde-onde* (small rice cakes rolled in grated coconut). The flavor of coconut at all its stages is savored throughout the region in recognizably compatible ways.

Spices, Herbs, Relishes

Southeast Asian tables generally bear not only serving platters with dishes to be shared and individual plates or bowls but also little satellite dishes for dipping sauces, spices, chopped herbs, and relishes like shrimp paste and fish sauce. The meal may be prepared by great cooks or chefs, but each diner has the right and freedom to fine-tune the dish to his or her individual taste by dipping, pouring, mixing, and sprinkling and thus giving the dish its final grace.

Among the possibilities are the Indonesian *sambal* and *sambel*, hot and spicy relishes served with food. They feature red and green chilies, hot bird peppers, *terasi* (shrimp paste, which is made by salting and mashing tiny shrimp and allowing them to ferment), lemon, lime, soy sauce, shallots, chili powder, tamarind water, salted yel-

low beans, and more, depending on the dish they are to accompany. Others are *serundeng* (roasted grated coconut) and *goreng bawang* (crisp-fried onions) to sprinkle on particular dishes.

In the Philippines dipping sauces are called *sawsawan* and could be basic vinegar, soy sauce, *patis* (fish sauce, made by salting and fermenting small fish); *calamansi* (lime) juice; combined vinegar-soy or *patis-calamansi*; or enhanced with herbs and spices, such as crushed peppercorns, ginger, garlic, chili peppers or seeds, coriander leaves, pork or crackling bits, and salted black beans. *Achara*, such as pickled papaya, mangoes, heart of palm, and chilies, are accompaniments as well. These make it possible to satisfy individual palates or to make each mouthful a different delight.

Parallels exist in Malaysian and Singaporean cooking, including prawn and shrimp pastes (*blacan terasi* and the mild Chinese liquid *hei-ko*); dried anchovy and fish sauce; the *rempah* spice mixture of *sambal* and *achar* (mangoes, mixed vegetables); and *goreng bawang* (crisp-fried onions). The famous Hainanese chicken rice of Malaysia and Singapore may come with *sambal belacan* (red chilies, shrimp paste, limes) or at least three sauces, a fresh-made chili sauce, finely crushed ginger and oil, and soy sauce. *Nasi lemak*, the Nonya-Malay rice steamed in coconut milk, and its satellite dishes constitute the traditional festal dish for the twelfth day of a wedding. The accompaniments may include *sambal udang* (shrimp), *ikan kuning* (small fried fish), cucumber slices, and sliced red chilies.

The renowned Indonesian *rijsttafel* (rice table), although based on feasts of yore, has become largely a Dutch custom. Rice, the central dish, is surrounded with smaller dishes and relishes. Popular in Indonesia is a miniature *rijstaffel* called *nasi rames* with some seven side dishes, like *dendeng ragi* (beef and grated coconut), *sayur lodeh* (spicy vegetable stew), *rendang* (beef cooked in spices and coconut milk), *kering tempe* (crisp-fried *tempe*), *kelia ayam* (Sumatran chicken curry), *sambal bajak* (mixed spice relish), and *krupuk* (prawn crackers). Each spice-enhanced dish introduces a flavor or flavors to harmonize with the rest in a whole Asian experience.

The sauces include fish, oyster, *hoisin*, chili, plum, black bean, yellow bean, chili bean, red bean, shrimp paste, sesame paste, and soybean; the cooking fats and oils are peanut, rape seed, coconut, sesame seed, palm, and chili; and the vinegars are rice, coconut, palm, sugar cane, and fruit. Combining all with the *sambals* and other made-up cooked or mixed combinations creates a repertoire of unnumbered possibilities, all Asian or Southeast Asian, a kaleidoscope of flavors and flavor makers.

Chinese and Other Foreign Influences

All three countries have significant Chinese populations, which even make up a full third of the population in Malaysia, that may or may not have integrated successfully in the cities and villages. Consequently all have strong Chinese dietary strains in their cuisines. Even during racial conflicts—riots in Malaysia, wars and ghetto burning in the Philippines, discrimination and segregation in Indonesia—the foods melded and the Chinese presence became a matter of fact, even of pride.

Nonya cooking in Malaysia originated among Chinese immigrants who settled in Malacca in the fifteenth century. Daughters of well-to-do Nonya women were trained in household and cooking skills from early childhood. The cuisine uses chilies, shrimp paste, coconut milk, and aromatic roots and leaves as in the Malaysian and Indonesian traditions but also retains pork and noodles from its Chinese past.

The *popiah* or spring roll is often served in its separate pieces—the wrapper pancakes; fillings, possibly including eggs, sausages, bean curd, bean sprouts, prawns, cucumber sticks, spring onions, lettuce leaves, pork, crab meat, bamboo shoots, and water chestnuts; and sauces and relishes—on a round table at which each diner creates a spring roll to taste. The Nonya pork *sate* is a compromise between a Muslim prohibition and a Chinese

taste for pork. The resulting taste is Malay, with chilies, coconut milk, lemon grass, and coriander.

In the Philippines the first public eateries were Chinese establishments that served indigenized *comida China* (Chinese food) in restaurants called *carinderia*, a Spanish formulation from a native word *cari* or *kari*, cooked food. To accommodate the Spanish patrons, the food had Spanish names, such as *aletas de tiburon* (shark fins), *tortilla de cangrejo* (crab omelet), *camaron rebozado* (batter-coated shrimps).

Widely popular and variegated is the *lumpia*, a vegetable or pork spring roll in a thin flour wrapper, the local edition of the Malay *popiah*. The noodle dishes, generically called *pansit* from the Hokkien word for that which is quickly cooked, vary from region to region, indeed family to family, cook to cook. *Char kway teow* is the most popular Malay-Singaporean noodle, but in the Philippines the most popular is *pancit palabok*, noodles shaken in water or broth and covered with a sauce of shrimp, pork, vegetables, bean curd, and sometimes squid, oysters, crumbled crackling, and flaked smoked fish. In Indonesia it may be *mie jawa*, which includes *bakmie goreng* (fried noodles) or *bakmie godog* (noodle soup), egg noodles with beef or pork, shrimp or prawns, carrots, bean sprouts, shallots, candlenuts, and other seasonings.

Each country's colonial and social histories left deep imprints on its cuisine, the roots of many regional differences. The Spanish-Mexican and American colonial regimes, building on the indigenous and Chinese food already in place, shaped what is now known as Philippine cooking. Native to the soil are dishes like *sinigang*, a sour stew of meats, crustaceans, fish, or fowl soured with tamarind, *bilimbi*, green mango, or other sour fruits and leaves. Sour broths are cooling to the skin, especially in tropical weather. Indigenous too are fresh meat, fish, and fowl, steamed, simmered, boiled, or roasted, and vegetables cooked in coconut milk or steamed and flavored with shrimp paste or fish sauce.

Filipinos indigenized Chinese, Spanish-Mexican, and American dishes through the use of native ingredients and cooking by native cooks with homegrown taste buds. Among those dishes are Spanish stews (*cocido, puchero*) with eggplant or squash relishes; the Mexican tamale transformed from a corn snack wrapped in corn husks into a rice snack wrapped in a banana leaf; a Chinese porridge cooked in the Philippines with chicken and *kasubha* (a saffronlike spice) or including unhatched eggs; beef hamburgers with soy and chopped onions; and steaks marinated in soy sauce and lime juice before grilling. The foreign food has been accepted but adapted to local tastes.

The colonial experience gives Philippine dishes a European-American dimension, just as British colonization colored Malay-Singapore food and Dutch domination redefined Indonesian cooking. Of the latter two, however, the Dutch influence is the lightest, because the colonizers

OTHER REGIONAL CUISINES

Most Southeast Asian societies have been in contact with each other and with other societies, such as India and China, for many centuries. Within Southeast Asia food serves as an ethnic and national marker, distinguishing one group from another. The region is characterized by a great diversity of cuisines that have been shaped by local geography, ecology, religion, and history. Despite the diversity, distinct commonalities exist. Ingredients like coconut milk, lemon grass, galingale, ginger, Asian basil, mint, fish sauce, and shrimp paste are used throughout the region. However, cooking techniques and the ways these ingredients are combined vary greatly and give each cuisine its distinctiveness.

Lao People's Democratic Republic
Rice, especially the glutinous variety, is the staple for Lao meals. Other frequently used ingredients include fresh vegetables, freshwater fish, poultry, duck, pork, beef, or water buffalo. Lime juice, lemon, fresh coriander, and various fermented fish sauces give Lao food its characteristic flavor. *Pla daek,* a highly pungent fermented fish sauce, is often considered an ethnic marker. Additionally its heavy use throughout the country and the consumption of *laap* are indicators of the cultural and historical links with Northeast Thailand. Hot chilies, garlic, mint, ground peanuts, tamarind juice, ginger, and coconut milk are other seasonings that link Lao cuisine to others of the region. A soup, such as *kaeng nor mai* (bamboo shoot soup) or *kaeng het bot* (mushroom soup), is a common feature of Lao meals. One popular dish eaten by the Lao is *feu,* a noodle dish of Vietnamese origin. Another noodle dish, *klao poun,* is served cold with a variety of raw chopped vegetables and a flavored coconut milk sauce and is often a part of celebrations. *Or lam,* a regional dish in Luang Prabang, combines lemon grass, sweet basil, dried buffalo meant and skin, chilies, and eggplant.

Myanmar (Burma)
Myanmar is a diamond-shaped country bounded by China, Laos, and Thailand in the east, by Bangladesh and India in the north, and by the Indian Ocean in the west and south. The landscape is mountainous, and only about one-sixth of the country is considered arable. Of the arable land, approximately one-tenth is irrigated, mostly for rice agriculture. The cuisine is considered a blend of Burman, Mon, Indian, and Chinese influences, and hot and spicy dishes particularly show the influence of Indian and other Southeast Asian cuisines. Rice, the core of most meals, is often eaten with curries of fish, chicken, or prawns, and noodles and vegetables are common local ingredients. Taste combinations of onion, ginger root, garlic, turmeric, and chili pepper give the cuisine its distinctive flavor. The curries in Myanmar are the mildest in Southeast Asia, but the heat level can be intensified by adding *balachaung,* a condiment made from chilies, tamarind paste, and dried shrimp, or *ngapi kyaw,* a hot and pungent shrimp paste fried in oil with garlic and onions.

Kampuchea (Cambodia)
Kampuchea shares borders in the north with Laos and Thailand, in the east with Vietnam, and in the southwest with the Gulf of Thailand. Khmer is Cambodia's official language, and Theravada Buddhism is the dominant religion. Fish, rice, coriander, and lemon grass are common dish ingredients. A Cambodian meal almost always includes a soup, which is eaten with the other dishes. As elsewhere in Southeast Asia, freshwater fish is a mainstay. Some dishes reflect the influence of French cooking, as does the use of bread.

were not too interested in changing the native culture of the colonized. However, Spanish colonization of the Philippines, which meant Christianization as well, was much more deeply engaged in culture change, as was American colonization, which made its impact through language and education. In Malaysia, the Indians, Chinese, immigrant elites from East and Southeast Asia, and Europeans influenced food more strongly than did the British.

Southeast Asian Cuisine in the Twenty-first Century
Although it is logical and true to speak of the individual sister cuisines of Southeast Asia, they are variations on regional themes. A common repertoire of spices, rice, coconuts, vegetables, fish, fowl, and animals exists. The lands and waters and the trade and interaction have made that inevitable. Thus the cuisines have compatible attitudes, common practices, and recognizable similarities. However, the differences wrought by history, especially the colonial experiences and the strategies of survival; social forces, including war, peace, trade, and population; and the countries' cultures, that is, the way people think, work, survive, and express themselves, have resulted in the kaleidoscope of tastes and dishes in Southeast Asia.

The Indonesian *pisang goring*, bananas mashed with sugar and flour, and the Philippine *linupak*, green bananas mashed with sugar and coconut, and *pinasugbu*, green banana slices dipped in molasses syrup, are variations on a theme. The Nonya pancake, a teatime snack filled with palm sugar and served with chocolate sauce, and the Philippine *piaya*, a flat cake filled with brown sugar and sprinkled with sesame seeds, are also variations. The similarities are clear, but regional circumstances gave them particular characteristics. On warm afternoons Indonesians enjoy *es cendol*, short strands of two kinds of flour sieved, flavored, and served with sugar syrup, coconut milk, and ice crushed or cubed. Malaysians have *bubor cha-cha* with yam and sweet potato cubes, tapioca, sweet coconut milk, and ice shavings. Filipinos serve instead *halo-halo* (literally mix-mix) with palm fruit, gelatin cubes, banana slices, sweetened coconut strands, milk, and crushed ice. The mixtures are analogous because the weather and the habits of refreshment are too.

The famous dishes of each cuisine may have tastes familiar and acceptable to the whole region, but they are different and make a rich repertoire. In Malaysia celebrations may include chili crab, *satays*, a steamboat, the Nonya *sambal sotong* (squid) or *sambal udang* (prawns), *bakwan kepiting* (a Nonya must for Lunar New Year's and birthdays), the Hokkien-Nonya *ngoh hiang* (five-spice rolls with prawns, pork, and crab meat), *rebong masak lemak* (chicken and bamboo shoots), *sambal kim chiam* (a salad of banana buds), Indian-based vindaloo (chicken or duck), and clay pot dishes and soups of Chinese origin. Malaysians and Singaporeans consider many other dishes connected to their multicultural family feasts and traditions.

Philippine feasting often features colonial food, such as Spanish stews (*cocido*, *puchero*) with sausages (chorizo, *morcilla*); sugar-glazed Christmas hams (*jamon en dulce*); stuffed turkeys and capons (*pavo embuchado*, *capon rellenado*); and American salads, pies, and cakes, once considered elite and thus appropriate for celebrations. To these time and custom have added specialties of Chinese origin, especially noodles, roast duck, roast pig, steamed fish chosen live from a tank, bird's nest and shark fin soups, and delicate dumplings and buns. The indigenous rice cakes, rolls, and desserts; stews like *kari-kari* (oxtail); and special dishes like *lechon* (tamarind leaf– or lemon grass–stuffed suckling pig skewered and roasted on an open fire) are the local contribution to a cuisine that combines the indigenous, the indigenized, and even the imported.

Indonesia, with so many regional traditions, has one of the richest cuisines, and the Western world, which has sent more scholars to Indonesia than to any other Southeast Asian country, has explored it. The names sound rare and enticing, like the famous beef *rendang*; the hearty *gado-gado* salad of cooked vegetables; the different *gulai* (vegetables like *pako*, fiddlehead fern) cooked in coconut milk; fish and fish cakes; *sates* of lamb, beef, and chicken; *bebek dengan bumbu betutu* (duck breasts in Balinese spices); *bubur ayam* (rice porridge with spicy chicken soup); and sweets like *rujak* (a spiced fruit salad), *marabak kubang* (Sumatran stuffed pancakes), and *lapis legit* (spiced

layered cake). Southeast Asian ingredients, spices, cooking methods, dishes traditional and new, meal patterns, and border-crossing food and foodways remind readers of cookbooks, menus, and travel, ethnographic, and anthropological accounts that the words are the merest keys to cultures deep and rich, starting points for meals, for cultural interactions, and for rich conversations with national identities, time, and traditions.

See also **China**; **Rice**.

BIBLIOGRAPHY

Brackman, Agnes de Keijzer. *Cook Indonesian.* Singapore: Times Books International, 1982.

Davidson, Alan. *The Oxford Companion to Food.* Oxford: Oxford University Press, 1999.

Fernandez, Doreen G. *Palayok: Philippine Food through Time, on Site, in the Pot.* Makati City, Philippines: Bookmark, 2000.

Goody, Jack. *Cooking, Cuisine, and Class: A Study in Comparative Sociology.* Cambridge: Cambridge University Press, 1982.

Ling, Kong Foong. *The Food of Asia.* Singapore: Periplus, 1998.

Morris, Sallie, and Deh-ta Hsiung. *The Practical Encyclopedia of Asian Cooking.* London: Lorenz Books, 1999.

Ng, Dorothy. *Dorothy Ng's Complete Asian Meals.* Singapore: Times Books International, 1979.

Oon, Violet. *Violet Oon Cooks.* Singapore: Ultra Violet, 1992.

Owen, Sri. *The Classic Asian Cookbook.* London: Dorling Kindersley, 1998.

Owen, Sri. *Indonesian Food and Cookery.* London: Prospect Books, 1986.

Owen, Sri. *Indonesian Regional Food and Cookery.* London and New York: Doubleday, 1994.

Owen, Sri. *The Rice Book: The Definitive Book on the Magic of Rice Cookery.* London: Transworld, 1993.

Robson, J. R. K., ed. *Food, Ecology, and Culture: Readings in the Anthropology of Dietary Practices.* New York: Gordon and Breach, 1980.

Simonds, Nina. *Asian Noodles.* New York: Hearst Books, 1997.

Solomon, Charmaine. *South East Asian Cookbook.* Sydney: Hamlyn, 1972.

Steinberg, Rafael. *Pacific and Southeast Asian Cooking.* New York: Time-Life Books, 1970.

Yoshida, Yoshiko. *Tropical Cookery.* Manila, Philippines: National Book Store, 1981.

Doreen Fernandez

THAILAND

Thailand is situated in the heart of mainland Southeast Asia. Located between latitudes 5° and 21° north and longitudes 97° to 106° east, it borders the Lao People's Democratic Republic (Lao PDR) and Myanmar (formerly Burma) to the north, Cambodia to the east, Myanmar to the west, and Malaysia to the south. Tropical temperature and rainfall patterns predominate throughout much of the country and influence its culinary traditions. Thailand, once called Siam, is distinguished from most other Southeast Asian countries by the fact that it has not ever been ruled by a European power. The monarch is a member of the Chakri dynasty, which has led the kingdom since 1782. Much of the Thai cuisine evolved in the central region during the Sukhothai period (1238–1350 B.C.E.). The rise of Ayutthaya in the fourteenth century brought an increase in trade, and outside influences became more pronounced. China, India, Indonesia, and Cambodia exerted strong influences, as did some European countries. After the fifteenth century domesticates from the Americas, such as the chili pepper and the tomato, were introduced. The complex of seasonings and dishes regarded as Thai cuisine was probably well established by the 1800s.

Staples, Specialties, and Etiquette

Rice and fish were first used as metaphors for prosperity and security in the inscription from King Ramkhamhaeng (1283 C.E.): "In the water there are fish, in the paddies there is rice" (*nai nam mee pla—nai na mee khao*). Rice, fish, and local fruits and vegetables form the centerpiece of Thai cuisine. Considerable evidence suggests that the domestication of wild rice occurred in the Yangtze Valley in China and later spread to Thailand and other areas in Southeast Asia. Rice is more than just a culinary staple. Rice agriculture is the primary farming activity nationwide, an integral way of life often portrayed in songs, poems, novels, and films. Rice is so central in the Thai diet that the most common term for "to eat" is *"kin khâo,"* literally "eat rice," and a common greeting is *"Kin khâo láew réu yang?"* literally "Have you eaten rice yet?" Regional distinctions exist in the type of rice consumed. Sticky or glutinous rice (*khâaw nĩaw*) is consumed widely in the north and the northeast, and plain white rice (*khâaw jâo*), especially jasmine rice, is popular in the central and southern regions (see "Thai Regional Cuisine" below). Glutinous or sticky rice is a variety (*Oryza sativa*) that requires a shorter growing season and contains a large amount of amylopectin starch. The high propor-

Garlic harvest at Mae Hong Song, Thailand. © JOHN HUME; EYE UBIQUITOUS/CORBIS.

tion of amylopectin causes the kernels to disintegrate when boiled. Consequently glutinous rice is usually soaked and then steamed in a container above the water.

Eating in Thailand is usually done in a social context rather than alone. In Thai the word for "meal" is *"meu,"* and meals usually consist of rice accompanied by various side dishes that are not eaten in any specific order. Frequently meals include a soup, a curry (*kaeng*), a salad, a steamed or fried dish, and at least one dipping sauce, such as fish sauce *nam pla* or one of the various forms of the hotter *nam prik*. Dessert usually consists of fruits, although various sweets called *kanome*, which are sometimes eaten as snacks, can also be served at a meal. Specific foods are seldom limited to certain times of the day, and distinctive breakfast, lunch, or dinner dishes do not exist. Some Thai food is eaten with the fingers, especially in certain regions of the country or specific foods such as sticky rice. The use of a fork and spoon predominates in urban areas, where the fork is used to push

Thai cooking is noted for its elaborate presentation. This expert carver is sculpting fruit for the Sala Rim Restaurant in Bangkok. © RICHARD T. NOWITZ/CORBIS.

food onto the spoon rather than to bring food to the mouth. Knives are not commonly used because food is usually cut into small pieces before it is cooked.

Traditionally some distinction is made between food eaten by royalty (*ahaan chow wang*) and village food (*aahan chow bâan*). The primary difference lies not so much in the ingredients as in the use of serving dishes, in the variety and number of side dishes, and in the presentation style as food is transformed by carving, shaping, or decorating to change its appearance. In addition to an artistic presentation, palace food has often required many hours of preparation. Traditional palace food is served in Bangkok at restaurants specializing in this type of cuisine. Some royal desserts such as *foi thong* (golden threads), a dessert made from egg yolks and sugar, and *luk choob*, small mung bean paste sweets, similar to marzipan, shaped into small replicas of various fruits, colored with vegetable dyes, and glazed in the gelatin-like agaragar. These sweets also can be obtained in many large grocery stores and from some street vendors.

A twentieth-century development, especially in the urban areas, was the rapid rise in Thai street food. Sometimes considered a culinary form in its own right, street food is characterized by rapid preparation methods and includes a wide variety of categories. Snacks, such as sliced fruits or sweets, are common, as are noodle dishes and main dishes. Usually each vendor concentrates on one of these categories of food. Sidewalk food vendors are regulated by official authorities in each city. This form of culinary activity clearly fills an important niche in the cosmopolitan Thai lifestyle.

The Tastes and Flavors of Thai Food

The consumption of meals is guided by the qualities of taste, smell, and texture. Often these are the same qualities that guide health-promoting behavior. Foods are classified and categorized in a variety of ways. The ingredients selected for cooking frequently have medicinal properties. Penny Van Esterik (1988, p. 753) notes that the taste relationship is so close to concepts of health that the head teacher of the Traditional Medical College identified medicine (*ya*) as "anything which can be eaten to improve one's health." The basic taste qualities overlap with the medicinal tastes of traditional Thai medicine, which is related to the Indian Ayurvedic system. These taste contrasts guide the combination of ingredients or the combination of dishes with rice. The tastes are primarily derived from local plants, resins, oils, roots, insects, and algae, many of which are gathered wild from forests, ponds, and rice paddies.

Flavoring is a defining characteristic of Thai cuisine that imparts regional or ethnic identification, a sense of familiarity, and a sense of tradition. Most Thais speak of five important tastes as the hallmarks of Thai food, sweet, sour, salty, bitter, and hot-spicy. The ideal meal is often designed to include these tastes, and sometimes several of the tastes are subtly combined in an individual dish. Despite regional differences, much of Thai food is characterized by a combination of *naam plaa* (predominantly in the central, northern, and southern regions) or *plaa daek* (in the northeast), lemongrass, ginger, galingale, Thai basil, garlic, and chili peppers. A wide variety of chili peppers is used, different types imparting distinctive

REGIONAL CUISINES OF THAILAND

Thailand is divided into four regions, the North, Northeast, Central, and South, which vary in geography, natural resources, culture, and history of contact with outer societies. Consequently each is characterized by its own foods and style of eating, although the increase in communication and extensive internal migration has been accompanied by the movement of regional dishes into different areas within the country.

The North
Northern Thailand, site of the early Thai city-states Lanna, Chiang Mai, and Chian Saen, borders Myanmar, Laos (Lao PDR), and China. Consequently the food of the North is an amalgamation of cuisine from these areas. The importance of sticky rice in the North is a reflection of dietary influences from Laos. The use of pork, tamarind, and turmeric belies the influence of Myanmar, as does the regional specialty *kaeng hang le* (a pork curry). Mild-hot, salty, and sour tastes predominate, and local dishes contain bitter acacia leaf, eggplants known for their bitterness, sour tamarind juice, and pickled bamboo shoots. A traditional form of a meal in this region is the *khantok* (*khan* means bowl, *tok* means low, round table), during which diners sit on the floor around a low table.

The Central Region
The Central region dominates the nation politically and economically. Hot, salty, sweet, and sour tastes predominate there. The cuisine of Central Thailand is characterized by curries made with coconut milk and spices, such as *kaeng phèt* (red curry) and *kaeng khĭaw wăan* (green curry). Stir-frying with basil and curry paste *(phàt phèt)* is also common, as are the well-known soups *tôm yam gôong* (spicy shrimp soup) and *tôm khà gaì* (chicken coconut soup). *Yam,* the hot and tangy salad, is most popular served with squid or barbecued beef or pork.

The Chinese community has had a large influence on Central Thailand as can be seen in *Kŭaytĕow,* noodle dishes, and the clear bitter soups made with green squash, bitter gourd, and ground pork. The eastern seaboard region is increasingly gaining attention as a separate region characterized by its reliance on seafood and distinctive fruits.

The Northeast (Isan)
Isan is characterized by hot, spicy, salty, and sour tastes. Food in this region reflects its relationship and similarity to neighboring Lao PDR. Some of the earliest archaeological sites in Asia with evidence of agriculture, pottery, and bronze work are located in the Northeast. Consumption of glutinous rice is a distinctive characteristic of Isan. The food is frequently flavored with *pla daek,* a fermented fish sauce. One special dish from the region is *laab* or *kôy.* This dish is a blend of minced meat, fish sauce, herbs such as cilantro and mint, scallions, lime juice, ground roasted sticky rice, and chilies either fresh or in powdered form. *Sôm tam,* a spicy green papaya salad, and grilled chicken are also characteristic of Isan.

The South
South of Bangkok the country rapidly narrows to a strip of land connecting Thailand with the Malay Peninsula. Culturally the South is distinctive, with a large Muslim and Chinese population. Hence much of the food of the South combines Thai, Malay, and Chinese elements, and the prevailing tastes are hot, spicy, salty, and sour. Curries in the Indian style, such as Massaman curry, are the predominant features of southern meals. Additionally influences from the Middle East and Pakistan are evident, for example in *roti* (flat Indian bread). The use of a pungent, flat bean, *sato (Parkia speciosa),* which imbues a bitter taste is also favored in this region.

---

tastes, colors, and levels of hotness, such as the small and extremely hot *prik ki nu.* In addition mint, coriander, lime, and kaffir lime leaves (*Citrus hystrix DC.)* are also frequently used.

Food in Thai Celebrations, Rituals, and Religion
Food plays an important role in the personal, social, and religious aspects of Thai life. Most Thais are Buddhists, and the daily offering of food to monks, called *tham boon tak bàat,* is one of the most important Buddhist acts. Every day throughout the country, in urban and rural communities, Thai Buddhist monks receive their daily food during a practice known as *bintábàat.* Walking through the streets and paths in the early morning, the

monks are met by people offering food. Food is also offered at numerous religious shrines and is an important part of most Thai Buddhist ceremonies. Houses, office buildings, hotels, and rice fields have a spirit (*phii*) house (*san pra poom*), where daily offerings are placed. The spirit houses, originating from past Brahman influences, may be elaborate and look like small temples or may be modestly constructed of plain wood or concrete. Thais give offerings to feed the spirits occupying the spirit house who protect the place from harm. As in secular life, rice has a central role in Thai spiritual life. The most common type of offering at spirit shrines is a small amount of rice, however, other food, such as fruits or sweets, may also be provided.

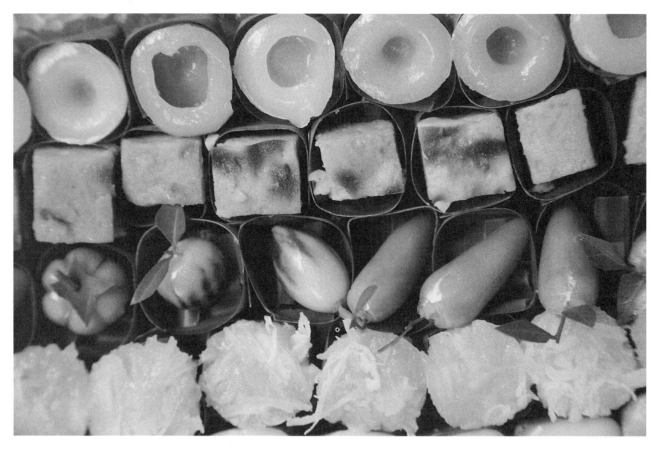

Thai candies are often made of exotic tropical ingredients. These confections were displayed in a shop in Bangkok. © DAVE BARTRUFF/CORBIS.

Buddhist monks perform many different ceremonies in which food offerings are integral. These include funeral rites, weddings, house consecrations, and inductions of new monks. Sweet offerings predominate at engagement and wedding ceremonies. The names of such sweets often signify a special aspect of the occasion. For example, *kanome* (sweet) *thong* (gold) *ake* (best) signifies bestowing wealth to the couple. The preparation and offering of food for religious ceremonies and rituals bestows merit on the person who provides the food. In preparing and giving ritual food individuals gain merit, and food is integrated into the spiritual and ceremonial fabric of Thai life.

See also **Buddhism**; **China**; **India**; **Rice**.

BIBLIOGRAPHY

Boontawee, Kampoon. *A Child of the Northeast.* Translated by Susan Fulop Kepner. Bangkok: Duang Kamol, 1988.

Cummings, Joe. *World Food Thailand.* Victoria, Australia: Lonely Planet Publications, 2000.

Higham, Charles. "The Transition to Rice Cultivation in Southeast Asia." In *Last Hunters—First Farmers: New Perspectives on the Prehistoric Transition to Agriculture*, edited by T. Douglas Price and Birgitte Gebauer, pp. 127–156. Santa Fe: School of American Research Press, 1995.

Krauss, Sven, Laurent Ganguillet, and Vira Sanguanwon. *The Food of Thailand: Authentic Recipes from the Golden Kingdom.* Singapore: Periplus Editions, 1995.

Moreno-Black, Geraldine. "Cooking Up Change: Transforming Diets in a Rural Thai Village." In *Cultural and Historical Aspects of Food*, edited by M. W. Kelsey and Z. A. Holmes, pp. 146–166. Corvallis: Oregon State University, 1999.

Na Songkla, Vandee. *Thai Foods from Thai Literature.* Book 2. Bangkok: Chotivej Compas, n.d.

Poladitmontri, Panurat, and Judy Lew with William Warren. *Thailand, the Beautiful Cookbook.* Bangkok: Asia Books, 1992.

Smith, Bruce. *The Emergence of Agriculture.* New York: Scientific American Library, 1995.

Van Esterik, Penny. "To Strengthen and Refresh: Herbal Therapy in Southeast Asia." *Social Science and Medicine* 27 (1988): 751–759.

Yee, Kenny, and Catherine Gordon. *Thai Hawker Food.* Bangkok: Book Promotion and Service, 1993.

Geraldine Moreno-Black

VIETNAM

The Vietnamese cuisine has been described as one of the most colorful and diverse in the world. The country's geography, climate, and history all play influential roles in creating its culinary range. The Vietnamese often describe their country as resembling a shoulder pole laden with two rice baskets. In fact, both the northern Red River delta and the southern Mekong River delta are rice-producing regions. The long coastline, rivers, and tributaries have ensured the place of seafood throughout the country, while the distinctive climates and cultures found in the North, Middle, and South, along with Vietnam's mountain-lowland ecologies have produced regional variation in the diet. Finally, Vietnam's relations with China (which controlled it for a thousand years, beginning in 111 B.C.E.), its Southeast Asian neighbors, India, France, and the United States have affected what the Vietnamese have chosen to eat, or been forced to eat, throughout their history.

Food Beliefs

Philosophy. Taoism, Buddhism, and Confucianism play an important role in Vietnamese food beliefs, but rural pragmatics are part of even the most cosmopolitan individual's belief system. According to Vietnamese from the countryside, there are two important qualities in food: quantity and taste. The elderly and guests, including spiritual ones, also require more prestigious food than is commonly eaten by everyone else. While the majority of Vietnamese profess a belief in Buddhism, relatively few adhere to Buddhist dietary prohibitions against meat and alcohol. The foods preferred in ancestor worship, and usually placed on an altar with incense and wine, were chicken and rice. These are the same foods that are served to company when possible. Pork is usually served at feasts.

Science. The Vietnamese regard two distinct health systems as scientific: Western medicine as practiced by the French and Western–trained physicians, and *thuoc bac,* literally "northern medicine," but colloquially "Chinese medicine." According to most sources, *thuoc bac* incorporates Chinese and Indian (Ayurvedic) traditions, and was possibly influenced by the humoral pathology of the classical Greek physician Galen (129–199 C.E.). In this frame of reference, health reflects a balance of two basic elements, *am* (the Chinese *yin*)—often translated as "cold"—and *duong* (Chinese, *yang*), or "hot." Ill health is the disequilibrium of these forces brought about by incorporating too much *am* or *duong* in the body. Foods share these designations, and can either upset the balance through deficit or overindulgence, or be used therapeutically.

A Vietnamese interpretation of the life cycle is that following childbirth, the mother and infant are both cold. As the infant develops, he or she becomes warmer. This warmth peaks in adolescence (teenagers are the hottest), and then the adult begins to cool down, maintaining neu-

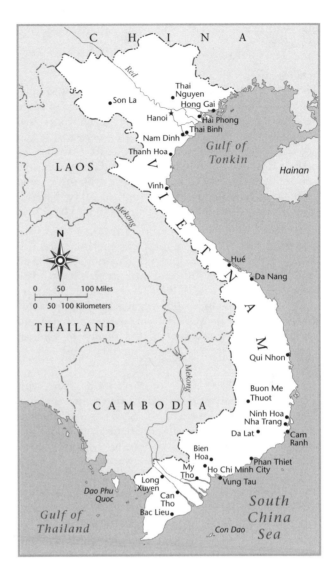

trality (the desired state) through maturity. The body becomes cool again in old age. Foods are recommended according to these life stages. Immediately following birth, for example, the mother is given hot foods and treatments (which are shared with the infant through breast milk). Infants and young children, while frequently troubled by cold illnesses such as diarrhea and stomachache, are naturally warm, with a tendency toward rashes, fevers, and constipation. Adults can acquire hot or cold illnesses that need to be counterbalanced by treatments and diet. The elderly tend to be cold, and frequently require therapeutic warming. Cigarette smoking used to be advocated for the elderly (the Vietnamese term for tobacco is *thuoc la,* or "medicinal leaves").

As is true in all humoral systems, the food's temperature has little to do with its qualities of *am* and *duong,* boiled water being the exception (water boiled, then cooled, is warming, whereas cool water is cold. Ice is hot!). Most green vegetables are considered cooling; fatty foods such as meat, sugary foods, and red or orange fruits (such as papaya, mango, or watermelon) are considered heating.

A Vietnamese Meal

The majority of Vietnamese cuisine is relatively simple, relying on fresh fish, vegetables, fruit, and steamed white rice. Rice is so important in the diet that the words used to enquire if someone has eaten are *an com roi*, or, "eaten rice yet?" Fish sauce (*nuoc mam*) made from fermented anchovies is used much like soy sauce in Chinese cuisine. Few Vietnamese dishes do not include a drop or two, and Vietnamese have often subsisted on little more than fish sauce on rice, when they were lucky enough to have rice.

A typical Vietnamese meal requires rice, soup (with greens), a fried dish of fish, meat, or vegetables, and fish sauce on the side for additional flavoring. This meal would be prepared in sufficient quantity that it would be consumed for lunch and dinner. The primary factors normally taken into consideration when preparing a meal include the number of people needing to eat, their ages and associated needs (according to the theory of *am* and *duong*), taste preferences, cost of the foods, and ease of preparation.

The Vietnamese like to eat three meals a day, with breakfast often consisting of a thick rice soup (*chau*) like the Chinese congee, bread products, or foods identical to those consumed at other times of the day. The Vietnamese appreciate coffee, preferring a dense, slow-dripped preparation mixed with sweetened, condensed milk. Noodles (with or without soup); fresh or dried fruits; salted, roasted seeds; dried squid; and just about any salty, chewy food makes up the snack world.

Tea, various infusions of seeds or herbs (particularly lotus roots or seeds), soft drinks, and beer (usually drunk with ice) are consumed throughout the country, with beer (including the artisanal variety *bia hoi*) edging out the other drinks in terms of popularity among men in the South. Everyone drinks water, preferably rainwater collected in large earthenware jars. Water is also consumed from local ponds and streams, although much of it carries a heavy parasitic load.

Holiday Food

While rice is the "pearl of heaven," plain cooked rice is not a prestige food. Celebratory foods gain their prestige because of the limited availability of their ingredients or the difficulty of their preparation. Often rice flour cooked into sheets is the basis for delicate preparations, or pounded rice is used to make sumptuous cakes filled with bean paste, pork, or other delicacies. The principal holiday is Tet, the Vietnamese lunar New Year; it usually occurs in February. A child's first birthday (at which time he or she is considered to be two years old) is celebrated to mark survival of the perilous first year of life, when many infants die. Foods common in Vietnamese restaurants in the United States, such as *cha gio*, which require a lot of preparation, are normally reserved for Tet and first-year celebrations. Coca-Cola (seemingly the only U.S. contribution to Vietnamese cuisine) or beer are the accompanying beverages of choice. Urban birthday meals include colored rice cakes and purchased French layer cake with frosting. And the urban way of celebrating a wedding is to take the entire extended family and other guests to a Chinese restaurant. There eight to ten courses of meat, fish, and poultry, and very little rice, are served.

Regional Variation

The North of Vietnam, with its colder climate and proximity to China, is the home of *pho*, the famous beef broth with noodles and thin slices of meat. Accompanying herbs such as mint, basil, green onions, and bean sprouts grow in the northern climate. Grilled meat and stir-frying are more common food-preparation methods here. There are fewer vegetables and fruits available.

Central Vietnam has an important historical heritage that adds chili peppers, other spices and characteristic presentation style to the cuisine. A "kingly" table consisted of many small dishes instead of a common bowl, which is the "common" (and ubiquitous) way to serve the family. The cuisine of Hue, the ancient capital, is also more seasonal than in the North or South, reflecting not only the availability of vegetables, fruits, fowl, and seafood, but the humoral qualities of people at this time of year as well as the food. The sweet pudding *chè*, usually made with beans or lotus seeds, hails from this region.

The South's hot and humid climate produces a year-round, changing supply of vegetables, fruits, and livestock. The South is also the social pressure cooker of Vietnam, with a fourteenth-century origin as an Indianized Khmer region, followed by Vietnamese sovereignty in the eighteenth century. The French occupied the region from the nineteenth through the middle of the twentieth century, when the Vietnamese took power again. Dishes such as *bánh xèo* have been described as a Vietnamese crepe, or an Indian *dhosa*, depending on how far

Women taking breakfast in front of their house in Vietnam. Socializing with neighhbors is an important feature of this early morning meal. © JOHN R. JONES; PAPILIO/CORBIS

Laotian serving basket for sticky rice. Laos, ca. 1975. Reed grass on wooden base. This server holds enough sticky rice for one person. The rice is eaten with the fingers instead of using chopsticks. These baskets are also made in regions of Vietnam and Thailand that border on Laos. ROUGHWOOD COLLECTION. PHOTO CHEW & COMPANY.

back in time the form is thought to have originated. Curries, asparagus, avocado, little white potatoes, French bread, and mayonnaise all make their way to the table in Ho Chi Minh City (formerly Saigon). Many dishes combine fish with vegetables or sour fruits, such as tamarind or pineapple. And "pâté" can refer to anything from a mixture of ground pork used to fill the famous Vietnamese spring roll (*cha gio*) to a shrimp paste spread on French bread.

The hill tribes of Vietnam, such as the Hmong, are fewer in number today due to their collaboration with South Vietnamese and U.S. forces during the Vietnam War; many were evacuated to the United States at the end of the war. Tribal groups, however, respect national borders less than altitude, and move somewhat freely between Thailand, Laos, and Vietnam. They practice slash-and-burn agriculture, raise and consume pigs, and prefer glutinous (sticky) rice, which can be eaten with the fingers, to the long-grain variety preferred by lowlanders, which is always consumed in a small bowl with chopsticks. They trade the products of poppies (seeds; opium)

and their renowned silverwork and embroidery for food products from the lowland areas.

It is impossible to not mention that millions of Vietnamese, highland and lowland alike, have known starvation throughout their history. Vietnam's struggle with the Chinese, with the French, with Japanese occupiers at the end of World War II, and with the Americans have resulted for varying periods in outright food shortages or broken distribution systems. Ho Chi Minh was able to gain support for his version of communism in part because of inequalities in the rice trade and widespread hunger in the North. The colonial system introduced many French delicacies to urbanites, but the rural poor subsisted on what they could grow on rented plots or fish from the irrigation canals of the plantations on which they worked for minimal wages.

Global economic downturns aside, Vietnam in the early twenty-first century appears to be well on the way to a stable economy. North-South differences in cuisine are still distinctive, even though the country has been unified since 1977. The hotel restaurant training school in Hanoi is bustling with noontime clients daily, with avocados and French onion soup prominent on the menu. Tens of thousands of Vietnamese now live outside the country, with most settled in the United States, Australia, France, and Canada. Expatriate Vietnamese have brought their cuisine to these countries, where it continues to evolve, incorporating a few local items into the rich Vietnamese culinary inventory.

See also **Buddhism**; **China**; **Fasting and Abstinence: Buddhism and Hinduism**; **Rice**.

BIBLIOGRAPHY

Fishman, Claudia. "Vietnamese Families in Philadelphia, an Analysis of Household Food Decisions and Dietary Outcomes for Vietnamese Women and Children Living in Philadelphia: 1980–1984." Dissertation in Anthropology, University of Pennsylvania. University Microfilms, Ann Arbor, Mich., 1986.

Fishman, Claudia, R. Evans, and E. Jenks. "Warm Bodies, Cool Milk: Conflicts in Post Partum Food Choice for Indochinese Women in California." *Social Science Medicine*, 1988, 26(11):1125–1132.

Ha, D. B. *An Uong va Suc Khoe (Nutrition and Health)*. Garden Grove, Calif.: VCP Printing, 1981.

Hickey, Gerald C. *Village in Vietnam*. New Haven: Yale University Press, 1964.

Manderson, L., and M. Mathews. "Vietnamese Behavioral and Dietary Precautions during Pregnancy." *Ecol. Food and Nutr.* (1981): 11:1–8.

Sterling, Richard. *Vietnam (World Food* series). Hawthorne, Victoria, Australia: Lonely Planet, 2000.

Tran, V. "Nutritional Value and Composition of Foodstuffs of the Diet of the Vietnamese Rural Adult." *American Journal of Clinical Nutrition*, 24 (1971): 38.

Claudia C. Parvanta

SOUTH PACIFIC. *See* **Pacific Ocean Societies.**

SOUTHWEST, THE (UNITED STATES). *See* **United States.**

SOY. The symbiosis between the soy plant and Rhizobium bacteria in the soil underlies the soybean's success as a major source of protein for human populations in Asia and domesticated animals in many countries, as well as an important renewer of land fertility in traditional agriculture. Rhizombium bacteria enter the root hairs of the soy plant (and those of other legumes), helping to form nodules where they feed on the plant's carbon supply. In exchange, the bacteria convert atomospheric nitrogen gas in the soil to ammonium, rendering the nitrogen accessible to the soy plant for use in protein synthesis. The resulting soybean is high in amino acids in ratios that make it, when compared to other known plant sources of protein, strikingly "complete" as a human food. Additional benefits are imparted when legumes such as soy decay. Bioavailable nitrogen is released into the soil, becoming accessible to other plants that lack symbiotic relationships with nitrogen fixing bacteria. Soy and other legumes have therefore played a crucial role in crop–rotation farming, contributing to the growth of other crops and pasturelands. Soybeans are also high in oil content, and in the latter twentieth century became the world's top source of edible oil.

Physical Characteristics of the Soy Plant

Erect and bushy, the soybean plant can grow to over six feet high. It has ovate leaflets in groups of three; white, purple, or pinkish self–fertilizing flowers; and one to five beans in each pod. As with other legumes, at maturity the pod bursts open on both sides to expose the beans. Beans range in size from 1 to 3.5 centimeters or more and can be yellow, green, brown, black, reddish, or bicolored; their variations offer mute testimony to generations of selective breeding. The beans are 15 to 20 percent oil, and 35 to 45 percent protein, depending on the variety and farming conditions.

Timing of the soy plant's maturation is highly sensitive to day length; each variety requires a specific span of darkness to induce flowering. Known as photoperiodicity, this phenomenon makes the optimal choices of varieties different for each latitude where soybeans are grown. Soy's extreme photoperiodicity, along with its vulnerability to frost, probably slowed the early spread of its cultivation in China. Under the right conditions for any given variety, however, soy is a reliable crop that tolerates poorer soils. For this reason, in ancient China it was deemed invaluable as protection against famine should other crops fail.

Soy also has nutritional virtues beyond its protein and oil. Although their nutritional value varies with the growing conditions, in general the beans provide modest levels of vitamin A, vitamin E, thiamine, riboflavin, other B–complex vitamins, potassium, phosphorus, magnesium, calcium, and iron.

Origins, Domestication, and Diffusion of Soy

The soybean, *Glycine max*, is a cultigen that apparently does not exist in the wild. Botanists believe its wild ancestor was *Glycine ussuriensis*, a vine native to Taiwan, Korea, Japan, the north–central and far northern areas of eastern China, and adjacent areas of Russia. Chinese legend has it that sometime between about 2800 and 2400 B.C.E., the Emperor Shen Nung, father of Chinese agriculture, first extolled the virtues of the soybean in writing. Contemporary sinologists believe, however, that Shen Nung's famous treatise—indeed, Shen Nung himself—are the inventions of a much later era. As Theodore Hymowitz details in his "On the Domestication of the Soybean," botanical, archaeological, and linguistic research suggest instead that the trial-and-error process of domesticating soy began during the Shang Dynasty (circa 1600 B.C.E.–1027 B.C.E.), and that *Glycine max* did not emerge as a successful domesticate until the eleventh century B.C.E., probably in the north-central section of eastern China.

Soy cultivation gradually spread; evidence suggests that by the first century C.E., it had reached northern Manchuria, Korea, central and south China, and northern Vietnam. The expansion and contraction of Chinese dynasties was probably instrumental in this spread, as were the activities of Buddhist missionaries, who encouraged soybean cultivation as an expression of their vegetarianism. Buddhists were also the likely agents of early soy cultivation in Japan, beginning around the sixth century C.E. The emigration of ethnic Thais from China during the seventh century C.E. spread soy agriculture to present-day Thailand; traffic along the Silk Road brought soy to the northern Indian subcontinent in the eleventh and twelfth centuries. Between the first century C.E. and the sixteenth, soy was also introduced to Indonesia, the Philippines, Malaysia, Burma, and Nepal.

In the twentieth century, the bulk of the world's soybean production shifted to the New World. Although soy was first cultivated in what is now the United States in 1765, it was not a leading U.S. crop until World War II. In the 1970s, South American nations also began expanding soy production. Today the primary growers are the United States, which produces about half the world's supply, Brazil, China, and Argentina.

Developments in Soy Agriculture— Demand and Supply

Demand. Unless adequately processed, mature soybeans are difficult for humans to digest and contain antinutritive components. In early centuries, the Chinese considered soybeans important yet undesirable—poor man's food. But once they learned to make palatable and nutritious processed soy products, beginning around the third century B.C.E., demand for soy increased. For centuries, however, the demand for soybeans in Asia had little influence elsewhere.

In the 1920s, soy oil was used in the United States for industrial purposes; by the late 1930s, research was improving its flavor for American palates. At that time, the oil was lucrative; the protein meal was a cheap by-product fed to animals. During World War II, with imports of foreign vegetable oils cut off, the U.S. government promoted a huge expansion of soybean harvesting. Although the oil commanded a higher price per pound, the enormous surplus of meal came to provide more overall profits as Americans—and gradually people in developed countries worldwide—began to eat far more meat than ever before.

Today some 95 percent of the soy meal used in the United States is consumed by meat-, egg- or dairy-producing animals. This pattern is repeated in numerous countries that import soy from the United States, such as Mexico and in Europe. Even in Japan, where soy protein is an integral part of human diets, more soy is used for animal feed than for human consumption.

Supply. Early in the twentieth century, the development of tractors and combines made profitable, large-scale soy farming possible in America. A system was developed for storing soybeans at the right conditions of temperature and moisture at processing plants and in giant grain elevators; the Mississippi River became a crucial artery for soy exports. Soy agriculture worldwide has benefited as well from research on managing pests and diseases, including programs for breeding pest-resistant varieties.

Breeding programs have also been critical to the success of soy farming in varying growing conditions and for various desired traits (for example, higher oil or protein content), beginning with Asian farmers' patient work over centuries. More recently, plant breeders developed varieties tolerant of equatorial latitudes, making cultivation of soy in tropical Brazil profitable.

Since 1996, soy genetically modified with a gene from bacteria has become popular among farmers in the United States and Argentina. This soy is engineered to tolerate the Monsanto company's herbicide, Roundup, enabling farmers to use the herbicide easily without killing their crop. In the year 2000, over 50 percent of soy acreage in the United States was planted with "Roundup Ready" (RR) soy; it is currently the most grown genetically modified (GM) crop in the world.

RR soy is present in minute quantities in a wide array of American processed foods. Nutritionist critics worry that it could provoke allergic reactions in sensitive individuals, although to date there is virtually no scientific evidence of such a problem. Environmentalists fear that the gene for resistance to Roundup could "jump" to other plants, creating superweeds. Although some scien-

Crates of tofu (soybean curd) await shipping in Kyoto, Japan. Water hoses are used to keep the tofu moist until it is delivered. © MICHAEL S. YAMASHITA/CORBIS.

tific evidence may support this concern, so far the problem has not materialized. Prestigious organizations such as the National Academy of Sciences have called for more government supervision of GM crops, however. There is, as well, a small but growing market for organic, non–GM soy used to make foods high in soy protein ("soyfoods"), both in the United States and in other developed nations.

Modern Trade in Soy

In the early twentieth century, Europe and the United States imported Manchurian soybeans for oil. Beginning in 1930, however, tariffs protected the American soybean industry. Gradually, soybeans (whole, as meal, and as oil) became the America's primary agricultural export; currently almost half the U.S. crop is sent abroad. This trade is controlled by a handful of powerful international grain companies. The expansion of U.S. (and Argentine) soy exports for human consumption is, however, hampered by concern in Europe (and to a lesser extent Japan) over the safety of GM soy; Brazilian soy is often preferred in these markets. Meanwhile, U.S. soy is making major inroads in the Chinese market, particularly with the entry of China into the World Trade Organization.

Processing Soy for Different Cuisines

Processing whole soy. In Asia, soy is prepared in many forms. Immature soybeans simmered in their pods (Japanese *edamame*) and sprouts from soybeans germinated in darkness are two vegetable uses. Soymilk is made by adding water to the beans, grinding and heating them, and filtering out the "milk"; in recent decades it has become quite popular in parts of Asia as a noncarbonated soft drink. Yuba is the thin protein film that forms on the surface of hot soymilk; skimmed off and sold in sheets, it is a delicacy in China and Japan. Tofu is made by curdling hot soymilk with a salt or acid coagulant and then pressing the whey out of the curd. Subsequent processing

Farm workers grading soybeans by hand in Vietnam, 1997. © TIM PAGE/CORBIS.

of tofu can include freezing, freeze-drying, deep-frying, or grilling, yielding different textures, flavors, and nutrient profiles. Okara is the pulp that remains after filtration of soymilk. It can be pickled or cooked with meat in stews. Soynuts are whole roasted soybeans consumed as a snack; when ground into a powder, they are used in pastry-making (China, Japan) or eaten with rice (Japan, Indonesia).

Asian societies have also developed many fermented soy products, including fermented tofu (sufu, or "Chinese cheese") and fermented okara. Fermentation increases soy's digestibility, preserves soy for long periods, and, crucially, provides flavoring to stimulate the appetite. Many fermentation processes use *Aspergillus* fungi, salt-loving yeasts, and lactic acid bacteria. Products include soy paste fermented with or without wheat, barley, or rice (for example, jiang in China; red, white, yellow, or brown miso in Japan); soy sauce, which is made from soy and wheat (either by fermentation or chemically); fermented soy nuggets ("salted black beans"); tempeh, an Indonesian soy cake fermented with *Rhizopus* mold, served as a main dish, and—when prepared in the traditional manner—often high in vitamin B_{12} from bacteria exposure during processing; and natto, a sweet, slippery, bacteria–fermented Japanese soybean dish served with soy sauce, mustard, and rice for breakfast or dinner.

In North America there is a small but growing market for soy products. Among those made from whole soybeans, the popularity of flavored soymilks and tofu is complemented by the marketing to vegetarians and health-conscious consumers of Western-style soyfoods such as soy yogurt, frozen soy desserts, and (unfermented) imitation cheese made from soy. In addition, full-fat soy flour is widely used commercially to bleach wheat flour and to condition doughs for Western-style breads.

Processing soy oil. Oil is extracted from soybeans either via chemical solvents such as hexane (the modern technique usually employed in developed countries) or by screw press (a lower-yield technique used at small extraction plants worldwide). Large processors refine the oil using techniques developed beginning in the 1940s. The removal of lecithin (itself used in many food applications—for instance as an emulsifier in chocolates) and other impurities is followed by bleaching and deodorization. The oil is then ready for use in salads and for home cooking. If hydrogenation is performed to enhance solidity and shelf life, soy oil can be blended with other oils to make margarine stock or shortening, including shortening for commercial deep-fat frying. Soy oil is also widely used in American prepared salad dressings and mayonnaises. Indeed, in the United States soy is by far the most commonly used oil in each of these applications. It is becoming increasingly popular worldwide because of its cheap price and high quality.

Processing defatted soy protein. Use of defatted soy protein has gone hand in hand with the development of large-scale hexane extraction of oil from the beans. Hexane, an organic solvent, dissolves the oil, thereby separating it from the soy protein. The hexane is then steamed out of the protein. Once desolventized, the protein is suitable for further refinement and processing into food-grade soy flakes, grits, defatted flour, concentrates (containing at least 70 percent protein), and isolates (containing at least 90 percent protein). Such products are used (1) in very small quantities as "functional" ingredients to improve the textures of a vast array of processed foods, including baked goods, soups, whipped toppings, and lunch meats; (2) as meat extenders in dishes for institutions such as schools and the armed forces; (3) as nutrition enhancers in products touted for their health benefits, such as protein-fortified breakfast cereals, weight-loss beverages, and "energy bars"; and (4) as the primary ingredient in dairy and meat substitutes ("analogs"). While some brands of dairy analogs are made directly from whole soybeans, others are made from defatted soy protein ingredients (or both). Those using defatted soy protein include some imitation cheeses, some frozen soy desserts, and soy infant formulas. American-style meat analogs, pioneered by scientists working for Henry Ford and by vegetarian Seventh Day Adventists, include soy burgers, steaks, "chicken," hot dogs, sausage, "bacon" bits, and lunch meats.

National Differences in Amounts of Soy Protein Consumed

Data from the United Nations Food and Agriculture Organization indicate that in 1999, North Koreans derived more daily protein per capita from soy than people in any other country (9.4 grams), followed by the Japanese (8.7 grams), Indonesians (7.2 grams), South Koreans (6.5 grams), and Chinese (5.1 grams). The many thousands of small tofu shops scattered throughout Japan, similar to bakeries in France, illustrate the dietary and cultural importance of soy protein to that society.

The rest of the world for which data are available had much lower rates of consumption in 1999, although some developing countries (for example, Libya, Uganda, Nigeria, and Costa Rica) have significantly increased their consumption in recent years. Average U.S. daily intake during that year was tiny but growing rapidly. Market studies suggest that soyfood sales are currently increasing at a rate of 30 percent per year in the United States.

Research on Soy's Health Benefits

Soy is the only commonly eaten food containing high levels of isoflavones—compounds similar to human estrogen that have hormonelike effects. In the past decade, hundreds of scientific studies have examined the potential of isoflavones and other components of soy to reduce cancer risks, reverse tumor growth, prevent osteoporosis, mitigate unpleasant symptoms of menopause, and decrease the risk of heart disease. Findings in many areas are still equivocal, but results have been promising with regard to prostate cancer and, especially, heart disease. In 1999, the U.S. Food and Drug Administration permitted manufacturers of foods meeting certain criteria to make claims on food labels linking consumption of soy protein to a potentially reduced risk of heart disease.

Ironically, while soy protein holds promise as a disease-fighting food of the future, and although natural, unhydrogenated soy oil has healthful properties, the hundreds of millions of pounds of hydrogenated soy oil used yearly in the United States to deep-fry fast foods contribute to high cholesterol levels and a national epidemic of obesity.

Future Directions for Soy

Many new varieties of soy are being developed, as conventional breeders and biotechnology companies focus on improving soy to benefit not only farmers, but also processors and consumers. Desired characteristics include improved shelf life and flavor of the oil; enhanced functional qualities of the oil for commercial food processing; improved nutritional profile for the oil or the protein; elimination of antinutritive elements and flatulence causing compounds; and reduction of soy's "beany" flavor. The new varieties are in differing stages of development; for some strains, the economic motivator is the improvement of animal feed or even the mitigation of environmental pollution caused by waste from animals fed conventional varieties. But much of the research has potential application to human foods.

Cultivating soybeans as a protein source for human foods is a significantly more efficient way to provide a population with protein than is raising mammals for meat: in the late 1990s, a pig raised in the United States required over three pounds of feed to produce a single pound of meat; a chicken required about two pounds. For this reason, soy has much greater potential than meat to provide critical protein to the world's hungry. The only flesh foods that currently approach soy's efficiency for protein production are farmed fish.

Development workers have labored, with varying degrees of success, to introduce soybeans into the cuisines of protein-deficient populations. For example, the International Soybean Program (INTSOY) of the University of Illinois has worked extensively in Egypt, the U.S. Peace Corps has introduced soyfoods in Malawi, and the Mennonite Central Committee has had a long-term soyfoods project in Bangladesh. Since according to United Nations estimates world population will grow by some four billion in the twenty-first century, such efforts will surely increase.

See also **China**; **Dairy Products**; **Genetic Engineering**; **Japan: Traditional Japanese Cuisine**; **Vegetarianism**.

BIBLIOGRAPHY

Carter, T. E., Jr., and S. Shanmugasundaram. "Vegetable Soybean (Glycine)." In *Pulses and Vegetable*, edited by J. T. Williams. New York: Chapman & Hall, 1993. Discusses soy, including such agronomic characteristics as photoperiodicity.

Du Bois, Christine M. "A Specific Legume Case: History of Soy and Soy Protein Products in the USA." Presentation for the Johns Hopkins University Center for a Livable Future's "Dietary Protein: Options for the Future" conference, 2001. Published online with references and bibliography available at http://www.jhsph.edu/environment/CLF_conferences/Dietary_Feb01.html.

Food and Agriculture Organization of the United Nations. www.fao.org. "Food Balance Sheets" indicating consumption levels can be found in the "Statistical Databases" section available at http://apps.fao.org/.

Huang, Hsing-Tsung. *Fermentations and Food Science.* Volume 6, Part 5 of *Science and Civilisation in China*, edited by Joseph Needham. Cambridge, U.K.: Cambridge University Press, 2000. This volume contains 86 pages on the history of soyfoods in China, drawing on literary texts, archaeology, and comparisons with present-day techniques.

Hymowitz, Theodore. "On the Domestication of the Soybean." *Economic Botany* 24 (1970): 408–421. Uses genetic data, literary sources, and archaeology to trace the history of soy's domestication. Available online at http://www.nsrl.uiuc.edu/GeneralInfo/historybeans.html.

Hymowitz, Theodore, and C. A. Newell. "Taxonomy of the Genus Glycine, Domestication and Uses of Soybeans." *Economic Botany* 35(3) (1981): 272–288. Covers history of taxonomic research and deliberations, domestication and diffusion of soybeans, and food uses in Asia and the West.

Johnson, L A., D. J. Myers, and D. J. Burden. "Soy Protein's History, Prospects in Food, Feed." *International News on Fats, Oils, and Related Materials* 3(4) (1992): 429–444. History of how soy protein has been used in the West.

Liu, KeShun. *Soybeans: Chemistry, Technology, and Utilization.* New York: Chapman & Hall, 1997. Covers agronomy; marketing; biochemistry; nutrition and health benefits; storage; preparation of Asian and Western soyfoods; genetic engineering.

Mintz, Sidney W., and Chee Beng Tan. "Bean-curd Consumption in Hong Kong." *Ethnology* 40(2) (2001): 113–128. Ethnographic survey. Details types of bean curd and related products, their production and retailing, and consumption patterns.

Shurtleff, William, and Akiko Aoyagi. *The Book of Tofu.* New York: Ballantine Books, 1979. Revised edition. Covers history, cultural importance, processing techniques, and recipes for tofu, okara, soymilk, and yuba.

Soya & Oilseed Bluebook. Bar Harbor, Maine: Soyatech, Inc., 2000. Annual directory of companies in soy and other oilseed industries.

Warnken, Philip F. *The Development and Growth of the Soybean Industry in Brazil.* Ames, Iowa: Iowa State University Press, 1999. Covers place of soy in the overall economy, production trends and programs, and future directions.

World Soybean Research Conference VI Proceedings. Chicago, Ill.: University of Illinois, Urbana–Champaign and Soybean Research & Development Council, 1999. Compiled by Harold E. Kauffman. Covers the state of soybean industries worldwide; biotechnology; breeding; and health issues.

Christine Madeleine Du Bois
Sidney W. Mintz

SPAIN. *See* **Iberian Peninsula.**

SPICES. *See* **Herbs and Spices.**

SPIRITS. Distillation is the process of separating a liquid from a solid by boiling the liquid and condensing the vapors in another container to reform the liquid. The solid material that did not boil off is left behind. To the alchemist, the essence—or the spirit—of the thing was in the condensed vapors.

One can observe distillation in action when the steam from a teakettle condenses on a surface, such as the side of a refrigerator. The products of the distillation are the drops of water on white enamel and the mineral sludge that is left in the bottom of the kettle. (The word "distillation" is derived from the Latin *distillare*, 'to drip', and modern Italian retains the sense of the word as a 'concentration of the essentials'.)

Distillation can also be used to sort out mixtures of liquids that have different boiling points. If a mixture of alcohol and water is heated to more than 174°F but less than 212°F, the alcohol will boil and the water will not. If the vapors from the boiling are condensed and the condensate is collected, the collecting vessel will contain alcohol and the original cooking pot will contain water.

Imagine that the teakettle on the stove contains some boiling wine. (Wine is essentially a mixture of alcohol and water, the alcohol being derived from fermentation, by yeast, of the sugar in the grape juice.) If the temperature is kept below 212°F, the substance that boiled off would be mostly alcohol.

The social ramifications of absinthe and its powerful mind-altering effects were captured in this painting of a late–nineteenth-century Paris café by Edgar Degas (1834–1917). © MUSÉE D'ORSAY, PARIS/ART RESOURCE

The simplest kind of alcoholic distilling apparatus is not much different from a teakettle. It is called a pot still, and it consists of a kettle loaded with a mixture of alcohol and water. The alcoholic steam, however, is not released into the air. Instead, the steam leaves the boiling chamber and goes into a long, downward-spiraling tube, where it cools and condenses back into a liquid. This liquid, called the distillate, is a mixture of alcohol, water, and substances called congeners, which are by-products of fermentation. However, as the alcohol evaporates, the boiling temperature of the mixture rises, and by the end of the batch, a lot of water vapor has boiled off and been condensed along with the alcohol. Thus, the by-products of fermentation—congeners—end up in the distillate. In the twelfth century an Italian physician, Salernus, discovered that the cooling action could be facilitated by spraying the tube with cold water or building an external tube through which a stream of cold water could flow.

Historically, there has been no liquid that is at once as ordinary and as precious as wine. Arnold de Vila Nova, a thirteenth-century alchemist, wrote of distilled wine

ABSINTHE

Ancestor of anise-based pastis, absinthe was the most popular and most notorious liquor in the nineteenth century, and possibly this combination of traits served to establish its reputation as the most notorious in history. Finally banned by the French government in 1915 because it was considered so harmful to one's health—it was 72 percent alcohol, or 144 proof—absinthe is inextricably linked to the artistic and literary life of Paris during the second half of the nineteenth century.

A favorite drink of Henri de Toulouse-Lautrec, Vincent van Gogh, Arthur Rimbaud, and Paul Verlaine, absinthe was popularized by French soldiers returning from Algeria in the 1830s. While stationed there, they had been prescribed the plant-based alcohol as an antiviral, antifever remedy, which they mixed in their drinking water. Upon returning to France, their taste for "*la fée verte*" (the green fairy), so named because of the drink's yellowish-green hue, soon spread throughout France to the general public, who sipped it sweetened with a lump of sugar in cafés. Crossing socioeconomic as well as gender lines, absinthe was enjoyed by all, from the top-hatted, well-fed factory owner to the penniless, tubercular laundress.

Absinthe was generally sipped as an aperitif between 5 o'clock and 7 o'clock in the evening. But those who were addicted drank it at any hour of the day, often consuming up to a dozen glasses in a single day. Part of the appeal of absinthe surely stemmed from the ritual surrounding its consumption. Unlike cognac, whiskey, gin, or eau-de-vie, which were imbibed in ordinary, shot-type glasses, absinthe was enjoyed in stemware designed expressly for the liquor. With an elongated cup measuring about four inches in height, the narrow, footed glass had a small depression at the bottom used to measure a dose of absinthe.

The liquor itself was clear, but when mixed with water, which was the customary way of drinking it, it turned cloudy and opalescent. First the absinthe was poured into a glass, and a perforated spoon was laid across the rim of the glass. Onto this spoon a lump of sugar was placed. Water was poured slowly over the sugar, which would melt into the glass and sweeten the drink. The long-handled spoon would then be used to stir the contents of the glass, at which point the drink turned cloudy.

With the increasing industrialization of alcohol as the century wore on and the subsequent lowering of prices, alcohol consumption of all kinds rose rapidly in France, making it the most "alcoholic" of all nations in the world by the end of the nineteenth century. Absinthe came under attack by the French Temperance Society and was the only alcoholic beverage officially banned in France. But the ban referred only to consumption and not to production, and in the late twentieth century some distilleries resumed production, but for export purposes only.

By the early twenty-first century about thirty brands of so-called absinthe were produced in countries where production was still legal. In addition to France, the Czech Republic, Bulgaria, and Spain distilled it. The Old Absinthe House in New Orleans, with its great, ornate water fountain in the center of the room, is a vestige of America's absinthe culture, which was introduced by the Louisiana French. After enjoying a certain degree of popularity at the turn of the century, the drink was banned in the United States in 1914, around the time most European countries also made it illegal.

The world's only absinthe museum (Le Musée de l'Absinthe), owned and operated by Marie-Claude Delahaye, is in Auvers-sur-Oise, France, an hour from Paris in the village where Van Gogh died and is buried. The tiny museum displays authentic glasses, spoons, absinthe fountains, and bottles with period posters advertising various brands of this unique liquor.

BIBLIOGRAPHY
See also Barnaby Conrad III, *Absinthe: History in a Bottle* (San Francisco: Chronicle Books, 1988); and Wilfred Niels Arnold, *Vincent van Gogh: Chemicals, Crises, and Creativity* (Boston: Birkhäuser, 1992).

Alexandra Leaf

and its restorative properties, calling it *aqua vitae* or "water of life." Chinese sources from about the same time mention a "wine" that could be ignited.

The chronology of distilling is not settled firmly, for there is archaeological evidence that the Minoans and Egyptians practiced distillation, which may suggest a very early understanding of the process. It can be said with certainty that by the fifteenth century distillation had spread across Europe. Every region that had sufficient wood to fire a still developed a distilled version of its own wine or beer.

The simple still described by Salernus, called an "alembic" or pot still, was refined to permit redistillation and continuous loading and operation. The modern column still is capable of producing an almost pure and relatively tasteless alcohol.

The "Ohio Whisky War" made national headlines when the women of Logan, Ohio, carried the cause of Temperance to the doorsteps of local taverns. They are shown here singing Temperance hymns. From *Frank Leslie's Illustrated Newspaper,* 21 February 1874. ROUGHWOOD COLLECTION.

All of these early alcoholic substances were taken as medicines, if they were consumed at all, or were used to dissolve medicinal ingredients. They probably tasted unbearably harsh unless moderated with a dosage of sugar (another medieval novelty). It would be a century or two before refinements in the distillation process and the introduction of aging produced spirits that could be consumed in a pure form.

Aging

When spirits age in wooden barrels, maturation results from an interaction of the original mix of alcohol and congeners with the wood and the small amount of oxygen that enters the barrel. The more intense the original flavors, the greater need there is to moderate the effects of wood and air. Once spirits are removed from

the breathable casks and put into bottles, no further maturation takes place. A bottle of ten-year-old rum purchased five years ago is still ten years old on the inside.

In the United States, small, new oak barrels are the norm for aging sprits in this manner. The wood has lots of extract to contribute to the finished flavor. Scotch whiskey, cognac, and rum are typically aged in older, larger barrels that have less oak flavor. When they were new, these barrels may have been used for storing wine.

Some governments specify storage time for spirits. The United States and Canada require a two-year storage period for most whiskey. Scotland and England mandate three years and Ireland five. Aging is never required for gin and vodka: In the case of these spirits, the problem of harsh flavors is addressed through precise column distillation and charcoal filtration. Brandies are typically aged for three to five years, but some are held in cask for twenty-five years or more.

Aging in dry warehouses promotes the evaporation of water, thereby increasing the alcohol content; humid storage encourages the opposite. After aging, spirits are diluted to the strength at which they will be sold, blended to achieve their final taste profile, and colored for uniform appearance.

Alcohol

Ethyl alcohol is the natural by-product of yeast acting on sugar in a water solution. This process is called fermentation, and it proceeds until either the yeast runs out of sugar, the alcohol concentration rises to the point where the yeast can no longer work, or the fermentation is artificially halted. The alcohol that most people drink is an organic chemical, C_2H_5OH. In 1536 the German alchemist Paracelcus first used the word "alcohol" in its modern sense.

Of great concern to alcohol producers and consumers is "how much alcohol is in this drink?" In the United States, containers of spirits are required to display the alcohol concentration of the drink as a percentage by volume. Alternatively, the strength of alcohol can be expressed as "proof," which is twice the percentage by volume: for example, 100-proof spirits are 50 percent alcohol by volume.

Alcohol and the brain. There are two reasons that alcohol has been so popular for so long. The first is that aside from wine or beer, alcohol was one of the few drinks upon which early civilized humankind could rely. A large sedentary population pollutes its own streams and ground water, deadly typhoid and cholera bacteria thrived in drinking water. Milk was unreliable and, for many adults, not digestible. Fruit juice, in the days before preservatives, was either turned into vinegar through bacterial activity or turned into wine by fermenting through its own yeasts. Only wine, which does not support any bacteria harmful to man, was consistently safe for consumption.

In places where grapevines did not grow, a hot-water extract of sprouted barley grains was used to make alcoholic beverages. The heating process activated enzymes that converted starch to sugar and sanitized the water from which it was made. This solution of barley sugar would also ferment in the presence of airborne yeast. When it did ferment, it was called beer. This beer probably did not resemble the modern beverage of the same name, but it was certainly safer to drink than water.

Of course, ancient cultures did know of other technologies that could have possibly sanitized the beverage supply. For example, the Chinese boiled water and infused it with herbs as both a culinary and sanitary device. However, the manufacture of alcoholic beverages triumphed over all of them for reasons that had nothing to do with sanitation. Alcohol's ability to demolish inhibi-

tions, inspire enthusiasm, and encourage sociability lies at the heart of and accounts for the transcendence of the beverage business. People drink in company because both the drink and the company become more pleasant in the process.

Prohibition. Like other milestone inventions, alcohol is not entirely a blessing. In addition to the lightened spirits and occasional hilarity of moderate drinking are the recklessness of excessive drinking and drunkenness.

Some people deny some of alcohol's manifest virtues. Many people find the altered state of consciousness that alcohol induces to be threatening. Such a state brings out things in themselves and other people that they would rather not have called forth. People consuming alcohol are more likely to be sexual and boisterous. They are also more likely to be aggressive or otherwise obnoxious.

It is a short step from being repelled by one's own impulses to wishing to eradicate or at least camouflage them in others. In the United States that impulse, coupled with a prejudice against wine- and beer-drinking immigrants, led to the adoption of the Volstead Act in 1919, which made the sale and possession of alcoholic beverages illegal.

Prohibition was the thirteen-year period during which there was no legal beer, wine, (apart from that used in religious services), or spirits consumed in the United States. This movement had profound and lasting effects on the U.S. beverage industry. It changed U.S. tastes and created a nation of whiskey drinkers. Since it is easier to traffic in small volumes of a highly concentrated illegal substance, distilled spirits became more available and more desired.

Brandy

Brandy is a spirit distilled from wine. The source of the wine is usually grapes but it can be derived from any fruit. Dutch and English merchants in the seventeenth century promoted the production of brandy in the areas around the little towns of Cognac and Armagnac. Cognac produced an almost flavorless wine that yielded a relatively clean distilled product. Armagnac had no wine-growing tradition, but it did have large forests to fuel the alembics (used for distillation), as well as local farmers who saw the value of commerce.

Cognac at one time was a fiery, intensely flavored drink that combined complexity and power. It has since been tamed to compete with the smooth whiskeys in the American market, and brandy drinkers looking for intensity increasingly order Armagnac.

Whiskey (Whisky)

Whiskey (Whisky) is distilled from beer, which is itself a fermented drink made by converting the starch of grains into sugar and then introducing yeast. If the conversion process involves sprouting the grain and then toasting it, it is called "malting," and the result can be labeled "malt

COGNAC DECANTERS

Anything as rare and fine as cognac is bound to be surrounded by some paraphernalia. One of the nicest accessories in the liquor business is the lead crystal decanter filled with amber-gold liquid. Set on a white tablecloth, the crystal catches and refracts the room light and turns the cognac ritual into a ballet of sparkles. The colors and the magnificent weight of the decanter make the drink (and by extension, the host) seem very important.

Alas, researchers have discovered that the lead that makes the decanter weighty and sparkly dissolves in the cognac over a period of time and ends up inside the consumer. Unfortunately, this lead is also poisonous.

whisky." If the whisky is bottled unblended as the product of a single malt house, it can legally be called "single malt."

The word "whiskey" or "whisky" is derived from a direct translation into Gaelic (*uisge beatha*) of Vila Nova's *aqua vitae*. It is fitting that a Gaelic word is used here, since the spiritual home of whisky is Scotland and Ireland. The characteristic smoke and iodine flavors that are introduced during the making of the malt have created a peculiar and distinctive spirit that was at the height of fashion at the end of the twentieth century.

It is easy to account for the rise of Scotch whisky in general and single malts in particular: They are both expensive and exotic. Both types of whisky are produced almost by hand, in very small amounts, in two countries to which many Americans have a romantic attachment. Single malts are also expensive and the very epitome of an acquired taste. It is also easy to see the cause of their eventual downfall in the popular mind: They do not taste very good. Often they are described as having a taste between seaweed and peat smoke.

In colonial America, West Indian molasses was abundant, and the coastal drink was rum. Westward expansion after U.S. independence allowed for the cultivation of corn well in advance of a transport system that could carry it cheaply to market. Farmers on the frontier (then in Allegheny County, Pennsylvania) saw rye and corn-based whisky as a condensed and easily transportable cash crop. Their iron-free water supply helped to make that whisky appealing, and tax disputes with the new federal government in 1794 only entrenched the drink as part of an ongoing culture of rebellion.

Bourbon whisky is the product of Kentucky refugees from federal taxation. Their rye crops failed, but their corn whisky, called bourbon after the county where it originated, triumphed. Its cult is threatened only by the generalized decline in the spirits market.

Gin

Gin was the first industrially produced spirit. The same Dutch traders who created cognac developed this continuously produced neutral spirit (one without a flavor characteristic). Gin was distilled from grain through a matrix of crushed juniper berries, called *genever* in Dutch. In England, a government that did not tax grain or distillation encouraged the availability of cheap gin. In the mid-eighteenth century, gin's availability not only undermined local brewing, but it encouraged a wave of drunkenness among the newly urbanized poor that upset the gentry.

Gin remains the spirit of choice in England, where it is mixed with tonic or served "on the rocks" (over ice). In the United States, the martini dominates the gin market. Officially, it is a mixture of gin and vermouth shaken over ice and decanted to a dedicated, triangular martini glass. In practice, the vermouth is vestigial and save for differences in serving temperature and glassware, the martini is not much different from the plain gin that scandalized Georgian London.

Vodka

The key to vodka-making is the charcoal filtering of the distillate to remove any traces of flavor. The original starch that supplies the sugar for fermentation can come from grain, potatoes, or even directly from sugar itself.

Vodka is defined in U.S. law as a flavorless beverage, but that has not stopped the marketing of more and more expensive "flavorless" vodkas or the development of an army of flavored variations. One brand, Absolut of Sweden, has recognized that in the absence of any real difference, it is important to make distinctions among brands; to this end, the manufacturer has created a long-running ad campaign that presents its distinctively shaped bottles as interpreted by various artists.

Tequila

Young Americans have enthusiastically embraced tequila, an icon of Mexican culture, as a "bad-boy" drink. Cheap tequilas, distilled from pulque, the fermented sap of the blue agave plant, are allowed to contain up to 49 percent alcohol. More expensive versions are wood-aged and based entirely on agave starch. In Mexico there is a delimited tequila district. Any distilled pulque made outside of this area is simply called "mescal."

Rum

Sugar cane was being planted in Puerto Rico, Cuba, and Hispaniola a few years after Columbus arrived. The Spanish had learned about cane when they were an Arab

Nuts Cashew nuts in the market of Guatemala City, Guatemala. © Dave G. Houser/CORBIS.

Top left: **Onions and Other Alliums** A Welsh bunching onion in the Roughwood Seed Collection. Photo by L. Wilbur Zimmerman.

Top right: **Onions and Other Alliums** The earliest color depiction of the poor man's leek or Welsh bunching onion. From *Curtis's Botanical Magazine* (London, 1809). Some of the most accurate depictions of heirloom vegetables can be found in this annual, which is still published today. Roughwood Collection.

Below: **Onions and Other Alliums** Shallots poached in Madeira. Food styling by William Woys Weaver. Photo by André Baranowski.

Top: **Pastry** Marzipan mold depicting fruits and nuts. South German, circa 1750. Collection of Charles Thomas.

Below: **Pastry** A selection of Tuscan pastries. Photo by André Baranowski.

Russia *Merchant's Wife at Tea* (1918) by Russian painter Boris Kustodiev. In this portrait of contented overabundance, Kustodiev depicts all of the symbols of Russian culture. Courtesy of The Russian Museum, St. Petersburg.

Inset: **Russia** Caviar has been considered a luxury food since Byzantine times, although the eggs of several different species of fish have been employed in making it. The black Beluga caviar from sturgeon is the most highly prized by connoisseurs. It is served here Polish style with new potatoes and sour cream. Photo by André Baranowski.

Bottom: **South America** Market scene in Sucre (formerly Chuquisaca), Bolivia. Photo by R. E. Salazar.

Top right: **Tomato** Still life with tomato by Philadelphia painter Raphaelle Peale, circa 1795. This work is noteworthy not only because Peale's painting is one of the earliest depictions of the tomato in American art, but the tomato itself is a rare variety from the Amazon basin. Courtesy of Wadsworth Atheneum, Hartford, Connecticut. The Ella Gallup Sumner and Mary Catlin Sumner Collection Fund.

Top left: **Tomato** Detail of the so-called "Reisetomate" from the former botanical collection of the Duke of Braunschweig. This tomato, depicted in the Peale still life, was collected in Brazil during a botanical expedition in 1836. The Roughwood Seed Collection. Photo by Rob Cardillo.

United States/Pennsylvania Dutch Food Duck Pond at Ronks, Lancaster County, Pennsylvania. A typical Old Order Mennonite farmstead in the heartland of the Pennsylvania Dutch region. Photo by William Woys Weaver.

Top left: **Utensils** The "Colonial Breakfast Skillet" made by the Griswold iron foundry in Erie, Pennsylvania, circa 1910. In this skillet the Victorian idealization of an entire colonial meal was condensed into an iron serving utensil that foreshadowed the TV dinner. Roughwood Collection.

Bottom: **Utensils** Earthenware food vessels from ancient China. From left to right: late Anyang period *jue,* eleventh century B.C.E.; Han Dynasty jar with textile impressions, 206 B.C.E.–220 C.E.; Eastern Han Dynasty spoon, 25–220 C.E.; Machang phase of Majiayao culture jar with snakes, late third millennium B.C.E.; Western Han Dynasty two-handled jar, second century B.C.E.; Western Han Dynasty *ding,* 206 B.C.E.–24 C.E. © Royal Ontario Museum/CORBIS.

Top right: **Wheat** Cypriot family making *trachanás,* cracked wheat cooked in goat's milk, then dried in the sun for use in soups during the winter. Photo by Charalambos Christodoulou.

Wine Rows of bottles of vintage wine in storage, like books on the shelves of an ancient library, or rows of crops ripening before harvest, symbolize both the cultivation and the eventual enjoyment of the fruits of labor. © Charles O'Rear/CORBIS.

colony, and they brought cuttings from the few small cane gardens to these areas from the homeland.

Sugarcane becomes sugar when it is crushed and its juice is extracted. The juice is reduced through boiling, and the sugar then crystallizes. The liquid left behind is called molasses, which contains about 5 percent sugar. Along with the fermentable sugar, this molasses contains the concentrated flavor of the cane itself and the flavor of sugar caramelized during the reduction of the original juice.

Fermented molasses is, with a few exceptions, the raw material of rum. Traditionally, molasses was fermented by wild yeasts in a slow fermentation process that introduced its own complex flavors. This is still the practice for most premium rums. Most modern-day rum is produced by distilling molasses in large column stills that operate continuously. These stills turn out a high-proof, highly refined, and neutral-tasting product that can be as much as 190 proof (95% alcohol). This is the rum that is mixed with three different kinds of fruit juices and served with a little paper umbrella on the edge of the glass. It is sometimes wood aged and sometimes very good. It is certainly an excellent foil for juices and sodas.

A small amount of the world's total rum production is made in pot stills. These stills are loaded with a batch of fermented molasses, which is then distilled at a fairly low 140 to 160 proof (70–80 percent alcohol). The rum is then aged in old wooden barrels. The results are said to rival cognac in complexity.

See also **Beer; Cocktail Party; Cocktails; Fermentation; Fermented Beverages Other than Wine or Beer; Whiskey (Whisky); Wine.**

BIBLIOGRAPHY

Brown, Gordon. *The Whisky Trails: A Traveler's Guide to Scotch Whisky*. London: Trafalgar, 2000.

McCusker, John J., and Russel Menard. "Rum." In *The Economy of British America 1607–1789*. Chapel Hill, N.C.: University of North Carolina Press, 1991.

McGee, Harold. "Distilled Liquors." In *On Food and Cooking*. New York: Macmillan, 1984.

Noorrman, Ola. *Home Distillation Handbook*. Malmoe: Bokforlaget Exakt, 2001.

Root, Waverly, and Richard de Rochemont. "Bourbon." In *Eating in America*. New York: Norton, 1981.

Serjeant, Richard. *A Man May Drink: Aspects of a Pleasure*. London: Putnam, 1964.

Lynn F. Hoffman

SQUASH AND GOURDS. Cucurbitaceae is a highly specialized and unique family of mainly trailing plants of subtropical or tropical, moist or dry habitats. Plants bear mostly palmately lobed, alternate, and simple leaves and have spiraling tendrils. Plants are mostly monoecious with yellow flowers, but sometimes with white petals, and inferior ovaries. The fruits are specialized berries called pepos and are of variable size. Some are among the largest fruits produced by any plant group. Because of their ability to produce large fruits, they lend themselves to competition. By the early twenty-first century the largest recorded fruit, which weighed a phenomenal 1,140 pounds (517 kilograms) was grown by Dave Stelts of Leetonia, Ohio, in 2000.

Plant Descriptions
Cucurbit is a general term used to describe all members of the Cucurbitaceae family, which includes the common vegetables cucumber, melon, and watermelon as well as the focus of this section, squash, pumpkin, and gourd. The common names in the three genera and seven species that represent the subject of this essay overlap considerably.

Products commonly called squash, pumpkin, or gourd are found in four of the seven species. The gourds are the source of least confusion since they are more or less readily identified by appearance regardless of species. Squash and pumpkin are used interchangeably depending on local custom. The sole exception is the decorative or Halloween pumpkin *Cucurbita pepo*, which is always referred to by that name. Defining characteristics of the cultivated *Cucurbita* species are in Table 1. Within squash it is useful to differentiate between summer and winter types. The summer types (yellow, zucchini, or scallop) are fast maturing, have soft rinds, are consumed when the fruit is immature, and are quite perishable. On the other hand, the winter squash take longer to mature, one hundred days versus fifty days, have a long storage life, several months versus two weeks, are consumed when the fruits and seeds are fully mature, and have durable rinds. Any confusion that may exist is among academics who quibble over nomenclature. Retailers, consumers, and cooks generally differentiate among squash, pumpkin, and gourd, and if not little damage is done.

History, Ethnography, and Symbolism of Production and Consumption
The word "pumpkin" is derived from the Old English *pompion* (originally Latin *pepo* and Greek *pepon*) and refers to a large melon or gourd. It was originally applied to the genus *Legenaria* but was later transferred to the New World *Cucurbita*. The more general word "squash" is a derivation of a New England Native American term *"askutasquash,"* meaning vegetables consumed while green, in other words, a summer squash. Cucurbits have cultural and economic significance cross-culturally. Ralf Norrman and Jon Haarberg (1980) examined the symbolic place of cucurbits in Western literature and culture and further extended their analysis to selected non-Western cultural settings. They noted that cucurbits have complex semiotic associations with sex and sexuality, fertility, vitality, moisture, creative power, rapid growth, and sudden death. Cucurbits also figure prominently in the symbolism and cosmologies of many non-Western societies.

TABLE 1

Some defining characteristics of the cultivated *Cucurbita* species

Species	Seed	Leaf	Stem	Peduncle	Fruit flesh
C. argyrosperma	Large, white, prominent margin that may be scalloped	Moderately lobed, short, soft pubescence	Hard, angular	Hard, corky, sometimes swollen	Very coarse, pale yellow
C. ficifolia	Black or tan, smooth margin	Deeply lobed, smooth margin, round, prickly	Hard, grooved	Hard, angled, slightly expanded at fruit attachment	Coarse, stringy, white
C. maxima	White to brown, oblique seed scar	Almost round, unlobed prickly	Soft, round	Round, corky, not flared at fruit attachment	Fine, not fibrous, deep orange
C. moschata	White to brown, rough margin, oblique seed scar	Shallow lobes, almost round, soft pubescence	Hard, ridged	Hard, angled, flared at fruit attachment	Fine, not fibrous, deep orange
C. pepo	Light tan, prominent smooth margin, rounded seed scar	Deeply lobed, very prickly	Hard, ridged	Hard, angled, ridged	Coarse, orange

Squash was domesticated in a variety of New World sites, including central Mexico, Peru, and the eastern United States, as early as 10,000 B.P. (Smith 1997). The more specific timing, locations, and hypothetical dynamics of the domestication processes of the five principal species of domesticated squash are reviewed in a number of texts. Squash, along with maize (corn) and beans, formed the staple carbohydrate cores of Mesoamerican crop complexes that were the basis for state formation in the region (Scarre and Fagan, 1997). These cultigens were also significant food sources for precontact Native Americans in North America. Squash diffused to the Old World after 1492 through the networks of trade, migration, and commodity chains linked to colonialism and the expansion of global capitalism.

Squash is cultivated in the twenty-first century throughout the Americas, Europe, Africa, the Middle East, China, India, and Indonesia. Virtually all parts of domesticated squash, including fruits, seeds, flowers, and leaves, can be eaten. Cross-cultural culinary uses are quite varied. The fruits are typically boiled, sometimes fried or added to soups or curries. Squash is also the basis of candy and fermented beverages in Latin America. The seeds of squash are consumed raw or are cooked in various forms in China, India, and Mexico. Some Native Americans, most notably the Sioux of the Great Plains, traditionally flattened strips of fresh pumpkins, dried them, and made them into mats. Squash seeds are also used in a number of traditional folk medicine applications.

Pumpkins have an important place in the social history, folklore, and cultural symbolism of the United States. In early colonial New England settlers sliced off the tops of pumpkins, removed the seeds, filled the insides with honey, milk, and spices or fruit and then baked

the pumpkin in the hot coals of an open fire. Pumpkins were therefore the crust and not the filling of the early precursors of pumpkin pie. Settlers also used pumpkins in beer, breads, puddings, cookies, and many other foods, including pumpkin sauce, that is, pumpkins stewed with butter, vinegar, and spices. Many of these uses of pumpkins continue in the North American diet in the twenty-first century. The most common nonfood use of pumpkins in the United States is for decorative purposes, including the carving of Halloween jack-o'-lanterns.

Gourds are among the world's oldest domesticated plants, dating back to at least 8000 B.P. Three principal genera of gourds, *Legeneria* (including the bottle gourd), *Trichosanthes* (including the snake gourd), and *Momordica* (including the bitter gourd), originated in the Old World tropics. They have a wide range of economic, symbolic, ritual, and artistic functions cross-culturally. For example, Sally Price, in her ethnographic study of the Saramaka of Suriname, analyzes how elaborately carved and decorated calabashes (in this case the tree gourds *Crescentia cujete*, which are not cucurbits) figure prominently in women's labor, production, artistic expression, ritual exchanges, status, and power relationships in this Maroon society (Price, 1993).

Snake gourds are cultivated in the humid tropics and subtropics of Asia, Latin America, and Africa. The young fruits are consumed boiled or in curries, the stem tips and leaves may also be eaten, and the roots and seeds have a wide range of uses in traditional medicine throughout Southeast Asia. Bitter gourds were domesticated in Asia and diffused to the New World via the transatlantic slave trade. They are popular vegetables throughout India, China, Asia, Africa, the Middle East, Latin America, and the Caribbean. As with snake gourd, the plant is used both as food and in a range of medicinal applications cross-culturally.

Bottle gourd was widely distributed as an early cultigen throughout the New World but is generally believed to be of African origin. It remains unclear as to how the bottle gourd diffused from Africa to the New World, although both human agency and oceanic drift currents have been proposed as mechanisms. Bottle gourd is principally used as a "bottle or container for both liquid and dry materials" (Heiser, 1979, p. 71) but also for food, floats, musical instruments, medicine, artistic expression, and in some cultures penis coverings. Among the Dani, an indigenous culture of highland western New Guinea (Irian Jaya), "from the age of four or five, males wear a *holim* or penis gourd at all times except when urinating or having sexual intercourse" (Heider, 1979, p. 56). Karl Heider notes that each Dani man owns "whole wardrobes of penis gourds of different lengths and shapes . . . and the gourd itself is not a focus or symbol of masculinity or sexuality." In the late twentieth century, Dani men continued to wear penis gourds in public, in defiance of Indonesian government attempts to ban the coverings, as a symbolic resistance to Indonesian state control over the region. In many societies bottle gourds have generally been displaced by the use of plastic and other industrially manufactured materials except in poorer regions or where gourds continue to have local cultural, ritual, or artistic significance.

Horticulture

Squash, pumpkin, and gourd are produced worldwide in temperate, subtropical, and tropical climates. They constitute an important but not life-sustaining part of the diet for many cultures. Production data is probably not reliable because these products do not usually enter into international commerce and are relatively minor in importance. For example, production data became available in the United States for these crops only in 2000. Michigan and New York are the leading producers of decorative pumpkins, and Georgia and Florida are the leading producers of summer squash. The available world data show that in the early twenty-first century Asia was the principal producer of these cucurbits and that China and India accounted for nearly half of the reported world production.

The nutritional value of these cucurbits on the whole is not exceptional since they are mostly water. Pumpkin fruits, flowers, and leaves and winter squash fruits are, however, good sources of vitamin A, which may be scarce in the diets of those in some developing countries. Pumpkin seeds are rich in protein, fat, and carbohydrate but usually are not consumed in large quantities. Many cucurbits are low in fat and carbohydrates, which makes them useful in diets of those concerned with weight control in developed countries.

The principal *Cucurbita* species may be further grouped according to horticultural traits (Table 2). Fruit

The white-flowering *zucca rampicante* (vining gourd) or *zucca a tromba* (trumpet gourd) is an Old World cucurbit (*Lagenaria siceraria*) that has been grown in the Mediterranean region since ancient times. The edible baby gourds, shown here, were known as *zucchette* or *zucchini* in Italian and were the breeding model for the New World squash grown today under the name of zucchini. PHOTO WILLIAM WOYS WEAVER.

shape and color and rind durability are the main discriminating characteristics. Some of the types are arbitrary and of historical interest only. For example, cushaw squash, winter crookneck squash, and marrow squash are not commonly grown, but they may be regionally important. The gourds and pumpkins of *C. pepo* are mostly grown for ornamental rather than culinary purposes and are increasing in economic importance in the United States. Show pumpkins are grown exclusively for competition in the heaviest-fruit contests held in various parts of the United States. Note that the word "pumpkin" or "squash" has been attached to each type. Some may disagree with these designations. The hard-rind types are generally called winter squash, whereas the soft-rind types (cocozelle, crookneck, scallop, straightneck, vegetable marrow, and zucchini) are generally referred to as summer squash. Winter squash are mostly indeterminate

ENCYCLOPEDIA OF FOOD AND CULTURE

TABLE 2

Horticultural types in *Cucurbita* spp.

Species	Type	Description	Typical Cultivars
C. argyrosperma	Cushaw squash	Striped, green or white hard rind. Pear shaped or with a straight or curved neck.	Green Striped Cushaw (Figure13), Japanese Pie, Tennessee Sweet Potato
C. moschata	Tropical pumpkin	Round, oblate, or irregular shape. Green, buff, yellow, or piebald hard rind.	La Primera, Seminole, Solar, Borenquin
	Cheese pumpkin	Variable shape, smooth, hard, buff-colored hard rind.	Dickinson, Kentucky Field
	Neck squash	Long curved or straight neck. Smooth hard rind fruit, usually buff.	Golden Crookneck, Winter Crookneck, Waltham Butternut, Zenith, Ultra
C. maxima	Banana squash	Elongated fruit pointed at the ends. Orange or pink moderately hard rind.	Banana, Pink Banana
	Delicious squash	Top shaped. Orange or green hard rind.	Delicious, Golden Delicious
	Hubbard squash	Round in the middle tapering at each end. Blue, orange, or green hard warty rind.	Hubbard, Blue Hubbard, Golden Hubbard
	Marrow squash	Lemon-shaped with orange hard rind.	Boston Marrow
	Show pumpkin	Very large globular, sutured, light orange fruit. Moderately hard rind.	Atlantic Giant, Big Max
	Turban squash	Turban shaped with a large button. Hard rind.	Turks Turban, Warren, Turks Cap
C. pepo	Acorn squash	Acorn-shaped, grooved fruit. Dark green, orange, or white hard rind.	Table Ace, Tay Belle, Heart of Gold, Table Gold
	Cocozelle squash	Long, cylindrical, bulbous blossom end. Striped or variegated green soft rind.	Cocozelle, Long Cocozelle
	Crookneck squash	Elongated with narrow curved neck. Yellow soft rind.	Dixie, Yellow Summer Crookneck, Supersett
	Ornamental gourd	Variously shaped and colored. Smooth or warty hard rind.	Egg, Striped, Pear, Bicolor, Spoon, Orange Ball, Crown of Thorns, Warted
	Pumpkin	Large, round, oval oblate shape. Mostly orange, sometimes white relatively soft rind.	Connecticut Field, Small Sugar, Howden, Jack-Be-Little
	Scallop squash	Flattened with scalloped margins. White, yellow, green, or bicolored soft rind.	White Bush Scallop, Peter Pan, Sunburst
	Straightneck squash	Long, cylindrical, yellow soft rind.	Enterprise, Goldbar, Early Prolific Straightneck, Multipik
	Vegetable Marrow	Short, tapered, cylindrical. Light green to gray soft rind.	Clarita, Goya, Zahra, Caserta
	Zucchini squash	Uniformly cylindrical. Green or yellow soft rind.	Dividend, Revenue, Spineless Beauty, Gold Rush

---

or vining in growth habit, and summer squash are mostly determinate or have a bush growth habit.

Squash and pumpkin are frost sensitive, so field establishment by seeds or by transplants two to four weeks old is made when no threat of frost remains. Summer squash plants are spaced three feet (one meter) apart in rows six feet (two meters) apart, and winter squash plants are spaced six feet apart in rows six to nine feet (two to three meters) apart. Local recommendations for crop management should be followed. Wild or domesticated bees are necessary for pollination and subsequent fruit enlargement since separate staminate (male) and pistillate (female) flowers occur on these plants. Baby squash, harvested when the flower opens or shortly thereafter, do not require pollination.

With good growing conditions, summer squash should be ready for harvest in about forty days from establishment. Fruit should be harvested about six to eight days after pollination, when they are small and the rind has a distinctive sheen. The rind becomes dull in overmaturity with a concomitant loss of quality. Summer squash should be consumed soon after harvest for best quality but may be kept in a plastic bag in a home refrigerator for a few days. Summer squash fruits should be harvested every day or two in warm weather.

Winter or hard-shelled squash, because they are grown to maturity, require much longer to produce a marketable product, 80 to 110 days, depending on weather and cultivar. Fruits should be harvested when fully mature (when seeds are fully developed) but before they are injured by frost. Winter squash, unlike summer squash, have a long life after harvest. Storage at or near 50°F (10°C) and 50 percent relative humidity retains quality for several months. For instance, the tropical pumpkin (*C. moschata*) fruits have remained in good condition for two to three months in a garage in Florida in uncontrolled conditions.

Plant Improvement

The economically important types showed marked genetic improvement in the last half of the twentieth century. Previously improvement had been mainly by selection, first from wild types and later from landraces.

The use of F$_1$ hybrids allows incorporation of dominant genes from two parents into the hybrid. For example, earliness in one parent can be combined with high culinary quality in the other parent to produce a superior hybrid. Often cited advantages of hybrids include uniformity, earliness, disease resistance, and intense fruit color. The *B* gene, originally obtained from an ornamental bicolor gourd, has been used to obtain bright yellow color in many *C. pepo* types. Exclusivity is usually not listed among the advantages of hybrids, but since the developer controls both parents, the hybrid cannot be duplicated by others. This fact provides the economic incentive for private development and competition among seed companies. Hybridity has been exploited most fully in cultivar development in summer squash, especially zucchini squash, and in decorative pumpkins.

Traditional plant-breeding techniques are most commonly utilized for improvement of these cucurbits. However, transgenic summer squash with resistance to cucumber mosaic virus, watermelon mosaic virus, and zucchini yellow mosaic virus have been developed and are used in areas where these diseases are a severe threat.

See also **Cucumbers, Melons, and Other Cucurbits**; **Fruit**; **Mexico and Central America, Pre-Columbian**; **Vegetables**.

BIBLIOGRAPHY

Andreas, Thomas. "Cucurbitaceae Families." Available at http://www.cucurbit.org/family.html.

Bates, David M., Richard W. Robinson, and Charles Jeffrey, eds. *Biology and Utilization of the Cucurbitaceae*. Ithaca, N.Y.: Cornell University Press, 1990.

Comer, James. "The History and Culture of Food and Drink in the Americas: North America from 1492 to the Present." In *The Cambridge World History of Food*, edited by Kenneth F. Kiple and Kriemhild Coneè Ornelas, vol. 2. Cambridge, U.K.: Cambridge University Press, 2000.

Decker-Walters, Deena, and Terrance W. Walters. "Squash." In *The Cambridge World History of Food*, edited by Kenneth F. Kiple and Kriemhild Coneè Ornelas, vol. 2. Cambridge, U.K.: Cambridge University Press, 2000.

Food and Agriculture Organization of the United Nations. Available at http://www.fao.org.

Heider, Karl G. *Grand Valley Dani: Peaceful Warriors*. New York: Holt, Rinehart, and Winston, 1979.

Heiser, Charles B. *The Gourd Book*. Norman, Okla.: University of Oklahoma Press, 1979.

McClung de Tapia. "The Origins of Agriculture in Mesoamerica and Central America." In *The Origins of Agriculture: An International Perspective*, edited by C. Wesley Cowan and Patty Jo Watson. Washington, D.C., and London: Smithsonian Institution Press, 1992.

Nee, M. "The Domestication of *Cucurbita* (Cucurbitaceae)." *Economic Botany* 44, no. 3 (1990): 56–68.

Norrman, Ralf, and Jon Haarberg. *Nature and Language: A Semiotic Study of Cucurbits in Literature*. London: Routledge and Kegan Paul, 1980.

Paris, Harry S. "Summer Squash: History, Diversity, and Distribution." *HortTechnology* 6 (1996): 6–13.

Pearsall, Deborah M. "The Origins of Plant Cultivation in South America." In *The Origins of Agriculture: An International Perspective*, edited by C. Wesley Cowan and Patty Jo Watson. Washington, D.C., and London: Smithsonian Institution Press, 1992.

Price, Sally. *Co-Wives and Calabashes*. Ann Arbor: University of Michigan Press, 1993.

Robinson, R. W., and D. S. Decker-Walters. *Cucurbits*. New York: CAB International, 1997.

Scarre, Christopher, and Brian M. Fagan. *Ancient Civilizations*. New York: Longman, 1997.

Scarry, C. Margaret, ed. *Foraging and Farming in the Eastern Woodlands*. Gainesville: University Press of Florida, 1993.

Smith, Bruce D. *The Emergence of Agriculture*. New York: Scientific American Library, 1995.

Smith, Bruce D. "The Initial Domestication of *Cucurbita pepo* in the Americas 10,000 Years Ago." *Science* 276 (1997): 932–934.

Smith, Bruce D. "Prehistoric Plant Husbandry in Eastern North America." In *The Origins of Agriculture: An International Perspective*, edited by C. Wesley Cowan and Patty Jo Watson. Washington, D.C., and London: Smithsonian Institution Press, 1992.

Tapley, William T., Walter D. Enzie, and Glen P. Van Eseltine. *The Vegetables of New York: The Cucurbits*. Albany: State of New York, Education Department, 1937.

U.S. Department of Agriculture. *Vegetables 2000 Summary*. Washington, D.C.: Government Printing Office, 2001.

U.S. Department of Agriculture, Agricultural ResearchService. 2001. USDA Nutrient Database for Standard Reference, Release 14. Nutrient Data Laboratory Home Page, http://www.nal.usda.gov/fnic/foodcomp

Whitaker, Thomas W., and Glen N. Davis. *Cucurbits: Botany, Cultivation, and Utilization*. New York: Interscience Publishers, 1962.

David Maynard
Donald N. Maynard

SQUID. *See* **Mollusks.**

SRI LANKA. *See* **India.**

STAPLES. Staple foods are those that appear most often in a given diet and provide its highest energy content. Satiety is the state sought from their consumption. A good example of an optimum staple are the loaves made from thick red sorghum porridge (*Sorghum caudatum*

[Hack Stapf]) that the Masa in northern Cameroon consume. The flour is unsieved on purpose so that it takes longer to digest. Insufficient staples in the diet leave the consumer unsatiated; it is when staples are lacking that famines occur.

Ambiguity of the Concept

The concept of a staple can be considered in two ways: (1) as the raw food material that is most often consumed and that brings the highest energy contribution to the diet and (2) as the most common dishes made from it. In Europe, wheat is a staple. For the French, bread is the wheat staple, and for the Italians, pasta is the usual foodstuff produced from it. In Africa, sorghum is a staple, and the Masai use it to make daily loaves.

It should be mentioned that staple foods are typically accompanied by a relish providing palatability and flavor. In Chinese culture, the idea of food is illustrated by the combination of two words: *fan*, meaning grain (or rice), and *tsai*, meaning relish (Chang, p. 7). This association of a staple with a relish may be observed in many cultures.

In traditional societies, the primal cuisine consists of preparing and making palatable the staple foods according to local criteria. In Senegal, pearl millet is cooked in many ways, using various kinds of flour and semolina. It can be steamed, or cooked in water or oil. In Mexico, maize used as grain or flour permits the preparation of countless dishes.

Types of Staples

In many societies, staple foods are of plant origin. However, among the Inuit, meat and fat can be considered staples (Robbe, pp. 101, 184), and for pastoralists like the Ariaal, Turkana, and Maasai of East Africa, milk is a dietary staple, representing over 50 percent of food calories (Little et al., p. 74). Similarly, milk may be regarded as a staple commodity for Mongolian herders (Accolas and Aubin, pp. 55–83).

Among most hunter-gatherers, plant foods provide the highest amount of calories in the diet and, according to their seasonal availability, many species therefore assume the role of a staple. In the Central African Republic, pygmies rely on wild yams (*Dioscorea* spp.) for this purpose. The mongongo nut (*Ricinodendron rautanenii* Schinz) may be similarly regarded as a staple among the !Kung San of Botswana (Lee, p. 307).

Most fishing societies, although depending on predatory activities for their livelihood, use a carbohydrate as their staple—rice (*Oryza sativa* L.), for instance, in southern Asia (Firth 1966, p. 3).

Storage

Since the Neolithic period, agricultural societies have produced and stored the elements of their diet. This is, for the most part, an easy matter with tubers, which re-

main planted in the fields and are only dug out as needed. Cereals and pulses, on the other hand, have to be protected from moisture, fungi, insects, and rodents. This is done by using granaries, some of which quite cleverly repel the pests. For instance, the *horreos* of northern Spain repose on pillars with an overhang, which prevents rodents from reaching the crop. In the Old World, where invasions were common, silos were dug into the ground and the opening hidden to avoid plundering (Gast and Sigaut). There are no optimal traditional solutions, however, and losses amounting to a quarter of the crop may sometimes be observed.

Main Staples

Among staples, one is usually prevalent. This is the case of wheat (*Triticum aestivum* L.) in Europe, rice in Asia, maize (*Zea mays* L.) in Central America, cassava (*Manihot utilissima* Crantz) in South America or Africa. Yams (*Dioscorea* spp.) are a main staple in the Pacific (Pollock) and Africa. In 2001 the production figures for the main commodities used as staple foods on a worldwide basis were as follows: maize, 604 metric tons (Mt); rice (paddy), 585 Mt; wheat, 578 Mt; potatoes, (*Solanum tuberosum* L.), 304 Mt; cassava, 176 Mt; barley, (*Hordeum vulgare* L.), 138 Mt; sweet potatoes, (*Ipomoea batatas* [L.] Lam) 136 Mt; sorghum, 57 Mt; and pearl millet, (*Pennisetum* spp.), 28 Mt (information available at the Food and Argricultural Organization, or FAO website).

Secondary Staples

Secondary staples, whose role is more seasonal, should also be mentioned. Some have been abandoned, others are still in use. For example, in Europe and the Near East, typical secondary staples include buckwheat (*Fagopyrum sagittatum* Gilib.), barley, true millet (*Panicum miliaceum* L.), and rye (*Secale cereale* L.), and also pulses such as broad beans (*Vicia faba* L.), lentils (*Lens culinaris* Medik.), and chick peas (*Cicer arietinum* L.). Common beans (*Phaseolus vulgaris* L.), which originated in America, also continue to flourish in Europe, where they often contribute protein to the diet of the poorest in society.

African secondary staples include hungry rice (*Digitaria exilis* [Kipp. Stapf]), finger millet (*Eleusine coracana* [L.] Gaertn.), cowpeas (*Vigna unguiculata* [L] Walp.), and bambara groundnuts (*Voandzeia subterranea* [L.] Thouars). Soya beans (*Glycine max* [L.] Merr.) are the usual secondary staple in Asia.

In many tropical areas around the world, the plantain banana (*Musa paradisiaca* L.), tubers like the American cocoyam (*Xanthosoma* spp.), and taro (*Colocasia esculenta* L.) are consumed as secondary staples. Breadfruit (*Artocarpus altilis* [Parkinson] Fosberg) and jackfruit (*Artocarpus heterophyllus* Lam. L.) fulfill the same role in southern Asia and Oceania. The starch made from the pith of the sago palm (*Metroxylon* spp.) is also popular for a similar reason among various tribes in New Guinea.

Other secondary staples, though no longer in popular or widespread use, include the following: the European chestnut (*Castanea sativa* Mill.), a farinaceous fruit, consumed in southern Europe (Bruneton-Governatori, *Le pain de bois*), and the acorns of various oaks, for example, the California white oak (*Quercus virginiana* Mill.), that served as an important staple food for Native Americans (Hedrick, p. 480).

Diffusion

Staple foods are not necessarily indigenous to the place where they are today most frequently consumed (Garine, p. 240). For instance, maize, which has spread to southern Europe, Africa, and Asia, is native to Central and South America (Estrella, p. 72; Messer, pp. 97–112). Cassava, which found its way to Africa, southern Asia, and Oceania, also originated in South America. And, rather unexpectedly, potatoes and maize, which are nowadays staple foods for some Nepalese populations, are in addition of South American origin.

The routes and methods of diffusion for such staples is still a matter of discussion (Purseglove, p. 1; Chastanet, p. 265). It is likely that the way by which rice (native to southern Asia) reached the Mediterranean basin in ancient Rome will never be known, or why it only began to be cultivated in Lombardy in the sixteenth century (Barrau, p. 291), or how sorghum, native to tropical Africa, reached China (Simoons, p. 75).

The discovery of America contributed to the establishment of many new staple crops (Lewicki, p. 50) in the Old World after Christopher Columbus's voyage in 1492. For instance, maize was introduced at the beginning of the sixteenth century in Spain and especially Portugal, where it rapidly became a main staple. It also enjoyed widespread popularity in Turkey (in fact, maize was commonly known as "Turkish wheat" in Europe) and spread to Africa through the Nile Valley. It was later transported to the west coast of Africa by Spanish and Portuguese merchants.

More extensively documented was the introduction of potatoes (*Solanum tuberosum* L.), native to South America, to Europe around 1540 by the Spaniards. At first a medicinal product, they later became a food in Ireland, France, the Netherlands, and Germany during times of famine and a cheap source of nourishment for industrial workers in the nineteenth century (Messer, p. 191). They are now a staple in many Eastern European countries.

The slave trade contributed to the development of maize and cassava production in Africa as high-yielding crops to feed the slaves on their way to America (Bahuchet and Philippson, p. 92). Colonial America later focused on the development of staples (Firth, "Sociological Study") that were easily produced and drought-resistant, such as cassava, or easy-to-store and prepare, like rice, in order to feed cheap labor engaged in cash cropping, industrial manufacturing, and mining (Chrétien, p. 76).

In 2001 the export of staples from countries with sophisticated technology and powerful means of commercialization, as in the United States and Europe, motivates harsh competition in their sale to developing countries (Barrau, p. 300). Low price, widespread availability, easy preparation, and prestige in adopting the tastes of thriving industrialized countries are underlying factors in such food changes. The French, for instance, promoted the importation of wheat into Africa. The urban elite in many African nations developed an interest in French cuisine as a result. Today, bread is widely consumed in French-speaking Africa, and in Senegal it is even delivered by car to small villages.

Prestige

In agricultural societies, the successful production of a staple formerly conferred prestige because it demonstrated technological skill and benevolent protection from supernatural powers. At harvest time, the display of vast quantities of yams still conveys success in the Trobriand Islands (Schiefenhoevel and Bell-Krannhals, p. 244) as it did seventy years ago (Malinowski, p. 171).

Staples and Cultural Superfood

As previously indicated, in most cultures one staple food is dominant. Some populations are restricted to a small number of staples, as is the case with the Masai population already mentioned. They consume their thick sorghum porridge loaves at 90 percent of their meals. Most traditional societies nonetheless have to adjust their range of staples according to the season and the habitat. This enables the Tamang, who live in the middle hills of Nepal, occupying a watershed ranging from 1,400 to 4,000 meters, to consume a wide range of basic foods: rice, maize, taros, potatoes, barley, and wheat.

It should be stressed, however, that a single staple normally becomes a key symbol in most traditional societies. This is certainly the role of rice among the Tamang and in most of India, of maize in Central America, and of wheat in Europe. Such a staple is what Jelliffe (p. 279) very adequately termed "cultural superfood" and it exists in a poulation's food supply as a "central core food," as described by Passin and Bennett (p.113).

Religious Aspects

Besides providing most caloric intake, a central staple also elicits emotional reactions in relationship to food: it is the "daily bread." Among the Masai, "to be alive" means eating the sorghum loaf. Its use is therefore strongly imbedded in their religious beliefs and mythologies.

Among the Serer of Senegal, pearl millet was considered a gift from god to prevent human starvation. Bread, made from wheat, is constantly referred to in the bible: It is a symbol of the body of Jesus Christ and also plays an important part in the Jewish Shabbat (Erlich, p. 227).

As such, staples are considered sacred foods to be handled with care and respect. The Kanaks of New Caledonia formerly carried yams in their arms like infants, since the crop grew on the land in which their ancestors are buried (Leenhardt, p. 83).

Staples are also often associated with particular deities. In Mexico, among the Aztecs, Tlaloc, one of the central deities, was linked to maize. In Greek and Roman mythology, Demeter, Mother Earth (Ceres for the Romans), is associated with agricultural products, especially wheat, symbolizing the resurrection of Persephone (or Proserpine).

Although a staple may be a revered food in a culture and is consequently to be respected, it may also elicit other responses during certain periods. For instance, in many rural societies, the harvest, marking the end of an annual cycle of food production, is an important time of celebration. Among the Koma of northern Cameroon, while sexual promiscuity is to be avoided during the maturation of staples, the threshing activities provide an opportunity for boisterous celebration, setting the stage for more permissive behavior.

Staples are additionally used in most religions as offerings to supernatural beings. In rural European societies, first-fruit offerings were formerly made with wheat, which has also been identified in Egyptian tombs dating from the dynastic period (Darby et al., p. 486). Offerings prepared with maize are presented to the deceased on All Saints Day in Mexico. Millet and sorghum are offered to deities in the form of grain, porridge, or beer in many African cultures.

Adaptability and Nutrition

Staple foods, the foodstuff to which infants are first introduced, are considered to be safe during weaning. They contribute to the development of a palate and organoleptic expectations. This can have important consequences in terms of food education and food relief programs, which might be more sucessful if they tried to provide the populations concerned with their own staples rather than those readily available or popular elsewhere.

In traditional societies, a staple is not necessarily chosen because it is the highest-yielding species with the best nutritional value. Many factors determine its selection. The elected staple might even provide little else than energy, as is the case with the false banana (*Ensete ventricosum* [Welw.] E. E. Cheesm.) among the Gurage of Ethiopia (Shack). In many areas of Africa, at the limit between the tropical savanna and equatorial forests, the cultivation of both maize and cassava is possible. Although the former is more nutritionally complete, it requires more work than the latter. Sometimes societies opt for the staple easiest to produce.

Since the staple, generally considered the safest food to consume, is also the first solid item offered to a child, its nutritional value may have important consequences

during the weaning period. In this respect, cereal staples, which contain proteins, provide better nutrition than tubers. Relying on a single staple food in a monotonous diet amplifies its nutritional weakness. The lack of the amino acid thiamine can provoke beriberi among rice eaters, and pellagra occurs among maize consumers through an inadequate amount of tryptophane (FAO, *Maize* and *Amino-Acid Content*). Cassava contains toxic cyanide, which has to be carefully eliminated before consumption to avoid health risks. The pulse *Lathyrus sativus* L., which is consumed mainly by the poorest in Central India, can cause a paralytic disease called lathyrism (Kaul and Combes).

The Present Situation

Because of the significant progress in food production, distribution, and commercialization, it is possible today for anybody with financial means to consume any food, in any quantity, at any time of the year. The range has no limits. This minimizes the material importance of staple foods and the nutritional risks related to their exclusive consumption. What is the staple food of a European today? There has been a general worldwide decrease in the consumption of carbohydrates. As a result, someone living in present-day France is likely to eat only half the amount of bread an individual consumed in 1955, 63 kg per year as opposed to 122 kg. In France cereals represent only 23 percent of food energy, whereas in Italy that number is 32 percent (Collet-Ribbing and Decloitre). This difference is probably due to the maintenance of a very old style of eating in Italy, which combines an energy-rich staple like pasta with a relish of varied composition.

The globalization process has had a positive impact on food distribution worldwide by making a very wide range of foods and dishes available, but the choices made in some cultures as a consequence are not necessarily nutritionally sound. The greater consumption of white rice over brown rice and traditional staples, which contain more proteins, minerals, and vitamins, may have unforeseen negative nutritional consequences such as protein malnutrition and beriberi (FAO, *List of Foods* and *1972 Food Composition Table*).

Today staples retain some of their religious and symbolic value. This is the case of bread among Christians, and rice among many populations of Asia. Consuming one's traditional staple food is also psychologically satisfying. This is why a number of emblematic dishes involving a cultural superfood are still consumed on social occasions, especially by immigrants. They exist as a token of the past, a demonstration of a lasting cultural authenticity.

BIBLIOGRAPHY

Accolas, J. P., and F. Aubin. "Les produits laitiers." *Études Mongoles* 6 (1975): 55–83.

Bahuchet, S., and G. Philippson. "Les plantes d'origine américaine en Afrique bantoue: Une approche linguistique." In

Plantes et paysages d'Afrique, edited by M. Chastanet. Paris: Karthala, 1998.

Barrau, J. *Les hommes et leurs aliments.* Paris: Temps Actuel, 1983.

Chang, K. C. *Food in Chinese Culture: Anthropological and Historical Perspectives.* New Haven: Yale University Press, 1977.

Chastanet, M. "Plantes et paysages d'Afrique: Une histoire à explorer." In *Plantes et paysages d'Afrique*, edited by M. Chastanet. Paris: Karthala, 1998.

Chrétien, J-P. "L'histoire de longue durée de la consommation alimentaire en Afrique." In *Les changements des habitudes et des politiques alimentaires en Afrique*, edited by I. de Garine. Paris: UNESCO/Publisud, 1991.

Collet-Ribbing, C., and F. Decloitre. "Consommation alimentaire en France et dans quelques pays occidentaux." In *Alimentation et cancer: Evaluation des données scientifiques*, edited by E. Riboli, F. Decloitre, and C. Collet-Robbing. Paris: Lavoisier Technique et Documentation, 1996.

Darby, W. L., P. Ghalioungui, and L. Grivetti. *Food, the Gift of Osiris.* 2 vols. New York: Academic Press, 1977.

Erlich, J. *La flamme du Shabbath.* Paris: Plon, 1970.

Estrella, E. *El pan de America: Etnohistoria de los alimentos aborigenes en el Ecuador.* Madrid: Centro de Estudios Historicos, 1986.

FAO. *Maize and Maize Diets.* Rome: FAO, 1953.

FAO. *Amino-Acid Content of Foods.* Rome: FAO, 1970.

Firth, R. *Malay Fishermen: Their Peasant Economy.* New York: W. W. Norton, 1966 (reprinted in 1975).

Garine, I. de. "The Diet and Nutrition of Human Populations." In *Companion Encyclopedia of Anthropology: Humanity, Culture and Social Life*, edited by Tim Ingold, Chap. 9, pp. 226–266. London: Routledge, 1994.

Gast, M., and F. Sigaut, eds. (with the collaboration of A. Bruneton-Governatori). *Les techniques de conservation des grains à long terme, leur rôle dans la dynamique des systèmes de culture et des sociétés*, tome 2. Paris: Centre National de la Recherche Scientifique, 1981.

Hedrick, U. P., ed. *Sturtevant's Edible Plants of the World.* New York: Dover, 1972.

Jelliffe, D. B. "Parallel Food Classifications in Developing and Industrialized Countries." *American Journal of Clinical Nutrition* 20 (1967): 279–281.

Kaul, A. K., and D. Combes, eds. *Lathyrus and Lathyrism.* New York: Third World Medical Research Foundation, 1985.

Lee, R. B. "Mongongo: The Ethnography of a Major Wild Food Resource." *Ecology of Food and Nutrition* 2, no. 4 (1973): 307–322.

Leenhardt, M. *Do Kamo, le mythe de la personne dans le monde mélanésien.* Paris: Gallimard, 1947.

Lewicki, T. (with the assistance of M. Johnson). *West African Food in the Middle Ages according to Arabic Sources.* Cambridge, U.K.: Cambridge University Press, 1974.

Little, M. A., S. J. Gray, and B. C. Campbell. "Milk Consumption in African Pastoral Peoples." In *Drinking: Anthropological Approaches*, edited by Igor and Valerie de Garine. Oxford, U.K.: Berghahn Books, 2001.

Magnien, V. *Les mystères d'Eleusis.* Paris: Payot, 1950.

Malinowski, B. *Coral Gardens and Their Magic: A Study of the Method of Tilling the Soil and of the Agricultural Rites in the Trobriand Islands.* London: G. Allen and Unwin, 1935.

Messer, E. "Maize." In *The Cambridge World History of Food*, vols. 1 and 2, pp. 97–112. New York: Cambridge University Press, 2000.

Passin, H., and J. W. Bennett. "Social Process and Dietary Change." *1941–1943 National Research Council Bulletin*, 108 (1943): 113–123.

Pollock, Nancy J. *These Roots Remain.* Honolulu: Institute for Polynesian Studies, and University of Hawaii Press, 1992.

Purseglove, J. W. *Tropical Crops.* 2 vols. London: Longmans, Green and Co., 1968.

Robbe, P. "Les Inuit d'Ammassalik, chasseurs de l'Arctique." *Muséum National d'Histoire Naturelle* 159 (1994): 1–389.

Schiefenhoevel, W., and I. Bell-Krannhals. "Of Harvests and Hierarchies: Securing Staple Food and Social Position in the Trobriand Islands." In *Food and the Status Quest*, edited by P. Wiessner and W. Schiefenhoevel. Oxford, U.K.: Berghahn Books, 1995.

Shack, W. *The Gurage, a People of the Ensete Culture.* London: Oxford University Press, 1966.

Simoons, F. J. *Food in China: A Cultural and Historical Enquiry.* Boca Raton, Fla.: CRC Press, 1991.

Wheeler, E. F. "Do Processed Societies Have Staple Foods?" *Oxford Symposium on Food and Cookery 1989*, pp. 24–26. London: Prospect Books, 1990.

Igor de Garine

STARCH

STARCH. Starch is a highly organized mixture of two carbohydrate polymers, amylose and amylopectin, which are synthesized by plant enzymes and simultaneously packed into dense water-insoluble granules. Starch granules vary in size (1 to 100 microns [μ m] in diameter) and shape, which are characteristic of their specific plant origin. Starch is the major energy reserve for plants; it is located mainly in the seeds, roots or tubers, stem pith, and fruit. Starch amylose is primarily a linear chain of glucose units. Amylose chains can coil into double helices and become insoluble in cold water. Amylopectin also is composed of chains of glucose units, but the chains are branched. This branched structure renders amylopectin soluble in cold water. The molecular architecture of the amylopectin and amylose within the granules is not entirely understood, but the granules are insoluble in cold water. The functional properties of native starch are determined by the granule structure. Both the appearance of the granules and their functional properties vary with the plant source.

Physical and Functional Properties

In home cooking and in commercial food processing native starches are used for their thickening properties. Starch granules when heated in water gradually absorb water and swell in size, causing the mixture to thicken. With continued heating however, the swollen granules

Starch is not only a food thickener but is itself the focal point of numerous recipes. The introduction of cornstarch led to the popularity of cornstarch pudding during the nineteenth century, as shown by the picture on this 1883 pamphlet cookbook. ROUGHWOOD COLLECTION.

fragment, the mixture becomes less thick, and the amylose and amylopectin become soluble in the hot mixture. This process of granule swelling and fragmenting is called gelatinization. Once gelatinized the granules cannot be recreated and the starch merely behaves as a mixture of amylose and amylopectin. Because of the larger size of the swollen granules compared to the size of amylose and amylopectin, the viscosity of the swollen granule mixture is much higher than the viscosity (the resistance to flow or a liquid or semi-liquid mixture) of the amylose/amylopectin mixture. Starches from differ-

ent plant sources vary in their gelatinization temperatures, rate of gelatinization, maximum viscosity, clarity of the gelatinized mixture, and ability to form a solid gel on cooling.

The texture of heat-gelatinized starch mixtures is variable. Some gelatinized starch mixtures have a smooth creamy texture, while others are more pastelike. Some starches form gels after cooking and cooling. These starch gels may lack stability and slowly exude water through the gel surface. A similar breakdown of the gelatinized starch occurs in some frozen foods during thawing and refreezing. Although amylose is soluble in the hot gelatinized starch mixture, it tends to become insoluble in the cooled mixture. This phenomenon is called retrogradation and it occurs when the amylose chains bind together in helical and double helical coils. Retrogradation affects the texture of the food product and it also lowers the digestibility of the product. The proper starches must be employed for the different food products to minimize these problems. Certain starches are good film formers and can be used in coatings or as film barriers for protection of the food from oil absorption during frying.

Native and Modified Starches
The predominant commercial starches are those from field corn (maize), potato, cassava (tapioca), wheat, rice, and arrowroot. Field cornstarch (27 percent amylose and 73 percent amylopectin) is the major commercial starch worldwide. Genetic variants of field corn include waxy maize, which produces a starch with 98 to 100 percent amylopectin, and high-amylose starches, which have amylose contents of 55 percent, 70 percent, and higher. Waxy starch does not form gels and does not retrograde readily. High-amylose starches retrograde more extensively than normal starches and are less digestible. Their linear structure enables them to form films.

From the 1940s on the demand for convenience foods, dry mixes, and various processed foods has led to the modification of starches for food use and for other commercial products. These modified starches improve the textural properties of food products and may be more suitable for use in modern processing equipment. The Food and Drug Administration regulates use of the various modified food starches by stipulating the types of modification allowed, the degree of modification, and the reagents used in chemical modification. However, the food label is required only to state that "modified starch" is present. Only a small fraction of the sites available for modification of the food starches are actually modified. Although the degree of modification is small, the properties of the starches are significantly improved. This small degree of modification is sufficient to give a more soluble and stable starch after cooking. The clarity of the gelatinized starch as well as the stability of the cooked starch and starch gels are improved. The modification procedures are carried out under mild conditions that do not cause gelatinization of the native starch granules, and therefore the functional properties of the granule are preserved. The emulsifying properties of starch also may be improved by proper modification, improving the stability of salad dressings and certain beverages.

Physically modified starches include a pregelatinized starch that is prepared by heat-gelatinization and then dried to a powder. This instant starch is water-soluble and doesn't require further cooking. Because of its lower viscosity resulting from loss of granule structure, the starch can be used at higher concentrations. Certain confectionaries require high levels of starch to give structure to their products. These gelatinized instant starches serve this role. Cold water swelling starches represent a different type of instant starch. They are made by a proprietary process that retains the granule structure but lowers the granule strength. These cold water swelling starches give higher viscosities than the other instant starches. They are used in instant food mixes and for products such as low-fat salad dressings and mayonnaise.

Plant breeding has led to specialty starches with atypical proportions of amylose and amylopectin. Waxy maize starch with nearly 100 percent amylopectin is inherently stable to retrogradation. Chemically cross-linked waxy maize starch is a very high-quality modified starch. High-amylose starches have become available more recently and have led to lower caloric starches. Because of the crystallinity of these starches they are partially resistant to digestion by intestinal amylases and behave as dietary fiber when analyzed by the official methods of analysis for dietary fiber. Some of these high-amylose starches contain as high as 60 percent dietary fiber when analyzed.

The nutritional value of uncooked (ungelatinized) starchy foods (cereal grains, potato, peas, and beans) is relatively poor. Our digestive enzymes do not readily convert the native granular starch of uncooked fruits and vegetables into glucose that would be absorbed in the small intestine. Undigested starch passes into the large intestine where, along with dietary fiber, it is broken down to glucose and fermented to short-chain fatty acids. Some of these short-chain acids are absorbed from the large intestine resulting in recovery of some of the caloric value of the native starch.

Starch-Derived Dextrins and Corn Syrups

Modified starches as described above were developed to improve starch functionality in foods as well as their ability to withstand the physical forces of modern food processing systems. In addition to the food applications of starches and modified starches, the native starches are also converted into other products that serve food and other industries. These products do not require the granular character of native starches, which is lost by chemical or enzymic action during processing of the starch.

Dextrinization, a process requiring high temperatures and acid that has been in use since the early 1800s,

converts native starch into dextrins that are composed of amylose and amylopectin chains of smaller sizes and altered structure. Consequently, food and nonfood industries have access to a range of dextrins of varying molecular sizes, solubility, and viscosity, but without the granular characteristics described above. Corn syrups are made in the same way as the dextrins, but they are converted to a higher degree such that glucose is a major ingredient. The more recent availability of an enzyme that converts glucose into fructose has led to a new industry in high-fructose corn syrups, which have found a strong market in beverages.

See also **Fats; Frying; Oil.**

BIBLIOGRAPHY

Frazier, Peter J., Peter Richmond, and Athene M. Donald, eds. *Starch Structure and Functionality*. Cambridge, U.K.: Royal Society of Chemistry, 1997.

Light, Joseph M. "Modified Food Starches: Why, What, Where, and How." *Cereal Foods World* 35 (1990): 1081–1092.

Murphy, Pauline. "Starch." In *Handbook of Hydrocolloids*, edited by Glyn O. Phillips and Peter A. Williams. Cambridge, U.K.: Woodhead Publishing; Boca Raton, Fla.: CRC Press LLC, 2000.

Thomas, David J., and William A. Atwell. *Starches*. St. Paul, Minn.: Eagan Press, 1999.

Betty A. Lewis

STEW. A stew has been described as an assortment of foods cooked in liquid within a container with a lid. Stews are usually made from several ingredients and may be named for the most important of these, for example, beef stew; for its point of origin, as in Irish stew; or for the pot in which it is cooked, as in Rumanian *ghiveci*, named for the Turkish *güveç*, an earthenware pot in which the stew is cooked.

The word "stew" is said to come from the old French word *estuier*, meaning to enclose. Most cultural groups have created a recipe for a special stew, and there are as many versions of them as there are cooks to make them.

In the Western world, meat stews are categorized as "brown" or "white." This means that the meat is browned in fat before liquid is added for the brown stew; meat for the white stew is not cooked in fat before liquid is added. Stews may contain meat, fish, or poultry; many of them, however, are meatless. There is also sometimes a fine line between stews and soups. Stews are usually thick, some so thick that they must be served on a plate and eaten with a fork. Others are served in soup bowls. Stews most often have several solid food ingredients. An exception is a seafood stew such as oyster or lobster stew, which contains fresh seafood, milk, and frequently butter.

Stews are commonly regarded as "comfort" foods, everyday dishes served to family or close friends in an intimate setting, rather than as fare in a more public setting or at special occasions. An exception would be *boeuf à la bourguignonne*, usually referred to as beef burgundy in the United States, a dish that is considered exceptional enough to be served to a guest. This stew is made with beef, tiny onions, mushrooms, wine, and herbs. M. F. K. Fisher once wrote that stews can be good enough to be haute cuisine, or the opposite, a meal fit for the lowest echelon of society, the imprisoned.

There are several important advantages to stews: Less tender cuts of meat can be tenderized with the long, moist cooking; more expensive ingredients that may be available only in small amounts can be stretched by adding less expensive foods; meat cut in small pieces cooks faster; and one-pot cooking conserves fuel and makes cleanup easier. Stews may be cooked on top of a range, in an oven, over an open fire, or in an electric Crock Pot.

In addition to being versatile in their ingredients, stews are versatile in their uses. Suggested uses include as filling for tarts or patty shells, or over mashed potatoes, rice, or biscuits.

Usually considered dishes that must be cooked for long periods, stews are, in fact, cooked quickly in countries where fuel is scarce. There are Asian chicken stews, made with young and tender chickens, that cook quickly, but are even more worthwhile because they conserve energy since the entire meal can be cooked in one pot.

Because stews are apt to use protein- and carbohydrate-containing food, as well as ingredients high in vitamin and mineral content, they are good sources of nutrients. Combining certain ingredients, for example, rice and beans, can enhance the nutrients in each food, making them more usable by the human body. Water-soluble nutrients are consumed in the sauces, or gravies, that are part of stews.

Kinds of Stew

Europe. In the eighteenth century, the term "made dish" was used to distinguish between a roast and various mixtures of ingredients. The made dishes in both France and England were often French stews, or ragouts, many still commonly served today. The term *daube* is more often used to describe beef stews in France. Patricia Wells's *Bistro Cooking*, published in 1989, contains a recipe for a *daube* containing wild mushrooms and oranges. An Alsatian meat stew (beef, pork, and lamb cooked with vegetables) is a tradition on Monday, washday, in certain regions. A family's stew pot is taken to the neighborhood bakery where the stew is cooked until noon, when a member of the family arrives to retrieve the meal.

Navarin is a popular French stew made with mutton, potatoes, and onion. In *The Food of the Western World*, Theodora Fitzgibbons tells us that if root vegetable are added, the stew should be called *ragout à la printanière*.

Bouillabaisse, the renowned Mediterranean fish stew of France, has its counterparts in the fish stews of Greece, Italy, and Spain. There is also a less well-known bouillabaisse made with monkfish and aioli, the French garlic mayonnaise. The reader should, in addition, be mindful that the terminology can sometimes be misleading: There is a *bouillabaisse de Tante Paulette*, which is actually a chicken stew flavored with fennel, saffron, and Pernod or another licorice-flavored liqueur, and was frequently served at a legendary Parisian bistro, and a rabbit bouillabaisse.

The German *Eintopf* is another one-pot meal or stew. In the 1930s Hitler urged Germans to return to the austere meals of former days. It became law in 1933 that one Sunday a month, from October to March, was *Eintopfsonntag*, one-pot Sunday. Money saved from not eating more lavishly was to be donated to the poor. *Eintopfs* are still popular in Germany, especially in the north. *Linsentopf*, lentil stew, and *Pichelsteiner*, made with beef, veal, lamb, and pork, are popular forms of *Eintopfs*.

Said to be Poland's national dish, *bigos*—hunter's stew—has ancient origins. It was first made of vegetables such as cabbage (fresh or as sauerkraut), mushrooms, and onions, along with prunes or apples and leftover game. It was a staple for hunters and was reheated frequently over outdoor fires. Some say a poorly made *bigos* will improve with reheating due to the condensation of flavors, but that a well-made *bigos* is delicious the first day. The meat used may be fresh pork or ham, sausages, poultry—goose or duck are considered best—and any game available. Madiera wine may be added as flavoring. Over the years, *bigos* has assumed greater importance at Polish New Year's Eve celebrations.

Waterzooi is a well-known Flemish stew of fish or chicken, vegetables, and white wine. It is associated with the city of Ghent in East Flanders, Belgium. Most food experts claim the original stew was prepared with fish. Whether fish or chicken, the stew contains cream and is thickened with egg yolk.

Africa. Stews are used in some cultures for dipping bread or a type of porridge. The mainstay of the Ethiopian diet is *injera*, a pancakelike bread made from the nutritious grain *tef*. Pieces of *injera* are broken off and used to scoop up stew. *Wat* is the usual name for an Ethiopian stew, frequently seasoned with *berbere*, a dried spice and herb mixture that can be made hot with peppers. Milder Ethiopian stews are called *alechos*. Although meats, fish, and chicken are all used in preparing *wats*, the stew is more likely to be vegetarian because of the many meatless fast days required in the Ethiopian orthodox religion. Legumes are therefore often used in these stews.

The main carbohydrate for Nigerians is *fufu*, a thick pasty that may be made from cassava, plantain, or from a grain. Nigerian immigrants in the United States sometimes use Cream of Wheat cereal to make *fufu*. A diner will scoop up some *fufu* in his or her fingers, deftly roll it into a ball, and then use that to dip up some stew. Nigerian stews are often vegetarian dishes, but they may contain meat, fish, or poultry, and are usually made hot with peppers.

Zambians use pounded millet for their starchy dipping porridge. As in many cultures, meat stews are frequently preferred, but vegetarian stews are more likely to be readily available.

Asia. The ancient Chinese cooked *keng*, meat and/or vegetable stews, in cauldrons. Ceramic, and later bronze, cauldrons have been found in archaeological digs; some of these cauldrons are thought to be eight thousand years old. In *The Food of China*, E. N. Anderson describes the Chinese process of preparing and cooking a stew as a gentle, subtle, and slow art. The cook typically worked with a set of well-seasoned sand pots (sand-tempered earthenware); now metal woks with lids are used for cooking stews.

Tubu-tchigae, or bean curd stew, is a Korean meal that remains nostalgically popular. The dish is made with firm bean curd, pork, garlic, ginger, soy sauce, sesame oil, and *kochujang* (a red pepper, soybean, and glutinous rice paste).

The Japanese *iri-dori*, a one-pot chicken stew seasoned with mirin, sugar, and soy sauce does not require the long cooking times generally needed if a young chicken is used. A variation on this stew uses fish in place of poultry.

Filipinos make *adobo* from pork, chicken, and perhaps shellfish or fin fish. Seasonings include garlic, vinegar, and soy sauce, providing the sour-cool-salty taste the Filipinos desire. Another favorite stew in the Philippines is *puchero*, the traditional Sunday dinner. It is prepared with chicken, beef, tomatoes, sweet potatoes, and garbanzos and sometimes is served with a sauce made from eggplant.

South America. Argentineans cook their beef stews with fruits, perhaps peaches, and sometimes chunks of corn-on-the-cob. These stews may be baked in a pumpkin or squash shell. Stews are also everyday fare in Bolivia, Paraguay, and Uruguay. One is more likely to find fish stews in Chile than in other South American nations because of that country's long coastline.

North America. Traditional Mexican cooking included many stews because the meat and poultry used in that location were often not tender and they required the long, moist cooking characteristic of stews. In spite of the improved quality of meat and poultry in modern times, stews have prevailed as a favorite food. One stew, *mancha manteles de cerdo*, is prepared with three varieties of red chilis and tomatoes.

Mexico's *pozole de lujo* is often described as a "luxurious" pork stew. The recipe calls for a pig's head and pig's feet, with pork loin, chicken, and hominy. Mexican *caldos* (stews or soups) are traditionally served with tortillas.

First Nations in Canada and Native Americans in the United States made stews in birch bark containers or hollowed-out trees before Europeans introduced metal containers. Some tribes left a stew on the fire for hours; its members would then add gathered plants or hunted game as they returned to camp.

The culinary history of both Canada and the United States includes numerous examples of stews brought by European settlers. Beef stews have been the most popular recipes among this legacy.

On the Canadian prairies, chuck-wagon cooks made stews from less tender cuts of meat. In the Laurentian Mountains of Quebec, a stew would typically be placed inside a wood-stove oven; the fire was then allowed to die down. The stew cooked in the waning fire. Ontario Mennonites still prepare stews in iron kettles.

Stews have been important food for most of the world's people for thousands of years, and there is no indication that this will change any day soon. They are wonderful concoctions, savored for their flavorful combinations as well as their reminders of home and family.

See also **Chicken Soup; Lamb Stew; Porridge; Soup.**

BIBLIOGRAPHY

Anderson, E. N. *The Food of China.* New Haven, Conn.: Yale University Press, 1988.

Armstrong, Julian. "A Taste of Quebec." In *Northern Bounty: A Celebration of Canadian Cuisine,* edited by Jo Marie Powers and Anita Stewart. Toronto: Random House, 1995.

Barer-Stein, Thelma. *You Eat What You Are: People, Culture and Food Traditions.* Buffalo: Firefly Books, 1999.

Barss, Beulah. "The Chuckwagon Traditions in Prairie Culture." In *Northern Bounty: A Celebration of Canadian Cuisine,* edited by Jo Marie Powers and Anita Stewart. Toronto: Random House, 1995.

Doi, Masaru. *Cook Japanese.* Tokyo: Kodansha International, 1964.

Fitzgibbon, Theodora. *The Food of the Western World: An Encyclopedia of Food from North America and Europe.* New York: Quadrangle/The New York Times Book Company, 1976.

Kittler, Pamela Goyan, and Kathryn P. Sucher. *Cultural Foods. Traditions and Trends.* Belmont, Calif.: Wadsworth/Thomson, 2000.

Millow, Marc, and Kim. *Flavours of Korea.* London: Andre Deutsch, 1991.

Montagné, Prosper. "Larousse Gastronomique." In *The Encyclopedia of Food, Wines and Cookery,* translated by Nina Frond, Patience Gray, Maud Murdock, and Barbara Macrae Taylor. New York: Crown, 1961.

Root, Waverly. *The Cooking of Italy.* New York: Time-Life Books, 1968.

Staebler, Edna. "The Old-Order Mennonites in Waterloo County." In *Northern Bounty: A Celebration of Canadian Cuisine,* edited by Jo Marie Powers and Anita Stewart. Toronto: Random House, 1995.

Tanttu, Anna-Maija, and Juha Tanttu. *Food from Finland*. Translated by Martha Gaber Abrahamsen. Helsingissa: Kustannusosakeyhtio Otava, 1988.

Wells, Patricia (assisted by Judy Kleiber Jones). *Bistro Cooking*. New York: Workman Publishing, 1989.

Wells, Patricia. *Patricia Wells at Home in Provence*. New York: Scribners, 1996.

Zelayeta, Elena. *Elena's Secrets of Mexican Cooking*. Garden City: Doubleday, 1968.

Mary Kelsey

STIMULANTS.   Foods and drinks (and other substances) that stimulate the consumer to enhanced mental alertness, increased or prolonged physical activity, uninhibited conviviality, or fierce fighting are called "stimulants." This definition is intentionally a narrow one. It excludes the great majority of nourishing foods, for example, because a nourishing meal in itself produces, alongside a feeling of well-being, somnolence (sleepiness) rather than alertness and activity. It also excludes substances such as cannabis and opium (both occasionally taken as foods) that depress mental and physical activity: these are sedatives, not stimulants. We must distinguish enhanced mental alertness from hallucination, the tendency to see what isn't there; hallucinogens are, therefore, also excluded. Other exclusions include appetizers, which stimulate the appetite for food, and aphrodisiacs, which (to the extent that such foods really exist) stimulate sexual appetites and energies.

Using foods that have a stimulant effect provides ways of intentionally adjusting the body's metabolism, which carries risks. There is a good reason why a nourishing meal produces sleepiness: after such a meal, the body is occupied with digestion. Postponing or interrupting that activity may produce digestive disturbance. In any case, increased alertness and physical activity will eventually be paid for in greater-than-usual exhaustion, and there may be other undesirable aftereffects. For example, it may be necessary to compensate for the aftereffects of stimulants by using them again. If the desired effect lessens after frequent use, increased quantities might be needed. In this way, regular use turns into dependence and addiction.

It is even more true of stimulants than of foods in general that their use is not independent of its social context, but no simple generalization is possible. Some of the foods discussed here are nearly always taken in company, as part of a social ritual. Some are nearly always taken as part of, or immediately before or after, a meal. Some, however, are customarily taken when one is not in company and not eating a meal; such habits may vary from one culture to another. External observers focusing on individual psychology may see the solitary use of stimulant foods as posing a personal, social, or criminal problem, while social use might be perceived as no problem or as a different kind of problem. Furthermore, observers focusing on social groups will find users of these stimulant foods to be unexpectedly protective, even nationalistic, about the preferred means of preparing them, which may vary widely.

Stimulant foods have been identified, like nearly all other foods and like many thousands of medicinal plants, in the course of very long-term unrecorded experiments: each human community explores its environment, notes animals and plants that may be of use, finds ways to use them, sometimes begins to farm them, and to trade in them. The stimulant effects of these foods were discovered empirically, as were their associated side-effects and dangers. In the last two centuries, chemists and nutrition scientists have identified their active constituents, making possible for the first time a scientific explanation of their effects.

In general, stimulant foods and drinks are either taken in a neutral vehicle, such as hot water, or they are slowly extracted by chewing. Nonfood stimulants are often taken as smoke or snuff. These various methods all ensure gradual absorption with relatively little interference from other foods. Alcoholic drinks are unusual because they are frequently taken without admixture and often contain strong flavorings: however, water is the principal constituent of most alcoholic drinks, and more water is often added.

Most traditional cultures had one, or at the most two, familiar stimulants. Globalization has changed this, producing such effects as the worldwide fashion for coffee; the worldwide marketing of chocolate, instant coffee, and the "cola" drinks; and the complex social interplay between alternative stimulants of almost equal status, neatly symbolized by the ritual question at breakfast in a French hotel, *"Café? Thé? Chocolat?"* (Coffee? Tea? Hot chocolate?)

Caffeine

Caffeine is among the commonest of stimulants worldwide. It is the chief active constituent in coffee and tea, which are familiar in practically every country, and in maté, guaraná, and cola nut, which are popular in South America and West Africa. It is present in smaller quantities in some other stimulant foods, including chocolate.

Coffee.   Coffee consists of the roasted, ground beans of *Coffea arabica*. Native to Ethiopia, its use spread in late medieval times to Yemen; from there it rapidly became popular around the Mediterranean. Both Arabs and Europeans encouraged its further spread. Details of its use vary. Boiling water is added; commonly sugar is used as a flavoring, and sometimes milk or cream. Often coffee is drunk after meals, but it is also often taken between meals, both by groups as a social drink and by workers as a stimulant. Several substances have been used as coffee substitutes. Most of them had the advantages of being cheap and of tasting somewhat like coffee but the

TABLE 1

Traditional stimulants: Origin and spread

	Usual botanical source	Active constituent	Spread and current use	Analogues and substitutes
South America				
maté	*Ilex paraguariensis*	caffeine	Argentina, Paraguay, Uruguay, and southeastern Brazil	yaupon (*Ilex vomitoria*), cassine (*I. cassine*), American holly (*I. opaca*), and other Ilex species provide stimulant and narcotic beverages, mainly in North America
guaraná	*Paullinia cupana*	caffeine	Brazil only	
coca	*Erythroxylum coca, E. novogranatense*	cocaine	Western South America only. The derivative, cocaine, is widely used as an illicit drug.	*Erythroxylum cataractum, E. fimbriatum, E. macrophyllum* used locally in South America
Central/North America				
chocolate	*Theobroma cacao*	theobromine, caffeine	Central America. Worldwide; spread began in 16th century	Pataxte (*Theobroma bicolor*) used locally in Central America
tobacco	*Nicotiana tabacum*	nicotine	Eastern North America. Worldwide; spread began in 16th century	Wild tobacco (*Nicotiana rustica*) used locally in North America and elsewhere
Mormon tea	*Ephedra nevadensis*	pseudoephedrine	Western North America only	
West Africa				
cola	*Cola nitida, C. acuminata*	caffeine, theobromine	West Africa. Now an ingredient in some soft drinks worldwide	
East Africa/Arabia				
khat	*Catha edulis*	cathinone	Southern Arabia and northeastern Africa only	
coffee	*Coffea arabica*	caffeine	Ethiopia, then Yemen. Worldwide; spread began in 15th century mainly in Europe; instant coffee (*Coffea robusta*) now worldwide	Chicory root (*Cichorium intybus*) and other coffee substitutes
Western Asia				
wine	*Vitis vinifera*	alcohol	Northwestern Iran or southern Caucasus. Worldwide; spread began in 3d millennium B.C.E.	Also made from other fruits and other sources of sugar
beer	*Hordeum sativum*	alcohol	Mesopotamia; perhaps developed independently elsewhere	Also made from other cereals
South and East Asia				
tea	*Camellia sinensis*	caffeine	Southern China. Worldwide; spread began c. 9th century	There are many herbal teas, often sedative or medicinal, less often stimulant
betel	*Areca catechu*	arecoline	South and Southeast Asia only	
kratom	*Mitragyna speciosa*	mitragynine	Thailand only	
Australia				
pituri	*Duboisia hopwoodii*	nicotine	Australia only	
Oceania				
kava	*Piper methysticum*	kavalactones	Oceania only	

disadvantage of containing little or no caffeine. These substitutes have now been overtaken in popularity by instant coffee, a soluble product manufactured from the beans of *Coffea robusta*, which does contain caffeine.

Tea. Tea is made from the dried leaves of *Camellia sinensis*, native to southern China. The use of tea was already spreading beyond China in the ninth century; like coffee, it became popular in Europe in the seventeenth century and its use then spread worldwide. Again, like coffee, details of its use vary. Boiling water is usually poured onto the leaves, which are then allowed to steep for a few minutes. The resulting liquid is much lighter in flavor and color than coffee. Some add sugar to it: fewer, notably the British, add milk; some drink it iced. Tea is more often taken between meals than during meals; like coffee, it is used both as a social drink and by workers as a stimulant.

Caffeine beverages in South America. Maté, also called Paraguayan tea, is made by pouring boiling water onto the dried and roasted leaves of yerba maté (*Ilex paraguariensis*). Most of the leaves that are used come from wild trees gathered from the forests of southern South America. Maté is traditionally a social drink, made in a gourd or a silver pot and sucked through a shared straw or

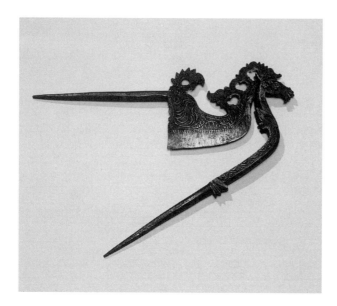

Betel nut sheller, Sri Lanka, nineteenth century. Wrought iron. The sharp blade cracks open the nut while the pointed handles serve as nut picks. ROUGHWOOD COLLECTION. PHOTO CHEW & COMPANY.

silver tube. It is drunk while still extremely hot, so added pleasure is provided by watching the reactions of unskillful foreigners who burn their lips and mouths while trying to drink it. It is usually taken without sugar, but sometimes orange zest is added as a flavoring. Maté is the national beverage of Argentina and Paraguay but has never spread beyond the region. The plant is a relative of European holly (*Ilex aquifolium*), whose leaves have occasionally been used to make a narcotic drink; more importantly, it is related to yaupon or Carolina tea (*Ilex vomitoria*) and other species that have been used to make stimulating and narcotic drinks by North Americans both before and after European settlement.

Guaraná (*Paullinia cupana*) is a tropical plant native to Brazil. Its seeds are traditionally roasted, pounded, and made into cakes called "Brazilian chocolate." They have this name not because they can be eaten solid, like modern chocolate bars, but because in pre-Columbian Mexico travelers used to carry similar cakes of powdered cacao for use in making an instant chocolate drink. Like those, cakes of guaraná are traditionally crumbled into water by tired travelers in Brazil, making a stimulating drink particularly rich in caffeine. Guaraná is now also used as a flavoring for soda, candy, and liqueurs.

Caffeine in Africa.   The cola nut, a rich source of caffeine, is the usual native stimulant of West and Central Africa. It might rather be called a seed, since eight or ten of them are found in each fruit of the trees *Cola nitida* and *C. acuminata*. These seeds are white, pink, or red: the white ones are said to be the best. They are customarily chewed before meals: they have a bitter flavor but, per-

haps as a result of this, foods and drinks taken afterwards seem sweet (water, taken after cola, tastes "like white wine and sugar," according to one observer). Apart from this effect as an appetizer, cola nuts have a high reputation among their traditional users, as stimulant, digestive, and aphrodisiac. Alongside caffeine, they contain theobromine (as does chocolate) and kolanin, a heart stimulant. Cola nuts can also be ground into powder and mixed with water as a drink, and cola extract is used to flavor sodas and candies: the names of Coca-Cola and Pepsi-Cola allude to cola nuts, which may well be an ingredient in these products.

Theobromine
Theobromine is the chief active ingredient in cacao beans, the seeds of the tropical tree *Theobroma cacao*. These beans, fermented, roasted, and ground, are the raw material for chocolate, the traditional stimulant of Mexico, familiar worldwide. In pre-Columbian civilizations, chocolate was used as a drink: the ground cacao was mixed into hot water, which was then poured from a height into the serving cup to produce the much-desired foam. Flavors (chili, vanilla, or others) and color (notably annatto) might be added. Popularized in Europe by the Spanish, chocolate became successively a sugary drink and a milky drink; many other flavorings were tried, including the cinnamon now favored in Mexico. Eventually (in the nineteenth century) chocolate was made into bars to be eaten solid, and in many countries this is now its most familiar form. In the Maya and Aztec civilizations, chocolate was a social drink, taken after dinner, serving as a stimulant (and, according to some, an aphrodisiac). Whole chocolate contains caffeine as well as theobromine, and it is also rich in cocoa butter, making it an extremely nourishing food and, therefore, unlikely to produce aftereffects such as exhaustion.

Nicotine
Tobacco, the fermented leaf of *Nicotiana tabacum*, is usually smoked; in that form it cannot be classified as a food. It can be chewed, however. In Western cultures, chewed tobacco has been typical of sailors and other manual workers subjected to extreme weather conditions that make smoking difficult. Tobacco's active ingredient, nicotine, a deadly poison in the pure state, acts as a stimulant when slowly absorbed.

In Australia, another plant, *Duboisia hopwoodii*, has leaves and flowers very rich in nicotine. Aborigines dry and grind the leaves, mix them with the ash of certain other plants, and roll them into balls, called "pituri," for chewing. These are used by solitary workers and travelers as a stimulant to stave off tiredness and hunger; they are also exchanged as a sign of friendship. They are, or were, used by warrior groups in preparation for a battle. There is a definite advantage in chewing ash in pituri (and also with coca and betel nut), because alkalis in the ash detach the active stimulant substance, in this case nicotine, from the plant acids, allowing it to be more rapidly absorbed. The use of ash in this way has developed, apparently independently, in Australia, southeastern Asia, and South America.

Cocaine

Coca is the dried leaf of a plant species native to western South America, *Erythroxylum coca*, and of a second species, *E. novogranatense*, which developed under cultivation. Coca leaves were known as a stimulant to the pre-Columbian peoples of the Andean region, and continued to be used by them and their Spanish conquerors. Their use is extremely widespread in South America. As with the nicotine plants, the principal use of coca leaves has been as a stimulant for workers and travelers. The usual way is to take some leaves, mix them with the ash of burnt coca or another wood, roll the mixture into a ball, and chew it. Coca leaves, like chocolate, are really nourishing, a property that tends to reduce the severity of the exhaustion that usually follows the use of stimulants. The active constituent of coca leaves was isolated (and named cocaine) in 1860. When taken in the pure form, cocaine was found to be a useful medicinal drug but also highly addictive. It was among the first stimulants to arouse strong medical and governmental disapproval. In the early twentieth century, many countries made it illegal. The name of Coca-Cola alludes to coca, and the early recipe for the product contained cocaine, like other soft drinks of the period.

Some other species of genus *Erythroxylum* contain cocaine or similar compounds and are used as stimulants by various South American peoples: *E. cataractum* by the Cubeo of Colombia; *E. fimbriatum* and *E. macrophyllum* by the Bora and Huitoto of Peru.

Other Stimulants

Betel. The commonest traditional stimulant of southern and southeastern Asia is betel. Like pituri and coca, betel is customarily made up as a chewing packet that includes ash. The active ingredient, arecoline, is contained in the areca nut or betel nut (the nut of the palm *Areca catechu*), which is cut into long narrow pieces and placed inside the packet along with a "lime" made from burnt coral and oyster shells. The packet is formed from a leaf of the betel pepper vine (*Piper betle*). In traditional households, the betel chews are made up each day from fresh supplies; as with pituri, it is a sign of friendship and hospitality to offer a chew to any visitor. The habitual chewing of betel eventually stains the mouth red and the teeth black. When it is first tried, betel can produce feelings of anxiety, excitement, and vertigo; to those who use it regularly, it is a mild stimulant.

Khat. Coffee, when it was introduced to Yemen from across the Red Sea, was not the country's first stimulant. That position belongs to khat (or qat), the leaf of *Catha edulis*. Khat is used in Yemen, Saudi Arabia, and a large area of East Africa from Ethiopia and Somalia to Mozambique and South Africa. It had not spread outside the region until some Americans acquired the taste for it while they were in Somalia with United Nations troops during the early 1990s. Khat is often taken as a tea, made by pouring boiling water onto the dried or fresh leaves. Fresh leaves can also be chewed; in this form its effect is said to be stronger than coffee but not as strong as alcohol. When chewed, khat is often used socially because it enlivens conversation. The principal active constituent in khat is cathinone, now classified as an illegal drug in the United States; however, cathinone is only present in fresh leaves. The second active constituent, cathine, which is still present in the dried leaves, is an appetite suppressant.

A milder stimulant of the same general type is Mormon tea, the leaf of *Ephedra nevadensis*. These leaves contain the active ingredient pseudoephedrine, and are made into a tea with boiling water.

Kava. The root of the plant kava-kava, *Piper methysticum*, is the source of kava, a familiar stimulant used in Hawaii and other Pacific islands. The fresh root is chopped or ground and then soaked and squeezed in water to produce a milky, spicy liquid, which is traditionally served in half coconut shells. Kava is a social drink whose effect is to produce a condition physically resembling drunkenness, though with apparent clarity of mind. The principal active constituents are known as kavalactones.

Kratom. Kratom, a stimulant indigenous to Thailand and little known elsewhere, consists of the leaves of *Mitragyna speciosa*. These leaves can be smoked or made into a tea. The active constituent is mitragynine, which, like cocaine, is a stimulant at low doses but a narcotic at higher doses.

Alcohol

Alcohol is an atypical stimulant because it is not naturally present in any fresh plant. It is produced from the fermentation by yeast of plant sugars. One starting point is a fruit juice. Grape juice makes wine; apple juice makes (hard) cider; pear juice makes perry. Several other fruits are used in various parts of the world. A second starting point is malted cereal: barley is the commonest choice, and the result is beer. Plant saps can be used if they contain sufficient sugar: liquid cane sugar is so used in India, while pulque, a Mexican alcoholic drink, is made from the sap of the maguey (*Agave atrovirens*). Finally, honey, mixed with water, can be used, and the result is mead (a beverage that figures importantly in the Old English epic *Beowulf*). There are two common adjustments to the process: adding cane or beet sugar to the original juice gives the yeast more raw material to work with, producing more alcohol; distilling the final product achieves much greater concentrations of alcohol, resulting in "hard liquor."

Wine and beer are both ancient inventions, going back to southwestern Asia several thousand years B.C.E.

But yeasts are naturally present in the air; therefore, alcoholic drinks might have been invented or discovered many times in human history; certainly, the origin of pulque is independent of those of wine and beer.

Alcoholic drinks have most generally, in traditional societies, been used as social drinks, and they have commonly been used in a ritualistic way as well. Their production is linked with the seasons (in general the required juices are available only when fruit is ripe, and the fermentation process takes time); therefore, by contrast with most other stimulants, the discovery of alcoholic drinks and the annual vintage (especially of wine) tend to be celebrated in major festivals. In many cultures, the ordinary, everyday consumption of alcohol follows precise rules, tending to ensure, for example, that everyone drinks equally. Both in the major festivals and in everyday social drinking, it is commonly the case that drunkenness is aimed at, at least to the extent of the loss of inhibitions, but sometimes going all the way to unconsciousness.

Like kava—and unlike many stimulants—alcohol tends to produce enhanced mental activity accompanied by physical incapacity. In traditional societies, travelers used coca, maté, guaraná, pituri, and other stimulants to keep them going; they would not use alcohol or kava till they had arrived. Likewise, coffee, tea, and some similar stimulants may enhance one's ability to drive safely, for a certain period, while kava and alcohol impair it.

See also **Alcohol**; **Chocolate**; **Cocktails**; **Coffee**; **Mexico and Central America, Pre-Columbian**; **Spirits**; **Tea**.

BIBLIOGRAPHY

Bibra, Ernst von. *Plant Intoxicants*. Edited by Jonathan Ott. Rochester, Vt.: Healing Arts, 1995. Originally published as *Der Narkotischen Genussmittel und der Mensch*. Nürnberg, Germany: Wilhelm Schmid, 1855. The 1995 edition is a major revision and expansion of Baron von Bibra's work, with an up-to-date bibliography that should be the starting point for further study.

Coe, Sophie D., and Michael D. Coe. *The True History of Chocolate*. London and New York: Thames and Hudson, 1996.

Henman, A. R. "Guaraná (*Paullinia cupana* var. *sorbilis*): Ecological and Social Perspectives on an Economic Plant of the Central Amazon Basin." *Journal of Ethnopharmacology* 6 (1982): 311–338.

Kennedy, J. G. *The Flower of Paradise: The Institutionalized Use of the Drug Qat in North Yemen*. Dordrecht, Netherlands: Reidel, 1987.

Lebot, Vincent, Mark Merlin, Lamont Lindstrom. *Kava: The Pacific Drug*. New Haven, Conn.: Yale University Press, 1992. Reprinted as *Kava: The Pacific Elixir*. Rochester, Vt.: Healing Arts Press, 1997.

Lewin, Louis. *Phantastica: Narcotic and Stimulating Drugs, Their Use and Abuse*. Translated by P. H. A. Wirth. New York: Dutton, 1964. Originally published as *Die Pfeilgifte; nach eigenen toxikologischen und ethnologischen Untersuchungen*. Leipzig: J. A. Barth, 1923.

Plowman, Timothy. "The Origin, Evolution, and Diffusion of Coca, *Erythroxylum* spp., in South and Central America." In *Pre-Columbian Plant Migration*, edited by Doris Stone, pp. 125–163. Cambridge, Mass.: Peabody Museum, 1984.

Watson, P. L. *The Precious Foliage: A Study of the Aboriginal Psycho-Active Drug Pituri*. Sydney, New South Wales, Australia: University of Sydney Press, 1983.

Andrew Dalby

STORAGE OF FOOD. Civilizations are built upon a stable and reliable source of food that is provided by a combination of current production, imports, and the preservation of seasonally abundant crops. Preagricultural, nomadic people followed herds of migrating animals or periodically visited traditional locations to slaughter animals and gather fruits, vegetables, and grains as they matured during the year. Locally cultivated crops became the predominant source of food once agriculture became established and farmers tilled specific plots of land. Food that was locally abundant for only a short period of time had to be stored against times of scarcity. A poor harvest or the appropriation of food by marauding brigands could produce local famine. However, the most common and recurring cause of famine resulted from the farmer's inability to store enough food to last from one harvest to another. Summer was often not an idyllic time of plenty for primitive agrarian societies, but a time when many went hungry. It is not surprising then that the fall harvest festivals were such joyous times, for they heralded the end of the seasonal famine and ushered in a time of plenty.

Primitive storage techniques were well developed in prehistoric times. Early storage methods included the selection and growth of naturally dormant crops, and the drying, parching, smoking, and salting of meats, fruits, and vegetables. Mature grains, nuts, roots, and tubers have a period after harvest when they do not sprout and can easily be stored with the simplest of technologies and protective structures. Many cultivars of temperate fruits and vegetables such as apples, pears, and cabbage were selected for their natural storability. More perishable foods (meat, fruits, and vegetables) were sliced into thin sections and dried and/or smoked, or pickled in brine. Some of these techniques, such as sun drying (e.g., raisins), smoking (e.g., ham, fish), and pickling (e.g., dill pickle, pickled pig's feet) are still used today. The storage of food became more sophisticated as the population increased and more concentrated as demand for fresh fruits and vegetables increased. Storage was also used to provide planting materials or propagules for the next season.

The growth of large urban centers and the establishment of large standing armies at the end of the eighteenth century provided an impetus for the development of better storage methods. Canning was developed in 1809 in response to a competition sponsored by Napoleon to provide a better supply of food for his armies. A tin-plated metal canister (from which the term "can" is derived) was filled and a lid hand-soldered in place after the can was heated in a water bath for a specified time. Canned food has a very long storage life, especially when stored under low temperatures. Food in century-old cans that were discovered at an arctic base was not spoiled, although it did contain viable bacteria and was unappetizing as a result of flavor and textural changes. Like canning, many storage technologies such as fermentation remained an unpredictable art until Pasteur identified microorganisms as the scientific cause of spoilage and decay in the 1860s.

With the Industrial Revolution, storage became increasingly important as the population increased dramatically and people moved into dense urban areas. As an affluent middle class developed, commodities that had once been luxuries available only to the nobility became widely available because of increasingly better storage and transportation technologies. For example, meat from Australia and Argentina appeared in European butcher shops, while tropical fruit such as bananas, citrus, and pineapples became available in grocery stores. Increased concern for a healthy diet and a better understanding of the link between diet and health prompted public demand for higher quality food.

Food quality encompasses a remarkable number of attributes. Although all food is made up of the same elementary constituents (carbon, hydrogen, oxygen, nitrogen, potassium, sulfur, etc.), the atoms it contains are arranged into molecules of diverse size, shape, and function. The idea that foods differed in molecular structure developed in the 1830s as food was found to contain the three major components of carbohydrates, proteins, and fats. Since then, more discovery of minerals, vitamins, and amino acids has increased to more than fifty, the essential nutrients found in food. Animals are incapable of many of the elementary syntheses performed by plants and therefore rely on them for many complex molecules such as vitamin C and the twenty-four essential amino acids. Many foods are consumed because of their pleasant aroma, taste, or texture, others because of their presumed medicinal properties. Storage technologies are devised and selected to preserve those specific characteristics that are most important to the consumer.

Limits to Storage Life

The storage life of food is usually limited by the loss of acceptable visual appearance, palatability, or food value, and these criteria of quality are often lost in the reverse order listed. Food provides both nutrition and quality to our diet. Often a commodity can be physically preserved longer than the traits for which it is being stored. For example, the flavor, texture, and nutrition of many fruits and vegetables are reduced before visual appearance of spoilage. Many storage technologies have been devised to retain an acceptable appearance or taste while ignoring changes in food value. This is understandable since

TABLE 1

Useful storage life of plant and animal foods

Food produce	Storage life (Days at 59° F [15° C])
Meat, fish, poultry	1 - 2
Leafy vegetables	1 - 5
Fruits	2 - 20
Root crops	7 - 90
Dried, salted, smoked meat or fish	>360
Dried fruit	>360
Grain and dried seeds	>360

appearance and palatability can be easily assayed by examining and eating the commodity, while measuring food value requires sophisticated laboratory assays.

Food spoilage results from three main causes: chemical changes from ripening and senescence processes, growth of unwanted microorganisms such as bacteria and fungi, and insect and rodent pests. However, many of the processes that cause food spoilage in one commodity are often necessary for high quality in another. Ripening of bananas and tomatoes harvested at a mature but unripe stage is necessary, but excessive ripening leads to poor quality. Insects are needed for the pollination of many crops, but they can also eat the plant and spread disease. Microorganisms cause spoilage, but yeast ferment wine, beer, and sauerkraut, while bacteria are needed for production of pickles and yogurt.

Often more than one series of reactions affects storage life. For example, the major factor influencing the storage life of fresh meat is microbial growth and fat oxidation. Meat is normally marketed after *rigor mortis* and a period of aging. The most common preservation methods for fresh meat are cooling (three to six weeks at 32°F [0°C]) and freezing (nine to fifteen months at −4°F [−20°C]). Fish is far more perishable than meat because it is an excellent substrate for microbial growth. Fish lipids are largely unsaturated and therefore very susceptible to oxidation.

Chemical deterioration. Many chemical reactions contribute to the loss of storage life. The majority are enzymatically driven while others are chemical reactions that occur because of the close proximity of reactive molecules within food. Maillard browning involves color, flavor, and odor changes that result from a chemical reaction between proteins and carbohydrates. The rate of this spontaneous reaction is rapid at baking temperatures, as in the browning of bread, much slower at room temperature, as in the browning of applesauce, and very slow at refrigerator temperatures. Removal of water during dehydration concentrates the reactants and accelerates Maillard browning.

Hydrolysis is the splitting of molecules, usually polysaccharides such as complex sugars, starches, and pectins with the chemical addition of water. During the processing of some fruits, the hydrolysis of sucrose into its components of glucose and fructose greatly affects the sweetness of the product. Storage of potatoes at too cold a temperature (32°F; 0°C) promotes the hydrolysis of starch to sugar. Sugars accumulating during this "sweetening" process turn dark brown when heated (i.e., Maillard browning), making the potatoes unsuited for the production of potato chips and French fries. Modification of amylopectins by hydrolysis contributes to textural changes and the formation of gels.

Oxidative rancidity is a chemical change in the unsaturated bonds of a fat or oil that produces chemicals giving food off-odors and off-flavors. Exclusion of oxygen and light combined with the addition of antioxidants retards rancidity. Vitamins C and E, which are antioxidants, can be destroyed by oxidation. Vitamin C, or ascorbic acid, is used as a reducing agent to prevent oxidative browning of cut fruits and vegetables. Both enzymatic and nonenzymatic reactions contribute to lipid oxidation. Blanching destroys enzymes responsible for rancidity reactions in fruits and vegetables. One of the functions of packaging is to exclude oxygen and light from processed foods. Cooked meats can become rancid within a day, but proper packaging or freezing can delay the process by several months. However, not all oxidation is detrimental; oxidative bleaching of pigments in flour during storage results in whiter flour.

Microbial contamination. Bacteria and fungus are everywhere in our environment, and most foods provide an excellent substrate for their growth. Packaging, whether natural (banana peel, seed coat, or egg shell) or artificial (glass bottle, metal can, or foil pouch) protects the enclosed food from microbial contamination. Some foods contain natural antimicrobial chemicals (for example, the tannins in unripe fruit), while other antimicrobial compounds, such as the fungicide in wax coatings, can be applied to food. Many foods are sterilized, pasteurized, or fumigated before packaging and storage to control microbes. Storage conditions of low temperature and humidity retard microbial growth. However, once these protective barriers are breached, microbial growth is often unchecked and rapidly destroys the commodity.

Food can be a vector and provide a growth medium for many pathogenic microbes (e.g., *Campylobacter jejuni, Escherichia coli, Listeria monocytogenes, Salmonella, Shigella, Vibrio cholerae*). However, common spoilage organisms (e.g., *Botrytis, Colletotrichum, Erwinia, Fusarium, Penicillium, Rhizopus*) are not human pathogens, although some bacteria (e.g., *Clostridium botulinum, Staphylococcus aureus*) and fungi (e.g., *Aspergillus flavus*) can produce potent toxins.

Insect and rodent pests. The major insect pests in stored food are moth (Lepidoptera) larva and beetle (Coleoptera) larva and adults. Insects have been controlled in stored food using physical methods for thousands of

years. Neolithic farmers in the Nile Delta kept seeds cool and dry by storing them in clay jars buried in the ground. Exposure to high temperatures has been used since the sixteenth century to control insects in stored grain. Under many circumstances the easiest, most rapid, and most economical method of controlling insects is with insecticides, often in the form of fumigants. Fumigation has been the method of choice since the late 1940s, but the unwanted side effects of some of the chemicals used (for example, toxicity to other species, depletion of stratospheric ozone, acquired resistance by the pest) have promoted interest in physical control measures. Many physical conditions such as temperature, relative humidity, moisture content, and atmospheric composition can be manipulated to affect insect survival. The structure containing the commodity (granaries, elevators, bags, and packaging), forces on the commodity (compression and impaction), and irradiation are also used in controlling insect infestation.

In general, insect survival in stored food is dependent on temperature, relative humidity, and gas composition. Temperatures lower than 55°F (13°C) or higher than 95°F (35°C) dramatically reduce survival. Sublethal temperatures also have effects; for example, at 68°F (20°C), most insects survive but stop feeding. Additional reductions in survival occur when stressful temperatures are combined with reduced moisture or oxygen levels. Drying affects insect population directly by reducing survival and indirectly by causing cracks that increase the susceptibility of the commodity to insect attack. The respiration by large numbers of insects produces heat and moisture, favoring both mold and further insect growth.

Physical movement of grain increases insect mortality. Moving grain by auger or pneumatic conveyer increases mortality of larva and adults. Impacts from dropping grain six meters resulted in up to 90 percent mortality. Moving can directly kill or injure insects by crushing them, or it can prevent feeding and mating by disrupting the microecological niches required by some insects. However, handling can also increase the amount of cracked seeds and grain dust, which are the preferred diet of some insects.

Biological control with insect pathogens, predators, or parasites is an important component of integrated pest management strategies. Unlike other treatments, biological control agents can reproduce, so one inoculation may be sufficient to establish lasting control. In contrast, many physical treatments such as cold, heat, fumigation, and irradiation have no lasting effect, and reinfestation must be controlled by proper storage and packaging.

Over the centuries, feral rodents have adapted to living in or near houses and farms. The most common rodents are the brown or Norway rat (*Rattus norvegicus*), the black rat (*Rattus rattus*), and the house mouse (*Mus musculus*). Food storage facilities provide ideal conditions for rodents to multiply very rapidly with food, shelter, and a lack of predators. Common signs of a rodent problem are fecal droppings, tail and footprints in dust, droppings and urine stains in feeding areas, gnawing marks on wood, plastic, metal, pipes, and food containers, spilled food, smear marks from rodents' fur (distinctive dirty marks, particularly along skirting boards and around doors), rat holes, nesting sites, rat runs, and the rodents themselves. Constant gnawing is necessary to keep rats' teeth ground down; their gnawing of electrical wires has caused structural fires.

Rodents eat a lot of food, particularly in grain stores, but far more food has to be discarded because it has been contaminated with hairs and droppings. Apart from *salmonella* food poisoning, rats may carry as many as thirty-five diseases including rabies, plague, typhus, leptospirosis, rat bite fever, and hantavirus. Disease may be spread by eating food contaminated by rodent droppings or urine, contact with rat urine, parasites that live on rodents, and rodent bites.

There are biological factors, behavioral factors, and environmental factors to be considered in designing a rodent control program. Rats normally range no more than 150 feet from the nest; a male mouse will control an area of ten to twenty feet from the nest. Rats will migrate on their own; mice are often carried in boxes or crates into new locations. Rodents begin reproducing at a very young age, have large litters, and breed year around. A 90 percent population reduction may be replaced in as little as nine months. Rodents have a well-developed sense of taste and can remember foods that made them sick in the past. They are very cautious and wary of new objects introduced into their surroundings (such as bait boxes or traps) and of changes in the surroundings. Rodents can be controlled by using poisons and traps. Positioning of control measures can be optimized by using tracking powder to locate runs and nesting areas.

Storage Technologies

Storage technologies manipulate the extrinsic factors of temperature, water activity, and oxygen availability to control the rate of quality loss by stored commodities. Examples of these treatments include drying, salting, brining, fermentation, canning, cooling, freezing, altering storage gases, and ionizing radiation.

Temperature. Temperature is the key factor influencing the storage life and safety of fresh and processed food. Living organisms are best adapted to a narrow range of temperature. As the temperature diverges from this optimum range, the organism is first retarded in growth and then killed (Table 2). Most of the physiological changes that shorten the storage life of fruits and vegetables, as well as many of the reactions in meat, eggs, and dairy products, are enzymatic. Other reactions are purely chemical. The effect of temperature is usually much greater for enzymatically driven reactions than for purely chemical reactions. Each 50°F (10°C) drop in tempera-

TABLE 2

Response of insects that are found in stored product to temperature

Area	Temperature °F	Temperature °C	Effect
Lethal	140 to 122	60 to 50	Death in minutes
	122 to 113	50 to 45	Death in hours
Sub-optimal	113 to 95	45 to 35	Development stops
	95 to 91	35 to 33	Development slows
Optimal	91 to 77	33 to 25	Maximum development
Sub-optimal	77 to 68	25 to 20	Development slows
	68 to 50	20 to 10	Development stops
Lethal	50 to 41	10 to 5	Death in days (un-acclimated)
	41 to 14	5 to -10	Death in weeks to months (acclimated)
	14 to -13	-10 to -25	Death in minutes

SOURCE: Modified from Fields and Muir, 1996.

ture halves the rate of most chemical reactions (i.e., a Q_{10} or temperature quotient of 2). In contrast, biological reactions often have Q_{10} values between 3 and 5, meaning that the reaction is decreased to a third or fifth by an 18°F (10°C) fall in temperature.

Thermal processing. Food is not stored at elevated temperatures, but high temperatures such as those involved in canning and pasteurization are often used to arrest microbial growth, denature enzymes, and alter the structure of food prior to storage. Temperatures above 140°F (60°C) inhibit and kill growing microorganisms. Resting stages require much higher temperatures.

Canning is the heating of prepared food in hermetically sealed metal, glass, or foil containers to a specific temperature for a specified time to destroy disease-causing microorganisms, denature enzymes, and prevent spoilage. Low-acid foods such as meats and vegetables are heated to 240–265°F (116–129°C), while acidic foods, such as fruits and tomatoes, are heated to about 212°F (100°C). The length of heating depends on the type and size of the container, the food being canned, and the method of heating. Flat foil packets may require less than ten minutes, while large metal containers may require over forty minutes. The aseptic container keeps out oxygen and contaminating microorganisms. Canned food is very stable and can be stored for many months at ambient temperatures; however, storage life is extended when the food is stored at low temperatures. Once opened, canned food is prone to spoil rapidly and should be stored under refrigeration.

Pasteurization is the heating of a liquid such as milk, wine, or beer to between 131 and 158°F (55 and 70°C), to destroy harmful bacteria without substantially altering the liquid's composition, flavor, or nutritive value. In addition to destroying potential disease-causing bacteria, pasteurization can greatly increase the storage life of milk by inactivating enzymes that reduce quality. There are two basic methods of pasteurization, batch or continuous. In the batch method a vat of liquid is heated to 145°F (63°C) for thirty minutes, rapidly cooled, and stored below 50°F (10°C). This method is used for milk and its by-products (e.g. creams, chocolate). Beer and wine are pasteurized at about 140°F (60°C) for twenty minutes. Water can also be pasteurized at 149°F (65°C) for six minutes, or to a higher temperature for a shorter time, to kill germs, viruses, and parasites. In contrast, the most common continuous processing method uses high temperature, short time (HTST) pasteurization. Milk is heated to 161°F (72°C) for fifteen seconds, while beer and wine are heated to 158°F (70°C) for about thirty seconds, and bottled under sterile conditions. The continuous process has several advantages over the vat method, the most important being time and energy saving. Radiation pasteurization of foods uses low doses of gamma rays, X-rays, and electrons to control foodborne pathogens on beef, pork, lamb, and fish.

Refrigerated storage. Cold storage. Most food stores best at temperatures near 32°F (0°C) because chemical and biological processes are slowed down. Maximum storage life for meat, eggs, dairy products, and all processed food is at 32°F (0°C). Most fresh fruits and vegetables are also best stored at 32°F (0°C). They include apples, berries, broccoli, cabbage, carrot, corn, grapes, lettuce, and pears. However, some fruits and vegetables are sensitive to low temperatures and are damaged if stored below 50°F (10°C). These chilling-sensitive commodities include asparagus, avocado, banana, beans, cucumber, eggplant, grapefruit, melons, peppers, potatoes, squash, sweet potato, tomato, and watermelon.

Best product quality is maintained under constant temperatures. Typically the storage temperature should vary no more than ±1.8°F (1°C) from the desired temperature, but even this variability may be excessive if it allows the temperature to fall below the freezing point of the commodity. Large swings in temperature can result in unwanted freezing or chilling injury, condensation of water on the product that promotes microbial growth, accelerated water loss, and reduced storage life. All fresh fruits and vegetables lose water in storage and must be properly packaged and/or stored under high relative humidity to prevent excessive water and weight loss.

Freezing. Living cells are mainly dilute aqueous solutions of salts, sugars, organic acids, proteins, and lipids. These solutes lower the freezing point of pure water from 32°F (0°C) to 31.6°F (−0.2°C) for lettuce, 30.6°F (−0.8°C) for bananas, 29.5°F (−1.4°C) for carrots and sweet potatoes, 26.6°F (−3°C) for beef, fish and poultry, and 17.6°F (−8°C) for peanuts. Most frozen foods can be kept at 0°F (−18°C) for a year with little loss of quality. Both free and bound water exist in foods. Bound water exists in combination within an insoluble matrix such as cellulosic cell walls and muscle protein. As the temperature falls, ice crystals first form where the water is the purest and therefore has the highest freezing point. Growing ice crystals remove pure water from the solution, and it becomes more concentrated. Slow freezing produces large ice crystals and highly concentrated solutions, both of which are detrimental to quality retention. Rapid freezing retains quality by either producing small ice crystals or a vitrified solid. The differential effects of freezing on bound and free water give rise to the complex freezing pattern of foods.

Water activity and humidity. Drying is perhaps the oldest method used to store food. Drying fish, meat, fruits, and vegetables in the sun or over a fire or by ventilation with heated air is still used to prolong storage life. Both the harvested food and the spoilage organism (microbe or insect) need water to live. Removal of water by drying, brining, salting, cooling, or freezing prevents the growth of microorganisms and insects, deactivates enzymatic pathways, and reduces the many chemical reactions that accompany a reduction in quality during storage.

Different foods can have different equilibrium moisture contents under the same relative humidity and different microbial stability under the same moisture content. The idea of water activity (a_w) was introduced to better understand how water availability in foods affects microbes. The water activity (a_w) of pure water is 1.00. The a_w of an aqueous solution is calculated by dividing the vapor pressure of solution by the vapor pressure of water at a given temperature. Under steady state conditions, water activity in food can be approximated by dividing the relative humidity of the ambient air by 100.

Few spoilage and pathogenic bacteria can grow below a_w's of 0.90, while levels below 0.70 prevent the growth of most yeasts and molds. An a_w that influences microbial growth is usually lethal to grain, fruits, and vegetables. Food quality can still deteriorate at a_w's below 0.60 from the enzymatic and nonenzymatic oxidation of lipids, vitamins, and pigments.

For most fresh fruits and vegetables, a relative humidity of 90 to 95 percent is recommended during storage. A relative humidity close to 100 percent or the condensation of water on a commodity that frequently accompanies such high humidity may cause cracking of the skin. Surface condensation may also accelerate the growth and spread of microorganisms. Large evaporator surfaces will improve the relative humidity in direct expansion refrigeration systems. A 41 to 50°F (5 to 10°C) temperature split, as commonly designed, will maintain 70 percent to 80 percent relative humidity; a 32.9°F (0.5°C) split would be required to maintain 95 percent relative humidity. In practice, supplementary humidification with fogging nozzles, spinning disc humidifiers, or steam humidifiers is often used to maintain high humidity in the storage of fruits and vegetables.

Dry cereal grains have an extremely low respiration rate and show only slight reduction in total sugars and quality even after years at a cool temperature and low oxygen concentration. In general, grain in equilibrium with 30 percent and 50 percent relative humidity air has a moisture content of about 8 percent and 12 percent, respectively. Grain respiration is particularly affected by moisture, increasing as the water content of the seed rises above 14 percent. Respiration produces heat and water, both of which contribute to increased respiration and an accelerated loss of quality. Warm temperatures and higher humidity also facilitate the growth of insects and molds. The moisture requirement for the growth and reproduction of different insect species in grains varies from 8 percent to 12 percent.

Controlling the moisture content is extremely important in preventing spoilage. Grains (e.g., wheat, rye, oats, barley, soybeans, corn, and sorghum) must be dried to around 12 percent moisture for safe storage during warm weather. Most grains are dry enough to store when harvested. Artificial drying of grains that are harvested before they are dry enough can be accomplished in a few hours with heated forced air. Longer times are required using dry (>70 percent relative humidity) ambient air. Rice storages must have driers since rice is customarily harvested before it is dry enough for storage. Temperature differences and air movement within grain stored at the proper moisture level can redistribute moisture and cause local increases conductive to spoilage. Respiration of the grain and associated pests (e.g., mold and insects) produces water that promotes their growth. Periodic ventilation and turning can remove or redistribute moisture to maintain proper storage conditions.

Low oxygen and/or high carbon dioxide. Researchers in the 1920s showed that altered concentrations of oxygen and carbon dioxide in the storage atmosphere retarded the germination and growth of microorganisms on fruits, vegetables, and meat. Low oxygen and moderately elevated carbon dioxide atmospheres retard respiration and the synthesis and action of the plant hormone ethylene and extend the storage life of fruits and vegetables. High carbon dioxide levels are more effective in prolonging the storage of meat.

Modified atmospheres have many advantages for the storage of both living and processed food, but the long treatment period may be incompatible with the marketing system. If crops sensitive to ethylene are to be stored together with crops that produce large amounts of ethylene, then either periodic or continuous venting may be necessary to prevent deleterious concentrations of ethylene from accumulating.

Fermentation. Oxygen is necessary for respiratory metabolism. Exclusion of oxygen causes a shift from aerobic to anaerobic metabolism and the production of many fermentative products such as ethanol and lactic acid. Fermentation is an ancient, low technology method of preserving food. When Ch'in Shih Huang Ti was constructing the Great Wall of China in the third century

METHODS USED TO STORE FOOD

Natural methods
Harvest as needed (field storage)
  Slaughter animals as needed
  Keep plants in the ground (carrots, cassava)
  Keep fruit on the tree (avocados, citrus)
Harvest and keep alive
  Selection of naturally dormant plants
   (grains, nuts, bulbs, tubers)
  Store in field or natural
   (clamps, curing, root cellars)

Technological methods
Harvest and keep alive
  Cold storage   Controlled atmosphere
  Curing   Ionizing radiation
Harvest and process
  Additives   Aseptic packaging
  Brining   Canning
  Cold storage   Controlled atmosphere
  Curing   Drying
  Fermentation   Freeze-drying
  Freezing   Fumigation
  Ionizing radiation   Pasteurization
  Refrigeration

B.C.E., the laborers were given mixed fermented vegetables as part of their rations. Fermentation is a complicated anaerobic process in which naturally present bacteria hydrolyze sugars to organic acids (e.g., acetic acid) or ethanol. Salt may be added to the initial mix to draw water from the vegetables and encourage brine formation. Brine promotes the growth of desirable bacteria; acid (vinegar or acetic acid) may be added to rapidly lower the pH and discourage the growth of undesirable bacteria.

Ionizing radiation. Ionizing radiation from gamma rays or electron beams is a cost-effective method of preparing food for storage. Low-dose irradiation controls insect infestation of grain and flour (0.2 to 0.7 kGy), food-borne parasites (1 kGy), and inactivates non-spore forming pathogenic bacteria (3 to 5 kGy). Higher dosages (20 to 50 kGy) are required to inactivate enzymes, kill spores and sterilize products. Levels of 0.2 to 1.0 kGy are not immediately lethal, and irradiated insects can survive for several weeks, but they feed less and are usually infertile. Higher dosages cause immediate mortality, but they can also reduce vitamin content and alter textural properties of grains. There is no residual effect of irradiation, so re-infestation must be controlled by appropriate handling

Storage basket for potatoes and onions made of willow and cherry branches, France, twentieth century. French farmhouse pantries were often furnished with several baskets of this type in varying sizes, the smallest for garlics, shallots, and fingerling potatoes. Food was removed through the trough at the bottom. ROUGHWOOD COLLECTION. PHOTO CHEW & COMPANY.

and packaging. Low doses inhibit sprouting of potatoes and onions, but higher doses stimulate wound responses in fresh fruits and vegetables that lead to reduced quality. Spices and vegetable seasoning are the products most commonly irradiated. Aseptically packaged irradiated meat can be stored without refrigeration for many months. The U.S. military has used irradiated food for a number of years. Consumers view irradiated food either as being adulterated or as being additionally protected against spoilage.

Sanitation, fumigation, and quarantine treatments. Since the leading cause of food spoilage is pests such as insects, fungi, and bacteria, storage life can be extended by removing these organisms. Using acceptable cultural practices during production of the raw material and sanitation practices during harvest and preparation for storage significantly decreases the initial number of pests present in stored food. Since many pests increase rapidly under favorable storage conditions, a significant reduction in their initial number can greatly extend the storage life of a commodity before expensive control measures are needed. Once stored, there are only a few techniques available to eliminate pests already present in raw and processed food.

Some of the most important control measures are fumigation, heat treatments, and controlled atmospheres. The anaerobic storage of grains in airtight containers can reduce the need for chemical fumigation to control insects and mold and does not require the technical sophistication required for the safe application of toxic fumigants. The hermetic storage of living tissue such as grains, fruits or vegetables is a form of modified atmosphere storage that has been used for centuries. The respiration of the commodity creates an atmosphere rich in carbon dioxide and deficient in oxygen. Some of these fast-acting treatments can be used as quarantine treatments. Many production areas throughout the world contain pests that importing countries do not want introduced into their production areas. Increasing international trade in staples and exotic foods and the elimination of effective, commonly used fumigants (e.g., methyl bromide) are promoting the development of new quarantine treatments that are not only environmentally safe, but also fast-acting and effective on a wide range of commodities.

Methods of Storage

Food can be stored alive (apples, cows, tomatoes, wheat), or dead (applesauce, beefsteak, spaghetti sauce, flour). Storage technologies must produce drastically different environments to effectively store these many kinds of food. Cereal grains store best at a relative humidity below 50 percent to reduce respiration, while fresh fruit and vegetables need humidity above 90 percent to prevent excessive weight loss. Some ripening fruits (bananas and tomatoes) are injured if stored below 10°C (50°F), while others (apples and pears) store best at 0°C (32°F). Carbon dioxide levels above 50 percent reduce the spoilage of meat, and exclusion of oxygen prevents rancidity of potato chips and nuts, but most fruits and vegetables will not tolerate oxygen levels below 2 percent or carbon dioxide above 3 percent. Although the word "storage" may conjure up images of large grain elevators, warehouses, and sophisticated refrigeration technology, there still exists a range of less sophisticated techniques that are widely used today.

Storage before slaughter or harvest. Animals can be slaughtered as necessary where the climate is mild or protective structures exist, and where animal feed is available or can be stored. However, animal products (eggs and milk) may need to be collected periodically to maintain production.

For most perishable food, maturity occurs over a short period of time, and harvest must take place during that period. However, a range of crops can be left on the plant (or in the ground) for up to a few months. The storage of potatoes and other root crops in the ground and the storage of citrus and avocados on the tree are good examples of this. Storage on the plant overcomes the need for capital investment in storage facilities and delays exposure of the commodity to water and nutritional loss encountered during storage. It also reduces the damage and disease inevitably associated with harvesting, handling, and storage. Problems include exposure of the commodities to environmental disasters (hail, frost, diseases, and sunburn), the cost of keeping the land idle (for field crops) or of reducing the following seasons' yield (for tree crops).

Storage after slaughter or harvest. Food can be stored after slaughter or harvest as fresh, still-living commodities (fresh fruits and vegetables), or as a processed, dead product (cured meat, canned tomatoes, etc.). Low humidity and temperature are two traditional means of facilitating the storage of naturally dormant crops such as grains (wheat, corn, and rice), bulbs (onions and garlic) and, roots and tubers (carrots, potatoes, and yams). The rates of the many chemical reactions that reduce quality are naturally suppressed in these crops. Using chemicals or treatments that interfere with those physiological processes that naturally terminate dormancy can lengthen the duration of storage.

Common (unrefrigerated) storage. One of the oldest methods of storage of perishables is the use of "clamps," which are basically piles of a commodity laid in the field and then covered with straw and soil to insulate and waterproof the clamp. This method is still in use for the storage of potatoes, turnips, parsnips, celeriac, rutabagas ("Swedes") and other "hard" vegetables. In large clamps, ventilation with chimneys and perforated channels through the stack are needed to remove the heat of respiration, and reduce the risk of anaerobiosis or CO_2 toxicity.

A step in sophistication above field clamps is storage in rooms dug into the ground, such as root cellars, and natural or man-made caves, and buildings that are often heavily insulated. Temperatures in caves and underground (1 m) are fairly stable at 10 to 15°C (50 to 59°F) throughout the year. They have the advantage of low maintenance costs, stable temperatures, and high relative humidity. These unrefrigerated stores are best suited for long-lived commodities like potatoes, onions, and winter squash. But these structures are only effective in climates where the ambient temperatures during the storage period are low enough to maintain product quality for a reasonable length of time. Old-fashioned storage of apples, cabbage, and pumpkins in root cellars is a good example of this type of storage. This technique is still used for potatoes, particularly those intended as propagation material.

Grain storage facilities come in a number of sizes and shapes: rectangular wood-framed bins; cylindrical prefabricated metal structures; flat, ground-level piles on concrete floors in warehouse-type buildings; and overhead bins above driveways. One of the most common storage and processing facilities is the granary or grain elevator; a tall (c. 30 meters tall) cylindrical building equipped with machinery for unloading, weighing, cleaning, mixing, storing, and loading grain. Livestock farms may have a number of small granaries to store feed grain at locations adjacent to feedlots. Every town in a grain producing area has an elevator to accumulate grain from farmers and store it for a short period of time while it is cleaned, conditioned, dried, and graded. Larger elevators are located at terminal grain markets and shipping centers where the grain is stored for use by millers or to await shipment. Grain arriving by truck, railroad car, or ship is unloaded and moved by auger, or belt, bucket, or pneumatic conveyer to an area above the cylindrical storage bins where it is cleaned and weighed. A number of bins can be built side-by-side to form facilities that can store millions of bushels of grain. Governments in some countries subsidize the long-term storage of grain to stabilize prices and protect against famine. In contrast to a granary or elevator that stores grain, a silo is any structure or container used for the storage of large masses of high-moisture forage or silage for animal feed.

Once processed, food is more physically stable than the original living material, but it is also a better source of nutrients to microbes. Processed food can be preserved for extended periods by a combination of aseptic packaging such as canning or bottling to exclude microbes and oxygen and moderate to low temperatures.

Night air storage. In warmer climates, a modification of common storage can be used if there is a substantial difference between day and night temperatures during the storage season. The technique used is termed "night air ventilation." The produce is placed in a common storage room, which is well-insulated and supplied with a ventilation system to enable air to be drawn into it and distributed through the produce during the coolest part of the night. This technique can be used to remove field heat and cool produce before refrigerated storage. It can also be used to maintain produce at the proper storage temperature when the nights are cold. In modern stores of this type, microprocessor technology can be used to regulate the ventilation system to optimize the storage environment.

Refrigerated storage. By far the largest proportions of fresh commodities are stored in insulated rooms provided with mechanical refrigeration. At low temperatures, the biological activity (and deterioration) of the product is dramatically slowed, and the growth rate (and sometimes the viability) of microorganisms is reduced, as is the rate of water loss.

Several methods are employed to provide cold storage in the absence of mechanical refrigeration. In some areas, cold well or lake water may be used. The air of the store may be cooled to near the water temperature with a good heat-exchange system. In cold climates, ice harvested from lakes and ponds during winter can be stored and used for summer refrigeration.

In areas where the relative humidity is low, an evaporative cooler may reduce the temperature of the air sufficiently to be an economical source of refrigeration. In the western United States, for example, the mean wet bulb temperature in growing areas ranges from 8 to 21°C (46 to 79°F) during the harvest season. A well-designed evaporative cooling system will provide cooling air at one or two degrees above the wet bulb temperature. Chilling-sensitive commodities can be cooled very satisfactorily by this technique. An additional advantage is that the high relative humidity produced during cooling significantly reduces water loss from the commodity.

Mechanical refrigeration. Without a doubt, the invention of mechanical refrigeration in the 1850s and its commercial application starting around 1875 was crucial to the modern storage of perishable food. Mechanical refrigeration relies on the basic principle that substantial amounts of energy (i.e., heat) are absorbed during the vaporization of a liquid and released during the condensation of a gas. Using a mechanical pump, a gaseous refrigerant is compressed, cooled, liquefied, and stored in the receiver. When cooling is needed, the liquid refrigerant is allowed to enter the evaporator where it evaporates into a gas as it absorbs heat from the cold storage enclosure. Fans blow air warmed by the commodity over the cold evaporator coils where heat is transferred from the air to the refrigerant. Repeated cycles of condensation and evaporation of the refrigerant "pumps" heat from the cold storage enclosure. Ammonia was the first and most commonly used refrigerant for many years. The development of Freons has produced refrigerants that are less toxic to plants and humans but that are being reassessed for their environmental impact.

There are a number of different techniques for using mechanical refrigeration in the cold storage of food. In the direct expansion method, the evaporator coils are in the cooled space. This system is simple, but it results in low relative humidity. Special and expensive modifications are necessary to provide high humidity for the storage of fresh fruits and vegetables. However, low relative humidity is beneficial for the storage of some commodities such as grains and onionsand for canned or packaged processed food.

See also **Cereal Grains and Pseudo-Cereals; Frozen Food; Preparation of Food; Seeds, Storage of.**

BIBLIOGRAPHY

Abeles, Frederick B., Page W. Morgan, and Mikal E. Saltveit. *Ethylene in Plant Biology.* 2nd ed. San Diego: Academic Press, 1992.

Calderon, Moshe, and Rivka Barkai-Golan, eds. *Food Preservation by Modified Atmospheres.* Boca Raton, Fla.: CRC Press, 1990.

Council for Agricultural Science and Technology. *Foodborne Pathogens: Risks and Consequences.* Report No. 122. Ames, Iowa: Council for Agricultural Science and Technology, 1995.

Diehl, Johannes F. *Safety of Irradiated Foods.* 2nd ed. New York: M. Dekker, 1995.

Fields, P. G., and Muir, W. E. "Physical Control." In *Integrated Management of Insects in Stored Products*, edited by Bhadrivaju Subramanyam and David W. Hagstrum, pp. 195–221. New York: M. Dekker, 1996.

Gould, G. W., ed. *New Methods for Food Preservation.* New York: Chapman and Hall, 1995.

Hardenburg, Robert E., Alley E. Watada, and ChienYi Wang. *The Commercial Storage of Fruits, Vegetables, and Florist and Nursery Stocks.* Agriculture Handbook No. 66 (revised). Washington, D.C.: U.S. Department of Agriculture, Agricultural Research Service, 1986.

Kilcast, D., and Persis Subramaniam, eds. *The Stability and Shelf-life of Food.* Cambridge, U.K.: Woodhead, 2000.

Ooraikul, B., and M. E. Stiles, eds. *Modified Atmosphere Packaging of Food.* New York: Ellis Horwood, 1991.

Saltveit, Mikal E. "Discovery of Chilling Injury." In *Discoveries in Plant Biology*, edited by Shain-Dow Kung and Shan-Fa Yang, vol. 3, pp. 423–448. Singapore: World Scientific Publishing, 2000.

Saltveit, Mikal E., ed. *Physiological Basis of Postharvest Technologies.* International Society for Horticultural Science *Acta Horticulturae* 343 (1993).

Taub, Irwin A., and Singh, R. Paul *Food Storage Stability.* Boca Raton, Fla.: CRC Press, 1998.

VanGarde, Shirley J., and Margy Woodburn. *Food Preservation and Safety: Principles and Practice.* Ames: Iowa State University Press, 1994.

Mikal E. Saltveit

STROKE. *See* **Health and Disease; Salt; Sodium.**

STYLING OF FOOD.

The styling of food, usually referred to as "food styling," is the art of preparing food to be photographed or filmed. The preparation, or styling, involved can be as deceptively simple as shopping for the perfect apple or as extreme as re-creating an elaborate, twelve-course belle epoque dinner party for fourteen. The creation of appealing images of food is a complex process. Whether the food is to be photographed for packaging, an advertisement, a cookbook, or a magazine, or to be filmed as part of a television commercial, cooking show, or movie, the styling of the food is an integral part of the process.

The People Who Do It: Food Stylists

Generally, those who work in the field of food styling are known as "food stylists." Since there is no formal training available for food styling, the particular skills and techniques required are usually learned while apprenticed to or assisting an established food stylist. While most people entering the field have a background in the culinary arts, additional skills that are invaluable include a knowledge of basic food chemistry, the principles of design, and the ability to improvise. Until the late twentieth century, courses on food styling were rarely offered, even at

Food styling is sometimes more complex than preparing a dish of food for the camera. In this instance, the subject is a model and an entire shopping cart full of food. Shot on a platform in a studio, the final image gave the impression that the shopper was walking through a store. Also note that in 1949, when this picture was taken, women dressed to go shopping, even for groceries. © Bettmann/CORBIS.

the top cooking schools. Where offered, these courses are primarily an introduction to the field.

While the term "home economist" is sometimes used, this is basically a holdover from the era when home economists on staff at women's service magazines (such as *Good Housekeeping, Ladies' Home Journal*, and *McCall's*), and large food corporations were responsible for the styling of food. Curiously, home economist is the term frequently used in the film industry.

Today, very few companies and magazines have food stylists on staff. Food stylists usually work on a freelance basis. The photographer, director, or production company hires them as needed, sometimes choosing a stylist that specializes in a certain area such as ice cream, chocolate, fast food, or baked goods.

Is The Styling of Food Necessary?
The need for food styling is a question that is often raised. The photographing or filming of food is very involved, and many techniques are employed to stabilize, sustain, and, if necessary, enhance the food to be photographed. Most important is that the food look as fresh and appetizing as possible until the image is captured on film, but

this process can take hours. During that time, the food needs to be kept "alive," or replaced as often as needed, sometimes very often. For example, it is difficult to take a photograph of a barbecue grill with flames lapping up through an arrangement of jumbo shrimp, because the flames will char the food within minutes. The food might need to be replaced a dozen times and look identical each time so as not to affect the lighting or camera framing. Or to shoot a commercial that features a slice of pie with a piece being broken off by a fork, twenty takes with twenty perfect slices might be needed before the director gets the shot in which the crust looks flaky enough. Even a bowlful of salad greens demands a unique knowledge and set of skills to keep it looking crisp and moist. This knowledge and these skills are essential to successful food styling, and ensure that the process of capturing the needed image on film is efficient and cost-effective.

While there is a trend toward a more documentary style of photographing food that shuns food styling, this seemingly straightforward approach still involves many of the same considerations that go into typical food photography: props, lighting, camera angle. While food photographed straight out of the kitchen might have an inherent honesty about it, the end result is not always attractive. Most consumers, and more importantly the clients, still expect to see images of appealing food.

The Process and Techniques Involved

Each project a food stylist undertakes is unique and has its own set of demands. The approach the stylist takes in preparing the food—even the same food—varies greatly depending on how the image is to be seen and used.

But before the food is prepared, there are several preliminary steps involved. The stylist meets with the photographer/director, and sometimes the client, to discuss what will be shot. The appropriate recipes, layout, or storyboards are reviewed. And from this, the necessary food, material, and equipment are determined. While the stylist is responsible for the shopping and purchasing of the needed food, actual product to be used is usually sent by the client. Often the shopping involves locating out-of-season or difficult-to-find items. The stylist then confers with the prop stylist (the person responsible for providing the tableware, linens, flowers, etc.) to make sure the props selected are suitable.

The first step in the actual preparation of the food is to create a "stand-in." The stand-in is a close approximation of the finished food, and gives the photographer/director the time needed to compose and light the shot without worrying about the food "dying" on the set. Another important reason for preparing a stand-in is that it allows the client to make recommendations the stylist can incorporate into the final, or "hero," food.

The preparation of the hero food involves any number of specialized techniques food stylists have developed to deal with the demands of photographing food. The overriding concern of the stylist is to keep the food looking fresh and alive. Moisture is critical.

Depending on the food, moisture is retained (or replenished) by brushing or spraying the surface with water or a thin coat of vegetable oil, and keeping the food under cover until needed. This is probably the most basic technique employed by the food stylist. It not only creates the appearance of freshness but can also make the food look juicy or even hot, since it is often cold and undercooked when photographed. (Heat will cause the food to continue cooking, then wilt and appear dried out.) For instance, vegetables are undercooked and kept in cold water until needed to retain their color. Poultry and meats are also undercooked, or cooked at lower than normal temperatures, to prevent them from shriveling or shrinking. A finished, roasted look is then added to the surface by brushing on gravy coloring, or browning the surface with a blowtorch. For a grilled look, grill marks are branded onto the surface using red-hot skewers.

Stabilizing delicate foods is a common challenge. This can be as straightforward as using toothpicks, straight pins, or hairpins to hold things in place. Or it can simply be a matter of placing a thin piece of cardboard under a slice of cake, or even meatloaf, to keep it from breaking. More complicated stabilizing techniques involve the use of thickening agents such as gelatin or food starches. These can be used to keep sauces in place, or a slice of pie from collapsing.

Foods that oxidize easily (such as cut fruit) are dipped in lemon juice. Commercial antioxidants are also used; they are especially good for keeping leafy greens crisp or preventing the surfaces of sliced meat from turning gray.

Occasionally, substitutes for the actual food are used. This is done when the technical requirements of the photography or filming make it difficult or even impossible to use the real thing. A model might be made of a candy bar or a piece of cereal. Sometimes ice cream is made out of a mixture of confectioner's sugar, vegetable shortening, and corn syrup. Hair tonic might be used in place of milk in a bowl of cereal.

In short, these examples represent just some of the basics of what is involved in the styling of food. More than the mere ability to prepare an attractive plate of food, successful food styling is a demanding occupation that requires resourcefulness, skill, and artistry.

BIBLIOGRAPHY

Bianco, Marie. "Dressing Up." *Newsday* (5 October 1988): Food, 6-7.

Carafoli, John F. *Food Photography and Styling.* New York: Amphoto, an imprint of Watson-Guptill Publications, a division of BPI Communications, 1992.

Foderaro, Lisa W. "A Food Beautician Reveals How a Nectarine Grew Fuzz." *The New York Times* (7 September 1996): Metro 27.

Kleiman, Dena. "Food Styling: The Art of Making the Basil Blush." *The New York Times* (7 November 1990): C1.

O'Neill, Molly. "All Tarted Up." *The New York Times Magazine* (19 September 1999): 137.

Simone, Luisa. "Food for Thought." *Photo/Design* (November/December 1989): 45-55.

Rick Ellis

SUGAR AND SWEETENERS. There are many sugars and sweeteners. Sucrose—the sugar obtained chiefly from sugar cane and sugar beets (see "Sugar Crops and Natural Sweeteners")—is the most important sweetener and the substance usually meant when people speak of sugar. In 2000, world consumption of cane and beet sugar marketed by industrial-scale processors reached almost 120 million metric tons (132 million short tons), in white quality terms, equivalent to roughly 20 kilograms (about 44 pounds) per inhabitant. In addition, upwards of 10 million metric tons of indigenous types of cane and palm sugar of different qualities—the product of small rural enterprises—were consumed, mainly in Asia and Latin America. Globally, sugar supplies around 9 percent of the total human dietary energy intake, as all but a small amount produced ends up in food and drink. At the country level, average annual per capita sugar consumption ranges from less than 5 kilograms to more than 60 kilograms, depending on economic factors—price, income, and availability—as well as national customs, habits, and tastes.

Sucrose

Ordinary refined, or white, sugar is at least 99.7 percent sucrose and is one of the purest products in common use. Like other carbohydrates, it is a stored form of energy, providing nearly 4 kilocalories (slightly more than 16 kilojoules) per gram. In the eyes of some Western food writers, this makes sugar merely "empty calories." If that were all there is to it, sugar would not play the dietary role it does. Without its sweetness and other functions, the fact that sugar generally tends to be one of the cheapest sources of dietary energy might not, by itself, enable it to compete against starchy foods—even if these did not, in addition to energy, provide other nutrients. What basically makes sugar a staple food is that it enhances the beverages and other foods in which it is ingested. Sugar cannot be consumed by itself in significant volume. Potatoes or rice can be eaten by the plateful with barely anything else; it is difficult to ingest a teaspoonful of granulated sugar without at least dissolving it in water. Even as a source of energy, sugar rides piggyback on whatever else we eat and drink. It can be consumed in large quantities because, while satisfying the innate human disposition for sweetness, it is sweet in a not very intense way, far less so than numerous other substances.

Nowadays, global sugar consumption grows roughly in line with the increase in world population. In high-income industrial countries, per capita usage tends to stagnate and even decline. In poorer and less developed countries, on the other hand, sugar remains, as a study at the beginning of the 1960s found, one of the first foods to respond to a rise in personal incomes, its chief appeal lying not in its function as a source of energy—often still expensive, compared with locally grown cereals and root crops—but in its ability to make a frequently drab and monotonous diet more appetizing.

Functional properties. Sugar provides not only energy and sweetness. It caramelizes on heating to form complex coloring and flavoring substances, and part of it is inverted (converted by acid hydrolysis or enzyme into a mixture of glucose and fructose) during food preparation, the resultant monosaccharides reacting with other recipe components to lend aroma and browning to the final article. This increases the color, luster, and flavor of bread crust, for example. Well-known, too, is sugar's antimicrobial effect—as in fruit preserves, marmalades, jellies, and jams—where the high concentration of sugar in solution inhibits the growth of spoilage microorganisms by raising the osmotic pressure.

In developed countries, the sugar used at home and in communal catering establishments represents only a minor portion of total consumption. German statistics

for 1999/2000, for instance, show 71.7 percent of total domestic sugar sales going directly to industry (principally food manufacturers), 22.9 percent to wholesale and retail traders, 0.2 percent straight to end users, and 5.2 percent to unknown recipients. Even in the United States, where sucrose has been widely replaced by high fructose syrup in food processing (especially in soft drinks, previously the largest single outlet), direct industrial receipts accounted for 58.5 percent of total sugar deliveries for human consumption in 2000. Producers of baked goods and cereals are now in first place among industrial sugar users, followed by makers of sweets and manufacturers of ice cream and dairy products. In addition to its nutritional value, sweetness, and other sensory functions (taste and aroma, texture and appearance), and preservative action, sugar fulfills the specific requirements of different food industries for a binder, bulking agent, fermentation substrate, or stabilizer. This does not exhaust the list of its functional properties, and the fact that sugar always acts in more than one way explains its wide use in food and beverages.

The many types and grades of sugar available in the marketplace reflect the multiple uses to which it is put in households and in industry. More than a dozen different kinds could be encountered in 2002 in a single British supermarket, for example: white beet or refined cane sugar—granulated, caster, icing, and cubes; unrefined cane sugar—golden granulated and caster, Demerara granulated and cubes, light and dark brown soft, light and dark muscovado, and molasses sugar; specialty items—amber sugar crystals, preserving sugar (large crystals), jam sugar (with pectin and citric acid), and a reduced-calorie mixture of sugar and the high-intensity synthetic sweeteners aspartame and acesulfame-K. Several kinds were available also in "organic" versions. One important distinction is the size of crystal. Finer sugar tends to dissolve more rapidly than coarser sugar. Also, the smaller the crystal, the greater the total surface area of crystals per unit of mass or volume. In raw and recoated white or refined sugars, each crystal is surrounded by a film of molasses or syrup containing nonsucrose substances that, while nutritionally insignificant, have technical and sensory effects such as taste. Therefore, the smaller the crystal, the greater the proportion of syrup or molasses in the product, a desirable characteristic in making things like dark fruitcake and gingerbread.

Still other types of sugar reflect national or regional processing technologies, customs, and tastes. So-called amorphous sugar features prominently in Brazil, as does white soft sugar in Japan. The loaves of the sugar bakers, which in their blue wrappers graced the shelves of nineteenth-century grocers' shops before cubing processes were invented, live on in Germany, where they are required on festive occasions for the preparation of mulled wine. Loaf sugar also remains popular in North Africa and the Near East, a legacy attributed to the fact that the loaves were easy to transport hung from the backs of camels. More importantly, altogether millions of tons of sugar, the product of boiling cane juice or the sap of palms in open pans, are still consumed, notably in the countries of the Indian subcontinent and Southeast Asia, China, and Colombia.

Granulated sugar going to processing industries is shipped in bulk or bagged in sacks, for the greater part directly from the factory or refinery, and often tailored to customers' specifications, especially concerning grain size. Many applications, however, require an aqueous solution. Dissolving batches of granulated sugar stands in the way of continuous manufacturing operations. Hence, beginning in the United States in the 1920s, large sugar users have increasingly obtained bulk delivery in liquid form. What is known generically as liquid sugar comes in many guises, in accordance with industry demands: colorless and colored; uninverted sucrose or partially or totally inverted (converted into glucose and fructose); unblended or mixed with glucose syrups and other components. Depending on type, liquid sugar contains 67 to 77 percent dry substance.

Nutritional, health, and safety aspects.

Whether robbing wild bees of their honey, as did our ancestors, or extracting sucrose from sugar cane or sugar beets, humans take easily assimilable energy from the environment because we are heterotrophs or feeders on others and cannot fix carbon dioxide from the air. Instead, we have to obtain our carbon in a more elaborate form. Nutritionally, we utilize sugar, like other carbohydrates, as a fuel to obtain the energy to function. Under normal physiological conditions, sucrose must be enzymatically hydrolyzed in the small intestine before it can be absorbed across the intestinal wall. Glucose is the body's preferred fuel and the only one that powers the brain.

As a food, sugar is now subject to international and national standards and public health regulations, on top of the quality assurances and specifications of producers and industrial users. Compliance is underpinned by a large body of sensitive analytical methods.

The Codex Alimentarius, drawn up by a joint commission of the Food and Agriculture Organization and the World Health Organization of the United Nations, recommends international standards for white, powdered, and soft sugars, among other products. The basic white sugar standard lays down the minimum content of sucrose and the maximum contents of invert sugar, conductivity ash, sulfur dioxide (a processing aid), and the contaminants arsenic, copper, and lead. Binding regulations impose similar specifications across the European Union. The U.S. Food Chemical Codex is an example of controls at the national level. Since sucrose is used in pharmaceutical preparations as a binder, bulking agent, and taste corrective, it is also included in international and national lists of drugs and medicinal preparations.

Virtually a pure carbohydrate—even raw sugar supplies practically no minerals or vitamins, no fiber, and no protein—sugar is widely attacked on nutritional and health grounds. The safety aspects of sugar and its impact on human health have been extensively examined by scientists and reviewed by expert committees such as the U.S. Food and Drug Administration (FDA) Sugars Task Force and the British Nutrition Foundation's Task Force on Sugars and Syrups. On the evidence, the consumption of sugar and other fermentable carbohydrates contributes significantly to the incidence of dental caries, which have multiple causes, however. Other than that, no conclusive proof has been found that dietary sugars pose a health hazard to the general public. They are not related to diabetes, except as a nonspecific energy source, nor to behavioral changes. They do not have a unique role as a cause of obesity or constitute an independent risk factor in cardiovascular disease, gallstones, cancer, or hypertension.

History.

The word "sugar," like its cognates in many languages, comes ultimately from Sanskrit. Crystalline sugar has been made in northern India since the fifth century B.C.E., if not earlier. Sugar in solid form, possibly imported from Indochina, was also known in China by the third century C.E. To the west, however, the comparatively short move of the industry from India into Persia did not take place until c.600 C.E. From there, it rapidly diffused westward across the Middle East in the train of Arab expansion.

For the better part of 900 years between 700 and 1600, sugar production outside of Asia flourished on the islands and around the shores of the Mediterranean, with Venice initially the foremost center of refining and trading. The second half of the period saw the first exports to central and northern Europe, triggering what Sidney Mintz has called "the conquest of honey by sucrose," albeit that sugar was still a rare and expensive luxury, its use confined to kings and nobles. The Mediterranean industry began to decline from about 1450 onwards, in parallel with the appearance of more efficient producers in the new Portuguese and Spanish colonies in the eastern Atlantic and the Americas, although that was not the sole reason. For a while, Madeira, the Canaries, and São Tomé figured prominently in the burgeoning international sugar trade, forerunners of the West Indian "sugar colonies" and "sugar islands" that Adam Smith spoke of in his *Wealth of Nations*. But, like the Mediterranean industry, they, too, could not match the natural conditions and space for growing sugar cane that lay waiting in the Western Hemisphere.

When Christopher Columbus carried sugar cane to the Americas on his second voyage in 1493, shortly followed by other Spanish and Portuguese explorers with their cargoes, the seed was sown for a vast expansion of the industry. Within a few decades, supplies doubled and doubled again, prices fell, and consumption extended to the middle classes. Still, about a century and a half after sugar from Brazil and Hispaniola became the first example of profitable agricultural exports from the Western

Hemisphere, average per capita sugar consumption in Britain in the first decade of the 1700s is estimated to have amounted to just four pounds a year, less than two kilograms, or about a teaspoonful a day. On the other side of the Atlantic, the growth of the sugar industry had lasting political, economic, social, and cultural consequences: based on plantation agriculture and slavery on a scale many times greater than previously seen in the Old World, it was instrumental in the formation of new nations.

Until the early 1800s, cane sugar had the field to itself, leaving aside sweeteners of no more than regional significance. Honey was a competitor only so long as sugar was still a costly rarity. Even then, the two products complemented as much as competed with each other. All that changed with the arrival of beet sugar early in the nineteenth century, a historically significant event aptly described by Timoshenko and Swerling as "the earliest example of the market for an important tropical product being seriously eroded by the application of modern scientific methods in relatively advanced countries." Extraordinarily, the challenge came not from a substitute but from what was, for all practical purposes, the identical substance, obtained from an entirely different plant. High-grade refined sugar from beet or cane is indistinguishable except by analytical methods that find the difference in the carbon isotope ratio ($^{13}C/^{12}C$).

Beet sugar added another dimension to the world sugar economy. It allowed temperate zone countries to produce their own sucrose and greatly increased global availabilities, so that sugar could become a staple item of consumption for all classes of society. By 1880, Austria-Hungary, France, Germany, and Russia were turning out beet sugar on a scale comparable to the largest cane sugar producers. Europe's beet sugar industries contributed enormously to its economic development in the second half of the nineteenth century. The Germany of the 1890s, for instance, had around 400 beet sugar factories, producing roughly one-and-a-half million metric tons of beet sugar a year, and sugar briefly headed the list of German merchandise exports. In his work *Der moderne Kapitalismus*, the German economist Werner Sombart wrote: "The sugar and distilling industries were the industrial sectors through which Germany developed into a great capitalist power, rather as the cotton and iron industries laid the basis for England's greatness."

Nowadays, most countries cover their requirements at least partially with homegrown sugar, and some that do not, such as New Zealand, possess a refinery to process raw sugar imports. The bulk of the world's sugar is today consumed in the countries where it is produced. Not surprisingly, in view of its sundry roles, sugar has become deeply embedded in politics over the centuries, and how much is produced and where is heavily influenced by tariffs, taxation, and subsidies.

Several industry-specific factors have favored the growth of sugar production and consumption through-

out history. Sugar's multiple functions, from its first uses as a medicine and condiment, have clearly been an advantage in boosting consumption. So was its long-time association in Europe with wealth and standing—demonstrated, for instance, by its conspicuous display in molded table decorations. In modern parlance, sugar enjoyed "snob appeal." Economists would say that it had a high positive-income elasticity of demand and confirmed Say's law that supply creates its own demand. Even as sugar becomes an inferior good in highly developed countries, consumption is sustained by increased demand for things like ice cream, sweets, and soft drinks, so long, of course, as these continue to be made with sugar and not other sweeteners.

On the production side, the by-products of sugar processing have always played a significant role in the viability of the industry. Sugar mills in many parts of tropical America survived deforestation and the scarcity of firewood because sugar cane brought its own fuel in the form of bagasse, the fibrous processing residue. Indeed, a modern raw cane sugar factory normally produces more bagasse or steam than it needs. The corresponding residue in the beet sugar industry—pulp—provides valuable fodder. Molasses, a by-product in both industries, is likewise utilized directly or in mixed feeds, or as a raw material for fermentation products. Students of U.S. history will be familiar with John Adams's statement in 1775: "I know not why we should blush to confess that molasses was an essential ingredient in American independence. Many great events have proceeded from much smaller causes."

The very nature of the industry facilitated its diffusion to and growth in new territories. A state-of-the-art sugar factory, operating at top technical efficiency, is an extremely sophisticated business—science-inspired, instrument-controlled, and automated. In essence, however, the methods of sugar processing are simple and robust. Although economies of scale have led to ever larger plants, sugar can be made in a wide range of plant sizes. The processes involved are easily scaled up, and factories can be enlarged and updated piecemeal by retrofitting new equipment. Right down to the present, the world cane sugar industry exhibits a technological diversity ranging from back-yard producers of a few tons of sugar, similar to that made centuries ago, to huge installations, pouring out hundreds of thousands of tons a year of high-grade product.

Technology. Sugar processing is basically a series of solid-liquid separations. The core processing stages are: (1) extraction of the juice, with bagasse or pulp the residue; (2) purification of the juice, removing nonsucrose substances; (3) concentration of the purified juice to syrup by evaporating water; (4) crystallization of the sucrose in the syrup by further evaporation; (5) separation of the crystals from the syrup. The methods employed after juice extraction determine the end product. One way leads to raw sugar, which is refined—on site or in a separate plant—by washing and redissolving the crystals and further clarifying and decolorizing the resulting solution. The clear syrup is then again boiled until crystals form, or made into liquid sugar. Much of the world's cane sugar is produced in this way. The alternative is to make white sugar directly after complex purification of the juice, the procedure followed in some cane-sugar factories and throughout the beet-sugar industry.

For two thousand years, machinery, apparatus, and processes underwent a slow and gradual evolution, highlighted by the crucial seventeenth-century innovations of the three-roller mill and the battery of cauldrons, which, once fitted with a single furnace and continuous internal flue, became known as the Jamaica train and survives to this day among small-scale producers of open-pan sugars (not made in closed vessels under vacuum). Development accelerated with the introduction of steam and the rise of industrial chemistry in the nineteenth century. By about 1880 the basic tool kit of the sugar industry was virtually complete, and that date marks the beginning of the modern era in sugar production.

Nonsucrose Sweeteners

High fructose syrups (HFS) and other caloric sweeteners.
Sucrose substitutes fall into two categories: nutritive or caloric substances, which, like sucrose, provide energy and bulk, and high-intensity sweeteners, used principally for their sweetening power, although that is not their only property. The discovery of how to convert starch into sugar (saccharification) in 1811 was the first step toward the development of serious commercial competitors to cane and beet sugar of the first kind. Still, the glucose syrups produced over the next 150 years were less sweet than invert sugar syrup, which restricted their range of industrial applications. That limitation was lifted by the invention of isomerization processes leading to high-fructose syrup, known as high-fructose corn syrup in North America and isoglucose in Europe. While glucose syrups continued to be made, world HFS production rose in less than forty years from zero to an estimated 13.1 million tons, dry weight, in 2001/2002. The United States accounted for 73 percent of global output; another 18 percent was shared by Japan, the European Union, Turkey, South Korea, Canada, and Argentina, and the remainder by more than a dozen other countries.

Location and volume of HFS production are conditioned by several factors:

1. Price: World sugar price booms in 1963, 1974, and 1980 greatly stimulated development. In the United States and Japan, two large sugar importers, HFS progressed under the umbrella of protective sugar regimes that kept sugar prices at an artificial level and ensured that, however much HFS manufacturers undercut the price of sucrose, displacement of the latter reduced sugar imports and did not impair domestic sugar production;

2. Starch supply: Ample supplies of starch at a competitive cost, net of by-product proceeds;

3. Consumer demand: Sufficient sweetener consumption in the form of processed foods and beverages, and the existence of bulk-handling facilities for liquid products;

4. Money: Financial resources for investment in research and development as well as in capital-intensive plants and equipment;

5. Political climate: Supportive, or at least permissive, government policies; in the European Union, however, isoglucose manufacture—and, more recently, also that of insulin syrup—has been restrained, first by a levy, then by production quotas.

Besides syrups, starch saccharification leads to dextrose or crystallized glucose. Sold in anhydrous (at least 98 percent solids) or monohydrate (at least 90 percent solids) form, dextrose is used in food and other industries.

Also employed industrially as bulking, humectant (moisturizing), and texturizing agents and in diabetic foods are various sugar alcohols or polyols. These have lower calorific values than sucrose and, with the exception of xylitol, only about half the sweetening power. The main one, sorbitol, occurs naturally in many plants—as does its isomer, mannitol—and is used, among other things, to synthesize ascorbic acid (vitamin C). It is commercially obtained by the hydrogenation of glucose or of invert sugar, the latter yielding equimolar amounts of sorbitol and mannitol from the fructose and sorbitol only from the glucose. Other members of this class are maltitol, produced by hydrogenation from high-maltose syrup; isomalt, for which sucrose is the feedstock; xylitol, made from xylose-containing materials, such as corncobs and birchwood sawdust; and erythritol, found in lichens and made from glucose by fermentation.

High-intensity sweeteners.
Artificial or natural substances with many times the sweetening power of sucrose, but no or negligible calorific value as used, are known as high-intensity sweeteners. Saccharin, the oldest of the kind, is about 300 times as sweet as sucrose. A derivative of the tar product toluene, it first achieved some market significance during the sugar shortages caused by World War I, when it began to be used as a substitute by people besides those who were unable to tolerate sugar. Newer sweeteners have, to a considerable extent, displaced saccharin, but it continues in demand, particularly in Asia, because it costs a small fraction of the price of sugar in terms of sweetness equivalence. Another older artificial sweetener, cyclamate, roughly thirty times as sweet as sugar, was discovered in 1937 and became popular after World War II, usually in combination with saccharin. Together, each masks the unsatisfactory taste of the other, producing an overall taste profile thought to approximate that of sugar.

Such blending of different sweeteners, nutritive as well as high-intensity, is a striking feature of sweetener usage in processed foods and beverages. One advantage lies in the resultant synergism—the sweetness effect of the mixture is greater than the sum of the sweetening powers of the individual components, enabling manufacturers to save costs and label certain products "reduced calorie." Blends may also produce other taste synergies and enhance the stability of the product.

The scope for blending was greatly increased in recent decades with the introduction of aspartame and acesulfame–K. Aspartame, a methylated amino acid dipeptide, actually has the same calorific value as sugar, but is about 180 times sweeter. Its taste profile closely resembles that of sucrose and, unlike saccharin, it has no bitter aftertaste. Widely used as a tabletop sweetener, aspartame is not suitable for all processed products because it can lose sweetness, depending on temperature, moisture, and degree of acidity. In contrast, acesulfame-K, the potassium salt of methyl oxathiazinone dioxide roughly 200 times as sweet as sugar, while more expensive, is very stable, blends well with other sweeteners, and is highly synergistic.

The latest artificial sweetener to acquire significant market presence is sucralose, which is 600 times sweeter than sugar. Technically trichloro-galactosaccharose, sucralose is actually made from sugar. It has the advantages of a good taste profile and of being acid and temperature stable. Several other substances, some with many thousand times the sweetness intensity of sugar, are waiting in the wings. High-intensity sweeteners are classified as food additives and require approval by national food safety authorities. Gaining approval tends to be a lengthy procedure and, once given, can be withdrawn. In the United States, for instance, cyclamate was banned in 1970, but it is allowed in many other countries.

Summary

Sucrose remains the benchmark against which the quality and price of substitutes are judged, but it has lost its former virtual monopoly as the sweetener and conditioner of food and drink. Not all the growth of nonsucrose sweeteners has been at the expense of sugar. Some of it reflects the development of new products, such as diet soft drinks. In certain applications, sugar and other sweeteners have to be blended in order to achieve the desired texture and consistency. Moreover, nonsucrose sweeteners compete not only against sugar, but also among themselves: aspartame against saccharin, and diet soft drinks sweetened with high-intensity sweeteners against regular soft drinks sweetened with HFS. Only in the United States was sucrose no longer the dominant sweetener at the beginning of the twenty-first century. Globally, sucrose still accounted for 70 percent or more of world sweetener consumption.

See also **Caribbean; Codex Alimentarius; FAO (Food and Agriculture Organization); Sugar Crops and Natural Sweeteners; Syrups; United States: Hawaii.**

BIBLIOGRAPHY

Ballinger, Roy A. *A History of Sugar Marketing*. Agricultural Economic Report No. 197. Washington, D.C.: United States Department of Agriculture, Economic Research Service, 1971.

Baxa, Jakob, and Guntwin Bruhns. *Zucker im Leben der Völker: Eine Kultur- und Wirtschaftsgeschichte*. Berlin: Albert Bartens, 1967.

Bruhns, Jürgen, Heinz-Peter Hochgeschurz, and Karsten Maier, eds. *Sugar Economy Europe 2002*. Berlin: Albert Bartens, 2001.

Deerr, Noel. *The History of Sugar*. London: Chapman and Hall, 1949–1950.

Galloway, J. H. *The Sugar Cane Industry: An Historical Geography from its Origins to 1914*. Cambridge: Cambridge University Press, 1989.

International Sugar Organization. *Sugar Year Book 2000*. London: ISO, 2001.

McGee, Harold. *On Food and Cooking: The Science and Lore of the Kitchen*. New York: Scribner's, 1984.

Mintz, Sidney W. *Sweetness and Power: The Place of Sugar in Modern History*. New York: Viking, 1985.

Mintz, Sidney W. "The Conquest of Honey by Sucrose: A Psychotechnical Achievement." In *Essays to Mark the 125th Anniversary of F. O. Licht*. Ratzeburg, Germany: F. O. Licht, 1989.

Nabors, Lyn O'Brien. "Sweet Choices: Sugar Replacements for Foods and Beverages." *Food Technology* 56, no. 7 (July 2002): 28–34, 45.

Timoshenko, Vladimir P., and Boris C Swerling. *The World's Sugar: Progress and Policy*. Stanford: Stanford University Press, 1957.

United States Department of Agriculture, Economic Research Service. *Sugar and Sweetener Situation and Outlook Yearbook*. (SSS-231). May 2001.

van der Poel, P. W., H. Schiweck, and T. Schwartz, eds. *Sugar Technology: Beet and Cane Sugar Manufacture*. Berlin: Albert Bartens, 1998.

Vettorazzi, Gaston, and Ian Macdonald, eds. *Sucrose: Nutritional and Safety Aspects*. (ILSI Human Nutrition Reviews). Berlin and Heidelberg: Springer-Verlag, 1988.

Viton, A., and F. Pignalosa. *Trends and Forces of World Sugar Consumption*. (Commodity Bulletin Series). Rome: Food and Agriculture Organization of the United Nations, 1961.

"World HFS—Back on the Growth Path?" *F. O. Licht's International Sugar and Sweetener Report* 134, no. 18 (31 May 2002): 279–284.

G. B. Hagelberg

SUGAR CROPS AND NATURAL SWEETENERS.

Chemically, the substance in the breakfast sugar bowl comes to us unchanged from the living organism in which it was manufactured. The familiar crystals are virtually pure sucrose, an organic chemical belonging to a large family of compounds classified as sugars. These, in turn, are members of a still larger group—the carbohydrates—that also includes starch and cellulose. The breakdown of carbohydrates into monosaccharides, oligosaccharides, and polysaccharides points to the relationship.

Carbohydrates are a product of photosynthesis, the complex biochemical process whereby green plants use light energy to combine aerial carbon dioxide and hydrogen from soil water, forming rings of carbon atoms to which atoms of hydrogen and oxygen are attached, usually in the ratio in which these elements occur in water (hence the name), surplus oxygen being released as free gas. Stripped of all detail, the photosynthetic reaction that produces the basic monosaccharide glucose may be summarized by the equation:

$$6CO_2 \text{ (carbon dioxide)} + 6H_2O \text{ (water)} + light = C_6H_{12}O_6 \text{ (glucose)} + 6O_2 \text{ (oxygen)}.$$

Affinities

Various carbohydrates are made in the course of photosynthesis. Sugars are the simplest. Glucose, also called dextrose and grape sugar, is the most prevalent sugar in nature. It occurs in the free state in fruits, plant juices and honey, as well as in blood. Polymerization of glucose leads to starch and cellulose—the one a form of energy storage, the other the main structural material of plants—both nothing but chains of glucose units. Conversely, natural starches can be saccharified by acid hydrolysis and enzymes to yield different types of sweet syrups or crystalline dextrose. Another monosaccharide, fructose (also called levulose and fruit sugar), occurs in the free state notably in honey. Sharing the same chemical formula but differing in structure, glucose and fructose are in fact interconvertible by chemical and biological reactions.

Fructose and glucose combine to form the oligosaccharide — more precisely, disaccharide — sucrose, $C_{12}H_{22}O_{11}$, shedding a molecule of water in the process. Sucrose is found in the sap of many plants and like starch functions as a storage product. It is easily hydrolyzed by acid or enzyme to equimolar amounts of glucose and fructose, and the mixture is then called invert sugar.

A family trait of many mono- and oligosaccharides is their sweet taste. Fruits, young vegetables, the nectar of flowers, and the sap of certain plants and trees taste sweet because they contain saccharides. Sucrose is generally used as the standard for relative sweetness, but this also depends on concentration, temperature and other factors affecting the physiology of taste. Approximate relative sweetness values for the sugars mentioned are:

Fructose	120	Invert sugar	95
Sucrose	100	Glucose	65

Sucrose, almost all of which is obtained from sugar cane and sugar beet, is commercially by far the most important sweetener. Its origin in photosynthesis explains how two wholly dissimilar botanical sources can furnish a practically identical product. Sugar cane—currently providing roughly three-quarters of the world's sucrose supply—is a perennial monocotyledon, propagated from cuttings, except in the breeding of new varieties, and capable of giving repeated harvests. In contrast, sugar beet is a biennial dicotyledon, harvested in the first season and replanted annually from seed. Cane grows in the tropics and subtropics, beet in temperate climates. The cane's sucrose comes from the stalk, the beet's from its root. Sugar cane has been exploited industrially for more than two millennia, sugar beet for just two centuries.

The origin of sugars in photosynthesis also explains the exploitation of other, more or less important sweetener sources, some going back to ancient times, for example boiled-down grape juice, fig and date syrup, the sap of palms, the maple tree, and sweet sorghum, and the exudations from certain trees and shrubs. Like the sugar from cane and beet, honey—the first concentrated sweetener known to humans—is ultimately a product of photosynthesis. In essence, bees making honey and humans processing cane or beet to crystal sugar are doing the same thing—both extract dilute sugar solutions from plants and convert them into forms that are easier to handle and storable by evaporating unwanted water.

Sugar Cane

Physical characteristics. Sugar cane is a giant perennial grass that tillers at the base to produce clumps of solid unbranched stems up to six centimeters in diameter and typically two to three meters long at maturity. It is grown for these thick stems which, stripped of tips and leaves, weigh between 500 and 2000 grams and, as a rule, contain 10–15 percent sucrose and 11–16 percent fiber. Each stem is divided into a number of joints comprising a node and an internode up to twenty-five centimeters in length. A node consists of a lateral bud in a leaf axil, a band containing root primordia, and a growth ring. Sword-shaped leaves, consisting of a sheath and a blade, are attached to the stem at the base of the nodes, alternating in two rows on opposite sides of the stem. The stems range in color from green or yellow to red, purple, violet, or striped, and have a hard wax-covered rind that reduces loss of water by evaporation. Depending on variety, plant age, and natural conditions, sugar cane may flower, producing plumelike panicles known as arrows or tassels that bear hundreds of small spikelets with inconspicuous flowerets. For sugar production, however, sugar cane is propagated vegetatively from stem cuttings or setts bearing at least one bud. Planted in moist soil, the bud develops into a primary stem, the basal buds of which form secondary stems, and so on, while rootlets sprout from the root primordia band on the sett. In time, the tillers throw out their own roots and, in favorable soil conditions, an established cane stool develops an elaborate root system of widely spreading superficial roots that absorb water and nutrients and buttress roots to provide stability, as well as a few vertical roots that may penetrate deep into the soil where moisture is available even during a severe drought.

Origin and geographical spread. All forms of sugar cane are species or hybrids of the genus *Saccharum*, a member of the large family of Gramineae in the tribe Andropogoneae, the sorghum tribe. Six *Saccharum* species are now recognized. Historically, sugar canes are derivatives of what is known as the *Saccharum* complex, which comprises the interbreeding genera of *Saccharum*, *Erianthus*, *Sclerostachya*, *Narenga*, and *Miscanthus*. The most primitive *Saccharum* species, *S. spontaneum* L., a highly variable and vigorous, but thin-stemmed, fibrous cane low in sugar, is believed to have originated in northern India. Subsequent modification, movement, and hybridization generated various Asian, Pacific, and African forms. Still being debated is the botanical lineage of *Saccharum officinarum* L., clones of which—so-called noble canes—furnished the raw material of plantation-based sugar industries from the latter part of the eighteenth century until the early 1900s. This species—thick-stemmed, soft-rinded, rich in sugar, and originally selected for chewing—is generally thought to have evolved in eastern Indonesia or New Guinea from the wild cane *Saccharum robustum* Brandes and Jeswiet ex Grassl. An alternative theory has *S. officinarum* derived from the Chinese sugar cane, *S. sinense* Roxb. emend. Jeswiet, which was carried to the Philippines, making that area the likely site of initial hybridization and development of *S. officinarum*. In any event, *S. officinarum* probably became a cultivated food plant about 5000 or 6000 years ago. In the course of time, sugar cane of one form or another spread eastward across the Pacific and northwestward to India, and thence via Persia and the Mediterranean basin to the Atlantic seaboard, finally reaching the New World in 1493 on the second voyage of Columbus.

The first cultivars grown in the Western Hemisphere were male-sterile, and the possibility of deliberately breeding new varieties was not generally recognized until the late 1800s after the fertility of cane seed was definitely established simultaneously in Barbados and Java. Finding that adaptability to less-than-optimal ecological conditions and, above all, resistance to diseases was unobtainable within the genetic variability of *S. officinarum*, breeders eventually began to cross noble canes with other *Saccharum* species and cross the progeny back with noble canes, a process called nobilization. Today, most cane-growing countries in the world pursue their own breeding programs. In addition to disease resistance and high yields in the local conditions over several seasons, the aim is to obtain varieties tailored to modern production methods such as suitability for mechanized harvesting and herbicide tolerance.

Environment and cultivation. Sugar cane is grown in about eighty countries between roughly 30° latitude north and 30° latitude south. Often described as a tropical crop, much cane is actually grown in subtropical areas. The ten leading producers are India, Brazil, China, Thailand, Australia, Mexico, Cuba, the United States, Pakistan, and South Africa. Sugar cane is a very adapt-

Early engraving by Theodore de Bry showing Caribbean Indians working as slaves in a Spanish sugar mill. COURTESY OF THE LIBRARY OF CONGRESS.

able plant that can be grown successfully on a wide range of soils. It grows best under ample sunlight in moist hot climates where a period of heavy rainfall is followed by a cool and dry season to increase sugar content and facilitate harvesting, or with controlled irrigation. Depending on location and other factors, the crop is ready for harvesting ten to twenty-four months after planting. In a harvesting period lasting between three and eleven months, again depending on location, the stems are cut, topped, and stripped of leaves by hand or machine. Yields vary widely from less than forty metric tons to more than one hundred metric tons of cane per hectare, equivalent, after processing, to upwards of four metric tons of sugar per hectare. Cut cane deteriorates rapidly and must be processed promptly to avoid heavy loss of sucrose. After the first harvest, underground buds on the stool throw out new shoots, and the plant develops a new root system. This allows the production of second, third, or more crops, known as ratoons, in a similar or shorter growth period and at less cost. The complete crop cycle usually lasts three to ten years, the field being replanted when the yield drops below an economic level.

Structural and economic aspects. As a perennial ratooning grass, sugar cane does not easily lend itself to crop rotation and is usually grown in monoculture. Extremely labor-intensive until mechanization, particularly at harvest time, sugar cane has been regarded as the archetypal plantation crop, produced in large enterprises employing many low-skilled workers under the supervision of a few skilled managers. Broadly speaking, this was true for the export-oriented sugar cane industries of the colonial period and lies at the heart of the historical association of sugar with slavery. However, the organizational structures of sugar cane agriculture have long exhibited great diversity, even in territories described as plantation economies, and range globally from small-holders with less than two hectares to miller-planter complexes in which a centralized management controls thousands of hectares as well as a factory.

Throughout the world, cane farming operations from soil preparation to harvesting and transport are increasingly mechanized. A bulky crop of low unit value, sugar cane presents formidable materials-handling problems. Until the 1960s, Hawaii, Louisiana, and Queensland were the only cane-growing areas to have mechanized both cutting and loading. Despite the arduous nature of the work, growers have tended to retain manual harvesting using heavy machete-type knives as long as economically feasible because mechanized harvesting systems entail extensive field reforms and modifications of transport equipment and factory reception facilities and because of the increased extraneous matter content in mechanically harvested cane, at least in the early years. Rising labor costs and better machines, however, have led to the progressive mechanization of harvesting operations in one country after another. In some areas, mechanization proceeded in stages, starting with the piling and loading of hand-cut cane or wholestalk harvesters; other areas have gone straight to combines that cut, chop into billets, clean, and load in a continuous operation.

Sugar Beet

Physical characteristics. The root of sugar beet, in which sucrose accumulates, consists, from the top down, of the epicotyl or crown, the hypocotyl or neck, and a swollen taproot. Roots vary greatly in size but average about 600 grams. The crown is the part above the lowest leaf scar; it is stem tissue with leaf buds and supports a rosette of leaves, the botanical engines that put the sucrose into the root. The hypocotyl, the region between crown and tap root and the thickest part of the root, extends from the lowest leaf scar to the uppermost lateral roots. Epicotyl and hypocotyl make up the part of the root that rises above ground. Depending on variety, plant population, and the various factors affecting growth, these two sections account for about 20 percent of the length and weight of the entire root. The white-fleshed tap root has two grooves on opposite sides from which lateral roots emerge. It tapers off to a tail less than one centimeter thick that with the hairlike ancillary roots often extends two meters or more deep into the soil.

The sucrose and nonsucrose constituents of sugar beet are not distributed uniformly in the root; sucrose content and purity are higher in the middle of the root than in the crown and tail. Hypocotyl and taproot together contain 14 to 20 percent sucrose. In harvesting, the beet is topped below the green leaf stalks of the epicotyl, a certain margin in the upper hypocotyl being allowed, while the tail usually breaks off in the lifting and subsequent handling of the root. A biennial, sugar beet flowers and bears seed in the second season, but is harvested for sugar in the first.

Origin and geographical spread. Sugar beet, *Beta vulgaris* L., is a member of the Chenopodiaceae or goosefoot family. Four distinct types of the species are cultivated: sugar beet, garden (red) beet, leaf beet and Swiss chard, and fodder beets. Sugar beet, the second major source of the world's sugar supply, is commercially by far the most important of the four types. Wild forms from which the crop could have been derived are widely distributed throughout the Mediterranean region and the Middle East. It is not known when the beet was taken into cultivation, but use of the plant medicinally and as a vegetable was already well established in Greek and Roman times. Cultivars with swollen roots, the result of human selection, are recorded in northern Europe from the sixteenth century onwards. The French agriculturist Olivier de Serres (1539–1619) compared the liquid from cooked red beet to sugar syrup. In 1747, Andreas Sigismund Marggraf (1709–1782), a member of the Berlin Academy of Sciences, reported having extracted from red and white beets a substance identical with cane sugar. Towards the end of the 1700s, another academician, Franz Carl Achard (1753–1821), began to grow white beets for sugar production, first near Berlin and then in Silesia where in 1802 he opened the first beet sugar factory. Achard's beets had a sugar content of up to 6 percent, but this was raised by simple mass selection to about 9 percent by the 1830s. Since then, thanks to advances in breeding methods, the sugar content in beets has roughly doubled. Average German beet yields per hectare have also more than doubled, so that a hectare of beets now produces approximately four times as much sugar as it did in the mid-1800s.

Environment and cultivation. Sugar beet is currently grown in nearly fifty countries, all save Chile in the northern hemisphere and most enjoying moderate summer temperatures and at least 250 millimeters of rainfall during the growing season except in areas where irrigation is available. Beet is successfully cultivated in many soils, but a deep loam, moist yet well-drained, is best. Member countries of the European Union, the United States, Turkey, Poland, Ukraine, Russia, and China are the leading producers. Sown in spring, the crop is lifted before the first frosts are expected. Different from cane, harvested beet can be stored for months under suitable conditions without intolerable loss.

Structural and economic aspects. Unlike cane, beet is grown in rotation with other crops and is closely integrated in the farming systems practiced in the regions where it is cultivated. As a root crop, it improves soil conditions. The beet tops can be used for fodder or, when plowed in, provide organic manure. The beet pulp remaining after sugar extraction is also used for animal feed, in contrast to bagasse, the fibrous residue of cane processing, which mainly ends up as factory boiler fuel. Like cane, beet was formerly an extremely labor-intensive crop. In the case of beet, however, not harvesting but thinning out the seedlings after emergence to create space between plants was the operation most resistant to the reduction of labor requirements. Until the advent of monogerm varieties with single flowers at each inflorescence node, sugar beet bore clusters of flowers which gave rise to multigerm seed balls. Even where animal- or tractor-drawn implements replaced the hand hoe in blocking out excess seedling clusters, the final singling to one plant per clump had to be done manually. Labor shortages in the United States during World War II spurred the introduction of mechanically segmented seed (followed after the war by decorticated seed) with a large proportion of single germs, better suited for precision drilling but at the risk of poorer germination and an uneconomic plant population in the field. The same drawbacks adhered to the seed of early genetically monogerm varieties, and the total elimination of manual labor in sugar beet agriculture did not become possible until the arrival of improved forms since the late 1960s.

Other Natural Sweetener Sources

Polysaccharide-bearing plants. In 1811, a Russian-German chemist, K. S. Kirchhof, working in St. Petersburg, discovered that adding diluted sulfuric acid to cooked potato starch produced a sweet syrup containing glucose. A year later, the first starch sugar factory was established in Germany. While the technological details would vary depending on the source of starch—cereals, roots and tubers, or stem pith—the door was opened to obtaining sweeteners from a wide range of plants. Syrup from corn (maize), rather than potatoes, has been made in the United States since the mid-1800s. Elsewhere, the raw materials could be sweet potatoes, tapioca (cassava, manioc), rice, wheat, and sago. But while such starch-based syrups could compete to some extent with cane and beet sugar in processed foods and drinks, their application was constrained by the fact that glucose is markedly less sweet than sucrose. This disadvantage was overcome in the second half of the 1960s and early 1970s by a new process of continuous enzymatic isomerization of glucose to fructose. (In essence, a glucose solution is passed through columns or beds containing immobilized enzyme, which changes the atomic arrangement of glucose into that of fructose.) The result is high-fructose corn syrup (HFCS), called isoglucose in Europe. Unlike the older glucose syrups, an equilibrium fructose–glucose syrup compares in sweetness and in other respects to invert sugar syrup made from sucrose. This greatly widened the possibilities of using starch sweeteners in industries such as the soft-drink industry, that were major users of sucrose. In the second half of the 1970s, further technological advances brought onto the market second-generation syrups with higher fructose contents, which deliver more sweetness with fewer calories, thanks to the fact that fructose is sweeter than sucrose. Since 1985, consumption of HFCS, glucose syrup, and dextrose, on a comparable dry basis, has exceeded that of beet and cane sugar in the United States, but this is so far the only country in which sucrose is no longer the leading sweetener.

Certain plants lay down fructose polymers as energy reserves in place of or in addition to starch. Inulin—found in, among other plants, chicory and Jerusalem artichoke—belongs to this category of polysaccharides. Inulin syrup is produced on an industrial scale in the European Union and falls under the EU's sugar and sweetener market regime.

Palms. Various species of palms have for centuries been tapped—notably in southern and southeastern Asia—for their sweet sap, which is drunk fresh or fermented. Alternatively, the sap has been boiled down until it sets to a solid mass of fudgelike consistency, called gur or jaggery, or is distilled to produce arrack. Among palm species exploited in these ways are the palmyra (*Borassus flabellifer*), the toddy fishtail or jaggery palm (*Caryota urens*), the coconut palm (*Cocos nucifera*), the nipa palm (*Nipa fruticans*), and a wild date palm (*Phoenix sylvestris*) related to the palm of commercial date production (*P. dactylifera*), the fruits of which are also a source of sugar.

Maples. Several species of the maple family, as well as birch and elm, can be tapped to make syrup and sugar, but the main source is the sugar maple, *Acer saccharum*. Maple syrup has been made in North America since before the arrival of the first European settlers. It was an important sweetener in the northern United States and Canada until overtaken by beet and cane sugar. A peculiarity of the maple sap run is that it takes place when the tree is still dormant. The sap that will make syrup differs from that circulating in the growing tree. Its flow is triggered by a thaw following a hard frost. The mechanics of the run are believed to involve changes in osmotic, water and gas pressures caused by the translocation of sugar stored in trunk xylem tissue the previous summer as the trunk warms up on a sunny late-winter day. Fresh sap contains up to 3 percent sucrose. Evaporation by boiling in open pans, which also adds color and the characteristic maple syrup flavor, raises the sucrose content to around 62 percent and reduces the water to 35 percent in the final product. At higher concentrations, the sugar crystallizes when the syrup cools. Thirty to 40 liters of sap make one liter of syrup.

Production methods have improved over the years. The Indian technique of cutting a wide gash in the trunk was hard on the tree. The colonists introduced the practice of making a small hole with an auger—now done with power drills—and fitting a spout from which a bucket was suspended. In recent times, plastic tubing has been adapted to collect the sap from an entire stand of trees, and central evaporator plants, with instruments to monitor boiling temperature and syrup concentration, now serve whole producer communities.

Sorghum. A near relative of sugar cane, sweet sorghum or sorgo (*Sorghum vulgare*), a native of Africa, was, for a while in the second half of the eighteenth century, thought to have the potential for becoming a mainstream source of sugar in the United States. Although it could not compete against the growing availability of beet and cane sugar from about 1880 onwards, sorghum syrup is still produced on a small scale.

Mahua or Mowrah Tree. Several trees of the genus *Madhuca* or *Bassia* (Sapotaceae) bear sweet fleshy edible flowers. Those of *M. indica,* also named *M.* or *B. latifolia,* were mentioned in Indian medical writings as a source of sugar as early as the third to seventh centuries A.D.

Manna. The word "manna" has various meanings. The biblical manna may have been wind-borne edible lichens, *Lecanora* (*Sphaerothallia*) *esculenta* or other species of the same genus. Two Middle Eastern shrubs, *Alhagi maurorum* and *A. pseudalhagi,* exude a sweet resin that hardens and can be collected by shaking the bushes over a cloth spread on the ground. Insect punctures in the stem of the French tamarisk, *Tamarix gallica,* of the same region produce drops of a honeylike exudation called manna. The word is also used for the incrustations formed by the sap that flows when incisions are made in the bark of the Sicilian flowering ash, *Fraxinus ornus* L. (Oleaceae). Numerous other sources of resinous mannas are listed in herbalist and pharmacological literature. Although not in all cases, the principal chemical constituent of such mannas is mannitol, also called mannite, a colourless sweet-tasting crystalline alcohol.

Stevia. The leaves of *Stevia rebaudiana* Bertoni, a wild shrub of the Compositae family that is native to Paraguay, contain a complex mixture of sweet diterpene glycosides. Stevioside, a high-intensity sweetener 250 to 300 times sweeter than sucrose, is extracted from the leaves and used as a sweetener in South America and Asia. Because of unresolved toxicological concerns, Stevia and stevioside cannot be sold as food or food ingredients in the European Union.

Protein sweetener sources. A number of plants yield taste-modifying proteins that function as natural sweeteners of very high intensity (thousands of times sweeter than sucrose). Some are believed to have been used for centuries by indigenous peoples to improve flavor and suppress bitterness in food and drink. The most widely known, thaumatin, is contained in the aril of the seed of *Thaumatococcus daniellii* Benth. (Marantaceae), a West African shrub. Monellin from the berries of the West African *Dioscoreophyllum cumminsii* Diels (Menispermaceae) is another example.

See also **Candy and Confections**; **Syrups**.

BIBLIOGRAPHY

Achaya, K. T. *Indian Food: A Historical Companion.* Delhi: Oxford University Press, 1994.

Blackburn, Frank. *Sugar-cane* (Tropical Agriculture Series). London and New York: Longman, 1984.

Blume, Helmut. *Geography of Sugar Cane.* Berlin: Albert Bartens, 1985.

Daniels, John, and Christian Daniels. "Sugarcane in Prehistory." *Archaeology in Oceania* 28 (1993): 1–7.

Deerr, Noel. *The History of Sugar.* London: Chapman and Hall, 1949–1950.

Fauconnier, R. *Sugar Cane* (Tropical Agriculture Series). London: Macmillan, 1993.

Galloway, J. H. *The Sugar Cane Industry: An Historical Geography from its Origins to 1914.* Cambridge: Cambridge University Press, 1989.

Institut für Zuckerrübenforschung, Göttingen, ed. *Geschichte der Zuckerrübe: 200 Jahre Anbau und Züchtung.* Berlin: Albert Bartens, 1984.

McGee, Harold. *On Food and Cooking: The Science and Lore of the Kitchen.* New York: Scribner's, 1984.

McGinnis, R. A., ed. *Beet-Sugar Technology.* 3rd ed. Fort Collins, Colo.: Beet Sugar Development Foundation, 1982.

Smartt, J., and N. W. Simmonds, eds. *Evolution of Crop Plants.* 2nd ed. Harlow, Essex: Longman Scientific & Technical, 1995.

van der Poel, P. W., H. Schiweck, and T. Schwartz, eds. *Sugar Technology: Beet and Cane Sugar Manufacture.* Berlin: Albert Bartens, 1998.

G. B. Hagelberg

SUPERMARKET. *See* **Retailing of Food.**

SUPPLEMENTS. *See* **Nutrient Supplements.**

SUSTAINABLE AGRICULTURE. From a technological and economic standpoint, agriculture today represents one of the success stories of the modern era. Despite an ever increasing global population, and a corresponding gradual decrease in the availability of nonrenewable natural resources such as energy, land, and water, farmers throughout the world have responded to the challenge by increasing total and per area production levels every year. This agricultural miracle is due to a long tradition of farmer self-reliance, ingenuity, and perseverance, and to the support provided to farmers by many private and public institutions. Especially noteworthy is the support provided by a network of agricultural research universities in North America and Europe. Furthermore, crop productivity has improved in the developed world, and in many Third World countries as well. By the 1970s, many Third World countries in Asia and Latin America had actually reached self-sufficiency with respect to several primary staple grains.

The race toward increased crop yields began in the mid- to late 1800s in precapitalist England. Ever since then, scientists, environmentalists, and economists have issued words of caution concerning environmental and social issues arising from modern agriculture. By the mid- to late twentieth century, some of the more negative en-

SOME KEY UNDESIRABLE SIDE EFFECTS OF MODERN AGRICULTURE

- Unsustainable irrigation programs throughout the world are resulting in an undesirable buildup of salinity and toxic mineral levels in one out of five hectares under irrigation. Thus, agricultural water, a nonrenewable resource whose use has tripled globally since 1950, has to be used more efficiently to minimize salinization problems.
- Excessive soil erosion, in the range of fifteen to forty tons per hectare annually, results in the loss of productive farmland in many parts of the world. Forested areas, a refuge for wildlife and biodiversity (biological diversity), are then often turned into agricultural fields to compensate for the loss of the abandoned eroded areas.
- The indiscriminate use of pesticides is affecting human health and wildlife populations, as first reported to the population at large in Rachel Carson's book *Silent Spring* (1962).
- The increased concentration of farms into larger and larger farm holdings is reducing the number of small family farms, believed by many to represent the heart of rural communities and to be key stewards of the environment.
- The trend toward larger farms and plantation-type monocultures is leading to a loss of global biodiversity. Biodiversity, many argue, may be a critical ecological feature that allows the continued survival of humans on earth.
- The excessive reliance on synthetic fertilizers, and the improper use and disposal of animal wastes is leading to the breakup of natural nutrient cycles. This causes an undesirable buildup of nutrients and salts in aquifers, affecting wildlife in aquatic habitats.

vironmental and economic side effects of modern capital-intensive agriculture became evident in many parts of the world. The increased realization that modern agriculture had serious side effects, resulting in reduced environmental quality, health concerns, and economic insecurity for the traditional family farm, led in part to what is known today as a global "Sustainable Agriculture" movement.

Definition

Because agricultural systems are so diverse, based on farm size, location, crop being grown, socioeconomic background, among many other factors, and because the

movement has become so widespread globally, sustainable agriculture has come to represent different things to different people. Nevertheless there are some common threads, concepts, and beliefs. In the most general terms, sustainable agriculture describes systems in which the farmer reaches the goal of producing adequate yields and good profits following production practices that minimize any negative short- and long-term side effects on the environment and the well-being of the community. The major goals of this approach are thus to develop economically viable agroecosystems and to enhance the quality of the environment, so that farmlands will remain productive indefinitely.

Why Sustainable Agriculture? History and Future Prospects

Ancient history, ranging from the Egyptians to the Romans to the Mayans, indicates that poorly managed agriculture can lead to the eminent decline of entire civilizations. By the midpart of the twentieth century, symptoms began to appear, documented by scientists, that some aspects of modern agriculture were unsustainable, leading in many cases to a decline in environmental quality and human quality of life. The undesirable side effects of modern agriculture, some believed, were threatening

WHAT IS SUSTAINABLE AGRICULTURE? SOME KEY DEFINITIONS

Sustainable agriculture involves farming systems that are environmentally sound, profitable, productive, and compatible with socioeconomic conditions (J. Pesek, in Hatfield and Karlen, *Sustainable Agriculture Systems*).

Agroecology is a field of research used to implement sustainable systems. It is the application of ecological concepts and principles to the study, design, and management of sustainable systems.

A *systems* approach is used to study and research sustainable systems. The goal is to study the farm as an entity made up of all its components and their interrelationships, together with relationships between the farm and its environment.

Key components of sustainable systems include enhanced internal nutrient cycling on the farm; improved soil quality through additions of organic matter and reduced soil erosion; increased vegetational diversity to promote natural systems of pest control; and alternative marketing programs that increase profits and minimize overhead costs.

BASIC FEATURES AND CONCEPTS OF SUSTAINABLE SYSTEMS

1. The need to maintain or improve soil quality and fertility. This is often attained by increasing the organic matter content of the soil, and by minimizing losses from soil erosion.
2. Production programs are designed to improve the efficiency of resource utilization. This will result in the most cost-effective use of water, fertilizers, and pesticides.
3. An attempt is made to improve internal nutrient cycles on the farm, which will reduce the dependence on external fertilizers.
4. Efforts are made to improve biological diversity on the farm. This will result in improved natural suppression of pests, and may also help to improve internal nutrient cycling within the farm.
5. Farm management and marketing programs are designed to minimize overhead costs and to increase returns, often by following alternative marketing schemes.

the lands and the very livelihood that farmers were trying to sustain. In contrast, from a historical perspective, scientists knew that civilizations that did follow sustainable practices were indeed able to thrive for centuries. Thus, by incorporating the use of production techniques developed by the latest agricultural research, along with some of the farming practices that proved effective through centuries of farming in many areas, a set of recommended management practices was established in individual production regions.

The future goal of farming communities is to strive to use current sustainable practices and to utilize the latest production techniques to remain competitive in the global agricultural market. For this to take place, a close communication link has to be maintained between rural communities, researchers, and society at large. This link gives urban communities a better understanding of issues affecting farmers, including the farmers' role as stewards of the environment, and of the economic realities of providing the public with a consistently healthy and safe food supply.

Implementing Sustainable Systems

An important aspect of sustainable agriculture is that it does not represent a specific set of agricultural practices that farmers need to follow step by step, like one would a recipe, to reach a specific goal. Instead, the concept rep-

resents more of a paradigm shift that encourages farmers to seek their own path, one that best fits the farm's particular conditions, and leads toward a more environmentally friendly approach without sacrificing yields or profits. Similarly, sustainable agriculture is not a specific target, but instead is more of a process that every farmer pursues as part of the daily farm operations. Thus, because agricultural systems are so diverse, farmers may choose among a myriad number of agricultural practices and techniques available to produce crops more effectively.

See also **Agriculture since the Industrial Revolution; Agronomy; Crop Improvement; Ecology and Food; Environment; Green Revolution; Greenhouse Horticulture; High-Technology Farming; Horticulture; Organic Agriculture; Organic Farming and Gardening; Organic Food; Tillage; Water: Water as a Resource.**

BIBLIOGRAPHY

Carson, Rachel. *Silent Spring*. Greenwich, Conn.: Fawcett Crest, 1962.

Collins, Wanda W., and Calvin O. Qualset, eds. *Biodiversity in Agroecosystems*. Boca Raton, Fla.: CRC Press, 1999.

Gliessman, Stephen R. *Agroecology: Ecological Processes in Sustainable Agriculture*. Chelsea, Mich.: Sleeping Bear Press, 1998.

Gliessman, Stephen R. *Agroecosystem Sustainability: Developing Practical Strategies*. Boca Raton, Fla.: CRC Press, 2001.

Hatfield, J. L., and D. L. Karlen, eds. *Sustainable Agriculture Systems*. Boca Raton, Fla.: Lewis Publishers, 1994.

National Research Council. *Sustainable Agriculture and the Environment in the Humid Tropics*. Washington, D.C.: National Academy Press, 1987.

Powers, L. F., and R. McSorley. *Ecological Principles of Agriculture*. Albany, N.Y.: Delmar, 2000.

Hector Valenzuela

SWEETENERS. *See* **Sugar and Sweeteners.**

SWEET POTATO. Sweet potato (*Ipomoea batatas*) is in the botanical family Convolvulaceae along with common plants, such as bindweed and morning glory. The generic name *Ipomoea* comes from the Greek words *"ips,"* meaning bindweed, and *"homoios,"* meaning similar. Sweet potatoes should not be confused with ordinary potatoes (*Solanum tuberosum*) as they are entirely unrelated, although their uses can be similar. Orange-fleshed sweet potatoes are often known as yams, especially in the southern United States, but they are quite different from true yams (*Dioscorea* sp.) in growth habit and use. Furthermore, unlike true yams, the greens of sweet potatoes are edible and provide an important source of food in Africa and Asia.

Identification

Sweet potato is a perennial that is usually grown as an annual. It grows from underground tuberous roots with trailing, twisting stems that can be as long as twenty feet (six meters). Leaves are variable in shape, size, and color but are generally more or less heart-shaped and green with purple markings. The single flowers are funnel-shaped and white or pale purple but are rarely seen in temperate regions. Roots grow where stem nodes touch the ground, and most develop into the edible storage roots, usually four to ten storage roots per plant.

Diversity

The International Potato Center (CIP) in Peru holds the largest sweet potato gene bank in the world with more than 6,500 wild, traditional, and improved varieties. Many of these are unique to a particular country or region. For example, an anthropologist in Irian Jaya found forty different cultivars of sweet potato growing in just one community garden. In contrast, Stephen Facciola's *Cornucopia II* (1998) lists only twenty-five different varieties available for the whole United States. Sweet potato flesh can be white, yellow, purple, red, pink, violet, and orange, while skin color varies among yellow, red, orange, and brown. Varieties with pale yellow or white flesh are less sweet and moist than those with red, pink, or orange flesh. They also have little or no beta-carotene and higher levels of dry matter, which means their textures are drier and more mealy and they stay firmer when cooked. Sweet potatoes also vary enormously in size, shape, taste, and texture, although all are smooth-skinned with roots always tapered at both ends.

Nutrients

All varieties of sweet potato are good sources of vitamins C and E as well as dietary fiber, potassium, and iron, and they are low in fat and cholesterol (see the Table for more detail). The orange- and red-fleshed forms of sweet potato are particularly high in beta-carotene, the vitamin A precursor.

Origins

Scientists debate the exact place of origin of *I. batatas*, although the evidence points toward Central America rather than South America. They are no longer found growing in the wild, but it is possible that the wild Mexican sweet potato *I. trifida* is an ancestor. Sweet potatoes have been cultivated for more than five thousand years, and fossilized remains found in the Andes have been dated at about 8,000 years old. Genetic studies suggest the likelihood that in early times sweet potatoes were carried by the local people from island to island, spreading gradually across the Pacific from Central and South America to eastern Indonesia, New Guinea, Polynesia, and New Zealand. Christopher Columbus is credited with taking sweet potatoes from the New World back to Spain, from where they spread through the warmer regions of Europe and were transported to other parts of

Asia and to Africa by Spanish and Portuguese explorers and traders. Sweet potatoes were grown in gardens by North American Indians and were an important staple food during the American Revolutionary War and the American Civil War. They were also an essential part of the diet of the slave population in southern states. Most large plantations had a sweet potato plot and root cellars beneath cabins for potato storage.

Popularity

At the beginning of the twentieth century sweet potatoes were the second most important root crop in the United States. In 1920 the per capita consumption of sweet potatoes was thirty-one pounds (fourteen kilograms), but consumption steadily declined. In 1999 consumption was only 4 pounds (1.8 kilograms) per person (U.S. Department of Agriculture, 2000).

TABLE 1

Constituents of the sweet potato: values per 100g (3.5 oz.) edible portion

	Units	Raw sweet potato	Cooked, baked in skin	Cooked, boiled without skin
Water	g	72.84	72.84	72.84
Energy	kcal	105	103	105
	kj	439	431	439
Protein	g	1.65	1.72	1.65
Total lipid (fat)	g	0.30	0.11	0.30
Carbohydrate by difference	g	24.28	24.27	24.28
Fiber, total dietary	g	3.0	3.0	1.8
Ash	g	0.95	1.06	0.95
Calcium Ca	mg	22	28	21
Iron Fe	mg	0.59	0.45	0.56
Magnesium Mg	mg	10	20	10
Phosphorous P	mg	28	55	27
Potassium K	mg	204	348	184
Sodium Na	mg	13	10	13
Zinc Zn	mg	0.28	0.29	0.27
Copper Cu	mg	0.169	0.208	0.161
Manganese Mn	mg	0.355	0.560	0.337
Selenium Se	mcg	0.6	0.7	0.7
Vitamin C	mg	22.7	24.6	17.1
Thiamin B_1	mg	0.066	0.073	0.053
Riboflavin B_2	mg	0.147	0.127	0.14
Niacin B_3	mg	0.674	0.604	0.64
Pantothenic acid B_5	mg	0.591	0.646	0.532
Vitamin B_6	mg	0.257	0.241	0.244
Folate, total	mcg	14	23	11
Vitamin B_{12}	mcg	0	0	0
Vitamin A, IU	IU	20,063	21,822	17,054
Vitamin A, RE	mcg-RE	2,006	2,182	1,705
Vitamin E	mg-ATE	0.280	0.280	0.280

SOURCE: U.S. Department of Agriculture. Agriculture Research Service Nutrient Database for Standard Reference, Release 14, 2001.

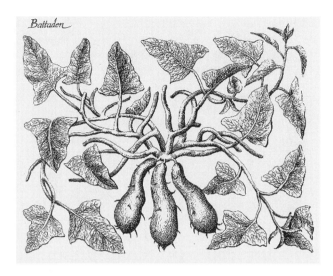

A sweet potato plant depicted in Johann Sigismund Elsholtz's *Diaeteticon* (1682), one of the first works to discuss the health and medical value of this New World vegetable. ROUGHWOOD COLLECTION.

Sweet potatoes grow in all warm, humid areas of the world and at the beginning of the twenty-first century were the seventh largest world food crop, 95 percent of which is produced in developing countries. They are typically grown by small farmers, often on marginal ground. This crop plant has a long history of saving lives. It matures fast, is rich in nutrients, and is often the first crop planted after a natural disaster, providing abundant food for otherwise starving populations. In eastern Africa the sweet potato is known as "the protector of children" or *cilera abana* because it is often the only food that stands between a child's survival and starvation.

Growing Sweet Potatoes

Sweet potatoes are tropical plants that can also be grown in the summer in temperate regions as long as they have at least five frost-free months combined with fairly warm days and nights. They can be grown from vine cuttings or by planting pieces of the roots. To grow new plants, place one or more sweet potatoes in a bed of sand and cover with a couple of inches of moist, sandy soil. When the sprouts reach about 10 inches (25.4 centimeters), detach by twisting and transplant to the place they are to grow. Push sprouts about 3 inches (7.6 centimeters) into the ground and water well. Leave a distance of about 1 foot (30 centimeters) between plants and 3 feet, 3 inches (1 meter) between rows. Sweet potatoes do best in full sun with fertile, open sandy-loam soils. They also like some added manure (well rotted) and compost, although they should not be given too much nitrogen as this encourages leaf growth at the expense of root growth. They benefit from regular additions of potash. Roots will be bigger and easier to harvest if sprouts are planted into raised mounds about 1 foot (30 centimeters) high. This is particularly important in heavy or wet soil. Once established, apart from occasional weeding, sweet potatoes need little care.

Harvesting

Roots are harvested as the leaves begin to yellow in the fall. They are then brushed clean and left to cure. Traditionally curing involved stacking the potatoes in the field or garden, covering them with sand, and leaving them for several weeks. Sweet potatoes in commercial production are cured in rooms with humidity between 75 percent and 80 percent and temperatures between 80°F and 86°F (27°C and 30°C). Curing heals cuts and reduces decay and shrinkage during storage, and it converts some starches to sugars, improving the flavor. Once cured, sweet potatoes can be stored for several months, and white-fleshed varieties last as long as ten months.

In the United States most of the sweet potato crop is canned. These are usually the smaller roots. Roots of good size are sold fresh, and any that are too large are generally processed into baby food.

Buying

When buying sweet potatoes, always choose ones that are firm with even skin coloration and no signs of decay. They should never be stored in the refrigerator. Keep them in a cool, dry, well-ventilated container (a basket is ideal) at about 55°F to 60°F (13°C–16°C). Generally they should be used within two to three weeks of purchase because it is not possible to determine how long they have already been stored before purchase.

Who Grows Sweet Potatoes?

According to figures released by CIP, more than 148.77 million short tons (135 million metric tons) of sweet potatoes are grown worldwide. China is by far the largest producer with about 87 percent of the crop, nearly half of which is fed to animals. The rest of Asia accounts for 6 percent, Africa 5 percent, Latin America 1.5 percent, and the United States 0.45 percent. In most developing countries, where the sweet potato is part of the staple diet, the white- or cream-fleshed forms with a bland taste are usually grown. These potatoes have a high dry matter content, which means they are a good energy source, which is vital for a staple food. In developed countries, where the sweet potato is used more as a vegetable or for sweet dishes, the red- or orange-fleshed types are preferred for their moist flesh and sweet flavor. The U.S. sweet potato crop was worth $214,980,000 in 1999, and just under a third of the crop was grown in North Carolina. Louisiana, Mississippi, and California also grow significant quantities. The largest European producer is Portugal with only .02 percent of world production. These figures clearly illustrate that sweet potatoes are an important crop in third world countries but are a secondary foodstuff in first world countries.

Preparing and Eating

Sweet potato roots can be boiled, steamed, baked, and fried. They are also canned or dried and made into flour, cereal, and noodles. Like pumpkins, sweet potato roots are often used in sweet dishes, such as pies, puddings, biscuits, cakes, and desserts. In some countries roots are processed to produce starch and fermented to make alcohol. Cooked red- or orange-fleshed sweet potato roots are sweet, soft, and starchy with a flavor that resembles roasted chestnuts and baked squash. Sweet potatoes are prepared by scrubbing and cutting into appropriately sized pieces. Leave the skin on if they are to be baked, boiled, or steamed; peel before frying. Cooking in the skin preserves more of the nutrients. Once the roots are cooked (when a knife can be easily inserted), they can be served whole or peeled and mashed, pureed, or sieved and served as a sweet or savory vegetable, depending on what is added.

In the United States sweet potatoes are probably best known for their use in pies and as a candied vegetable. They are a traditional accompaniment to Thanksgiving dinner and often appear on the menu at other festival times, such as Christmas and Easter. Sweet potatoes can be substituted for potatoes, apples, or squash in almost any recipe. Cooked, mashed sweet potatoes are also used to replace some of the wheat flour in breads, cakes, muffins, and cookie recipes, as is sweet potato flour. Sweet potatoes cooked in their skins can be frozen. Wrap each piece in aluminum foil or freezer wrap, place into a freezer bag, and freeze.

In third world countries sweet potatoes are processed into starch, noodles, candy, desserts, and flour. This allows the farm household to extend the availability of the crop. In China, for example, sweet potato starch production has become an important cottage industry, while in Uganda sweet potatoes are sliced and dried, which allows them to be kept for about five months. The dried pieces are also ground into flour, which is then rehydrated and eaten as a thick porridge known as *atapa*.

Although usually the roots are eaten, young leaves and the tips of vines can be harvested, washed, and boiled as a green vegetable or added to stir-fries. All parts of the sweet potato are used as stock feed, although the roots are often cooked first.

As a Medicine

Sweet potato roots and leaves are used in folk remedies to treat illnesses as diverse as asthma, night blindness, and diarrhea. Easily digestible, they are good for the eliminative system. It is believed they bind heavy metals, so they have been used to detoxify the system.

Sweet Potatoes in Africa

In eastern and southern Africa some 3 million children under the age of five suffer from xerophthalmia or dry eye, which causes blindness. Dry eye is caused by a lack of vitamin A in the diet, and many of the affected children die within a few months of becoming blind. The yellow- and orange-fleshed varieties of sweet potatoes are high in beta-carotene, which can be converted into vitamin A in the intestines and liver. It has been shown that even small amounts of these sweet potatoes as a regular part of the diet will eliminate vitamin A deficiency in adults and children. African countries have traditionally grown white-fleshed sweet potatoes, which are low in vitamin A. A ten-year research project concluded that varieties high in beta-carotene could compete with production levels of the white-fleshed varieties and would be acceptable to local tastes. Consequently CIP and related organizations launched a regional effort to encourage African women to also grow orange-fleshed varieties.

At the same time researchers at CIP have combined parental clones of sweet potatoes to yield a group of yellow and orange potatoes with high dry matter (a characteristic of the white-fleshed forms of sweet potato) that they believe will be more acceptable to African consumers. In Kenya sweet potatoes are mostly grown in the densely populated Western Province, where often more than half the crop is destroyed by a virus. In 2000 the Kenyan Agricultural Research Institute released genetically modified sweet potatoes with increased disease resistance and assured the public that these potatoes would be largely resistant to the virus.

Twenty-first Century Changes

In the last four decades of the twentieth century the uses of sweet potatoes diversified beyond their classification as subsistence, food security, and famine-relief crops. In particular the last decade of the century saw a concentrated, coordinated effort to fully realize the potential of this crop. The hoped for result is that millions of subsistence landholders in Africa, Asia, and Latin America will be able to use sweet potatoes for food, stock food, and processed products and to generate income.

The United States is also exploring the potential of sweet potato products. A patent was granted for the production of bread made from 100 percent sweet potato flour. It is hoped that these products will appeal to consumers who are allergic to grain breads and flours. Also scientists at two different institutes in the United States have developed genetically modified sweet potatoes containing edible vaccines. One of these vaccines works against hepatitis B and the other against the Norwalk virus found in food that has not been handled or stored correctly. Edible vaccines such as these may provide cheap protection for some of the poorest people in the world.

See also **Columbian Exchange**; **Potato**; **Tubers**; **Vitamins**.

BIBLIOGRAPHY

Facciola, Stephen. *Cornucopia II: A Sourcebook of Edible Plants.* Vista, Calif.: Kampong Publications, 1998.

Herklots, G. A. C. *Vegetables in South-East Asia.* London: George Allen and Unwin, 1972.

International Potato Center. Available at http://www.cipotato
.org.

Musau, Z. "Genetically Modified Sweet Potato Launched in
Kenya." *Nation*, 19 August 2000.

North Carolina Sweet Potato Commission. Available at http://
www.ncsweetpotatoes.com.

Onstad, Dianne. *Whole Foods Companion: A Guide for Adventurous Cooks, Curious Shoppers, and Lovers of Natural Foods.*
White River Junction, Vt.: Chelsea Green Publishing,
1996.

U.S. Department of Agriculture, Agriculture Research Service.
Nutrient Database for Standard Reference, Release 14. Washington, D.C.: Government Printing Office, 2001.

U.S. Department of Agriculture, Economic Research Service.
Situation and Outlook, Vegetables and Specialties. Washington, D.C.: Economic Research Service, 2000.

Woodward, Penny. *Asian Herbs and Vegetables.* Flemington, Victoria: Hyland House Publishing, 2000.

Penny Woodward

SWEETS. *See* **Candy and Confections.**

SWIDDEN. Swidden is an agricultural strategy that
necessitates the slashing, cutting, felling, and burning of
forested areas for the planting of impermanent garden
plots or agricultural fields, and that has been the mainstay of horticulturalists and peasant farmers in the tropics and primeval forests of the world for the better part
of the past four to eight thousand years. This method of
agricultural intensification, more widely known as "slash-
and-burn" agriculture, is called *tlacolol* or *milpa* agriculture in Mesoamerica. It is often associated with patterns
of shifting cultivation or extensive agriculture via which
soil exhaustion or weed intrusion necessitates plot rotation and fallow cycles.

Tropical soils are extremely fragile, and agriculture
in the tropics tends to deplete soil-based nutrients
rapidly, resulting in decreasing yields from such parcels
after just a few seasons. In order to stimulate the regeneration of soil nutrients through the growth and decay of
tropical vegetation, swidden agriculturalists typically
abandon or fallow such plots for as many as twenty-five
years. These cycles of slash-and-burn field preparation,
cultivation, and fallow, and the necessity of shifting or
relocating cultivation to adjacent or new fields on a cycli-
cal basis, play a key role in the social, economic, and political configurations of those societies that resort to such
strategies of agricultural intensification in tropical or otherwise forested environments.

Swidden and Shifting Cultivation
According to cultural ecologist Robert Netting, a broad
spectrum of agricultural systems exists within traditional
or otherwise "technologically simpler" societies in what
today constitute some of the nations of the Third World.
Such systems range from those that require a constant
shifting from field to field within virgin forests to intensive agriculture supported by irrigation works in year-
round production. Within this spectrum can be identified
a variety of swidden system strategies that include short-
term as opposed to long-term fallowing, sectorial fallowing, forest-fallow, bush-fallow, and short-fallow
cultivation (pp. 65–66). The latter three types, originally
identified by agricultural economist Esther Boserup, are
defined on the basis of land-use types and the total period of cultivation as opposed to periods of fallow.
Whereas forest fallow may see the cultivation of a single
swidden parcel for a period of one to two crop years, that
same field may then lie dormant (fallow) for a period of
twenty to twenty-five years. On the other hand, bush fallow may encompass a period of one to eight successive
years of cultivation, and only six to ten years of fallow.
Finally, the short-fallow system may range from a very
short or variable period of months or seasons of cultivation to a one-to-two-year fallow cycle. In each of these
systems, the extent to which productive yield is maintained or enhanced by the regeneration of tropical vegetation and its subsequent slashing and burning is key to
the nature of the system employed. Similarly, in those areas where population growth and settlement place constraints on the availability of viable forest parcels,
agricultural intensification may necessitate an increase in
the number of parcels devoted to short-fallow cropping.

Origins and Development
Archaeologist Richard E. W. Adams has noted broad similarities in the nature of settlement patterns and artifact
distributions between the ancient Maya swidden farmers
of Mesoamerica and early Danubian swidden agriculturalists of Europe. According to Adams, the expansion of
Danubian farmers into western Europe at 5000 B.C.E. resulted in the rapid and extensive spread of Danubian settlements and traditional arts and technologies across a
vast area. Adams attributes this pattern to the use of slash-
and-burn (swidden) agricultural systems in the primeval
forests of Europe. Such a pattern resulted in the rapid
establishment, abandonment, and reoccupation of villages over vast areas in a pattern reminiscent of that identified with swidden agriculturalists the world over (p.
119). According to Robert Gary Minnich, similar demographic and cultural patterns have been identified with
swidden practices introduced by the Slavs to the eastern
Alps and northern Balkans in the sixth century (pp.
96–98). Such practices, in fact, persisted well into the
twentieth century in the hilly and forested regions of
Slovenia (p. 221).

Similarly, Myrdene Anderson has documented the
introduction of swidden agricultural strategies into Norwegian Lapland from Finland at the beginning of the
eighteenth century. In fact, a further review of swidden-
related documents in the eHRAF Collection of Ethnog-

raphy (the online version of the Human Relations Area Files) will readily produce references to some forty-eight societies the world over whose cultural histories center on swidden agriculture or similar forms of agricultural intensification. Those societies range across the length and breadth of Africa, Asia, Europe, Middle America and the Caribbean, North America, Oceania, and South America.

Traditional Crops and Agriculturalists

Swidden agriculture is practiced by diverse societies across a broad range of habitats, with the result that the methods, settlement patterns, cropping cycles, and traditional crops also vary widely. For instance, Bernard Sellato reports that the Dayak peoples of Borneo practice a range of agricultural pursuits, swidden being but one of many adaptive strategies. Among those Dayak groups that engage in swidden agricultural practices, crops consist of a variety of plant foods that are multicropped (planted within the same fields). According to Sellato, while the customary Dayak practice centers on the swidden cultivation of hill or dry rice in rain-forest clearings, such fields are seldom used to cultivate any more than a single crop of rice per year. However, while two crops of rice may be harvested on some occasions, cassava or manioc is sometimes cultivated within the same fields after the rice harvests. Once harvested, such fields are left to fallow for ten to twenty years. Sellato has also observed that the declining productivity of those swidden gardens closest to the communal dwelling place or longhouse often necessitates the relocation of village settlements and, thereby, accounts in large part for the shifting or semisedentary nature of the Dayak communities of Borneo, as is typical of other swidden farming communities the world over (p. 13).

In addition to hill or dry rice plantings in swidden parcels, Dayak communities also cultivate cassava, taro, yams or sweet potatoes, maize, sugarcane, beans, cucumbers and leaf greens, and various semiwild fruits. Despite a reliance on swidden crops, Dayak farmers nevertheless supplement their diets with fishing, hunting, and a pattern of animal husbandry centered on the consumption of dogs and cats, as well as chickens, pigs, and some ducks. While traditional Dayak swidden agriculture is largely reliant on the aforementioned crops, other cash crops include pepper, cloves, coffee, cocoa, coconut and oil palms, and rubber. In other contexts, permanent year-round garden plots and irrigation agriculture have displaced swidden practices in those contexts where population growth has resulted in the abandonment of traditional swidden patterns.

Swidden Ecology and Its Consequences

Cultural ecologist Roy Ellen provides a detailed analysis of the cultural and ecological benefits and constraints posed by swidden agriculture. According to Ellen, declining crop yields identified with swidden farming are largely the result of pest infestations, plant disease, weeds,

the deterioration of soil nutrient content and composition, topsoil erosion, and changes in the number and composition of soil organisms or root biomass in any given parcel (p. 36). Because tropical soils are typically low in organic matter, slash-and-burn agriculture enriches soils to a limited extent and for a limited period of time by adding phosphorous, nitrogen, and potassium from the burned vegetation.

On the other hand, H. J. Albers and M. J. Goldbach found a correlation between the duration of cropping periods in swidden systems and the onset of species competition, resulting in an irreversible ecosystem transformation away from forest cover to grassland ecological regimes (pp. 262–263). In such instances, deforestation was the inevitable result of poor choices made by swidden farmers who were not concerned with the long-term benefits of longer fallow cycles.

In sum, despite the inherent challenges of farming in the tropics or primeval forests of the world, swidden remains a relatively efficient, and ecologically sound, system of agricultural production and resource management for the peoples of the Third World. This is particularly so when compared to those labor- and resource-intensive permanent and irrigation-based systems that dominate the nation-states of the First World. While the latter systems are ultimately more productive in terms of total crop yields, such productivity comes at great cost. The massive investment in agricultural equipment, fertilizers, pesticides, and personnel necessary to sustain intensive farming systems often outweighs the viability of such agricultural systems for the majority of those farmers whose only access to potentially viable agricultural land is largely restricted to the tropical and primeval forests of the Third World.

See also **Agriculture, Origins of; Inca Empire; Mexico and Central America, Pre-Columbian.**

BIBLIOGRAPHY

Adams, Richard E. W. *Prehistoric Mesoamerica*. Boston: Little, Brown, 1977.

Albers, H. J., and M. J. Goldbach. "Irreversible Ecosystem Change, Species Competition, and Shifting Cultivation." *Resource and Energy Economics* 22 (2000): 261–280.

Anderson, Myrdene. "Saami Ethnoecology: Resource Management in Norwegian Lapland." eHRAF Collection of Ethnography, Document Number 18, EP04. New Haven, Conn.: HRAF, 1996. Available at http://etx.umdl.umich.edu/cgi/e/ehraf/ehraf

Boserup, Esther. *The Conditions of Agricultural Growth*. Chicago: Aldine, 1965.

Ellen, Roy. *Environment, Subsistence, and System: The Ecology of Small-Scale Social Formations*. New York: Cambridge University Press, 1982.

Johnson, Allen W., and Timothy Earle. *The Evolution of Human Societies: From Foraging Group to Agrarian State*. Stanford, Calif.: Stanford University Press, 1987.

Minnich, Robert Gary. "Homemade World of Zagaj." eHRAF Collection of Ethnography, Document Number 30, EP04. New Haven, Conn.: HRAF, 1997. Available at http://ets .umdl.umich.edu.cgi/e/ehraf/ehraf

Netting, Robert M. *Cultural Ecology.* 2nd ed. Prospect Heights, Ill.: Waveland, 1986.

Porter Weaver, Muriel. *The Aztecs, Maya, and Their Predecessors: Archaeology of Mesoamerica.* 2nd ed. San Diego, Calif.: Academic, 1981.

Sellato, Bernard. *Nomads of the Borneo Rainforest: The Economics, Politics, and Ideology of Settling Down,* translated from the French by Stephanie Morgan. Honolulu, Hawaii: University of Hawaii Press, 1994.

Ruben G. Mendoza

SWITZERLAND. *See* **France; Germany, Austria, Switzerland; Italy.**

SYMBOL, FOOD AS. A symbol is an object, image, or action that is conventionally understood to represent something else. Food is particularly powerful as a symbol because it is so deeply embedded in everyday as well as celebratory life, and can therefore be read in many ways. Because it fulfills physical as well as emotional and psychological needs, it may be intentionally utilized as a symbol in some instances but not in others. And because food engages all the senses, it tends to evoke strong sensory and emotive as well as cognitive associations. This range of association adds to the potential symbolic power of food.

Three properties of symbols as defined by anthropologist Victor Turner are clearly demonstrated in food. The first is condensation: many ideas or actions are represented in a single formation. For example, turkey represents the American holiday of Thanksgiving, standing for the family gatherings, feasts, specific menus, and football games that commonly occur with the celebration. A second property is unification: symbols link disparate references. The turkey as symbol evokes abundance of natural resources, a romanticized New England heritage, patriotism, family harmony, and the fall season. The final property of symbols is polarization of meaning: they contain both ideological meanings (representing values, ethos, social norms) and sensory meanings (related to the objective properties of the symbol and representing physical aspects of life), merging these two poles and grounding conceptual references in felt experience. For example, apple pie is an American symbol of both patriotism and maternal nurturing, strengthening the referential power of each yet also lending the emotional associations of each to the other.

Foods become symbolic either through the presence of analogous qualities or by association in fact or thought with a particular reference. Analogous, or like, qualities include the physical structure or appearance of the item, its texture, color, flavor, and even its nutritional components. For example, bananas are commonly used to represent a phallus; apples used to represent wholesomeness and innocence, as in "apple-cheeked children"; peaches to represent female attributes; caffeinated drinks to represent energetic and fun-filled personalities or activities.

Symbolic references for foods are also developed by association in fact or thought. Cherry blossoms bloom in early spring and are therefore used as a symbol to celebrate the change in season. Similarly, other crops ripen in the fall and become associated with that season. In the United States, pumpkins, corn, and apples are used to celebrate both autumn and the harvest-based holidays falling within that season.

Symbolic foods that develop their meanings through use and practice over time are "organic" symbols; they emerge from everyday usage, and their meanings are seemingly logical and inevitable within that cultural context. Symbols can also be created and imposed upon a culture. For these "invented symbols," individuals or institutions intentionally attach particular meanings to a food and attempt to control the interpretation given to that food.

As communicative tools, symbols can be manipulated for a multitude of purposes, on a personal as well as a cultural level. Food symbols are commonly exploited in marketing and advertising. Restaurant chains frequently attempt to associate themselves with a particular food item, for example, Red Lobster and Long John Silver with seafood, Wendy's with chili and square hamburgers, MacDonald's or Burger King with hamburgers and french fries. Similarly, advertising symbols can become attached to particular foods: the Jolly Green Giant with vegetables, Aunt Jemima with pancakes, the dignified Quaker with oatmeal.

Food's symbolic potential is also utilized for national, ethnic, and regional identity and pride. Americans rally around hot dogs, Spaniards around ham, Koreans around kimchi. Conversely, specific foods may be held up as distinguishing one group from another and as demonstrating that group's lesser worth.

Food symbolism occurs in all the activities surrounding the procurement, preservation, preparation, presentation, and performance of food as well as the food product itself. "Foodways" refers to this network of activities.

Procurement refers to the processes of obtaining food. Hunting, for example, can function as a symbol of manhood, of family tradition, of regional heritage. Purchasing groceries from specialty shops or catalogs rather than a local supermarket can signify economic status. Similarly, procurement can affect the referential meanings of a food item. Even though the food items are structurally identical, a bagel bought from the local corner deli can carry completely different emotional associations from one bought from the frozen bread aisle of a chain supermarket.

Preservation includes the means by which food is stored and kept for later use, the material forms used, the types of foods selected for specific types of preservation, and the physical arrangement of preserved goods. Smokehouses used for curing hams can reference a southern U.S. heritage; similar structures for smoking fish represent a Midwestern background.

The size and design of refrigerators can symbolize social status (custom-designed to fit kitchen decor represents up-scale wealth), ethnicity (Americans tend to use large refrigerators and frequently possess an additional freezer to allow for the weekly or monthly shopping habits in the United States), or even occupation (university students use half-size ones to fit their smaller dorm rooms).

Preparation refers to the actual processes of turning the raw ingredients into a cultured and edible food. This involves methods of cutting, cooking, mixing of ingredients, selecting of ingredients, and adapting of the recipe. The process may be as simple as picking an apple from a tree or taking a handful of raisins from a box to complex and sophisticated techniques requiring refined skills and extensive experience.

Presentation refers to how food is physically arranged and presented for consumption. Presentation can frame the act of eating as a social event and as a meal genre and can also communicate the emotional responses intended to occur. Candlelight implies romance; fine china a formal, celebratory event; paper plates an informal and casual occasion.

Performance includes two aspects. First is the manner in which the food is consumed, the utensils used, and the immediate context: the time and place of consumption and other people present. Performance also refers to the cultural use of food, to the meanings intentionally attached and elicited to the food item or meal, and the occasion for consumption.

Foodways can be performed as symbol in any number of arenas—cookbooks, festivals, restaurants, cooking competitions, family holiday meals. Each of these offer sites for the articulation and manipulation of the meanings of the foodways. Similarly, food symbols occur in a variety of forms: as objects, activities, relationships, events, gestures, and spatial units within a ritual.

Food as a symbol can refer to any aspect of a culture's or individual's history and identity. Commonly recognized and articulated referential domains include ethnicity, region, gender, religion, ethos, social status, and social relationships

Ethnicity is one of the most common references for food. These foods become symbolic frequently because they stand in contrast to host foods and mark the ethnic group as different and separate. This marking is frequently, though not always, negative, emphasizing the strangeness of the ethnic group, and the particular foods

Food has always served as a potent symbol of identity, religious preference, festivities, even nationalism. This 1907 postcard celebrates apple pie as the ultimate symbol of American patriotism. ROUGHWOOD COLLECTION.

functioning as symbols depend on the specific cultural context of that group.

Foods may also become symbolic of ethnicity because of their ubiquitousness in the cuisine of that ethnic group—rice in Asian cultures, beans and tortillas in Mexican cuisine, curry spices in Indian cuisine. Through their consistent use, these foods become associated with that identity; however, they may or may not be felt by members of that ethnic group to symbolize their heritage. Symbols of ethnicity are frequently ascribed by primary cultures or institutions.

Food can be used to refer to another ethnic group, frequently in a derogatory manner—French are called "frogs," Germans "krauts." Again, the food used as symbol represents the difference between two cultures and is often an item considered inedible, or at least, unpalatable to one culture, stigmatizing the other as less civilized or even less human.

Region is another major referential domain of food. As with ethnicity, regional foods are frequently those that stand in contrast to foods found in other regions, therefore marking differences rather than representing the culture. American regional food symbols include grits for the South, lobsters for Maine, cheese for Wisconsin, meat and potatoes for the Midwest. Region and ethnicity can be closely connected. For example, much historical Southern cooking is derived from African American traditions; the upper Midwest is closely associated with Scandinavian foods.

Religion and ethos are emotionally powerful references for food, representing individuals' and cultures' worldviews and value systems. Some food symbols invoke an entire foodways system and its underlying ethos: Kosher foods embody Judaism; meatless meals reference vegetarianism; diet foods may represent a status-quo valuing of physical appearance and traditional gender roles. Specific foods may also symbolize ritual acts or occasions within a belief system: bread and wine represent the body and blood of Christ and the ritual of communion in Christianity.

Gender is another referential domain, with some cultures designating particular foods as symbolizing specific genders and maintaining strict taboos to ensure social and psychological distance between genders. Other cultures demonstrate less formalized perspectives; having stereotypes rather than taboos. In the United States, large portions of any food, thick slabs of meat, beer, and "hearty" foods are associated with masculinity, while foods thought to be light—salads, quiche, poultry, and fish—are associated with femaleness.

Food as symbolic of social relationships includes status and place within a social group as well as relationships between individuals. Food can be used to mark one's socioeconomic standing, since certain items are associated with particular classes: for example, caviar, fine wine, and gourmet cooking with upper classes; beer, white bread, and junk food with lower classes. Some foods, such as hot dogs, apple pie, chili, and barbecue, cut across class divisions and are sometimes used to intentionally signify a democratic and "all-American" event or institution.

Individuals can also use food as social capital, in that by demonstrating competence with a particular food, they demonstrate a mastery of knowledge needed to belong to a particular social group. For example, being able to discern quality of wine can signify membership in an upper class; being able to ingest extremely spicy peppers can signify masculinity. Food can also be used to signify relationships between individuals. The referential meaning, however, is situational and frequently tied to celebrations or rituals. A box of chocolates often represents romance, particularly on Valentine's Day; however, it can also be a gesture of thanks for hospitality.

Overall, food is a rich resource for symbolic communication, expression, and action.

See also **Art, Food in; Gender and Food; Humor, Food in; Icon Foods; Language about Food; Literature, Food in; Metaphor, Food as; Presentation of Food; Proverbs and Riddles; Sacrifice; Sex and Food; Sin and Food; Taboos; Thanksgiving.**

BIBLIOGRAPHY

Bauman, Richard. "Conceptions of Folklore in the Development of Literary Semiotics." *Semiotica* 39 (1982):1–20.

Douglas, Mary. *Implicit Meanings: Essays in Anthropology.* Boston: Routledge and Kegan Paul, 1975.

Jakobson, Roman. *Language in Literature.* Cambridge, Mass.: Harvard University Press, 1987.

Levi-Strauss, Claude. "The Culinary Triangle." *Partisan Review* 33, no. 4 (1966):586–595.

Turner, Victor. *The Forest of Symbols: Aspects of Ndembu Ritual.* London: Cornell University Press, 1967.

Lucy M. Long

SYRUPS. Syrup is essentially sugar dissolved in water, with or without flavors. Candy making relies almost exclusively on the special qualities of hot sugar syrups. Other foods which use them as ingredients are ice creams, baked items, drinks, and preserved fruit.

Maple syrup, made in eastern Canada and in the northeastern part of the United States, is a special product, made by boiling down sap from maple trees. It is made in early spring, and the special flavor of this product is much appreciated on pancakes and waffles and in frostings, desserts, and candies. Other countries also make syrups from fruit juices or tree sap. Grape juice syrup is known as *pekmez* in Turkey and *dibs* in the Arabian Gulf states (*dibs* can also be based on date juice). Pomegranate juice is boiled down to make syrup for drinks and cooking in Syria, Iran, and neighboring areas, and carob pod syrup is used in Cyprus, Lebanon, and Asia Minor. Honey, although regarded as a different commodity entirely because of the production method, is chemically related to syrups and shares similar characteristics.

In some countries, residues from sugar refining are called syrup, notably Golden Syrup, a branded product sold in the United Kingdom. It has a blander flavor than molasses and is a light gold color. In China and Japan, rice is mixed with malt, whose enzymes break down starch from the grain to give sugar. Corn syrup, produced from maize by a similar method, is an industrial product, important in candy, baking, and drinks manufacture.

Sugar Syrup
Sugar syrups are simple to make but have no agreed formula. Cooks and pastry chefs prepare "stock syrup" us-

ing the proportions of sugar to water that are demanded by specific recipes. A basic formula is five cups sugar to four cups water (one kilo to one liter). The two are stirred together until dissolved, brought to the boil, then cooled and refrigerated. Old recipes sometimes call for "light syrup" or "heavy syrup"; only experiment shows what quantities are best. This hit-and-miss system is inadequate for industry, so methods for measuring syrup density (and therefore its sugar content and properties in food) have been devised. The saccharometer, a weighted glass bulb that floats upright in the syrup so that a figure can be read off a scale, has been used since the early nineteenth century. Two types of scale—degrees Baumé (devised by the French chemist Antoine Baumé, 1728–1804) and a modern decimal system—are used. Special thermometers were devised for candy makers in the late nineteenth century. Modern industry relies on more complex devices.

Maple Syrup

This runny brown syrup with a wonderful flavor is produced from the sap of various maple species, especially the hard or rock maple, *Acer saccharum*, and the black maple, *Acer nigrum*. The trees are tapped in early spring when the sap runs in large quantities, especially after a very cold winter and when there are relatively high daytime temperatures and cold nights. A small hole is bored in each trunk and fitted with a spout; the sap is collected in buckets underneath. Several gallons can be collected from a tree without damaging it.

Maple sap contains about 3 percent naturally occurring sugar (sucrose). The accumulated sap is concentrated by boiling until the sucrose content is about 62 percent. It takes between thirty and forty gallons of sap to produce a gallon of syrup. The heating process leads to reactions between the sucrose and amino acids contained in the sap, which produces the color and unique flavor of the syrup. Until the late nineteenth century, the sap was concentrated to a point at which it would form crystals of sugar. This has left a legacy of terms such as "sugar house," "sugar bush," and "sugaring off" that are still in use. However, most production is now aimed at making syrup and maple candy.

Native Americans had their own methods for making maple syrup since they had only flammable birch bark or fragile clay vessels. One method they used for concentrating the sap was heating it with hot stones. Another was allowing it to freeze so that some of the water could be lifted off the top as a block of pure ice, leaving syrup with a higher sugar concentration. European settlers introduced metal kettles, which made boiling easier.

Pure maple syrup has an excellent flavor but is expensive because production is affected by the weather, and it is a labor-intensive cottage industry. Several grades varying in flavor and color are produced, and pale syrup is considered the best quality. The containers bear a controlled symbol of a maple leaf as a guarantee. "Maple-flavored syrup," made by stretching a little true maple syrup with corn syrup, is much cheaper.

Maple syrup is considered very much a North American product, but there were old-world precedents for the idea. Birch sap was collected and used in parts of Europe to make syrup or alternatively, fermented to make "wine." In the Middle East and India, the sap of date palms is still used to make syrup and sugar.

Corn Syrup

Corn syrup is produced by soaking maize kernels. This extracts the starch, which consists of long chains of glucose molecules. Acid or an enzyme is used to break the starch down into shorter lengths, including maltose (the sugar which provides sweetness in malt, two glucose units linked together) and individual glucose molecules. The process can be halted at different stages to give a thick texture (many long chains of glucose molecules) or a sweeter one (more individual molecules); taste and texture can therefore be tailored to the needs of the food industry.

Another enzyme is used to "invert" the glucose to become fructose for high-fructose corn syrup. This has an identical chemical formula but a different molecular structure and tastes intensely sweet. The process is called inversion because glucose rotates a beam of polarized light to the right (hence its alternative name of dextrose), whilst fructose (also known as levulose) rotates it to the left.

Thick corn syrups are much used in candy making because their long-chain molecules help to inhibit the formation of crystals in soft candies without making them overly sweet. Fructose syrups, significantly cheaper than ordinary sugar and more convenient to use, are increasingly important in the soft drinks industry. Other uses for corn syrups include cakes, cookies, pie fillings, jellies, and various composite food products.

The process for making corn syrup is known as hydrolysis. It was discovered by the German-Russian chemist K. S. Kirchhof in 1811 when he heated potato starch in the presence of sulfuric acid and found that it yielded sweet crystals and a syrup. The technique was developed into an industrial process. In 1865 the Union Sugar Company of New York began manufacturing corn syrup.

Uses of Syrup

Syrups of sugar and fruit juice or other essences are used to make drinks and are diluted as required at home or in bulk to make branded drinks at a bottling plant. This use echoes the origin of the word "syrup." It is derived from the Arabic *sharab*, which originally meant a sweet drink ("sherbet" also comes from this root). Simple sugar syrup is an important ingredient in other drinks such as juleps, a word that has an equally exotic derivation from the Persian *golab*, meaning rosewater. Fruit syrups are also used as dessert sauces and, when poured over crushed ice in a paper cone, are essential to that summer favorite, the snow cone.

Concentrated syrups are much used in cooking and preserving fruit. They add a sweet flavor and inhibit the growth of spoilage microorganisms. Weak syrups sweeten fruit salads and compotes. Stronger ones are used in canning although concerns about excessive sugar consumption led to the substitution of fruit juices in the late twentieth century. Fruit is candied or crystallized by steeping it in increasingly concentrated syrups. Starting with a light syrup, osmosis allows the sugar to penetrate the cells of the fruit. The syrup strength is concentrated progressively over several days until enough sugar has been absorbed to prevent the fruit from rotting. This technique was brought to North America by the earliest European settlers. Compotes and candied fruit represent a cooking and preserving spectrum which goes back to medieval Europe.

The chemical and physical properties of syrups make them exceptionally useful in industrial baking. Many syrups are hygroscopic, that is, they attract water. Because of this, corn syrup is added to cakes and cookies, where it softens the texture and extends shelf-life. Honey has long been used in this way, for example, in *Lebkuchen*, the traditional German gingerbread.

Many cultures use syrups in traditional baking. The English use sugar syrup to glaze the hot cross buns made for Good Friday and put golden syrup into treacle tarts, distant relations of shoofly pies, which are made with molasses. Babas, small rich yeast cakes of eastern European origin, are soaked in rum-flavored syrup. In the eastern Mediterranean and the Middle East, many pastries require syrup as a sweetener. A well-known example is baklava, made of layers of thin pastry with a nut filling, over which syrup is poured after baking (sugar syrup sometimes substitutes for the traditional honey). *Jellabies* (also *jalebi*), deep-fried batter spirals widely made in the Middle East, and *gulab jamun*, Indian confections of flour and reduced milk, are sweetened and stored in syrup. Chinese and Japanese cultures use malt syrup in traditional desserts and candies.

Nutritionally, syrups provide concentrated energy but little else. They also tend to be used in energy-dense foods such as candies, desserts, and baked goods, all of which are considered undesirable for good health in large quantities. Diets high in sugars and other carbohydrates are also less likely to be high in essential nutrients. Particular worries are expressed by nutritionists over soft drinks. They are consumed in large amounts by certain sectors of the population in the developed world, and they are thought to be especially bad for the teeth. However, the food and drink industries consider syrups of enormous value in enhancing the flavor and texture in numerous foods and drinks. Corn syrup in particular is simple to use and relatively cheap, so it is likely that syrups will continue to be used in large quantities.

See also **Candy and Confections; Fruit; Sugar and Sweeteners; Sugar Crops and Natural Sweeteners.**

BIBLIOGRAPHY

Densmore, Frances. *Uses of Plants by the Chippewa Indians: How Indians Use Wild Plants for Food, Medicine, and Crafts.* Washington, D.C.: U.S. Government Printing Office, 1928. Reprint, New York: Dover, 1974. Also published in Canada as *Indian Use of Wild Plants for Crafts, Food, Medicine and Charms.* Oshweken, Ontario: Indian Reprints, 1993.

Fussell, Betty. *The Story of Corn.* New York: Knopf, 1992.

McGee, Harold. *On Food and Cooking: The Science and Lore of the Kitchen.* New York: Scribners, 1984.

Nearing, Helen, and Scott Nearing. *The Maple Sugar Book.* New York: Schocken, 1950.

Laura Mason

TABLE DÉCOR. *See* **Presentation of Food; Styling of Food.**

TABLE MANNERS. *See* **Etiquette and Eating Habits; Table Talk.**

TABLE TALK. All human societies take advantage of the fact that meals are physically necessary, normally frequent, and often eaten with others. They turn dinnertimes into opportunities to express and to practice "culture." Because talking is the primary mode of human communication, mealtimes commonly provide occasions for conversation. Every culture has its own ideas about the management of verbal interaction or of silence at meals.

When to Talk

Most of the time human beings who are sharing a meal prefer to eat without saying much. They simply concentrate on what they are doing, appreciating and enjoying their food. When talking takes place, it is often socially regulated, its timing clarified by rules. In some societies talk is completed before dinner. The meal then serves as a contented celebration of togetherness and agreement, after the discussions that have preceded it (Ortner, 1978; Fitzgerald, 1941). In others the eating comes first, and only when hunger is satisfied should talk break out (Chao, 1956). Formal meals might require silence, conversation being reserved for intimacy among family and friends (Toffin, 1977, ch. 4). In modern Europe and North America the opposite is the case. On formal occasions or when invited out, people should talk; it is rude not to. For this very reason eating together in "companionable" silence can be a sign of great intimacy. On the other hand, everybody eating without talking might be the expression of an oppressive tension.

The Japanese begin a banquet in silence but warm up as time goes on. Barriers fall, and discourse increases accordingly (Befu, 1974). Sometimes it is thought proper that only elders and important people should speak (Okere, 1983). Although it is commonly accepted that mealtimes are excellent opportunities for small children to learn to talk, in many places and times older children

have been forbidden to speak during meals taken with adults. In the modern West, middle-class children are likely to be encouraged to talk during meals. Such family meals have even been described as "class[es] in oral expression" (Bossard and Boll, 1966, p. 141).

Until the early twentieth century in the United States and until the late twentieth century in Britain, it was thought proper at formal upper-class meals to send the women away from the dining room table into the drawing room, originally called a "withdrawing" room, owing to this practice. They took tea and engaged in conversation, leaving the men behind to move together around the table to drink port and discuss politics and other "male" subjects. (The men had been separated during the meal owing to "promiscuous" seating, men and women alternating around the table.) The host decided when the segregation should cease and then shepherded the men to "join the ladies" again (Post, 1922, pp. 223–224).

Often entertainment is laid on, and then of course talking is minimal. Watching television during meals is a modern instance of an ancient tradition that includes entertainers dancing and juggling during pauses between courses (as in the medieval and Renaissance entremets), someone reading aloud as monks eat silently in the refectory, musicians performing, and even the host dancing, singing, or playing a musical instrument for his or her guests.

Drama and Dialogue

At aristocratic ancient Greek dinner parties, talk was mostly limited, during the actual eating, to reaching a decision about what subjects to discuss afterward. Later the wine drinking began, the *symposion* or "drinking together," and then people were expected to be able to sing in turn and to have something intelligent to say about the topics proposed. From this custom a literary genre developed in which an imaginary dialogue after dinner is reported by the author. Plato's *Symposium* (on the subject "What is love?"), Xenophon's *Symposium*, Plutarch's *Symposiacs* and *Banquet of the Seven Sages*, Macrobius's *Saturnalia*, and Athenaeus's fifteen-volume *The Sophists at Dinner* are surviving examples of the type. They are ancestors of collections of table talk or *propos de table* that have continued as a minor tradition of European and American belles lettres down the centuries.

Meals have often been the locus of drama, the eating companions filling the roles of both actors and audience. Every organized feast has a theatrical aspect, and what is said on the occasion is at least as memorable as what is eaten or what is done. Where it is that people sit (and therefore who will most easily talk to whom) is often decided by the host, the "producer" of the performance. In many cultures it is incumbent upon the host before, during, or after the meal to give a speech. Dramatic rituals requiring speech have often been inserted into mealtime festivity. One highly developed and still surviving custom in this class is that of drinking toasts with the eloquence traditionally required (Dickson, 1981). In medieval Europe a rich feast was incomplete without a nonpartaking audience looking on.

All religions include ritual eating events, usually with important speaking roles for those present. Examples are the Jewish seder (Quesnel et al., 1999, pt. 1) or the Javanese *slametan* (Geertz, 1960). During the last supper that Jesus ate with his friends, he instituted the Eucharist and asked that his disciples repeat his words and actions. In the course of the meal his betrayer was revealed. The discourses of Jesus during this meal are of central importance to Christian belief (John 13–17; Luke 22). Prayer, either before meals, or after meals, or both, is common the world over.

Rules of Behavior

Modern Western societies make talking an important component of a formal meal and of many other eating events as well. (These very societies have rigid requirements about eating silently, with mouths shut. The necessity of nevertheless talking constitutes the kind of complication that is typical of manners in general.) Where people talk, everybody should do so. Not talking is not joining in, where conviviality is the aim. The silence of one individual in these cultures and in others can be interpreted as hostility, incompetence, or even greed, a plot to take advantage of the others' conversation in order to eat more than anybody else.

It is forbidden at a dining room table to reach past people, and especially across their plates, for what one might need. It is therefore necessary to ask and then to thank the neighbor who obliges. Before helping himself or herself to more food, the polite diner first asks others whether they want some more. Such simple exchanges, made mandatory by table manners, create a ready-made, basic fabric of verbal interaction with others.

Since all have the duty, all should also have the opportunity to talk. Politeness therefore commonly demands, to varying degrees in different cultures, no drowning out of others' words by shouting and no interrupting. All the manners governing conversation may apply even more strictly than is usual. Where the guests are seated around a table, on view to all those present, it

GOOD MANNERS

Let Noise of lewd Disputes be quite forborn,
No Maudlin Lovers here in Corners Mourn,
But all be Brisk, and Talk, but not too much.
On Sacred things, Let none presume to touch,
Nor Profane Scripture, or sawcily wrong
Affairs of State with an Irreverent Tongue.
Let Mirth be Innocent, and each man see
That all his Jests without Reflection be.
(*The Rules and Orders of the Coffee House,* 1674)

The turning of the table is accomplished by the hostess, who merely turns from the gentleman (on her left probably) with whom she has been talking through the soup and the fish course, to the one on her right. As she turns, the lady to whom the "right" gentleman has been talking, turns to the gentleman further on, and in a moment everyone at table is talking to a new neighbor. [To refuse to change partners is to cause the whole table to be blocked,] leaving one lady and one gentleman on either side of the block, staring alone at their plates. At this point the hostess has to come to the rescue by attracting the blocking lady's attention and saying, "Sally, you cannot talk to Professor Bugge any longer! Mr. Smith has been trying his best to attract your attention." (Emily Post, 1922, p. 221)

I knew a man who had a story about a Gun, which he thought a good one and that he told it very well; he tried all means in the world to turn the conversation upon Guns—but if he failed in his attempt, he started in his chair, and said he heard a Gun fired, but when the company assured him that they heard no such thing, he answered, perhaps then I am mistaken, but however, since we are talking of Guns,—and then told his story, to the great indignation of the company. (Lord Chesterfield, Letter to his Godson, no. 141)

is bad manners to talk, whisper, and laugh with one companion to the exclusion and possible covert ridicule of others. A guest should not be singled out and so closely questioned that he or she has no time to eat the food.

It is rude, the etiquette books repeatedly remind their readers, to upset people with descriptions of what might disgust them or shock them (the last thing people want while eating is to be perturbed or "put off their food"). Dinnertime conversationalists are often advised against controversial or overly important subjects like politics or religion. Talking shop is frowned upon and also long-winded technical explanations nobody wants to hear. There should be no holding forth so that only one person is heard from. The host in particular is enjoined not to praise the culinary excellence of the meal or otherwise to put himself or herself forward. He or she should concentrate instead on encouraging the guests to shine (Morel, 1977; Staffe, 1899).

At a Japanese *cha no yu* or tea ceremony, the host goes to great trouble to make the dining space beautiful with flower arrangements and utensils chosen to express appreciation for the season of the year. The host might deliberately and delicately absent himself at a certain point to give guests the opportunity to comment, without embarrassing the host with too much praise, on the tea bowls, their beauty and their perfect taste, and the room and its furnishings. Contemplation, heightened sensitivity, and admiration are the aim of the ceremony. Spoken expression of people's responses is an essential aspect of the experience (Kondo, 1985).

Wit, Creativity, Social Bonding

Among people prosperous enough to eat in company for pleasure and entertainment, meals have often been occasions for the display of wit. Brilliant conversation was what writers of "table talk" attempted to recapture. Table talk is different with every gathering; it is on each occasion the group's own improvised creation. The conversation may range from the boring or unpleasant to a memorable art form, as may the preparation of the meal itself. At times dinnertime discourse can become artificial and competitive and even part of power struggles, since being invited to the right dinner parties and so consorting with important people has often been essential to an ambitious career. Dinner guests invited in order to dazzle others with their famous wit have frequently prepared themselves with stories ready to insert into the conversation, have sharpened their sallies in advance, and have polished their bons mots and their paradoxes.

Dinnertime conversation of course takes time. This has often meant that it was, as a social skill, highly developed only among people with money, leisure, and servants as well as verbal polish. In modern society, where time is money or "at a premium," table conversation may be forced into a minor role in people's lives. Yet it is often still customary for people to make time for talking at meals. Conversation after dinner is an institution in Hispanic cultures, with its own name, *hacer la sobremesa*, "doing the over-the-table" or "doing the tablecloth." The dishes are removed for this part of the event. Such conversations knit families and groups of friends together, ensuring contact, constant negotiation, and understanding. They are important occasions for identity building and for self-expression.

"It's not what's on the table that matters but what's on the chairs." The adage expresses what has been an almost universal insistence among human beings, that we people should strive not to let the material necessities dominate our their lives, that the food should not be the only attraction when we people sit down to eat together.

See also **Etiquette and Eating Habits; Greece, Ancient.**

PLUTARCH'S *SYMPOSIACS*

Examples of subjects for discussion at a symposium:

- "Whether the host should arrange the placing of his guests or leave it to the guests themselves."
- "Why men become hungrier in autumn."
- "Why we take pleasure in hearing actors represent anger and pain but not in seeing people actually experience those emotions."

BIBLIOGRAPHY

Anonymous. *The Rules and Orders of the Coffee-House*. 1684. Published in Colin Clair, *Kitchen and Table*. London: Abelard-Schuman, 1964.

Befu, Harumi. "An Ethnography of Dinner Entertainment in Japan." *Arctic Anthropology* 11, (Supplement, (1974): 196–203.

Bossard, James H. S., and Eleanor Stoker Boll. "Family Table Talk." In *The Sociology of Child Development*. New York: Harper and Row, 1966.

Chao, Buwei Yang. *How to Cook and Eat in Chinese*. London: Faber and Faber, 1956.

Chesterfield, Lord. *The Letters of Philip Dormer Stanhope, Fourth Earl of Chesterfield* (1777). Edited by Bonamy Dobrée. Six vols. London: Eyre and Spottiswoode: 1932. Vol. 6, *Letters to His Godson*. Number 141.

Dickson, Paul. *Toasts: The Complete Book of the Best Toasts, Sentiments, Blessings, Curses, and Graces*. New York: Delacorte, 1981.

Fitzgerald, C. P. *The Tower of Five Glories*. Chapter 9. London: Crescent Books, 1941.

Furnivall, Frederick James. *The Babees' Book*, edited by Edith Rickert. London: Chatto and Windus, 1908.

Geertz, Clifford. *The Religion of Java*. Glencoe, Ill.: Free Press, 1960.

Kondo, D. "The Way of Tea: A Symbolic Analysis." *Man* 20 (1985): 287–306.

Morel, J. "La Politesse à table au XVIIe siècle" [Politeness at Table in the Seventeenth Century]. *Marseille* 109 (1977): 93–98; 96.

Okere, L. C. *Anthropology of Food in Rural Igboland, Nigeria*. Lanham, Md.: University Press of America, 1983.

Ortner, Sherry B. *Sherpas through Their Rituals*. Chapter 4. New York: Cambridge University Press, 1978.

Plutarch, *Symposiacs* [Table-Talk]. *Plutarch's Moralia*, vols. VIII and IX. The Loeb Classical Library. Cambridge: Harvard University Press, 1961.

Post, Emily. *Etiquette: In Society, in Business, in Politics, and at Home*. New York: Funk and Wagnalls, 1922.

Quesnel, Michel, Yves-Marie Blanchard, and Claude Tassin. *Nourriture et repas dans les milieux juifs et chrétiens de l'antiquité: Mélanges offerts au Professeur Charles Perrot* [Food and Meals in Jewish and Christian Circles in Antiquity: Collected Essays in Honor of Professor Charles Perrot]. Paris: Cerf, 1999.

Staffe, Baronne. *Usages du monde* [Manners in Polite Society]. Paris: G. Havard Fils, 1899.

Toffin, G. *Pyangaon, communauté newar de la vallée de Kathmandou: La vie matérielle* [Pyangaon, a Newar Community in the Katmandu Valley: The Materials of Everyday Life]. Chapter 4. Paris: CNRS, 1977.

Visser, Margaret. *The Rituals of Dinner: The Origins, Evolution, Eccentricities, and Meaning of Table Manners*. New York: Grove Wiedenfield, 1991.

Margaret Visser

TABOOS. A food taboo is a prohibition against consuming certain foods. The word "taboo" (also spelled "tabu") is Polynesian and means 'sacred' or 'forbidden'; it has a quasi-magical or religious overtone. The term was introduced in the anthropological literature in the second half of the nineteenth century. In the field of food and nutrition, food taboos are not necessarily connected with magical-religious practices, and some nutritionists prefer to speak of "food avoidance." In this article these terms are used interchangeably.

Food is a culturally specific concept. In general, anything can function as food if it is not immediately toxic. But what is edible in one culture may not be in another. The concept of food is determined by three factors: biology, geography, and culture. Certain plants and animals are not consumed because they are indigestible. Geography also plays a role. For example, dairy products are not part of the food culture of the humid tropical regions since the geographical conditions for keeping cattle are unfavorable. Milk is often a taboo food in such cultures. Insects are not considered food in Europe and most of the United States despite attempts to introduce them in the late twentieth century. This is because there are few edible insects in regions with temperate climates. In Mexico, by contrast, insects are packaged in plastic sachets, cans, or jars for sale. Cultural reasons for food taboos often have a geographical basis—unknown or exotic foods will be rejected as unfit for consumption.

It is of interest to note that food avoidance most frequently relates to animal meat, since in most cultures human beings have an emotional relationship with animals they have to kill to eat. One of the few taboos of a food of vegetable origin is the prohibition against alcohol for Muslims and some Christian denominations.

Food may establish a cultural identity of an ethnic group, religion, or nation. Food taboos in a society function also as a means to show differences between various groups and strengthen their cultural identity. Refraining from eating pork is not only a question of religious identity but is likewise an indication of whether or not one belongs to the Jewish or Muslim cultural community. In order to better understand the range of food taboos, it is useful to distinguish between permanent and temporary food taboos or food avoidances.

Permanent Food Taboos

Foods that are permanent taboos or avoidances are always prohibited for a specific group. The classic example of a permanent food taboo is the prohibition against pork by Jews and Muslims. The Jewish prohibition against pork is found in Leviticus 11:1. Some anthropologists point out that food taboos are based on the failure of these foods to fit into the usual systems of classification. Foods that do not fit into these classifications are unsuitable for consumption, or unclean. According to the Qur'an (2, 168), Muslims should not only avoid pork, but also blood, non-ritually slaughtered animals, and cadavers and alcohol. In the case of both Jewish and Muslim food taboos, the foods themselves are considered unclean. A different concept of food avoidance is found in Hinduism. Hindus abstain from eating beef because cows are considered sacred. Various arguments have been used to explain the origins of such food taboos or food avoidance including religion, culture, and hygiene.

Marvin Harris has rightly pointed out that when people reject certain foods, there must be a logical and economical reason for doing so. The pig is an animal of sedentary farmers and unfit for a pastoral way of life because pigs cannot be herded over long distances without suffering a high rate of mortality. Herdsmen generally despise the lifestyle of sedentary farming communities.

In Western society cats and dogs are not consumed because of the emotional relationships developed with these pets. Increasingly pets are being "humanized" in such a way that eating them is seen as an act of anthropophagy or cannibalism. The feeling of closeness to certain animals can also be found in the savannah regions of West Africa. Certain West African clans consider dogs clan animals, based on the fact that they have been beneficial to the clan in the past; as clan animals they are unfit for consumption. Hippocrates (460–377 B.C.E.) regarded dog meat favorably as a light meal, but in later antiquity, dogs were considered unclean and unfit to eat. This is still the case in the Mediterranean area and the Middle East. By contrast, dog meat is popular in China and the mountainous regions of the Philippines. From a nutritional point of view, dog meat is an excellent source of animal protein, and dogs do not require the grazing area demanded by cattle or other large ruminants.

Temporary Food Taboos or Avoidances

Some foods are avoided for certain periods of time. These restrictions often apply to women and relate to the reproduction cycle.

The times of temporary food avoidances related to particular periods of the life cycle include:

- Pregnancy
- Birth
- Lactation
- Infancy
- Initiation
- Periods of illness or sickness

From a nutritional point of view, temporary food avoidances are of great importance as they concern vulnerable groups: pregnant women, breast-feeding women, and infants and children during the period of weaning and growth. Food regulations and avoidances during these periods often deprive the individual of nutritionally valuable foods such as meat, fish, eggs, or vegetables. In a number of African countries pregnant women avoid green vegetables. They also do not consume fish. When asked why, women say the unborn child might develop a head shaped like that of a fish. Some of these avoidances may seem odd from a scientific point of view, but there is often an unnoticed logic behind it. In the first place, women are aware of the critical period and know that much has to be done to ensure the successful delivery of a healthy child. Observing the rules of avoidance will give her the strength of knowing that everything possible has been done for the benefit of the child.

In Central Africa nutritionists observed that young children did not eat eggs. They were worried that a nutritious food was not available for this vulnerable group. The village elders gave a convincing explanation of why eggs should be avoided by children. In the past the wise ancestors were much concerned about young children roaming around the villages searching for eggs and even chasing the brood hens away from their eggs. In order to avoid a depletion of the poultry stock, the elderly decided that eggs were harmful to young children and should be avoided.

A different form of temporary food avoidances involves the rules of fasting. In medieval Christianity the most important period of fasting was Lent (the period from Ash Wednesday to Holy Saturday), during which meat and animal products were forbidden. There were also other days (Ember Days, Fridays, etc.) on which people were required to abstain from eating meat. The Reformation broke the tradition of fasting to a large extent. The Ethiopian Orthodox Church has a wide and complicated system of dietary rules and fasting, as does the Eastern Orthodox Church. In the Muslim world, Ramadan, the ninth month of the Muslim year, means strict fasting, even from beverages, from sunrise to sunset (Sakr).

Do Food Taboos Change and Disappear?

Food taboos may seem rather stable, but they are often under pressure because the society is changing. Migration is a powerful factor in the process of changing food culture. In Europe and North America, most Muslim migrants from the Middle East and South Asia try to maintain their food habits, but some cannot fully resist the food culture of their new home country. A substantial number of Muslims begin drinking beer, wine, and even stronger spirits. Women tend to be less inclined to give up the avoidance of alcohol. The fear of pollution from pork often remains strong, however. In some European countries Muslims refrain from eating in factory canteens out of fear that meals may be polluted with pork fat or pork meat. In contrast, many Jewish Europeans and Americans eat pork from time to time, or even on a regular basis.

Nutrition and health education have reduced the temporary food avoidances of the vulnerable groups in a great number of countries. In the humid tropical countries of Africa and Asia, where the raising of dairy animals is unfavorable, the rejection of milk as a food is diminishing. Despite the occurrence of lactose intolerance among the population, the use of milk and milk products has extended since colonial times. Primary lactose intolerance occurs from an apparent decrease in the intestinal enzyme lactase and can occur between the ages of two and five years. This condition is present in about 75 percent of the world population. However, small but significant quantities of milk consumed throughout the day can be tolerated among ethnic groups known to be lactose intolerant. At the beginning of the twenty-first century, milk products and a little fresh milk are available for the upper and middle classes. This availability seems to have increased due to dairy exports from Western countries and dairy food aid during the 1950s through the 1970s. In a country without a dairy tradition such as Indonesia, the importation of canned sweetened condensed milk can be traced back to around 1883. In the high lands of Java, the Dutch introduced dairy farming on a small scale in the nineteenth century. From the colonists, a modest use of milk spread gradually among the emerging Indonesian upper and middle classes.

In the United States and other countries with Anglo-Saxon traditions, horsemeat is not part of the food culture. This is in contrast to continental Europe, in particular France, where horsemeat is a well-known and appreciated food. The history of horsemeat gives insight into how attitudes toward food avoidance change over the course of time. In Europe it started with a decree by Pope Gregory III (d. 714) that the Christian communities of Germany and the Low Countries refrain from eating horsemeat because the horse played an important role in pagan rituals. The purpose of the decree was that the Christian community should distinguish itself from the pagans by avoiding a typical pagan symbol, horsemeat. Gradually the consumption of horseflesh disappeared. The meat was considered to be unfit for consumption. In the nineteenth century the attitude toward horsemeat changed dramatically. Food emergencies connected with war and promotion of horsemeat as a food were the driving forces for change. During the Napoleonic Wars, hungry soldiers were forced to eat their horses. To their surprise, the meat was fit to eat and even had a reasonably good taste. French pharmacists promoted the idea that horsemeat was suitable for consumption, and from a scientific point of view no threat at all to health. Discarded workhorses became a source of good and cheap meat for the growing working classes in urban France. The concept of horsemeat as food spread to other European countries, but not to the United Kingdom, where the horse remained a noble animal, and the idea of eating horsemeat was viewed with disgust.

In periods of emergency, dietary rules including food avoidances can be temporarily ended. The West African Fulani pastoralists avoid the consumption of fish. During the dry season the herdsmen have to move with their cattle from the northern savannahs to the land along the Niger River in the south. Because of the seasonal food shortage, herdsmen are more or less forced to turn to eating fish. In rural areas with a dry and a rainy season, people will collect in the period of seasonal food shortage the so-called hungry foods. Hungry foods are mainly wild foods, often not very attractive and tasty and as such normally avoided. They are consumed only in an emergency.

See also **Africa; Anthropology and Food; Christianity; Fasting and Abstinence; Feasts, Festivals, and Fasts; Hippocrates; Hinduism; Islam; Judaism; Lent; Middle Ages, European; Ramadan; Religion and Food; Shrove Tuesday.**

BIBLIOGRAPHY

Brothwell, Don, and Patricia Brothwell. *Food in Antiquity*. London: Thames and Hudson, 1969.

De Garine, Igor. "The Socio-cultural Aspects of Nutrition." *Ecology of Nutrition* 1 (1972): 143–163.

Den Hartog, Adel P. "Acceptance of Milk Products in Southeast Asia. The Case of Indonesia as a Traditional Non-dairying Region." In *Asian Food. The Global and the Local*, edited by Katarzyna Cwiertka and Boudewijn Walraven. Richmond, Va.: Curzon Press, 2002.

Douglas, Mary. *Purity and Danger: An Analysis of Concepts of Pollution and Taboos*. London: Routledge and K. Paul, 1966.

Gade, Daniel W. "Horsemeat as Human Food in France." *Ecology of Food and Nutrition* 5 (1976): 1–11.

Grivetti, Louis E., and R. M. Pangborn. "Origin of Selected Old Testament Dietary Prohibitions." *Journal of the American Dietetic Association* 65 (1974): 634–638.

Harris, Marvin. *Good to Eat. Riddles of Food and Culture*. New York: Simon and Schuster, 1985.

Kilara, A., and K. K. Iya. "Food and Dietary Habits of the Hindu." *Food Technology* 46 (1992): 94–104.

Sakr, A. H. "Fasting in Islam." *Journal of the American Dietetic Association* 67 (1971): 17–21.

Shack, William A. "Anthropology and the Diet of Man." In *Diet of Man, Needs and Wants*, edited by John Yudkin. London: Applied Sciences Publishers, 1978.

Simoons, Frederick J. *Eat Not This Flesh: Food Avoidances from Prehistory to Present*. Madison: University of Wisconsin Press, 1994.

Adel P. den Hartog

TAILLEVENT. Taillevent (c. 1315–1395), whose real name was Guillaume Tirel, was employed in the kitchens of the French court from the 1320s to until his death in 1395. The recipes from the manuscript cookbook with which his name is associated, *Le Viandier*, were copied and widely disseminated both during and long after Taillevent's lifetime and had an enormous influence on French cookery, as evidenced by the different versions to be found in various existing manuscripts. Toward the end of the fifteenth century, as the first cookbook to be printed in France, a greatly enlarged version of *Le Viandier* remained in circulation for over a century and had an enormous influence on French cookery. Because of the success of his cookbook, Taillevent can rightfully be called the first chef to achieve "star" status in France, where his name became synonymous with "master chef."

Taillevent's recipes, destined principally for festive occasions, give us a glimpse of the kind of cuisine practiced in the aristocratic households from the fourteenth to the sixteenth century. Characterized by the use of a wide range of spices—in keeping with the dietetic principles of the time that demanded that the cold, wet "humors" of meats, fish, and vegetables be tempered by the hot, dry "virtues" of spices—they call for such familiar ingredients as veal, capon, or pike, as well as much more exotic foods like crane, swan, or sturgeon, prized for the beauty of their feathers (placed back over them to serve), or for their sheer size. Among the new recipes included in the printed *Viandier* at the end of the fifteenth century, the importance of pâtés and tarts in the French culinary landscape is documented for the first time.

BIBLIOGRAPHY

Hyman, Philip, and Mary Hyman. "Le Viandier de Taillevent." In *Les fastes du Gothique: Le siècle de Charles V*. Paris: Editions de la Réunion des musées nationaux, 1981.

Hyman, Philip. "Les livres de cuisine et le commerce des recettes en France aux XVe et XVIe siècles." In *Du Manuscrit à la Table*. Carole Lambert (ed.). Paris: Slatkine, 1992.

Laurioux, Bruno. *Le règne de Taillevent*. Paris: Publications de la Sorbonne, 1997.

Mary Hyman
Philip Hyman

TAKE-OUT FOOD. Take-out food is food prepared for consumption away from the location where it is purchased. As a term, its first appearance was in James Cain's novel *Mildred Pierce* (1941), in which the main character expressed her desire to sell pies to the take-out trade. Synonyms for "take-out" include "carry-out," "take-away," and "food to go."

Origins of Take-out Food

From Roman antiquity onward, people have been buying foods to consume elsewhere that have already undergone some form of preparation. Roman cook shops, early precursors to restaurants, were an early example of today's modern gourmet to-go shop. A variety of production kitchens were available to the Romans. Not only did the Roman soldiers get food from a centralized kitchen, but large towns such as Rome had areas where food was prepared for eating on the premises or to take out. Cooks in ancient Greece and Rome were often itinerant, bringing their prepared foods to theater audiences, predating ballpark hot-dog vendors by millennia. In ancient Rome, according to historian Maguelonne Toussaint-Samat, prepared foods were available for sale to be consumed in the markets or elsewhere. In fact, Trajan's Forum in Rome could be viewed as an extension of the idea of the Greek agora, where all kinds of goods were freely exchanged.

Cooked-meat vendors date back to ancient Mesopotamia, where a wide variety of foods were available to take out, from roasted meats to fish to almond paste–based desserts.

The custom of buying ready-cooked food was found, as recorded by historian Reay Tannahill, in twelfth-century London, where

> you may find viands, dishes roast, fried and boiled, fish great and small, the coarser flesh for the poor, the more delicate for the rich, such as venison, and birds both big and little. If friends, weary with travel, should of a sudden come to any of the citizens, and it is not their pleasure to wait fasting till fresh food is bought and cooked….they hasten to the river bank, and there all things desirable are ready to their hand (Tannahill, p. 164).

Even in late-sixteenth-century France, more than two hundred years before the term "restaurant" takes on the meaning now associated with it, prepared foods were available from "the roasters and the pastrycooks, [who] in less than an hour, will arrange a dinner for you, or a supper," to eat on the premises or to take out to consume elsewhere. Only from 1786 onward did Parisian caterers and restaurateurs open their doors to the public for consumption of meals. It was at this time that the custom of the table d'hôte ("host's table") took hold, an expression that meant that paying customers were invited to partake of foods in the caterer's place of business at the very table where the caterer dined, instead of having to take the meal out to eat elsewhere.

Across the English Channel, a hundred years later, fast-food eating shops had become London institutions, frequented by members of all classes. In 1671 in Munich, Germany, the luxury food store Dallmayr opened, purveying box lunches to the noblemen of the day. The tradition continued with the founding of Fortnum and Mason in London in 1707. By 1788 Fortnum's was selling foods to go, including boned portions of poultry and game in aspic jelly, decorated with lobsters and prawns, all prepared so as to require no cutting, for a distinguished clientele that resided nearby. By 1851 ready-to-eat dishes had become all the rage: to sustain life during such ceremonies as the Coronation festivities, the new queen's review of 6,000 troops in Hyde Park, and the Great Exhibition of 1851. Harrods in 1849 began purveying high-quality foodstuffs to royalty and upper-class Londoners alike.

Hédiard (founded in 1854) and Fauchon (1886) brought a taste of what were then considered exotic foods to the Parisian elite. The German-born Leonardo Peck opened an epicurean delicatessen in Milan, Italy, in 1883, specializing in artisanally prepared smoked and cured meats and cheeses. The large department store Kaufhaus Des Westens (KaDeWe) in Berlin, Germany, established in 1907, devoted considerable space to foods to go. These and other stores featured imported fruits, spices, teas, and coffee; foods prepared on the premises for take-out set new standards in elegance and luxury that retailers in the United Sates wished to emulate.

Packaging

Packaging is an essential component of foods to go. In the United States, paper bags for holding purchases were introduced around the 1860s, a significant development that catalyzed the growth of carry-out foods. Prior to this, clerks had often placed small purchases for customers who were without baskets, bags, or other containers into cones made of rolled paper, twisting them at the bottom to create a kind of primitive bag. By the 1860s the process of making paper containers was becoming mechanized. By 1875, a full-scale manufacture of paper bags was under way. Coupled with stepped-up mechanized production of food, improved refrigeration technology, and transportation of food by rail, a multiplicity of food choices was becoming available nationwide.

The late nineteenth century saw the establishment of grocery store chains. A&P was established in 1869, Kroger in 1882, and Gristede Brothers in 1891. Department store food halls, such as New York City's Macy's food department of 1908, would eventually serve as a model for Dean & DeLuca (founded in 1977 in lower Manhattan), a specialty-foods store with boutiquelike departments, each of which specialized in a different category of food (cheese, meats, prepared foods, pastries) displayed artfully.

Convenience and Education

In one of a number of attempts to educate the working class about healthful eating habits, Ellen Richards, a founder of domestic science who was a chemist and the first woman appointed to the faculty at the Massachusetts

Take-out food has been a feature of urban cookery for centuries, but industrialization and mechanization have altered many sectors of this market, especially in the area of fast foods. This is a scene from McDonald's in Moscow. © AP/WIDE WORLD PHOTOS.

Institute of Technology (1884), helped open the New England Kitchen in 1894 as a place where neighborhood people could purchase foods to take home. Through it, she intended to promote the values of home and family life over the trend toward eating out. Ahead of its time, Richards's effort could be seen as the precursor to the delivery of prepared meals by the then new automobile. In the early 1900s, food delivery services in New Jersey (an offshoot of a communal dining experiment) and Illinois lasted only a few years but served as early models for the pizza delivery services that dominated the take-out food market from the 1970s onward. In the period after World War I, small independently owned grocery stores sprung up in cities and in their surrounding bedroom communities throughout the country, offering prepared foods to the carriage trade. One such operation, William Poll in New York City, started out as a grocery and catering establishment in 1921. Offering some of the earliest prepared take-out of the modern era (1951), a marvel of freezer and packaging technology in the form of shish kebab, cooked and ready for reheating, Poll continued into the twenty-first century. In 1934 the Zabar family started what was to become one of the largest delicatessen-prepared food establishments in New York City; its take-out operations have continued to the present.

In the modern era of food retailing, from the 1960s onward, in the United States the rise of two-career couples created a demand for fast food and prepared foods, available for take-out or delivery. Those early revolutionaries of the Boston experiment such as Ellen Richards, who said that home cooking as traditionally defined would soon be a thing of the past, were more prescient than they may have realized, given how much modern industrialized society has come to depend on sources for ready-to-eat food outside of the home. Among the upwardly mobile and working-class alike, a once weekly pilgrimage to the local Chinese restaurant, a phenomenon

begun in the 1950s, defined take-out for many Americans. The growing ethnic diversity of populations nationwide in the succeeding fifty years enabled Americans to experience the cuisines of other countries, including Mexico, Thailand, Vietnam, and the Middle East. Restaurants with limited seating often capitalized on the demand for convenience and offered their complete menus "to go." Take-out food was no longer limited to pizza, burgers, or fried chicken. From the late 1980s, the percentage of take-out foods purchased increased year by year. Take-out and delivery of foods accounted for 57 percent of all restaurant traffic, with more than nine out of ten table-service restaurants offering take-out options. In the last three decades of the twentieth century, Americans strayed far from the nightly ritual of eating a home-cooked meal with all members of the family congregating around the dinner table. In 2001, according to the National Restaurant Association, 47 percent of Americans aged eighteen to twenty-four said purchasing take-out food is essential to the way they live, with 29 percent of all age groups in agreement. With convenience and variety in increasing demand, the trend is not likely to cease.

See also **Fast Food; Fauchon; Food Politics: U.S.; French Fries; Hamburger; Hédiard; Marketing of Food; Places of Consumption; Preparation of Food; Restaurants; Retailing of Food; Sandwich.**

BIBLIOGRAPHY

Du Vall, Nell. *Domestic Technology: A Chronology of Developments.* Boston: G. K. Hall, 1988.

Levenstein, Harvey. *Revolution at the Table: The Transformation of the American Diet.* New York: Oxford University Press, 1988.

Paston-Williams, Sara. *The Art of Dining: A History of Cooking and Eating.* London: National Trust, 1993.

Revel, Jean-Francois. *Culture and Cuisine.* New York: Doubleday, 1982.

Tannahill, Reay. *Food in History.* New York: Crown, 1989.

Toussaint-Samat, Maguelonne. *History of Food.* Cambridge, Mass.: Blackwell, 1993.

Wheaton, Barbara Ketcham. *Savoring the Past: The French Kitchen and Table from 1300 to 1789.* Philadelphia: University of Pennsylvania Press, 1983.

Robert Wemischner

TEA.

This entry includes two subentries:
Tea as an Icon Food
Tea (Meal)

TEA AS AN ICON FOOD

The origins of tea drinking are shrouded in historical obscurity and legend. While some scholars maintain that tea drinking began in ancient India, most place its beginnings in China as early as 2700 to 3000 B.C.E. A commonly cited account is more recent, however (Qin dynasty, c. 221–206 B.C.E.). According to the story, tea was created one day when the Emperor Shen Nung was boiling water next to a fragrant bush when a gentle breeze blew a leaf from the bush into the pot, creating a pleasing aroma—and tea. Although this story is probably apocryphal, it is likely that plain boiled water or rice water were most commonly drunk in ancient China, and that tea was used occasionally and boiled in combination with other ingredients such as ginger, shallots, orange peel, and mint. The first documented reference to tea occurs in a Chinese dictionary, in 350 B.C.E.

More important than any exact date, however, is the idea of tea as a linchpin and iconic food type in Chinese and other Asian and world cultures. Tea has had social, medicinal, economic, political, and class implications for centuries, being used as a chew, a beverage, a vehicle for familial and business bonding, a curative, a preventative, a stimulant, and a soporific. The preferred drink of many nation's ruling classes, and a measure of economic prosperity among all classes, it is also associated with the British opium trade and the Opium Wars in China, the economic development of the Indian subcontinent and the North American continent, and the beginnings of the American Revolution.

Tea and Chinese Culture

Published accounts of tea cultivation and enjoyment surfaced in the sixth century B.C.E. when Lao-tzu (c. 604–520 B.C.E.), author of the Tao Te Ching and founder of Taoism, is reputed to have proclaimed tea an "elixir of immortality." That description is supported by tales of a monk who extended his lifespan considerably by drinking forty cups of tea a day. While Chinese drink the beverage with meals and at numerous other points throughout the day, consistent with a culture deeply committed to an ideal life of balanced opposites, they also recommend against drinking too much because overindulgence might have negative effects.

Factual accounts of tea as a bona fide drink surface most convincingly in China during the Han dynasty (c. 206 B.C.E. to 220 C.E.), when it became a widely popular drink, and lacquered cups, manufactured specifically for the use of tea ("tea cups"), appeared. Tea has continued to be popular in China throughout its history, but most notably during a high point of Chinese civilization, the Tang dynasty (c. 618–907 C.E.). During this period, the rituals of tea preparation and drinking were codified and spread throughout northern China and Asia, along with other aspects of China's culture. Tea was also taxed during this period, eventually becoming a valuable asset in Chinese households, where it was used as currency and referred to as "green gold." Tea bricks (compressed tea leaves) were used to buy horses (and, for example, in the case of the British, were exchanged only for precious metals such as silver and later for opium).

Preparing tea from a samovar, Baghdad, Iraq, circa 1920. The tea is drunk hot from small glasses. ROUGHWOOD COLLECTION.

During the same period, the poet and philosopher Lu Yü (d. 804 C.E.) wrote the Ch'a Ching (c. 780 C.E.; later translated as *The Classic of Tea*). Respected among tea enthusiasts, connoisseurs, and amateurs alike it became a definitive book on the subject. Concisely and beautifully written, it describes various forms and types of tea, explaining the selection and use of proper utensils, and discussing the water used for brewing. Water collected from natural springs located near Buddhist monasteries was believed to possess spiritual qualities, for example. Lu Yü also recommended water from the mouth of Szechuan's Yangtze River (where some of the best teas in China are cultivated) and mountain water. The precise instructions of Lu Yü raised tea drinking to an art form, earning him the status of tea "divinity." It is likely that his *C'ha Ching* became the basis for the highly ritualized and formal Japanese *chado* ("tea ceremony"). Teahouses were also established during the Tang dynasty, where people could enjoy pungent bitter tea with savory and sweet bite-size morsels or dumplings, early snack foods. (The popular Chinese expression *yam cha* literally means "drink tea," but figuratively it refers to eating *dim sum* ["touch of the heart"], steamed or fried dumplings stuffed with a variety of fillings, for example, bean paste.)

Two women perform a tea ceremony in a traditional home in Kyoto, Japan. © CATHERINE KARNOW/CORBIS.

The appearance of teahouses further ritualized tea drinking as an essential component of Chinese life, connecting it to business negotiations, social encounters, relaxation, and other facets of Chinese culture. In this sense, it parallels the use of alcohol and other stimulants as social lubricants in other cultures. Tea is also a preferred drink at wedding banquets, and is traditionally presented to the bride and groom as a symbol of unification. Additionally, tea, along with fruit, is used as an offering at ancestral altars. It is also customary, if not mandatory, in Chinese culture to offer a cup of tea to a guest at any time of the day.

Tea in Japan

While the date of tea's introduction to Japan is difficult to pinpoint, Okakura Kakuzo, the great twentieth-century Japanese philosopher and tea master, wrote that the Japanese Emperor Shomu (c. eighth century C.E.) offered tea brewed from Chinese leaves sent by Japanese ambassadors to the Tang court to one hundred monks. The Japanese monk Saicho (767–822 C.E.), who had spent time in China, is believed to have offered a cup of tea to the Emperor Saga in 815 C.E. Saga was said to be so fond of the drink that he ordered the planting of a bush in order to establish tea as the beverage of choice

in Japan. The tea proved to be too strong for many Japanese, however, and its popularity has proven less consistent than with the Chinese. Nonetheless, Japanese tea cultivation began during this period and was well established by the thirteenth century C.E.

Revivals of interest occurred during the thirteenth century, and reached a plateau during the sixteenth century (a period of cultural consolidation and political reunification), when tea cultivation spread, making the drink widely available. With this cultural shift came the traditional teahouse, a small bamboo hut created by tea master Sen Rikyu, who developed the *chado* (*cha-no-yu*, "hot water for tea"), or tea ceremony. The Japanese came to consider tea a way of life, and, like the Chinese, saw it as a symbol of hospitality, relaxation, and consolation. The *chado* both reflected and extended the preparation and drinking of tea as a ritual, codifying the preparation, serving, and drinking of tea according to strict rules. This codification is sometimes tellingly referred to as "the law of tea," and is closely associated with the principles of Japanese Zen Buddhism.

The Japanese ceremony involves the whipping and frothing of powdered green tea (*matcha*) with a slit bamboo brush while introducing hot water. It derives from a

JAPANESE TEA CEREMONY

The rituals known collectively as the Japanese tea ceremony are based on practices brought to Japan from China by Zen priests in the 1200s. Their style of tea preparation became popular among military and merchant elites, and these practices were later codified by Sen no Rikyuu (1521–1591). The art is organized by "schools," such as Ura-senke and Omote-senke.

Finely powdered green tea is put in a bowl, hot water is added, and the tea is whipped into a suspension with a bamboo whisk. The tea is prepared by a host for guests, who are expected to know the elaborate etiquette. For the first several years, students tend to focus on performance aspects, learning when to bow or how to carry utensils into the room. For elite practitioners, however, the key to the art lies in their connoisseurship of the many art pieces used in the ritual, such as the tea bowl, the hanging calligraphy, or the lacquered tea container. Hosts manipulate the symbolism of utensils to create complex themes for each gathering, and guests are expected to read these allusions.

The most complex ritual, called *chaji*, lasts four or more hours and involves the serving of an elaborate meal. The food should be simple and seasonal yet arranged with casual artistry on understated, elegant dishes. After the meal, sake is served. Moist sweets (*omogashi*) are served before the preparation of thick tea (*koicha*) and dried sweets (*o-higashi*) before the preparation of the thin tea (*usucha*).

BIBLIOGRAPHY

Anderson, Jennifer L. *An Introduction to Japanese Tea Ritual*. Albany: State University of New York Press, 1991.

Castile, Rand. *The Way of Tea*. New York: Weatherhill, 1971.

Holland, James-Henry. "A Public Tea Gathering: Theater and Ritual in the Japanese Tea Ceremony." *Journal of Ritual Studies* 14, no. 1 (2000): 32–44.

Tanaka, Sen'ō, and Sendō Tanaka. *The Tea Ceremony*. Rev. ed. Tokyo: Kodansha International, 1998.

James-Henry Holland

Chinese Sung Dynasty (c. 960–1279 C.E.) tradition in which steamed and formed tea cakes are pounded into a fine powder. (The Japanese serve *kaiseki-ryori*, a meal masterfully prepared and eaten prior to the tea ceremony.) Due to its rather complex preparation, *matcha* is usually reserved for tea ceremonies or special occasions. Japanese *sencha*, loose tea leaves, was brought from China during the seventeenth century, and remains a more convenient and common form of tea. While the tea's popularity eventually waned, it was revived in the twentieth century, and the Japanese people have come to perceive it as a convenience food, ideally suited to their fast-paced lifestyle, something to accompany a light meal carried in a Japanese lunch box.

Tea and Europeans

While the Portuguese were the first Europeans to trade and drink Chinese tea in their Macao colony during the early sixteenth century, the Dutch established the Dutch East India Company during the same period and were the first to import tea to Europe. It was the British, however, who most took tea to heart, making it an integral part of their culture, trading it under the English East India Company out of Java, popularizing it globally, and mastering its cultivation.

The first public tea sale in Britain took place in the mid-1600s, beginning a commerce that would increase in volume to several million pounds annually by the late 1700s. The suspicious, protective (and perhaps wise) Chinese successfully denied information about the cultivation of tea to the British for so long that they did not fully understand that green, black, and oolong teas came from the same bush until the late nineteenth century. Tea plants were eventually discovered in Assam (between Burma and India) in the early nineteenth century, enabling the British to circumvent the Chinese and establish tea cultivation in India shortly thereafter, and in Ceylon during the later nineteenth century.

Tea services developed by the British were known as high tea or low tea and were common throughout their empire by the late seventeenth century. Low tea was served during the afternoon, usually around four o'clock, with sweets and bite-size sandwiches. High tea was served as an early dinner with a hot entrée and other tidbits. A tradition among the aristocracy, English teas are rather complex and precise rituals, employing a tea strainer (to hold back the brewed leaves) while pouring the infusion into the cup. Tea service was popularized in Hong Kong during its British colonization, and one of the best remaining examples of formal British tea service can still be experienced at the Peninsula Hotel, located in Kowloon, Hong Kong.

Tea in India

Some Indian scholars argue that, like Buddhism, tea originated in India. This is often connected with the idea that wild tea plants were discovered in ancient Assam and then transplanted to China. While this is possible, the first records of the Indian aristocracy drinking tea date back only to the seventeenth century. Tea cultivation flourished in India under the British, however, and today India is the largest exporter of tea in the world.

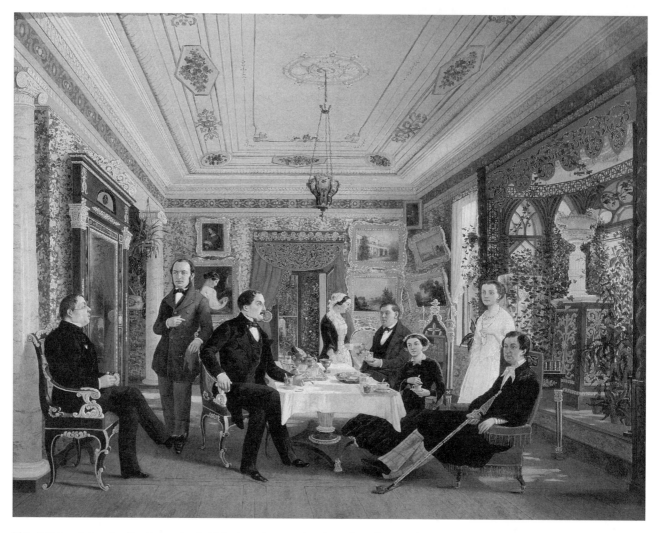

This 1851 painting by Russian artist A. Voloskov shows a family gathered around a tea table for an elaborate afternoon repast. © ARCHIVO ICONOGRAFICO, S. A./CORBIS.

Darjeeling tea, for example, is grown in the foothills of the Himalayas, and is a prized Indian black tea. The use of milk and sugar in tea is also linked to India: while the Chinese and Japanese believe that the only way to drink tea is pure—without milk and sugar—Indians drink theirs with both. This convention may have originated with the British, who enjoy tea "light and sweet" to this day. It is also possible, however, that the Indians, who had enjoyed the milk of their sacred cows as a favorite beverage, developed it on their own and passed it on to the British.

Tea in North America

Tea has frequently been associated with political turmoil historically. One well-known event has been credited with precipitating the American Revolution. The mid-eighteenth century was a time of both illegal Dutch tea smuggling and economic exploitation of the tea trade by the British in their North American colonies. The noto-

rious Tea Act of 1773 epitomized British manipulation of the tea market and pointed the way to possible future British abuse of American colonial tax law. Protests erupted in New York, Charleston, South Carolina, and, most famously, in Boston, Massachusetts, culminating in the Boston Tea Party of December 1773. Boston merchants marched to Griffin's Wharf disguised in Mohawk headdresses, smashing and dumping tea chests from British East India boats into the water as an act of political defiance, instigating broader rebellion and, eventually, the American Revolution (1775–1782), which secured the independence of America from the British Empire.

Americans were able to plant and cultivate their own tea in the South, with particularly large plantations in South Carolina. It is said that tea, as part of that state's overall agricultural wealth, allowed South Carolina to finance the Confederacy substantially during the American Civil War. The Charleston Tea Plantation in South

Carolina was established in 1799, eventually growing teas crops that originated in China, India, and Ceylon. It remains the only tea plantation in America today, producing an excellent orange pekoe black tea under the label American Classic Tea.

Varieties of Tea

Tea can be broadly divided into three common types: green (unfermented), oolong (semi-fermented), and black (fermented). These are usually sold as loose whole leaves, pearled, crushed, powdered, cakes (preferred by Tibetans), and—beginning in modern times—the twentieth century, as individual tea bags. The Chinese prefer the green varieties for their unique and delicate floral notes. Understood to be the healthiest of all teas, fresh green tea is sometimes recommended as a modern cancer preventative and curative, primarily because of its high concentrations of antioxidants. The best of the green teas are considered to be those produced in the province of Szechuan, including a highly regarded, fragrant, and semisweet type variety called "Dragon's Well." The fresh varieties require a bit of fussing in their preparation and, for this reason, are usually reserved for both formal and informal social rituals as a result. Fermented teas were developed as a means of preservation, especially preservation related to early international trade and shipping, when long sea voyages would have caused the leaves to rot. Accordingly, black teas have enjoyed greater historical popularity in the West, where they were the prevalent type most readily available.

The price of tea—essentially its value—is determined by the quality and rarity of the leaf. As such a pound of tea can range from roughly ten dollars to one thousand dollars, with the best most expensive teas usually being those in the green tea category. Today's quality teas come from China (Gunpowder, Pu'erh, Lapsang Souchong, Dragon's Well), Taiwan (Imperial Oolong, Formosa White Tip, Jasmine), Japan (Sencha, Bencha, Matcha, Genmaicha), India (Assam, Darjeeling), and Sri Lanka (Ceylon). The word "blend" is used to describe teas composed of various tea leaves from different locales. Good examples of blended teas include English and Irish Breakfast teas. Scented teas are perfumed with ingredients such as oil of bergamot, magnolia, cassis, and other fruits or herbs. Examples of classic scented teas include Earl Grey and Jasmine tea.

Tea as a Cooking Ingredient

Tea is also used as a cooking ingredient, imparting a bitter, sweet fragrance to dishes. Classic Chinese recipes include tea-boiled eggs, Hunan tea-smoked duck, and shrimp cooked with tea leaves—a specialty of the Imperial Court of Beijing. In Southeast Asia, especially Burma, pickled tea leaves—steamed, pressed into bamboo culms, and then buried until the tea is properly aged—are a popular snack, these having been steamed and pressed into bamboo culms, which are then buried until the tea is properly aged.

Tea in the Contemporary World

Tea has spread throughout the world, becoming an important part of Southwest Asian, Central Asian, African, European, North and South American, and Australian culinary cultures. International tea drinking has been affected by invention and innovation. Ice (or "iced") tea was invented early in the twentieth century, introduced by an Englishman, Richard Blechynden, at the 1904 World's Fair, Louisiana Purchase Exposition, in St. Louis, Missouri, and helped to sustain the beverage's popularity. Since then, ice tea is offered in private homes, public events, diners, fast-food chains, and restaurants the world over.

Tea bags were invented by Thomas Sullivan in 1908, which made it convenient to brew single servings of tea in individual cups quickly and simply. (It also kept the leaves from spreading into the drink, at once solving a problem and stripping the beverage of some of its ritual.) Tea bags rapidly became the most popular form of making tea. Fruit-flavored, sweetened teas have become increasingly popular, too, not only as stimulants but satisfying the American (and increasingly international) taste for sweet drinks. Powdered, "instant" ice teas also exist, a cultural counterpoint to periodic revivals of more complex teas such as Indian milk-based chais.

See also **British Isles: England; China; Coffee; India; Southeast Asia; Stimulants.**

BIBLIOGRAPHY

Butel, Paul. *Histoire du thé*. Paris: Les Editions Desjonquères, 1997.

Chang, K. C., ed. *Food in Chinese Culture: Anthropological and Historical Perspectives*. New Haven: Yale University Press, 1977.

Dutta, Arup Kumar. *Cha Garam! The Tea Story*. Guwahati, India: Paloma, 1992.

Ishige, Naomichi. *The History and Culture of Japanese Food*. London: Kegan Paul, 2001.

Japan Culture Institute. *A Hundred Things Japanese*. Tokyo: Japan Culture Institute, 1975-1978.

Kiple, Kenneth F., and Kriemhild, Coneè Ornelas. *The Cambridge World History of Food*. Cambridge: Cambridge University Press, 2000.

McGee, Harold. *On Food and Cooking: The Science and Lore of the Kitchen*. New York: Collier, 1984.

Okakura, Kakuzo. *Le Livre du thé, d'Okakura Kakuzo*. Paris: Bibliophiles du Faubourg, 1930.

Podreka, Tomislav. *Serendipitea: A Guide to the Varieties, Origins, and Rituals of Tea*. New York: Morrow, 1998.

Sen, Soshitsu. *Chado: The Japanese Way of Tea*, translated and edited by Masuo Yamaguchi. New York and Tokyo: Weatherhill, 1979.

Simoons, Frederick J. *Food in China: A Cultural and Historical Inquiry*. Boca Raton, Fla.: CRC, 1991.

Tannahill, Reay. *Food in History*. New York: Crown, 1989.

Toussaint-Samat, Maguelonne. *History of Food*, translated from the French by Anthea Bell. Cambridge, Mass.: Blackwell, 1993.

Windridge, Charles. *The Fountain of Health: An A–Z of Traditional Chinese Medicine*, consultant editor Wu Xiaochun. Edinburgh, Scotland: Mainstream, 1994.

Yü, Lu. *The Classic of Tea: Origins and Rituals*, translated by Francis Ross Carpenter. Hopewell, Va.: Ecco, 1974.

Wilkinson, Endymion Porter. *Chinese History: A Manual*, rev. and enl. ed. Cambridge, Mass.: Harvard University Asia Center, 2000.

Corinne Trang

TEA (MEAL)

The year 1840 is a landmark in culinary history. Antoine's restaurant had its beginnings in New Orleans, San Francisco consumed the first vintage of commercially produced California wine, and London society imitated Anna, the seventh Duchess of Bedford (1788–1861), with her cure for what she described as "a sinking feeling" she suffered each afternoon. It was then customary in England for the aristocracy to eat a huge breakfast, make do with a small lunch, and sit down to a substantial meal for dinner at eight o'clock or after. Milady's late afternoon discomfort was shared by many another and so was her cure: She ordered tea and a collation of sandwiches and cakes to complement the tea to be served daily at the stroke of five and invited friends to join her.

From the 1840s on, the tradition of afternoon tea with sandwiches and pastries trickled down from the aristocracy to enter English life at large. By the year of Anna's death, the conservative Mrs. Beeton's authoritative *Household Management* pronounced afternoon tea— "a meal of elegant trifles"—to be obligatory in any well-run Victorian household. Not long after Anna's death, the novelist George Gissing was to write, as if in tribute to her, "Nowhere is the English genius for domesticity more notably evidenced than in the festival of afternoon tea." As it began, so it remained essentially a female ritual, but gradually two distinct "teas" evolved.

Aristocratic homes served what was called "low tea" in the afternoon. This was a repast of "elegant trifles" like cucumber sandwiches and other finger foods rather than solid nutrition; the emphasis was placed upon presentation of the foods and socializing over the delicacies. This "terribly, terribly nice" affair became known as "low tea" in contrast to the petty bourgeois and working class custom of "high tea," which has also been called "meat tea" or "farmhouse tea." These are family affairs—hearty, lavish spreads to satisfy the appetites of workers home from toiling and children hungry after school. High tea serves the humbler classes in Britain as the evening meal and often consists of such left-overs as cold joints of mutton, with fresh baked scones, buns, or biscuits and tea in abundance to warm the belly and banish fatigue. "High tea" is not parallel to "high church"; the more elegant

and ceremonious the tea, the further it departs from high tea. In Britain during Victoria's later years, teatime migrated from five o'clock to four, and its ceremonial aspects attained the very height of ostentation. Besides the evidence of Oscar Wilde's play *The Importance of Being Earnest* and Saki's short story "Tea," we have historical accounts of these excesses. Margot Asquith, second wife of the British Liberal prime minister Lord Herbert Asquith (1852–1928), writes in her autobiography how the Rothschild family kept great state in, among other places, their home in Waddesdon, where one day Prime Minister Asquith was waited on at teatime by the butler. "Tea, coffee, or a peach from the wall, sir?" "Tea, please." "China, Indian or Ceylon, sir?" "China, please." "Lemon, milk, or cream, sir?" "Milk, please." "Jersey, Holstein, or Shorthorn, sir?" Volumes could be written.

See also **British Isles; Coffee; Dinner; India; Lunch; Meal; Restaurants; Stimulants.**

BIBLIOGRAPHY

Asquith, Margot. *The Autobiography of Margot Asquith*. Abridged edition, edited by Mark Bonham Carter. London: Weidenfeld & Nicholson, 1995.

Burnett, John. *Plenty and Want: A Social History of Diet in England from 1815 to the Present Day*. London: Scolar Press, 1979.

Hartley, Dorothy. *Food in England*. London: MacDonald and Jane's, 1954; Little, Brown, 1996.

Wilson, C. Anne, ed. *Luncheon, Nuncheon, and Other Meals: Eating with the Victorians*. Stroud, U.K.: Alan Sutton, 1994.

James Norwood Pratt

TELEVISION. *See* **Art, Food in.**

THANKSGIVING. The classic representation of Thanksgiving—a crowded dinner table set in the open air on a golden autumnal afternoon in Plymouth Colony, 1621—might include some anachronisms such as apples, potatoes, corn-on-the-cob, and cranberry sauce, but the gathered Pilgrims and their Wampanoag Indian guests are sure to have one of the "great store of wild turkeys" if not the geese, ducks, and venison that founded the historic feast, bowls of assorted root vegetables, and pumpkin pies. It is an idyllic scene, but it has nothing to do with how the Thanksgiving holiday historically began in America.

There never was a true "first" American Thanksgiving from which all subsequent celebrations derived. Thanksgiving did not originate in America at all, but arrived with the intellectual baggage of New England's Puritan colonists. Having banished the medieval roster of holidays including Christmas and saint's days, the reformers admitted only three holy days: the Sabbath, fast days, and Thanksgivings. Fasts and Thanksgivings subsequently appeared independently in each of the New England colonies (except Rhode Island). Each was like an extra Sabbath during the week, requiring church attendance and sober activity, but a big dinner following the meeting was customary on days of thanksgiving and praise. Eventually, fast days were relegated to the spring (when there was nothing to eat) to petition God for a successful season, while autumnal Thanksgivings celebrated the cumulative blessings of the year, including the fruits of the harvest.

As Puritans metamorphosed into Yankees, the social and gustatory character of the day overtook and then equaled the religious observation in consequence. The preparation for the feast began weeks before with Sunday readings of the governor's proclamation. Apples, spices, suet and lean beef were chopped for mincemeat. Massive numbers of pies and tarts were baked of mince, pumpkin, apple, cranberry, and other fillings, intended to last well beyond the holiday. Livestock and fowl were slaughtered and prepared for the spit, pot, or chicken pie (which might take six birds, bones and all). The requisite turkey was gotten from the barnyard, market, or turkey shoot where poor shots underwrote the costs of better marksmen. Charity was an important holiday element. Food supplies, unprepared (including flour, rice, sugar, and even turkeys) or cooked, were given to the poor by prosperous families and sent to prisons by town officials.

As Thanksgiving approached, family and friends assembled at the patriarchal homesteads. Thanksgiving balls were very popular, and women made sure that their clothes were the best and newest possible, despite grumbling about impious frivolity among the more devout. On the day itself, the more respectable attended morning service in the meetinghouse, before returning for the customary feast prepared by the women and servants of the household. The significators of a true New England Thanksgiving dinner were firmly established by the time of the American Revolution: the all-important turkey in place of honor, the massive chicken pie flanked by ducks, geese, and cuts of "butcher's meat," plum pudding, bowls of vegetable and fruit "sass" (sauce), and of course the pies. Following the dinner, the company might relax around the fire with wine or cider, dried fruits, and nuts to play games, tell stories, or in more pious households, to continue their religious exercises in the private sphere and welcome the minister's evening call. Alternately, sleighing visits to other households were popular, as were dances and weddings.

Even before 1800, many households got their holiday foodstuffs not from the family farmstead but in the marketplace. The food was processed, prepared, and served by the housewife to as many family, friends, and dependents as could be accommodated. Later, the emphasis shifted to kin rather than community, but the classic Thanksgiving bill of fare, based on what was available in November in colonial New England, remained sacro-

Thanksgiving dinner is one of the most important occasions for American families of all faiths and ethnic backgrounds to come together and enjoy a large home-cooked meal. © STEVE CHENN/CORBIS.

sanct. Over the years the ideal of a home-prepared meal and informal family gathering has sent generations of women seeking the advice of experts from Catherine Beecher to Martha Stewart. Regional and ethnic variations were allowed, but the iconic turkey, cranberry sauce, and pumpkin (or squash) pie consecrated all true Thanksgiving meals.

The first of ten national Thanksgivings was declared by the Continental Congress in 1777. After 1815, there were no further presidential proclamations despite annual editorial pleadings by Mrs. Hale in *Godey's Magazine*, but the popularity of the holiday grew apace. By the 1850s, Thanksgiving was celebrated in almost every state and territory, its national character assured. Abraham Lincoln declared two Thanksgivings in 1863, the second in November being the first of our modern national holidays, but it was not until 1941 after Roosevelt fiddled with the date with an eye to Christmas sales that Congress established the fourth Thursday as a legal holiday. Aside from packaged versions of traditional foods, expenses associated with holiday travel, and a moderate amount of decorative kitsch, the holiday also escaped the exploitive commercialism of other American holidays. Restaurants take advantage of the holiday to sell turkey dinners, and those dedicated purveyors of classic Thanksgiving fare, the armed services, do their best, but Thanksgiving retains its strongly domestic focus.

In light of their modern importance as the symbols of the holiday, it might be asked. "What about the Pilgrims?" The fact is that the famous description of the 1621 harvest festival in Mourt's Relation had been entirely forgotten before being rediscovered in 1822 and identified as the "First Thanksgiving" by Alexander Young in 1841.

No one had associated the Plymouth colonists and Indian guests with the holiday before. However, in 1841 the event resembled contemporary Thanksgivings, even if it had not been so regarded by the original participants. The concept took time to catch on, as the Pilgrims had other symbolic burdens to bear, and Thanksgiving still implied family reunions, turkeys, and Yankee homesteads to most people. It wasn't until a fictional account appeared in the bestselling *Standish of Standish* (1889) that the Plymouth association gained widespread popularity, and only after World War II did the Pilgrims become the primary significators of the holiday.

See also **American Indians; Christianity; Fasting and Abstinence; Feasts, Festivals, and Fasts; Holidays; Icon Foods; Religion and Food; United States: New England.**

BIBLIOGRAPHY

[Abbott, Jacob.] *New England and Her Institutions by One of Her Sons.* Boston: John Allen, 1835.

Appelbaum, Diana. *Thanksgiving: An American Holiday, An American History.* New York: Facts on File, 1984.

Austin, Jane G. *Standish of Standish.* Boston: Houghton, Mifflin, 1889.

Beecher, Catherine. *Miss Beecher's Domestic Receipt-Book.* New York: Harper and Brothers, 1846.

DeLoss Love, William. *Fast and Thanksgiving Days of New England.* Boston: Houghton, Mifflin, 1895.

Hale, Mrs. Sarah Josepha. *Northwood; or, Life North and South,* 2d ed. New York: Long, 1852.

Heath, Dwight B., ed. *A Journal of the Pilgrims at Plymouth (Mourt's Relation).* New York: Corinth Books, 1963.

Hooker, Richard J. *Food and Drink in America.* Indianapolis: Bobbs-Merrill, 1981.

Howland, Mrs. E. A. *The New England Economical Housekeeper.* New London: Bolles and Williams, 1848.

Sickel, H. S. J. *Thanksgiving: Its Source, Philosophy and History with All National Proclamations and Analytical Study Thereof.* Philadelphia: International Printing, 1940.

Stow, Harriet Beecher. *Oldtown Folks.* Boston: Fields, Osgood, 1869.

Young, Alexander. *Chronicles of the First Planters of the Colony of Massachusetts Bay.* Boston: Little, Brown, 1846.

James W. Baker
Peggy M. Baker

THIAMINE. *See* **Vitamins.**

THIRST. Thirst is a conscious sensation that results in a desire to drink. Although all normal humans experience thirst, science can offer no precise definition of this phenomenon because it involves numerous physiological responses to a change in internal fluid status, complex patterns of central nervous system function, and psychological motivation. Three factors are typically recognized as components of thirst: a body water deficit, brain integration of central and peripheral nerve messages relating to the need for water, and an urge to drink. In laboratory experiments, thirst is measured empirically with subjective perceptual scales (for example, ranging from "not thirsty at all" to "very, very thirsty") and drinking behavior is quantified by observing the timing and volume of fluid consumed.

Psychologists classify thirst as a drive, a basic compelling urge that motivates action. Other human drives involve a lack of nutrients (for example, glucose, sodium), oxygen, or sleep; these are satiated by eating, breathing, and sleeping. Clark Hull published a major, relevant theory describing the nature of human drives in 1943. He observed that learned habits, in addition to the thirst drive, influence drinking strongly. If a behavior reduces thirst, that behavior is reinforced and learned as a habit. Irrelevant behaviors (for example, sneezing, grooming) provide no reinforcement, have no effect on drinking, and do not become habits. Further, Hull realized that external incentives, such as the qualities or quantity of a fluid, also influence fluid consumption. On a hot summer day, for example, a cold beverage is more attractive than a cup of hot tea. Yet when chilled to a very low temperature, a cold beverage becomes an aversive stimulus to drinking behavior. Physiologists have popularized the term *alliesthesia* (from Greek root words referring to altered sensation) to describe the fact that the sensation of thirst may have either pleasant or unpleasant qualities, depending on the intensity of the stimulus and the state of the person.

Numerous investigations have verified that thirst and drinking behavior are complex entities. For example, drinking behavior (that is, the timing and the amount of fluid consumed) is not linearly related to the intensity of perceived thirst. Nor should we infer that individuals experience thirst simply because they drink. These facts indicate that thirst and drinking behavior are distinct entities that influence each other and are influenced by numerous internal and external factors.

Physiological Components of Thirst
Thirst is often viewed by physiologists and physicians as a central nervous system mechanism that regulates the body's water and minerals. The significance of the thirst drive is emphasized by three facts: 50 to 70 percent of adult body weight is water, the average adult ingests and loses 2.5 liters of water each day, and body weight is regulated within 0.2 percent from one day to the next. Clearly, water is essential to life and the body responds in a manner that ensures survival.

In 1954, Edward Adolph and colleagues proposed a multiple-factor theory of thirst that has not been refuted to date. This theory states that no single mechanism can account for all drinking behavior and that multiple mechanisms, sometimes with identical functions, act concurrently. Because water is essential to life, the existence of redundant mechanisms has great survival value. Among these, thirst appears to be regulated primarily by evaluation of changes in the concentration of extracellular fluid, measured as the osmolality of blood plasma. (Osmolality is a measurement that describes the concentration of all dissolved solids in a solution, that is, dissolved substances per unit of solvent. In research and clinical laboratories, the unit for osmolality of blood is mOsm/kg or milliosmoles per kilogram of water.)

Below a certain threshold level of plasma osmolality, thirst is absent. Above this threshold, a strong desire to drink appears in response to an increase of 2 to 3 percent in the level of dissolved substances in blood. The brain's thirst center lies deep within the brain, in an area known as the hypothalamus. This anatomical site contains cells that respond to changes in the concentration of body fluids. When the thirst center is stimulated by an increased concentration of blood (that is, dehydration), thirst and fluid consumption increase.

As the brain senses the concentration of blood, it allows a minor loss of body water before stimulating the drive to drink. This phenomenon has been named voluntary dehydration. Specifically, several research studies since the 1930s have observed that adults and children replace only 34 to 87 percent of the water lost as sweat, by drinking during exercise or labor in hot environments. The resulting dehydration is due to the fact that thirst is not perceived until a 1 to 2 percent body weight loss occurs. Interindividual differences, resulting in great voluntary dehydration in some individuals, have caused them to be named reluctant drinkers.

Reduced extracellular fluid volume, including blood volume, also increases thirst. Experiments (for example, reducing blood volume without altering blood concentration) have demonstrated that volume-sensitive receptors in the heart and blood vessels likely regulate drinking behavior by increasing the secretion of hormones. This effect is relatively minor, however. Animal research suggests that a change in extracellular fluid concentration accounts for most (for example, 70 percent) of the increased fluid consumption that follows moderate whole-body dehydration, whereas a decrease of fluid volume per se plays a secondary role.

Thus, thirst is extinguished when body fluid concentration decreases and fluid volume increases. Osmolality-sensitive nerves in the mouth, throat, and stomach also play a role in abating thirst. As fluid passes through the mouth and upper gastrointestinal tract, the sense of dryness decreases. When this fluid fills the stomach, stretch receptors sense an increase in gastric fullness and the thirst drive diminishes.

As dehydration causes the body's extracellular fluid to become more concentrated, the fluid inside cells moves outward, resulting in intracellular dehydration and cell shrinkage, and the hormone arginine vasopressin (AVP,

Down through the centuries, potters, glassblowers, and metalsmiths have devised clever and decorative ways to quench thirst. These Roman glass tumblers, discovered at Pompeii, were made by blowing the glass into wooden molds in order to create the raised patterns. Raised patterns helped the drinker hold the glass more firmly, thus lessening the likelihood of having it slip through the fingers when tipsy on wine. © MIMMO JODICE/CORBIS.

also known as the antidiuretic hormone) is released from the brain. AVP serves two purposes: to reduce urine output at the kidneys and to enhance thirst; both serve to restore normal fluid balance. Other hormones influence fluid-mineral balance directly and thirst indirectly. Renin, angiotensin II, and aldosterone are noteworthy examples. As dehydration reduces circulating blood volume, blood pressure decreases and renin is secreted from blood vessels inside the kidneys. Renin activates the hormone angiotensin II, which subsequently stimulates the release of aldosterone from the adrenal glands. Both angiotensin II and aldosterone increase blood pressure and enhance the retention of sodium and water; these effects indirectly reduce the intensity of thirst. Angiotensin II also affects thirst directly. When injected into sensitive areas of the brain, it causes a rapid increase in water consumption that is followed by a slower increase in sodium chloride consumption and water retention by the kidneys.

Host Factors

Repeated training sessions in cool or hot environments alter fluid consumption in four ways. First, physical training increases the secretion of the hormone AVP, which stimulates drinking and body water retention. Second, exercise-heat acclimation (that is, adaptations due to exercise in a hot environment over eight days) increases the volume of fluid consumed and the number of times that adults drink during exercise. Third, frequent rest periods, in the midst of labor or exercise, will increase fluid replacement time and enhance fluid consumption.

FACTORS THAT ALTER THIRST

Increase Thirst

- increased concentration of blood
- decreased blood volume
- decreased blood pressure
- mouth and throat dryness
- increased angiotensin II

Decrease Thirst

- decreased concentration of blood
- increased blood volume
- increased blood pressure
- increased stomach fullness
- decreased angiotensin II

Humans tend to drink less when they are preoccupied or are performing physical or mental tasks. Fourth, learned behaviors can enhance fluid consumption when thirst is absent. This phenomenon is widely appreciated among military personnel and athletes who are trained to consume water at regular intervals, whether they are thirsty or not.

Several research groups have reported that chronological age influences thirst and drinking behavior. Elderly men experience a blunted thirst drive and reduced fluid intake, perhaps due to their brains' reduced ability to sense changes in plasma osmolality or blood volume. Further, elderly individuals experience a decrease in the ability of their kidneys to conserve water. This suggests that the elderly are predisposed to dehydration when illness increases water loss (that is, vomiting, diarrhea) or when physical incapacity prevents access to water.

Fluid and Environmental Characteristics

Many fluid characteristics stimulate or enhance drinking, during or after exposure to a hot environment. Fluid temperature (consumption is greatest at 14 to 16°C, reduced above 37°C), turbidity, sweetness, fruit flavorings (for example, cherry, grape, orange, lemon), addition of citric acid which imparts a citrus flavor, and addition of sodium chloride or other minerals are examples. These components enhance palatability and increase fluid consumption. The addition of a small amount of salt (sodium chloride), besides enhancing palatability, may result in thirst and increased drinking, due to the specific action of sodium on fluid movements. An increased sodium concentration outside of cells causes water to leave cells via osmosis. The resulting cellular dehydration is an important stimulus for drinking. Increased beverage carbonation tends to reduce the palatability of a fluid as well as the volume of fluid consumed, without an increase in thirst. In addition, intakes of food and water are closely related. During 24-hour observations of fluid intake, most studies report that the majority of fluid (69 to 78 percent) is consumed during meals. The foregoing characteristics, therefore, tend to reduce the magnitude of voluntary dehydration.

Conversely, fluid characteristics may influence drinking behavior negatively, regardless of the intensity of thirst. Experiments conducted during mild prolonged exercise have shown that the following qualities are perceived as undesirable: nausea, bloating, an objectionable feeling in the mouth, excessive viscosity, and excessive sweetness (see Passe, 1996). Exercise and high ambient temperature may independently alter an individual's perception of fluid palatability. For example, drinking behavior increases when air temperature exceeds 25°C. Fluid consumption can also be enhanced by changing the shape of a fluid container, proximity of fluid containers to the drinker, volume of fluid that is available, and time allowed for drinking.

Societal customs may influence fluid consumption, as evidenced by cross-cultural differences in beverage preferences. Even rituals, such as accepting the friendly offer of a beverage in a social setting, may enhance fluid intake beyond that driven by physiological cues. These factors usually involve learned habits. Similarly, when people repeatedly drink fluids with initially unfamiliar flavors, the palatability of the fluids is enhanced.

Although a comprehensive theory of thirst and fluid balance eludes description, it is likely that the thirst drive increases and diminishes because multiple factors (for example, oral dryness, gastric distension, osmolality, volume, fluid qualities) are integrated concurrently by the brain's thirst center.

See also **Alcohol**; **Appetite**; **Beer**; **Cocktails**; **Coffee**; **Grapes and Grape Juice**; **Sensation and the Senses**; **Tea**; **Water**; **Wine**.

BIBLIOGRAPHY

Adolph, Edward F., June P. Barker, and Patricia A. Hoy. "Multiple Factors in Thirst." *American Journal of Physiology* 178 (1954): 538–562.

Armstrong, Lawrence E., Roger W. Hubbard, Patricia C. Szlyk, William T. Matthew, and Ingrid V. Sils. "Voluntary Dehydration and Electrolyte Losses During Prolonged Exercise in the Heat." *Aviation, Space and Environmental Medicine* 56 (1985): 765–770.

Armstrong, Lawrence E., and Carl M. Maresh. "Fluid Replacement During Exercise and Recovery from Exercise."

In *Body Fluid Balance in Exercise and Sport*, edited by Elsworth R. Buskirk and Susan M. Puhl. Boca Raton, Fla.: CRC Press, 1996.

Cabanac, Michel. "Physiological Role of Pleasure." *Science* 173 (1971): 1103–1107.

Engell, Diane, and Edward Hirsch. "Environmental and Sensory Modulation of Fluid Intake in Humans." In *Thirst: Psychological and Physiological Aspects*. edited by David J. Ramsay and David Booth, pp. 382–389. London: Springer-Verlag, 1991.

Fitzsimons, J. T. "Thirst and Sodium Appetite in the Regulation of Body Fluids." In *Control Mechanisms of Drinking*, edited by G. Peters, J. T. Fitzsimons, and L. Peters-Haefeli. New York: Springer-Verlag, 1975.

Fitzsimons, J. T. "Angiotensin, Thirst, and Sodium Appetite." *Physiological Reviews* 78 (1998): 583–675.

Greenleaf, John E. "Problem: Thirst, Drinking Behavior, and Involuntary Dehydration. *Medicine and Science in Sports and Exercise* 24 (1992): 645–656.

Greenleaf, John E., and Taketoshi Morimoto. "Mechanisms Controlling Fluid Ingestion: Thirst and Drinking." In *Body Fluid Balance: Exercise and Sport*, edited by Ellsworth R. Buskirk and Susan M. Puhl, pp. 3–17. Boca Raton, Fla.: CRC Press, 1996.

Hubbard, Roger W., Barbara Sandick, William T. Matthew, Ralph P. Francesconi, James B. Sampson, Michael J. Durkot, Maller Owen, and Diane B. Engell. "Voluntary Dehydration and Alliesthesia for Water." *Journal of Applied Physiology: Respiratory, Environmental, Exercise Physiology* 57 (1984): 868–875.

Hubbard, Roger W., Patricia C. Szlyk, and Lawrence E. Armstrong. "Influence of Thirst and Fluid Palatability on Fluid Ingestion During Exercise." In *Perspectives in Exercise Sciences and Sports Medicine: Fluid Homeostasis During Exercise*, pp. 39-96. Indianapolis, Ind.: Benchmark Press, 1990.

Hull, Clark. "Primary Motivation and Reaction Potential." In *Principles of Behavior*. New York: Appleton-Century-Crofts, 1943.

Passe, Dennis H. "Physiological and Psychological Determinants of Fluid Intake." In *Sport Drinks: Basic Science and Practical Aspects*, edited by Ronald J. Maughan and Robert Murray. Boca Raton, Fla.: CRC Press, 1996.

Lawrence E. Armstrong

TILLAGE.

Farmers perform tillage when they prepare soil for the raising of crops. Soil tillage has three primary purposes. Prior to planting, farmers use tillage to mix compost, manure, and other fertilizers into the root zone where growing plant roots may reach it. Tillage also aids seed germination by creating a smooth, uniform soil surface for planting. After planting, farmers use tillage to control weeds between crop plants—including vegetable, fruit, forest, medicinal, and farm crops. Since early agriculture, tillage has been the first step in the process that makes it possible to harvest food from plants. However, soil tillage has come under close scrutiny since soil is recognized as a natural resource that deserves pro-

tection. Agronomists (scientists who study crop production and soil management) are concerned because erosion (soil loss) from tillage is one of the most significant problems in agriculture. If left unchecked, soil erosion leads to loss of soil productivity, as well as off-site deposition of sediments and farm chemicals that pollute surface and groundwater.

Early History of Tillage

Soil tillage had its beginnings ten to twelve millennia ago in the Near East, as early farmers used a digging stick to loosen the soil before planting seeds. The tool evolved from digging stick to spade to triangular blade, and was made of wood, stone, and ultimately metal. One or more people likely used their bodies to pull the first wooden plows. Animals began pulling plows around 3000 B.C.E. in Mesopotamia. Jethro Tull (1674–1741), a pioneering British soil physicist, was the first to recognize that loosening soil helps to supply plant roots with nutrients.

In North America, agricultural innovators copied European trends. Charles Newbold patented the first cast-iron plow in the late 1700s. In 1837, John Deere and Leonard Andrus began manufacturing steel plows. By the 1840s, the growing use of manufactured equipment had increased the farmers' need for cash, thus encouraging the rise of commercial farming. Agriculture, society, and economics were closely linked, as George Marsh said in an address delivered in 1847 to the Agricultural Society of Rutland County, Vermont: "Pure pastoral life, as I have said, advances man to but an humble stage of civilization, but when it is merged in agriculture, and the regular tillage of the soil commences, he is brought under the dominion of new influences, and the whole economy of domestic and social life is completely revolutionized." Marsh explained that once cultivation of soil begins, all aspects of society are affected by changes: "Hence arises the necessity of fixed habitations and store houses, and of laws which shall recognize and protect private exclusive right to determinate portions of the common earth, and sanction and regulate the right of inheritance, and the power of alienation and devise, in short the whole frame work of civil society."

Horses and mules had taken over the work of draft oxen by the late 1800s. As agriculture became increasingly mechanized and commercialized, tractors became more common and replaced most draft animals by the early to mid-1900s. Until then, the size of most family farms was restricted to the land that a man could work using several horses. With the advent of the light, gasoline-powered tractor, both family and commercial farms added crop area and prospered.

The Dust Bowl

Tractors helped to create farm fields that stretched far westward, setting the stage for the Dust Bowl in the 1930s. Open grassland in the southwestern Great Plains region of the United States was settled and farmed by

Tilling with draught animals is a dying art, for both farmer and team must be well-trained to accomplish plowing in the quickest and most efficient manner. This elderly farmer is using a horse team in fields near Melk, Austria. © ADAM WOOLFITT/ CORBIS.

homesteaders who planted row crops and grazed their cattle. Before farmers came, the region was covered by hardy grasses that held the soil in place despite long droughts and torrential rains. Tillage combined with drought left the soil exposed to wind erosion. Lightweight soil components—organic matter, clay, and silt— were carried great distances by the winds, while sand and heavier materials drifted against houses, fences, and barns. This drifting debris buried farm buildings and darkened the sky as far as the Atlantic coast. Over a period of ten years, millions of acres of farmland became useless, and hundreds of thousands of people were forced to leave their homes.

The Dust Bowl gave impetus to the soil conservation movement; nevertheless, mechanization continued to spread. In 1938, Hugh Bennett and Walter Lowdermilk of the United States Soil Conservation Service wrote in the *Yearbook of Agriculture*: "Soil erosion is as old as farming. It began when the first heavy rain struck the first furrow turned by a crude implement of tillage in the hands of prehistoric man. It has been going on ever since, wherever man's culture of the earth has bared the soil to rain and wind."

Conservation Tillage and Sustainable Agriculture

By 1954, the number of tractors on farms exceeded the number of horses and mules for the first time. The increasing availability of agricultural chemicals in the mid- to late-1900s, including weed killers that did not harm crop plants, further changed crop and soil management practices. "Conservation tillage"—a broad spectrum of farming methods that help to reduce soil erosion due to wind and water and help to reduce labor and fuel—gained a following among farmers in the 1980s. Early methods of conservation tillage, such as no-tillage, were *un*sustainable since they relied heavily on chemical weed killers

called herbicides. The no-tillage method worked well to control both soil erosion and weeds, while requiring less energy. However, herbicides were highly toxic to people and wildlife and their manufacture and use caused environmental pollution. Tillage reduction methods were fine-tuned to suit local conditions throughout the United States.

By 1989, a far-sighted handful of new-generation farmers became interested in lowering costs, avoiding agricultural chemicals, and saving soil. They started the agricultural movement that became known as "sustainable agriculture." Low-input methods meet the needs of more farmers each year. They are promoted by a program of the United States Department of Agriculture called Sustainable Agriculture Research and Education (SARE). Farmers practicing sustainable agriculture produce food and fiber while enhancing environmental quality and natural resources, make the most efficient use of nonrenewable resources and on-farm resources. Further, they integrate natural biological cycles and pest controls and sustain the economic viability of farm operations.

Today's tillage practices reflect society's concern with environmental quality, and the farmer's need to reduce costs while preventing soil erosion and compaction. However, significant amounts of soil are still lost annually around the world where soil is not protected.

See also **Agronomy**; **Greenhouse Horticulture**; **Horticulture**; **Organic Farming and Gardening**; **Sustainable Agriculture**.

BIBLIOGRAPHY

Blann, K., review of Coughenour, C. M., and S. Chamala, "Conservation Tillage and Cropping Innovation: Constructing the New Culture of Agriculture," in *Conservation Ecology* 5 (2): 2 (2001). Ames: Iowa State University Press.

Hillel, Daniel. *Environmental Soil Physics*. San Diego: Academic Press, 1998.

Jasa, P. J., D. P. Shelton, A. J. Jones, and E. C. Dickey. *Conservation Tillage and Planting Systems*. Bulletin G91-1046. Lincoln, Neb.: Cooperative Extension, Institute of Agriculture and Natural Resources, University of Nebraska, Lincoln, 1997.

Library of Congress. *The Evolution of the Conservation Movement 1850–1920*. Library of Congress: Washington, D.C.

Robinson, Clay. *Dr. Dirt*. Online notes for courses in soil science. Canyon, Tex.: West Texas A&M University.

United States Department of Agriculture, Economic Research Service. *A History of American Agriculture 1776–1990*. Washington, D.C.: U.S. Government Printing Office, n.d.

Patricia S. Michalak

TIME. "Time" may not spring to mind immediately when one thinks of food, but time is always a factor. After all, recipes generally incorporate an element of time (for example, "let rise for four hours" or "bake for forty-five minutes"), cooking preparation involves time, and various demands drive the length of meals. Thus, time has an impact on one's daily food and food-preparation routine, and this impact is a particularly gendered process.

In nearly all parts of the world, cooking is a female task (Murdock and Provost, 1973). Women's time is bounded by food-preparation tasks, particularly if they must perform those tasks several times a day (for example, tasks such as tortilla preparation, millet pounding, and the preparation from scratch of several meals a day). Alteration of a daily routine, for example, the intrusion of a more "urban" or fast-paced schedule, can alter food-preparation patterns. If women enter a market economy, they have less time to prepare food, which leads to, among other things, increased purchases of prepared food and more business for the fast-food industry. Time and food preparation are also markers of rank or class, since elaborate meals are generally costly in terms of time preparation as well as ingredients—in most societies, only the well-to-do, who have either time or help or both, can prepare elaborate meals. These widespread changes in food-preparation patterns are part of urban Western culture, where convenience and fast-food items (the names of which indicate their purpose) are replacing daily meal preparation. The Italian "slow food" movement is counterpoised against this trend.

Food Preparation

The preparation of foods—the transformation from a raw or unprocessed state to one suitable for consumption—occupies a major portion of many women's time throughout much of the world. For rural women and those in developing nations, preparation of meals may take up the major portion of a woman's waking life. Since staple foods must undergo a lengthy preparation process, women can spend much of their time processing grain, nuts, or tubers, in addition to meal preparation itself. (This pattern has antecedents in the West, as well: consider the time needed to make bread and churn butter.)

Accompanying this ongoing preparation of staples is the routine of meal preparation. For example, Andean Ecuador meal preparation, which is performed from scratch twice a day, generally involves two to three hours of potato peeling, water boiling, and construction of the soup that constitutes the staple meal (Weismantel, 1988). In southern Mexico, rural Maya women may prepare up to two hundred tortillas per day, grinding and cooking them at each of two or three meals (Eber, 2000). In rural Africa, women farmers grind the standard grains, usually millet or sorghum, into flour for porridge or soup on a daily basis. Pounding millet, as this process is called, occurs at least once a day, and sometimes more often as needs demand. African women are also responsible for preparing and assembling meals. In Western urban settings, the food-preparation process may be slightly less rigorous, but often remains time-consuming, since the cook must peel, chop, and cook.

Scheduling and Meals

The timing of meals is culturally determined and is linked to preindustrial work patterns, particularly the agricultural cycle. Throughout Latin America, the main meal of the day traditionally falls in mid-afternoon. The siesta, stereotypically seen by North Americans as a sign of indolence, is actually the main meal of the day. This pattern remains intact in smaller cities and rural areas, though the demands of global business are increasingly pushing urban workers into the short noon lunch typical of the United States. Among rural indigenous peoples, however, mealtimes may differ, following much more closely the requirements of subsistence farming. Breakfast is eaten very early in the morning, and a second, larger meal follows in the late morning or early afternoon. Another meal occurs in early evening, with an occasional snack before bedtime (which also occurs early, often shortly after sundown). At the same time, much of the urban world has already adopted a meal schedule that better conforms to the demands of industrialism. Such changes may alter or eliminate traditional meals or reduce the time families spend together (Rotenberg, 1992).

Food, Time, and Class

Social standing shapes the ways in which food and time intersect. For those with sufficient income, only one member of a family need work, leaving the other family members at home to prepare traditional meals. Another alternative to preparing food for oneself is to hire a professional cook, who is also able to prepare meals from scratch.

For those with little money and little time, the options decrease. Convenience and fast-foods are expensive for what they provide, and they are often limited to single or perhaps two servings. Time, money, and class intersect in other ways that affect meals, as well. For the working poor, hours of overtime, or even two jobs, may take up the time that would otherwise be spent preparing and eating meals; meager wages may also reduce one's housing choices. In her book on the working poor, *Nickel and Dimed*, Barbara Ehrenreich describes this housing process: Unable to afford housing with a kitchen, the worker cannot purchase foods to prepare in bulk and cannot store or freeze these foods. Such workers are sometimes entirely dependent on meals they can purchase and eat immediately, such as fast-food or the kinds of overpriced but affordable snack food sold in convenience stores.

Changing Time and Changing Food

The impact of urban work patterns has affected mealtimes, food choices, and diet throughout the world. As workers move from an agrarian life to one driven by waged work, they shape their mealtimes to that of the workplace rather than the farm. The kinds of foods workers choose to eat are likely to be those that can be taken to the workplace or eaten on the run. The rise in sales of prepared foods appears to inevitably accompany women's entry into the workforce, and sometimes women themselves enter the workforce to provide the prepared food, a pattern seen in Peru (Babb, 1998), rural Africa (Clark, 1994), and elsewhere. The ability to bring home prepared food enables women to spend longer periods of time working in a pattern that parallels western women's purchase of fast-food dinners for the family. For the westerner and the rural worker alike, elaborate meals requiring lengthy preparation become increasingly associated with ritual and holiday feasting. The role of time in the preparation of holiday foods rather than (or in addition to) the use of special ingredients marks them as special treats. This stands in contrast to the faster and less elaborate meals consumed during a regular workweek. Sidney Mintz, in his work *Sweetness and Power*, has further suggested that the increasing consumption of sugar in tea allowed the shift of displaced rural English into industrial labor—they could consume cheap quick meals of tea and bread and spend much of their time working.

The speedy meal is familiar also in the form of the fast-food industry that the demands of postindustrial capitalism shaped. The busy worker can order, pick up, and pay for a quick and generally tasty meal, all without ever leaving the car. Eric Schosser has described in-depth the quite extensive impact of the fast-food industry on diet, food production, and meal patterns in his book *Fast Food Nation*. While answering the demand for quick, easily consumed meals, the fast-food industry has also shaped marketing, taste preferences, and even agricultural practice.

The "slow food" movement has arisen in opposition to the pervasiveness of the fast-food industry. Founded in Italy, "slow food" promotes local and organic foods, family mealtimes, and the role of food in social life. In general, this movement opposes the increasingly mechanized and driven work life that the fast-food industry and North American culture represent (Inouye, 2001).

See also **Class, Social; Division of Labor; Fast Food; Preparation of Food; Slow Food.**

BIBLIOGRAPHY

Babb, Florence. *Between Field and Cooking Pot: The Political Economy of Marketwomen in Peru.* 2nd ed. Austin: University of Texas Press, 1998.

Clark, Gracia. *Onions Are My Husband: Survival and Accumulation by West African Market Women.* Chicago: University of Chicago Press, 1994.

Eber, Christine. *Women and Alcohol in a Highland Maya Town: Water of Hope, Water of Sorrow.* 2nd ed. Austin: University of Texas Press, 2000.

Ehrenreich, Barbara. *Nickel and Dimed: On (Not) Getting By in America.* New York: Metropolitan Books, 2001.

Inouye, Brenda. "Slow Food." *Alternatives Journal* 27, no. 1 (Winter 2001): 4.

Mintz, Sidney. *Sweetness and Power: The Place of Sugar in Modern History.* New York: Viking, 1985.

Murdock, G. P., and Catarina Provost. "Factors in the Division of Labor by Sex: A Cross-Cultural Analysis." *Ethnology* 9 (1973): 122–225.

Rotenberg, Robert. *Time and Order in Metropolitan Vienna: A Seizure of Schedules.* Washington, D.C.: Smithsonian Institution Press, 1992.

Schlosser, Eric. *Fast Food Nation: The Dark Side of the All-American Meal.* New York: Houghton-Mifflin, 2001.

Weismantel, M. J. *Food, Gender and Poverty in the Ecuadorian Andes.* Philadelphia: University of Pennsylvania Press, 1988.

Robin O'Brian

TOMATO. The *Lycopersicon* genus of the Solanaceae family originated along the coastal highlands of western South America. The genus is composed of nine generally accepted species, of which only two are used for culinary purposes: *L. esculentum*, the common tomato, and, to a much smaller extent, *L. pimpinellifolium*. Ripe, raw tomatoes consist of approximately 93 percent water. Consuming one hundred grams of raw tomatoes provides seventeen grams of carbohydrates, three grams of protein, twenty-three grams of vitamin C, or about forty percent of the adult recommended daily allowance (RDA), and about nine hundred international units of vitamin A, or about 30 percent of the adult RDA. Today, the tomato is one of the most commonly eaten foods in the world with almost every cuisine employing them in some form.

In the United States, tomatoes are second only to potatoes in U.S. vegetable consumption. During the 1980s and 1990s, U.S. annual per capita use of tomatoes and tomato products has increased by nearly 30 percent, reaching an annual total fresh-weight equivalent of 91 pounds per person by 1999. By that date, the total world production was 111.1 million short tons. Until recently, the United States was the world's largest tomato producer. However, during 1999 China was ranked the largest tomato producer with 18 million short tons, followed by the United States (12.7 million short tons), Turkey, Egypt, and Italy.

The Spread of the Tomato

Although the tomato originated in South America, little evidence has surfaced indicating that indigenous peoples in South America ate tomatoes before the Spanish conquest in the sixteenth century. In pre-Columbian times the tomato migrated by unknown means to Central America, where it was domesticated by Mesoamerican peoples. When the Europeans arrived, tomatoes were consumed only in a narrow geographical area from Central America to Mexico City. This lack of widespread diffusion has led observers to conclude that tomatoes were a late addition to the culinary repertoire of Mesoamerica. The Spanish first encountered tomatoes after their conquest of Mexico began in 1519. Tomato plants were disseminated first to the Caribbean, and then to Spain and Italy. From Central America, domesticated tomatoes were introduced into South America by the Spanish Conquistadors. Toward the end of the sixteenth century, tomatoes traveled west to the Philippines, from where they were introduced into Indonesia and later onto the Asian mainland.

Tomatoes were consumed in southern Italy and Spain by the mid-sixteenth century. The first published record of the tomato appeared in an 1544 Italian herbal. By the late seventeenth century, the first known tomato recipes appeared in the cookbook *Lo scalco alla moderna* (Naples, 1692), by Antonio Latini. By this time, tomatoes were also consumed in the eastern Mediterranean and North Africa. Tomato cookery took off in southern France late in the eighteenth century and tomato recipes appeared in French cookbooks by the early nineteenth century. Tomatoes were cultivated in England by 1597; however, little evidence for British consumption has been found prior to the mid-eighteenth century.

Beginning in the seventeenth century, Spanish colonists introduced tomatoes into their settlements in Florida, New Mexico, Texas, and California. As English settlers visited and occupied territories previously controlled or influenced by Spain and Mexico, they were exposed to tomato cookery. Some American colonists ate tomatoes as early as the mid-eighteenth century, although only one colonial cookery manuscript is known to have contained a tomato recipe. From the Southern states, tomato culture slowly spread up the Atlantic coast and into rural areas. By the early nineteenth century, tomato recipes frequently appeared in American cookery manuscripts and cookbooks. By the mid-nineteenth century, tomatoes were a common part of cookery throughout western Europe, the Mediterranean and the Americas. Tomato cookery later expanded into Northern and Eastern Europe, and finally spread to sub-Saharan Africa, and South and East Asia.

Procurement

Traditionally, all aspects of tomato sowing, growing, and harvesting were accomplished by hand. Beginning in the late nineteenth century, machinery began to assist farmers in planting, sowing, and weeding. Although all fresh tomatoes continue to be picked by hand today, tomatoes used for processing are picked by mechanical harvesters, which were first successfully employed in California during the 1950s.

Beginning in the early nineteenth century, tomatoes were bottled by the Frenchman Nicholas Appert. In the United States, tomato canning and bottling began in New Jersey during the 1840s. It expanded during the Civil War, and by 1870 tomatoes were among the top three canned products in America. Tomato cultivation increased in northern states, such as Maryland, Delaware, Pennsylvania, and Ohio, and spread south and west after the war. Today, California grows the largest number of tomatoes, with about 80 percent of total U.S. production.

THE FIRST KNOWN AMERICAN TOMATO RECIPE

To Keep Tomatoos for Winter use

Take ripe Tomatas, peel them, and cut them in four and put them into a stew pan, strew over them a great quantity of Pepper and Salt; cover it up close and let it stand an Hour, then put it on the fire and let it stew quick till the liquor is intirely boild away; then take them up and put it into pint Potts, and when cold pour melted butter over them about an inch thick. They commonly take a whole day to stew. Each pot will make two Soups.

N.B. if you do them before the month of Oct they will not keep.

SOURCE: Harriott Pinckney Horry Papers, 28. The Collections of the South Carolina Historical Society.

Tomato Canning

The major use of tomatoes is the canning of four major products: whole tomatoes, tomato sauce, tomato paste, and tomato soup. The first canneries processed whole tomatoes. These efforts began in the 1850s and were labor-intensive operations. The fruit were skinned, cored, and trimmed. Cans were fashioned by hand, and the seams were soldered on. These were then boiled in water. The cans were hand-filled, then given to the cappers, who soldered on the lids one at a time. A few days later the cans were hand labeled, loaded onto wagons, and carted to stores.

Before long, every stage of the canning operation had a machine associated with its operation. Devices for capping, filling, scalding, topping, and wiping were introduced, as were power hoists and cranes. Wrapping and boxing machines also soon came into use. Equipment manufacturers developed lines of interconnected equipment. New machinery was released about 1903, providing for the fully automated manufacture of sanitary cans. By the 1920s, the process of canning tomatoes was fully automated. From the time tomatoes arrived by truck until the canned goods were shipped out the back door, the tomatoes were never touched by human hands. Subsequent developments in machinery sped up the process and made it more efficient.

During the 1950s, evaporators originally developed for the dairy industry were adapted for use in tomato processing. The evaporators rapidly remove water and concentrate the pulp to forty-two percent solids. Some concentrate is frozen via flash coolers, which remove water and heat, as the paste falls through the machine. The chilled concentrate is then stored in drums and used when

The Tomato: Vegetable or Fruit?

The edible portion of the tomato is botanically a fruit (defined as a ripened ovary!) as is the edible portion of melons, cucumbers, eggplants, and hot and sweet peppers. However, these plants are considered vegetables both horticulturally and in common English usage. A vegetable in the culinary sense is thought of as an edible herbaceous (soft-stemmed) plant of which some part is eaten, often in the main part of a meal; this includes the fruit as in tomato, the leaves in lettuce, the stem in asparagus, the root in beet, and the seed in the garden pea. The edible portions are also referred to as vegetables. Fruit plants in the horticultural sense are plants in which a more or less succulent fruit or closely related structure is eaten (but usually as a dessert or a snack). In this case the edible portion is also called a fruit, even if it is not clearly a fruit botanically. We call a strawberry a fruit, but it is the hard little seeds that are the botanical fruits (one-seeded fruits called achenes). Fruit plants are most often perennial and usually woody (exceptions include strawberry and banana, which are not truly woody). Fruit plants with fruits borne on trees are termed tree fruits, fruits borne on low-growing plants are called small fruits, and those on vines are called vine fruits. Nuts are a special subcategory of fruits characterized by having a hard shell separating the inner kernel of the seed. There is no precise distinction that can be made between the terms "fruit" and "vegetable." In the case of tomato, confusion can be avoided by referring to it as a "vegetable fruit." In 1893 the U.S. Supreme Court ruled that the tomato was legally a vegetable in a decision resolving a dispute concerning import duties, making an important legal point that the meanings of terms used in laws and statutes refer to common everyday meanings, not necessarily the scientific meanings.

See also **Fruit: Temperate Fruit; Horticulture; Naming of Food; Nuts.**

Jules Janick

needed. Other concentrate is pumped into aseptic bags, which exclude outside air. Framed in collapsible wooden boxes, the bags are placed on trucks and shipped to factories for conversion into tomato products.

Ketchup Production

Another major use of tomatoes in the United States is in the production of ketchup. Initially, ketchup production began as an attempt to use leftovers from the canning

process. These scraps were placed in barrels during the high canning season in September and October and were saved for later conversion into ketchup. As tomato ketchup became more popular, factories emerged that specialized solely in its production. Because the bright red color of the ketchup was an important selling point, ketchup was placed in bottles so that the consumer could see its color. Long narrow-nosed bottles with small holes were employed to reduce contact with air, which oxidized ketchup and turned it a deep dark color. Early ketchup bottlers had great difficulty preventing the introduction of air through the cap. In the early part of the twentieth century researchers developed improved glass bottles that would not shatter during the manufacturing process. Corks were covered with a metal cap that effectively sealed the bottle from contact with outside air. As capping technology improved, screw caps replaced corks.

Early ketchups were thin and were easy to pour out of the small hole at the top of the bottles. After the passage of the Pure Food and Drug Act in 1906, thick ketchup became the norm in order to meet the new federal standards. Thick ketchups were difficult to pour through the narrow spout, but consumers were already familiar with the narrow nosed bottle and commercial manufacturers had invested time, effort, and funds in creating an image for their bottle.

Packaging changes since the 1970s have greatly increased ketchup usage. The H. J. Heinz Company, the largest ketchup producer in the world, introduced the Vol-Pak, a plastic bag filled aseptically with ketchup. Designed for foodservice operators, restaurants placed the bag on a rack and refilled plastic bottles. The Vol-Pak soon replaced cans. During the 1980s, two additional packaging revolutions occurred: the single-serve ketchup pouch, for which production increased from half a million cases to five million cases in just ten years; and the squeezable plastic ketchup bottle, which was easier to use, and almost unbreakable. By the 1990s, sixty percent of all U.S. ketchup was sold in plastic containers.

Preparation and Consumption

Tomatoes were employed by pre-Columbian Aztecs and other indigenous peoples of Central America for making sauces, particularly in combination with chili peppers and ground squash seeds. After the Spanish conquest, vinegar was added to the tomato and chili peppers to produce salsa. Numerous other uses for the tomato were developed in Mexico and Central America. In Europe, the first tomato recipe appeared in an 1544 Italian herbal, which recommended that tomatoes should be fried in olive oil and seasoned with salt and pepper. Variations of this recipe were published regularly in Europe and later in the Americas. Within a hundred years, tomatoes were well established in southern Italian cookery. The first tomato recipe appeared in a British cookbook in the late eighteenth century. The first known American tomato recipe appeared in Harriott Pinckney Horry's cookery manuscript, dated 1770.

Tomato recipes regularly appeared in American cookbooks by 1792. Early recipes fell into several major categories; the most important was tomato sauce, which originated in Italy and Spain and had migrated to southern France before 1800. Tomato sauce was used on beef, veal, fowl, chicken, rabbit, sweetmeats, pork, macaroni, fish, shrimp, and pigeon. Tomatoes were used to make marmalades, soups, gumbos, gazpacho, ketchups, sweetbreads, jumbles, dumplings, puddings, jelly, figs, omelets, and many other dishes. Tomatoes were stewed, baked, fried, stuffed, hashed, pickled, broiled, scalloped, forced, pickled, and preserved. Green tomatoes were consumed from the beginning, and sometimes were used for seasoning and gravy. Tomatoes were combined with many other vegetables to be consumed as side dishes, including okra and potatoes. Tomatoes were served raw at all meals. Raw tomatoes were seasoned with sugar, molasses, vinegar, salt, pepper, mustard, or milk. The most common way to eat raw tomatoes was sliced and seasoned, like cucumbers, with vinegar, salt, and pepper. Others plucked them from the vine and ate them like ripe fruit, without seasoning.

American restaurants were opened toward the end of the eighteenth century, mostly by French refugees. Their clientele consisted of businessmen and an increasingly affluent upper class. Tomatoes were served in these restaurants at least by the 1820s and probably much earlier. From their inception, restaurants offered a variety of tomato dishes. Tomatoes were noted on hotel menus by 1825. By the 1840s the diversity of tomato dishes dramatically increased.

Tomatoes were also employed to make beverages. The earliest beverages were alcoholic: beer, whisky, champagne, and wine, none of which were particularly successful. The drinking of tomato juice was a mid-twentieth-century phenomenon. According to several accounts, tomato juice was the creation of the American-born French Chef Louis Perrin, who in 1917 served tomato juice to his guests at a resort in French Lick Springs, Indiana. However, none of the early products yielded juice with just the right color and flavor. The reason for the failure of canned tomato juice was that tomato solids settled at the bottom of the can or in the glass when poured out. In 1928, this problem was solved by Ralph Kemp of Frankfort, Indiana, who used a viscolizer previously employed in the manufacture of ice cream. Tomato juice was an instant hit with the American public. Heinz and the Campbell Soup Company moved into high gear to produce tomato juice. One reason that tomato juice was so successful was the end of prohibition. A cocktail made of tomato juice and vodka was probably first developed at Harry's Bar in Paris by Ferdinand "Pete" Petiot, who moved to New York in 1933 and introduced his new creation. After experimentation, he added Worcestershire sauce and called it a Bloody Mary.

Another tomato product was V8 vegetable juice, a blend of eight vegetables along with several flavor-

The "Quarter Century Tomato" introduced in 1901 by Philadelphia seedsman William Henry Maule. During the fifty-year period from about 1875 to 1925, American seed companies vied with each other to develop newer and better tomatoes every year, owing to the popularity of tomatoes among home gardeners. Cover graphics from the Maule 1901 seed catalog. © CYNTHIA HART DESIGNER/CORBIS.

enhancers. It had been conceived in 1933 by W. G. Peacock of Evanston, Illinois. Several people worked on the formula. Peacock interested three investors, and the New England Products Company was created. The product was first created in 1936 under the name "Veg-min" juice. At the first store that sold it, a clerk suggested that they change its name to "V-8," which Peacock did. Later the hyphen was removed and the product was marketed as V8 Cocktail Vegetable Juices. Peacock's entire operation was accomplished by hand, and he only had the ability to produce twenty-five cases per day. V8 juice was a success, but he did not have sufficient manufacturing capability to meet the demand. Peacock sold the V8 formula, and in 1948 the product ended up at the Campbell Soup Company, which is the largest tomato user in the world.

Relation to Human Biology

While there are many reasons for identifying the tomato as a healthy vegetable, the specific attributes that have generated the latest interest are the carotenoids, a family

LOVE APPLES

I gather love-apples very ripe, when they have acquired their beautiful colour. Having washed and drained them, I cut them into pieces, and dissolve them over the fire in a copper vessel well tinned. When they are well dissolved and reduced one third in compass, I strain them through a sieve sufficiently fine to hold the kernels. When the whole has passed through, I replace the decoction on the fire, and I condense it till there remains only one third of the first quantity. Then I let them become cool in stone pans, and put them in bottles, &c. in order to give them one, good boiling only, in the water-bath.

SOURCE: Nicholas Appert, *The Art of Preservation.* New York: D. Longworth, 1812. pp. 53–54.

of pigments found in yellow, orange, and red vegetables and in green leafy vegetables. There are over six hundred carotenoids, but the predominant one in tomatoes is lycopene, a pigment that gives tomatoes their red color. The human body cannot manufacture Lycopene or other carotenoids. Some studies have offered evidence that foods rich in antioxidants and carotenoids may play a role in preventing certain types of cancer. Dr. Edward Giovannucci, an assistant professor in the Department of Nutrition at Harvard School of Public Health and the Department of Medicine at the Harvard Medical School, examined responses of fifty thousand participants in the Harvard University Professionals Health Study that began in 1986. He concluded that the consumption of four vegetables and fruits were associated with lower prostate cancer risk: three of the foods he cited were tomato sauce, tomatoes, and pizza. Lycopene is present in each of these. The risk of prostate cancer was one third lower in men who ate tomato-based products. In another study in northern Italy, a high correlation was drawn between tomato consumption and the lack of cancers of the digestive track. Of the 2,700 respondents, those who consumed seven or more servings of raw tomatoes every week had 60 percent less chance of developing cancer of the colon, rectum, and stomach.

Diets with abundant tomatoes cooked in oil were more readily absorbed than other forms of tomato. Pizzas and raw tomatoes were also protective against prostate cancer, but tomato juice was not. Giovannucci believed that cooking broke down the tomatoes' cell walls, releasing more lycopene, and that the oil enhanced absorption of the fat-soluble carotenoid. In the case of raw tomatoes, salad oil may have contributed in a similar manner.

Symbolism

The tomato has become deeply entwined with popular culture throughout the world. In Japan a bank is named for it. In America tomato is slang for an attractive woman. Perhaps the most universal activity has been tomato throwing, a tradition that dates from the mid-nineteenth century. This tradition started in rural areas and moved to theaters to express lack of appreciation. Recently politicians have been the favorite target of tomato throwers. During the late 1940s, tomato throwing became an organized event in Bunyol, a town 25 miles west of the Mediterranean city of Valencia, Spain. The Tomatina festival, held on the last Wednesday in August, has been officially sponsored by the city since 1979. More than 30,000 people pelt each other and the city with tomatoes for a hour.

Other tomato festivals are held in other countries, including the United States. The Reynoldsburg Tomato Festival in Ohio attracts 35,000 residents who engage in tomato contests and consume tomato cookery. The Kendall-Jackson Heirloom Tomato Festival, held just north of Santa Rosa, California, featured tastings from more than 100 heirloom tomato varieties.

Contemporary Issues

Beginning in the 1950s, botanists induced genetic mutations with X rays and chemicals. These mutants were mainly of interest to researchers. The research, however, encouraged further investigations into the chromosomal structure of the tomato, making more sophisticated alterations possible. During the late twentieth and early twenty-first centuries, this research began to be productive. In a project funded by Campbell's Soup Company, Calgene, Inc., in Davis, California, genetically engineered the first tomato, called MacGregor's, which was slow-ripening and transportable over great distances.

Calgene had conducted research concluding that the rapid softening of ripe tomatoes was caused by an enzyme called Polygalacturonase, or PG. Calgene spliced into the tomato's genes an extra one to cancel out the effect of the PG enzyme, and thus created the Flavr Savr. Thus, the tomato remained firmer in its last week and could be left on the vine to ripen for extra days. After a week or so of extra firmness, the Calgene tomato softens and decays like other tomatoes. The company voluntarily presented their genetically altered tomato to the U.S. Food and Drug Administration (FDA) for approval. The genetically engineered tomato was approved by the FDA's Food Advisory Committee. Since 1994, genetically altered tomatoes have been sold in grocery stores. Other genetically engineered tomatoes are under development. Other companies with strong biotech programs include DNA Plant Technology, Petroseed, Monsanto, Pioneer, and Dupont.

Many critics have strongly opposed genetic engineering of the tomato as presenting an unacceptable risk for humans. Some grocery stores have refused to sell genetically engineered tomatoes, while others have agreed to identify them as genetically engineered. Restaurants have announced that they will boycott the new "mutant" tomatoes. A major concern is that there is no requirement that the genetically altered foods be labeled as such. Many critics believe they have the right to know which products have been altered and which are natural.

See also **Fruit; Genetic Engineering; Packaging and Canning, History of; Potato; Vegetables**.

BIBLIOGRAPHY

Collins, Douglas. *America's Favorite Food: The Story of Campbell Soup Company.* New York: Harry N. Abrams, 1994. The history of Campbell Soup Company, the largest tomato user in the world, and the largest producer of tomato soup.

Gould, Wilbur. *Tomato Production, Processing and Technology.* 3d ed. Baltimore, Md.: CTI Publications, 1992.

Livingston, Alexander. *Livingston and the Tomato.* Reprint. Columbus: Ohio State University Press, 1998.

Nevins, Donald J., and Richard A. Jones, eds. *Tomato Biotechnology.* New York: Alan R. Liss, 1987.

Rick, Charles, "Genetic Resources in Lycopersicon," in Donald J. Nevins and Richard A. Jones, *Tomato Biotechnology.* New York: Alan R. Liss, 1987.

Smith, Andrew F. *Pure Ketchup: The History of America's National Condiment.* Columbia: The University of South Carolina Press, 1996.

Smith, Andrew F. *Souper Tomatoes: The Story of America's Favorite Food.* New Brunswick, N.J.: Rutgers University Press, 2000.

Smith, Andrew F. *The Tomato in America: Early History, Culture, and Cookery.* Columbia: University of South Carolina Press, 1994.

Tracy, Will W. *The Tomato Culture.* New York: Orange Judd Co., 1907.

Andrew F. Smith

TOOTH DECAY. *See* **Dentistry; Fluoride.**

TORTILLA. *See* **Maize.**

TOURISM. Food has always been a component of tourism. As a physical necessity and as a prominent arena for expressing creativity and for embodying cultural and individual identity, food has functioned as destination, venue, and vehicle for tourism. As destination, food is the primary experience sought. The preparation, consumption, and even the viewing of a foreign dish gives the tourist a sense of otherness and the exotic. As vehicle, food offers an entry point for viewing another culture. The sensory attributes of food enable consumers to feel a deeper level of experiencing; by ingesting food representing another culture, they can feel that they ingest that

culture. As venue, food offers a site from which a culture can be explored. These aspects can be commercial or domestic, public or private, festive or ordinary. Restaurants, festivals, cookbooks, grocery stores, private festive food events, cooking classes, cooking shows, advertising, literature, films, tourism brochures, food tours, and other such sites are physical loci for experiencing tourism. They also offer a tangible, knowable base from which other facets of culture—history, religion, artistic traditions, customs—can be understood and experienced.

Tourism is generally thought of as an activity in which individuals explore a culture that is foreign to them. Valene Smith defines a tourist as "a temporarily leisured person who voluntarily visits a place away from home for the purpose of experiencing a change" (*Hosts and Guests*, p. 1). The theme of tourism as spiritual and emotional quest appears frequently in scholarly works. Dean MacCannell sees tourism as a modern phenomenon in which tourists are on a quest to recover lost authenticity: it offers a way for modern man to explore the "real life" of others (*A New Theory of the Leisure Class*, p. 91). Mark Neumann suggests that "tourism is a metaphor for our struggle to make sense of our self and world within a highly differentiated culture" ("Wandering Through the Museum: Experience and Identity in a Spectator Culture," p. 22). Most scholars of tourism now see tourism both as a state of mind in which anything, including the everyday and the local, can be subjected to the "tourist gaze"—to borrow John Urry's book title—and as a continuum of types of experiences involving otherness. Erik Cohen offers a typology of tourists based on their concept and concern with authenticity: existential, experimental, experiential, recreational, and diversionary tourists ("Authenticity and Commoditization in Tourism"). Valene Smith, in *Going Places*, outlines a typology of tourists based on aspects of culture being explored and on the motivations of the tourist: ethnic, cultural, historical, environmental, recreational. Maxine Feifer adds the "post-tourist" who sees tourism as a game and inherently inauthentic in its experiencing of another culture.

Culinary tourism is a theoretical framework for analyzing the role of food in tourism. It refers to the "intentional, exploratory participation in the foodways of an Other." It is voluntary and consciously contains an element of curiosity—that is, people eating out of choice, not only physical need.

The term "foodways" involves all the other aspects of food, referring to the network of activities and systems—physical, social, communicative, cultural, economic, spiritual, and aesthetic—surrounding the product itself: procurement, preparation, preservation, presentation, consumption, clean-up, and conceptualization. In this sense, culinary tourism can occur in any aspect of foodways, from purchasing familiar ingredients from a new grocery store to adding exotic ingredients to a familiar recipe. It can also include behaviors connected to thinking and talking about food: collecting recipes, watching televised cooking shows or films incorporating food, conversing about restaurants, reading cookbooks and food columns, reminiscing about food experiences.

The culinary Other is simply anything different from the known and familiar. It can be broken into six overlapping categories. National or cultural identity is the most commonly perceived category and includes "ethnic" foods as well as "foreign" foods. Foods become a cultural Other by being placed in a context in which they are different. Thus, kimchi is standard fare in Korea, but is ethnic and foreign in the United States.

Region is the second category of Other and refers to groupings within a culture, differentiated by geographic location and physical resources. Within the United States, regional foods from areas such as the South (grits, fried chicken, hominy, corn bread), New England (baked beans, lobster, boiled suppers), the Southwest (chili peppers, Mexican-based foods), the Mid-Atlantic states (crab and seafood), and even the Midwest (meatloaf, mashed potatoes); and from specific cities, such as New Orleans (gumbo, jambalaya), Kansas City and Memphis (barbecue), and San Francisco (nouvelle cuisine) are advertised as culinary Others appropriate for tourism.

Time as Other refers to both past and future. Foods from the past are commonly found in museums, reenactment events, and cookbooks, and are used as a way of touring a historical era. Similarly, visions of the future can be translated into foodways—astronaut foods, freeze-dried ice cream, foods compressed into pills and vitamins. Ethos and religion as Other offer foods representing different or novel worldviews and value systems. Religions specifying food taboos or guidelines, such as Judaism, Islam, and Hinduism, can be explored as tourism by experiencing their foodways. Vegetarian foods—textured protein, veggie burgers, and foods commonly used in the United States as meat substitutes, such as bean curd and tempeh—are frequently tried out of curiosity rather than ethical belief.

Socioeconomic class is another category of Other. Gourmet foods, fine wine, and expensive restaurants are associated with the upper class, and individuals can get a taste of that lifestyle through these foodways. Conversely, foods associated with lower classes—white bread and bologna sandwiches, junk foods, processed "cheese food," opossum meat or roadkill, meager portions—can be tried in order "to see how the other half lives."

Gender represents the final Other. Although strict taboos do not exist in the United States, there are certain foods associated with each gender: women eat salads, "light" foods, poultry and fish, dainty portions; men eat red meat, large portions, hearty foods. By trying the foods associated with another gender, an individual can try out that identity.

Culinary tourism involves three realms or continua of experience: the exotic, the edible, and the palatable.

Based on the perceptions of consumers, the exotic ranges from those food experiences that are familiar and commonplace to those that are strange, new, and different. The edible-to-inedible continuum represents concepts of which items are physically, conceptually, and morally possible for ingestion. These concepts are culturally constructed but also draw upon the consumer's personal ethos. Palatable refers to pleasant and satisfying tastes, and represents individual preferences as well as social trends identifying desirable foods and designating their symbolic associations. Since the placement of foods and food experiences within these continua is a matter of perception and experience, this placement can shift over time or place and between individuals. Foods, therefore, that are perceived as appropriate for culinary tourism can become mundane and familiar, and then may be eaten out of hunger or taste preference rather than curiosity. For example, in the United States, foods that were recently touristic but have become standard fare in many American diets include Japanese sushi; Thai noodles with peanut sauce; Chinese chop suey, chow mein, and egg rolls; Mexican tacos and burritos; and Middle Eastern pita. These and other foods range in the extent of their adaptation to American tastes and resources. As these foods become more familiar, those eaters seeking more touristic experiences tend to seek more authenticity and depth of understanding of a foreign cuisine.

Food will be a part of tourism as long as people are curious about the world around them, but both are multivocal and multivalent domains of activity. And it is important to remember that although foodways can offer an entry into another realm of Other, culinary tourism is frequently not as much a window into other cultures as a mirror on our own.

See also **Comfort Food; Gender and Food; Travel; United States: Ethnic Cuisines.**

BIBLIOGRAPHY

Cohen, Erik. "A Phenomenology of Tourist Experiences." *Sociology* 13 (1979): 179–201.

Cohen, Erik. "Authenticity and Commoditization in Tourism." *Annals of Tourism Research* 15 (1988): 371–386.

Feifer, Maxine. *Going Places.* London: Macmillan, 1985.

Long, Lucy M. "Culinary Tourism: A Folkloristic Perspective on Eating and Otherness." Special Issue of *Southern Folklore* 55/3 (1998):181–204.

Long, Lucy M., ed. *Culinary Tourism: Eating and Otherness.* Special Issue of *Southern Folklore* 55/3 (1998).

MacCannell, Dean. *The Tourist: A New Theory of the Leisure Class.* Berkeley and Los Angeles: University of California Press, 1973.

Mintz, Sidney. *Tasting Food, Tasting Freedom: Excursions into Eating, Culture and the Past.* Boston: Beacon, 1996.

Neumann, Mark. "Wandering Through the Museum: Experience and Identity in a Spectator Culture." *Border/Lines* (Summer 1988):19–27.

Smith, Valene. *Hosts and Guests*. Philadelphia: University of Pennsylvania Press, 1989.

Urry, John. *The Tourist Gaze*. London: Sage, 1990.

Lucy M. Long

TOXINS, UNNATURAL, AND FOOD SAFETY.

Toxins may be released into the environment through industrial processes and agricultural products. These toxins are unnatural and may become harmful when they enter the food chain through crop and animal uptake.

Many agricultural products are known to contain heavy metals and other contaminants. In fact many, such as fertilizers, pesticides, fumigants, sludge, liming agents, animal feed supplements, and soil amendments, are known or are suspected to be derived from industrial waste. Waste disposed in this manner includes but is not limited to that generated by leather tanneries, steel mills, coal-fired power plants, mines, film processors, nuclear fuel processors, pulp and paper, tire incinerators, and petroleum refineries.

Little regulation and even less oversight is devoted to this method of disposal. If the waste contains just one of the macronutrients or micronutrients or if it possesses a soil-amending quality, industry can call it a product. Theoretically, anything can go into fertilizer. It is frequently contaminated with arsenic, mercury, cadmium, lead, dioxin, radionuclides, nickel, beryllium, and more. The only requirement for these wastes is that they meet the standard for disposal in a lined hazardous waste landfill. In other words, they are too toxic for standard disposal, but because of a loophole in the law, they are not too toxic for disposal on farmland. Even mined fertilizers, such as phosphate rock, may contain high levels of toxic metals.

Fertilizers, soil amendments, and liming materials are of particular concern since they are applied to agricultural soils in high volume. Over 110 billion pounds of fertilizer are land-applied each year in the United States, approximately 90 percent of it on farmland. The Environmental Protection Agency, whose charge it is to regulate hazardous waste disposal, admits that it does not know how much hazardous waste is disposed as fertilizer or the fate of these chemicals in the environment.

It is the fate of these chemicals that is cause for greatest concern. Increased soil concentrations, differing soil types, and pH levels can affect plant uptake of contaminants. Sandy soils and low pH, for example, increase plant uptake, while clay soils and high pH reduce it. Many of these contaminants have half-lives of hundreds of years and can change form in the environment as new chemicals are added. These new compounds may differ from the originals in toxicity, solubility, and plant availability.

In addition to crop uptake, these contaminants may also pollute waterways and become available for uptake

A TOXICITY GLOSSARY

Arsenic—Known carcinogen. Highest concentrations are in seafood, rice and rice cereal, mushrooms, and poultry. Root crops, such as carrots, onions, and potatoes, are the most vulnerable.

Cadmium—Low levels are found in all foods. Largest dietary contributors are grains and cereal products. Highest levels are found in leafy vegetables, potatoes, and other root crops. Long-term exposure to low levels may cause kidney disease, cancer, lung damage, and fragile bones.

Dioxin—Endocrine disruptor. Causes birth defects, developmental problems, and cancer.

Lead—Neurotoxin. Lowers IQ and damages the immune system. Fruits, grains, cereal products, and legumes contain the highest concentrations. Fetuses and pregnant women are most at risk.

Mercury—Possible carcinogen. May cause brain, kidney, or fetal damage. Highest concentration is in fish. Grains and meat account for half of the dietary intake.

Macronutrients—Examples include nitrogen, phosphorous, potassium, sulfur, calcium, magnesium.

Micronutrients—Examples include boron, molybdenum, copper, manganese, zinc, selenium, iron chloride.

by other plant and animal species. Forty percent of waterway pollution is attributed to runoff. Additionally, some of these wastes, such as zinc from steel mill flue dust, are used as animal feed supplements. Animals ingest thirteen toxic metals, which concentrate in organ meats, such as liver and kidney, and dioxin, which is stored in fat.

These toxins find their way into the food supply, as documented by the Food and Drug Administration (FDA) Total Diet Study. Since 1961 the Total Diet Study has monitored the U.S. food supply for industrial contaminants, toxic elements, radionuclides, essential minerals, and pesticides. The study has found that, on a body-weight basis, infants and toddlers consume on average two to three times as much cadmium, arsenic, and mercury and three to four times as much lead as do teens and adults.

Infants, toddlers, and developing fetuses are the most vulnerable populations. Many toxins pass from the mother to the fetus, potentially altering the developing brain, nervous system, and orderly development of the body.

See also **Agronomy; Crop Improvement; Ecology and Food; Food Safety; Government Agencies; Government Agencies, U.S.; Health and Disease; High-Technology Farming; Inspection; International Agencies; Water: Safety of Water.**

BIBLIOGRAPHY

Agency for Toxic Substances and Disease Registry (ATSDR). "Toxicological Profiles for Heavy Metals." Available at http://www.atsdr.cdc.gov/toxpro2.html.

Gunderson, Ellis L. "FDA Total Diet Study." *Journal of AOAC International* 71, no. 6 (1988): 1204–1207; 78, no. 6 (1995): 1353–1363.

Raven, K. P., and R. H. Loeppert. "Trace Element Composition of Fertilizers and Soil Amendments." *Journal of Environmental Quality* 26 (1997): 551–557.

U.S. Environmental Protection Agency. *Background Report on Fertilizer Use, Contaminants, and Regulation.* Washington, D.C.: National Program Chemicals Division, Office of Pollution Prevention and Toxics, U.S. Environmental Protection Agency, 1999.

Wilson, Duff. *Fateful Harvest: The True Story of a Small Town, a Global Industry, and a Toxic Secret.* 1st ed. New York: HarperCollins, 2001.

Patricia Martin

TRACE ELEMENTS. Early in the twentieth century, scientists were able to qualitatively detect small amounts of several elements in living organisms. At the time, these elements were often described as being present in "traces" or "trace amounts." This apparently led to the term "trace elements," which today is usually defined as mineral elements that occur in living systems in micrograms per gram of body weight or less. A majority of elements of the periodic table probably could be considered trace elements. However, the presence of most of these elements in higher animals quite likely is just a manifestation of our geochemical origin or the result of environmental exposure. Only eight trace elements are generally accepted as being essential for health and well-being in higher animals through the consumption of food and beverages; these are cobalt, copper, iodine, iron, manganese, molybdenum, selenium, and zinc. Persuasive evidence has recently appeared that indicates two other trace elements, boron and chromium, may also be essential; however, general acceptance of their essentiality is still lacking. Based on findings with experimental animals and lower life forms, numerous other trace elements have been suggested as being essential for higher animals including aluminum, arsenic, fluorine, lithium, nickel, silicon, and vanadium. However, conclusive evidence for essentiality, such as a defined biochemical function, is lacking for these elements. Thus, their nutritional importance remains to be determined. Of the elements mentioned, assuring the consumption of foods providing adequate amounts of iodine, iron, and zinc is of greatest practical concern for human health. Evidence is emerging, however, suggesting that the amount of cobalt (as vitamin B_{12}), copper, selenium, boron, and chromium provided through foods should be considered a practical nutritional concern in assuring or promoting health and well-being. These eight elements will be emphasized in this review.

Physiological Roles of Trace Elements
Trace elements have several roles in living organisms. Some are essential components of enzymes where they attract substrate molecules and facilitate their conversion to specific end products. Some donate or accept electrons in reactions of reduction and oxidation, which results in the generation and utilization of metabolic energy. One trace element, iron, is involved in the binding, transporting, and releasing of oxygen in higher animals. Some trace elements impart structural stability to important biological molecules. Finally, some trace elements control important biological processes through such actions as facilitating the binding of molecules to receptor sites on cell membranes, altering the structure or ionic nature of membranes to prevent or allow specific molecules to enter or leave a cell, and inducing gene expression resulting in the formation of proteins involved in life processes.

Homeostatic Regulation of Trace Elements
The ability of the body to maintain the content of a specific substance such as a trace element within a certain range despite varying intakes is called homeostasis. Homeostasis involves the processes of absorption, storage, and excretion. The relative importance of these three processes varies among the trace elements. The homeostatic regulation of trace elements existing as positively charged cations (for example, copper, iron, zinc) occurs primarily during absorption from the gastrointestinal tract. Trace elements absorbed as negatively charged anions (for example, boron, selenium) are usually absorbed freely and completely from the gastrointestinal tract. Thus, they are homeostatically regulated primarily by excretion through the urine, bile, sweat, and breath. Storage of trace elements in inactive sites or forms is another mechanism that prevents inappropriate amounts of reactive trace elements to be present, for example, storage of iron in the form of ferritin. Release of a trace element from a storage site also can be important in preventing deficiency.

Iodine
This trace element has one known function in higher animals and humans; it is a constituent of thyroid hormone (thyroxine, T_4) that, after conversion to triiodothyronine (T_3), functions as a regulator of growth and development by reacting with cell receptors, which results in energy (adenosine triphosphate, ATP) production and the activation or inhibition of synthesis of specific proteins.

Recognition that iodine was nutritionally important began in the 1920s when it was found that iodine pre-

410

vented goiter, and increased iodine intake was associated with decreased endemic cretinism, the arrested physical and mental development caused by the lack of thyroid hormone. Today, the consequences of iodine deficiency still are a major public health problem in the world. In fact, iodine deficiency is the most prevalent global cause of preventable mental retardation. Briefly, the spectrum of iodine deficiency disorders is large and includes fetal congenital anomalies and perinatal mortality; neurological cretinism characterized by mental deficiency, deaf mutism, spastic diplegia (spastic stiffness of the limbs), and squint; psychomotor defects; goiter; and slowing of the metabolic rate causing fatigue, slowing of bodily and mental functions, weight increase, and cold intolerance.

Although homeostatic mechanisms allow for a substantial tolerance to high intakes of iodine, iodine-induced hyperthyroidism has been recognized for nearly two centuries. People who have had a marked iodine deficiency and are then given high amounts of iodine as part of a preventative program are at risk of getting hyperthyroidism with clinical signs including weight loss, tachycardia, muscle weakness, and skin warmth.

Iodide, an anion, is rapidly and almost completely absorbed from the stomach and upper gastrointestinal (GI) tract. Most other forms of iodine are changed in the GI tract to iodide and completely absorbed. When thyroid hormone is ingested, about 80 percent is absorbed without change; the rest is excreted in the feces. Absorbed iodide circulates in the free form; it does not bind to proteins in blood. Iodide is rapidly removed from circulation by the thyroid and kidney. Urinary excretion is a major homeostatic mechanism. If iodine intake has been adequate, only about 10 percent of absorbed iodide appears in the thyroid, the rest appears in the urine. However, if iodine status is inadequate, a much higher percentage, up to 80 percent, can appear in the thyroid. The thyroid gland is essentially the only storage site for iodine, where it appears mostly as mono- and diiodotyrosine and T_4, with a small amount of T_3.

The recommended intakes of iodine for various age and sex groups are shown in Table 1, which shows that the recommended dietary allowance (RDA) for adults is 150 μg/day. Iodized salt has been the major method for assuring adequate iodine intake since the 1920s. Other sources of iodine are seafood and foods from plants grown on high-iodine soils.

Iron

This trace element is a component of molecules that transport oxygen in blood. Numerous enzymatic reactions involving oxidation and reduction (redox) use iron as the agent through which oxygen is added, hydrogen is removed, or electrons are transferred. The classes of enzymes dependent on iron for activity include the oxidoreductases, exemplified by xanthine oxidase/dehydrogenase; monooxygenases, exemplified by the amino acid oxidases and cytochrome P450; dioxygenases, exempli-

fied by amino acid dioxygenases, lipoxygenases, peroxidases, fatty acid desaturases, and nitric oxide synthases; and miscellaneous enzymes such as aconitase.

Among the trace elements, iron has the longest and best described history. By the seventeenth century, a recognized treatment for chlorosis, or iron deficiency anemia, was drinking wine containing iron filings. Despite the extensive knowledge about its treatment and prevention, and the institution of a variety of effective interventions, iron deficiency is the primary mineral deficiency in the United States and the world today. The physiological signs of iron deficiency include anemia, glossitis (smooth atrophy of tongue surface), angular stomatitis (fissures at the angles of the mouth), koilonychia (spoon nails), blue sclera, lethargy, apathy, listlessness, and fatigue. Pathological consequences of iron deficiency include impaired thermoregulation, immune function, mental function, and physical performance; complications in pregnancy, including increased risk of premature delivery, low birth weight, and infant mortality; and possibly increased risk of osteoporosis.

Concerns have been expressed about high intakes of iron being a health issue. This has come about through epidemiologic observations associating high dietary iron or high body iron stores with cancer and coronary heart disease. Further experimental studies, however, are required to confirm whether the high intakes of iron increase the risk for these diseases. The toxic potential of iron arises from its biological importance as a redox element that accepts and donates electrons to oxygen that can result in the formation of reactive oxygen species or radicals that can damage cellular components such as fatty acids, proteins, and nucleic acids. Antioxidants are enzymes or molecules that prevent the formation of oxygen radicals or convert them to nonradical products. When not properly controlled by antioxidants, reactive oxygen damage can lead to premature cell aging and death. An iron overload disease known as hereditary hemochromatosis is caused by a defective regulation of iron transport with excessive iron absorption and high transferrin (transport form) iron in plasma. Clinical signs appear when body iron accumulates to about 10 times normal and include cirrhosis, diabetes, heart failure, arthritis, and sexual dysfunction. Hemochromatosis also increases the risk for hepatic carcinoma. The treatment for hereditary hemochromatosis is repeated phlebotomy.

Absorption from the GI tract is the primary homeostatic mechanism for iron. Dietary iron exists generally in two forms, heme and non-heme, that are absorbed by different mechanisms. Heme iron is a protoporphyrin molecule containing an atom of iron; it comes primarily from hemoglobin and myoglobin in meat, poultry, and fish. Non-heme iron is primarily inorganic iron salts provided mainly by plant-based foods, dairy products, and iron-fortified foods. Heme iron is much better absorbed and less affected by enhancers and inhibitors of absorption than non-heme iron. Iron absorption is regulated by mucosal cells of the small intestine, but the exact mechanisms in the regulation have not been established. Both iron stores and blood hemoglobin status have a major influence on the amount of dietary iron that is absorbed. Under normal conditions, men absorb about 6 percent and menstruating women absorb about 13 percent of dietary iron. However, with severe iron deficiency anemia (functionally deficient blood low in hemoglobin), absorption of non-heme iron can be as high as 50 percent. Iron loss from the body is very low, about 0.6 mg/day. This loss is primarily by excretion in the bile and, along with iron in desquamated mucosal cells, eliminated via the feces. Menstruation is a significant means through which iron is lost for women. It should be noted, however, that nonphysiological loss of iron resulting from conditions such as parasitism, diarrhea, and enteritis account for half of iron deficiency anemia globally. Excess iron in the body is stored as ferritin and hemosiderin in the liver, reticuloendothelial cells, and bone marrow.

The recommended intakes of iron for various age and sex groups are shown in Table 1, which shows that the RDA for adult males and postmenopausal women is 8 mg/day; and that for menstruating adult women is 18 mg/day. Meat is the best source of iron, but iron-fortified foods (cereals and wheat-flour products) also are significant sources.

Zinc

This trace element is the only one that is found as an essential component in enzymes from all six enzyme classes. Over 50 zinc metalloenzymes have been identified. Zinc also functions as a component of transcription factors known as zinc fingers that bind to DNA and activate the transcription of a message, and imparts stability to cell membranes.

Signs of zinc deficiency in humans were first described in the 1960s. Although it is generally thought that zinc deficiency is a significant public health concern, the extent of the problem is unclear because there is no well-established method to accurately assess the zinc status of an individual. The physiological signs of zinc deficiency include depressed growth; anorexia (loss of appetite); parakeratotic skin lesions; diarrhea; and impaired testicular development, immune function, and cognitive function. Pathological consequences of zinc deficiency include dwarfism, delayed puberty, failure to thrive (acrodermatitis enteropathica infants), impaired wound healing, and increased susceptibility to infectious disease. It has also been suggested that low zinc status increases the susceptibility to osteoporosis and to pathological changes caused by the presence of excessive reactive oxygen species or free radicals.

Zinc is a relatively nontoxic element. Excessive intakes of zinc occur only with the inappropriate intake of supplements. The major undesirable effect is an interference with copper metabolism that could lead to copper deficiency. Long-term high zinc supplementation can reduce immune function and high-density lipoprotein (HDL)-cholesterol (the "good" cholesterol). These effects are seen only with zinc intakes of 100 mg/day or more.

A primary homeostatic mechanism for zinc is absorption from the small intestine. Absorption involves a carrier-mediated component and a nonmediated diffusion component. With normal dietary intakes, zinc is absorbed mainly by the carrier-mediated mechanism. Although absorption can be modified by a number of factors, about 30 percent of dietary zinc is absorbed. The efficiency of zinc absorption is increased with low zinc intakes. The small intestine has an additional role in zinc homeostasis through regulating excretion through pancreatic and intestinal secretions. After a meal, greater than 50 percent of the zinc in the intestinal lumen is from endogenous zinc secretion. Thus, zinc homeostasis depends upon the reabsorption of a significant portion of this endogenous zinc. Intestinal conservation of endogenous zinc apparently is a major mechanism for maintaining zinc status when dietary zinc is inadequate. The urinary loss of zinc is low and generally not markedly affected by zinc intake.

The recommended intakes of zinc for various age and sex groups are shown in Table 1, which shows that the RDA for adult males is 11 mg/day and for adult females is 8 mg/day. The best food sources for zinc are red meats, organ meats (for example, liver), shellfish, nuts, whole grains, and legumes. Many breakfast cereals are fortified with zinc.

Cobalt (Vitamin B$_{12}$)

Ionic cobalt is not an essential nutrient for humans. Cobalt is an integral component of vitamin B$_{12}$, which is an essential nutrient for nonruminant animals and humans. Vitamin B$_{12}$ is a cofactor for two enzymes, methionine synthase which methylates homocysteine to form methionine, and methylmalonyl coenzyme A (CoA) mutase which converts L-methylmalonyl CoA, formed by the oxidation of odd-chain fatty acids, to succinyl CoA.

In the nineteenth century, a megaloblastic anemia (functionally deficient blood containing primitive large red blood cells) was identified that was invariably fatal and thus called pernicious anemia. The first effective treatment for this disease was 1 pound of raw liver daily. In 1948, the anti–pernicious anemia factor (vitamin B$_{12}$) in liver was isolated and found to contain 4 percent cobalt. Vitamin B$_{12}$ deficiency most commonly arises when there is a defect in vitamin B$_{12}$ absorption caused by such factors as atrophic gastritis, *Helicobacter pylori* infection, and bacteria overgrowth resulting from achlorohydria and intestinal blind loops. Because vitamin B$_{12}$ only comes from foods of animal origin, absolute vegetarianism will lead to deficiency in vitamin B$_{12}$ after 5 to 10 years. The physiological signs of severe vitamin B$_{12}$ deficiency are megaloblastic anemia, spinal cord demyelination, and pe-

TABLE 1

Recommended Dietary Allowances for Selected Trace Elements Established by the Food and Nutrition Board, Institute of Medicine, National Academy of Sciences (see bibliography).

	Recommended Dietary Allowance					
	Copper (µg/day)	Iodine (µg/day)	Iron (mg/day)	Selenium (µg/day)	Vitamin B_{12} (cobalt) (µg/day)	Zinc (mg/day)
0–6 months	—	—	—	—	—	—
7–12 months	—	—	11	—	—	3
1–3 years	340	90	7	20	0.9	3
4–8 years	440	90	10	30	1.2	5
9–13 years	700	120	8	40	1.8	8
14–18 years	890	150	11 M/15 F	55	2.4	11 M/9 F
19–50 years	900	150	8 M/18 F	55	2.4	11 M/9 F
51 years and greater	900	150	8	55	2.4	11 M/8 F
Pregnancy						
18 years or less	1,000	220	27	60	2.6	13
19–50 years	1,000	220	27	60	2.6	11
Lactation						
18 years and less	1,300	290	10	70	2.8	14
19–50 years	1,300	290	9	70	2.8	12

Abbreviations: F, female; M, male.

ripheral neuropathy. The pathological consequences of deficiency include pernicious anemia, memory loss, dementia, an irreversible neurological disease called subacute degeneration of the spinal cord, and death. Recently, mild vitamin B_{12} deficiency has been cited as a cause of high circulating homocysteine, which has been associated with an increased risk for cardiovascular disease. Vitamin B_{12} is essentially nontoxic. Doses up to 10,000 times the minimal daily adult human requirement do not have adverse effects.

Vitamin B_{12} absorption is a relatively complex process. Digestion by the saliva and acid environment of the stomach releases vitamin B_{12} from food, then it is bound to a haptocorrin called R protein that carries it into the duodenum. A binding protein, called intrinsic factor, released by gastric parietal cells binds vitamin B_{12} after the stomach acid is neutralized in the duodenum, and digestive enzymes remove the R binder from the vitamin. The intrinsic factor–bound vitamin B_{12} is carried to a specific receptor in the ileum called cubilin and internalized by receptor-mediated endocytosis. Because vitamin B_{12} is water-soluble, excessive intakes are efficiently excreted in the urine.

The recommended intakes for vitamin B_{12} for various age and sex groups are shown in Table l, which shows that the RDA for adults is 2.4 µg/day. Food sources of vitamin B_{12} are of animal origin and include meats, dairy products, and eggs. Fortified cereals have also become a significant source of vitamin B_{12}.

Copper

Copper is a cofactor for a number of oxidase enzymes including lysyl oxidase, ferroxidase (ceruloplasmin), dopamine beta-monooxygenase, tyrosinase, alpha-amidating monooxygenase, cytochrome C oxidase, and superoxide dismutase. These enzymes are involved in the stabilization of matrixes of connective tissue, oxidation of ferrous iron, synthesis of neurotransmitters, bestowal of pigment to hair and skin, assurance of immune system competence, generation of oxidative energy, and protection from reactive oxygen species. Copper also regulates the expression of some genes.

Although copper is a well-established essential trace element, its practical nutritional importance is a subject of debate. Well-established pathological consequences of copper deprivation in humans have been described primarily for premature and malnourished infants and include a hypochromic, normocytic, or macrocytic anemia; bone abnormalities resembling scurvy by showing osteoporosis, fractures of the long bones and ribs, epiphyseal separation, and fraying and cupping of the metaphyses with spur formation; increased incidence of infections; and poor growth. The consequences of the genetic disorder Menkes' disease (copper deficiency caused by a cellular defect in copper transport) in children include "kinky-type" steely hair, progressive neurological disorder, and death. Other consequences have been suggested based upon findings from epidemiological studies, and animal and short-term human copper deprivation experiments;

these include impaired brain development and teratogenesis for the fetus and children, and osteoporosis, ischemic heart disease, cancer, increased susceptibility to infections, and accelerated aging for adults.

Copper toxicity is not a major health issue. The ingestion of fluids and foods contaminated with high amounts of copper can cause nausea. Because their biliary excretion pathway is immature, accumulation of toxic amounts of copper in the liver could be a risk for infants if intake is chronically high; this apparently caused cases of childhood liver cirrhosis in India.

Intestinal absorption is a primary homeostatic mechanism for copper. Copper enters epithelial cells of the small intestine by a facilitated process that involves specific copper transporters, or nonspecific divalent metal ion transporters located on the brush-border surface. Then the copper is transported to the portal circulation where it is taken up by the liver and resecreted in plasma bound to ceruloplasmin. Transport of copper from the liver into the bile is the primary route for excretion of endogenous copper. Copper of biliary origin and nonabsorbed dietary copper are eliminated from the body via the feces. Only an extremely small amount of copper is excreted in the urine. The absorption and retention of copper varies with dietary intake and status. For example, the percentages of ingested copper absorbed were 56 percent, 36 percent, and 12 percent with dietary intakes of 0.8, 1.7, and 7.5 mg/day, respectively. Moreover, tissue retention of copper is markedly increased when copper intake is low.

The recommended intakes for copper for various ages and sex groups are shown in Table 1, which shows that the RDA for adults is 900 μg/day. The best sources of copper are legumes, whole grains, nuts, organ meats (for example, liver), seafood (for example, oysters, crab), peanut butter, chocolate, mushrooms, and ready-to-eat cereals.

Selenium

Selenium is a component of enzymes that catalyze redox reactions; these enzymes include various forms of glutathione peroxidase, iodothyronine 5′-deiodinase, and thioredoxin reductase.

Although selenium was first suggested to be essential in 1957, this was not firmly established until a biochemical role was identified for selenium in 1972. The first report of human selenium deficiency appeared in 1979; the subject resided in a low-selenium area and was receiving total parenteral nutrition (TPN) after surgery. The subject and other selenium-deficient subjects on TPN exhibited bilateral muscular discomfort, muscle pain, wasting, and cardiomyopathy. Subsequently, it was discovered that Keshan disease, prevalent in certain parts of China, was prevented by selenium supplementation. Keshan disease is a multiple focal myocardial necrosis resulting in acute or chronic heart function insufficiency,

heart enlargement, arrhythmia, pulmonary edema, and death. Other consequences of inadequate selenium include impaired immune function and increased susceptibility to viral infections. Selenium deficiency also can make some nonvirulent viruses become virulent.

Recently, however, not only selenium deficiency, but effects of supranutritional intakes of selenium have become of great health interest. Several supplementation trials have indicated that selenium has anticarcinogenic properties. For example, one trial with 1,312 patients supplemented with either 200 μg selenium/day or with a placebo found the selenium treatment was statistically associated with reductions in several types of cancer including colorectal and prostate cancers.

Selenium is a relatively toxic element; Intakes averaging 1.2 mg/day can induce changes in nail structure. Chronic selenium intakes over 3.2 mg/day can result in the loss of hair and nails, mottling of the teeth, lesions in the skin and nervous system, nausea, weakness, and diarrhea.

Selenium, which is biologically important as an anion, is homeostatically regulated by excretion, primarily in the urine but some also is excreted in the breath. Selenate, selenite, and selenomethionine are all highly absorbed by the GI tract; absorption percentages for these forms of selenium are commonly found to be in the 80 to 90 percent range.

The recommended intakes for selenium are shown in Table 1, which shows that the RDA for adults is 55 μg/day. Food sources of selenium are fish, eggs, and meat from animals fed abundant amounts of selenium and grains grown on high-selenium soil.

Boron

Recent findings with this trace element suggest that it may be of nutritional importance, although a clearly defined biochemical function for boron in higher animals and humans has not been defined. It has been hypothesized, however, that boron has a role in cell membrane function that influences the response to hormones, transmembrane signaling, or transmembrane movement of regulatory cations or anions. Human studies suggest that a low boron intake can impair cognitive and psychomotor function and the inflammatory response, as well as increasing the susceptibility to osteoporosis and arthritis.

About 85 percent of ingested boron is absorbed and excreted in the urine shortly after ingestion. Because boron homeostasis is regulated efficiently by urinary excretion, it is a relatively nontoxic element. A tolerable upper level intake of 20 mg/day was determined for boron by the Food and Nutrition Board of the United States National Academy of Sciences.

An analysis of both human and animal data by a World Health Group suggested that an acceptable safe range of population mean intakes for boron for adults could be 1 to 13 mg/day. Foods of plant origin, especially fruits, leafy vegetables, nuts, pulses, and legumes are rich sources of boron.

Chromium

A naturally occurring biologically active form of chromium called chromodulin has been described that apparently has a role in carbohydrate and lipid metabolism as part of a novel insulin-amplification mechanism. Chromodulin is an oligopeptide that binds four chromic ions and facilitates insulin action in converting glucose into lipids and carbon dioxide.

The nutritional importance of chromium is currently a controversial subject. Chromium deficiency has been suggested to impair glucose tolerance, which could eventually lead to diabetes. Supranutritional chromium supplementation (1,000 μg/day) has been found beneficial for some cases of type II diabetes. Supplements containing supranutritional amounts of chromium in the picolinate form have been promoted as being able to induce weight loss and to increase muscle mass. However, most ergogenic (work output) oriented studies have found chromium picolinate supplementation to be ineffective for increasing muscle mass, strength, and athletic performance, and there are no data from well-designed studies to support the claim that chromium picolinate supplementation is an effective weight loss modality. Chromium in the +3 valence state is a relatively non-toxic element.

Chromium homeostasis is regulated by intestinal absorption, which is low. Estimates of absorption range from less than 0.5 to 2 percent. Absorbed chromium is excreted in the urine.

The Food and Nutrition Board of the United States Academy of Sciences determined that there was not sufficient evidence to set an estimated average requirement of chromium. Therefore, an adequate intake was set based on estimated mean intakes. The adequate intake for young males was set at 35 μg/day, and that for young females was set at 25 μg/day. Some of the best food sources of chromium are whole grains, pulses, some vegetables (for example, broccoli and mushrooms), liver, processed meats, ready-to-eat cereals, and spices.

Conclusion

It is likely that not all the essential mineral elements for humans have been identified. Moreover, numerous biochemical functions for trace elements most likely remain to be identified. Thus, the full extent of the pathological consequences of marginal or deficient intakes of the trace elements has not been established. Furthermore, some trace elements such as selenium, fluoride, and lithium in supranutritional amounts are being found to have therapeutic or preventative value against disease. Thus, the determination of the importance of trace elements for human health and well-being should be considered a

work in progress with some exciting advances likely in the future.

See also **Antioxidants; Bioactive Food Components; Dietary Assessment; Dietary Guidelines; Iodine; Iron; Microbiology; Minerals; Nutrient Bioavailability; Nutrition; Proteins and Amino Acids; Vitamins.**

BIBLIOGRAPHY

Bowman, Barbara A., and Robert M. Russell, eds. *Present Knowledge in Nutrition.* 8th ed. Washington, D.C.: ILSI Press, 2001.

Food and Nutrition Board, Institute of Medicine, National Academy of Sciences. *Dietary Reference Intakes for Thiamin, Riboflavin, Niacin, Vitamin B$_6$, Folate, Vitamin B$_{12}$, Pantothenic Acid, Biotin, and Choline.* Washington, D.C.: National Academy Press, 1998.

Food and Nutrition Board, Institute of Medicine, National Academy of Sciences. *Dietary Reference Intakes for Vitamin A, Vitamin K, Arsenic, Boron, Chromium, Copper, Iodine, Iron, Manganese, Molybdenum, Nickel, Silicon, Vanadium, and Zinc.* Washington, D.C.: National Academy Press, 2001.

Nielsen, Forrest H. "Trace Mineral Deficiencies." In *Handbook of Nutrition and Food,* edited by Carolyn D. Berdanier, pp. 1463–1487. Boca Raton, Fla.: CRC Press, 2002.

World Health Organization. *Trace Elements in Human Nutrition and Health.* Geneva: World Health Organization, 1996.

Forrest H. Nielsen

TRAVEL. During the course of history, the impact of travel on the relationship between food and man has been manifold. Encounters with new foods have often caused reactions of dissociation or of rejection—not only of the foods themselves, but also of the people eating them. The widespread idea that the food consumed by a group of people is closely connected with their level of civilization has been a way to express and underscore differences between neighboring populations. Food being an inoffensive category, it readily lends itself to becoming a means of distinguishing between "us and them," both geographically, in relation, for instance, to regions or countries, and socially, setting "us" apart from people within the same region we consider to be at a lower level in the social hierarchy.

Food habits are closely linked to a person's conception of identity. The acceptance of different foodstuffs, or their avoidance—taste or distaste—is a mixture of cultural conditioning and personal idiosyncrasies. It is natural, therefore, that the food consumed by one's own group is considered to be the "proper food," whereas the food of the others encountered during one's travels is accepted with some reluctance. Foods associated with a higher status are more easily adopted, as are those associated with lifestyles one wishes to share.

Obviously the reason for traveling will have some bearing on the attitude toward the food encountered.

American railroad fare is not much better today than in the nineteenth century. Travelers on the Chesapeake & Ohio line were obliged to buy their bad coffee, railroad cakes, hardtack, and Sally Lunns from vendors who congregated at stations along the way. FROM JOHN BACHELDER'S POPULAR RESORTS (BOSTON, 1875). ROUGHWOOD COLLECTION.

People who have been forcibly displaced (through war, disasters, slavery [but see below], economic hardships, or religious persecution) are more likely to maintain earlier food habits, where possible—partly through lack of means, partly from nostalgia for a lifestyle that has been lost. If, on the other hand, travel is undertaken on a voluntary basis, especially for pleasure (most notably tourism), people are more likely to try new foods.

Historically, little is known about travelers' food. It may be said that in general those who could took their food (and even people in charge of preparing it) with them, which meant that they tried to emulate their usual food habits. Others would make do with the local fare at wayside inns or the tables of hospitable notables. After the emergence of restaurants at the beginning of the nineteenth century in Europe, an internationalized bourgeois cuisine became available to travelers. Regional cooking did not start to come into focus for the general public until the period between the two World Wars, alongside the emergence of automobile tourism. And only recently has local and regional food become a focus of scientific as well as of touristic discourse. To better understand the role of food in travel one needs to distinguish different categories of travelers. Professional travelers of the past, such as sailors and military men, would in the main take their own food with them; however, at the same time, they were often adventurers and would typically experi-

ence extremely foreign foods, though they would only rarely bring these back with them.

In many instances on the other hand, food became the very reason for travel: explorers set out from Europe to reach the homelands of desirable foods, particularly spices. In a second phase, explorers were followed by tradesmen, civilian officials, and others establishing colonies on other continents. From these activities came sugar, tea, coffee, and many fruits, vegetables, and grains (for example, pineapples, potatoes, and rice), now everyday commodities in the Western world. Their history is intertwined with that of major empires. In some cases, myths have been constructed around them (for instance, the one claiming that Marco Polo brought pasta to Italy from China—belied by the fact that there was a flourishing commerce of pasta in the Mediterranean before the time of his travels). The rise and fall of food trends is clearly reflected in more general world history, as exemplified by the passion for spices in the Middle Ages and Renaissance leading to journeys of exploration, or the court culture of Italy and France, which, through traveling notables, influenced the food habits in many European countries from the sixteenth century onward.

For immigrants, the acquisition of new food habits is dependent on the time spent in the new environment (usually it is a matter of generations). As for any traveler, the reaction to the different food habits experienced will be related to the scope and duration of the travel. A special case is that of the American Pilgrims adopting the food of Native Americans, with the event evolving into a national commemorative meal: the Thanksgiving dinner. On the other hand, the slaves brought to America from Africa, who had no possibility of either maintaining their own food habits or having a free choice among those they met in the new country, have developed a very different symbolic food: soul food.

However, food habits may also be affected in the opposite direction. Colonies of foreign nationals have introduced new items in the diet of the new environment. Thus, for example, in the Middle Ages, gingerbread spread throughout Europe with German immigrants, and more recently Chinese food has become a familiar food in Western countries. Following the rise of charter tourism in the 1950s, pizza and pasta started to become a familiar food in many countries outside Italy, having in some places even replaced potatoes as an everyday staple food.

During the second half of the twentieth century, food began to play a significant role in tourism. In the meeting with the unfamiliar that takes place during travel, food plays a central role, since everybody has to eat every day, and so the deviation from what is habitual and accepted cannot be avoided or disregarded. Travel thus brings about an awareness of differences between the self (the learned and shared culture at home) and others (notably, their culture and habits), as it forces the individual to venture into the realm of sensory experiences that belong to the others. In parallel with the increased movement of people we see in recent times, the establishment of international restaurants and sale of foreign foodstuffs means one no longer needs to travel to experience foreign foods. This highlights some of the paradoxes of the international world today, where tourists may oscillate between the attraction of what represents "other" and adventure, and the unchallenging ease of familiarity and security. Tourists typically want to escape boredom, but to do so while staying within their comfort zone.

See also **Comfort Food; Herbs and Spices; Thanksgiving; Tourism; United States,** subentries on **African American Foodways** and **Ethnic Cuisines.**

Renée Valeri

TRUFFLES. *See* **France.**

TUBERS. Tuber is a loan word deriving from the Latin verb *tumere* (to swell). It was introduced into colloquial English via botanical Latin during the Renaissance and retains a number of related meanings: a swelling, a growth resembling a knot, or even a truffle. When applied to vegetables, tuber is now understood to mean a fleshy underground swelling on root strands that normally contains varying proportions of starch. In reality, this definition is quite imprecise given the huge diversity of tuberous-like roots and stems that exist in nature.

For example, taro (*Colocasia sp.*), is sometimes referred to as a tuber and sometimes as a corm since it straddles the definition of both. Other vegetables, like the arracacha (*Arracacha xanthorrhiza*) of South America, are often classified as "tuberous rooted" since the swollen part is not distinctly separate from the crown or herbaceous (above-ground) parts of the plant. The potato is considered a classic example of a common tuber, since the swollen part forms along various root strands and is only connected to the rest of the plant in this fashion. However, it is possible to induce this feature in any number of wild tuberous-rooted plants once domesticated and carefully selected.

Most true tubers are capable of reproducing themselves vegetatively and when reproduced in this manner, they become true genetic clones of their parents. This reproduction technique allows beneficial characteristics, such as flavor, texture, storing qualities, or resistance to certain pests and diseases to be preserved from one generation to the next. It would appear, however, that most tubers originally appealed to humans for their starch or sugars, especially tubers that could be consumed raw. Only later did cookery expand the list of choices, since many tubers like cassava are toxic until exposed to heat or some other processing step.

Nutrient rich and relatively easy to gather, tubers have played a major role in the history of human diet,

since they could be collected from the wild and stockpiled against times of food shortage. This dietary shift from happenstance to organized gathering, which required calculations regarding collection, storage, and distribution, brought about profound changes in human social organization and development, even more so after tubers were brought under cultivation.

Pre-agricultural societies relied heavily on foraged tubers, especially those that required little or no processing. Bog potatoes or groundnuts (*Apios tuberosa*) supplied the hunter-gatherers of eastern North America with an easy to collect source of small, starchy tubers that could be stored in pits for later use and eaten like nuts. Even for societies that later turned to intensive agriculture, such wild tubers remained an important supplement to the diet. However, many tuberous vegetables like the water parsley (*Oenanthe sarmentosa*) and wood sunflower (*Helianthus strumosus*) of North America, the bagana (*Amorphophallus abyssinicus*) of Ethiopia, and the kudzu (*Pueraria lobata*) of New Guinea, were never brought under cultivation by the native peoples of those areas, but simply gathered from the wild and traded, or allowed to grow in patches kept free of competing weeds. These managed plants were the preliminary steps toward gardening and primitive agriculture.

There is no precise record of when the first tubers were brought under cultivation on an organized basis, but in all likelihood the taros of India (if we allow that *Colocasia* and *Alocasia* are tubers) were among the first since they are mentioned in Sanskrit sources and terms for them are known in pre-Sanskrit languages. Doubtless they were followed or even preceded by potatoes in the high Andes, the yam bean (*Pachyrrhizus erosus*) in Central America, and the chufa (*Cyperus esculentus*) of the Mediterranean region. Vestiges of many tuberous plants have been found in caves, but this does not mean they were cultivated. Unless there are corroborating written records, or artifacts depicting tuberous vegetables, archeology cannot safely establish that a tuber was in fact cultivated since traces of pollen, preserved seeds, or actual dried tubers can originate from wild as well as cultivated sources. Furthermore, even where there are physical depictions of the plant, as in the case of chufa and coco grass (*Cyperus rotundus*) in ancient Egyptian paintings of pleasure gardens, this only proves that they were appreciated as ornamentals.

Yet, over time, many tuberous vegetables were indeed brought under cultivation in order to increase the supply and the reliability of the harvest. The highest percentage of indigenous cultivated tubers of different species is found in South America, where there is presently a concerted attempt to analyze and promote their uses. Elsewhere, many tubers gathered from the wild have fallen into neglect even where this nutritional diversity supplied a more balanced diet. Additionally, except for the Pacific islands, almost all of the lesser sorts of cultivated yam, such as the White Yam (*Dioscorea rotundata*), and the Buck Yam (*Dioscorea pentaphylla*), have decreased in production because of the introduction of commercially improved sweet potatoes. No tubers have done more than the potato and sweet potato (*Ipomoea batatas*) to alter human agriculture and diet, since both of these plants can be grown in a wide variety of soils and microclimates on a large commercial scale.

In the tropics, however, taros and yams (*Discorea sp.*) remain key food crops, followed by the New World cassava (*Manihot esculenta*) and to a limited extent malanga or yautia (*Xanthosoma sp.*). Consumption patterns vary from country to country and from one cultural group to the next, and practical growing considerations should not be overlooked. For example, in some areas, cassava and malanga have become important agricultural supplements since they will grow where taro will not and like sweet potatoes, they yield a ready supply of nutritionally rich greens. Since the 1500s, Old and New World tubers have moved out of their original habitats to such an extent that there is often a great deal of confusion as to where the plants came from. The inventory that follows deals with tubers based on their continent of origin, but with brief comments on how they have spread to other parts of the world, or how they are employed in local cuisines.

Africa (Sub-Sahara)

When we consider that yams, taros, sweet potatoes, and cassava are all exotics introduced from other continents, the range of indigenous tuberous vegetables available to Africans is extremely small. The African landscape is rich in leafy vegetables, but until the introduction of yams about 1000 C.E., there was no large tuberous vegetable serving as a staple on a continent-wide scale. Only here and there, locally occurring tubers provided limited food supplies for those willing to gather them. Most of Africa's indigenous tubers are small in size and few of them have ever been brought under cultivation. Furthermore, to date, there are no complete continent-wide inventories of native tuberous plants, a task made doubly difficult because of so many common synonyms that exist in the numerous languages of Africa, not to mention the political instability in several key countries.

While there has been a large amount of research devoted to African foodways and tribal cultures, little has been devoted to traditional gardening. The growing, gathering, and cooking of traditional plants is largely a woman's task in Africa, and in the past, this has been treated as an activity of low status. Fortunately, there is now a shift of interest in promoting the conservation and use of underutilized and neglected foods, particularly in Botswana, Ethiopia, Kenya, and Nigeria.

Many of the native tubers listed below are presently being inventoried for study and evaluation for possible breeding programs in conjunction with sustainable agriculture. However, very few of them are mentioned in cookbooks. Aside from these, *Arisaema schimperianum*, *Campanula edulis*, *Commelina benghalensis* and *latifolia*, *Cyperus esculentus*, *Dioscorea quartiniana*, and *Dioscorea schimperiana* all provide a source of indigenous tubers that are collected from the wild in several parts of Africa.

***African yam bean* (Sphenostylis stenocarpa).** This plant produces protein-rich seeds, edible leaves, and a large spindle-shaped tuber that can be cooked like a potato. The yam bean is mostly consumed by villagers in West Africa and even appears in cookbooks from that region.

***Anchote* (Coccinia abyssinica).** This perennial occurs as a wild vine in several parts of East Africa. The small tubers are cooked like potatoes in Ethiopia. Coccinia grandis and Coccinia triloba, both relatives of anchote, are gathered by some tribes in Kenya.

***Hausa potato* (Solenostemon rotundifolius).** Formerly classified *Coleus rotundifolius*, these black tubers are prepared like potatoes and may be eaten either raw or cooked. This plant has been introduced into Southeast Asia, where it is employed in curries or eaten with coconuts.

***Jacob's Coat or Sayabana* (Coleus blumei).** Both the leaves and tubers are eaten. The leaves are also added to fermented beverages. Now introduced into tropical Asia.

***Livingstone potato* (Coleus parviflorus).** Also known as the country potato and African potato, this handsome tuber is widely cultivated in the dry regions of East and West Africa. The tubers resemble the crosnes of east Asia, but have yellow skin and white flesh. They are also dried and then ground to make a flour for dumplings. The Arabs are thought to have introduced this into India. From there the Portuguese introduced it into Malaysia and Indonesia.

***Serendipity berry* (Dioscoreophyllum cumminsii).** Known as *utobili* in Nigeria, this shrub produces a number of products useful to the native peoples of West Africa. The tubers are employed in soups, especially as thickeners and are considered one of the distinctive ingredients in regional Nigerian cookery.

Eurasia (Including the Mediterranean Basin and Pacific Islands)

The Eurasian land mass represents a huge diversity of tuberous plants, and some of the earliest ones brought into cultivation. This includes all the cultivated taros (two species each of *Alocasia* and *Colocasia*, one species of *Cyrtosperma*), most of the agricultural yams (roughly ten species out of 600), and innumerable lesser tubers such as the kudzu (*Pueraria lobata*), which has become an invasive pest in the southern part of the United States. Historical information on many of the tubers from this part of the world is good, since their cultivation is often noted in the records left by peoples residing in ancient China, India, the Near East and Mediterranean Basin. It should be noted, however, that most of the Eurasian staple tubers are of tropical origin.

Adder's grass (**Dactylorhiza maculata**).   This is technically an orchid whose tuber was ground to yield a starchy powder employed in the preparation of *salep*. *Salep*, a word of Turkish and ultimately of Arabic origin, was a beverage served cold during hot weather and hot during cold weather. The actual drink is of Byzantine origin (or perhaps even Lydian as some historians have suggested), since the orchid tubers with which it is made are found primarily in Asia Minor and Armenia. The starch was also used to thicken milk and more recently to make a line of elastic ice creams popular in the Middle East.

Historically, salep was also popular in seventeenth- and eighteenth-century England and America, especially in coffeehouses, but in general it was regarded as a health drink. It was also thought to contain aphrodisiac qualities. It has been replaced by cornstarch or arrowroot.

Asphodel (**Asphodeline lutea**).   A native of the Mediterranean, the Egyptians, Greeks, and Romans prepared it like a potato. It prefers sandy soil and was probably a minor crop in some parts of North Africa during classical antiquity. It also yields a starch that was highly valued as a food thickener for making medieval blancmanges, sauces, and thickened soups.

Chufa (**Cyperus esculentus**).   Chufa is found throughout the Mediterranean Basin and in parts of sub-Saharan Africa. It has been taken to most parts of the world where it is either maintained as a garden plant or has managed to escape into the wild (as in the case of North America). Wild chufa, which is often called nut grass in English speaking countries, produces small tubers resembling brown shriveled peas. Their flavor is similar to almonds and when pressed, they yield an oil similar to almond milk. The tubers of cultivated chufa are much larger, sometimes the size of a lima bean, and much easier to employ in cookery.

Chufa was domesticated thousands of years ago and was probably an important food source for the ancient Phoenicians. The Egyptians grew it both for its ornamental leaves and its tubers. The Byzantine Greeks used it both in cookery and medicine. It is still employed in modern Spain in the preparation of *horchata*, a milky beverage popular in the fall. The British Isle imitation was called orgeat in eighteenth century cookbooks.

Crosnes (**Stachys affinis**).   Generally harvested during the winter months when the tops are dead, the tubers are knobby and white. The plant resembles nettle and prefers moist, shady soil; thus, it is ideal for marginal ground. It is also extremely hardy, and has been cultivated as an important supplement crop in China and Japan for many centuries. The tubers are pickled or eaten in stir-fries. The plant was introduced into France in the 1880s and takes its European name from the village of Crosnes (Seine-et-Oise), the site of a large experimental farm

Crosnes (*Stachys affinis*) is a tuberous rooted relative of mint native to Asia. The nutty tubers are extremely popular in China and Japan both in stir-fries and pickles. The plant was introduced into Europe in the early 1880s and takes its name from the village of Crosnes, France, where it was first grown. PHOTO BY L. WILBUR ZIMMERMAN. ROUGHWOOD SEED COLLECTION.

where crosnes were first trialled. Crosnes are also grown in the United States and are now commonly seen in farm markets.

Devil's tongue (**Amorphophallus rivieri**).   A native of Southeast Asia that is now very important in Japanese and Korean cooking, the tubers yield a starch that is solidified into a gel called *konnyaku* (yam cake). Noodles called *shirataki* are made from this. Yam cake is also commonly added to Korean hot-pot dishes.

Elephant's foot or telinga potato (**Amorphophallus campanulatus**).   Mentioned in Sanskrit, this is one of the most ancient cultivated plants of tropical Asia. In India, the tuber (also called a corm) is prepared in curries, fried, added to stews, and cooked in syrup. It is also sold in cans and is imported in this form to the United States. The plant is now cultivated in East Africa, especially in areas where Indians have settled.

Giant swamp taro (**Cyrtosperma camissonis**).   A native of the Pacific Islands and Indonesia. It grows well on the difficult soils of coral atolls, thus it is much favored by Polynesians. The tuber requires several years to mature, so cultivation is continuous, with some being dug while others are being planted.

Kembang Bangké (**Amorphophallus variabilis**).   A near relative of devil's tongue mentioned above, this is also used to make the starchy gel known as *konnyaku*.

Korean bellflower root (**Platycodon grandiflorus**).   This is the east Asian counterpart of the European rampion. Called *toraji* in Korean, is it employed in stir-fries and kimchee, or pickled like crosnes.

Kudzu (**Pueraria lobata**).   Kudzu originates in China and Japan, and its common name is of Japanese origin.

It grows wild in the grasslands of the Pacific Islands, and because all parts of the plant are edible, it was formerly important in the agriculture of India, Malaysia, and Southeast Asia. Because the tubers, which can reach a length of three feet (1 meter) require several years to mature, the plant is slowly losing ground to sweet potatoes as a staple even though the tubers contain roughly 27 percent starch. The vines grow anywhere from 24 (8 meters) to 36 feet (12 meters) in one season and will overwhelm any plants nearby.

Polynesian Arrowroot or Tacca **(Tacca leontopetaloides).** Grown mostly on the Pacific Islands, this is an ancient source of starch, which has long been sold under the name of pia flour. The plant is cultivated throughout Oceania as well as in India and Sri Lanka. Cultivation is now declining in favor of cassava, which is easier to grow.

Rampion **(Campanula rapunculus).** The tubers resemble tiny potatoes and were once popular in salads and as a table vegetable. It is still cultivated to some extent in France, Germany, and Switzerland. Historically, it was grown as a garden vegetable even during Roman times, with the center of cultivation in the Rhine Valley. Its Latin name means little turnip, and it was evidently an important food among the Gauls and early Germans, perhaps with some now lost sacred connections. Numerous folk legends survive dealing with personifications of this tuber, including the famous Grimm fairy tale about Rapunzel, and the story of the first king and queen of ancient Poland—the queen's name was rampion.

Soldier orchid **(Orchis militaris).** Found in temperate regions of Europe and Asia, this tuber was often gathered and prepared like a small potato. It was also used in medicine and in the preparation of *salep* (see adder's grass). Because the tubers resemble testicles, they were thought to enhance male sexuality. As the common name implies, the tuber was often employed as a forage food by armies on the move.

Taro **(Colocasia sp.).** This group of tubers includes two cultivated species as well as the closely related genus *Alocasia*, all of which appear to originate in southern India. Some Indian historians claim that taro was brought under cultivation over 10,000 years ago, although this is not firmly established. Whatever the date, it is clear that taro is one of the most ancient of the cultivated Old World tubers. It spread to Egypt by the first century C.E. and then to many parts of the Mediterranean. The Spanish and Portuguese brought it to the New World. The history of taro and its many forms is taken up in further detail below.

Yam **(Dioscorea sp.).** Yam is a loose term covering some 600 species, of which about ten are cultivated for food. Many member of this genus are poisonous or require processing to remove toxins in order to make them safe for consumption. The common name derives from a West African word nyami, but the botanical origin is

thought to be Sri Lanka or Southeast Asia. Since this is such a large and economically important group, yams are treated separately below. Yams are now found in tropical regions throughout the world.

North America (United States and Canada)
In terms of naturally occurring and domesticated native tubers, North American biodiversity is relatively sparse. Most of the edible tuberous plants that exist here were employed by native populations prior to European contact. Very few of these plants were acculturated by Europeans except under frontier conditions or during times of scarcity. The introduction of the sweet potato in the South and the potato in cooler parts of the continent more or less preempted the domestication of potentially important native tuber crops that might offer nutritional alternatives better adapted to soil and climate. Only the Jerusalem artichoke (*Helianthus tuberosus*) has played a minor role doubtless because of its similarity to the potato when cooked. The following list is by no means complete, but it does list the primary tubers known to native peoples.

Arrowhead **(Sagittaria sagittifolia).** Found all over continental United States and Canada, it is known by many Indian names, the most common being wapatoo. The tuber tastes like a potato and can be sun-dried for use in the winter. A closely related species, sessile-fruited arrowhead (*Sagittaria rigida*) is found only in the eastern North America. Both plants are aquatic. It is also important to note here that European and Asian arrowhead, formerly treated as separate species, are now grouped together, thus this plant is in fact found throughout the Northern Hemisphere.

Bush morning glory **(Ipomoea leptophylla).** A native of the Great Plains, this was once collected for its tuber, which resembles a sweet potato. The tuber has also been classified as a root, although the distinction here is hazy. Some plants produce unpleasantly bitter or tough tubers, while others are starchy or even pleasantly sweet. These differences may be environmental. The tuber may be eaten raw or cooked and is excellent when sliced and sun-dried.

Groundnut or bog potato **(Apios americana).** Sweet and starchy, these small tubers contain about 17 percent crude protein and are therefore among the most nutrient rich of all the New World tubers, more so even than the potato. They can be eaten raw or prepared like potatoes, or added to soups and stews like beans or peas. There is considerable breeding being undertaken to develop commercially feasible crops, with over ten named cultivars in circulation among experimental growers at the present time. The commercial advantage of this tuber is that it can be grown on marginal land and it is not subject to a large number of pests.

Jerusalem artichoke **(Helianthus tuberosus).** First noted by Europeans about 1605, the Jerusalem artichoke has experienced numerous cycles in popularity over the ensuing centuries. It was promoted by French agricultural writers Antoine Parmentier (1789) and especially by Victor Yvart (1790) who wrote a treatise on the subject, and is even mentioned by American cookbook author Amelia Simmons in 1796. Rich in inulin, the Jerusalem artichoke was widely cultivated by native peoples in North America, especially in the Midwest where it is thought to have originated.

There are five basic tuber types and a wide range of skin colors, from pure white, to red, purple, even brown. There are also discernible differences in flavor, but nearly all of the known varieties share in common a strong resemblance to the flavor of cooked artichokes, hence the name: artichoke of New Jerusalem. Most native peoples referred to the plant as a "sun root," which is botanically more correct. The Jerusalem artichoke has been hybridized with the sunflower to yield the Sunchoke, which is high in sugar and may eventually serve as a commercial source for sugar.

A number of Jerusalem artichoke cultivars are considered improvements over the knobby, hard to pare wild sorts. These include Challenger, French Mammoth, Skorospelka (developed in Russia), Stampede (developed by Ontario Indians), and Fuseau, a tapered sort resembling a sweet potato in shape which was developed in Egypt about 1913.

Maximilian's sunflower (**Helianthus maximilianii**). This is a near relative of the Jerusalem artichoke, which produces tubers or thick tuberous roots prepared and eaten in the same manner. It is native to the dry prairies of the Great Plains, where it was first identified by Prince Maximilian of Wied-Neuwied during a trip up the Missouri River between 1815 and 1817.

Water parsley (**Oenanthe sarmentosa**). An aquatic tuber with black skin and starchy white flesh tasting of parsley. It was highly esteemed by the native peoples of the Pacific Northwest.

Wild potato (**Solanum fendleri** *and* **Solanum jamesii**). These are small, marble-size potatoes found in the Southwest. They were gathered mostly by the Navajo, Hopi, and other native groups. The Fendler Wild Potato is said to taste like a chestnut when cooked. The Colorado Wild Potato (*Solanum jamesii*) was eaten raw, baked or boiled and can be stored for long periods of time. It was also dried and ground to make flour. Both species contain bitter toxins that can be neutralized when cooked with an alkaline substance.

Wild sweet potato (**Ipomoea pandurata**). This is in most ways similar to the Bush Morning Glory, except that it has a vining habit and grows in the eastern regions of North America rather than on the Great Plains. It was considered an important food source by Eastern Woodlands peoples.

Wood sunflower (**Helianthus strumosus**). A near relative of the Jerusalem artichoke, the tubers are less well formed, more elongated and knobby. The flavor is similar to a Jerusalem artichoke. The plant grows in forest clearings in eastern North America and has become relatively rare. It is cultivated on a very limited basis by specialists interested in heirloom crops.

South America (Including Central America and Mexico)

This region of the world possesses the richest natural diversity of tuberous species, yet nowhere is the literature more confusing than from this continent. As the late Sophie Coe pointed out "the treachery of common names" can transform comparative research into linguistic nightmares, especially when it comes to cookery. Local names for plants change not only across national borders, but from one region to the next, and even among neighboring native languages. All of these aliases show up in regional cookbooks, which must be read with great care. The *ocumo* of Venezuela is the *malanga* of Puerto Rico and the *quequisque* of Nicaragua. Not all of the multitudes of local names are listed below, just those that are most commonly mentioned in culinary literature. Nor are all of the South American tubers included, since many of the minor ones like swamp lily (*Thalia geniculata*) are consumed primarily or exclusively by indigenous ethnic groups. The tubers included here are those that play an important role in agriculture and kitchen gardens, and many of them are now commonly grown in other parts of the world.

Arrowroot (**Maranta arundinacea**). Some botanists refer to the root of this plant as a tuber when it is round and as a rhizome when it is long, even though the genetic material is identical. This difference in shape is owing to physical changes as the plant matures, but for the purposes of cookery, it is treated here as a tuber. This is a plant that grows on boggy ground or along steams, and in the West Indies where it originates, it was grated, boiled, or baked in the manner of a potato by the native peoples. Because it is so rich in starch, arrowroot became an article of trade by the eighteenth century, the starch being an ideal thickener in sauces as well as a basis for soupy gruels in invalid cookery. It also became one of the base thickeners for *budín*, and a key ingredient in delicate *galletas*. Arrowroot is now grown mainly as a source of culinary starch, but its culture has spread to several parts of the world. In Asia, it is planted along the borders of rice fields, so it is an important secondary crop for small-scale farming. It is also employed in the manufacture of noodles.

Cassava (**Manihot esculenta**). Also called manioc and yuca, cassava has become on of the most important food crops in the tropics, particularly in sub-Saharan Africa. The nutrient-rich leaves are boiled like spinach, the tuber cooked like potatoes, and the starch used for making tapioca. The genetic origin of the plant is tropical South

America, most likely northeastern Brazil. It was brought under cultivation about 3,000 B.C.E., but had spread to many areas of Central America, Mexico, and the Caribbean by the time Columbus first saw it in 1492. It became an important military ration for the conquistadors because it could be stored for a long period of time. Since the 1500s, cassava has been introduced and thoroughly integrated into the agricultures of Asia and Africa. In South America entire cookbooks, such as Enrique Tercero Hoyos's *Casabe* (Bogotá, 1996), are devoted to the preparation of this vegetable. A more complete discussion of cassava and its complex history are provided in a separate article.

Cush-cush or Indian yam **(Dioscorea trifida).** Also called Mapuey. Compared with the more popular yams introduced from the Old World, this may be considered a minor crop limited to the northern coast of South America, parts of Central America, and the Caribbean. It has not received much attention in scientific literature, although it is the only New World yam raised for food. In Afro-Caribbean cookery, it is treated like the sweet potato and is superior in quality. The texture is very fine and creamy when mashed. There are several landraces, most with white flesh, others with rose or purple flesh.

Dahlia **(Dahlia pinnata).** The common garden dahlia now grown as an ornamental was not noticed by European horticulturists until it was sent to Spain in 1787. Prior to that, its tubers were cultivated or gathered from the wild by the native peoples of southwest Mexico. The dahlia is still considered one of the native ingredients in the cookery of Oaxaca, and the petals make a colorful addition to salads. Today, there are several cultivars raised especially for their large, sweet potato-like tubers. There the similarity stops, since these tubers do not cook soft, but rather retain a certain celery-like crispness that is ideal for vegetable stir-fries. The flavor is complex, something akin to steamed pumpkin with overtones of sunflower seeds and a hint of spinach. Dacopa, an intensely sweet extract from the tubers, is used to flavor beverages in Central America. This extract tastes like strong mocha.

Madeira vine **(Andredera cordifolia).** This fine ornamental vine, which was a popular verandah plant in Victorian America, is actually a very good garden vegetable with many overlooked qualities. Its succulent, fleshy leaves may be eaten raw or cooked, and its white, nutty tubers make excellent additions to a meal, especially because they retain their crispness if not cooked too long. Otherwise, when cooked soft, they resemble potatoes. This is a relative of Malabar spinach and ulluco, which is still commonly found in Central American markets. It originates in the tropical parts of South America, but outside the western hemisphere it is not widely dispersed as a food plant except for a few places in Asia, such as Japan and the Philippines.

Malanga **(Xanthosoma sp.).** Christopher Columbus encountered this plant during his voyages to the New World but no one yet has established a universally accepted name. It was called *taia* in Carib, but goes by *yautia* or *malanga* in Spanish, *ocumo* in Venezuela, *chou caraibe* in the French West Indies, *tannia* and *calaloo* in the English-speaking islands, and *quequisque* in Nicaragua. The confusion is even greater since these names refer to specific species in some localities, while in others they are just general monikers to differentiate the plant from taro, which it resembles. The *yautia amarilla* of the Dominican Republic is *Xanthosoma atrovirens* and not any other yellow-tubered species, while the *yautia morada* of Puerto Rico is the same species as Nicaraguan *quequisque* (*Xanthosoma violaceum*). To get it right in the marketplace, it is almost necessary to bring a botanist along. Confusion arises from the fact that within each species there are numerous varieties and indeed many named cultivars. To the subsistence farmers of the Caribbean and South American tropics where this plant originates, all of this does not matter; it is only how it tastes that counts.

The most commonly grown species is the white tubered sort called *yautia blanca* or *malanga blanca* (*Xanthosoma saggittifolium*), a key ingredient in Cuban and Puerto Rican cookery. The differences between malanga and taro are very noticeable when subjected to comparative taste-testing. The malanga is finer textured, easier to digest, and contains more starch. The leaves, which are cooked like greens, are also richer in protein and minerals, and the Haitians believe they taste a bit like mild cabbage. The underground parts harvested are the lateral tubers, which means that by digging beside the plant, it is possible to remove tubers as needed without killing it. This low maintenance, perennial food supply is one reason that the vegetable is so popular among the rural poor in the tropics. It also grows in areas with less rainfall than required by taro and will even grow in well-drained uplands. For this reason, its cultivation has also spread to Hawaii, Malaysia, the Philippines, Indonesia, and much of Southeast Asia, where it is used like taro.

Mashua **(Tropaeolum tuberosum).** Also known as Añu, this species of the garden nasturtium has been cultivated since ancient times in the Andes and has no known ancestral forms. It grows like a typical vining nasturtium and produces red and yellow flowers during the summer, but requires day lengths of twelve to nine hours for tuberization. The tubers are cone-shaped and thickened toward the bottom. There are two distinct varieties, a white skinned tuber flushed with violet, and a red-speckled one with pale yellow skin. Both are cooked before they are eaten and taste much like Jerusalem artichokes. Like oca and ulluco, the plants are highly productive and easy to harvest. Historically, Inca generals shipped large quantities of the tuber along with their armies under the belief that it would suppress venery so that the soldiers would forget their wives and devote themselves more energetically to fighting. It does not seem to have this effect on the Spanish.

Oca (**Oxalis tuberosa**).   Next to potatoes, oca was—and still remains—one of the most important tubers raised in the high Andes. It forms an historical triumvirate with the potato and ulluco, and speaks for the genius of the farmers who figured out how to coax prolific tuberization from plants that in the wild would never have supported the complex societies that later evolved in that part of the world. In fact, oca has been cultivated for so long that the ancestral plant is now lost.

Oca is rather hardy, with fleshy leaves and stems, and a multitude of colorful tubers that form very late in the season, when the days grow exceptionally short. In the Northern Hemisphere, this means that oca will not tuberize until late November; therefore, it must be grown in cold frames, polytunnels, or cool greenhouses in order to produce a crop. This is not a problem in the oca-growing regions of the Andes, where frosts come late, but it has hindered the spread of oca to other parts of the world. The French and English, for example, experimented with oca in the 1820s, but it remained a curiosity, more ornamental than culinary.

Ocas are sold by color in Andean markets, and there seem to be at least 60 variant forms, from snowy whites to bright, waxy reds, even black. In spite of this biodiversity, which certainly excites the eyes of experimental chefs, ocas are essentially of two sorts: the sweet ones that are eaten raw or sun-dried like figs to make *caui*; or the bitter ones that are boiled, and boiled again, then freeze-dried to make *ckaya*. Dried ocas are more nutritionally rich than freeze-dried potatoes (*chuño*), and therefore form an important supplement to the Andean diet. Fresh ocas resemble miniature potatoes, even to the "eyes," which can be planted like potato eyes in the early spring. Europeans find them bland-tasting, but when added to soups or raw to salads, they greatly enhance the visual appeal of the dish. Furthermore, the Indians of the Andes consider oca a potent aphrodisiac, so there may be unsung benefits to promoting oca beyond its old native borders.

Potato (**Solanum tuberosum**).   Known as papas in Quechua and in Spanish, potatoes have been cultivated in the Andes roughly since 3700 B.C.E. (there are scholars who argue for an even older date of domestication). Seven distinct species of potato are still cultivated in South America, although only *Solanum tuberosum* is presently grown worldwide. The long tubered species *Solanum ajanhuiri* was introduced to France from Peru about 1815. It is still cultivated by potato connoisseurs, especially the black variety called Negresse or Truffe de Chine, which has become popular with Parisian chefs because of its truffle-like flavor. A detailed discussion of the potato and its history and near relatives may be found in a separate article.

Sweet potato (**Ipomoea batatas**).   This tuber was brought under cultivation along the western coast of South America about 2800 B.C.E. It spread to nearly all parts of South and Central America, but never reached Mexico proper. The early Spanish likened its flavor to marzipan, and it was this potato, not the Peruvian potato, that was first sent to Europe. Sweet potatoes were grouped into two basic types by indigenous peoples: a mealy, starchy type used for bread making, and the fine-grained sweet types known today. Since the Spanish preferred only the sweet types, the starchy types have become extinct, except for a small pocket of "relic" cultivars found in parts of the Pacific and among the Maori of New Zealand.

The history of the sweet potato is complex, for it is one of the few New World plants that spread beyond the hemisphere prior to European contact. For a fuller treatment of the sweet potato, refer to the article by that name.

Ulluco (**Ullucus tuberosa**).   A relative of the tropical Malabar spinach, ulluco prefers growing conditions quite the opposite: short day length, high humidity, cool weather, ample rainfall. In the high Andes it has been interplanted with potatoes for thousands of years and is still grown in a region stretching from Bogotá, Colombia, into northern Argentina. It is one of the most frost-resistant of all the Andean tubers. Its native names are many, including *lisas, papa lisas, chuguas, rubra, timbos,* and *melloca*. The smooth-skinned tubers resemble miniature potatoes and are quite startling visually, coming in a rich array of yellows, purples or magentas, vibrant greens, and varieties that are speckled. There are six named cultivars which vary in sweetness or starch content. Some find the tubers bland when boiled, but when boiled and then fried, they taste like potatoes. They are also eaten raw with vinegar or dried in the sun to make *lingli*, an Andean snack food.

Yacon (**Smallanthus sonchifolius**).   A near relative of the sunflower, yacon (pronounced ha-KON) has been cultivated in the Andes for almost 2,000 years and perhaps much longer. The name is a Spanish combination of Quechua *yacu* and *unu*, both of which mean water in the language of the Incas. This refers to the fact that the tubers are juicy like apples and will yield a pleasant beverage when pressed. This juice is also cooked down until thick to make a type of molasses called *chancaca*. The plant itself is a handsome ornamental, with large palmate leaves resembling tithonia. The leaves are used in medicinal teas and are considered antidiabetic. The long, smooth, sweet-tasting tubers were treated as fruit by all Andean peoples and are still sold among fruits in the country markets of Peru, Bolivia, and Ecuador.

Images of yacon tubers and leaves dating from 500 C.E. have been found on cloth fragments at Nazca in Peru, direct evidence that the plant was already considered an important food source. Genetic evidence of long cultivation is also evident, since many strains have been reproduced from cuttings for such a long time that the flowers have become infertile. It is known from early Spanish accounts that yacon was mostly planted along the margins of fields and that its cultivation was spread over a wide area of the Andes by the Incas in the period immediately preceding Spanish conquest. Because yacon is day-length sensitive, many species cannot be grown outside their native habitats. There is some effort at present to breed out this sensitivity so that yacon can be grown more easily in North America and Europe. Since yacon's sugars can be tolerated by diabetics and it is nutritionally very low in calories, the plant offers a number of interesting possibilities for further development.

Aside from the yacon discussed here, there are at least 20 other species of yacon found in Mexico, Central and South America. Only a few of these have been brought under cultivation, although several types were treated as "managed" plants by native peoples. That is, they were maintained in the wild rather than cultivated in fields. Many of the Central American yacons produce edible seeds that resemble small, black sunflower seeds. They make excellent bird feed and would probably appeal to humans if they could be bred to grow larger. The seed also yields an oil which is highly valued for its medical properties.

***Yam bean* (Pachyrrhizus erosus).** Also known as *ahipa*, *xiquima*, and *jicama*, this is often described as a mono-tuberous root rather than a true tuber. Native peoples treated it as a tuber, and the Mayans included it in many of their food riddles, mentioning both yellow and white sorts. The plant is indeed a bean with a highly ornamental vine, but the beans themselves are toxic and narcotic. Only the tuber is eaten, and generally, if we are to judge by Aztec codices and early Spanish accounts, this meant eaten raw for its refreshing crispness.

The plant is native to tropical America, although its center of biodiversity appears to be Central America where other species are commonly found. The archeological record has not been helpful, but it is likely that the yam bean was domesticated in that part of the New World first, and then spread to other cultures. It was exported to the Philippines by the Spanish, and from there spread to other parts of Asia during the 1600s. It is now also grown in East Africa, where it has become quite common, although it is generally cooked.

It is also being marketed in the United States and Europe under the Mexican name *jicama* and plays an important role in Mexican and Central American cookery to this day.

See also **Africa; Aphrodisiacs; Cassava; Iberian Peninsula; Japan; Potato; South America; Sweet Potato.**

BIBLIOGRAPHY

K. T. Achaya, *Indian Food* (Delhi: Oxford University Press, 1994); Emilii Bretschneider, *History of European Botanical Discoveries in China* (London: Samson Low, Marston, and Co., 1898); Sophie D. Coe, *America's First Cuisines* (Austin: University of Texas Press, 1994); L. Guarino, ed. *Traditional African Vegetables* (Rome: International Plant Genetic Resources Institute, 1997); U. P. Hedrick, ed. *Sturtevant's Notes on Edible Plants* (Albany: J. B. Lyon, 1919); G. A. Herklots, *Vegetables in Southeast Asia* (New York: Hafner Press, 1972); M. Hermann and J. Heller eds., *Andean Roots and Tubers* (Lima, Peru: Centro Internacional de la Papa, 1995); Udelgard Körber-Grohne, *Nutzpflanzen in Deutschland* (Stuttgart: K. Theiss, 1987); Janet Long, ed., *Conquista y Comida: Consecuencias del Encuentro de dos Mundos* (Mexico City: Universidad Nacional Autónoma de Mexico, 1996); Lucia Rojas de Perdomo, *Cocina Prehispanica* (Bogotá: Voluntad Interes General, 1994); Anna C. Roosevelt, *Prehistoric Maize and Manioc Subsistence along the Amazon and Orinoco* (New York: Academic Press, 1980); Alix Wilkinson, *The Garden in Ancient Egypt* (London: The Rubicon Press, 1996).

William Woys Weaver

TURKEY. *See* **Poultry.**

TURKEY. *See* **Middle East.**

TWELFTH NIGHT. *See* **Epiphany.**

U

UNITED KINGDOM. *See* **British Isles.**

UNITED STATES.

This entry includes twelve subentries:
African American Foodways
Cajun Cooking
California and the Far West
Ethnic Cuisines
Hawaii
The Middle Atlantic States
The Midwest
New England
Pennsylvania Dutch Food
Pioneer Food
The South
The Southwest

AFRICAN AMERICAN FOODWAYS

A discussion of African American food must include the cultural patterns associated with how, where, when, with whom, and why certain foods are consumed and the patterns of food procurement, preparation, presentation, and dispensation. Studies of food as part of a cultural system should consider dietary behavior, the environmental conditions in which foods are grown, the meanings associated with food, the social structure and material culture affecting food, and the historical factors that contribute to the persistence or change in food behavior. Food meets a host of human needs—political, economic, communal, cognitive, and affective as well as nutritional—and it has a role in power relations, stereotypes, and assumptions.

Before discussing African American foodways, it is important to first clarify what is meant by the term "African American." *Webster's Encyclopedic Unabridged Dictionary of the English Language* (1996) defines "African American" as "a black American of African descent." This discussion narrows that definition to focus on black persons of African ancestry whose lineal relatives (parents, grandparents, great grandparents) have resided in the United States for several generations. The focus on lineal relatives for establishing African American foodways is based on the assumption that most children grow up in households with adult lineal relatives (parents and grandparents) and/or with adult collateral relatives (aunts, uncles, cousins), who in turn grew up in households with their lineal and/or collateral relatives. Where adults in the household grew up is important because they influence the initial foodways of children. Black parents who grew up in Africa or the Caribbean pass on preferences for foods from those cultural areas that are different from the preferences of black parents who grew up in the United States. Parents and close relatives also pass on many of the cultural patterns that surround dietary content. For the purposes of this discussion "foodways" are products of multigenerational historical process, reproduction, and change.

Soul Food: A Metaphor of Group Identity

Linda Keller Brown and Kay Mussell, in *Ethnic and Regional Foodways in the United States: The Performance of Group Identity* (1984), discussed foodways as a metaphor of group identity and included contributions on Jewish Americans, Italian Americans, Russian Americans, Mexican Americans, Cajun Americans, Hindu Americans, and Florida Seminole Indians. However, no contribution focused on African American foodways even though during the 1960s soul food was adopted by millions of African Americans as a marker of ethnic identity, and soul food restaurants emerged wherever significant numbers of African Americans resided.

The concept of soul food emphasizes both content and preparation styles. Whitehead commented:

> Pork is a favorite soul food meat that must be fixed in a certain way. In addition, soul food requires the use of pork fat ("fat back," salt pork, streak-o-lean) as a seasoning in the cooking of vegetables in a slow stewing manner (vegetables such as collard and turnip greens, black-eyed and field peas, green and lima beans), and in the frying of other favorite foods such as chicken, fish, and [white] potatoes. (1992, p. 28)

William Wiggins has written that soul food restaurants include:

> down-home breads (cornbread, cracklin' bread, and biscuits), vegetables (collard, turnip, and mustard greens, candied yams, black-eyed peas, red beans and

425

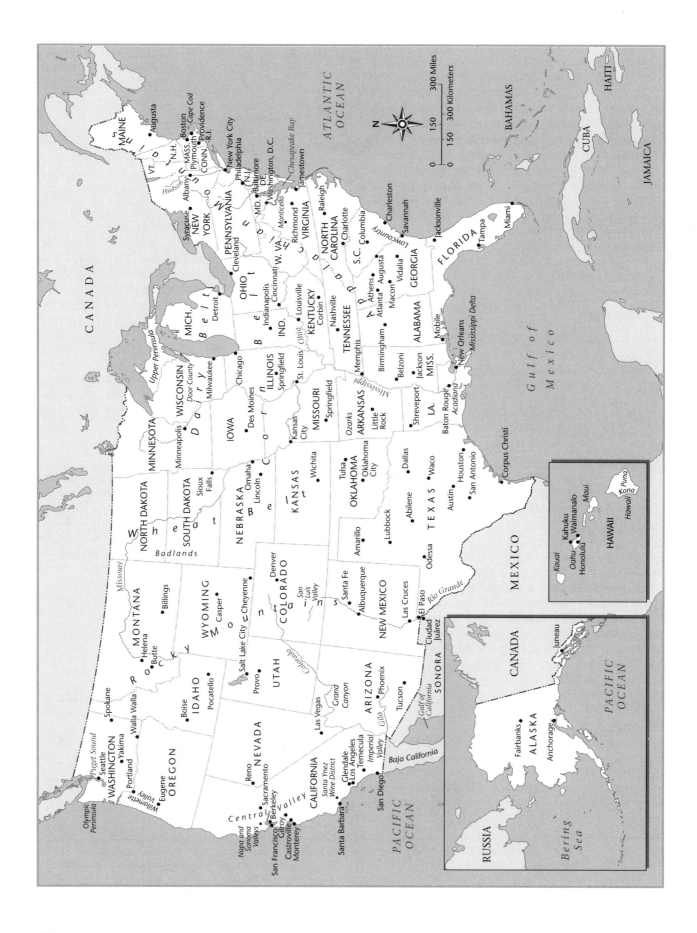

rice, fried okra, fried green tomatoes, green beans, pigeon peas, and squash), meats (fried chicken, shrimp, oysters, white buffalo, and catfish, neckbones, chitterlings, ham, gumbo, burgoo, and barbecue), and desserts (apple, peach, and cherry cobblers, sweet potato, transparent, pecan and apple pies). (1987, p. 81)

Some African Americans include rice on the soul food menu. Delilah Blanks (1984) found older African Americans in the South added wild animals, such as squirrels, rabbits, opossums, and deer. Flour-based gravies are a favorite with meats and rice. According to Wiggins, slaves began New Year's Day festivities as early as 27 or 28 December for ample celebration. They ate hoppin' John and attended watch night services to ward off family separations in the new year (Wiggins, 1987, p. 26). Many African Americans still eat hoppin' John or rice and black-eyed peas on New Year's Day for good luck in the upcoming year.

Among the soul food preparation styles are foods high in fat, salt, and sugar. Meats and other foods are fried, and most vegetables are stewed with pork fat. Whitehead reports that while dining with one of his study families in eastern North Carolina, at a single meal he was served fish, slices of country ham, corn bread, and white potatoes fried in pork fat and green vegetables stewed with salt pork as a seasoning. Country ham, preserved in a heavily salted brine, is a salt-laden favorite in the soul food menu (Whitehead, 1992, p. 98). Soul food is also spiced with red pepper (cayenne), malegueta peppers, hot pepper sauces, mace, allspice, cinnamon, cloves, sesame seed (benne), filé powder from sassafras leaves, thyme, and vinegar.

First-time patrons at soul food restaurants often find the drinks and desserts overly sweet. Heavily sweetened iced tea is the traditional drink, but unsweetened tea is often available. Whitehead observed that iced tea, lemonade, and Kool Aid, made with one cup of sugar to seven cups of water, were the favorite summer drinks of his study households. Fat (butter) and sugar are also used liberally in the preparation of favorite side dishes, such as candied "yams," a sweet potato dish, and desserts, such as apple or peach cobblers or pies; sweet potato pie and pudding; banana pudding; and chocolate, pineapple, coconut, lemon, and pound (plain) cakes.

With the increased awareness of heart disease, stroke, and diabetes, many African Americans have felt the need to reduce their consumption and preparation of these traditional soul foods, though they have not found it easy to change. Studies indicate that canned greens, frozen fried chicken, macaroni and cheese, corn or bread pudding, and sweetened tea are high in cholesterol, sodium, and saturated fat. Consequently public health agencies like the National Cancer Institute and cookbooks like *The New Soul Food Cook Book* (1996) by Wilbert Jones suggest ways to maintain flavors and diminish unhealthy habits.

The Southern Flavor of African American Culture and Foodways

The emergence of soul food was part of a cultural revitalization resulting from the black identity sentiments many blacks expressed in the 1960s. Most revitalization movements initiated by people of African ancestry in the Western Hemisphere, such as the Rastafarians of Jamaica, the Black Muslims in the United States, and Kwanzaa participants, seek to revive African cultural trends.

Evidence also suggests that various components of African American foodways have their origins in Africa. For example, the soul foods black-eyed peas, collard greens, okra, and benne or sesame seeds probably came from Africa. Archaeological discoveries indicate that "the meals the black women prepared for themselves and their families . . . readily could have used techniques and ingredients important in West African cookery" (Yentsch, 1994, p. 196). Anne Elizabeth Yentsch admits, however, that raising the point of African origins opens a Pandora's box because determining origins is "complex and tricky." The predominant cultural source of African American foodways is not Africa but the American South, involving a multiple-generation creolization process with contributions from Europeans and Native Americans as well as from Africans.

Pork and chicken are the dominant soul food meats, derived from animals the Europeans brought to the Americas. The Europeans, as maritime and colonial powers, were responsible for the movement of foods from continent to continent. For example, Europeans brought sugar cane to the Americas and thus contributed to the sweet foods in southern and soul food menus. Europeans brought foods from the Caribbean and Central and South America, "sometimes by circuitous routes through Europe and Africa and Asia," that became part of the southern and soul food diet, including "hot and sweet peppers, peanuts, tomatoes, lima beans, white potatoes, and sweet potatoes," chocolate, pineapples, lemons, and coconuts. (Egerton, 1987, p. 13). Europeans also brought rice to the lowlands of South Carolina and Georgia, from where it spread to Louisiana and Arkansas (Egerton, 1987, p. 307).

These foods Europeans brought to the American South became inextricably linked to the enslavement of Africans. For example, the slaves ate yams, peanuts, corn, and rice during the middle passage. Citrus fruits, like limes and lemons, hot malegueta peppers, herbs, and spices were provisioned during the middle passage for medicinal purposes. West African or Gold Coast slaves, who had centuries of experience, cultivated rice in the lowlands of South Carolina and Georgia (Egerton, 1987). Sugar cane traveled the circuitous route "North Africa to Spain and Portugal with the Moors; from Portugal to Madeira with the Portuguese; from Madeira to the Canary Islands with the Spaniards; and from the Canary Islands to Santo Domingo with Columbus . . . [and finally] to Louisiana in 1751" with the Atlantic slave trade (Mintz,

An upper-class African American family eating dinner in their home during the early 1900s. COURTESY OF THE LIBRARY OF CONGRESS.

1991, pp. 117–126). The Atlantic slave trade also introduced West African yams, which were replaced by sweet potatoes, millet, sorghum, rice, plantains, bananas, corn, cassavas, and palm oil.

Native Americans contributed maize or corn; a variety of peas and beans; fish, such as catfish and trout; and seafood, such as herring and shrimp, to southern diets. Indians taught white southern colonists and black slaves to hunt wild animals, such as opossums, deer, rabbits, and squirrels, which were still soul food items in the 1980s. Slaves quickly adopted bird hunting from Native Americans. European travelers' accounts noted that guinea fowl and other birds were a source of meat in West Africa. African Americans in the low country and Virginia were particularly shrewd "chicken merchants" (Yentsch, 1994, p. 203; Morgan, 1998, p. 367).

Archeological evidence suggests that African and Native American cultures were intertwined primarily in methods of consumption and in preparation of foods like rice and corn. During the colonial period, African meals consisted of a starchy main course accompanied by vegetables and a small serving of meat. Customarily the food was prepared in a large container and was eaten with hands or spoons (Ferguson, 1992, p. 97 *n*). Gourds were used as eating utensils and musical instruments. Leland Ferguson noted that the shards of cooking pots suggest commonalities among the foodways of Africans from several countries and Native Americans. Europeans influenced African and Native American food-related material culture, most notably in the adoption of such items as iron pots and wooden buckets. But Ferguson and others suggest that the manner of their use was adapted to African familiarity.

Given the contributions of Europeans and Native Americans, whites and Native Americans with cultural roots in the South could just as well view soul food as their own. Yet African contributions to southern foodways were considerable, as for centuries Africans and African Americans dominated the food scene through the

preparation of these foods and thereby claimed the tradition. During the antebellum period, the slave cook was the primary food preparer for both the white plantation owner and the black slave families. For slaves

> the kitchen was one of the few places where their imagination and skill could have free rein and full expression, and there they often excelled . . . one of the few places where either blacks or women could let their guard down and be themselves. Almost everywhere else, they had to conform to binding roles that stifled expression and killed creativity; but in the kitchen, they could be extravagant, artistic, whimsical, assertive, even sensuous . . . . herein may lie the ultimate explanation for the natural superiority of Southern food. (Egerton, 1987, pp. 15, 17)

In its "natural superiority," southern food tends to be more spicy than foods from other regions of the United States. The slave cooks took advantage of the spices that came into North America from Africa, the Caribbean, and Central and South America. These spices not only stimulated the taste buds of the planter class but also made the lowly food items given to the slaves, such as the excess fat, snouts, tails, ears, and intestines of the pig and the bland and sometimes bitter greens, more tasty.

Of course the majority of African Americans with cultural roots in the South do not eat the same foods or prepare them the same way their ancestors did. However, the South has historically had the largest presence of African Americans. Even with the mass migration of blacks to the urban centers of the North and West during the first three-quarters of the twentieth century, the percentage of African Americans who remained in the South never dropped below 50 percent. As economic and political opportunities in the South improved, there came a reverse migration: a large number of African Americans returned, and by 2000 the South recorded a higher increase in African American population than in any other region in the United States. Consequently there has been a continual evolution of an African American culture in the South that includes African American foodways.

Even for the blacks who migrated out, the South retained its important cultural influence as ties continued with family members "back home," through holiday visits, attendance at church revivals and homecomings, and shared network functioning such as child and parental care (Stack, 1974). Migrants returned to get some of that "old down home cooking." Moreover, when African Americans moved to urban areas of the North and West, they took their food traditions with them along with their religions, which tended to perpetuate their foodways (Whitehead, 1992).

The foregoing should not be read as an argument for a synchronic view of southern or African American foodways—that is, one that ignores historical antecedents. Neither system has endured unchanged. Certain foods are consumed in all regions of the country and by members of most if not all ethnic groups. Consequently some argue that a truly "southern" diet and a truly African American diet do not exist (Fitzgerald, 1979). The notion that American food habits and preferences are national is based on supermarket and fast-food chains, mass media marketing, and the spread of ethnic groups and their traditional food preferences to all regions of the country. For example, Italian pastas, particularly spaghetti, and pizza have long been eaten in all regions, and Mexican and Chinese foods have become American favorites (Gabaccia, 1998).

A Cultural Ecological Approach to Foods and Foodways

The argument against specific southern and African American foodways parallels the argument that a southern culture does not exist because nationwide communication and transportation networks have incorporated southern components into a national, multiethnic American culture. However, these arguments focus narrowly on what people eat rather than on foodways as part of a larger biocultural system or what many foodways scholars refer to as a cultural ecological approach (Jerome et al., 1980). In this approach, the question is not to what extent other American foodways have permeated southern or African American food habits but rather to what extent southern and African American foodways have permeated the food habits of other Americans.

Thomas R. Ford described culture as a "historical production of environmental adaptation" (1977, p. 4). With regard to the study of food and foodways, five theoretical principles might be considered in a cultural ecological approach.

(1) Culture is a process of historical reproduction, and foodways as part of a cultural system are reproduced from generation to generation.

(2) Food is necessary for biological survival, thus the nutritional status of an individual or population is related to the availability and accessibility of food.

(3) The availability and accessibility of food is not only a function of the nutritional capacity of the physical environment but also a function of social and cultural influences.

(4) Social and cultural adaptations are made to factors related to the availability and accessibility of food.

(5) The persistence of factors related to the availability and accessibility of food contributes to the continuity of social and cultural adaptations developed in response to such factors.

The Historical Foundation of the African American Traditional Core Diet

The cultural roots of African Americans in the South were firmly established during more than two hundred years of slavery. Because slavery was a "total institution,"

TASTE PREFERENCES FOR FATS AND SWEETS: THE U.S. SOUTH VERSUS THE FRENCH

Tony Whitehead spent the 1987–1988 academic year working with the noted French nutritional anthropologist Igor de Garine. Before Whitehead left for France, the owner of Dip's Country Kitchen, a soul food restaurant in Chapel Hill, North Carolina, implored him, "During your research in France, would you find out for me why is it that the French love fat foods and sweets as much as we [black people] do, but they don't seem to get as fat we do?" While Whitehead did not have the means to empirically explore this question, from his observations he concluded that fat, in particular butter and cream, was quite present in the French diet and preparation styles and that the French loved desserts. However, their desserts and drinks did not taste as sweet as the ones he was familiar with as a native and food researcher in the American South. And the French did not snack frequently on sweets, which were relegated to specific times of the day, the afternoon, equivalent to the English tea, and the evening. The French would just as likely have cheese for dessert. Even though the French have multiple courses at meals, they eat small quantities of each course. Finally, eating for the French seems to be a social event, with much talking and social interaction with wine, rather than an eating event.

it influenced the availability and accessibility of food and slaves' responses to these conditions (Stampp, 1956). Most of the foods available to slaves were passed on to them by their owners. African Americans in the South in the twenty-first century use preparation styles similar to those developed by slaves.

Plantation records, slave narratives, and archaeological examinations of slave quarters provide information on the diets of both blacks and whites. The planter class in the South consumed the "better" parts of hogs, chickens, and cattle; fresh milk; butter; and cheese. They passed to slaves the feet, necks, ears, and tails of hogs; hog chitterlings, kidneys, livers, and brains; chicken feet, livers, and gizzards; and buttermilk. Slaves were frequently allotted cornmeal, salt, pork, molasses, and herring, as these foods could be stored in bulk by the planters (Gibbs et al., 1980).

Many planters encouraged slaves to cultivate gardens for their own subsistence (Singleton, 1999, pp. 20–21). However, the foods slaves were allowed to produce for themselves varied. On some plantations slaves raised chickens and ducks and grew cabbage, collard and turnip greens, white potatoes, sweet potatoes, and a variety of beans and peas. Other planters prohibited slaves from producing such foods in fear that the slaves would sell them to earn money to buy their freedom or trade them for whiskey (Gibbs et al., 1980). According to Todd Lee Savitt (1975), planters often used slave produce to pay certain debts, and the slaves were allowed to keep the remaining produce for themselves.

Frequently slaves had to supplement their diets by gathering plants and wild berries; hunting small game, such as squirrels, rabbits, opossums, and raccoons; fishing; and stealing. Some scholars have placed these methods of food procurement within the context of plantation power dynamics and resistance, arguing that slaves in some instances exercised a modicum of autonomy by resisting planter attempts to control their diets. Fishing, hunting, and gathering gave slaves some sense of autonomy, but true acts of resistance involved theft of livestock and other foodstuffs, such as smoked meats, eggs, chickens, and vegetables (Yentsch, 1994).

Many of these food items are included in the African American traditional core diet that was characterized by Whitehead (1992) and Delilah Blanks (1984). In separate studies in North Carolina in the 1970s and 1980s, Whitehead and Blanks found that most were still regularly eaten in African American households. Presumably this traditional core diet has persisted over a number of generations.

Whitehead and Blanks found that other foods in the core diets of their study families were not a regular part of slave diets according to historical accounts. Among these foods are pork products, such as hams, ribs, chops, loins, and shoulders; whole chickens and chicken breasts, thighs, legs, and wings; beef products, such as ground beef, roasts, and steaks; fresh fruit; desserts, such as fruit pies, cobblers, cakes, and cookies; and beverages, such as sweet milk, coffee, tea, and lemonade. This does not mean that some slaves and some black free persons did not eat such foods, but according to historical accounts most African Americans did not eat them frequently during the slave period. It is likely that after emancipation more African Americans raised their own food and traded for or bought a wider variety of foods.

African Americans consumed other foods added to their diets by the twentieth-century mass food delivery and marketing systems. Whereas many African American traditional core foods were fresh produce, most of the foods were processed, canned, prepackaged, or frozen. Whitehead's research was motivated by the high fat and low fiber content of traditional core foods, which public health professionals blamed for the higher incidence of heart disease, hypertension, stroke and other cardiovascular conditions, diabetes, and rectal and colon cancers among blacks and whites in the southeastern United States. However, in a study published in 1996, Barry M.

AN EXPERIMENT TO TEST SOUTHERN PREFERENCE FOR SALT AND SUGAR

While Tony Whitehead's research in North Carolina was only exploratory, his findings were suggestive. Whitehead's original sample was the membership of 43 total households of 193 African Americans 10 years of age and above. A nutritionist on Whitehead's research team, Judith Katona Apte, created two simple instruments to explore sugar and salt preferences. The first was five water and sugar mixtures with the amount of water evenly calibrated between each. Mixture 1 had the least amount of sugar, and mixture 5 had the greatest. The second instrument was similar, consisting of broth-type mixtures with five different calibrated amounts of salt. These mixtures were first administered to ten graduate students at the University of North Carolina who were asked which mixture they preferred in their foods. Mixture 3 was selected by eight out of the ten students. The mixtures were then administered to the study participants. It was a methodological error to not pretest these instruments on research participants from the study community and adjust based on their preferred tastes. Nevertheless it was instructive that the most frequently stated preference of both salt (97 out of 141 cases) and sugar (111 out of 140 cases) concentrations was mixture 5. Even with the methodological error, the finding at least suggests that African Americans residing in this southern study community preferred higher concentrations of salt and sugar in their foods than did the ten graduate students, seven of whom were not originally from the southeastern United States. Whitehead observed that the favorite summer drinks among his study group had what might be considered higher concentrations of sugar (one cup) to water (seven cups) than what most Americans whose foodways are not southern would prefer. This also suggests that southerners and African Americans prefer foods higher in these ingredients.

Popkin and Anna Maria Siega-Riz found that between 1965 and 1991 many traditional foods like sweet potatoes, greens, and black-eyed peas had decreased significantly in the diets of poorer blacks. The study noted that, among all socioeconomic classes, consumption of fast-food items, including "pizza, tacos and pasta dishes loaded with hidden fats" increased (Popkin and Siega-Riz, 1996, p. 718). These foods contribute to the fact that proportionately more African Americans, especially women, are overweight than white Americans (Kumanyika, 1997).

430

FOODS ACCESSIBLE TO SLAVES: THE AFRICAN AMERICAN TRADITIONAL CORE DIET

Meats, Poultry, and Seafood

Pork Extremities
Chicken Extremities
    wings, necks, backs, and feet
Chicken Organs
    livers and gizzards
Wild Game
    rabbits, squirrels, deer, and
    opossums
Seafood
    dried and salted herring; fresh-
    water fish, such as trout, catfish,
    kingfish, croaker, black and red
    drum, and flounder; and shellfish,
    such as crabs, clams, and mussels

Vegetables, Legumes, Tubers, and Grains

Green Vegetables
    okra; collard, mustard, and turnip
    greens; poke salad, cabbages; and
    pumpkins
Legumes
    cowpeas and lima beans
Tubers
    white potatoes, sweet potatoes,
    onions, and turnips
Grains
    rice, corn, and wheat
Wild Berries

Breads, Sweets, and Beverages

Breads
    cornbread and biscuits
Desserts
    sweet breads made with
    molasses or honey
Beverages
    buttermilk and teas made from
    roots and herbs, such as
    sassafras

The African American participants in a study by Psyche Williams-Forson (2001) complained that the grocery stores in their communities did not provide enough variety in fish, fruits, vegetables (all items in the African American traditional core diet), and soy products. Rather, the perception of all African Americans preferring primarily pork and beef products and low dietary fiber foods still exists.

Ecological Factors in the Post emancipation Continuity of African American Traditional Core Foodways

The content of the African American traditional core diet became more entrenched after emancipation because the Civil War left the economy of the South devastated. Blacks and many whites resorted to the means of acquiring food that slaves and poor whites had learned during the slavery period, including gardening, hunting, fishing, gathering edibles, and for those who could afford it, raising chickens and pigs. However, lifestyle differences by race and class, including foodways, continued into the postslavery period.

Although slavery formally ended in 1864, the political economy of the plantation system did not. Sharecropping and tenant farming were the only forms of employment available to most blacks, and the economy maintained the marginal status of African Americans well into the twentieth century. African American foodways continued, particularly the modes of food acquisition. Gardening, hunting, and fishing remained significant forms of food procurement (Cussler and de Give, 1952). Blacks still got some food from "the white man," but now they had to pay cash or receive it on credit. For sharecroppers and small farmers, this frequently meant turning over a good portion of their pay from a good crop. The landlords who owned the farms allowed their tenants to garden and keep animals on these properties, similar to the pattern during slavery. Some foods and other goods could be purchased from stores in the nearest town or on the plantation, but usually with a credit line made out to the landlord. Thus workers saw little cash return for their labor as the landlords paid the accounts out of their wages.

Along with persistent poverty, the ecology of the region supported the continuity of the African American traditional core diet. The same foods grew wild or were cultivated, and African American families continued the food producing behaviors practiced during slavery with the exception of receiving rations from the planter (Gibbs et al., 1980). They raised many of the vegetables, legumes, and tubers they had consumed during slavery, and they continued to hunt and fish. Hogs and chickens were rather inexpensive to raise, partially because these animals ate pretty much anything the fertile area offered them.

These patterns of food acquisition continued in the twentieth century. Scholars of southern and African American foodways have noted that, although most foods were acquired from grocery and fast-food chains in the twentieth century, many African Americans in predominantly rural southern counties fished, hunted, and gardened; were involved in networks that killed hogs and shared pork products; and bought fresh produce from roadside stands and truck farmers who sold their produce in neighborhoods.

SOUTHERN "HOSPITALITY" IN BLACK AND WHITE

John Egerton noted that the concept of "southern hospitality" grew out of a "grand style . . . of gracious and elegant living" that was made possible because of the "platoon of black cooks and servants" that made the "elegant service and distinctive cookery" associated with the social events of the higher southern (white) classes possible (1987, pp. 14–15). He commented that while "white mistresses may have had favorite recipes they prepared themselves . . . one of the most fascinating and ironic indicators of the pervasiveness of this social pattern was the spate of post–Civil War cookbooks aimed at white women who found themselves quite literally helpless after the Civil War" (1987, p.16). Mary Titus has suggested that the concept and its ideological attachments are rooted in a complex cultural legacy of conflict. Two of the primary indicators of hierarchy and markers of separation coded in southern hospitality as practiced by southern whites were table manners and etiquette books, which emerged out of a social institution shaped by racial complexities. Thus for southern whites this notion of southern hospitality was also practiced as a symbolic gesture or code demonstrating the social distance between cook and consumer. Yet while the white practice of southern hospitality was a code for the elegance (or superiority) of southern (white) cuisine, it was also complicated by the adoption of the idea of southern hospitality by black southerners. However, during his North Carolina research, Tony Whitehead observed that the southern hospitality practiced by African Americans was not about southern manners that southern whites used to construct some sense of false superiority. The southern hospitality practiced by African Americans maintained the frequent practice of inviting acquaintances to social events in which food is a primary component. Whitehead (1988) also found that those who accepted such invitations were incorporated subtly into the social network of the person doing the inviting. Certain obligations and rights are associated with such network inclusions, which may then be functionally operational during times of need or may simply lie dormant if no need arises.

Taste Preferences and the Continuity of Foodways

One of the primary contributors to the persistence of foodways, in particular food content and preparation styles, is human taste preferences and how they evolve over time. Preferences for fat, salt, and sugar are widespread in human societies, but in the United States,

especially in the South, the preferences for these ingredients are arguably the highest in the world. Methods of preserving and preparing foods have contributed greatly to taste preferences. For example, the preservation of pork in salt brine and the use of this salted pork and pork fat in the preparation of other meats and vegetables created a preference for salty, fatty foods.

Sweetened foods figure in the southern culinary tradition. Sugar was first brought to the West from the Orient, but it was only available to the well-to-do. Eventually sugar became the primary crop of West Indian plantations, production began in the American South, and sugar was available to the masses in colonial America. By that time the South had discovered other, less-expensive sweeteners, such as molasses; maple syrup, a technology borrowed from Native Americans; honey from bees brought by the Europeans; and sorghum syrup, also brought by the Europeans. Molasses was especially popular and was used in desserts, in drinks, and to flavor vegetable and meat dishes (Mintz, 1991, p. 125). Slaves worked in the sugar cane fields, where they sucked the cane and stole some for their own use. Sugar, a source of quick energy, may have contributed to the productivity of plantation labor, and fat and salt also may have been adapted for long hours of work in the hot fields.

Slave cooks influenced southern foodways and contributed to the southern preference for foods high in fat, salt, and sugar. Elizabeth Fox-Genovese commented:

> The talents deployed in the kitchens owed much to the slave women's special way with herbs and spices and to recipes developed and handed down among themselves. They brought similar skills and even greater ingenuity to the preparation of foods for their own families and friends. Regularly resisting the masters' preference for communal kitchens, slaves pressed for raw rations that they could prepare for themselves. On some plantations, one woman would cook for all the slaves in a kitchen built specifically for the purpose, but even then, the last meal of the day usually was prepared individually in the family cabins. (1988, pp. 160–161)

Most of the foods passed on to the slaves, such as pig and chicken feet, necks, and livers; pig fat, ears, chitterlings, and brains; and chicken hearts and gizzards, may not be considered "food" by many Americans. However, the tastes the slave cooks created made them delicacies to many.

Slave cooks prepared food for their families and other slave families, and they also prepared much of the food for the families of their white owners. Most plantation owners had at least one female slave who prepared the family meals, and on large plantations even the overseer had a female slave who prepared his meals. Consequently slave cooks shared their taste preferences with the whites (Gibbs et al., 1980). However, the whites on the plantation ate ham, biscuits, relishes, and pies, while the slaves ate fatback, greens, and corn bread (Walter,

ROMANTICIZING SOUTHERN FOODWAYS

Some years ago Tony Whitehead heard a nationally known journalist state humorously in a speech at the University of North Carolina at Chapel Hill, "The worst thing about the North is that there is nothing good to eat up there." Whitehead found the comment interesting because it was similar to many sentiments he had heard from a number of his study participants during his five years of food-related research in the area. Southerners think northerners "mess up" food. One study participant (SP) told Whitehead about being invited to a barbecue by a transplanted northern friend who was going to cook pork ribs on a gas grill. The SP told his friend the total purpose of cooking ribs was to cook them slowly over charcoal. His friend said such a procedure was too slow. The SP responded that you have to cook them slow so you can drink a lot of beer while they are cooking: "A barbecue is no good without drinking a lot of beer." The SP had to go further into the analogies and metaphors that characterize the speech narratives of many southerners to convince his friend to cook the ribs properly. He finally won his case with an analogy between food and sex:

> The enjoyment of good food is similar to the enjoyment of good sex. You have a long period of foreplay to build your anticipation. This raises the actual act [eating or copulation] to the highest level of pleasure. Then afterwards, you fall into a nice pleasurable sleep—feeling very satisfied with the world and your place in it.

1971). The availability of slave cooks allowed white masters to entertain frequently, giving rise to the concept of "southern hospitality." Poor whites outside the plantation most likely adopted the preparation styles of slave cooks because they consumed the same less-desirable foods (Hilliard, 1972). These tastes for salt, fat, and sugar contributed to the notion of the "natural superiority of southern food" mentioned earlier.

The superiority of southern or African American foods over those of the North may not be an exaggerated romantic notion, however. In fact southern foodways have permeated the foodways of Americans in other regions of the country. The diffusion of southern preferences may be attributable to the human preference for foods made more tasty with fat, salt, and sugar and their availability to early American colonists in the North as well as in the South.

John Egerton pointed out that many mass food delivery systems, including the supermarket chains Winn-

Dixie and Piggly Wiggly and the fast-food outlet Krystal, originated in the South (1987, p. 39). These food delivery systems were successful in part because they responded to their clientele's taste preferences, including many items in the traditional African American core diet. Food outlets in other parts of the country emulated these pioneers in their high salt, high fat, and sweetened wares. Making foods more "tasty" makes them more attractive to consumers. While supermarket chains in other parts of the country did not initially stock popular southern items, such as pork fat, salt pork, ham hocks, and pig feet, eventually they discovered a market for those foods. Restaurants outside of the South added Creole and Cajun dishes and deep-fried catfish when they realized that southern tastes existed in their regions. Egerton stated, "Anyone who grew up on the [southern] food can attest, life without a little South in your mouth at least once in a while is a bland and dreary prospect" (1987, p. 49).

Social Networks, Festive Occasions, and the Persistence of African American Foodways

Even as the foodways of African Americans changed with upward mobility, broader ethnic diversity in all regions

JUNETEENTH

Juneteenth (19 June 1865) is one of the oldest-known celebrations to commemorate the end of enslavement. It is celebrated primarily in Texas as that was the day many enslaved Texans learned that they had been freed. Numerous tales attempt to explain the two-year delay between Abraham Lincoln's Executive Order of 1 January 1863 and the day the Texans heard the news. Many continue to make the annual pilgrimage to Galveston, the city where General Gordon Granger of the Union made the freedom announcement, to celebrate the day. While not as popular as Kwanzaa, Juneteenth is celebrated by African Americans throughout the United States with numerous cultural events. Because of its Texas roots, most menus for the event include barbecue spareribs or chicken. William Wiggins recorded that his first Juneteenth celebration included many foods familiar to African American southerners, "platters of barbecued chicken, long link sausages and brisket-sized chunks of beef, bowls of steaming brown beans seasoned with hunks of jowl bacon, a cold apple, lettuce, and mayonnaise salad, trays of white 'store-bought' bread, frosty pitchers of red lemonade, jugs of homemade blackberry wine, and a pan of peach cobbler" (1987, p. 3).

MALE FOOD PREPARERS

Tony Whitehead found that, in most of the households in his study, meals and the food served at church suppers were prepared primarily by the females. However, he found that, particularly among African Americans, men often did take to the kitchen. This was particularly true for some special meal. One of type of food at both small and grand feasts is the pig barbecue, which in North Carolina is referred to as a "pig picking." When a pig picking is "done right," it is a ritual in which males are responsible for preparing and cooking the pig, which begins the night before the feast. Males kill and clean the pig so it can be placed on the hot grill at midnight. It is grilled through the night, and the host and other males apply the barbecue sauce. Through the night the men carry out other important male activities, such as gossiping, telling tall tales, and drinking. Whitehead reported that in the historically racially segregated county of his research, an African American pig picking was one of the few places where he saw black and white males socialize, probably because of the absence of white women. Shortly before the feast the host may cut up portions of the pig, or the guests may "pick" pieces from the well-cooked animal until nothing is left but the carcass, thus the name "pig picking." Through the pig picking males become noted for their "special" barbecue sauces and their abilities to season the pig. As guests eat the pig they also applaud the cooks' abilities and extol their reputations among the best barbecue chefs in the state. The pig picking can become a male competition when a number of noted barbecue chefs (whether anointed by self or by others) are invited to cook the pig and to bring their own sauces. They are given a portion of the pig, to which they apply their respective sauces. At the feast the guests are told which male was responsible for which portion, and they give their opinions about which was the best.

of the country, and greater concerns about health issues, the traditional core foods and foodways were preserved through festive occasions that bring members of a group together in celebration or recognition of some event of social significance. These occasions also reaffirm social ties crucial to the biological and psychological survival of the group and its members. This reaffirmation has been particularly crucial for African Americans. It was impossible for slaves to continue the social structures related to kinship, marriage, and family that they had known in Africa. However, slaves developed new social ties based on family and kinship systems, churches, and voluntary organizations that survived into the twenty-first century.

Whitehead (1988) divided festive occasions into two types, impromptu and institutionalized. Impromptu occasions, such as a party or barbecue, are not related to any significant event. Institutionalized occasions are of three types, life cycle, calendrical, and communal, and correspond to three significant levels of social organization, the individual, the community, and the social network.

Life cycle occasions, such as births, initiations, weddings, and funerals, are celebrations of transitions or stages in the lives of individuals. Calendrical occasions are periodic celebrations recognized by the wider community, such as national holidays, like Independence Day, Memorial Day, Labor Day, or Presidents' Day, or annual religious events, like Easter, Christmas, and Thanksgiving Day. African Americans have created others, such as Kwanzaa and Juneteenth, which celebrates the termination of slavery. Communal occasions are celebrations of the social network, such as family reunions, church homecomings, and club or office celebrations.

Although life cycle occasions are celebrations of individual transitions, they are just as important for the network because they mark a change in status for both. For example, the network must adjust to the addition of a new member as a consequence of marriage or birth or to the loss of a member as a result of death. Similarly calendrical events are celebrated by the wider community, but networks take the opportunity to come together and reconfirm their ties. Food is central to festive occasions. In his North Carolina work (1992), Whitehead identified four types of African American food events: the meal, the petite feast, the small feast, and the grand feast.

Whitehead's study participants in a predominantly rural area defined a "meal" as a sit-down affair with others present. In other words, a meal is a communal occasion, not something one does alone. While meals are a day-to-day routine, the other three types of food events bring together household or network members into a festive occasion, and thus are referred to as "feasts." Feasts vary according to the number of network members present. A petite feast is best exemplified in the Sunday prechurch breakfast, which includes members of the household, and the Sunday postchurch dinner, which might include household and extended family members, the itinerant minister, and other guests. A small feast, such as a church or club dinner or an office picnic, includes network members from several local households. A grand feast, such as a family reunion or a church homecoming, includes extended network members, some from beyond the local setting.

In rural southern counties African Americans eat traditional core foods at evening meals. For morning breakfast and midday lunch some, particularly the young, take advantage of prepared and fast foods. These households usually have traditional core foods on certain days of the week, such as for Friday or Saturday night dinner or for Sunday breakfasts, dinners, and suppers.

For African American families involved in church, Sunday breakfast and dinner are frequently petite feasts. The Sunday morning petit feast or big breakfast might be eggs; grits; sausage, bacon, country ham, fried chicken, or pork chops and rice smothered with gravy; and biscuits or rolls. The petite feast dinner, served after church at around 2:00 P.M., has similar foods in larger quantities with side dishes, such as macaroni and cheese and candied yams; drinks, such as lemonade, Kool Aid, and tea; and desserts, such as peach or apple cobbler or pie and pound, chocolate, pineapple, or coconut cake.

Traditional core foods are also served at small and grand feasts. Whitehead found that to be known as a "good cook" was important to the women of the church, who display their cooking skills at church dinners on Friday nights, Sunday afternoons, or Sunday evenings. Whitehead observed a functional aspect to the concept of "southern hospitality." He suggested that a cook invites a new acquaintance to a food event, usually a petite or small feast, in part to broaden the affirmation of her or his status as a good cook.

African Americans raised in the South but living outside southern rural counties do not eat traditional core foods often, but many include them in feasts. African Americans with southern cultural roots gather on holidays for cookouts, picnics, or barbecues and share foods similar to those from home. In Washington, D.C., the staffs of representatives of some southern states have small feasts at which foods from their states are served. Sometimes a favorite restaurant from the home state caters the food, for example, North Carolina barbecue.

African Americans outside the South go "back home" on other holidays to have petite feasts with their relatives there, and they are expected to come home for family reunions and church homecomings. Family reunions usually last two or three days and involve several feasts. Subfamily units may hold petite or small feasts in addition to the grand feast or banquet dinner for all who attend the reunion. A church homecoming invites members who have moved away back for a celebration. Church members invite their ministers to their family reunions, but Whitehead found that some churches organized homecomings around the family reunions of several church members to broaden the occasion for those returning and to lessen concerns about making too many trips. Feasts are central to all of these occasions, and African American traditional core foods are the primary fare. Whitehead (1989) observed that the greatest incentive for traveling a long distance is to get one's fill of that "good old down home cooking." The more feasts during these visits, the better the time. Moreover, family members in the South know that food is an incentive and prepare enough so visitors can take a little back North with them.

Gulla basket for storing dried okra. Made of long needle pine and reed grass in South Carolina, circa 1880. The hooplike handle was designed so that the basket could hang from a hook in the kitchen ceiling. This style of basket weaving was brought to South Carolina from West Africa. ROUGHWOOD COLLECTION. PHOTO CHEW & COMPANY.

As mass food delivery and marketing systems change the diets of all Americans, the feasts that bring together African Americans, particularly those with cultural roots in the South, provide continuity in African American traditional core foods. As long as festive occasions and the rituals that accompany them continue, those foods will continue as well.

See also **Barbecue; Fats; Feasts, Festivals, and Fasts; Kwanzaa; Pig; Poultry; Salt; Sugar and Sweeteners; Sugar Crops and Natural Sweeteners; Tea; Thanksgiving.**

BIBLIOGRAPHY

Anyike, James C. *African American Holidays.* Chicago: Popular Truth, 1991.

Blanks, Delilah. "Cultural Continuity and Change in Food Habits in Southern Black Families." Ph.D. diss., University of North Carolina, Chapel Hill, 1984.

Brown, Linda Keller, and Kay Mussell, eds. *Ethnic and Regional Foodways in the United States: The Performance of Group Identity.* Knoxville: University of Tennessee Press, 1984.

Clark-Hine, D. "Black Migration to the Urban Midwest: The Gender Dimension, 1915–1945." In *The Great Migration in Historical Perspective*, edited by Joe William Trotter Jr. Bloomington: Indiana University Press, 1991.

Copage, Eric V. *Kwanzaa: An African-American Celebration of Culture and Cooking*. New York: Morrow, 1991.

Cussler, Margaret, and Mary L. de Give. *'Twixt the Cup and Lip: Psychological and Socio-Cultural Factors Affecting Food Habits*. New York: Twayne, 1952.

Deetz, James. *In Small Things Forgotten: An Archaeology of Early American Life*. Garden City, N.Y.: Anchor Press and Doubleday, 1977.

Egerton, John. *Southern Food: At Home, on the Road, in History*. New York: Knopf, 1987.

Fairbanks, C. H. "The Kingsley Slave Cabin in Duval County, Florida, 1968." In *Conference on Historic Sites, Archaeology Papers* 7 (1971): 62–93.

Ferguson, Leland. *Uncommon Ground: Archaeology and Early African America, 1650–1800*. Washington, D.C.: Smithsonian Institution Press, 1992.

Fitzgerald, Thomas. "Southern Folks' Eating Habits Ain't What They Used to Be . . . if They Ever Were." *Nutrition Today* (July–August 1979): 16–21.

Flanders, Ralph Betts. *Plantation Slavery in Georgia*. Chapel Hill: University of North Carolina Press, 1933.

Ford, Thomas R. "Contemporary Rural America: Persistence and Change." In *Rural USA: Persistence and Change*, edited by Thomas R. Ford. Ames: Iowa State University Press, 1977.

Fox-Genovese, Elizabeth. *Within the Plantation Household: Black and White Women of the Old South*. Chapel Hill: University of North Carolina Press, 1988.

Gabaccia, Donna R. *We Are What We Eat: Ethnic Food and the Making of Americans*. Cambridge, Mass.: Harvard University Press, 1998.

Genovese, Eugene D. *Roll, Jordan, Roll: The World the Slaves Made*. New York: Pantheon Books, 1974.

Gibbs, T., K. Cargill, L. S. Lieberman, and E. Reitz. "Nutrition in a Slave Population: An Anthropological Examination." *Medical Anthropology* 4, no. 2 (Spring 1980): 175–262.

Graven, A. O. "Poor Whites and Negroes in the Antebellum South." *Journal of Negro History* 15 (1930): 14–25.

Hall, Robert L. "Savoring Africa in the New World." In *Seeds of Change: A Quincentennial Commemoration*, edited by Herman J. Viola and Carolyn Margolis. Washington, D.C.: Smithsonian Institution Press, 1991.

Harris, Jessica B. *Iron Pots and Wooden Spoons: Africa's Gifts to New World Cooking*. New York: Ballantine-Random, 1989.

Harris, Jessica B. *A Kwanzaa Keepsake*. New York: Simon and Schuster, 1995.

Harris, Jessica B. *The Welcome Table: African-American Heritage Cooking*. New York: Simon and Schuster, 1995.

Hess, Karen. *The Carolina Rice Kitchen: The African Connection*. Columbia: University of South Carolina Press, 1992.

Hilliard, Sam Bowers. *Hog Meat and Hoecake: Food Supply in the Old South, 1840–1860*. Carbondale: Southern Illinois University Press, 1972.

Jaynes, Gerald David, and Robin M. Williams Jr., eds. *A Common Destiny: Blacks and American Society*. Washington, D.C.: National Academy Press, 1989.

Jerome, Norge W., Randy F. Kandel, and Gretel H. Pelto, eds. *Nutritional Anthropology: Contemporary Approaches to Diet and Culture*. Pleasantville, N.Y.: Redgrave Press, 1980.

Jones, Wilbert. *The New Soul Food Cookbook: Healthier Recipes for Traditional Favorites*. New York: Birch Lane Press and Carol Publishing Group, 1996.

Joyner, Charles. "Soul Food and the Sambo Stereotype: Folklore from the Slave Narrative Collection." *Keystone Folklore Quarterly* (Winter 1971): 171–178.

Kumanyika, Shiriki K. "The Impact of Obesity on Hypertension Management in African Americans." *Journal of Health Care for the Poor and Underserved* 8, no. 3 (1997): 352–365.

Mintz, Sidney W. "Pleasure, Profit, and Satiation." In *Seeds of Change: A Quincentennial Commemoration*, edited by Herman J. Viola and Carolyn Margolis. Washington, D.C.: Smithsonian University Press, 1991.

Morgan, Philip D. *Slave Counterpoint: Black Culture in the Eighteenth-Century Chesapeake and Lowcountry*. Chapel Hill: University of North Carolina Press, 1998.

Popkin, Barry M., and Anna Maria Siega-Riz. "A Comparison of Dietary Trends among Racial and Socioeconomic Groups in the United States." *New England Journal of Medicine* 335, no. 10 (September 1996): 716–720.

Rawick, George P., ed. *The American Slave: A Composite Autobiography*. 19 vols. Westport, Conn.: Greenwood Press, 1972–1976.

Savitt, Todd Lee. *Sound Minds and Sound Bodies: The Diseases and Health Care of Blacks in Ante-Bellum Virginia*. Charlottesville: University of Virginia Press, 1975.

Singleton, Theresa A., ed. *I, Too, Am America: Archaeological Studies of African-American Life*. Charlottesville: University of Virginia Press, 1999.

Stack, Carol B. *All Our Kin: Strategies for Survival in a Black Community*. New York: Harper and Row, 1974.

Stampp, Kenneth M. *The Peculiar Institution*. New York: Knopf, 1956.

Viola, Herman J., and Carolyn Margolis, eds. *Seeds of Change: A Quincentennial Commemoration*. Washington, D.C.: Smithsonian Institution Press, 1991.

Wagner, Mark. "The Introduction and Early Use of African Plants in the New World." *Tennessee Anthropologist* 6, no. 2 (1981): 112–123.

Walter, Eugene. *American Cooking: Southern Style*. New York: Time-Life Books, 1971.

Whitehead, Tony L. "Family, Black." In *Encyclopedia of Southern Culture*, edited by Charles Reagan Wilson and William Ferris. Chapel Hill: University of North Carolina Press, 1989.

Whitehead, Tony L. "Festive Occasions and Network Dynamics in a Southern Community." Unpublished manuscript, 1988.

Whitehead, Tony L. "In Search of Soul Food and Meaning: Culture, Food, and Health." In *African Americans in the South: Issues of Race, Class, and Gender*, edited by Hans A.

Baer and Yvonne Jones. Athens: University of Georgia Press, 1992.

Wiggins, William H., Jr. *O Freedom! Afro-American Emancipation Celebrations.* Knoxville: University of Tennessee Press, 1987.

Williams-Forson, Psyche A. "Suckin' the Chicken Bone Dry: African American Women, Fried Chicken, and the Power of a National Narrative." In *Cooking Lessons: The Politics of Gender and Food*, edited by Sherrie A. Inness. Lanham, Md.: Rowman and Littlefield, 2001.

Yentsch, Anne Elizabeth. "West African Women, Food, and Cultural Values." In *A Chesapeake Family and Their Slaves.* Cambridge and New York: Cambridge University Press, 1994.

Tony L. Whitehead
Psyche Williams-Forson

CAJUN COOKING

Cajun cooking is a regional cuisine native to South Louisiana. Traditional Cajun cooking developed in a diverse and abundant natural environment and a multiethnic though predominantly French Catholic social environment. In the narrowest sense the word "Cajun" refers to descendants of eighteenth-century Acadian settlers expelled from Canada who eventually settled in South Louisiana among a multiethnic French-speaking population, including people of French, African, Spanish, German, Native American, and other descent. Eventually the Cajuns (short for Acadians) dominated twenty-two parishes of South Louisiana, now called Acadiana. They lived in relative isolation until the twentieth century, when the outside world came to Cajuns in the form of compulsory English education, the oil industry, World War II, mass media, and an influx of outsiders bearing a standard American mass culture. Like immigrants from foreign shores, Cajuns found themselves in a new world of change. Cajun culture was a source of scorn by outsiders and an embarrassment for many insiders, and French speaking declined.

However, a revival of Cajun culture gained steam in the 1970s with the creation of French programs in the schools, a general attention to cultural expressions (music, food, and so forth), and a rise in pride in being Cajun. Part of this pride of identity is as a people who are highly sociable, who know how to enjoy life (joie de vivre), including the enjoyment of food, and who know how to prepare food that is exceptionally good. It is fitting that Cajun cooking has become a major cultural export and Cajun chefs have become high-profile media personalities.

Ingredients

In the past, small farms produced pork and poultry, while beef was more common in the southwestern part of the region. People raised corn, greens, okra, peppers, mirliton (chayote), seasoning vegetables (onions, peppers, gar-

Jambalaya is the great classic of Cajun cooking. Its main ingredients are rice, sausage, and chicken. © OWEN FRANKEN/ CORBIS.

lic), and more. Rice, the preferred grain, was raised in some areas and imported in others. Native Americans taught the use of filé powder, made from sassafras trees, for gumbo. Hunting, fishing and gathering in the bayous, swamps, and Gulf waters provided ingredients such as crawfish, crab, shrimp, finfish, turtle, alligator, venison, squirrel, and other game.

In the past it was necessary for Cajuns to be competent in the various environments to acquire food, and it was necessary to know how to process it for cooking. Today, most food is purchased at grocery stores, yet the traditional subsistence skills are symbolically valued and often practiced as recreation (hunting, fishing, gardening) or shown off at festivals (skinning furs, opening oysters, butchering a hog).

Cooking Aesthetics

The aesthetics of traditional Cajun cooking demand that foods have strong, intense flavors. Strong flavoring comes from the use of seasoning vegetables (onion, bell pepper, garlic, celery) and from the careful browning of ingredients. Gumbo and other sauce-based dishes begin with a flour-based roux that is slowly browned to a dark color. Seasoning vegetables are browned. Coffee is dark-roasted. The use of cayenne and other hot peppers intensifies flavor. The proportion of hot pepper varies throughout the region and among cooks.

Cajuns say good food takes time, and many dishes require long simmering that follows slow browning. For example, gumbo, a soup, or stew that will be served over

Cooked crayfish, known locally as crawfish (or sometimes "crawdads"), are a Louisiana bayou specialty. They are traditionally served on newspaper. © NATHAN BENN/CORBIS.

rice, is simmered for hours until the ingredients soften and break down.

Major dishes reflect the practice of combining a flavorful multi-ingredient item with a bland staple, usually rice. Gumbo (of many varieties), étouffée, sauce piquant, and fricassee are served over rice. Jambalaya and rice dressing contain rice. The pattern occurs in less obvious forms, such as rice-containing boudin sausage (the "Cajun fast food"), corn bread dressing, boulettes (rice and meat or seafood balls), vegetables stuffed with seasoned meat and corn bread, and crawfish bisque, which contains cleaned crawfish heads stuffed with a dressing mixture.

Community Food Events

Community food events include boucheries, cochon de laits, rural Mardi Gras, and festivals dedicated to certain foods. At old-fashioned boucheries families took turns butchering a hog, then cooking or distributing the perishable meat for quick use. A modern family boucherie is a party at which a hog is butchered, cleaned, and converted to various dishes, including boudin sausage, cracklings, hogshead cheese, backbone stew, chaudin (stuffed stomach), rice dressing, and cuts for the freezer. A party called a cochon de lait is a pig roast, a scaled-down version of a boucherie. Rural Mardi Gras involves gathering the ingredients for gumbo, including live chickens, by riding horses or trucks from house to house, begging for ingredients, and performing antics. Women cook the gumbo for the night's dance at a community kitchen. Throughout Acadiana festivals are dedicated to food as prepared dishes or major ingredients, such as crawfish, gumbo, sauce picquant, boudin, shrimp, rice, and so forth. Festivals usually include eating contests and food preparation demonstrations.

In both traditional and modern Cajun culture, food is a center of attention, something to brag about, something to enjoy, and something to center social events around. Both men and women cook, and men are often the star cooks at larger social events. A man's outdoor kitchen is as elaborate and well equipped as the owner can afford.

Crawfish Boils

The quintessential Cajun food event is the backyard crawfish boil. In spring people catch or buy live crawfish and boil them outdoors with cayenne pepper and vegetables (corn on the cob, potatoes, carrots). The hot crawfish and vegetables are poured onto newspaper-covered tables. People peel the crawfish by hand to extract the tail meat and often suck the heads for additional flavored juices. Crawfish boils are extended family events but also events that outsiders to the region are likely to be invited to. At a crawfish boil food is a boundary marker that positively shows that Cajuns are competent and sociable. Outsiders often have difficulty peeling the crawfish or tolerating the hot pepper, and many are squeamish about boiling live animals or about eating what looks like an insect. The outsider (in the past often the more powerful or wealthier immigrant from the dominant American culture) is the novice, and the Cajun is the skilled one, a friendly yet superior host teaching how to peel and eat crawfish. Once a poor people's food, scorned by outsiders, the crawfish has become a symbol of Cajuns as well as a relatively high-priced ingredient sometimes used in nontraditional dishes such as crawfish Newburg or crawfish pizza.

Cajun Cooking Gains Fame

In the 1980s trained chefs raised on Cajun cooking, such as Paul Prudhomme and Alex Patout, brought their food to the nation though restaurants, cookbooks, television, and public appearances. Cajun cooking became famous, even faddish. Cajun dishes appeared on menus far from Louisiana with varying quality. Fast food chains featured "Cajun" items. The number of food manufacturers in Louisiana multiplied, as did the number of restaurants catering to tourists. Internet sites sell Cajun ingredients and prepared dishes for overnight shipment. The non-Cajun Emeril Lagasse promotes Cajun dishes on television and in cookbooks, and tourism advertising focuses on Cajun cooking as a major reason to visit Louisiana.

See also **Crustaceans and Shellfish; Fish; Game.**

BIBLIOGRAPHY

Ancelet, Barry Jean, Jay D. Edwards, and Glen Pitre. *Cajun Country*. Jackson: University Press of Mississippi, 1991.

Gutierrez, C. Paige. *Cajun Foodways*. Jackson: University Press of Mississippi, 1992.

Prudhomme, Paul. *The Prudhomme Family Cookbook: Old-Time Louisiana Recipes*. New York: Morrow, 1987.

Ten Eyck, Toby A. "Managing Food: Cajun Cuisine in Economic and Cultural Terms." *Rural Sociology* 66, no. 2 (2001): 227–243.

C. Paige Gutierrez

CALIFORNIA AND THE FAR WEST

California mirrors the history and culture of many states in the Far West. Like the states in the Southwest, California was first settled by the Spanish from what is now Mexico, but it received many of its subsequent settlers from the eastern United States during the Gold Rush of 1849. California's population includes descendants of Russian settlers, as do the states of Oregon and Washington. Like Idaho, Nevada, Colorado, Wyoming, and Montana, California is home to Basque families, many of them sheepherders, whose ancestors came from the Pyrenees Mountains of northeast Spain and southwest France. Chinese laborers who came to the West to build railroads settled in many small towns and founded businesses, eventually creating the great California Chinatowns of San Francisco and Los Angeles. California also encompasses many of the agricultural activities of other Western states, including citrus growing, also found in Arizona, and wine making, a prominent industry in Oregon and Washington. Fruits and vegetables that are grown in the Imperial Valley of California in winter hit their peak growing seasons somewhat later farther north in the San Joaquin and Sacramento valleys; Oregon and Washington follow even later. The American West could be said to begin where the Great Plains meet the mountains of the Continental Divide. From that point west, all streams flow in the general direction of the Pacific Ocean. From there ranges of mountains separated by broad, fertile valleys or deserts stretch across the land until, after the final range, the land, moist from winter storms and fog and rich from the great river bottoms, drops gently to the Pacific Ocean.

The great majority of the population in the West is concentrated along the Pacific Coast, yet cities like Denver, Salt Lake City, and Las Vegas grow each year, as the population of the United States moves into the Sun Belt in ever-greater numbers. The states of the West adjacent to California and the Pacific Northwest contribute greatly to the character of the Far Western states, because it is through them that many of the settlers migrated from the East on their way to the Pacific's shores. This region is also home to its first settlers, the Native American nations, whose ancestors, in prehistoric times, are thought to have crossed the land bridge from Asia into what is now Alaska. These nations and tribes have made a significant contribution not only to the development of foods in the region, but also to its artistic and spiritual elements.

It is misleading to categorize the food and culture of the Far West by state lines or even by cities or small communities. Cultures rarely start and stop at administrative boundaries. Traditions and tastes spread with far greater subtlety as groups move from one community to another, not only taking with them food that has always been a part of their lives but also adopting foods and flavors along the way. The largest cities of the West are cosmopolitan places where many ethnic groups practice a broad variety of food traditions. Most towns and villages have food and culture practices similar to those of larger cities. In addition, many families of specific ethnic descent do not eat the foods of their own tradition every day, but enjoy exploring the foods of other cultures or foods generally considered "American." It is most often at various festival times that ethnic groups celebrate their heritage, whether it is the festivals of individual pueblos in northern New Mexico or a Greek Orthodox festival held for the entire community on a specific saint's day. The Far West can be grouped into four general areas for the purposes of discussing food and culture: The Mountains, the Great Southwest, California, and the Pacific Northwest. (The Southwest is also covered in more detail in a separate article by that title.)

The Mountains

The states of Montana, Wyoming, Idaho, Nevada, Utah, and Colorado are punctuated by broad expanses of plains at the easternmost extent, leading to ranges of mountains separated by broad expanses of farming or ranch country. The food of the region is reflected in the activities that once took place there or in current lifestyles. After the Native Americans, the first settlers were trappers seeking furs. They were followed by settlers who came west in the mid-1800s following the Lewis and Clark Expedition (1804–1806). Mining exploration took place throughout the region in the nineteenth century. At the height of mining activity, larger mining towns possessed hotels and restaurants with menus to rival those in long-established cities, and the finest performers played in the local opera houses.

Large ranches, which raised cattle and sheep, were established in the nineteenth century followed by the smaller farms of homesteaders. Food in the ranch house or farmhouse was simple, reflecting both the Yankee origins of the settlers and the distance consumers lived from the sources of supplies. Early settlers subsisted on salt pork and beans, supplementing their diets with fresh foods if they could find them. Quick breads were made either using a kind of baking powder called *saleratus* or from a sourdough starter. When a steer or sheep was slaughtered, every part of the animal was put to good use. The huge extent of large ranches dictated the use of portable, compact camp kitchens called chuck wagons, which could be moved from one place to another to feed cowboys while they were working away from the main ranch buildings. The Dutch oven played a versatile role both in the home and in chuck wagon cooking. Over the coals of a fire it was an excellent vessel for making all kinds of stews. Buried in the coals, the Dutch oven served literally as an oven capable of producing biscuits, cobblers, and other shortbreads.

What marks the region today are foods that can be enjoyed in the outdoors while hiking, fishing, river rafting, skiing, or camping. Freshwater fish, especially trout, and game are plentiful. While camp food tends to be the simple fare like beef stew inherited from the English, Welsh, and Yankee settlers, it is sometimes enhanced by experienced camp cooks, who produce creative dishes like lasagna made with dried spfoglia pasta sheets and reconstituted dried shitake mushrooms in Dutch ovens over their campfires. Restaurants in major cities of the Mountain region offer many different kinds of cuisine to sophisticated diners.

The Southwest

The Southwest encompasses New Mexico, Southwest Texas, Arizona, and the southern part of Colorado settled by the Spanish. The distribution of what is considered "traditional food" of the Southwest (a combination of Native American food and food adapted from Old Mexico) is not uniform, but instead is reflected in the areas that have been settled the longest. For greater detail on this area, see the separate article on the Southwest.

One aspect in the history of the Southwest that affected the growth of food culture throughout the West by introducing refinement in menu offerings and service was the Harvey House restaurant chain established along the line of the Santa Fe Railroad. Here entrepreneur Fred Harvey established restaurants that served train passengers at scheduled stops. A sophisticated menu was offered, and passengers made their choices en route. The orders were forwarded by telegraph to the restaurant so that the food was ready to be served when the train arrived. Passengers were served in the restaurant dining rooms by uniformed young women who had been recruited from respectable eastern families. This effort led to greater expectations for quality food and service throughout the West. In addition, many of the young women stayed and married business and professional men, contributing to the character of many of the cities in the area.

California

Contemporary California is a land of dramatic contrasts, from the richly populated coastline to the sparsely settled inland deserts; from the highest point of land in the contiguous United States (Mount Whitney) to the lowest (Death Valley); from the hot dry interior to the cool, moist, and sometimes foggy seacoast. In the San Joaquin and Imperial valleys, where fields are irrigated, vast amounts of produce are grown for markets throughout the United States. Lettuces with names like red leaf, oak leaf, and curly leaf grow near other table greens with names like radicchio, trevise, and arugula, reflecting their French and Italian ancestry.

Table corn and table grapes are grown in California's Central Valley for consumption in several western states. In the microclimates near the coast, delicate produce is raised for sale at local farmers' markets. Some communities are known for specialized crops: Gilroy claims the title of Garlic Capital of the World, and Castroville, near the coast above Monterey Bay, boasts proudly of its artichokes. Ingredients indigenous to California's land and seacoasts include soft fruit, stone fruit, nuts, grain, game, cattle, poultry, fish, shellfish, and olives. Also grown are avocados, figs, pomegranates, persimmons, citrus, almonds, asparagus, strawberries, and dates.

The settlement of California. Spanish settlement in California began in the sixteenth century with military and missionary expeditions from what is now Mexico. Spanish missionaries often resettled Native Americans near their new missions, sometimes giving a tribe a new name to match the name of the mission. Civilians came with these expeditions and established the great land-grant ranches of early California, bringing with them food traditions of Spain, tempered by years in Mexico.

Some settlers came by sea. Russian families settled in Northern California and farther north in Oregon and Washington. Basques from the Pyrenees mountains of northwestern Spain and Southwestern France settled to grow sheep in eastern mountains of the state, bringing with them their special versions of sheepherder's bread and oxtail stew. With the discovery of gold in 1849, people of all backgrounds moved west, many staying to take up some activity other than mining. Many Chinese provided labor for the construction of the railroads.

In the twentieth century, California's population grew tremendously, and cities like Los Angeles, San Francisco, and, somewhat later, San Diego expanded to accommodate larger numbers of people and their needs. Today the state is home to a considerable portion of the aeronautical industry, film and television production, some large military installations and a great diversity of technical development, especially in the field of computing. New residents came from Asia, eastern Europe and the Middle East. Chinatown in San Francisco is one of the largest in the United States, bringing with it much excellent food and sources for ingredients. Los Angeles has its own Chinese community as well as a well-established Vietnamese community. The Los Angeles suburb of Glendale is host to a large Armenian enclave with its own supermarkets and its own hospital.

California foods. Food availability in California makes cooking at home and dining out a pleasure. The broad, year-round availability of good fruits and vegetables, seafood, poultry, locally grown rice (including exotic types), and many other products gives cooks and chefs enormous inspiration. Fine fresh ingredients have always been appreciated in California, as is evident from California cookbooks published in the late nineteenth and early twentieth centuries. In the last quarter of the twentieth century, a champion of these products, Alice Waters of the restaurant Chez Panisse in Berkeley, launched a renewed appreciation of locally grown ingredients acquired directly from producers, a move that ultimately inspired the growth of local green markets across the entire United States. The emphasis on freshness and proximity to the buyer is reflected in the cuisine of many of California's restaurants, now emphasizing the uncomplicated flavors of ingredients in season.

Some traditional dishes in California reveal the origins of its inhabitants. *Cioppino* (a tomato-based seafood soup) is the child of Italian immigrants who became fishermen in San Francisco and the Monterey Peninsula. Another dish, a product of nineteenth-century San Francisco in gold-rush days, is hangtown fry (a combination of fried oysters, crisp bacon, and scrambled eggs often served as a special breakfast). Mexico's influence, both old and new, can be seen in the Mexican food of Southern California, where flavors and textures of the food of the Mexican state of Baja California are reflected in such simple but excellent fare as shrimp or fish tacos wrapped in soft, warm tortillas and garnished with shredded cabbage.

Despite a frequent focus on the coastal cities of California because of their large populations, there is much to California that is neither coastal nor urban. The deserts along the borders of Arizona and Nevada are dry and desolate. Where water is available, ranches like those in the Mountain States and in the Southwest continue to flourish, raising cattle and sheep. Where Basque families have settled, they have established restaurants featuring the traditional foods of their culture. Food is served in many courses, family-style, and includes hearty stews with sweet peppers and Basque sheepherder's bread. Major inland agricultural centers are large farm-oriented operations. Others, catering to the demand for organically grown produce or specialty items, employ methods imported from Asia and other countries and do much of their work by hand.

In the northwestern part of California, where giant redwoods populate the forests, the rainfall may exceed one hundred inches a year, too wet for most farming but an exceptional climate for fresh wild mushrooms, which are gathered by experts who have their own special spots that only they know. The mushrooms are then passed on to produce brokers to sell.

Wine. The California wine industry produces wines to complement the breadth of California food. Although the wine industry in California burgeoned after World War II, it actually was begun in the early twentieth century, surviving the effects of Prohibition. The state's many hills and valleys are home to microclimates that give unique character to the many varieties of wine grapes grown locally. Best known of the regions are the Napa, Sonoma, and Russian River valleys of California north of San Fran-

California should be called the Salad State, for it has created a whole health cuisine based on fresh greens and vegetables. Its most famous salad is Caesar Salad, which is now found on menus throughout the United States. When properly made, Caesar Salad is prepared with great flourish by a waiter at tableside. PHOTO BY ANDRÉ BARANOWSKI.

cisco, and the Santa Ynez Valley north and east of Santa Barbara, but other vineyards abound in Monterey County and even as far south as Temecula, near San Diego. Wines made in the state have won many awards in "blind" tastings against some of the finest wines in the world.

The Pacific Northwest: Oregon and Washington
Like California, both Oregon and Washington are dry in the eastern portion and more humid in the west and along the seacoast. And, as with California, these states are rich in fresh fruits and vegetables, excellent fish and shellfish, quality meats and poultry, and outstanding wines. Each state has its own special character, dictated by the climate and latitude.

Oregon was founded at the end of the Oregon Trail, a two-thousand-mile route from Missouri that was followed by thousands of emigrants, primarily from the 1840s to the 1860s. From the mouth of the trail poured settlers from the Midwest and the East, bringing with them architecture and foods of their previous homes. Foods learned along the way also became a part of the culinary repertoire, with desserts like cobblers, popular because of the ease of producing them and the abundance of berries in the area. Cherries, blackberries, loganberries, raspberries, and blueberries appear as summer progresses. Occasionally, blueberries and quail are raised together, the berries providing some of the food for the quail while also enhancing the taste of the flesh of the bird as well. Oregon's eastern farms and orchards produce extraordinary pears and other cool-weather fruit.

Some prominent restaurants in Oregon have chosen to celebrate local foods and wines on their menus, featuring the excellent oysters that are harvested in the area, or farmstead cheeses and local wines.

Aquaculture plays a large role in the production of oysters, mussels, and Atlantic salmon in the Pacific Northwest. Restaurants and stands offering shellfish may have four or five varieties of oysters available for tasting.

Oregon's and Washington's wines are almost as well known to many Americans as the wines of California. Many of the smaller productions rarely leave the state or are eagerly purchased by knowledgeable wine shop proprietors and sommeliers (restaurant wine stewards). Oregon wines include exceptional ones made largely from the pinot noir grape and the cabernet sauvignon grape, both of which develop well in cooler climates.

Like Oregon, Washington's coastal area is home to growers of all kinds of crops, including a rich supply of soft fruit, that require a mild climate. The eastern part of the state is famous for its apples. Washington is also well known for its salmon production and nearly as well known for its smoked salmon as its fresh fish. The Ballard area of Seattle is home to many Scandinavians, whose emigrant parents brought with them the skills for both hot and cold smoking.

While New England Yankees, Scandinavians, and Russians were some of Oregon and Washington's first settlers, the Asian population has contributed greatly to the area in terms of food culture. One historian referred to the region as less a melting pot than a stir-fry. New residents to the region have come from Southeast Asia and also from Hong Kong during the period when it was becoming a Special Administrative Region (status conferred in 1997) of China.

Native American food traditions have considerable influence in Washington and Oregon, where salmon is split open, stretched on wood racks, and roasted before an open fire. The salmon plays a similar sacred role in the Pacific Northwest as corn does for the Native Americans of the American Southwest.

Also a part of the tradition of Native Americans in the Pacific Northwest is the "potlatch" gathering, celebrating wealth sharing, prosperity, and overabundance. The word "potlatch" comes from the Nootka-Chinook *patshal* ("gift"). The largesse demonstrated at these gatherings is a demonstration of success as well as an attempt to outdo the host of the previous potlatch feast.

While permanent and temporary markets abound in the coastal regions of Washington and Oregon, no place represents the bounty of the area quite like the Pike Place Market in Seattle. This open market is active every day, featuring the freshest of fish and shellfish, vegetables and fruits in season, and other ingredients, as well as flowers and crafts. Permanent indoor shops in the complex sell many items other than those related to food, and shops around the market have expanded into blocks to the east, but the array of ingredients for the dishes of many cultures remains a main attraction and represents a microcosm of the food culture of the region.

See also **Crustaceans and Shellfish; Farmers' Markets; Fish; Fish, Smoked; Fruit; Herding; High-Technology Farming; Organic Agriculture; Organic Food; Vegetables; Wine.**

BIBLIOGRAPHY

Bertolli, Paul, with Alice Waters. *Chez Panisse Cooking.* New York: Random House, 1996. The original edition was printed in 1988.

Brown, Helen. *Helen Brown's West Coast Cook Book.* Boston: Little, Brown, 1952.

Conlon, Joseph R. *Bacon, Beans, and Galantines.* Reno and Las Vegas: University of Nevada Press, 1986.

Cox, Beverly, and Martin Jacobs. *Spirit of the West: Cooking from Ranch House and Range.* New York: Artisan, 1996.

Fussell, Betty. *I Hear America Cooking.* New York: Viking, 1986.

Hibler, Janie. *Dungeness Crabs and Blackberry Cobblers.* New York: Knopf, 1991.

Rex-Johnson, Braden. *Pike Place Public Market Seafood Cookbook.* Berkeley, Calif.: Ten Speed Press, 1997.

Skott, Michael, with Lori Mckean. *Pacific Northwest Flavors.* New York: Clarkson Potter, 1995.

Van Loan, Sharon, and Patricia Lee with Mark Hoy. *Thyme and the River: Recipes from Oregon's Steamboat Inn.* Portland, Oreg.: Graphic Arts Center, 1988.

Madge Griswold

ETHNIC CUISINES

"Ethnic food" has been used colloquially for a wide variety of foodstuffs, virtually any that can be identified in the public mind with a foreign source or a American minority group. In the narrower ethnographic meaning, which will be employed here, however, it pertains only to food prepared or consumed by members of an ethnic group as a manifestation of its ethnicity. Thus it would not be an appropriate term for most foreign food eaten in a foreign land, fusion food as prepared by some innovative chef, Italian food as prepared by Greek restaurateurs, sushi prepared by a non-Japanese American housewife, or food purchased from Taco Bell or Pizza Hut, though it is sometimes extended to all these. Unfortunately, there is no clear cut universally accepted definition. In the end ethnic food is food that members of an ethnic group consider their own and that others attribute to them.

Most social scientists agree that the ethnic group is a social category defined by any one of a variety of criteria, including country of origin, physical features such as skin color, ancestral language, religion, or some combination of these. Ultimately ethnicity is a matter of identity—recognition of the social distinction by both members of the group and outsiders. Although ethnicity has to do with social not cultural categories, members of each group inevitably participate in a subculture that is more or less different from that of those outside the group. Food and foodways (by which is meant that entire complex of ideas and behaviors associated with food) is a particularly important component of these cultural differences.

Cultural Adaptations

Ethnic foodways, like other American foodways, are in constant flux. Changes in immigrant foodways are part of a larger process of social and cultural change.

The process by which immigrants become ethnic Americans is long, gradual, and complex. One can think of this as ethnogenesis or the creation of a new social group. Along with the development of a new ethnic group is a parallel development of a new subculture, including new foodways, that both symbolizes the group's uniqueness to its members and marks off its social boundaries. The new subculture is created in the American context, altered to a greater or lesser degree from what was known in the homeland. Polish Americans (and any other ethnic group can be substituted here) are not the same as Polish in Poland, and Polish American culture is different from the culture(s) found in Poland. Neither do Polish Americans belong to some culture somewhere between American and Polish, as might be surmised from the overly simplistic models of acculturation that have so often dominated thinking on the subject. Ethnicity exists only in specific contexts where one sort of people (Us) is brought into regular and intimate contact with people of other sorts (Them).

It is impossible to re-create exactly in America the foods of one's homeland, no matter where that might have been. Ingredients as basic as flour are different in the United States, yielding different results. Many ingredients are unobtainable here. The white cheese *(beli sir)* of Bosnia that Bosnian refugees require for one of their most common dishes, *sirnjaca* (a sort of cheese pie), is not available in the United States. Many Bosnians say *sirnjaca* is the food they miss most. They cannot even make cheese or the many other milk products that were an important part of their diet in Bosnia, because unpasteurized milk is unobtainable in the United States.

The same is true of the equipment and implements of cooking. The national dish of Bosnia, *Bosanski lonac*, is a stew of combined meats and vegetables slow cooked in

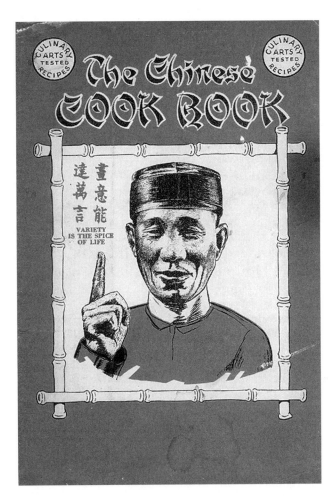

Foreign cuisines are often altered once they are transplanted to the United States. This Chinese-American cookbook by M. Sing Au published in 1936 features many dishes unknown in China, such as Lantern Party Salad and Chop Suey Soup. ROUGHWOOD COLLECTION.

a special earthenware pot. The special pot is so much a part of the dish that it is named after it; *lonac* means pot in Serbo-Croatian. These are used for no other purpose and are often treasured heirlooms. One Bosnian American housewife related that hers was a gift from her father, who had given each of his daughters one he had brought back from a distant market where they were sold. She had been forced to abandon hers when she fled Bosnia. One might cook a similar combination of meats and vegetables in an aluminum stew pot, but it is not the same.

But these sorts of problems get worked out, just as they do for other aspects of life. Adjustments are made. Substitutions are found. One accepts that some favorite foods of one's homeland can now exist only as fond memories. It is this process of adjustment, the culinary dimension of an immigrant becoming an ethnic American, that is of significance here.

The process by which immigrants become ethnic begins as soon as they board the boats and planes that carry them to the New World. The incentives are somewhat different for refugees than for willing immigrants, but the process remains pretty much the same. No group of emigrants from any country represents a cross section of that country's population. They are always drawn from some regions more than others, some social strata more than others, and some communities more than others. Since each of these groups possesses a recognizable subculture (including distinctive foods and foodways), it is logical that immigrant communities cannot replicate exactly their old national culture in the New World. If most of the Italians who settle in a particular community are from Calabria, then Italian cooking in that community will surely reflect the regional cuisine of Calabria, at least in the earlier phases.

Out of immigrant culture develops an ethnic culture that differs from it in significant ways. There are several primary sources on which this developing subculture draws. The first is the culture of the homeland. One aspect of the process is an amalgamation of the local, regional, and class-related subcultures that are represented in the new community. These processes have both a public and a private face, and it may well be that they work faster in the public. In the Detroit area, Lebanese, Yemeni, and Chaldean restaurants are rapidly developing a common Arab-American menu at the same time that housewives of these same groups continue to cook distinctive national cuisines. Even though the proprietors and cooks of many Mexican restaurants have come directly from Mexico, their menus feature the same standardized combination plates of the stereotypic "Mexican" restaurant derived primarily from Texas-Mexican cuisine. This is so even when a significant proportion of their customers are also recent arrivals from Mexico. Some regional recipes or cooking techniques may be preserved as family traditions, but in general the community will reach some consensus.

A second source in the creation of an ethnic culture is the culture of mainstream America, such as it is experienced by immigrants and ethnics. An important part of the accommodation process is finding ingredients in the United States to substitute for those from the homeland that are no longer available. Hmong find aluminum foil an acceptable substitute for banana leaf when wrapping food. Serbian American cooks, like other Balkan immigrants, attempt to replicate the white cheese so important in their cuisine with some combination of cottage cheese, feta, sour cream, or cream cheese. Different combinations may be used for different purposes, but nothing tastes quite right. Other substitutions are for the sake of convenience. Norwegian Americans making *lefse* may replace freshly peeled potatoes with dried potato flakes, especially when cooking in quantity. Many Asian Indians quickly replace labor-intensive flatbreads with store-bought white bread. Still other changes have to do with

higher standards of living. Dark flour may be replaced by white flour, considered desirable but less affordable in the Old Country. Meat becomes much more prevalent in the diet of most immigrant groups.

Creolization

The third source—too often overlooked—is the cultures of other immigrant and ethnic groups encountered in the United States. Most often immigrants settling in multi-ethnic environments will move into neighborhoods and will work in occupations associated with earlier immigrant groups. Finns, Croatians, and Italians who went to northern Michigan to work in the iron and copper mines replaced Cornishmen, some of whom became their foremen and bosses. These earlier immigrants from Cornwall became their model for American culture, and the Cornish national dish, pasty, was soon adopted by all. New Yemeni immigrants in Detroit, Michigan, moved into houses vacated by Poles, Romanians, and Lebanese who were ready to move uptown or to the suburbs. Their foreman at the auto plant is likely to have been hired from one of these previous waves of immigrants. These people of different ethnic cultures establish models of American life for the new immigrant. The Mexican immigrant who is hired to work in the kitchen of an Italian restaurant is surely affected by that experience. And when he or she takes home extra food to share with members of his or her family, they too will be affected.

The creation of ethnic culture from these various sources takes place within the particular constraints of minority life: the homesickness, the prejudice, the sense of being different, the urge to assimilate or to resist assimilation, the need to recreate the Old World in the New or to reject all possible reminders of the life that was. All these factors shape the specific form taken by the new culture. Many have come to call this process "creolization" after the term for a similar linguistic process, both of which refer to the creation of a new cultural configuration out of parts of several other preexisting cultures. Creolization may be regarded as the defining characteristic of ethnic food.

One can observe creolization in any aspect of ethnic culture, but it is particularly significant in food and foodways. There are a number of reasons for this. First, cooking and eating are expressive behaviors relatively easy to observe and, most important, heavily laden with symbolic meaning. A particular dish can evoke memories of home, family, better times, one's own place in the world. Familiar food is very much the natural way of things. In a sense, for an immigrant all the food of one's homeland is "comfort food." African Americans outside the South may pointedly eat soul food as an expression of who they are. A single dish may become the most important expression of ethnic identity, symbolizing the group and signaling to other members this common bond and by extention others, thereby reinforcing an individual's own sense of belonging. Crawfish among Cajuns and kielbasa among Polish Americans of pre–World War II immigration serve as examples. Because cuisine is especially responsive to new environments, where some ingredients are unavailable, and because new social settings bring new ways of eating and cooking, foodways are especially quick to adapt and change. At the same time, however, perhaps no aspect of culture is so resistant to change, so tenaciously held. After all, eating is a daily reaffirmation of who you are. Generations after the loss of their mother tongues, ethnic Americans are still likely to be cooking and eating some version of the family's "mother cuisine," even though it may be significantly changed from food in their homelands.

The social structure of an American ethnic group is often reflected in its foodways. Some groups were ethnic minorities in the nations from which they came to the United States. Examples include Jews and Roma from eastern Europe, Hmong from Vietnam, Germans from Russia. Such groups usually develop distinct communities in the United States with foodways that are distinctive, albeit usually closely related to those of others who came from the same country. Ethnic groups are often nested, one identity subsumed within another. A person might be Sephardi in the company of Ashkenazim and Jewish when with a group of Gentiles. A Hmong might be so categorized when with other Vietnamese and Vietnamese when with other Americans. All such social differences are replicated by differences in cuisine, and these take on great symbolic importance.

Foodways serve to demonstrate ethnic community in more instrumental ways as well. Eating together at an ethnic picnic or banquet is a manifestation of group solidarity. Borrowing a start of yogurt in the Armenian-American community or for *viili* (another soured milk product) among Finnish Americans is an expression of the network of relationships that constitutes community. Receiving needed ingredients from relatives or friends still living in one's homeland demonstrates the link to homeland that is another aspect of the ethnic community. These might be foodstuffs unavailable here, at least in the locale where the recipient resides. Similar social relationships may be enacted when foodstuffs are sent between different American communities, as when Arab Americans in Detroit's large community send basic ingredients to relatives living in northern Michigan, where the Arab-American community is small and even the basics are unavailable.

Often foodstuffs are sent from abroad, not because the item is unavailable in the United States but because the item from one's homeland is thought to be superior in quality. Most Lebanese Americans, for example, prefer spices and *kishik* (dried yogurt) from Lebanon. In some cases the item sent from abroad is not even considered superior but is laden with symbolic meaning. An Austrian American who receives annually a box of walnuts from home knows that they do not taste better than American walnuts and that sending them costs more then buying them in the United States. But they come from the tree in the family homestead where he or she grew up, and no American walnut really suffices.

Diffusion

Diffusion is rarely a one-way street. Just as members of an ethnic group are influenced in their foodways by those they live among, members of the majority population (including members of other ethnic groups) adopt ethnic foods, usually changing them in the process. Most often this involves commercialization, often initiated by ethnic entrepreneurs from within the community itself. As the process proceeds, changes in the foodstuff often transform it into something far different from the original; pizza, yogurt, and bagels come to mind.

Ethnic food has existed in America since colonists first encountered the exotic foods of local Native Americans and vice versa. But as a field of study, ethnic food attracted little interest until just prior to World War II. Most earlier commentary on ethnic food had to do with hastening its demise in the interest of assimilation. Some of the earliest work on the subject was done by Margaret Mead and her colleagues at the National Research Council's Committee on Food Habits during the early 1940s. Their goal was to develop profiles of cultural food preferences in the United States in an attempt to better shape national policy to fit particular local situations. At first they planned to exclude ethnic food from their studies, but soon, most likely under impetus of the new world war, they began to include study of what was then called "the food habits" of "foreign background groups in the U.S." By the time the committee was disbanded in 1942, it had produced a series of mimeographed memoranda on ethnic food.

The Federal Writers Project (1935–1943) generated further study of ethnic foodways as one part of its studies of regional cultures. America Eats, more specifically devoted to foodways, was a spinoff. The goal was to publish a book by that title comprising a comprehensive account of the history and ethnography of culinary traditions in the United States. Although it was to be regionally organized, research inevitably included ethnic foodways. A tentative table of contents included such items as Minnesota's lutefisk dinners, Mexican backyard barbecues, and North Dakota's Scandinavian picnics. Due to increasing concern with the war effort, the project was abandoned in 1942, and little of the research was ever published.

Nearly all of the work on ethnic cuisines up to this period was descriptive in nature and applied in purpose. One of the first analytic papers on the intersection of food and ethnicity was by John Bennett, Harvey Smith, and Herbert Passin in 1942, "Food and Culture in Southern Illinois," in which they demonstrate how diet is shaped by culture in a region shared by Germans, African Americans, and old-stock Americans.

The revitalization of ethnicity in the United States initiated by the African-American civil rights movement and further stimulated by activities surrounding the bicentennial brought ethnicity to the fore of American consciousness, both within and outside ethnic communities. As a multicultural model of America developed and ethnic pride was manifested, retention of traditional foodways came to be regarded as a positive rather than a negative attribute. Ethnic food was further popularized during the explosion of interest in food during the 1960s, 1970s, and 1980s and the general search for new and exotic foods. This surge of interest was felt at both the popular and scholarly levels. Ethnic food continues to be a frequent and important research topic for folklorists, cultural anthropologists, and culinary historians.

See also **Combination of Proteins; Foodways; Icon Foods; National Cuisines, Idea of.**

BIBLIOGRAPHY

Abraham, Nabeel, and Andrew Shryock, eds. *Arab Detroit: From Margin to Mainstream.* Detroit: Wayne State University Press, 2000.

Belasco, Warren J. "Ethnic Fast Foods: The Corporate Melting Pot." *Food and Foodways* 2 (1987): 1–30.

Gabaccia, Donna R. *We Are What We Eat: Ethnic Food and the Making of Americans.* Cambridge, Mass.: Harvard University Press, 1998.

Goode, Judith, Janet Theophano, and Karen Curtis. "A Framework for the Analysis of Continuity and Change in Shared Sociocultural Rules for Food Use: The Italian-American Pattern." In *Ethnic and Regional Foodways in the United States: The Performance of Group Identity,* edited by Linda Keller Brown and Kay Mussell. Knoxville: University of Tennessee Press, 1984.

Goode, Judith, Karen Curtis, and Janet Theophano. "Meal Formats, Meal Cycles, and Menu Negotiation in the Maintenance of an Italian-American Community." In *Food in the Social Order: Studies of Food and Festivities in Three American Communities,* edited by Mary Douglas. New York: Russell Sage Foundation, 1984.

Gutierrez, C. Paige. *Cajun Foodways.* Jackson: University Press of Mississippi, 1992.

Gvion-Rosenberg, Liora. "Telling the Story of Ethnicity: American Cookbooks, 1850–1990." Ph.D. diss., State University of New York, Stony Brook, 1991.

Kalcik, Susan. "Ethnic Foodways in America: Symbol and the Performance of Identity." In *Ethnic and Regional Foodways in the United States: The Performance of Group Identity,* edited by Linda Keller Brown and Kay Mussell. Knoxville: University of Tennessee Press, 1984.

Kaplan, Anne R., Marjorie A. Hoover, and Willard B. Moore. *The Minnesota Ethnic Food Book.* Saint Paul: Minnesota Historical Society Press, 1986.

Lockwood, William G., and Yvonne R. Lockwood. "Ethnic Roots and American Regional Foods." In *A Conference on Current Research in Culinary History: Sources, Topics, and Methods: Proceedings.* Higham, Mass.: Culinary Historian of Boston, 1986.

Lockwood, Yvonne R., and William G. Lockwood. "Pasties in Michigan: Foodways, Interethnic Relations, and Cultural Dynamics." In *Creative Ethnicity,* edited by Stephen Stern and John Allan Cicala. Logan: Utah State University Press, 1991.

Lockwood, William G., and Yvonne R. Lockwood. "Continuity and Adaptation of Arab-American Foodways." In *Arab Detroit: From Margin to Mainstream,* edited by Nabeel Abraham and Andrew Shryock. Detroit: Wayne State University Press, 2000.

Magliocca, Sabina. "Playing with Food: The Negotiation of Identity in the Ethnic Display Event by Italian Americans in Clinton, Indiana." In *Studies in Italian American Folklore,* edited by Luisa Del Giudice. Logan: Utah State University Press, 1993.

William G. Lockwood

HAWAII

Located almost dead center in the North Pacific Ocean—2,500 miles west of California—Hawaii consists of a string of 132 coral and volcanic islands extending some one thousand miles from the Big Island to Wake Island. Centuries of volcanic activity have deposited layers of ash that have enriched the soil. Strong sun combined with moderate temperatures and plenty of rain have produced a long growing season in the midst of a tropical paradise—a paradise that lured nineteenth-century European and American merchants and adventurers interested in exploiting Hawaii's natural resources. One result was an economy dominated by King Sugar, which employed waves of immigrants to do the backbreaking work refused by native Hawaiians.

This successive importation of workers left Hawaii with a thriving mélange of cultures, each of which made its own contribution to the twentieth-century phenomenon known as Local Food. A Creole mixture of different cuisines (including Polynesian, Japanese, Chinese, Portuguese, Korean, and American), Local Food is centered on carbohydrates—an ancient Hawaiian quest.

The First Polynesian Immigration

When human beings originally landed on Hawaiian shores between 300 and 500 C.E., having probably sailed roughly two thousand miles from Samoa, they encountered over a hundred species of birds, including large fowl, abundant fish and shellfish in shoreline reefs and lagoons, a few fruit trees at high altitude, ferns, several kinds of *limu* (seaweed), and nearly a thousand flowering plants. These species had arrived gradually on trade winds or sea currents and had evolved in isolation over hundreds of thousands of years.

But the same geologic conditions—deep canyons, high cliffs, forests, bogs, and a wide variation in barometric pressure, rainfall, temperature, and wind—that produced Hawaii's unique flora and fauna had also lim-

Taro is one of the most important food plants in traditional Hawaiian cookery. The root is used in making *poi*, while the stems (shown here) can be cooked as a green vegetable. © DOUGLAS PEEBLES/CORBIS.

ited its native foods. Hawaii's astonishing diversity included almost no edible vegetation and no source of edible carbohydrates. Luckily, the early Hawaiians brought at least twenty-seven kinds of foodstuffs, including the coconut, breadfruit, sweet potato, banana, sugarcane, arrowroot, wild ginger, mountain apple, and taro—much revered by the ancient Hawaiians, who pounded the roots into a paste, *poi*, that remains a starchy staple today. In addition, they imported pigs, chickens, and dogs. By mistake, they brought along rats.

They lived well on their isolated islands. They ate many foods raw, including some fish. Other food was cooked in *imus*, earthen pits lined with *kiawe* wood and lava rock. They prepared for bad weather by drying and salting fish. While they had no distilled liquors, they used the roots of *awa* (kava) and ti (a lily relative) to brew narcotic drinks.

The Second Polynesian Immigration
The early Hawaiians were legendary seafarers who had sailed thousands of miles using the stars, sun, winds and currents, shifting cloud masses, and bird flights. There is some evidence that they continued to sail their hundred-foot-long outrigger canoes to distant islands in the Pacific, bringing back food, plants, and spouses.

Between the eleventh and thirteenth centuries, aggressive, roaming Polynesians from Samoa and Tahiti settled in Hawaii and established a feudal regime overseen by their nobles and priests. The new feudal lords protected the ancient stonewalled fishponds, which yielded five thousand pounds of fish daily, and they enhanced traditional irrigation systems by building elaborate rock terraces.

They allocated property rights fairly widely, enabling most Hawaiians to eat well. The new rulers also enforced many complex *kapus*, or taboos, some of which helped manage scarce resources. Their system of land division is cited by biologists for its habitat protection. The huge freshwater and seawater fishponds were integrated with agriculture, and river valleys were managed as unified systems. The upland forest, left uncut by taboo, helped supply rivers with nutrients for downstream fields and fishponds. Seasons for gathering or catching scarce food or game were strictly enforced. Some taboos were exclusionary, particularly toward women, who were barred from preparing food for or eating with men. They were not allowed to eat the best foods, such as coconuts, shark meat, and pork. Breaking the taboos was punishable by death.

The Arrival of Westerners
By the time Captain James Cook landed on Kauai in 1778, Hawaiians had developed a comfortable economic system overseen by a feudal government. The Westerners would soon change all that.

Cook was the first of many seamen to use Hawaii as a way station to refuel and resupply ships in the middle of the ocean. He was renowned for having solved the

The warm waters off the Hawaiian islands offer a large variety of colorful tropical fish that are prized in local cookery. © DOUGLAS PEEBLES/CORBIS.

immense problem of scurvy among sailors, which he concluded was due to a lack of fresh fruits and vegetables. At every port he sought out fruit (particularly citrus), vegetables (including onions and new potatoes), fish, and meat.

The lush islands had much to offer Cook, who ruthlessly took immense amounts of food on his first trip, exploiting Hawaiian generosity. While Hawaiians had welcomed him with a lavish feast on his first visit, they knifed him to death when he returned in 1779.

Cook gave Hawaiians the first specimens of Western flora and fauna—goats, English pigs, and melon, pumpkin, and onion seeds. Close behind him came whalers and traders at the end of the eighteenth century, then the American missionaries, mainly Congregationalists, in 1820.

The missionaries introduced the church, school, printed word, woolen clothes, wood houses, and many foods. They sought to clean, clothe, and feed Hawaiians according to Christian standards to make them more responsive to the gospel. Beef was already available because cattle had been imported in 1793 by Captain George Vancouver, who had convinced King Kamehameha to permit women as well as men to eat it, as long as they ate from different cows.

The Congregationalists brought their prized New England foods—potatoes, apples, salted cod, corned beef, butter, and cheese. Food became a vital tool in Christianizing Hawaiians and turning them away from their traditional practices. When Queen Regent Kaahumanu converted to Christianity in 1824, she held a service at the edge of the Halemaumau fire pit sacred to the goddess Pele. Declaring her allegiance to Jehovah, she ate ohelo berries, which were both sacred to Pele and taboo to women. Not a murmur was heard from the volcano goddess.

Dominance by Plantations

Meanwhile, Westerners had also introduced their diseases, which reduced the native Hawaiian population from an estimated 300,000 at Cook's arrival to 60,000 by the mid-1800s and 40,000 by the end of the century. The rapidly expanding sugar industry—many plantations were owned by missionaries and their descendants—imported thousands of Chinese and then Japanese laborers to replace the Hawaiians. Just as the arrival of Westerners nearly wiped out native Hawaiians, the domination of agriculture first by sugar and later by pineapples wiped out the Hawaiian system of small farming overseen by religious laws, which regulated both hunting and farming.

Although wealthy whites received important administrative posts in the Hawaiian government, thereby governing indirectly, they became increasingly unhappy with the monarchy, which they deemed corrupt and inefficient. They wanted secure property rights to build their plantations and they wanted no restrictions on their importation of labor. They overthrew the monarchy in 1893. (Hawaii became a U.S. territory in 1900 and the fiftieth state in 1959.)

Between 1852 and 1930, Chinese, then Japanese, Okinawans, Norwegians, Germans, Koreans, Puerto Ricans, Portuguese, and Filipinos were imported by the immensely powerful factors that supplied plantations with all their needs, including workers. The workers wanted their own food, and the plantation stores procured it from abroad if it could not be grown locally. What could be grown was. Thus rice became Hawaii's third most important crop, after sugar and pineapples. Most immigrants brought seeds with them, though they could not always get them to grow. Manufacturers sprang up to produce tofu, noodles, kimchi, and sake.

Into this diversity came yet another set of missionaries—home economists, most trained by Columbia University's Teachers College. Convinced of the legitimacy of their field, the home economists taught at the newly established University of Hawaii, a land-grant university. Working with the electric and gas companies in the 1920s, they developed recipes that required the new appliances—stoves, ovens, and refrigerators. They promulgated the nutritional messages and agricultural advice of the Extension Services. They catalogued locally grown tropical foodstuffs and analyzed the nutritive values of the Hawaiian diet. They encouraged the consumption of American food, including milk, which many adult Hawaiians were unable to digest properly. They trained school cafeteria managers to produce Salisbury steak, mashed potatoes, and creamed corn. And they wrote the first cookbooks on Local Food.

The Development of Local Food

Hawaii's sad story of colonial exploitation is tempered by its exuberant ethnic diversity, nowhere to be found more clearly than in food. Calling themselves "locals," Hawaiians call the food they eat "Local Food," a term that most food writers now capitalize. Identified in the 1920s as a distinct phenomenon, Local Food mixes dishes from each of Hawaii's ethnic groups into unique forms, most famously the plate lunch served at diners and lunch wagons. This includes two scoops of sticky rice, meat cooked Asian style, and macaroni or potato salad—all eaten with chopsticks. Local Food includes shaved ice, SPAM wonton, *malasadas* (Portuguese donuts), saimin (noodle soup), crack seed (Chinese preserved plum), and butter *mochi* (a rice confection).

Except for indigenous coconut and banana trees, most foods associated with Hawaii are imported. The first immigrants, the Canoe People, brought with them twenty-four different plants. Since about 1800, a large number of additional plants, including pineapples, papaya, avocado, guava, sugar cane, coffee, and macadamia nuts, were introduced. Even the Kiawe tree—a variety of the family that includes mesquite, and is now rampant throughout the islands—was introduced.

Hawaii's premier agricultural product in modern times, the pineapple, is a native of Paraguay. Although introduced in the early 1800s, it was not commercially successful until the early twentieth century, when it was canned and sold to U.S. markets. By the early 1950s, almost 75 percent of pineapple on the world market was Hawaiian, thanks to inspired advertising. Hawaii has no canneries left today. Its entire crop is distributed fresh, accounting for about one million tons of fruit, or one-third of the world's consumption.

The highly prized Kona coffee, imported by Don Francisco de Paulay Marin in 1828, thrived in Hawaii's volcanic soil, enhanced by local altitude and climate. Simultaneously mellow and robust, Kona beans became renowned worldwide after the market crash of 1899, when the large plantations began leasing their lands to families of workers, who greatly improved the methods and quality of production. Many of those families are now in their fifth generation, producing some two million pounds a year. In the 1990s, coffee began to supplant the sugar cane plantings on several other islands, including Kaua'i, Maui, Moloka'i, and O'ahu—which now surpass Kona in total production. Most Hawaiian beans are sold for blends. Coffee marketed as a Kona blend must be at least 10 percent Kona.

Theobroma cacao, a variety of criollo, was able to take advantage of the same volcanic soil and climate and thrive. Though originally equatorial, Hawaiian crossbreed cacao, which has a nutty flavor and low acidity, grows quickly in open sun. (Its equatorial competitors need shade.) Its pods are harvested early—in two years rather than five—and its trees are more productive than elsewhere, averaging a hundred pods each, or five times the world's average. The chocolate is premium grade.

While macadamia nuts were brought to Hawaii as ornamentals in the nineteenth century, they did not become a commercial crop until the 1920s. Because the nut is very hard to crack, it is normally sold shelled. And because its production is labor intensive—one hundred pounds of harvested nuts yield only ten to fifteen lbs of edible meats—macadamias garner a premium price. Hawaii has some twenty thousand acres planted with macadamia trees today. The trees have a fifty-year lifespan.

Sugar cane, now displaced as a commercial crop, was introduced by the Polynesians. In the nineteenth century it became the islands' most significant commercial crop; it was for sugar cane that the Western economic interests eventually overthrew the monarchy.

Bananas were both indigenous and imported. With seventy varieties now grown on the island—and prestige accorded to some—Jean-Marie Jossellin likens the Hawaiians' distinctions among bananas to the Eskimos' distinctions of the varieties of snow.

Making Sense of Tourism

Since Hawaii's resident population of 1 million serves some 6 million tourists annually, the influence of outsiders on Hawaiian food can hardly be overstated. Until the late twentieth century that influence was baleful, with Honolulu having perhaps the worst restaurants of any major Western city. Even once elegant hotels like the Royal Hawaiian serve wretchedly bad meals in the name of traditional luaus—originally religious feasts of genuine importance degraded to farce by commercial exploitation.

But it is also true that many foods thought to be Hawaiian are not. Much of the so-called Hawaiian food served at Polynesian restaurants on the American mainland was invented in California and promulgated by Trader Vic's and other restaurateurs. Fried rice, satays, curries with coconut milk, rum-based drinks garnished with flowers and paper parasols, and dishes named after the goddess Pele or King Kamehameha have no real connection with Hawaii.

Since the early 1990s, however, a genuine Pacific Rim cuisine emphasizing cross-cultural influences but using local ingredients has developed. This has benefited small farmers, giving them outlets for superb fruits and vegetables—Maui onions (comparable to Vidalias), Manoa lettuce, Kahuku watermelon, Waimanalo corn, Kona oranges (a Valencia competitor) and avocados, Puna papayas, and an amazing range of seaweeds and ferns.

Meanwhile, native Hawaiians have reversed their population decline—about one-fourth of Hawaii's resident population of one million at the start of the twenty-first century claims some Hawaiian ancestry. Who is a native? One definition is that a native Hawaiian is someone who eats *palu*, a condiment made of chopped bits of fish head and stomach mixed with tiny amounts of *kukui* (candlenut) relish, chili peppers, and garlic. Not many fraudulent Hawaiians are likely to come forward to win this credential.

See also **Coffee; Fruit; Pacific Ocean Societies; Sugar and Sweeteners; Sugar Crops and Natural Sweeteners.**

BIBLIOGRAPHY

Corum, Ann Kondo. *Ethnic Foods of Hawai'i.* Honolulu: Bess Press, 1983.

Costa-Pierce, Barry A. "Aquaculture in Ancient Hawaii." *Bioscience* 320 (1987): 320–331.

Daws, Gavan. *Shoal of Time: A History of the Hawaiian Islands.* Honolulu: University Press of Hawaii, 1974.

Eyre, David L. *By Wind, by Wave: An Introduction to Hawai'i's Natural History.* Honolulu: Bess Press, 2000.

Grimshaw, Patricia. *Paths of Duty: American Missionary Wives in Nineteenth-Century Hawaii.* Honolulu: University of Hawaii Press, 1989.

Juvik, Sonia P., and James O. Juvik, eds. *Atlas of Hawai'i.* 3d ed. Honolulu: University of Hawai'i Press, 1998.

Laudan, Rachel. *The Food of Paradise: Exploring Hawaii's Culinary Heritage.* Honolulu: University of Hawaii Press, 1996.

Julia Vitullo-Martin

THE MIDDLE ATLANTIC STATES

The waves of European ethnic settlement in the mid-Atlantic colonies in the United States prior to the Revolution produced regional culinary patterns that have influenced American cookery down to the present day. These areas of settlement have been described as "culture hearths" by folklore scholar Henry Glassie because they created a continuous emanation of influences. The cumulative effect of these culture hearths has been twofold: an evolution of distinctive mid-Atlantic foods and foodways, and a spread of this coastal culinary identity into the interior of the country, especially into the Midwest.

The succession of settlement begins with the Holland Dutch, who in 1624 carved New Netherlands out of the Hudson Valley of New York and adjoining parts of New Jersey, with significant settlements in Delaware (direct from Holland), and in Pennsylvania in the form of migrations from New York and New Jersey. The Swedes and Finns settled among the Dutch in the Delaware Valley beginning in 1638 with the foundation of New Sweden (over Dutch legal objections). All of this initial settlement, which was represented by relatively small numbers of people, was later numerically overwhelmed by large immigrations from the British Isles, headed principally by the English Quakers who founded New Jersey, Pennsylvania, and Delaware.

The Quakers themselves represented a mixture of English, Welsh, Scots, Irish, and Ulster Scotch-Irish elements, and each of these groups brought Old World foods and foodways to the region. The Quaker policy of extending settlement opportunities to continental Europeans suffering from religious persecution virtually threw the entire region open to a vast mélange of new settlers from Germany, Switzerland, Alsace, Austria, and

New Year's cake print issued by Thomas Y. Watkins of New York to commemorate a dinner given at the Waldorf-Astoria Hotel by the Pilgrims of the United States in honor of Field Marshal Viscount Kitchener of Khartoum on April 18, 1910. The field marshal is depicted on horseback. ROUGHWOOD COLLECTION. PHOTO CHEW & COMPANY.

France. These non-English-speaking settlers created in the Middle Colonies a cultural diversity that has come to represent American food culture as a whole. Yet each group has left its legacy, the most important perhaps being the German-speaking element, which gave rise to the present-day Pennsylvania Dutch. In terms of area, the so-called Pennsylvania Dutch settlement region was about the same size as modern Switzerland and just about as varied. Close behind the Pennsylvania Dutch were the Scotch-Irish who settled the hill country of Appalachia and who created a regional culinary culture known as Cohee.

From a historical standpoint, the most recent treatment of the foods and foodways of the New Netherlands Dutch is Peter G. Rose's translation of *The Sensible Cook* (1989), which explores Hudson Valley Dutch foodways via an old Holland Dutch cookbook. The original *Sensible Cook* (*De Verstandige Koek*) appeared in 1667, at a time when Dutch gardening was undergoing a horticultural revolution. The Dutch infatuation with exotic plants and kitchen gardening was transplanted to the New World, especially through the medium of Dutch Mennonite seed and plant merchants, who controlled much of the trade with New Netherlands and the Quaker colonies to the South.

The Dutch Cuisine

In spite of persistent Old World contacts, New Netherlands Dutch evolved into a dialect of its own with a large

450

array of food concepts fully unknown to the Old World Dutch. These dishes would include *suppawn* (a type of cornmeal mush) and pumpkin pancakes, but intermingled with such Old World dishes as *olie-koecken* (a type of fat cake), soft or yeast-raised waffles, and *kool sla* (cabbage salad), served hot or at room temperature. Modern American coleslaw is probably the best known legacy of this old Dutch cooking tradition. However, the small Dutch New Year's cake called a *kookjie* has also entered standard American English under the more generic form of cookie (small cake). The true New Netherlands *kookjie* was in fact the so-called New Year's Cake, which evolved into a high art form in New York and Philadelphia. Many elaborately carved molds survive as a silent testimony to this lost art of ornamental pastry. The New York atelier of baker and mold maker John Conger produced some of the most elaborately carved molds to survive from the 1830s and 1840s.

The English Cuisine

By contrast, the English cuisine in the Middle States, as illustrated by the Quakers of Philadelphia and Baltimore, was basically a British Isles cookery adjusted to New World ingredients and climate. Nineteenth-century Quaker cookbook authors such as Elizabeth Ellicott Lea (Sandy Spring, Maryland), Elizabeth Nicholson (Philadelphia), and Hannah Widdifield (Philadelphia) mention a number of dishes associated not only with their religious group, but with the general population at large: white sweet potato pie (Quarterly Meeting Pie to Quakers), lemon butter and rusks, and the ubiquitous dried beef gravy. This last dish, which was served over toast, was often known as "Quaker gravy" throughout the region. Its chopped beef and onion version has survived to this day under the rubric of the Philadelphia cheese-steak sandwich.

The Quaker element was especially well known for its dairy culture in the form of substantial spring houses for the production of high quality butter and cheese. Philadelphia cream cheese (a soft cheese resembling French brie) was famous in the nineteenth century, although today it lives on in name only in the form of a processed cheese spread. The rich milk and cream that produced the popular cheeses and butters of the region also served as a major ingredient in Philadelphia ice cream, at one time a highly sought-after food on the American luxury market.

Quaker farmers were also skilled gardeners and orchardists, and some, like the Bartrams of Philadelphia, Humphrey Marshall, and William Darlington, studied native plants and trees and exchanged seeds with their European contacts. The Quakers also kept up an English preference for tea-drinking over coffee. Among the urban Friends of the nineteenth century, Quaker Tea Parties were synonymous with catered balls, a menu heavy with rich cakes and fancy side dishes, and a beverage selection awash with the best wines and champagne.

A New Year's cake made from the Thomas Y. Watkins print (facing page). The cake would have been further ornamented with colored icings and gilding. PHOTO WILLIAM WOYS WEAVER.

In total opposition to this show of opulence, were Friends who promoted vegetarianism and abstinence from alcohol long before these themes became commonplace in American culture. In fact, the first health food stores were opened in Philadelphia by the Quaker Martindale family during the 1860s.

The Pennsylvania Dutch element introduced food concepts found in the traditional peasant cookeries of southwest Germany, Switzerland, and Alsace-Lorraine. The pioneer generation ate simple, one-pot meals like sauerkraut and pork or *Schnitz-un-Gnepp* (dried apples and dumplings with ham and ham stock) reproduced from the homeland. They consumed more soups than their English-speaking neighbors, as well as numerous flour-based preparations like noodles and filled dumplings. Since the Pennsylvania Dutch farmers settled in what soon became the colonial wheat belt, a vast array of pies, cakes, breads, and festive cookies were added to the immigrant menu. Outdoor bake ovens were once a common feature on nearly every farmstead in the region, and travelers through the area never fail to mention the popularity of *Lotwarrick* (apple butter), salads with hot dressings, and *Schmierkees* (cottage cheese), especially *Schmierkees* flavored with chives.

In spite of the culinary quiltwork that once represented the region, most ethnic groups did not initially like or adopt the cuisines of their neighbors, except out of necessity. Thomas Hill, a New Jersey Quaker passing through eastern Pennsylvania on his way to settle along

Watercolor of the interior of La Panetière, a 1980s Philadelphia restaurant that employed the setting of an elegant turn-of-the-century townhouse to create an intimate atmosphere. ROUGHWOOD COLLECTION. PHOTO CHEW & COMPANY.

the west branch of the Susquehanna River, remarked in reference to the Germans: "My breakfast this morning, two cups of coffee without sugar, and three eggs; bread baked hard, and crust wet." For another meal: "Salad with milk, oil, vinegar, bonny clabber and bread; good God! How can they work so hard on such food!" A melting-pot effect did eventually overtake such aversions, especially in urban areas and in families in which intermarriage between ethnic groups occurred. This kind of hybrid mixing resulted in such regional specialties as pop-robin pudding (grated dough baked with cinnamon and butter), mush muffins (cornmeal Welsh muffins), and chicken salad served with fried oysters—to name a few.

Due to religious tolerance, this part of the United States was the first to witness many charitable food-related events, such as the church supper, fund-raising cookbooks, camp meeting dinners, and Sunday school picnics. The spread of these blue-collar social institutions was due in part to the publishing industry that once characterized Philadelphia's literary scene. Writers like Eliza Leslie and Sarah Josepha Hale gained national prominence through *Godey's Lady's Book*, a prominence the city maintained into the early 1900s with *The Confectioners' Journal*, Wilmer Atkinson's *Farm Journal*, Sarah Tyson Rorer's *Table Talk*, as well as Curtis Publishing's *Ladies' Home Journal* and *Country Gentleman*. Every one of these publications is chock-full of recipes reflecting trends in

American cookery during this period. Sarah Tyson Rorer in particular managed to take her culinary agendas well beyond the walls of her once-famous Philadelphia Cooking School. Her crossover into product promotional literature and specialized recipe books for everything from ice cream to vegetables made her a household name by 1900.

From a historical standpoint, colonial New York and southeastern Pennsylvania have left a lasting impression on American cookery via such foods as coleslaw, crullers, shoofly pie, soft pretzels, and rye whisky, not to omit New Jersey's once famous apple brandy known affectionately as "Jersey Lightning." Much of this emphasis on regionalisms has been revitalized through the efforts of the Kutztown Folk Festival, founded in the early 1950s and considered the first of its kind in the country. While the festival may attract New Yorkers in search of rural roots, the movie *The Age of Innocence* has recaptured the sumptuousness of the culinary scene during New York's Gilded Age. This was an era when American food as social display by the robber barons reached its ultimate apotheosis, since the grand dinners were also social events staged as much for the participants as for a spectacle-hungry public. In this exchange the seeds of many mythologies were sown.

The Origin of Current Trends

It is often forgotten today that the cowboy in American mythology and the "chow" cookery now associated with cowboy fare were not created from scratch on the Great Plains, but in the townhouse study of blue-blood Philadelphia author Owen Wister. His romantic novel *The Virginian* (1902) was a launching point for this very pervasive image in American culture. Immigration has also contributed to an ongoing evolution of more recent icon foods, such as New York's bagels and Reuben sandwich and Philadelphia's hoagies (known elsewhere as grinders or submarines).

New York has evolved into a truly international metropolis with a fascinating food story that would consume all the pages of this encyclopedia. Its position on the international scene was firmly fixed after World War II with the establishment of the United Nations headquarters in Manhattan. But it was New York's role in the American culinary revolution that has had its most lasting effect on our food. The transformation of the classic French cookery of such restaurants as Le Pavillon (which opened in 1941) into the likes of The Four Seasons and the celebrated Windows on the World in the World Trade Center is the story of an Americanization process in *haute cuisine* that emanated primarily from New York City. Added to this were the TV personalities of James Beard and Julia Child, whose impact on American cookery has been fundamental. The James Beard Foundation, with its annual awards for chefs and food writers, has continued to focus on New York's leadership in many branches of American food and culture.

As a counterpoint to this, Philadelphia and Baltimore have managed to retain a regional American character, especially in terms of culinary identity. Philadelphia established itself as the American culinary capital in the early nineteenth century, with roughly one-fourth of its immigrant population either European or Caribbean French. This contributed to a Caribbean accent in its urban cookery, hence the turtle soup and pepperpot vendors. It was also the cultural mecca where the Old South wintered. Pre–Civil War Philadelphia was indeed a city whose lifeblood was derived from Southern money and shipping, which brought to its larders vast quantities of foodstuffs from Asia, the Caribbean, and South America. Its economic rival was sister-city Baltimore, which today has preserved much of its Federalist Era culinary culture as defined by the Chesapeake Bay.

Both Philadelphia and Baltimore became centers of manufacturing after the Civil War, which changed elegant streets of stately row houses into smoke-congested corridors of noise, shuffling foreign labor, and crime. The rich left for the suburbs; thus, in both cities, dining culture retreated to country houses or into the hands of dining club managers and African-American caterers. In Philadelphia, the Augustin family (originally from Haiti) became the most important catering family on the East Coast and prided itself on such specialties as oyster fritters, creamed terrapin, and rasped rolls. At one time the Augustins owned railroad cars with kitchens so that elegant meals could be served as far away as Boston, Chicago, and Washington.

It was the Chesapeake Bay that eventually saved Baltimore, because the city has revived its culinary identity within the last thirty years on such local Bay specialties as soft-shell crab, beaten biscuits, stuffed ham, sweet potato pie, and Lady Baltimore Cake (another Owen Wister invention). With the restoration of historic Society Hill, Philadelphia culinary culture was revived in the 1970s by La Panetière, the haute-cuisine launchpad for what has become a culinary renaissance in that city. Philadelphia's annual spring food festival called Book and the Cook (created by White Dog Café owner Judy Wicks) has done much to bring national attention to the City of Brotherly Love. Unlike New Orleans, which depends primarily on tourism for its restaurant business, Philadelphia's success story has been the result of a grassroots appreciation of good food paired with its old loyalty to farm markets and regional produce.

The anomaly for the entire region is Washington, D.C., which for its first century was largely an artificial city carved out of Maryland farmland. Aside from the White House, where lavish dinners were *de rigueur*—but not under every administration—Washington was a boardinghouse town for congressmen and not noted for its good food. By the early 1900s, the city evolved into a more cosmopolitan place, yet retained a provincial Southern character well into the 1960s, when the Kennedys brought a new kind of flair to the capital, and George-

town and northwest Washington underwent a cultural revitalization. However, there were always a few popular restaurants, such as Marjorie Hendrick's Watergate Inn, which served regional American specialties, even a respectable Pennsylvania Dutch menu. More recently, the influx of Vietnamese immigrants and the renovation of numerous downtown buildings have led to an exciting new mix of culinary choices.

See also **Foodways; Germany, Austria, Switzerland; Low Countries; Restaurants**.

BIBLIOGRAPHY

Bodle, Wayne. "The 'Myth of the Middle Colonies' Reconsidered: The Process of Regionalization in Early America." *The Pennsylvania Magazine of History and Biography* 113:4 (1989): 527–548.

Ferris, Benjamin. *A History of the Original Settlements on the Delaware*. Wilmington, Del., 1846.

Glassie, Henry. *Pattern in the Material Folk Culture of the Eastern United States*. Philadelphia: University of Pennsylvania Press, 1968.

Hill, Thomas. "A Journey on Horseback from New Brunswick, N.J. to Lycoming County Pennsylvania, in 1788." *Now and Then: A Quarterly Magazine of History and Biography* (Muncy, Penn.) 4, no. 6 (1931): 176–179.

Hines, Mary Ann, Gordon Marshall, and William Woys Weaver. *The Larder Invaded: Reflections on Three Centuries of Philadelphia Food and Drink*. Philadelphia: The Library Company of Philadelphia and the Historical Society of Pennsylvania, 1987.

Kuh, Patric. *The Last Days of Haute Cuisine*. New York: Viking, 2001.

Lemon, James. "Household Consumption in Eighteenth Century America and its Relationship to Production and Trade: The Situation among Farmers in Southeastern Pennsylvania." *Agricultural History* 41 (1967): 59–70.

Lemon, James T. *The Best Poor Man's Country: A Geographical Study of Early Southeastern Pennsylvania*. Baltimore: Johns Hopkins Press, 1972.

Moonsammy, Rita Zorn, David Steven Cohen, and Lorraine E. Williams, eds. *Pinelands Folklife*. New Brunswick, N.J.: Rutgers University Press, 1987.

Rose, Peter G. *The Sensible Cook: Dutch Foodways in the Old and the New World*. Syracuse, N.Y.: Syracuse University Press, 1989.

Tangires, Helen. *On Common Ground: Public Markets and Civic Culture in Nineteenth-Century America*. Baltimore: Johns Hopkins University Press, 2002.

Thompson, Peter. "The Friendly Glass: Drink and Gentility in Colonial Pennsylvania." *The Pennsylvania Magazine of History and Biography* 113, no. 4 (1989): 549–573.

Tinker, Edward Larocque. *Gombo Comes to Philadelphia*. Worcester, Mass.: The American Antiquarian Society, 1957.

Wacker, Peter O. *Land and People: A Cultural Geography of Preindustrial New Jersey: Origins and Settlement Patterns*. New Brunswick, N.J.: Rutgers University Press, 1975.

Weaver, William Woys. *A Quaker Woman's Cookbook: The Domestic Cookery of Elizabeth Ellicott Lea.* Philadelphia: University of Pennsylvania Press, 1982.

Weaver, William Woys. *Pennsylvania Dutch Country Cooking.* New York: Abbeville Press, 1993.

Weaver, William Woys. *Sauerkraut Yankees: Pennsylvania Dutch Foods and Foodways* 2d ed. Mechanicsburg, Penn.: Stackpole Books, 2002.

Weigley, Emma S. *Sarah Tyson Rorer: The Nation's Instructress in Dietetics and Cookery.* Philadelphia: American Philosophical Society, 1977.

Woodward, Carl Raymond. *Ploughs and Politicks: Charles Read of New Jersey and His Notes on Agriculture, 1715–1774.* New Brunswick, N.J.: Rutgers University Press, 1941.

Yoder, Don. *Discovering American Folklife: Essays on Folk Culture and the Pennsylvania Dutch.* 2d ed. Mechanicsburg, Penn.: Stackpole Books, 2001.

Don Yoder

THE MIDWEST

The term "Midwest" first appeared in print in 1880 to describe the Kansas-Nebraska region and was enlarged by 1910 to include all twelve of what are now considered the midwestern states: Illinois, Indiana, Iowa, Kansas, Michigan, Minnesota, Missouri, Nebraska, North Dakota, Ohio, South Dakota, and Wisconsin. Geographic features of what are now considered the midwestern states include wide and fertile river valleys, limestone bluffs overlooking rivers and lakes, broad expanses of grasslands, the Great Lakes, the dry and rocky Badlands of the Dakotas, the deciduous woodlands of the northern Midwest and southern Missouri, the sandhills of Nebraska, and wetlands.

According to the geographer James R. Shortridge, "midwestern" connotes pastoralism, small town life, hospitality and friendliness, traditional values, farmers, yeoman society, and the Jeffersonian ideal. "The Midwest is America's pastoral face," he says, "etched into our consciousness as a permanent physical location, despite the presence of industrial cities" (Fertig, 1999, p. 30).

The most prominent geographic feature of the Midwest is rolling grassland or prairie. But of the 400,000 square miles of prairie that once stretched from central Ohio westward to the foothills of the Colorado Rockies and from Alberta, Manitoba, and Saskatchewan in Canada south to central Texas, less than 1 percent has remained natural prairie (Fertig, 1999, p. 166).

Native Foods

Before European settlement of the Midwest, Native American tribes gathered wild foods, such as native persimmons, papaws, berries, nuts of all kinds, and prairie turnips (Wilson, 1987, p. 119). Wild rice, really an aquatic grass, not a true rice, is the only grain native to North America, and it was a staple food of the Sioux and Chippewa tribes. Wild rice grows in the lakes and rivers of Minnesota, upper Michigan, northern Wisconsin, and lower Canada (Fertig, 1999, p. 223).

Wild game included venison, rabbit, elk, antelope, quail, migrating geese and ducks, prairie chickens, wild turkeys, and the American buffalo (bison). Certain tribes also planted many different varieties of corn, beans, squash, and sunflowers (Wilson, 1987, pp. 16, 58, 68, 82–84). Dakota Sioux Indians pounded buffalo fat, dried meat, parched cornmeal, and dried berries together to make "wasna," a high-calorie trail food (Episcopal Church Women, 1991, vol. 2, p. 21). Native Americans also fished for walleyed pike, bass, and perch from the lakes and catfish and trout from the rivers and streams.

Most of the prairie ultimately became productive farmland, small towns, cities, and suburbs. It is rangeland to the American cattle industry and is recognized as the nation's breadbasket. The eastern or short-grass prairie in Ohio, Indiana, Illinois, and Iowa has become the corn belt. The western or tall-grass prairie in Kansas, Nebraska, the Dakotas, and Canada has become the wheat belt. The central mixed-grass prairie in the hilly grasslands of southern Indiana, Illinois, and southwestern Wisconsin has become the dairy belt (Fertig, 1999, p. xi).

Midwestern Cooking

Midwestern cooking reflects both the bounty of the land and the ethnic diversity of the population. Favorites include wheat and honey buns, kolaches (fruit-filled sweet yeast dough pastries, originally *kolače*), traditional breads of all kinds, steaks, hamburgers, fried chicken, and pot roast. Locally brewed wheat beers are enlivened with a squeeze of lemon and accompany a bowl of chuck wagon chili zipped with the heat of peppers. Crisply roasted pheasant and other game delicacies are autumn treats. A piece of homemade pie and a cup of coffee welcome a newcomer, provide a warm and homey occasion for catching up with all the gossip, or bring a sweet ending to a family dinner.

City dwellers start the day with a cup of coffee and a bagel or a piece of toast. For farm families a hearty breakfast of bacon or sausage, eggs, biscuits or toast, and hash browns is more common. Lunch is a sandwich or salad and soup, perhaps a favorite bean soup. For dinner farm families might enjoy a slow-simmered pot roast or stew that has cooked all day. Midwesterners are also fond of casseroles, known as "hot dishes" in Minnesota, that can be assembled early in the day and baked later on. City households might have pasta, grilled chicken, or steak.

From barbecue competitions in the warmer months to ethnic food festivals throughout the year, midwesterners proudly affirm their culinary traditions. Residents of Milwaukee, Wisconsin, enjoy traditional Friday night fish fries at restaurants and churches. Catholic churches in rural parts of eastern Indiana and western Ohio offer chicken dinners throughout the summer and fall months,

Main Dining Room looking west, as seen from the balcony of Private Dining Room "B." Avenue of Palms is to the left; the windows to the right overlook Lake Shore Drive and Lake Michigan.

The main dining room of the Drake Hotel on Lake Shore Drive, Chicago in 1928. During its heyday, the Drake and its famous menus represented the ultimate in fine dining in the Midwest. ROUGH-WOOD COLLECTION.

featuring chicken fried in lard, garden vegetables, and homemade pies and cakes. The Door County Fish Boil is an ongoing summer ritual in Wisconsin in which whitefish, potatoes, and onions are boiled to overflowing in an outdoor cauldron.

Culinary Traditions
During the late 1700s and early 1800s settlers from the original thirteen American colonies began to move westward into Ohio, Indiana, Illinois, and Michigan. French settlers had already established villages along the Mississippi River in what is now Illinois, Missouri, and Iowa, and along the Missouri River in what is now Missouri and Kansas. These small settlements began to grow as the Louisiana Purchase, acquired by President Thomas Jefferson in 1803, opened up vast tracts of land for settlement. Between 1865 and 1880 Kansas attracted more immigrants than any other place in the nation. The promise of virtually free land and a chance to start over drew thousands to the rolling prairie. The first Homestead Act, passed by Congress in 1862, enabled the head of a family to claim 160 acres of land in Kansas for only a small filing fee and a residency requirement of five years (Fertig, 1999, p. 29).

As the Homestead Acts continued to be revised, new land was opened up in North and South Dakota, Iowa, and Nebraska that attracted new groups of immigrants, including Poles, Irish, Czechs or Bohemians, and Austrians. Each adult in the family could claim 160 acres, up to 480 acres per family, on the prairie. For a small filing fee the families could farm the land providing they built a homestead and lived there for a certain number of months a year. Women as well as men filed claims and lived on the land until it was theirs after the residency requirement had been completed (Fertig, 1999, p. 29). Each ethnic group brought its own unique culinary traditions to the melting pot of the Midwest.

Czech. Immigrants from what became Czechoslovakia brought their love of sweet and sour flavors, dumplings of all kinds, dried fruits and mushrooms, and kolache. Wild duck or jackrabbit was marinated in a vinegar and spice mixture, then roasted in the oven. The gravy was thickened with sour cream. Dumplings made from flour, bread crumbs, or potatoes were cooked on top of simmering stews or soups. Dried fruits and mushrooms were plumped in liquid and made into sweet or savory soups. Barley filled out stuffed cabbages or added depth to wild

The Midwest is home to numerous ethnic communities. One of the largest is the Polish community in Chicago and around Detroit. Polish foods are available in many parts of the Midwest, and the best known are pirogi. PHOTO BY ANDRÉ BARANOWSKI.

mushrooms in a baked dish. Cold weather vegetables like cabbage, carrots, potatoes, and parsnips also feature in Czech cooking. Kolache, tiny individual coffeecakes made of buttery yeast dough and filled with fruit butters or preserves, are a favorite fresh and hot in Nebraska, South Dakota, and Kansas kitchens.

German. The Heartland welcomed Germans from many different culinary traditions, and each group brought a different cooking style. The Volga Germans enjoyed a tradition of bierocks, verenicke, and other dishes similar to those of the Russian Mennonites. The "border people" from Bavaria loved homemade noodles and sweet-sour dishes, such as sweet-sour heart, liver, and tongue. Most of their cuisine was centered around cabbage and pork of all kinds. Smoky flavors combined with sweet and sour flavors, and onions and herbs. Homemade sauerkraut simmered with pork, potato pancakes, tortes, braised cabbage, sausage cooked in beer, honey, and spice cookies entered mainstream American cuisine thanks to German immigrants.

Russian Mennonite. Wheat-farming Russian Mennonites, who brought the first Turkey red winter wheat seeds to Kansas in 1875, are credited with transforming this part of the prairie into the nation's breadbasket (Fertig, 1998, pp. 47–57). Their foodways were influenced by so-

journs in the Netherlands, Germany, and the Ukraine. A Protestant sect advocating a simple life and a firm commitment to the ideas of the church, much like the Amish, the Mennonites kept searching for a place where they could work and worship in peace. Fleeing religious persecution for their pacifist views, the Mennonites brought their favorite foodways with them to each new homeland. One specialty, a fruit soup or *moos* (pronounced "mose"), is thickened with flour. Verenicke, a ravioli-like pasta filled with dry-curd cheese, is served with sour cream ham gravy, jelly, or syrup. Homemade bread is a staple in most households, but the traditional favorite is zwieback, a brioche-type sweet yeast bread often served on Sundays. When sliced and toasted in the oven, it takes on a nutty, delicious flavor and keeps for weeks. Immigrant families often brought baskets of toasted zwieback to last until they reached the prairie.

Swedish. Pure, clean flavors combine with rich, buttery baked goods and creamy, mild tastes to form the constellation of Swedish foods of the Midwest. The flavors and colors of sillsalat, pickled herring, and pickled beets offer a taste counterpoint to the mild flavors of Swedish potato sausage, baked brown beans, and Swedish yellow pea soup. Fresh dill turns up in potato dishes and pickles of all kinds. But the highlight of a meal is always the baked goods: hard and crispy knackebrod with soup, almond-flavored kringler or saffron-flavored Lucia buns (for Saint Lucia Day on 14 December) and tea rings with breakfast, mellow limpa rye bread with dinner. Mellow and milky desserts like ostakaka and rice pudding are often served with a red fruit sauce as much for a color contrast as for a taste complement. Indeed deep red is a favorite punctuation mark in Swedish meals, whether is appears in the spiced gluhwein on special occasions, beet dishes and sillsalat, or lingonberry and red currant sauces for everything from lacy Swedish pancakes to roast goose.

Polish. Without the traditional "seven sours" of pickled vegetables, no deluxe Polish meal would be complete. Centered around hearty peasant food, the cooking of Poland is full of thick soups, dried mushrooms, sauerkraut, potatoes, ground and spiced meats, fish with horseradish sauce, sour rye bread, and buttery baked goods. The Easter tradition of "breakfast all day long" and the Christmas tradition of the multicourse Vigilia hold firm in Polish families. Sour cream, vinegar, plums, horseradish, beets, cabbage, potatoes, poppy seeds, caraway seeds, and allspice configure and reconfigure in countless recipes. Buttery baked goods flavored with almonds and poppy seeds, smoked sausages of all kinds, poached pike with horseradish sauce, marzipan baked apples, and herring in sour cream reflect the diversity of this cuisine.

Italian. Italians, mainly from Sicily, were one of the last immigrant groups to arrive in the Midwest, in the early 1900s. Many Italian immigrants became market gardeners or opened restaurants or produce businesses in places like Des Moines, Chicago, St. Louis, Cincinnati, and Kansas City. Varieties of Italian cookies, some made with pine nuts or fig preserves, star in Italian bakeries and festivals throughout the Heartland. *Amogio*, a marinade of white wine, garlic, and herbs, flavors chicken and beef, which is then rolled in *modiga* or flavored breadcrumbs and grilled. Zesty tomato sauce tops pasta dishes and baked eggplant.

Barbecue. Traveling up from South America, the barbeque tradition is rooted in the foodways of rain-forest Indians, who smoked meats over green wood to preserve them for later use. Over time this technique spread to the American South and from there to Missouri, where black residents used pit barbeques to smoke lesser and cheaper cuts of meat like spareribs and brisket. In 1916 the Kansas City resident Henry Perry began selling barbequed turkey, duck, pig, and goose, and by 1929 he had three separate barbeque stands. His fame spread, and he taught others, including Charlie Bryant, the secrets of slow smoking. Bryant and his brother Arthur Bryant eventually took over Perry's business, calling it Charlie Bryant's. When Charlie died in 1952, it became Arthur Bryant's, whose barbeque rose to fame when Calvin Trillin extolled it. By the early twenty-first century Kansas City had over one hundred barbeque joints, from the basic shack to the high-style restaurant (Stein and Davis, 1985, pp. 11–20).

State Fairs

The region's agricultural roots are celebrated every year in state fairs held in late summer and early fall. During the 1850s, when the region was predominately agricultural, state fairs were established throughout the Midwest. The first was the Ohio State Fair, held in Cincinnati in 1850. Even though most state economies changed from mainly agricultural to businesses of other kinds, the tradition continued into the twenty-first century. They usually include the butter cow or other object or person sculpted from butter, a traditional attraction that began at the Ohio State Fair in 1903. Concessions offer unique state fair food, such as pork chop dinners in Iowa, barbecued rib dinners in Missouri, fried chicken dinners in Ohio, Indian tacos in Nebraska, and anything you want on a stick, including cheese, bamboo beef, smoked turkey legs, roasted corn, and corn dogs (Fertig, 1999, p. 60).

See also **Barbecue; Beer; Bread; Dairy Products; Maize.**

BIBLIOGRAPHY

Episcopal Church Women of the Saint James Episcopal Church, comps. *Our Daily Bread.* Enemy Swim Lake, Waubay, South Dakota. 1991.

Fertig, Judith M. "America's Wheat." *Saveur Magazine* 20 (June 1998): 47–57.

Fertig, Judith M. *Prairie Home Breads.* Boston: Harvard Common Press, 2001.

Fertig, Judith M. *Prairie Home Cooking.* Boston: Harvard Common Press, 1999.

Shortridge, James R. *Peopling the Plains: Who Settled Where in Frontier Kansas.* Lawrence: University of Kansas Press, 1995.

Stein, Shifra, and Rich Davis. *All About Bar-B-Q Kansas City–Style.* Kansas City, Mo.: Barbarcoa Press, 1985.

Wilson, Gilbert L. *Buffalo Bird Woman's Garden: Agriculture of the Hidatsa Indians.* St. Paul: Minnesota Historical Society Press, 1987.

Judith M. Fertig

NEW ENGLAND

New England's early foodways set a pattern for the common, everyday cookery that would be carried across the American continent and endure through time to the present. Many dishes considered today particularly American—pumpkin pie, johnnycake, pork and baked beans, apple pie, among others—evolved in New England from the yeoman English cookery of the seventeenth century colonist who came to the region.

Early Preferences

English settlers arrived in New England with a decided preference for beef and beer, wheat bread, peas and root vegetables, tree fruits, particularly apple, and well-developed dairying practices. Their seasoning habits were close to the rich and complex flavorings of the late medieval era. They ate fish on fast days, regarded it appropriately as light fare, but often associated it, especially salted fish, with poverty. Venison hunting and consumption was, for these people, restricted in Old England as sport and fare for the gentry. Within a few decades, settlers had considerably altered some of these habits to accommodate the climate and growing conditions of their new home, the variable supplies of still-developing trade networks, and economic realities of a colony as a joint stock company.

Climate and Cash Flow

New England's weather was much colder, particularly in winter, than the English were accustomed to in the Gulf Stream–moderated British Isles. The colonial period and early nineteenth century were, as well, affected by what weather historians have characterized as a mini ice age. Still summers were shorter, hotter, and more humid than English growing seasons, conditions that adversely affected wheat and pea growing in particular. A recurring mildew attacked wheat, gradually impelling a switch from wheat flour bread to one made with rye and the Native American's cornmeal, which settlers named "Indian" to produce a loaf called "rye and Indian." New England's climate favored the native beans that ultimately fared better than peas as a field crop and helped urge the shift to the beans pottage that would evolve into baked beans.

New England's climate limited natural abundance. Compared to other colonies in North America, settlers in the north were limited to gathering greens in early spring,

The icon food of New England is baked beans—one of Boston's nicknames is "Beantown"—and many families pride themselves on heirloom recipes, some tracing to the 1600s. Baked beans were originally prepared in earthenware cookpots. Slow simmering is one of the cooking secrets for a successful recipe. © BECKY LUIGART-STAYNER/CORBIS.

and wild fruits and nuts in two to three months of summer and early fall. Deer, moose, and small animals were most toothsome in the fall before they had spent cold months grazing on evergreens and mosses. Settlers near water could hunt wild fowl, as well as catch fish. But cold weather hunting and fishing was often strenuous and yielded uncertain results with at least as great an expenditure of energy finding food as would be gained from eating it. Besides the issue of dubious food value, early settlers viewed hunting and gathering as the sport of the gentry and idle, and, more to the point, they faced economic realties which mitigated against that activity.

Of first importance was establishing an economic base for the colonies settled all through southern New England. As joint stock companies, they owed money, and much effort was expended to raise it and to create some business that would yield profit. From the start, this impulse created a market economy that skewed settlers' activity toward lumbering, fishing, and producing the most merchantable crops and agricultural products, and away from growing experimental foodstuffs or from indulging in hunting and gathering with potentially unreliable results. New England's gentry farmers in later years took up the gentlemanly farming found earlier in the South and the Middle Atlantic colonies, growing experimental crops, vegetables, conducting animal husbandry, and cultivating fruit trees—quince, pears, cherries, apricots, and even peaches, but chiefly apples. By the later nineteenth century even middle-class professionals spent their leisure growing everything from strawberries to pumpkins in gentile competition, but for the first century and anywhere on New England's frontiers, Yankees

preferred the tried, true, and reliably abundant. This conservatism in taste and preference for reliability endured through the centuries.

Food from the Native Americans

New England's settlers adopted a limited range of food stuff and agricultural practice from the Native Americans. As most cultures do when encountering new foods, the English accepted those that most resembled the familiar and preferred. Practicality drove the adoption of what the Native Americans called the Three Sisters: corn, squash and pumpkins, and beans.

Corn grew and yielded well. Cornmeal behaved culinarily like the familiar oatmeal and was handled as oatmeal had been in England in the unleavened bread bannock. Bannock was also known in the North of England as jonniken. The corruption of the term jonniken accounts for the name johnnycake, best seen in the Rhode Island spelling of jonnycake, which is to this day an unleavened mixture of cornmeal, salt, water, sometimes thinned with milk, and baked over fire on a flat pan in traditional bannock fashion. Cornmeal was also cooked as a mush or hasty pudding, as had been oatmeal. Similarly, Indian meal was used in place of the customary coarse oatmeal to make the milk-based, molasses-sweetened Indian pudding, ultimately named for the cornmeal used to make it.

Squash and pumpkins worked in recipes like apples did, so they were stewed as a sauce or sliced in pie form as apples were in the seventeenth century. Later, in the eighteenth century, they would be used like the similarly textured sweet potato in the sweet puddings often baked in pastry shells, and thus gradually evolved into pumpkin pie.

For many centuries, the most commonly used bean in Europe was a large flat bean of which the modern fava is a kind. Settlers encountered the smaller, rounder, kidney-shaped beans of North America that could be used as peas had always been used in potages and soups, often with salted meat, or even sometimes ground to be combined with grains for a coarse bread. Most of the early potages were stewed dishes, but toward the end of the eighteenth century, New Englanders took advantage of still warm brick bake ovens to bake slowly a pot full of beans with salt pork. Baked beans were barely sweetened in the early era, the most usual proportion being one large spoonful of molasses to a quart of dried beans. Industrially produced beans of the later nineteenth and early twentieth centuries were notoriously and popularly sweet, and many homemakers followed the example to create the sweet baked beans we know today.

Reform and Beer and Bread

Uncertainty with grain crops together with the relative ease of apple growing gradually brought about a slight shift from beer and ale to apple cider drinking. Still for the first two centuries of New England's history, housewives continued the paired activities of baking and brewing, both of which used and generated yeast. The advent of the Temperance movement, the earliest of the food-ways-related reforms to take hold of New England, gradually eliminated brewed beverages from widespread daily and family consumption and replaced them with tea and coffee, and eventually for festive occasions, lemonade. Some people continued to drink wine, and beer and cider, but the Temperance influence was widespread in New England, and broke the bread-making and brewing connection, opening the way for commercial yeast-making and the wider acceptance and manufacture of chemical leavenings such as pearlash, later saleratus, and eventually baking soda and cream of tartar, and baking powder.

New Englanders reverted to making bread with wheat after the Eire Canal opened in the 1820s, and lower cost wheat flour came on the market. The old rye-and-Indian gradually disappeared, but in the mid-nineteenth century the combination could be found in Boston brown bread, which continued to use rye, cornmeal, and sometimes wheat flour as well, mixed with chemical leavenings, milk, sweetened with molasses, and steamed—more pudding than bread, but eaten as bread would be, often accompanying baked pork and beans. This combination continues even to our time, and was carried across the country anywhere New Englanders settled.

Fish, Molasses, and Industry

New England was the earliest region to industrialize. In the late eighteenth and early nineteenth centuries, Boston and Providence capitalists converted money from trade and shipping into textile manufacture. Some of this wealth had been originally generated by the salt cod trade with Europe and the West Indies, where it formed a leg of the well-known triangle trade that included molasses and slaves. Settlers engaged in cod fishing early, utilizing one of the regions natural resources, in order to produce an income for repayment of investments in colonies. The codfish that hangs in the Massachusetts State House has little to do with gastronomic preferences of New Englanders, but honors instead the source of much wealth.

New Englanders certainly did consume salt codfish, often on Saturday, often in the form of a boiled dinner with root vegetables, and a sauce of fried salt pork or butter and chopped boiled eggs. This dish gained the derisive nickname Cape Cod Turkey, variously Block Island Turkey. Chowder, another dish with strong New England associations, came ashore from the fishing fleets. Earliest versions of it were comprised of fishermen's provisions, salt pork and hardtack, to which fish was added. When Yankees added potatoes to their everyday diet, they were used in the chowder, too, eventually replacing hardtack as a thickener.

The molasses was made into rum, and provided an inexpensive sweetening characteristic of many of New England's early dishes. Wherever saltwater access made

The Maine lobster dinner is one of New England's most popular tourist attractions. The menu may vary from restaurant to restaurant, but the basics are universal: boiled lobster, corn on the cob, cornbread, and coleslaw. Many menus include oysters or quahogs (a type of clam) for starters. © BOB KRIST/CORBIS.

shipping possible molasses, brown sugar, and refined white sugar were available to cooks, even in the hinterlands. Two other sweeteners, commonplace in interior New England, were a thick, molasses-like syrup made from boiled down sweet apple cider, and maple sugar. Produced mostly as a commodity, partly for home consumption, sugar-making from maple tree sap became a widespread activity in the middle to late eighteenth century, and grew steadily through the nineteenth. The goal was sugar production, though in more recent times, the syrup has become more desirable.

The industrialization of New England promoted urban growth and transformed many New Englanders from food producers to food consumers only. Urbanization created a stronger market for dairy products—cheese, milk, and butter—and changed many New England farms from producing varied crops to focusing on a specialty such as dairying, orchards, or raising poultry for meat and eggs. By the mid-nineteenth century, grain and even beef and pork were brought into New England's cities from the West by way of railroads and artificial refrigeration.

New England has many distinctive cookeries, from the shipboard fare of the old whaling ships to the rustic cookery of Maine logging camps. This cook in the Fletcher Field Logging Camp (Washington County, Maine) is shown preparing bread in a 1948 photograph taken by Leland J. Prater. © CORBIS.

Factory work also changed the daily patterns of meals for many New Englanders. The old rural pattern of a morning breakfast, noon dinner, and a smaller meal called tea or supper in the evening gave way to breakfast, a lunch carried to work, and a supper or dinner in the evening at the end of the work day. For many laboring families, however, dinner became a Sunday phenomenon, placed in the middle of the day. People in farming communities would continue the old pattern well into the twentieth century.

Immigration

Industrialization encouraged immigration from the French Canadian north and Europe and gradually introduced ethnic flavors to the region. The same reformist impulse that gave Temperance such a strong footing in New England also worked toward mainstreaming the newcomers' diets. Scientific cooking and cooking schools, such as the well-known Boston Cooking School, made as their missions both to educate middle-class women in healthful and aesthetically pleasing cookery, but also to

uplift the poor, often immigrant, populations caught in the economic vicissitudes of industrialization. This combined readily with many immigrants desire to meld into American life, which they accomplished by giving up some of their traditional dishes to eat more meat. Many ethnic groups living in neighborhoods nevertheless managed to continue many familiar foodways and supported local groceries, butchers, fish markets, and green grocers. In the twentieth century, with the culmination of nearly a century of exposure to Italians, Portuguese, Eastern Europeans, French, and Asians, Yankee cooks ate in ethnic restaurants and experimented with foreign dishes at home.

Thanksgiving

The national holiday Thanksgiving owes it origins to the sustained custom of autumn harvest festivals brought to and continued in New England. Originally a moveable feast that could occur almost anytime at the conclusion of the growing season, early New Englanders preferred to conclude butchering season before celebrating the harvest, usually at the end of November or beginning of December. Individual colonial, later state, governors declared what day, usually a Thursday, the holiday would be observed. A holiday of family reunion, feasting, and recreation, Thanksgiving's menu has been much mythologized, starting with the event considered the first Thanksgiving, described by Edward Winslow in *Mourt's Relation*: "so we might after a special manner rejoice together after we had gathered the fruit of our Labors." Winslow reported that they had wild fowl and venison, and William Bradford writing in *Of Pilmoth Plantation* about the same event, referred to fish, turkeys, and Indian meal.

In the nineteenth century when the story of founding settlers of Plymouth was romanticized, the association of turkeys and the so-called Pilgrims at Thanksgiving assured that dish would appear on the table along with roast pork, chicken pies, fall-harvested vegetables such as squash, potatoes, and turnips. Cranberry sauce and pickles and other preserves accompanied the meal, and pies followed made of pumpkin, apple, and mincemeat. This menu, with very few substantial changes, spread across the country with settlers, and has continued to the present along with the habit of observing the day. While nearly every state in the nation observed Thanksgiving in some form, the day became a nationally declared holiday when Abraham Lincoln, at the urging of Sarah Josepha Hale, set the holiday at the last Thursday in November. Franklin Roosevelt changed the date to the fourth Thursday, where it rests today.

See also **Fish: Sea Fish**; **Foodways**; **Maize: Maize as a Food**; **Squash and Gourds**; **Sugar Crops and Natural Sweeteners**; **Thanksgiving**; **Wheat: Wheat as a Food.**

BIBLIOGRAPHY

Albion, Robert, William A. Baker, and Benjamin W. Labaree. *New England and the Sea*. Mystic, Conn.: Mystic Seaport Museum, 1972.

Bradford, William. *Of Plimoth Plantation*. Edited by Samuel Elliot Morison. New York: Knopf, 1952.

Child, Mrs. Lydia Maria. *The American Frugal Housewife*. (Reprint of 12th ed. Boston: Carter, Hendee, and Company, 1833) Worthington, Ohio: Historical Society, 1965.

Dwight, Timothy. *Travels in New England and New York*. Edited by Barbara Miller Solomon. 4 vols. Cambridge, Mass.: Belknap Press of Harvard University Press, 1969.

Farmer, Fanny Merritt. *The Boston Cooking-School Cook Book*. Boston: Little, Brown, 1895.

Hazard, Thomas Robinson. *The Jonnycake Papers of "Shepherd Tom" together with Reminiscences of Narragansett Schools of Former Days*. Boston, 1918.

Oliver, Sandra L. *Saltwater Foodways: New Englanders and Their Food at Sea and Ashore in the 19th Century*. Mystic, Conn.: Mystic Seaport, 1995.

Parloa, Maria. *Miss Parloa's New Cookbook and Marketing Guide*. Boston: Estes and Lauriat, 1880.

Russell, Howard S. *A Long Deep Furrow: Three Centuries of Farming in New England*. Hanover, N.H., and London: University Press of New England, 1976.

Shapiro, Laura. *Perfection Salad: Women and Cooking at the Turn of the Century*. New York: Farrar, Straus, and Giroux, 1986.

Simmons, Amelia. *American Cookery: Or, the Art of Dressing Viands, Fish, Poultry and Vegetables* (1796). Introduction by Mary Tolford Wilson. New York: Dover, 1984.

Travers, Carolyn Freeman, ed. *The Thanksgiving Primer*. A Plimoth Plantation Publication. Plymouth, Mass.: Plimoth Plantation, 1991.

Winslow, Edward. *Mourt's Relation*. Edited by D. B. Heath. Cambridge, Mass.: Applewood Books, 1986.

Sandra L. Oliver

PENNSYLVANIA DUTCH FOOD

Also referred to as Pennsylvania German and incorrectly as Amish, this rural style of regional American cookery underwent its greatest flowering during the nineteenth century. It became one of the primary regional cookeries of the Middle Atlantic and Midwestern states, encompassing communities scattered throughout Pennsylvania, Maryland, Virginia, North Carolina, Ohio, Indiana, Illinois, Iowa, and Wisconsin, and of Ontario, Canada. Each area of settlement developed its own regional specialties or regional interpretation of shared culinary themes. The heartland of the cookery, however, is southeastern Pennsylvania, where it first evolved in the eighteenth and early nineteenth centuries. Because they represent a composite of several German-speaking cultures that settled in colonial America, Pennsylvania Dutch foods and foodways are remarkably diverse, incorporating elements of Swiss, Southwest German, and North German cuisines but transformed into something essentially American.

If a unifying thread once existed, it was in characteristics shared with the regional cookery of Alsace, France, as exemplified by the cookery books of George Girardey (1842) and William Vollmer (1856). The differences between Alsatian and Pennsylvania Dutch cuisines are much more acute, since a large number of the Pennsylvania Dutch shifted from daily wine consumption before the Civil War to near total abstinence. Wine was replaced by sugar, especially in the tourist fare styled as Amish or Pennsylvania Dutch. Also opinions vary over what to call this ethnic cookery, reflecting an evolution both of the group's self-perceptions and how it is seen by outsiders.

The term "Pennsylvania Dutch," the oldest label, derived from the colloquial English use of "Dutch" to designate anyone from the Rhine Valley, be they Hollanders, Germans, or Swiss. Even William Shakespeare used the word in this sense. The term was given popular currency by the travel writer Phebe Earle Gibbons in *Pennsylvania Dutch and Other Essays* (1872). One body of American scholars who study this culture prefers the term "Pennsylvania Dutch" since it implies a native hybrid that

Fish mold for the New Year. Berks County, Pennsylvania, circa 1810. Yellow glaze on pale earthenware. This ancient symbol of the New Year traces to the sacred salmon of the Rhineland Celts, which swam into the Rhine in vast numbers in early March (old New Year). By chasing its tail, the fish is symbolically chasing the old year, since its head represents the new. ROUGHWOOD COLLECTION. PHOTO CHEW & COMPANY.

evolved in North America as opposed to German American cuisine. An opposing body prefers to use the term "Pennsylvania German," a label that came into vogue during the 1890s among a group of scholars, mostly Germanophiles, who viewed the culture as a pure, uncreolized European transplant. These two opposing points of view, an American-centered definition and cultural vision defined by Europe, remained in tension into the twenty-first century.

With the ascendancy of Adolf Hitler in the 1930s, the term "Pennsylvania German" fell into disfavor due to anti-German sentiments in the United States. This shift was exemplified by J. George Frederick's *Pennsylvania Dutch and Their Cookery* (1935), which struck a patriotic note by highlighting famous individuals from the culture and the very Americanness of the cuisine. At the same time the Amish Mennonites, whose agrarian lifestyle represents a co-mingling of Old and New World themes and whose pacifist beliefs were fully opposite to those espoused by Hitler, provided a new and convenient symbol for the culture as a whole. Numerically, at the end of the twentieth century the Amish represented less than 5 percent of the total Pennsylvania Dutch population, yet tourism after the late 1940s exploited them to such an extent that "Amish" became a muddied synonym for both "Pennsylvania Dutch" and "Pennsylvania German."

A stylized and highly limited menu format created by the Pennsylvania Dutch Folk Festival at Kutztown, Pennsylvania, and its many spin-offs during the early

1950s led to a canonized cuisine, including chow-chow pickles, whoopie pies, chicken corn soup, and red velvet cake, that most restaurants claim is Dutch. The foods on this limited menu neglect the wide range of cooking styles prevalent in the community, emphasizing only peasant roots or once-popular Victorian farm fare, cracker pudding for example, at the expense of the more sophisticated ethnic dishes. The term "Amish" is also commonly misapplied to this menu and serves as an advertising gimmick for such dubious products as Amish Polish pickles, Amish tortillas, or Amish friendship bread. The implication is that, since the Amish live close to the land, foods associated with them convey values of purity, integrity, simplicity, and homemade goodness, commercial connotations formerly associated with the term "Quaker" in the nineteenth century. Thus the Amish theme has given rise not only to a type of interior decoration (the Amish are forbidden to decorate their homes) but also to a spate of Amish-style cookbooks promoting those values.

Historically, the best Pennsylvania Dutch cooks and cookbook authors, like Mrs. J. A. Keller, Edith Bertels Thomas, Ruth Hutchison, Ann Hark, John Levan, and Preston Barba, came from the ranks of the mainstream groups, such as the Lutherans, Reformed, or Moravian.

GINGERKRAUT (*IMBERGRAUT*)

This is a Christmas dish generally eaten with turkey or roast goose. It is also served at New Year's.

Yield: 6 to 8 servings

¼ cup (60 ml) walnut oil (olive oil may be substituted)
2 Tablespoons (15 g) white mustard seed
2 medium onions (300 g), sliced
2 cups (500 ml) turkey or chicken stock
2 pounds (1 kg) sauerkraut, drained of liquid
3 Tablespoons (50 g) coarsely shredded fresh ginger root
15 juniper berries
3 Tablespoons (15 g) chopped red bell pepper

Heat the oil in a deep nonreactive saucepan. Add the mustard seed and sizzle until they pop and begin to turn gray (about 1 minute). Add the sliced onions and cover. Let the onions sweat for 10 minutes, then add the turkey or chicken stock, sauerkraut, ginger, and juniper berries. Cover and simmer over a low heat for 1 hour. Add the chopped pepper as a garnish and serve immediately.

SOURCE: Weaver, *Pennsylvania Dutch Country Cooking*, p. 174

Professionals from that segment of the community operated the inns, the once-numerous wineries, the hotels, the bakeries, and the confectionery shops. The plain sects, like the Amish, were the farmers who provided the cuisine with high-quality, fresh materials, keeping alive a system of farm markets that survived into the twenty-first century. But due to their religious restrictions, they could not indulge in fine cookery, such as goose liver pie or wine noodles, of the sort taught in Moravian girls' schools. This dichotomy of cuisines based on differences in income and religion is perhaps best exemplified by Moravian sugar cake, a rich pastry served with coffee, and the various kinds of *Botboi* (potpie) eaten by farmers for Sunday dinner. Both dishes are of medieval origin.

Moravian sugar cake is a festive bread sweetened with brown sugar and cinnamon. It originally was baked in large, round loaves that were broken apart and served during Moravian love feasts, a congregational celebration. The *Botboi* (pronounced BOT-boy), originally an English colonial one-pot meal boiled in an iron pot lined with dough, gradually evolved a Pennsylvania Dutch identity by replacing the dough, which the English made with suet, with flat egg noodles. The concept of layering ingredients between noodles, similar to lasagna, traces to classical antiquity and may represent a technique preserved in the medieval cookeries of southern Germany and Alsace. In any case, *Botboi* further evolved among the Pennsylvania Dutch so that each Pennsylvania region could claim its own identifying dish, such as the chicken-and-saffron *Botboi* of Lancaster and Lebanon Counties, the pea *Botboi* of the Cumberland Valley, and the peach *Botboi* of Somerset County.

Other types of Pennsylvania Dutch dishes include the *Schales* (pronounced SHAH-less), a species of baked casserole normally made with legumes and shredded vegetables; the *Gumbis* (pronounced GOOM-biss), a deep-dish casserole consisting of layered ingredients; and various distinctive types of meat dishes and sausages. The most popular form of *Gumbis* is a dish called *Schnitz-un-Gnepp* (pronounced SHNITS-oon-NEPP), a baked or stewed mixture of dried apples, ham, and dumplings. Among the meat dishes, *Panhas* (pronounced PAN-haas), a word derived from ancient Belgic *pannas*, is sold in most farm markets as a breakfast dish. The word "scrapple" is replacing the dialect name *Panhas*. Of Lower Rhineland origin, *Panhas* was eaten as a porridge on butchering day but became a pot pudding, made with the leftovers of pork butchering, that is sliced, fried, and eaten with a variety of condiments. The primary thickeners are buckwheat and cornmeal.

Among the Pennsylvania Dutch, *Seimawe* (pronounced ZEI-maa-eh) is considered a "national" dish. A pork stomach is stuffed with potatoes, sausage, bread, and various herbs, poached, then baked. Served with great fanfare, the best are those that can be sliced like sausage. The origin of this dish is quite ancient and probably traces to pre-Germanic cultures in the Rhineland. Other

Broadside print for Adam and Eve Day (December 24), an old Pennsylvania Dutch folk observance that associated the Tree of Knowledge with the Christmas tree. Printed by Heinrich Sage, Reading, Pennsylvania, circa 1820. ROUGHWOOD COLLECTION.

signature foods are sauerkraut, de rigueur for New Year's dinner; summer sausage, also called Lebanon bologna; and shoofly pie, a molasses crumb cake baked in a pie shell that was first introduced commercially at the U.S. centennial in 1876. Of all the Pennsylvania Dutch contributions to American culture at large, the most lasting have been the Christmas panoply of gingerbreads, candies, and pastries; pretzels of all kinds; and vegetable gardening, which has persisted as a symbol of biodiversity and small-scale sustainable agriculture.

See also **Christmas; Germany, Austria, Switzerland; Sustainable Agriculture.**

BIBLIOGRAPHY

Girardey, George. *Höchst nützliches Handbuch über Kochkunst.* Cincinnati, Ohio: n.p., 1842.

Hark, Ann, and Preston A. Barba. *Pennsylvania German Cookery*. Allentown, Pa.: Schlechter, 1950.

Vollmer, William. *The United States Cook Book*. Philadelphia: J. Weik, 1856.

Weaver, William Woys. *Pennsylvania Dutch Country Cooking*. New York: Abbeville Press, 1993.

Weaver, William Woys. *Sauerkraut Yankees*. 2d ed. Mechanicsburg, Pa.: Stackpole Books, 2002.

William Woys Weaver

PIONEER FOOD

Pioneer foods can be defined as the emergency foods and the makeshift methods of food preparation employed by European settlers in the Americas, Africa, Australia, and other parts of the world to which European culture was transplanted en masse. While work has been done on such scattered themes as the Australian Germans (Heuzenroeder, 2001), the German settlers on the Russian steppes (Kloberdanz and Kloberdanz, 1993), and the Portuguese experience in Brazil (Camara Cascudo, 1967), research on pioneer cultures has largely concentrated on particular ethnic groups rather than looking at overall patterns and themes. This essay attempts to outline some general observations on the pioneer food culture of the continental United States. These foods have played an important role as symbols in traditional culture and as continuing images in modern mass culture. The Fort restaurant outside of Denver has become a national symbol of this genre of cookery, and its owner, Samuel Arnold, has been a keen supporter of research on this subject. Jacqueline Williams's *Wagon Wheel Kitchens* (1993) is especially noteworthy for its treatment of pioneer foods along the Oregon Trail.

Faced with the double problem of establishing new economic and social communities to replace the ones left behind, early American settlers were forced to make compromises on what they served on their tables. The primitive, log-cabin-in-the-clearing style of life was indeed rugged and different from later stages of more settled food production and consumption. In wooded areas fields had to be cleared before farming and gardening could commence. European methods of slash-and-burn agriculture were employed to make new ground amid the stumps of trees later removed. On the Great Plains the log cabin became the sod house, but on all frontiers the initial dependence was significantly on wild foods to supplement the diet. This included game, such as wild turkey, jackrabbit, quail, pigeon, venison, squirrel, groundhog, bear, and, of course, buffalo.

County histories are rich in stories of pioneer foodways, especially in noting wild plant foods that are no longer consumed. Cattail flapjacks, the wapatoo or swamp potato (*Sagittaria latifolia*), prairie breadroot (*Psoralea esculenta*), the pond apple (*Annona glabra*) of Florida, the buffalo pea (*Astragalus crassicarpus*), the cabbage palm

(*Sabal palmetto*) of the coastal South, and the miner's lettuce (*Montia perfoliata*) of the West Coast all carry names that allude to their substitute uses in settlers' diets. Some native plants, like miner's lettuce and Mormon tea (*Ephedra viridis*), are still widely consumed in the twenty-first century, while others, like the mayhaw (*Crataegus aestivalis*) of the Deep South, have become symbols of regional cooking (mayhaw jelly). Many wild food plants, like camass (*Comassia quamash*) of the Northwest, are grown mostly as garden ornamentals.

Aside from wild plants, the principal food source derived from the Native Americans was corn (maize), which became the primary grain raised by backwoods farmers, taking precedence over wheat and other cash crops. Corn products eaten at the pioneer table were many. Corn on the cob was a favorite summer dish once corn attained the milk stage in midsummer. It was commonly roasted in ashes downhearth rather than boiled. In fact, in the twenty-first century is still called "roasting ears" in many parts of Appalachia.

Cornmeal mush or suppawn was a common winter dish normally eaten with milk or syrup. The solidified residue was sliced and fried the next day for breakfast. Dried corn was also a winter dish, along with hominy or samp. The latter was of two kinds: large hominy hulled in lye water, then boiled and served whole; or small hominy (grits), which was ground to create several grades of texture, depending in part on the type of corn used. Small hominy is a popular dish in the South, although it was once widely eaten in other parts of the country.

Another pioneer grain, this one brought from Europe, was buckwheat, which could thrive in poor soils on hilly or mountainous land and provided bees with a local source for buckwheat honey. An English traveler through early America once referred to the ubiquitous buckwheat cake as a popular American breakfast preparation. Buckwheat was also combined with cornmeal to make various types of pork or venison scrapple known by such regional names as panhas (Pennsylvania and Ohio), poor-do (Upper South), and liver mush (Appalachia). Because of its dark color, buckwheat dishes fell out of fashion during the late nineteenth century in favor of foods made with wheat.

The prevalent method of cooking in pioneer settlements was in open fireplaces, where primitive breads, such as johnnycakes and corn dodgers, could be baked on hanging griddles or in Dutch ovens. The Dutch oven, a straight-sided iron bake kettle with a tight-fitting lid, became a symbol of frontier one-pot cooking because it could be used for baking, frying, boiling, and braising. Among the Mormon settlers of Utah, the Dutch oven represented their religious trek through the wilderness, and in the twenty-first century Dutch oven cooking remains a central feature of Mormon outdoor gatherings.

Undoubtedly the frontier diet was monotonous by any standard, especially during the winter, when greens were few. Such was the observation of the Methodist circuit rider Marmaduke Pearce, who traveled through the thinly settled areas of western New York in 1811: "O the cold houses, the snow, the mud, the sage tea, the baked beans!" (Peck, 1860).

See also **Cake and Pancake; Game; Hearth Cookery; Maize.**

BIBLIOGRAPHY

Arnold, Samuel P. *The Fort Cookbook.* New York: HarperCollins, 1997.

Arnow, Harreitte Louisa Simpson. *Seedtime on the Cumberland.* New York: Macmillan, 1960.

Camara Cascudo, Luis da. *Historia de Alementação no Brasil.* Sao Paulo, Brazil: Companhia Editoria Nacional, 1967.

Cox, Beverly, and Martin Jacobs. *Spirit of the West.* New York: Artisan, 1996.

Harrington, H. D. *Edible Native Plants of the Rocky Mountains.* Albuquerque: University of New Mexico Press, 1991.

Heuzenroeder, Angela. "Bread in the Wilderness." *Petits Propos Culinaires* 68 (November 2001): 90–101.

Kloberdanz, Timothy J., and Rosalinda Kloberdanz. *Thunder on the Steppe.* Lincoln, Nebr.: American Historical Society of Germans from Russia, 1993.

Medsger, Oliver Perry. *Edible Wild Plants.* New York: Macmillan, 1967.

Peck, George. *Early Methodism within the Bounds of the Old Genessee Conference.* New York, 1860.

Wagenen, Jared van, Jr. *The Golden Age of Homespun.* Ithaca, N.Y.: Cornell University Press, 1963.

Williams, Jacqueline. *Wagon Wheel Kitchens.* Lawrence: University Press of Kansas, 1993.

Don Yoder

THE SOUTH

One of the most popular books written about the American South, Margaret Mitchell's *Gone with the Wind* (1936), begins with a barbecue. To the 80 million people who live in the region, it would seem only appropriate. Food, like music or a syrupy drawl, has always been one of the cultural touchstones that sets the South apart.

Some of the best-known regional dishes in American cookery come from the great crescent that stretches from Virginia to eastern Texas. The South is home to a groaning table of famously down-home foods, like fried chicken, skillet cornbread, pork barbecue, pecan pie, catfish and hushpuppies, bourbon whiskey, and greens and pot likker (which refers not to real liquor but to the aromatic juices of boiled greens).

When Americans speak of the South, they usually mean the eleven states of the old Confederacy (Alabama, Arkansas, Florida, Georgia, Louisiana, Mississippi, North Carolina, South Carolina, Tennessee, Texas, and Virginia) plus parts of border states, like Kentucky and Maryland,

ALL THE KING'S PONE

Back in the 1930s Huey Long, the pot-bellied potentate of Louisiana, tried to show his common touch by talking up the health benefits of cornbread and pot likker, a modest dish enjoyed by southerners everywhere. "The Kingfish" decreed that it was classier to dunk the bread into the likker, the savory juice left behind by boiled greens, instead of crumbling it. Julian Harris, the editor of the *Atlanta Constitution,* disagreed. Thus started the Great Corn Pone Debate of 1931.

For weeks the mock controversy raged in newspapers, as Harris accused Long of closet crumbling and Long charged Harris with yellow-corn journalism in telegrams fired off to the *Constitution*'s Pot Likker and Corn Pone Department. Long even offered a jesting recipe called Pot Likker à le Dictator.

The future president Franklin D. Roosevelt eventually weighed in, proposing that the important question be referred to the 1932 Democratic National Convention. "I must admit that I crumble mine," he wrote, perhaps belying a bias from all the time he spent at the spa in Warm Springs, Georgia.

that lean toward Dixie culturally. It is a varied landscape that takes in multiple mountain ranges, a spacious swath of hill country, broad coastal plains, vast alluvial flatlands, and three thousand miles of shoreline. Historians have called it the closest thing to a nation within a nation in the United States, and it has spawned a collection of foods and foodways as varied as the landscape.

The First Southerners

When Europeans began to arrive during the 1500s, they found the land well populated by American Indians whose ancestors had dwelled there for thousands of years. The natives fished, hunted game, gathered berries and nuts (like the indigenous pecan), and cultivated crops, especially beans, squash, and maize (corn). Early European settlers were struck by the bounty. Captain John Smith, who helped found the first permanent English colony at Jamestown, Virginia, in 1607, wrote of "an abundance of fish, lying so thicke with their heads above the water, as for want of nets . . . we attempted to catch them with a frying-pan" (quoted in Ketchum, 1964). The place-names spoke of plenty; for example, Chesapeake is an Indian word meaning "great shellfish bay."

At least one of the cornerstones of southern food was already in place when the Europeans came, that is, corn. The Powhatan tribe of Virginia showed the English how

Not the actual South, but the nostalgic South brought north and served forth in this New York club menu featuring "stimulating" Southern Comfort, fried chicken dinners ($2.00), mint juleps, and a place to party until 4 A.M. Menu cover, 1946. ROUGHWOOD COLLECTION.

to plant, harvest, soak, and hull the native grain, which they ground into a gritty meal called rockahominy. They also made a bread of it, *appone*. Both names stuck, and southerners have enjoyed corn pone and hominy grits ever since.

Many of the foods that came to be associated with the South are not native. The Spanish, who explored the region during the 1500s and colonized Florida, introduced oranges, peaches, sugar cane, pigs, and chickens. The French, who planted their tricolor along the Gulf Coast from Mobile to New Orleans, brought their cooking techniques and used local ingredients to create new dishes like gumbo and jambalaya. The Scotch-Irish, who poured into the southern Appalachian mountains, squeezed a new distilled spirit out of corn. According to legend, a Baptist preacher by the name of Elijiah Craig was the first to make bourbon whiskey in the 1780s in Bourbon County, Kentucky.

But the dominant strains of southern cooking, as of southern life, are English and African. The English who settled the region brought their own livestock and fruits (apples chief among them), a direct, earnest style of cooking, and a taste for stews, puddings, and pies.

The African slaves who were imported to work the fields starting in the 1620s brought some of the most quintessentially southern foods with them, including okra, peanuts, watermelons, and black-eyed peas. Some of these foods, peanuts, for instance, actually originated in South America but did not take root in North America until they were taken to Africa and brought back across the Atlantic in the slave trade. Slave cooks also enlivened the southern kitchen by using peppers and spices they had either known in Africa or picked up in the Caribbean, the first stop in the New World for many of them. This forced collaboration between black and white newcomers laid the foundation for the region's cooking.

Southern Hospitality

By the time of the American Revolution in the 1770s, the southern Atlantic colonies were developing an economic system dominated by the large-scale cultivation of single cash crops, such as tobacco and rice. The plantation system spread west after independence, as cotton bolls blanketed the region and sugar cane sprouted through the lower Mississippi River valley.

The plantations developed a reputation for lavish entertaining that led to one of the enduring legends of the young country, southern hospitality. In 1746 a correspondent for *London* magazine compared the Virginia planters' lifestyle to that of English country squires: "All over the Colony, a universal Hospitality reigns; full Tables and open Doors, the kind Salute, the generous Detention, speak somewhat like the old Roast-beef Ages of our Forefathers. . . . Strangers are sought after with Greediness, as they pass the Country, to be invited."

Company was so routine at Mount Vernon, George Washington's estate, that the first president once complained in a letter that he and Martha had not dined by themselves in twenty years. The first lady evidently made a custom of large meals. The recipe for Martha Washington's Great Cake in the files at Mount Vernon begins "Take 40 eggs."

The apotheosis of this grand spirit was Thomas Jefferson, the third president and first epicure, who brought vanilla, macaroni, and wine making to the hills of the Virginia Piedmont. Jefferson loved to entertain at the White House and at his neoclassical mansion Monticello. His lavish entertaining was largely responsible for his dying $40,000 in debt.

Hard Times

Few southerners could afford to set a table like Jefferson or Washington. Before the Civil War the great majority were slaves or yeoman farmers. After the war ended slavery and bankrupted the plantation system, millions became tenant farmers or sharecroppers, working fields they rented by giving landlords a large portion of what they grew.

These new American peasants were fueled by a monotonous diet of salt pork, cornbread, molasses, and whatever vegetables they were able to grow or gather. The most commonly eaten vegetables were green beans, black-eyed peas, and leafy greens (turnips in the Upper South, collards in the Lower South), usually boiled for at least an hour with ham hocks or some other pork flavoring. Sweet potatoes joined the plate in late summer, when they were harvested and stored in earthen mounds for consumption through the winter.

Humble though these foods may have been, they could summon powerful emotions among those raised on them. In Ralph Ellison's novel *Invisible Man* (1952) the narrator, a young man from the South, practically bursts into homesick tears when he smells Carolina sweet potatoes roasting at a vendor's stand on the sidewalks of New York.

Decades after the devastation of the Civil War, hunger and malnutrition lingered in the South. In the early 1900s federal doctors investigated the widespread listlessness—some called it laziness—that many had noticed among the region's poor. Much of it was blamed on pellagra, a disease of vitamin deficiency caused by a grossly unbalanced diet. Pellagra did not recede until a nutritional campaign was launched during the 1930s and cornmeal, the bulk of so many diets, was enriched with vitamin B_{12}.

Many southern foods have long been linked with poverty. Mark Twain makes the connection in his masterpiece *The Adventures of Huckleberry Finn* (1884), when Huck tells Jim he would rather eat wheat bread because that's "what the quality eat—none of your low-down corn pone."

Indeed, southerners used to regard wheat bread as somehow elevated, calling it "light bread" to distinguish it from run-of-the-mill cornmeal. Baking with wheat did not catch on until commercially milled flour and baking powder became widely available in the late 1800s. Then southern cooks made up for lost time, making light, fluffy biscuits part of their daily routines, especially at breakfast. Kinky Friedman, a country musician from Texas, once wrote a song titled "Get Your Biscuits in the Oven and Your Buns in Bed." Most of his listeners no doubt approved of his priorities. In the South, hot bread always comes first.

Some Special Foods

Many distinctively southern dishes are associated with special events, including holidays, family reunions, community fundraisers, and the like. On New Year's Day, for example, a peas and rice dish called hoppin' John is eaten for good luck, often with a side serving of greens to fore-

tell money. Reunions bring out cauldrons of Brunswick stew, Frogmore stew, burgoo, or muddle—hearty concoctions made in particular areas of the South with vegetables and pork, seafood, mutton, or fish respectively. Churches and athletic leagues raise money with plates of catfish and hushpuppies, fried dollops of cornmeal whose name probably derives from the way cooks used to keep dogs at bay by tossing them some batter. Funerals and homecomings produce an amazing variety of pies and cakes, a reflection of the region's pronounced sweet tooth. And some people think it would not be Christmas without ambrosia, a dessert made of grated coconut and orange sections that is virtually unseen the rest of the year.

No matter what the occasion or month, it is considered perfectly normal to accompany any meal with iced tea. Given its hot, humid climate, the South has a powerful thirst for cold beverages. Among the many soft drinks that originated in the region are the world's two most popular, Coca-Cola and Pepsi, both created by pharmacists (the first in Georgia, the latter in North Carolina) in the late 1800s.

Fried chicken, perhaps the most renowned of southern dishes, may have begun as a seasonal specialty. Its genealogy is uncertain. Among the settlers of the South, both Africans and Scots have a tradition of frying poultry. However it got there, fried chicken was already established by 1828, when Mary Randolph included a recipe for it in one of the earliest American cookbooks, *The Virginia House-wife*. She specified all the essentials, chicken parts dredged in flour, seasoned, and fried in hot fat.

In the nineteenth century fried chicken was usually eaten during the warm months, when hens hatched the chicks that grew into tender young fryers. By the mid-1900s a huge poultry industry that could supply fryers year-round had developed in Georgia, Arkansas, and the Carolinas. Poultry consumption rose throughout the calendar.

Traditionally fried chicken was a Sunday treat reserved for after-church dinners and special company, like the preacher or the in-laws. The dish gradually spread into other days of the week, spurred on by the rise of fast-food franchising after World War II. The first and largest of the chicken chains, Kentucky Fried Chicken, once advertised "Sunday dinner seven days a week." Harland Sanders, who went by the honorary title "colonel," started the business in the 1930s at a roadside cafe in Corbin, Kentucky. By the end of the twentieth century the empire that bears his goateed image was selling a taste of Dixie at nearly eleven thousand outposts around the world.

An Enduring Love Affair

Another food that strongly evokes the South is barbecue. While much of the rest of the United States uses the term to refer to a backyard cookout, southerners use it quite particularly to mean the slow smoking of meat over hardwood coals. The meat is almost always pork.

Green glaze collards were introduced in South Carolina by Philadelphia seedsman David Landreth in 1820. Landreth developed this unique variety of worm-resistant cabbage so that southern gardeners would enjoy larger yields. Boiled collard greens and the pot broth are one of the cornerstones of southern cooking. PHOTOGRAPH BY L. WILBUR ZIMMERMAN. ROUGHWOOD SEED COLLECTION.

Southerners have long had a thing about swine. William Byrd, a Virginia planter, observed in the early 1700s that his neighbors were eating so much pig flesh that they "seem to grunt rather than speak." Before refrigeration became common, pigs were usually slaughtered when the weather turned cold in late autumn—"hog-killing time"—and the meat was preserved as bacon, sausage, salt pork, or hams rubbed in spices and allowed to cure for months in a smokehouse. Little of the hog was wasted. The small intestines were breaded and fried or boiled as chitlins, and the fat was rendered into cracklins that flavored cracklin cornbread.

Of all the uses of pork, barbecue is probably the most popular. In the beginning the dish was usually served at political rallies and other community get-togethers. By the end of the twentieth century it was more commonly served at casual restaurants, universally known as barbecue joints, where everyone from blue-collar laborers to white-collar professionals sit cheek by jowl mopping barbecue sauce from their lips.

Southerners love to argue the merits of different barbecue styles. Two areas are particularly known for their expertise. In the Carolinas pit masters smoke whole hogs at gatherings called "pig pickin's" and serve the meat pulled from the bone with a spiced vinegar sauce that, unlike most barbecue dressings, contains no tomatoes or ketchup. In parts of South Carolina the sauce is mustard-based. Meanwhile in Memphis, Tennessee, the self-described "pork barbecue capital of the world," pork ribs or chopped pork shoulders are served in sandwiches with creamy coleslaw. People in Memphis love barbecue so much that some restaurants serve barbeque-topped pizza and barbecue spaghetti, pasta tossed with barbecue sauce.

Changing Tastes

The last half of the twentieth century brought rapid change to the South. The civil rights movement engineered a revolution in race relations, business and government invested heavily in the region, and air conditioning made it more comfortable to live there. Millions of outsiders moved south for jobs or retirement, bringing their tastes and customs with them. In fast-growing areas like Atlanta, Georgia, or Charlotte, North Carolina, it is almost as easy to find a bagel as a biscuit.

In the midst of this evolution southern cooking enjoyed something of a revival, as natives and newcomers alike came to regard it as another ethnic cuisine to be discovered or rediscovered. Native sons and daughters like Craig Claiborne, Edna Lewis, and Nathalie Dupree celebrated the region's foods in cookbooks and television cooking shows. A new generation of chefs lavished their talents on the old cuisine at high-end restaurants from Arkansas to Virginia. Popular road-food guides told travelers where to find the best barbecue joints, seafood shacks, produce stands, ladies' tea rooms, and meat-and-three-plate lunch emporiums.

Even so, traditional southern home cooking seemed to be fading. Fewer people had time to make messy, demanding dishes like fried chicken. Some avoided them altogether out of concern for fat and cholesterol. Old-fashioned southern food was increasingly left to restaurant kitchens or rolled out only on special occasions.

Yet southerners remain deeply attached to their foods and rituals. In a nation that relentlessly wears down regional distinctions, their shared foodways are one of the few things that knits them together and reminds them who they are. How else to explain the enduring appeal of grits, the unremarkable cornmeal porridge that is one of the region's most joked about icons?

Shelby Foote, the Mississippi-born novelist and historian, takes his culinary heritage seriously. Once, when he was staying in a hotel, he hung a breakfast order on his doorknob asking for grits. Room service brought him hash browns instead. Yankees eat hash browns with breakfast. He put out the card again, this time with a note: "This morning you brought me potatoes. Do not commit this outrage again."

See also **Barbecue**; **Biscuits**; **Chitlins (Chitterlings)**; **Maize**; **Pig**; **Sensation and the Senses**.

BIBLIOGRAPHY

Belk, Sarah. *Around the Southern Table.* New York: Simon and Schuster, 1991.

Dabney, Joseph E. *Smokehouse Ham, Spoon Bread, and Scuppernong Wine: The Folklore and Art of Southern Appalachian Cooking.* Nashville: Cumberland House, 1998.

Egerton, John. *Southern Food: At Home, on the Road, in History.* New York: Knopf, 1987.

Ketchum, Richard M., ed. *The American Heritage Cookbook.* New York: Simon and Schuster, 1964.

Rogers, Mara Reid, and Jim Auchmutey. *The South the Beautiful Cookbook: Authentic Recipes from the American South.* San Francisco: Collins, 1996.

Taylor, Joe Gray. *Eating, Drinking, and Visiting in the South.* Baton Rouge: Louisiana State University Press, 1982.

Walter, Eugene. *American Cooking: Southern Style.* New York: Time-Life Books, 1971.

Wilson, Charles Reagan, and William Ferris, eds. *Encyclopedia of Southern Culture.* Chapel Hill: University of North Carolina Press, 1989.

Jim Auchmutey

THE SOUTHWEST

The Southwest encompasses New Mexico, southwestern Texas, Arizona and the southern part of Colorado that was settled by the Spanish. Although all of Texas is sometimes considered part of the Southwest, much of east Texas is more closely related to the Southeast and much of north Texas is more related to the Midwest and the West.

Southwestern foods in the United States are a product of the foods of the Native Americans and the foods of Spanish and Spanish-Indian settlers from Mexico. This tradition appears in the areas that have been settled the longest. Its distribution follows a roughly north–south line starting in southern Colorado, especially along the San Luis Valley, and proceeding southeast along the Rio Grande River, including the cities of Santa Fe, Albuquerque, and Las Cruces, New Mexico. In Arizona, the line is roughly an east–west one, marked by the Gila River, below which are long-established Spanish-Mexican settlements. In Texas the Southwest can be described as being south and west of San Antonio. Traditional food is also found in other communities in the region, as individual families have moved to establish new homes.

Outside of the traditional areas, communities of the Southwest reflect a food tradition that is more Eastern or Midwestern than Southwestern. In some cases it may also represent the simple ranch cooking of the Mountain States of Colorado and Utah. Inhabitants of larger cities in the Southwest represent many different cultures, as is the case with cities elsewhere in the United States. Asians, Africans, Europeans, Latin Americans, and people from many countries in the Middle East and the Indian subcontinent all have their own enclaves, giving rise to a broad variety of markets and restaurants. Tucson, Arizona, far from the largest of the cities in the Southwest, boasts a cultural and food festival each October that regularly has more than fifty different ethnic food booths. While some families cling to their ethnic food traditions, especially in isolated communities, others are more likely to celebrate their inherited food culture on special holidays. It is not unusual in the Southwest to find a family enjoying its own native cooking one evening, while exploring flavors from another on the next.

Traditional Foods in the Southwest

Traditional Southwestern food is commonly viewed by persons living outside the Southwest as consisting of tamales, tacos, enchiladas, tostadas, and burritos. While these dishes are extremely popular in many restaurants, they are referred to in the culinary repertoire as *antojitos* (snacks).

Traditional to the old Southwest are slow-cooked stews and slow-grilled foods, served with beans, rice, and corn tortillas. Vegetables used include squashes, *nopales* (pared and trimmed pads from the prickly pear cactus), jicamas (spherical tubers that, when pared, have a crisp texture and a faint taste of apple or water chestnut), purslane, and tomatillos (tart fruit that resemble tomatoes with husks but are related to the cape gooseberry). Avocados are used to make guacamole (a thick sauce of crushed avocado with seasonings). Fresh cilantro (also known as coriander), is used frequently to season fresh, quick-cooked dishes. Many of these foods existed in the diet of the Native American before the arrival of the Spanish. Opinions differ on whether chilies were grown in the Southwest before the arrival of the Spanish from Mexico, but the variety of spices that create the chili-based dishes today, both within the Native American culture and outside, arrived with the Spanish.

Food specialties of the Southwest differ from region to region. The burrito (a soft flour tortilla wrapped around a hot, savory filling) originated in the area north of the state of Sonora, where the flour tortilla originated. Stacked enchiladas (corn tortillas prepared as for rolled enchiladas but layered flat with savory fillings) are a specialty of New Mexico, although their popularity has spread throughout the region. *Salpicon* (a shredded-beef salad with vegetables) is a hallmark of southwest Texas.

Elements of Traditional Southwestern Cooking

Tortillas, beans, rice, vegetables, and some meat and cheese are the mainstays of traditional Southwestern cooking. In areas within driving distance of the Gulf of California, fish and shellfish increase the choices. Apart from the well-known *antijitos* mentioned earlier lie the true gems of Southwestern cuisine: red chili con carne (chili with meat) made with meat simmered in a sauce of reconstituted dried red chilies, cumin, dried coriander and oregano; and green chili con carne made from meat simmered in fresh green chilies, onions, garlic, and tomatoes. Beef, pork, lamb, and goat are all used, although beef is the most common in restaurants. Chicken is also cooked with sauces made from either red chilies or green chilies. These dishes vary from town to town and family to family. Beans are usually served separately, not as a part of the chili stews. While chili stews are slow-cooked, fish and shellfish may be quickly grilled. Chicken is marinated in a mixture of orange juice and spices before being grilled, and steak is often marinated, then grilled for *carne asada* (literally translated as "roasted meat"). The cheese used in many popular Southwestern restaurants is either Longhorn cheddar or Monterey Jack, with sour cream used as a garnish. In the barrios (the Hispanic-Mexican neighborhoods) and in the homes of serious Southwestern cooks, Mexican *queso fresco* (literally "fresh cheese") and commercially made Mexican *crema* (similar to sour cream) are used instead.

Chili. The dish known as "chili," much beloved in the region, is a creation of U.S. cooks. True aficionados eschew tomatoes or beans in their chili, preferring to have their meat, either cubed or coarsely ground, simmered only in a sauce made from reconstituted dried red chilies, spices, and other flavorings. Contests are held throughout the region to determine the best chili. Private cooks and restaurants often take liberties with this tradition, producing their own variations.

Tortillas. Tortillas in the Southwest were traditionally made with either yellow or white corn, and sometimes with the more exotic red or blue corn. These corn tortillas are made from corn that has been soaked in slaked lime and then ground. They require no fat of any kind

and are cooked on an ungreased *comal* (griddle). The tortilla acts as a wrapper or as bread. Occasionally, wedges of tortilla are crisped as a snack. Nachos (crisp wedges of corn tortilla topped with cheese and other garnishes) are a recent invention. While crisp, folded corn tortillas are served with fillings as tacos, the more authentic style for a taco is simply a soft, warm tortilla.

The flour tortilla native to the Mexican state of Sonora, sometimes as much as eighteen inches in diameter, is a more recent addition to traditional foods. The traditional flour tortilla of northern Sonora is a thin disc made from flour, water, and lard patted into shape by hand, than cooked quickly on a large hot griddle. These large tortillas are used to wrap foods, but they also are spread with butter and crisped before cheese and occasionally other toppings are added to form a crisp snack that resembles pizza. Flour tortillas are also made into quesadillas (tortillas folded over cheese and other fillings and grilled or fried). Small flour tortillas used in place of corn tortillas are an addition of the twentieth century, as is the inclusion of baking powder in the dough to give the flour tortilla a puffy quality.

Tamales. A *tamal* (plural, *tamales*) is a packet of corn-based dough that is stuffed, wrapped in softened corn husks, and steamed. The corn husks are removed at the table before the tamales are eaten. While tamales are served throughout the year in restaurants in the Southwest, beef and red chili tamales are traditional for Christmas when families and friends gather to assemble dozens of tamales. A traditional Christmas *tamal* is made from *masa* (a dough of corn treated with slaked lime, which is whipped with lard or shortening to make it fluffy), with a filling of shredded beef that has been stewed with red chilies and spices. Fillings used throughout the year may be made from slow-cooked chicken, beef, pork, lamb, or goat, which have been seasoned with reconstituted dried chilies and with spices.

The green corn *tamal* is a specialty of midsummer and best known in southern Arizona, although green corn tamales are also made in New Mexico. Although the green corn *tamal* is now available frozen year round, it is best fresh when corn is in season. The best green corn *tamales* are made from field corn, the kind given to animals for fodder. The fresh corn dough is filled with cooked green chilies and cheese, and the *tamales* are traditionally prepared as above.

Chilies. Many chilies, both red (which is the ripe form) and green, are grown in the Southwest, but the variety of chilies available, however, is not as diverse as it is in Mexico. Each variety of chili has its own special use, alone or in combination. Green chilies appear in fresh salsas (sauces) but also appear in stewed dishes, depending on the flavor desired. Red chilies are dried for use throughout the year and are reconstituted for use in cooked salsas and slow-cooked dishes. The combination of different red chilies with spices and herbs such as ground coriander seed, ground cumin seed, and oregano or fresh coriander leaves (cilantro) gives each dish its special character. Chilies, even those from the same plant, can vary in piquancy. Traditionally, the piquancy has been rated in Scoville units, where higher readings indicate a higher degree of piquancy. Some experts now question the value of that practice as different humans react somewhat differently to levels of piquancy.

Beans. Simmered dried beans, the mainstay of traditional Southwestern cooking, are usually *charro* beans (cowboy beans), but beans may be simmered or baked with various flavorings. "Refried" beans are not fried twice but are cooked beans mashed into shortening and seasoned with onion, garlic, and other seasonings.

Barbacoa and grilled foods. While not as widespread as the ubiquitous red or green chili-flavored stews, pit-cooked meats and grilled meats, chicken, and fish are also elements of Southwestern cooking. Slow pit barbecuing traditionally was done using the head of the animal, although today other cuts are used. Grilled meats include *carne asada* and chicken marinated in orange juice and spices and then grilled.

Fried breads and sweets. *Sopaipillas* (made from quick dough of wheat flour and baking powder, rolled out, cut, and deep-fried so that they puff up) are served as a savory bread with meals in parts of New Mexico. In Arizona, these are occasionally served with savory seasonings, but are more likely to be served as a dessert with honey. Southwestern desserts are fairly simple, serving as a soothing and cooling finish to a meal. A favorite is flan (a molded baked custard). Another is *almendrado* (an almond-seasoned mixture of egg white and gelatin served with a custard sauce). *Bizcochitos* (anise cookies) and *buñuelos* (deep-fried wheat-flour pastries) are popular as well.

Drinks. While the Margarita (a mixture of Tequila, lime juice, and orange liqueur) is popular in Southwestern restaurants, Mexican beers are more often drunk with foods in the Southwest if an alcoholic beverage is desired. Many nonalcoholic drinks are available in Hispanic-Mexican neighborhoods shops and restaurants, including *tamarinda* (a sweetened drink made from tamarind pulp), *horchata* (sweetened rice drink), and *aguas frescas* (literally "fresh waters") made from various fresh fruits.

The Food and Culture of the Southwestern Native American

The importance of corn in the food life of Native Americans cannot be overemphasized. Corn is essential and sacred; corn is life itself. In many pueblos the day begins with a sacrifice of corn. Corn originated in Mexico in about 2500 B.C.E., but required hybridization before it was useful as a food. Contemporary Pueblo Indians plant corn with great ceremony and care. Corn appears in the Native-American diet today in the form of tortillas. It

The meeting of Mexican and Navajo Indian come together in this southwest invention, the fry-bread taco. PHOTOGRAPHED AT CANYON DE CHELLY NATIONAL MONUMENT, ARIZONA.

also appears as hominy and *posole* (corn kernels that have been treated with slaked lime so that they swell and release nutrients bound inside). *Posole*, sold dried and made of yellow, white, red, or blue corn, refers to a soupy stew that is made with simple ingredients, including seasoning of chilies for everyday fare and with meat for festival occasions. Another significant part of the diet of the Southwestern Native American, beans are planted with the same kinds of sacred observances as corn. While the most common bean in the Southwest today is the pinto bean, a wide variety of beans, some extremely flavorful, were a part of the Native American diet in the past. As seed savers work to isolate some of these "heirloom" beans and grow them, some of the old varieties are again becoming available not only to the Native American but also to the general public.

While the hunting, gathering, or growing of food take on a sacred aspect, the act of preparing food is an important and time-consuming activity. Among the Pueblo Indians and other nations, the act of stringing red chilies to dry each autumn takes on a special significance, for there must be a string of chilies equal to the height of each person in a family to sustain the demand for the coming year.

The popularity of foods such as Indian fry bread, (dough cooked on a hot stone) came with the increased availability of refined flour and commercially prepared shortening or lard. From a culinary standpoint, fry bread and *sopaipillas*, mentioned earlier, are essentially the same. The "Navajo taco" employs fry bread rather than a tortilla as its wrapper. While this increased used of fat and flour has provided flavorful alternatives to the corn tortilla, the consumption of significant quantities of these ingredients has altered the diet of the Southwestern Native American to the extent that obesity and diabetes are rampant. Efforts of such organizations as Native Seeds Search to preserve the original foods of these peoples are intended to at least partially encourage a return to a more healthy diet.

See also **American Indians; Central America; Chili Peppers; Combination of Foods; Legumes; Maize; Mexico; Squash and Gourds; Stew.**

BIBLIOGRAPHY

Dent, Huntley. *The Feast of Santa Fe.* New York: Simon and Schuster, 1985.

Frank, Lois Ellen, with Cynthia J. Frank. *Native American Cooking.* New York: Potter, 1991.

Hughes, Stella. *Chuck Wagon Cookin'.* Tucson: The University of Arizona Press, 1974.

Johnson, Ronald. *The Aficionado's Southwestern Cooking.* Albuquerque: University of New Mexico Press, 1968.

Newsom, Lynn. *Authentic Southwestern Cooking.* Tucson, Ariz.: Southwest Parks and Monuments Association, 1999.

Niethammer, Carolyn J. *American Indian Food and Lore.* New York: Collier and Macmillan, 1974.

Madge Griswold

UTENSILS, COOKING. Among professional cooks, cooking implements in the kitchen are referred to collectively by the French term *batterie de cuisine*. This includes all utensils involved in the preparation of food regardless of specific function or type of material (ceramic, metal, glass, wood). The range of utensils in any given kitchen speaks volumes about the elaborateness of the cooking that takes place there as well as the type of food prepared. There are also large cultural differences in the implements deemed necessary for food preparation, so the *batterie de cuisine* of a Chinese kitchen is quite different from that of of a kitchen of medieval Syria, ancient Rome, or a modern American hotel. From the standpoint of culinary history, the study of cooking utensils falls under two broad categories: archaeology for the ancient and medieval utensils, and material culture for objects of more recent date. Because of their beautiful design, cooking implements are also of interest to certain branches of decorative arts and antique collecting.

Archaeologists rely almost exclusively on utensils in their attempt to reconstruct cuisines of the past, especially when there are no written records to provide working recipes. It is known that the Roman cookery book of Apicius was originally illustrated with pictures of utensils because there are a few scattered references to these pictures in the surviving text. Medieval scribes did not bother to copy those pictures. If they had, modern food historians would have a better idea of what some of the mysterious implements mentioned in Apicius looked like. But the fact that the original cookbook contained pictures of unusual utensils is evidence in itself that certain recipes in Apicius were not familiar even to most educated Romans.

The Austrian food ethnographer Anni Gamerith revolutionized the study of cooking utensils during the 1970s when she published her studies about the relationship among food types, utensils, and heat source (open hearth or enclosed cook stove). Heat source determined the design of the utensils, and this functional reality determined the range of dishes that could be accomplished with that technology. To be certain, the *batterie de cuisine* of a typical farm kitchen or even of a well-equipped kitchen in an urban townhouse not only reflected the type of dishes made there but also inventoried the economic level of the household, where it fit into the larger social picture. The kitchen and its implements thus become critical keys in understanding the foods of the past.

Cooking utensils can be organized into several categories depending on their function and the kind of cooking that is done. The categories include preparation equipment; pots, pans, frying pans, and cauldrons; griddles and equipment for roasting and baking; utensils for tabletop cooking; and utensils used for charcuterie.

Preparation Equipment

Preparation equipment includes spoons, spatulas, meat forks, knives, cutting boards, scissors, and shears. Grinding, crushing, straining, sifting, and sieving implements are also part of this group, as are whisks and beating devices that range from the most primitive handful of twigs bound together with string to the most powerful food processors and blenders. Ceramic, glass, and stainless steel bowls fit into this category as well. Measuring devices vary from country to country, depending on the weight system used. Most countries use a metric system for measurement of both liquids and solids, although the actual number of units to the measure may vary. Home cooks in the United States use a system developed in the late nineteenth century that employs measuring spoons and measuring cups (different kinds for dry or liquid measuring), but the body of measurements used in American cookery (pounds, ounces, quarts, and so forth) dates to Elizabethan England and represents a system of measure that is both archaic and at odds with that of the rest of the world.

Pots, Pans, Frying Pans, and Cauldrons

Pots, pans, kettles, skillets, cauldrons, and frying pans are included among items that are placed on an open flame or directly over a heat source. These utensils have the longest history of use, as they were first used over open fires. There were also critical differences in their designs. A kettle, for example, was characterized by straight or outwardly splayed sides. It was generally used uncovered for boiling foods or reducing them to another consistency, as in the case of large copper apple butter kettles. On the other hand, a traditional pot bulged on the sides and featured a neck below the rim. It was often used for cooking several things at once and invariably included a wooden or tin lid. Pot lids were normally sold separately from the pot itself but were usually numbered to match the number on the pot, such as "5" for five gallons, or "10" for ten gallons. Cookpots (one word in colloquial American usage) were generally small and made of ceramic. They were employed in cooking foods that would be spoiled in color or flavor if they came in contact with an iron pot or kettle. Classic New England baked beans were originally baked in ceramic cookpots set on a trivet among the hot coals.

Frying pans were known in ancient Greek and Roman kitchens: *téganon* to the Greeks, *patella* to the Romans. The Roman *patella* survived in modern Spanish as *paella* and in modern Italian as *padella*. Frying pans were probably also used to prepare grain dishes, the antecedents of paella made with rice. Skillets were originally deep, much like modern sauce pans, but the term is used interchangeably with frying pan. It is common practice among American cookbook writers to forego the use of "frying pan" altogether in favor of "skillet," as in the phrase, "brown lightly in a skillet" rather than "brown lightly in hot fat in a frying pan." This word manipulation is an attempt to make the recipe sound more appealing and less fatty although the ingredients remain the same. Frying pans with legs, once common in open hearth cookery, were generally called spiders both in England and in America.

"Pan" is a term of truly ancient origin, deriving from Celtic *panna*. The feature that distinguished it from other utensils was its flat bottom. This is why sauce pans and sauté pans, while very different in shape, are nonetheless called "pans." A versatile pan that combines the best of both the sauté pan and the frying pan has higher, sloping sides that are often slightly curved. This pan is called a *sauteuse* (literally a sauté pan in the female gender), an *evasée* (denoting a pan with sloping sides), or a *fait-tout* (literally "does everything"). Most professional kitchens have several of these utensils in varying sizes.

The cauldron evokes a vision of a huge pot boiling fiercely over an open fire. Actually the traditional cauldron was used in much more diverse ways, sometimes containing several different foods in smaller, sealed containers or wrapped in cloth. It is far more likely that the cauldron gently simmered than rapidly boiled. The word itself is of Celtic origin, and this one hearth utensil was universal throughout Celtic-speaking Europe. It was the symbol of hospitality, was used in religious rituals, and was often mentioned in Irish myths. Judging from archaeological evidence, the most ancient cauldrons were shaped like bowls. The Belgic Celts used cauldrons in the preparation of fish stews, which they made on board their fishing boats. These stews, called "chowders," were adopted by the Roman navy, survived through the Middle Ages, and have many counterparts. One unifying feature of all chowders prepared in a cauldron was the lining of cabbage leaves (later coarse dough) that separated the food from the metal, thus preventing it from taking on the taste of the pot.

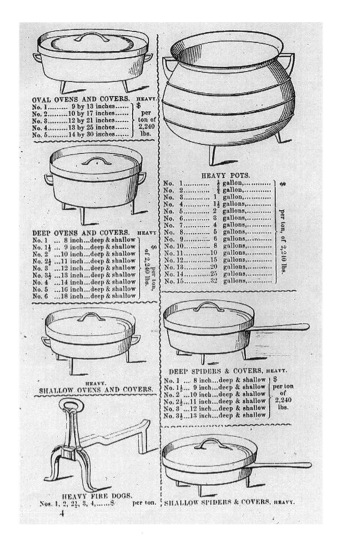

Detail of a page from the 1857–1858 catalogue of cast iron utensils manufactured by Savery & Company of Philadelphia. Note the careful terminology given to each of the different shapes: oval oven (top left), deep spider and shallow spider (bottom right), and pot (top right). Pot is synonymous with cauldron and by strict definition must have a bulging body and neck or rim as shown in the catalog. Pots were sold with or without lids. ROUGHWOOD COLLECTION.

Griddles and Equipment for Roasting and Baking

Griddles, grill pans, and irons for baking and toasting fall into another category of cooking utensil that also includes open outdoor and indoor grills and rotisseries. In one of the most effective rotisseries, the flame is arranged vertically, and the food is arranged on rods before the fire. These are most often used in commercial environments, including permanent food stalls in some countries. Griddles are used for pan grilling and for hearthside baking in much of the world, from the crumpets of England to the tortillas of Mexico, and the Hopi Indians used a special stone griddle to make *piki* bread. Irons are used for forming special cookies, but they also include hinged

An assemblage of utensils showing how an Appalachian dish of squirrel, potatoes, and maize would be baked on the hearth in the 1830s. A brown stoneware baking dish has been placed on a hanging griddle. The tin bonnet reflects heat from the hearth back towards the food so that it cooks evenly. ROUGH-WOOD COLLECTION.

irons for making waffles, hinged and ridged irons for producing *panini* (a grilled sandwich that originated in Milan), and the characteristic shell design of the iron to form the French *croque monsieur* (a grilled ham and cheese sandwich).

Roasting pans and equipment include spits, dripping pans, and roasting pans for use in ovens. Skewers also fall into this category, as when they are used in a tandoor oven, although they may also be used for grilling.

Baking and pastry work calls for yet another set of equipment. Such items include plaques (baking sheets) and pans and dishes especially designed for this use. This category includes frozen and chilled desserts as well, bringing into play molds of various kinds. Bread baking often employs flat baking stones that permit the retention of heat and, in combination with steam, produce a crisp crust. Loaf pans are also employed in bread baking and dessert making.

Utensils for Tabletop Cooking
One classification that crosses over into table service is equipment for tabletop cooking. This includes fuel sources, such as spirit lamps, alcohol burners, Sterno (a commercial fuel), or butane. Tabletop or tableside cookware includes the chafing dish, in which a sauté pan is set over simmering water over a heat source, the oval skillet for finishing dishes over a flame at table side, and the Mongolian firepot. The latter is a device, frequently made from brass, in which a central chimney is set above a heat source. Liquid, usually broth of some kind, is heated and added to the pan that surrounds the chimney. Guests then cook their own food, such as a variety of meats, poultry, and vegetables, in the simmering liquid. Fondue pots, pottery for cheese fondue and metal for meat or fish fondues, are also used to cook at the table.

Utensils Used for Charcuterie
A final category of cooking utensils is those used for making charcuterie (pâtés, terrines, galantines, and sausages). These include grinding and stuffing equipment for sausages and specialized baking dishes for various kinds of charcuterie loaves. A terrine, as a utensil for baking the dish of the same name, may be pottery or enameled cast iron. Forms for *pâté en croûte* (loaves baked in pastry of some kind) often have designs in the sides to make the pastry case more attractive when baked.

Materials Used in Cooking Utensils
While fired clay, bronze, and iron pots were used for many centuries, copper pots were also found in the Middle East, Europe, and North Africa. In addition, porcelain, aluminum, stainless steel, and glass have become common, and newer materials develop as stove technologies change.

As hearths evolved, so did the designs for various kinds of utensils. As a wider variety of materials became available, some were judged better for specific kinds of cooking. Thus, although cooking utensils are sold in sets of different shapes and sizes but all made of the same material, some usually are better fitted to a specific cooking function than others. The function also depends on how well the metal conducts heat. Sometimes a great deal of heat is required, as in sautéing or searing meats. In some cases, slower heating but fine heat retention is needed. Utensils made of certain metals are preferred by expert cooks for the superior results they produce. For example, where it is important to conduct heat quickly and remove it just as quickly, as in sautéing to just the right degree of doneness, copper lined with tin, stainless steel, or nickel is excellent, and aluminum is a close second. That is not to say that utensils of other metals cannot be used for those purposes; they simply are not as effective.

For long, slow cooking, heavy cast iron holds heat evenly and permits simmering at relatively low temperatures, as does clay (although, except in the case of the Japanese *donabe* cooking pot, clay utensils cannot be used over a direct flame). Steel, on the other hand, has low conducting properties and is useful for foods to be cooked in a large amount of boiling water, for example blanching vegetables. Ceramic and glass materials may be used for baking and are also used in tempered-glass double boilers.

Some metals, notably copper, aluminum, and iron, interact with foods cooked in them and must be lined with another metal to be used safely with food. Copper can be used unlined for boiling water, melting sugar, and beating egg whites. Since acid and eggs interact with copper, pans used to cook them are generally lined with tin, nickel, or stainless steel.

Iron and aluminum, like copper, interact with some foods. Unlined cast iron or aluminum interacts with eggs and acidic foods like tomatoes. Cast iron is often enameled to reduce this problem. Aluminum can be lined with stainless steel, which is nonreactive. Some aluminum is treated to make its surface nonreactive.

One of the finest materials for slow simmering in ovens remains low-fired clay. It holds heat well and even imparts a flavor or quality that metals cannot provide to a dish. For higher-heat work, such as soufflés, highly fired porcelain is preferred by some cooks, although others use glass or tinned steel.

The thickness of the material used in a utensil also affects the quality of the results. Thin metal utensils tend to warp easily over heat. Thin pottery, porcelain, or glass breaks easily and does not hold heat. Thickness, however, also implies weight. Professional-weight copper utensils are heavy, especially in larger sizes, as are cast iron ones. This is one of the reasons lined or anodized aluminum is preferred by some cooks.

Form and Function in Cooking Utensils

Function determines the shape of a pot or pan nearly as much as the material from which it is manufactured. In sautéing, for example, a wide pan with three-inch straight sides and a long handle permits the food to be shaken and tossed easily without falling from the pan. Moisture evaporates quickly, preventing food from being steamed rather than sautéed. Pots used for long braisings, on the other hand, have higher sides to concentrate the contents and prevent evaporation. Such vessels have closely fitting lids as well. Stockpots are traditionally tall in proportion to the diameter to minimize evaporation during the long, slow simmering process. Some stockpots in professional use for restaurant work, however, are wider than they are tall to allow evaporation of a large amount of liquid and concentration of flavor.

Professional kitchens also have the challenge of handling large amounts of food that make enlarged utensils heavy and awkward. Giant stockpots either turn on gimbals for easy pouring or have spigots at the bottom to draw off liquid. Braising devices for banquet work are often large, rectangular devices, four feet long and two feet

wide or more, and are arranged on gimbals so the pan can be tilted easily. Overall, the utensils and cooking equipment of the large, professional kitchen have a far more industrial appearance than cooking utensils used in a home.

Differentiation of Use in Forms of Cooking and Cooking Utensils

The anthropologist Claude Lévi-Strauss notes, in both *The Raw and the Cooked* (1969) and *The Origin of Table Manners* (1968), that in certain tribes, some cooking functions were reserved for men and others for women. In his example, the roasting function (representing something that was somewhere between raw and cooked) was reserved in certain tribes to men, while boiling (which represented something that was well cooked and was even associated with the start of decay) was reserved to women. Lévi-Strauss also mentions that roasts are more often served to guests or at feasts, while boiled or simmered foods are considered everyday food. In the Middle East, cooking methods associated with hunting, roasting, or grilling over a campfire were reserved for men. The tradition has become common among Americans, where many men handle outside grilling at home.

Cooking utensils sometimes are reserved for special functions related to religion. The Jewish laws of kashruth dictate that separate utensils be used for dairy meals and for meat meals. They further direct that either a completely different set of utensils be used for the feast of Passover or the utensils be ritually prepared for Passover by a special boiling process. This grouping of utensils by food type was also practiced by many peasant societies in Europe, especially in areas where ceramic utensils predominated. Since pottery absorbs food flavors (onions and fats in particular), many households maintained separate utensils for fish, meat, and milk preparations.

See also **Ancient Kitchen; Apicius; Cooking; Cuisine, Evolution of; Etiquette and Eating Habits; Gamerith, Anni; Greece, Ancient; Hearth Cookery; Iron Cookstove; Kitchen Gadgets; Preparation of Food; Rome and the Roman Empire.**

BIBLIOGRAPHY

Beard, James, Milton Glaser, and Burton Wolf. *The International Cooks' Catalog.* New York: Random House, 1977.

Bridge, Fred, and Jean F. Tibbetts. *The Well-Tooled Kitchen.* New York: Morrow, 1991.

Campbell, Susan. *Cooks' Tools.* New York: Morrow, 1980.

David, Elizabeth. *English Bread and Yeast Cookery.* London: Penguin, 1979.

Davidson, Alan, ed. *The Cook's Room.* New York: HarperCollins, 1991.

Grigson, Jane. *The Art of Making Sausages, Pâtés, and Other Charcuterie.* New York: Knopf, 1981.

Hartley, Dorothy. *Food in England.* London: Macdonald and Jane's, 1954.

Lévi-Strauss, Claude. *The Origin of Table Manners.* Translated by John Weightman and Doreen Weightman. Chicago: University of Chicago Press, 1990.

Lévi-Strauss, Claude. *The Raw and the Cooked.* Translated by John Weightman and Doreen Weightman. New York: Harper and Row, 1969.

Luard, Elisabeth. *The Old World Kitchen: The Rich Tradition of European Peasant Cooking.* Toronto: Bantam Books, 1987.

Marks, Gil. *The World of Jewish Cooking.* New York: Fireside, 1996.

O'Driscoll, Dairmud. "An Experiment in Bronze Age Cooking: The Fulacht Fiadh, Castlemary 1993." *Petits Propos Culinaires* 45 (November 1993): 43–50.

Rai, Ranjit. *Tandoor: The Great Indian Barbeque.* Woodstock, N.Y.: Overlook Press, 1995, 2001.

Redon, Odile, Françoise Sabban, and Silvano Serventi. *The Medieval Kitchen: Recipes from France and Italy.* Chicago: University of Chicago Press, 1998.

Solomon, Charmaine. *The Complete Asian Cookbook.* New York: McGraw-Hill, 1996.

Walden, Hilaire. *North African Cooking.* Edison, N.J.: Chartwell Books, 1995.

Wolf, Burt, Emily Aronson, and Florence Fabricant, eds. *The New Cooks' Catalog.* New York: Knopf, 2000.

Madge Griswold

VEAL. *See* **Cattle; Mammals; Meat.**

VEGETABLES. Vegetables are plants considered fit for human consumption, although they may also double as fodder crops for domesticated animals. As cultural metaphors, they are firmly embedded in all languages and emerge in such expressions as "hot tomato" for an attractive woman, "cabbage head" for someone who is not too bright, or "cool as a cucumber" in reference to extremely calm nerves. However, from a scientific standpoint, the use of the term "vegetable" is highly subjective and is a term of convenience rather than one based on a neatly ordered scientific classification. This ambiguity evolved out of horticultural practice and to some extent out of cultural bias hinging on the key question: what is fit to eat? The vegetable of one culture may be repulsive to another, as, for example, the cannibal's tomato *(Solanum uporo Dunal)* of Melanesia and Polynesia, which was formerly used in salsas for human flesh. On Fiji, the berry was actually cultivated near sites designated for human sacrifice.

Vegetable classification as defined by Western culture derives in part from prescientific attitudes about the mythic world to which those plants belonged in antiquity. Both the Greeks and Romans—and most other ancient Mediterranean peoples—differentiated between two types of edible plants, *holera* or *olera* (cultivated plants) and *horta* (wild plants gathered as food). This dichotomy was presided over by different sets of deities who represented fundamental attitudes about human society and its relationship to nature. We have inherited this structural framework insofar as vegetables are now exclusively defined as oleraceous or esculent herbs, as cultivated in the *hortus oleritus* (kitchen garden). Thus the formal botanical term for growing vegetables is "olericulture."

The idea that certain vegetables were suitable for boiling (or conversely that only boiling plants were "vegetables") was highly developed even in ancient Greece. The implication arising from this was that these plants were also worthy of domestication. The ancient Greek physician Diocles of Carystus even went so far as to note that, among the *horta*, beet greens, mallows, sorrel, net-

tle, orach, iris corms, truffles, and mushrooms were the most suitable for boiling. His beet greens were the ones found growing near the sea, not those cultivated in gardens, presumably the wild ancestor *(Beta vulgaris* L. spp. *maritima)* of the present-day cultivated sorts.

In most romance languages this association with boiling or poaching is further reinforced by such cognates of *oleritus* as Spanish olla (a cook pot or stewing pot), implying that the kitchen garden is designed to produce plants mostly earmarked for treatment in hot water. This connotation is clear in the word *Gemüse*, the German term for vegetables that derives from the medieval German *Gemüsz*, a mush or porridge. The idea of cooking or boiling the plants is preeminently expressed in the French term *jardin potager*, literally 'a garden for pot dishes: soups and stews.'

The French have also provided English with the word "vegetable." Its most literal meaning is plain: edible vegetation. The accepted origin of the word is that it derives from Medieval Latin *vegetare* via Old French *vegeter* (to vegetate). The classical Latin root is generally given as *vegetus* (lively or active), although this line of linguistic evolution may be subject to revision as more research on French links to Gaulish comes to light. In any case, the old meaning of "vegetate" did not imply something in decline, a common modern connotation, but rather something that was springing to life, a profusion, a natural bounty expanding from seed almost to the extent that it could be heard rustling as it grew—the complete opposite of the gardens of Adonis discussed later in this essay. This concept of vegetal fecundity is quite in line with Celtic ideas about food and nature and is especially characteristic in the obvious lack of definition between the cultivated and uncultivated worlds. Thus, in its root meaning, the English word is more all-inclusive than the Mediterranean concepts of *holera* and *horta*.

This ambiguity is best exemplified by the vast range of plants that are called vegetables in the English language. Tomatoes are berries, yet they are called vegetables. Garlic is considered a vegetable, yet one does not eat the leaves. And what about rhubarb stems, which are treated like a fruit (the leafy part is poisonous), or the sunflower, which is consumed as a seed or as oil? Where does edible vegetation fit in? Most garden books define

Ceramic vegetable steamer with deep red glaze by Virginia potter David Norton. The concept is based on the Yunnan pot of China, which features a cone in the center and holes for admitting steam. Roughwood Collection. Photo Chew & Company.

vegetables as annuals because they are grown to crop for one season only, yet many of these plants are true biennials (celery, carrots, cabbage, leeks, turnips), and some are even perennial (rhubarb, horseradish, sweet potatoes, asparagus, sorrel, peppers).

Another method for defining vegetables was based on the part of the plant considered most esculent for consumption. Here we have the rather simplistic division of the plant world into root vegetables (such as parsnips), pod vegetables (cowpeas, for example), and leaf vegetables (spinach and chard to name two). Again, while it is easy to imagine carrots as root vegetables, lima beans as pod vegetables, and collards as leaf vegetables, the unending discovery of edible plants from exotic locales such as Africa and South America has challenged all Old World definitions of this classification.

In this category is the East African oyster nut (*Telfairia pedata*), a rampantly vining cucurbit that is normally planted at the base of trees large enough to support the heavy fruit. In fact, several vines—both male and female—are grown on the same tree and will produce large squash-like fruit for up to twenty years. But it is the seed, not the fruit itself, that is eaten. Once established, the vines are not given much attention. While oyster nuts are intentionally planted around trees conveniently located near dwellings, this is a vegetable crop based more on passive intervention than on formal horticultural practice. This is a pattern once common in hunter-gatherer societies, where certain patches or stands of useful wild plants were periodically tended and encouraged through selective weeding to produce higher yields.

The yacon (*Smallanthus sonchifolius*) of South America is similarly outside the norm, for it produces crunchy, sweet-tasting tubers that are eaten like fruit. It has been cultivated in the High Andes for so many centuries and reproduced by root division for such a long time that many varieties can no longer produce fertile seeds. They are utterly dependent on humans for survival. Since it is low in calories, the tuber has been recently reevaluated as a possible diet food.

This continuing botanical revelation has also altered dietary schematics. Old peasant foraged foods like dock have been rediscovered as biodynamic or macrobiotic, synonyms for well-being, longevity, and psychological balance. In this way the vegetable has repeatedly inserted itself into the most radical of lifestyle movements—but this is hardly new, since vegetarianism and the dietary signification of plants has played a key role in philosophical approaches to nutrition since the days of Pythagoras or even since Adam and Eve, the original vegetarians.

Vegetables in the Fertile Crescent

Eden was said to be somewhere in ancient Mesopotamia. About the original garden we know little, but the Mesopotamian peoples left vast heaps of cuneiform tablets that reveal detailed information about the vegetable plants they once cultivated. As the climate grew hotter and drier many thousands of years ago, a vivid visual distinction evolved between cultivated and uncultivated ground. In fact, the vegetable gardens of that era were enclosed by walls both as protection from wandering livestock and as a means to contain and define the area where precious water would be distributed. Furthermore, it is clear from most of the records, whether Assyrian, Babylonian, or of any of the other cultures sharing the Fertile Crescent, that vegetables were commonly grown around date palms or fruit trees. The palms filtered the blasting sunlight and gave the garden the appearance of a welcoming grove. Thus the garden was also a place where socialization took place and indeed became a place sanctified by its own gods and protective forces.

Archaeological remains (mostly seeds) from this region also support what is documented in clay tablets. The range of vegetables included many still familiar: cucumbers, chards, gourds, onions, garlics, leeks, melons, chickpeas, lentils, cress, kales, and sesame—both for the seeds and for the oil. Colocynth melons, which resemble small watermelons, were grown primarily for medical applications. Some modern Arabic words, such as *kurrat* for a type of leek, can be traced to ancient texts from this period, proof of the long continuity of many of these vegetables. Indeed, even the Arab word for vegetables, *baql*, traces to ancient Aramaic *buqul*.

Tablet inscriptions also point to another feature of vegetable culture that suggests highly developed horticultural practices: specialization. There are numerous references to the "cucumber place" or to the "garlic place," which implies that entire beds were devoted to one type of vegetable and that in many cases this was the sole crop raised by the grower. Garlic was especially valued in this respect and even was used as collateral in financial agreements. In texts where a year-to-year continuity can be reconstructed, it is evident that a garlic place may change into a chard place, so some system of crop rotation must have been in effect. This concept of agricultural specialization was thought to have been perfected by the Phoenicians and codified by Mago, whose great work on agriculture (lost in the original Punic) was highly respected by the Romans.

The Phoenicians were also great middlemen in trading vegetables and seeds throughout the Mediterranean. They are thought to have spread the culture of shallots and artichokes well beyond the eastern Mediterranean, and are known to have introduced the intensive cultivation of saffron into North Africa and southern Spain—saffron was primarily a dyestuff and secondarily a ritual herb. Many Punic words for specific vegetable varieties reflected this plant exchange, as, for example, in *koussimezar* (the Mezar melon or Egyptian "cucumber"), an egg-shaped melon, one of the earliest types to come out of Africa.

Vegetables in Egypt

There is a large body of published material on the history of gardening in ancient and pre-Islamic Egypt, but there are no books per se devoted exclusively to vegetables. Orchards, trees, flora, landscape gardening, and even aquatic plants have received thorough coverage, yet the vegetable stands alone in this curious neglect. Vegetables in general have been viewed as poverty food by most cultures, especially when they form a large portion of peasant diet. Egypt was no different in this regard.

The fine gardens of ancient Egypt were enclosed like those of Mesopotamia and contained trees, flowers, even ponds for fish and ducks. The gardens of the peasants were mostly simple agricultural plots devoted to a specific mix of vegetable crops associated with the local economy, as, for example, lentil or onion growing for absentee landlords in large urban centers like Alexandria. On the other hand, vegetable gardens within temple precincts were often quite elaborate and were intended to supply the priesthood with a full range of food as well as offerings for the deity. Lettuce, for example, was important to the cult of Amun-Min, thus its cultivation held both culinary and religious significance. Indeed, temple gardens were considered to be part of heaven, like the temple itself, so vegetables from those gardens achieved a purity unlike those from the common world.

Papyri and tomb paintings have provided a rich array of material dealing with the common vegetables of the day, although not much is known about their actual preparation as food. The most commonly mentioned vegetables were lentils, leeks, lotus, melons, gourds, garlic, asphodel (grown for its bulb), fava beans, chickpeas, fenugreek (ground as flour), garland chrysanthemum

(now popular in Asian cooking), cucumbers, onions, lettuce, and mallow. Egypt also served as a conduit for the introduction of watermelons from tropical Africa and, during the late Ptolemaic Period, for the introduction of rice, taro, and sugar cane from Trapobane (ancient Sri Lanka). Due to their dependence on specialized irrigation and cultivation techniques, none of the last three plants spread beyond the eastern Mediterranean until after Arab conquest.

The Greek occupation of Egypt under the Ptolemys radically altered the Egyptian vegetable garden, both with new introductions and in lasting terminologies. *Molókhe* or mallow (*Malva parviflora*), which was once so important to Greek cookery both as a green sauce and as an ingredient in complex recipes, also supplied leaves used like grape leaves for making dolmas. The Egyptians transferred the Greek name to a native wild plant now known as Jews mallow (*Corchorus olitorus*), which was similarly used in green sauces. It is still called *molkhia* in Egyptian Arabic. The use of the same name for plants of a different genus or species is one of the lasting ambiguities inherited from the ancients, who were more apt to lump vegetables together according to how they were used, as in the case of the Roman propensity for treating carrots, parsnips, and parsley root as *pastinaca*.

The Vegetables of Ancient Greece and Rome

There are few surviving writings from the Greeks and Romans that do not mention food and vegetables in some manner. It is known from quotes and citations in works like the *Deipnosophists* of Athenaeus that many books on gardening and agriculture once existed but are now lost. Athenaeus himself lavished considerable attention on foodstuffs, none the least being vegetables. His interests ranged from toasted chickpeas (still a snack food in the Mediterranean) to the medical applications of beets and carrots as vermifuges or a good dish of cabbage to treat a hangover. He even cited the known varieties of lettuce, garlic, fava beans, and many other garden plants in an effort to differentiate which were the best from a connoisseur's point of view.

The surviving Roman work most easily accessible to the general reader is also by another connoisseur, an eccentric called Apicius, whose detailed recipes give specific hints about the role vegetables played in the haute cuisine of imperial Rome. For example, asparagus was baked in eggy casseroles called *patinae*, mallow was commonly added to barley soup, celery made a good stuffing for suckling pig, and turnips marry well with baked duck. There is also scattered advice on when to harvest certain vegetables, as in the case of stinging nettles, which only loose their prickly character when cooked or dried.

Many other works could be cited, such as Columella's *On Agriculture* and especially Pliny's monumental *Natural History*, but the medical writings of the imperial physician Galen are perhaps the richest in detail, since there is considerable commentary on the diet of peasants and farmers and the sorts of vegetables they ate. The aristocratic tone and intended readership of most of the writings that have survived from this period do not provide the kind of firsthand observations one might expect from a true master gardener, although Pliny's eye was in fact well nuanced to such details—yet some of his botanical "facts" are obviously scrambled and second-hand. And while it is true Columella certainly knew how to run an estate, he was not the vegetable gardener.

Furthermore, aside from comments about asparagus and cabbage, Cato's treatise *On Agriculture* makes only passing reference to vegetables—be certain to grow them near cities. While this allusion does confirm the existence of well-organized market gardening, Cato's treatise is so loaded with ideology about salty Romanness *(Romanitas)* and the purity of certain rigorous lifestyles that any conclusions drawn from him must be done so with definite reservations. However, it is fairly clear from these and other ancient authors that quite a few cities had developed market gardening to a high degree and even specialized in the cultivation and export of vegetable produce to Rome and other large urban centers.

For example, Cyrene in present-day Libya was well-known in ancient times for its silphium, fragrant saffron, and a mild-tasting tuber now generally identified as taro. It was also the center for the export of the so-called wild artichoke (*Cynara cornigera* Lindl.), whose domestication was introduced early into Cyprus, Libya, and Carthage from the Levant. This handsome plant is depicted on surviving mosaics in the House of Dionysios at Paphos, Cyprus, and in a mosaic in the Bardo Museum at Tunis. The Roman farmers of Spain and Italy evidently adapted the novel idea of harvesting the flower bud as a delicacy to their local wild cardoons because the artichoke of the western Mediterranean is a subspecies derived genetically from the cardoon (*Cynara cardunculus* L.), not from a wild artichoke ancestor. Buds of the milk thistle, blessed thistle, and safflower were also similarly harvested and eaten.

The dissemination of the artichoke, or at least of the horticultural technology required to cultivate it for food, brings up the larger question of plant exchange during the height of the Roman Empire. Commerce flowed to and from the far-flung provinces in a manner only replicated by the European Union. Archaeology has indeed confirmed that foodstuffs moved quite easily from one place to another, with such exotics as rice turning up in sites in Germany and England. There is also indisputable evidence that, among the aristocracy at least, country life on the great estates attempted to imitate the court life of imperial Rome. Gardens excavated from villa sites have confirmed this.

On the local level, however, Mediterranean cuisine and Mediterranean vegetables were not readily assimilated among the general populace. Joan Alcock's study of food in Roman Britain (2001), based on overwhelming archaeological evidence, reached the conclusion that assimilation was selective, and it was this selectivity that gave rise to the regional cookeries that eventually provided a link of continuity with the regional cookeries of the Middle Ages. This is also the growing consensus of archaeologists in other parts of Europe. Thus, the old saw that "the Romans introduced it" must be requalified, especially since quite a number of vegetables were cultivated in some regions long before the Romans arrived. Cabbage, especially the kales, originated in northern Europe, and in fact, the English words for kale and cabbage are Celtic in origin, as are the German words *Kabbis* and *Kohl*, not to mention the Latin *brassica* and *caulis*. This is evidence in itself that the vegetable exchange during Roman times was complex and two-way, with the Romans themselves learning new things from conquered peoples.

A broader look at Roman literature of all types is especially useful in drawing general conclusions about the state of vegetable gardening from that time. For example, Pliny parodied "gastronomic prodigies," monster vegetables and fruits valued for their size alone. This would suggest that some market gardeners were well acquainted with horticultural practices based on careful seed selection, cold frame techniques, and the manuring of plants at critical periods of growth, much like the modern-day cult of the monster pumpkin or watermelon. There is also a great deal of information concerning value judgments about the role of vegetables in the diet and their cultural significance. Many Roman satires mention garlic as a food only fit for galley slaves and peasants or as something eaten only by soldiers going off to war (garlic heats up the body and therefore creates a warlike spirit). The general drift is that anything flavored with garlic is therefore rustic and unrefined and as much an antidote to poison as it is to the consuming flames of love (what sweet kiss is not withered by the scorpion sting of garlic breath?). Likewise, fava beans are eaten by jurymen in order to stay awake during trials, their noisy flatulency providing an echoing thunder of divine approval or of legal derision.

The most commonly mentioned vegetables in Roman literary sources include many still known, although in shape and habit they probably did not resemble modern varieties. The list includes turnips, radishes, rocket (arugula to American grocers), leeks, lentils, lettuce, orach, Old World gourds (eaten young like zucchinis), cabbage, onion, peas, chickpeas, fava beans, cucumbers, asparagus, cowpeas, beets, beet chards, sprouting broccoli, watermelon, garlic, mallow, dock, chickling vetch, and blite—otherwise known as purple amaranth (*Amaranthus lividus*).

A number of scholars have taken the liberty of translating *blitum* (blite) as spinach (Gowers, 1996), and this has greatly added to the confusion about the culinary history of spinach because *blitum* is not true spinach. However, something called *barbaricum bliteum* (barbarian blite) also surfaces in Roman literature. This is either true spinach as cultivated by the Armenians and Persians or else good-king-henry, so important to the ritual cookery of the ancient Gauls—the leaves of both plants are similarly shaped. In any case, this mystery vegetable was considered insipid eating and was equated with crudeness and stupidity (insipid people were people who lacked "flavor").

Some of these vegetables also carried a great deal of symbolic baggage, especially in connection with religious cults. Mallow (molóche) was considered one of the purest sacrifices for Apollo Genétor at Delos, and Pythagoras himself was said to have lived on it as part of his vegetarian dietary regime because it "washes" the stomach.

Lettuce was associated with the gruesome death of Adonis, the prepubescent lover of Aphrodite, who hid among lettuce before he was gored to death by a wild boar. Thus lettuce was associated with male sterility, effeminacy, and cowardice, and generally was viewed as a suppressant of sexual performance (Detienne, 2000). Gardens of Adonis were planted in pots or baskets during the heat of summer and then allowed to die prematurely on the roofs of houses during the feast of Adonia (19 July during the Roman Empire) as symbolic evidence of the boy's sexual prowess, which produced no "seed" or fruit. Significantly, these little gardens consisted of barley, wheat, lettuce, and fennel, each plant highly symbolic of some aspect of fertility yet a total inversion of what was understood to be garden abundance.

Interestingly, a distinctive lettuce dedicated to Gauas (the Cypriot Adonis), and later known as "Cyprian" during the Byzantine period, was discovered in a Serbian monastery by the U.S. Department of Agriculture in the early twentieth century and is preserved in several American seed banks. It is physically similar to the pointed-leaf lettuce depicted in the medieval *Tacuinum Sanitatis* (Arano, 1976) of the eleventh-century Syrian Christian physician Ibn Botlân. By virtue of this continuity, at least in form and appearance, Cyprian lettuce is a true heirloom variety, a category of vegetable that will be dealt with later in this discussion.

Vegetables in the Early Christian Period
The early Middle Ages is a murky period for the study of vegetables, but a copy (in the Austrian State Library at Vienna) of the *Codex of Dioskorides* dating from 500 to 511 C.E. is illuminated with pictures of plants. The drawings are fairly accurate and convey the important physical characteristics of the vegetables and herbs shown. Thus it is possible to determine that a leek on folio 278 belongs to the Kurrat Group, an ancient type of salad leek mentioned earlier and still grown in the Near East.

The *Codex of Dioskorides* is medical in nature, dealing with the health and dietary aspects of the plants discussed. For a horticultural companion, the *Gheoponika* of Kassianos Bassos, a tenth-century reworking of several older agricultural treatises, provides rules for the cultivation of garden vegetables, thus offering some insights into the seasonal food cycle, both horticultural and culinary, in the old Byzantine East. More specifically, the role of the *Gheoponika* in the provisioning of Constantinople with fresh vegetables has been studied by several historians, most importantly by Johannes Koder (1993). When taken together with the *Book of the Eparch* (prefect of Constantinople) regulating merchants and guilds during the reign of Leo VI (886–912), a relatively detailed picture of market gardening falls into place. It is perhaps significant to note that by the 1100s many villages in Bulgaria were given imperial privileges that freed them of military duty in exchange for producing food for the court. It is for this reason that the Bulgarians have long been called the gardeners of the Balkans, a status they maintained even under later Ottoman rule.

In the West, the eighth century *Capitulare de villis* of the Holy Roman Emperor Charlemagne is quite valuable for its references to gardens. For example, the *ravocaulos* of that document is believed to refer to a variety of kohlrabi. However, the most priceless garden record is a parchment drawing of the garden plan of the Cloister of St. Gall in Switzerland surviving from the early 800s. It provides a detailed look at how the Roman kitchen garden became transmogrified into a source of both food and medical plants. Sixteen plants are discernible on the plan, including cucumbers, melons, cowpeas, bottle gourds, and smallage (celery resembling parsley). Most important, they are organized into rectangular raised beds. This is one of the earliest references extant to this common garden practice, but it was not unique.

The *Hortulus* of Walahfrid Strabo, abbot (from 838 to 849) of the Cloister of Reichenau on an island in Lake Constance, makes reference to a similar number of plants, again arranged in raised rectangular beds. Strabo's Latin poems about his garden discuss the uses of both herbs and vegetables and is the oldest surviving source on gardening written in Europe during the Middle Ages. Most interesting of all, archaeological exploration of the abbey site has revealed that it was constructed from the recycled ruins of an abandoned Roman villa and that the layout of the garden more or less followed the outlines of the ancient one. The implication is that the Roman gardening tradition maintained by the wealthy during imperial times did not fully disappear at the outset of the Middle Ages. Many estate gardens disappeared completely due to wars and pillaging, but in some regions they simply became fewer in number and passed into non-Roman hands (Percival, 1976). Château Ausone near Saint-Emilion in Bordeaux is a famous example of this continuity, although its fame rests on wine not gardens.

The archaeological link is not as clear when it comes to the vegetables themselves, since botanical residues, especially seeds, impose certain limitations on what can be retrieved for science. A carrot seed is indistinguishable from a wild carrot seed and will not tell how the root was shaped or even its color. Unfortunately, seeds are mostly what one has to work with from medieval sites, although some inferences can be revealing. Cucumber seeds show up in Polish sites in the 900s, thus establishing a bottom line for a vegetable much associated with Polish national cookery. Carbonized fava bean plants from North Germany from the same period reveal that, after the beans were harvested (as winter fare), the plants were used as straw in barns. Seeds, however, do help untangle dates of introduction, and one thing that scholars have learned from medieval archaeology is that the vegetable world was not static, as historians have led us to believe in the past.

The broad, flat fava bean, which is the preferred sort for modern cookery, did not appear until the 800s in Spain. This is only one example of vegetable breeding (probably through highly controlled selection) that took place during the Middle Ages, although innovation was indeed slow by present-day standards. Some agricultural historians have suggested that it was the Arabs who created these new types of vegetables—the cauliflower, for example. What can be documented from surviving Arab literary sources is rapid dissemination, but the westward movement of plants in general and vegetables in particular was far more complex than hitherto presumed and remains an area of research ripe for future exploration.

Vegetables and the Arab Diaspora

The agricultural historian Andrew Watson has long promoted the idea that an agricultural revolution took place under early Islamic rule in the eastern Mediterranean, a revolution that was carried westward into North Africa and Spain (Watson, 1983). This has important implications for the movement of vegetable plants. However, other scholarship has questioned this thesis. There is growing evidence that the revolution was already taking place during the late Byzantine period and that it consisted of newer ways of irrigating land and reclaiming marshes so more intensive forms of agriculture could be undertaken. Without entering the question of who invented what, two critical points are undeniable: the technology came out of Persia and South India (the vast irrigation systems in Sri Lanka were well known even to the Greeks), and its spread westward was made possible by the political stability that Arab conquest brought to the regions under its control. It is easy to point to the concentration of wealth in bright spots such as Syria (Damascus and Baghdad in particular), Egypt, and al-Andalus in Spain, but there was an economic implosion in other parts of the newly formed empire. The family papers of the Ibn'Awkal merchants of eleventh-century Egypt reveal a great deal about industrial crops like Egyptian flax or high-profit goods like black pepper, indigo, and sal ammoniac, but information on common garden vegetables is rather limited. That is, unless one looks at medical literature and cookery books.

The most heavily used culinary source is also one of the oldest: the *Kitab al-tabikh*, otherwise known as the Baghdad cookery book. It was written down in 1226, although internal evidence clearly indicates that the material was compiled from several much earlier sources, some

of which were not Arabic. This ambiguity is one of the difficulties in using cookbooks to pinpoint the introduction of new vegetables. But that said, there are other Arabic cookery manuscripts equally rich in detail surviving from the Middle Ages, such as the *Manuscrito Anónimo* of Moorish Spain, and all of the recipes no matter what the source are fairly clear about the role vegetables played in the diet of the times.

There is certainly no ambiguity in the Baghdad cookery book about the use of eggplants and no doubt at all that the sort discussed had dark black skin (there are directions for removing it). The book also makes ample reference to fava beans, cardoons, rhubarb, leeks, the ridged cucumber (Armenian snake melon), carrots, gourds, taro, cultivated purslane, turnips, sweet fennel, and spinach. There are also references to a form of cabbage commonly translated into English as cauliflower. Without a picture, one cannot be sure (it could be a type of broccoli), but since true cauliflower evidently evolved in the Dead Cities region of northwestern Syria, it is quite likely that this luxury vegetable migrated during the early 800s with its growers when they resettled elsewhere—a small group of those Syrian Christians emigrated to the Karpasia district of Cyprus, where cauliflower was first observed by pilgrims to the Holy Land later in the Middle Ages. The cauliflower is not mentioned in European scientific works until specimens are discussed by Dodonaeus in 1560. By that time Cypriot seed was being exported to northern Europe via Venice.

One is also treated with a rich array of vegetables in another work called *Kitab Wasf al-At'ima al-Mu'tada* (Description of Familiar Foods) written in 1373. Of particular interest is the differentiation of several types of leeks, indicating not only distinct varieties but also distinct culinary uses at different stages of development—indirect evidence of a highly evolved sense of market gardening. Four sorts of leek are mentioned: the vegetable leek (*kurrath baql*), the Nabatean leek, the table leek, and the Syrian leek. The first is not a variety but rather a spring leek, young greens similar in character to Chinese garlic chives. The Nabatean leek may be equated with the modern salad leek of Iraq, a member of the Kurrat Group, short in height and rather deep-rooted. The table leek is a blanched leek similar to the Catalan Calçot onion, and indeed the cultural technique of burying them in deep trenches may be the same. The Syrian leek is the *kephalotón* of medieval Cyprus, a Greek word derived from Syrian *quaflot*, a leek with an unusually large bulb. This plant is the genetic ancestor of the modern elephant garlic. Under the name *Porrum Syriacum*, it was first illustrated in European botanical literature by Tabernaemontanus in 1588.

Arab books dealing with cookery exhibit an undeniable passion for elegant preparations, even with simple vegetables. But such food was the privilege of the aristocratic few, and the wealth that sustained that lifestyle was soon to fade with the economic upheavals caused by the

Crusades. Until the late twentieth century, historians have greatly underestimated the exchanges that took place after the establishment of Latin footholds in the Levant and Byzantium or the role of large Christian minorities that persisted in Egypt and Syria during the early Muslim period.

The Nestorian or East Syrian Church, which spread into Persia, established strong trading communities in China and Malabar as well as in Cyprus, where the Nestorian Lakhan family became extremely powerful based on trade in medical aloes. One line of trade and plant exchange went through Tabriz in Persia overland to the Caucasian kingdom of Georgia and the Greek Empire of Trebizond on the north coast of modern Turkey, all to circumvent the Arabs. That this Black Sea entry was an important route for the movement of Asian food plants westward may be inferred from an eleventh-century Byzantine reference to the "citrons" of Anatolia, a variety of lemon introduced via Georgia and Armenia and still preserved in Georgian botanical collections. Eggplants also followed this route.

European contact with foods of the Arab world was not limited to the crusading troops that went to the Holy Land and returned. The Latin Kingdom of Jerusalem (1099–1291), the Principality of Achaea (1205–1430), a French feudal state established in Greece with its capital at Mistra, a Catalan principality centered on Athens, various Venetian and Genovese ports, and the sister kingdoms of Cilicia (1080–1375) in Asia Minor and on Cyprus (1192–1489) were all characterized by colonial aristocracies with highly orientalized foodways.

The last kingdoms, especially that of Cyprus due to a Papal Bull, served as conduits for the spice trade with the Muslim world. In the case of Cyprus, the kingdom lent its name to an international style of cookery mentioned in numerous medieval cookbooks. More important, the intermarriage of wealthy Latins in the Levant with European nobility, particularly with families in Aragon and in northern Italy, brought to Europe a constant influx of personal cooks, gardeners, and retainers schooled in eastern Mediterranean ways. It is not surprising that some of the earliest references to exotic vegetables like eggplants, cauliflowers, okra, and numerous sorts of Near Eastern melons show up in late medieval Italy.

Vegetables in the Renaissance

The *Carrara Herbal* (British Library, Egerton MS 2020), created sometime before 1403, was one of the first late medieval herbals to depict plants and vegetables accurately, although it may have been based on a now lost Byzantine prototype. Such illustrated handbooks of health, as well as numerous herbals, offer a rich visual record of the sorts of vegetables deemed worthy for the table in that period. The beautiful gardens witnessed by travelers through the Latin East were now replicated in Italy but with the goal for reattaining a glorious Roman

Hands holding a variety of vegetables: beet chards, carrots, turnips, spring onions, and radishes. © CRAIG LOVELL/CORBIS.

past. The Italian pleasure gardens of this period so impressed Casimir the Great of Poland that he installed one in Cracow during the 1360s, complete with cold frames for forcing Mediterranean vegetables. In short, the vegetable garden once again becomes an object of status.

The discovery of printing, followed quickly by the discovery of the New World and the heady harvest of its vegetable riches, only accelerated a quest for new and exotic things to ornament the gardens of the rich and powerful. Tomatoes, peppers, potatoes, sunflowers, beans, sweet potatoes, new sorts of pumpkins, and a new kind of wheat called maize fill the pages of botanical treatises and plant books of the period. The 1500s may be characterized as a century during which botanists attempted to organize the vegetable world into some type of scientific order, although that "order" by modern standards was quite chaotic. For example, a confusing observation is that the Jerusalem artichoke from North America (not from Jerusalem and not an artichoke) is known as *Flos solis Farnesianus* (Farnese sunflower) in reference to the fact that the gardens at the Villa Farnese in Rome provided several botanists with the first known specimens. Sorting out such conflicting nomenclature has plagued garden historians ever since.

However, botanical gardens were established in this century, the first in 1545 at the University of Padua, and some of the greatest botanical works of the Renaissance were issued during this era, especially those devoted to cataloging the gardens of such important plantsmen as Conrad Gesner in Switzerland (1561), Georg Fabricius in Meissen, Germany (1569), and Camerarius in Nürnberg (1588). All of these books contain valuable woodcuts depicting vegetables, and many medieval favorites like skirret *(Sium sisarum)* and monk's rhubarb *(Rumex patientia)* are shown for the first time. Vegetables also figured prominently in Renaissance art and paintings, especially the still life genre. Among the most whimsical vegetable compositions are those by the court painter Giuseppe Arcimboldo (c. 1527–1593), who used vegetables and fruits to create faces and other conceits.

The most significant body of literature, however, was the garden guides that discussed not only specific vegetable varieties but also how to grow them. The French work known as *L'agriculture ou la maison rustique*, first published in Latin (1535) by the Paris printer Charles Estienne, was soon translated into most major European languages. Marco Bussato's *Giardino di agricultura* (Venice, 1592) was also extremely influential, as was Johann Coler's *Oeconomica ruralis et domestica* (Wittenberg, 1597). The great classic, however, was Oliver de Serre's *Théatre d'agriculture* (Rouen, 1600), which became a standard garden book for much of the next century. This great outpouring of garden knowledge was capped in many ways by the lavishly illustrated *Hortus Eystettensis* assembled by Basilius Besler in 1613 for his patron plant collector, the bishop of Eichstätt in Bavaria. Not only did the good bishop own prize specimens of rare eggplants, balsam apple *(Momordica balsamina)*, tomatoes, and domesticated asparagus, his potted prickly pear cactus from the New World required a wooden superstructure to hold the monster plant in place.

Vegetables in the Baroque Period

The seventeenth century witnessed a revolution in botanical science and the proliferation of books devoted to illustrating plants and vegetables from many parts of the world, including new introductions from Asia and the Americas. Francisco Hernandez's *Nova Plantarum* (Rome, 1651) was devoted almost exclusively to the foods of Mexico and included native names for the plants. His woodcut illustrations offer a priceless look at the characteristics of common vegetables then grown in New Spain, including the lowly miltomatl or tomatillo *(Physalis ixocarpa)* now popular in Southwest American cooking. Other books containing strange designations like *Pomum amoris majus fructu luteo* (large yellow fruited love apple or, more simply, yellow tomato) remind one how much lack of order prevailed in the scientific naming of newly discovered vegetables and how much has changed since Linneaus imposed order on the world of plants in the eighteenth century. Names like *bamia Aegypitiaca* (Egyptian okra—*bamya* is actually a Syrian word) of one author might become "ladies' fingers" of the next. Likewise the *lactuca hispanica* (Spanish lettuce) of one author was the

Cos or Roman lettuce of another, the names more often than not reflecting the source of seed rather than the true origin and history of the vegetable. One of the most fashionable cabbages of the period was the so-called *Brassica tophosa*, better known as black Tuscan palm tree kale, "rediscovered" by American seedspeople under the new moniker "dinosaur kale." The penchant for fanciful names has not changed.

If a generalization can be made about the seventeenth century, it is that the rare and exotic vegetable of the previous century gradually became the daily fare of the urban middle class by 1700. Plant breeding, especially in Holland, brought many new sorts of vegetables onto the market. Named varieties of potatoes, carrots, celery, chicory, peas, and turnips soon proliferated in kinds and colors. Added to this roster were newly discovered Asian foods, like Malabar spinach *(Basella alba)*, introduced from Java in 1688. Handbooks on plant breeding were even published, one of the earliest in English being Walter Sharrock's *History of the Propagation and Improvement of Vegetables* (1660). From this time on, the vegetable undergoes a steady refinement with emphasis on greater delicacy of flavor, more beautiful shape, and increasing tenderness.

Much of this was directly connected with shifts taking place in cookery, especially the use of vegetables in sauces and elaborately prepared dishes. Vegetables were also given ornamental value with paring knives, so turnips feathered out into birds, carrots unwound into golden fish, and the cookbooks of the day are full of illustrations showing how to do this. Most notably, however, the vegetable became a prized market commodity; growing of vegetables, a respectable line of work for the honest laborer; and period depictions of market scenes never fail to convey the impression that only the best has been laid before the eye.

Aside from shifts in cookery, the virtues of country life and the pursuit of its simple pleasures helped elevate vegetable gardening as a worthy and genteel pastime. Jan van der Groen's *Den Nederlandtsen Hovenier* (Amsterdam, 1669) was extremely influential in this respect, as were Nicolas de Bonnefon's *Les delices de la campagne* and *Le jardinier françois* in France. All of these works were translated into several languages and included specific discussions of vegetable varieties and cooking tips. Under fava beans, for example, Bonnefon recommended several different methods of preparation, including fricassees like peas or boiled plain with slices of bacon, noting that fresh green savory went "marvelously well" with any fava bean dish.

Not the least important, from the standpoint of vegetables, was John Evelyn's *Acetaria: A Discourse on Sallets* (London, 1699), which discussed most of the popular types of vegetables of the day, especially ways to employ them raw or semicooked in salads. Of earth chestnuts *(Bunium bulbocastanum)* he remarked: "the Rind par'd off, [they] are eaten crude by Rustics, with a little Pepper; but are best when boil'd like other Roots, or in Pottage rather, and are sweet and nourishing."

Vegetables in the Enlightenment

The idea that vegetables recaptured the original wholesomeness of Eden became an underlying theme for many of the more offbeat cookbooks of the eighteenth century, with *Adam's Luxury and Eve's Cookery* (London, 1744) considered one of the most typical. The underlying philosophies expressed in these books may be said to represent the intellectual forerunners of true vegetarianism, which was indeed practiced in colonial North America by the so-called White Friends, a group of Quakers who wore clothing of unbleached cloth. The most highly organized vegetarians in early North America, however, were the Bible Christians, who expanded from England in 1816. Martha Brotherton's *Vegetable Cookery* (London, 1833) became the dietary handbook for this group.

The European penchant for country life was quickly transferred to England during the 1600s and from there to colonial America. Doubtless it achieved its American apotheosis in such famous estates as William Penn's "Pennsbury Manor" along the Delaware River, Thomas Jefferson's "Monticello" in Virginia, William Hamilton's "Woodlands" near Philadelphia, and Charles Carroll's "Mount Clare" in Baltimore. Jefferson's personal garden account book, published by the American Philosophical Society in 1944, remains a lasting testimony to the central role that kitchen gardens—and vegetables in particular—played in this manorial lifestyle.

It was on such estates as these that many of the Old World exotics were first introduced to North America. Charles Norris of Philadelphia, for example, is known to have raised black-skinned eggplants, since a letter survives from 1763 imploring him for seed. Many of the most popular vegetables of this period can be found in Philip Miller's *Gardener's and Botanist's Dictionary* (London, 1759), and remarkable as it may seem, some of Miller's vegetables are extant, among them red celery, Spotted Aleppo and Silesia lettuces, spinach beets, and domesticated sea kale.

The Vegetable in the Nineteenth Century

The Industrial Revolution in England and Europe created the need for a new type of gardener and, indeed, new sorts of vegetable varieties. Market gardening had always existed to some extent in and around urban centers, but the huge new concentration of landless workers packed into the cities meant someone else would have to act as a surrogate kitchen gardener to supply their tables. Thus vegetable horticulture underwent rapid specialization with growers focusing on such basic food crops as cabbages and onions, or turnips and potatoes.

New demands were placed on vegetable breeders for vegetables that would travel well and that gave a good appearance even after rough handling. The old-time requirements of the country kitchen gardener for vegetables that dried or pickled well were overthrown by cold frame and hot-house horticulture that could deliver such tender things as fresh peas and lettuce all winter. Furthermore, most of the old medieval vegetables like skirrets, rampion, orach, sow thistle, and nettles dropped out of mainstream diet and by the mid-nineteenth century were largely associated with rural poverty, those "rustics" mentioned by Evelyn in his treatise on salads. So thorough has industrialization distanced the consumer from the *horta* of old traditional northern European diet that the wild greens of Mediterranean culture, indeed any unusual food plants from Asia or Africa, are embraced as an antidote to a diet adrift of its "natural soul."

The two bibles of nineteenth-century American kitchen gardening are arguably Bernard M'Mahon's *American Gardener's Calendar* (Philadelphia, 1806) and Fearing Burr's *Field and Garden Vegetables of America* (Boston, 1863). Both of these works were reprinted in the twentieth century because they contain long, valuable lists and detailed descriptions of many nineteenth-century vegetables. Burr even included small woodcut illustrations. M'Mahon's book is a cultural bridge with the past, for it contains much on the old types of vegetables still eaten by traditionalists of his day. His is also a book written for the person who gardens, in particular a person who employs a staff, thus his vegetables fall into that category of food destined for genteel tables. Fearing Burr's book was quite another sort.

Burr's primary interest was to catalog the best commercially available vegetable varieties so gentlemen farmers and market gardeners would be guided in their selection of the best seed for the best investment. The book was arranged like a scholarly encyclopedia, and it was not cheap, two points against it from a farmer's standpoint. Its New England stodginess was quickly overtaken by Peter Henderson's *Gardening for Profit* (New York, 1865), an inexpensive handbook that became a best seller and the blueprint for true truck farming. Henderson was a seedsman, and he was not blind to the fact that small-scale farming for urban markets would require yet another type of vegetable; indeed, his book marks the birth of the so-called commercial vegetable grower.

Henderson's effect on vegetable breeding was immediate, and nowhere in the United States did it manifest itself more than in the explosion of newfangled high-profit tomatoes. The Paragon tomato was introduced in 1870 along with the canning jar of the same name—the connection was not coincidental. The leading tomato breeder of the time was Alexander Livingston (1822–1898) of Ohio. His Acme tomato (1875), Golden Queen (1882), Beauty (1885), and Stone (1891) are still grown and are considered among the classics of American commercial garden vegetables. But Livingston was only one of a number of seedspeople actively engaged in creating newer and better vegetables for the market. Perhaps the dean of them all was W. Atlee Burpee of Philadelphia, who even went so far as to offer large monetary rewards for backyard discoveries worthy of commercialization. Many of Burpee's best vegetable introductions came from housewives and farmers who happened to have an eye for the unusual, of which the Montreal Market Melon is a prime example. Burpee's sense of marketing was also shrewdly sophisticated, because he hired Sarah Tyson Rohrer, owner of the Philadelphia Cooking School, to create a cookbook called *How to Cook Vegetables* (Philadelphia, 1891), thus insuring that even the most helpless beginner would feel confident in buying his seeds. After all, they received the cookbook as a bonus.

The second half of the nineteenth century witnessed a large increase in the number of vegetables developed solely for manufacturing purposes not only in the United States but in Europe as well. In France, the tiny cornichon pickles were introduced in the 1880s. In England, the Marrowfat pea became the ubiquitous pea of the canneries, both as a canned vegetable and as pea soup. Whole communities grew up around the production of one vegetable. In Germany, Zittau became famous for its monster onions and Tetlow for its dwarf turnips; Poitou in France became famous for its golden leeks. In the Austro-Hungarian Empire, at Znaim in what is now the Czech Republic, a pickling industry was established in 1852 based entirely on the Znaim cucumber, a mutation of a cucumber brought from Asia in 1802. This pickle capital of central Europe remained in business until 1945, when it collapsed under ethnic cleansing. Today the Znaim cucumber is extinct.

The need for fresh breeding stock to supply growers with newer and better varieties of plants lay behind the establishment of several experimental gardens in the late 1800s. The most famous was at Crosnes (Seine-et-Oise) in France, a place-name now attached to a tuberous vegetable *(Stachys affinis)* from China first trialed there in the 1880s. The heads of that garden were Auguste Paillieux (1812–1898) and his assistant Désiré Bois. The two of them coauthored a garden classic known as *Le Potager d'un curieux* (Paris, 1885), and Bois later published his own masterwork, *Les Plantes alimentaires* (Paris, 1927). These men were responsible for a large number of new vegetable introductions, and they were interested as well in their histories. They valued the research of such botanists as Emilii Bretschneider, whose history of plant exploration in China (1898) remains one of the milestones of nineteenth-century horticultural writing. They were also keenly aware of the value of biodiversity.

The greatest collector of vegetables and edible plants in general specifically for their genetic interest was Nikolai Vavilov (1887–1943) of Russia. The Vavilov Institute, founded at St. Petersburg in 1905, became a model for similar gene banks established in other countries, including the United States. Vavilov's collections gathered from all parts of the world are considered priceless, and they have taken on much greater importance since the development of hybrids and genetically engineered foods.

In the past the hybrid vegetable was viewed as a worthless mule, and most growers disdained them because they were not fixed in their characteristics, thus they would not grow true from seed. A revolution took place in this thinking during the 1940s as seed companies began to promote the benefits of controlled crosses to yield vegetables with specific traits. Such plants are known as F1 hybrids, the label standing for "first generation." This concept has further evolved with the idea that the precise genetic mix to create that plant may be patented and thus owned in perpetuity. Genetic engineering has added one more element to the mix: traits borrowed from near species or from other life-forms to create vegetables that would not have occurred in nature. This type of vegetable dominates agribusiness, but it has also come under attack from many quarters under the moniker of "Frankenfood" (a word combination of "Frankenstein" and "food").

The primary argument against the hybrids is that, since seed cannot be saved, growers are forced to purchase new seed each year. For large-scale farmers, this increases the debt side of the ledger at the cost of seed-saving convenience. Another argument is that hybrids on the whole lack the same vigor as open-pollinated plants, that there is some long-term genetic decline at play. The patented vegetable has been criticized on moral grounds (who owns Nature?) and because it is easy to circumvent the patent by creating renegade varieties with slightly different genetic compositions. Furthermore, the ownership issue resembles the sort of complex economics of old tithes and quitrents that eventually changed medieval agriculture from a tenant system to serfdom. This New Feudalism is based not on class privilege but on farms mortgaged to banks, fertilizer companies, and seed suppliers.

While the pros and cons of these arguments are primarily limited to the farming side of the equation, it is an issue that ultimately affects the consumer and the price of vegetables on the shelf. These issues are also more polarized in developed countries like the United States than in Africa, Asia, or Latin America, where small-scale farming is the norm, and the economics of farming are different and are not necessarily based on cash flow or cash crops. However, the financial success of hybrids, patented varieties, and genetically engineered food is predicated on cheap oil for transportation, not to mention the chemical by-products of oil translated into herbicides and pesticides required to maintain these specialized vegetable crops. Oil, not politics or environmentalism, may ultimately determine the future of such vegetables. But there is also another revolution taking place. It is known as artisanal agriculture, its technology is increasingly organic, and it is based on open-pollinated vegetables, many of which are also heirloom varieties.

The Heirloom Vegetable and the Ten-Acre Farm

The discovery of vitamins and the role they play in human nutrition raised the status of the vegetable from an adjunct to the meal to a much more centralized role. When it became clear that legumes could deliver much of the same nutritional value as meat, a new look at all sorts of vegetables seemed to be in order. On hindsight, the appearance of Eleanour Sinclair Rohde's *Uncommon Vegetables* (London, 1946) and John Organ's *Rare Vegetables* (London, 1960) should have served as warnings that a shift was taking place in the food world and that this shift was the harbinger of something new. Several elements appear to have converged and to have begun working in conjunction with one another.

The first was a general setting of rapid economic growth, especially in the 1980s, and the flow of some of this new-made wealth into dining out. The second was the mainstreaming of vegetarianism and more broadly of healthy lifestyles, which placed new demands on the market (and on restaurants) to come up with a more challenging and nutritionally satisfying range of vegetable choices, although not necessarily inexpensive choices. The third was the American Bicentennial in 1976, which spawned a renewed look at historical foods and foodways and which gave rise to a number of grassroots organizations devoted to studying and preserving foods of the past. The most important plant organization, and one with enormous continuing influence, is Seed Savers Exchange in Decorah, Iowa, the high temple of what is known as the heirloom vegetable.

The fourth and perhaps the most significant development was the growth of small or artisanal farms devoted to supplying high-end urban markets with the vegetables demanded for a new American cuisine variously styled California cuisine and championed by such activist restaurants as Chez Panisse in Berkeley, California, and the White Dog Café in Philadelphia. The core concept of California cuisine was the use of locally grown food products with an emphasis on freshness, originality, and organic horticultural methods. This type of model could be replicated anywhere in the country, and thus a real interest in heirloom vegetables was born.

The heirloom vegetable is a variety that has been handed down from the past. It may be an old commercial variety like Conover's Colossal Asparagus (1863), a garden classic like Victoria Rhubarb (1837), or a symbol of American gardening genius like the Brandywine tomato (1889). Whatever their role, these are plants that have been preserved more or less intact since they were developed. Their historical and cultural genealogies may be impressive, and this alone appeals to many people who sense a loss of cultural identity and who are looking for a means to recover their "natural souls." Native American heirlooms are extremely potent in this regard.

From an economic standpoint, the heirloom vegetable is free of the ownership issues inherent in hybrid, patented, and genetically engineered food. The heirloom belongs to the community, and an exchange of this food (as well as its seeds) is viewed as a strong link in the commensality of people and a link with nature, especially since the plants are pollinated by natural means out under the sky. On a less philosophical level, heirloom vegetables were developed to meet the agricultural needs of specific soils and environments and therefore do not require the same economic investment in fertilizers and insecticides as hybrid varieties. They are also strengthened by an inherent genetic diversity lacking in hybrid sorts—a built-in mechanism to prevent massive crop failure. This appeals to organic growers, and the surprisingly rich flavors of plants raised in this manner have gained many converts in the food community at large. Politically, the heirloom vegetable represents an alternative to the type of market control and genetic expropriation associated with agribusiness. In developing countries, this means local control of local food resources, a theme championed by the Food and Agriculture Organization of the United Nations.

When the astronauts first set foot on the moon, they looked back to behold a blue orb in the darkness of space. That view changed humanity, because it said as no words could express that Earth is indeed an Eden and perhaps, for all its vicissitudes, our only reward. The philosophies that have guided us in the past are seriously challenged. While it is true that vegetables are not perceived by humans to react to pain, fear, or anxiety and while they do not have red blood, who is to say they are not our protectors?

See also **Cannibalism; Gardening and Kitchen Gardens; Genetic Engineering; Legumes; Maize; Onions and Other *Allium* Plants; Organic Farming and Gardening; Peas; Pythagoras; Tubers; Vegetarianism; Vitamins.**

BIBLIOGRAPHY

Anthimus. *Anthimus De observatione ciborum*, edited and translated by Mark Grant. Totnes, U.K., Prospect Books, 1996.

Athenaeus. *The Deipnosophists* [The Sophists at dinner]. 7 vols. Translated by Charles Burton Gulick. Cambridge, Mass.: Harvard University Press, 1969.

Bois, Désiré. *Les Plantes alimentaires.* Paris: Lechevalier, 1927.

Bowman, Alan K., and Eugene Rogan, eds. *Agriculture in Egypt.* Oxford: Oxford University Press, 1999.

Braund, David, and John Wilkins, eds. *Athenaeus and His World.* Exeter, U.K.: University of Exeter Press, 2000.

Brotherton, Martha. *Vegetable Cookery.* London: E. Wilson, 1833.

Burr, Fearing. *Field and Garden Vegetables of America.* Boston: Crosby and Nichols, 1863.

Cogliati Arano, Luisa. *The Medieval Health Handbook Tacuinum Sanitatis.* New York: Braziller, 1976.

Dannenfeldt, Karl H. *Leonhard Rauwolf.* Cambridge, Mass.: Harvard University Press, 1968.

Detienne, Marcel. *The Gardens of Adonis: Spices in Greek Mythology.* Princeton: Princeton University Press, 1994.

Facciola, Stephen. *Cornucopia II: A Source Book of Edible Plants.* Vista, Calif.: Kampong, 1998.

487

Gale, Rowena, and David Cutler. *Plants in Archaeology*. London: Westbury and Royal Botanic Gardens, 2000.

Gowers, Emily. *The Loaded Table: Representations of Food in Roman Literature*. Oxford: Clarendon, 1996.

Grant, Mark, ed. and trans. *Galen: On Food and Diet*. London: Routledge, 2000.

Guarino, L., ed. *Traditional African Vegetables*. Rome: International Genetic Plant Resources Institute, 1997.

Hanelt, Peter, ed. *Mansfeld's Encyclopedia of Agricultural and Horticultural Crops.* Berlin: Springer, 2001.

Hunt, John Dixon, and Erik de Jong. *The Anglo-Dutch Garden in the Age of William and Mary*. London: Christie's, 1988.

Jabs, Carolyn. *The Heirloom Gardener*. San Francisco: Sierra Club Books, 1984.

Jardin, Claude. *List of Foods Used in Africa*. Rome: Food Consumption and Planning Branch, Nutrition Division, Food and Agriculture Organization, 1970.

Koder, Johannes. *Gemüse in Byzanz*. Vienna: Fassbaender, 1993.

Körber-Grohne, Udelgard. *Nutzpflanzen in Deutschland*. Stuttgart: Theisis, 1988.

Langkavel, Bernard August. *Botanik der Späteren Griechen*. Amsterdam: Adolf M. Hakkert, 1964. Facsimile reprint of Berlin edition of 1866.

Meyer, F. "Food Plants Identified from Carbonized Remains at Pompeii and Other Vesuvian Sites." In *Studia Pompeiana et Classica in Honor of Wilhelmina Jashemski*, edited by Robert I. Curtis, pp. 183–230. New Rochelle, N.Y.: Caratzas, 1988–1989.

Miller, Naomi F., and Kathryn L. Gleason, eds. *The Archaeology of Garden and Field*. Philadelphia: University of Pennsylvania Press, 1994.

Percival, John. *The Roman Villa*. Berkeley: University of California Press, 1976.

Prest, John. *The Garden of Eden: The Botanic Garden and the Re-Creation of Paradise*. New Haven, Conn.: Yale University Press, 1981.

Rohde, Eleanour Sinclair. *Uncommon Vegetables*. London: Country Life, 1943.

Sampson, H. C. *Cultivated Crop Plants of the British Empire and the Anglo-Egyptian Sudan*. London: H.M. Stationary Office, 1936.

Sharrock, Walter. *History of the Propagation and Improvement of Vegetables by the Concurrence of Art and Nature*. Oxford: A. Lichfield, 1660.

Smith, Bruce D. *The Emergence of Agriculture*. New York: Scientific American Library, 1995.

Sweeney, Del, ed. *Agriculture in the Middle Ages*. Philadelphia: University of Pennsylvania Press, 1995.

Tindall, H. D. *Vegetables in the Tropics*. London: Macmillan, 1983.

Varisco, Daniel Martin. *Medieval Agriculture and Islamic Science*. Seattle: University of Washington Press, 1994.

Waters, Alice. *Chez Panisse Vegetables*. New York: HarperCollins, 1996.

Watson, Andrew M. *Agricultural Innovation in the Early Islamic World*. Cambridge: Cambridge University Press, 1983.

Weaver, William Woys. *100 Vegetables and Where They Came From*. New York: Algonquin Books, 2000.

Weaver, William Woys. *Heirloom Vegetable Gardening*. New York: Henry Holt, 1996.

Westmacott, Richard. *African-American Gardens and Yards in the Rural South*. Knoxville: University of Tennessee Press, 1992.

Wilkins, John, David Harvey, and Mike Dobson, eds. *Food in Antiquity*. Exeter, U.K.: University of Exeter Press, 1999.

Wilkinson, Alix. *The Garden in Ancient Egypt*. London: Rubicon, 1998.

William Woys Weaver

VEGETARIANISM. The dietary practice and philosophy of vegetarianism dates back to the views of Pythagoras in the fifth century B.C.E., as well as to religious practices associated with Hinduism, Janism, Zoroastrianism, and Buddhism. Historically, support for a vegetarian lifestyle has been grounded in both health and ethical and moral arguments. However, in the United States and Canada health arguments have dominated, and ethical and moral arguments typically have taken a lesser role. While many people become vegetarians because of concern for the treatment of animals raised in factory-like conditions, North Americans more commonly become vegetarians because they believe that it will help them lose weight, have more energy, or ameliorate such health conditions as high blood pressure or heart disease.

While the percentage of North Americans practicing vegetarianism has remained rather consistent at about one percent of the total population (and about 5 to 6 percent in the United Kingdom), social acceptance of this lifestyle increased dramatically in the late twentieth century. In large part, recognition by medical and nutritional authorities that vegetarian diets can be healthful and even desirable when appropriately planned has led to the legitimacy of vegetarian diets and to fewer fears regarding nutritional deficiencies. While the increasing scientific and cultural acceptance of vegetarian diets has not led to a greater percentage of the population adhering to vegetarian diets, more people are experimenting with "semi-vegetarianism," adding more meatless meals to their weekly menus.

Varieties of Vegetarianism

A wide range of dietary practices falls under the rubric of "vegetarianism." People who practice the strictest version, veganism, do not use any animal products or by-products. They do not eat meat, poultry, or seafood, nor do they wear leather or wool. They avoid foods that contain such animal by-products as whey and gelatin and do not use products that have been tested on animals.

Other vegetarians limit their avoidances to food. For example, ovo-lacto vegetarians consume eggs and dairy products but not meat, poultry, and seafood. Ovo vegetarians do not consume dairy products, and lacto vegetarians consume dairy products but not eggs. Semivegetarians occasionally consume some or all animal products and may or may not consider themselves vegetarians. Studies suggest that semivegetarians outnumber "true" vegetarians by about four to one.

These terms define the various types of vegetarians by what they do not consume. Consequently, many vegetarians are concerned that nonvegetarians view vegetarian diets as primarily prohibitive and restrictive. They emphasize that following a vegetarian diet often leads people to consume a wider variety of foods than many meat eaters do, as vegetarians often include a wider range of fruits, vegetables, grains, and legumes in their diets.

A Brief Historical Perspective

Vegetarianism arrived in the United States in the early 1800s as primarily a religious practice associated with the Bible Christian Church of Philadelphia. The church's leader, William Metcalfe, advocated abstinence from meat as a form of spiritual temperance. In 1830 the Bible Christian Church hired Sylvester Graham, who had been studying medicine in Philadelphia, as a temperance lecturer. Graham soon branched out on his own, turning elements of a religious philosophy into a more secular set of practices in which he advocated abstinence from alcohol, sex, coffee, tea, spices, and of course meat.

Graham's philosophy was rooted in a deep distrust of the emerging industrial revolution of the 1830s and 1840s. He expressed concern that the marketplace was supplanting the role of "hearth and home" in developing moral character and stressed the importance of individual efforts to restore a moral balance in an increasingly chaotic social world. With Metcalfe and such vegetarian advocates as William Alcott and Russell Trall, Graham helped form the American Vegetarian Society in 1850. Many early suffragists and abolitionists, such as Susan B. Anthony, Lucy Stone, and Horace Greeley, attended the early meetings of this organization.

The vegetarian legacy continued with the efforts of John Harvey Kellogg, who developed cornflakes in 1894. The Seventh Day Adventist Church hired Kellogg in the 1870s to run its Battle Creek Sanatorium, where popular treatments included exercise, hydropathy (water cure), and a vegetarian diet. The Seventh Day Adventist Church continued to endorse and promote vegetarian diets in the twenty-first century, although it did not require its members to adopt them.

Interestingly, although early vegetarianism was strongly associated with religion (first with the Bible Christian Church and then with Seventh Day Adventism), vegetarianism has been primarily a secular rather than a spiritual practice in North America. Even the early vegetarians were encouraged to adopt vegetarianism as a means to good health that would enhance their individual capacities, including their capacity to experience the Divine,

Early eighteenth-century engraving of Benjamin Lay, a Quaker vegetarian and hermit in Pennsylvania. Lay and other Quaker vegetarians known as "White Friends" (they wore only undyed cloth) were heavily influenced by Thomas Tryon's *The Way to Health* (London, 1683). Tryon's discourse contained material on Pythagoras and his vegetarian philosophies. Later editions were expanded with recipes for seventy-five "noble dishes" prepared without "eating flesh and blood." Lay is shown holding Tryon's book in his hand. ROUGHWOOD COLLECTION.

and vegetarianism has rarely been promoted as a spiritual path in and of itself. Consequently, despite its historically religious underpinnings, the health aspect of vegetarianism has predominated in the United States and Canada.

Characteristics of Contemporary Vegetarians

While vegetarians probably exhibit more differences than similarities, researchers have discerned several patterns regarding their social backgrounds and statuses. Vegetarians tend to come from predominantly middle-class backgrounds, and a substantially smaller percentage comes from lower social classes. This can be explained by the fact that people who have less money view meat as desirable and associate it with upward social mobility. Therefore, when they have discretionary income, they are likely to use it to purchase meat products. In North America meat is often associated with success and social status. People are only likely to reject meat once they have the opportunity to consume as much as they want.

Gender is another patterned feature of vegetarians in North America. Studies have consistently found that about 70 percent of all vegetarians are female. Several explanations are possible. First, the foods embraced by vegetarian diets are those already symbolically linked with feminine attributes, that is, foods that are light, low-fat, and not bloody (as people often equate blood with strength). For many people meat and masculinity are inextricably linked; therefore it is easier for women than for men to escape cultural expectations. In addition, women tend to be more concerned with weight loss, and many pursue a vegetarian diet as the means to that end. Finally, some researchers hold that women are more likely than men to hold a compassionate attitude toward animals, leading them to have more concern about killing animals for food. All of these factors contribute to the reality that women are more likely than men to become vegetarians.

Studies have suggested that vegetarians may share a variety of other characteristics as well. For example, while vegetarians are less likely than the general population to follow a conventional religion, they are more likely to describe themselves as spiritual and to practice some form of yoga or meditation. They are more likely to describe themselves as "liberal" and less likely to adhere to traditional values that embrace upholding the existing social order. They are also less likely than the general population to smoke cigarettes and drink alcohol. Yet it is important to point out that vegetarians are more different than similar in their social backgrounds, political beliefs, and health practices.

Reasons for Vegetarianism

People become vegetarians for a variety of reasons, including personal health, a concern for the treatment of farm animals and the environment, spiritual beliefs, and sometimes simply a physical disgust toward meat. Most commonly North Americans follow a gradual path toward vegetarianism that starts with a health motivation. They perceive that a vegetarian diet will give them more energy, will help them lose weight, or will assuage a health condition, such as heart disease or cancer. Other people become vegetarians out of a concern for the rights of animals or a belief that meat production causes devastating effects to the environment. Some grew up with or adopted a religion (for example, Hinduism, Jainism, Seventh Day Adventism) that encourages or requires a vegetarian diet. Still others are concerned with world hunger and take the view that many more people can be fed on a vegetarian diet than on a meat-based one.

People tend to first stop eating the foods they view as the most offensive or unhealthy. For most gradual vegetarians this is red meat. The typical path for a new vegetarian is to stop eating red meat first, then poultry, and then fish. Some move to further prohibitions by adopting a vegan lifestyle as they eliminate eggs, dairy products, and other animal by-products. As people progress along the vegetarian "path," they tend to adopt new rea-

sons to support their lifestyle practices. Most commonly people begin with a health motivation and gradually become concerned with the humane treatment of animals and protecting the environment, and many develop a disgust response to meat products.

Scientific Controversy and Gradual Acceptance

After the mid-1800s, the medical establishment responded to advocates' claims that vegetarian diets are healthful and desirable. In the 1800s vegetarians were primarily labeled as "quacks" and were characterized in the popular press as weak, sallow, and emaciated. The notion that vegetarians are weak and lack energy persisted throughout the twentieth century.

In the 1970s dietitians and nutritional scientists focused much attention on vegetarian diets, and many considered them a medical problem. These nutritionists were particularly concerned that vegetarians did not consume adequate protein. During the 1970s and 1980s many articles in nutrition journals debated whether or not vegetarian diets were desirable and gave advice about how to deal with obstinate vegetarian clients. Over time, however, dietitians accepted the idea that vegetable protein derived primarily from grains and legumes is not of lesser quality than protein from meat and other animal-based foods. Eventually dietitians accepted their clients' vegetarian lifestyles and began to help them improve those diets instead of trying to convert them to meat eating.

By the early twenty-first century the American Dietetic Association and the U.S. Department of Agriculture both endorsed the healthfulness of vegetarian diets when they are appropriately planned (just as any diet should be). However, new controversies have arisen, particularly regarding the necessity and desirability of consuming milk and other dairy products. This controversy was spurred in the late 1990s in large part by the view of the renowned pediatrician Benjamin Spock that children should be fed a vegan diet after age two. This stance has generated much debate, as it challenges the deep-seated cultural notion that milk is necessary to build strong bones and to foster physical development.

The Vegetarian Movement

Most people adopt vegetarian diets at least in part as a result of interactions with other practicing vegetarians. People rarely become vegetarians in isolation. Through social interactions, people learn the reasons for adopting vegetarian diets and how to successfully follow them. For example, they learn how to cook vegetarian meals and where to buy foods that will ensure that their new diets are both nutritionally sound and personally satisfying. Consequently, vegetarianism is typically much more of a social experience than an individual experience.

Numerous vegetarian organizations facilitate this social learning. Although they are largely distinct from animal rights and environmental organizations, they sometimes share leadership and other resources. At the national level the American Vegan Society, the North American Vegetarian Society, and EarthSave hold conferences, distribute literature on vegetarian diets, and help form local vegetarian societies. In these local groups people interact, share potluck meals, listen to speakers, and sometimes distribute vegetarian literature to the public at local events.

Other national vegetarian organizations, such as FARM, Vegan Action, and Vegan Outreach, encourage vegetarians to take a more activist stance. The Vegetarian Resource Group distributes well-documented, scientifically oriented literature to the public and works with governmental and professional organizations to advance the movement's goals. All of these groups primarily promote vegetarianism through education and embrace the varied reasons for adopting vegetarian diets.

See also **Kellogg, John Harvey**; **Organic Food**; **Pythagoras**; **Vegetables**.

BIBLIOGRAPHY

Amato, Paul R., and Sonia A. Partridge. *The New Vegetarians: Promoting Health and Protecting Life.* New York: Plenum, 1989. A sociological work based on a survey of vegetarians.

Fox, Michael Allen. *Deep Vegetarianism.* Philadelphia: Temple University Press, 1999. A philosophical examination of vegetarianism.

Jabs, Jennifer, Carol M. Devine, and Jeffery Sobal. "Personal Factors, Social Networks, and Environmental Resources." *Canadian Journal of Dietetic Practice and Research* 59 (1998): 183–189. A qualitative investigation of the social aspects of maintaining a vegetarian diet.

Marcus, Erik. *Vegan: The New Ethics of Eating.* Ithaca, N.Y.: McBooks Press, 1998. A vegan's perspective that includes interviews with vegetarian leaders.

Maurer, Donna. *Vegetarianism: Movement or Moment?* Philadelphia: Temple University Press, 2002. An analysis of the contemporary vegetarian movement in the United States and Canada.

Melina, Vesanto, Brenda Davis, and Victoria Harrison. *Becoming Vegetarian: The Complete Guide to Adopting a Vegetarian Diet.* Summertown, Tenn.: Book Publishing, 1995. A guide to vegetarian diets written by three dietitians.

Spencer, Colin. *The Heretic's Feast: A History of Vegetarianism.* Hanover, N.H.: University Press of New England, 1995. A global historical analysis of vegetarianism focusing on its philosophical aspects.

Stepaniak, Joanne. *The Vegan Sourcebook.* Los Angeles: Lowell House, 1998. A compendium of vegan information, including recipes.

Donna Maurer

VITAMIN C. Vitamin C is also known as ascorbic acid, because it is the "anti-scorbutus" vitamin (*scorbutus* being the Latin name for the disease of scurvy). Unlike other vitamins, it is only required by a few species, particularly humans, but also guinea pigs and bats. Others, such as dogs and cats, make it for themselves by oxidiz-

ing glucose. Species that require the vitamin have lost the key enzyme that manufactures vitamin C because of a genetic mutation during evolution, in a period when the natural diet was vitamin C–rich, resulting in no disadvantage. The empirical formula of the vitamin is $C_6H_8O_6$; it is a white crystalline powder, freely soluble in water and pleasant tasting, but easily destroyed by heat and oxidation. A daily intake of as little as 7 milligrams (mg) has been found to be sufficient to prevent the development of signs of scurvy, but the usual recommendation is that adults should aim to take some 70 mg per day, partly as a safety factor. One school of thought recommends much higher intakes, of perhaps 1,000 mg, on the grounds that its antioxidant properties will increase resistance to infections, aging, and cancer. This assertion remains controversial, however. The Institute of Medicine recommends 2,000 mg/day as the tolerable upper intake level for adults. High levels may have a laxative effect, but this is welcomed by many people. The main natural sources of the vitamin are fresh fruits and vegetables. One of the first fruits valued for its antiscorbutic activity was the orange—each one containing some 50 to 75 mg of the vitamin. In contrast, an apple of similar size has only 7 mg. Potatoes have been an important source of the vitamin in some cultures, not because they are particularly rich, but because they have been consumed in large amounts.

The value of potatoes as a source of vitamin C is influenced by the way in which they are prepared. Thus, one large potato cooked in its skin in a microwave oven may supply 30 mg of the vitamin, but the same quantity may supply only a third of that or even less when boiled, mashed, and reheated on a buffet table. One problem has been to understand how Eskimos, in their traditional lifestyle, managed to obtain enough vitamin C when they had no access to fruits or vegetables. Although fully cooked meats have lost essentially all their vitamin C, the scarcity of fuel meant that the Eskimos could only bring a piece of meat just to the boil in water. They then drank the vitamin-rich broth and ate the meat, thus meeting their need for vitamin C. Liver cooked in this way is richer than muscle meats in vitamin C. Cows' milk too loses most of its vitamin C when heat-sterilized or "condensed," and infantile scurvy has been a problem where mothers have economized by using canned milk as a complete food for their infant.

See also **Beriberi**; **Niacin Deficiency (Pellagra)**; **Nutrient Bioavailability**; **Nutrients**; **Nutrition**; **Scurvy**; **Vitamins**.

BIBLIOGRAPHY

Counsell, J. N., and D. M. Hornig, eds. *Vitamin C (Ascorbic Acid).* London: Applied Science Publishers, 1981.

Institute of Medicine. *Dietary Reference Intakes for Vitamin C, Vitamin E, Selenium, and Carotenoids.* Washington, D.C.: National Academy Press, 2000.

Packer, Lester, and Jürgen Fuchs, eds. *Vitamin C in Health and Disease.* New York: M. Dekker, 1997.

Kenneth John Carpenter

VITAMINS.

OVERVIEW

The word "vitamin" came from the term *vita mines* (vital amines), which was introduced by Casimir Funk, who, in 1912, isolated a growth factor from rice polishings that contained an amine (a compound incorporating a nitrogen atom with two hydrogen atoms) and could cure the disease beriberi. Several other growth factors were identified early in the twentieth century as well, and these substances were also called vitamins even though they did not contain an amine. Vitamins are classified into two major groups: fat-soluble and water-soluble. (See the Appendix for a complete chart of vitamins.)

Fat-Soluble Vitamins

Vitamin A. In the early 1900s, Sir Frederick Hopkins demonstrated that animals would not grow if lard was provided as a sole dietary lipid. When a small quantity of milk containing fat was added to the diet, the animals thrived. The fat-soluble factor was isolated and designated as vitamin A, later called retinol or retinal; these and similar compounds are referred to as retinoids. Carotenoids, which are essentially two retinoids joined tail to tail, are inactive forms of vitamin A and are called provitamin A. They are converted to vitamin A in the intestine and liver. Vitamin A and carotenoids are absorbed in the chylomicron (a lipoprotein particle that transports lipids from the intestine) fraction and stored in the liver. Some foods such as milk are fortified with vitamin A. Rich sources of carotenoids include carrots, leafy green vegetables, and pink grapefruit.

Vitamin A is, chemically, a subgroup of retinoids, which are defined as a class of compounds that consist of a six-membered ring and a side chain with four conjugated double bonds (four isoprenoid units). The term vitamin A is used to describe retinoids exhibiting qualitatively the biologic activity of the retinoid, retinol.

Vitamin A binds to a retinol-binding protein that transports the light-sensitive vitamin to various target tissues, including the eyes, skin, and gastrointestinal track. The major functions of vitamin A include vision and regulation of cellular proliferation and differentiation. Vitamin A functions on vision by interacting with the rod and cone cells in the retina. It is responsible for absorbing light. The 11-*cis* form of vitamin A (retinal) combines with the protein opsin to form rhodopsin in the rod cells and iodopsins in the cone cells. The rhodopsin and iodopsins absorb light at various wavelengths and trigger a nerve impulse to the visual cortex in the brain that is ultimately perceived as black-and-white and color vision, respectively.

Vitamin A's other major physiologic function is to maintain the health of skin and mucous-secreting cells by regulating their cellular activity and maturation. The dietary requirements depend on age.

The major consequence of vitamin A deficiency, which continues to be a serious nutritional problem among millions of schoolchildren in southern and southeastern Asia and parts of Africa and South America, is night blindness. Vitamin A deficiency can lead to complete blindness and severe damage to the outer covering of the eye (the cornea), often causing it to perforate, with loss of the fluid from inside the eye (keratomalacia). Vitamin A deficiency also produces changes in the skin that are related to the inability of the skin cells to mature and produce keratin properly. This leads to follicular hyperkeratosis and phrynoderma (a condition characterized by rough, dry skin). Vitamin A deficiency has also been linked to increased mortality in early childhood.

Acute and chronic ingestion of excessive amounts of vitamin A can cause a multitude of symptoms and consequences. The most serious is that it can cause severe birth defects, spontaneous abortions and learning defects, and skin and epithelial-cell exfoliation. Inexperienced white explorers of the Arctic who ate polar-bear liver in excess developed severe vitamin A intoxication that caused a total sloughing of their skin and mucous-secreting cells in the upper airway and esophagus, bringing on painful death. (This is in contrast to the indigenous Inuit, who specifically avoid eating polar-bear liver.)

Vitamin D. One of the consequences of the industrial revolution was the high incidence of the bone-deforming disease rickets. It was estimated, at the turn of the twentieth century, that more than ninety percent of children living in the industrialized cities of northern Europe and the northeastern United States had rickets. It had been known that cod-liver oil possessed a factor that had antirachitic activity. Originally, it was thought that the antirachitic factor was vitamin A. However, Hopkins heated cod-liver oil to destroy the vitamin A activity and demonstrated that it still possessed antirachitic activity. This new fat-soluble vitamin was labeled vitamin D. It was also recognized that exposure of food, animals, and humans to ultraviolet radiation also prevented and cured rickets.

There are two principal forms of vitamin D: Vitamin D_2 comes from the precursor ergosterol found in yeast and plants, and vitamin D_3 comes from the cholesterol precursor 7-dehydrocholesterol that is found in the skin of reptiles, birds, mammals, and humans. Vitamin D_2 and vitamin D_3 are essentially equally active in most birds and in most mammals, including humans. Chickens and New World monkeys, however, cannot utilize vitamin D_2. There are very few foods that naturally contain vitamin D. Fatty fish, such as salmon and mackerel, and fish-liver oils, such as cod-liver oil are good sources of vitamin D. Cow's milk and human milk have very little vitamin D. However, in the United States and Canada, milk and some breads and cereals are fortified with vitamin D. In Europe, fortification of foods with vitamin D was outlawed when sporadic cases of vitamin D intoxication were observed in children in the 1950s. Today some margarine and cereals are fortified with vitamin D in Europe, but milk is not.

Vitamin D_3 is made by the action of sunlight on the skin. Provitamin D_3 (7-Dehydrocholesterol) absorbs solar ultraviolet B radiation (wavelengths 290–315 nm) and is transformed into previtamin D_3. Previtamin D_3 is unstable at body temperature and isomerizes (rotates its double bonds) to vitamin D_3. Once formed, vitamin D_3 leaves the skin and enters the circulation, bound to the vitamin D binding protein. It travels to the liver where it is activated to 25-hydroxyvitamin D [25(OH)D]. This form, however, is biologically inert at physiologic concentrations and is the major circulating form of vitamin D. It is, nevertheless, the form that is measured to determine the vitamin D status of an individual, because it represents a summation of dietary and skin sources of vitamin D. 25(OH)D is transported on the vitamin D binding protein to the kidney, where it undergoes its final activation on carbon 1 to form 1,25-dihydroxyvitamin D [1,25(OH)$_2$D], the biologically active form of vitamin D.

The principal function of vitamin D is to maintain blood calcium and phosphorus in the normal range in order to promote neuromuscular function and to maintain metabolic activities. It accomplishes this by enhancing the efficiency of intestinal calcium transport in the small intestine and by stimulating precursor cells of osteoclasts to become mature osteoclasts. Among the functions of osteoclasts is to remove calcium from bone. Serum calcium and phosphorus are in the form of $Ca_x(PO_4)$. When these compounds are in the normal range, they are in a supersaturated state that can thus be deposited in the skeletal matrix as calcium hydroxyapatite.

1,25(OH)$_2$D interacts with a receptor in the nucleus of cells, known as the VDR (vitamin D receptor). It also complexes with the "retinoic acid x" receptor in that cellular structure. These receptor-activated vitamin D complexes find their way to genes that have responsive elements known as the vitamin D-responsive element. These elements in turn unlock genetic information that is responsible for various biologic functions in intestine and bone. It is recognized that a wide variety of tissues including the brain, parathyroid glands, breast, prostate, stomach, and skin also have VDR. Although the exact physiologic function of 1,25(OH)$_2$D in these non-calcium-regulating tissues is not well understood, 1,25(OH)$_2$D inhibits cellular proliferation and induces terminal differentiation of a wide variety of cells, including bone, skin, skeletal muscle, breast, and prostate. The dietary requirement depends on age.

Vitamin D deficiency results in a decrease in the efficiency of intestinal calcium absorption that in turn leads to a decrease in unbound or free calcium concentrations in the circulation. This is recognized by the parathyroid gland and results in an increase in the production and secretion of parathyroid hormone (PTH). PTH enhances calcium reabsorption by the kidney and causes increased output of phosphate in the urine. PTH also stimulates the kidney to produce more 1,25(OH)$_2$D. The net effect of vitamin D deficiency is a low-normal serum calcium and a low serum phosphorus (due to the PTH-induced phosphate wasting in the kidney). Thus calcium and phosphorus concentrations fall below supersaturating levels, thereby resulting in poorly mineralized bone. In children, this causes rickets and, in adults, osteomalacia. In addition, vitamin D deficiency in adults can precipitate and exacerbate osteoporosis. In winter, little if any vitamin D can be made in the skin of people who live above 40° north or below 40° south of the equator. An increase in the zenith angle of the sun due to latitude, time of day, and season of the year will dramatically reduce the production of vitamin D_3 in the skin. Moreover, aging and sunscreen use can markedly reduce the production of vitamin D by more than 60 percent and 99 percent, respectively. Rickets due to vitamin D deficiency in children may include bowlegs or knock-knees, widening of the ends of the long bones, growth retardation, and muscle weakness. In adults, in addition to osteomalacia and increased risk of osteoporosis, it causes bone pain, muscle weakness, and fractures.

The safe upper limit for Vitamin D is 2,000 units a day. Although it is difficult to ingest enough to cause vitamin D intoxication, it can occur. Usually, oral ingestion of 10,000 units a day and greater will cause vitamin D intoxication. This intoxication causes an elevation in the blood levels of calcium and phosphorus, which results in the calcification of soft tissues, including the kidney and major blood vessels, and may also cause the formation of kidney stones.

Vitamin E. The discovery of vitamin E (tocopherols—from *toc-* meaning 'childbirth', *phero-* meaning 'bringing forth', and *-ol* representing the alcohol portion of the molecule) was due to the observation that supplementation of the diet with vitamin E prevented fetal death in animals that were fed a diet containing rancid lard. There are eight naturally occurring vitamin E compounds. Four of them are known as tocopherols and four are known as tocotrienols. The most abundant form of vitamin E is alpha-tocopherol. One of the major functions of vitamin E is to act as a biologic antioxidant to protect the sensitive cellular membranes from oxidative destruction. The major sources of vitamin E consumed by Americans are vegetables and seed oils, such as corn oil, soybean oil, and safflower oil. Wheat germ is a rich source of vitamin E. Although butter contains very little vitamin E, American margarine contains a significant amount of this antioxidant vitamin.

Vitamin E, like the other fat-soluble vitamins, is absorbed in the chylomicron fraction into the lymphatic system and is transported into the venous blood. The dietary requirements depend on age.

There have been difficulties in defining a clinical syndrome that correlates with vitamin E deficiency in humans. Vitamin E deficiency is associated with anemia in newborns.

Toxicity from excess vitamin E has been associated with increased bleeding tendency in adults and impaired immune function, decreased levels of vitamin K-dependent clotting factors, and impairment of leukocyte function.

Vitamin K. Vitamin K was discovered by Henrik Dam in Copenhagen in 1929. He observed that chicks fed a fat-free diet developed severe bleeding under the skin and in the muscle and other tissues. He named this new fat-soluble vitamin, vitamin K (for "Koagulation vitamin"). Vitamin K is distributed widely in both animal and vegetable foods as well as in milk. It comes in several forms: vitamin K_1 comes from plants and is known as phylloquinone, and vitamin K_2, first isolated from fish meal and in animal foods, comprises a group of compounds known as menaquinones. In addition, bacterial flora in the intestine synthesize menaquinones that are bioavailable.

Vitamin K, like other fat-soluble vitamins, is absorbed in the chylomicron fraction and then appears in the lymph and subsequently in the venous circulation. The major physiologic function of vitamin K is to activate blood-clotting proteins. This is accomplished by the modification of a substance, glutamate, found in several precoagulant factors, including factors II, VII, VIIII, and X, that are produced in the liver. Vitamin K is also responsible for the modification of other proteins, including the major noncollagenous protein in bone. The dietary requirements depend on age.

Vitamin K deficiency is rare because of the widespread distribution of the vitamin in plant and animal foods and because microbiotic flora in the normal gut synthesize menaquinones. However, vitamin K deficiency in breast-fed newborns remains a major worldwide cause of infant morbidity and mortality. Infants have very little stored vitamin K at birth, and the gut is nearly sterile during the first few days of life. As a result, infants can develop a severe bleeding condition known as hemorrhagic disease of the newborn if they do not obtain vitamin K during the first few days of life from an exogenous source, particularly since mother's milk contains little vitamin K and few bacteria other than those it picks up from maternal skin as an infant suckles. Adults who have intestinal malabsorption syndrome and who are taking antibiotics can become severely vitamin K-deficient. This can lead to generalized bleeding from all orifices.

There are no reported cases of intoxication due to excessive ingestion of phylloquinone. Ingestion of excessive amounts of menadione, a vitamin K precursor, can cause anemia secondary to the destruction of red blood cells, and an alteration in bilirubin metabolism causing hyperbilirubinemia in infants (kernicterus).

Water-Soluble Vitamins

Thiamine (vitamin B_1). Beriberi is a disease with a constellation of systems affecting the nervous and cardiovascular systems. It was first described by the Chinese in 2697 B.C.E. In 1926, B. C. P. Jansen and W. F. Donath identified a factor from rice-bran extracts that prevented beriberi. The antiberiberi factor was identified chemically and called thiamine (vitamin B_1). Thiamine is found in yeast, lean pork, and legumes. It serves as a receptor for high-energy pyrophosphate. It is this form of the vitamin that provides its chemical function. Pyrophosphate is extremely important for the generation of energy in the cell. However, it cannot enter the cell unless it is attached to thiamine. Thiamine is absorbed by the small intestine and transported to the liver. The major biochemical function of thiamine is to act as a coenzyme (that is, to provide a transfer site) in the alpha-keto acid carboxylation pathway. The dietary requirements depend on age.

Thiamine deficiency causes beriberi. Anorexia, neuritis, gastrointestinal dysfunction, cardiac irregularities, and muscle atrophy are present. There are three types of this disorder: wet, dry, and infantile. Wet beriberi is associated with body fluid retention (edema). Dry beriberi is related to neurologic abnormalities. It is recognized that alcoholics who have poor nutrition and thiamine deficiency, when receiving intravenous fluids, for example in the emergency room of a hospital, can develop severe altered mental states known Wernicke's and Korsakoff's syndromes. Wet beriberi is associated with heart abnormalities; dry beriberi is associated with neurological abnormalities that can cause permanent confusion if not treated in a timely manner.

Excessive ingestion of thiamine is cleared by the kidneys. There is no evidence that ingesting excessive amounts causes toxicity.

Riboflavin. In the 1920s, another water-soluble vitamin was discovered; it exhibited antipellagra activity and was termed vitamin B_2. The substance was found to be yellow in color and was identified as a coenzyme, riboflavin 5'-phosphate (flavin mononucleotide or FMN).

The more abundant form of this vitamin is a complex flavin-adenine dinucleotide (FAD) that also participates as a coenzyme. Usually, the FMN and FAD are associated loosely with proteins and are released in the acidic gastrointestinal juices. The vitamin is absorbed by the proximal small intestine. Sources of riboflavin include eggs, lean meats, milk, broccoli, and enriched breads and cereals.

The physiologic function of riboflavin is to participate in oxidation-reduction reactions in numerous metabolic pathways and in energy production via the respiratory chain in the mitochondria. The dietary requirements depend on age.

Riboflavin is distributed widely in foodstuffs, and therefore deficiency is not common. However, there are reported cases of deficiency that are characterized by sore throat, hyperemia and edema of the pharyngeal and oral mucosal membranes, cheilosis (abnormal scaling and fissuring of the lips), angular stomatitis (surface inflammation of the mouth), glossitis (inflammation of the tongue), seborrheic dermatitis (an inflammation of the skin involving oversecretion by the oil-producing cutaneous glands), and anemia. Severe riboflavin deficiency can affect the conversion of vitamin B$_6$ to its coenzyme and reduce the conversion of tryptophan, an amino acid found in proteins of animal and plant origin, to niacin (see next section). Deficiency is principally due to abnormal digestion, abnormal absorption, or both. People who are lactose-intolerant—a condition that is most common among blacks and Asians—often limit consumption of milk (as noted above, an excellent source of riboflavin); they may therefore be at increased risk for riboflavin deficiency. Intestinal malabsorption syndromes, including tropical sprue celiac disease, small bowel resection, and gastrointestinal and biliary obstruction can lead to riboflavin deficiency.

There is no evidence that toxicity can occur as a result of excessive ingestion of riboflavin. The most likely reason for this is that riboflavin is cleared rapidly by the kidney and is not stored in the body.

Niacin. In the mid-1700s, a Spanish physician, Gaspar Casal, recognized a disease known as pellagra that caused diarrhea, dementia, and dermatitis in maize-eating (corn-eating) populations throughout the world. In 1937, Conrad Elvehjem and his colleagues observed that nicotinic acid was an effective treatment for pellagra. Nicotinic acid is synonymous with both niacin and nicotinamide. It is associated with ribose lyphosphate to form nicotinamide adenine dinucleotide (NAD) and NAD phosphate. Most niacin in food is present as a component of NAD or NADP and is relatively stable to cooking and storage. Good sources of niacin include meats (especially liver), fish, legumes such as peanuts, some nuts, and some cereals. Both coffee and tea also contain reasonable amounts of this vitamin. Niacin is unique among the B vitamins because its precursor amino acid, tryptophan, can help meet the daily niacin requirement.

Niacin has a multitude of physiologic functions in a wide variety of metabolic pathways that are related to energy production and biosynthetic processes. At least two hundred enzymes are dependent on NAD and NADP. Both of these substances act as electron acceptors or hydrogen donors. Most NAD-dependent enzymes are involved in catabolic reactions, whereas NADP is used more commonly for reductive biosyntheses of fatty acids and steroids, for example. The dietary requirements depend on age.

Niacin deficiency causes pellagra. This condition is associated with diarrhea, dementia, and dermatitis. It is endemic in India and in parts of China and Africa. The classic appearance of pellagra is a pigmented rash that develops symmetrically in areas of the skin exposed to sunlight. The tongue can become bright red and there is often vomiting and diarrhea. Patients can also exhibit

anxiety or sleeplessness, and can become disoriented and delusional.

Nicotinic acid is now used to treat hypercholesterolemia. Side effects of large amounts of nicotinic acid include flushing of the skin, abnormalities in liver function, and hyperglycemia. At extremely high ingestion levels, nicotinamide causes death in rats.

Pyridoxine (vitamin B$_6$). Vitamin B$_6$ was identified in the 1930s. Like many of the water-soluble B vitamins, vitamin B$_6$ includes a group of compounds that act as a coenzyme phosphate donor. These include pyridoxal 5'-phosphate (PLP), and pyridoxamine 5'-phosphate (PMP). Plants foods contain predominantly pyridoxine, whereas animal products contain primarily pyridoxal and pyridoxamine. Vitamin B$_6$ is absorbed mainly by the lower small intestine (jejunum).

Like many of the other coenzyme B vitamins, vitamin B$_6$ has numerous biologic functions that are related to metabolism. B$_6$ is critically important for the production of glucose. PLP is also necessary for the conversion of tryptophan to niacin, which is why the two are often associated. The dietary requirements depend on age.

As with many of the other B vitamins, there are a wide variety of clinical symptoms associated with vitamin B$_6$ deficiency including an abnormal electroencephalogram, convulsions, stomatitis, cheilosis, glossitis, irritability, depression, and confusion.

High doses of pyridoxine have been used to treat premenstrual syndrome and other neurological diseases. Such uses have resulted in neurotoxicity and photosensitivity.

Pantothenic acid. Pantothenic acid was one of the more difficult vitamins to isolate and separate from the other water-soluble B vitamins. Finally in the 1940s, it was synthesized and was found to be associated with coenzyme A (CoA). CoA is an essential cofactor for biologic acetylation reactions and participates in the respiratory tricarboxylic acid cycle, fatty-acid synthesis and degradation, and a wide variety of other metabolic and regulatory processes. The dietary requirements depend on age.

Pantothenic acid deficiency affects the adrenal gland, nervous system, skin, and hair adversely. Pantothenic acid deficiency in humans is rare, but has been associated with fatigue and depression.

High doses of calcium pantothenate have not been found to be toxic in humans.

Folic acid and cobalamin (vitamin B$_{12}$). In the mid-1800s, several physicians recognized that a severe form of anemia was associated with disorders of the digestive system. In 1934, William Castle and his associates observed that normal human gastric juice contained an intrinsic factor (IF) that combines with an extrinsic factor in animal-protein food, resulting in the absorption of a vitamin that

VITAMINS: OVERVIEW

prevents anemia. Vitamin B_{12} was isolated in 1948 and was shown to be the extrinsic antianemia factor.

Vitamin B_{12} absorption is unique among the B vitamins, in requiring an IF to help its absorption. Folate, on the other hand, is absorbed directly by the upper (proximal) small intestine.

Whereas vitamin B_{12} is found only in animal protein, folates are common in nature and present in nearly all natural foods. The dietary requirements depend on age.

Vitamin B_{12} deficiency can occur either because of inadequate vitamin B_{12} ingestion or because of the loss or inadequacy of production of intrinsic factor in the stomach. The two most notable clinical signs of vitamin B_{12} deficiency include megaloblastic anemia and neurological deficits. Vitamin B_{12} deficiency can cause paresthesia (especially numbness and tingling in the hands and feet); the diminution of vibration and position sense; unsteadiness; poor muscular coordination with ataxia (loss of muscular coordination); moodiness; mental slowness; poor memory; confusion; agitation; depression; and central visual loss. Delusions, overt psychosis, and paranoid ideas may occur in severe deficiency.

Folate deficiency also causes megaloblastic anemia and can cause neurological abnormalities as well, including irritability, forgetfulness, and hostile and paranoid behavior. For adults, ingestion of ten thousand times the minimum requirement for B_{12} and several hundred times that for folic acid has not been associated with toxicity.

Biotin. Biotin was identified in the 1940s. It, like many of the other B vitamins, acts as a coenzyme. Biotin is plentiful in foods such as liver, egg yolk, soybeans, yeast, cereals, legumes, and nuts. With the exception of cauliflower and mushrooms, vegetables, fruits, and meats, however, are poor sources of biotin. Biotin is also present in human and cow's milk. The major physiologic functions of biotin are related to carbohydrate and lipid metabolism. The dietary requirements depend on age.

Biotin deficiency causes mental-status changes, myalgia (muscle pain), hyperesthesia (abnormal sensitivity to pain, touch, cold, etc.), localized paresthesia, and anorexia with nausea. Dermatitis can also be associated with deficiency. The immune system is impaired in biotin-deficient animals. Neurological disorders including seizures and developmental delays have been reported in children. There have been no reports of intoxication due to excessive biotin ingestion.

Vitamin C. Scurvy is recognized as a deficiency disease that has taken a high toll in human suffering and death. The disease, which is caused by vitamin C deficiency, was recognized in ancient times by the Egyptians, Greeks, and Romans. It was especially prevalent among sea explorers of the sixteenth to eighteenth centuries. Typically, sailors developed bleeding and rotting gums, swollen and inflamed joints, dark blotches on the skin,

and muscle weakness that occurred within months when at sea. It was the loss of 1,051 sailors in 1774 that prompted the British Admiralty to seek a cure for this devastating disease. They found that lemon or lime juice could prevent the disease. In the late 1920s, Albert Szent-Györgyi and Glenn King isolated vitamin C and identified it as hexuronic acid. Vitamin C is water-soluble and is absorbed efficiently by the small intestine. Its major physiologic function is to provide reducing activity for a wide variety of metabolic steps. It is important for the modification of lysine and proline—two amino acids that are common components of collagen. These modifications result in the cross-linking of collagen strands providing structural support for this essential component of bone and fibrous tissues. The dietary requirements depend on age.

As noted, vitamin C deficiency causes scurvy, which is associated with a wide variety of abnormalities, including hemorrhages under the skin, black-and-blue marks, hyperkeratosis, joint discomfort, edema, weakness, fatigue, lassitude, depression, and hysteria.

It was suggested by the Nobel Prize Laureate Linus Pauling that extremely high doses of vitamin C could prevent cancer. With the exception of excessive amounts of vitamin C causing bowel impaction via a large number of vitamin C tablets ingested, there are very few serious consequences from an overingestion of vitamin C, though it can increase the risk of kidney stones and other renal diseases.

Other nutrients. Other nutrients that are essential could be considered vitamins. These include choline, carnitine, inositol, and taurine.

See also **Beriberi; Choline, Inositol, and Related Nutrients; Inuit; Maize; Niacin Deficiency (Pellagra); Nutrients; Vitamin C; Vitamins: Water-soluble and Fat-soluble Vitamins; Appendix: Dietary Reference Intakes.**

BIBLIOGRAPHY

Frisell, W. R., ed. *Human Biochemistry.* New York: Macmillan, 1982.

Holick, Michael F. "Vitamin D: New Horizons for the 21st Century" (McCollum Award Lecture, 1994). *The American Journal of Clinical Nutrition* 60 (1994): 619–630.

Institute of Medicine. *Dietary Reference Intakes for Vitamin A, Vitamin K, Arsenic, Boron, Chromium, Copper, Iodine, Iron, Manganese, Molybdenum, Nickel, Silicon, Vanadium, and Zinc.* Washington, D.C.: National Academy Press, 2001.

Institute of Medicine. "Vitamin D." In *Dietary Reference Intakes for Calcium, Phosphorus, Magnesium, Vitamin D, and Fluoride*, pp. 250–287. Washington, D.C.: National Academy Press, 1997.

Shils, M. E., J. A. Olson, and M. Shike, eds. *Modern Nutrition in Health and Diseases.* 8th ed. Philadelphia: Lea and Febiger, 1994.

Michael Holick

VITAMINS.

WATER-SOLUBLE AND FAT-SOLUBLE VITAMINS

Vitamins are among the nutrients found to be essential for life. Unlike other classes of nutrients, vitamins serve no structural function nor do they provide significant energy. Their various uses tend to be highly specific. Common food forms of most vitamins require some metabolic activation into a functional (active) form. Although vitamins share these general characteristics, they show few close chemical or functional similarities. For example, some vitamins function as coenzymes, others function as antioxidants, and two vitamins, A and D, function as hormones.

Fourteen substances are now generally recognized as vitamins. Vitamins are frequently described according to their solubility; they may be either fat-soluble or water-soluble. This method of classification dates back to the history of their discovery as labeled by McCollum as "fat-soluble A" and "water-soluble B."

Other sections in this encyclopedia describe the chemistry, biochemistry, and physiology of the vitamins. This article provides additional information that is focused on dietary requirements, upper levels (to avoid toxicity from supplementation), and food sources. (See sidebar for definition of terms, and see Appendix for a complete chart of vitamins.)

Water-Soluble Vitamins

Thiamin. Thiamin was the first vitamin to be identified. In modern times, thiamin deficiency is seen most commonly in association with chronic alcoholism. Only a small percentage of large doses are absorbed, and elevated serum levels result in its active urinary excretion. After an oral dose of the vitamin, peak excretion occurs in about two hours (Davis et al., 1984). Total body thiamin content in adults is approximately 30 milligrams with a half-life of 9 to 18 days (Ariaey-Nejad et al., 1970).

The recommended dietary allowance (RDA) for thiamin in adult women is 1.1 mg/day and in adult men it is 1.2 mg/day. The RDA for pregnancy and lactation is 1.4 mg/day (FNB, 1998). It should be noted that increased needs exist in persons being treated with hemodialysis or peritoneal dialysis, individuals with malabsorption syndrome, women carrying more than one fetus, and women nursing more than one infant.

There are no reports of adverse effects from the consumption of excess thiamin consumed in food or supplements. No upper level (UL) can be set due to the lack of reported findings associated with adverse effects. Supplements that contain up to 50 mg/day are available over-the-counter with no reported problems.

Food sources from which most of thiamin in the United States is derived include enriched, fortified, or whole-grain products, such as bread, bread products, mixed foods that contain grain, and ready-to-eat cereals. Foods that are especially rich in thiamin include yeast,

DIETARY REFERENCE INTAKES

See Appendix for full chart of Dietary Reference Intakes.

Recommended Dietary Allowance (RDA)—the dietary intake level that is sufficient to meet the nutrient requirement of nearly all (97 to 98 percent) healthy individuals in a particular life stage and gender group.

Adequate Intake (AI)—a recommended intake value based on observed or experimentally determined approximations or estimates of nutrient intake by a group (or groups) of healthy people that are assumed to be adequate—used when an RDA cannot be determined.

Tolerable Upper Intake Level (UL)—the highest level of nutrient intake that is likely to pose no risk of adverse health effects for almost all individuals in the general population. As intake increases above the UL, the risk of adverse effects increases.

SOURCE: Food and Nutrition Board, Institute of Medicine. *Dietary Reference Intakes* (FNB, 2000, p. 3).

lean pork, and legumes. Thiamin is absent from fats, oils, and refined sugars. Milk, milk products, seafood, fruits, and vegetables are not good sources.

Riboflavin. The second vitamin discovered was named vitamin B_2 or riboflavin. Most dietary riboflavin is consumed as a complex of food protein. Signs of riboflavin deficiency are sore throat, redness, and edema of the throat and oral mucous membranes, cheilosis (cracking of the skin around the mouth), and glossitis (red tongue). Vitamin B_2 deficiency most often occurs in combination with other nutrient deficiencies. The B vitamins are quite interrelated; for example, niacin requires riboflavin for its formation from the amino acid tryptophan, and vitamin B_6 requires riboflavin for conversion to the active coenzyme form (McCormick, 1989).

The RDA for riboflavin has been set at 1.3 mg/day for men and 1.1 mg/day for women through age seventy years and older. For pregnancy, the RDA for riboflavin is set at 1.4 mg/day and it is 1.6 mg/day for lactation (FNB, 1998).

When riboflavin is absorbed in excess, very little is stored in the body tissues. Excess is excreted via the urine, and the amount varies with intake, metabolic events, and age (McCormick and Greene, 1994). No adverse effects associated with riboflavin consumption from food or supplements have been reported. No adverse effects were reported from a single dose of up to 60 milligrams and 11.6 milligrams of riboflavin given as a single intravenous (IV) dose (Zempleni et al., 1996).

The greatest contribution of riboflavin from the diet comes from milk and milk drinks, followed by bread products and fortified cereals. Especially good food sources of riboflavin are eggs, lean meats, milk, broccoli, and enriched breads and cereals. Recall that riboflavin loss occurs when it is exposed to light, so store milk in opaque containers or away from the light.

Niacin. The term "niacin" refers to nicotinamide and nicotinic acid. The coenzymes, the active form of niacin in the body, are synthesized in all tissues of the body. The amount of niacin in the body is the result of absorbed nicotinic acid and nicotinamide, as well as conversion of the amino acid tryptophan (60 milligrams of tryptophan = 1 milligram of niacin; Horwitt et al., 1981). Excess niacin is excreted through the urine.

Pellagra is the classical manifestation of niacin deficiency. Pellagra has been seen in areas where corn (low in niacin and tryptophan) is the dietary staple. Enrichment and fortification of grain has virtually eliminated pellagra from the United States and Europe.

The RDA for adult men is 16 mg/day of niacin equivalents, and the RDA for women aged nineteen to over seventy is 14 mg/day. In pregnant women the RDA is 18 mg/day of niacin equivalents and in lactating women it is 17 mg/day (FNB, 1998).

Niacin, given as nicotinic acid in doses from 4 to 6 g/day, is one of the oldest drugs used in the treatment of hyperlipidemia, which consists of elevated blood levels of triglycerides and cholesterol. Niacin lowers low-density lipoprotein (LDL) cholesterol and triglyceride concentration. This therapeutic effect is not seen with nicotinamide. Nicotinic acid in therapeutic doses can cause flushing and headache in some people. These side effects are not harmful.

An upper limit for niacin was set at 35 mg/day for adults, if the niacin is obtained from supplements, not foods. Individuals who take over-the-counter niacin to "self-medicate" may exceed the UL on a chronic basis. The UL is not intended to apply to those receiving niacin under medical supervision.

Dietary intake of niacin comes mainly from mixed dishes containing meat, poultry, or fish, followed by enriched and whole-grain breads, and fortified cereals. Significant amounts of niacin are found in red meat, liver, legumes, milk, eggs, alfalfa, cereal grains, yeast, and fish.

Vitamin B$_6$. Vitamin B$_6$ is a coenzyme for more than 100 enzymes involved in the metabolism of amino acids, glycogen, and nerve tissues (FNB, 1998). Microcytic anemia, reflecting decreased hemoglobin synthesis, can be seen in deficiency states. The interaction of vitamin B$_6$ and folate (another B vitamin discussed below) has been shown to reduce the plasma concentrations of homocysteine and decrease the incidence of cardiovascular disease (CVD) risk (Rimm et al., 1998). Subjects with the highest intake of folate and vitamin B$_6$ had a twofold reduc-

tion in CVD as compared to the group with the lowest intake.

In the 1970s there was quite a bit of discussion about the status of vitamin B$_6$ in women using oral contraceptives. This was probably an artifact of hormonal stimulation of tryptophan catabolism rather than vitamin B$_6$ deficiency. At the time these studies were conducted, estrogen concentrations were three to five times higher in contraceptive agents than they are today.

The RDA for vitamin B$_6$ is 1.3 mg/day for adult men and women up to age fifty years. The RDA for people over fifty years of age is 1.7 mg/day for men and 1.5 mg/day for women. For pregnant women the RDA is set at 1.9 mg/day and for lactating women, 2.0 mg/day (FNB, 1998).

No adverse effects have been associated with intakes of vitamin B$_6$ from food. However, large doses of pyridoxine used to treat carpal tunnel syndrome and premenstrual syndrome have been associated with sensory neuropathy (Schaumburg and Berger, 1988). These findings were noted with dosages from 2 to 6 g/day. It appears that the risk of developing sensory neuropathy decreases quite rapidly at dosages below 1 g/day. Thus, the UL for adults is set at 100 mg/day of vitamin B$_6$ as pyridoxine.

Food sources of vitamin B$_6$ include fortified, ready-to-eat cereals; mixed foods with meat, fish, or poultry as the main ingredient: white potatoes, starchy vegetables, and noncitrus fruits. Vitamin B$_6$ is widely distributed in foods; good sources are meats, whole-grain products, vegetables, and nuts.

Folate. Folate is a B vitamin that exists in many chemical forms (Wagner, 1996). Folic acid, the most stable form of folate, occurs rarely in food, but is the form used in supplements and fortified food products. Folate coenzymes are involved in numerous reactions that involve DNA synthesis, purine synthesis, and amino acid metabolism. The most well known is the conversion of homocysteine to methionine. It is this reaction that reduces the concentration of homocysteine in the plasma, and may lower the risk of cardiovascular disease (Rasmussen et al., 1996).

The metabolic interrelationship between folate and vitamin B$_{12}$ may explain why a single deficiency of either vitamin leads to the same hematological changes. In either folate or vitamin B$_{12}$ deficiency, megaloblastic changes occur in the bone marrow and other replicating cells.

Pregnant women are at risk for developing folate deficiency because of the heightened demands imposed by increased synthesis of DNA. Low folate status is associated with poor pregnancy outcome, low birth weight, and fetal growth retardation (Scholl and Johnson, 2000). Because of the possible incidence of neural tube defects (NTDs) during the preconception period (that is, just be-

498

fore and during the first 28 days of conception), the Food and Nutrition Board recommends that women who are capable of becoming pregnant should consume 400 μg/day of synthetic folic acid, derived from dietary supplements or fortified food, in addition to their usual dietary intake (FNB, 1998). NTDs are the most common major congenital malformations of the central nervous system.

Recommendations for intake of folate are dependent on variation in bioavailability. Supplemental folate is nearly 100 percent absorbed, while absorption of folate found in foods is only about 50 percent. Fortified foods approach the level of bioavailability of folate found in supplements. This has led to the term Dietary Folate Equivalents or DFEs. Thus, dietary recommendations for folate intake are based on "folate equivalents." One μg of folate equivalents = 1 μg of food folate = 0.5 μg of folic acid taken on an empty stomach or = 0.6 μg folic acid with meals. The RDA for women is 320 μg dietary folate equivalents and for men it is 400 μg. During pregnancy 600 μg/day of folate is recommended and 500 μg/day is recommended during lactation (FNB, 1998).

No adverse effects have been associated with the consumption of normal folate-fortified foods. However, the risk of neurological effects that result from vitamin B_{12} deficiency that are masked with high doses of folate caused the FNB to set a UL. The UL for adults, nineteen years and older, is set at 1,000 μg/day of folate from fortified food or supplements.

Folates are found in nearly all natural foods. Protracted cooking or processing may destroy folate. Foods with the highest folate content include yeast, liver, other organ meats, fresh green vegetables, and some fruits (oranges, for example). Most of the dietary intake of folate in the United States comes from fortified ready-to-eat breakfast cereals followed by a variety of beans and peas, fresh and dried. As of 1 January 1998, all enriched cereal grains, pasta, flour, and rice are required to be fortified with folate at 1.4 mg/kg of grain.

Vitamin B_{12}. Cyanocobalamin is the compound we call vitamin B_{12}. This is the only vitamin B_{12} preparation used in supplements. An adequate supply of vitamin B_{12} is essential for normal blood formation and neurological function. The absorption of vitamin B_{12} is dependent on several physiological steps. In the stomach, food-bound vitamin B_{12} is dissociated from proteins in the presence of stomach acid. Vitamin B_{12} then binds with protein and in the intestine the vitamin B_{12} binds with intrinsic factor for absorption. If there is a lack of sufficient acid in the stomach or intrinsic factor in the intestine, malabsorption occurs and the resulting condition caused is pernicious anemia.

The anemia of vitamin B_{12} deficiency (completely reversed by addition of B_{12}) is indistinguishable from that seen with folate deficiency. Because up to 30 percent of people older than fifty are estimated to have atrophic gastritis with low stomach acid secretion, older adults may

have decreased absorption of B_{12} from foods. Thus, it is recommended that most of the vitamin B_{12} consumed by adults greater than fifty-one years of age be obtained from fortified foods or supplements.

The RDA of vitamin B_{12} for men and women is 2.4 μg/day, most of that amount coming from fortified foods or supplements in those over fifty years of age. During pregnancy, the RDA is 2.6 μg/day and it is 2.8 μg/day during lactation (FNB, 1998). No adverse effects have been associated with excess B_{12} intake from food or supplements. After reviewing the literature, the FNB found insufficient evidence for determining a UL.

Vitamin B_{12} is present in all forms of animal tissues. It is not present in plants and thus does not occur in fruits or vegetables. Because a generous intake of animal foods is customary in the United States, B_{12} intake from foods is usually adequate. People who avoid eating animal products may obtain most of their requirement through fortified foods.

Vitamin C. Ascorbic acid (the chemical name for vitamin C) is a potent antioxidant in animals and plants. Vitamin C is important in the synthesis of collagen. Some evidence indicates that vitamin C reduces virus activity by inhibiting viral replication (Johnston, 2001). Many anecdotal reports support a role for vitamin C supplementation to reduce the severity of cold symptoms.

Some epidemiological evidence indicates that supplemental vitamin C protects against risk for myocardial infarction. However, large-scale epidemiological studies do not suggest a benefit of vitamin C supplementation on cardiovascular health risks (Kushi et al., 1996).

Non-heme iron absorption from food is enhanced two- to threefold in the presence of 25 to 75 mg of vitamin C, presumably because of the ascorbate-induced reduction of ferric iron to ferrous iron, which is less likely to form insoluble complexes in the intestine. However, vitamin C has no effect on increasing iron absorption from heme iron (Johnston, 2001). Unlike most animal species, humans lack the ability to synthesize ascorbic acid; thus, the diet is the sole source for this vitamin.

The current requirement of vitamin C is 90 mg/day for adult men and 75 mg/day for adult women. During pregnancy the RDA is 85 mg/day, and 120 mg/day during lactation. The UL for vitamin C was set at 2 g/day (FNB, 2000). This level was set as a guideline for people using dietary supplements and was based on reports of gastrointestinal symptoms reported when too much vitamin C was taken.

Almost 90 percent of vitamin C in the diet comes from fruits and vegetables, with citrus fruits, tomatoes, tomato juice, and potatoes being the major contributors. It is also added to some processed foods as an antioxidant.

Pantothenic acid. Pantothenic acid was named after the Greek, meaning "from everywhere," because it is so widespread in foods. Pantothenic acid is essential in the diet because of the inability of animals and humans to synthesize the pantoic acid moiety of the vitamin. Pantothenic acid plays a primary role in many metabolic processes, such as oxidative metabolism, cell membrane formation, cholesterol and bile salt production, energy storage, and activation of some hormones (Miller et al., 2001).

Pantothenic acid deficiency in humans is rare because of its ubiquitous distribution in foods. Many health claims are made regarding the role of pantothenic acid in ameliorating rheumatoid arthritis, lowering cholesterol, enhancing athletic performance, and preventing graying of hair (Miller et al., 2001). However, sufficient information is lacking at this time and so firm recommendations may not be made. No reports of adverse effects of oral pantothenic acid in humans have been reported.

The Food and Nutrition Board (1998) established an adequate intake level (AI) for pantothenic acid of 5.0 mg/day for adult men and women, 6.0 mg/day during pregnancy, and 7.0 mg/day during lactation. As mentioned above, pantothenic acid is found in a wide variety of both plant and animal foods. Because of its thermal lability and susceptibility to oxidation, significant amounts are lost during processing. Rich food sources include chicken, beef, liver, and other organ meats, whole grains, potatoes, and tomato products.

Biotin. In mammals, biotin serves as a coenzyme for reactions that control such important functions as fatty acid metabolism and gluconeogenesis. Biotin is recycled upon degradation of enzymes to which it is bound. Biotin from pharmaceutical sources is 100 percent bioavailable. Deficiency is rare but has been seen in patients on parenteral nutrition without biotin supplementation (Zempleni and Mock, 1999). Lipoic acid and biotin have structural similarities, thus competition potentially exists for intestinal or cellular uptake. This may be of concern in settings where large doses of lipoic acid are administered or taken as supplements (Zempleni et al., 1997).

The Food and Nutrition Board established an AI for biotin due to insufficient data to set an RDA. Adult men and women have an AI of 30 μg/day (FNB, 1998). It is the same for pregnancy and increases to 35 μg/day during lactation. No adverse effects of biotin have been reported. Toxicity has not been reported in patients receiving up to 200 mg orally daily or up to 20 mg intravenously.

Biotin is distributed widely in natural foods. Those rich in biotin include egg yolk, liver, and some vegetables. It is estimated that individuals in the United States consume between 35 and 70 μg/day.

Choline. Choline has been considered a nonessential nutrient because humans can synthesize sufficient quantities. However, when hepatic function is compromised, hepatic choline synthesis is decreased and thus choline is

now considered "conditionally" essential. In a 1998 report from the Food and Nutrition Board, choline is considered an essential nutrient (FNB, 1998). The Food and Nutrition Board noted that additional studies on the essentiality for human nutrition are needed. Specifically, the 1998 Food and Nutrition Board study suggested that graded doses of choline intake be studied regarding their effects on organ function, plasma cholesterol, and homocysteine levels.

Choline functions as a precursor for phospholipids and acetylcholine, and betaine. The AI for adult men was set at 550 mg/day and for women at 425 mg/day. For pregnancy, the AI was increased to 450 mg/day and during lactation, to 550 mg/day (FNB, 1998). Due to reports of hypotension (low blood pressure) from excess intake, a UL was set at 3.5 g/day for persons nineteen years and older. Choline and choline-containing lipids, mainly phosphatidylcholine, are abundant in foods of both plant and animal origin. Rich sources include muscle and organ meats and eggs. To date there are no nationally representative estimates of choline intake from food or supplements.

Fat-Soluble Vitamins

Vitamin A. The active forms of vitamin A participate in three essential functions: visual perception, cellular differentiation, and immune function. A number of food sources are available for vitamin A. Preformed vitamin A is abundant in animal foods and provitamin A carotenoids are abundant in dark-colored fruits and vegetables. With a 2001 report from the Food and Nutrition Board (FNB 2001), there has been recognition of a change in equivalency values of various carotenoids to vitamin A. Retinol activity equivalents (RAEs) for dietary provitamin A carotenoids—beta-carotene, alpha-carotene, and beta-cryptoxanthin—have been set at 12, 24, and 24 μg, respectively (see Table 1, below). This decision is based on an extensive review of studies, which are summarized in the FNB report (2001) (see Table 1).

A number of factors affect the bioavailability of carotenoids (Castenmiller and West, 1998). Percent ab-

TABLE 1

Dietary forms of vitamin A and provitamin A carotenoids

Consumed	Absorbed	Bioconverted
Dietary or supplemental Vitamin A (1 µg)	Retinol	Retinol (1 µg)
Supplemental beta-carotene (2 µg)	beta-carotene	Retinol (1 µg)
Dietary beta-carotene (12 µg)	beta-carotene	Retinol (1 µg)
Dietary alpha-carotene or beta-cryptoxanthin (24 µg)	alpha-carotene or beta-cryptoxanthin	Retinol (1 µg)

SOURCE: Adapted from FNB 2001

sorption decreases as the amount of dietary carotenoids increases, and the relative carotene concentration absorbed increases when consumed with oil or associated with plant matrix material. That is part of the plant vitamin source, not separated out as a supplement. The presence of dietary fat stimulates the secretion of bile acids and improves the absorption of carotenoids.

Recommended dietary allowance for men is 900 μg/day of vitamin A and for women 700 μg/day. During pregnancy, RDA is set at 770 μg/day and 1,300 μg/day during lactation. Human infants consume about 400 μg/day of vitamin A in the first six months of life (FNB, 2001).

Based on the literature review, the FNB used liver abnormalities as the critical adverse effect for setting the UL for adults. Issues of carcinogenicity were considered for women of childbearing age. The UL varies slightly with age between 2,800 and 3,000 μg/day of preformed vitamin A in food or supplements for adolescents and adults. Note that alcohol intake enhances the toxicity of vitamin A.

The richest sources of vitamin A are fish oils, liver, and other organ meats. Whole milk, butter, and fortified margarine and low-fat milks are also rich in the vitamin. In the United States carrots, fortified spreads, and dairy products are the leading contributors of vitamin A to the diet.

Vitamin D. Vitamin D is essential for life in higher animals. It is one of the most important regulators of calcium homeostasis and was historically considered the "anitrachitic" factor. The biological effects of vitamin D are achieved only by its hormonal metabolites, including two key kidney-produced metabolites: 1,25(OH)$_2$ vitamin D and 24,25(OH) vitamin D. In addition to its role in calcium metabolism, research has identified that vitamin D plays an important role in cell differentiation and growth of keratinocytes and cancer cells and has shown that it participates in the process of parathyroid hormone and insulin secretion (Bouillon et al. 1995).

Vitamin D$_3$, the naturally occurring form of the vitamin, is produced from the provitamin, 7-dehydrocholesterol, found in the skin under the stimulation of ultraviolet (UV) irradiation or UV light. Vitamin D$_2$ is a synthetic form of vitamin D that is produced by irradiation of the plant steroid ergosterol. A requirement for vitamin D has never been precisely defined because vitamin D is produced in the skin after exposure to sunlight. Therefore, humans do not have a requirement for vitamin D when sufficient sunlight is available. The fact that humans wear clothes, live in cities where tall buildings block the sunlight, use synthetic sunscreens that block UV rays, and live in geographical regions of the world that do not receive adequate sunlight contributes to the inability of the skin to synthesize sufficient vitamin D (Holick, 1995). Exposure to the sun sufficient for humans to obtain enough UV radiation to synthesize adequate vi-

tamin D can be as little as three weekly exposures of the face and hands to ambient sunlight for 20 minutes (Adams et al., 1982).

A substantial proportion of the U.S. population is exposed to suboptimal levels of sunlight during the winter months. Under these conditions, vitamin D becomes a true vitamin and must be supplied regularly in the diet. The Food and Nutrition Board recommend an AI or adequate intake of vitamin D at 200 IU/day (5 μg) for adults up to fifty years of age (FNB, 1997). For adults over fifty-one, the AI is set at 400 IU/day (10 μg).

To prevent life-threatening hypercalcemia, an upper level (UL) for vitamin D has been set at 2,000 IU/day (50 μg) for adults over age eighteen. The use of 1,25 (OH)$_2$ vitamin D for treatment of hypoparathyroidism, vitamin D–resistant rickets, renal osteodystrophy, osteoporosis, and psoriasis opens the door for potential toxicity because this form of the vitamin is much more toxic and the body's metabolic controls are bypassed. When this medication is being used, careful monitoring of plasma calcium concentrations is required.

Salt-water fish are good unfortified sources of vitamin D. Small quantities are derived from eggs, beef, butter, and vegetable oils. Fortification of milk, butter, margarine, cereals, and chocolate mixes help in meeting the dietary requirements. Excessive amounts of vitamin D are not available in usual dietary sources. However, excessive amounts can be obtained through supplements that result in high plasma levels of 25(OH) vitamin D.

Vitamin E. Vitamin E (also called tocopherol) is found in cell membranes and fat depots. Because of their chemical structure, there are eight stereoisomers of each of the tocopherols. In addition to each of the stereoisomers, each occur in alpha, beta, gamma, and delta forms (FNB, 2000).

Its most recognized function is to protect polyunsaturated fatty acids (PUFA) from oxidation. PUFAs are particularly sensitive to oxidative damage, and the protective role of vitamin E is supported by a similar antioxidant protection from vitamin C and selenium. One tocopherol molecule can protect 100 or more PUFA molecules from autoxidative damage (Pryor, 2001).

The various forms of vitamin E have different biological activity, with the natural source isomer—*R,R,R*,-alpha-tocopherol—being the most active. In supplements you may see this isomer called by its former name, *d*-alpha-tocopherol. Synthetic vitamin E is called *all-rac*-alpha-tocopherol or *dl*-alpha-tocopherol in supplements. Biological activities of vitamin E are given in the older international units (IU) or alpha-tocopherol equivalents (alpha-TE). Because of the many forms of vitamin E in plants and available synthetically, the relative activities of each form is complex. Current evidence indicates that vitamin E from natural sources has approximately twice the bioactivity in humans that the *all-rac* (synthetic) vitamin does (Burton et al., 1998).

Based on the literature review, FNB used hemor-rhagic (bleeding) effects for the criteria to set the UL. For adults nineteen years and older the UL is 1,000 mg (2,326 mol)/day of any form of supplementary alpha-to-copherol. There is no evidence of adverse effects from intake of vitamin E naturally occurring in foods.

The RDA for vitamin E is 15 mg/day of naturally occurring alpha-tocopherol for adults above nineteen years of age (FNB, 2000). During pregnancy 15 mg/day is recommended and 19 mg/day for lactation.

The tocopherol content of foods varies widely de-pending on storage, processing, and preparation. The best sources of vitamin E are the common vegetable oils and products made from them. However, most of the to-copherols may be removed in processing. Wheat germ and walnuts also have high amounts of tocopherols.

Vitamin K. Vitamin K was named after the first letter of the German word *Koagulation*. For many years blood coagulation was assumed to be the sole physiological role for vitamin K. We now know that vitamin K plays an es-sential role in the synthesis of proteins including pro-thrombin and the bone-forming protein, osteocalcin (Vermeer et. al., 1995).

Dietary vitamin K absorption is enhanced by dietary fat and is dependent on bile and pancreatic enzymes. The human gut contains large amount of bacterially produced vitamin K, but its contribution to the maintenance of vi-tamin K status has been difficult to assess (Suttie, 1995). The vitamin K produced by bacteria in the gut is less bi-ologically active even though it is stored in the liver and present in blood. Current understanding supports the view that this vitamin K source may partially satisfy the human requirement but that the contribution is much less than previously thought.

The drug warfarin, widely prescribed as an antico-agulant, functions through inhibition of vitamin K. As a result, alterations in vitamin K intake can influence the efficacy of warfarin. The effective dose of warfarin varies from individual to individual, as does the dietary intake of vitamin K. The best solution appears to be to estab-lish the necessary dose of warfarin and urge patients to maintain a constant intake of foods high in vitamin K in their diets. Only a small number of food items contribute substantially to the dietary vitamin K.

The recommended intake is based on an AI or ade-quate intake of 120 μg/day for men, 90 μg/day for women, and 90 μg/day during pregnancy and lactation (FNB, 2001). No adverse effects have been associated with vitamin K intake in humans from food or supple-ments. Thus, no UL is set for vitamin K.

Collards, spinach, and salad greens are high in vita-min K. Broccoli, Brussels sprouts, cabbage, and Bib let-tuce contain about two-thirds as much, and other green vegetables contain even less. Vitamin K is also found in plant oils and margarine, with soybean and canola oils having the highest amounts. U.S. food intake surveys in-dicate that spinach, collards, broccoli, and iceberg lettuce are the major contributors of vitamin K in the diet.

See also **Additives; Assessment of Nutritional Status; Di-etary Guidelines; Immune System Regulation and Nutrients; Microbiology; Nutrient Bioavailability; Nutrient–Drug Interactions; Nutritional Biochem-istry; Appendix: Dietary Reference Intakes.**

BIBLIOGRAPHY

Adams, J. S., T. L. Clemens, J. A. Parrish, and M. F. Holick. "Vitamin D-Synthesis and Metabolism after Ultraviolet Ir-radiation of Normal and Vitamin-D-deficient Subjects." *New England Journal of Medicine* 306 (1982): 722–725.

Bouillon, R., W. H. Okamura, and A. W. Norman. "Structure-Function Relationships in the Vitamin D Endocrine Sys-tem." *Endocrine Reviews* 16 (1995): 200–257.

Burton, G. W., M. G. Traber, R. V. Acuff, W. Walters, H. Kayden, L. Hughes, and Ku Ingold. "Human Plasma and Tissue Alpha-Tocopherol Concentrations in Response to Supplementation with Deuterated Natural and Syn-thetic Vitamin C." *American Journal of Clinical Nutrition* 67 (1998): 669–684.

Castenmiller, J. J., and C. E. West. "Bioavailability and Con-version of Carotenoids." *Annual Reviews of Nutrition* 18 (1998): 19–38.

Davis, R. E., G. C. Icke, J. Thom, and W. J. Riley. "Intestinal Absorption of Thiamin in Man Compared with Folate and Pyridoxal and Its Subsequent Urinary Excretion." *J Nu-tritional Science and Vitaminology (Tokyo)* 30 (1984): 475–482.

Food and Nutrition Board (FNB). *Dietary Reference Intakes for Calcium, Phosphorus, Magnesium, Vitamin D, and Fluoride.* Washington, D.C.: National Academy Press, 1997.

Food and Nutrition Board (FNB). *Dietary Reference Intakes for Thiamin, Riboflavin, Niacin, Vitamin B6, Folate, Vitamin B12, Pantothenic Acid, Biotin, and Choline.* Washington, D.C.: National Academy Press, 1998.

Food and Nutrition Board (FNB). *Dietary Reference Intakes for Vitamin C, Vitamin E, Selenium, and Carotenoids.* Washing-ton, D.C.: National Academy Press, 2000.

Food and Nutrition Board (FNB). *Dietary Reference Intakes for Vitamin A, Vitamin K, Arsenic, Boron, Chromium, Copper, Io-dine, Iron, Manganese, Molybdenum, Nickel, Silicon, Vana-dium, and Zinc.* Washington, D.C.: National Academy Press, 2001.

Holick, M. F. "Environmental Factors That Influence the Cu-taneous Production of Vitamin D." *American Journal of Clinical Nutrition* 61 (Suppl) (1995): 638S–645S.

Horwitt, M. K., A. E. Harper, and L. M. Hendersen. "Niacin-Tryptophan Relationships for Evaluating Niacin Equiva-lents." *American Journal of Clinical Nutrition* 34 (1981): 423–427.

Johnston, C. S. "Vitamin C." In *Present Knowledge of Nutrition*, 8th ed., edited by B. A. Bowman and R. M. Russell, pp. 175–183. Washington, D.C.: ILSI Press, 2001.

Kushi, L. H., A. R. Folsom, R. J. Prineas, P. J. Mink, Y. Wu, and R. M. Bostick. "Dietary Antioxidant Vitamins and

Death from Coronary Heart Disease in Postmenopausal Women." *New England Journal of Medicine* 334 (1996): 1156–1162.

McCormick, D. B. "Two Interconnected B Vitamins: Riboflavin and Pyridoxine." *Physiological Reviews* 69 (1989): 1170–1198.

McCormick, D. B. "Riboflavin." In *Modern Nutrition in Health and Disease*, edited by M. E. Shils, J. E. Olson, and M. Shike, pp. 366–375. Philadelphia: Lea & Febiger, 1994.

Miller, J. W., L. M. Rogers, and R. B. Rucker. "Pantothenic Acid." In *Present Knowledge of Nutrition*, 8th ed., edited by B. A. Bowman and R. M. Russell, pp. 253–260. Washington, D.C.: ILSI Press, 2001.

Pryor, W. A. "Vitamin E." In *Present Knowledge of Nutrition*, 8th ed., edited by B. A. Bowman and R. M. Russell, pp. 156–163. Washington, D.C.: ILSI Press, 2001.

Rasmussen, K., J. Moller, M. Lyngbak, A.-M. Pedersen, and L. Dybkjaer. "Age- and Gender-Specific References Intervals for Total Homocysteine and Methylmalonic Acid in Plasma before and after Vitamin Supplementation." *Clinical Chemistry* 43 (1996): 630–636.

Rimm, E. B., W. C. Willett, F. B. Hu, L. Sampson, G. A. Colditz, J. E. Manson, C. Hennekens, and M. J. Stampfer. "Folate and Vitamin B6 from Diet and Supplements in Relation to Risk of Coronary Heart Disease among Women." *Journal of the American Medical Association* 279 (1998): 359–365.

Schaumberg, H. H., and A. Berger. "Pyridoxine Neurotoxicity." In *Clinical and Physiological Applications of Vitamin B6*, pp. 403–414. New York: Alan R. Liss, 1988.

Scholl, T. O., and W. J. Johnson. "Folic Acid: Influence on the Outcome of Pregnancy." *American Journal of Clinical Nutrition* 71 (Suppl) (2000): 295S–303S.

Suttie, J. W. "The Importance of Menaquinones in Human Nutrition." *Annual Review of Nutrition* 15 (1995): 399–417.

Vermeer, C., K.-S. G. Jie, and M. H. J. Knapen. "Role of Vitamin K in Bone Metabolism." *Nutrition* 15 (1995): 1–22.

Wagner, C. "Symposium on the Subcellular Compartmentation of Folate Metabolism." *Journal of Nutrition* 126 (1996): 1228S–1234S.

Zempleni, J., J. R. Galloway, and D. B. McCormick. "Pharmacokinetics of Orally and Intravenously Administered Riboflavin in Healthy Humans." *American Journal of Clinical Nutrition* 63 (1996): 54–66.

Zempleni, J., and D. M. Mock. "Biotin Biochemistry and Human Requirements." *Journal of Nutritional Biochemistry* 10 (1999): 128–138.

Ann M. Coulston

VITICULTURE. *See* **Grapes and Grape Juice; Wine.**

W–Z

WAFFLES AND WAFERS. Waffles and wafers are like many other foods of ancient origin in that the name and the food described have separate histories that eventually merge into one. The wafer traces its origin to ancient Egypt, but the descriptive terms applied to it are generally of medieval origin. In Latin, *oblatao* and *oblatum* were used to denote cakes made with unleavened flour and water worked into a thin flat round or square sheet of pastry and baked until crisp. This Latin root meaning is still employed in many European languages, but with varied interpretations. In modern German, *Oblaten* are both communion wafers and sheets of paper-like material laid under gingerbreads or baked meringues to keep them from sticking to the baking sheet. In Polish, *oplatki* are communion wafers or any wafers resembling them in shape and texture.

In English, however, the root word stems from medieval German and Anglo-Saxon: *weben*, "to weave," in reference to the crisscrossed pattern on the surface of the wafer. It appears in medieval Frankish as *wafel* and later in medieval French as *waufre*, now written *gaufre*, with the diminutive *gaufrette*. *Gaufre* can also be a honeycomb and in that sense may refer to an ancient pattern imprinted on certain wafers. This same honeycomb design is found on Coptic ritual breads in Egypt and may relate to an extinct votive wafer or flat bread sweetened with honey. Its modern survival may be the Swiss *Tirggel*, a type of honey wafer imprinted with a wide variety of ornamental images.

The wafers of ancient Egypt were prepared from only the finest wheat flour (actually the flour of emmer, a species of primitive wheat). Athenaeus of Naukratis attributed the origin of the wafer's name (*obelias*) to the fact that it cost one *obel* (a thin Greek coin). Since this "fact" was drawn from a literary source, it may well be pure folk etymology. As Otto Meinardus has pointed out repeatedly in his seminal work on early Coptic Christianity, there is a far more fundamental dimension to the wafer since the grain from which it was made was treated as the actual "body of Osiris" (Meinardus 1964 and 1999); thus those who partook of the ritual wafers were said to live by the body of their god. This concept was carried over into Christianity in two forms: in the *oblata hosta* employed as the bread of communion in the Latin church

(due perhaps to its similarity in shape and function to ritual bannocks), and in the *fetir* (leavened flat bread), *duhn* (unleavened flat bread), and *qurban* (communion loaf) of the Coptic church. All three Coptic breads may be stamped, although it is mainly the *qurban* that serves as the ritual link to pre-Christian Egypt by virtue of its employment as communion bread. This bread, prepared only by monks from the finest wheat flour, is stamped with a wooden form to create the honey-comb pattern also found on wafers. This pattern is sometimes described by art historians as interlocking crosses.

In addition to the New Testament associations of the communion bread, the Copts also believe that Adam received grains of wheat from the Archangel Michael and therefore must honor god with bread offerings. The Feast of St. Michael on 12 Hatur (21 November) is one of the major Coptic feasts for which a large number of ritual breads are prepared. Thus, some of the earliest depictions of both wafers and round loaves stamped with wafer patterns can be found in Coptic art honoring this saint.

The introduction of the ritual wafer into the West cannot be accurately dated, although in the form taken over by Christians, it may have arrived in connection with the cult of Osiris once found throughout the Roman Empire. It survived solely as a key element of the Latin Eucharist and remained a point of contention with Eastern Orthodoxy, which claimed that the Christ intended leavened bread for the Eucharist. Jacobite Christians even claim to preserve the original sourdough starter.

During the Middle Ages, communion wafers were made by monasteries, which also sold them as a form of fasting food, since they contained no animal fats, eggs, or dairy products. It is evident, however, that the composition of wafers could be elaborated with expensive ingredients like saffron, sugar, and various spices for the benefit of the nobility and other classes of society willing to pay a higher price for a more pleasurable form of self-denial. By the 1200s wafers were well integrated into courtly cuisine and form one of the standard dessert foods served at banquets. One of the earliest references to this appears in the 1285 Anglo-Norman "Treatise of Walter of Bibbesworth," which includes dinner menus set to verse. In one menu, the meal ends with "plenty of wafers" (*oubleie a fuissun*). These were probably sweetened with

Wafer iron for stove-top baking. Made by the Werle Iron Foundry, Ottweiler (Saarland), Germany, ca. 1840–1870. Cast iron. The underside of the wafer depicts the traditional *waben* or "woven" texture while the topside is ornamented with snails, flowers, and hearts. ROUGHWOOD COLLECTION. PHOTO CHEW & COMPANY.

sugar from Cyprus and flavored with saffron, since sweet saffron wafers are mentioned many times in medieval manuscript cookery books.

Wafers also played a significant role in localized religious observances in many parts of Europe. In Franconia (a subdivision of modern Bavaria), wafers were especially important on Ascension Day and Pentecost. On Ascension, for example, the Auswerfung des Himmelbrots (showering the manna) was practiced, whereby priests threw wafers and other treats down from the "sky" painted on the church ceiling in imitation of manna falling from heaven—this after a figure of Christ was hoisted up through a trap door as though rising into the clouds. In Alsace, communion wafers were purchased from monasteries and used to ornament the earliest known Christmas trees. In most cases, these wafers were ornamented with religious pictures, Christian symbols, or a simple cross.

Since wafers could be consumed as fasting fare, there was considerable demand for them in towns and cities. This demand led to the secularization of wafer manufacture as a specialized craft organized into guilds. Wafer makers also altered the pictorial imagery employed on wafers, introducing scenes from fables, classical antiquity, coats-of-arms, or symbols of love. Thus the wafer moved from a purely religious context to a middle-class form of dessert, especially for festive occasions. By the 1600s, the irons used to make wafers were commonly found in the homes of well-off burghers, and many Dutch, French, German, Spanish, and Italian still life paintings show wafers, especially those rolled into tubes, scattered among the foods on richly appointed tables. These festive wafers acquired numerous names all over Europe, such as *pizzelle* in Italy, *Eiserkuchen* (iron cakes) in some parts of Germany, or in Holland *Nijarskouk* (New Year's cake). Elsewhere they were called Twelfth Night wafers and were even stamped with fantastic masks or printed with molds to resemble playing cards—this latter motif popular in Switzerland.

Wafers rolled into tubes were not an invention of the Renaissance even though they became popular at that time. The concept is said to trace to the Christians of Syria who were especially well known for their filled pastries during the Byzantine period. One type of wafer was first wrapped around sticks of sugar cane to dry, then removed, filled with various rich mixes of mashed fruit or cheese, and fried or baked. These confections were taken to India by the Syrian Christians who settled there and were continued by the exiled Syrians living in Cyprus during the de Lusignan dynasty (1291–1489). Wafers filled with jelly or used sandwich style for fruits cooked in wine and mashed, continued to be popular as Christmas confections in Europe well into the nineteenth century. Bent into cones, they were used to hold various sweets, and this idea was the basis for the now ubiquitous ice-cream cone commercialized at the U.S. Centennial in 1876.

The waffle is a later offshoot of the basic wafer idea, but taking it to an opposite extreme. Where the wafer served as a metaphor for fasting and self-denial, the waffle became the Protestant symbol of festive luxury. Made with eggs, cream, and other rich ingredients originally forbidden during fast days, the waffle evolved as a type of fat cake baked between irons in imitation of *pain perdu* or French toast. It first appeared in the Low Countries in connection with Christmas, New Year's, Twelfth Night, and Carnival, employing the distinctive honeycomb pattern to render it crispier than a deep-fried slice of toast. Like wafer irons, waffle irons were often given as wedding gifts, and it was the Dutch who settled in New York who brought the waffle custom to North America, for it was otherwise not well known to the English.

In the United States, waffle irons appeared in many eighteenth-century household inventories, especially those of well-to-do families. The popularity of waffles as a special occasion dish (for Sunday breakfast, for example) or as Christmas and New Year's confections gradually spread so that by the Civil War, waffles were available in most hotels, especially as a breakfast or supper food served plain or in combination with various meat fricassees. Ham gravy, chicken gravy, waffles made with a sweet potato batter, all of these and many more permutations appeared on hotel menus. By the early 1900s, once the automobile and the Sunday drive came into fashion, such main course waffle dishes were integrated into the menu of local tourist destinations catering to the Sunday clientele. Waffle dinners of the 1920s and 1930s even become a form of fund-raising for churches and fire companies.

Hot coffee and waffles are popular high-energy breakfast fare in both Europe and America, especially at ski resorts. PHOTO TAKEN AT A FARM KITCHEN OPEN TO SKIERS IN HAFJELLET, NORWAY. © ADAM WOOLFITT/CORBIS.

The electric waffle iron, which first appeared in the 1890s, became a popular tool of the home economics movement, and a popular wedding gift by the end of World War I. It brought the eat-out experience full circle into the home not just for its convenience, but by lowering the perceived cost through boxed waffle mixes, canned gravy preparations, and the like. The processed waffle, entirely pre-made and frozen so that can be cooked in toasters or the microwave oven, is now the supermarket descendant of the rich confection of former times. The fat-free waffle with its New Age ingredients and designer flavors may not evoke a breakfast fit for kings. On the other hand, the costly honey drizzled over it, now imported from the Amazon jungle, can only provoke wonder from the gods of old, whose honeycombed cakes were once a metaphor for eternal life.

See also **Bread**; **Breakfast**; **Christianity**; **Christmas**; **Epiphany**; **Fasting and Abstinence**; **Wheat: Wheat as a Food.**

BIBLIOGRAPHY

Meinardus, Otto. "Das Brot bei den Kopten," *Brot und Gebäck*. Ulm: Deutsches Brot Museum, October 1964.

Meinardus, Otto. *Two Thousand Years of Coptic Christianity*. Cairo: American University in Cairo Press, 1999.

Pechstein, Klaus, and Ursula Ellwart, *Festliches Backwerk: Holzmodel, Formen aus Zinn*. Nuremberg: Das Nationalmuseum, 1981.

Tenschert, Helga. *Engelsbrot und Eisenkuchen mit Oblaten*. (Munich: BLV Verlagsgesellschart, 1983.

Thiele, Ernst. *Waffeleisen und Waffelgebäcke*. Cologne: Oda-Verlag, 1959.

Weaver, William Woys. *The Christmas Cook: Three Centuries of American Yuletide Sweets*. New York: HarperPerennial, 1990.

Wiswe, Hans. *Kulturgeschichte der Kochkunst: Kochbücher und Rezepte aus zwei Jahrtausenden*. Munich: H. Moos, 1970.

William Woys Weaver

WAITERS AND WAITRESSES.

The career of the waiter and waitress begins with the industrialization of food. Prior to that, women dominated food preparation and serving in most cultures, and this may have reinforced the suspicions of them as dangerous. Polluted or poisoned foods have been a style of murder favored by women. A notorious poisoner was the Marquise de Brinvilliers (1630–1676) who claimed that half the French court of Louis XIV was engaged in attempted murder. Before her, there was Agrippina (15–59 C.E.), Lucrezia Borgia (1480–1519), and Catherine de' Medici (1519–1589), who have each been associated with such acts.

The Trusted Sex

In court societies, before the regulations introduced by the modern bureaucratic state, chefs, waiters, and food handlers were appointed by the monarch, and this served as an endorsement of trust. In the modern era, with refrigeration and scientific forensics, the incidence of food pollution and poisoning has dramatically dropped. At the same time, men have entered the food business and become celebrated chefs and restaurateurs. This is not to imply a causal relationship, but an interesting association of gender and status, borne out with examples from the formal restaurants of the late nineteenth century, where respectable women were not allowed as guests but could work—in lowly positions—and where only males were trusted with the job of waiter. They were required to justify that trust by wearing white gloves while serving to demonstrate that their fingers had not slipped into the sauce and then been licked clean.

Waiters and Power

Many pleasures of dining out relate to service and luxury. In the formal restaurant, diners have temporary possession of elegant silverware, crystal and tableware, and

TIPPING

The origins of the term may be the phrase—To Insure Promptitude—or from the slang "tip," to give. Tipping now operates as a tacit rule in most restaurants other than the fast-food chains and large-scale, self-service canteens. However, even though tipping is almost universal, the rules governing it are not. In the early part of the twentieth century, etiquette manuals offered lengthy advice about it, thereby indicating that it was a problematic exchange in a new, liberal era. Current tourist guides simply state that it is expected, even when there is a service charge already included. The iconic metropolitan comedian, Jerry Seinfeld, tells his urbane New York City audience that we tip in order to prevent violence, such as having our heads smashed into the glass-top table or being chased up the street by the "stiffed" waiter.

the command of others. George Orwell (1933) declares that one should never feel sorry for the waiter who stands by, watching and attending to the pleasures of diners. The waiter is a snob and thoroughly understands the attractions of the experience and wishes only for the opportunity to act exactly as the diner is doing.

There are various contests for power and privilege going on in this setting. Orwell gives the example of personal appearance: the chef wears a moustache to display rank and show contempt for the waiters who do not wear a moustache, who in turn show their superiority by refusing to allow the *plongeur* or dishwasher to wear a moustache. Gerald Mars and Michael Nicod (1984) note the many strategies and tactics employed by waiters, diners, and management to gain advantages over one another. Each of them struggle, using tipping, fiddling (pilfering), and cutting corners, to display their superior status and power to one another.

Service

The great divide between American and European restaurant styles emerges with the industrialization of food, dating from the end of the nineteenth century, when grocery stores (then, supermarkets), factory production, mass marketing of snack foods, and fast-food and chain restaurants began to transform a minor retail activity into a major economic market. American women worked in restaurants after the 1940s (Pillsbury, 1990), making them less formal and more relaxed. Dolores Dante, a waitress of twenty-three years (Terkel, 1972) reported on the pride she took in her work despite the

508

Final exam for a waiters' school in Berlin, from a wood engraving circa 1880. The parents of the young men watch as they are clocked to set a banquet table in five minutes. ROUGHWOOD COLLECTION.

taunts and insults received from male clients, who mistakenly used the threat of not tipping as a way of gaining her attention and service.

The role of the waiter and waitress has held constant fascination for novelists and social investigators, all of whom comment on the highly charged relationship between the diner and waiter. In formal restaurants, knowledgeable waiters can intimidate diners they consider out of place or presumptuous. Lone women diners, or those with young children, for example, may find the formal restaurant inhospitable because the waiter expects a negligible tip and judges them not to be worth their effort. In short, the pleasures of dining out rest largely on the performance of the waiter.

American Economics vs. European Craft

Americans mostly favor small diners, self-service, or fast-food chain restaurants where the level of service is low and the expectations of customers limited. At the other end of the spectrum, there are prestigious, celebrated, and expensive restaurants where the waiter is required to indulge the demands of diners. Between these extremes is the increasingly popular range of casual restaurants and bistros that often advertise themselves as emulating the

more luxurious restaurants. However, in doing so, they create expectations in their customers which, in reality, they cannot deliver. The waiter (and more often waitress) in such restaurants is caught between the efficiencies demanded from the restaurant management and the customers' expectations. In this gap, waiters and waitresses learn short cuts; they may finger the food in order to improve the presentation on the plate; wipe off dirty dishes and cutlery rather than replace them; dilute coffee by making two from one serve and so on. The waiter is caught in a perennially conflict-infused relationship with the management, chef, and diner over presentation, quality, and speed of service (Hughes, 1958; Whyte, 1949).

Dining in America can be theatrical, with gimmick and theme restaurants that require waiters and waitresses to deliver food on roller-skates or to dress in colorful uniforms or theme costumes. With such attractions and diversions, the American restaurant locates itself within the entertainment industries. Accordingly, the waiter or waitress is a performer, spruiking the attractions of the menu, providing amusement, and creating the illusion of service. (Spruiking is a style of advertising in which the waiter is trying to convince his customer about the delights of a certain portion.) Included in the job might be salary incentives for selling the greatest numbers of desserts or menu specials. The European waiter does not traditionally work in such an environment where the numbers of clients and settings determine his salary. The waiter's interests are to enhance the pleasures of eating; thus a European diner in a formal restaurant expects the waiter to demonstrate impeccable manners and elegant style, and not to promote certain dishes. A greater degree of informality exists between the American diner and waiter; more conversation takes place that has little to do with the food and menu and more to do with the sociability of the event. The displays of food craft from waiters such as carving meats, serving portions at the table, and setting cutlery, have largely vanished from the restaurant scene in America, and only re-emerge now and then as part of the entertainment of dining in expensive, formal, elegant restaurants.

See also **Delmonico Family; Kitchens, Restaurant; Places of Consumption; Restaurants.**

BIBLIOGRAPHY

Hughes, Everett C. *Men and Their Work.* Chicago: Glencoe Free Press, 1958.

Mars, Gerald, and Michael Nicod. *The World of Waiters.* London: Allen and Unwin, 1984.

Orwell, George. *Down and Out in London and Paris.* Harmondsworth, U.K.: Penguin, 2001. Original edition, 1933.

Pillsbury, Richard. *From Boarding House to Bistro: The American Restaurant Then and Now.* Boston: Unwin Hyman, 1990.

Terkel, Studs. *Working: People Talk about What They Do All Day and How They Feel about What They Do.* New York: Pantheon, 1972.

Whyte, William Foote. "The Social Structure of the Restaurant." *American Journal of Sociology* 54, no. 4 (January 1949): 302–310.

Joanne Finkelstein

WALES. *See* **British Isles.**

WASTE. *See* **Food Waste.**

WATER.

This entry contains three subentries:
Water as a Beverage and Constituent of Food
Water as a Resource
Safety of Water

WATER AS A BEVERAGE AND CONSTITUENT OF FOOD

The human body has a water content that represents from 65 to 70 percent of its total mass. This means that a 70-kilogram (154-lb.) adult male has a fluid content of 45 to 50 liters of water. Only 3.6 to 4.0 liters or 8 percent of

this fluid is in the bloodstream. Of the body's total water content, 60 to 70 percent is within the cells, and an additional 20 percent is in the intercellular space. These fluid compartments differ with respect to certain important constituents such as ions (electrolytes) that play an important role in cell function. The maintenance of homeostatic balance in each of these fluid compartments requires finely tuned interactions of the endocrine system and the organs involved in the absorption and excretion of minerals and other nutrients. The chemical properties of the food and water consumed can have profound effects on the function of the organs maintaining this balance. An extreme example of imbalance with fatal consequences is the dehydration that follows the consumption of salty seawater. When this occurs, the kidneys are forced to increase urine production to rid the body of the excessive salt, with the result that blood and intercellular fluid volume are reduced. In extreme cases such loss can disrupt fluid homeostasis sufficiently to result in death.

Hydration
Humans differ from other primates in relying heavily on evaporative cooling achieved through the sweat response to maintain normal body temperature under increased heat loads. Sweat contains proteins and minerals in addition to water. Heavy, sweat-inducing exercise, especially under warm, humid conditions and in untrained individuals, can result in the loss of excessive salt in sweat. Water loss exceeding twenty liters per day, sometimes as much as three liters per hour, can result from vigorous exercise under desert conditions. Replacement of fluids under such circumstances often requires forcing fluids since the human thirst response lags behind actual requirements, resulting in what has been termed "voluntary dehydration."

Athletes engaged in ultra endurance competition are especially subject to the risk of dehydration, since they typically do not satisfy their fluid requirements while exercising. On the other hand, forced consumption of plain water can, under such circumstances, result in overhydration. Insufficient salt intake can also produce a serious impairment of performance. Under such circumstances, fluids containing electrolytes are necessary to sustain performance. In addition to electrolytes, glucose, or glucose-containing carbohydrates, can enhance water absorption as well as supply supplemental energy for muscle metabolism. However, a carbohydrate concentration exceeding 5 percent weight per volume may actually reduce the rate of water absorption (Rehrer, 2001). Athletic training for endurance competition routinely includes emphasis on increasing the ability to consume sufficient fluids.

Minerals in Water
In addition to their needs for energy, proteins, and fats, humans require a number of vitamins and minerals. Some of these nutrient requirements, especially those for minerals, can be partially and sometimes totally satisfied

through the consumption of drinking water (Costi et al., 1999). The water people drink varies greatly from one area to another. Some communities rely on surface water drawn from rivers and lakes, often stored in reservoirs. Other communities rely on groundwater drawn from subterranean aquifers. Both surface water and groundwater can bear significant loads of salts and other minerals. Water purification systems are usually designed to keep the salinity of drinking water within prescribed limits in areas where water supplies tend to be salty. However, sodium can be detected in most water supplies, sometimes in surprisingly high concentrations. In cities such as Jiddah, Saudi Arabia, that depend entirely on desalinated seawater, the salinity of the drinking water is quite noticeable to the visitor.

Because of its unique chemical properties, water is seldom if ever found in its pure state. Even rainwater contains contaminants absorbed from the atmosphere while in the vapor phase and during its descent to Earth in its liquid phase. However, rainwater is generally considered to be "soft water," since its mineral content is lower than that of most other sources. Water "hardness" is often associated with its calcium content, since drinking water is drawn from aquifers associated with limestone deposits in many parts of the world. In these areas precipitated water percolates through topsoil rich in organic compounds, becoming increasingly acidic in the process. When this acidic water comes into contact with the calcium carbonate of the limestone bedrock, it gradually dissolves the rock and carries its soluble constituents with it into the aquifer. Depending upon the length of time over which this process occurs, the water that finally finds its way into the aquifer can carry a substantial load of calcium and carbonates. Such water may require "softening" if it is to be used to launder clothing, since it tends to precipitate soaps. However, hard water of this sort is potable and may indeed be considered quite desirable as drinking water.

Sources of Drinking Water

While the palatability of drinking water is literally a matter of taste, it is unlikely that pure, distilled water would be considered a desirable beverage. When comparisons of drinking water are made, the samples generally considered most desirable are invariably ones that bear a significant mineral content. For example, the drinking water of New York City, piped in from reservoirs in upstate New York, is considered of superior taste as a result of its mineral content. In other parts of the United States, groundwater drawn from ancient deposits is considered a precious but diminishing resource. A case in point is that of Tucson, Arizona, where Pleistocene water deposits are being withdrawn at a rate faster than normal recharge. Consequently the growing needs of this urban area are projected to be satisfied through increasing use of Colorado River water diverted to Phoenix and Tucson by the Central Arizona Project (CAP). Community resistance to the use of Colorado River water has resulted in a program focused on the "blending" of groundwater

The Water Carrier, nineteenth-century painting by Mexican artist Edouard Pingret. In the age before indoor plumbing, the water carrier was the primary source of drinking water in most cities and towns. Private Collection, Mexico. © ARCHIVO ICONO-GRAFICO, S.A./CORBIS.

with CAP water in an effort to avoid an abrupt change in the perceived quality of the drinking water.

The features of CAP water that have most troubled the Tucson Water Authority are the substantial load of sediment it bears as well as its different mineral composition. The expense of purification to achieve a standard comparable to that of the Pleistocene groundwater long taken for granted has been prohibitive. In an initial attempt to convert to exclusive use of CAP water in a number of Tucson neighborhoods, tap water was found to be turbid, and according to many residents, it had a distinctly unpleasant flavor. It was eventually determined that part of the problem arose from the release of mineral deposits from the water pipes both within and outside residences subsequent to sustained exposure to water having a significantly different chemical profile. The release of these deposits sometimes caused leakage that resulted in property damage and claims for compensation. The problems encountered by the Tucson Water Authority were the result of an unusual set of circumstances coupled with concern for the damage that could occur if the depletion of the local groundwater supply should progress to a point where subsidence caused structural damage to buildings. Concern for the risk of subsidence was

Traditional *cantaro* or water jar. Nicaragua, twentieth century. Brownware pottery. This ancient Mediterranean form was brought to the New World by Spanish settlers. It is still common in Central America. ROUGHWOOD COLLECTION. PHOTO CHEW & COMPANY.

well-founded, since parts of Interstate 10 less than fifty miles from Tucson have required repeated repair due to damage directly attributable to subsidence.

The problem of subsidence is of concern in many parts of the world where increasing need for drinking water has led to the depletion of aquifers. It is a concern in the central United States, for instance, in an extensive area overlying the Ogalalla Aquifer. Although the falling water table in this region is largely the result of agricultural use of water, urban growth has had a deleterious impact on aquifer recharge with the result that drinking water supplies are increasingly drawn from surface water sources. The long-term consequence is a decline in both the quality and quantity of drinking water in a number of cities. In coastal areas, depletion of aquifers has led to saltwater incursions that seriously impact the quality of drinking water. As is sometimes the case in midcontinental regions, damage to aquifers in coastal areas can be irreversible, necessitating reliance on alternative sources of drinking water. In the event of a rise in sea level associated with global warming, such reliance will become increasingly widespread. In almost every case the mineral profile of the alternative source will differ from that of the original groundwater, often in ways that alter the taste of drinking water.

Contaminants

Reliance on surface water sources for drinking-water supplies presents numerous problems. Surface water is subject to forms of contamination not usually found in groundwater. During the time it takes for water to percolate from the surface into the aquifer, most of its organic contaminants are left behind. Generally minerals take their place. The array of minerals present in the soil and bedrock determine the character and taste of the groundwater. As a rule the oldest deposits are the deepest. Therefore water pumped up from deep wells is less likely to bear organic contaminants. Additionally, deep wells provide a more stable supply of water since they draw on supplies that are less dependent upon recharge to maintain a constant flow. Shallow wells, such as the tube wells in many parts of Asia, for the most part trap surface water during a rainy season for use during the dry season. Water from such wells resembles surface water more than groundwater and may therefore contain a substantial load of organic contaminants.

The organic contaminants found in the surface water in many parts of the world include agricultural fertilizers and pesticides. Agricultural runoff, which finds its way to the larger streams and rivers before eventually reaching the oceans, contaminates freshwater bodies at all points along the line. In many cases the rich mixture of organic fertilizers entering lakes and rivers stimulates the growth of microorganisms, such as algal blooms. Eutrophication, the overgrowth of algae and other plant life, depletes the water of oxygen. Oxygen depletion limits the range of aquatic species that can inhabit these bodies of freshwater. The eutrophication of freshwater lakes is a serious problem in many parts of the world. It has a serious impact on the quality and quantity of drinking water wherever it occurs.

At least in part because of general distrust in the quality of drinking water, the consumption of bottled water has increased. The commoditization of the drinking-water supply is a fairly recent phenomenon in many parts of the industrialized world. The quality of water available from this source is highly variable. Some is drawn from mountain springs, where the mineral content is consistent and organic contaminants are virtually absent. Other commercially marketed bottled water comes from more dubious sources and may contain a variety of contaminants, including pathogenic organisms in unacceptably high concentrations.

Certain mineral waters, especially those purported to have therapeutic value, have long had a market. These mineral waters were originally consumed at their sources, often at spas, where hot springs produced highly mineralized, often sulfurous water thought to have medicinal properties when consumed or used as a bath. The Romans sought thermal springs throughout the areas they occupied in Europe, and they constructed baths that served as focal points of the communities.

The Romans were well aware of the benefits of a reliable supply of pure drinking water even in the absence of thermal springs, as the many aqueducts in Europe attest. The Romans did not face the problems associated with chemical contamination that accompany modern agricultural methods. However, they were aware of the risk of disease associated with contaminated drinking water and consequently preferred to draw their water supplies from mountain sources whenever possible. To what extent this preference reflects awareness of superior taste as a beverage is not known with certainty, but Roman literature includes many references to the desirable properties of the drinking water in specific parts of the empire.

The widespread marketing of drinking water in industrialized countries reflects in part an increasing awareness of the risks of contamination of conventional sources. This awareness comes at a time of increasing concern for the future supply of potable water for a steadily growing world population. Clearly, water is a basic requirement of life. Freshwater is not evenly distributed over the face of the planet. It is most abundant in places where few people live, and the transport of large amounts of water to the arid and semiarid areas of high population density presents a serious technological challenge. Contamination, both by chemical agents and by pathogenic organisms, is a problem that requires serious attention at every governmental level. Even in the United States, where the safety of the drinking water supply is usually assumed to be assured, occasional events, like the outbreak of a waterborne disease in Milwaukee, point up the fact that surface water supplies in particular are vulnerable. However, recognition of the urgency of the problem has increased public awareness of the necessity of preserving and protecting a fundamental resource, and it appears that drinking water is receiving the level of appreciation it deserves.

See also **Food Supply, Food Shortages.**

BIBLIOGRAPHY

Ayo-Yusuf, O. A., J. Kroon, J. and I. J. Ayo-Yusuf. "Fluoride Concentration of Bottled Drinking Waters." *Journal of the South African Dental Association* 56 (2001): 273–276.

Berkow, Robert , ed. *Merck Manual*, pp. 664–676. New York, Pocket Books, 1997.

Buclin, T., M. Cosma, M. Appenzeller, A. F. Jacquet, L. A. Decosterd, J. Biollaz, and P. Burckhardt. "Diet Acids and Alkalies Influence Calcium Retention in Bone." *Osteoporosis Int.* 12 (2001): 493–499.

Coen, G., D. Sardella, G. Barbera, M. Ferrannini, C. Comegna, F. Ferazzoli, A. Dinnella, E. D'Anello, and P. Simeoni. "Urinary Composition and Lithogenic Risk in Normal Subjects Following Oligomineral versus Bicarbonate-Alkaline High Calcium Mineral Water Intake." *Urologia Internationalis* 67 (2001): 49–53.

Colussi, G., M. E. De Ferrari, C. Brunati, and G. Civati. "Medical Prevention and Treatment of Urinary Stones." *Journal of Nephrology* 13 (2000): S65–S70.

Costi, D., P. G. Calcaterra, N. Iori, S. Vourna, G. Nappi, and M. Passeri. "Importance of Bioavailable Calcium Drinking Water for the Maintenance of Bone Mass in Post-Menopausal Women." *Journal of Endocrinological Investigation* 22 (1999): 852–856.

Drobnik, M. "Evaluation of Pharmacodynamic Properties of Medium-Mineralized Alkaline Water Designed for Distribution as Bottled Natural Mineral Water." *Roczniki Panstwowego Zakladu Higieny* 5 (2000): 379–384.

Kessler, T. and A. Hesse. "Cross-Over Study of the Influence of Bicarbonate-Rich Mineral Water on Urinary Composition in Comparison with Sodium Potassium Citrate in Healthy Male Subjects." *British Journal of Nutrition* 84 (2000): 865–871.

Lalumandier, J. A., and L. W. Ayers. "Fluoride and Bacterial Content of Bottled Water vs. Tap Water." *Archives of Family Medicine* 9 (2000): 246–250.

Misund, A., B. Frengstad, U. Siewers, and C. Reimann. "Variation of 66 Elements in European Bottled Mineral Waters." *The Science of the Total Environment* 243 (1999): 21–41.

Musaiger, A. O., and A. A. Khunji. "Chemical Quality of Drinking Water in Bahrain." *Journal of the Royal Society of Health* 10 (1990): 104–105.

Parry, J., L. Shaw, M. J. Arnaud, and A. J. Smith. "Investigation of Mineral Waters and Soft Drinks in Relation to Dental Erosion." *Journal of Oral Rehabilitation* 28 (2001): 766–772.

Rehrer, N. J. "Fluid and Electrolyte Balance in Ultra-Endurance Sport." *Sports Medicine* 31 (2001): 701–715.

Ritter, L., K. Solomon, P. Sibley, K. Hall, P. Keen, G. Mattu, and B. Linton. "Sources, Pathways, and Relative Risks of Contaminants in Surface Water and Groundwater: A Perspective Prepared for the Walkerton Inquiry." *Journal of Toxicology and Environmental Health Part A* 65 (2002): 1–142.

Rudzka-Kantoch, Z., and H. Weker. "Water in Children's Diet." *Medycyna Wieku Rozwojowego* 4 (2000): 109–115.

Sichert-Hellert, W., M. Kersting, and F. Manz. "Fifteen-Year Trends in Water Intake in German Children and Adolescents: Results of the DONALD Study. Dortmund Nutritional and Anthropometric Longitudinally Designed Study." *Acta Paediatrica* 90 (2001): 732–737.

Sohn, W., K. E. Heller, and B. A. Burt. "Fluid Consumption Related to Climate Among Children in the United States." *Journal of Public Health Dentistry* 61 (2001): 99–106.

Toumba, K. J., S. Levy, and M. E. Curzon. "The Fluoride Content of Bottled Drinking Waters." *British Dental Journal* 176 (1994): 266–268.

Willershausen, B., H. Kroes, and M. Brandenbusch. "Evaluation of the Contents of Mineral Water, Spring Water, Table Water and Spa Water. *European Journal of Medical Research* 5 (2000): 251–262.

Wynckel, A., C. Hanrotel, A. Wuillai, and J. Chanard. "Intestinal Calcium Absorption from Mineral Water." *Mineral and Electrolyte Metabolism* 23 (1997): 88–92.

William A. Stini

WATER AS A RESOURCE

The central role played by water in the origin of life has long been acknowledged. As early as the seventeenth century, geologists recognized the extent to which water shaped and reshaped the landforms on the earth's surface. More recently, it has been argued that water plays a fundamental role in the formation of stars (Nisini, "Water's Role in Making Stars"). According to this account of the process of star formation, water may be present in two of its physical states, ice (a solid), and water vapor (a gas) in the earliest stages of the birth of a new star. During this phase, ice on the surface of dust particles contributes to the cooling of circumstellar gases by removing excess energy released during protostellar collapse. At the same time, water vapor serves as a reservoir of oxygen in the warmer sectors of accumulating mass. Certain of the peculiar physical and chemical properties of water to be discussed later make water uniquely qualified to participate in this seminal cosmological event.

Since stars form as the result of the gravitational collapse of dense molecular clouds, almost all of the water present in its earliest stages is found in the ice coats of dust grains. A small amount, however, is produced as vapor through a series of reactions beginning with H_3^+ and O and resulting in the formation of H_2O and O_2. As star formation proceeds and gravitational collapse accelerates, increasing amounts of radiation energy are released. Consequently, the ambient temperature rises dramatically, and the temperature of the dust grains attains a level where water is released by evaporation. As the temperature continues to rise, all available atomic oxygen is rapidly transformed to water by the following reactions:

1. $O + H_2 \longrightarrow OH + H$
2. $OH + H_2 \longrightarrow H_2O + H$

As the process of star formation moves into its later stages, these equations are reversed with the release of OH and atomic oxygen. However, some of the water produced is deposited on dust grains in the form of ice, where it may remain while planets are formed. Thus, newly formed planets have continued access to water during their evolution. Within our own solar system, there is considerable evidence that liquid water was abundant at some earlier stage in the history of Mars. The erosion patterns still visible on the planet's surface bear a striking resemblance to some found on earth. Many astronomers are also convinced that liquid water is still present on Saturn's moon, Titan, and under a deep layer of ice on Jupiter's moon, Europa.

The Reshaping of Landforms

Geologists have long been aware of the role water plays in the reshaping of the earth's surface. The uniformitarian theory of the earth's history explicated by Charles Lyell in the early nineteenth century recognized that the surface of the earth is essentially a chronicle of its reshaping by water erosion. Some of the most informative strata for the reconstruction of past events are those that contain sedimentary deposits. These deposits, formed in lake beds and ocean floors, often contain fossils of species extant at a specific time, and can therefore be used, along with chronometric methods, to estimate the age of a given deposit and its contemporaneity with other deposits bearing similar fossils.

The formation of sedimentary deposits provides one of the bases for determination of relative dating sequences through the comparison of fossil inclusions. However, it is the gradual wearing down of mountains and other landforms by rain and snowfall and the transport of particles of rock and soil to the sea that are continually altering earth's topography. Water erosion, combined with tectonic forces at work beneath the earth's crust, is ultimately responsible for environmental changes that occasionally trigger major evolutionary events. In some areas, such as the Grand Canyon of Arizona, long sequences of the earth's history can be reconstructed through examination of strata exposed by the action of Colorado River water.

When major geological events such as the collision of tectonic plates occur, marine deposits sometimes end up in mountains, while other segments of the sea floor may be returned to the magma layer in zones of subduction. Mountain building may have profound effects on rainfall patterns. Under the appropriate circumstances, alterations in atmospheric conditions associated with major events such as the collision of the plates that joined the Indian subcontinent to the Asian landmass have the potential to trigger significant climatic changes. Changes in rainfall patterns, glaciations, and altered temperature gradients may be implicated in the onset of epochal events such as the Pleistocene "Ice Age," with worldwide effects on the evolution of plant and animal species.

Water and Weather

The possibility of a worldwide change in climate associated with the rapid building of a major mountain range arises from the central role that the oceans of the earth play in the distribution of heat energy received from the Sun. Approximately 70 percent of the earth's surface is covered by water. Because of the tilt in the earth's axis, the waters of the equatorial zone receive the Sun's radiation more directly than areas in the higher latitudes. Consequently, more of the wavelengths of solar radiation that are subject to reflection, scatter, or absorption in the atmosphere actually reach the earth's surface in the tropics. Much of their energy serves to warm the oceans. The energy so received sets up warm ocean currents that flow away from the equatorial zone. Ultimately, the warm currents flowing out of the tropics mix with colder currents originating in the polar regions, but not before heat energy has been widely distributed over the oceans and landmasses of the temperate zones.

The warming of the oceans in the equatorial zone has the additional effect of evaporating ocean water.

Thus, water vapor enters the atmosphere. In the tropics, some of the moisture-bearing warmed air rises until it is sufficiently cooled to form precipitation. The result is the return of fresh water to the surface. The circulation of moisture-bearing atmosphere through the action of thermal gradients and prevailing winds allows some of it to flow to the cooler, drier areas at higher latitudes as well. Thus, the supply of fresh water is continuously replenished on the continental landmasses of both the Northern and Southern Hemispheres. The large number of plant and animal species that require access to fresh water for survival is evidence that the distribution of fresh water through the atmosphere has played a major role in the evolutionary process.

The mixing of ocean waters and the direction of currents produce a complex pattern that is influenced by factors beyond the dissipation of heat energy absorbed in the tropics. The salinity of seawater varies from one area to another according to the amount and composition of the silt emptied into the oceans by rivers and streams. Since very salty water is heavier than fresh water, streams of water flowing away from the mouths of rivers tend to sink. This tendency sets up a network of crosscutting currents that affect the temperature of water at various depths. Temperature and salinity both affect the mix of marine organisms present in the ocean biome (ecological community). Generally, estuaries are some of the richest and most diverse of the marine habitats. Exploitation of fisheries such as the one that formerly produced abundant catches of sardines in the Mediterranean Sea off the mouth of the Nile River provided local human populations with an important source of dietary protein for many millennia. Other areas, such as the zone of nutrient upwelling off the west coast of South America, are illustrative of the way in which the combination of geological factors and ocean currents can create a major source of food for human populations that have learned how to exploit them.

Although the vast majority of the earth's water is too salty to drink for many animals, including humans, evaporation and precipitation provide a constantly renewing source of fresh water. In addition, the atmospheric recirculation of water modifies the climate in the higher latitudes to such an extent that life can exist in areas that would otherwise be uninhabitable. Moreover, along with rainfall, atmospheric circulation plays an important role in the carbon cycle and nitrogen fixation, both essential to the maintenance of life.

The Physical and Chemical Properties of Water

Through its role in the formation of stars, the reshaping of the earth's surface, the absorption and release of solar energy, and the provision of marine and aquatic habitats, water is essential for the existence of life as we know it. However, as important as each of these factors has been in shaping the evolutionary pathways that produced contemporary species, the physical and chemical properties of water have resulted in a much more intimate relationship between water and the processes of life than the mere provision of an appropriate environment. Water molecules and the molecules of living organisms interact in ways that would make the existence of life, as we know it, inconceivable in the absence of water. Understanding the nature of certain properties of water provides important insights into the nature of life itself, since organisms can quite properly be categorized as aqueous chemical systems.

Water has an unusually high boiling point, melting point, and heat of vaporization. Thus, the transition from solid to liquid and liquid to gaseous phases requires a high energy input. Functionally, this attribute makes water an effective heat absorber. The aforementioned capture and distribution of solar energy by the oceans is one result of this attribute. Moreover, the density of water is greatest when it is in its liquid phase. Therefore, ice floats. The formation of a layer of ice on the surface of a lake or pond serves as insulation for the water beneath it, with the result that aquatic life can continue even through the long, cold winters of the higher latitudes. While it is certainly possible for small bodies of water to freeze solid during prolonged periods of severe cold, most large, deep lakes and rivers sustain a thriving population of fish and other aquatic species through even the most severe winters.

Water molecules have a strong attraction for each other. Therefore, water has surprisingly high surface tension and exhibits the properties of cohesion and adhesion. Its ability to form hydrogen bonds is extraordinary. This ability comes into play in a variety of ways during many biochemical reactions. Water's tendency to adhere to a surface and to attract other molecules underlies the biologically important process of capillary action whereby water has the capability of moving against the force of gravity under certain circumstances. An illustration of this capability is seen in the capillary action that pulls water from soil through the roots and ultimately to the leaves of even the tallest trees.

Water is also a very effective solvent. In fact, it is so effective in the dissolution of other substances that it is only rarely present in the pure, unadulterated state. The solvent properties of water have significance in both the geochemical and biochemical context. The nature and rate of erosion occurring in different kinds of rock will produce changes in the physical geography of the land as well as the chemical nature of silt borne by rivers and streams. The dissociation of mineral compounds can be of special significance when the solute is one of a number of salts that dissociate into ions in water. Ionization of salts converts water into an effective conductor of electricity. Many biological processes, including transmission of nervous impulses and contraction of muscle fibers, depend upon a mild salt solution's ability to conduct an electrical current under controlled conditions.

The explanation for the extraordinary properties of water can be found in its previously mentioned unparalleled ability to form hydrogen bonds. Structurally, an individual water molecule is made up of two hydrogen atoms covalently bonded to one oxygen atom. That is, each hydrogen atom shares a pair of electrons with the oxygen atom. As a result, the molecule has a nonlinear shape and has electrical polarity because of a net positive charge on the hydrogen atoms and a net negative charge on the oxygen atom, creating a dipole moment. Water can serve as both a hydrogen donor and a hydrogen acceptor during hydrogen-bond formation, with each water molecule having the potential to form four hydrogen bonds. The intermolecular attraction inherent in this property accounts for water's high boiling point, melting point, heat of vaporization, and surface tension. The hydrogen bonds between water molecules are relatively weak and are continually broken and reformed with different partners. In liquid water, the average lifetime of the hydrogen bond between two water molecules is only 9.5×10^{-12} seconds (Garrett and Grisham, 1999). As a result, there is dynamism in a water solution that intensifies the diffusion of the products of dissociation. This continuous movement of water molecules enhances its solvent effect. Water also forms hydrogen bonds with a wide range of polar solutes. This permits nonionic but polar molecules such as sugars also to dissolve effectively in water.

Certain nonpolar substances, categorized as hydrophobic, interact with water much differently than the hydrophilic ones discussed up to this point. When such substances are dissolved in water, the surrounding water molecules reorganize to encapsulate the solute molecules in a hydration shell. Hydrophobic molecules trapped in these structures are attracted to each other. The tendency of fats and oils, both hydrophobic in nature, to form closed aggregations when submerged in water arises from this tendency. On the other hand, the tendency for oil to spread out into a thin film when poured on the surface of water reflects its hydrophobic nature in a situation where the lowest free energy state occurs when each molecule has minimum contact with neighboring water molecules. The composition of cell membranes, which characteristically combine a hydrophobic phospholipid bilayer with hydrophilic protein and carbohydrate receptors, provides an example of the manner in which the presence of an aqueous environment can be used to govern the movement into and out of the cell's interior.

Life Requires the Presence of Water

All living organisms require the presence of water to satisfy their metabolic needs. Even in such simple organisms as bacteria, metabolic processes requiring maintenance of solute concentrations inside the cell membrane that differ from those outside are essential to survival. In more complex organisms, the ability of water to absorb and diffuse solutes, create a potential electrical charge, and diffuse heat energy involves a variety of tissues, organs, and organ systems. These systems must communicate and support each other to satisfy the demands created by greater size and differentiation. Each organism, whether simple or complex, is dependent upon the unique properties of water to metabolize, survive, and reproduce. So intimate is the relationship between water and the structure and function of living organisms that the phenomenon of life as found on this planet is inconceivable in the absence of water. There is no concrete evidence of life anywhere else at this time. However, there is good evidence that water is abundant in the universe. Therefore, it is likely that if living organisms are ever found elsewhere, they will share many characteristics with those found here on earth, because of the inextricable relationship between life and water.

See also **Biodiversity; Evolution; Fish; Nutrients**.

BIBLIOGRAPHY

Brown, James H., and Lomolino, Mark V. *Biogeography*. 2d ed. Sunderland, Mass.: Sinauer, 1998.

Calvin, Melvin. *Chemical Evolution: Molecular Evolution Towards the Origin of Living Systems on the Earth and Elsewhere*. New York: Oxford University Press, 1969.

Garrett, R. H., and C. M. Grisham. *Biochemistry*. 2d ed. Fort Worth, Tex.: Saunders, 1999.

Hochachka, Peter W., and Somero, George N. *Biochemical Adaptation: Mechanism and Process in Physiological Evolution*. Oxford: Oxford University Press, 2002.

Hunten, Donald M. "Clues to the Martian Atmosphere." *Science* 294 (2001): 1843–1844.

Kauffmann, Guinevere, and Frank van den Bosch. "The Life Cycle of Galaxies." *Scientific American* 286, no. 5 (2002): 46–58.

Krasnopolsky, Vladamir, and Paul D. Feldman. "Detection of Molecular Hydrogen in the Atmosphere of Mars." *Science*. 294 (2001): 1914–1917.

Martini, Frederic. *Fundamentals of Anatomy and Physiology*. Englewood Cliffs, N.J.: Prentice Hall, 1989.

Nisini, Brunella. "Water's Role in Making Stars." *Science* 290 (2000): 1513–1514.

Ridley, Mark. *Evolution*. 2d ed. Cambridge, Mass.: Blackwell Scientific Publications, 1996.

Strickberger, Monroe W. *Evolution*. 3d ed. Sudbury, Mass.: Jones and Bartlett, 2000.

William A. Stini

SAFETY OF WATER

The understanding that some water caused disease while other water sources did not has long prompted human civilizations to attempt to make water safe to drink. Sanskrit medical lore from around 2000 B.C.E. mentions boiling foul water, exposing it to sunlight, and filtering through charcoal. It is possible that the Asian custom of drinking tea made with boiling water was an early method to make water safe to drink. Cyrus the Great in the sixth century B.C.E. took vessels of boiled water with his troops when they traveled to do battle. Residents of Alexandria, Egypt in 50 B.C.E. drank Nile River water brought to the city through a series of underground aqueducts to cisterns where it was clarified by sedimentation. Other parts of the Egyptian empire used single, double, and even triple filtration to purify water. Sextus Julius Frontinus, water commissioner of Rome in 97 C.E., wrote the first detailed description of a public water system in his *Two Books on the Water Supply of the City of Rome.* While these early water engineers had no understanding of bacteria and were probably treating water to decrease its cloudiness and improve its looks and taste, they nevertheless developed the earliest water treatment systems.

In one of the earliest cases to link a specific disease to the water supply, Dr. John Snow demonstrated in 1855 how cholera spread through water pumps during a large outbreak of the disease in London. He noticed that people who obtained their water from a particular well were more likely to become ill than those drawing their water from another well. He persuaded city officials to remove the pump handle from that particular well, forcing inhabitants to draw water from another well, and the number of cholera cases dropped immediately.

The U.S. Water Supply

In 1799 Philadelphia became the first U.S. city with a public water system that pumped water from a surface source and distributed it through a series of pipes to residents. By 1900 there were more than 3,000 public water systems in the United States. Rather than guaranteeing a safe water supply, some of those systems actually contributed to major disease outbreaks in the early 1900s. If the water supplies were contaminated, the pumped and widely distributed water provided a means for spreading bacterial disease throughout communities. Federal regulation of the nation's drinking water began in 1914 when the U.S. Public Health Service (PHS) imposed bacteriological standards for drinking water. These standards were revised in 1925, 1946, and 1962 and were eventually adopted by all fifty states. After World War II, industrialization and the use of fertilizers on crops began to pollute the quality and safety of the nation's water. A 1969 survey showed that only 60 percent of water systems delivered water that met PHS standards. A study in 1972 detected thirty-six chemicals present in already treated water taken from the Mississippi River. This increased awareness of the problems with the water supply led to the passage of federal environmental and health laws dealing with polluted water, hazardous waste, and pesticides.

Current water use in the United States averages about 100 gallons per person per day, more than just about any other country. A very small proportion of this, approximately two gallons, is actually used for drinking and cooking. Drinking water comes from either surface water or groundwater. Surface water includes rivers, lakes, and reservoirs, while groundwater is pumped up

BOTTLED WATER

As news reports of contaminated municipal water supplies proliferate, more and more Americans are purchasing bottled water. Between 1976 and 1997 yearly sales of bottled water skyrocketed from 500,000 gallons to almost 3.5 million gallons. Even though the cost of bottled water is 240 to 10,000 times more per gallon than that of tap water, the industry continues to grow at a rate of 8 to 10 percent per year. Many people buy bottled water with the assumption that it is safer than regular tap water.

Bottled water is considered a food and as such is regulated by the FDA under the Code of Federal Regulations Title 21, Part 165, Section 110. FDA considers carbonated water and seltzer water to be soft drinks, and thus regulates them as such. FDA regulations only apply to products that are sold in interstate commerce. Therefore, FDA does not regulate bottled waters that are packaged and sold within the same state, an estimated 60 to 70 percent of all bottled water sold in the United States. States regulate bottled water to varying degrees. One-fourth of bottled water is actually bottled tap water, which may or may not be further treated. EPA regulates tap water.

In its 1999 report, *Bottled Water: Pure Drink or Pure Hype?*, the Natural Resources Defense Council (NRDC) found that, while most of the bottled waters they tested were of high quality and safe, some brands were contaminated. The NRDC also believes that EPA regulations governing tap water are more stringent than the FDA regulations for bottled water. The NRDC concluded that bottled water is not always safer than tap water.

FDA has also established current good manufacturing practice (CGMP) regulations for processing and bottling drinking water, which apply to all waters sealed in bottles, packages, or other containers. Under the CGMP regulations for bottled water, the water to be bottled must be from an approved source and must be processed, packaged, transported, and stored under safe and sanitary conditions. The International Bottled Water Association has also produced a voluntary model code for use by its members.

from wells drilled into aquifers, underground geologic formations that contain water. Over half the nation gets its drinking water from groundwater sources.

The more than 170,000 water systems in the United States are either private or public. Private water systems do not draw water from a public water supply and serve only one or a few homes. Public water systems include community water systems and those at schools, factories, campgrounds, and some restaurants that have their own water supply. Community water systems deliver water to people year-round in their homes. In most community water systems, a network of underground pipes transports water under pressure to smaller pipes that then enter individual homes.

Hazards to the Water Supply and Treatment Methods

Because water is the universal solvent, many chemicals and other materials easily dissolve in it. Water supplies become contaminated through many different channels—chemicals can migrate from disposal sites; animal wastes and pesticides may be carried to lakes and streams by rainfall runoff; human wastes may be discharged to receiving waters that ultimately flow into water used for drinking. Other sources of contamination include discharge from industry, erosion of natural deposits, corrosion of household plumbing systems, and leaching from septic tanks. Nitrates, inorganic compounds that can enter water supplies from fertilizer runoff and sanitary wastewater discharges, are especially harmful to young children. Naturally occurring contaminants are also found in drinking water. For example, the radioactive gas radon-222 occurs in certain types of rock and can seep into groundwater. It would be impossible to remove all contaminants from our water supply. It would also be unnecessary since at very low levels many contaminants are generally not harmful.

Most outbreaks of waterborne disease are due to contamination by bacteria and viruses, mostly from human or animal waste. Two pathogens commonly associated with drinking water are *Cryptosporidium parvum* and *Giardia lamblia*. Both are protozoa that cause gastrointestinal illness and have cysts that are difficult to destroy. *Cryptosporidium* in particular may pass through water treatment filtration and disinfection processes in sufficient numbers to cause health problems. *Cryptosporidium* was first documented as posing a threat of infection to humans in 1976. A 1993 outbreak of cryptosporidiosis in Milwaukee, Wisconsin, is the largest outbreak of waterborne disease to date in the United States. Milwaukee's water supply, which comes from Lake Michigan, is treated by filtration and disinfection. Due to an unusual combination of circumstances during a period of heavy rainfall and runoff, water treatment was ineffective. An estimated 403,000 persons were affected by the disease, 4,400 were hospitalized, and at least 50 died. The original source of contamination is still unknown. Although *Cryptosporidium* had previously been found in surface water, it was not expected to appear in treated water from a municipal water supply that met state and federal standards for acceptable water quality. Increased awareness of the parasite has led to increased testing for it, and, not surprisingly, increased prevalence has been discovered. In

addition to drinking-water outbreaks, *Cryptosporidium* is associated with swimming pools and amusement park wave pools. This is particularly important as *Cryptosporidium* is highly resistant to chlorine and other chemical disinfectants. This is a new parasite showing up in new environments with new resistance capabilities.

Runoff from farms is another source of hazards to the nation's drinking water. In 1994 the Environmental Working Group released *Tap Water Blues*, a report in which the group identified over ten million individuals who had been exposed to five herbicides at levels above the Environmental Protection Agency's (EPA) negligible cancer risk standard of one additional case per million individuals. A second report in 1995, *Weed Killers by the Glass*, analyzed herbicides in the tap water of twenty-nine Midwestern cities. Again, their results show that Americans are exposed to harmful pesticides in their drinking water at levels far above federal health standards.

The Centers for Disease Control (CDC), the EPA, and the Council of State and Territorial Epidemiologists collaborate to maintain a surveillance system that collects data on waterborne disease outbreaks (WBDOs) from drinking and recreational water. This program seeks to determine what pathogens in the water supply cause illness, how many people become ill, and how and why outbreaks occur. The data are submitted on a voluntary basis and most likely underestimate the true incidence of WBDOs. More WBDOs occur in the summer months, and the cause is often unidentified. WBDO outbreaks peaked between 1979 and 1983 and have been declining ever since. This decrease could be due to improved implementation of water treatment regulations, increased efforts by many water utilities to produce drinking water substantially better than EPA standards require, and efforts by public-health officials to improve drinking-water quality. Of the waterborne disease outbreaks reported to the CDC from 1974 to 1996, about 12 percent were caused by bacterial agents, 33 percent by parasites, 5 percent by viruses, 18 percent by chemical contaminants, and 31 percent by unidentified agents.

During 1997 and 1998 there were seventeen outbreaks in drinking water, resulting in 2,038 people becoming ill. Six (35.3 percent) of the illnesses were caused by parasites (4 by Giardia, 2 by Cryptosporidium); four (23.5 percent) by bacteria (three by *E. coli* O157:H7 and one by *Shigella sonnei*); five (29.4 percent) were of unidentified origin; and two (11.8 percent) were attributed to chemical poisoning. Both chemical poisonings were from copper. Eight (47.1 percent) of the seventeen WBDOs were associated with community water systems. Of these eight, three were caused by problems at water treatment plants, three were the result of problems in the water distribution systems and plumbing of individual facilities, and two were associated with contaminated, untreated groundwater. Five (29.4 percent) of the seventeen WBDOs were associated with noncommunity water systems; all five were from groundwater (i.e., a well or spring) systems. The four outbreaks (23.5 percent) associated with individual water systems were also from groundwater.

Also during 1997 and 1998, eighteen outbreaks associated with recreational water caused 2,138 people to become ill. Nine (50 percent) were caused by the parasite *Cryptosporidium*. The other outbreaks were due to *E. coli* O157:H7 (three outbreaks or about 16.7 percent), *Shigella sonnei* (one outbreak or 5.6 percent), Norwalk-like viruses (two outbreaks or 11.1 percent), and unknown causes (three outbreaks or 16.7 percent). Slightly over half (55.6 percent) occurred in treated water—pools, hot tubs, or fountains; the others occurred in fresh-water lakes, rivers, or hot springs.

Depending on the conditions and types of contaminants likely to be found in a particular water source, most water suppliers use a combination of two or more treatment processes. Major water treatment processes are:

Flocculation/sedimentation. Flocculation is the process of getting small particles to combine into heavier particles called floc. The heavier particles can then be removed by letting them settle out as sediment. Once settled, the particles combine to form a sludge that is later removed.

Filtration. Filtration removes particles from water by passing the water through a permeable fabric or porous bed of materials. Groundwater is naturally filtered as it flows through porous layers of soil. Some filtration processes can remove very small particles, including microorganisms.

Ion exchange. Ion exchange processes remove inorganic constituents such as arsenic, chromium, excess fluoride, nitrates, radium, and uranium if they cannot be removed adequately by filtration or sedimentation. Electric current is used to attract negative and/or positive ions to one side of a treatment chamber for removal.

Adsorption. Adsorption involves making organic contaminants that cause undesirable color, taste, or odor stick to the surface of granular or powdered activated carbon.

Disinfection. Disinfection refers to killing harmful microorganisms. The three most commonly used methods of disinfection are chlorination, ozonation, and ultraviolet treatment. Chlorination is the method most often used in the United States while ozonation is very common in Europe.

    Chlorination. Chlorine kills bacteria by forming hypochlorus acid, which attacks the respiratory, transport, and nucleic acid activity of bacteria. Most bacteria are very susceptible to chlorine while viruses are less so. Cysts from *Giardia lamblia* are very resistant to chlorine, and *Cryptosporidium* cannot be readily killed by chlo-

rination. Of concern with this method of disinfection are the by-products (DBPs), particularly trihalomethanes (THMs), formed when chlorine reacts with organic matter that is in the water. Long-term exposure to some DBPs may increase the risk of cancer or have other adverse health effects. THMs are cancer group B carcinogens, which means they have been shown to cause cancer in laboratory animals. EPA regulations limit the amount of these by-products allowed in drinking water.

    Ozonation. Ozone is created by passing air through an electric current. The ozone gas is then dissolved in water, where it acts as an oxidant to destroy microorganisms. The ozone is removed before the water is used. As there is no residual antimicrobial effect, it is still necessary to chlorinate the water after ozone treatment. Ozone has received increased attention because it appears to be the only disinfectant that is effective against *Cryptosporidium*.

    Ultraviolet light. Ultraviolet light (UV) does not actually kill bacteria. Instead, it effectively sterilizes them, making it impossible for them to reproduce. The use of ultraviolet light is only practical for small water systems due to the need for the microorganisms to be close to the radiation source. UV does not inactivate *Giardia* or *Cryptosporidium* cysts.

With so many different bacteria that can cause illness, it is not possible to test the water supply for each of them separately. Instead, indicator organisms are used. Coliform bacteria are the most popular indicator organisms for drinking water as they are easily detected in water. Coliforms are a group of bacteria common in the environment and in the digestive tracts of humans and animals. While these organisms are themselves harmless, their presence indicates possible contamination with human and/or animal waste. The effectiveness of disinfection is judged by analyzing water supplies for total coliform bacteria. Presence of coliform bacteria is not acceptable in public water supplies and is a sign that disinfection is required.

Regulation

Local governments, public water systems, the states, and the EPA work together to ensure that all public water supplies are safe. Local governments have a direct interest in protecting the quality of their drinking-water source, be it groundwater or surface water. Part of the governments' job in protecting the water supply is to oversee land uses that can affect the quality of untreated source water. State public health and environmental agencies have the primary responsibility for ensuring that federal drinking-water quality standards, or more stringent ones required by the state, are met by each public water supplier. Municipal water systems test their own water systems for residues but do not regulate or test private wells. For households on private wells, state and local health departments usually have some standards for the drinking water, but it is generally up to the homeowner to maintain the quality of the drinking water.

An increased awareness of the vulnerability of the nation's water supply led to the passage of the 1974 Safe Drinking Water Act (SDWA). Prior to 1974 each state ran its own drinking-water program and set local standards. As a result, drinking-water protection standards differed from state to state. The act authorized the EPA to establish national enforceable health standards for contaminants in drinking water, encouraged federal-state partnerships in protecting the nation's water supply, and required notification to alert customers to water-system violations. In 1986 the act was strengthened through the Surface Water Treatment Rule, which requires public water systems to filter and disinfect all surface-water supplies. In 1996 amendments to the act extended the protection of drinking water from source to tap. Provisions in the 1996 amendment include the following:

- Consumers must receive more information about the quality of their drinking-water supplies. Water suppliers must notify customers within twenty-four hours of violations of EPA standards "that have the potential to have serious adverse effects on human health as a result of short-term exposure." If such a violation occurs, the system must announce it through the media and provide information about potential adverse effects on human health, steps taken to correct the violation, and the need to use alternative water supplies (such as boiled or bottled water) until the problem is corrected. When microorganisms such as those that indicate fecal contamination are found in drinking water, water suppliers may be required to issue "boil water notices." At least 725 communities, including New York City and the District of Columbia, have issued boil water notices affecting over 10 million people.

- The SDWA amendments also require public water systems to prepare Consumer Confidence Reports. These are to inform consumers about the source of their water supply, contaminant levels detected in their water, and the health effects of contaminant levels that are above the established safety limit. Beginning in 1999, systems are to prepare and distribute the reports annually.

- Under the new amendments, each state must develop a program to identify potential contamination threats and determine the susceptibility of drinking-water sources to activities that may harm the source water.

- The 1996 SDWA Amendments provides up to $9.6 billion over six years to improve drinking-water in-

TABLE 1

Sample monitoring schedule

Contaminant	Minimum monitoring frequency
Acute Contaminants	
Bacteria	Monthly or quarterly, depending on system size and type
Protozoa and Viruses	Continuous monitoring for turbidity, monthly for total coliforms, as indicators
Nitrate	Annually
Chronic Contaminants	
Volatile Organics (e.g., benzene)	Groundwater systems, annually for two consecutive years; surface water systems, annually
Synthetic Organics (e.g. pesticides)	Larger systems, twice in three years; smaller systems, once in three years
Inorganics/Metals	Groundwater systems, once every three years; surface water systems, annually
Lead and Copper	Annually
Radio nuclides	Once every four years

General requirements may differ slightly based on the size or type of the drinking-water system.

SOURCE: Environmental Protection Agency (EPA). July 1997. *Water on Tap: A Consumer's Guide to the Nation's Drinking Water.* Washington, D.C.: Environmental Protection Agency, Office of Water, 1997. Available at http://www.epa.gov/OGWDW/wot/ontap.html

frastructure. Water systems can apply for low- and no-interest loans to upgrade their facilities and ensure compliance with drinking-water standards. Other sources of funding are also available to water systems through the U.S. Department of Agriculture's Rural Utility Service (RUS). As part of the Water 2000 initiative, which is aimed at providing clean, safe, and affordable drinking water to all rural homes, RUS administers a water and wastewater loan and grant program. Under the RUS programs, rural areas and small cities and towns can receive loans or grants to restore a deteriorating water supply, upgrade a water or wastewater facility, or develop new systems.

The EPA Office of Water sets standards for pesticides and other chemicals in drinking water and issues Maximum Contaminant Levels (MCLs), which limit the amount of each substance that can be present in drinking water, for more than eighty contaminants. Scientists use a process called risk assessment to set drinking-water quality standards. When assessing the cancer and noncancer risks from exposure to a chemical in drinking water, the first step is to measure how much of the chemical could be in the water. Next, scientists estimate how much of the chemical the average person is likely to drink. This amount is called the exposure. In developing drinking-water standards, the EPA assumes that the average adult drinks two liters of water each day throughout a seventy-year life span. MCLs are set at levels that will limit an individual's risk of cancer from that contaminant to between one in 10,000 and one in 1,000,000 over a lifetime. For non-cancer effects, risk assessment provides an estimate of an exposure level below which no adverse effects are expected to occur. The EPA also takes into account the ability of various technologies to remove the contaminant, their effectiveness, and the cost of treatment.

To comply with MCLs, public water systems may use any state-approved treatment. According to 1996 statistics, 7 percent of community water systems, or 4,151 systems, reported one or more MCL violations, and less than 2 percent (681 systems) reported violations of treatment technique standards. The table shows the major groups of contaminants and the minimum frequency with which water systems must test for them.

Finally, Healthy People 2010, a national health-promotion and disease-prevention initiative, has two goals for water quality:

1. Increase the proportion of persons served by community water systems who receive a supply of drinking water that meets the regulations of the Safe Drinking Water Act. The current baseline is 73 percent; 2010 goals are to increase that to 95 percent.

2. Reduce waterborne disease outbreaks from drinking water among persons served by community water systems. Currently an estimated six outbreaks per year originate from community water systems. The goal is to decrease that to two outbreaks per year.

See also **Food Safety.**

BIBLIOGRAPHY

Baker, M. N. *The Quest for Pure Water: The History of Water Purification from the Earliest Records to the Twentieth Century*. New York: American Water Works Association, 1948.

Carson, Rachel. *Silent Spring*. Boston: Houghton Mifflin, 1962.

Environmental Protection Agency (EPA). *25 Years of the Safe Drinking Water Act: History and Trends*. Washington: Environmental Protection Agency, December 1999. Available at http://www.epa.gov/safewater/sdwa/trends.html

Environmental Protection Agency (EPA). *Water on Tap: A Consumer's Guide to the Nation's Drinking Water*. Washington: Environmental Protection Agency, July 1997. Available at http://www.epa.gov/OGWDW/wot/ontap.html

Environmental Working Group (EWG). *Just Add Water*. Washington: Environmental Working Group, May 1996. Available at http://www.ewg.org/pub/home/reports/JustAdd Water/jaw_short.html

Environmental Working Group (EWG). *Weed Killers by the Glass*. Washington: Environmental Working Group, September 1995. Available at http://www.ewg.org/reports/Weed_Killer/Weed_home.html

Food and Drug Administration. *What Guidance Does FDA Have for Manufacturers of Bottled Waters?* Available at http://www.cfsan.fda.gov/dms/qa-ind4c.html

Frerichs, Ralph R. *Snow on Cholera. Part 2: Broad Street Pump Outbreak*. Internet slide show. Los Angeles: UCLA School of Public Health, 1999. Available at http://www.ph.ucla.edu/epi/snow/Snowpart2_files/frame.htm

Government Printing Office. Code of Federal Regulations, 21CFR165.110, pp. 521–537. Bottled water. Available at http://www.accessdata.fda.gov/scripts/cdrh/cfdocs/cfPCD/ShowCFR.cfm?FR=165.110

International Bottled Water Association. The IBWA Model Code. 2000. Available at http://www.bottledwater.org/

National Drinking Water Clearinghouse. *Tech Briefs*. Morgantown, W.Va.: National Drinking Water Clearinghouse, 1996-1999.

Natural Resources Defense Council. *Bottled Water: Pure Drink or Pure Hype?* March 1999. Available at http://www.nrdc.org/water/drinking/nbw.asp

Cynthia A. Roberts

WEDDING CAKE. Wedding cakes are elaborate constructions, each standing for a particular marriage and each used in the wedding that establishes it. The link between cake and wedding, the distinctiveness of its form, its derived uses, and the meanings attached to it have all been most complexly and influentially developed in the English-speaking world. A classic form was commercially established in Britain and the United States in the early years of the twentieth century. An exceptionally large, rich fruit cake, as much as twelve inches in diameter and twenty pounds in weight, was used as a base for pillars supporting a similar but smaller cake. A third, still smaller cake layer was mounted on another set of pillars above that. The three tiers were each covered with hard white "royal" icing, which also was used for a characteristically formal decoration of piped icing. The whole was crowned with flowers, natural or in a variety of artificial materials, or a limited range of other appropriate ornamentation that might also adorn the sides. This form traveled widely in the course of the twentieth century and was modified locally in relation to changing tastes and the development of new decorative potentials and uses. Though the classic form was especially tenacious in Britain, the knowledge of alternatives, contributed by different European traditions, spread with increasing rapidity. The significance of the cake shifted from representing marriage as a fixed reality into which each couple entered to representing the individuality and even originality of the couple celebrating.

Historic Sources

The classic form had three sources, the use of loaves at Christian marriage rites, the appearance of "subtleties" and later sugar sculpture in medieval and Renaissance banquets in Europe, and the development of the English form of the substance "cake," mainly in the seventeenth century. Decorated loaves had been carried to the church in pre-Reformation wedding processions to be blessed

The royal wedding cake created at Windsor Castle in 1871 for the marriage of Princess Louise and the Marquis de Lorne. This cake, which stood over five feet tall, is crowned with a figure of a vestal virgin. It was one of the first wedding cakes to introduce the idea of tiers and height and became a prototype of the many-tiered wedding cakes of today. Wood engraving from the *Illustrated London News,* 1 April 1871. ROUGHWOOD COLLECTION.

and then returned to be eaten at a popular celebration following. Possibly earlier, and certainly later, there were baked but unleavened items more like Scottish oatcakes and shortbread: the "infare cake" is well known in the literature. These cakes were to be broken over the bride's head and/or eaten at the marriage feast. How widespread such practices were is not known, but these were among the variety of things to which the term "bride cake" has been applied over the centuries.

A clearer continuity is represented by the rich fruit-cake developed in England by a process of enriching breads with sugar, spices, and dried fruits. The transformation was achieved by the mid-seventeenth century, providing a luxury that might be baked for wedding celebrations in the homes of the wealthy. Icing for cakes followed, and in 1769 a Manchester confectioner, Elizabeth Raffald, included the recipe for an iced "bride cake" in her cookery book, *The Experienced English Housekeeper.* This recipe was for a distinctive rich fruitcake covered with two layers of icing, a naturally pale yellow almond icing encased in a hard outer layer of plain white icing. Over the next century this became the distinguishing formula for British celebration cakes of increasing variety.

The subtleties of medieval Europe were, like modern wedding cakes, display items designed to impress and amaze as well as to be at least marginally consumable as food. The tradition culminated in the production of sugar sculpture for some of the greatest court festivities of the Renaissance period. They had no specific link with wedding feasts, but when revived in the enthusiasm for historic forms and styles in the nineteenth century, they acquired it. Led by the British royal establishment, for the weddings of Queen Victoria's children superstructures of sugar architecture and sculpture were raised on bases of cake, transforming them into tall centerpieces for the tables of wedding banquets. The decoration was characteristically white, and made symbolic references to the royal alliance. By the end of the century their example had stimulated leading baker-confectioners and enthusiasts for the art of piping into commercial developments leading directly to the three-tier classic. Typically only wealthy customers could initially afford the product, but in the course of the following half-century it became the standard for all.

Meanings and Uses

The classic form of the cake was impersonal, excluding written inscriptions or any direct reference to the personal tastes or interests of the couple marrying. Decorative motifs were confined to the most genteel of references to love and constancy. White, and if not white, silver, predominated. The cake was indeed a prime component of the white wedding. This, though it has not been well studied, appears to have developed at a period when public attention was increasingly drawn to sex and when, among the respectable classes, embarrassment on this score in the context of marrying was strong. The formality of the white wedding and of the style of the classic cake with it was, it has been argued, a strategy for diverting attention from the sexual implications of marrying to the decorous purity of the bride.

The cake acquired a particular relationship with the bride in two ways. It was heir to popular traditions that centered weddings on the transition the bride was making. As noted above, this sometimes involved breaking baked items over the heads of brides. Unmarried young

Traditional wedding cakes baked in the shape of floral wreaths. Rethymnon, Crete, 1996. Most very old types of wedding cakes like these were little more than enriched bread, although elaborately ornamented. © GAIL MOONEY/CORBIS.

people often obtained fragments to dream on to discover their own life partners. The second link arose when cakes spread more widely in the social scale in the midnineteenth century, from the aristocratic wedding banquet to the modest domestic wedding breakfast. In this new context, the bride in her new married status was called on to cut the cake for her guests. Cut pieces could then take on the old use for divination. In the twentieth century cake cutting became one of the major popular rites of marrying, but it developed into a joint action by the new husband and wife together. In Japan this theme was developed to the exclusion of edibility. The joint insertion of a knife into a slot in an enormous wax cake provided a striking photo opportunity as part of a complex sequence developed in commercial wedding halls. In the United States a mutual feeding of cake by bride and groom extended the symbolic use in another direction.

More esoteric meanings have at times been discovered for the wedding cake and its uses. The complexity of the classic form and its apparently traditional nature often encouraged speculation on the contrast between the dark interior and the whiteness of the exterior and on the meaningfulness of ingredients and their flavors. The almond, appearing in one layer of icing as well as in the mixture inside, attracted particular attention. Most spectacular has been the identification of the white, tiered cake with the bride in her wedding costume and the joint cutting of the cake as a symbolic consummation of the marriage. As forms have diversified, the scope for such symbolic interpreting has declined.

See also **Bread**; **Cake and Pancake**; **Candy and Confections**; **Epiphany**; **Weddings**.

BIBLIOGRAPHY

Charsley, Simon R. "Marriages, Weddings, and Their Cakes." In *Food, Health, and Identity*, edited by Pat Caplan. London and New York: Routledge, 1997.

Charsley, Simon R. *Wedding Cakes and Cultural History*. London and New York: Routledge, 1992.

Goldstein-Gidoni, O. "The Production of Tradition and Culture in the Japanese Wedding Industry." *Ethnos* 65 (2000): 33–55.

Henisch, Bridget Ann. *Cakes and Characters*. London: Prospect Books, 1984.

Simon Charsley

WEDDINGS. Weddings are a universal life cycle event where rituals and ceremony display a group's interest, whether conspicuously or obscurely, in economics, organizational balance, power, and social forms. Nuptials allow families and couples to establish a new status in society; this is especially true for the bride as she is now an adult woman, belonging to her husband's family and responsible for perpetuating his (and now her) lineage. Upon marrying, the groom also gains a new status of respectful adulthood, a full member of society.

One major role of food in this rite of passage is the show of opulence and social status. For example, the

My small-leaf basil
and my marjoram
it is you who will separate me
from my mother
Come to the window
girl, the one with the glass pane
to see your face
[which is as white as] flour
The stairs you ascend
[I wished] I ascended too
and at every step
to give you sweet kisses

Traditional song sung by village musicians reserved for the women as part of the nuptial festivities (Argyrou, Tradition and Modernity in the Mediterranean, p. 69).

English nobility of the late Middle Ages had their own ideas regarding the proper wedding feast: boar and lamb were served as a first course, followed by venison in broth and antelope served with a spiced, sweet pudding containing rice flour. The third course contained fish and a baked meat and began with lozenge and almond cream in syrup; cheese, hot bread, a sweet, and other dishes were the fourth course.

Weddings in Greece

As Vassos Argyrou writes in *Tradition and Modernity in the Mediterranean* (pp. 60–110), weddings in Cypriot and other small villages of Greece were five- to six-day affairs in the 1930s. The nuptial rites customarily began on a Friday or Saturday with the preparation of the *resi*, a dish particular to the Limassol and Paphos areas. The communal preparation of the *resi* is the first of many fertility rituals; here the crushed wheat, pork, chicken, and other meats represent the abundance and fertility of the land upon which the couple would make their home. First, a group of village women cleaned the wheat by removing inedible portions and stones. Then, having placed the cleaned wheat in large wooden vessels, *skafes*, and covered these bowls with red shawls, the women, led by musicians, proceeded to the village fountain. After washing the wheat seven times in a step called *efta plimmata*, the wheat was returned to the bride's house in the same processional fashion, where it was pounded until crushed by using a *faouta*, a rectangular paddle with rounded edges. While the *resi* would not be served until the Sunday feast, the lengthy preparation process customarily started on Friday, and the dish was cooked on Saturday.

After the church ceremony, *stefanoman*, on Sunday, the couple and their guests returned to the newlyweds' home to perform one of the many rituals of that day. In response to good wishes from guests, the couple sprinkled the guests' hands with rosewater. Afterwards, men were served a glass of homemade wine, while the women were given a dish of fruit preserved in syrup, *ghliko*. An elaborate feast followed, attended by many people of the village. They dined on the traditional *resi*, potatoes *yakhni* (cooked in tomato sauce), *kolokasi* (a root vegetable similar to a sweet potato), salads, beets, and meats. The traditional beverage selection was limited to homemade wine and *zivania* (grappa).

On Monday, food such as *kanishia*, potatoes, olive oil, cheese, pasta, chicken, and wine was brought by people of the community to the couple's home. These gifts would unofficially set the guest list for the dinner served later that evening; in addition, they served as a hospitality gift to the couple's families with implications of future reciprocity.

The final rituals of the week were *to kopsimon ton makarounion* (the cutting of the pasta) and *to sinaman ton ornithon* (the collection of the chickens). These events took place on Tuesday and were attended by those who could not participate in Sunday or Monday's festivities. Accompanied by live musicians at the couple's home, the women rolled small pieces of dough between their palms, producing long, thin pieces which they then cut into small pieces. The collection of the chickens began after cutting the pasta, where young men gathered chickens from various village households (usually homes of invited guests). Also part of a musical procession, the youths brought the chickens home to be slaughtered and prepared with the pasta for the evening meal.

Greek weddings in the 1930s were not a small family affair; weddings were public celebrations, as almost all community members were considered friends and members of the family. Fathers of the bride and groom also felt their family name required a worthy nuptial celebration; thus, in Paphos, weeks before any actual celebrations, the two families distributed a special bread called *yiristarka* as an invitation.

Weddings in India

In an 1899 article titled "The Hill Tribes of the Central Indian Hills," William Crooke describes the Hindu-based wedding customs of several tribes. These customs emphasize the role of food in carrying out rites promising fertility, happiness, and abundance. An initial marital rite takes place when the parents of the newly betrothed couple drink together out of vessels made from the leaves of a holy tree. For brides of the Majhwâr tribe, entry into the couple's new home is forbidden until she and her husband eat rice boiled in milk. A young Dhobi male will not consume boiled rice before his wedding feast so as to preserve the sacred meaning of this ritual. Some Bengali tribes practiced a custom where blood was drawn from the husband's finger and mixed with betel and eaten by the bride. Rice also enters the nuptial customs as five mounds of rice are placed on a stone and the bride is made to knock them down with her foot symbolizing her departure from her natal family and her entry into the family of her husband.

Grains continue to represent fertility across the world's cultures as special wheaten cakes are prepared for the newlyweds to walk on; women throw betel and barley over the groom as he enters his new home; and the bride's brother pours wheat, rice, or barley over the bride as she turns around.

Boiotian Weddings

Ancient Boiotian weddings were secondarily presented and analyzed in the nuptial iconography of several vases found in the Kanapitsa cemetery of Thebes. Researchers believe the fertility ritual of *katachysmata*, where the bride and groom are showered with cakes, figs, apples, nuts, and other fruits, is depicted, as well as the practice of the bride consuming a quince, apple, or other fruit to signify her public transition into her new role as a married woman.

In Greek Orthodox wedding ceremonies, the bride and groom sip wine from the same cup as a symbol of the shared cheer and unpleasantness they will experience in their life together.

Chimbu Weddings

The Chimbu of the New Guinea highlands live in a world where transactions define all relationships and interpersonal interactions. These dynamic operations—gifts, tolls, assistance—carry many implicit meanings which test loyalty and create intergroup balance. Chimbu weddings provide opportunities for groups to participate in transactional gift-giving and feasting; sweet potatoes are given or exchanged at weddings, as are bean roots and nuts when available. Marriages often occur at the height of a pig ceremony where numerous pigs are sacrificed, *bulga kande*, and cooked at a ceremonial ground; also at this time, male dancers enact a fertility rite, blessing the women, pigs, and sweet potato vines. Along with the gift of vegetable produce, the widely traditional cooked pig meat is distributed among those who cooked it and individual kinsmen.

Nias Weddings

The wedding feasts of the Nias people—Nias is the largest chain of islands off the west coast of Sumatra—also include a large amount of pork. Preparation for the traditional feast at the bride's house begins when the groom's party begins a procession over the hills involving gongs and drums and a small herd of about six pigs. Upon arrival at the bride's house, the men are served betel. Many hours and ritual transactions later, two pigs (*bawi huku*, law pig, and *bawi vangovalu*, wedding pig) are slaughtered by an elder or member of the bride's party to commence the main attraction of the feast. Provided by the groom, the raw pig is ceremoniously and carefully butchered into portions; the lower jaw, the most prized

The state wedding feast of Peter I of Russia is detailed in this 1712 engraving by Alexei Zubkov. © THE STATE RUSSIAN MUSEUM/ CORBIS.

portion, is divided into four. The bride's father and his close relatives and elders of the bride receive a portion running the whole length of the pig. A small quantity is cooked for the bride's relatives, and the remaining raw portions are given to the chief, wife-givers, and butchers.

The host reciprocates the gift of the wedding pig with another larger pig, *bawi daravatö*. Once again the pig is split among the guests; the groom takes one leg and a hind-part (about one-quarter of the animal) home to his village, the groom's speaker receives one back section, and the host is entitled to a leg and the lower jawbone as a token of the evening. The remaining parts are cooked and served to all other guests. The groom and his family members receive the lower jaw, belly, and heart served on a large mound of rice, while he and his bride eat from the same plate. Status determines the size and type of portion; thus, only the elders of each group are entrusted with the duty of distributing the meat.

The betrothal of a Nias couple is solidified with *fea-manu*, the eating of the chicken. Provided that specific omens which can break the contract are not encountered, the couple will eat the cooked chicken as their first meal together, and a small pig will accompany the meal. Raw and cooked portions, especially the lower jaw, are cut and given to the groom's father.

Weddings in China

The marriage customs observed in 1938 of the Chinese in the town then known as I Chang, located on the north bank of the Yangtse River, required preparations to begin at least one year in advance. During this time, pigs must be fattened, rice and other foods accumulated, and goats and chickens prepared. About one week before the wedding ceremony, final preparations for the wedding

A Hungarian immigrant wedding held near Wilkes-Barre, Pennsylvania, about 1906. The bride and groom are standing behind the bride's parents on the right. ROUGHWOOD COLLECTION.

feast began. The feast, which lasted four hours, included nine courses; the first course was cuttlefish or sea slugs and wine; the roundness of the meatballs of the fifth course represented a coming together of the groom greeting his guests; the ninth course also included fish, *yü*, which also means surplus, ending the meal with an omen to abundance in the couple's future.

In *The Wedding Day in All Ages and Countries* by Edward J. Wood published in 1869, Wood writes on the various wedding rituals throughout the world. In Athenian tradition, sweetmeats, symbolic of abundance, were gingerly thrown upon the couple as they walked into a house for the nuptial feast. Later on, a quince was shared by the pair in hopes that their marriage would be agreeable. A man in Algiers placed fish at his new wife's feet for good luck. Past Chinese tradition called for a quilt, held by her relatives, to be placed in front of the bridal chair and as the bride sat there, four bread cakes were thrown into the air so that they would land on the quilt; this ritual also represents good luck.

Later in the course of this days-long elaborate marriage ritual, tea and poached eggs with sugar were served three times to the guests. The groom and his party only feign partaking of these refreshments since actual consumption would violate social etiquette. Numerous tea ceremonies take place, often followed by a serving of tobacco.

While preparing the nuptial bed, two women selected by the groom's family place cakes, dried *lungan* nuts, red-stained peanuts, and ginko nuts in the bed. Young girls search for these goods and eat them in hopes of future fertility. In a ceremony to finalize the marriage, the bride and groom are each given a glass of wine; they drink half the contents, exchange the cups, and finish consuming the rest of the wine; the same ritual is done with pieces of candy after the wine.

To ensure that as a wife the bride will be thorough in completion of her duties, she places a pre-prepared fish in the stove with the head pointing toward the front of the stove, and the tail in the back. This ritual, *yu tou yu wei*, says that she will be thoroughly dutiful. In addition, a dish of steamed vegetables mixed with rice flour, *chêng tsai*, is prepared by the bride, symbolizing abundance.

Contemporary Hindu Rituals

Contemporary Hindu wedding rituals also involve food at almost every stage in the ceremony. In a prenuptial rite at the bride's and groom's homes, male and female guests heat the couple's bodies to ready them for sexual intercourse by rubbing them with turmeric. In another preliminary ritual, the groom's party is served a light *pakka* (fried) meal at the bride's house, then the bride sits behind a mound of rice, and the groom's father places coconuts and sweets (believed to be auspicious) and money in her lap.

During the main nuptial ritual, the priest pours rice into a small tray held in the bride's right hand. The groom places his arm around her shoulders and knocks the rice onto the ground seven times. After the ceremony is completed, *Muhajayana* takes place. During this rite, the bride fills a metal tin with uncooked rice and holds it on the ground for the new husband to kick over seven times. The disturbance of the raw grain by the male in these two practices places him in an active role for reproduction.

Also during *Muhajayana*, the wife cooks a mixture of rice and pulse, *khichri*, for the groom and his younger brothers. When the husband is full from his portions, he hands the leftovers to her for her to eat. This act embodies the belief that the leftovers of a superior confer a blessing on the subordinate who consumes them.

See also **Anthropology and Food; Feasts, Festivals, and Fasts; Nutritional Anthropology; Wedding Cake.**

BIBLIOGRAPHY

Argyrou, Vassos. *Tradition and Modernity in the Mediterranean.* New York: Cambridge University Press, 1996.

Beatty, Andrew. *Society and Exchange in Nias.* New York: Oxford University Press, 1992.

Brown, Paula. "Chimbu Transactions." *Man, New Series 5* (1970): 99–117.

Charsley, S. R. *Wedding Cakes and Cultural History.* New York: Routledge, 1992.

Crooke, William. "The Hill Tribes of the Central Indian Hills." *Journal of the Anthropological Institute of Great Britain and Ireland* 28 (1899): 220–248.

Han-yi, Feng, and J. K. Shryock. "Marriage Customs in the Vicinity of I chang." *Harvard Journal of Asiatic Studies* 13 (1950): 362–430.

Sabetai, Victoria. "Marriage Boiotan Style." *Hesperia* 67 (1998): 323–334.

Wood, E. J. *The Wedding Day in All Ages and Countries.* Vol. I. London: Richard Bentley, 1869.

Dalila Bothwell

WHEAT.

This entry includes two subentries:
The Natural History of Wheat
Wheat as a Food

THE NATURAL HISTORY OF WHEAT

Wheat's beginnings can be traced to a clan of wild grasses called *Triticeae*, the seeds of which had a flavor that was pleasing to primitive people. *Triticeae* included wheat,

barley, rye, their wild relatives, and a number of important wild grasses. The Fertile Crescent, at the core of western Asia and northern Africa, is the center of origin and early diversification of this clan. Wild einkorn and emmer, which have been known for roughly 75,000 years, are credited as wheat's earliest ancestors. The ripple effect of these grains has been immense, since wheat is the most widely produced and consumed cereal grain in the world.

Through the archeological evidence left by nomadic humans in west Asia, researchers have learned that humans adapted from hunting animals to also gathering seeds for food. Periods of glaciers no doubt inspired this move by reducing available game. The early gatherers were also the first millers and selected grains that could be most easily released from their glumes or husks and prepared. People parched, simmered, and ground these grains and prepared flat cakes. Thus, using grains as food changed the way early ancestors lived their daily lives, in addition to providing basic sustenance. The evolution of agriculture and cultivating seeds for harvest (which occurred about 9,000 to 10,000 years ago) changed not only the available food supply but how people moved about. Human beings' ability to process (mill), store, cultivate, and trade grain marked the beginnings of civilization.

Beyond Grass: The Early Use of Wheat

As mentioned earlier, early wheat was part of a clan called *Triticeae* and is classified under the Old World genus *Triticum*. Wheat's early relatives had seed heads that were brittle and easily broken apart and the hulls clung to the grains. This made the seeds better for re-seeding but also difficult to thresh.

Primitive women who were responsible for the tasks of gathering, threshing, grinding, and cooking would have selected heads with the largest grains and sought out those that were easiest to thresh or separate from the hulls. Some early wheat species grew as tall as six feet, but modern varieties average two to three feet in height. Domestic wheat is selected and bred for strong seed heads that do not shatter easily and that release the glumes or hulls so the kernels are bare.

Einkorn (*Triticum monococcum*) is considered to have been the first wheat gathered and cultivated. Its centers of early distribution were Armenia, Georgia (in the former Soviet Union), and Turkey, where it is still grown and eaten. Impressions of einkorn are found in Neolithic pottery as far north as Great Britain and Ireland, but there are no prehistoric records of it in India, China, or Africa.

All plants are identified by their chromosomes. Every variety of wheat grown today has arisen from wild, fourteen-chromosome wheat, undoubtedly einkorn. Einkorn and fourteen-chromosome wild grass crosses created twenty-eight-chromosome (tetraploid) wheats. Only one twenty-eight-chromosome species can be found in nature: wild emmer (*T. dicoccoides*). It grows in

EARLY BEGINNINGS

Archeologists look for certain evidences of early agricultural society. These include tools for pounding or grinding grain; pottery or means of quantity grain storage; remains of a permanent settlement; tools for planting, sickles or scythes for harvest; and related religious symbols. Some of the earliest finds include the following.

Pre-agriculture (Early wheat ancestors—wild einkorn and emmer—are gathered and ground.)

- 75,000 years ago—Simple roundish stones one-and-one-quarter-inch thick and four inches across, with flat working surface, such as the Arugnacian combination grinding stones, found in La Combe, France.
- 20,000 years ago—Mortar stones are an improvement, such as a dip to contain the product while grinding/pounding, found in Magdalenia, Vezere valley, France.
- 12,000 years ago—Pounder-rubber for grain and possible sickle-like blade from Azilian culture, found in Mas d'Azil, France; also found in Danish Maglemose period.
- 10,000 years ago—Pounder-rubbers—found in Pinto Basin, Riverside County, Calif., and Oak Grove Natives, Santa Barbara, Calif.

Early agricultural period

- 10,000 years ago (Stone Age)—Einkorn cultivated in southeastern Turkey.
- 9,500 years ago—Clustered mud-brick houses, cultivation tools, saddle stones (found in Abu Hureyra village, northern Syria).
- 8,700 years ago—Swiss cave dwellers provide evidence of eating wheat in flat stone-baked cakes.
- 8,050 years ago—Sickle blades coated with silica patina from grain stems; sandstone milling stones and mortars, baked pottery (Ghar-I-Kamarband or Belt Cave, northern Iran).

- 8,000 years ago—Goat grass (*Aegilops tauschii*) and wheat (*Triticum turgidum*) cross for the rise of bread wheats.
- 7,500 years ago—Pottery is invented.
- 7,000 years ago—Pottery is used in grain storage and cooking; tools—Natufian culture, Palestine and Sialk, northern Iraq; sickle, Fayum, Egypt; einkorn found in Jarmo, northern Iraq.
- 6,000 years ago—Unbaked clay grain bins—Hassuna, west of Sialk; planting tools, pottery, grain drying kilns, grain storage—Jericho, Dead Sea, and Abydos, Egypt.
- 3000 B.C.E.–2,737 B.C.E.—First plows depicted on monument in Egypt and China.
- 2600 B.C.E.—Egyptians develop fermentation and bread-baking.
- 2500 B.C.E.—Bread wheat emerges in Mohenjo-Daro India, Hungary, and China.
- 2470 B.C.E.—Tomb bas-reliefs of royal bakery and baking pottery remnants are placed in the Old Kingdom pyramids, Giza, Egypt.
- 2000–1100 B.C.e—Old Testament refers to Joseph overseeing Egyptian grain stores (1800 B.C.E.), Hebrew people enslaved in Egypt (1700–1250 B.C.E.), and Ruth on the threshing floors (1210 B.C.E.).
- 1100 B.C.E.—Iron plowshares used.
- 700 B.C.E.—In Greece, Solon's constitution develops agriculture and "Bread and Soil" cult under goddess Demeter; raised barley; imported wheat from Sicily, shores of Black Sea and Egypt; quern mill in use in Egypt and Far East.
- 200 B.C.E.—Flour milling methods improved lever mills, Greece and Roman hourglass mills, using two rotary stones turned by slaves and animals.
- 150 B.C.E.—Roman bakers' guilds formed.
- 100 B.C.E.—Roman water mills evident in Pontus and Thessalonica, Asia Minor.

---

the region comprising northern Israel, west Jordan, Lebanon, and adjoining southern and southeastern Turkey, western Iran, northern Iraq, and northwestern Syria.

Emmer (*T. dicoccum*), which closely resembles wild emmer, is the oldest and was once the most widely cultivated twenty-eight-chromosome wheat. Well-preserved spikelets of emmer have been found in Fifth Dynasty Egyptian tombs—the bread bakeries from that period in Egypt's history used emmer flour. Remains and impressions are also common in Neolithic sites in continental Europe, Great Britain, and Ireland. Durum wheats that

are grown today for pasta and couscous are derived from emmer wheat crosses.

The Emergence of Bread Wheat

Varieties of wheat that have forty-two chromosomes are the most recently evolved and most used types of wheat. All of these varieties have been cultivated by humans (as opposed to growing wild). They are hybrids of twenty-eight-chromosome wheats and wild fourteen-chromosome wheats or grasses. Early bread wheat was the result of the crossing of goat grass (*Aegilops tauschii*) with *Triticum turgidum*. Modern bread wheat varieties have forty-two chromosomes and evolved from crosses between emmer and goat grass, which is the source of the unique glutenin genes that give bread dough the ability to form gluten. Goat grass grows abundantly in the region stretching from Greece to Afghanistan. Descriptions of the fourteen species of wheat that yield the thousands of wheat varieties grown today are provided here.

The Diffusion of Wheat

The fact that prehistoric people accomplished selective breeding of wheat is a testament to their powers of observation and curiosity. Through their efforts and, much later, through the development of the laws of heredity by nineteenth-century Moravian monk Gregor Mendel, wheat began to diversify.

Up through the Middle Ages and into the seventeenth century, the varieties of wheat grown in different parts of the world were often "landrace" (native wheat or wheat grown for centuries in a region) varieties. People carefully selected the biggest and best grains at harvest for seeding the next crop. Through trade routes and immigration, new varieties of wheat were sold or shared by people from different regions. If a type of wheat grew well (in other words, if it resisted soil or airborne diseases, insects, and variations in rainfall or climate), people were likely to continue growing it.

As people emigrated to the Americas and Australia, the varieties of wheat grown in their mother countries were the first seed stock cultivated in the new frontiers. If these crops failed, people tried raising other crops or experimented with wheat seed others had from another region.

Six Wheat Classes

The wheat foods that we enjoy today are all produced from varieties of wheat bred from the first fourteen species. The wheat industry divides the thousands of varieties available today into six wheat classes: hard red winter, hard red spring, soft red winter, durum, hard white, and soft white wheat. Each wheat class has qualities that millers and food processors seek for specific products. Farmers grow varieties from classes that will grow in their location.

Spring wheat classes (hard, soft, and durum) are planted in the spring and harvested in the summer. Winter wheat is planted in the fall, grows several inches, and may even be grazed by livestock before the grain head develops. Winter wheat lies dormant through the winter, continues growing in the spring, and is harvested in the summer months. Sometimes varieties of spring wheat are planted in the fall, as is the practice in some locations in China.

In general, the hard wheat classes (spring and winter) contain higher quantities of the proteins needed to

DISTINCT SPECIES OF WHEAT

The thousands of wheat varieties grown today rose from crosses in these fourteen species (Mangelsdorf, pp. 2–11).

Fourteen chromosomes
- *Triticum aegilopoides* (wild einkorn)
- *T. monococcum* (einkorn)

Twenty-eight chromosomes
- *Tritcum dicoccoides* (wild emmer)
- *T. dicoccum* (emmer)
- *T. durum* (macaroni wheat; first appeared first century B.C.E., Greco–Roman period)
- *T. persicum* (Persian wheat; of no great commercial importance today)
- *T. turgidum* (rivet wheat; of no great commercial importance today)
- *T. polonicum* (Polish wheat; of no great commercial importance today)
- *T. timopheevi* (has no common name; grown on only a few thousand acres in western Georgia [in former Soviet Union])

Forty-two chromosomes (First three species—true bread wheats—account for about 90 percent of all wheat grown today.)

- *Triticum aestivum* (common wheat)
- *T. sphaerococcum* (shot wheat)
- *T. compactum* (club wheat)
- *T. spelta* (spelt; grown on only a few thousand acres in western Georgia [former Soviet Union]; once the principle wheat of central Europe)
- *T. macha* (macha wheat; grown on only a few thousand acres in western Georgia [former Soviet Union])

SOURCE: Mangelsdorf, Paul C. "Wheat." *Scientific American* (July 1953): 2–11.
CONTRIBUTIONS: W. J. Raupp, Senior Scientist. Kansas State University, Wheat Genetic Research Center. Available at http://www.oznet.ksu.edu/wgrc.org.

produce bread, buns, pasta (durum), pizza crust, and other bread products. Soft wheat contains lower quantities of protein than hard wheat, and it is conducive to producing tender cookies, cakes, pastries, crackers, Asian noodles, and steam breads.

The white wheat classes are desirable because they lack a red gene in the bran that contributes to a darker color and a slightly bitter flavor to the whole grain. Hard and soft varieties of white wheat are grown increasingly in the United States and Australia.

New Varieties of Wheat

Developing and planting wheat varieties that resist diseases and insects is essential for a secure food supply, human health, and reducing the use of chemical controls. For example, fungal diseases like Karnal bunt, leaf rust, or smut will ruin entire wheat crops. In the Middle Ages European rye hosted a disease called ergot and was the cause of a horrible plague when the rye was mixed with wheat flour in breads. In more recent times, problems with Karnal bunt have rendered large portions of India's wheat harvest useless, and thousands of acres of Minnesota spring wheat were tilled under due to plant-disease damage.

Wheat hybridization occurs naturally and through human assistance. Wheat breeding has been practiced since people first selected the biggest seeds that were easiest to thresh and stored them for planting. In a formal sense, favorable characteristics such as disease resistance, large kernels, short straw, and cold hardiness are selected in two parent wheats, which are then crossed to form a hybrid.

For example, northern wheat hybrids were first made in Ontario, Canada, in 1885. North Dakota followed this trend in 1892. The early spring wheat varieties that were brought to North America had heads that shattered easily, and farmers needed them to ripen faster. Dr. William Saunders, organizer and first director of the Dominion Experimental Farms, produced a Canadian cross between an Indian wheat (Red Calcutta) and a popular Polish spring wheat (Red Fife) that gave rise to Marquis, a hard spring wheat. Marquis was put into production in 1909 and was soon grown over 90 percent of the northern United States and Canadian plains. It helped alleviate food shortages during World War I.

Another source of many new varieties of wheat is Turkey Red, which was hand-picked and carried to Kansas in 1874 by Mennonites from Crimea, Russia. Turkey Red wheat once covered over 90 percent of wheat acreage in the Great Plains. Winter-wheat research at Kansas State University has given rise to new winter wheat varieties and crosses grown all over the world.

Wheat breeders in centers around the world collect, conserve, and utilize wheat plant materials. Japan first began collecting wheat plant material in the early 1900s. Since the 1960s, wheat research centers have been formed (through private and government funding) in wheat regions all over the world.

It takes ten to twelve years of lab and field tests at a cost of around $500,000 per new variety of wheat before a seed wheat can be released to farmers for production. There are perhaps 100,000 unique varieties of wheat derived from the six classes worldwide. A variety will commonly be grown for about ten years before a new variety may be needed.

Genetically modified (or GM) wheats were not to be released until the early twenty-first century. The primary benefit of GM wheat technology is the precision it allows in adding desired wheat characteristics located at specific points on wheat's chromosomes. With wheat breeding or hybridization, all the genetic material from both parents is present in the cross. The resulting variety must be grown in order for researchers to see what attributes are included in the cross. Through genetic mapping, specific traits may be added, such as disease resistance to wheat streak mosaic or the addition of nutritive elements. With GM wheat technology, the testing time for new varieties of wheat may be reduced to as little as two years versus the ten to twelve years needed in traditional breeding programs.

Centers for wheat research also preserve early wheat and grass germplasm while new crosses and genetic research are performed. Wheat research is shared for the improvement of agriculture and food-production systems in all countries.

Wheat Production

Through centuries of seed selection and modern wheat breeding, wheat can be grown in every temperate climate in the world. World wheat production is perennial, that is, wheat is being harvested in some part of the world in every month of the year.

Wheat is seeded anywhere from sea level to elevations of ten thousand feet. A ninety-day growing season is needed for wheat growth, and a period of dry, sunny weather is preferred for the ripening period. Rainfall between ten and thirty inches annually is required, and soils that range from sandy loam to clay are used to grow wheat. The plant averages between two to three feet in height, and some varieties reach five to six feet.

Advances in Wheat Production

From 7500 B.C.E. to 1840 C.E. there were surprisingly few mechanical advances in the production of wheat. The invention of the iron plowshare, sickles for cutting ripe wheat, and the use of oxen or horses for tilling and threshing are considered the main advances during this time. With their reliance on human and animal labor and without the availability of machines, agricultural practices greatly limited how much wheat was produced. Fields were left fallow (unplanted) for a year to improve their moisture, and animal manure was used to enrich the soil. Many fields were planted to hay in order to feed essential work animals. Eventually soils were exhausted in Europe, Asia, and other regions where grains had been cultivated for thousands of years.

Three major advances were vital in the expansion and development of wheat production and consumption. First, in the early 1800s, the first soil-chemistry studies were performed. European soil chemists Sir Humphry Davy (from England), Albrecht von Thaer (from Prussia), and Justus von Liebig (from Germany) provided farmers with evidence that the soil had been "robbed" or depleted and that fresh sources of specific chemicals were

PERENNIAL WORLD WHEAT HARVEST

Wheat is harvested somewhere in the world every month. The world's top wheat producers are China, United States, Romania, Czech Republic, Slovakia, Russia, Canada, Germany, and France.

- January: Argentina, Chile, Australia, New Zealand
- February and March: Egypt and India
- April: Egypt, Asia Minor, Mexico
- May: Algeria, Central Asia, China, United States
- June: Turkey, Spain, France, United States, Italy
- July: Romania, Czech Republic, Slovakia, Austria, Russia, Germany, Switzerland, France, England, Denmark, Poland, United States, Canada, Italy
- August: Holland, Belgium, England, Denmark, Poland, United States, Canada
- September: Scotland, Sweden, Norway, Russia
- October: Scotland, Sweden, Norway, Russia
- November: Peru, South Africa
- December: India, Argentina

needed for crops to flourish again. The manure that farmers were using was not enough for healthy crop production. The inorganic minerals the researchers identified as essential were nitrogen, potassium, lime, and phosphoric acid. By 1843, Dawes in England began producing chemical fertilizers for the exhausted soils of Europe.

The second advance surrounding wheat production involved major improvements in milling technology. James Watt invented the steam engine in 1769. Oliver Evans began automating the milling process in 1785, and by 1834 steam-driven steel roller mills had been introduced in Europe. Steel roller mills were capable of milling the harder spring and durum wheats grown in Canada and the United States. By 1870, superior flour production and a new process called middling purification (created by Edmond La Croix) had created growing wheat demands.

A third major advance, convenient to the homesteading of vast expanses of untilled land in North America in 1862, was the mechanization of U.S. agriculture. In 1842, the Pennock brothers launched a mechanical sower called a drill, and the McCormick reaper was rolling out of factories in 1861. The invention of steam-driven threshing and self-binders meant that, by 1940, producing a bushel of wheat took only sixteen minutes, whereas in 1850 manual labor produced a bushel in four and a half hours. This meant there was no longer a risk of losing crops that were waiting to be harvested by hand. With machines, more ground could be seeded to wheat

instead of animal feed as long as there was adequate rainfall. Delivery of wheat was greatly improved by the advent of cross-continental railroad service. Between 1866 and 1900 U.S. wheat production increased from 175 million bushels to 655 million bushels. Exporting wheat became a new trade opportunity.

Challenges in the Wheat Industry

For thousands of years, all wheat, regardless of variety, was grown, harvested, and co-mingled in storage. As milling and the wheat food industry became increasingly sophisticated, companies became aware of the uniqueness and importance of wheat varieties. They now wanted to keep different classes and varieties of wheat separate at harvest and to identify which were best for what end use. For example, millers, bakers, and farmers all looked for different qualities in wheat. Thus, wheat manufacturers asked the question: Who should determine what qualities would be developed in new varieties?

Milling. Early millers were the first to begin to distinguish the unique qualities of different wheat species. They could tell in the milling process that all wheat was not the same. For example, some varieties of wheat were difficult to mill, produced less usable flour, and produced more "animal feed." Their customers also had increasingly sophisticated needs as baking became more mechanized. Cereal science isolated specific wheat and flour characteristics, and milling as a science and food technology had begun.

Baking and wheat food industry. Those who bake or prepare pasta, Asian noodles, crackers, tortillas, cakes, steam breads, and many other wheat foods long ago determined that all flour is not the same. Certain characteristics in various flours performed better when producing specific end products. Food companies need dependable flour for consistent products. After thousands of years, baking and wheat food industries have their specifications down to a science in regard to starch and protein content and a wide variety of other performance factors in various types of flour.

Agriculture. The farmer recognizes and needs wheat varieties that are resistant to plant, and soil, and airborne diseases and insects, that are suited to certain climates, and that are able to produce adequate bushels for the cost of production. There is very little monetary incentive provided by the food industry for specific wheat attributes. A farmer's source of profit is the production of the quantity of bushels that generate profitability for the farming operation.

Gauging wheat quality. Solutions to the various tensions surrounding wheat quality began in 1937. Under the bipartisan leadership of Mennel Milling in Michigan and Nabisco in New York, legislation was written that formed four wheat quality laboratories in the United States. These Agricultural Research Service laboratories

Goatgrass wheat is an ancient relative of cultivated wheat. PHOTO COURTESY OF THE WHEAT GENETIC RESEARCH CENTER AND KANSAS STATE UNIVERSITY.

operate under the direction of the U.S. Department of Agriculture. Their goal is to guide the development of new wheat varieties to meet functional and nutritional needs of food processors while considering agricultural parameters for the growing regions they serve. In addition, representatives from milling, wheat food production and agriculture collaborate through the Wheat Quality Council.

Changes in World Wheat Production

The world's yield per acre of wheat continually improves with the evolution of better wheat varieties and practices. World wheat production has nearly tripled since 1955 and has grown an average of 2.3 percent annually since 1951 (World Wheat Facts and Trends, 1998–1999).

Wheat needs continue to change. Great Britain traditionally grew soft wheat and once needed to import 2.75 million tons of higher protein wheat for bread flour from North America. Through wheat breeding, Great Britain now grows varieties suitable for bread flour and imports only 300,000 tons.

Many developing countries seek to be self-sufficient in their wheat needs. Over the past fifty years, India has achieved self-sufficiency and is now a wheat exporter. China, with nearly the same number of wheat-growing acres as India, has boosted its yields over a span of fifty years, becoming less dependent on imports. It is now the leading wheat producer in the world. Yields have increased from eight bushels per acre to thirty-five to sixty bushels per acre.

In past century in the United States there has been a dramatic decline in the number of farmers. In 1840, 70 percent of all Americans were engaged in farming. That number dropped to 12 percent by 1950 and to less than 2 percent by 2002. The cost of wheat production is simply not matched by returns in the marketplace. Despite having fewer farmers than it once did, the United States is second in world in production with Canada, Australia, the European Union, and Argentina being other major wheat contributors. Even thought the faces involved in wheat production have changed, world wheat production continues to meet population growth and steady consumption demands.

The Wheat Trade

The wheat trade reflects the unique ability of wheat to produce a wide variety of staple foods within diverse cultures. Wheat has come a long way from stone ground flat cakes baked on hot rocks, or gruel simmered over a fire. Asian noodles and steamed breads, chapattis, naan, baguettes, bagels, pasta, buns, crackers, biscuits, tortillas, and more all sustain the world's strong daily demand for wheat.

The wheat trade is not driven by market demand for wheat as an animal feed. Only an average of 16 percent of wheat is fed to animals worldwide. This number falls to less than 4 percent in developing countries and may be as much as 35 percent in developed countries. Other commodities tend to fuel new industrial uses of wheat, such as ethanol and plastics production.

Early wheat trade. The early wheat trade followed trade routes in the Mediterranean, with Greece and Roman civilizations being some of the earliest importers of wheat from west Asian countries and Egypt. Wheat was undoubtedly carried on trade routes throughout those empires and into China via the Silk Road. Evidence of wheat in sunken cargo ships, religious writings, on pottery, and in the agriculture of northern Europe and Asia indicates the existence of an early wheat trade.

In the Middle Ages, the wheat trade became tied more closely with milling. For example, in Great Britain, the value of wheat was in its edible form, starting with flour. This tie was very pronounced from the ninth to eleventh centuries. Tenant farmers were compelled to mill their grain at their landlord's mill, and a "soke" of one-sixteenth of the production was kept by the landlord. Until the soke system died out in 1791, wheat was not sold much beyond the landlord's domain. Millers were tied to buying the varieties of wheat that were grown in their region. They welcomed the end of the soke system so they could import the wheat of their choice. In modern times some governments still restrict wheat imports by requiring their millers to buy domestic wheat, even if these varieties do not perform well in the end product.

The English Magna Carta (1215), borrowing from moral law, influenced the measures used in dealing in wheat over time. European countries had various systems of controlling the sale of wheat through warehousing, fixed prices, loans, and speculation (futures).

Developing a world wheat trade. After having wheat bread as a staple in Europe for thousands of years, settlers in the New World found no wheat upon their arrival. These setters were dependent on imported flour from Europe, most often England, until they were able produce wheat on their own. Though maize or Indian corn saved the early settlements, many English settlers viewed it with disdain. Out of necessity they would bake a bread called "thirds" to extend the precious imported wheat flour. This bread was prepared from one-third wheat flour, one-third rye, and one-third cornmeal.

Unlike silk or spices, shipping wheat throughout the world was not considered profitable. By the 1740s the United States was successfully exporting wheat to England from the northern fields of New York, New Jersey, and Pennsylvania. Shipments of wheat and flour were also sent, against British regulations, by defiant colonists to British, Dutch, and French colonies in the West Indies.

The role of the United States as a wheat exporter rose substantially after the American Revolution. Euro-

TABLE 1

Per capita wheat consumption (1994–1996), in pounds per year

Kazakhstan	1,023
Bulgaria and Czech Republic	772
Turkey	705
Ukraine	683
France	666
Ireland/Canada	584/593
Israel	487
Australia/United Kingdom	439/443
Italy	403
Argentina/Chile	306
United States	276
China	207
South Korea	163
India	148
Japan	117
Mexico/Central America	112
World average	220

pean countries needed U.S. wheat due to crop failures in 1790 and 1807, and later in 1860–1862. Napoleonic wars and, later, World Wars I and II created record wheat demands.

Government trade practices and agreements. U.S. wheat exports experienced the largest decline in seventy years during the Great Depression and Dust Bowl era in the early twentieth century. Exports rebounded somewhat in the late 1930s until the rebuilding of Europe following World War II. As wheat production rose worldwide, wheat demand slackened.

The second half of the twentieth century saw enormous changes in world wheat production and the resulting wheat trade. Countries that were once centers in wheat production, self-sufficient for their wheat needs, became wheat importers. For example, west Asian countries, which were the cradle of wheat production (Afghanistan, Iran, Iraq, Saudi Arabia, Syria, Turkey, Yemen) and the earliest exporters of wheat to the Mediterranean and other early trade routes, imported 9.7 million tons of wheat in 1997. Countries such as India, not formerly known for wheat production, became notable wheat exporters. A new era began in the United States once wheat surpluses occurred. The U.S. government began to assume new importance in balancing the wheat trade.

All major wheat exporters employ a variety of trade-enhancement programs to maintain or increase their market share. Politics are an extremely important aspect of the functioning of these programs. Just one example is the grain embargo the United States placed on the Soviet Union in the 1970s. The United States watched its 49 percent market share of exports steadily fall to about 28 percent in 1998.

EXAMPLES OF U.S. TRADE ENHANCEMENT PROGRAMS

- 1938: The U.S. government price-support program, the Commodity Credit Corporation, was formed.
- 1949: The International Wheat Agreement specifies quantities of wheat that could be sold abroad at a fixed range of prices.
- 1954: Agricultural Trade Development and Assistance Act or Public Law 480 allowed the U.S. government to make agreements for wheat sales or barter.
- 1959: Public Law 480 was amended to include long-term agreements and credit extensions for sales of surplus farm products.
- 1990: Export Enhancement Program (EEP) created.

How Wheat Is Traded

Trade begins just after the wheat is loaded onto a grain truck or cart at harvest. Trade may even begin before the crop is grown if it is sold on futures or by contract. The following are the steps wheat takes in the market.

Field to elevator or bin storage. Wheat travels from the combine harvester in the field via truck or grain cart to storage bins on farm or a grain elevator (it may be a country cooperative elevator or a terminal elevator). Elevators are large storage facilities named for the moving belts used to move or "elevate" the grain. The elevator operator may purchase the grain or the farmer may store it for future sale. The wheat will be purchased according to its test weight, dockage, and grade.

Grain inspection. A seller would not want a buyer to refuse his or her grain due to a high level of moisture (14 percent maximum) or the presence of foreign material

TABLE 2

Top five wheat exporters

	Wheat production	2000 exports (in millions of tons)
United States	69 4	31.9
Canada	29	19.2
Australia	21.6	17.6
European Union	104.2	16.5
Argentina	12.3	12.5

SOURCE: U.S. Wheat Associates. www.uswheat.org.

TABLE 3

Top importers of wheat (1995–1997, in millions of tons):

China	9
Belarus	6.9
Brazil	6.8
Thailand	5.8
Indonesia	4.3
Mexico	1.5

SOURCE: May 2002, www.CIMMYT.org.

(FM). If either of these things occurs, the price paid will be "docked" and it will have to be cleaned prior to storage or sale. These factors also promote insect infestation, decay, and other problems in shipment or storage.

Government or private inspectors examine samples from each load of wheat to record the wheat class, protein, moisture, and percentage of FM in the sample. Inspectors also grade the wheat for quality.

Trade options: Cash for export or domestic use or futures contracts, government price supports. A variety of wheat sales methods exists in the world. In the United States, wheat is traded on the floor of a grain exchange, which is where U.S. grain buyers and sellers meet. The grain exchange does not buy or sell wheat; rather, grain exchange members represent either the buyers or individuals or companies that sell grain. Buyers include millers, brewers, feed manufacturers, and exporters. The largest grain exchanges are in Chicago, Minneapolis, and Kansas City. Wheat is then purchased on either a cash or a "futures" basis. Futures markets originated with the Dutch tulip bulb trade in the 1600s. In the United States futures trading developed in Chicago prior to the U. S. Civil War. Selling wheat on a futures basis provides the producer a guaranteed price for a contracted future grain delivery date.

In many countries, if the price a farmer receives is too low to cover the cost of production it may be subsidized through a government agreement. Some governments subsidize grain transportation. In the United States, the subsidization is called a "deficiency payment." An average cost of production is calculated and the difference between market price and the cost of production is the amount that the government will subsidize, within pre-set limits.

Transporting grain to the customer. After it is purchased, wheat will be moved out of or across the country to its destination via ship, train, or truck. Prior to delivery and upon arrival, the wheat is inspected for the specific tolerances of FM, moisture, and the class and grade listed in the contract. The wheat must be of a single class—no buyer will want wheat classes that have mingled.

Fair trade practices. International trade agreements are written by representatives from the trading nations involved. Representatives from trading countries negotiate trade practices through the General Agreement for Tariffs and Trade (GATT). The North American Free Trade Association (NAFTA) set guidelines for fair trade practices in that region. The European Union has laws and policies for fair trade. The agreements are meant to avoid the "dumping" of low-priced grain or price support practices that give one country an unfair advantage in the marketplace.

The Future of Wheat

Ongoing wheat research and technological developments continue throughout the world. New wheat foods emerge weekly. Nutrition research continues to support wheat's role as a food staple. Wheat components, such as fiber, starch, and gluten, are used in a wide variety of food products and pharmaceuticals. Wheat holds an important food-security role in a growing world population.

Ongoing wheat research includes many industrial applications in packaging, plastics, horticulture, and ethanol production, to name just a few. One of grain producers' highest research priorities is finding a way out of the world's reliance on petroleum.

See also **Bagel; Barley; Biscuit; Bread; Rice; Russia; United States.**

BIBLIOGRAPHY

Conrat, Maisie, and Richard Conrat. *The American Farm. A Photographic History.* Boston: Houghton Mifflin, 1977.

Davis, Sharon. *From Wheat to Flour.* Washington, D.C.: North American Millers' Association and Parker, Colo.: Wheat Foods Council, 1997.

Dondlinger, Peter Tracy. *The Book of Wheat. An Economic History and Practical Manual of the Wheat Industry.* New York: Orange Judd, 1908.

From Wheat to Flour. Chicago, Ill.: Wheat Flour Institute, 1956.

Horder, Lord, Sir Charles Dodds, and T. Moran. *Bread: The Chemistry and Nutrition of Flour and Bread, with an Introduction to Their History and Technology.* London: Constable, 1954.

Jacob, H. E. *Six Thousand Years of Bread: Its Holy and Unholy History.* Garden City, N.Y.: Doubleday, Doran, 1944.

Jaradat, A. A. *Triticeae III.* Enfield, N.H.: Science Publishers, 1998.

Koehnke, Marx. *Kernels and Chaff: A History of Wheat Market Development.* Lincoln, Neb.: Marx Koehnke, 1986.

Mangelsdorf, Paul C. "Wheat." *Scientific American* (July 1953): 2–11.

Molleson, Theya. "The Eloquent Bones of Abu Hureyra." *Scientific American* (August 1994): 70–75.

Murdock, Victor. *It May Chance of Wheat.* Kansas City, Mo.: Lowell Press, 1965.

Storck, John, Walter Dorwin Teague, and Harold Rydell. *Flour for Man's Bread. A History of Milling.* Minneapolis: University of Minnesota Press, 1952.

"The 320 Year-Old U.S. Wheat Trade." *Milling* 141, no. 24 (13 December 1963): 618.

Sharon Davis

WHEAT AS A FOOD

The development of civilization may be directly connected to the cultivation of wheat. When humans no longer needed to roam the land to find animals, wild berries, and grains, villages arose. People could grow wheat in the warm months, store it throughout the winter for food, and set some aside for planting the next spring. It is not certain when civilization and the cultivation of wheat began, but anthropologists speculate it may have started in the Fertile Crescent of western Asia around 6000–8000 B.C.E. or earlier. This area between the Tigris and Euphrates Rivers is home to modern-day Iraq.

History of Wheat as a Food

In about 17,000 B.C.E., human ancestors' consumption of wheat consisted of chewing the hard kernels for sustenance. Eventually, they doubtless soaked whole or cracked wheat in water until it softened and swelled, making a porridge of sorts or providing the basis for a mixed dish much like tabbouleh salads. Pastes made from flour and water or milk were most likely one of the first staples of the early human diet. In about 10,000 B.C.E., the earliest recipe for a type of flat bread was invented: "pound wheat into flour, add water and bake." Similar flat breads are still made in India (chapati), Mexico (tortillas), and in the Middle East (pita bread).

Einkorn, an ancient relative of wheat, was eventually domesticated and was popular until about 4000 B.C.E. There is evidence that more emmer (a wheat cousin) than wheat was grown at that time; emmer can still be raised in poor-quality soil in France, Italy, Turkey, and Yugoslavia. Einkorn and emmer were most likely eaten as a porridge before bread making was developed. After bread making became increasingly important, *Triticum vulgare*, another type of wheat, replaced einkorn and emmer. *Kamut*, which was found in King Tut's tomb and is thus nicknamed "King Tut's wheat," was also cultivated in the Fertile Crescent area. It is still grown in limited quantities in the United States and is a registered trademark. *Kamut* is an ancient Egyptian word meaning "wheat."

Egyptians are credited with having invented leavened bread. Archaeologists discovered what might be one of the oldest bakeries in the Giza Plateau of Egypt, dating back to around 4500 B.C.E. In his article "The Lost City of the Pyramids," Mark Lehner speculates that such bakeries might have served workers building the pyramids. Honey was eventually added to bread for sweetening, and other flavorings such as salt, herbs, and seeds were also

Wheat becomes food when it is milled; thus, mills have been a center for wheat processing since ancient times. In colonial America, the miller acted as banker, since wheat was also used instead of cash for transacting business. This shows the old millstone in the restored nineteenth-century Murray Mill in Catawba County, North Carolina. COURTESY OF THE CATAWBA COUNTY HISTORICAL ASSOCIATION.

added. A form of this traditional bread recipe is often used to make sourdough breads either by airborne yeast or by adding yogurt with live active cultures.

The Romans discovered leavened bread long after the Egyptians. During the Second Punic War (218–201 B.C.E.) wheat was imported to Italy, and in the first century B.C.E. public bakeries were common. Wealthy Romans ate bread made from very finely ground flour, while the common people and soldiers survived on very coarse flour that was usually blended with other grains and broad bean flour.

Religious Significance of Wheat

There are more than twenty references to bread in the Old Testament and over thirty in the New Testament. The first Biblical reference to wheat appears in Genesis 18: when three angels visit Abraham, he runs to his tent to ask his wife, Sarah, to make "cakes" of "fine meal." (Fine meal probably referred to wheat flour that had been finely ground between stones.) Grinding stones have been found throughout the Middle East, as have sieves made from horsehair. References to wheat and bread also appear in sacred texts of Judaism, Hinduism, and Islam.

The Jewish people celebrate the eight days of Passover with unleavened bread, in the form of matzoh, to commemorate the Exodus from Egypt when they took only unleavened dough in their haste to flee. The Haggadah (a Jewish prayer manual) instructs its followers to declare: "This is poor man's bread; the bread our forefathers ate when they were enslaved in Egypt." During the rest of the year, every Jew is required to eat three meals on Shabbos, or the Sabbath: one on the night when Shabbos begins and two the following day, each of which must contain bread over which a specific blessing called the *motzi* is made. The traditional bread used at Shabbos is challah, an egg-enriched braided loaf (Fohrman, personal correspondence).

The Roman Catholic and Protestant churches usually use unleavened bread and wafers for the sacrament of Holy Communion; however, some churches (such as the Greek Orthodox Church) use leavened bread. In Islam, although they are not required by the Qur'an, the bulgur wheat-based soups *Jary* and *Shorobat Il-Jereesh* are traditionally used to break the fast during the observation of Ramadan (Solley).

Worldwide Consumption of Wheat

Wheat is the most consumed grain in the world, with rice being a close second. China is the world's largest producer of wheat. Almost every country in the world has some form of wheat-based bread, soup, or mixed dish in its culture. Numerous products overlap various countries and cultures because of migration. The following is by no means a complete list of all wheat-based foods that are available, rather it is a list of only some of the more well-known wheat products.

Asia. *Chapati*, a tortilla look-alike, is common in northern India and is usually made from whole-wheat flour and cooked on a *tava*, which resembles a grill. *Naan* is also an Indian bread that can be found in the Middle East and surrounding countries. It is a very soft round bread that is often coated with flour.

Asian noodles are often made from wheat, although they can also be made from buckwheat and rice as well. They do not contain egg and can be broadly divided into Japanese and Chinese types. Japanese noodles use regular salt whereas Chinese noodles use alkaline salt. Pot stickers are a popular Japanese dish whose base is wheat flour. They are small envelopes containing minced meats and vegetables and are fried or steamed.

Europe. Bagels originally came from Austria in 1683. Folklore says a baker was grateful to the King of Poland for saving Austria from invading Turks. He reshaped a local bread into the shape of the king's stirrup and called it a *beugel*, derived from the German word for stirrup, *Bügel*. As bagels were brought to America, the word was changed to bagel.

Cookies came from the Dutch word *koekje*, meaning 'little cake'. The British adopted them in the nineteenth century and call them biscuits. Cookies eventually became a favorite in American diets.

English muffins are flat rounds of yeast-raised breads that are chewy with air pockets. One of its ancestors may have come from tenth-century Wales, called *bara maen*. English muffins are now popular throughout the Western world.

Gyro bread is a Greek pita bread that is wrapped around meats and vegetables to make the popular gyro sandwiches.

Pasta is an Italian word meaning paste, since it is made from durum wheat and water. The dough is then put through a variety of shaped sieves (there are over four hundred shapes worldwide) and cooked until dry. It can be served fairly plain with butter or olive oil or have any numbers of sauces piled on top. It can also be made into soups or casserole dishes such as lasagna. There is some controversy in regard to where pasta originated. Some have credited Marco Polo with bringing pasta back from China in 1255 C.E.; however, there is evidence that it was a staple in Italy before that time. Thomas Jefferson brought pasta to America, where it has also become a staple, in the late eighteenth century.

Pizza may have originally come from Italy, but it is no longer a strictly Italian product. Italian pizzas are much simpler than those found in the British Isles, Australia, New Zealand, and the United States. While traditional Italian pizza is not much more than a crust, tomato sauce, and sometimes cheese, the rest of the world heaps numerous meats, vegetables, and a variety of cheeses on their pizza crust.

Rye bread is a popular product in Northern and Eastern Europe. Rye crispbread is an essential part of Finnish army life and family diet even today. Soft, round, flat loaves with a hole in the middle, which in the old days were stored on horizontal poles under the ceiling in farmhouses, are made from rye through a fermentation process. The specialties of southwestern Finland and the archipelago are the soursweet loaf and malt bread. Island-baked bread is dark in color, and its northern counterpart may also have animal blood as an ingredient.

The Middle East. A variety of flat breads and bulgur soups are commonly eaten in the Middle Eastern countries. Bulgur (bulgar) is cracked, pre-cooked wheat that has about 5 percent of bran removed in processing. However, bulgur is still considered a whole grain product. It is the basis for tabbouleh salad and many stews and soups, and it can be eaten as a breakfast cereal. Bulgur can also be added to breads and muffins for extra texture and nutrition.

Fatayer are small bread-dough pies filled with meat, spinach, cheese, tomato, or onion. These are made especially for parties (Abourezk, p. 26). *Fettoush* was originally created to use up stale pita bread, but is now made from fresh, toasted pita bread. It is a salad of lettuce, tomatoes, peppers, radishes, onions, squares of pita bread, olive oil, lemon juice, and several spices (Abourezk, p. 59).

Lagymat is a sweet mixture of flour, oil, leavening, yogurt, spices, and water. The batter is fermented and then spoonful portions are deep-fried. The golden brown products are cooled and dipped into syrup, which is usually flavored with cardamom and saffron.

Pita bread is a yeast-leavened flat bread that contains an internal pocket formed when steam puffs the bread up and then collapses before baking. Pita is often used as a "scoop" for dips or for stuffing with vegetables and/or meats as a sandwich.

Tabbouleh is a popular salad in the Middle East that has found a home in the Western world. It contains cooked bulgur, tomatoes, parsley, onions, and spices. Tabbouleh is often made as a social group activity as it requires a lot of chopping.

Africa. Couscous is very common in northern Africa but is not usually eaten in the rest of the continent. Couscous is a small, round product made from the same ingredients as pasta: semolina and water. It is precooked and needs only soaking in hot water to be ready to eat. Its bland flavor is often enhanced with spices and vegetables. It can be eaten as a breakfast cereal. Couscous is also becoming quite popular in North American restaurants.

Kishk (*kashk*) is often eaten in northern Africa and in the Middle East. It is a dried mixture of ground wheat and a heavily fermented dairy product. It is added to a variety of meals for taste and flavor. Moroccan whole-wheat bread is yeast leavened and actually is part white flour and is made into a round, flat bread.

North America. Biscuits were originally made in Europe and were twice-cooked, hard cakes that were the staple of sailors and soldiers for centuries. They are now a popular staple throughout southern United States and are light and flaky because of the fat content and the air beaten into the dough.

Cakes are popular sweet desserts and are used in traditional celebrations of birthdays and anniversaries. There are two basic types of cakes: those with fat (butter cakes) and those without (foam cakes). Angel food cake is the most common foam cake, whereas there are numerous popular butter cakes: chocolate, carrot, layered, and even some that contain frozen ice cream.

Corn bread is a favorite in the southern United States and Mexico. It usually contains some wheat flour as well as the cornmeal for volume and texture. It is often cooked in a hot iron skillet or corn bread mold for a darker, crisper crust.

Fry bread is a Native American bread that is still eaten in various parts of the country. The yeast-leavened bread dough is cut into squares and fried in hot oil and served with butter and sometimes honey.

The Roman goddess, Ceres, who was deemed protector of the grain, gave grains their common name today—cereal.

*

The Chinese are more likely to steam or boil wheat foods rather than bake them. Steamed breads, pao, cakes, dumplings, and noodles are prepared in steamers or boilers rather than ovens.

*

Even though airborne yeast was used as the leavening agent for thousands of years, it was not until the 1800s that yeast was actually identified as the organism that provided the leavening.

*

A bushel of wheat weighs about 60 pounds (27 kg) and contains approximately one million individual kernels.

Pancakes are thin flat cakes made from a batter of water, flour, eggs, and leavening (usually baking powder or soda or a combination of the two). Pancakes are usually eaten for breakfast and sometimes called flapjacks, wheatcakes, or griddlecakes. Some form of pancakes can be found in most cultures.

Pies are a favorite dessert and come in all sizes and flavors. Fruit pies, such as apple, peach, and cherry are made in a pastry flour crust. They are usually eight inches in diameter and baked in a pie pan in the oven. Cream pies such as chocolate, coconut or banana are generally made in a flour crust or graham cracker crust.

Quick breads, such as zucchini, carrot, and banana breads, are sweet loaves that are leavened with baking powder and/or soda and appear to be native to the United States. Muffins are also considered a quick bread although they are made in individual muffin pans or paper cups for single servings.

Sourdough became a staple for the gold miners and other pioneers in the west and northern parts of North America. These individuals could carry a "starter" of yeast, flour, and water from camp to camp and then add water and warmth at the next campsite to make bread. From each batch they would save a starter for the next batch. This practice earned miners, sheepherders, and mountain dwellers the nickname "Sourdoughs."

Tortillas are probably the fastest growing wheat product in North America. The original unleavened flat bread was made from corn in Mexico and Central and South America. Wheat tortillas are now the largest category sold in the United States. The word tortilla comes from the Spanish word *torta*, which means 'round cake'.

White pan bread, hamburger, and hot dog buns are the major wheat products sold in North America. One hundred percent whole-wheat products consist of less than five percent of sales, but sales of whole wheat and partial whole grain products are growing faster than white breads.

Australia and New Zealand. In this part of the world, wheat flour is used in the production of many Western products in addition to their unique meat pies and sausage rolls. Meat pies are usually about three to four inches in diameter, may be square or round, and consist of a pastry base and cover that encloses a filling of cooked minced meat (often beef) and gravy. Sausage rolls are usually about four inches long and about one-and-a-half inches wide and consist of seasoned sausage filling that is rolled in flaky pastry and then baked.

South America. *Alfajores* are desserts popular in Peru and Chili. They are made from wheat flour and vegetable shortening and baked. When served, they are layered with *manjar blanco* and topped with confectioner's sugar. *Manjar blanco* is condensed milk that is slowly cooked until it thickens and becomes brown.

Empanadas are baked or fried and filled with a variety of meats, cheeses and vegetables. Empanada literally means 'wrapped in bread', although it is often a pastry dough rather than a bread dough.

The South American *paneton* is similar to the Italian Christmas cake. It is a wheat bread containing pieces of citron and sugar-glazed on top. In Peru, it is eaten on Christmas Eve with hot chocolate beverages.

Classes of Wheat

A variety of wheat classes are grown throughout the world, but six major varieties are grown in the United States. They are:

Hard red winter wheat—This is primarily grown in the "bread basket," the Midwestern states of Kansas, Nebraska, Oklahoma, Texas, Colorado, and Wyoming. South Dakota and Minnesota also raise some hard red winter wheat. It is primarily used for breads and all-purpose flour.

Hard red spring wheat—This type of wheat is grown mostly in the upper, colder states such as North Dakota, Minnesota, and Montana. It is primarily used for breads and croissants.

Durum wheat—Durum wheat is grown primarily in North Dakota, with additional supplies coming from Montana, South Dakota, and Minnesota. Arizona and California grow a desert durum variety. Durum is used primarily for pasta.

Hard white wheat—This is the newest class of wheat grown in the United States. It is raised to some extent in all of the major wheat states and is used for breads and Oriental noodles.

Soft white wheat—This wheat is grown primarily in the northwest states of Washington, Idaho, and Oregon. This wheat is used for pastries, crackers, cereal, cakes, cookies, and Oriental noodles.

Soft red wheat—Soft red wheat is grown in eastern parts of the United States, it is used in cakes, cookies, and crackers.

Kinds of Wheat Flours

Commercial bakers require several types of flours to be milled to specification for use in the end products they will produce. Home bakers are most likely to use all-purpose, cake, bread, and whole-wheat flour. Serious bakers will even use pastry and semolina in their baking.

All-purpose flour—This is the finely ground endosperm of the wheat kernel and is often a blend of hard and soft wheat that produces a flour suitable for many types of products. All-purpose flour is usually bleached, which does not affect the nutritional value, but it does improve the baking qualities for cakes and cookies.

Bread flour—This flour comes from hard wheat, because of its strong gluten strength that will hold the framework of a loaf of bread. Bread flour is usually unbleached.

Cake flour—Cake flour is the finely ground endosperm of soft white and soft red wheat. It is usually bleached and is used for cakes, cookies, crackers, quick breads, and some pastries. It has a lower gluten content, which makes the products more tender.

Durum flour—The finely ground endosperm of durum wheat, durum flour is usually found in specialty sections of supermarkets or health food stores. It is used primarily for making noodles.

Gluten flour—Gluten flour is milled from hard wheat and is a high-protein (gluten) flour. It contains about 45 percent protein, whereas bread flour is usually about 12–14 percent protein. Gluten flour is added in small amounts, one tablespoon per one pound loaf, when making bread at home. Commercial bakeries use it to strengthen their bread flour if necessary.

Pastry flour—This type of flour is not as common for the home baker as it is for the wholesale baker. It also is made from soft wheat to make a tender, fluffy pastry crust.

Self-rising flour—Self-rising flour originated in the southern part of the United States and is the oldest "mix" found in America. It is an all-purpose flour with appropriate amounts of leavening and salt added to make quick breads. A cup contains one-and-a-half teaspoons of baking powder and a half-teaspoon of salt.

Semolina—Semolina is a coarsely ground endosperm of the highest quality durum wheat and is used for making pasta, although it can be used for making bread because of its high gluten quality.

Whole-wheat flour—Whole-wheat flour is also called graham flour and stone-ground flour. Whole-wheat flour is ground from the entire kernel containing the bran, germ, and endosperm.

Nutritional Value of Wheat

Wheat is the most consumed grain in the world, providing both calories and nutrients for the growing population. Wheat is a significant source of complex carbohydrates, dietary fiber, plant protein, phytochemicals, antioxidants, vitamins, and minerals. On a per-capita basis in 1995, Germans consumed 187 pounds of bread, while U.S. citizens ate only 53 pounds each. Many countries consume a considerable amount of wheat each year. The United States eats about 150 pounds of wheat flour per person annually, whereas Chile consumes 214 pounds; Pakistan consumes 334 pounds; the European Union averages 160 pounds; the East Africa region eats about 250 pounds; and China consumes an average of 221 pounds per person annually.

Whole-wheat products such as cereals, breads, pastas, tortillas, English muffins, and other products are extremely healthy. The American Dietetic Association recommends consuming three servings a day of whole-grain product foods (wheat, barley, oats, corn, rye, etc.).

In July 2000, the following whole-grain health claim was approved by the U.S. Food and Drug Administration (FDA) Center for Food Safety and Applied Nutrition: "Diets rich in whole grain foods and other plant foods low in fat, saturated fat and cholesterol may reduce the risk of heart disease and certain cancers." In addition to helping to prevent heart disease and some cancers, preliminary research shows that whole grains might also help prevent the onset of type II diabetes.

In some countries throughout the world, refined grains are offered to the consumer without any nutrient enrichment. This is a disservice to the public since the product, in that state, has fewer nutrients to offer. In some countries, however, vitamin A is added to help prevent blindness in children. In several Western countries, three B vitamins—thiamine, riboflavin, and niacin—and iron are added in the same amounts found in whole-wheat flour. In 1998, the United States required that enriched grains also be fortified with folic acid, a B vitamin that (among other benefits) may reduce the chances of certain birth defects. Between 1998 and 2001, after the mandatory fortification of wheat was put into effect, neural tube birth defects dropped 19 percent in the United States (Honein et al.). Preliminary studies have also shown that folic acid is effective in reducing homocysteine levels in the blood. High levels of homocysteine are believed to contribute to heart disease, strokes, and Alzheimer's disease. Although more research must be done, there is positive indication that folic acid may also be effective in helping to prevent cleft lip and palate, Down's syndrome, and several cancers.

Enriched flours are often bleached for two reasons: to lighten the flour and to improve baking qualities. Bleaching oxidizes the gluten slightly and therefore makes cakes and pastries more tender. Breads, on the other hand, need strong gluten, so bread flour and gluten flour are rarely, if ever, bleached. When flour is bleached, it is exposed to chlorine gas and benzoyl peroxide. No residues of these substances are left in the flour, however, so there is no nutritional difference between unbleached and bleached flour.

A small percentage of people cannot tolerate the gluten (protein) in wheat because they lack the enzymes to digest it. This disease is known as non-tropical celiac sprue, and those who have it cannot eat wheat, rye, or barley. Some experts recommend they eliminate oats also; however, the latest thinking is that oats may be safe.

Biotechnology and Wheat

As of the start of the twenty-first century, no genetically engineered wheat was available on the market, but such products were in development. The first genetically engineered wheat would primarily benefit the farmer and the consumer by using fewer pesticides during the growing period.

See also **Bagel; Bread; Noodle in Asia; Noodle in Northern Europe; Pasta; Pastry.**

BIBLIOGRAPHY

Abourezk, Sanaa. *Secrets of Healthy Middle Eastern Cuisine.* New York: Interlink Publishing Group, 2000.

Davis, Sharon P. *From Wheat to Flour.* Parker, Colo.: Wheat Foods Council/North American Millers' Association, 1996.

Fohrman, Rabbi David. "Wine, Matzah and Tchaikovsky." 2002. Available online at http://www.torah.org/features/holydays.

Global Gourmet Finland. *Bread: A Firm Favorite.* 2002. Available at www.globalgourmet.com/destinations/finland/fin-bread.html.

Honein, M. A., L. J. Paulozzi, T. J. Matthews, J. D. Erickson, and L. C. Wong. "Impact of Folic Acid Fortification of the U.S. Food Supply on the Occurrence of Neural Tube Defects." *Journal of the American Medical Association* 285, no. 23 (20 June 2001): 2981–2986.

Jacob, H. E. Six *Thousand Years of Bread: Its Holy and Unholy History.* New York: Doubleday, 1944.

"Kiddush and the Shabbos Meals." 2002. Available online at http://www.torah.org/learning/halacha. 2002.

Lehner, Mark. "The Lost City of the Pyramids." Available online at http://www.egyptontheweb.com/omar_sherif/pyramids.html.

Roberts, David. "Rediscovering Egypt's Bread Baking Technology." *National Geographic* (1995): 32–35.

Solley, Pat. "Soup of the Evening." 1997. Available online at http://www.s2f.com/psolley.

Judi Adams

WHISKEY (WHISKY). The spelling "whiskey" is common for Irish whiskeys and the vast majority of U.S. whiskeys. The spelling "whisky" is sometimes used for Scotch, Canadian, and other whiskeys and occasionally for some U.S. whiskeys. The word "whisky"/"whiskey" is derived from the Irish and Scottish Gaelic *usquebaugh* or *uisge beatha*, meaning 'water of life' (compare the French *eau-de-vie*). Whiskey is of course a high-alcohol beverage ("spirit") produced by the distillation of grain-based lower-alcohol fermentations.

Origins and Social History

The art of distillation of various fermented brews, most often wine-based, dates back to ancient civilizations, including Chinese, Indian, and Egyptian. Much of the European Middle Ages saw distilled alcohol used medicinally, but undoubtedly a proportion of early distillations was consumed as a warming, mood-uplifting drink. It is likely that whiskey-type distillation originated in Ireland, possibly as early as 500 to 800 B.C.E. and mainly within monastic communities. Irish Gaels emigrated to western Scotland and beyond, and it is likely they took their craft with them. Distilling the brews of grains, usually from their own land, was largely a home-based craft among Highland clans for personal consumption. What is referred to as Scotch whisky was first specifically listed in print around 1500.

Home distilling for personal consumption remained legal until 1784, but long before then whisky was sold or traded illicitly. However, greater problems developed with the introduction of taxes on spirits. Following the "union of the Crowns" in 1603 (King James VI of Scotland inherited the English throne as King James I of England and Scotland), whisky distilled in Scotland became more popular in England. However, England and Scotland maintained separate Parliaments with individual legal systems and laws. The "republican" English government (the Commonwealth years of Oliver Cromwell) imposed the first tax on spirits in 1643. Under duress, the Scottish Parliament followed suit the following year and levied an additional high duty in 1693. The British monarch Charles II also attempted to tax Irish whiskey in 1661 but with little success.

The Act of Union (the union of the Scottish and English Parliaments to become the British government in London) in 1707 brought more serious problems for Scottish (and, to a lesser extent Irish) whisky in the eighteenth century. More duties were levied, but the vast majority of distillers avoided paying taxes. The numerous excisemen found collection difficult as most distilling was still small scale, often in remote Highland glens, and illegal stills were easy to dismantle and relocate. Smuggling, often undertaken during darkness, was widespread. Even when illicit distillers were brought to court, magistrates were often sympathetic and lenient, imposing low fines.

A selection of American whiskies distilled in or near Bardstown, Kentucky. PHOTO BY PHILIP GOULD, 1991. © PHILIP GOULD/CORBIS.

Robert Burns, Scotland's national bard worked as an exciseman for some eight years before his death in 1796. He was a devotee of whisky and its warm, merry, and creative effects. He wrote several poems and songs in praise of whisky, such as "The Deil's Awa' Wi' th' Exciseman" (The devil's away with the exciseman). A few choice lines give the flavor (English equivalents of Scots words are in parentheses).

> We'll mak [make] our maut [malt], and we'll brew our drink,
>> We'll laugh, sing, and rejoice, man, . . .
>> . . . There's threesome reels, there's foursome reels,
>> There's hornpipes and strathspeys [dances] man,
>> But the ae [one] best dance e'er [ever] cam [came] to the land
>> Was the deil's awa' wi' th' Exciseman.

By 1823 new legislation completely altered the development of Scotch whisky distilling. The change from heavy taxation, calculated by volume, to a reasonable license fee encouraged larger distilleries in more permanent locations.

A somewhat similar history applies to American whiskey. Following the English Pilgrims, further immigrants included Scots and Irish, who spread westward to farm. As their yields of grains increased, many settlers made their own whiskey from barley, rye, and upon further expansion west, corn. British taxes were introduced as early as 1684, with little success in collection. In 1791 Pennsylvania passed a law requiring registra-tion of all distilling equipment. A few years later an outright rebellion erupted in Pennsylvania, including destruction of property and capture of excisemen, that was only quelled by the militia. As in Scotland, larger commercial distilleries, including those in Pennsylvania, Tennessee, and Kentucky, began to take over during the nineteenth century.

Raw Materials and Basic Processes

Scotch whisky can be divided into two basic types, malt whisky and blended whisky. The former, original type uses barley exclusively, whereas blended whisky combines malt whisky with spirits from other cereals.

Malt whisky. The harvested and dried barley is first "malted," that is, the grain is allowed to germinate to a certain point. This is achieved by soaking in water for a controlled period (two to three days), draining the water, and airing and turning the germinating grains at a controlled temperature (around 60°F). The last process usually involves large revolving drums. The grains are soft, and germination is stopped. During germination, enzymes convert insoluble starch to soluble. This "green malt" is dried, which in most cases includes various periods of peat-fire smoke (peat originates from the decomposition of vegetable matter). The dried malt is coarsely ground, and hot water is added. This process of "mashing" converts soluble starch to the sugar maltose. The liquid is drawn off, cooled to around 70°F, and run into fermentation vessels along with yeast, mainly from brewers but often including cultures of selected strains.

Distilling *poteen* (illegal whiskey). The home distiller is shown here straining the mash. Photo by Michael St. Maur Sheil, taken at an undisclosed location in the Republic of Ireland, 1996. © MICHAEL ST. MAUR SHEIL/CORBIS

Fermentation is vigorous and rapid, usually thirty-six to forty-eight hours, with the yeast converting sugars to alcohol (7 to 8 percent).

This liquid is then distilled in pear-shaped copper ("pot") stills, first in large stills to produce crude "low wines" with around 30 percent alcohol. This is redistilled in smaller stills with precise care to minimize impurities (such as alcohols higher than ethanol), producing pure but immature spirits of around 70 percent alcohol. A few Scotch and most Irish spirits are distilled a third time, finishing as lighter whiskeys.

These "rough" spirits require maturation and are transferred to oak barrels, often with water added to reduce the alcohol content to around 63 percent. Various types of oak barrels, such as bourbon, sherry, and Madiera casks, contribute color and flavor from the wood. Although by law the minimum storage is three years, five years is more common (mainly for blending), and most superior malts are matured ten to fifteen years or longer.

Blended whisky. This type added enormously to the amount of Scotch produced in the nineteenth century with the design of a much larger still. The blends are a mixture of a wide variety of malt whiskies with "grain whisky," which is distilled from a range of grains, including corn, rye, wheat, and barley, mainly unmalted. The large stills used are modified versions of the Coffey stills (patented in 1830), which distill continuously and produce a purer 90 percent alcohol. Blending the many types of malt whiskies is a skilled occupation, accomplished by an experienced nose. Generally lighter- to fuller-flavored blends are related to the increasing proportion of malt whiskies used.

Twentieth-Century Developments

Apart from new varieties of barley and other cereals, centralized and mechanical maltings, and novel designs of Coffey stills, whiskey production is essentially traditional. In the twentieth century prohibition in the United States provided opportunities for increased production of Scotch, Irish, and Canadian whiskeys. Whiskey production has spread to many countries, especially Japan, which already had a traditional base and which offers brands that are prized among the world's elite. Larger companies and mergers have also resulted in conglomerates. Surprisingly, given the long tradition, production and marketing of single malt Scotch whiskies increased strongly only since the 1960s. Quite a number of malt whisky distilleries in Scotland are owned by U.S., Canadian, and Japanese companies, for example, Jim Beam, Seagrams, and Suntory respectively.

See also **Alcohol; Barley; Cereal Grains and Pseudo-Cereals; Fermentation; Spirits**.

BIBLIOGRAPHY

Arthur, Helen. *Whisky: Uisge Beatha, the Water of Life*. London: Apple Press, 2000.

Brown, Gordon. *Classic Spirits of the World: A Comprehensive Guide*. London: Prion Books, 1995.

Daiches, David, and Alan Daiches. *Scotch Whisky: Its Past and Present*. 3rd ed. London: Deutsch, 1978.

Jackson, Michael. *Scotland and its Whiskies*. London: Duncan Baird, 2001.

Murray, James. *Classic Bourbon, Tennessee and Rye Whiskey*. London: Prion Books, 1998.

Wisniewski, Ian. *Classic Malt Whisky*. London: Prion Books, 2001.

John Johnston

WIC (WOMEN, INFANTS, AND CHILDREN'S) PROGRAM.

The Special Supplemental Nutrition Program for Women, Infants, and Children, commonly referred to as WIC, is a Federally funded nutrition-intervention program administered by the Food and Nutrition Service of the U.S. Department of Agriculture. WIC began as a two-year pilot program in 1972 under an amendment to the Child Nutrition Act of 1966, and was made permanent in 1974. Its mission is to provide supplemental food, nutrition education, and health-care referrals to low-income pregnant or postpartum women, their infants, and children up to the age of five, to improve their health outcomes.

WIC is available in all fifty states, the District of Columbia, thirty-two Indian Tribal Organizations, Puerto Rico, the Virgin Islands, American Samoa, and Guam. WIC is the third-largest national food assistance program, following the Food Stamp and National School Lunch programs, and accounts for 12 percent of total Federal expenditures in this area. In fiscal year 2001, WIC served an average of 7.3 million participants per month, 75 percent of whom were infants and children; annual expenditures exceeded $4 billion (see Table 1). WIC does not guarantee participation for all eligible women, infants, and children who apply, and the number of people the program serves is determined by annual levels of Federal funding. In recent years, WIC has been fully funded, and all eligible persons have been able to participate.

To qualify for WIC, applicants must first meet income guidelines and a state residency requirement, and they must be at nutritional risk as determined by a doctor, nurse, or nutritionist. Guidelines state that the gross income of the applicant must fall at or below 185 percent of the Federal poverty-guideline figure, although each state can reduce income-limit standards. Participants in other benefit programs such as the Food Stamp Program, Medicaid, or Temporary Assistance for Needy Families automatically meet income requirements. To be at nutritional risk for WIC, one must have either a medically based risk such as underweight, anemia, or previous poor pregnancy outcomes, or a diet-based risk such as a dietary pattern deemed inadequate compared with U.S. Dietary Guidelines.

Participants in WIC receive benefits in the form of checks, vouchers, or electronic benefits transfer (EBT) cards that are redeemable monthly at certain retail food stores. In 2001, average monthly benefits per person were about $34. Participants may use these benefits to purchase specific foods designated as important to supplementing the diet of this population. Only nutrient-dense foods that are high in one or more of particular nutrients—protein, calcium, iron, and vitamins A and C—are included, although the food package is not intended to fulfill all of the nutrient needs of the participants. Examples of foods available using WIC include iron-fortified infant formula, iron-fortified infant and adult cereals, fruit or vegetable juice rich in vitamin C, eggs, milk, cheese, peanut butter, dried beans or peas, tuna fish, and carrots. Foods are substituted where there are medically necessary dietary modifications. Participants also receive nutrition education and necessary referrals to health-care services.

WIC is one of the most cost-effective and successful nutrition-assistance programs in U.S. history. Several studies have concluded that, for every $1 spent on pregnant women under WIC, between $1.77 and $3.13 in Medicaid costs were saved over the first sixty days after childbirth. Research consistently shows that WIC participation results in improved birth outcomes and savings in health-care costs, improved diet and diet-related outcomes, improved infant-feeding practices, increased immunization rates, and improved cognitive development for children.

WIC Program Participation and Costs

Fiscal Year	Total Participation (Thousands)	PROGRAM COSTS (Millions of Dollars)			Average Monthly Benefit Per Person (Dollars)
		Food	NSA	Total	
1974	88	8.2	2.2	10.4	15.68
1975	344	76.7	12.6	89.3	18.58
1980	1,914	584.1	140.5	727.7	25.43
1985	3,138	1,193.2	294.4	1,489.3	31.69
1990	4,517	1,636.9	478.7	2,122.2	30.20
1995	6,894	2,516.6	904.9	3,441.4	30.41
2000	7,192	2,852.2	1,102.6	3,971.1	33.05
2001 (P)	7,306	3,007.8	1,114.3	4,153.0	34.31

NSA = Nutrition Services and Administrative costs. Nutrition Services includes nutrition education, preventative and coordination services (such as health care), and promotion of breastfeeding and immunization. In addition to food and NSA costs, Total (under Program Costs) includes funds for program evaluation, Farmers' Market Nutrition Program (FY 1989 onward), special projects, and infrastructure.

SOURCE: Data as of 25 April 2002. Fiscal year (FY) 2001 data are preliminary; all data are subject to revision.

See also **Class, Social; Food Pantries; Food Stamps; Government Agencies, U.S.; Poverty; School Meals; Soup Kitchens.**

BIBLIOGRAPHY

United States Department of Agriculture, Economic Research Service. *Food Assistance Landscape.* Available at http://www.ers.usda.gov/

United States Department of Agriculture, Food and Nutrition Service. *Women, Infants, and Children.* Available at www.fns.usda.gov/wic

United States Department of Agriculture and United States Department of Health and Human Services. *Nutrition and Your Health: Dietary Guidelines for Americans.* Home and Garden Bulletin No. 232. Washington, D.C.: U.S. Government Printing Office, 2000.

United States General Accounting Office. *Early Intervention: Federal Investments Like WIC Can Produce Savings.* Document HRD92-18. Washington, D.C.: U.S. Government Printing Office, April 1992.

Jamillah Hoy Rosas
L. Beth Dixon

WINE.

This entry includes five subentries:
Overview
Wine in the Ancient World
Wine from Classical Times to the
    Nineteenth Century
Wine in the Modern World
Wine, Nongrape

OVERVIEW

Wine is an alcoholic beverage made by fermenting grape juice. Although the juice of other fruit, berries, and vegetables can be fermented to create alcohol, fruit wines are generally qualified by the name of the produce used, such as gooseberry wine and blueberry wine. The word "wine" when used alone refers to an alcoholic beverage made from grapes. Wines come in various colors (red, white, rosé) and many types, which include dry and sweet, still and sparkling, and wines fortified with grape spirit (brandy). There are also many wine-based drinks, such as wine coolers and sangria.

Grape Varieties

Although wine can be made from any kind of grape, not all grape varieties are suitable for making good quality wine—wine with acceptable taste and capable of lasting in good condition for several years. Most of the world's wine is made from one species, *Vitis vinifera* (meaning "a wine-bearing vine"), which is native to Europe and the Middle East. Most of the grapes used for making commercial wine are members of this species, and they include such common varieties as Chardonnay, Riesling, Sauvignon Blanc, Merlot, Pinot Noir and Cabernet Sauvignon, and Syrah/Shiraz.

Other grapes also used for making wine include varieties such as Concord, Alexander, and Catawba, which are members of the *Vitis labrusca* species that is indigenous to North America. Additional varieties have been created by breeding two varieties of the same species (called crosses) and by breeding two varieties of different species (called hybrids). Thus the Dornfelder variety was bred from two *Vitis vinifera* varieties and is a cross, while Baco Noir, bred from a variety of *Vitis vinifera* and a *Vitis riparia*, is a hybrid.

The many reasons for breeding new varieties include creating grapes with particular flavor profiles, grapes that ripen early (important in regions with short growing seasons), or vines that are tolerant of colder climates. In addition to crosses and hybrids, vines generate clonal variations spontaneously, with each clone having slightly different growing, taste, or other characteristics.

Many hundreds of grape varieties can successfully be used for making wine, and the list seems even longer because some varieties can have different names in different places. For example, the grape known as Syrah in France is called Shiraz in Australia, while the Malbec variety has many alternative names, including Cot, Pressac, and Auxerrois. Some variations in name simply reflect language (Pinot Gris is known in Italy as Pinot Grigio) while others reflect the origins of the grape (Burgundy's Pinot Noir is known in Germany as Spätburgunder).

It is likely that wine was originally made (in the Neolithic period, 7,000 years ago) from wild grapes, and that when farmers began to cultivate vines for wine, they selected grapes that seemed particularly suitable. The selected grapes would have had a high ratio of pulp to seeds and might have given better flavors than other grapes.

Characteristics of the Grape

Grapes contain or bear everything that is needed to produce wine; each grape is effectively a microwinery. The most important parts of the grape are the pulp, which contains water, sugar, fruit acids, and pectin, and the skin, which contains color pigments, flavors, and tannins. The skin also carries wild yeasts that occur naturally in the vineyard. The other parts of the grape, which are less often important for winemaking, are the stem (which contains tannins) and the seeds or pips (which contain tannins and bitter oils).

Tannins are compounds that occur naturally in grapes and other products and that give a drying feel when they come into contact with the mouth. Swishing cold, strong black tea, which is high in tannins, will make the mouth and gums feel as if they are contracting with dryness. Tannins are preserving agents (used to tan skin and turn it into leather), and in wine they are a natural preservative that allows a wine to age without degrading. Young wines meant for long-term cellaring can be high in tannins and, over time, the feel of tannins softens.

Although the winemaking process is very important, such that the same grapes made into wine by two different winemakers can taste significantly different, the grape variety is the single most important factor. Like other fruit, varieties of grapes differ from one another in a many ways. Some have thick skins and some have thin, which can be important for their relative ability to withstand disease and for the degree of flavor and tannins they have. Some varieties develop a higher ratio of acid to sugar (just as more acidic Granny Smith apples differ from the sweeter Red Delicious variety). Some grapes (such as Cabernet Sauvignon) naturally have more tannins than others (such as Gamay). The sum of each grape variety's characteristics is the primary influence on the character and flavor of the finished wine it makes.

Environment

A second set of influences on wine is the environment in which the grapes grow: especially the soil and climate. The total environment is sometimes referred to as the *terroir*, a term that includes the composition of the soil (topsoil, bedrock) and its nutrient, drainage and heat-retention properties; climate (annual temperature, hours of sunshine, precipitation, frosts, winds); geographical features (such as forests, mountains, rivers, bodies of water) that influence climatic patterns; the slope of the vineyards (on steep or gentle slopes or on plains); and aspect (angle to the sun, direction of slope).

Slope can be important because the most interesting and complex grapes seem to grow on vines that are stressed, which is to say that they must struggle for water and nutrients. The best soils for vineyards are not the rich, fertile humus suitable for other produce, but often hard, stony or sandy soils that are well drained (which is why slopes are often ideal). Vines can also be stressed by planting them closer together so that each has to compete with others.

Terroir has become an article of faith for many producers, who argue that the flavors and other qualities of a wine express the *terroir* in which the grapes were grown. Some producers (particularly in regions like Burgundy) insist that wines made from vines grown a few feet apart taste distinctly different. Some ardent advocates of *terroir* include in it not only the physical and environmental character of a specific site, but also the tradition of vine growing and the soul of centuries of winemakers.

Viticulture

Cultivation practices (viticulture) are also very important in that they can modify the environment. Density of plantings and types of trellising can have an impact on the exposure of vines to nutrients and sunshine. Canopy management, the removal of some foliage, can increase the ripening potential of grapes. Irrigation (which is not universally permitted) can make up for shortages in natural water supply, while excess water can be dealt with by burying drainage tiles to increase the flow of water away from vine roots. Some viticulturalists even modify the soil by digging in rocks (which absorb heat during

Wine is not only a beverage but is also used as an ingredient in cookery. This nineteenth-century American cake tin was used for making Madeira cake, a popular food for teas and fancy suppers. ROUGHWOOD COLLECTION. PHOTO CHEW & COMPANY.

the day and radiate it at night) and spreading dark soil, which attracts more heat than lighter-colored soils.

Yield

An important influence on grape character is yield, which is often expressed as the number of tons of grapes harvested per acre of vines or the number of hectoliters (one hectoliter is 100 liters) of wine per hectare (about 2.4 acres) of vines. In general terms, the lower the yield, the more flavorful and complex the wines. Yields are often reduced by "green harvesting," which involves picking (and throwing away) a proportion of the bunches of grapes on each vine before they begin to ripen. This allows the smaller number of bunches remaining to benefit from all the nutrients the vine absorbs. Some national and regional wine laws (see below) set maximum yields on vines.

The same principle underlies the value attributed to "old vines," a quality that is sometimes shown on labels. As vines age, they begin to bear fewer bunches so that, without human intervention (like green harvesting), their fruit tends to be of higher quality. There is, however, no regulated definition of what constitutes an old vine, and, depending on varietal and producer, it can mean a vine from fifteen to eighty and more years old.

Pests and Diseases

Finally, viticulturalists have to decide on what methods to use to deal with vineyard pests and diseases. Pesticides and other chemicals (notably sulfur) are widely used to control insect infestation and vine diseases but, for environmental and financial reasons, their use is declining in many regions. Some producers have adopted organic practices and, depending on wine or agricultural law, can label their wines organic.

Climate

Clearly *terroir* and cultivation practices interact with grape variety in that some varieties do best in specific climatic and other growing conditions. Riesling, for example, does best in cool climates that preserve the acidity so highly valued in Riesling wines, even if the alcohol level is often below 12 percent. Zinfandel, on the other hand, thrives in warm regions where it produces wines high in alcohol (often 14 percent and higher) with rich, ripe fruit flavors and relatively low acidity.

All these characteristics have an important bearing on the quality of the grapes grown in any specific region. In general terms, warmer regions (like South Africa and many regions in California) produce riper grapes with higher sugar content that have the potential of producing deep-colored, high-alcohol wines (13% and higher). Cool climate regions with shorter growing seasons (like Germany and northern France) tend to produce paler, more acidic wines that are lower in alcohol (12.5% and less). Vines on south-facing slopes in the Northern Hemisphere benefit from more sun, but there are some places (in Greece, for example) where vines are grown on north-facing slopes so as to moderate the effect of the sun's heat.

Terroir is not constant. Although soil characteristics change very slowly over time (unless there is human intervention), climate experiences annual variations that range from modest to dramatic. One summer in a given region might be dry and hot, the next cool and wet. There might be a late frost, a summer hailstorm, and an early winter or Indian summer. These variations can affect and make diseases of the vines more or less likely. Hot, humid conditions can lead to molds and mildews. Weather conditions can lead to lower or higher yields and can affect the ability of grapes to ripen and develop the desired levels and balance of sugars, acids, tannins, and other properties.

Annual weather variation is the reason that so much attention is paid to vintage. The vintage of a wine is the year the grapes were harvested, and knowledge of the weather conditions in a region in a given year will reveal much about the potential quality of the wine made in that region that year. Some years stand out for the quality of the wine produced, whether it is good or bad. For example, 1997 is considered to be an excellent year for Tuscan wines (including Chianti) but a poor year for most of the districts in Bordeaux. But weather conditions that might be negative for one grape variety can be less so for another. So in a region like Bordeaux, where three principal red grape varieties are grown, and where the red wine is a blend of up to five different varieties, producers can consider the quality of each variety when deciding on the blend.

Harvesting

Decisions about vine variety, vineyard location, and cultivation practices are made so as to maximize the quality of the fruit at the point that it is judged optimal for harvesting. Harvesting itself involves myriad decisions. Grapes can be harvested by hand or by machine, by bunch or by individual berry. Some vineyards are entirely harvested in one go, while others are harvested in several runs (*tris*) over a period of days, with only the ripest bunches or grapes being picked each time. Most harvesting is done during the day, but some producers practice night harvesting, when the cooler temperatures allow grapes to be picked and transported to the winery in temperatures that help preserve their freshness.

It is a cliché among winemakers that "wine is made in the vineyard." This means that good quality wine can be made from only good quality fruit, and that what goes on in the vineyard is more important to wine quality than what happens in the winery. Yet just as the quality of the grapes results from scores of decisions related to grape variety, vineyard site, and cultivation practices, so the winemaker makes scores of decisions that affect the quality and character of the finished wine. It takes an able winemaker to make high-quality wine from even the best quality grapes.

Fermentation

Wine is made by crushing the grapes so that the yeasts on the skin (or cultured yeasts introduced by the winemaker) come into contact with the sugars in the pulp. This initiates fermentation, the process by which the yeasts consume the sugar and produce alcohol and carbon dioxide. Fermentation is the central part of winemaking but it is preceded and followed by several other stages, and the methods of carrying them out influence the taste and character of the finished wine.

The grapes are first crushed or pressed so as to extract the juice. Old methods of treading grapes by foot or pressing them in manually operated screw presses have virtually disappeared, and most commercial wines are made from grapes crushed in mechanical presses. Many producers prefer pneumatic bladder presses, which crush the grapes gently and do not release the bitter oils in the pips.

If white wine is being made from black or other dark-skinned grapes (nearly all of which have pale-colored pulp), the must (unfermented grape juice) is quickly drawn off the skins and other solids so that the color pigments they contain do not dye it. For red wine (which can be made only from dark-colored grapes), the must is left in contact with the skins so as to draw color from them. Winemakers who want to make very dark wines (which are increasingly popular) sometimes use enzymes to extract all possible color from the skins so as to dye the juice deep red.

Naturally occurring yeasts can be used for fermentation, but because they tend to be unpredictable (in terms of when they start fermentation and the speed of fermentation), many producers use more reliable and predictable cultured yeasts. Length of fermentation can affect the flavor of wine, as can the temperature. Fermentation is a naturally hot process, and some wines are "cool fermented," meaning that the fermentation tanks or barrels are artificially cooled during fermentation. Cool fermentation tends to preserve the fresh, fruity flavors in wine.

Most fermentation takes place in stainless steel vats, but some wines are fermented in oak barrels. This adds additional flavor to the wine although it does not, as many people expect, make the finished wine taste "oakier" than wines that are simply aged in oak barrels. Whether in vat or barrel, the carbon dioxide produced during fermentation is allowed to dissipate into the air.

Fermentation is generally complete when the yeasts have consumed all the sugar, resulting in a wine that is "dry" because it contains no residual sugar. But fermentation can also terminate when the alcohol level in the wine reaches a level that kills the yeasts, generally at an alcohol level of about 16 percent. Any sugar not fermented by that stage remains in the wine, giving it a degree of sweetness depending on the percentage of residual sugar. In some specific wines, fermentation is deliberately terminated before all the sugar is fermented. For example, Port and some other sweet, fortified wines are made by adding grape spirits (brandy) during fermentation. This raises the alcohol level and kills the yeasts before they ferment all the sugar in the must, resulting in a wine that is sweet and has a higher alcohol level than it would have achieved without the added spirits.

Wines can also undergo secondary fermentation. The most common is malolactic fermentation (MLF) in which the harsher malic acid in the wine is turned into softer lactic acid. This is commonly used for white wines and produces the softer feel of the wine in the mouth that is sometimes described as "buttery." Some red wines also undergo malolactic fermentation.

Champagne and sparkling wines made in the "Champagne method" or traditional method undergo secondary fermentation in the bottle. Sugar and yeast are added to a base wine in the bottle so that fermentation re-starts, but the bottle is capped so that the carbon dioxide produced during the process is trapped inside rather than dissipating. Unable to escape, the gas is dissolved into the liquid. Later, the dead yeast cells are removed and the bottle is topped up and corked, all without releasing the gas. It finally escapes, in the form of bubbles, when the cork is removed.

The sugar level of the grapes at the time of harvest determines the potential alcohol level of the finished wine. Several different scales are used to measure the concentration of grape sugars (the must weighty). A widely used (American) scale is Brix, and in approximate terms, grapes make wine with a percentage of alcohol roughly half the Brix level. More precisely, grapes with 23.7 Brix will make wine with a potential alcohol of 12.5 percent. Other scales for measuring must weight are degrees Oechsle (used most widely in Germany) and Baumé.

In many wine regions, producers can supplement low levels of sugar in their grapes by adding sugar or concentrated (and naturally sweet) grape juice, called *Süssreserve* in Germany. The addition of sugar is often known as chaptalization after Chaptal, one of Napoleon's ministers who advocated (but did not invent) the technique, but it is increasingly called enrichment. Wine laws generally regulate the degree of permitted enrichment. In Burgundy, sugar may be added to raise potential alcohol by about two percent.

In addition to sugar, producers can (depending on wine law) add acid and tannins to make up for deficits in the grapes. Just as sugar is added to compensate for low sugar concentrations in cool climate regions, acidification is practiced in warm climate regions where grapes ripen well and have high levels of sugar but have low acidity. Without some correction the wines would be unbalanced. Wine laws forbid both enrichment and acidification of the same wine.

Aging

Beyond sugar, acid, and tannin, additives are not permitted and the only nongrape flavoring comes from wood. This is generally added during the aging process in oak barrels, but in one specific case, the production of Retsina wine in Greece, pine resin is added to the must during fermentation. It gives the Retsina an aroma and taste reminiscent of turpentine or pine.

Following fermentation, wine is generally racked (drawn off any remaining solid matter) and aged. Some wines, however, are left on the lees, the dead yeast cells that fall to the bottom of vat or barrel when fermentation is complete. Perhaps the best known of these *sur lie* ("on the lees," or sediment) wines, which often have a yeasty note to their flavors, is Muscadet sur lie from the Atlantic coastal region of the Loire Valley in France.

Depending on the wine and the prevailing wine law, aging before bottling can be a short process of a few weeks or as long as several years. In general, white wines are aged for shorter periods than reds, although some reds get little aging and are bottled very soon after fermentation is complete. This is the case with *primeur* or *nouveau* wines that are put on the market within months of the harvest. The best known is Beaujolais Nouveau, a light, fruity wine from southern Burgundy that is released throughout the world on the third Thursday of November each year, only two months after the grapes are picked. It now has many imitators from other wine regions throughout the world.

Other wines sold young include the *Heurigen* (literally, "the season's") wines of Austria, spritzy wines that can officially be sold after November 11 of the vintage year.

But there are also wines that are sold for consumption while they are still fermenting, like Austrian *Sturm* or German *Federweiss* ("white feather" from the cloudy appearance of the still-fermenting beverage in the glass).

Such young wines are the exception, however, and most wine undergoes a period of aging for at least a couple of months to give the flavors and other properties of the wine (like acids and tannins) an opportunity to integrate. Depending on the varietal and style, wine can be aged in an inert vessel (such as a concrete or stainless vat that imparts no additional flavor to the wine) or in a wooden container that might add flavors and tannins to the wine it contains. Some varietals, such as Riesling and Sauvignon Blanc, are almost always made and aged in stainless steel. Others, such as Cabernet Sauvignon and Pinot Noir, are almost always aged in wood. Varieties like Chardonnay are aged in stainless steel or wood, depending on the style the winemaker is aiming for.

Most barrel-aged wine is kept in small 225-liter barrels called *barriques*, whose size ensures a high ratio of wood to wine. There are, however, barrels that hold tens of thousands of liters of wine. New barrels give the greatest flavor and tannins to wine, and barrels contribute less and less with each year of use until, after about five years, they become effectively inert. The insides of barrels are "toasted" by direct flame during construction and the degree of toasting (light, medium, heavy) influences the degree to which the wood can flavor the wine.

Although barrels have been made of various kinds of wood, the most favored is oak because of the flavors it contributes and because the tightness of the grain makes oak less porous than other wood. It thus holds the wine in and keeps the air out, although wine in barrels does experience loss through evaporation and absorption, and must be topped up now and again when aged over a long period. The two principal sources of oak are France and the United States, but there is increasing use of eastern European and Russian oak, too.

The flavors oak barrels give to wine vary according to the wine itself and to the provenance, age, and toasting of the barrel. In general, American barrels are said to give sweeter, vanilla notes to wine, while French barrels contribute more savory flavors. Both may contribute toasted notes to a wine's flavor profile.

Because of the cost of barrels, barrel aging is an expensive proposition, and producers of mass-produced wines have devised less expensive methods of giving oak flavor to their wine. One is to use oak chips, small particles of oak that are mixed into the wine and then filtered out. Some tasters believe that oak chips give the wine an oily texture. An alternative method is to age the wine in steel tanks and to suspend oak planks into it. This has some of the same effect as barrel aging, but it does not expose the wine to oak in the same ratio and nor does it bring the wine into contact with small amounts of air as barrel aging does.

Some aged wines are known as Reserve wines and in Spanish, Italian, and Greek wine law Reserve (*Riserva* or *Reserva*) wines must be aged for specified minimum periods in oak and bottle. The word "Reserve" on the labels of most countries and regions has no regulated meaning, but is generally intended to signify a premium wine that had had a longer period of aging that its non-Reserve counterparts.

Fining and Filtering

Other processes in winemaking include fining and filtering. Fining involves clarifying and stabilizing wine by dropping into it substances like egg whites, fish bladders, or specific clay deposits. Particles adhere to these substances and fall to the bottom of the container. Solid particles may also be removed by filtering, usually by forcing the wine through paper filters. Some wines are not filtered because the process not only removes unwanted particles but can also remove some color and flavor compounds.

Blending

Before or after barrel aging, wines may be blended. A blend may combine wines of different varieties so as to make, for example, a Cabernet Sauvignon Merlot or a Semillon Chardonnay blend. (In any declared blend, the predominant variety is stated first.). Most of the world's great wines are blends of more than one variety. Red Bordeaux, for example, must be a blend of between two and five specific grapes, Châteauneuf-du-Pape can include up to thirteen varieties, and Australia's premier cult wine, Penfold's Grange, is almost all Shiraz with a little Cabernet Sauvignon. Blends are designed to create an integrated, harmonious wine that is greater than the sum of any of its constituent varieties.

Blending can also involve bringing together wines that have been aged differently. Many Chardonnays are blends of wines that have variously been aged in French and American oak, or that have been partly aged in stainless steel, partly in oak.

Aging can also take place in the bottle (bottle aging), and some Spanish and Italian wine laws regarding wines such as Rioja and Barolo require a minimum period of barrel and bottle aging before the wine can be released for sale. Most wines, however, are ready for sale as soon as they are bottled (or, in some cases, put into plastic bladders and sold as "box wine" in large formats).

Bottling

Wine intended for long-term cellaring (*vin de garde* or "keeping wine") is kept in bottles. Depending on the wine, it may be cellared for decades and its components will continue to integrate over the long term. Bottles should be kept on their side so that the cork does not dry out, in an environment that is, ideally, dark and with a constant temperature between 50°–57°F (10°–14°C). Over time, tiny amounts of air do get through the cork, and it is believed that this is important to the aging process. Wines kept over the very long term (as in the libraries of wine producers) have their corks renewed about every twenty-five years.

There has been increasing concern about the rate at which corks are vulnerable to infection and contaminate the wine they are in contact with. Estimates of corked wine range from 5 to 10 percent. Producers are increasingly substituting corks (which are made from the bark of the cork tree) with synthetic stoppers and even screw caps. Such closures seem ideal for wines intended for consumption while young (the vast majority of wines), but it is thought that a wine with a synthetic stopper would not allow the air that seems crucial to proper aging.

Standard wine bottles hold three-quarters of a liter (75 cl or 750 ml) of wine, but common alternatives are half bottles (375 ml) and magnums (two-bottle size, or 1.5 liters). Magnums of premium wine generally cost a little more than twice the price of a single bottle, partly because it is believed that wine ages better in the magnum volume than in standard bottle format.

Bottle shape does not affect aging, but it can be an important part of a wine's branding or image. There are two major bottle types: the Burgundy bottle with long, sloping shoulders, and the Bordeaux with more square shoulders. Much German wine is sold in long, slender flutes, while wine from Germany's Franken region is bottled in a squat green bottle called a Bockbeutel. Beyond patterns such as these, individual producers sometimes develop bottles with distinctive shapes and colors to identify their brands.

Appellation

Bottles are labeled so as to indicate their contents, but not all labels carry the same information because they reflect the prevailing wine law. The great majority of wine-making regions and countries have wine laws that govern such things as food safety (additives that may be used) and what must be shown on a wine label. Laws vary, sometimes radically, but almost all regulate what is broadly called appellation. The appellation is a wine-producing region whose geographical boundaries are legally defined such that only wine made from grapes grown in the region can use the name. Thus a sparkling wine can be called Champagne only if it is made from grapes from the Champagne region of France (and if it has been made according to the rest of the Champagne wine law).

The word "appellation" comes from the French practice of regulating the names of products according to where they are made. Thus a St. Emilion wine from the Bordeaux region must be made of grapes from St. Emilion, and Camembert cheese can only be made in Camembert. Through a series of agreements, European appellations have now obtained near-monopolies over

their names, such that sparkling wines made outside Champagne cannot be called Champagne. Wines made in Australia, California, and New Zealand that used to be called Burgundy or Chablis (both French appellations) have been renamed. Sherry and Port (Spanish and Portuguese appellations respectively) will eventually follow.

Many European wines are labeled only by appellation. Examples are Burgundy, Rioja, and Chianti. But because the wine laws of each appellation specify the varieties of grapes that can be grown in the regions, the appellations are a kind of coded grape variety. Thus red Burgundy can be only Pinot Noir, white Burgundy can be only Chardonnay, Rioja is mostly made from the Tempranillo variety, and Chianti is mostly Sangiovese. In most of the non-European wine world, however (and parts of Europe), wine is labeled by variety (these are varietal wines) because wine laws do not limit the kinds of grapes that can be grown. Italy is a mixture of appellation and varietal labeling, as is Spain, but most German wine is labeled by variety.

Appellation regulations take different forms in different countries. Legally defined appellations in the United States are called American Viticultural Areas (AVAs), while in Australia they are called Geographical Indications (GIs). In order to identify a wine by an AVA, such as Napa Valley, Willamette Valley or Bell Mountain, a wine must be made of grapes 75 percent from that AVA. Countries such as Australia and Canada (Ontario) require 85 percent grown in the stated wine region. In addition, wines laws require a varietal wine to be a minimum percentage of that variety. A California Chardonnay must be at least 75 percent Chardonnay and it can be up to 25 percent of the other varieties.

Vintage and Alcohol Level

Vintage years and alcohol levels stated on labels can be equally flexible. A New Zealand wine labeled 1999 needs only be 85 percent of that vintage (there could be 15 percent of 1998 or an earlier vintage). And the alcohol level needs be only within one percentage point either way of the stated level, so that a wine labeled 12.5 percent can have between 11.5 percent and 13.5 percent alcohol. Almost all wine laws allow this kind of flexibility.

Some wine laws also differentiate among different quality levels. In Europe there are three: a basic table wine (French *vin de table*, Italian *vino di tavola*) made according to few restrictions; regional wines (like French *vin de pays* and Spanish *viño de la tierra*) made with more restriction and meant to reflect the wines of a specific region; and quality wine (French *Appellation d'Origine Contrôlée* and German *Qualitätswein*), which is the highest rank of all. In reality these are only guidelines: some table wines are of higher quality than so-called quality wines, but do not qualify for the highest rank because they use grapes not permitted by wine law for that category.

Styles of Wines

There are many different styles of wine, allowing wine to satisfy a wide range of individual tastes and occasions, and permitting wine to accompany many styles of food. Most table wines are dry in the technical sense that they contain no residual sugar because all the sugar that was in the grapes (or added to the must) has been fermented out. Even so, wines can feel sweet in the mouth because of their fruit flavors, and many varietals like Chardonnay, Shiraz, and Zinfandel have a sweet fruit dimension to them. (Alcohol also tastes sweet, and a high alcohol level adds to the sweet sensation.)

Wine should be assessed in terms of the way all its component parts fit together. A white wine whose acidity and fruit flavors are balanced tastes better than one where there is an imbalance. Many inexpensive Chardonnays are so heavily oaked that it is difficult to detect the fruit. For many reds, it is a matter of achieving a good relationship among acidity, fruit, tannins, wood, and alcohol. Too high alcohol can ruin an otherwise good fruit-acid balance, as can too much oak.

But wines that are intended for long-term cellaring are often unbalanced when young, and the purpose of aging them is to allow time for them to integrate. Many new Bordeaux reds, for example, have such strong tannins that they are undrinkable for the first few years. But the great bulk of commercial wine is made for early drinking (within four or five years of vintage) and they are more likely to deteriorate rather than improve if kept much longer.

Food and Wine

Matching food and wine has preoccupied wine and food writers for centuries. Rules of thumb such as "white wine with fish, red wine with meat" used to be popular, but current thinking is much more flexible. In general there are two ways of thinking about the wine-food relationship. One is to match their flavors, so that dishes high in acid are accompanied by similar wines. Thus, tomato-based dishes (tomatoes being acidic) often pair well with many Italian wines that have high acidity. The second approach is to contrast food and wine. Thus a dish with a heavy, creamy sauce would not be paired with a heavy, buttery Chardonnay but with a substantial but leaner, even crisp wine whose acidity will cut through the fat in the dish and refresh the diner's palate.

Although there are no rigid rules for matching wine and food, useful principles are to match the weight of each and to consider the dominant flavors of the food. Just as some foods feel lighter or heavier in the mouth (compare sole and steak) so all wines fall on a spectrum of light to full bodied. Many young white wines (like Soave and Verdicchio) feel light, whereas older Semillons and Shirazes are full bodied. Matching the weight of the wine to the food creates a balance.

As for matching flavors, it is important to consider the dominant flavors in a dish. Roasted chicken with sage stuffing, barbecued chicken, chicken marsala, and chicken tandoori all have quite different flavors because of the herbs, spices and other ingredients used in their preparation, even though chicken is common to them all. Generally it is not the meat or fish that gives a dish its main flavors, and advice to match a particular wine to fish or chicken is not very useful. Instead, it is desirable to match wine to the strength, intensity, and quality of the ingredients that provide the main flavors.

Finding a perfect match of wine and food (called a marriage) is often a matter of trial and error, but there are some classic matches. They include Sauvignon Blanc with oysters or goat cheese, full-bodied red wine with simply prepared steak or full-flavored game, and Eiswein (ice wine) with strong blue cheese. Some foods are difficult to match with wine, including dishes whose flavors are heavily influenced by vinegar or citrus juice.

Advice on wine to accompany a meal at a restaurant should be available from the sommelier or server. A sommelier (who historically was employed by a king or noble to look after the pack-animals—the *bêtes de somme*—who carried the food and wine) should have full knowledge of the way a restaurant's dishes are prepared and should be familiar with all the wines on the wine list. He or she should know how hot or spicy a dish is and what the strongest flavors are.

A sommelier's tasks include developing a wine list appropriate for the restaurant's cuisine, and ensuring that the wine is properly kept and served. Once a diner has selected a bottle, it should be brought unopened to the table and presented to the diner to ensure that it is the correct one. The bottle should be opened and a small amount of the wine poured for the diner to taste. The purpose is to ensure that the wine is in good condition and not corked or flawed in any other way.

Drinking Wine

Flaws can generally be detected by smell alone, but it is a good idea to taste the wine, too, if only to check its temperature. White wines are often served too cold and reds too warm. There are no hard-and-fast rules about serving temperature, but white wines should not be so cold that they have no taste or so warm that they lose their feel of fresh acidity. And although it is a rule of thumb that red wine should be served at room temperature, many modern rooms are so warm that wine served at their temperature taste coarse and alcoholic. Although there is commonly a difference of about 15 degrees in the serving temperature of whites (wine straight from a refrigerator is about 39–43°F [4–6°C]) and reds (rooms are commonly 68°F [20°C] and warmer), the difference between them should be much narrower. In broad terms, white wine can be served at ideal cellar temperature (about 53°F [12°C]), while most reds do well at about 60–64°F (16–18°C), a difference of only four to six degrees.

Although many people insist on opening wine an hour or two before serving so that it can breathe, experiments show that merely removing the cork makes little difference to the taste or quality of the wine. Exposing some wines to air can improve and soften them, but this is best done by decanting the wine beforehand or simply swirling it in the glass. Special care should be taken with very old wines, which can begin to degrade very soon after they are opened.

The size and shape of the glass can make a difference to the experience of a wine. There are now glasses designed for every varietal and style of wine by companies such as Riedel. For ordinary use, the most satisfactory glasses have a mouth smaller than the widest point of the bowl, so that the aromas are trapped. The stem should be long enough that the glass can be held comfortably by it; holding a wineglass by the bowl can warm the wine and dirty the bowl.

Health Benefits

Beyond the sheer pleasure that wine can give, it appears to have health benefits if consumed in moderation. Historically, wine has been attributed myriad therapeutic properties, but for much of the twentieth century the stress was on its toxic properties and its ability to inebriate consumers. The discovery of the "French Paradox" revived interest in the relationship between wine and health. The paradox is that, given their level of wine consumption, the French ought to have a higher rate of heart disease than they do. An explanation was that wine actually protected against coronary disease. The weight of current research supports that conclusion, but doctors stress that it applies only to moderate consumption: about one or two glasses a day by men, one glass by women. More than that neutralizes the health benefits.

There are many guidelines for the maximum enjoyment of wine but, in the end, each individual finds the relationship with wine that she or he is comfortable with. Individuals have different taste preferences and varying tolerance of tannins and acids. Food and wine pairings that repel some, delight others. The great thing is that wine, the result of the complex interplay of work by countless humans and a seemingly infinite combination of natural circumstances, comes in such a wide range of styles that there is a wine to please everyone, to match any dish, and to suit any occasion.

See also **Fermentation; Food Production, History of; France; Fruit; Germany, Austria, Switzerland; Harvesting; Iberian Peninsula; Italy; Pleasure and Food.**

BIBLIOGRAPHY

Dominé, André. *Wine*. Cologne: Könemann, 2000.

Halliday, James, and Hugh Johnson. *The Art and Science of Wine*. London: Mitchell Beazley, 1997.

Immer, Andrea. *Great Wine Made Simple*. New York: Broadway Books, 2000.

MacNeill, Karen. *The Wine Bible*. New York: Workman, 2001.

Robinson, Jancis. *The Oxford Companion to Wine*. 2d ed. Oxford: Oxford University Press, 1999.

Vine, Richard P. *Wine Appreciation*. 2d ed. New York: Wiley, 1997.

Rod Phillips

WINE IN THE ANCIENT WORLD

The earliest evidence of wine dates to about 5000 B.C.E. in the Middle East, where archaeologists have discovered earthenware jars and other vessels containing grape seeds and stems. Others contain deposits of tartaric acid and calcium tartrate that are almost certainly the residue of grape liquid because grapes are rare among fruit in that they accumulate tartaric acid. Any grape juice not consumed very quickly would have soon fermented into wine in the warm temperatures of the region.

The earliest known wine jar (dated to 5000 B.C.E.) was found in the Zagros Mountains of modern western Iran. Excavations elsewhere in the region located 30- and 60-liter (7.92- and 15.85-gallon) earthenware jars, all with wine deposits, dating from 3500 to 3000 B.C.E. Similar evidence of wine-making at this time has been found at many locations in the Fertile Crescent (the region south of the Caspian and Black Seas and including parts of modern Turkey, Armenia, Georgia, and Iran).

Many scholars speculate that the first vintage was an accident, the result of fresh wild grapes being crushed accidentally and fermenting spontaneously. Over time, people began to crush the grapes deliberately and also began to select and cultivate varieties that produced better wine (such as grapes with a high pulp-to-pip ratio).

Many ancient accounts of the origin of wine stress its accidental character. One refers to the Persian king Jamsheed, who was so fond of grapes that he stored them in jars so as to have supplies out of season. When one lot

Winemaking in ancient Egypt, as depicted in the Tomb of the Nobles in the Valley of the Kings near Cairo. © OTTO LANG/ CORBIS.

Wine shops were common throughout the Roman Empire. This bas-relief from the Museo Nacional de Arte Romano shows a shop owner pouring wine into a carafe in much the same way as beer is kept on tap today. © ARCHIVO ICONOGRAFICO, S.A./CORBIS.

fermented, he thought they had gone bad, and had the jar labeled "poison." When a woman from his harem, suffering headaches so bad that she wanted to die, drank the wine with the intention of killing herself, she fell asleep under the effect of alcohol. When she awoke, her headache was gone, and thus was born wine and its ancient reputation as a medicine.

Wine played a part in the diet and culture of all ancient societies from the Neolithic period onward. For the most part, it was a privileged beverage of the elites, while beer was the drink of the masses. A relief from seventh-century-B.C.E. Nineveh shows King Assurbanipal and his queen resting under a trellis of vines and drinking wine from cups. In Nimrud, a ration of wine was given to all six thousand members of the royal household. The basic male ration was 1.8 liters (3.81 pints) for ten men each day, while skilled laborers got twice that. The queen and her retinue received 54 liters (14.26 gallons) a day, but we do not know how many individuals shared it.

One reason for the special status of wine was its scarcity. Grain grew far more widely and easily than grapes, and beer (really liquid bread) could be made year-round as long as grain was available. But grapes grew only in certain localities and ripened only once a year, so that there was limited scope for wine-making. Moreover, each year's wine had to last a year, until the next vintage was ready for drinking. In regions where grapes did not grow, wine had to be imported, thus adding to its cost.

One of the earliest wine trade routes ran a thousand miles down the Tigris and Euphrates rivers from the vine-clad mountains of northern Mesopotamia to southern Mesopotamian cities like Ur, Babylon, and Sumer. This trade route lasted for thousands of years, and it appears that many regions began by importing wine and then proceeded to cultivate grapes and make their own wine. There is clear but uneven evidence of viticulture and wine making from 5000 to 3000 B.C.E., but they probably spread in a number of directions from the Fertile Crescent, one track taking them to the eastern seaboard of the Mediterranean and then south toward Egypt. The Middle Eastern climate around 3000 B.C.E. seems to have been wetter than today, allowing for cultivation is regions where it is no longer possible.

Egypt provides the most coherent image of an ancient wine culture. Hundreds of clay jars of wine (with a total volume of some 4,500 liters (118.78 gallons) were buried with one of the first Egyptian kings, Scorpion I (about 3150 B.C.E.). Analysis of the clay shows that the jars were made in the modern Israel-Palestine region.

Between 3000 and 2500 B.C.E., Egyptians began to grow their own grapes, mainly in the Nile Delta (where the earth was fertile and the heat was moderated by the Mediterranean), but also further south. The vines were owned by royalty and great officials and by priests, and a census taken about 1000 B.C.E. listed 513 vineyards owned by temples alone throughout the country.

Vines were often trained on trellises, irrigated, and fertilized with pigeon droppings. Wall paintings show the wine-making process in great detail. The grapes (almost always depicted as black) were trod by slaves in a vat and the juice was run off into fermenting jars. The must (unfermented juice) is usually colored red or black, which suggests there might have been some period of skin contact. The residual skins and other solids were squeezed in a sack to extract every drop of juice.

Fermentation took place in large clay jars that were sealed, apart from a small hole that allowed the carbon dioxide to escape. Each jar was identified with a clay seal, the forerunner of the label, that might give information on the year, the vineyard and the name of the winemaker.

The aroma, taste and texture of Egyptian wines are lost to us, but in any case the wine was often flavored with herbs and spices before being consumed. But they cannot have been very stable because the grapes were picked and crushed in August, were slowly crushed and pressed and then rapidly fermented, all in the summer heat. Moreover, the clay jars were slightly porous (unless they were coated with resin or oil), which would have led to a degree of oxidation. There was no premium on aging wine here, and there are records of wine going bad after twelve to eighteen months.

Wine cost about five times more than beer, the staple beverage of the Egyptian masses. It was consumed by powerful and wealthy individuals and by priests attached to temples that owned vineyards, who received wine as part of their salary. The elite status of wine is indicated by its prominence in the burial chambers of the kings. Thirty-six jars of wine were buried with the young King Tutankhamen.

Wine played an important role in Egyptian religion, as it did in religions in other parts of the ancient world, and it was poured as a libation or offering to the gods as prayers were said. Ramses III claimed to have presented 59,588 jars of wine to the god Ramon-Re. Some texts present wine as divine in origin: as the perspiration of Re, the sun god, or as the eyes of the god Horus. Wine was also used for medical purposes. Physicians prescribed it to increase the appetite, purge the body of worms, and treat asthma. It could also be applied externally to bring down swelling and to treat wounds.

By the time wine reached Egypt it had come to occupy a privileged place in the diet and culture of the elites. It is possible that viticulture was transferred from Egypt to Crete and from there to the European mainland. The ancient world thus established practices and attitudes that were adopted and adapted by later societies.

See also **Ancient Kitchen, The; Greece, Ancient; Mesopotamia, Ancient; Rome and the Roman Empire**.

BIBLIOGRAPHY

Lesko, Leonard H. *King Tut's Wine Cellar*. Berkeley, Calif.: B. C. Scribe Publications, 1978.

McGovern, Patrick, S. J. Fleming, and Solomon H. Katz, eds. *The Origins and Ancient History of Wine*. Luxembourg: Gordon and Breach, 1996.

Phillips, Rod. *A Short History of Wine*. New York: Harper-Collins, 2001.

Poo, Mu-chou. *Wine and Wine-Offering in the Religion of Ancient Egypt*. London: Kegan Paul International, 1995.

Unwin, Tim. *Wine and the Vine: An Historical Geography of Viticulture and the Wine Trade*. London: Routledge, 1991.

Younger, William. *Gods, Men and Wine*. London: Michael Joseph, 1966.

Rod Phillips

WINE FROM CLASSICAL TIMES TO THE NINETEENTH CENTURY

In the more than two thousand years between the Classical period and the nineteenth century, wine underwent changes in almost every respect. The geographical extent of viticulture (the cultivation of grapes), vine cultivation, wine making, trade, and the culture of wine consumption were all transformed as part of broader political, social, economic, and cultural transformations.

Wine-Making in Ancient Greece

The beginnings of wine-making in Greece by about 1000 B.C.E. were an important step in the history of wine. Until that point, wine had been a marginal product, made in relatively small volumes and consumed only by social elites. This had been the case in ancient societies like Mesopotamia and Egypt. In Greece, however, vineyards expanded rapidly from their initial sites near main population centers and markets to more distant islands like Thasos, Lesbos, and Chios, and by the third century B.C.E. there was a veritable wine industry in the region.

Wine was consumed at all levels of society and it became, along with oil and grain, one of the three main products of Mediterranean agriculture and commerce. Greek wine could be found in locations as diverse as France, Egypt, around the Black Sea, and in the Danube region. Moreover, the Greeks introduced viticulture to France (with limited plantings near modern Marseilles), southern Italy, and Sicily.

The extent of the Greek wine trade is evident in the many wrecked ships along the Mediterranean coast. One ship carried an astonishing ten thousand amphoras (six- to seven-gallon earthenware jars) that would have contained as much as 66,000 gallons of wine, or 400,000 standard modern bottles. It is estimated that 2.2 million gallons of Greek wine were shipped to France each year through the port that is now Marseilles.

The Greeks not only supplied foreign markets with wine, but they also consumed vast quantities domestically. Far from being an elite beverage, wine was consumed at all levels of society. This was an example of an egalitarian approach to drinking expressed by Euripides, who wrote that Dionysus (the Greek god of wine) had given "the simple gift of wine, the gladness of the grape" to "rich and poor" alike. Yet there were significant variations in the quantity and quality of wine consumed at different social levels. The affluent drank wine that was described as quite full-bodied and sweet. The poor drank a thin, low-alcohol, bitter solution made by soaking the skins, seeds, and stalks left over after the final pressing of the grapes.

Greek males of the upper social strata developed a specific institution for consuming wine: the symposium, meaning "drinking together." A dozen or more men, all wearing garlands on their heads, reclined on couches and drank diluted wine while conversing, being entertained by young men and women, and playing games that often involved wine. Symposia were idealized as occasions for elevated discussion and cultural activities, but often they were merely boisterous drinking sessions. Greek wine cups were often decorated with scenes of drunkenness and sexual activities at symposia.

Women were excluded from symposia (except as servers, entertainers, and prostitutes) and there is evidence in Greek writings of male anxiety about women drinking wine. Women were believed to become intoxicated more quickly than men and to behave immorally once in that state. These became persistent themes in Western culture, and they underpinned lower consumption rates of all forms of alcohol by women.

Although it was apparently a not uncommon occurrence in symposia, drunkenness was generally frowned upon in ancient Greece. Homer highlighted the dangers of drunkenness in the *Odyssey*, in which several characters meet their deaths in accidents caused by drunken men. Yet moderate consumption of wine was viewed as beneficial. Hippocrates, regarded as the founder of Western medicine, wrote extensively on the effects of different types of wine on the digestion. He criticized "dark and harsh" wines as difficult for the body to digest and expel, but praised "soft dark wines . . . they are flatulent and pass better by stool."

As for wine production, the Greeks paid serious attention to viticulture and wine-making. They adopted techniques of growing vines along trellises and up stakes to make the grapes more accessible during harvest. Vine-dressers, who were responsible for the vital pruning operations in the vineyard, became a recognized profession. It was the Romans, however, whose empire superseded that of the Greeks, and it was they who left the most coherent documentation on wine in the Classical period.

Wine-Making in Ancient Rome

A host of writers, including Cicero, Pliny, and Cato, described viticultural and wine-making practices in Rome and wrote extensively about the wines available to them in the last centuries B.C.E. In about 65 C.E., Columella described the principles of viticulture, including the recommended density of vines, the importance of selecting appropriate sites for vineyards, and the economics of vine-growing. For his part, Cato stressed the importance of sunlight to grape-ripening and outlined the basic principles of canopy management.

Roman writers also focused on wine-making and gave recipes for wines that would appeal to Roman tastes. Unlike modern wine-making methods, where additives are minimal, Roman wine was a grape-based concoction that might include sea-water, honey, and all kinds of herbs and spices. Additional flavors might be contributed by the pitch and resin sometimes used to seal the insides of earthenware jars, and sweetness could be added by boiling the grape juice in a lead vessel. Lead not only sweetened wine, but it also preserved it by killing some bacteria. (Lead's potential toxicity was recognized but was largely ignored until the seventeenth century.)

Roman wine writers paid attention to the quality of wines. They gave particular value to color, body, and sweetness, but they also noted wines that they believed had special medical properties. Athenaeus praised wines from Alexandria, which he thought were excellent, fragrant, not likely to go to the head, and which had diuretic effects. Strabo gave high marks to wines from

Turkey and Aegean islands like Cos, Chios, and Lesbos. In the first century C.E., Pliny the Elder provided a catalogue of wines from various parts of the empire: ninety-one varieties of wine, fifty kinds of quality wine, and thirty-eight varieties of foreign wine. His list is notable for its stress on varieties rather than just provenance.

The engine of the Roman wine industry was Rome itself, which grew from 300,000 to over one million inhabitants between 300 B.C.E. and the beginning of the first century C.E. By that time, Romans were consuming an estimated 39.6 million gallons of wine a year, which was about seventeen fluid ounces a day for every inhabitant. Not only did the region around Rome provide this wine, but many other parts of the Italian peninsula shipped it as well.

The prominence of wine in the Roman diet was threatened when Mount Vesuvius erupted in 79 C.E., burying the wine port of Pompeii and destroying many vineyards and two vintages of wine (one in warehouses, the other still on the vines). The immediate shortage of wine led to such a rush to plant new vineyards that there was a glut several years later. The Emperor Domitian tried unsuccessfully to limit the land under viticulture in Italy and to reduce vineyards in Rome's overseas provinces such as Gaul. The ostensible reason for the policy was that vineyards were taking over land needed for grain production, but it is thought that Domitian was as much concerned with protecting Roman wine producers from competition.

Despite any pressure there might have been from wine producers in Italy who wanted to protect their export business, the Romans extended viticulture throughout Europe as their empire expanded. By the first century C.E., most of the famous French wine regions (including Bordeaux, the Rhône, and Burgundy) had been planted, as had areas in England, Germany, Hungary, and other parts of southeastern Europe. The Romans were thus responsible for the beginnings of the European wine industry.

As was the case in Greece, Rome's wine culture was generally inclusive, and everyone from the elites to slaves consumed wine. Cato proposed that slaves in chains should receive about 1.3 gallons of wine a week—not for pleasure but to give them strength to work. (The ration allotted to a sick slave was half that of a healthy, working slave.) Also as in Greece, in Rome there were vast differences in the quality of the wine consumed by different social groups.

In Rome there was also concern about wine consumption by women. One myth told of a husband who beat his wife to death with a stick for drinking wine, a punishment said to have been praised by Romulus, one of Rome's founders. For a brief time, Roman law allowed a man to divorce his wife for drinking wine, and women were associated with the cults centered on Bacchus, the Roman god of wine. The authorities concocted stories of wild, drunken orgies (Bacchanalia) in order to suppress the cults, which had become implicated in opposition to the government.

Drunkenness, whether on the part of women or men, was broadly condemned by Roman commentators. Cicero frequently labeled his opponents drunkards and alleged that his main rival, Mark Antony, started drinking early each morning. Others cautioned against excessive drinking for a variety of physical and mental reasons. Lucretius argued that wine could disturb the soul and weaken the body, while Seneca wrote that wine revealed and magnified character defects. Pliny the Elder praised quality wines, but he warned that many of the truths spoken under the influence of wine were better not expressed.

On the other hand, Classical medical opinion generally held that wine, alone or with other substances, had curative properties, particularly for gastric and urological ailments. Cato recommended certain flowers soaked in wine as effective for snakebite, constipation, gout, indigestion, and diarrhea.

If wine had achieved a privileged status at the center of the Roman Empire, some non-Roman populations on the margins of Roman control carved out their own relationship with the beverage. For Jews, wine was a powerful expression of divine power. When Moses sent out scouts to survey the Promised Land, they returned with a bunch of grapes so massive that it took two men to carry it. Grapes and wine were such important signs of the bounty provided by God to the Jews that the Old Testament frequently threatens that God will make the vines barren if Jews disobey God's word.

This intense symbolism of wine carried over to Christianity. The first miracle performed by Christ was to turn water to wine at the wedding at Cana. Wine became an integral part of Christian theology, ritual, and tradition. In the Christian sacrament of the Eucharist, wine represents the blood of Christ, and there are many representations of "Christ in the wine press," where Christ's blood, flowing from wounds inflicted during the crucifixion, mixes with the red juice flowing from the grapes as they are crushed.

Because the Eucharist required wine, Christianity and wine became so intimately connected that in the first centuries C.E., conversion from beer to wine became a sign of conversion from paganism to the new religion. Many religious houses had their own vineyards. Monasteries were centers of learning, not only in theology but also in the practical sciences, and for hundreds of years religious orders were at the forefront in developing new techniques in viticulture and wine-making.

Wine-Making in the Middle Ages

The invasion of the western region of the Roman Empire by tribes from central and eastern Europe from the fifth century C.E. did not affect European viticulture as

dramatically as once thought. It is possible that some vineyards were abandoned, but overall it seems that Europe's new rulers were as interested in protecting viticulture as the Romans had been. What did suffer was the wine trade, as the single Roman Empire was broken up into smaller political units, each dominated by one of the invading tribes.

It is a mistake, then, to think of a Dark Ages of wine, and certainly misleading to suggest, as some scholars have done, that viticulture survived only because of the vineyards owned by the Christian Church and various religious houses. They were undoubtedly important and some were extensive: the Abbey of St.-Germain-des-Prés near Paris had 1–1.5 square miles of vineyards in 814 C.E. The Church also sponsored the expansion of vineyards in the important Rhine region and in Austria and Switzerland. Even so, many vineyards had secular owners, and viticulture and wine was not particularly threatened in this period. However, with a decline in trade, many regions began to cultivate their own grapes.

The real threat to wine (and alcoholic beverages generally) emerged not in Europe, but in the Middle East, the birthplace of wine. There the Islamic religion took hold in the seventh century, and within a hundred years it had extended its control across northern Africa, the Iberian Peninsula, and, for a short time, parts of southwestern France. The Prophet Muhammad forbade his followers the consumption of alcohol. Although he acknowledged that wine could make people happy and sociable, he believed that its threats to social order and morality were so great that alcohol should be banned. Wine production practically dried up in many parts of the Islamic empire, but in some parts (like Spain) it was generally tolerated and even acknowledged in so far as it was taxed by Muslim authorities.

Wine production and trade in Christian Europe began to boom around the year 1000 C.E. One reason was the creation of a large political unit in Europe under the Emperor Charlemagne. This not only encouraged commerce, but Charlemagne himself encouraged wine production. He is said to have given the hill of Corton (in Burgundy) to the Abbey of Saulieu; the wines from this estate are known as Corton-Charlemagne.

A further reason for the expansion of wine production from 1000 was the growth of population, cities, and trade that took place in Europe between 1000 and 1300. In northern Europe, northern Italy, and elsewhere, new urban middle classes of entrepreneurs and merchants emerged, all with a thirst for wine. Wine regions close to these new urban markets (like those in Tuscany and other regions of northern Italy) prospered. However, many of the new cities were in areas unsuitable for viticulture, and wine trade routes developed to serve them. Among the most important were the sea route from southwestern France (now the Bordeaux region) to England and the northern European ports, and the wine trade

The interior of a German wine cellar as depicted in a Renaissance woodcut from the 1500s. COURTESY OF HANS WEISS. ROUGHWOOD COLLECTION

Wine-Making Advancements and Expansion

During the sixteenth to the nineteenth centuries, there were many varied developments in viticulture and winemaking. Lead was abandoned as a means of sweetening wine, and adding sugar to raise the alcohol level of wine became a common practice. (It was later known as chaptalization, after Napoleon's minister of the interior, Chaptal, who recommended it to compensate for grapes that did not ripen fully.)

New styles of wine emerged, too. The technique of making sparkling wine evolved, and bottles and stoppers developed so that it could be conserved more reliably. Starting in the late seventeenth century there was increasing recognition of the individuality of wines from specific estates. The first wine to be marketed as an estate wine was Haut Brion from Bordeaux, which appeared on the London market in the 1660s.

Wine was, in this period, part of the daily diet in many parts of Europe. Reliable statistics on per capita consumption are hard to come by (because the information was not collected) but common estimates range from 17–101 fluid ounces a day. The impact of these volumes depends on the alcohol content of the wine, which was often diluted with water.

Wine was also part of some people's income or entitlement. Artisans employed by the Duke of Lorraine received an allotment of wine as part of their daily wages, and wine was a standard element in military rations. In 1406, the six men who guarded the Château de Custines each received two liters of wine a day.

It was during this period, too, that Europeans extended viticulture beyond Europe itself. The first major advance was the invasion of Central and South America by Spain in the sixteenth century. Vines were planted in Mexico in the 1520s, and viticulture rapidly spread down the west coast of South America in the wake of the invading Spanish armies and Jesuit missionaries. As mission stations were established, vineyards were planted, and the connection was so strong that the grape commonly planted became known as the Mission variety. By the 1550s, major vineyards had been established in Peru, Chile, and Argentina. During the 1600s, the Dutch established vineyards in what is now South Africa, and in 1788 the first vines were planted in Australia.

Viticulture in North America was far less successful. Settlers tried to make wine from native grapes from the 1600s and later tried unsuccessfully to grow European varieties. A combination of climate and disease condemned most of these attempts to failure, and even though Franciscan missionaries established vineyards in California in the eighteenth century, it was not until the nineteenth century that wine was produced in America in meaningful volumes.

The nineteenth century was a turning point for wine, in many respects. From the 1860s onwards, vineyards throughout Europe and other parts of the world were

down the Rhine River from the vineyards of central and southern Germany to the North Sea and Baltic ports.

This boom period for the medieval wine industry ended with the Black Death that struck Europe from the mid-fourteenth century. The European population declined by as much as a third, and as markets contracted and vineyard workers died or fled the plague, many vineyards were abandoned. Production and trade began to recover as population and markets grew again in the sixteenth century. There were slight setbacks in this period, when religious reformers like Calvin and Luther accused the Church of Rome of being morally lax, including being tolerant of drunkenness. The Protestant religions tended to be hostile to social drinking, and it is interesting that the only European wine region to become Protestant was Switzerland.

devastated by a North American aphid called *Phylloxera vastatrix*. Unable to eradicate the pest, vine-growers began to graft their vines onto the roots of native American vines that were tolerant of the aphid. The *Phylloxera* disaster affected European wine production for several decades, but it gave a boost to production elsewhere. California vineyards, which had expanded after the end of the Gold Rush, grew rapidly as producers eyed the disaster in Europe and imagined California taking over the world wine market.

The advent of the railroad was a boon to production in many countries. It made eastern markets available to California wine and enabled producers in the south of France to get their inexpensive wine to France's northern industrial cities.

At this same time, a wave of anti-alcohol sentiment swept across many countries. Temperance and abstinence movements had varying success in having alcohol laws tightened, and some American states introduced Prohibition. These movements were reinforced by the discovery (some scholars refer to it as the construction) of alcoholism in the mid-nineteenth century, which seemed to confirm the dangers of drinking any alcohol, including wine.

During the two millennia that separated the Classical period from the end of the nineteenth century, wine had changed from being an elite beverage to one shared by all sectors of many societies. It had spread globally, and it had sensitively reflected broad shifts in economies, societies, and culture. There were also continuities. Voices across this long period spoke to the dangers of excessive drinking, and others praised the health benefits of wine. The experience of wine in this period confirms the importance of understanding wine in its historical and cultural contexts.

See also **Beer; Christianity; Fermentation; Fermented Beverages Other than Wine or Beer; Grapes and Grape Juice; Greece, Ancient; Mesopotamia, Ancient; Middle Ages, European; Rome and the Roman Empire.**

BIBLIOGRAPHY

Brennan, Thomas, *Burgundy to Champagne: The Wine Trade in Early Modern France.* Baltimore: Johns Hopkins University Press, 1997.

Johnson, Hugh. *The Story of Wine.* London: Mitchell Beazley, 1989.

Phillips, Rod. *A Short History of Wine.* New York: HarperCollins, 2001.

Pinney, Thomas. *A History of Wine in America from the Beginnings to Prohibition.* Berkeley: University of California Press, 1989.

Seward, Desmond. *Monks and Wine.* New York: Crown, 1979.

Unwin, Tim. *Wine and the Vine: A Historical Geography of Viticulture and the Wine Trade.* London: Routledge, 1991.

Rod Phillips

WINE IN THE MODERN WORLD

At the start of the twentieth century wine was a beverage with a very limited range. Essentially it was made as a bulk product by peasants in southern Europe and was consumed by all classes in the country of origin. A small amount of premium wine found its way to the tables of the rich in the capital cities of Europe and the European diaspora. Some outposts of production existed in the United States and the colonies of Europe, but they were insignificant both qualitatively and quantitatively. The Bordeaux vintage of 1900 was highly regarded, but the production and consumption of that style of wine was marginal to the substantive function of the drink.

The Years of Decline

Despite the great opening vintage, the first decades of the century were not happy ones for wine producers. By 1900 phylloxera had completed its devastation of the European viticultural landscape, often leaving vineyards replanted with low-quality hybrid vines that brought viral disease in their wake. Algeria was widely planted and produced large amounts of cheap *vin ordinaire* (ordinary wine). Agricultural depression and the flight of the population to the cities exacerbated the situation; then came World War I. Meanwhile, for the producers of prestige wines a continual flood of impostors from poor-quality viticultural regions seeking to gain the premium offered by reputation devalued that reputation and reduced their profits.

The response was to define a system that, it was argued, would protect both the producer and the consumer. By defining the boundaries of a given region and allowing only wine from grapes grown there to carry the name of the region, producers could maintain a price premium, and consumers could have certainty about the nature (and by extension the quality) of what they were drinking. The first nationwide appellation system was developed in Portugal, but it was perfected in France from 1935 onward in the *appellation controlée* system with the legal enshrinement of the definitions of "quality wine" and "table wine."

This codification of a classification system helped producers in prestigious regions but did little for the bulk producers, still almost all agricultural peasantry with little capital to invest in the technical advances in the winery. In these regions a strange combination of corporatist government and anarcho-syndicalism produced wine cooperatives that were controlled by local small-scale grape growers and to which they could sell their produce. Cooperatives in turn could raise the necessary capital to invest in production facilities.

The Technological Revolution

The development of both the science of biochemistry and the technology of agricultural engineering started a revolution in wine production that expanded even more rapidly after World War II. Originating in the work of Louis Pasteur in the second half of the nineteenth century, enology

A visitor to the Robert Mondavi Winery in Napa, California, attends a weekly class on wine tasting. Wine tastings have become an important tool for educating the public about wine and its different aromas and flavors. © CHARLES O'REAR/CORBIS.

and viticulture developed a rational, scientific base. It was no longer enough to continue practices merely because they had been adopted by one's forebears. Universities like Bordeaux and Montpellier in France and later the University of California at Davis and Adelaide in Australia began both to research wine and to teach those who would grow grapes and make wine. As the science developed, so did the wines. Control of yeast and bacteria meant that off-dry and medium-dry wines could be safely marketed. This allowed massive expansion of styles like German liebfraumilch, which dominated the white wine market in the United Kingdom until the 1980s. This technological change came late to wine, perhaps because it was an agricultural, often peasant-based product, but it became crucial as, with the development of the railways and the new markets of industrialized nations, wine had to travel some distance and had to remain stable enough to be drinkable.

Technical development involved three key areas. First was the understanding of the importance of anaerobic handling, the need to control oxygen contact both to preserve fruitiness in wine and to avoid bacterial spoilage. Second was the recognition of the significance of hygiene during wine making and handling, again to avoid spoilage. Underpinning both of these was an increased control of all stages of the process: temperature control, specially cultured yeasts, prepared bacteria to stimulate the malolactic fermentation, and the addition of enzymes that enhance the development of "natural" aromas in the wine (such as pectinase and apiosidase). A

modern winery could be a tank farm with a central computerized control room that monitored what each batch of wine was doing.

Viticulture developed at the same time. Spurred originally by the need to combat phylloxera, then by the requirements of rapid new plantings in the Americas and Australasia, pest control, soil management, irrigation, and controlling the canopy of the vine to maximize sun exposure have been led by science. The result has been to raise the quality of the most basic wines, so even at the cheapest end of the market the consumer can expect to get a fruity, fault-free wine rather than one dominated by oxidative flavors and coarse tannins. The converse, some critics claim, has been to make wines more homogeneous. This, they argue, means that wines have lost their personalities, and wines from across the world increasingly resemble each other. Certain wine makers have reacted against such a clinical approach to let the wine develop in its own way. But even when producers indulge in so-called "dirty wine making" in pursuit of individuality, they do it from a position of knowledge, not faith, as their predecessors would have done.

A New World of Wine
At the start of the twentieth century the production of wine was firmly European. This was not so by the start of the twenty-first century. Although France, Italy, and Spain still dominated in quantitative terms, together producing over 50 percent of all the world's wine, their international reputations increasingly were challenged by

the "new producing" countries, those of the New World. In the U.K. market, something of a yardstick, Australia became the second most popular country of origin after France.

This growing international reputation for the new producing countries reflected a rapid increase in their production. Consumption in the wine producing countries of Europe dropped dramatically, and at the same time national governments and the European Union pursued policies designed to reduce production, particularly in the bulk wine producing regions around the Mediterranean. In the new producing countries the reverse was true. From a low base, consumption rose, but production of wine grapes rose even more dramatically, driven not just by domestic demand but by the desire to penetrate new markets in northern Europe, North America, and eastern Asia.

The newer wine producing countries have been at the forefront of structural changes in the industry. In the early twenty-first century Australia had over 56,000 grape growers, each with an average holding of 1.25 hectares (3 acres), making the industry highly fragmented. In New Zealand, the most concentrated of all producing nations at that time, the largest company (Montana) was responsible for over 60 percent of all wine made. The California producer E. & J. Gallo made more wine in a year than the whole of Australia or the whole of the Bordeaux region. This does not mean that Europe does not have large companies. At the beginning of the twenty-first century the French-based Louis Vuitton Moët–Hennessy produced more wine each year than any other company in the world. Nevertheless, Europe does have a more fragmented industry.

Wine production in the new producing countries tends to be dependent on access to capital rather than inheritance. This has had another consequence, for access to capital facilitates greater use of the equipment modern technology offers. The focus on control and hygiene mentioned above is particularly significant—some would say obsessively so—in these countries. Again it is not true that wine producers in Europe disdain technology, as some in the erstwhile colonies would claim. Some Bordeaux châteaus have state-of-the-art equipment, and the *champenois* (people of Champagne) are world leaders in the production of sparkling wine. Crucially, however, fragmentation makes widespread access both to the technology and the attitudes that accompany it less likely.

Changing Market

As the geography of production has changed, so has the geography of consumption. Changes in income patterns, reflected in the development of consumer culture, as well as travel, both voluntarily with holidays and forced in migration or war service, have made wine more accessible to many. Technology allows better wine to be made cheaper, and the blurring of class difference means wine is perceived less as the drink of the elite in many coun-

FIGURE 1

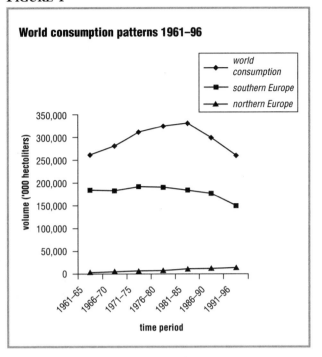

FIGURE 1

tries. A nascent wine culture in East Asia has offered the world's producers yet more opportunity to sell their wares and, with that region's focus on the label as a status symbol, has generated a rapid escalation in price of the world's most prestigious wines.

Wine in Society

While the consumption of wine has spread widely, so too have the forces opposed to it multiplied. Historically, opposition to wine was limited to the religion of Islam. Before about 1800, moderate consumption of alcohol was almost universally accepted in western Europe, although the religious maintained that drinking to excess was wrong. However, two social movements combined to change that widespread tolerance. The social anomie of industrialization and the shift to the city resulted in widespread abuse by the poorer classes. At the same time a new religious conservatism, allied to socially concerned evangelicalism, saw in alcohol the work of the devil. Temperance is a misnomer. It means restraint rather than prohibition, but the temperance movements came to work for prohibition. The movements were most successful in the United States with the passing of the Eighteenth Amendment to the Constitution in 1919. But the impact of temperance movements was felt in strict limits on alcohol use in places as diverse as New Zealand, Wales, Canada, and Scandinavia.

Formal prohibition failed, but its influence lived on in a neoprohibitionist approach, mainly in North America and to a certain extent in Scandinavia. Justifiable concern about the effects of driving under the influence of

Viticulture continues to spread outside the traditional wine growing regions. It has become a major source of agricultural income for South Africa. This vineyard is located on the Cape Peninsula. © LANZ VON HORSTEN; GALLO IMAGES/CORBIS.

alcohol is confused with an absolute need to protect people from themselves and to deny them the possibility of moderate enjoyment of wine.

At the end of the twentieth century, however, another factor came in into play, the relationship between wine and health. While abuse of alcohol contributes to a range of diseases, most notably cirrhosis, science has rediscovered what doctors have known down the centuries, that moderate consumption of wine can have positive health effects. Scientists have also provided the objective evidence for this, for instance, showing the impact red wine can have on improving the balance the beneficial high-density lipoprotein component of cholesterol in the vascular system. This change in outlook was typified by the broadcasting of "The French Paradox" on television in the United States in 1991. Sales of red wine jumped dramatically overnight, followed by a prolonged battle between the wine industry and the Bureau of Alcohol, Tobacco, and Firearms about the health labeling on bottles of wine.

The Twenty-first Century

What does the twenty-first century hold for the wine industry and the wine consumer? The pace of technological change is increasing. Disputes have developed over gene modification and the possibility of creating new varieties in the laboratory. Perhaps ultimately great wines will be recreated in test tubes. The mass production of 1961 Chateau Lafitte would horrify some but could please many.

The geography of production continues to change. The quality of wine produced in southern Europe has improved gradually, but many poor-quality sites have been abandoned because of a lack of markets for the wines. Meanwhile, as long as demand in the English-speaking and East Asian countries rises, the new producing countries will probably continue to raise their production. However, in the short term it is possible that they will suffer a glut of grapes for which no market exists. Then what happens when China begins to select appropriate sites for the production of high-quality wine?

Historically wines were sold on the basis of their geographic origins. Increasingly they are sold by the variety of grape used, and it seems likely that this trend will continue. Chardonnay and cabernet sauvignon currently dominate worldwide, but previously sherry and lambrusco reigned. The balance could yet shift to, for example, nebbiolo and manseng.

The current catchphrase is, people drink less but better. That probably hides the true shift in consumption, but it is a useful rule of thumb for how consumption changes. Critically in the late twentieth century, wine, like every other production industry, was taken over by marketing. That is not necessarily a bad thing, as part of the marketing manager's job is to ensure that consumers are satisfied with what they get. If that means more palatable wine, then consumers benefit. On the other hand, the tendency of marketing to "segment" its customers into large groups means that those who seek the unusual or the different may find it increasingly hard to find the grape variety or region of their choice in price-point driven supermarkets that command up to three-quarters of the retail market in many Western countries. The signs, however, indicate that the gradual shift back is to greater diversity.

See also **Alcohol; Beer; Fermentation.**

BIBLIOGRAPHY

Berger, Nicholas, Kim Anderson, and Randy Stringer. *Trends in the World Wine Market, 1961 to 1996: A Statistical Compendium.* Adelaide, Australia: Centre for International Economic Studies, 1998.

Brook, Stephen, ed. *A Century of Wine.* London: Mitchell Beasley, 2000. Separate chapters provided by individual experts cover the development of the wine industry over the twentieth century.

Fuller, Robert C. *Religion and Wine.* Knoxville: University of Tennessee Press, 1996. The relationship of wine and religion, including prohibition, in an American context.

Johnson, Hugh. *The Story of Wine.* London: Mitchell Beasley. 1989. A readable, popular introduction to the subject.

Loubère, Leo A. *The Wine Revolution in France.* Princeton, N.J.: Princeton University Press, 1990. A century of developments in the world's most important wine producing country.

Phillips, Rod. *A Short History of Wine.* New York: Ecco, 2000.

Robinson, Jancis. *The Oxford Companion to Wine.* 2d ed. New York: Oxford University Press, 1999. An invaluable and comprehensive work on wine.

Unwin, Tim. *Wine and the Vine.* London: Routledge, 1996. The most comprehensive academic introduction to the history of wine and wine production.

Steve Charters

WINE, NONGRAPE

Winemaking is one of the most ancient of human endeavors. Archaeological evidence suggests that early winemakers began practicing their art nearly eight thousand years ago. Since then, efforts have been largely directed toward controlling the fermentation of the grape. United States regulatory agencies classify nongrape wines by their primary component into apple or pear, fruit or berry, citrus and agricultural wine. The latter includes wines made from honey, root crops, flower parts, cacti, and rice.

Successful fermentation of nongrape materials presents a variety of challenges. Most important is increasing the sugar content in the fruit or other component. At optimal maturity of any fruit, the sugar content is insufficient to yield a wine of 10+ percent alcohol. As a result, winemakers are allowed to add sugar, a process called chaptalization. A winemaker also needs to control acidity since fruit and vegetables are often deficient. The deficiency is corrected by addition of either citric or malic acids or by blending higher acid fruit or wine. In contrast, citrus and some berries may be too high in acidity,

a defect that can be corrected by the practice of amelioration or regulated addition of water. Nitrogen deficiencies may arise from the fruit and/or processing and, if critically low, result in interrupted or stuck fermentation. Such fermentations require addition of exogenous nitrogen, typically in the form of diammonium phosphate (DAP). With the exception of berries, processing of fruit and vegetable products generally results in very poor juice yields. Pectinase enzyme preparations may be used to attack cell wall structure, liberating fluid. Alternatively, the fruit may be frozen and thawed before processing. Formation of ice crystals ruptures cell walls, which then release fluid and increase juice yield. However, this may result in premature oxidation and diminished fruit character. An alternative, fermentation of macerated pulp, rather than of expressed juice, will trap heat of fermentation and increase the probability of stuck fermentation. In contrast, fermentation of larger volumes of juice requires cooling capable of dissipating heat.

When making mead or honey wine, the principal component, honey, is typically 70 percent sugar or more, with the compositional balance reflecting type and origin of the flowers. Honeys may range in color and flavor from light, mild, and fragrant to darker and more strongly flavored. Since refined honeys have reduced character, due to thermal processing, mead producers prefer to purchase unprocessed or minimally processed honey. While intensified in flavor and aromatics, natural honey is prone to crystallization when stored at refrigeration temperatures. Although sensorially unapparent, honey is acidic (average pH 3.9). The primary acid is gluconic (5.7 g/L) with lower concentrations of other common acids, which reflect the honey's origins.

Pulque is fermented from the sap (*aguamiel*) of the Agave (Maguey), a succulent plant indigenous to the desert highlands of central Mexico. Bacteria, primarily *Zymomonas mobilis*, and yeasts have historically been responsible for alcoholic fermentation; however, modern producers use commercial yeast (*Saccharomyces cerevisiae*). Wine made from melons is not as successful as those made from other products. Unless cofermented or blended with more highly flavored fruits, melon wines are generally insipid. Further, color is colloidal: A variety of melon that is red when fermenting will become straw-yellow upon clarification and bottling.

Dandelion wine is probably the best-known example of wine made from flower parts. Although most view dandelions as a nuisance, the flower has a long history as a medicinal herb and teas. Petals are excised, boiled, and extracted in various formulations of sugar and acid (citrus fruit or juice) for several days prior to straining and addition of yeast. Since petals are typically low in available nitrogen, supplementation is required.

Berry fermentations from cultivated and native berries are relatively simple. Most have adequate to excess acidity and juice/wine yields are acceptable. Apple wine (cider, hard cider, apple jack) is also an ancient beverage, and consumption of fermented apple juice is well over two thousand years old. English colonists brought apple seeds to north America where both "hard" and nonalcoholic juice became their most popular drink. Pear wine, also known as perry or *poire*, has its origins in both the England and Normandy region of northern France. Compared with ciders, perrys have more refined and ephemeral aromas. Perry also contains a high level of the nonfermentable sugar-alcohol, sorbitol, resulting in a more full-bodied presentation.

Included in the stone fruits category are wines made from numerous varieties of peaches and nectarines, plums, apricots, and cherries. Each presents unique challenges. As noted above, the most significant issue is juice yield. Enzyme additions are helpful. Produced from either cultivated or native species, cherries yield a relatively distinctive and easily managed fruit wine. Cherry pits contain organic cyanides either as cyanogenic glycosides or hydrocyanic acid. Therefore, any cracked seeds should be separated from the pulp prior to fermentation. Among commercially available varieties, sour cherries, such as Montmorensay, are sought after due to their already high acidity. However, sweet cherries may also produce excellent wine upon blending or with acid supplementation. "Wild" or chokecherries are common to much of North America. Chokecherries derive their name from their extraordinary acidity or "sourness" compared with cultivated cherries.

See also **Alcohol; Apple; Beer; Berries; Fermentation; Fermented Beverages Other than Wine or Beer; Flowers; Fruit; Sugar and Sweeteners; Wine.**

K. C. Fugelsang

WOMEN AND FOOD. Although the subject of women and food is of vast importance, it is difficult to document. Unfortunately for women's history in general, early historians customarily focused on public events (usually male), and most women's records have been discarded or lost. Further, the material we have in greatest abundance is that of the wealthy, who were literate, had large properties and kitchens to manage, and kept records. If one generalization can be made from this uneven data, it would probably be the concept that family cooking was universally associated with women and was shaped by location, period, culture, and class. Because most changes in women's relationship to food are found in the middle status range, it will be the focus of this essay.

Women's Early Association with Food and Agriculture

From the earliest days of prehistory, women have not only nurtured society with their own kinds of cookery but also figured predominantly in the agricultural innovation that, to this day, feeds much of the world. Women's place in a pervasive gender food dichotomy has defined their

THE CORN GODDESS

Nearly all New World tribes had a Corn Goddess or Corn Maiden, an Earth Goddess who taught them how to grow food from her body. Often her body was sacrificed, as she demanded, so that her children could grow food on it. This became a constant reminder to her descendants to treat the land as their Mother. One of the most famous Corn Mothers was Central American Chicomecoatl, who also guarded women who had died in childbirth.

power and status for millennia. In the earliest nomadic societies that subsisted on foraging and hunting, the foragers were almost always females. Men's contribution was through the hunt. Recent archaeological findings suggest that the diet was largely vegetative (female) and was not nearly as meat-centered (male) as surviving bone remains once seemed to indicate. Nevertheless, this diet sustained extremely healthy people. The extent of women's knowledge must have been vast, as they knew where, in their wanderings, specific plants were to be found at different times of the year and which parts of the plants were edible in different stages of their life cycle. This early gender-based pattern still exists, and survives in such nomadic cultures as the African Bushmen.

It has been suggested that the division of food responsibility was a consequence of women's limited mobility, resulting from childbearing and extended periods of childcare. In any case, their familiarity with plants and their own identification with creating new life (the male role having been as yet unrecognized) were undoubtedly factors in their monumental innovation, the formation of the first organized agriculture (c. 8000 B.C.E.).

Evidence of the high regard women earned is reflected cross culturally in the stories of universal origin even up to and including subsequent patriarchal systems. For example, in ancient Greco-Roman mythology, the story of Demeter (Ceres), the goddess of agriculture and fertility, and her daughter Persephone (Proserpina) acknowledge women's responsibility for developing agriculture, the origin of growing seasons, and the agrarian skills that they taught people. In distant Mexico people worshiped Ceres' counterpart, the pre-Aztec Great Corn Mother known as Chicomecoatl; variants of her story abound in tribes and nations throughout the hemisphere.

The new agriculture did more than feed people—it changed basic human society. Food could now be produced in one place and stored there for year-round avail-

Pictures of markets the world over reveal one common theme: women selling food. In nations where agriculture is small-scale, women are usually both food producers and food retailers. The twist in this nineteenth-century woodcut is that folk costume is being exploited as a marketing ploy to call attention to the agricultural products. Woodcut from the *Neues Illustriertes Schweizer Kochbuch* [New Illustrated Swiss Cookbook] published at Zurich in 1876. ROUGHWOOD COLLECTION.

ability, and it enabled the formation of permanent settlements that preceded the growth of civilizations.

Women's agricultural revolution was followed by men's parallel development of domesticated herds and large animal husbandry, today practiced by nomadic Masai of East Africa and the sheepherders of Central Asia. Their herds supplied not only food but also a reservoir of a different commodity—wealth and status.

During this time, women continued their long-established custom of cooking privately indoors to strengthen family ties and health. When men cooked, it was usually outdoors for other men, serving the religious, political, and social needs of the community. Each gender had its own kind of pots and specific areas of cuisine. Women slow-cooked moist dishes of grain and vegetable (sometimes flavored with small amounts of meat) in clay stewpots. Men tended to roast or grill meats with iron equipment. A vestige of this remains today in women's daily cooking and men's backyard barbecues. This sim-

ple division of food tasks by gender has changed very little with the centuries; the distinctive roles have blurred only as society itself has undergone major changes.

Women in Ancient Greece and Rome

One of these changes happened with the appearance of patriarchal societies. Gender food divisions among the ancient civilizations indicate not only women cooking at home, but also some men forming a professional class of chefs that cooked for the most privileged. In Greece and Rome, for example, these chefs were noted for their elaborate presentations for upper-class banquets and epicurean occasions. At the same time, the taverns and street vendors that provided a substantial amount of food to all levels of urban society were staffed by both men and women of lower status, but with unclear gender divisions. Women of all classes were considered by men to be inferior and were restricted to "lesser" domestic duties and family service at home, but they were still credited for

THE RIGHT TO COOK

In 1677, Beatrice Plummer found herself in the Salem, Massachusetts, courthouse. She complained that her husband had denied her not only food provisions but also the right to perform her household responsibilities by cooking properly for the household. The court fined her husband for his "abusive carriages and speeches." The unequal division of spheres sometimes had its ironic side.—Cited in Laurel Thatcher Ulrich, *Good Wives* (1982).

their cookery. Women's place in the middle-class kitchens sometimes became more supervisory, as slaves were easily available, but their earlier place of power and honor was gone. Under ongoing patriarchal control, such gender divisions continued to be established and enforced for centuries.

The Middle Ages through the Early Modern Centuries

During the Middle Ages and the Renaissance, the gender divisions were increasingly reinforced by a growing system of secular and religious laws. Upper- and middle-class women remained relatively powerless at home under the rule and protection of male relatives and had no possibility of developing their own careers. There were, as always, a different set of culinary standards for male cooks, who sometimes achieved the prestigious positions denied to women. Manuscripts of their compiled recipes were written for other chefs and ultimately became the first cookbooks. Women who cooked in the urban marketplace were still working at lower-status work and may have filled a variety of positions, depending on fortune or skill. At one end of the gamut, they may have been hired as cooks in modest homes, and at the other as scullery maids. Like men, they also worked in taverns or as street vendors, perhaps as the ubiquitous and fanciful "Gingerbread Women" who sold spicy goodies at local fairs and festivals.

The rural world has always lived by its own code of gender rules. Like working-class women, farm women often participated in the workplace. In much of urban middle-class Europe, only men were permitted to function in public, where they represented their families' interests and worked to keep the community strong. Married middle-class urban women lived more privately under the umbrella of male authority and representation. However, women commonly functioned more independently within the rural corporate family, where they traditionally contributed to family decision-making and

income. Their labors, beyond the customary cooking, kitchen gardening, preserving, caring for barnyard animals, etc., included the local sale of their own products, among them butter, eggs, cheese, fruit and vegetables, poultry, and perhaps cooked wares in season. They secured much-needed funds, as farm capital is usually tied up in buildings, stock, equipment, and cash is invariably scarce. Thus, farm women, even those of means, were early food entrepreneurs in the public market.

It should also be mentioned, in the interest of thoroughness, that women with high positions were rarely in the kitchen, apart from supervising menus or preparing occasional delicacies in honor of a special guest or occasion.

One of the few sources of material about women in this period is the world of art. Although such works are too sparse to provide a conclusive picture, they nevertheless suggest some parameters of gender roles. Many paintings from the sixteenth century show women cooking, but rarely in positions of authority. In a German print of 1507, a male chef adjusts flavorings, while a lower-status scullery maid washes (or peels) food. A Dutch image from 1510 shows important-looking men conducting business in the hall in the foreground while a woman cooks in the kitchen in the background. In eighteenth-century France, Chardin painted a series of female kitchen servants in low circumstances, depicting their fatigue and perhaps boredom. However, in the same period we see evidence of change: a Spanish painting shows two authoritative women in an elaborate Valencian kitchen, cooking and handing their platters to liveried butlers, presumably for an important feast. Likewise, the frontispiece of Eliza Smith's cookbook (London, 1727) shows in the foreground three women in charge of the kitchen, while in the background one sees the suggestion of a butler carrying a tray into the dining room beyond. This is consistent with an event in the American colony of Virginia, in which the English Governor Bottetourt hired a woman (unnamed in the records) to replace his retiring steward William Marshman. Over a century later, Isak Dinesen's short story "Babette's Feast" centered on a French female chef who embodied Dinesen's youthful professional dreams, perhaps indicating that such careers for women were becoming more conceivable. These isolated examples in themselves give suggestions of possible circumstances but obviously wield more clout when combined with sources such as cookbooks.

Women and Cookbooks

The printing press and other incipient technologies made a new genre of cookbooks possible, this time for a widening audience of middle-class urban women. They had begun to work with this audience by the late 1500s. In a field dominated by men, the first published works, under male *noms de plume*, guided affluent and literate women who presided over privileged estates and well-appointed home kitchens. Cookbook writing was essentially done in private; anonymity hid its entrepreneurial aspect and circumvented the social code. More often, male writers, such as Gervase Markham (*The English Housewife*, 1615) and Richard Bradley (*The Country Housewife and Lady's Director*, 1732), writing for this female audience used recipes from women's manuscripts without noting their sources.

By the eighteenth century, middle-class women driven by economic need began publishing cookbooks for other women under their own names. They often incorporated the knowledge and experience of their own kitchens with more complex hospitality food. In a few cases they were the work of the more privileged, who wrote as a social service. These cookbooks appeared in differing numbers throughout European cultures: England's strong middle class produced many, while France, with a different social and economic system, produced relatively few. Women of other established traditions, among them German, Polish, Dutch, Spanish, and Scandinavian, were also represented.

Many of these early cookbooks were carried around the world by emigrating colonists. For example, Eliza Smith's *The Compleat Housewife* (London, 1727) and Hannah Glasse's *Art of Cookery* (London, 1747) were used extensively in North American settlements. Amelia Simmons, author of *American Cookery*, the first American cookbook (1796), followed their lead with her commonly used English-American cuisine. Those who followed her were, interestingly enough, women of stature who were justly famous for their works on women's affairs and social and political reform. These culinary pioneers of the new American democracy presented a new public female image of independence, competence, and enterprise. By the mid-nineteenth century, growing literacy and lowering book prices made cooking manuals available in increasing numbers and by the century's end, they were owned in large numbers throughout the nation. Noted authors such as Marion Harland, Maria Parloa, Sarah Tyson Rorer, and Fannie Farmer also ran cooking schools, wrote newspaper and magazine columns, and lent their names and reputations to new product endorsements and advertisements. Their influence helped to mold a unified national American cuisine, and sometimes they used their culinary forum to support women's social or religious issues.

The changing nature and proliferation of women's cookbooks unwittingly documented a shift in women's general social and economic position. Many cookbooks were prefaced with dedications to brides and young matrons of the urban middle class, with the comment that young women were no longer learning housekeeping at home and were unprepared to run their own homes. The early years that girls had traditionally spent learning these tasks were now dedicated to education in public school, perhaps followed by finishing school or college, and then by jobs that lasted until marriage. Women were nevertheless expected to acquire domestic skills and to aspire

ACTIVIST COOKS

Capable women who wrote cookbooks were often noted for their other public activities. Lydia Maria Child, author of *The Frugal Housewife* (1832) also wrote widely on social and political issues; Sarah Josepha Hale (1849) edited Godey's *Lady's Book*—the preeminent women's periodical of the time; and Catharine Beecher, who published *Domestic Receipt* in 1846, also campaigned widely for strong women's professions in education and the home.

to the idealized Victorian separation of gender responsibilities, the "Doctrine of Separate Spheres," under which women avoided involvement in the public world of work. One of their sanctioned spheres, that of service to the community, revealed indications of the changes to come.

Women in the Public Sphere
The growing female philanthropic movement used home-cooking skills to produce fund-raising cookbooks, church suppers, food festivals, and bake sales. Women's Exchanges supported middle-class women in straitened circumstances by selling their home-cooked foods, often in special lunchrooms. These educational and charitable activities taught basic business skills, which had hitherto been held only by men. By the early 1920s, their example (and the new automobile) inspired female tearooms and luncheonettes, run by and geared to women, and serving a feminine "dainty" cuisine. It is entirely likely that this major step in women's progress toward economic equality succeeded because it utilized the familiar, accepted, and integral bonds between women, food, and community service.

Cookbook writing was only one activity related to the growth of cities in the early nineteenth century. Yeoman farm women had spent much of their time in food work, but once transplanted to the city they found alternative opportunities in the emerging middle class, the cash economy, and entrepreneurism. For example, Pearl Rivers (whose real name was Elizabeth Jane Poitevent Nicholson), the first woman publisher of a major newspaper (*The Picayune*, New Orleans), used her position to organize field research, collect local home-based recipes, and preserve the disappearing but cherished Creole cuisine in *The Picayune Creole Cookbook*, 1900.

The amalgam of cultures in the United States allowed for differing women's roles. New England's separate spheres doctrine, promoted in women's writings nationally, kept middle-class urban women out of the marketplace, while New Orleans's internationally based culture encouraged them. For example, Madame Begue, an accomplished Bavarian chef relocated in New Orleans, earned an impressive reputation with her Creole food as both restaurateur and cookbook author (1900). She was, in many ways, like the skillful French matriarchs drawing on their own home cooking and running bistros. Some women ran boardinghouses and competed on the merits of their kitchens. They are credited with molding a generation of young farm men relocating in growing cities, and in many ways directing the course of the emerging middle class. Other work opportunities opened in higher education with the establishment of federally mandated land grant colleges (1862) and the developing schools of home economics at which food study was elevated to a more academic level. They trained middle class women for significant food careers in nutrition, social work, and education.

The Late Twentieth Century

The Great Depression, the World Wars, and the postwar return to normalcy did relatively little to change basic American cuisine or women's home responsibility for it. However, in the 1970s the women's movement began to weaken traditional gender divisions, and women at home were exposed to a new wave of highly visible professional female cooks and authors. Julia Child and Alice Waters familiarized homemakers with innovative food, and incidentally offered a model of the professional female. Inspired by such luminaries, a succession of TV cooking shows, and the growing feminist emphasis on business careers, numbers of capable young women began to operate their own restaurants, bakeries, and publications. Female journalists such as Mimi Sheraton, Gael Greene, and Ruth Reichl found a niche as food essayists, critics, and restaurant reviewers. In academia food became a more acceptable subject for professional attention as the social sciences began the study of women as foodgivers through the perspectives of history, sociology, anthropology, archaeology, and folklore.

The Twenty-first Century

While a good part of the undeveloped and developing world still identifies women with traditional home cooking, the food role of women in developed nations is in a period of change, a logical response to shifting economic opportunities and family structure. As women increasingly work away from home, they have, of necessity, reduced their customary domestic food preparations. Many men have accepted some of the responsibility for daily cooking (a new role for them), perhaps continuing to cook a special (often gourmet) menu for weekend guests.

As traditional domesticity becomes more scarce, Martha Stewart's style of home cookery has vindicated the ancient female role for those at home, assuring her female audience of renewed status and satisfaction. Many women know far less about cookery than their mothers did and have asserted their perceived liberation from household drudgery with the proud statement, "I don't cook." Fortunately or not, their daughters often lack basic skills and culinary understanding. Having experienced neither instruction nor the memory of food cooked from natural ingredients, they tend to associate good dining with the elusive processes of restaurants. As women establish a respected place in the professional work force and prepare the food that had been associated with men since antiquity, the old dichotomy of men's food and women's food has begun to slip. At the same time, fast food, convenience, and "take-out" foods, which are, in a sense, the traditional male cuisine, are replacing the comfort foods associated with women's home cooking. It would seem that economic progress has weakened associations between gender and cuisine and the link between women and food, leaving us to ponder the consequences.

See also **Anthropology and Food; Apicius; Child, Julia; Cookbooks; Fisher, M. F. K.; Food and Gender; Home Economics.**

BIBLIOGRAPHY

Avakian, Arlene Voski, ed. *Through the Kitchen Window: Women Writers Explore The Intimate Meanings of Food and Cooking.* Boston: Beacon Press, 1997.

Cowan, Ruth Schwartz. *More Work for Mother: The Ironies Of Household Technology From The Open Hearth To The Microwave.* New York: Basic Books, 1983.

Curtin, Deane W., and Lisa M. Heldke. *Cooking, Eating, Thinking: Transformative Philosophies of Food.* Bloomington: Indiana University Press, 1992.

Douglas, Mary, ed. *Food in the Social Order: Studies of Food and Festivities in Three American Communities.* New York: Russell Sage Foundation, 1984.

Farb, Peter, and George Armelagos. *Consuming Passions: The Anthropology of Eating.* Boston: Houghton Mifflin, 1980.

Humphrey, Theodore C., and Lin T. Humphrey, eds. *"We Gather Together:" Food and Festival in American Life.* Ann Arbor: UMI Research Press, 1988.

Longone, Janice B., and Daniel T. Longone. *American Cookbooks and Wine Books 1797–1950.* Ann Arbor: Clements Library and The Wine and Food Library, 1984.

Reed, Evelyn. *Woman's Evolution: From Matriarchal Clan to Patriarchal Family.* New York: Pathfinder Press, 1975.

Shapiro, Laura. *Perfection Salad: Women and Cooking at the Turn of the Century.* New York: Farrar, Straus and Giroux, 1986.

Strasser, Susan. *Never Done: A History of American Housework.* New York: Pantheon, 1982.

Ulrich, Laurel Thatcher. *Good Wives: Image and Reality in the Lives of Women in Northern New England.* New York: Knopf, 1982.

Alice Ross

WRAPS. *See* **Sandwich.**

YEAST, BREAD AND BREWER'S. *See* **Baking; Beer; Fermentation; Microorganisms.**

ZOROASTRIANISM. The prophet Zarathushtra (known to the Greeks as Zoroaster) founded Zoroastrianism, one of the world's oldest living religions, in northeastern Iran, probably between 1800 to 1000 B.C.E. Zoroastrianism became the state religion of the first Persian Empire in the sixth century B.C.E. after which its influence waxed and waned until finally it was supplanted by Islam in the seventh century C.E. In the tenth century B.C.E. a small group of Zoroastrians migrated to the Gujurat region of northwest India where they became known as Parsis (Persians). Today, the number of adherents is estimated at 274,000 worldwide with the largest community centered around Bombay and a smaller number in the Iranian homeland. Zoroastrians follow the creed of "good thoughts, good words, good deeds" and uphold virtues of honesty, charity and hospitality.

Ruins of ancient Persian fire altars at Naqch-E-Rostem, Iran. © Charles and Josette Lenars/CORBIS.

Role of Food in Zoroastrian Tradition
Dietary laws and food proscriptions are not part of original Zoroastrian teachings. Nevertheless certain ritual and symbolic uses of food have evolved over time, based on later Zoroastrian writings and as a consequence of interaction with other cultures and religions. For example, Zoroaster abolished the tribal custom of animal sacrifice, though it quickly reemerged and became incorporated in Zoroastrian rituals. Today it survives only amongst Iranian Zoroastrians during the festival of Mehregan, when meat and bread are distributed. Generally all foods are permitted and are consumed according to personal preference and local custom. For example, Zoroastrians often forgo pork and beef in deference to their Hindu and Moslem neighbors, or are vegetarian by choice. Certain foods may still be avoided because they belong to the evil counter creation. These include birds of prey and "hideous fish." Carrion is regarded as impure as is any food coming into contact with it.

The concept of purity versus impurity is central to Zoroastrianism. Cleanliness is highly regarded and purification rites are a part of most ceremonies. Formerly there were elaborate codes to preserve food from impurities such as skin, nail clippings, sweat, blood, and excreta. It was forbidden to eat or drink from a common cup, and priests would not accept food from non-Zoroastrians. Although cleanliness and purity remain as important values, ritual practices have declined amongst ordinary Zoroastrians. Constraints of contemporary urban life, and differing interpretations by orthodox and reform groups within the faith also contribute to variations in actual practice. It is also notable that fasting—a common religious discipline—plays no part in the faith. Asceticism and renunciation, of which fasting is an integral part, are forbidden.

Symbolism and Sacred Foods
Rituals are important in Zoroastrianism. They establish a connection between the material and spiritual universes. Food plays a part in rituals, as a thanksgiving to God and as a symbol of fellowship created through sharing of material bounty. There are certain foods that are symbolic of the various creations of Ahura Mazda and are therefore regarded as being superior and thus suitable for use in religious rituals and ceremonies. These include bread (*dron*), milk, water, ghee, rice, dates, and pomegranates. *Dron* is an unleavened bread made from wheat flour and ghee. It may be prepared only by a member of a priestly family. During the preparation of the bread the words *humata, hukhta, hvarshta* (good thoughts, good words, good deeds) are intoned three times, accompanied by placing a mark on the bread, for a total of nine marks. This bread of life is a source of spiritual strength. Haoma (*hom*) juice extracted from the haoma plant is used in a number of rituals. It contains a mild narcotic.

The pomegranate, being an evergreen, is a symbol of everlasting life and of the fecundity of nature. It is also a symbol of prosperity and plenty because of its numerous seeds. Pomegranate leaves are chewed during purification rituals at initiation ceremonies, marriages, after childbirth and by those who have come into contact with corpses. (There has been a modern decline in the latter practice). Rice, as in the Hindu tradition, represents happiness and prosperity.

Ceremonies and Ritual
Yasna is the most important of the Zoroastrian ceremonies. It is celebrated daily, but only in Iranian and Indian fire temples and only by qualified priests. Yasna is an "inner" ceremony, which only Zoroastrians may attend and is often specially commissioned by community members. Ritual materials used include haoma with pomegranate twigs, goat's milk, *dron* with ghee, water, and a presanctified mixture known as *parahom*. The water signifies health and wellbeing, while the milk represents the presence of Vohu Manah, the protector of the animal kingdom. The haoma twigs and pomegranate leaves are pounded with consecrated water and milk is

TABLE 1

Zoroastrian festivals

Name	Season	Description	Creation link	Dates
Maidh-yo-zarem	mid-spring	Fresh vegetables in plenty	Sky	April 30–May 4
Maidh-yo-shema	mid-summer	Time for harvesting corn	Water	June 29–July 3
Paiti-Shahem	early autumn	Harvesting of fruit	Earth	September 12–16
Aya-threm	mid-autumn	Sowing of winter crops	Plants	October 13–17
Maidh-ya-rem	mid-winter	Period of perfect rest	Cattle	January 1–5
Hamas-path-maedern	pre-spring	Equality of heat and cold	Man	March 16–20
Nou Rouz	spring	Renewal of life	Fire	March 21

The Zoroastrian year is based on a solar calendar and starts at the exact time of the vernal equinox.

SOURCE: Adapted from the website of the Ancient Iranian Cultural and Religious Research and Development Centre (www.ancientiran.com).

added to the mixture, some of which is then poured out into a well from whence it will flow out to strengthen the whole of creation. The remainder of the mixture is offered first to those present who endowed the ceremony and then to other observers.

One of the main Zoroastrian "outer" ceremonies, Afrinagan, may be performed in any suitable clean place and can be witnessed by Zoroastrians and non-Zoroastrians alike. Its purpose is to praise the bounty of Ahura Mazda and to request His blessings on members of the community. Ritual objects include a tray of food, usually fruit, wine, eggs, milk and water, which serves as a visible sign of Ahura Mazda's generosity and care for the wellbeing of his people. The main feature of the ritual is a threefold exchange of flowers between the officiating priests.

After giving birth, a woman should be confined with her baby for a period of forty days in order to allow the impurities she has contacted to dissipate. For modern urban Zoroastrian women this requirement not to leave the house for nearly six weeks is extremely difficult to fulfill. As a compromise the woman eats separately from the rest of the family. After forty days she takes a ritual bath that allows her to rejoin the wider community. The new baby may be given a drop of consecrated *hom* from a Yasna ceremony as a "strengthening drink." If this is not possible a drink may be made from *hom* twigs, pomegranate leaves and water.

Children are initiated into the Zoroastrian faith at age seven to eleven years (Parsi) or twelve to fifteen years (Iranian), at which time they become responsible for fully observing Zoroastrian practices. At the initiation ceremony (Naojote) the child receives a sacred white shirt (*sudra*) and a sacred cord (*kushti*). A ceremonial tray prepared for the ceremony contains a mix of rice, pomegranate, raisins, almonds, and slices of coconut. The officiating priest who blesses the child pours these over the head of the child. A banquet for family and friends follows the initiation ceremony.

Marriage ceremonies take place at the house of the bride or in public places where large crowds can congregate. Prior to the actual marriage ceremony the bridegroom, with family friends and priests, arrives at the bride's house. While the others enter the house the groom remains on the threshold where he is greeted with traditional symbols of welcome. An egg, a coconut, and a dish of water are successively passed around his head, then dashed to the floor. The groom may then enter the house and the marriage ceremony commences. During the ceremony the priest sprinkles rice on the bride and groom who also sprinkle each other with rice. A feast for family and friends follows the marriage ceremony.

After a death, consecrated food, such as *dron* or eggs is offered to sustain the soul of the newly departed. The family of the deceased may not eat meat for three days, a practice that may be linked to fear over impurities or to the idea that flesh food is more suitable for celebratory occasions. On the anniversary of a death the souls of the departed are offered cooked foods, milk, water, and fresh fruit. This food is subsequently given to charity. These observances, like others, may be in decline.

Holidays and Festivals

Zoroaster established a series of holy days and also assimilated existing traditional festivals and celebrations. There are six seasonal festivals known as Gahambars, which celebrate the six creations of Sky, Water, Earth, Plants, Cattle, and Man. Traditionally each lasted for five days, though now much curtailed, and included feasting, prayer and rejoicing. The most important festival is that of Nou Rouz—the New Year. Held at the spring equinox it celebrates the rejuvenation of nature and the beginning of new life, and is linked to fire—the seventh and most sacred creation of Ahura Mazda. It is marked by family and community gatherings, religious services, feasting, and gift giving. The ten days prior to Nou Ruz are for commemoration of the departed. A variety of grains and lentils are soaked so that they will germinate in time for the holiday. These green sprouts are added to a thanksgiving table that also holds a variety of other symbolic objects and foods such as bread, fruit, fresh vegetables, sugar cones, and decorated eggs.

Each day in the Zoroastrian calendar is dedicated to a particular divine being or important event, twelve of which also has its own month. Name-day feasts are held when month name and day name coincide. Adar, the ninth day of the ninth month, is celebrated as the birthday of fire and is a time to give thanks for warmth and light. Traditionally food is not cooked in the home, to give the fire a rest. Other festivals include the birth and death anniversary of the prophet and the feast of all souls (Muktad) for remembrance of departed family members.

See also **Death and Burial; Feasts, Festivals, and Fasts; India: Northern India; Iran; Middle East; Religion and Food**.

BIBLIOGRAPHY

Boyce, Mary. *Zoroastrians*. London: Routledge and Kegan Paul, 1979.

Clark, Peter. *Zoroastrianism. An Introduction to an Ancient Faith*. Brighton: Sussex Academic Press, 1998.

Dhalla, Homi B. "Social Dimensions of the Zoroastrian Jashan Ceremony." *Dialogue and Alliance* 4, no. 11 (1990): 27–36.

Nigosian, Solomon A. *The Zoroastrian Faith: Tradition and Modern Research*. Montreal: McGill-Queens University Press, 1993.

Paul Fieldhouse

APPENDIX: DIETARY REFERENCE INTAKES

The table on the pages that follow lists vitamins, their food sources, and adverse effects of over-consumption. The table gives recommended intake (RDA) and—a feature not available in previous RDA lists—shows tolerable upper levels that readers can use as a guideline to prevent excess consumption.

The reference values are referred to collectively as the Dietary Reference Intakes (DRIs) and include Recommended Dietary Allowance (RDA), Adequate Intake (AI), and the Tolerable Upper Intake Level (UL). A requirement, which can vary depending on age, gender, and life stage, is defined as the lowest continuing intake level of a nutrient that will maintain a defined level of nutriture in an individual. (The nutrient levels published in the DRI reports apply to the healthy general population. They are not expected to be sufficient for individuals who are already malnourished, nor would they be adequate for disease states known to have increased nutrient requirements.)

The table was developed by the Institute of Medicine's Standing Committee on the Scientific Evaluation of Dietary Reference Intakes, in cooperation with Health Canada. In 1995 the Food and Nutrition Board of the Institute of Medicine—part of the National Academy of Sciences—appointed the committee to replace the tenth (1989) edition of the Recommended Dietary Allowances (RDAs) document.

Dietary reference intakes: Vitamins

Nutrient	Function	Life stage group	RDA/AI*	UL[a]	Selected food sources	Adverse effects of excessive consumption	Special considerations
Biotin	Coenzyme in synthesis of fat, glycogen, and amino acids	Infants	(µg/d)		Liver and smaller amounts in fruits and meats	No adverse effects of biotin in humans or animals were found. This does not mean that there is no potential for adverse effects resulting from high intakes. Because data on the adverse effects of biotin are limited, caution may be warranted.	None
		0–6 mo	5*	ND[b]			
		7–12 mo	6*	ND			
		Children					
		1–3 y	8*	ND			
		4–8 y	12*	ND			
		Males					
		9–13 y	20*	ND			
		14–18 y	25*	ND			
		19–30 y	30*	ND			
		31–50 y	30*	ND			
		50–70 y	30*	ND			
		> 70 y	30*	ND			
		Females					
		9–13 y	20*	ND			
		14–18 y	25*	ND			
		19–30 y	30*	ND			
		31–50 y	30*	ND			
		50–70 y	30*	ND			
		> 70 y	30*	ND			
		Pregnancy					
		≤ 18 y	30*	ND			
		19–30 y	30*	ND			
		31–50 y	30*	ND			
		Lactation					
		≤ 18 y	35*	ND			
		19–30 y	35*	ND			
		31–50 y	35*	ND			
Choline	Precursor for acetylcholine, phospholipids, and betaine	Infants	(mg/d)	(mg/d)	Milk, liver, eggs, peanuts	Fishy body odor, sweating, salivation, hypotension, hepatotoxicity	Individuals with trimethylaminuria, renal disease, liver disease, depression, and Parkinson's disease may be at risk of adverse effects with choline intakes at the UL.
		0–6 mo	125*	ND			
		7–12 mo	150*	ND			
		Children					
		1–3 y	200*	1000			
		4–8 y	250*	1000			
		Males					Although AIs have been set for choline there are few data to assess whether a dietary supply of choline is needed at all stages of the life cycle, and it may be that the choline requirement can be met by endogenous synthesis at some of these stages.
		9–13 y	375*	2000			
		14–18 y	550*	3000			
		19–30 y	550*	3500			
		31–50 y	550*	3500			
		50–70 y	550*	3500			
		> 70 y	550*	3500			
		Females					
		9–13 y	375*	2000			
		14–18 y	400*	3000			
		19–30 y	425*	3500			
		31–50 y	425*	3500			
		50–70 y	425*	3500			
		> 70 y	425*	3500			
		Pregnancy					
		≤ 18 y	450*	3000			
		19–30 y	450*	3500			
		31–50 y	450*	3500			
		Lactation					
		≤ 18 y	550*	3000			
		19–30 y	550*	3500			
		31–50 y	550*	3500			

[continued]

Dietary reference intakes: Vitamins

Nutrient	Function	Life stage group	RDA/AI*	UL[a]	Selected food sources	Adverse effects of excessive consumption	Special considerations
Folate Also known as: Folic acid Folacin Pteroylpoly- glutamates Note: Given as a dietary folate equivalents (DFE). 1 DFE = 1 μg food folate = 0.6 μg of folate from fortified food or as a supplement consumed with food = 0.5 μg of a supplement taken on an empty stomach.	Coenzyme in the metabolism of nucleic and amino acids; prevents megaloblastic anemia	Infants 0–6 mo 7–12 mo Children 1–3 y 4–8 y Males 9–13 y 14–18 y 19–30 y 31–50 y 50–70 y > 70 y Females 9–13 y 14–18 y 19–30 y 31–50 y 50–70 y > 70 y Pregnancy ≤ 18 y 19–30 y 31–50 y Lactation < 18 y 19–30 y 31–50 y	(μg/d) 65* 80* 150 200 300 400 400 400 400 400 300 400 400 400 400 400 600 600 600 500 500 500	(μg/d) ND[b] ND 300 400 600 800 1,000 1,000 1,000 1,000 600 800 1,000 1,000 1,000 1,000 800 1,000 1,000 800 1,000 1,000	Enriched cereal grains, dark leafy vegetables, enriched and whole-grain breads and bread products, fortified ready-to-eat cereals	Masks neurological complication in people with vitamin B_{12} deficiency. No adverse effects associated with folate from food or supplements have been reported. This does not mean that there is no potential for adverse effects resulting from high intakes. Because data on the adverse effects of folate are limited, caution may be warranted. The UL for folate applies to synthetic forms obtained from supplements and/or fortified foods.	In view of evidence linking folate intake with neural tube defects in the fetus, it is recommended that all women capable of becoming pregnant consume 400 μg from supplements or fortified foods in addition to intake of food folate from a varied diet. It is assumed that women will continue consuming 400 μg from supplements of fortified food until their pregnancy is confirmed and they enter prenatal care, which ordinarily occurs after the end of the periconceptional period—the critical time for formation of the neural tube.
Niacin Includes nicotinic acid amide, nicotinic acid (pyridine-3-carboxylic acid) and derivatives that exhibit the biological activity of nicotinamide. Note: Given as niacin equivalents (NE). 1 mg of niacin = 60 mg of trytophan; 0–6 months = preformed niacin (not NE).	Coenzyme or cosubstrate in many biological reduction and oxidation reactions—thus required for energy metabolism	Infants 0–6 mo 7–12 mo Children 1–3 y 4–8 y Males 9–13 y 14–18 y 19–30 y 31–50 y 50–70 y > 70 y Females 9–13 y 14–18 y 19–30 y 31–50 y 50–70 y > 70 y Pregnancy < 18 y 19–30 y 31–50 y Lactation ≤ 18 y 19–30 y 31–50 y	(mg/d) 2* 4* 6 8 12 16 16 16 16 16 12 14 14 14 14 14 18 18 18 17 17 17	(mg/d) ND ND 10 15 20 30 35 35 35 35 20 30 35 35 35 35 30 35 35 30 35 35	Meat, fish, poultry, enriched and whole-grain breads and bread products, fortified ready-to-eat cereals	There is no evidence of adverse effects from the consumption of naturally occuring niacin in foods. Adverse effects from niacin-containing supplements may include flushing and and gastrointestinal distress. The UL for niacin applies to synthetic forms obtained from supplements, fortified foods, or a combination of the two.	Extra niacin may be required by persons treated with hemodialysis or peritoneal dialysis, or those with malabsorption syndrome.

[continued]

Dietary reference intakes: Vitamins

Nutrient	Function	Life stage group	RDA/AI*	UL[a]	Selected food sources	Adverse effects of excessive consumption	Special considerations
Pantothenic Acid	Coenzyme in fatty acid metabolism	Infants	(mg/d)	(mg/d)	Chicken, beef, potatoes, oats, cereals, tomato products, liver, kidney, yeast, egg yolk, broccoli, whole grains	No adverse effects associated with pantothenic acid from food or supplements have been reported. This does not mean that there is no potential for adverse effects resulting from high intakes. Because data on the adverse effects of pantothenic acid are limited, caution may be warranted.	None
		0–6 mo	1.7*	ND[b]			
		7–12 mo	1.8*	ND			
		Children					
		1–3 y	2*	ND			
		4–8 y	3*	ND			
		Males					
		9–13 y	4*	ND			
		14–18 y	5*	ND			
		19–30 y	5*	ND			
		31–50 y	5*	ND			
		50–70 y	5*	ND			
		> 70 y	5*	ND			
		Females					
		9–13 y	4*	ND			
		14–18 y	5*	ND			
		19–30 y	5*	ND			
		31–50 y	5*	ND			
		50–70 y	5*	ND			
		> 70 y	5*	ND			
		Pregnancy					
		≤ 18 y	6*	ND			
		19–30 y	6*	ND			
		31–50 y	6*	ND			
		Lactation					
		≤ 18 y	7*	ND			
		19–30 y	7*	ND			
		31–50 y	7*	ND			
Riboflavin Also known as: Vitamin B$_2$	Coenzyme in numerous redox reactions	Infants	(mg/d)	(mg/d)	Organ meats, milk, bread products, and fortified cereals	No adverse effects associated with riboflavin consumption from food or supplements have been reported. This does not mean that there is no potential for adverse effects resulting from high intakes. Because data on the adverse effects of riboflavin are limited, caution may be warranted.	None
		0–6 mo	0.3*	ND			
		7–12 mo	0.4*	ND			
		Children					
		1–3 y	0.5	ND			
		4–8 y	0.6	ND			
		Males					
		9–13 y	0.9	ND			
		14–18 y	1.3	ND			
		19–30 y	1.3	ND			
		31–50 y	1.3	ND			
		50–70 y	1.3	ND			
		> 70 y	1.3	ND			
		Females					
		9–13 y	0.9	ND			
		14–18 y	1.0	ND			
		19–30 y	1.1	ND			
		31–50 y	1.1	ND			
		50–70 y	1.1	ND			
		> 70 y	1.1	ND			
		Pregnancy					
		≤ 18 y	1.4	ND			
		19–30 y	1.4	ND			
		31–50 y	1.4	ND			
		Lactation					
		≤ 18 y	1.6	ND			
		19–30 y	1.6	ND			
		31–50 y	1.6	ND			

[continued]

Dietary reference intakes: Vitamins

Nutrient	Function	Life stage group	RDA/AI*	UL[a]	Selected food sources	Adverse effects of excessive consumption	Special considerations
Thiamin	Coenzyme in the metabolism of carbohydrates and branched-chain amino acids	Infants	(mg/d)		Enriched, fortified, or whole-grain products; bread and bread products, mixed foods whose main ingredient is grain, and ready-to-eat cereals	No adverse effects associated with thiamin from food or supplements have been reported. This does not mean that there is no potential for adverse effects resulting from high intakes. Because data on the adverse effects of thiamin acid are limited, caution may be warranted.	Person, who may have increased needs for thiamin include those being treated with hemodialysis or peritoneal dialysis, or individuals with malabsorption syndrome.
		0–6 mo	0.2*	ND[b]			
Also known as: Vitamin B1 Aneurin		7–12 mo	0.3*	ND			
		Children					
		1–3 y	0.5	ND			
		4–8 y	0.6	ND			
		Males					
		9–13 y	0.9	ND			
		14–18 y	1.2	ND			
		19–30 y	1.2	ND			
		31–50 y	1.2	ND			
		50–70 y	1.2	ND			
		> 70 y	1.2	ND			
		Females					
		9–13 y	0.9	ND			
		14–18 y	1.0	ND			
		19–30 y	1.1	ND			
		31–50 y	1.1	ND			
		50–70 y	1.1	ND			
		> 70 y	1.1	ND			
		Pregnancy					
		< 18 y	1.4	ND			
		19–30 y	1.4	ND			
		31–50 y	1.4	ND			
		Lactation					
		< 18 y	1.4	ND			
		19–30 y	1.4	ND			
		31–50 y	1.4	ND			
Vitamin A	Required for normal vision, gene expression, reproduction, embryonic development and immune function	Infants	(μg/d)	(μg/d)	Liver, dairy products, fish	Teratological effects, liver toxicity	Individuals with high alcohol intake, pre-existing liver disease, hyperlipidemia, or severe protein mal-nutrition may be distinctly susceptible to the adverse effects of excess preformed vitamin A intake.
		0–6 mo	400*	600			
Includes provitamin A carotenoids that are dietary precursors of retinol		7–12 mo	500*	600		Note: from preformed Vitamin A only.	
		Children					
		1–3 y	300	600			
		4–8 y	400	900			
		Males					
Note: Given as retinol activity equivalents (RAEs). 1 RAE = 1 μg retinol, 12 μg ß-carotene, 24 μg α-carotene, or 24 μg ß-crytoxanthin. To calculate RAEs from REs of provitamin A carotenoids in foods, divide the REs by 2. For preformed vitamin A in foods or supplements and for provitamin A carotenoids in supplements, 1 RE = 1RAE.		9–13 y	600	1,700			ß-carotene supplements are advised only to serve as a provitamin A source for individuals at risk of vitamin A deficiency.
		14–18 y	900	2,800			
		19–30 y	900	3,000			
		31–50 y	900	3,000			
		50–70 y	900	3,000			
		> 70 y	900	3,000			
		Females					
		9–13 y	600	1,700			
		14–18 y	700	2,800			
		19–30 y	700	3,000			
		31–50 y	700	3,000			
		50–70 y	700	3,000			
		> 70 y	700	3,000			
		Pregnancy					
		≤ 18 y	750	2,800			
		19–30 y	770	3,000			
		31–50 y	770	3,000			
		Lactation					
		≤ 18 y	1,200	2,800			
		19–30 y	1,300	3,000			
		31–50 y	1,300	3,000			

[continued]

Dietary reference intakes: Vitamins

Nutrient	Function	Life stage group	RDA/AI*	UL[a]	Selected food sources	Adverse effects of excessive consumption	Special considerations
Vitamin B$_6$ Vitamin B$_6$ comprises a group of six related compounds: pyridoxal, pyridoxine, pyridozamine, and 5'-phosphates (PLP, PNP, PMP)	Coenzyme in the metabolism of amino acids, glycogen and sphingoid bases	Infants 0–6 mo 7–12 mo	(mg/d) 0.1* 0.3*	(mg/d) ND[b] ND	Fortified cereals, organ meats, fortified soy-based meat substitutes	No adverse effects associated with Vitamin B$_6$ from food have been reported. This does not mean that there is no potential for adverse effects resulting from high intakes. Because data on the adverse effects of Vitamin B$_6$ are limited, caution may be warranted. Sensory neuropathy has occurred from high intakes of supplemental forms.	None
		Children 1–3 y 4–8 y	 0.5 0.6	 30 40			
		Males 9–13 y 14–18 y 19–30 y 31–50 y 50–70 y > 70 y	 1.0 1.3 1.3 1.3 1.7 1.7	 60 80 100 100 100 100			
		Females 9–13 y 14–18 y 19–30 y 31–50 y 50–70 y > 70 y	 1.0 1.2 1.3 1.3 1.5 1.5	 60 80 100 100 100 100			
		Pregnancy ≤ 18 y 19–30 y 31–50 y	 1.9 1.9 1.9	 80 100 100			
		Lactation ≤ 18 y 19–30 y 31–50 y	 2.0 2.0 2.0	 80 100 100			
Vitamin B$_{12}$ Also known as: Cobalamin	Coenzyme in nucleic acid metabolism; prevents megaloblastic anemia	Infants 0–6 mo 7–12 mo	(μg/d) 0.4* 0.5*	(μg/d) ND ND	Fortified cereals, meat, fish, poultry	No adverse effects have been associated with the consumption of the amounts of Vitamin B$_{12}$ normally found in foods or supplements. This does not mean that there is no potential for adverse effects resulting from high intakes. Because data on the adverse effects of vitamin B$_{12}$ are limited, caution may be warranted.	Because 10 to 30 percent of older people may mal-absorb foodbound vitamin B$_{12}$, it is advisable for those older than 50 years to meet their RDA mainly by consuming foods fortified with vitamin B$_{12}$ or a supplement containing vitaming B$_{12}$.
		Children 1–3 y 4–8 y	 0.9 1.2	 ND ND			
		Males 9–13 y 14–18 y 19–30 y 31–50 y 50–70 y > 70 y	 1.8 2.4 2.4 2.4 2.4 2.4	 ND ND ND ND ND ND			
		Females 9–13 y 14–18 y 19–30 y 31–50 y 50–70 y > 70 y	 1.8 2.4 2.4 2.4 2.4 2.4	 ND ND ND ND ND ND			
		Pregnancy ≤ 18 y 19–30 y 31–50 y	 2.6 2.6 2.6	 ND ND ND			
		Lactation ≤18 y 19–30 y 31–50 y	 2.8 2.8 2.8	 ND ND ND			

[continued]

Dietary reference intakes: Vitamins

Nutrient	Function	Life stage group	RDA/AI*	UL[a]	Selected food sources	Adverse effects of excessive consumption	Special considerations
Vitamin C Also known as: Ascorbic acid Dehydroascorbic acid (DHA)	Cofactor for reactions requiring reduced copper or iron metalloenzyme and as a protective antioxidant	Infants 0–6 mo 7–12 mo	(mg/d) 40* 50*	(mg/d) ND[b] ND	Citrus fruits, tomatoes, tomato juice, potatoes, brussel sprouts, cauliflower, broccoli, strawberries, cabbage, and spinach	Gastrointestinal distrubances, kidney stones, excess iron absorption	Individuals who smoke require an additional 35 mg/d of vitamin C over that needed by non-smokers.
		Children 1–3 y 4–8 y	15 25	400 650			Nonsmokers regularly exposed to tobacco smoke are encouraged to ensure they meet the RDA for vitamin C.
		Males 9–13 y 14–18 y 19–30 y 31–50 y 50–70 y > 70 y	45 75 90 90 90 90	1,200 1,800 2,000 2,000 2,000 2,000			
		Females 9–13 y 14–18 y 19–30 y 31–50 y 50–70 y > 70 y	45 65 75 75 75 75	1,200 1,800 2,000 2,000 2,000 2,000			
		Pregnancy ≤ 18 y 19–30 y 31–50 y	80 85 85	1,800 2,000 2,000			
		Lactation ≤ 18 y 19–30 y 31–50 y	115 120 120	1,800 2,000 2,000			
Vitamin D Also known as: Calciferol Note: 1 μg calciferol = 40 IU vitamin D The DRI values are based on the absence of adequate exposure to sunlight.	Maintain serum calcium and phosphorus concentrations	Infants 0–6 mo 7–12 mo	(μg/d) 5* 5*	(μg/d) 25 25	Fish liver oils, flesh of fatty fish, liver and fat from seals and polar bears, eggs from hens that have been fed vitamin D, fortified milk products, and fortified cereals.	Elevated plasma 25 (OH) D concentration causing hypercalcemia	Patients on glucocorticoid therapy may require additional vitamin D.
		Children 1–3 y 4–8 y	5* 5*	50 50			
		Males 9–13 y 14–18 y 19–30 y 31–50 y 50–70 y > 70 y	5* 5* 5* 5* 10* 15*	50 50 50 50 50 50			
		Females 9–13 y 14–18 y 19–30 y 31–50 y 50–70 y > 70 y	5* 5* 5* 5* 10* 15*	50 50 50 50 50 50			
		Pregnancy ≤ 18 y 19–30 y 31–50 y	5* 5* 5*	50 50 50			
		Lactation ≤ 18 y 19–30 y 31–50 y	5* 5* 5*	50 50 50			

[continued]

Dietary reference intakes: Vitamins

Nutrient	Function	Life stage group	RDA/AI*	ULᵃ	Selected food sources	Adverse effects of excessive consumption	Special considerations
Vitamin E	A metabolic function has not yet been identified. Vitamin E's major function appears to be as a non-specific chain-breaking antioxidant.	Infants	(mg/d)	(mg/d)	Vegetable oils, unprocessed cereal grains, nuts, fruits, vegetables, meats	There is no evidence of adverse effects from the consumption of vitamin E naturally occurring in foods.	Patients on anti-coagulant therapy should be monitored when taking vitamin E supplements.
Also known as: α-tocopherol		0–6 mo	4*	NDᵇ			
		7–12 mo	5*	ND			
Note: As α-tocopherol. α-Tocopherol includes RRR-α-tocopherol, the only form of α-tocopherol that occurs naturally in foods, and the 2R-stereoisomeric forms of α-tocopherol (RRR-, RSR-, RRS-, and RSS-α-tocopherol) that occur in fortified foods and supplements. It does not include the 2S-stereoisomeric forms of α-tocopherol (SRR-, SSR-, SRS-, and SSS-α-tocopherol), also found in fortified foods and supplements.		Children				Adverse effects from vitamin E containing supplements may include hemorrhagic toxicity.	
		1–3 y	6	200			
		4–8 y	7	300			
		Males				The UL for vitamin E applies to any form of α-tocopherol obtained from supplements, fortified foods, or a combination of the two.	
		9–13 y	11	600			
		14–18 y	15	800			
		19–30 y	15	1,000			
		31–50 y	15	1,000			
		50–70 y	15	1,000			
		> 70 y	15	1,000			
		Females					
		9–13 y	11	600			
		14–18 y	15	800			
		19–30 y	15	1,000			
		31–50 y	15	1,000			
		50–70 y	15	1,000			
		> 70 y	15	1,000			
		Pregnancy					
		≤ 18 y	15	800			
		19–30 y	15	1,000			
		31–50 y	15	1,000			
		Lactation					
		≤18 y	19	800			
		19–30 y	19	1,000			
		31–50 y	19	1,000			
Vitamin K	Coenzyme during the sythesis of many proteins involved in blood clotting and bone metabolism	Infants	(μg/d)	(μ/d)	Green vegetables (collards, spinich, salad greens, broccoli), brussel sprouts, cabbage, plant oils and margarine	No adverse effects associated with vitamin K consumption from food or supplements have been reported in humans or animals. This does not mean that there is no potential for adverse effects resulting from high intakes. Because data on the adverse effects of vitamin K are limited, caution may be warranted.	Patients on anti-coagulant therapy should monitor their vitamin K intake.
		0–6 mo	2.0*	ND			
		7–12 mo	2.5*	ND			
		Children					
		1–3 y	30*	ND			
		4–8 y	55*	ND			
		Males					
		9–13 y	60*	ND			
		14–18 y	75*	ND			
		19–30 y	120*	ND			
		31–50 y	120*	ND			
		50–70 y	120*	ND			
		> 70 y	120*	ND			
		Females					
		9–13 y	60*	ND			
		14–18 y	75*	ND			
		19–30 y	90*	ND			
		31–50 y	90*	ND			
		50–70 y	90*	ND			
		> 70 y	90*	ND			
		Pregnancy					
		≤ 18 y	75*	ND			
		19–30 y	90*	ND			
		31–50 y	90*	ND			
		Lactation					
		≤ 18 y	75*	ND			
		19–30 y	90*	ND			
		31–50 y	90*	ND			

[continued]

Dietary reference intakes: Vitamins

Note: The table is adapted from the DRI reports, see www.nap.edu. It represents Recommended Dietary Allowances (RDAs) in **bold type**, Adequate Intakes (AIs) in ordinary type followed by an asterisk (*), and Tolerable Upper Intake Levels (ULs)[a]. RDAs and AIs may both be used as goals for individual intake. RDAs are set to meet the needs of almost all (97 to 98 percent) individuals in a group. For healthy breastfed infants, the AI is the mean intake. The AI for other life stage and gender groups is believed to cover the needs of all individuals in the group, but lack of data prevent being able to specify with confidence the percentage of individuals covered by this intake.

[a]UL = The maximum level of daily nutrient intake that is likely to pose no risk of adverse effects. Unless otherwise specified, the UL represents total intake from food, water, and supplements. Due to lack of suitable data, ULs could not be established for vitamin K, thiamin, riboflavin, vitamin B_{12}, pantothenic acid, biotin, or carotenoids. In the absence of ULs, extra caution may be warranted in consuming levels above recommended intakes.

[b]ND = Not determinable due to lack of data of adverse effects in this age group and concern with regard to lack of ability to handle excess amounts. Source of intake should be from food only to prevent high levels of intake.

SOURCE:: *Dietary Reference Intakes for Calcium, Phosphorous, Magnesium, Vitamin D, and Fluoride* (1997); *Dietary Reference Intakes for Thiamin, Riboflavin, Niacin, Vitamin B_6, Folate, Vitamin B_{12}, Pantothenic Acid, Biotin, and Choline* (1998); *Dietary Reference Intakes for Vitamin C, Vitamin E, Selenium, and Carotenoids* (2000); and *Dietary Reference Intakes for Vitamin A, Vitamin K, Arsenic, Boron, Chromium, Copper, Iodine, Iron, Manganese, Molybdenum, Nickel, Silicon, Vanadium, and Zinc* (2001). These reports may be accessed via www.nap.edu.

Reprinted courtesy of the National Academy of Sciences.

SYSTEMATIC OUTLINE OF CONTENTS

This systematic outline provides a general overview of the conceptual scheme of the *Encyclopedia*, listing the titles of each entry and subentry. The outline is divided into twenty-seven parts.

Because the section headings are not mutually exclusive, certain entries in the *Encyclopedia* are listed in more than one section.

FOODS: STAPLE FOODS

Apple
Arthropods: Insects, Arachnids, and Crustaceans
Banana and Plantain
Barley
Berries
Botanicals
Cabbage and Crucifer Plants
Cactus
Cassava
Cattle
Cereal Grains and Pseudo-Cereals
Chili Peppers
Crustaceans and Shellfish
Cucumbers, Melons, and Other Cucurbits
Dairy Products
Eggs
Fish
       Overview
       Freshwater Fish

Nutrients
Phosphorus and Calcium
Proteins and Amino Acids
Sodium
Starch
Sugar and Sweeteners
Trace Elements
Vitamins: Overview
Vitamins: Water-Soluble and Fat-Soluble Vitamins
Vitamin C

CONDITIONS, DISORDERS, AND DISEASES

Allergies
Anorexia, Bulimia
Beriberi
Disease: Metabolic Diseases
Health and Disease
Malnutrition
Malnutrition: Protein-Energy Malnutrition
Niacin Deficiency (Pellagra)
Obesity
Scurvy

HUNGER

Codex Alimentarius
Distribution of Food
Food Banks
Food Pantries
Food Riots
Food Stamps
Food Supply and the Global Food Market
Food Supply, Food Shortages
Homelessness
Hunger, Physiology of
Hunger Strikes
Malnutrition
Malnutrition: Protein-Energy Malnutrition
Meals on Wheels
Political Economy
Rationing
Soup Kitchens
WIC (Women, Infants, and Children's) Program

POLICY

Agricultural Research
Botulism
Climate and Food
Commodity Price Supports
Cost of Food
Ecology and Food
Extension Services
FAO (Food and Agriculture Organization)
Food as a Weapon of War
Food Consumption Surveys

Food Politics: United States
Food Safety
Food Security
Food Stamps
Food Trade Associations
Government Agencies
Government Agencies, U.S.
Grain Reserves
Herbicides
Inspection
International Agencies
Labeling, Food
Pesticides
Political Economy
Population and Demographics
School Meals
Toxins, Unnatural, and Food Safety
Water: Safety of Water
WIC (Women, Infants, and Children's) Program

FOOD AND SOCIETY

Aphrodisiacs
Chef
Class, Social
Comfort Food
Consumer Protests
Death and Burial
Folklore, Food in
Food, Future of: A History
Food Politics: United States
Fusion Cuisine
Gender and Food
Health Foods
Homelessness
Intake
Luxury
Macrobiotic Food
Myth and Legend, Food in
National Cuisines, Idea of
Political Economy
Poverty
Professionalization
Sex and Food
Slow Food
Table Talk
Taboos
Tourism
Travel
Vegetarianism
Waiters and Waitresses
Women and Food

RELIGION

Ancient Mediterranean Religions
Bahá'í

Nutritionists
Sociology

BIOGRAPHIES

Apicius
Arcimboldo, Giuseppe
Beard, James
Beeton, Isabella Mary
Birdseye, Clarence
Brillat-Savarin, Jean Anthelme
Carême, Marie Antoine
Child, Julia
Delmonico Family
Epicurus
Escoffier, Georges-Auguste
Fauchon
Favre, Joseph

Fisher, M. F. K.
Gamerith, Anni
Goodfellow, Elizabeth
Grimod de la Reynière
Hédiard
Herodotus
Hippocrates
Kellogg, John Harvey
La Varenne, Pierre François de
Leslie, Eliza
Medici, Catherine de'
Parkinson, James Wood
Pasteur, Louis
Petronius
Platina
Pythagoras
Rabelais, François
Taillevent

DIRECTORY OF CONTRIBUTORS

Michael Abdalla
University of Agriculture,
Poznan, Poland
> Myth and Legend, Food in

Judi Adams
Wheat Foods Council,
Parker, Colo.
> Wheat: Wheat as a Food

Ken Albala
University of the Pacific
> Dietary Systems: A Historical
> Perspective

Gary Allen
Author of The Resource Guide for Food
Writers
> Caramelization
> Education about Food
> Sausage

E. N. Anderson
University of California,
Riverside
> China: Ancient and Dynastic
> Cuisine
> China: Beijing Cuisine
> China: Guangzhou Cuisine
> China: Zhejiang Cuisine
> China: Sichuan Cuisine

Jean Andrews
Author of Peppers: The Domesticated
Capsicums
> Chili Peppers

Mahadev Apte
Duke University (Emeritus)
> Humor, Food in

Gertrude Armbruster
Cornell University (Emerita)
> Frozen Food

Lawrence E. Armstrong
University of Connecticut
> Salt
> Thirst

Alice Arndt
Food Historian and Editor of Culinary Biographies
> Favre, Joseph
> Pasteur, Louis

Charles J. Arntzen
Arizona Biomedical Institute,
Arizona State University
> Biotechnology

Hea-Ran L. Ashraf
Southern Illinois University,
Carbondale
> Health Foods

Jim Auchmutey
The Atlanta Journal-Constitution
> United States: The South

Joëlle Bahloul
Indiana University
> Judaism

Stephen M. Bailey
Tufts University
> Combination of Proteins

James W. Baker
Former Senior Historian,
Plimoth Plantation, Plymouth, Mass.
> Thanksgiving

Peggy M. Baker
Pilgrim Society, Plymouth, Mass.
> Thanksgiving

Enrique Balladares-Castellón
> Central America

David Dwight Baltensperger
University of Nebraska Panhandle
Research and Extension Center,
Scottsbluff
> Cereal Grains and Pseudo-
> Cereals

Lewis A. Barness
University of South Florida
> Disease: Metabolic Diseases

David R. Bauer
Cornell University
> Eating: Anatomy and
> Physiology of Eating

Warren Belasco
University of Maryland,
Baltimore County
> Food, Future of: A History

David John Bell
Staffordshire University,
Stoke-on-Trent, U.K.
> Diaspora

Amy Bentley
New York University
> Baby Food
> Food Riots
> Food Studies
> Rationing

Margaret E. Bentley
University of North Carolina
> Household

Jennifer Berg
New York University
> Food Studies
> Icon Foods
> Pizza

Rob Berg
University of Colorado
Health Sciences Center
Fluoride

Irene Berman-Levine
University of Pennsylvania
Artificial Foods

Linda Murray Berzok
Food Historian and Writer,
Stephentown, N.Y.
Cookbooks, Community
Food Archaeology
Gelatin
Jell-O
Poisoning
Potato
Royal Tasters
Sex and Food

Bruce Ryan Bistrian
Harvard Medical School
Enteral and Parenteral
Nutrition

Fritz Blank
Deux Cheminées, Philadelphia
Gastronomy
Intestinal Flora

Roberta Bloom
Independent Mental Health and
Macrobiotic Counselor, Gainesville, Fla.
Macrobiotic Food

John Blundell
University of Leeds, U.K.
Appetite

Phyllis Bober †
Bryn Mawr College
Apicius
Platina

Barry Bogin
University of Michigan, Dearborn
Paleonutrition, Methods of

Loring Davena Boglioli
Culinary Arts Educator, Islip, N.Y.
Professionalization

Kristen Borré
East Carolina University
Arctic
Mammals, Sea

Paul W. Bosland
New Mexico State University
Leaf Vegetables

Dalila Bothwell
New York University
Weddings

George Bray
Louisiana State University Medical Center
Hunger, Physiology of
Obesity

Leslie Brenner
Author of The Art of the Cocktail Party
Cocktail Party

Barrett P. Brenton
St. John's University,
Jamaica, N.Y.
American Indians:
Contemporary Issues

Paul B. Brown
Purdue University
Agricultural Research
Aquaculture
Choline, Inositol, and Related
Nutrients
Fishing

Bill Brown
Cutlery Historian,
Beckenham, Kent, U.K.
Cutlery

Lynn R. Brown
World Bank, Washington, D.C.
Food Security

Marjo Buitelaar
University of Groningen,
The Netherlands
Africa: North Africa

Barbara A. Burlingame
Food and Agriculture Organization of the
United Nations
Food, Composition of

Charles Camp
Maryland Institute College of Art
Foodways

Susan Campbell
Kitchen Garden Historian, London
Gardening and Kitchen
Gardens

Geoffrey Campbell-Platt
University of Reading, U.K.
Fermentation

Kenneth John Carpenter
University of California, Berkeley (Emeritus)
Beriberi
Niacin Deficiency (Pellagra)
Nutrient Bioavailability
Proteins and Amino Acids
Scurvy
Vitamin C

Irene Casas
California State University,
Monterey Bay
Maize as a Food

Elisabeth Giacon Castleman
Food Writer and Cookbook Translator,
Frederick, Md.
Arcimboldo, Giuseppe
Italy: Northern Italy

Simon Charsley
University of Glasgow
Wedding Cake

Steve Charters
Edith Cowan University,
Perth, Western Australia
Wine in the Modern World

Shirley C. Chen
Unilever Bestfoods North America,
Baltimore
Margarine

Shirley E. Cherkasky
Food Historian, Alexandria, Va.
Birthday Foods

Terrie Wright Chrones
Food Historian, Eugene, Ore.
Ancient Kitchen, The
Fads in Food
Marinating and Marinades

Miguel Civil
Oriental Institute, Chicago (Emeritus)
Mesopotamia, Ancient

Mark Nathan Cohen
State University of New York at Platts-burgh
Agriculture, Origins of

Nancy Cotugna
University of Delaware
Food Banks

Ann M. Coulston
Nutrition Consultant, Woodside, Calif.
Vitamins: Water-Soluble and
Fat-Soluble Vitamins

Carole M. Counihan
Millersville University
Gender and Food

Karen A. Curtis
University of Delaware
Food Pantries

Katarzyna J. Cwiertka
University of Leiden, The Netherlands
Japan: Contemporary Issues in
Japanese Cuisine
Korea

Andrew Dalby
*Historian and Linguist,
Saint-Coutant, France*
Byzantine Empire
Epicurus
Etymology of Food
Food in Ovid's *Art of Love*
Greece, Ancient
Herodotus
Luxury
Petronius
Rome and the Roman Empire
Stimulants

Jonathan C. David
Writer and Folklorist, Philadelphia
Art, Food in: Literature
Folklore, Food in

Alan Davidson
*Editor of The Oxford Companion to
Food*
Crustaceans and Shellfish
Fish: Overview
Fish: Sea Fish
Fish, Smoked
Mollusks

Mitchell Davis
*The James Beard Foundation,
New York*
Kitchens, Restaurant

Sharon Davis
*Family and Consumer Sciences
Consultant*
Wheat: The Natural History of
Wheat

Teresa de Castro
University of Adelaide, Australia
Couscous
Iberian Peninsula: Overview

Igor de Garine
*Centre National de la Recherche
Scientifique, Paris (Emeritus)*
Staples

Cara De Silva
Food Historian, New York
Pizza

Wesley R. Dean
Texas A&M University
Kitchen Gadgets
Larousse gastronomique

Raja Deekshitar
*Independent Research Scholar,
Chidambaram, India*
Fasting and Abstinence:
Hinduism and Buddhism

Luise Del Giudice
*Italian Oral History Institute,
Los Angeles*
Pasta
Slow Food

Dominique-André Demers
Biobest Canada Ltd.
Greenhouse Horticulture

Adel P. den Hartog
*International Commission for Research
into European Food History*
Packaging and Canning,
History of
Taboos

Jean-Philippe Derenne
Groupe Hospitalière Pitié-Salpetrière, Paris
Nouvelle Cuisine

Daphne L. Derven
*Copia: The American Center
for Wine, Food, and the Arts,
Napa, Calif.*
Organic Agriculture
Preserving

Jonathan Deutsch
Kingsborough Community College
Lamb Stew

L. Beth Dixon
New York University
Food Stamps
Poverty

Jessica Rae Donze
Georgetown University Medical Center
Medicine

Mary Douglas
University College London (Retired)
Disgust

R. Keith Downey
*Agriculture and Agri-Food Canada
Research Centre, Saskatoon,
Saskatchewan*
Mustard

Christine Madeleine Du Bois
Johns Hopkins University
Soy

Darna L. Dufour
University of Colorado
Arthropods: Insects, Arachnids,
and Crustaceans
Cassava
Crushing

John T. Dunn
University of Virginia
Iodine

Johanna Dwyer
Tufts University
Dietary Assessment
Mediterranean Diet

Boyd Eaton
Emory University
Prehistoric Societies: Stone Age
Nutrition: The Original
Human Diet

John T. Edge
University of Mississippi
Chitlins (Chitterlings)

Lolis Eric Elie
Author of Smokestack Lightning
Barbecue

Rick Ellis
Food Stylist and Historian, New York
Styling of Food

Erika A. Endrijonas
Santa Barbara City College
Betty Crocker

Luis L. Esparza Serra
El Colegio de Michoacán, A.C., Mexico
Food Supply and the Global
Food Market

Nina L. Etkin
University of Hawaii
Ethnopharmacology

David W. Everett
*University of Otago, Dunedin,
New Zealand*
Dairy Products
Phosphorus and Calcium

Doreen Fernández
Ateneo de Manila University
Southeast Asia: Indonesia,
Malaysia, and the
Philippines

Judith M. Fertig
Food Writer and Cookbook Author, Overland Park, Kans.
Breakfast
United States: The Midwest

Paul Fieldhouse
University of Manitoba
Bahá'í
Islam: Shi'ite Islam
Islam: Sufism
Islam: Sunni Islam
Ramadan
Zoroastrianism

Erin Fields
University of North Carolina
Household

Gary Alan Fine
Northwestern University
Mushroom Collectors

Joanne Finkelstein
Author of Dining Out
Waiters and Waitresses

Chad Elliott Finn
*U.S. Department of Agriculture–
Agricultural Research Service,
Horticultural Crops Research Lab*
Berries

Sara Firebaugh
New York University
Cheese

Christina Maria Fjellström
Uppsala University, Sweden
Natural Foods

Cornelia Butler Flora
Iowa State University
Cattle

John D. Floros
Pennsylvania State University
Packaging and Canning,
Modern

Stella Fong
*Asian Food Expert,
Billings, Mont.*
Noodle in Asia

Steven Foster
*Steven Foster Group, Inc.,
Fayetteville, Ark.*
Botanicals

Richard L. Frank
*Olsson, Frank and Weeda, P.C.,
Washington, D.C.*
Adulteration of Food
Labeling, Food

Peter S. Franklin
*PeterBread Consulting, Inc.,
Marblehead, Mass.*
Bread

K. C. Fugelsang
California State University, Fresno
Wine, Nongrape

Gordon William Fuller
Author of Food, Consumers, and the
Food Industry
Additives

Ellen B. Fung
*Children's Hospital and Research
Center, Oakland, Calif.*
Nutrition

Betty Fussell
Food Historian, New York
Beard, James
Brillat-Savarin, Jean Anthelme
Child, Julia
Grimod de la Reynière
Medici, Catherine de'

Víctor Galán Saúco
*Instituto Canario de Investigaciones
Agrarias, Tenerife, Canary Islands*
Banana and Plantain
Fruit: Tropical and Subtropical

David F. Garvin
*U.S. Department of Agriculture–
Agricultural Research Service,
Plant Science Research Unit*
Barley

Kurt Genrup
Umea University, Sweden
Lapps

Ed Gibbon
Compiler of CongoCookbook.com
Africa: Central Africa

Hallgerður Gísladóttir
National Museum of Iceland, Reykjavik
Horse

Maja Godina-Golija
*Institute of Slovenian Ethnology,
Ljubljana, Slovenia*
Balkan Countries

Irwin L. Goldman
University of Wisconsin
Onions and Other *Allium*
Plants

Peter Goldsbrough
Purdue University
Genetic Engineering

Darra Goldstein
Williams College
    Caviar
    Russia

Judith Goode
Temple University
    Retailing of Food

Jack Goody
St. John's College,
Cambridge University (Emeritus)
    Civilization and Food

L. J. Grauke
U.S. Department of Agriculture–
Agricultural Research Service,
Pecan Breeding
    Nuts

Madge Griswold
Independent Scholar, Tucson, Ariz.
    United States: California and
        the Far West
    United States: The Southwest
    Utensils, Cooking

C. Paige Gutierrez
Author of Cajun Foodways
    United States: Cajun Cooking

Barbara Haber
Author of From Hardtack to
Home Fries
    Cookbooks
    Male Cooks in the Mid-
        Twentieth Century

Jean-Pierre Habicht
Cornell University
    International Agencies

G. B. Hagelberg
Canterbury, Kent, U.K.
    Sugar and Sweeteners
    Sugar Crops and Natural
        Sweeteners

Robert A. Hahn
Olsson, Frank and Weeda, P.C.,
Washington, D.C.
    Adulteration of Food
    Labeling, Food

Oliver M. Haid
University of Innsbruck, Austria
    Festivals of Food

Maha N. Hajmeer
University of California, Davis
    Fish, Salted
    Meat, Salted

Sabrina H. B. Hardenbergh
Southern Illinois University,
Carbondale
    Ecology and Food
    Health Foods

Jessica B. Harris
Culinary Historian, New York
    Brazil
    Kwanzaa

Christine A. Hastorf
University of California, Berkeley
    Inca Empire

Corinna Hawkes
Food Policy Consultant, New York
    Geography
    Population and Demographics

Brian Hayden
Simon Fraser University,
Burnaby, British Columbia
    Hunting and Gathering

Sarah Wolfgang Heffner
Mennonite Heritage Center,
Harleysville, Pa.
    Apple

Susan Sykes Hendee
CULACON (Culinary Arts Concepts),
Islip, N.Y.
    Professionalization

Bridget Ann Henisch
Author of Cakes and Characters
    Christmas Drinks
    Epiphany

Constance Hieatt
University of Western Ontario (Emerita)
    Medieval Banquet

Thomas Jefferson Hoban IV
North Carolina State University
    Consumer Protests
    Sociology

Edith Hörandner
University of Graz, Austria
    Gamerith, Anni
    Gingerbread

Lynn F. Hoffmann
Drexel University
    Spirits

David Gerard Hogan
Author of Selling 'em by the Sack
    Fast Food

Michael Holick
Boston University School of Medicine
    Vitamins: Overview

James-Henry Holland
Hobart and William Smith Colleges
    Japan: Traditional Japanese
        Cuisine
    Japanese Tea Ceremony

Heather Holmes
Author of As Good as a Holiday
    Advertising of Food
    Biscuits
    British Isles: Scotland

Marvine Howe
Former New York Times
Correspondent, based in Portugal
    Iberian Peninsula: Portugal

Nancy R. Hudson
University of California, Berkeley
    Nutritionists

Gwen Hyman
Cooper Union for the Advancement of Science and Art
    Lunch

Mary and Philip Hyman
Coauthors of The Oxford Companion to
French Food
    Carême, Marie Antoine
    France: Food and Cuisine in
        France
    France: Northern French
        Cuisines
    France: Southern French
        Cuisines
    France: Tradition and Change
        in French Cuisine
    France: Wine and the French
        Meal
    La Varenne, Pierre François de
    Taillevent

Maryam Imbumi
*Kenya Resource Centre for Indigenous
Knowledge*
 Africa: East Africa

Susan L. F. Isaacs
Union College, Barbourville, Ky.
 M. F. K. Fisher

Jules Janick
Purdue University
 Crop Improvement
 Fruit: Temperate Fruit
 Hippocrates
 Horticulture
 Tomato: Vegetable or Fruit?

Rachel K. Johnson
University of Vermont
 Carbohydrates

John Johnston
*University of Strathclyde,
Glasgow (Emeritus)*
 Whiskey (Whisky)

Carol Zane Jolles
University of Washington
 Inuit

Christopher Justinich
Alfred I. DuPont Hospital for Children
 Allergies

Barbara E. Kahn
*Wharton School,
University of Pennsylvania*
 Marketing of Food

Wilhelmina Kalt
*Atlantic Food and Horticulture
Research Center, Kentville,
Nova Scotia*
 Nutraceuticals

Judit Katona-Apte
*United Nations World Food
Programme, Bangkok*
 Italy: The Italian Meal
 Italy: Southern Italy
 Italy: Tradition in Italian
  Cuisine

Solomon H. Katz
University of Pennsylvania
 Cuisine, Evolution of

Mary Anne Katzenberg
University of Calgary
 American Indians: Prehistoric
  Indians and Historical
  Overview

Alice Kehoe
Marquette University
 Potlatch

Mary Kelsey
Oregon State University (Emerita)
 French Fries
 Silverware
 Stew

Eileen Kennedy
U.S. Department of Agriculture
 Dietary Guidelines

Mark Kern
San Diego State University
 Physical Activity and Nutrition

Jean D. Kinsey
University of Minnesota
 Cost of Food
 Distribution of Food
 Grocery Cart

Barbara Kirshenblatt-Gimblett
New York University
 Bagel
 Passover

Pamela Goyan Kittler
Coauthor of Food and Culture:
A Nutrition Handbook
 Goat

Robin Kline
*Food and Nutrition Writer and
Consultant, Des Moines*
 Mammals

Ria Kloppenborg
University of Utrecht, The Netherlands
 Fasting and Abstinence:
  Hinduism and Buddhism

Aglaia Kremezi
Journalist and Author of The Foods of
Greece
 Greece and Crete

David Kritchevsky
Wistar Institute, Philadelphia

 Cholesterol
 Eggs
 Lipids
 Margarine

Robert R. Krueger
*U.S. Department of Agriculture–
Agricultural Research Service,
National Clonal Germplasm Repository
for Citrus and Dates*
 Dates
 Fruit: Citrus Fruit

Klara Kuti
Hungarian Academy of Sciences
 Central Europe

Kyra Landzelius
Cambridge University
 Body
 Hunger Strikes

Ruth A. Lawrence
*University of Rochester School
of Medicine*
 Lactation

Alexandra Leaf
Author of The Impressionists' Table
 Absinthe

Adrienne Lehrer
University of Arizona (Emerita)
 Language about Food
 Naming of Food

Joanna C. Le Noury
University of Leeds
 Appetite

Rodney E. Leonard
*Community Nutrition Institute,
Minneapolis*
 Codex Alimentarius
 Food Supply, Food Shortages

William R. Leonard
Northwestern University
 Energy

Walter Levy
Pace University, New York
 Picnic

Betty A. Lewis
Cornell University
 Starch

Wendy Hunnewell Leynse
New York University
Metaphor, Food as

Jiming Li
Cornell University
Rice: The Natural History of
Rice
Rice: Rice as a Food
Rice: Rice as a Superfood

Charles S. Lieber
*Bronx V.A. Medical Center and Mount
Sinai School of Medicine*
Alcohol

Leslie Sue Lieberman
University of Central Florida
Caloric Intake

David Ming Lin
Cornell University
Genetics

Doric Little
University of Hawaii
Places of Consumption

Michael Little
*State University of New York
at Binghamton*
Cannibalism
Climate and Food
Herding

Phoebe Lloyd
Texas Tech University
Art, Food in: Painting and the
Visual Arts

Richard L. Lobb
Food Writer, Fairfax, Va.
Botulism
Broasting
Broiling
Food Production, History of
Government Agencies, U.S.
Green Revolution
How to Roast
Meat, Smoked
Military Rations
Oil
Poultry
World Health Organization

Julie Locher
University of Alabama, Birmingham
Comfort Food

Fusion Cuisine
TV Dinner

William G. Lockwood
University of Michigan (Emeritus)
United States: Ethnic Cuisines

Alexandra W. Logue
New York Institute of Technology
Aversion to Food

Lucy M. Long
Bowling Green State University
Symbol, Food as
Tourism

Janet Long-Solís
Universidad Nacional Autónoma de México
Columbian Exchange

Dan Looker
Successful Farming Magazine
Pet Pigs of New Guinea
Pig
Sheep
Spam

Ilya V. Loysha
*Food Historian, Limassol, Cyprus,
and Tomsk, Siberia*
Siberia

Stephanie Lyness
Cookbook Author
Soup

Patricia Lysaght
University College Dublin
British Isles: Ireland
Death and Burial
Seabirds and Their Eggs
Shrove Tuesday

Glenn Mack
University of Texas
Asia, Central

David Magnus
*Associate Editor, American Journal
of Bioethics*
Genetically Modified
Organisms: Health and
Environmental Concerns

Julie O'Sullivan Maillet
*University of Medicine and Dentistry
of New Jersey*
Dietetics

Alan Mann
Princeton University
Evolution

Jeffrey W. Mantz
Vassar College
Caribbean

Lourdes March
Food Consultant, Madrid
Paella Valenciana

James L. Marsden
Kansas State University
Fish, Salted
Meat, Salted

Patricia Martin
*Safe Food and Fertilizer,
Quincy, Wash.*
Toxins, Unnatural, and Food
Safety

Marty Martindale
*Host of FoodSiteoftheDay.com,
Largo, Fla.*
Birdseye, Clarence

Homero Martínez
*Instituto Mexicano del Seguro Social Coor-
dinación de Investigación en Salud*
Malnutrition: Protein-Energy
Malnutrition

Laura Mason
Food Historian, Yorkshire
Baking
British Isles: England
Butter
Candy and Confections
Custard and Puddings
Pastry
Sherbet and Sorbet
Syrups

Maryam Matine-Daftary
Human Rights Advocate, Paris
Iran

Konstantinos I. Matsos
The Pennsylvania State University
Packaging and Canning, Modern

Patrick M. Maundu
*Author of Traditional Food Plants
of Kenya*
Africa: East Africa

Donna Maurer
Author of Vegetarianism: Movement or Moment?
    Vegetarianism

David Maynard
State University of New York at Stony Brook
    Cucumbers, Melons, and Other Cucurbits
    Squash and Gourds

Donald N. Maynard
University of Florida
    Squash and Gourds

Charles Chipley W. McCormick
Cornell University
    Minerals

Francis McFadden
Drexel University
    Grilling
    Meat, Smoked
    Roasting

Wm. Alex McIntosh
Texas A&M University
    Class, Social

Debra Coward McKenzie
University of Vermont
    Carbohydrates

Rebecca J. (Bryant) McMillian
Nutrition Scientist, Raleigh, N.C.
    Antioxidants
    Malnutrition

Ruben G. Mendoza
California State University, Monterey Bay
    Maize: Maize as a Food
    Maize: The Natural History of Maize
    Swidden

Stephen Mennell
National University of Ireland, Dublin— University College Dublin
    France: French and British Cooking Compared

Lorraine Stuart Merrill
Writer on Agriculture and the Environment, Stratham, N.H.
    Environment
    Livestock Production

Simone Meyer
Technical University, Munich
    Food Consumption Surveys

Patricia S. Michalak
Writer, Kempton, Pa.
    Agricultural Workers
    Cereals, Cold
    Extension Services
    Grain Reserves
    Pesticides
    Tillage

Katharine Milton
University of California, Berkeley
    Animals: Primate Diets

Sidney W. Mintz
Author of Tasting Food, Tasting Freedom
    Soy

Geraldine Moreno-Black
University of Oregon
    Southeast Asia: Thailand

Brad Morris
U.S. Department of Agriculture– Agricultural Research Service, Grand Forks Human Nutrition Research Center
    Legumes

Patricia McGrath Morris
Social Policy Researcher, Falls Church, Va.
    Homelessness
    School Meals
    Soup Kitchens

Lucie Morton
Viticulturist, Broad Run, Va.
    Grapes and Grape Juice

Mark Morton
University of Winnipeg
    Proverbs and Riddles, Food in

Hyde H. Murray
Agricultural Attorney
    Commodity Price Supports

James R. Myers
Oregon State University
    Cabbage and Crucifer Plants

Gary Paul Nabhan
Northern Arizona University
    Biodiversity

Khursheed P. Navder
Hunter College, City University of New York
    Alcohol

Mary Kay Nelson
University of California Medical Center, San Francisco
    Food Waste

Marion Nestle
New York University
    Food Politics: United States
    Food Studies

Jacqueline M. Newman
Queens College, City University of New York
    China: Fujian Cuisine
    Escoffier, Georges-Auguste
    Home Economics

Forrest H. Nielsen
U.S. Department of Agriculture– Agricultural Research Service, Grand Forks Human Nutrition Research Center
    Trace Elements

Park S. Nobel
University of California, Los Angeles
    Cactus

Corrie E. Norman
Converse College
    Religion and Food
    Sin and Food

James Norwood Pratt
Author and Creator of The Tea Society, San Francisco
    Tea (Meal)

Henry Notaker
Literary Historian and Food Lecturer, Oslo
    Nordic Countries

Robin O'Brian
Elmira College
    Division of Labor
    Time

Sandra L. Oliver
Author of Saltwater Foodways
    United States: New England

Sven-Olle Olsson
Physiologist, Gastronomist, and
Praeses Academia Gastronomica
Scaniensis, Malmö, Sweden
    Beer: From Late Egyptian
        Times to the Nineteenth
        Century
    Beer: Origins and Ancient
        History
    Beer: Production and Social
        Use
    Beer: The Twentieth Century
    Fermented Beverages Other
        than Wine or Beer

Elisabeth Lambert Ortiz
Author of The Book of Latin American
Cooking
    South America

MM Pack
Food Writer and Culinary Historian,
Austin, Tex.
    Coloring, Food
    Fauchon

Athanasios P. Papadopoulos
Greenhouse and Processing Crops
Research Centre, Agriculture and Agri-
Food Canada, Harrow, Ontario
    Greenhouse Horticulture

Claudia C. Parvanta
Centers for Disease Control and
Protection, Atlanta
    Southeast Asia: Vietnam

Gretel Pelto
Cornell University
    International Agencies
    Nutritional Anthropology

Ramona Lee Pérez
New York University
    Metaphor, Food as

Thangam Philip
Institute of Hotel Management,
Catering, Technology, and Applied
Nutrition, Bombay
    Hindu Festivals
    Hinduism
    India: Moghul India

    India: Northern India
    India: Southern India

Rod Phillips
Author of A Short History of Wine
    Wine
    Wine from Classical Times to
        the Nineteenth Century
    Wine in the Ancient World

Jeffrey M. Pilcher
The Citadel, Charleston, S.C.
    Day of the Dead
    Mexico

Susan Pitman
Porter Novelli, Washington, D.C.
    Biotechnology

Fred Plotkin
Author of Opera 101
    Art, Food in: Opera

Liliane Plouvier
Brussels, Belgium
    Jam, Jellies, and Preserves

Lionel Poilâne †
Poilâne Bakery, Paris
    Bread, Symbolism of

Nancy J. Pollock
Victoria University, Wellington,
New Zealand
    Pacific Ocean Societies

Barry M. Popkin
University of North Carolina
    Nutrition Transition:
        Worldwide Diet Change

Gregory L. Possehl
University of Pennsylvania
    Indus Valley

Jo Marie Powers
University of Guelph, Ontario
(Retired)
    Canada
    Canada: Native Peoples

John Prescott
University of Otago, Dunedin,
New Zealand
    Acceptance and Rejection
    Sensation and the Senses

Sara A. Quandt
Wake Forest University
    Assessment of Nutritional
        Status

Jeri Quinzio
Writer on Food and Spirits, Boston
    Cocktails

Harsh Raman
NSW Agriculture, Wagga Wagga Agri-
cultural Institute, Australia
    Barley

Krishnendu Ray
Culinary Institute of America
    Political Economy

Joan Reardon
Author of M. F. K. Fisher, Julia Child,
and Alice Waters
    Boiling
    Nostalgia
    Poaching

Wendy Reinhardt
International Food Information
Council, Washington, D.C.
    Functional Foods

Alicia Ríos
Food Historian
    Iberian Peninsula: Spain
    Pleasure and Food

Cynthia A. Roberts
Author of The Food Safety
Information Handbook
    Food Safety
    Water: Safety of Water

Una A. Robertson
Author of The History of the Housewife
    Porridge

Susan Rodriguez
California State University, Fresno
    Microbiology

Harry Rolnick
Coauthor of The Chinese Gourmet
    Durian

Jamilla Hoy Rosas
New York University
    WIC (Women, Infants, and
        Children's) Program

Peter G. Rose
Food Historian, South Salem, N.Y.
Low Countries

Meryl S. Rosofsky
New York University
Aphrodisiacs

Alice Ross
Food Historian, Smithtown, N.Y.
Hearth Cookery
Iron Cookstove, The
Women and Food

Daniel J. Royse
Pennsylvania State University
Fungi

Paul Rozin
University of Pennsylvania
Meat

E. C. A. Runge
Texas A&M University
High-Technology Farming

Edward J. Ryder
Plant Geneticist, Salinas, Calif.
Lettuce

Daniel Sack
Author of Whitebread Protestants
Christianity: Western
Christianity

Mikal E. Saltveit
University of California, Davis
Agriculture since the Industrial
Revolution
Food as a Weapon of War
Harvesting
Pythagoras
Seeds, Storage of
Storage of Food

Barbara Santich
University of Adelaide,
Australia
Australia and New Zealand
Australian Aborigines
Renaissance Banquet

Jack Santino
Bowling Green State University
Feasts, Festivals, and Fasts
Halloween

Eleonore Schmitt
South Asia Institute,
Heidelberg, Germany
Bible, Food in the

Barbara O. Schneeman
University of California, Davis
Digestion
Fiber, Dietary

Edmund (Ned) Searles
University of Alaska, Fairbanks
Inuit

Hwai-Ping Sheng
University of Hong Kong
Body Composition
Electrolytes

Colin Sheringham
University of Western Sydney,
Australia
Rabelais, François

Andrew F. Smith
Culinary Historian,
Brooklyn, N.Y.
Chicken Soup
Condiments
Hamburger
Kellogg, John Harvey
Microwave Oven
Peanut Butter
Popcorn
Salad
Snacks
Tomato

Kevin P. Smith
University of Minnesota
Barley

Jeffrey Sobal
Cornell University
Class, Social
Food Waste

Mark F. Sohn
Pikeville College
Flowers
Frying

Rebecca L. Spang
University College London
Restaurants

Diane M. Spivey
Author of The Peppers, Cracklings, and
Knots of Wool Cookbook
Africa: West Africa

Peter W. Stahl
State University of New York
at Binghamton
Prehistoric Societies: Food
Producers

Virginia A. Stallings
Children's Hospital of Philadelphia
Nutrition

John Stanbury
Massachusetts Institute of Technology
(Emeritus)
Iodine

Rosemary Stanton
University of New South Wales,
Australia
Consumption of Food

Karel Steenbrink
University of Utrecht, The Netherlands
Fasting and Abstinence: Islam

Keith H. Steinkraus
Cornell University
Microorganisms

William A. Stini
University of Arizona
Water: Water as a Beverage
and Constituent of Food
Water: Water as a Resource

Martha H. Stipanuk
Cornell University
Calorie
Nutrients
Sodium

Patrick J. Stover
Cornell University
Fats
Folic Acid
Gene Expression, Nutrient
Regulation of
Iron
Nutritional Biochemistry

Adrienne Su
Author of Middle Kingdom
Art, Food in: Poetry

Mared Wyn Sutherland
Museum of Welsh Life, Cardiff
British Isles: Wales

Mona R. Sutnick
Food and Nutrition Writer,
Philadelphia
Dentistry

Joy Emilie Swanson
Cornell University
Bioactive Food Components

Michael Symons
University of Adelaide
Cooking
Dinner
Holidays
Last Supper
Mood
Preparation of Food
Presentation of Food
Recipe
Sacrifice
Sauces
Serving of Food

Helen Tangires
Author of Public Markets and Civic Culture in Nineteenth-Century America
Farmers' Markets

Hans-Jürgen Teuteberg
University of Münster, Germany
Germany, Austria, Switzerland

Louise Thibault
McGill University
Intake

Roy Thornton
California State University, Fresno
Microbiology

Katherine Thrasher
International Food Information Council, Washington, D.C.
Biotechnology

Camille Tipton-Allaband
New York Botanical Garden
Ethnobotany

Corinne Trang
Author of Authentic Vietnamese Cooking

Bento Box
Coffee
Tea: Tea as an Icon Food

Amy B. Trubek
Author of Haute Cuisine
Chef, The
National Cuisines, Idea of

Virginia Utermohlen
Cornell University
Anorexia, Bulimia
Eating: Anatomy and Physiology of Eating
Nutrient-Drug Interactions

Hector Valenzuela
University of Hawaii, Manoa
Organic Farming and Gardening
Organic Food
Sustainable Agriculture

Renée Valeri
Lund University, Sweden
Travel

Penny Van Esterik
York University, Toronto
Buddhism
Milk, Human

Connie E. Vickery
University of Delaware
Meals on Wheels

Margaret Visser
Author of The Rituals of Dinner
Etiquette and Eating Habits
Table Talk

Julia Vittulo-Martin
Freelance Writer, New York
United States: Hawaii

Tatiana Voronina
Institute of Ethnology and Anthropology, Moscow
Christianity: Eastern Orthodox Christianity
Magic

James J. Vorst
Purdue University
Agronomy

Gail E. Wagner
University of South Carolina
Anthropology and Food

John K. Walton
University of Central Lancashire, Preston, U.K.
Fish and Chips

Robert A. Waterland
Human Nutritionist, Durham, N.C.
Metabolic Imprinting and Programming

William Woys Weaver
Drexel University
American Biscuit, The
Cake and Pancake
Christmas
Chutney
Compote
Curds
Curry
Delmonico Family
FAO (Food and Agriculture Organization)
Germany, Austria, Switzerland
Goodfellow, Elizabeth
Gravy
Heirloom Potatoes
How to Read an Old (Handwritten) Recipe
How to Use Chopsticks
Ice Cream
Leslie, Eliza
Noodle in Northern Europe
Origins of Soup, The
Pantry and Larder
Parkinson, James Wood
Peas
Pie
Porridge, Pottage, Gruel
Sandwich
Tubers
United States: Pennsylvania Dutch Food
Vegetables
Waffles and Wafers

Gary Wedemeyer
Western Fisheries Research Center (Emeritus)
Fish: Freshwater Fish

Todd C. Wehner
North Carolina State University
Cucumbers, Melons, and Other Cucurbits

Doris Weisberg
City College, City University
of New York (Emerita)
Art, Food in: Film and
Television

John C. Wekell
National Oceanic and
Atmospheric Administration,
Northwest Fisheries Science Center
Algae, Toxic

Stephen C. Weller
Purdue University
Herbicides

Robert Wemischner
Coauthor of Cooking with Tea
Hédiard
Take-out Food

Tony Whitehead
University of Maryland
United States: African American
Foodways

Andrea S. Wiley
James Madison University
Geophagy
Health and Disease

Jennifer L. Wilkins
Cornell University
Food Cooperatives
Marketing of Food: Alternative
(Direct) Strategies

John Wilkins
University of Exeter, U.K.
Ancient Mediterranean
Religions

Psyche A. Williams-Forson
McDaniel College, Westminster
College, Westminster, Md.
United States: African American
Foodways

Warren M. Wilson
University of Calgary
Game

Johanna Maria van Winter
University of Utrecht, The Netherlands
(Retired)
Fasting and Abstinence:
Christianity
Middle Ages, European

Elliot R. Wolfson
New York University
Fasting and Abstinence:
Judaism

Yoke-Sum Wong
University of Alberta
Beeton, Isabella Mary

Robin Yeaton Woo
Ceres Forum, Alexandria, Va.
Food Trade Associations
Government Agencies
Inspection

Roy C. Wood
University of Strathclyde, Glasgow
Meal

Penny Woodward
Author of An Australian Herbal
Herbs and Spices
Sweet Potato

Karen S. Wosje
South Dakota State University
Calcium

Andrew R. Wyatt
University of Illinois, Chicago
Mexico and Central America,
Pre-Columbian

Don Yoder
University of Pennsylvania (Emeritus)
Carnival
Easter
Lent
United States: The Middle
Atlantic States
United States: Pioneer Food

Gregory R. Ziegler
Pennsylvania State University
Chocolate

J. Paul Zimmer
Wyeth Nutrition, Philadelphia
Immune System Regulation and
Nutrients

Sami Zubaida
University of London
Middle East

INDEX

Bold page numbers (e.g., **3:437–439**) refer to the main entry on the subject. Page numbers in italics refer to illustrations, figures, and tables. Page numbers followed by the abbreviation *tab* indicate a table within the article. The abbreviation *col. ins.* refers to the color inserts in each volume. (The color inserts are arranged in alphabetical order.)

References to contributors of articles in this encyclopedia may appear in the index, but the best way to find a writer's article(s) is to look in the Directory of Contributors that begins on page 589; articles are listed under the person's name.

about genetically modified foods, **1:**56; **2:**34, *113*
about mad cow disease, **1:***448*
cost of food, **1:**462–463
food riots, **1:**447; **2:3–5**
and genetically modified foods in the U.S., **1:**210
growing interest in purchasing directly from farmers, **2:**458
and use of recombinant DNA technology on plants, **1:**468–469
consumption of food, **1:449–452.** *See also* intake
factors determining food intake, **2:**275
food consumption surveys, **1:683–684**
food intake and climate, **1:**423
food riots and, **2:**5
levels of, **1:**419
nutritional anthropology and, **2:**596
contaminants
in drinking water, **3:**512–513
filth in food, **1:**15
foodborne illnesses, **2:**476
in locally harvested foods in the Arctic, **2:**281
Arctic trichinosis, **2:**451
standards established by Codex Alimentarius, **1:**428
in wine from corks, **3:**549
Continuing Survey of Food Intakes by Individuals (CSFII), **2:**594; **3:**129
food stamps and, **2:**15
controlled environment agriculture (CEA). *See* greenhouse horticulture
convenience stores, **1:**538
Cook, James, **3:**447
Cook, the Thief, His Wife, and Her Lover, The (film), **1:**116
cook, to, definition in English language dictionaries, **1:**460
cookbooks, **1:452–456**
Austrian, **2:**128–129
Betty Crocker, **1:**197
Bohemian, **1:**350–351
British, **2:**51
Christmas joke book, **2:***216*
for cocktail parties, **1:**425
on comfort foods, **1:**442
community, **1:456–458**
Dutch, **2:**390, 393
early jam recipes, **2:**318
by Elisa Leslie, **2:**374–375
engraved plates in early, **1:**320
French, **2:**33, 50–51
of French *chefs de cuisine*, **1:**365
fund-raising, **3:**452
gender and, **2:**107
German, **2:**126–127
in Germany, Austria, Switzerland, **2:**122
on horse meat, **2:**209
including methods for making ice cream, **2:**238

information about curds and curd-making, **1:**482
of Juana Inez de la Cruze, **2:***496*
Lenten, **2:**374
of the Middle Ages, **2:**519–520
national cuisines, **2:**551
noodles in, **2:**557
Nordic, **2:**559–560
pamphlet cookbook for corn starch, **3:***340*
on peanut butter, **3:**57
of Pennsylvania Dutch cooks, **3:**462
on picnic menus, **3:**67
Polish, **1:**350
professional, **1:**557
by restaurant chefs, **1:***177*, 365
in Russia, **3:**221
Swiss, **2:**130, 131–132
wartime
American, **1:**454–455
British, **1:**453–454
women and, **3:**564–565
"cooked dinner," concept of, **2:**462
and validation of women's roles in family and marital contexts, **2:**463
Cookery as It Should Be (an.), **1:**556; **2:**139, 148
cookies, **1:214–217,** *col. ins.;* **3:**291
Christmas cookie-cutter, **1:***414*
etymology, **3:**451, 536–537
in French cooking, **2:**44–45
in Iran, **2:**287
irons used for, **3:**473–474
snacks, **3:**290
cooking, **1:458–462**
archaeological evidence of, **2:**94
calorie intake and, **1:**570
cooking equipment, **3:**472–473, *473*
fiber content and, **1:**639
fish, **1:**644
with gas, **2:***292*
gender divisions in, **3:**563
hearth, **2:**96–97, 180–185
herbs and spices in, **2:***189tab1,* **190–195**
hunting and gathering and, **2:**223
nutrient bioavailability and, **2:**574
research on, **1:**458; **2:**592
syrups in, **3:**380
tea in, **3:**393
temperatures in stoves, **2:**291
using marinades, **2:**453
vocabulary of, **2:**351–352
Cooking, Cuisine, and Class (Goody), **3:**142, 167, 262
on preparation of a meal of the LoDagaa, **3:**147
cooking appliances. *See* kitchen gadgets; preparation of food; utensils, cooking
Cooking as Men Like It (Frederick), **2:**107
Cooking for Christ (Berger), **2:**374
Cooking in Old Creole Days (Eustis), **3:**110

cooking methods. *See also* baking; boiling; broasting; broiling; frying; grilling; pressure-frying; roasting
in East Africa, **1:**29
listed by Beeton, **1:**459
in macrobiotics, **2:**412
of rice in Middle East, **2:**523
in West Africa, **1:**44
cooking schools, **1:***5453*, 556–557
Boston Cooking School, **1:**557; **2:**207, 240; **3:**460
caricature, **1:***5453*
Cordon Bleu, Le (Paris), **1:**368, 556
École des Trois Gourmandes, **1:**368
James Beard Cooking School, **1:**171
London Cookery School, **1:**556
Miss Farmer's School of Cookery (Boston), **1:**454
Mrs. Goodfellow's cooking school, **1:**556
Philadelphia Cooking School, **3:**452
in Prague, **1:**350
replacing apprenticeship, **1:**366
run by women, **3:**565
Cook It Outdoors (Beard), **1:**170
cookpots, **3:**473
Cooks and Confectioners Dictionary (Nott), **2:**147
Cook's Dictionary, A (Beard and McKie), **2:**218
Coolidge effect, **3:**264
Coon, Carlton, **3:**78
Cooper, Ambrose, **1:***64*
Cooper, Peter, **2:**105
Cooperative Extension Service (CES), **1:599–600**
home economics and, **2:**207
cooperatives. *See* food cooperatives
Coordinated Program in Dietetics (CP), **2:**599
copal, **1:**506
copper, **2:**433, 532, 536; **3:**410, 413–414
in corn tortilla, **2:**426
function in body, **2:***581tab1*
importance of, **1:**532
Recommended Dietary Allowance (RDA), **3:***413tab1*
Coppola, Francis Ford, **1:**114
Coptic Christians, **3:**505
coral reefs, **1:**660
cordials, **1:**310
coriander. *See also* cilantro
added to beer, **1:**184
brought to Brazil by Portuguese, **1:**232
in Central Asia, **1:**133
in curry, **1:**484
use in Iberian Peninsula, **2:**227
corm crops, **2:**211–212
corn. *See* maize
corn, etymology of word, **1:**593–594
corn bread
in American South, **3:**467
in central Asia, **1:**134

diabetes and, **1:**531
in eating, **1:**549
ethnopharmacology and, **1:**585
exercise and, **3:**5
fatty acid synthesis and, **1:**622–623
in hunger, **2:**219
obesity and, **3:**2
onions and, **3:**13
insurance, dietetics and, **1:**524
intake, **2:274–276.** *See also* consumption of food
food consumption surveys, **1:683–684**
not equal in poor households, **3:**129
optimal daily adult iodine intake, **2:**282
theories of the mechanisms controlling, **2:**275
Integrated Pest Management (IPM) programs, **1:**60; **3:**61
for apple orchards, **1:**106–107
intellectual potential, effect of PEM on, **2:**440
Interamerican Society of Tropical Horticulture, **2:**77
Intergovernmental Group on Bananas and on Tropical Fruits, **2:**77
Intergovernmental Panel on Climate Change, **1:**423
international agencies, **2:276–278**
challenges of, **2:**277
International Association of Cooking Professionals (IACP), **1:**368
International Atomic Energy Agency (IAEA), **2:**276
International Bottled Water Association, **3:**517
International Cooperative Alliance, **1:**684, 685
International Covenant on Economic, Social and Cultural Rights, **2:**14
international cuisine, **3:**182–183
International Federation of Organic Agriculture Movements (IFOAM), **3:**18
International Flavors and Fragrances (IFF), **3:**148
International Food Information Council (IFIC), **2:**81
International Food Policy Research Institute (IFPRI), **3:**105
International Fund for Agricultural Development (IFAD), **2:**12, 276
International Labor Organization (ILO), **2:**276
International Monetary Fund (IMF), **2:**5
International Network of Food Data Systems (INFOODS), **1:**672, 674
International Obesity Task Force (IOTF), **2:**603
International Plant Protection Committee (IOOC), **2:**273
International Potato Center (Lima, Peru), **3:**116, 371
International Rice Research Institute (IRRI), **2:**156; **3:**196, 310

International Society for Horticultural Science (ISHS), **2:**77, 161, 212
International Soybean Program (INTSOY), **3:**325
International Task Force for Hybrid Rice, **3:**196
international trade
and agricultural subsidies, **3:**99
bananas, **1:**163
berries and, **1:**192
dumping, **2:**27–28
between England, New England, and the Caribbean, **1:**301
exporters of agricultural products, **2:***19tab1*
importers of agricultural products, **2:***19tab1*
of wheat, **3:**532–535
of wine, **3:**552
International Trade Center, **3:**15
International Whaling Commission, **1:**659
International Wheat Agreement, **3:**534
Internet
culinary information, **1:**557
e-commerce of food, **1:**538–559
and food advertising, **1:**17
grocery shopping on, **1:**539; **2:**455
health foods on, **2:**180
humor on, **2:**216
recipes on, **3:**171
Internet marketing, **2:**458
INTERSALT Cooperative Research Group, **3:**296
intestinal flora, **2:278–279**
intestines
in digestion, **1:**525–526
digestion/absorption in, **1:**551–552
drug interactions and, **2:**577, 578
in eating, **1:**547
fiber and, **1:**639–640
and regulation of whole body iron concentrations, **2:**289
sodium and, **3:**295–296
intolerances (to food), **2:**476. *See also* lactose intolerance
intravenous feeding. *See* parenteral nutrition
Inuit, **1:**110, 307; **2:279–281**
food related to identity, **2:**279
and sea mammals, **2:**450
technology of, **3:**38
traditional diet *versus* manufactured foods, **1:**306; **2:**280, 281, 451
traditional practices combined with modern convenience, **2:**280–281
inulin as fiber, **1:**638
invalid cookery, **2:**557
Invention of the Restaurant, The (Spang), **3:**151
Invisible Man (Ellison), **1:**399–400
on Southern food, **3:**467
"Inviting a Friend to Supper" (Jonson), **1:**125

Iocca, Pasquale, **2:**231
iodide, **2:**433
iodine, **2:281–283**, 532, 536; **3:**410–411
detecting endemic iodine deficiency, **2:**281
function in body, **2:***581tab1*
milk, **1:**500
Recommended Dietary Allowance (RDA), **3:***413tab1*
in salt, **2:**590
Iowa. *See also* Midwest
cattle producer, **1:**333
Iowa Beef Packing (IBP), **1:**334; **3:**147
Iran, **2:283–288.** *See also* Persia, ancient
dates and, **2:**76
fish in, **2:**525
goats in, **2:**136
livestock production, **2:**389
map, **2:***284*
pistachios in, **2:**612
rice in, **2:**523
Shi'ism in, **2:**293
Iraq
dates and, **2:**76
rice in, **2:**523
Ireland, **1:256–259.** *See also* British Isles
butter in Middle Ages, **1:**274
death and burial in, **1:**507, 508
Great Irish Potato Famine, **1:**447, *col. ins.*; **3:**111
griddle baking in, **1:**154
map, **1:***249*
milk consumption in, **1:**503
Samhain, **2:**167–168
seabirds and their eggs in, **3:**245
Shrove Tuesday in, **3:**276
wake, **1:***509*
whiskey-type distillation originating in, **3:**510
Irish moss, **1:**301
iron, **2:288–290**, 433, 477, 532, 535; **3:**410, 411–412
absorption, **2:**289
added to flour, **3:**539
added to grain products, **1:**241; **2:**289
in bananas, **1:**163
bioavailability of, **2:**575
in capsicums, **1:**369
in corn tortilla, **2:**426
daily needs for different people, **2:**289
deficiency, **2:**175, 290, 535
studies of effects of, **2:**441
ferric iron, **2:**289
function in body, **2:***581tab1*
and genetics, **1:**210; **2:**110
and immune system, **2:**246
importance of, **1:**532
in insects, **1:**130
in lamb, **3:**268
in meat products, **2:**289
in porridge, **3:**106
in potato, **3:**108

as condiment, **1**:446
fasting and abstinence from, **1**:613
giant-sized, **3**:*9*
introduced in Hawaii by Cook, **3**:448
in Korea, **2**:337
in the Middle Ages, **2**:518
in Middle East, **2**:525
in Newfoundland, **1**:300
onion soup, **3**:299
Peoples of the First Nations, **1**:307
polyphenols in, **1**:202
in southern Italy, **2**:306
Welsh bunching onion, **3**:*col. ins.*
in West Africa, **1**:44
Onions and Their Allies (Jones and Mann), **3**:8
On Right Pleasure and Good Health (Platine), **1**:367
Ontario, **1**:303–304
On the Corruption of Morals in Russia (Shcherbatov), **3**:219
"On the Domestication of the Soybean" (Hymowitz), **3**:322
On the Observance of Foods (Anthimus), **1**:276
On the Properties of Foods (Galen), **3**:211
Opera (Scappi), **1**:121
opera, food in, **1**:**120–121**
Opera dignissima (et) utile per chi se diletta di cucinare (A both elegant and practical guide to cooking) (Maestro Giovane), **3**:90
Operation Harvest, **3**:221
opium poppies, **1**:583
Opium Wars, **3**:389
opoi, **3**:*447*
opossums, **2**:444
Oppenheim, Meret, **1**:124
optimal foraging theory, **1**:51; **2**:224; **3**:134
orach, **2**:363
oral tradition of Central American cookery, **1**:340
orange juice, **2**:65–66
scurvy and, **3**:243
orangeries, **2**:62, *63*, 100
orange roughy, **1**:660
oranges, **2**:62
bitter orange imported for English marmalade, **1**:253
blood oranges, **2**:311
in Byzantine Empire, **1**:275
fiber in, **1**:203, *638tab1*
health benefits of, **2**:83
introduced in American South, **3**:466
nutritive value, **2**:*66tab2*
producing countries, **2**:*71tab1*
types of, **2**:59, *60tab1*, 61
vitamin C in, **3**:491
Oregon, **3**:441–442
cole crops, **1**:285
Willamette Valley, **1**:194
Ore-Ida, **2**:55

Organ, John, **3**:487
organic agriculture, **3**:**14–19**, 60–61, 486
certification in, **3**:22–23
organic standards for, **1**:555–556
production of poultry, **3**:123
Organic Chemistry and Its Applications to Agriculture and Physiology (Liebig), **1**:46
organic farming and gardening, **3**:**19–21**
organic food, **3**:**21–24**. *See also* natural foods
apples, **1**:106
baby food, **1**:150
bananas, **1**:164
in England, **1**:255
farmers' markets and, **1**:606
fish, **1**:650
food cooperatives and, **1**:686–687
as food fad, **1**:601
health food and, **2**:179
Japan and, **2**:326
labeling on, **2**:346
lettuce, **2**:378
natural foods and, **2**:**551–553**
regulation of, **2**:3
symbolism of, **3**:376
Organic Foods Production Act (1990), **3**:14, 16–17
Organic Gardening Magazine, **2**:179; **3**:15
Organismo Internacional Regional de Sanidad Agropecuaria (OIRSA - International Regional Organization for Plant and Animal Sanitation), **2**:273
Organization International des Epizooties (OIE), **2**:273
organ meats
folate in, **3**:499
goat, **2**:137
in Nordic diet, **2**:560–561
vitamin A in, **3**:501
organosulfur compounds, **1**:202
Original Boston Cooking-School Kitchen Cook Book, The (Farmer), **1**:557
Origin of Species (Darwin), **1**:54
Origin of Table Manners, The (Lévi-Strauss), **3**:474
Origin of the Family, Private Property and the State (Engels), **3**:262
orlistat, **3**:5
ormer, **2**:540
Ornish, Dean, **3**:130
Orrorin tugenensis, **1**:596–597
Orwell, George, **2**:335; **3**:508
Orzoff, Jerry, **3**:227
osmolality, **3**:229
osteomalacia, **2**:534; **3**:493
osteoporosis, **1**:294; **2**:533, 534; **3**:493
bioactive food components and, **1**:202
and calcium deficiency, **3**:63
and changes in body composition, **1**:225
fluoride and, **1**:664

milk and, **1**:500
Österreichisches Festtagsgebäck (Austrian festive breads and pastries) (Burgstaller), **2**:129
Ostmann, Barbara Gibs, **3**:167
ostrich, **3**:128
Our Favorite Recipes, **1**:456
Our Sisters' Recipes, **1**:457
outdoor dining, **3**:89
Ouyang, Z., **1**:138
ovens
beehive, **1**:154
clay, **1**:459–460
and drying, **3**:153
Dutch ovens, **1**:155; **2**:*181*, 182, 183
and chuck wagons in the Far West, **3**:439
used by pioneers, **3**:464
used in Wales, **1**:265
earth oven in Pacific islands, **3**:27
enclosed, **1**:154
Gamerith on, **2**:96–97
in Mesopotamia, **2**:483, 486
in Middle East, **2**:522
moveable ovens, **3**:*142*
open hearth compared with, **2**:183–184
outdoor bake ovens of Pennsylvania Dutch, **3**:451
pot ovens used in Wales, **1**:265
tandoor, **1**:154, 459–460; **2**:254
seasoning of, **2**:254
overnutrition, **1**:449; **2**:433. *See also* obesity
medical risks resulting from, **2**:476
Ovid, **1**:125, 126, 242
ovo-lacto vegetarianism, **3**:488
ovo vegetarianism, **3**:489
Owades, Joseph L., **1**:180
Owen, Michael J., **3**:30
Owen, Richard, **2**:8
Owen, Sri, **3**:198
oxalic acid effect on calcium, **1**:293; **2**:533,**3**:63
Oxford Companion to Food, The, **1**:213
Oxford English Dictionary
on comfort food, **1**:442
on earliest use of "kitchen gadget," **2**:330
on picnic, **3**:66
spammy, **3**:79
Oxford Symposia on Food and Cookery, **1**:558; **3**:143, 145
oxidation, milk fat deterioration and, **1**:495
oxidation-reduction reactions, **2**:582
oxidative rancidity, **3**:350
oxygen
in body, **1**:221
consumption, **1**:567
in food storage, **3**:353
oyster houses, **2**:*col. ins.*; **3**:183

domestication, **3:**139
in Hawaii, **3:**447, 449
in history, **1:**583
introduced in American South, **3:**466
rum and, **3:**330–331
in South America, **3:**305, 360–361
in southern India, **2:***259*
wine, **1:**633
world consumption of, **3:**358
sugar crops and natural sweeteners,
	3:363–368. *See also* honey; sugar
	beets; sugar cane
sugar festival, **1:**616
sugar-palm wine, **1:**633
sugarplums, **1:**310
Sukup, Sophie, **1:***92;* **2:**125
sulfides/thiols in functional food,
	2:*82tab1*
sulfites
	as antioxidants, **1:**96
	salt and, **3:**230, 231
sulfur, **2:**433, 532
	as pesticide, **3:**60
sulfur dioxide (bisulfite), **2:**504
Sullivan, Thomas, **3:**393
Sully, Thomas, **2:***374*
sultanas, **2:**146–147
suman, **3:**310
Summer at Port Phillip, A (Murray),
	1:130
Summer Food Service Program, **2:**434
summer squash, **3:**333, 334
sumpweed, **1:**73
Sunbeam, **2:**333
Sunday dinner. *See* dinner
sunflowers
	and Canadian Native Peoples, **1:**308
	domestication, **3:**139, 140
	fat content of oil, **3:***17tab2*
	during Renaissance, **3:**483
Sunn hemp, **2:***371tab1*
Sunni Islam. *See* Islam
Sunset magazine, **1:**602
Super Bowl Sunday, **1:**626
supermarkets. *See* grocery stores
superstitions. *See* legends and myths
supertasters, **3:**97, 258–259
supper, **1:**530
	definition of, **2:**351
	sandwiches and, **3:**235–236
Supper at Emmaus (Carravaggio), **1:**122
Supper of the Lamb, The (Capon), **3:**224
Surface Water Treatment Rule (1986),
	3:520
surgery, obesity and, **3:**5
surplus food, **2:**3
	economic impact of, **2:**24–25
	global food market and, **2:**18–21
	luxury and, **2:**403–407
sushi, **2:**320; **3:**200
Sushruta Samhita, **2:**253
sustainability
	fishing and, **1:**658

livestock and, **2:**388–389
population and, **1:**676–678
sustainable agriculture, **3:368–370**. *See
	also* organic agriculture
tillage and, **3:**400
Sustainable Agriculture Research and
	Education (SARE), **1:**600; **3:**400
swallowing, **1:**549
swamp potato, **3:**464
swan, **3:**217
Swank Dinner Party, A (film), **1:**114
Swanson & Sons, **2:**57
sweating, **1:**565
	salt and, **3:**229–230, 233–234, *233tab3,*
	295
Sweden, **2:**558–567
	attempt to treat pigs more humanely,
	3:80
	Christmas in, **2:**566
	Lapps in, **2:**353–354
	lutefisk, **1:**641
Swedes
	in Middle Atlantic States, **3:**450
	in Midwest, **3:**456
Swedish American Cook Book (West Hart-
	ford Ladies Aid Society), **1:**456–457
sweeteners, **1:**12; **3:358–363**. *See also* ar-
	tificial sweeteners
sweet foods
	in American South, **3:**432
	and poisoning, **3:**96
sweet gale added to beer, **1:**184
Sweetness and Power (Mintz), **2:**17; **3:**402
sweet potatoes, **3:370–374**, 418, 429
	in American South, **3:**467
	arrival in China, **1:**384
	arrival in Europe, **1:**436
	in Brazil, **1:**232
	carotenoids in, **1:**203
	in China, **1:**389, 394
	depicted in Elsholtz's *Diaeteticon,* **3:**372
	greens consumed in Central Africa,
	1:23
	in Hawaii, **3:**447
	in Japan, **2:**318
	leaves consumed in East Africa, **1:**33
	in Mesoamerica, **2:**500
	in Oceania, **3:**25
	during Renaissance, **3:**483
	in South America, **3:**423
	as staple, **3:**336
	wild, **3:**421
sweets. *See also* pastry; desserts
	in Byzantine Empire, **1:**275
	in Central Asia, **1:**136
	in Greece and Crete, **2:**153
	in India, **2:**253, 254, 255
	in Karnataka, **2:**262
	in Moghul cuisine, **2:**251
	seasonality of, **2:**322
	in Sicily, **2:**306
sweet taste, **1:**1; **3:**250, 251–252
	in Ayurveda, **2:**253

babies' reaction to, **1:**3
pleasure derived from, **1:**1, 102
spicy food and, **3:**257
sucrose, **3:**359
sugar, **3:**364
swidden agriculture, **3:374–376**
Swift, Jonathan, **1:**126
Swift & Company, **1:**334
Swingle, W. T., **2:**59
Swiss chard, **2:**357, 358–359
	in antiquity, **3:**478
	nutritional constituents, **2:***360tab1*
Swiss influence
	on Brazilian food, **1:**233
	on Pennsylvania Dutch food, **3:**461
Switzerland, **2:122–132**
	breakfast, **1:**246
	household size in, **2:**214
	map, **2:***123*
	one-pot cooking, **1:**227
	potato recipes, **3:**113
swordfish, **1:**654
symbol, food as, **2:**221; **376–378**
	in Buddhism, **3:**174
	in every culture, **2:**414, 461
	in India, **2:**257–258; **3:**524
	during seder, **3:**42–43
	in Zoroastrianism, **3:**557
symbolism
	of amaranth, **1:**356
	of bagel shape, **1:**150
	of bananas, **1:**161
	of bivalves in China, **2:**541
	of bread, **1:241–244**
	Brillat-Savarin on, **3:**175
	of cattle, **1:**337; **3:**174
	of cauldron, **3:**473
	of Christmas drink, **1:**417
	cooking of the pot as feminine domain,
	1:227
	of cucurbits, **1:**478
	of egg, **2:**416
	of fish, **1:**641
	of flowers, **1:**661
	folklore and, **1:**668
	of food presentation, **3:**150
	of ghee, **3:**174
	in hunger strikes, **2:**221
	of *kimchi,* **2:**337
	of lettuce, **2:**377–378; **3:**481
	of maize, **2:**429
	of mallow, **3:**481
	of meals, **2:**461
	of *mochi,* **2:**318
	of noodles, **2:**557
	of peaches, **1:**212
	of pigs, **3:**76, 80
	of pomegranates, **2:**416; **3:**557
	of potato, **3:**114
	of poultry, **3:**123
	of pumpkins, **3:**332
	of regional cuisines, **3:**378
	religion and food, **3:**173–174